STATE AND CAMPUS

STATE AND CAMPUS

State Regulation of Religiously Affiliated Higher Education

Fernand N. Dutile

AND

Edward McGlynn Gaffney, Jr.

UNIVERSITY OF NOTRE DAME PRESS

Notre Dame & London

Library of Congress Cataloging in Publication Data

Dutile, Fernand N.
  State and Campus

  1. Church colleges—Law and legislation—United
States—States.   I. Gaffney, Edward McGlynn.   II. Title.
KF4124.Z95D87   1984   344.73'074   83-27366
ISBN 0-268-01711-5   347.30474

Manufactured in the United States of America

To Brigid Dooley Dutile
both good wife and good friend,
for giving me love, joy, and Irish descendants

Contents

Preface   ix

Introduction   1

PART I: OVERVIEW AND ANALYSIS

1. Corporate Status   5
2. State Support   9
3. Personnel Policies and Practices   14
4. Students   23
5. Facilities   34
6. Taxation   41
7. Fund Raising   49
8. Miscellaneous   52

PART II: STATE-BY-STATE

9. Alabama   57
10. Alaska   63
11. Arizona   69
12. Arkansas   75
13. California   80
14. Colorado   87
15. Connecticut   93
16. Delaware   100
17. Florida   106
18. Georgia   112
19. Hawaii   119
20. Idaho   125
21. Illinois   133

22. Indiana 140
23. Iowa 149
24. Kansas 154
25. Kentucky 160
26. Louisiana 167
27. Maine 174
28. Maryland 180
29. Massachusetts 187
30. Michigan 199
31. Minnesota 209
32. Mississippi 216
33. Missouri 223
34. Montana 229
35. Nebraska 234
36. Nevada 240
37. New Hampshire 245
38. New Jersey 250
39. New Mexico 256
40. New York 262
41. North Carolina 274
42. North Dakota 281
43. Ohio 288
44. Oklahoma 294
45. Oregon 299
46. Pennsylvania 306
47. Rhode Island 313
48. South Carolina 320
49. South Dakota 329
50. Tennessee 333
51. Texas 342
52. Utah 349
53. Vermont 358
54. Virginia 362
55. Washington 370
56. West Virginia 376
57. Wisconsin 382
58. Wyoming 388
59. Notes 393

Preface

This volume, completed under the aegis of the Center for Constitutional Studies at the University of Notre Dame, grew out of two prior Center research projects. The first, published by the University of Notre Dame Press under the title *Church and Campus*, explores the legal problems of religious groups engaged in higher education. The second, also published by the University of Notre Dame Press and entitled *Government and the Campus*, explores problems of federal regulation of church-related colleges. The present volume analyses the status of private religiously affiliated institutions of higher learning vis-à-vis state regulation.

Part I, the "Overview," takes a national look at eight different categories of state regulation: corporate status, state financial aid, personnel policies and practices, student admission and student discipline, use of publicly funded facilities, taxation and exemption from taxation, charitable solicitation and other forms of fund raising, and miscellaneous provisions regulating religiously affiliated colleges. To avoid awkward repetition, we refer to religiously affiliated colleges as RACs throughout the volume.

Part II provides a state-by-state analysis of each of these eight areas. It should be noted that none of the individual state sections contains a comprehensive discussion of the "state action" and "student discipline" issues. Since the analysis of the constitutional and common law dimensions of these themes is largely the same

for all states, these seemed better treated in the overview discussion in Part I.

Two caveats are in order. First, this volume deals with a wide range of issues arising in fifty states. Obviously, therefore, not every legal problem in its individual context has been anticipated, nor in the discussion of cases or legislation was the listing of every qualification possible without reproducing their every word. Moreover, the development of the law is never stayed. Therefore, in concrete cases, administrators and others involved in legal matters touched upon by this volume should consult legal counsel.

Second, this volume focuses on state—as opposed to federal—regulation. Any statement that religiously affiliated colleges are free to pursue a particular course of conduct is made in the context of state law only and does not purport to suggest that federal law authorizes that conduct. This is especially true in areas such as employment discrimination and public accommodations, in which federal statutes or regulations often proscribe practices allowed under state law. In this regard as well, legal counsel should be consulted.

Many thanks are due our Advisory Panel: Philip R. Moots, Esq., Chairman; Hon. Anthony Celebreeze; Dr. Frank E. Duddy, Jr.; Dr. Francis J. Michelini; Dr. Richard M. Millard; Dr. James Oliver; and Robert Stone, Esq.

We thank the following Notre Dame law students for their help: Leslie Allard, Bruce Baty,

Rebecca Butler, Jane Conley, Shawn Conway, Joseph Cosgrove, Roger Daley, John Ferroli, Doriana Fontanella, Cecelia Glacy, Antonia Greenman, Eileen Groves, David Halpin, Theresa Heamon, John Horak, William Klatt, Gregory Lodge, Lorelie Masters, Colleen McMullen, Grace Murgia, Michael Palumbo, Bruce Peterson, Marie Quinlivan, Mary Lou Solomon, Catherine Valcourt, Douglas Van Essen, Michelle Wendling, Steven Zarowny, and Jonathan Zischkau.

We also wish to thank the following persons for their invaluable aid in commenting on the manuscript: Margaret V. Tedone, Acting President, Connecticut Conference of Independent Colleges; Nancy Connic, Assistant Attorney General, Colorado; Roger A. Akin, Deputy Attorney General, Delaware; Dupree Jordan, Association of Independent Colleges and Universities in Georgia; George Freitas, Director of Taxation, Hawaii; Evelyn Nowaki, Deputy Attorney General, Hawaii; Richard W. Cosby, First Assistant Attorney General, Illinois; Eric M. Cavanaugh, Deputy Attorney General, Indiana; Donald B. Ruthenberg, President, Iowa Association of Independent Colleges and Universities; John W. Frazer, Executive Director, Council of Independent Kentucky Colleges and Universities; Bradley J. Smoot, Deputy Attorney General, Kansas; James J. Mingle, Assistant Attorney General, Maryland; Frank A. Trendinnick, Jr., Executive Vice President, Association of Independent Colleges and Universities in Massachusetts; Helen R. Bartlett, Assistant Attorney General, Michigan; Frank J. Kelley, Attorney General, Michigan; Charles T. Mottl, Special Assistant Attorney General, Minnesota; Marion L. Shane, Director, Minnesota Private College Research Foundation; Charles A. Marx, Assistant Attorney General, Mississippi; Mary Libby Payne, Professor of Law, Mississippi College School of Law; Robert A. Fazella, Deputy Attorney General, New Jersey; Howard B. Maxwell, President, Association of Independent Colleges and Universities in New Jersey; George D. Braden, Assistant Attorney General, New York; Wayne L. Benjamin, Assistant Attorney General, New York; Rufus L. Edmisten, Attorney General, North Carolina; Nancy K. Hoff, Assistant Attorney General, North Dakota; Rick D. Johnson, Assistant Attorney General, North Dakota; Michael E. Gurley, Chief, Charitable Foundations Section, Office of the Attorney General, Ohio; Jim Reid, President, Oklahoma Association of Independent Colleges and Universities; Edward Branchfield, Assistant Attorney General and Counsel, Oregon; Dave Frohnmayer, Attorney General, Oregon; William F. Hoelscher, Assistant Attorney General and Counsel, Oregon; Robert J. McKenna, Director, College and Community Relations, Salve Regina-The Newport College; J. Emory Smith, Jr., Assistant Attorney General, South Carolina; J. Lacy McLean, President, South Carolina College Council, Inc.; Robert D. Hunter, Acting President, Independent Colleges and Universities of Texas, Inc.; Frank V. Nelson, Assistant Attorney General, Utah; Paul J. Forch, Assistant Attorney General, Virginia; Jerald R. Anderson, Assistant Attorney General, State of Washington; Morton M. Tytler, Senior Assistant Attorney General, Washington State Human Rights Commission, State of Washington; Ronald K. Forren, Department of Health, West Virginia; Ben L. Morton, West Virginia Board of Regents; James L. Sankovitz, Vice President for Governmental Relations, Marquette University; Gordon B. Baldwin, Professor of Law, University of Wisconsin; Wendell Q. Halverson, Executive Director, Wisconsin Association of Independent Colleges and Universities; Harry F. Franke, Milwaukee, Wisconsin; Edgar Young, Assistant Attorney General, Wyoming.

We are indebted to Diana Smith who, with great cheerfulness, diligence, and accuracy, typed countless pages of text and footnotes. We appreciate also the help of the rest of the Notre Dame Law School staff, including Nancy Wesolowski, Darlene Carlson, Kathleen Bradley, and Elizabeth Eggleston.

The co-authors are deeply grateful to the Ford Foundation for its generous grant in support of this project. We thank also Dean David T. Link, of the Notre Dame Law School, for his encouragement and help in connection with this volume. The Center for Constitutional Studies also provided indispensable logistical and financial support.

Introduction

Religiously affiliated higher education provides our nation with an invaluable diversity, richness, and spice. Perhaps American higher education could survive without its religiously affiliated component, but it would not be the same. Nonetheless, this volume is not intended to be a brief for such institutions. Our aim is to provide an accurate, scholarly, and comprehensive assessment of state law regulating religiously affiliated higher education, an aim demanding that we point out the strengths and the weaknesses of that law and the security or vulnerability of these institutions under it.

We have reached several fundamental conclusions. First, a religiously affiliated college or university must be provided every means to promote its religious mission, including the right to select its faculty and students on a religious basis and to enforce its religious precepts within its community. Generally, the only issue that will arise is whether the members of that community were given appropriate notice of any nonobvious conditions applying to their status at the institution. The spirit of the First Amendment to the U.S. Constitution, in our view, *requires* public schools to remain nonsectarian in character and *entitles* private religious institutions generally to effectuate their religious goals as they see fit. Legislatures and courts should, therefore, view with equal suspicion any indoctrination in religious beliefs or mandatory attendance at worship ceremonies in the public college, and any limitation on a religiously affiliated college's exercise of its religious mission. This two-pronged legal approach to American higher education provides the best accommodation of the values and rights that our people cherish.

Second, we are also convinced that the First Amendment was not intended to provide religiously affiliated colleges immunity from generally applicable health and welfare regulations that are unrelated to the religious mission. A religiously affiliated college has no constitutional right—nor, we submit, any valid interest—in paying below subsistence wages, in maintaining unsafe buildings, or in serving unwholesome food. Like any other institution, these colleges are bound by governmental regulations covering such matters. Indeed, the occasional assertion that all regulation of religiously affiliated institutions is inappropriate dilutes and devalues the legitimate claim of these institutions for freedom vis-à-vis matters related to their religious purpose. To be sure, there will be rare occasions pitting the value of religious freedom against the public welfare argument. In such instances religious freedom should prevail unless the government must otherwise protect a solid and fundamental state interest.

Our third conclusion is that states must take a comprehensive look at their law to assess its impact on individual areas of endeavor and on institutions of various sizes. It is not clear that the same safety statute applying to a large manufacturing concern should apply as well to a college. Nor is it inevitable that the same regulatory and reporting scheme tolerable to a college of 40,000 students makes good sense when applied to a college of 400 students. Vol-

1

umes such as this one may present the occasion for assessing whether, at least in the area of religiously affiliated higher education, state regulation is appropriate or stifling, liberating or inhibiting. We trust, then, that this volume will be of value not only to administrators and counsel who serve in the more than eight hundred religiously affiliated colleges and universities in this country, but also to those who make public policy in the several states, whether in the executive, legislative, or judicial branch of government.

PART I
Overview and Analysis

1. Corporate Status

The American Law Institute's Model Nonprofit Corporation Act has been either adopted entirely or closely followed in twenty-eight states,[1] and therefore its provisions govern the creation, maintenance, and dissolution of religiously affiliated colleges (hereafter designated as RACs) in those states. In the others, these three steps will be governed by the state's business corporation statutes, many of which have special sections relating to nonprofit corporations,[2] by the regulations of the state's board of education or a similar body,[3] by special statutes which create the institution,[4] or by a combination of these.

The Model Act's provisions for the creation of a nonprofit corporation are formally similar to the steps for creating a for-profit corporation: one or more persons must sign and deliver articles of incorporation to the Secretary of State,[5] and when the Secretary issues the certificate of incorporation, the corporate existence begins.[6] The articles of incorporation must state the purpose of the organization. The section of the Model Act delineating allowable purposes is very broad, and charitable, educational, and religious purposes are specifically mentioned. Specifically excluded are labor unions, cooperative organizations, and "organizations subject to any of the provisions of the insurance laws" of the state.[7] The last exclusion, presumably intended to prevent insurance companies from forming as nonprofit organizations, could be read to exclude any organization obliged to pay insurance for its employees by state law, such as RACs, which are subject to such state insurance laws. Such an exclusion would not, however, seem to be the purpose of the language, and the purpose of most RACs, being educational, religious, or both, will be within the Act's requirements.

In California, which repealed its former Nonprofit Corporation Law in 1980, an RAC must choose between "public benefit" or "religious" purposes, the former making it easier for an RAC and its students to receive public assistance benefits, but the latter enabling it to exercise religious preferences in hiring under section 702 of the federal Civil Rights Act.[8] An RAC in Alaska faces a similar choice.[9] In states using the Model Act, however, nothing would prevent a corporation from stating its purposes as both educational and religious.[10] In North Dakota, if an RAC is designated a religious corporation, it may not acquire or use real estate of a value greater than five hundred thousand dollars, "unless used for educational purposes."[11] There the combination of educational and religious purposes erases a limitation which a solely religious purpose would cause to be imposed. In Illinois, an RAC may choose to be organized under the Not for Profit Corporation Act, or by a statute which deals specifically with educational institutions.[12]

The powers granted a nonprofit corporation under the Model Act are the usual business powers: to sue or be sued; to buy, receive, lease, take by gift or otherwise, own, hold, improve, use and otherwise deal in or with real or personal property; to make contracts and incur liabilities, borrow and lend money "for its corporate purposes," invest and reinvest its funds, and conduct its affairs generally.[13] The phrase "for its corporate purposes" demonstrates that it is important for an RAC to choose the broadest language for its purposes in its articles of incorporation. Consideration of the effect on its status under the state tax laws may also effect the choice of "purposes" language in the articles.

The Model Act gives a nonprofit corporation wide powers to manage its affairs as it chooses. Its main limitation comes from defining a nonprofit corporation as one "no part of the income or profit of which is distributable to its members, directors, or officers."[14] This does not preclude establishing pension plans for any and all directors, officers, and employees.[15] The corporation need not list its powers in its articles of incorporation unless they are to go beyond those enumerated in the Act.[16] This provision allows room for even broader powers to be given such corporations if the state and the corporation so wish.

A nonprofit corporation may make any amendments to its articles of incorporation needed or desired. If it has no members, such amendments may be made by a majority vote of the directors; if it has members, the directors may propose changes to the members, who must adopt the changes by a two-thirds majority.[17]

In some states, the creation and operation of degree-granting RACs come under the regulation of a board or commission for higher education, as well as under the regulation of either nonprofit or for-profit corporation statutes.[18] In others, like New Mexico, such regulation may not apply to RACs.

A significant body of state law which directly affects RACs sets guidelines for the management of investment funds held by certain nonprofit organizations. Twenty-six states[19] have adopted, with some variations, the Uniform Management of Institutional Funds Act[20] (UMIFA) as approved in 1972 by the National Conference of Commissioners on Uniform State Laws.

UMIFA is important because there are practically no cases or statutes pertaining to the legal authority and responsibility of trustees of eleemosynary institutions for the management of endowment funds.[21] RACs which manage funds in states that have adopted the legislation can be more certain of the scope of the powers and duties of their investment governing boards.

RACs are clearly included under the Act's definition of an "institution,"[22] to the extent that the RAC holds funds exclusively for its own "use, benefit, or purposes," with some exceptions.[23] The Act provides a standard for the use of appreciation in invested funds,[24] a method of releasing restrictions on the use of funds or selection of investments,[25] and specific investment authority for fund managers.[26] The salient feature of this model law is its standard of conduct for investment managers:

In the administration of the powers to appropriate appreciation, to make and retain investments, and to delegate investment management and institutional funds, members of a governing board shall exercise ordinary business care and prudence under the facts and circumstances prevailing at the time of the action or decision. In doing so they shall consider long and short term needs of the institution in carrying out its educational, religious, charitable, or other eleemosynary purposes, its present and anticipated financial requirements, expected total return on its investments, price level trends, and general economic conditions.[27]

RAC investment agents in all states must be cognizant of the institutional funds statutes because those statutes constitute virtually the only clear law on the subject and are specifically intended to affect colleges and universities.[28] The laws may benefit RAC fund managers,[29] but they also establish reasonable guidelines which limit the managers' freedom.[30] Endowment fund investment is a significant method of achieving growth for many RACs, and the enforcement of state institutional funds laws may have a substantial impact on that growth.

Another body of law affecting RACs is securities regulation legislation. All of the states require the registration of securities. Thirty-three states[31] also have blue-sky laws—i.e., laws imposing merit and prospectus requirements on securities offerings—which generally imitate the Uniform Securities Act.[32] States not adopting the uniform proposal have related statutes.[33]

These laws may affect the ability of RACs to issue or invest in securities, and securities legislation will certainly dictate the manner in which such offerings are made. However, the

Uniform Securities Act exempts from its registration and prospectus requirements "any security issued by any person organized and operated not for private profit but exclusively for religious, educational, benevolent, charitable, fraternal, social, athletic, or reformatory purposes, or as a chamber of commerce or trade or professional association."[34] This suggests that many RACs are exempt from compliance with state blue-sky laws[35] and are relatively free to issue securities and form investment contracts, which can be important tools for bolstering some RACs' financial structure.

The Model Act contains provisions governing the merger of nonprofit corporations.[36] Any two domestic nonprofit corporations deciding to merge may restate their articles of incorporation as necessary, subject to the same approval procedure as amendments.[37] There is a further provision for merger or consolidation of domestic corporations with foreign corporations.[38] Sale, lease, and exchange of assets of such corporations are similarly provided for.[39]

The dissolution of a nonprofit corporation under the Model Act may be voluntary or involuntary. A two-thirds approval of the corporation's members, or, if there are no members, a resolution by a majority of the board of directors is required for a voluntary dissolution.[40] The Act requires the corporation to distribute its assets in this order: first, all debts and liabilities must be discharged; second, any assets held conditionally must be returned or transferred in accordance with the original requirements; third, assets held subject to use for charitable or educational purposes must be transferred to another organization with similar purposes; and fourth, any remaining assets must be distributed as the articles of incorporation provide. In some cases, when it is not clear whether a donor has specifically restricted an asset, a court may have to make the final determination.[41] Usually, however, in states having the Model Act, the trustees will be able to dispose of the assets without going through the courts.

In states which have not adopted the Model Act, the common law doctrine of *cy pres* (Norman French for "as close as," meaning as close to the donor's intention as possible) is likely to be applied by the courts to direct the disposition of assets. Some states, such as Louisiana, have a *cy pres* statute. Forty-one states have either applied or recognized the doctrine of *cy pres*,[42] and two other states have adopted a rule that is functionally equivalent, such as approximation of the donor's intent.[43] The law tends to protect the terms of a trust and to resolve doubts in favor of the recipient. When no provision for distribution of assets is made, the assets may escheat to the state. In these forty-one states, however, the courts will usually apply *cy pres* and give the assets to a similar institution.

Involuntary dissolution can come about for various reasons: that a corporation has failed to file its annual report or has abused its authority, that fraud has been detected, or that the corporation has failed to maintain a registered agent, as the Model Act requires.[44] It can also happen for failure to meet the standards of a board of higher education in states where the educational corporation must be created or certified by such a board, as in Maryland.[45] In such a case a court may enter a decree dissolving the corporation.[46] Actions for the involuntary dissolution of a corporation are begun by the state Attorney General.[47] The court has the power to appoint a receiver to liquidate the corporation, if that is necessary.[48]

The Model Act gives the order in which assets are distributed: first, court costs are to be paid and expenses and all debts and liabilities of the corporation discharged; second, any assets the corporation held upon condition requiring return are to be so returned; third, assets held subject to being used for charitable, religious, eleemosynary, benevolent, educational, or similar purposes are to be transferred to organizations engaged in activities "substantially similar to those of the dissolving corporation as the court may direct;" fourth, other assets are to be distributed in accordance with the articles or bylaws of the corporation; and fifth, any remaining assets are to be distributed "as the court may direct."[49] In the forty-one states which acknowledge *cy pres*, assets in the fifth category would probably be given in the same way as those in the third.[50]

The Model Act also provides that dissolution either by certificate from the Secretary of State or by court decree, or by simple expiration of its corporate life, should not impair any remedy available to or against such a corporation, its directors, officers, or members, if action is commenced within two years after the dissolution.[51]

The most important choice for an RAC incorporating under the Model Act would seem to be its listing of purposes. This listing may affect its freedom to hire professional and other employees; to exercise religious preference in regard to its employees and to its students; to be free of property tax and sometimes of other taxes, such as meal, use, or sales taxes; to receive gifts; and to receive public benefits, both for itself and for its students.

2. State Support

In 1979 the Center for Constitutional Studies conducted an extensive survey of administrators at religiously affiliated colleges (RACs) concerning federal and state regulation.[1] Eighty-six percent of the responding institutions indicated that they accepted some form of direct financial aid from the federal government, and all but three of the respondents indicated that they admit students who receive some form of federal assistance in the form of grants or loans.[2] State aid is received by 40 percent of the responding institutions; all but two of the respondents indicated that they enroll students who receive financial assistance that is either granted to the student by the state or administered in some fashion by a state government agency.

Some of the RACs participating in this study reported that, as a matter of policy, they do not accept public financial assistance. The more obvious explanation of the dramatic difference between the number of RACs receiving federal aid and those receiving state aid is not the philosophical stance of some RACs. Rather the explanation lies in the fact that for a variety of reasons, including stricter prohibitions against state aid in state constitutions than that found in the Establishment Clause of the First Amendment to the federal Constitution, many states do not provide financial aid to independent institutions of higher education. Professor A. E. Dick Howard has provided a comprehensive analysis[3] of the history, constitutional provisions, statutes, case law, and administrative rulings relating to the constitutionality of public assistance

to private higher education in each state. His volume should be consulted by anyone interested in a more extensive study of this theme.

One difference in perspective between the work of Professor Howard and the present volume is that Howard studied in detail the legal problem of the permissibility of *state aid* to private higher education as an end in itself, while the present volume reports this theme briefly in order to focus on the major phenomenon explored in this volume, *state regulation* of RACs, which often arises as a condition of state financial assistance to these institutions. In order to appreciate the unique way in which state law governs both state aid to RACs and consequent regulation of these institutions, a comparison with the federal treatment of these themes is useful.

A. Federal Aid and Federal Regulation Under the Federal Constitution

In the leading case sustaining federal aid to RACs, *Tilton v. Richardson*[4] , the Supreme Court of the United States rejected the view that federal grants for the construction or renovation of academic facilities at RACs violated the Establishment Clause of the First Amendment. The statute challenged in the *Tilton* case required that for a period of twenty years after construction or renovation of a building with the assistance of federal funds, the college refrain from any use of the building for "sectarian instruction or as a place for religious worship."[5] The Court invalidated the twenty-year limita-

9

tion on the regulatory aspect of the funding, but sustained the funding itself.[6] One of the arguments made against the constitutionality of the federal program was that the policing of the grants or loans by the federal government would engender excessive entanglement of the government with church-related institutions. In his plurality opinion Chief Justice Burger rejected this contention, stating that various factors typically present in higher education but not in elementary and secondary education[7] diminish the risk that religion would "seep into the teaching of secular subjects"[8] at an RAC. As of mid-1982 there is no significant funding for the federal program sustained in *Tilton*, but at the direction of the Court the regulatory aspects of the statute must continue indefinitely.[9]

B. State Aid and State Regulation Under the Federal Constitution

After the *Tilton* decision several states enacted programs similar to the federal program sustained by the Court. One such program, enacted by the State of South Carolina, created the Educational Facilities Authority, distinct from the state itself, to issue revenue bonds "to assist institutions for higher education in the construction, financing and refinancing of projects."[10] Like the federal statute on which it was modeled, the state statute prohibited the bonding authority from financing any facility to be used for "sectarian instruction or religious worship."[11] The South Carolina statute authorized inspection of campus facilities to determine whether an RAC is in compliance with the regulatory aspect of the financing. Under the statute, however, contact between the state and an RAC is more attenuated than the contact between the federal government and an RAC under the federal statute. First, the state statute makes clear that bonds issued by the Authority shall not be deemed obligations of the state, directly or indirectly.[12] Second, none of the general revenues of the state may be used to support a project, since all the expenses of the Authority must be paid from the revenues of the various projects.[13] Third, as Professor Howard notes:

the bond issue contemplated the college's conveying the project to the authority, which would then lease

the property back to the college; the authority's regulations required that lease agreements contain a clause obligating the institution to honor the restrictions on religious uses and also permitting inspections by the authority.[14]

The application of this statute to RACs in South Carolina was challenged as a violation of the First Amendment in *Hunt v. McNair*.[15] The Supreme Court sustained the program, concluding that the purpose of the statute was manifestly secular, since its benefits are available to all colleges and universities in the state,[16] that it would not have the primary effect of advancing or inhibiting religion because of the regulatory provisions referred to above,[17] and that it would not engender an impermissible degree of entanglement between the state and the college.[18]

In the same year in which *Tilton* was decided, the State of Maryland enacted a program of noncategorical assistance to independent institutions of higher education in the state. The federal statute sustained in *Tilton* prohibited federal aid to any facility "used or to be used primarily in connection with any part of the program of a school or department of divinity."[19] The South Carolina statute sustained in *Hunt* contained a similar restriction. The parallel to these restrictions in the Maryland legislation excluded from participation institutions awarding only seminarian or theological degrees,[20] and the capitation grant formula used for determining the amount of aid each institution would receive excluded students enrolled in seminarian or theological programs.[21] After *Tilton*, the Maryland legislature amended the statute to provide that "none of the moneys payable under this subtitle shall be utilized by the institutions for sectarian purposes."[22] The state agency administering the statute determines eligibility for participation in the program and requires annual reports by recipients concerning the use of state funds.

The application of this grant program to RACs in Maryland was challenged as a violation of the First Amendment in *Roemer v. Board of Public Works of Maryland*.[23] The U.S. Supreme Court sustained the program. Justice Blackmun's plurality opinion emphasized that the statute had a valid secular purpose of "supporting private higher education generally, as an economic alternative to a wholly public system,"[24] that the primary effect of the statute was to assist only the secular aspects of the educational mission of the colleges,[25] and that the provisions for annual review of grants under the program did not foster an excessively entangling relationship between state and campus.[26]

C. Federal and State Aid to Students under The Federal Constitution

Beginning after World War II with the education benefits for veterans providing in the "G.I. Bill,"[27] the federal government has come to bear an increasingly significant share of the costs of higher education through a variety of grant and loan programs providing students with financial aid to enable them to attend an accredited college of their choice, including an RAC. Currently the federal government is the largest single source of student financial aid funds. The major federal programs currently providing student aid are the Pell Grant program (formerly Basic Educational Opportunity Grant or BEOG),[28] the Supplemental Educational Opportunity Grant (SEOG) program,[29] the College Work-Study (CWS) program,[30] the National Direct Student Loan (NDSL) program,[31] Guaranteed Student Loan (GSL) program,[32] and the State Student Incentive Grant (SSIG) program,[33] No successful challenge has ever been mounted under the First Amendment to this kind of financial aid for students attending RACs. *Committee for Public Education and Religious Liberty v. Nyquist,*[34] moreover, invalidating a modest state program of tuition grants to low-income families with children attending church-related elementary and secondary schools, does not compel the conclusion that federal tuition grants such as those enumerated above, "made available generally without regard to the sectarian-nonsectarian, or public-nonpublic nature of the institution benefitted," would "impermissibly advance religion in violation of the Establishment Clause."[35]

As the state-by-state analysis in this volume indicates, many states have enacted programs of student aid similar to the federal grant and loan programs referred to above. Constitutional challenges under the First Amendment were mounted against two such programs in *Smith v. Board of Governors of the University of North Carolina*[36] and in *Americans United for Separation of Church and State v. Blanton.*[37] In each instance the federal district court sustained the state student aid programs under the federal Constitution. The *Smith* court concluded that the RACs in North Carolina attended by students benefiting from the state aid program were not significantly different from the RACs in Maryland involved in the *Roemer* case, and ruled that these institutions "are not so pervasively religious that their secular activities cannot be separated from their sectarian ones."[38] The *Blanton* court found that the evidence "established that some, but not all, of the private schools whose students benefited from this program are operated for religious purposes, with religious requirements for students and faculty, and are *admittedly permeated with the dogma of the sponsoring religious organization.*"[39] Nonetheless, the court upheld the Tennessee student aid program, noting that under the Establishment Clause "total separation between church and state is not necessary. Instead, neutrality is what is required; incidental benefits conferred on religious institutions are not proscribed."[40]

The Supreme Court summarily affirmed the judgments of the district courts in both *Smith* and *Blanton.*[41] The importance of these cases is their suggestion that the Supreme Court, after reviewing several cases involving federal and state aid to RACs, has concluded that the federal Constitution does not prohibit such aid. This conclusion has some support in *Valley Forge Christian College v. Americans United for Separation of Church and State,*[42] in which the Court denied taxpayer standing to challenge the transfer of surplus federal property to an RAC that by its own description offers "systematic training on the collegiate level to men and women for Christian services as either ministers or laymen."[43] A more cautious conclusion based on the narrow holding of the courts in *Smith* and *Blanton* is that it is permissible under the federal Constitution to provide state aid to students to enable them to attend a "pervasively sectarian" RAC, even if direct institutional aid to such an institution might be deemed impermissible. This conclusion is sound in light of several decisions of the Court to the effect that a summary affirmance is a decision on the merits of the case and constitutes a binding precedent that must be followed by lower courts unless and until it is reversed by the Supreme Court.[44]

D. State Aid to RACS and Their Students under State Constitutions

Although state aid to RACs and to their students may be permissible under the Establishment Clause of the federal Constitution, such aid may be proscribed either under parallel religion clauses in state constitutions that are by their terms or by judicial construction more restrictive than the First Amendment, or under other stringent provisions in state constitutions prohibiting, for example, all forms of state aid to the private sector of higher education. As Professor Howard observes: "For draftsmen in most states, devising an aid program which complies with the First Amendment is likely to be a less troublesome matter than being sure that a program satisfies the state constitution."[45]

First, religion clauses in state constitutions may constitute a bar to various forms of aid to RACs even where the text of the state constitutional provision is virtually identical with the parallel provisions in the First Amendment. For example, providing public transportation of children attending nonpublic church-related schools is clearly permissible under the federal Constitution[46] but impermissible under the directly parallel provisions of Alaska's constitution.[47] The U.S. Supreme Court, moreover, generally declines to review cases decided by state courts construing the state constitution rather than grounding their decisions on a provision in the federal Constitution.[48]

Second, similarly disparate results under the federal and state constitutions occur where the text of the state provision is similar to but not identical with the federal provision. For example, the loan of secular textbooks to students attending church-related schools, which is clearly permissible under the federal Constitution,[49] has been held violative of similar provisions in the Missouri Constitution, construed to be "not only more explicit but [also] more restrictive than the Establishment Clause of the United States Constitution."[50]

Again, the U.S. Supreme Court often declines to review decisions by state courts grounded on state constitutional provisions. This discretionary abstention from review of state court decisions, however, does not mean that the Court will favor a state constitutional provision over a parallel federal constitutional provision, especially where the judgment is made by a lower federal court that both federal and state constitutional provisons are relevant to the outcome of a case. For example, the U.S. Supreme Court rejected the contention made by the attorneys representing the University of Missouri in *Widmar v. Vincent*[51] that the concededly more restrictive provision in the state constitution prohibiting an establishment of religion was a legitimate governmental interest sufficiently compelling to override the federally protected rights of students on a public campus to freedom of speech, freedom of association, and free exercise of religion.[52]

Third, state courts, in considering different kinds of state aid, have not always been consistent in construing state constitutional provisions that prohibit an establishment of religion. For example, in *California Educational Facilities Authority v. Priest,*[53] the California Supreme Court sustained a program, similar to the South Carolina program sustained in *Hunt,*[54] providing financial assistance for construction or renovation of facilities at independent colleges. The *Priest* court not only relied on the *Hunt* case in grounding its decision on the First Amendment to the federal Constitution,[55] but also construed very broadly several provisions in the state constitution viewed by opponents of the program as a bar to the program.[56] When confronted with a parallel to the Missouri case invalidating under the state constitution the loan of secular textbooks to children attending nonpublic church-related schools, the California Supreme Court ruled that the same provisions it had construed broadly in *Priest* should be construed narrowly to prohibit state aid at the elementary and secondary level.[57] This decision has provoked an attempt to overturn the state court's rationale by the adoption of an amendment to the state constitution that would allow the program invalidated by the court.

Finally, it should be observed that some state courts have sustained various programs of state aid to RACs and their students, despite state constitutional provisions that on their face would appear to prohibit any form of such public assistance. For example, the so-called "Blaine Amendment" in the New York Constitution prohibits the direct or indirect use of any public money in aid of "any school or institution of learning wholly or in part under the control or direction of any religious denomination, or in which any denominational tenet or doctrine is taught."[58] This seemingly clear prohibition against state aid to RACs in New York, however, has been construed liberally by New York courts to allow the operation of the so-called "Bundy Law," authorizing direct state aid to nonpublic institutions of higher education, including RACs, that meet the requirements set forth in the statute.[59]

E. Summary

All fifty states provide some form of aid to RACs or to students attending them. This is true, however, only because of the existence of the federal State Student Incentive Grant program, which was created to encourage the establishment of state scholarship programs for college students with substantial financial need, where no such program existed, and to encourage the expansion of existing programs. The SSIG program varies considerably from state to state, according to the commitment of each state to providing scholarship assistance to low-income students. The Reagan Administration, moreover, has announced that it will not support further federal incentives for states to maintain such programs. And in states such as

Colorado that have provisions in their state constitutions similar to the Blaine Amendment, even these modestly funded programs have now become subject to legal challenge under the state constitutions.[60]

These programs will withstand state constitutional challenges only if state courts construe their state constitutions as the New York courts have done with respect to the direct institutional aid at issue under the "Bundy Law," or as the Supreme Court has indicated is proper with respect to federal institutional assistance in *Tilton*, to state institutional assistance under the federal Constitution in *Hunt* and *Roemer*, and to state student aid programs under the federal Constitution in *Smith* and *Blanton*. State courts are free, however, to read state constitutional provisions narrowly to prohibit various forms of assistance to church-related schools and their students, as courts in Alaska, California, and Missouri have done.

In short, state legislation providing aid to RACs and their students will continue to be scrutinized under both federal and state constitutional standards. After *Tilton, Hunt, Roemer, Smith, Blanton,* and *Valley Forge Christian College*, however, it seems safe to predict that litigation over the permissibility of financial aid to RACs will focus more on state constitutional provisions than on the Establishment Clause of the First Amendment. In order to pass muster under the First Amendment, moreover, all forms of state aid to RACs will probably have to retain some of the regulatory features contained in the federal aid program sustained in *Tilton* and in the state programs sustained in *Hunt* and *Roemer*.

3. Personnel Policies and Practices

A. Religious Preference in Employment Policies

The principle of equal justice under law requires not only the federal government but all the states to be concerned about invidious employment discrimination based on factors usually irrelevant to job performance, such as race, national origin, religion, or sex. From the mid-nineteenth century to the early part of this century, religious discrimination by employers unfairly exluded from jobs thousands of people who were members of a disfavored religious minority.[1] Although religious bigotry is no longer as rampant or pervasive a phenomenon as it was in the past, vestiges of religious discrimination can still work in subtle ways to exclude persons from full and equal participation in the American economy.[2] It is, therefore, appropriate that the vast majority of the states have enacted civil rights legislation that, as a general rule, prohibits employers from discriminating against employees or prospective employees on the basis of their religion.[3]

This general rule, however, should yield to exceptions wherever the equally significant constitutional principle of religious freedom would be needlessly diminished. For example, it would clearly not be improper for a synagogue to exclude Christians from consideration to serve as its rabbi, just as it would clearly be permissible for a Christian denomination to restrict its ministers to members of that denomination. It would be frivolous to maintain that such distinctions, although based on religion,

constitute a civil rights violation. To the contrary, it would constitute a serious violation of the free exercise of religion to enact legislation that needlessly restricted religious corporations or groups from maintaining some form of religious preference in employment.

There is no standard or uniform policy of religious preference in employment exercised by the nearly 800 institutions that are commonly designated as church-related. For example, some might assert that the religious background or commitments of a prospective employee is a factor to be considered before that person is hired; others would deem it inappropriate to take religion into consideration in subsequent employment decisions such as promotion, tenure, or termination. Some might take the religious factor into consideration with respect to all positions; others would limit the consideration of the religious factor to positions clearly implicating the religious mission and purpose of the institution, such as top-level administrators or members of a theology department.[4]

The very fact that there is no single view among religious educators concerning religious preference in employment at their institutions, however, argues not for the imposition of a single, narrow rule of law governing all schools, but for broader latitude in this matter.

The right to exercise religious preference in employment, at least with respect to some employees of RACs, is regarded by many administrators and members of governing boards of RACs as crucial to preserving the distinct religious character of those institutions. This need has been voiced repeatedly by leaders in church-related higher education. For example, at a conference in Washington, D.C., in 1976, the spokesman for Saint Olaf College in Northfield, Minnesota, stressing the importance of the relationship between his college and the American Lutheran Church, concluded:

Most importantly of all, we hire people who are committed to these matters [the religious values identified with Lutheran Christianity]. All the programs and money in the world cannot help us achieve our stated ideals unless most of our faculty and administration embrace them out of conviction. When we hire, we try to hire the most capable chemists, artists or deans we can find; but we hire only those who convince us that they believe in our distinctness as a college of the Church, and who persuade us that they cherish our ideals even if they don't share our religious and ethnic heritage.[5]

Reverend James T. Burtchaell, C.S.C., forcefully restated this theme when as provost of the University of Notre Dame, he reminded his colleagues at a Mass celebrating the opening of an academic year:

At Notre Dame we have no task more important than to recruit and invite into our midst men and women who, beyond their being rigorously given over the profession of learning, are likewise dedicated to a life of intelligent belief. If we are to be a Christian University, we must have a critical mass of Christian teachers. If Notre Dame is to remain Catholic, the only institutional way for assuring this is to secure a faculty with prominent representation of committed and articulate believers who purposefully seek the comradeship of others to weave their faith into the full fabric of their intellectual life.

And we shall continue to need, as we have been blessed with it in the past, the companionship of believers from other religious traditions who sense and share the peculiar ambitions and hopes of Notre Dame. Indeed, it is of the very character of Notre Dame that teacher-scholars from so many religious traditions, and some who are not believers at all, share a common desire that this school retain its wonderful and special character. By no means need only Catholic or even Christian faculty be invited here. But by no means should anyone be invited here

unaware that it is a house dedicated to intelligent belief, or indifferent to this heritage. . . .

The predominating presence of Christian, Catholic scholars among our faculty, then, must be a priority of Notre Dame.[6]

The current Provost of the University of Notre Dame, Dr. O. Timothy O'Meara, when asked in 1978 how that university would try to maintain its Catholic identity, replied:

In several ways. By assuring that the faculty consists of people of all faiths who live by the spirit of Notre Dame. By assuring that committed Catholics predominate in the community. By promoting faculty members on the basis of their character and contribution to Notre Dame's values, in addition to their teaching and research achievements. By fostering religious life on campus, through campus ministry and in the residence halls. And by continuing to explore moral and spiritual questions.

At some universities, it's considered professionally unacceptable to consider such questions. We think they're important. And we think it's important that this school reflect its Catholic heritage. It's one of our greatest strengths.[7]

William Jewell College, an institution in Liberty, Missouri, affiliated with the American Baptist Church, utilizes a merit system in granting promotion and tenure. According to this system a professor being evaluated for promotion or tenure must demonstrate not only teaching competence, professional education, advisory effectiveness, scholarly achievement, and contribution to the college, but also "commitment to the Christian character of William Jewell College" as described in the college's official statement of purpose. That statement indicates that the college is committed:

To be an institution with unquestioned loyalty to the ideals of Christ, which includes a Christian philosophy in teaching and in daily living on the campus. The college aspires to be a community in which the Christian commitment of the members exemplifies the compatibility of sound scholarship and the Christian faith, and demonstrates its worthiness as a way of life. In keeping with this viewpoint the individual is challenged to develop a worthy code of conduct for his life which should inspire him to meaningful involvement with his fellow man.

To cooperate thoroughly with the Missouri Baptist Convention to offer the finest Christian education possible. As a church related institution, William Jewell College, founded in 1849 by the Baptists of Missouri, who have continued to provide financial support, aims to serve the denomination and to emphasize the best in its Baptist heritage. The college helps train leaders, both professional and nonprofessional, for the denomination and seeks new methods of communicating the Christian faith to each generation.[8]

These statements by administrators at Notre Dame and at William Jewell are fairly representative of a strong point of view asserted by many of the leaders of religously affiliated higher education in this country. These educators insist that no less than a fundamental religious freedom—the right of religious groups to preserve and to transmit their religious heritage in full integrity—is at stake in their employment practices. Because the First Amendment protects groups as well as individuals,[9] a strong case can be made that this claim of religiously affiliated higher education is protected by the Free Exercise Clause of that amendment.

For this reason, then, it is important to be somewhat discriminating about discrimination. The term "discrimination" is fraught with connotations of invidious unfairness and inappropriate attitudes. Hence the term is properly used to designate employment decisions unfairly based, for example, on the race or sex of an employee. Racial discrimination by the government and in many instances by private parties not only has no support in the text of the Constitution, it is positively interdicted by the commands of the Thirteenth, Fourteenth and Fifteenth Amendments as well as by a series of civil rights statutes enacted by Congress and by most state legislatures after the Civil War. Neither the text of the Constitution nor judicial construction of the Equal Protection Clause of the Fourteenth Amendment amount to as vigorous a prohibition against gender-based discrimination as that which obtains against racial discrimination; but the proposed Twenty-Seventh Amendment (ERA), several leading

equal protection cases, and many federal and state statutes in combination add up to a policy disfavoring irrational distinctions based on sex. As was suggested above, the First Amendment Religion Clauses protect the important constitutional value of religious freedom. To be sure, there may be instances where employment decisions based on religion would constitute invidious discrimination, but at least where religious employers are involved it is more appropriate to refer to their employment policies as religious preference rather than as religious discrimination. The insistence on the phrase "religious preference," then, is more than a linguistic nicety. It is a necessary mode o indicating the difference between legitimate exercise of a constitutionally protected right and invidious discrimination on the basis of race and sex.

Forty-three states prohibit employment discrimination, either by way of a civil rights clause in the state constitution or by a civil rights statute, sometimes designated a Human Rights Act or a Fair Employment Practices Act. Nearly all of these states also provide exceptions for religious preference by religious corporations or associations. Since these exceptions are typically patterned on provisions in the federal Civil Rights Act of 1964, as amended,[10] a brief discussion of the federal statute is helpful to understanding the parallel state statutes.

Federal Civil Rights Legislation

Title VII of the federal statute deals with unfair employment practices and generally prohibits an employer from failing to hire or from discharging any individual because of that person's religion.[11] Section 702 of the Act, as amended in 1972, now provides:

This title shall not apply to a religious corporation, association, educational institution or society with respect to the employment of individuals of a particular religion to perform work connected with the carrying on by such corporation, association, educational institution or society of its activities.[12]

An RAC is therefore free to exercise religious preference with respect to all of its employees without violating the federal civil rights statute.

A similar provision, section 703(e)(2) of the statute, declares:

[I]t shall not be an unlawful employment practice for a school, college, university, or other educational institution or institution of learning to hire and employ employees of a particular religion if such school, college, university, or other educational institution or institution of learning is, in whole or in substantial part, owned, supported, controlled, or managed by a particular religion or by a particular religious corporation, association, or society, or if the curriculum of such school, college, university, or other educational institution of learning is directed toward the propagation of a particular religion.[13]

A third provision in Title VII, available not only to church-related colleges but to all employers, allows consideration of the religion, sex, or national origin of a prospective employee "in those certain instances where religion, sex, or national origin is a bona fide occupational qualification reasonably necessary to the normal operation of [a] particular business or enterprise."[14] This provision, known as the bona fide occupational qualification (BFOQ) exception, has been construed narrowly both by the federal courts[15] and by the Equal Employment Opportunity Commission, the federal administrative agency that implements the acts.[16] For example, an RAC could not base a policy of religious preference with respect to all of its employees on the BFOQ exception, but could rely on this provision to support a policy of religious preference with respect to employees engaged in positions directly related to the religious mission or purpose of the college.

Model Anti-Discrimination Act

At its annual meeting in the summer of 1966 the National Conference of Commissioners on Uniform State Laws approved the Uniform Law Commissioner's Model Anti-Discrimination Act.[17] Chapter three of this Model Act deals with discrimination in employment. Section 302 defines discriminatory practices in language virtually identical to that of section 703(a) of the federal Civil Rights Act of 1964. The exemption found in section 702 of the 1964

version of the federal statute has its parallel in section 308 of the Model Act, which provides:

This chapter does not apply to a religious corporation, association, or society with respect to the employment of individuals of a particular religion to perform work connected with the carrying on by the corporation, association, or society of its religious activities.[18]

The exception for church-related schools found in section 703(e)(2) of the federal statute likewise has a parallel in the Model Act, but the latter does not include language concerning the curriculum of the school. Section 309(2) of the Model Act provides that it is not a discriminatory practice "for a religious educational institution or an educational organization operated, supervised, or controlled by a religious institution or organization to limit employment or give preference to members of the same religion."[19] Because of the elimination of the reference to curricular orientation, fewer RACs would qualify for the exception since not all of them are formally "operated, supervised, or controlled by a religious institution or organization."[20] Moreover, the limitation of religious preference to "members of the same religion" as that with which the college is affiliated would seemingly preclude a Roman Catholic college from giving preference to a Protestant theologian over a Catholic if it chose to do so.

The Model Act also contains a BFOQ exception that is virtually identical with the parallel provision in Title VII of the federal statute.[21]

Patterns in State Legislation

The Model Act, therefore, closely parallels Title VII of the federal civil rights statute, but is not a carbon copy of that statute. Similarly, the comprehensive state civil rights statutes that prohibit employment discrimination on the basis of religion or creed are basically similar to the federal statute, with some significant differences.

Of the forty-three states with civil rights statutes, all but ten states[22] provide for a BFOQ exception that would allow an RAC to take account of the religious background of an em-

ployee or prospective employee. Most states
define a BFOQ in language virtually identical
with section 703(e)(1) of the federal statute,
and section 309(1) of the Model, which speak
of a qualification "reasonably necessary to the
normal operation of a particular enterprise."[23]
However, twelve jurisdictions that provide for
a BFOQ offer no definition of that term in the
statute.[24] If state courts construing these provisions in state statutes were to rely on parallel
federal jurisprudence,[25] the BFOQ exception
would probably be interpreted very narrowly.
On this view an RAC could rely on the BFOQ
exception to prefer faculty members on the
basis of their religion if their employment
responsibilities were directly related to the
religious mission of the institution, as, for example, by teaching theology, religious studies,
or philosophy. If state courts were to adopt a
broader construction of the BFOQ exception
than that which prevails in federal jurisprudence, an RAC might rely on this provision for
a policy of religious preference with respect to
positions such as dean of students, counsellor,
or dormitory director. The Iowa statute would
apparently allow an RAC to practice religious
preference with respect to any of its administrators or teaching faculty. The BFOQ exception, however, does not appear to authorize religious preference with respect to employees
not directly engaged in the religious mission of
the college, such as housekeepers, janitors, or
groundkeepers.

A second pattern of state legislation affecting
the ability of RACs to exercise religious preference in employment is the provision included
in the majority of state statutes parallel to section 702 of the federal statute and section 308
of the Model Act, allowing religious corporations, associations, or societies to exercise religious preference.[26] For an RAC to qualify
under these provisions, it must be identified as
a religious corporation, perhaps not only in its
charter but also in current, operative governing
documents such as bylaws, bulletins, or cata-
logues. An RAC qualifying under this exemption
is typically able to exercise religious preference
only with respect to persons engaged in the religious activities of the RAC.[27]

A third pattern of state legislation is the exception found in most state civil rights laws,

parallel to section 309(2) of the Model Act,
allowing "a religious educational institution or
an educational institution or an educational
organization operated, supervised or controlled
by a religious institution or organization to limit
employment or give preference to members of
the same religion."[28]

Two problems for RACs arise under this sort
of statute. First, there is the definitional problem concerning control of an RAC by a religious organization. RACs have a variety of
structural relationships, some quite loose and
informal, with sponsoring religious bodies.
Neither state statutes nor cases construing the
statutes offer much guidance for determining
whether a particular institution is within the
statutory exception on the basis of its structural
relationship with a religious body. Some states
address this problem by granting the exception
to all colleges operated "in connection with" a
religious organization,[29] or "in affiliation with"
a religious group.[30] This looser statutory language may be of use to RACs that formerly
were connected with a particular religious
body, but currently are religious in character
without formal links with any particular denomination or religious society.

Second, even if an RAC qualified for this exception in the state civil rights law, it is
authorized by that provision to give preference
only to "members of the same religion," presumably that of the sponsoring religious body.[31]
On this model a Lutheran college could prefer
Lutherans, and a Southern Baptist college could
prefer Southern Baptists, but a Roman Catholic
college could not prefer Methodists, nor could
a Presbyterian college prefer a Jew. Some states
have addressed this difficulty by providing
RACs with much broader freedom of choice in
exercising religious preference. Some states,
for example, allow an RAC to use religious
criteria in their employment decisions if these
decisions are "calculated to promote religious
principles."[32]

As noted above, several jurisdictions have no
state civil rights law.[33] At least one state sets
forth a ringing policy declaration against any
employment discrimination on the basis of
race, religion, or sex, but provides no consequences for any violation of that policy statement.[34]

Some drafting errors occur in the state civil rights legislation. For example, the provision in the Ohio civil rights statute which refers to RACs is found in the housing section of the statute, but not in the employment section.[35] Similarly, the Minnesota legislators drafted a definition of a religious or denominational educational institution, but neglected to include the term in the section dealing with employment.[36] Even the Model Act shows an apparent discrepancy in allowing a broader choice for religious preference to employers relying on the BFOQ exception than to RACs relying on the provision expressly drafted with these institutions in mind.[37]

In short, careful consideration ought to be given to amending several of these statutes to enable RACs to exercise the kind of freedom in religious preference necessary or appropriate to the carrying out of their distinctive missions in a pluralistic society.

B. Wage and Hour Legislation

RACs are not explicitly mentioned either in the federal Fair Labor Standards Act[38] or in the parallel statutes that have been adopted by every state. But they are clearly subject to regulation under these statutes, which define "employment" and "employer" broadly. Moreover, RACs are bound to observe the more stringent requirement, whether federal or state.[39] For example, RACs in Maine are bound to observe the requirements of the federal statute, despite the exemption in the state statute for "any individual engaged in the activities of a public-supported nonprofit organization or in a program controlled by an educational nonprofit organization."[40] Similarly, RACs in Massachusetts, which are required by state law to pay a minimum wage but not to compensate at a higher rate for overtime work,[41] must nonetheless comply with federal requirements concerning compensation for overtime. Hence a brief review of federal wage and hour standards is useful for comparison with parallel provisions in state laws.

As of mid-1982 the federal Fair Labor Standards Act requires RACs to pay virtually all of their employees a minimum wage of $3.25 per hour. States can set a higher hourly rate, but not a lower rate.

Some employees of RACs are exempt from coverage under the federal statute. For example, the Department of Labor has issued an interpretive bulletin indicating that ordained ministers or members of a religious order serving in RACs pursuant to their religious duties are not "employees" within the meaning of the Act.[42] Although there is no authority for this ruling in the legislative history of the statute, the ruling is in accord with the rationale adopted by the Supreme Court with respect to collective bargaining at church-operated elementary and secondary schools.[43] Three states explicitly exclude members of religious orders from coverage under state minimum wage laws.[44]

There is clear warrant in the federal statute for an exemption for various "white collar" employees of RACs, such as executives, administrators, and professional employees who "customarily and regularly exercise discretion" in conducting the business of the college or university.[45] A number of states provide an exemption parallel to the "white collar" exemption in the federal statute referred to above.[46] Many states also exempt from their minimum wage laws volunteers performing services for any nonprofit organization, including an RAC.[47]

As of mid-1982, RACs are authorized under the federal regulations to employ full-time students at a minimum wage of $2.85 per hour, if the students are not beneficiaries of the federal College Work Study program.[48] The same regulations clarify whether an employment relationship exists between a college or university and a student. For example, no employment relationship exists where a university engages a graduate student to perform research primarily for the purpose of fulfilling requirements for an advanced degree, even though the institution awards a grant or stipend to the student for that research. If a graduate student's responsibilities under the grant include teaching, however, the student is regarded as an employee under the act and must be compensated at the minimum wage. If an institution pays a nominal sum to students to participate in extracurricular activities conducted primarily for the benefit of students, no employment relationship is created. If, however, students are hired to perform tasks that are not part of an educational program, for example, to work in a dining hall or bookstore, they must be paid the prevailing minimum wage. It may be difficult in some instances to be sure that a particular position is a component of the educational program of the institution rather than a commercial aspect, but one court has ruled that residence hall assistants are not employees within the meaning of the Fair Labor Standards Act.[49]

A number of states provide exemptions in their minimum wage laws for students. Nine states exempt students performing various services for a college or university in which they are enrolled.[50] Two states exempt part-time services performed by students.[51] One state does not exempt students, but provides that they need be paid only 85 percent of the minimum wage.[52]

C. Worker's Compensation

Worker's compensation is a statutory program enacted in all fifty states whereby employers are required to provide benefits to employees who sustain work-related injuries while carrying out the responsibilities of their employment. Workers are to be compensated for reasonable medical expenses and for lost work time due to injury or illness; dependents are to be compensated for the worker's death if it is job-related. Employers may elect to insure themselves to cover this business expense or they may obtain insurance coverage from private insurance companies and, in some instances, from state insurance companies. In some states, employers are required to post a bond with the state commission or agency that administers the worker's compensation program.

Congress declared in the Occupational Safety and Health Act (OSHA) of 1970 that worker's compensation should be "adequate, prompt, and equitable" because "the vast majority of American workers, and their families, are dependent upon workmen's compensation for their basic economic security."[53] In the same statute Congress established a National Commission on State Workmen's Compensation Laws to undertake a comprehensive evaluation of these state laws.[54] The Commission, completing its task in July of 1972, submitted to President Nixon and to the Congress a report that urged the federalization of the worker's compensation

program if the states had not made substantial improvements in their worker's compensation statutes by July of 1975.[55] If Congress decides to follow the recommendations of the Commission, coverage of employees would be broadened and benefits expanded. As of mid-1982, however, there is no indication that worker's compensation will be federalized soon; and it remains an aspect of state law.

All fifty states have enacted worker's compensation statutes, and RACs are included within the broad definition of an "employer" in all but three states.[56] The definition of a covered "employee" in four states is limited to workers engaged in "hazardous occupations," but the definition of such hazardous occupations includes at least some employees of RACs, such as maintenance workers and food service personnel.[57] In three states, volunteers working for a nonprofit institution are excluded from coverage unless they and their employer opt for coverage.[58] Unless executive officers of any corporation opt for coverage, they are exempt employees in five states;[59] ministers of religion are similarly exempt in five other states;[60] in one state teachers in a religious, charitable, or educational institution are likewise exempt unless they elect to be covered.[61] Casual workers are exempt employees in thirteen states.[62] The definition of "casual worker" varies from state to state, but generally includes persons who work less than a period of time stated in the statute during each quarter of the year, or those engaged "not in the usual course of the trade or profession of [their] employer." An employer, however, may elect to have casual workers covered if they consent and if adequate notice is given to the appropriate state commission or agency. Finally, students working to pay any part of their tuition expenses are exempted from coverage in at least one state.[63]

D. Unemployment Compensation

The Federal Unemployment Tax Act (FUTA) appeared originally as Title IX of the Social Security Act of 1935[64] and was enacted in response to the widespread unemployment during the "Great Depression." It called for a cooperative federal-state program of benefits to unemployed workers, who are covered during temporary, involuntary periods of unemployment. By 1937 all the states had enacted a state statute parallel to FUTA. The original act imposed a wage tax on "for-profit" employers only, and so did not include RACs. Coverage under the act has expanded steadily since the 1950s. In 1970 the federal act was amended to include nonprofit institutions within the statutory definition of an employer.[65] All state laws were then amended to conform to the federal statute. Hence, RACs are generally subject to regulation under this federal-state program.

The program works by imposing a wage tax on employers, and then allowing them a tax credit of up to 90 percent of their contributions to certified state unemployment funds.[66] Employers must make contributions to state unemployment compensation plans for their covered employees. In many states, however, RACs may make payments representing the benefits paid rather than the regular contributions.[67] These payments are usually equal to the full amount of regular benefits paid plus one half of the extended benefits. State laws are written to conform with the federal requirements so as to obtain the tax credit for employers in the state. For this reason they have been called "mirror images" of the federal law.

To understand some of the intricacies of the operation of FUTA, reference must be made to certain provisions in the Internal Revenue Code. For example, the wage tax provisions in the Internal Revenue Code[68] define employment to include services for any institution which is excluded from the term "employment" solely by reason of another provision in the Code, section 3306(c)(8), which excludes services performed "in the employ of a religious, charitable, educational, or other organization described in section 501(c)(3) which is exempt from income tax under section 501(a)."[69] Under sections 501(a) and 501(c)(3) of the Internal Revenue Code, corporations organized and operated exclusively for religious or educational purposes are exempt from federal taxes.[70]

Most state unemployment compensation laws define covered employers in part by reference to FUTA. For example, several state laws cover employment by religious, charitable, or educational organizations if services for those organizations are exempt from "employment" under FUTA solely because of section 3306(c)(8).[71]

Because most RACs are tax exempt because of sections 501(c)(3) and 501(a) of the Internal Revenue Code, they are within this category, and are therefore subject to regulation under the state unemployment compensation laws. Any doubt that RACs are covered under the State unemployment compensation statutes is removed altogether in six jurisdictions which explicitly include nonprofit organizations, and hence RACs, within the statutory definition of an "employer."[72] In a number of other states, RACs clearly fall within the broad definition of covered employers without being referred to explicitly.[73] Alaska, for example, defines a covered employer as "any unit employing one or more persons for some portion of the day within a year."[74]

Most state laws closely follow the exemptions found in FUTA for a variety of services not covered under the act.[75] Four of these exemptions found both in FUTA and parallel state legislation are of special relevance to RACs and exclude from coverage: (1) services for a church, an association of churches, or an organization operated primarily for religious purposes and operated, supervised, controlled, or principally supported by a church or association of churches; (2) services by a minister or member of a religious order in the exercise of his or her duties; (3) services by a regularly enrolled student at the RAC, and in some states by a student's spouse; and (4) domestic services in a college club, fraternity, or sorority if no more than $1,000 was paid for such services in any quarter during the current or preceding calendar year.[76]

Finally, it should be noted that in *St. Martin Evangelical Lutheran Church v. South Dakota*,[77] the U.S. Supreme Court ruled that schools that have no separate legal existence apart from a church or a convention or association of churches are not "employers" subject to regulation under FUTA. In *California v. Grace Brethren Church*,[78] the Court heard arguments on the issue whether FUTA constitutionally requires that participating state unemployment compensation programs cover employees of elementary and secondary schools that have a religious orientation, but are not controlled by a church or convention of churches.[79] Although the Court in *NLRB v. Catholic Bishop of Chi-*

cago[80] took the view that federal labor legislation should be construed so as to avoid potentially troubling questions of entanglement arising under the First Amendment,[81] that rationale
has been sharply criticized[82] and the precedential value of the case has been limited by the
National Labor Relation Board (NLRB) to the
fact pattern of that case, which involved church-
operated elementary and secondary schools
rather than RACs.[83] Hence it is unlikely that *St.
Martin* or *Grace Brethren* will have any significant impact on the coverage of RACs under
FUTA and parallel state unemployment compensation laws.

E. Collective Bargaining

The U.S. Supreme Court ruling in *NLRB v.
Catholic Bishop of Chicago*[84] that employees at
church-operated elementary and secondary
schools are not covered by the National Labor
Relations Act has not been extended to employees at RACs.[85]

No judicial authority supports the view of the
NLRB that members of a religious order should
be excluded from bargaining units at RACs,[86]
but the issue remains a thorny one.[87]

In *NLRB v. Yeshiva University*,[88] the U.S.
Supreme Court ruled that some faculty members participate so extensively in the management and operation of a college or university
that they should be classified as managers rather
than as employees under the National Labor
Relations Act. Like *Catholic Bishop*, the *Yeshiva*
case was narrowly decided and sharply criticized.[89] And as the NLRB narrowed *Catholic*

Bishop to its facts, so also has the General
Counsel of the Board indicated that the degree
of collegiality and participation in management
decisions by faculty members at Yeshiva University was not typical of the role played by
faculty members in the governance of most
American colleges and universities.[90] After
Catholic Bishop and *Yeshiva*, therefore, RACs
remain subject to the jurisdiction of the NLRB
in matters concerning the rights of their employees to bargain collectively over wages and
other terms and conditions of employment.

In addition, RACs are subject to state regulation of a similar nature in several states that
have enacted so-called "mini-Wagner Acts"
protecting under state law the right of workers
to organize and to bargain collectively.[91] RACs
are not explicitly excluded from the statutory
definition of an employer in these statutes.
Their employees, therefore, generally enjoy the
same rights as other employees in their state. At
least one state appellate court has ruled that a
state statute protecting the right to bargain collectively did not apply to employees at a nonprofit college, although there was no explicit
exemption for colleges in the statute.[92] Eleven
states have enacted not only a statutory provision protecting the right to bargain collectively,
but also some form of a "right to work" law,
which typically declares as public policy of the
state that the right of persons to work shall not
be denied or abridged on account of membership or nonmembership in a labor union or
labor organization.[93] Nine other states have
enacted "right to work" laws without any state
statute supporting or protecting the right to
organize and to bargain collectively.[94]

4. Students

A. General

State laws directly affecting an RAC's student admissions policies are rare. Twenty-four states have no legislation directly governing the admission of students to private colleges.[1] In these states, only the federal Civil Rights Act of 1964, prohibiting discrimination in institutions receiving federal financial assistance, will apply to admissions policies, and only with regard to RACs which receive such assistance; for these, discrimination on the basis of race, color, or national origin is prohibited.[2] As the federal law does not forbid religious discrimination in this regard, it leaves an RAC free to exercise any kind of religious preference in choosing its student body.

The receipt of state funds in states like Alaska, Alabama, Arkansas, California, Illinois, and Maryland,[3] however, could bar the receiving institution from using religion as a basis of choice. While these states may not have intended to restrict RACs from exercising religious preferences, RACs are not specifically exempted.

Several states having civil or human rights or equal educational opportunity statutes forbidding certain kinds of discrimination in certain educational institutions do not extend any prohibition against religious selectivity to RACs.[4] RACs in these states are, therefore, able to exercise selectivity on the basis of religion in admitting students. In some states, they may do so only in favor of students of the "same religion" as that of the college's affiliation;[5] in such states, a question may arise concerning what the "same religion" is. Can a Catholic school in such a state favor only Catholics or other Christians as well?[6]

In other states this restriction is followed by an enlarging clause such as New Hampshire's stating that an RAC should not· be prevented "from making such selection as is calculated by such organization to promote the religious principles for which it is established and maintained."[7] If these principles are broadly stated in the RAC's articles of incorporation, they may be interpreted to mean the institution needs a diversity of religions among its student body, allowing it to exercise a very broad religious preference. Such language in effect removes a restriction which otherwise could compel a Methodist college, for example, to prefer only Methodists. Even if this would be an RAC's natural use of its freedom of choice, such a restriction seems an undue limitation of the religious freedom RACs generally should have (and do have under federal law).

In Wisconsin, the statutory regulations on admissions are silent on the subject of religious selectivity, so RACs would probably have the freedom of choice the federal law grants them. In Montana and Oregon, anti-discrimination provisions include religion as a prohibited basis for discrimination unless "reasonable."[8] An RAC's preference for students of its own or certain other religions could be argued to be reasonable.

Indiana, Michigan and Minnesota[9] explicitly

allow for RACs to be single-sex. In other states, there seem to have been no problems with the general exemption of private colleges from the ban on sex discrimination in Title IX of the federal Education Amendments of 1972.[10]

The federal prohibition against discrimination on the basis of handicap in federally funded programs has generated inconclusive litigation concerning the extent to which schools receiving federal assistance must modify their facilities or programs to accommodate handicapped students, for example, by making buildings more accessible, by providing Braille collections, or by providing translators for hearing-impaired students. While some states have laws forbidding discrimination solely on the basis of a handicap, which would apply to the admission of students, these states do not require private colleges to modify their facilities to accommodate the handicapped.[11] Legislation does bar discrimination against the blind in Massachusetts and Vermont, and, in Missouri, state money is to be provided for readers for blind students.[12]

Laws governing places of public accommodation will affect RACs in states, such as Colorado, where any educational institution is by definition a place of public accommodation. (How such laws affect an RAC's campus generally is covered in the "Facilities" section.[13]) But the public accommodations or fair housing laws of some states, when no exception for religious or other private institutions is included, could be read as indirectly affecting student admissions policies: if, for example, facilities such as dormitories are limited only to enrolled students of a university, religious selectivity in the school's admissions could be considered a violation of the fair housing law of the state. Such a result would, however, presumably not have been the intention of the legislature.[14]

Many states have specifically excepted RACs, either as religious institutions, or distinctly private institutions, from the public accommodations laws. Washington is an example. Florida law excludes even university-run hotels and food service establishments. In South Dakota, the exemption provided for RACs for their admissions would surely prevent any argument that an RAC could not limit its housing to its own students, even though the South Dakota Housing discrimination law would technically bar such a limitation.

State regulations regarding requirements that buildings be modified for handicapped students are also covered in the "Facilities" sections.

B. Academic and Disciplinary Dismissals and Other Sanctions

Judicial Intervention Generally

In their dealings with students, RACs must now recognize the greater likelihood that courts (and other agencies) will be called upon to redress grievances.[15] Indeed, law has become an indispensable consideration in the daily professional lives of post-secondary administrators at all levels.[16] The procedural context for court action includes mandamus, specific performance, statutory decree, declaratory judgment, injunction, and action for damages.[17]

Nonetheless, courts "will not generally interfere in the operations of colleges and universities,"[18] and students rarely win.[19] Although the chief reason for this is the custom of deference to the educational institution's discretion, others include the concern that outside review will undermine the school's authority, the large number and often small importance of student complaints, the better ability of the institution to judge the situation involved and the delicacy of the issues.[20] The net result, especially for private colleges, is a broad disciplinary discretion.[21]

Despite the "historical independence of universities from intervention by outsiders,"[22] however, it is now recognized that a student's stake in a college education cannot be dismissed as a mere "privilege."[23] A college education may be seen as vital to social and economic advancement,[24] and a dismissal, academic or disciplinary, is a stigma that will hound one for life.[25] Courts, therefore, will not tolerate arbitrary and capricious dismissals even in private institutions.[26] Conversely, courts will probably intervene only when serious sanctions are at stake,[27] and "institutions of higher education are not yet in danger of an extensive or continuous examination of their judgments by the courts."[28] After all, even in cases as serious as dismissal, "[s]uits for reinstatement in a private college ask the court to examine the internal processes of an institution entitled by reason both of autonomy and of academic freedom to a special deference."[29]

Academic Versus Disciplinary

In any event, it is clear that courts will defer to institutional judgments more readily in purely academic matters,[30] e.g., the grading of a paper, than in disciplinary ones because the former are more directly tied to academic freedom and more clearly within the academic community's area of expertise.[31] Indeed, a purely academic dismissal may not require any formal hearing whatever[32] (although, in a certain sense, the reading of the student's papers by the instructor is the hearing in such cases), even in a public institution bound by the Fourteenth Amendment.[33] If, however, the student alleges bias or professional incompetence, some procedural device is in order for assessment of the claim since arbitrariness, capriciousness or bad faith will increase the chances for judicial intervention into even academic matters.[34]

It is not always clear into which category an issue falls, however. A plagiarism or other intellectual dishonesty case may have a foot in each camp.[35] Indeed, it has been suggested that fitness and moral standards might be academic criteria.[36]

In Loco Parentis

In loco parentis, the most prominent traditional doctrine employed by the courts in dealing with institutions of higher education, treated the college as the substitute parent, with a consequent broad discretion in discipline and the like. Although some courts imposed a reasonableness requirement on the device,[37] oftentimes no limits on the institution's power were recognized[38] even though a student above the age of twenty-one is not appropriately subject to paternalism and even though *in loco parentis* should rarely justify expulsion, which is in effect the severance of the parental relationship.[39] Moreover, a parental doctrine now seems especially anachronistic in light of the modern, impersonal university and the maturity of the present-day student.[40] In any event, courts have moved away from *in loco parentis*,[41] and today other doctrines are more significant.

Constitutional Rights in Private Institutions

The Fourteenth Amendment to the United States Constitution provides that no *state* shall "deprive any person of life, liberty, or property, without due process of law; nor deny to any person . . . equal protection. . . ."[42] One seeking to recover for a violation of due process or equal protection, therefore, must show "state action" since the Constitution does not in these respects guard against merely private conduct.[43]

Although federal regulation, in itself, of higher education is beyond the scope of this volume, the application of due process and equal protection through the state action concept requires attention to *state* involvement in the institution's workings, the main thrust of our inquiry. Moreover, the application of various protections under state constitutions may also depend on the presence of state action.[44] A brief discussion of the state action concept, at issue in most lawsuits filed against colleges,[45] is therefore in order.

The landmark state action case, for our purposes, arose in connection with a power company, not a college. The plaintiff in *Jackson v. Metropolitan Edison Company*[46] sued Metropolitan following the company's termination of electrical service to her. She claimed that prior to any such termination she was entitled, under the Fourteenth Amendment, to notice, a hearing and an opportunity to pay any amounts due. The trial court dismissed her complaint on the grounds that the termination did not constitute state action.[47] The United States Supreme Court recognized the difficulty of assessing whether conduct by a formally private party may be deemed action of the state:

While the principle that private action is immune from the restrictions of the Fourteenth Amendment is well established and easily stated, the question whether particular conduct is "private," on the one hand, or "state action," on the other, frequently admits of no easy answer.[48]

Although a monopoly situation is perhaps more likely to be state action, said the Court, heavy state regulation is not enough.[49] The crux of the inquiry is "whether there is a sufficiently close nexus between the State and the challenged action of the regulated entity so that the action of the latter may be fairly treated as that of the State itself."[50]

The Court also found insufficient the fact that Metropolitan Edison had filed with the Pennsylvania public utility commission, clearly a state agency, the electric company's termination procedure. The Court felt it significant that the commission had neither ordered that procedure nor even passed on it, but had merely failed to disapprove it.[51] The initiative came from the utility, not from the state.[52]

The Court in *Jackson* made clear that a detailed inquiry may be needed to resolve the state action inquiry.[53] With the *Jackson* case as a beacon, let us assess the possibility of a private institution of higher education being deemed the state for purposes of the Constitution.

Just as courts have reflected a general reluctance to intervene in matters of private higher education, they have demonstrated a specific reluctance to impose constitutional standards upon universities that are not state supported.[54] Indeed, "it is reasonably certain that the [United States Supreme] Court has adopted the general principle that private colleges, universities, and professional schools are somehow special, and should not be compelled to have all of their decisions judicially examined."[55] They have been rebuttably presumed not to be state actors lest they lose "their right of independent decision making which is their chief definitional characteristic, and is arguably their chief institutional end."[56]

The Threat to Diversity

As private schools take on more of the indices of public institutions, especially in terms of support, there is greater likelihood that this traditional hands-off doctrine will change. As Professor O'Neil has forcefully argued, the spectrum of universities today ranges from the purely private to the purely public.[57] "Some private universities are engaged in state action for all purposes and some for no purpose; most

of them fall, however, somewhere in-between, and should be judged by the fourteenth amendment under some but not all circumstances."[58] Whether one agrees with his conclusion, it is clear that considering private colleges to be the state for constitutional purposes could do serious harm to a valuable diversity in American education. Private higher education, a "vital and influential force in American intellectual history," has been able to respond to special concerns beyond the reach of public institutions because of legal or political constraints.[59] State action findings against private colleges might not only reduce diversity but also raise constitutional problems with regard to religious schools[60] which, to the extent they are the "state," might well lose their right to proclaim particular religious views or to exercise religious preference in the selection of faculty and students.

"Specific act" versus "General involvement"

It is not clear whether, in order for a private actor to be considered the state for constitutional purposes, the state must be associated directly with the particular act involved or merely have significant connections with the private actor generally, regardless of the act involved. In *Jackson*, it will be recalled, the Court said the question is whether there is a close enough nexus "between the State and the challenged *action* of the regulated entity so that the *action* of the latter may be fairly treated as that of the state itself."[61] Although ambiguous, the language is surely supportive of the view, as put by one court, that "the state's involvement must be . . . concerned with the activity which caused the injury, and must aid, encourage, or connote approval of the activity."[62] But in 1976, a United States District Court held that the "general state involvement" test was appropriate, not the so-called "particular act analysis of state action."[63]

It would seem, however, that neither test need be exclusive. An institution might be so pervasively controlled and financed by the state that any of its acts would constitute state action although the *act itself* was not particularly state-connected. On the other hand, if a state passes legislation authorizing a large and otherwise private agency to choose who will be admitted to a state university, that agency's act of selecting students seems state action even though the selection function is a minuscule part of the agency's work. In short, a less extensive involvement should suffice if it is in the very area giving rise to the plaintiff's claim.[64]

The Interest at Stake

Moreover, whatever the logic of it, courts may be willing to take into account the particular interest at stake in deciding whether there is state action.[65] All other things being equal, for example, state action may be easier to demonstrate in race or sex cases than in others.[66] Presumably, the courts are able to use the "state action" label to take cases of special interest and reject less welcome ones.[67] In the Supreme Court itself, however, this proposition has apparently not been specifically adopted.[68]

Specific Indices of State Action: State Control

In the detailed inquiry which the *Jackson* Court said may be needed to assess state action, the extent to which the state regulates the private party is clearly relevant. Many states exercise significant control over private educational institutions, with the extreme case being New York's Board of Regents.[69] The presence of public officials on the college's governing board[70] or in other positions[71] is relevant as well.

Significant regulation in itself, however, will not be enough. In *Jackson*, the Court found it insufficient for state action that the utility was a heavily regulated partial monopoly.

State Support

As early as 1819, in *The Trustees of Dartmouth College v. Woodward*,[72] Chief Justice Marshall suggested that public funding might make Dartmouth a public institution.[73] Today, it is recognized that the amount, source, and purpose of state financial support to the private entity must be considered in any state action assessment.[74] Professor O'Neil argues that such support in itself may be enough: "[T]he sheer extent and volume of public support for such universities as Harvard, Pittsburgh and Temple would without more render the private shell irrelevant for constitutional purposes."[75] Except perhaps in extreme situations, however, more than financial support will be needed for a state action finding.[76] Indeed, if financial support were the test, those government contractors who rely on the government for the bulk of their income would be considered state actors,[77] an unlikely result indeed.

In this connection, it should be noted that much government "support" is received by universities as private contractors for research and the like. Such support should be given very little consideration in state action assessments since the money is being exchanged for services between two independent parties. In such situations, the government is the buyer and the college the seller with no necessary suggestion of government endorsement and furtherance of the entity's continued existence or its policies. Such support is a purchase, not a subsidy. Outright grants and other subsidies (e.g., the donation of land or of buildings, interest-free loans, sales of property at less than market value) more surely denote a mutual interest and goal and more clearly reflect a partnership.

Taxation Benefits

Related to state support is the tax benefit, which also could suggest state action on the part of the recipient. This is especially true, it has been argued, where the tax exemption is not available to other nonprofit organizations,[78] or covers non-educational income, thereby more closely resembling a subsidy.[79] Most tax exemptions, however, may merely represent neutrality by the state[80] and, in any event, have been deemed essentially irrelevant in education cases.[81] Indeed, one United States District Court found tax concessions combined with support insufficient to make of a private university a governmental actor: "Although money and tax considerations are given to the defendant [university], this is a far cry from any influence on policy in decision-making or encouragement of any specific policy."[82]

Public Function

In *Jackson v. Metropolitan Edison Company*,[83] Justice Marshall suggested in dissent that the electric utility was a state actor because it supplied an essential public service which is supplied in many communities by the government.[84] Since education is so commonly thought of as a function of government, this "public function" argument could support state action claims against private institutions.[85]

Several points are marshalled to buttress the argument: the authority to award degrees belongs to the state, not the college;[86] education is affected with a public interest;[87] in many respects, college communities are like company towns,[88] which have been deemed to be state actors.[89] The argument is not hurt when public authorities make available funding for building facilities.[90] When the state has otherwise delegated to the institution a clearly governmental power, such as eminent domain, the thrust is still stronger,[91] especially if the conduct complained of is related to the use of that power.[92] Nonetheless, education cases have not generally been won on the public function theory,[93] courts being alert to the fact that "education has substantial roots in the private sector . . ."[94]

Justice Marshall has suggested the need for differing standards of state action for differing aspects of the "public function":

Private parties performing functions affecting the public interest can often make a persuasive claim to be free of the constitutional requirements applicable to governmental institutions because of the value of preserving a private sector in which the opportunity for individual choice is maximized . . . Maintaining the private status of parochial schools . . . advances just this value. In the due process area, a similar value of diversity may often be furthered by allowing various private institutions the flexibility to select procedures that fit their particular needs.[95]

It is interesting to note that Justice Marshall chose the educational area—and religiously oriented schools—to make his point.

Incorporation and Other Forms of State Involvement

Although incorporation under state law as a nonprofit tax-exempt educational institution has been looked to for state action purposes, courts have generally not been impressed.[96]

Other sorts of state involvement, some of which could be included within the state regulation category, might be relied upon in arguing state action on the part of a private institution: the college calling on the police to expel students from a building,[97] the inclusion of the institution in a state master plan for the provision of higher education,[98] the authorization or encouragement by state statute of certain institutional conduct,[99] the presence of state officers in nominal positions of the institution,[100] the conferral of peace officer status and statewide jurisdiction upon the institution's security officers,[101] a consortium arrangement of colleges,[102] relative lack of choice for a particular area of study,[103] and the leasing by the college of public property[104] are examples.

Two further points must be made. First, a private institution may be deemed a state actor in some of its actions and not in others. At Alfred University, for example, students in the Ceramics College were entitled to Fourteenth Amendment protection since that part of the University "was in actuality a state school administered by private individuals."[105]

Second, a defendant college may not be able to single out each element as in itself insufficient for state action.[106] "It is not enough to examine *seriatim* each of the factors upon which a claimant relies and to dismiss each individually as being insufficient to support a finding of state action. It is the aggregate that is controlling."[107]

Contract

A major theory underlying judicial intervention into campus disputes, especially at private colleges,[108] focuses on the contract relationship[109] between the student and the institution, as spelled out in the college catalogue and the student handbook.[110] Customs and usages are also relevant[111] and, in any event, courts will recognize, even without a written provision, the college's right to maintain order on campus.[112]

There are, however, problems with the contract model. One court has observed:

Contract theory is not wholly satisfactory, however, because the essentially fictional nature of the contract results in its generally being assumed rather than proved, because of the difficulty of its application, and because it forecloses inquiry into, and a balancing of, the countervailing interests of the student on the one hand and the institution on the other.[113]

Moreover, the student's bargaining position is so unequal[114] that the arrangement has been analogized to the yellow dog labor contract.[115] As a result, such "agreements" could be voided as against public policy or as unconscionable.[116] At the least, the "adhesion contract" concept could be used to interpret vague language against the contract "drafter," i.e., the college.[117]

In some cases, courts have given the institution "virtually unlimited power to dictate the contract terms, and the contract, once made, was construed heavily in the institution's favor."[118] The problem is aggravated by the use of broad "reservation clauses," through which the institution reserves the right to dismiss for any reason it sees fit.[119] Courts should be reluctant to enforce such clauses, at least absent conduct any student clearly should know is objectionable.

The contract theory may, of course, put limits on the college's power through implication.[120] If, for example, the catalogue specifies the conduct calling for expulsion, the contract may prohibit expulsion for other reasons.[121] Moreover, the university may waive its rights under provisions it continually fails to enforce.[122]

Commercial law contract principles should not be rigidly applied to the student-college relationship.[123] After all, "educational contracts have unique qualities" and are to be construed so as to give the institution sufficient educational discretion.[124] Professor Kaplin expects the contract theory to gain in importance.[125] While limiting the institution's authority, contract concepts can be creatively employed to enforce order and fairness within the institution and to maintain a nonjudicial, in-house grievance procedure.[126]

Tort

The common law tort doctrine may also authorize court review, although the tort may be difficult to name.[127] The tort device has not been prominent in college dismissal discussions and, in any event, private higher educational institutions have in the past enjoyed immunity from negligence and other tort suits through the doctrine of charitable immunity.[128]

Other Theories

Other theories yield possible court intervention into private college affairs. For example, statutes, both state and federal, have directly created enforceable rights,[129] and a "law of associations" concept[130] as well as a fiduciary analysis have also been advanced under which the faculty and administrators act in a fiduciary or confidential capacity with regard to students.[131]

Procedures

The procedures used by colleges for resolving serious allegations against students, for example those carrying suspension or expulsion as a possible consequence, are central. First, courts are more expert at,[132] and therefore more comfortable, dealing with procedure than with the substance of the institution's regulations. Second, a procedural resolution by the court may spare the institution any invasion of the academic "inner sanctum" or compelled testimony from administrators or faculty.[133] Indeed, courts are especially likely to defer to the college's judgments if a hearing was held,[134] and the fact that a hearing was held may be more important than its form.[135]

What kind of procedures should an RAC provide its students? It is important to note that a full-scale, legal trial-type process is not essential. For example, the exclusionary rule, which bars the use of illegally seized evidence in criminal trials, does not apply to disciplinary hearings.[136] Even when a state actor is involved, due process requires only that a balance be struck between the procedure involved and the interest at stake: the greater the potential loss, the more extensive the procedural protection.[137] Indeed, more process may be due in professional or graduate schools since the damage is more specific.[138] In short, a hearing may be fair without being complex.[139]

Whichever legal theory a court finds relevant to an RAC, whether state action, contract or other, some level of procedural protection may be required before serious penalties can be visited upon students.[140] Although there are no generally recognized guidelines applicable to student disciplinary hearings, there is judicial agreement that there must be notice and an opportunity to be heard "appropriate to the case."[141] It is submitted that RACs should carefully develop procedural protections not only to avoid, or prevail in, court action, but because fairness requires it. Educational institutions teach as well (better?) by what they do as by what they say. Not only do fair procedures teach fairness to the community, they also reassure it that no one will be subject to arbitrary or capricious action. After all, part of education involves learning to live in a democracy and summary dismissals or the like do not promote such learning.[142] A college has little to lose in providing fair procedures and, in any event, the "martyrdom" effect that can be created by arbitrarily imposed punishments may outweigh any bad effects of a good hearing.[143]

Moreover, the fact that an RAC has provisions for such hearings firmly in place does not mean that every incident of alleged serious misconduct will necessitate such a hearing. The RAC's procedural code should allow at least two separate by-passes to the full hearing procedure. First, if the alleged wrongdoer is freely and fully prepared to admit the misconduct, it makes little sense to *require* a full hearing. Once the violation is admitted in writing, the case may proceed directly to the penalty phase. Second, even a student who insists on a hearing should have the option to be heard by a specified official — for example, an assistant dean — rather than by the full hearing board. For a variety of reasons, among them a strong case against the student or an interest in privacy, many students will prefer such by-passes which, of course, should be spelled out in the student handbook along with the full hearing process.

The first requisite of a fair process is notice of what sanctions might accompany what situation. In sum, the RAC should spell out as clearly as possible what misconduct, what academic inadequacy and what medical unfitness may yield which serious consequence, be it probation, suspension, dismissal or other separation.

This notice will usually occur in a student handbook, in the college bulletin or perhaps even in a letter to the student at the time of his acceptance into the college. Although such

notice need not carry the specificity of penal statutes,[144] reasonable clarity is possible. Moreover, although the college may wish to insert a "reservation clause" (e.g., allowing dismissal for any other reason the college sees fit), it should not rely on such a clause both because courts might find it too vague or unfair to apply and because a student is entitled to more.

When an allegation[145] is made against a student that could yield serious consequences, the student should be given written notice setting out the factual allegations, the section of the student code allegedly violated, and the alternative procedures available to him in resolving the matter. The student should be given ample time to choose which procedure he will pursue and, if a hearing procedure is selected, to prepare any defense. Ideally, he should be given the names of at least the principal witnesses,[146] and the nature of the main evidence against him.

The hearing itself should be conducted by a neutral examiner, that is, one who played no part in the discovery, witnessing or prosecution of the alleged misconduct. (The hearing board may vary depending on the nature of the hearing. If, rather than misconduct, medical unfitness is the issue, perhaps a medically trained person, e.g., a psychiatrist, should hear the case. If plagiarism is the issue, then a scholar might well be the ideal examiner. For a violation of the community standards, a cross-section of that community may be appropriate.[147])

The student should be allowed "counsel" of his choice, although this need not be a lawyer unless the college is represented by a lawyer.[148] The student should be entitled to confront the witnesses against him through cross-examination, and to present witnesses and other evidence in his defense. Although formal rules of evidence are not in order, hearsay evidence (e.g., letters or other written accounts) should be avoided if possible. As complete a record as possible should be made of the hearing itself.

If the student is "acquitted" on the evidence,[149] the matter should end there; no appellate tribunal is in a better position to assess witness demeanor, credibility and the like.[150] If the student is "convicted," he should be allowed an appeal either on "legal" grounds — e.g., the law was too vague, his hearing was unfair — or on factual grounds if it can be said on the available record that the evidence was *insufficient* (not merely that the appellate tribunal would have reached a different result on evidence about which reasonable persons could differ).[151]

Any penalty assessed should be reasonably proportionate[152] to the offense and should be appealable for excessiveness. Confidentiality should be provided for throughout the process. It is crucial, in any event, that an institution follow the procedures set out in the bulletin or otherwise, for even a private educational institution "is bound by its own rules,"[153] absent unusual circumstances.[154]

Substance

As suggested earlier, courts will be less likely to intervene into the RAC's substantive regulations than into its procedural inadequacies. The college will probably be allowed to enact and enforce any regulation it is reasonably interested in as long as students are reasonably notified of the regulation and as long as the regulation is enforced in a procedurally fair way. This is especially true if the school is not a state actor for constitutional purposes.

Nonetheless, a school should avoid arbitrary regulations, i.e., those it has no legitimate interest in enforcing. It should calibrate its rules to the age and needs of its particular student body; regulations that are essential for tenth-graders may be ludicrous for college-age students.

Regulations should, therefore, bear a reasonable relationship to the purposes and values of the institution. Obvious among these are rules relating to academic performance, to order in the classroom and on the campus generally, to intellectual honesty in examinations and papers and the like. Surely, for example, an RAC has legitimate interest in proscribing theft, assault and drug sales on its campus.

More controversial is the regulation which in some way interferes with the "private life" of the student. Should an institution be entitled to prevent its students from legally drinking alcoholic beverages off-campus? From gambling? From smoking cigarettes or marijuana? To the extent that an activity is a crime, pre-sumably yes, since an institution has a legitimate interest in separating out criminal types from its law-abiding students.

In *Krasnow v. Virginia Polytechnic Institute,*[155] the Court of Appeals for the Fourth Circuit found constitutional the institution's rules against unlawful drug usage and any other criminal act, *on or off* the campus. "The university clearly has the prerogative to determine that any unlawful possession of drugs or criminal conduct on the part of students is detrimental to the university."[156] Conversely, schools should recognize a right to privacy among its students *as long as no significant interest of the school is at stake.*

This last provision is especially relevant to the RAC, which may wish to enforce certain moral or religious standards among its students. Especially in light of the First Amendment to the U.S. Constitution and of the legitimate value of a diversity of higher educational institutions, an RAC should be entitled to enforce any regulation, even one governing the "private life" of the student, if (1) that regulation is reasonably related to the school's values or purposes; (2) the student is made aware of the regulation prior to accepting admission into the college; and (3) the regulation is enforced through appropriate procedures, in light of any factual issues involved and of the severity of any penalty. Would anyone seriously contend that a Catholic university must sit idly by while one of its students runs an abortion clinic, even legally? On a less dramatic level, an RAC whose religious affiliation deems smoking immoral should, under the conditions listed above, be able to enforce a smoking ban upon its students, even off-campus.

This result is perfectly comprehensible if one recognizes that colleges purport to teach more than purely academic theory. RACs legitimately claim to teach moral and religious lessons as well and therefore a student violating one of these moral or religious lessons may be deemed to have failed just as much as one who failed regular examinations. After all, "the definition of education must be established by the school's own conception of its mission within the world of knowledge."[157] Moreover, neither the nation nor the student has anything to fear from this arrangement. The nation gains a healthy diversity and the student gets no less than he bargained for since he knowingly undertook the responsibility of adhering to the institution's rules.

Lexington Theological Seminary v. Vance[158] reflects a judicial willingness to take into account the institution's special interests. Holding that "reasonably clear standards concerning character were set forth in the catalogue,"[159] and that the Seminary therefore had the right to exercise its discretion in the matter of granting a divinity degree to an admitted homosexual, the Kentucky Court of Appeals observed that:

the questions of morality of homosexual Christian ministers must be of overriding importance to an institution . . . engaged in the business or calling of training persons for the Christian ministry . . . [T]he argument that Christian denominations or other religious groups should adopt the life style and morals of some segments of the population is ridiculous on its face . . . [The Seminary] has the most compelling interest in seeing that its graduates . . . shall be persons possessing character of the highest Christian ideals.[160]

This is not to espouse expulsion whenever any college rule is violated—the wise college will weigh the seriousness of the violation in light of the school's interests, the violation history of the offender and any prospect for reformation—but merely to assert the legitimate right of the RAC to implement doctrines it feels strongly about, especially on a religious basis.

In the landmark dismissal case directly involving religion, *Carr v. St. John's University*,[161] four Roman Catholic students who participated as principals or witnesses in an off-campus civil marriage ceremony were dismissed from the University. In the eyes of the Roman Catholic faith, an order of whose priests ran the University, such conduct was seriously sinful.[162] New York law declared it a "fundamental American right for members of various religious faiths to establish and maintain educational institutions exclusively or primarily for students of their own religious faith or to effectuate the religious principles in furtherance of which they are maintained."[163] Moreover, the University bulletin contained the following provision, of which the students conceded awareness: "In

conformity with the ideals of Christian education and conduct, the University reserves the right to dismiss a student at any time on whatever grounds the University judges advisable. Each student by his admission to the University recognizes this right."[164]

Despite the breadth and vagueness of this language, the New York court upheld the University's action. The dismissals of these students, who claimed no lack of understanding of their act or its consequences, were within the University's discretion. The court found that implied in the contract between student and University was a term or condition that the student would not act subversively to the discipline of the college or show himself to be morally unfit to remain a member.[165]

Three points about *Carr* must be borne in mind. First, it is not an essentially procedural but a substantive case. The students admitted the conduct involved. Therefore, fact-finding processes such as confrontation of witnesses and determination by a neutral examiner were not the issue. Second, and most important, *Carr* establishes the right of RACs to insist not only on academic standards but on conduct standards, and not only on conduct standards related to campus order, but on religious conduct standards. In this light, *Carr* assumes an incredible importance for the religious independence and viability of RACs. It is difficult to posit the continued existence of RACs if, for example, a Catholic college could not prohibit premarital sexual intercourse or if a Jewish college could not enforce its dietary laws.

The third point is a related one. *Carr* allows the RAC to enforce its religious conduct rules even with regard to the student's non-academic and non-campus life. *Carr* did not involve campus religious conduct (e.g., the requirement that resident students attend evening chapel or say a prayer in class). It involved a matter of considerable personal privacy which presumably occurred off the campus. Still, the court sustained the exercise of discretion. Indeed, the court was prepared to strain the terms of the University bulletin to do it, interpreting "Christian education and conduct" to mean *Catholic* education and conduct. (Obviously, not all Christians would object to the civil marriage.)

Some problems remain, however. For example, since St. John's University had non-Catholic students, could it enforce Catholic standards against them? Would it have to distinguish between requirements directly related to morality—for example, pre-marital sex—and those related to worship—for example, Sunday Mass attendance? If so, into which category would participation in the civil wedding fit? Presumably, the institution will be prepared to insist that all students honor the most fundamental moral precepts such as those against theft, assault and the like. Those that are peculiar to the religious affiliation of the institution are more likely to be relaxed vis-à-vis students not of that affiliation.

Is there a problem, however, in enforcing different laws against different students? The dissent in *Carr* argued:

The University is a public institution, chartered by the State, open to persons of all religious faiths, and engaged in providing secular learning leading to a general academic degree. Such a University may not enforce against the student an ecclesiastical law, the breach of which is not immoral according to the standards of society in general, or which it does not enforce equally against all students at the University, whether Catholic or non-Catholic.[166]

The argument misses the point. Nothing requires an institution to treat unequal things equally. A university may have different rules for seniors than for freshmen, for sick students than for well, for honor students than for others. What is illogical (or unfair) about a Catholic institution insisting that its Catholic students live up to Catholic requirements? Must Yeshiva enforce its dietary standards upon its non-Jewish students in order to be entitled to enforce them at all? Could not a Baptist school insist that students participate weekly in worship appropriate to each student's own religious affiliation? The dissent's view would unnecessarily and rigidly homogenize RACs.

Nonetheless, whatever course an RAC might choose to steer in this regard, it should make clear in advance, as specifically as possible, what it expects of all its students. If certain students are to have more (or less) stringent requirements than others, this too should be spelled out in the bulletin or perhaps even in the letter

of acceptance. The *Carr* court, after all, saw itself enforcing a contract and it is best for all parties that its terms be clear.

The result in *Carr* is buttressed by Professor Kaplin's assertion that "the religious beliefs and practices of private institutions are affirmatively protected from governmental interference by the free exercise clause."[167] Just as this clause protect RAC regulation of student conduct, so too must it protect the RAC's right to regulate expression on the campus. Since the typical RAC will not be a state actor under the constitution, it is not bound by the Constitution to honor any claimed right to free expression. Under its own rights as a private college, an RAC is entitled to protect its purposes and values from subversion. As Professor O'Neil has commented: "Queens or Brooklyn or City College must permit a campus Ku Klux Klan or Nazi youth group, however offensive its tenets may be to the vast majority of students, but is it equally clear that Brandeis or Yeshiva must shelter such an organization?"[168]

This is not to suggest that RACs enter into rigid control of student speech and campus speakers. An RAC and its students have a deep need for freedom of expression[169] and a too casual suppression of dissenting ideas may forfeit the institution's claim to be a true university or college. In short, although the RAC has the *power* to control pervasively, it would not be *wise* to do so. The prudent RAC will exercise the power only in the face of a serious threat to its values and purposes, only with a full appreciation of the value of academic freedom and diversity even on the private campus and only after a check of its charter for any limitation on its right to curb free expression.[170] It will be more justifiable, therefore, to control expression that threatens the religious values of the institutions than that which merely threatens its public relations.[171]

In summary, RACs should clearly promulgate their standards of conduct and of academic and medical fitness. The procedures for enforcing these standards should be spelled out as well. Any public pronouncements, however, whether in bulletins, student handbooks, or elsewhere, should not suggest a promise or commitment unless there is full intent to deliver.[172]

5. Facilities

State laws dealing with public accommodations, housing, and safety can have a substantial effect on an RAC's operation of its facilities. Conceivably, these laws might also impinge upon an RAC's freedom of selectivity in its student admissions policies. If an RAC is strictly held to a state fair housing law which prohibits religious discrimination, for example, then enforcement of that law could suggest state control over the RAC's admission policies. Thus, an evaluation of these laws and their potential impact on RACs is worthwhile.

Thirty-one states[1] had passed public accommodations laws prior to the passage of Title II of the Civil Rights Act of 1964,[2] which laid down the federal law against discrimination in places of public accommodation. To date, only ten states[3] have not enacted comprehensive public accommodations provisions, i.e., provisions which match the scope of Title II.

Title II prohibits discrimination based on race, color, religion or national origin in a wide variety of places of public accommodation which affect interstate commerce. The constitutionality of Title II was first established five months following its enactment in *Heart of Atlanta Motel v. United States*.[4] The Supreme Court in that case held that Congress had not exceeded its power to regulate commerce in passing the act. The case left the door open for a broad interpretation of the key words "affect commerce",[5] and strengthened the federal government's ability to enforce Title II against the states.

What is the effect of the federal public accommodations law on state laws? Under Title II, the aggrieved person must give written notice to appropriate state authorities thirty days before any action can be filed under the federal law, if that state has its own public accommodations law.[6] This provision suggests that Title II is "complementary," as one author put it, and is "not meant to supplant remedies available to citizens in states which have effective public accommodations statutes."[7] Of course, the federal statute and its judicial interpretations can have a bellwether effect on state statutory construction, especially in areas where Title II parallels the state laws.

For persons in states with no public accommodations law, a civil action for injunctive relief can be brought immediately under Title II. If an RAC is the alleged violator, the federal government will have no difficulty finding that its operations "affect commerce." The question for RACs in these states concerns the scope of Title II and the applicability of the private club exemption[8] to their facilities.

The vast majority of the states prohibit more types of discrimination in their public accommodations laws than the federal government does under Title II.[9] Thirty-three states (out of a total of forty with public accommodations laws) bar sex discrimination in addition to discrimination based on race, color, creed, and national origin or ancestry.[10] Fourteen of those states also outlaw age discrimination,[11] and eleven of those fourteen ban discrimination based on marital status.[12] Finally, twenty states include some form of prohibition of discrimination against the handicapped in their public accommodations laws.[13]

To what extent do these laws affect RACs? The primary way in which the states limit the applicability of their laws to RACs is in their statutory definitions of a "place of public accommodation." Many statutes define a public accommodation as any place which caters or offers its services, goods, or facilities to the general public.[14] Many laws will list specific examples of places of public accommodation in addition to such a general definition.[15] A good number of definitions contain clauses which specify the inapplicability of the public accommodations law to any place that is "in its nature distinctly private"[16] or is "not in fact open to the public."[17] A few laws consider any place which "solicits patronage" from the general public to be a public accommodation,[18] and two of those states also include any place which is "supported directly or indirectly by governmental funds."[19]

The very definition of a public accommodation may restrict the applicability of the state laws to a certain type of RAC-owned facilities, i.e., those places which are open to the general public. Campus cafeterias, bookstores, stadiums, and hotels will be covered by the laws, but "distinctly private" places such as dormitories, student dining halls, and classrooms normally are not thought to be places of public accommodation.

Other facilities, such as a campus church or a temple or a library, may qualify as public accommodations under certain circumstances. If a place of worship is located inside a dormitory or if a library is part of a classroom building, however, either place may be deemed to be a private place. The critical question is whether an RAC has "offered" a particular facility or service to the general public. Nothing would prevent an RAC from staging an activity (such as a commencement exercise) inside a building which is normally open to the public (such as a stadium) and to limit admission to students, faculty, and other invited guests. In such a case, the RAC has not held the facility open to the general public. Once an RAC has invited

the general public to use a certain facility, however, that facility becomes a place of public accommodation for purposes of the anti-discrimination laws. RACs can still admit persons to that facility (e.g., a stadium) on a selective basis—e.g., give special seating to students or alumni—even though such selectivity may *result* in favoring members of one religion or one sex.

State laws generally[20] do not list educational institutions as examples of places of public accommodation. In a sense, RACs do offer a service (education) to the general public, but most laws give no suggestion that either RACs as a whole or private RAC facilities (e.g., dormitories) come under such statutory provisions. The best solution that these laws can offer concerning the problem of defining a place of public accommodation is to attach a list of examples to their more general "places open to the public" definition. The principle of *ejusdem generis*[21] could then be invoked to delineate the extent of the statutory coverage. Even if a state law fails to provide examples of places of public accommodation, the examples set forth in Title II[22] and in other state laws can play an important role in judicial interpretation of such broad definitions.

A second way in which public accommodations laws are restricted in their applicability to RACs is through exemption clauses. A few states that specifically exempt RACs employ some form of "religious organization" exemption. New Hampshire's law, for example, states:

Nothing contained in paragraph V shall be construed to bar any religious or denominational institution or organization, or any organization operated for charitable or educational purposes, which is operated, supervised or controlled by or in connection with a religious organization, from limiting admission to or giving preference to persons of the same religion or denomination or from making such selection as is calculated by such organization to promote the religious principles for which it is established or maintained.[23]

Arguably, this type of clause only purports to grant qualifying RACs freedom in their *admis-*

sions policies ("such selection") and does not otherwise exempt them from the discrimination prohibitions of the law applicable to public accommodations. On the other hand, the clause may be intended to exempt RACs from *any* compliance with the law. The latter interpretation is less likely to be accepted as it seems to violate the spirit of the public accommodations laws. The "religious organization" exemption more frequently accompanies fair housing statutes, so the full implications of this clause (and its numerous variations) will be discussed later.

The main types of exemption clause found in the state laws is similar to the "private club" exemption clause of Title II:[24]

This act does not apply to a private club, or other establishment not in fact open to the public.[25]

Similar clauses specify the inapplicability of the public accommodations laws to any place that is "in its nature distinctly private."[26] Although these clauses seem merely to restate the usual definition of public accommodations, they do provide a greater indication of a legislative intent to exempt those accommodations which are not wholly "public."

Other types of exemption clauses include a few nonprofit corporation exemptions,[27] and certain limited exemptions for sectarian institutions,[28] some of which may not exempt any RACs in those states. Two states allow for an exemption from their public accommodations provisions as long as the discrimination is "reasonable."[29]

All of these clauses only open the possibility that RACs will be exempt from the respective anti-discrimination laws. The "religious organization" exemption may give RACs substantial leeway since its focus is most clearly on those types of institutions. As virtually all RACs are nonprofit organizations, they will be clearly exempt from public accommodations laws in a few states. Most of the exemption clauses—the "distinctly private" place exemptions—are subject to as much interpretation as the definition of a place of public accommodation itself. It seems unlikely that RACs will be exempt if they discriminate unreasonably or purposefully disregard the legislative intent behind the public accommodations laws.

A third way in which a state public accommodations law may have limited applicablity to RACs is through the *lack* of any positive indication that the law intended to affect facilities normally open only to enrolled students and indirectly, therefore, an RAC's admissions policies. In other words, state legislatures are not presumed to want to restrict admissions to these colleges. Some states[30] allow for RAC exemption from *other* anti-discrimination laws (e.g., fair housing laws) and these exemption clauses may also suggest that the state does not mean to control RAC admissions. Otherwise, this type of limitation is only seated in the assumption that if a state intended to govern RAC admission policies, it would purposefully and specifically have done so. Given the existence of this limitation, however, presumably places which are normally open only to enrolled students (e.g., dining facilities) are not intended to be covered by the law either, since the enforcement of the public accommodations law in those places would necessarily stymie selective enrollment policies.

What is the impact on RACs of public accommodations laws? The general rule seems to be that although RACs are not themselves places of public accommodation, those facilities which RACs hold open to the general public must adhere to the provisions of the public accommodations laws. This would include places like stadiums, bookstores, inns, and restaurants, as long as the public is invited to use them.

Ultimately, an RAC's freedom to be selective will not be unduly undermined. Since admissions policies are generally not regulated, an RAC can simply restrict the use of a certain facility to "students" or "alumni" and still comply with the anti-discrimination law, even though such a restriction results in the admission of a disproportionate number of members of a particular denomination and/or sex. More importantly, RACs may gain no real advantage by unlawfully discriminating in places of public accommodation. The facilities which the laws cover usually are revenue-producing and will benefit from as much patronage as possible. Finally, RACs which desire a good national image or a good rapport with the local community may have no interest in risking a soiled reputation by being accused of violating public accommodations laws. Thus, state public accommodations statutes do not seem to impinge unreasonably upon an RAC's freedom to select its student body or to operate its facilities.

State housing laws affect RACs in a way very similar to public accommodations laws. Through a strict enforcement policy, a state could require an RAC to maintain student housing which does not discriminate against members of a particular religion or sex. This would force the RAC to alter its admissions policies, if necessary, to satisfy the housing law. The law could thus restrict an RAC's freedom of selectivity and freedom to dictate its campus operating procedures.

Federal fair housing legislation can be found in two separate parts of the Code. The main provision, Title VIII of the Civil Rights Act of 1968,[31] outlaws discrimination on account of race, color, religion, sex, or national origin in the sale, rental, offer to sell or rent, terms or conditions, or advertisement, and the like, of any dwelling.[32] The law then outlines the familiar "religious organization or private club exemption."[33] Title VIII set the tone for subsequent state fair housing laws, and provides that no federal action can be initiated if the aggrieved person has an equivalent remedy under state or local law.[34]

The second piece of federal legislation is Title I of the Civil Rights Act of 1964,[35] relating to equal rights and property rights of citizens. It specifies the right of every citizen to inherit, purchase, lease, sell, hold, and convey real and personal property.[36] This legislation has been held to be "independent and concurrent" with regard to the Fair Housing Act of 1968 (Title VIII),[37] and a federal action for damages *can* be instituted under this act even though a similar remedy is available under state laws.[38]

Thirty-six states have enacted comprehensive, Title VIII-type housing laws. Only two of the state laws do not prohibit as many types of discrimination as does Title VIII,[39] while thirteen state laws ban age discrimination[40] and eighteen prohibit discrimination based on marital status[41] in addition to the standard pro-

hibitions, i.e., race, color, religion, sex, and national origin. Twenty-one states incorporate some form of handicap discrimination prohibition in their comprehensive laws,[42] and two states ban "source of income" (or welfare status) discrimination.[43] Most of the laws prohibit discrimination involving the same types of real estate transactions as does Title VIII.[44]

A few states have statutes which do not resemble Title VIII and seem limited or ambiguous.[45] Depending on judicial interpretation and/or state enforcement of these laws, they could affect an RAC's housing.

At least fourteen states[46] have adopted, with some variation, the Uniform Residential Landlord and Tenant Act (URLTA) as set forth by the National Conference of Commissioners on Uniform State Laws.[48] The major provisions of this act include landlord obligations (e.g., to maintain the premises), tenant obligations (e.g., to abide by state health codes), and restrictions on the use of certain types of lease agreements.[48] Other states have adopted a landlord-tenant law with respect to mobile home parks.[49] Virtually all of the states which have enacted a comprehensive URLTA-type statute *exempt* private educational institutions. This seems to leave RACs reasonably free to establish their own rental agreements with their students and to incorporate into housing contracts many terms and conditions which they deem both advantageous and fair.

To what extent do the state fair housing laws affect RACs? The majority[50] of states with fair housing legislation seems to exempt RACs by way of "religious organization" exemption clauses. The most inclusive version of this clause has been adopted by seven states:[51]

Nothing . . . in this section shall bar any religious or denominational institution or organization, or any charitable or educational organization that is operated, supervised or controlled by or in connection with a religious organization . . . from giving preference to persons of the same religion or denomination . . . or from making such selection as is calculated by such organization to promote the religious principles or the aims, purposes, or fraternal principles for which it is established or maintained.[52]

Some states omit the "charitable or educational organization" clause,[53] some omit the "or in connection with" phrase,[54] and some substitute "nonprofit organization" for "charitable or educational organization."[55] In the least inclusive version of this type of exemption, six states[56] (along with Title VIII) require that: a) the dwelling be owned or operated for other than a commercial purpose; b) the organization only limit sales or rentals to persons of the same religion; and c) the organization's membership not be restricted on account of race, color, or national origin.[57]

At its broadest, the "religious organization" exemption might exempt all RACs from such fair housing acts. Moreover, the final "as is calculated" clause of this form of the exemption is so broad that it seems to give RACs nearly total freedom to limit housing accommodations as they deem appropriate, e.g., through the segregation of students by sex or marital status in both dormitories and off-campus student apartments. An RAC may even lawfully exercise its preferences as regards an RAC-owned hotel or other guest lodgings, unless otherwise prohibited, for example under a public accommodations law.

Many RACs may win exemption under the more limited form of the "religious organization" exemption, but the range of preferences granted to those RACs is much smaller. For instance, an RAC affiliated with a Baptist denomination may not be able to grant housing preferences to students of other Christian denominations. Some RACs may not qualify for an exemption in states which omit the "in connection with" or "in conjunction with" phrase, because this phrase seems to reduce the degree of affiliation a religious organization must have with its educational institution for the latter to come under the exemption clause.

Other states, although not proffering a "religious organization" exemption, do provide some possibility of an RAC exemption. These exemptions more or less demand that a qualifying organization be a "religious corporation,"[58] and most RACs may find it difficult to fulfill such a requirement.

About ten states[59] provide no exemption for RACs from their fair housing laws. For the most part, the laws in these states nonetheless seem limited in their applicability to RACs inasmuch as there is no persuasive indication that any of the housing laws are intended indirectly to control RAC admissions policies. Some of these states specifically allow for single-sex housing,[60] and it is reasonable to presume that the other states would not bar such an arrangement. No state has any policy which manifests an intent to exercise direct state control over admissions to RACs. This is not to say that an RAC could legally exercise a religious preference in the *allocation* of student housing, which would constitute a *de jure* restriction. However, RACs may lawfully choose to limit housing accommodations to *students*, although this may result in a *de facto* restriction of housing to members of one denomination or one sex. One may argue that if a state intended to control RAC admissions via its fair housing law, it would have specifically established such a policy. If an RAC makes its admissions selections in good faith, i.e., not just to avoid the housing law, it should have no difficulty in giving housing preferences to its enrolled students.

Some states offer RACs the possibility of exemption from their public accommodations laws yet specify no such exemption from their fair housing laws.[61] Although these two pieces of legislation are separate—which reinforces the conclusion that private housing facilities are not places of public accommodation—it may be argued that such states have shown some intent not to indirectly affect admissions to RACs by enacting the housing statutes.

What types of housing facilities would come under the fair housing laws? Some laws bar discriminatory housing practices by "any person,"[62] while others only focus on the "owner" of the housing accommodation.[63] An owner is generally defined to include "any person having any legal or equitable right of ownership or possession or the right to rent or lease housing accommodations,"[64] with a "person" usually including any individual or group of individuals.[65] Under almost all of the fair housing laws, all RAC-owned housing facilities (e.g., dormitories) will be covered. Although hotels are usually thought of as places of public accommodation,[66] some statutory definitions of a "housing accommodation"—e.g., a "sleeping place"[67] or "sleeping quarters"[68] —are so broad as to encompass *theoretically* even them. Other scattered accommodations, such as apartments located in nonresidential campus buildings and intended for rental by student caretakers, would also be affected by the laws.[69]

Where states prohibit "any person" from engaging in housing discrimination, RACs may even be held responsible for certain illegal practices involving non-RAC-owned housing accommodations. For example, an RAC that distributes housing lists[70] (e.g., concerning the availability of privately-owned off-campus apartments) which are made unavailable to members of a certain race, religion, or sex may be subject to fair housing provisions even though the RAC is not an "owner" of the apartments.

Many states specifically prohibit the publication of a housing listing that expresses "directly *or* indirectly" some unlawful discrimination.[71] A few laws have a clearer scienter requirement, prohibiting the aiding or abetting or assisting of another in the violation of the fair housing law.[72] Thus, an RAC may be in violation of a housing statute where it publishes a housing listing which lists an owner who, the RAC knows or has reason to know, maintains some unlawfully discriminatory rental policy.

Thus, state fair housing laws probably have no significant impact on an RAC's admissions selectivity. Provisions barring discrimination on account of sex, religion, and marital status in real estate or housing transactions are potentially inapplicable to many RACs by reason of specific exemptions or by a lack of a legislative intent to control RAC admissions policies. Since an RAC is always free to limit its housing accommodations to or give preference to its own students, the arrangement of those housing facilities will normally be deemed a lawful product of the RAC's *admissions* procedures unless, at least, those procedures purposefully discriminate on the basis of race, color, or national origin. The effect of housing laws on RACs may ultimately be determined by the reasonableness of the RAC's selection policy, as well as by the effectiveness of state enforcement procedures. RACs generally have the freedom to manage their housing procedures in a reasonable manner, including the freedom to draft advantageous housing contracts, and to

limit housing accommodations to their students, and to maintain single-sex dormitories. This conclusion is partly predicated, of course, on the belief that states probably do not (and would not) intend to regulate admissions to RACs.

Beyond the comprehensive anti-discrimination laws, states may put restrictions on an RAC's use of its facilities whenever the states finance the construction or renovation of RAC-owned buildings. About half the states[73] constitutionally and/or statutorily prohibit distribution of any form of aid to denominational institutions. Some states, although they do not specifically bar state aid to religion, simply have never given any.[74]

At least eleven states[75] have passed higher education facilities construction acts, however, and many others have established similar aid programs.[76] Some states[77] give RACs only a slight hope or a future possibility that some kind of aid will be available to them.

Most of the states which suggest that they would support RAC-facility construction also place restrictions on the type of programs which are conducted in those facilities once the aid is given. Some laws state that such buildings are limited to secular uses,[78] while some ban sectarian instruction in them.[79] Some aid covenants, however, either directly or indirectly require religious nondiscrimination in RAC admissions.[80] RACs in those states may be induced to alter their admissions policies in order to benefit from the states' financing programs.

A group of state laws which may affect the cost of building and/or renovating RAC facilities are architectural barrier laws favoring the handicapped. Many of these statutes accompany state constitutional provisions which declare equal rights of access for the handicapped, and nearly all states have some barrier-free legislation.[81] Most of the barrier-free statutes apply only to facilities supported by the state or local governments,[82] however, and only three statutes[83] demand that existing facilities actually be modified to suit the handicapped. Thus, the impact of state handicap legislation on RACs may be minimal. Many states do specify the equal rights of the handicapped in their civil rights laws, but most of those states simultaneously allow RACs the possibility of exemption.[84] In

states where the handicap laws are strictly enforced, however, RACs may have to cater to
the handicapped by modifying campus housing
and places of public accommodation and by admitting the disabled on a nondiscriminatory
basis.

The existence and enforcement of state safety
laws can inflate an RAC's operating costs and
dictate the manner in which an RAC manages
its campus. The most comprehensive safety
laws are modeled after the federal Occupational
Safety and Health Act of 1970.[85] The Act
enables the Secretary of Labor to set safety
standards and places a duty on each employer
to "furnish to each of his employees employment and a place of employment which are free
from recognized hazards that are causing or are
likely to cause death or serious physical harm
to his employees."[86]

An "employer" for purposes of the federal
law is any person, excluding a state, engaged in
a business affecting commerce, who has
employees.[87] The most recent federal regulation concerning the OSHA's coverage states
that "[c]hurches or religious organizations, like
charitable and nonprofit organizations, are considered employers under the Act where they
employ one or more persons in secular activities."[88] Cited as an example of an employer-
religious organization is "a private school or or-
phanage owned or operated by a religious
organization."[89]

Although at least one-half of the states do not
have comprehensive occupational safety plans,
RACs in those states will still be subject to the
provisions of the federal safety law. Moreover,
most of the states that have not enacted OSHA-
type legislation have passed other laws which
generally codify the more limited duty of an
employer to exercise reasonable care for the
safety of his employees,[90] or which empower
the state Commissioner of Labor to make investigations and set some safety standards.[91] RACs
are not covered under two of these state laws.[92]

The policy behind OSHA, however, is to
assist the states in developing and enforcing
their own occupational safety plans.[93] The
federal law requires that states wishing to
regulate work safety submit a plan which must

be both initially and thereafter periodically approved by the Secretary of Labor.[94]

Twenty-four state plans (laws) have been
given initial approval[95] but apparently none of
them as yet has been given "final" approval,[96]
although supplements to ten state plans were
approved in 1980.[97] Most of the state plans
resemble the federal plan in content,[98] and in
only two states[99] are RACs exempt by definition from compliance with the laws. Thus, most
RACs are "employers" for purposes of the state
occupational safety laws and will be subject to
the provisions of both those laws *and* the
federal law, at least until the state plans receive
ultimate federal approval. This means that
RACs must meet the requirements of all relevant safety standards (at some cost) or risk a
civil or criminal penalty[100]for noncompliance.

Other state safety laws include food and
beverage health standards,[101] housing standards,[102] and fire safety laws.[103] All of these
laws are at least theoretically necessary for safe
and orderly living, and it is only reasonable that
RACs must comply with those provisions.
Landlord and tenant laws also create an obligation to maintain safe housing accommodations,[104] although RACs are usually exempt.
Architectural barrier laws can be viewed as
safety laws, too, especially with respect to handicapped persons.

The true impact of all of the state anti-
discrimination and safety statutes will always
be measured by the extent to which those laws
are enforced. This suggests a *de facto* limitation
on the applicability of facilities legislation to
RACs, i.e., a limitation which is not inherent in
the laws themselves. Enforcement will probably always be a difficult task for any comprehensive legislation, but the degree of compliance that is demanded will change over time.
Public support or pressure for all of these laws
may wane in one decade and wax in another.
On the other hand, the public interest in or sym-
pathy for the plight of private colleges may
similarly rise or fall with the passing of years.
The impact of all state facilities legislation on
RACs may ultimately depend on public desire
for stricter or more relaxed implementation.

6. Taxation

Charitable, religious, and educational institutions are often given special tax treatment in the form, for example, of exemptions from inheritance, income, property, and sales taxes. Moreover, personal and corporate income tax deductions and, more rarely, credits for contributions spur charitable giving in favor of these institutions.

The federal and most state authorities exempt transfers to RACs from gift, inheritance and estate taxes which the donor (or donee) migh otherwise have to pay, thus providing tax incentives for gifts to RACs. By not paying a tax the donor is able to retain or contribute anew the moneys that would otherwise have been paid in taxes. Moreover, knowledge that the donee will not be taxed encourages donors by making their total donation available to the RAC. For some, denying the government the amount that would have gone to taxes may create an incentive.

The government encourages such private support because the private institutions involved are either relieving the government of a burden it might have to assume in the institution's absence or because the institution is providing a service thought to be socially beneficial.

A tax concession, in some ways, presents the most desirable method of granting such support. Politically a more subtle method of encouraging socially desirable activity than a direct grant, tax concessions usually generate less public debate than appropriation of tax moneys. Furthermore, the tax concession device allows the marketplace, through the donor's selection of beneficiaries, to determine which institutions will receive how much help, sparing the government the necessity of selecting among potential donees.

This indirect method of assisting RACs also tends to mute the separation of church and state debate which might surround more direct methods of support. Conversely, tax exempt status for religious institutions also prevents any controversy from arising from a governmental attempt to tax such organizations. RAC and other private colleges certainly ease some of the governmental burden of providing higher education, and it is therefore neither unreasonable nor inappropriate for the government to provide support to them.

A. Income Tax

Perhaps most prominent among these subsidies is the income tax exemption afforded RACs and other religious, charitable and educational institutions by Section 501(c)(3) of the Internal Revenue Code. Under this provision, RACs need not pay any tax on any of their income which is related to or derived from their exempt endeavors. However, any income derived from a source unrelated to the institution's exempt purposes, called "unrelated business income," is subject to federal income taxation.[1]

To qualify for the federal income tax exemption, no part of the RAC's net earnings may inure to the benefit of any private individual or shareholder and no substantial part of the RAC's activities may involve the carrying on of propaganda or otherwise attempting to influence legislation.[2] RACs usually meet these two statutory criteria and the requisite public benefit test[3] since they are organized to benefit the general public and not just a limited group. Therefore, virtually all RACs qualify for the federal income tax exemption.

This tax exemption, once qualified for, remains a revocable privilege. A discriminatory admissions policy found contrary to public policy may be grounds for such a revocation of an RAC's tax exempt status.[4] Nonetheless, certain RAC admissions policies differentiating on the basis of religious background are not viewed as contrary to public policy and are therefore permissible.[5]

But how far should the government inquire into the RAC's founding religion and into its social desirability? By finding some beliefs more worthy of a tax exemption than others, the government would probably violate the establishment clause of the Constitution[6] by favoring one religion over another. The government, generally anxious to sidestep such delicate issues, is therefore generally quite liberal in granting tax exempt status to RACs.[7]

Generally, states with income taxes are also generous in granting RACs state income tax exemptions. Of the forty-six states with some form of state income tax, all but two, North Carolina and Maine, specifically exempt RACs and organizations like RACs from their income tax.[8] The states providing an exemption base it to some extent on the standards established for the federal exemption. Some states plainly provide that a state exemption depends on the tax-paying entity's federal tax exempt status.[9] Some provide an exemption by reference to the federal definitions of taxable income which, for an RAC, would be limited to its unrelated business income.[10] Others merely incorporate the federal requirements—no private benefit or excessive lobbying—without any specific reference to the organization's federal exempt status.[11] Still others focus on only one of the federal requirements: California, for example, stresses the no-private-benefit test and expands the concept to require that RAC assets be ir-

revocably dedicated to exempt purposes in the event of the RAC's dissolution.[12]

Most states also retain the federal "unrelated business income" concept, subjecting such income to taxation. A few states will exempt an RAC's unrelated business income but only if the moneys are put back into the organization for use in its exempt functions.[13]

Many states require that an annual report be filed concerning the RAC's continuation of its exempt activities.[14] Such requirements must be strictly complied with in order to preserve what is probably one of the RAC's most important financial assets—the income tax exemption.

B. Inheritance, Estate and Transfer Taxes

Transfers to RACs are deductible from a decedent's gross estate in arriving at the federal estate tax payable by the estate.[15] This exemption is based on the same policy justifications underlying the RAC's income tax exemption. The government wishes to encourage private benefaction to institutions which provide a socially beneficial educational service and private provision of higher education relieves some of the pressure on government to spend public moneys in order to provide it.

A federal estate tax deduction for transfers to RACs is allowed only when the recipient institution has received a Section 501 income tax exemption,[16] which virtually all RACs have received.

Every state, except Nevada,[17] also imposes some sort of death tax on their residents' estates through estate, inheritance, succession or transfer taxes. Since these terms are often used loosely, almost interchangeably, the reader is cautioned that the "inheritance" tax and "estate" tax labels may mean different things in different states.

Approximately two-thirds of the states still have an "inheritance" tax, i.e., a tax levied on the right to receive property by descent.[18] A true inheritance tax is paid by the donee,[19] although in many states the estate or its administrator is made primarily liable.[20] Payment of the tax is generally apportioned to each recipient's distributive share by virtue of the Unified Credit Act.[21]

In the absence of the decedent's express intention that his charitable bequests bear some of the taxes, charitable bequests, such as those to RACs, are not subject to apportionment of any of the estate's tax liability, since these bequests, deductible as they are, do not give rise to any estate tax liability in the first place. Almost all states imposing an inheritance tax exempt transfers to RACs from their tax.[22] They do so to encourage such private benefaction and to relieve the RAC from any financial burden imposed in those states which tax the recipient of the transfer.

All states, except Nevada, impose an estate tax. An estate tax differs from an inheritance tax in that it is imposed on the privilege of transmitting, not receiving, property by death.[23] The estate, rather than the recipient, must pay the tax. Sometimes a state estate tax is computed similarly to an inheritance tax, as either a straight or accelerating percentage of the taxable estate.[24] However, most states[25] compute their estate tax not as a percentage of the taxable estate but in relation to the amount of a credit for state death taxes allowed against the federal estate tax.[26]

These states impose death taxes in an amount equal to the allowable maximum federal credit merely to rechannel to the state moneys which would otherwise go to the federal government in estate taxes. Many states with existing inheritance and estate taxes took full advantage of the credit by imposing an additional estate tax,[27] in an amount which would oftentimes equal the unused portion of the federal credit after the pre-existing taxes had been computed and subtracted. Many statutes explicitly provided that imposition of this additional estate tax should not increase the tax burden on the estate by limiting the total amount of estate taxes to what they would have been in the additional tax's absence,[28] thereby guaranteeing a mere rechanneling of funds. Most states without this explicit provision accomplish the same purpose by imposing the additional tax in an amount equal to the residual of the federal credit after the other state death taxes have been computed.

Transfers to RACs are generally not exempted from this additional tax,[29] even though many states imposing the new tax exempt transfers to RACs from their other estate and inheritance taxes,[30] since no one bears a heavier

tax burden because of the additional tax; it is a mere rechanneling of federal estate taxes to the states.

Exemptions under state inheritance and estate tax schemes not based on the federal credit for state death taxes are still helpful to the extent the tax otherwise imposed would not be credited against the federal estate tax, for example, in estates too small to be subject to federal estate tax. This will more often be the case as the estate tax reforms of 1981 take effect. Moreover, in those states in which inheritance taxes are generally paid by the recipient, specific exemptions are most certainly beneficial to RACs.

C. Gift Tax

Only about fifteen states impose a gift tax and all exempt gifts to RACs.[31] These states usually effect their exemption by incorporating the federal definition of "taxable gift" into their state statute.[32] Since gifts to RACs are not federally taxable, they are not taxable under these state schemes as well.

D. Income Tax Deductions or Credits for Gifts to RACs

Since RACs receive a major portion of their revenues from private contributions, they are very interested in tax incentives to potential RAC contributors. Generally, contributions are deductible from a contributor's income in computing federal income tax when the organization contributed to is exempt from federal income tax under Section 501(c)(3) of the Internal Revenue Code. Since RACs are income tax exempt under Section 501, contributions to RACs are deductible on the contributor's federal income tax return.[33]

Special tax incentives for contributions to RACs and other exempt organizations are given for the same reasons underlying the organization's tax exempt status. Increasing the public's desire, incentive, and ability to support organizations such as RACs, tax incentives increase the flow of contributions to RACs, thus helping RACs provide educational services to the public and thereby relieving some pressure on the government to do so.

Contributors to RACs could be given favorable tax treatment through the use of either a deduction for the amount of the contribution from the taxpayer's income or through the use of a credit against the actual taxes due for some or all of the taxpayer's contribution.

Under the federal income tax system contributions to RACs are a deduction allowed against the taxpayer's income.[34] The tax saved through the taxpayer's charitable deduction reduces his cost of giving thereby making him more attracted and financially able to contribute. The taxpayer's cost of giving to organizations like RACs is even lower if his state allows a similar charitable deduction (or a credit) against state income taxes.[35]

Of the approximately forty-four states with income taxes,[36] only a few refuse special consideration to contributions to exempt organizations like RACs.[37]

About thirty-five states provide a deduction similar to the federal deduction for contributions to RACs. Generally, a deduction is allowed for both individual and corporate taxpayers, but some states with both corporate and individual income taxes provide a deduction only for corporations[38] or only for individuals.[39] Since policy reasons for permitting such a deduction are the same for both individual and corporate contributors, this dichotomy is, at best, difficult to explain.

The majority of states with a deduction explicitly tie it to the federal deduction in one of three ways. The state may use the federal definitions of adjusted gross income and taxable income[40] to determine state income tax liability.[41] Since these definitions already incorporate deductions for contributions to RACs, a state deduction is in effect provided in the computation of the state income tax. Other states permit a state deduction for contributions only if a corresponding federal deduction was actually taken on the taxpayer's federal return.[42] The third method of incorporating the federal deduction, exemplified by the Colorado statute, allows a deduction for contributions to RACs if a federal deduction could have been taken, whether or not it actually was.[43] This helps the contributor whether or not it was advantageous for him to itemize on his federal return.

At least three states, Idaho, Indiana, and Michigan, allow a credit against state income taxes due for a stated percentage of the taxpayer's contribution to an RAC.[44]

Indiana allows fifty percent of a taxpayer's contribution to be set off against state income tax, up to a limit of twenty percent of state tax liability. The credit may not exceed $100 for single returns and $200 for joint returns. Corporations are allowed to credit half of their contributions up to a $1000 credit or ten percent of the corporation's adjusted gross income, whichever is less.[45] Michigan provides a tax credit very similar to Indiana's.[46]

Idaho allows a fifty percent credit for contributions to RACs up to a maximum of $50 for individuals and $500 for corporations.[47] Idaho has also retained its traditional deduction for contributions in addition to the newly enacted tax credit mechanism.[48] Though the choice of which device will yield the greatest tax savings seems obvious — a $100 contribution would merit the maximum $50 credit for an Idaho taxable income of at least $6000, while a traditional $100 deduction for the contribution made by the taxpayer in this seven and one-half percent tax bracket would only yield a tax savings of $7.50 — certain generous contributors with large incomes could benefit from using a deduction which is limited only to a percentage of income and not by an absolute amount. A gift of $1000 could reduce the contributor's state tax liability $75 through the deduction, but only $60 through the credit.[49]

While tax credits for contributions are extremely beneficial, the lower the maximum limit on the credit, the greater the need for allowing a deduction-type alternative, particularly in the case of a large contributor in a state with a very progressive income tax.

Both types of contribution tax incentives are extremely important in channeling funds to RACs and RAC officials should familiarize themselves with state tax laws in order to inform their potential contributors of various tax advantages. In stating the tax advantage through specific examples, however, they should recall that any reduction in *state* income tax liability will, *pro tanto*, reduce the contributor's potential *federal* tax deduction for state income taxes, so that the state savings is partly nullified for the contributor who itemizes federally.

Property Tax

Historically, property used for educational or religious purposes has been specifically exempted from state property taxes.[50] The overwhelming majority of states provide such an exemption in their constitutions.[51] Others so provide by statute.[52] In any event, all states provide some sort of property tax abatement for religious and educational institutions and therefore for RACs.

RACs generally qualify for a property tax exemption as educational institutions. RACs and educational institutions in general may qualify for property tax abatement under other types of exemptions when a specific exemption for educational institutions is not provided. In Massachusetts, RACs can qualify under an exemption for scientific institutions[53] and, in Utah, under an exemption for charitable institutions.[54] States also provide property tax exemptions for religious institutions, but these exemptions are generally too narrowly defined to include RAC property beyond campus chapels, churches or monasteries, except perhaps at Bible colleges or seminaries.

When an RAC's property tax exemption emanates from its status as an educational institution, the property must be used for an educational purpose. "Educational purpose", however, is open to many different definitions. Consequently, states may apply different standards in determining when property owned by an educational institution is used for educational purposes so as to further the state's interest in education sufficiently to warrant a property tax concession.

Many state property tax exemptions for colleges specify that exempt property must be used "exclusively" for educational purposes.[55] Here again, however, various interpretations are possible. At the one extreme, Alaska gives "exclusive" its strictest interpretation.[56] Any technical deviation from a purely educational use of the exempt property could be grounds for revocation of the exemption. Michigan's equally demanding standard requires that the "solely for educational purposes" provision be strictly construed.[57]

Many other states interpret the "exclusively for educational purposes" standard loosely so that property used incident to traditional education and not used for buildings of instruction,[58] but nonetheless furthering the students' education[59] will qualify for an exemption. Under this looser standard, the property need only have an educational function as its main purpose or use or, to borrow Florida's phraseology, should be used "predominantly for educational purposes."[60] An incidental or minor type of noneducational use will not terminate this type of property tax exemption.

Other states set similar standards for the use of exempt RAC property by requiring that the property be used directly,[61] actually,[62] solely,[63] regularly,[64] primarily,[65] or purely[66] for educational purposes or to further the institution's educational purposes.[67] The vagueness of these statutory standards requires that case law be consulted in order to determine with some degree of certainty which RAC property used in which way warrants a state property tax exemption.

The actual use made of RAC property, not its stated function, determines the property tax exempt status.[68] A related principle, that the exemption is determined by the use of the property and not by the use of the profits realized,[69] emphasizes that the property itself must be used in an exempt purpose, not merely the profits from its lease or rental for a non-exempt purpose. Some states go so far as to say that no RAC property rented or leased so that any income is derived therefrom, warrants a property tax exemption.[70] Other states, taking a more tempered approach, exempt RAC-owned, income-generating property if the income from the property is used to further the RAC's educational purposes.[71] This gives RACs greater freedom to use their property in its most productive capacity and further promotes the states' purpose of indirectly assisting RACs.[72]

States try to prevent abuse of these income-generating property tax exemptions in several ways. Some states specify the use to which the funds derived from exempt property must be put. In Alabama, for example, the gate funds from RAC stadiums must be used to benefit the college's athletic associations or the stadiums will lose their tax exemption.[73] Other states guard against abuse by setting an upper limit on the amount of income which can be gotten from exempt property.[74] Some states set an absolute acreage limit on the exempt property an RAC may hold, regardless of income generation.[75] Although quantitative limits do not guarantee against abuse, they can help to minimize it.

Most states, recognizing that dormitories and other student housing further an RAC's educational purposes, exempt them from property taxation.[76]

Certain states exempt RAC-owned property used as housing for RAC faculty, administrators and even other RAC employees.[77] This type of exemption is generally allowed only when it can be shown that providing such housing furthers the RAC's general educational purposes, for example by promoting the efficient administration of the institution.[78] It has been argued, though less effectively, that housing provided to attract higher caliber faculty also furthers the institution's educational purposes.[79] Of course, residences for clergy serving as teachers may be property tax exempt under corresponding exemptions for religious institutions.[80] Specific statutes and case law must be consulted.

Some states do not require a present exempt use of the property by the RAC as a prerequisite for exemption, but are willing to exempt land held by an RAC for future expansion as long as the intended use of the land will further the RAC's educational or religious purposes. Land held as the site for a new college library is exempt under this type of provision. A few states will even exempt RAC property not currently being used, and held solely for investment purposes if the proceeds from such investment will be used for exempt purposes.[81] Most states, however, require a planned exempt use and will not exempt property held solely for investment.[82]

RACs also hold property in forms other than real property. Generally an RAC's personal property is exempt from property taxation either because the state's property tax (and therefore exemptions) cover both real and personal property,[83] or because personal property

is specifically exempted from a separate personal property tax under a provision parallel to the state's real property tax exemption.[84] States imposing an intangibles tax on items such as stocks, bonds, patents, and copyrights often exempt RACs from this tax, as well.[85]

F. Sales Tax

Many states raise a substantial amount of revenue by taxing the sale of goods within the state. With the exception of New Mexico and Alaska,[86] all states imposing a sales tax exempt sales made to RACs and to other nonprofit organizations.[87] Though some critics feel that exemptions unnecessarily complicate tax records and bookkeeping,[88] the states themselves obviously think that supporting the state's charitable, religious, and educational institutions through even such a minor exemption is worth the costs.

The method and magnitude of the sales tax exemption vary from state to state. Some states broadly exempt sales to and by RACs at the time of purchase and sale. Others, like North Carolina, use the refund method to return to exempt organizations sales taxes paid by them,[89] which is, of course, most cumbersome.

In order to qualify for an exemption, in most states, an eligible RAC must obtain a certificate of exemption from the state tax commission.[90] Most states also require that sellers to RACs keep a record of all tax-exempt sales.[91]

Virtually all states with a sales tax also have a compensating use tax, i.e., a tax on the consumption, use or storage within the state of goods purchased outside the state. The use tax, generally equal in amount to the sales tax, discourages out-of-state purchases made to avoid the state sales tax. Since RACs are usually exempt from the sales tax, they are usually given a parallel use tax exemption for their out-of-state purchases.

Each state puts some limit on the goods eligible under the exemption in order to ensure that persons not intended to be exempt, e.g., private individuals employed by RACs, not buy under the RAC's tax exemption. The most common limitation restricts the exemption to the purchase of goods used for the RAC's educational purposes. This fairly broad language will encompass an RAC's educational needs without affording a wholesale exemption which might be subject to abuse. Accurate record-keeping and documentation also prevent abuses, which could otherwise ultimately result in revocation of the RAC's sales tax exemption.

Other states further limit the exemption extended to RACs. For example, Hawaii's broad general excise tax exemption is not available when the goods will be used to produce income even though the income would be used for the RAC's generally exempt purposes.[92] Mississippi limits its exemption differently, extending it only to sales to RACs of those goods which will not be resold.[93]

Some statutes specify the items whose sale to RACs is exempted from sales and use tax. North Carolina,[94] for example, exempts the sale to RACs of building materials and supplies to be used in the construction, renovation or remodeling of buildings furthering the RAC's educational purposes. The most common limitation on such building materials exemptions is typified by Kansas' refusal to exempt buildings to be used for human habitation.[95]

Although there is generally no blanket exemption for all sales *by* RACs, sometimes the sale of certain fund raising items and items otherwise exempt by statute will qualify for an exemption. Also certain occasional sales by RACs are not subject to sales tax when they are limited to a certain number of days per year at certain specified intervals.[96]

Generally, the more an RAC appears to be engaged in the regular, commercial sale of goods at retail, the less likely a sales tax exemption will be allowed.[97] This not only protects local business from "unfair" competition, but also reflects the fact that the RAC was not originally exempted to carry on retail operations.

While sales *to* RACs are tax exempt because the *RAC* is the purchaser, sales *by* RACs are not generally sales tax exempt merely because the *RAC* is the seller. Certain items typically sold by RACs, however, may be exempt when sold by anyone, including an RAC.

Several states, for example, exempt the sale of all religious publications and writings;[98] others more broadly exempt "materials used for religious purposes."[99] West Virginia exempts the sale of textbooks[100] and Massachusetts the

sale of books required for instructional purposes within an educational institution.[101]

Tuition is generally not subject to sales tax. Indeed, most states exempt from the sales tax all services, or at least professional and personal services, and therefore either implicitly or explicitly exempt tuition as a service.[102]

The sale of food or food products, generally in the form of groceries to be consumed off the premises[103] with some additional preparation necessary, are sales tax-exempt in at least one-half the states having a sales tax.[104] This common food exemption generally excludes the sale of candy, soda pop, sandwiches, or any hot food which is served ready to eat.[105] Any foods packaged in a container or served with table service making it possible to consume the item immediately[106] are usually not exempted from the sales tax under a food or grocery exemption. (A meals tax exemption might apply[107] but a straight sales tax exemption probably will not.) Since each state carefully classifies this type of exemption in many different ways, a careful reading of the statute is essential to determine which food items served in which ways are exempt.[108]

Meals sold on a contract basis are exempt from sales tax in North Dakota[109] and New York.[110] A contract meal plan means the sale of meals with no cash being exchanged at the time the meal is served.[111]

RAC cafeterias and snack bars not open to the general public need not charge any sales tax in Nebraska,[112] while Indiana and Kentucky limit their exemption only to meals served to students.[113]

A few states grant a sales tax exemption to school meals. Some limit it to public schools.[114] Others extend it to both public and private schools, but only for primary and secondary grades.[115] Meals served at RACs obviously fall outside this type of exemption.

New Hampshire's meal tax does extend an exemption for meals served at RACs, as long as the profit from their sale helps further the RAC's originally exempted purposes.[116] This limitation appropriately furthers the state's objective of supporting education.

G. Other Taxes

Many states levy a tax similar to a corporate income tax on the privilege of doing business within their state. RACs are generally not subject to these taxes since providing educational services is not considered doing business in the usual sense.

West Virginia does not impose its business and occupation tax on RACs since RACs are not businesses organized for profit and therefore are not doing business within the state.[117] RACs are also exempted from the New York,[118] Virginia,[119] and Mississippi[120] corporate franchise taxes, which are generally imposed on the corporate franchise granted by the state to carry on business within the state.

Certain state taxes imposed on a more local basis provide special exemptions for RACs. Mississippi RACs are exempt from local privilege taxes,[121] as are Oregon RACs.[122] Wisconsin exempts RACs from their county tax.[123] New York extends this special local treatment by providing RACs with city services such as water, sewage and garbage pickup at no charge.[124]

Certain states, Nevada[125] for example, do not charge RACs the standard incorporation filing fees. Virginia exempts RACs from the payment of recording fees on newly acquired property[126] and Illinois exempts RACs from their real estate transaction tax.[127]

In many states, RAC-owned motor vehicles are exempt from the standard state licensing fees. Missouri provides a limited motor vehicle use tax exemption applicable to RACs when the vehicles have been purchased by a religious institution to be used primarily for regular religious functions.[128] Vehicles loaned to RACs in Virginia are given a limited exemption from that state's sales and use tax.[129]

Many states imposing entertainment-related taxes provide exemptions which apply to RACs. Admissions and amusement taxes are generally included within the ticket price of a sporting event, movie, or other place of amusement. In Maryland,[130] Connecticut[131] and Mississippi,[132] among other states, these taxes are not charged on admission to activities which are sponsored by an RAC and whose proceeds are used for the RAC's generally exempt purposes. South Carolina also grants RACs an admission tax exemption, but does not exempt the receipts from college athletic events under the state license tax on admissions.[133] Missouri's exhibition tax does not apply to shows and performances sponsored by RACs.[134]

State room and hotel occupancy taxes do not generally apply to RACs because the rental of dorm rooms does not meet the statutory requirement of offering sleeping accommodations to the public, the object of the tax.[135] Campus hotels open to the public, however, would generally be subject to such taxes. Nonetheless, some states, extending exemption beyond RAC dormitories, exempt even a hotel operated by an RAC for generally exempt purposes.[136]

7. Fund Raising

A. Charitable Solicitation

Charities play an important role in the community, a role that must be enlarged as the federal budget in such areas is decreased. Obviously, the public sector could not accept responsibility for or do justice to the numerous and varied tasks performed by the over 800,000 nonprofit organizations in the United States.[1] Conversely, charitable giving fills needs of donors as well as of recipients. Dedicating time or money to a cause one believes in is a good expression of individualism. Government sponsorship of social programs can reduce the individual's opportunities to direct extra resources autonomously. Giving of oneself to promote social ideals fosters a spirit of voluntarism and encourages exercise of discretion. Maintenance of charities improves community mental health.

In the past, charities performed a much broader function than they do today. Those Americans now subsidized by the government relied for survival on charity within their own community. Charity was not a panacea to ease the collective conscience of the upper middle class, an occupation for idle housewives, or just a nice thing to do; it was a necessity.[2] Indeed, charitable giving as it exists today, donations in response to an organization, institution or cause, dates at least from Benjamin Franklin, who espoused a "do-it-yourself habit of organized philanthropy."[3]

One indication of the importance of charities is the exemption of nonprofit organizations from taxation.

[O]ne stated reason for a deduction or exemption of this kind is that the favored entity performs a public service and benefit, and relieves the government of a burden which would otherwise belong to it. . . . [T]he government is compensated for the loss of revenue by its relief from a financial burden which would otherwise have to be met with appropriations from public funds and by the benefits resulting from promotion of the general welfare.[4]

Presently, Americans each year give to charity about half as much as they spend on food. In 1979, individuals donated at least $25 billion and about six billion hours of volunteer work to charitable organizations.[5] Bruce R. Hopkins, author of *Charity Under Siege: Government Regulation of Fund Raising*, writes that "rough extrapolation from available data indicates total receipts of the nonprofit sector to be in the range of $80 billion."[6] Of this sum, about $20.4 billion is given to religious organizations and $5.99 billion to educational institutions.[7]

Certain personal traits correlate with donation to charity:

College graduates give six times as much on the average as do those with only high school educations. Small town residents give more than city dwellers. The married give more than the single. The old give more than the young. The giving of time was found to correlate closely with the giving of money; the contributor of one is likely to be a contributor of the other.[8]

Individuals donating time and money to charities are naturally intolerant of charitable

49

fraud or other misuse of funds. Regrettably, incidents of fraud and misuse have recently come to light.

For example, "Stained Glass Watergate," a story in the July 1976 issue of *Esquire*, capsulized the case of the Pallotine Fathers. The Pallotines, a Catholic order based in Baltimore, Maryland, conducted direct mail solicitation of funds, collected $7.6 million in 1976, and spent approximately 2.5 cents of every dollar on missionary work. A grand jury found that the order owned extensive real estate and had helped finance the then state governor's divorce.[9] Widely publicized incidents such as this precipitated public scrutiny of charitable institutions.

Such incidents may be isolated. Probably only a small percentage of charitable funds are misused but, since this may amount to hundreds of millions of dollars, it is not surprising that the media, and consequently the public, become concerned and press for regulation and surveillance. Public response to charity fraud in turn activates legislatures to design and adopt regulatory frameworks for the supervision of private charities.

Regulation has advantages and a charity which manages funds scrupulously, honors commitments made to contributors, and establishes a good reputation has little to fear. Indeed, the deregulation of charities would presumably hurt contributions to reputable charities due to both the decrease in public confidence and the siphoning off of available funds by unsavory "charities."

The major objection to extensive regulation is the cost and trouble of preparing extensive records. A small charity may find a sizeable part of its money eaten up by costs of detailed reporting; the funds may never reach the intended beneficiaries. Protection of contributors may thwart the objectives they had in donating. Regulatory statutes must be sensitively drafted to provide adequate vigilance against fraudulent charities, without hassling credible and struggling ones. Nonetheless, there is certainly some percentage of contributions over some significant period of time that should go directly to the donors' purposes and legislation so requiring and applicable to most organizations is both reasonable and necessary.

Some forms of regulation may violate the constitutional rights of charities. Some states place a percentage ceiling on the amount a charity may spend on administrative expenses. Certain percentage approaches may be unfair to some charities with necessarily high operational expenses. Public advocacy organizations, for example, may expend almost all their donations on fixed costs. (The United States Supreme Court has ruled that an absolute percentage limitation on fund raising costs applied to advocacy-oriented groups that solicit door-to-door may be unconstitutional).[10] A new charity may spend most contributions on expenses. Finally, there is no universal way to compute the cost of fund raising. One group's records may reflect low fund raising costs while another's show expenditures far above the percentage limit. This disparity may reflect bookkeeping techniques more than substantive difference.

Charitable organizations enjoy First Amendment rights even though the speech involved may be nothing more than an attempt to raise money. They are entitled to exercise these First Amendment rights in public places. In addition, charitable groups are constitutionally guaranteed due process rights. In a recent case, a Hare Krishna group challenged, on grounds of overbreadth, a city official's power to decide whether to grant licenses to religious groups wanting to solicit funds. The federal district court, finding for the Hare Krishna group and holding such discretion in municipal authorities impermissible,[11] reaffirmed an earlier dictum that "[b]road prophylactic rules in the area of free expression are suspect. Precision of regulations must be the touchstone."[12]

In drafting regulatory schemes, states must observe certain guidelines. Bruce Hopkins suggests that:

where the purpose of the solicitation pursued by a religious organization is primarily religious, regulation of the activity must pass a test of strict scrutiny showing

1. the state has a compelling interest in undertaking this regulation
2. the statute has a secular purpose
3. the primary effect of the law neither advances nor inhibits religion [and]

4. the law does not foster extensive government entanglement in religion.[13]

In addition, Chief Justice Burger, in *Walz v. Tax Commissioner,* proposed a two-prong constitutional test for regulatory schemes: (1) Is the involvement excessive? (2) Is it a continuing one calling for official and continuing surveillance leading to an impermissible entanglement?[14]

Regulatory measures, then, should honor the Constitution, avoid excessively costly and time-consuming effort by soliciting organizations, and filter out fraudulent solicitors. This is, to be sure, no easy mandate. Nonetheless, conscientious regulators must strike this delicate balance. As Harvey Katz has stated, "Effective regulation of a particular system in the public interest requires laws prescribing proper conduct, authority to enforce those laws and people who use that authority wisely and energetically."[15]

Of the thirty-nine states which presently regulate fund raising, twenty-three exempt RACs. Where such exemptions are provided, the RAC may have to write a letter explaining its status and secure a letter of exemption. Twenty-five states require religious and educational organizations to register.[16] The trend is toward more regulation.

At present, regulatory schemes carry at least some of the following features:

1. definitions
2. registration and licensing requirements
3. annual report requirements
4. exemptions
5. registration requirements for professional solicitors
6. record keeping and public information requirements
7. percentage limitations
8. listing of prohibited acts
9. reciprocal agreement authorization
10. registered agent requirements
11. varied regulatory obligations
12. variety of sanctions.[17]

In short, the typical statute grants state agencies the authority to investigate, supervise, and maintain reports on organizations soliciting funds.

B. Games of Chance

Whether an RAC can raise money by running a bingo or a raffle for prizes depends entirely on state law. Some state laws, in turn, require the approval of the local municipality.[18]

Some states, such as Indiana and Hawaii, outlaw all gambling, with no exceptions. Others may outlaw gambling in general but make exceptions for charitable, religious, or nonprofit institutions (most RACs would fit into one or more of these categories). Even where such exceptions are made, the institution may be required to have been in existence for a certain number of years (e.g., three) before it can sponsor such games of chance. Moreover, the circumstances under which games such as bingo can be used for fund raising are themselves limited. Some states require licenses.[19] In Georgia, however, an RAC would not need a license if it operated such games only one day a year.

The regulations generally limit the value of the prizes; the location of the events and of their advertising; who can attend (New Jersey laws forbid the attendance of minors); and, perhaps most importantly, who can manage or operate the games (regulations may prohibit for example, the assistance of professional gamblers, or require that no one who manages or operates the games be paid for his services).

In Florida, the laws allow race tracks, for both dogs and horses, and *jai alai* stadiums to give a "charity day" for the benefit of certain nonprofit institutions, including RACs.

8. Miscellaneous

Probably thousands of state laws have a potential effect on RACs, but the nature of many of them makes classification futile. Delaware, for example, closes all colleges on election days.[1] Mississippi permits minors to enter RAC-owned billiard halls.[2] Although laws such as these are unique to certain states or affect RACs in a special way, others have the potential to regulate an RAC's daily operations as much as other more comprehensive laws.

One common provision among these "miscellaneous" laws is the Compact for Education which, as an interstate agreement, requires Congressional approval.[3] The vast majority of the states[4] have joined this Compact, which creates the Education Commission of the States as a forum for interstate disputes or problems involving educational matters. Many states have joined additional compacts like the New England Higher Education Compact[5] and the Southern Regional Education Compact.[6] RACs are included within the broad coverage of these compacts[7] and are open to recommendations issued by the Education Commission.

Some states[8] have coordinating boards which theoretically have the power to set standards for institutions of higher education. These boards usually deal with accreditation regulation, but some may have little real power to affect RACs.[9] Many states have college accreditation requirements, and some of these laws more or less coerce RAC compliance by threatening to curb student loan applications or scholarships or to abolish an RAC's tax-exempt status.[10]

State laws may also dictate an RAC's ability to establish life, disability, and liability insurance programs for its students or employees. Some states[11] may allow an RAC to create life insurance contracts—by naming the RAC as an irrevocable beneficiary—even though the RAC has no insurable interest in the life of the person insured. State laws may limit RACs to obtaining a certain form of disability insurance,[12] or they may allow RACs to acquire liability insurance to indemnify employees against their own work-related negligence.[13] At least one state[14] permits RACs to issue annuity policies (upon certification) and therefore receive money or property transfers. The various state insurance codes thus enable RACs to protect themselves, their students and employees, and even their alumni and financial contributors,[15] but insurance laws may also delimit the style and scope of policies procured by RACs.

Liquor control laws can affect RACs in some limited ways. Most liquor regulations and licenses are issued by state liquor boards and commissions,[16] but additional authority has been delegated to local executives to establish local rules.[17]

The sale of alcholic beverages near schools and places of worship is generally forbidden,[18] with some exceptions.[19] Some states do specifically include colleges within the meaning of the term "schools,"[20] but the scope of each law may otherwise be determined by varying state judicial interpretations or local enforcement of the law. In some states, an RAC's consent may enable a retailer to continue to sell liquor.[21] Other laws prevent fraternities and sororities from qualifying as retailers[22] and bar the sale or consumption at campus public events.[23] States frequently exempt from their restrictions wine used for religious ceremonies, but total freedom in this regard is unlikely as most states will employ some means to ensure continued compliance.[24] Educational institutions such as RACs may also be permitted to store and use alcohol for scientific or therapeutic purposes.[25] The enforcement of state liquor laws may well affect RAC students more than other RAC groups.

RAC placement offices may be affected by employment agency licensing laws and state fair employment practices statutes. For purposes of the fair employment laws, some states define "employment agency" to include persons who procure opportunities for others to work for compensation,[26] but most other states exclude the compensation requirement.[27] RAC placement bureaus may be exempt from some employment agency regulations,[28] but RACs are generally not exempt from prohibitions against minority bias in job referrals.[29]

RACs may also benefit from state immunity laws which reduce an RAC's liability for certain unlawful acts. Few states[30] grant RACs complete charitable immunity against tort liability, but more are willing to give qualified immunity to RACs (or RAC directors and trustees) for tort liability for student injuries[31] or other acts.[32]

The list of laws which may have some impact on RACs—lobbyist registration laws,[33] motor vehicle laws,[34] narcotics laws,[35] property laws[36] —is, of course, quite long. There are a few more state laws, however, which warrant special mention.

Mississippi has a law permitting the sale or lease of public school buildings for "church purposes."[37] This may be viewed as a form of state aid to RACs, depending on judicial or administrative interpretations of the law. Missouri requires RACs to give courses in American History and the U.S. and state constitutions, and demands that RAC students pass these courses in order to graduate.[38] Such requirements, which seem to go beyond any accreditation laws, could perhaps be satisfied more properly and effectively in the state's high schools rather than in post-secondary institutions.

Many states[39] have enacted campus disorder legislation, but it has been more than a decade since the nation's campuses spawned protest and violence, thus there is a lull in campus disorder laws and the future of existing statutes is uncertain.[40] These laws are special in the sense that their full effect may depend on the occurrence of an unusual sequence of social events, which ultimately generates campus disorder.

Finally, one Maine statute deserves a direct quotation:

The presidents, professors and tutors of colleges, the preceptors and teachers of academics and all other instructors of youth in public or private institutions, shall use their best endeavors to impress on the minds of the children and youth committed to their care and instruction the principles of morality and justice and a sacred regard for truth; love of country, humanity and a universal benevolence; sobriety, industry and frugality; chastity, moderation and temperance; and all other virtues which ornament human society; and to lead those under their care, as their ages and capacities admit, into a particular understanding of the tendency of such virtues to preserve and perfect a republican constitution, secure the blessings of liberty and to promote their future happiness and the tendency of the opposite vices, to slavery, degradation and ruin.[41]

PART II
State-By-State

9. Alabama

A. Corporate Status

Religiously affiliated colleges (RACs) incorporated in Alabama prior to 1955 may choose to maintain the corporate status granted to them in their charter or may re-incorporate under the Alabama Nonprofit Corporation Act enacted in 1955.[1] Since that year, however, new RACs must incorporate under the Act. The Act defines a nonprofit corporation as one in which no part of the income is distributable to its members, directors or officers.[2] The remainder of the act deals with such matters as who may incorporate,[3] the require content of articles of incorporation and bylaws,[4] the various filing fees,[5] the maintenance of a registered agent in the state,[6] and the inspection of the corporation's books.[7]

Management of the RAC is under the general supervision and control of its governing board,[8] subject to the regulations issued by the Alabama Commission on Higher Education,[9] which is empowered to authorize instructional programs at RACs.[10] The Commission's power applies "equally to all postsecondary institutions regardless of any authority that may be, or has been, conferred upon them by the Constitution or by statutes."[11] RACs are excepted, however, from an Alabama law which further regulates colleges in an attempt to provide students and educational institutions with added protection against fraud by maintaining recognized educational standards and practices.[12]

In Alabama each college governing board has the power to formulate rules governing the conferring of "academic and honorary degrees as are usually conferred by institutions of like character."[13] There are no stated exceptions for RACs.

Dissolution of a nonprofit corporation may be voluntary or involuntary. Voluntary dissolution takes effect upon the filing of the articles of dissolution in the office of the judge of probate in the appropriate county.[14] An RAC may be dissolved involuntarily by order of the circuit court in an action filed by the attorney general alleging fraud, abuse of authority, or failure to maintain a registered agent in the state.[15] Upon dissolution, the law requires that assets be distributed as follows: (1) all liabilities and obligations are discharged; (2) assets subject to a condition of return at the time of dissolution are returned; (3) assets that must be used for the purpose of the organization (but that are not subject to return) may be transferred to any organization of like purpose as provided in a plan of distribution; (4) assets are returned to members to the extent required by articles of incorporation or bylaws; (5) all other assets are distributed to any organization according to the plan for distribution.[16]

In addition, the doctrines of *cy pres* and approximation are means by which a court in Alabama can apply funds to another purpose or recipient as nearly as possible to that prescribed by the donor.[17]

B. State Support

The Alabama Private Colleges and Universities Facilities Authority Act[18] created a public corporation[19] to assist private colleges, including RACs, in the financing and refinancing[20] of the construction and remodeling[21] of structures and facilities "essential or convenient for the orderly conduct" of institutions of higher education.[22] The Authority is empowered "to finance projects for participating institutions of higher education through the issuance of authority revenue bonds and the lending of such revenue bond proceeds to the participating institution for higher education under such loan agreements or repayment contracts as the authority deems necessary or appropriate."[23] An RAC qualifies as a participating institution if it is an accredited "not-for-profit educational institution which is not owned or controlled by the state."[24] Paralleling the federal restrictions on the use of federally funded facilities, the Alabama legislation prohibits the use of a building constructed or renovated with state funds for sectarian instruction, as a place of religious worship or primarily in connection with any part of a school or department of divinity program.[25]

Although the Alabama Constitution of 1901 prohibits the lending of credit to private corporations,[26] the Alabama Supreme Court has sustained this kind of state aid on the ground that the Facilities Authority is an entity separate from the state and therefore not subject to the constitutional prohibition referred to above.[27]

In addition to providing this kind of institutional assistance, Alabama also has student grant and loan programs. The Student Grant Program,[28] which is administered[29] by the Commission on Higher Education,[30] gives financial assistance (currently $600 per year)[31] to residents who choose to attend an accredited independent college within the state.[32] These annually renewable grants[33] are available to both full-time and part-time eligible students[34] "without regard to place of residence within the state of Alabama, age, race, color, creed, sex, or national origin."[35] An eligible student includes any applicant who is (1) a high school graduate, (2) classified as an undergraduate student, (3) an Alabama resident, (4) a United States citizen, (5) enrolled in an approved institution and (6) *not* enrolled "in a course of study leading to an undergraduate degree in theology or divinity."[36] Students at an RAC

would, therefore, be eligible for these grants unless they were seminarians or divinity students.

An approved institution under the law includes any appropriately accredited[37] independent nonprofit postsecondary institution of higher learning within the state with

an academic curriculum which is not comprised principally of sectarian instruction or preparation of students for a sectarian vocation and which does not award primarily theologian or seminarian degrees. To the extent that any such institution may have a religious or denominational affiliation, it must perform essentially secular educational functions which are distinct and separable from religious activity.[38]

RACs would generally qualify unless they were seminaries or pervasively sectarian bible colleges.

The Commission on Higher Education enforces the regulations which will "ensure against the utilization of grants for religious or sectarian purposes.[39] In the case of students enrolled at RACs, the Commission must insure that the maximum amount of assistance available to a student does not exceed the per student costs for "nonsectarian secular educational purposes"[40] and that "under no circumstances shall any funds paid (under the grant) be utilized by an institution for religious, secular or denominational purposes."[41] In order to facilitate enforcement by the Commission, an RAC must segregate grant funds in a special revenue account; "identify nonsectarian expenditures of such funds in its budget;"[42] open its records to audits by authorized examiners "to the same extent, degree and scope as . . . other public educational institutions;" and annually submit to the legislature "a full accounting of its receipts, disbursements, assets, liabilities and other resources."[43]

Although the Supreme Court of Alabama issued an advisory opinion in 1973 to the effect that state aid to students attending church-related schools would be unconstitutional,[44] six years later in *Alabama Educational Association v. James*[45] the Justices sustained the Alabama statute authorizing grants for students at independent colleges because it met the three-pronged test relied on by the Supreme Court of the United States in *Roemer v. Maryland Public Works Board*.[46] The Alabama Supreme Court ruled that the statute had a secular legislative purpose and a primary effect that neither aided nor inhibited religion, and that it did not foster excessive government entanglement with religion.[47] The Court specifically held that the statute did not violate the Alabama Constitution, which states: "No money raised for the support of the public schools shall be appropriated to or used for the support of any sectarian or denominational school."[48] This was so, said the Court, because the statute does not appropriate money and the grants are not for the support of independent schools "but are for the benefit of individual students and the state educational system."[49]

Two years after enacting the Student Grant Program, the Alabama legislature established a Student Loan Program.[50] Residents of Alabama attending any postsecondary educational institution approved by the Alabama Commission on Higher Education may participate.[51] The statute defines a resident of Alabama as:

a person who attends an eligible institution within the state of Alabama, or who lives in Alabama and attends an eligible institution outside the state, or who obtains a guaranteed student loan from an approved lender.[52]

Part-time and full-time students[53] are eligible for loans.[54] Because of the broad statutory definition, students attending RACs are eligible for such loans. Unlike the Student Grant Program, this statute has no admission requirements for institutions whose students seek loans.

Another possible avenue for aid to nonpublic institutions is a provision in the state constitution that may be construed to allow, upon a two-thirds vote of the members of the Alabama legislature, appropriations of state funds to any private educational institution.[55] This section of the Constitution is in apparent conflict with another constitutional provision prohibiting appropriations to private corporations.[56] No litigation has developed to test the provision because the legislature has not appropriated funds under it.

The Commission on Higher Education also oversees Alabama's role in the Southern Regional Education Compact,[57] which provides residents with out-of-state graduate and professional instruction that is not available in Alabama. Alabama pays the student's expenses that exceed the probable costs if the program were available at an Alabama state-supported institution.[58] Public and private colleges, including RACs, are part of the Compact.[59]

C. Personnel

Hiring, Promoting and Firing

Under Alabama law the governing boards of institutions of higher education determine the "policies and procedures governing the employment, dismissal, promotion, and disciplining of university faculty and staff."[60] There is no state civil rights act nor is there a state fair employment practices law which would provide a general framework to guide employer-employee relations in Alabama.[61] Hence there is no state statute regulating or prohibiting religious preferences by RACs in their employment policies and practices. Such policies may be explicitly stated in the bylaws of an RAC or less formally adopted as a general practice of the institution. Like all employers in Alabama who affect interstate commerce, however, RACs are, of course, subject to the relevant federal discrimination and employment laws enacted under the Commerce Clause or the Fourteenth Amendment of the U.S. Constitution.

The personnel policies of RACs in Alabama must also take into consideration the Governor's Committee on Employment of the Handicapped Act[62] which promotes by rules and regulations the employment of the physically, mentally, emotionally, and otherwise handicapped citizens of Alabama.[63] Unlike the regulations issued under the federal act prohibiting employment discrimination against the handicapped, the Alabama statute does not specify that dependency on alcohol or on illicit drugs falls within the meaning of the term "handicap." Hence, RACs are presumptively free to adopt a policy that would for religiously based considerations exclude from employment at such institutions a person who consumes alcoholic beverages or uses illicit drugs.

Wages and Hours

Alabama has no minimum or overtime wage laws.[64] Alabama's few laws regulating maximum work hours for specific jobs do not directly affect RACs.[65] The governing boards of institutions of higher education in Alabama have broad discretion in fixing the salaries of faculty members and staff personnel.[66] RACs in Alabama are, of course, subject to relevant federal minimum wage laws.

Workmen's Compensation

The Alabama Workmen's Compensation Act[67] covers any corporation that has three or more employees.[68] Generally, RACs are covered unless some of their employees come within the exceptions for casual employment[69] or employment covered by another state or a federal worker's compensation law.[70] Injured employees not covered by the state's compensation law, however, may sue an RAC for damages.[71] To avoid potential suits, RACs may elect to include their exempted employees (except casual employees) within the state's compensation provisions by filing notice with the Department of Industrial Relations.[72] RACs must carry insurance or prove financial ability to compensate injured employees directly.[73]

Unemployment Compensation

The Alabama Unemployment Compensation Act[74] defines "employee" broadly as any individual who stands in a master-servant relationship to his employer.[75] The definition of "employing unit" is also inclusive, referring to "any individual or type of organization."[76] Included within the act's definition of "employer" is any employment unit that does not otherwise qualify as an employer:

a. [f]or which, within either the current or preceding calendar year, service is or was performed with respect to which such employing unit is held liable by the federal government for any federal tax against which credit may be taken for contributions required to be paid into a state employment fund;

b. [w]hich, as a condition for approval of this chapter for full tax credit against the tax imposed by the Federal Unemployment Tax Act, is required to be an "employer" under this chapter.[77]

Service performed for a religious, charitable, or educational organization constitutes employment if two conditions are satisfied.[78] First, the employees of the organization number four or more for a part of a day in each of twenty weeks.[79] Second, the service is excluded from coverage under the Federal Unemployment Tax Act. Except for service meeting these two conditions, the following do not constitute employment under the act:

service performed in the employ of a corporation, community chest, fund or foundation organized and operated exclusively for religious, charitable, scientific, literary or educational purposes, . . . no part of the net earnings of which inures to the benefit of any private shareholder or individual, and no substantial part of the activities of which is carrying on propaganda, or otherwise attempting to influence legislation.[81]

The act further exempts from the act's coverage employment services performed for a "church or convention or association of churches" or an organization whose purpose is primarily religious and whose control or support is derived from a church or convention or association of churches.[82] The services of a "duly ordained, commissioned or licensed minister of a church" or of a member of a religious order, performed in the exercise of his duties, remain outside the act's definition of employment.[83] Furthermore, the Act does not cover services provided to a school, college, or university by students who are regularly enrolled and attending classes[84] or who are participating in a program for credit that combines academic instruction with work experience.[85]

The option of electing to pay, in lieu of regular contributions, the amount of regular benefits plus one-half the amount of extended benefits paid is available to nonprofit organizations that are covered[86] by the Act.[87] This election becomes effective for a two-year period when an organization's timely written notice[88] is approved by the director of the Alabama Department of Industrial Relations and Labor.[89] Termination of this election requires the filing of a written notice with the department, effective only at the end of a calendar year.[90]

The Act does provide with some exceptions,[91] for election of coverage by employing units not otherwise subject to its provision.[92]

Collective Bargaining

Since 1943, Alabama's Bradford Act[93] has provided that every person shall be free to join or to refrain from joining any labor organization. Since there is no exemption in this act, RACs are subject to its coverage, at least to the same extent as other colleges and universities. Ten years later, moreover, the legislature enacted a Right to Work law declaring that a person's right to work shall not be denied or abridged because of membership or nonmembership in a labor organization.[94]

Indemnification and Bonding

Nonprofit corporations in Alabama, including RACs, may indemnify any present or former director or officer against expenses incurred in connection with the defense of any action or proceeding involving the person as an officer of the corporation except where negligence or misconduct in the performance of duty is found. An RAC may also indemnify any person who served at its request as a director or officer of another corporation whether for profit or not for profit. Indemnification is not exclusive of any other rights that the RAC may grant to the officer under its bylaws, by agreement, or by a vote of the board of directors or otherwise.[95]

Nonprofit corporations, including RACs, may also guarantee or stand surety for the debts or obligations of any other nonprofit corporation, provided that the articles of incorporation of the RAC include this power, and the governing board authorizes the guarantee or surety.[96]

D. Students

To be eligible for student grant and loan programs, an RAC "must not discriminate in its admissions practices on the basis of religious or denominational preference."[97] Grants are paid to approved institutions on behalf of eligible students "without regard to place of residence within the state of Alabama, age, race, color, creed, sex, or national origin."[98] In addition to these admission criteria for grant eligibility, RACs are also subject to admission regulations established by the Commission on Higher Education for postsecondary educational institutions.[99]

E. Facilities

Although Alabama has no comprehensive legislation relating to public accommodations or fair housing, two statutes do apply to facilities at an RAC. Alabama's only public accommodations law protects only the physically disabled:

The blind, the visually handicapped and the otherwise physically disabled are entitled to full and equal accommodations, advantages, facilities and privileges of all common carriers, airplanes, motor vehicles, railroad trains, motor buses, streetcars, boats or any other public conveyances or modes of transportation, hotels, lodging places, places of public accommodation, amusement or resort and other places to which the general public is invited, subject only to the conditions and limitations established by law and applicable alike to all persons.[100]

RAC hotels, motels, theaters, restaurants, and sport facilities as well as any other RAC facility to which the general public is invited are subject to the provisions of this law.

The other relevant statute relates to discrimination in housing:

For the promotion of the public peace, order, safety or general welfare, . . . municipal corporations may, within residential districts established pursuant to this article, further regulate as to the housing or residence therein of the different classes of inhabitants, but such regulations are not hereby authorized as will discriminate in favor of or against any class of inhabitants.[101]

This statute's reference to "any class of inhabitants" may be so broad as to be ineffective.

In any event, the statute does not exempt RACs from any housing regulations that may be established.

Alabama has not enacted a comprehensive OSHA statute. However, every employer is required to furnish "reasonably safe employment," to furnish and use safety devices and safeguards and to maintain a place of employment that is reasonably safe.[102] The statutory definition of an employer is all-inclusive: anyone who has "control or custody of any employment, place of employment or of any employee."[103] The only exclusion from the definition of employee is for agricultural workers and domestic servants. A federal district court has noted that "the effect of [this section] is to enlarge the common law duty of the employer."[104]

F. State Taxation

Despite the lack of a specific exemption, RACs are exempt from the payment of state income tax because they are "organizations not organized for profit but operated exclusively for the promotion of social welfare."[105]

RACs are exempted, moreover, from certain property taxes. The Alabama Constitution provides that "property devoted exclusively to religious, educational, or charitable purposes" is exempt from the *ad valorem* property tax.[106] On the authority of this constitutional provision, the legislature has exempted from payment of all state and local property taxes any property used in connection with the exempt purposes of a college.[107] But it imposed a tax on property owned by any educational, religious, or charitable institution, society or corporation "let for rent or hire or for use for business purposes—notwithstanding that the income from such property shall be used exclusively for educational, religious or charitable purposes."[108] Athletic stadiums owned and controlled by RACs which are used exclusively for the purpose of promoting intercollegiate athletics are also exempt from the *ad valorem* property taxes provided that the revenue received from the stadiums is used for the benefit of athletic associations at the college.[109] This exemption is extraordinary because it not only provides criteria for the exemption but also legislates how the RAC may spend moneys received from athletic events. It is difficult to discern any legitimate governmental interest that would warrant so specific a control over the financial management of a private institution of higher education.

Also exempt from taxation is all RAC property owned and used for the housing of students, faculty, and other employees.[110] Individuals, corporations,[111] and estates[112] may deduct from their income tax contributions and gifts made to RACs.

Alabama imposes an estate tax on the transfer of the net estate of every resident in an amount equal to the federal tax credit.[113] No specific exemption or credit is provided in the Alabama Code for property left to RACs.

Alabama has no inheritance or gift tax.

RACs engaged in the "business of selling at retail any tangible personal property whatsoever, including merchandise and commodities of every kind and character" must pay a sales tax.[114] RACs are also subject to the sales tax levied on corporations engaged in conducting places of entertainment, theaters, athletic events, skating rinks, golf courses, or any other such place which is open to the public or where an admission fee is charged.[115] RACs in the business of selling through coin-operated dispensing machines must also pay a sales tax.[116]

The only exemption from the use and consumption taxes imposed by the state of Alabama that would be available to an RAC in that state is the exemption from tax on the storage, use, or consumption of religious magazines and publications when distributed by churches or other religious organizations free of charge to students at RACs.[117]

G. Fund Raising

There is no charitable solicitation statute in Alabama.

Under Alabama law, games of chance, gambling[118] and lotteries[119] are criminal offenses.[120] There are no stated exemptions for RACs from this general prohibition.

10. Alaska

A. Corporate Status

The Nonprofit Corporation Chapter[1] of the Alaska Statutes allows the formation of a nonprofit corporation for educational purposes.[2] The Alaska Supreme Court has construed the term "educational purposes" to include "any and all branches of learning from which a substantial benefit is derived,"[3] so RACs in Alaska clearly may be organized as nonprofit corporations, with "all powers necessary or convenient to effect the purposes for which the corporation is organized."[4]

If preferable, an RAC in Alaska might be organized as a religious corporation, with the same powers as those enjoyed by a nonprofit corporation, but with a different statement of purpose, namely of "acquiring, holding or disposing of church or religious society's property, for the benefit of religion, for works of charity and education, and for public worship."[5] The emphasis in this statute is clearly on the religious character of the educational endeavor, implying a strong link between church and campus.[6] One advantage of incorporating under this statute would be to preserve the right to exercise religious preference in employment policies that is afforded to religious corporations by section 702 of the federal Civil Rights Act of 1964.[7]

As noted in the following section of this chapter, the Alaska Supreme Court has construed the state constitution to be more restrictive of aid to religiously affiliated schools than is the federal constitution.[8] Incorporators of a contemplated RAC and members of the governing board of an existing college should bear in mind that incorporation as a religious corporation could make it more difficult for the institution or its students to receive public financial assistance.

If an RAC is incorporated as a nonprofit corporation, its merger or consolidation with another institution, as well as its dissolution would be governed by Alaska's nonprofit corporation law,[9] which follows closely the provisions of the Model Nonprofit Corporation Act.[10] A merger, consolidation, or voluntary dissolution is subject to approval by the state Commissioner of Commerce.

The superior courts have jurisdiction to dissolve a college involuntarily in an action filed by the Attorney General alleging the college's (1) failure to file its annual report; (2) fraud in procuring its articles of incorporation; (3) abuse of authority; or (4) failure to name or change its registered agent.[11] A court of general jurisdiction in Alaska may involuntarily dissolve a college and supervise the distribution of its assets in a case properly brought by a member of the governing board or a creditor of an insolvent college.[12] The assets of a dissolving nonprofit corporation are to be distributed according to a schedule identical to that of the Model Nonprofit Corporation Act.[13]

B. State Support

The Alaska constitution contains language virtually identical to the religion clauses of the

First Amendment to the federal constitution.[14] It further provides that "No money shall be paid from public funds for the *direct benefit* of any religious or other private educational institution."[15] According to the Alaska Supreme Court, this provision is more restrictive of public assistance for religiously affiliated schools and for their students than the federal constitution. In *Matthews v. Quinton*,[16] for example, that court repudiated the child benefit theory articulated in *Everson v. Bd. of Education*.[17] It concluded that a program of school bus transportation designed as a safety measure for all children, whether attending public or nonpublic schools, was invalid as applied to children attending nonpublic schools, who, in the court's opinion, were directly benefited by the program.[18] The *Matthews* decision stood for nine years. As Professor Howard notes, however, "the Alaska legislature in 1972 enacted a statute virtually identical to the one struck down in that case,"[19] and the validity of the later statute has not yet been challenged.

In 1972 the legislature also adopted a program of scholarship loans available to Alaska residents attending any accredited college or university, including an RAC,[20] in Alaska. State loans to students are approved by the Commission for Post-Secondary Institutions, and the funds may be used only for tuition, books, fees, and room and board at an approved institution in Alaska.[21] Eligibility for participation in this loan program is based on merit and financial need.[22]

Alaska has also established a memorial scholarship revolving loan fund, which is administered by the executive secretary of the student financial aid committee at accredited colleges and universities in Alaska. The terms of this program prohibit discrimination in its administration on the basis of race, sex, creed, color, ancestry, national origin, or membership or nonmembership in fraternal or political societies.[23]

The legislature likewise adopted a tuition grant program available only to students attending accredited private colleges and universities in Alaska.[24] The purpose of this program is to facilitate choice among all institutions of higher education, public and private, by providing to students preferring to attend private colleges a benefit similar to the subsidy the state provides for public colleges and universities. Despite a 1977 ruling by the United States Supreme Court that a virtually identical Tennessee program does not offend against the Establishment Clause of the First Amendment to the federal constitution,[25] the Alaska Supreme Court, in *Sheldon Jackson College v. Alaska*,[26] ruled in 1979 that this tuition grant program violated the state constitutional provison prohibiting any "direct benefit" to any private educational institution.

In the *Sheldon Jackson College* case the court noted that the omission of the words "or indirect" from this provision of the state constitution demonstrated an intent to allow some forms of support for nonpublic education, and concluded that the "direct benefit" clause was "designed to commit Alaska to the pursuit of public, not private education without requiring absolute governmental indifference to any student choosing to be educated outside the public school system."[27] The court suggested three factors in determining the constitutionality of a legislative enactment under the direct benefit clause: the breadth of the beneficiary class, the nature of the use to which public funds are to be put, and the magnitude of the benefits conferred.[28]

The grant program at issue in *Sheldon Jackson College* was invalidated primarily because it benefited only students attending private colleges. If the legislature were to specify its intent to allow all Alaskans to pursue postsecondary education in the college of their choice, public or private, this difficulty might be overcome. The broadening of the beneficiary class to include all students attending college, moreover, is consistent with the articulated policy of the state not "to refuse, withhold, or deny to any person any local, state or federal funds . . . because of race, *religion*, sex, color, or national origin."[29]

Alaska is a member of the Western Regional Higher Education Compact,[30] which enables the Western Interstate Commission of Higher Education to contract with any institution in the region offering graduate programs. The Commission is empowered to act on behalf of Alaska in placing students in public or private colleges outside the state through payments of tuition and reciprocal benefits. Accredited

RACs may participate in this Compact on the same basis as any other private college.

The Governor's Code of Fair Practices[31] gives state agencies engaged in granting state financial assistance the power to deny assistance to a recipient engaged in discriminatory practices. Because the only aid programs currently affecting RACs are indirect, an argument can be made that if RACs are not eligible institutions for purposes of the student grant program, they ought not to be regarded as "recipient institutions" for purposes of the state regulations accompanying state financial assistance.[32] If, however, the direct benefit clause were to be construed otherwise than it was in the *Sheldon Jackson College* case, RACs would presumably be governed by the nondiscrimination provisions in the Governor's Code relating to employment practices and student admissions.

C. Personnel

Under Alaska's constitution the civil rights of a person may not be denied because of race, color, creed, sex, or national origin.[33] A State Commission for Human Rights has been established to investigate discrimination in the state and to order appropriate relief. The mandate of the Commission is to prevent and eliminate discrimination in the areas of employment, credit and financing, public accommodations, and housing.[34] The statutes creating the Commission declare the opportunity to obtain employment on a nondiscriminatory basis a civil right[35] and make it unlawful for an employer to refuse employment or discriminate in pay or terms of employment with regard to any person on the basis of race, religion, color, national origin, sex, age, marital status, changes in marital status, pregnancy, or parenthood.[36]

An exception is allowed if the "reasonable demands" of the position require a distinction on the basis of age, physical handicap, sex, marital status, changes in marital status, pregnancy, or parenthood.[37] In *McLean v. Alaska*, the state supreme court narrowly construed the "reasonable demands" exception to mean only "necessities of an urgent nature," and stated that exceptions should be construed very strictly against the person seeking to use them.[38]

If a particular RAC can be characterized as a nonprofit religious association, it is exempt from these general requirements because such associations are explicitly excluded from the definition of an "employer" under this statute.[39] Otherwise, however, the college may exercise religious preference in its personnel policies and practices only if the "reasonable demands" of a position, narrowly construed, required that a person of a particular religion fill that position.

Alaska's Wage and Hours Act[40] establishes minimum wage and overtime hours and compensation guidelines. RACs must follow these guidelines except when (a) service is rendered to a nonprofit religious or educational organization on a volunteer basis,[41] (b) the person employed is in a bona fide executive, administrative, or professional capacity, or that of an outside salesman (possibly including fund raisers for a college),[42] or (c) the employees are planting or tending trees, if fewer than twelve persons are so employed (possibly including groundskeepers).[43] This law and other labor laws are regulated by the state Department of Labor.

The Alaska Worker's Compensation Act[44] covers any person employing one or more employees.[45] RACs, then, are generally covered by the Act. The executive officers of an RAC are excluded from coverage,[46] but an RAC may elect to include these officers within the coverage of its insurance contract.[47] Other RAC employees excluded from coverage are part-time cleaning persons and "similar part-time or transient help."[48] RACs must carry insurance or prove financial ability to compensate injured employees directly.[49]

The state Employment Security Act[50] establishes a fund contributed to by employers out of which unemployment benefits are paid. RACs are clearly embraced within the broad definition of employer as "any unit employing one or more persons for some portion of the day within a year."[51] Nonprofit organizations may pay into the fund either contributions with respect to present wage accrual[52] or an amount equal to the full amount of regular benefits plus one-half the amount of extended benefits paid.[53] A nonprofit organization is defined by reference to the definition of a tax-exempt nonprofit corporation in the federal Internal Revenue Code: one operated exclusively for religious or educational purposes, none of whose net earnings goes to any private individual as profits, and which is not substantially engaged in propaganda or similar attempts to influence legislation.[54] Since most, if not all, RACs enjoy tax-exempt status under the federal Internal Revenue Code, they likewise qualify under this provision in the Alaska Employment Security Act.

The Act exempts domestic servants if the employer paid less than $1,000 for such services in any quarter within the current or preceding calendar year.[55] In addition, three other types of employees at an RAC are exempt from coverage: ministers or members of religious orders in the exercise of their duties, students enrolled at the RAC who are employed by the college, and individuals under 22 years of age who are enrolled at the RAC in a program which combines academic instruction with work experience.[56]

Although the public school system must be insured and indemnified by the district school board against financial loss due to liability for wrongful acts,[57] there is no parallel provision for private schools.

D. Students

The only provisions applicable to the admission of students in Alaska law refer specifically to the University of Alaska, where discrimination is prohibited on the basis of sex, color, or nationality.[58] As all colleges, including RACs, however, are "educational institutions" embraced within the definition of "places of public accommodation" by the state Commission for Human Rights, the statute forbids them to "deny any person any of its services, goods, facilities, advantages, or privileges because of sex, marital status, changes in marital status, pregnancy, parenthood, race, religion, color, or national origin."[59] Regulations issued by the Commission, however, explicitly grant to RACs a limited right to exercise religious preference, but not discrimination of any other kind.[60]

An RAC considered to be a direct recipient of

aid, as described in Section B above, would also have to comply with the provision in the Governor's Code of Fair Practices relating to nondiscrimination in student admissions.[61]

E. Facilities

Public accommodation law in Alaska is placed under the regulation of the Commission for Human Rights, with its mandate to eliminate discrimination in the state.[62] The owner of a place of public accommodation and any of his agents are forbidden "to refuse, withhold from, or deny to a person any of its services, goods, facilities, advantages, or privileges because of sex, marital status, changes in marital status, pregnancy, parenthood, race, religion, color, or national origin."[63] RACs are specifically included in the definition of "place of public accommodation," under the rules and regulations of the Commission, as "educational institutions."[64] However, RACs may be allowed to exercise religious selectivity by a further stipulation in the rules:

Any organization operated for charitable or educational purposes and supervised or controlled by or in connection with a religious organization is not prohibited from limiting admission to or giving preference to persons of the same religion or denomination or otherwise making a hiring decision that will promote the religious principles for which it is established or maintained.[65]

The rights of the handicapped under Alaska law include full and equal access to public buildings, facilities, places of public accommodation, and "other places to which the general public is invited."[66] Their rights are the same as those of other citizens,[67] and "handicapped" specifically includes the blind, the visually handicapped, and "otherwise physically disabled."[68] Architectural barrier regulations, under the control of the state Department of Public Works, insure that the public buildings and facilities in the state will be accessible to the physically handicapped, aged, or infirm.[69] These regulations apply only to those buildings which are "owned or controlled and held by the state for government or public use."[70] Because of the prohibition against any direct public benefit to RACs, Alaska does not provide assistance for the construction or renovation of facilities on those campuses. RACs, therefore, do not own buildings held by the state for public use; but whatever parts of their property are open to public use are subject to the laws ensuring access to these buildings by the handicapped.

Alaska has passed a civil rights statute which bars discrimination based on race, religion, color, national origin, age, sex, marital status, changes in marital status, pregnancy, or parenthood in the sale, lease, or rental of real property.[71] A more specific statute makes it unlawful for "the owner, lessee, manager, or other person having the right to sell, lease, or rent real property" to engage in any of a number of discriminatory real estate transactions.[72] RACs are not exempt from this provision, but regulations issued by the state Commission for Human Rights indicate that admissions would not be restricted.[73]

Residents at any educational institution[74] are excluded from coverage under the state's fair housing legislation, The Uniform Residential Landlord and Tenant Act.[75] This exemption applies to students, faculty, and staff persons using the housing facilities at any college. The statute explicitly excludes maintenance personnel living on campus from the laws regulating landlords and tenants.[76]

Student housing facilities on college campuses are regulated by the Commission on Post Secondary Education, and are required to be "appropriate, safe, and adequate."[77]

For any special events and facilities "open to the general public," whether the events are permanent or temporary, the public must be provided with toilet facilities.[78] There is no exemption for RACs from this regulation.

Alaska has enacted a comprehensive OSHA statute modeled after the federal act.[79] The purpose of the act is "to reduce the incidence of work related accidents and health hazards,"[80] and the Department of Labor is empowered to adopt and issue rules and regulations to carry out the legislative intent.[81] An employee is defined comprehensively as any person who works for an employer; and employer is defined as any person, including the state and all political subdivisions, with at least one employee.[82]

F. State Taxation

For-profit corporations in Alaska with income "derived from sources within the state" must pay a tax on net income.[83] Income from sources within the state is defined by statute as income from a business within the state or "any other activity from which income is received, realized, or derived in the state."[84] Nonprofit RACs are exempted from the payment of this tax; the exempt status under state law is defined by reference to Section 501 of the Internal Revenue Code.[85] A corporation which is required to make a return under the federal provisions must likewise file a return in Alaska.[86]

The Alaska constitution provides that "[a]ll, or any portion of, property used exclusively for non-profit religious, charitable, cemetery, or educational purposes, as defined by law, shall be exempt from taxation."[87] The constitution does not define the term "nonprofit," but the frequent reference to the Internal Revenue Code in other state tax legislation suggests that the state would follow the federal requirement that "no part of the earnings inures to the benefit of any private individual."[88]

In *McKee v. Alaska,*[89] the state supreme court construed the term "educational purposes" in the constitutional provision on property tax exemption to include "systematic instruction in any and all branches of learning from which a substantial public benefit is derived." The *McKee* case involved the training of journeyman electricians, and the court stated that the "lack of eleemosynary motives" on the part of the school's sponsors was "inconsequential" because the purpose of the exemption was "to encourage the establishment of privately supported non-profit educational institutions."[90]

RACs clearly qualify under the broad interpretation and are therefore exempt from payment of property tax unless their property is also being used for an income-producing activity. The statute describes property meeting the "exclusive use" standard as: property owned by religious organizations for residence of their ministers, or of the religious orders; structures used solely for public worship; religious administrative offices; nonprofit hospitals, and the lots adjacent to such properties, such as the parking lots required by local laws.[91]

The definition of "exclusive use" is strict. For example, even when the uses of a piece of property are closely related to an exempt activity such as a residence for teachers, such property is not exempt because the use of the property is not considered to be exclusively for an exempt purpose.[92] When a piece of property is used even in part by non-exempt parties for their private business purposes, the property is likewise not exempt.[93] Only that much of the property not used for business, rent, or profit is exempt, and a proration between the taxable and nontaxable portions is allowed.[94]

Alaska has no gift tax, but gifts made in contemplation of death or gifts which take effect at or after death are subject to the Alaskan estate tax.[95] As in many other states, the amount of the state estate tax equals the maximum allowable federal estate tax credit for state death taxes.[96] Alaska no longer has an inheritance tax.[97]

Alaska's sales tax applies only to cigarettes, real estate, fisheries, and real property deeds sales, with no exemption given to educational institutions.[98]

The state's Business License Act requires a license fee for any business engaged in within the state.[99] Educational or religious activities were formerly exempt, but this provision has been repealed.[100] Hence an RAC engaging in any form of business activity, such as the operation of a cafeteria, a gift shop, or a bookstore, must apply for a license to do so and pay the tax associated with this license.

G. Fund Raising

Alaska does not have a charitable solicitations statute. Religious corporations have the right to receive donations "to carry on or promote the objects of the corporation, but not for the purpose of obtaining revenue or profits from the property."[101] A nonprofit corporation is also allowed to take real or personal property by grant or devise.[102]

If an RAC in Alaska were to desire to raise funds by sponsoring games of chance or skill[103] it would be free to do so under Alaska law. Permits, granted annually by the Commissioner of Revenue for a $10 fee, must be obtained at least fifteen days prior to the gambling activity.[104] The institution must have been established for at least five years prior to applying for such a permit.[105] The RAC must file a report of its income and expenses,[106] and the proceeds must be used within a year for the publicized purpose.[107] The purposes for which the proceeds must be used include:

benefiting persons either by bringing them under the influence of education or religion or relieving them from disease, suffering, or constraint, or by assisting them in establishing themselves in life or by providing for the promotion of the welfare and well-being of the membership of the organization within their own community, or through aiding candidates for public office, or by erecting or maintaining public buildings or works, or lessening the burden on government but do not include the erection, acquisition, improvement, maintenance, or repair of real, personal or mixed property unless it is used exclusively for one or more of the uses stated.[108]

Most RACs would be able to conduct fund raising activities under these provisions.

11. Arizona

A. Corporate Status

Religiously affiliated colleges (RACs) may be incorporated in Arizona under that state's nonprofit corporation law, which is patterned after the Model Nonprofit Corporation Act.[1] A nonprofit corporation is a corporation "no part of the income or profit of which is distributable to its members, directors or officers."[2] The incorporation procedure follows the procedures generally required of for-profit corporations.[3] Nonprofit corporations may be organized for any lawful purpose, including educational or religious.[4]

Management of the corporation is in the hands of a board of directors whose qualifications must be set out in the articles of incorporation or in the bylaws.[5] The board of directors may include members of the religious order or group that controls the nonprofit corporation.[6] There must be at least three persons on the board of directors.[7]

Dissolution of the nonprofit corporation may be voluntary or involuntary. Voluntary dissolution may be accomplished by a vote of the membership upon resolution by the board of directors.[8] If there are no members entitled to vote, the dissolution may be achieved simply by authorization of the board of directors.[9] Upon dissolution, the statute requires that assets be distributed as follows: (1) all liabilities and obligations are discharged; (2) assets subject to a condition of return at the time of dissolution are returned; (3) assets that must be used for the purpose of the organization (but that are not

subject to return) may be transferred to any organization of like purpose as provided in a plan of distribution; (4) assets are returned to members to the extent required by articles of incorporation or bylaws; (5) all other assets are distributed to any organization according to the plan for distribution.[10]

Although the *cy pres* doctrine has not been formally adopted in Arizona, uncertainty and indefiniteness as to the ultimate recipients of a charitable gift would not by themselves cause the gift to fail.[11]

The provisions of Arizona's nonprofit corporations act are of general applicability. With minor exceptions, there are no provisions directed expressly towards religious organizations or toward RACs.

B. State Support[12]

The Arizona constitution prohibits the appropriation of public money for the support of any religious exercise, institution or establishment.[13] There are also constitutional prohibitions against the use of public funds for the aid of any church or private or sectarian school[14] and against the extension of credit of a political entity to any private association or corporation.[15]

The Supreme Court of Arizona has indicated, however, that the prohibition may not be absolute. In *Community Council v. Jordan*,[16] in which state funds had filtered through a local community social service agency to subsidize expenditures of the Salvation Army, the court stated that the issue was whether the state or any of its agencies could choose to do business with and discharge part of its duties through denominational or sectarian institutions without violating the state constitution. The court rejected a number of theories used by other jurisdictions to justify state aid to such institutions – the "doctrine of substitution," the "value received theory," the "full reimbursement plan" and the "limited full reimbursement plan." The court, however, ruled that the "partial matching plan" theory, relied upon in this case, did not violate the constitutional prohibition. The court stated:

The state constitutional provision must be viewed in light of contemporaneous assumptions concerning appropriate spheres of action for [the state and the church] . . . "[A]id" like the word "separation" must be viewed in light of contemporary society and not strictly held to the meaning and context of the past.[17]

In 1970, before the series of Supreme Court decisions in the past decade concerning the permissibility of various forms of aid to religiously affiliated schools and to children attending them, the Attorney General of Arizona suggested that a legislative proposal which provides for nondiscriminatory aid to children attending nonpublic schools, private or parochial, which include secular subjects in their curricula, would not violate the Arizona Constitution.[18]

Since then, the federal constitution has been construed both to permit some and to prohibit other federal and state programs aiding institutions of higher education[19] and their students.[20] The state constitution question, however, has not yet been squarely faced because the Arizona legislature has not enacted a general program of aid to students attending private schools. The only exception, a minor one, grants members of the National Guard a tuition fee reimbursement which can be used at any university in the state.[21]

One other program potentially provides an indirect benefit to RACs. Under the Industrial Development Program,[22] municipalities or counties may approve the development of projects sponsored under an Industrial Development Authority. The Authority is a political subdivision of the state.[23] Its purpose is the development of projects such as land, buildings, and real or personal property, suited for such purposes as the erection of convention or trade show facilities or for educational institutions operated by a nonprofit organization not otherwise funded by state moneys.[24] Projects developed by the Authority may be leased, sold, donated, exchanged, or otherwise conveyed.[25] Apparently, no funds from this program have yet benefited any RAC in Arizona.

C. Personnel

Hiring, Promoting, and Firing

The Arizona Civil Rights Act[26] prohibits discrimination in employment. It is an unlawful employment practice for an employer[27] to "fail or refuse to hire or to discharge or otherwise discriminate with respect to compensation, terms, conditions or privileges of employment because of an individual's race, color, *religion*, sex, or national origin."[28] It is also an unfair employment practice for an employer to indicate a preference in a notice or advertisement relating to employment[29] or to discriminate against an employee who has been involved, in any way, in the processing of an unfair employment practice charge.[30]

Three provisions allow RACs in Arizona to prefer employees on the basis of their religion without thereby violating the state civil rights law. First, the statute exempts from its application "a religious corporation, association, educational institution or society with respect to employment of individuals of a particular religion to perform work connected with the carrying on by such corporation, association, educational institution, or society of its activities."[31] Second, the statute excepts from its definition of an unfair labor practice religious preference in the hiring of members of a particular religion by an educational institution that is in whole or substantial part owned, supported, controlled, or managed by a particular religion or religious society or if the curriculum of the educational institution is directed toward the propagation of a particular religious belief.[32] Third, the statute also excepts religious preference by any employer where religion is a bona fide occupational qualification (BFOQ) reasonably necessary to the normal operation of the enterprise;[33] the statute also provides that it is not an unfair labor practice for an employer to indicate a religious preference in a notice or advertisement relating to employment when religion is a BFOQ.[34]

Like the federal civil rights legislation on which it is patterned, the Arizona statute contains some ambiguities and contradictions. The first of these exemptions[35] seems to grant to religious educational institutions the right to exercise religious preference in all hiring decisions regardless of the nature of the employment. This seems to be the intent of the use of the general word "activities," which is not modified by an adjective referring to a particular type of activity.[36] It is unclear, however, whether the statute allows the preference of a religion or denomination different from that of the sponsoring body or church with which the RAC is affiliated. On the one hand, the use of "a particular religion" implies "any" particular religion and is not limited to the religion or denomination of the church sponsoring the college. Indeed, if the legislature had intended a more restrictive understanding, it could easily have indicated this by using the definite article "the" before "particular religion," followed later in the section by "that" particular religion. An official in the Arizona Civil Rights Division, however, indicated that this interpretation might not be followed should the question arise.[37]

Second, there are problems with the two other exceptions provided in the statute. One of these appears in some respects at least to be duplicative of the exemption discussed above. It provides an exception for an educational institution if it is in whole or in substantial part owned, supported, controlled, or managed by a particular religion or religious society or if the curriculum of such educational institution is directed toward the propagation of a particular religious belief.[38] If this provision is meant to serve as a definition of the sort of institution to which both the exemption and the exception are applicable, RACs in Arizona that are managed by a board of trustees or that are supported substantially from sources outside a religion or religious society may not be within the exemption or the exception. Similarly, most RACs

would not be able to rely on the description of their curricular orientation as the basis for asserting religious preference in their employment practices, since most RACs do more than propagate a particular religious belief. Alternatively, if an RAC were to rely on either of these statutory definitions as the basis for its employment policies, it could be inviting litigation on the permissibility of public financial assistance to pervasively sectarian institutions.[39]

Finally, under the BFOQ provision, an RAC as an employer is clearly not limited in its religious preference to the religion affiliated with the institution. For example, a Catholic college might prefer a rabbi over a priest to teach a course on Judaism without violating the Arizona statute. On the other hand, given the generally restrictive interpretation of BFOQ that prevails in federal employment discrimination law, this exception is more limited than that available under the previously discussed sections, for it is applicable only when there is a nexus between the job and the educational activities of the institution. For example, RACs would find it much easier to prevail with a BFOQ defense where the position is in the administration or the faculty than if it were a secretarial or janitorial position.[40]

Arizona also prohibits discrimination in any manner, specifically including areas of employment, against a person who has been treated for a mental disorder.[41] A mental disorder is a disorder relating to a person's emotional processes, thought, cognition, or memory as distinguished from conditions primarily relating to drug abuse, alcoholism, or mental retardation.[42] Employers are also prohibited from denying equal employment opportunities because of developmental disability[43] unless the disability will significantly impair the person's ability to qualify for the position or the denial is based on a BFOQ.[44] Thus, it seems that Arizona law presents no problem for RACs religiously motivated to regulate the use of illicit drugs or the consumption of alcoholic beverages.

Wages and Hours

The Arizona minimum wage law was amended to apply only to minors when the equal wages law for men and women was passed. The

minimum wage law for minors[45] does not provide any exemptions for RACs. However,
special wage rates for learners and apprentices
and special licenses for minors whose learning
capacity is impaired by physical or mental deficiency, or injury authorizing less than the
minimum wage may be approved by the state
board.[46]

The equal wage law provides that no employer[47] shall pay a wage less than the wage
paid to a person of the opposite sex for the same
quantity and quality of the same classification
of work.[48] The prohibition relates to differentiation in pay scale solely on the basis of sex, and
wage differentiation may be based on a good
faith application of a bona fide job factor.[49]

Workmen's Compensation

The Arizona Workmen's Compensation
Law[50] covers every person with one or more
employees.[51] RACs are not specifically exempt. However, employees may elect to reject
coverage under the law by written notice to
their employer prior to injury and thereby retain the right to sue their employer.[52] Casual
employees are exempted from coverage under
the law.[53] RACs must carry insurance or file
proof with the Industrial Commission of their
financial ability to compensate injured employees directly.[54]

Unemployment Compensation

The Arizona Economic Security Act[55] includes within its definition of "employing unit"
any individual or type of organization.[56] The
statute then defines "employer" generally as
"any employing unit"[57] and more specifically as
an employing unit which, although not otherwise considered an employer under the statute,
is liable for tax under the Federal Unemployment Tax Act.[58] Any individual performing
services for an employing unit and subject to
the employing unit's control is considered an
employee under the statute.[59]

After stating that "any service of whatever
nature performed by an employee" constitutes
"employment,"[60] the statute extends its coverage to services performed for religious, charitable, or other organizations under certain con-

ditions.[61] First, the service must not qualify
as "employment" under the Federal Unemployment Tax Act.[62] Second, the organization must
have employed four or more people for some
part of a day in each of twenty weeks, within
either the current or the preceding year.[63] However, the statute's coverage does not reach services performed

(i) [i]n the employ of a church or convention or
association of churches, or an organization which
is operated primarily for religious purposes and
which is operated, supervised, controlled, or
primarily supported by a church or convention
or association of churches; or

(ii) [b]y a duly ordained, commissioned, or licensed
minister of a church in the exercise of his ministry or by a member of a religious order in the
exercise of duties required by such order.[64]

Services performed for a school, college, or
university by a student who is enrolled and
regularly attending classes[65] or by the student's
spouse[66] are exempt from coverage. Also excluded from coverage are services performed
by a student, twenty-two years of age or under,
who is participating in a program combining
academic instruction and work experience at a
nonprofit or public educational institution.[67]

Employing units exempt from coverage under
the Act may elect to become an employer[68]
and to be considered a consumer of services
constituting employment pursuant to the Act.[69]
This election is effective for a two-year period.
Religious, charitable, or educational institutions which qualify as employers under the
statute[70] lose this status if (1) the institution did
not operate for thirty-five weeks during the
previous calendar year,[71] or (2) it files with the
Arizona Department of Economic Security a
written application for termination of coverage.[72] Termination requires a finding by the
Department that "there were not twenty different days, each day being in a different calendar
week within the preceding calendar year, within
which such employing unit employed four or
more individuals."[73]

Certain nonprofit organizations[74] may make
payments in lieu of contributions.[75] Those
payments equal the amount of regular benefits
plus one-half of the extended benefits paid.[76]
The statute further provides that

[t]wo or more employing units that have become liable for payments in lieu of contributions, may file a joint application to the department for the establishment of a group account for the purpose of sharing the cost of benefits paid that are attributable to service in the employ of such employing units.[77]

Organizations which take advantage of this option, either individually or jointly, are subject to the law's provisions for a period of three years.[78]

Collective Bargaining

There is no "mini-Wagner Act" in Arizona. To the contrary, the Arizona constitution contains a "right to work" provision that declares that no person shall be denied the opportunity to obtain or retain employment because of nonmembership in a labor organization.[79] Under the authority of this provision the legislature has enacted "right to work" legislation.[80]

D. Students

No Arizona statute regulates RAC student admissions. However, since the employment laws allow selectivity on the basis of religion, it would seem a logical corollary that the legislature wishes RACs to be at least as free in student selection as in employment practices. Since student selection, moreover, is at the very core of the concept of academic freedom, it is unlikely that the legislature will enact legislation restricting the ability of RACs to assert such religious preference.

E. Facilities

The public accommodations section of the Arizona Civil Rights Act forbids discrimination in places of public accommodation for reasons relating to race, color, creed, national origin or ancestry.[81] Places of public accommodation include all public places for entertainment or recreation, places where food or beverage is sold for consumption on the premises, places for lodging of transients and all establishments which offer service to or solicit patronage from the general public.[82] Expressly excluded from places of public accommodation are residences

with fewer than five rental rooms, residential houses, private clubs, or any place "which by its nature is distinctly private."[83]

Arizona law also requires that places of public accommodation be accessible to and functional for the physically handicapped.[84] Construction standards and specifications are laid out in the statute.[85]

There are no exemptions for RACs with regard to either of these provisions. Not only would an RAC be required to admit persons to snack bars, restaurants, public cafeterias, arenas, and other places generally open to the general public without regard to the suspect criteria, it would also be required to adapt such places to the needs of the physically handicapped.

Educational institutions are exempted from the application of the Residential Landlord and Tenant Act,[86] which deals with the rental of dwelling units and governs terms and conditions of rental agreements, remedies for breach, and duties and liabilities of landlord and tenant.

An RAC is clearly an employer for the purposes of the Arizona Occupational Safety and Health Act, which includes any organization which employs one or more individuals.[87] Under the act an employee is any person performing services for an employer except household domestic laborers.[88]

F. State Taxation

A corporation is exempt from the state corporate income tax if it is organized and operated exclusively for religious, charitable, scientific, literary, or educational purposes, and if no part of its net earnings inures to the benefit of any private stockholders or individuals, and if no substantial part of its activities is directed toward influencing the legislative process.[89]

Any organization or church which is exempt from the state income tax is, however, subject to a tax on its "unrelated business income" as defined by the Internal Revenue Code.[90] A trade or business that is conducted primarily for the convenience of the members, students, or employees is not considered an unrelated business.[91] The income from the sale of most items in a campus bookstore would fall within this "convenience" exception and, therefore, would not be subject to taxation.

A tax-exempt organization may lose its tax-exempt status if it engages in certain prohibited transactions, which relate to the diversion of funds to insiders and away from the purpose of the organization.[92] There are no statutory provisions denying tax-exempt status for discrimination within the scope of the civil rights laws.

A new estate tax statute imposes a tax in the amount of the federal tax credit, with a credit for any transfer tax imposed by another state.[93] There is no special consideration given to transfers to RACs.

Arizona law allows a deduction, for corporate income tax purposes, for any contributions to organizations organized exclusively for religious or educational purposes if the contributions are used within the United States by a domestic organization for a purpose consistent with the organization's goals.[94] A parallel deduction is allowed for contributions from individuals; however, the provision relating to use by domestic organizations within the United States is not included.[95] These deductions will be disallowed if the organization has lost its tax exempt status for any reason.[96]

The Arizona Constitution permits the legislature to exempt the property of religious and educational institutions or associations from the state property tax if the property is not used or held for profit.[97] On the authority of this provision, the legislature has exempted public libraries, colleges, schoolhouses, and other buildings used for education[98] as well as churches and other buildings used for religious worship[99] and the land appurtenant thereto. However, the exemption is not applicable to property owned by these groups if it is primarily held or used by others whose use is not exempted.[100] The Arizona Supreme Court has stated that it is "the use of the property itself, not the use of the proceeds or income, which

is decisive in determining the tax-exempt status."[101]

A provision of the Intangible Property Tax Act exempting intangibles owned, held, or used exclusively for charitable, humanitarian, benevolent, scientific, educational, or religious purposes was declared unconstitutional by the Arizona Supreme Court as being beyond the scope of the exemptions permitted by the Arizona Constitution.[102]

Except for the sale of groceries, sales to and by RACs are subject to the state sales tax.[103] RACs are also subject to the use tax.[104]

G. Fund Raising

There are no general state statutes regulating charitable solicitations. An opinion of the state Attorney General states that such matters are within the purview of the local municipalities.[105] Referring to a provision of the Arizona Constitution dealing with toleration of religious sentiment,[106] the Attorney General stated that a city ordinance regulating the solicitation of charitable funds must bear a reasonable relationship to the avowed purpose of the ordinance and may not involve a religious test which would interfere with the free exercise of religion or present a prior restraint to such free exercise.

Bingo games are regulated by statute.[107] Qualified organizations[108] must apply for and obtain a license from the State Tax Commission.[109] In addition, approval must be obtained from the local governing body.[110] The net profits of the bingo games must be applied to a lawful purpose, i.e., "educational, charitable, patriotic or religious purposes which benefit persons by relieving disease or suffering, assisting themselves, or maintaining facilities that accomplish such purposes."[111] An alternative "small bingo" license, available on less restrictive terms, limits gross receipts to $300 per week.[112]

12. Arkansas

A. Corporate Status

Private colleges and universities in Arkansas are incorporated under a special chapter of the Corporations and Associations Law of that state dealing with institutions of learning.[1] The Act provides that "any number of persons, not less than six, nor more than thirty-three, may associate for the purpose of founding or maintaining an institution of learning" if they meet the other requirements of the Act.[2] These persons become the trustees of the proposed institution.[3] To secure legal existence by act of incorporation, the trustees must prepare a charter for the proposed institution and must present the charter to the State Board of Higher Education.[4] This charter, or articles of association, must specify the purpose for which the corporation is being established.[5] If the State Board of Higher Education approves the charter, it will issue a certificate stating that the charter is granted to the trustees and that they thereby constitute the board of directors of the corporation and are invested with all powers described in the charter.[6] A copy of the charter and certificate must also be filed with the Secretary of State.[7]

RACs incorporated under these provisions have the powers normally associated with a separate corporate entity.[8] However, the Act does not contain any detailed provisions concerning the creation, maintenance, or dissolution of an educational corporation. Although a literal reading of the terms of the Arkansas Nonprofit Corporations Act gives the impression that this section of Arkansas law is inapplicable to most private colleges,[9] the only legal basis for handling the merger, consolidation, or dissolution of an RAC is found in the provisions of the Nonprofit Corporations Act relating to merger and consolidation[10] and to dissolution.[11]

A merger, consolidation, or voluntary dissolution is subject to approval by the Secretary of State.[12] Either the Circuit Court or the Chancery Court has jurisdiction to liquidate the assets of a corporation in an action brought by the corporation,[13] a shareholder (or analogously by a member of the governing board in a nonstock corporation), a creditor, or by the Attorney General when it has been established that liquidation should precede a decree of involuntary dissolution by the court.[14] Actions may be brought by these parties only in circumstances similar to those described in the Model Act.[15]

The Dissolution and Liquidation chapter of the Corporations and Associations title does not provide a complete procedure for the distribution of assets belonging to a nonprofit college. The Chapter provides only for the distribution of the assets of a corporation to shareholders[16] and subscribers,[17] following the satisfaction of debts and liabilities. It must be noted, however, that the *cy pres* doctrine is applied in Arkansas when it becomes impossible or impracticable to administer a charitable trust according to its terms.[18]

B. State Support

Arkansas has no program of direct institutional assistance similar to the federal program sustained in *Tilton v. Richardson*[19] or the state program sustained in *Hunt v. McNair*.[20] It has, however, recently established a state scholarship program to assist all Arkansas residents to attend the institution of their choice.[21] Any state resident who satisfies the qualifications of financial need, academic achievement and full-time status at an approved institution, whether public or private, is eligible for a state scholarship.[22]

An approved private institution is defined as a nonprofit two or four year institution privately operated and under the control of an independent board of directors.[23] Public funds that are obtained by a private institution must be used only for secular purposes.[24] In addition, the aid is conditioned by the requirements that an eligible institution may not discriminate in admission of students upon the basis of race, color, religion, sex, or national origin[25] and that it must subscribe to the principles of academic freedom.[26]

The current minimum scholarship is $100, and the maximum is the lesser of one-half of the tuition and fees or $300 per year.[27] The award of the scholarship funds is made directly to the student, though any refund upon withdrawal is made by the institution to the state.[28]

The Arkansas Department of Higher Education administers the State Student Incentive Grant Program which coordinates requests for federal grants and funds under the Federal Student Incentive Grant Program.[29] Students at both public and private institutions of higher education who are eligible under the federal program are likewise eligible to participate in this federal-state program.

The Student Loan Guarantee Foundation of Arkansas is a nonprofit corporation organized to administer guaranteed student loans for state citizens attending approved institutions of higher education.[30] A qualified student is defined by the statute as "a student (1) who qualifies for a guaranteed student loan and (2) who is a resident of the state of Arkansas, or who has been accepted for enrollment at or is attending a participating institution within the state of Arkansas."[31]

Arkansas is a participant in the Southern Regional Education Compact, which was organized by several states to effectively utilize and plan educational facilities.[32] As Professor Howard describes it, "The Southern Regional Education Board, created by the compact, is authorized to act for Arkansas in placing and paying partial or full tuition for students in public or private institutions."[33]

C. Personnel

Hiring, Promoting, and Firing

The Arkansas Constitution states that "the equality of all persons before the law is recognized, and shall ever remain inviolate; nor shall any citizen ever be deprived of any right, privilege or immunity, nor exempted from any burden or duty, on account of race, color or previous conditions."[34] But this general constitutional principle, susceptible to application in employment practices, has never been expanded in a civil rights statute expressly prohibiting racially discriminatory practices in employment. There is a provision which explicitly prohibits wage discrimination on the basis of sex,[35] but the provision does not cover employees engaged in service for an educational or religious association.[36]

Wages and Hours

Under the Arkansas Minimum Wage Act, every employer in the state of Arkansas must pay to each of his "employees" a minimum wage, currently $2.70 per hour.[37] The definition of an employee for purposes of this act, however, does not include students performing services for any school, college, or university in which they are enrolled and are regularly attending classes,[38] or any individual engaged in the activities of any educational, charitable, religious, or nonprofit organization where the employer-employee relationship does not in fact exist or where the services are rendered to such organization gratuitously.[39] Thus, it would appear that RACs would not have to pay student employees the statutory minimum wage. However, RACs must conform to the wage requirements of the act with respect to other nonprofessional employees where an employer-employee relationship exists.[40] Handicapped individuals, moreover, may be granted a special exemption license authorizing the employment of such individuals at wages lower than the minimum statutory requirement.[41]

A recent amendment to the act provides that every employer in the state must pay employees equal compensation for equal services, and no employer can discriminate against any employee in wages or compensation solely on the basis of the sex of the employee.[42]

In addition, no employer may employ any of his employees for a work week longer than forty hours, unless such employee receives compensation for his employment in excess of forty hours at a rate not less than one and one-half times the regular rate of pay at which he is employed.[43] There is no mention of maximum work hours allowed outside the areas of sawing or planing mills.[44]

The Arkansas Workers' Compensation Law[45] covers any corporation[46] that has three or more employees[47] who are not expressly excluded from coverage.[48] Generally, then, RACs are covered. Some of their employees may come within the exception for casual employment.[49] Arkansas also exempts employment carried on by "institutions maintained and operated wholly as public charities."[50] The Workers' Compensation Law does not define this public charities exception and there are no reported cases citing it. However, the Arkansas Charitable Organizations Law defines charitable organizations as benevolent, philanthropic, patriotic, or eleemosynary corporations.[51] Therefore, if the exception in the Workers' Compensation Law is similarly construed, RACs would not come within this exemption from coverage. Employees may elect to waive the exemption for any or all excepted employees and become subject to the compensation provisions by giving adequate notice prior to any injury.[52] RACs must carry insurance or receive authorization from the Workmen's Compensation Commission to be a self-insurer after furnishing the Commission with satisfactory proof of financial ability to pay compensation directly to injured employees.[53] The Commission may require the self-insurer to deposit acceptable security before issuing such authorization.[54]

Under the Arkansas Employment Security Law[55] an "employing unit" is broadly defined to include any individual or organization.[56] With regard to RACs the statute includes within the definition of "employer" any employing unit that is a nonprofit organization for which services constitute employment.[57] According to the definition of employment, services performed for a religious, charitable, or educational organization[58] are covered by the statute, if at least one individual was working a portion of ten different days, in either the current or the preceding calendar year.[59] Excluded from the Act's definition of employment are services performed (1) in the employ of a church or group of churches; (2) in the employ of an organization which is operated primarily for religious purposes and which is operated, supervised, controlled, or principally supported by a church or convention or association of churches; or (3) by a duly ordained, commissioned, or licensed minister of a church in the exercise of his ministry or by a member of a religious order in the exercise of duties required by such order.[60]

Services performed for a school, college, or university by a student who is enrolled and regularly attending classes are exempt from coverage.[61] A final exemption relevant to RACs covers services performed by a student under the age of twenty-two who is participating in a program combining academic instruction and work experience at a nonprofit or public educational institution.[62]

The Arkansas statute offers to nonprofit organizations[63] that are liable for contributions under the Act the option of making payments in lieu of contributions.[64] These payments must equal the "amount of regular benefits and, to the extent that the unemployment compensation fund is not reimbursed for such extended benefits . . . , the extended benefits paid."[65] This election is effective for a two-year period and must be made at least thirty days prior to that year to which the election is applicable.[66] It is terminable only upon the filing of a written notice not later than thirty days before the start of the calendar year to which the termination applies.[67]

It is the expressed public policy of Arkansas that employers and employees have the right to bargain collectively through representatives of their own choosing in order to establish wages or other conditions of work.[68] In addition, no person, group of persons, firm, corporation, association, or labor organization may enter into any contract to exclude from employment persons who are either members of a labor union or affiliated with a union, or persons who are not members of, or who fail or refuse to join or affiliate with a labor union.[69]

D. Students

Arkansas does not directly regulate the process of admission of students to private institutions of higher education. As suggested above in the section of this chapter relating to state support, however, the statutes controlling scholarships and loans require that institutions accepting recipients must not discriminate in admission of students upon the basis of race, color, religion, sex, or national origin.[70] The conditioning of aid upon a policy of non-discrimination on the basis of race, color, and national origin has, of course, a strong parallel in Title VI of the federal Civil Rights Act of 1964,[71] and a similar ban relating to federally funded educational activities is found in Title IX of the Education Amendments of 1972.[72] But the prohibition of religious preference in student admissions at an RAC has no parallel in federal legislation[73] and appears to be an unwarranted interference with the measure of autonomy appropriate to RACs.[74]

No provision in Arkansas law impedes an RAC from disciplining a student who, contrary to the ethical standards of the religious body affiliated with the college, consumes alcoholic beverages or uses illicit drugs.

E. Facilities

As suggested above in the section on employment, Arkansas has not enacted any civil rights legislation governing access to public accommodations or to housing units on a non-discriminatory basis. In lieu of such state legislation, the relevant federal legislation, such as Title II of the Civil Rights Act of 1964[75] and Title VIII of the Civil Rights Act of 1968,[76] is, of course binding on RACs as well as on other parties.

Arkansas has enacted legislation affording the handicapped equal rights to public buildings and facilities, "and all other places to which the general public is invited."[77] The handicapped are also entitled to full and equal access to "all housing accommodations offered for rental, lease, or compensation."[78] No modification of any housing accommodation to favor handicapped persons is required,[79] but a violation of the law is a misdemeanor.[80]

The Industrial Health Services Act,[81] enacted in 1947, creates the Division of Industrial Hygiene, which investigates places of employment and studies conditions that could result in the ill health of the industrial worker.[82] The statute prohibits the use of any "material, process, or condition known to have an adverse effect on health."[83] The statute empowers the State Board of Health to promulgate reasonable rules and regulations to implement the act.[84] Because there is no statutory definition of an "industrial worker" that would suggest that the term refers solely to blue collar workers, one must assume that the Act could cover workers at a college or university as well.

F. State Taxation

Article XVI, §5 of the Arkansas constitution provides that "school buildings and apparatus [and] libraries and grounds used exclusively for school purposes" are exempt from property tax.[85] In *Hilger v. Harding College, Inc.*, the Arkansas Supreme Court construed this provision narrowly to exempt only property that is actually and directly used for the exempt purpose, not the rents and revenues of property owned by a charitable organization, even where such income is devoted to the exempt purposes of the organization.[86] In a late nineteenth century decision, however, the Arkansas Supreme Court ruled that the exemption from property tax applies to private schools as well as public schools.[87]

Building on these decisions, the Arkansas legislature has extended this exemption to "all buildings belonging to institutions of purely public charity, together with the land actually occupied by such institutions, not leased or otherwise used with a view to profit, and all moneys and credits appropriated solely to sustaining and belonging exclusively to such institutions."[88]

Arkansas taxes the gross receipts or proceeds from the sale of tangible personal property or services within the state,[89] but it exempts churches and charitable organizations from the payment of this tax except where such organizations are engaged in business for profit.[90] Also exempt are the "[g]ross receipts or gross proceeds derived from the sale of food in public, common, high school or college cafeterias and lunch rooms operated primarily for teachers and pupils, not operated primarily for the public and not operated for profit."[91]

Arkansas taxes the net income of for-profit corporations.[92] It exempts from the payment of this tax all corporations organized for religious or educational purposes, which are defined with reference to the federal Internal Revenue Code's requirement that no part of the net earnings of a nonprofit corporation accrue to the benefit of a private stockholder or individual.[93] In addition, the state income tax law provides that income "derived from investments made by nonprofit organizations, whether or not such organization is organized or exists under the laws of this State, shall be exempt from Arkansas Income Tax where such income is for the sole purpose of providing pension and annuity benefits to members of such nonprofit organizations."[94]

Contributions or gifts to educational institutions are eligible deductions under Arkansas Income Tax law if such gifts and institutions fulfill the requirements of §170 of the federal Internal Revenue Code of 1954. This section of the Internal Revenue Code has been adopted as Arkansas law.[95]

Arkansas has no gift tax.

Arkansas imposes a tax upon the privilege of storing, using or consuming tangible personal property within the state.[96] However, if the sale of tangible personal property was already taxed under the Gross Receipts Act or has been specifically exempted from the sales tax, such property would be exempt from the use tax.[97]

Arkansas taxes the transfer of real estate or personal property owned by a state resident and passing in their estate.[98] No estate taxes, inheritance taxes, or transfer taxes are imposed, however, on bequests of a state resident to a "religious, charitable or educational institution, organization or foundation, whether incorporated or unincorporated."[99]

G. Fund Raising

Arkansas regulates the charitable solicitation of charitable organizations, defined broadly to include all "benevolent, philanthropic, patriotic or eleemosynary" organizations.[100] All such organizations are required to register with the Secretary of State before soliciting contributions by any means.[101]

In addition, organizations must file annual reports either on or before March 1, or within 90 days after the close of its fiscal year.[102] The organization must maintain comprehensive records to facilitate provision of information to the Secretary of State.[103]

Professional fund raisers,[104] engaged by an RAC or other charitable organization,[105] must register with the Secretary of State each year, post a $5,000 bond, and pay a fee.[106] Employees of professional fund raisers must likewise register with the state.[107] Contracts between RACs and fund raisers must be in writing, with a copy retained both by the organization and by the fund raiser for at least three years. Fund raisers are limited to 25% of proceeds, and 75% of proceeds must be distributed to meet the charitable purpose for which the contribution is solicited.[108]

The Arkansas Criminal Code prohibits "betting any money or any valuable thing on any game of hazard or skill."[109] RACs and other charitable organizations may not, therefore, resort to sponsoring bingo games or other games of chance or skill to raise funds.

13. California

A. Corporate Status

The incorporation, maintenance, and dissolution of RACs in California are governed by the statutes governing nonprofit corporations[1] and private institutions of higher education.[2]

California repealed its former General Nonprofit Corporation Law in 1980 and replaced it with a new law that provides for two distinct categories, nonprofit public benefit corporations, which may be formed for any public or charitable purposes,[3] and religious corporations, which may be formed only if the purposes of the corporation are primarily or exclusively religious.[4] By requiring a religiously affiliated college to choose between the "public benefit" or "religious" designation of its corporate status, California has placed this kind of institution on the horns of a dilemma. If it opts for the public benefit designation, it enhances its eligibility for public assistance but presumably foregoes the exemption provided for "religious corporations" in section 702 of Title VII of the federal Civil Rights Act, as amended, and presumably falls within closer supervisory powers of the Attorney General. On the other hand, if it opts for designation as a religious corporation, it maintains its rights under section 702 of the federal statute and it distances itself further from the powers of the Attorney General, but presumably runs the risk of becoming ineligible for public financial assistance to itself or to its students.

Irrespective of which designation an RAC prefers, corporate status commences upon the filing of articles of incorporation with the Secretary of State, who forwards the articles to the Attorney General.[5] These articles must specify the public purpose, *viz.*, education, that the corporation intends to serve.[6] Designation as a nonprofit public benefit corporation is contingent and may be withdrawn if the purpose of the corporation is the realization of personal profit; any property held by the corporation and any incidental profits made by the corporation must be held in trust for the publicly beneficial purpose for which the corporation was authorized to exist.[7]

In addition to these requirements of corporation law, California has imposed on RACs further requirements in its education code. Application for certification as an institution of higher education must be made to the Superintendent of Education, who reviews the application and may grant or deny approval.[8] The certification statute contains an exemption for some RACs, but it is narrowly drawn and applicable only to educational institutions such as seminaries or Bible colleges that limit instruction to the principles of the church or denomination that owns, controls, operates, or maintains the institution.[9]

RACs and other private institutions of higher education are subject to supervision by the Council for Private Postsecondary Educational Institutions,[10] the Superintendent of Education,[11] and the Attorney General.[12] The statute establishing this process suggests that the purpose of such supervision is the provision of "leadership and direction in the continuing development of private postsecondary education as an integral and effective element in the structure of postsecondary education in California."[13] The detailed involvement of the state in the process of certification of private colleges,[14] however, raises a serious question of the autonomy and independence of these private institutions from state control.[15] In the case of RACs, the detailed monitoring of their operations by the state raises an additional question of excessive entanglement of the government with religion.[16]

California has enacted a strong consumer protection statute that subjects private colleges to loss of their certification, to refunding of money improperly taken from students, and in some instances to payment of treble damages for engaging in false or inaccurate advertising.[17]

A nonprofit college in California can dissolve voluntarily.[18] The plan of distribution of assets in the case of dissolution is as follows: payment of all just debts and liabilities, distribution of assets held with a condition requiring a specific disposition upon dissolution, and distribution of residual assets according to the articles of incorporation and bylaws.[19] A nineteenth century decision suggests that if the articles and bylaws make no provision for this distribution, the assets may vest in the state.[20] However, the doctrine of *cy pres* has subsequently been adopted in California courts,[21] so the net assets of a dissolving college would likely go to another private college or to another aspect of the work of the sponsoring religious body.[22]

Finally, an RAC can be dissolved involuntarily as a result of a complaint filed against the institution in a Superior Court by an aggrieved party or by the Attorney General.[23]

B. State Support

One year after *Tilton v. Richardson*[24] was decided in 1971, the California legislature enacted the California Educational Facilities Authority Act.[25] The purpose of this enactment is to provide, through that authority, assistance to private institutions of higher education in California "to expand, enlarge and establish dormitory, academic, and related facilities, to finance such facilities, and to refinance existing facilities."[26] Like the parallel federal legislation

sustained in *Tilton*, the California statute defines educational facilities broadly, but explicitly prohibits state financing of "any facility used or to be used for sectarian instruction or as a place for religious worship or any facility used or to be used primarily in connection with any part of the program of a school or department of divinity."[27]

A private college is eligible to participate in this program if it "neither restricts entry on racial or religious grounds nor requires all students to be instructed in the tenets of a particular faith."[28] It appears that an RAC which limits enrollment to its particular denomination or synod or which requires particular theology courses would not be eligible to participate in the grants and loans authorized under this act. Unless the phrase "restricts entry" is to be construed so broadly as to include employment policies as well as student admissions policies, however, the statute imposes no restrictions on an RAC's exercise of religious preference in employment.

The statute was challenged under the Establishment Clause of the First Amendment of the U.S. Constitution and under various provisions of California's constitution, but the California Supreme Court sustained the act in *California Educational Facilities Authority v. Priest.*[29] Article IX, section 8 of the California constitution prohibits the appropriation of public funds for the support of a sectarian or denominational school;[30] and Article XVI, section 5 prohibits public expenditures to "sustain any school, college, [or] university . . . controlled by any religious creed, church, or sectarian denomination."[31] Finding that neither provision was violated by this act, the court ruled that there was no appropriation of public funds and that the legislature had expressly determined that the support and improvement of the higher educational facilities was in the public interest and advanced "legitimate public ends."[32]

The Chairman of the Private Postsecondary Educational Institutions Council, as well as two representatives of independent California colleges and universities, sit as members of the California Postsecondary Education Commission,[33] which exists to promote the full utilization of the state-wide postsecondary education system, to plan and coordinate the resources of the institutions, and to develop state policy toward funding for postsecondary education.[34]

In 1976 the state adopted a pilot program of tuition grants to narrow the gap between student expenses at public institutions and those at private ones. It was hoped to encourage freedom of choice and "to help assure that independent colleges will continue to contribute to the overall quality and diversity of higher education in California."[35] There were no restrictions relating to religious preference written into the grant legislation. The only significant condition is that the student attend an accredited institution.[36] Although this program was a laudable attempt to equalize the cost of attending public and private institutions of higher education, funds for this program were never allocated by the legislature.

The scholarship and grant programs in California have been amalgamated within the California Grant Program. These awards are to be based upon financial need and past academic performances. The authorization allows state awards for tuition and fees to be utilized at any accredited California institution. The amount granted depends upon financial need, which is reviewed annually in some of the programs. California grants are awarded by the state without regard to race, religion, creed, sex, or age.[37]

In addition to authorizing grants for students attending RACs, California has established a Student Loan Authority whereby eligible students may obtain insured student loans through the state's participation in the federal loan program under the Higher Education Act of 1965.[38]

Although California has been a national leader in providing quality education as indicated by its extensive university and community college system, the passage of Proposition 13 in 1978 heralded a new and more parsimonious attitude, at least on the part of most voting taxpayers, towards governmental costs in general. This attitude has had its inevitable toll on the various educational components of the state budget, including the grant and loan programs described above.[39] With the spread of this attitude nationwide, moreover, as the results of the presidential election of 1980 would appear to indicate, scholarships, grants, and loans for students attending college can be expected to be a scarce commodity in the 1980s.[40]

C. Personnel

California was the first state in modern history to enact fair employment practices legislation, prohibiting discrimination on the basis of race, creed, or color in apprenticeships soon after World War II.[41] This legislation was expanded throughout the following decade, so that five years before the passage of the federal Civil Rights Act of 1964, California had created one of the first state Fair Employment Practices Commissions (FEPC) in the country. The statutory purpose of the FEPC was the enforcement of the "public policy of the state that it is necessary to protect and safeguard the right and opportunity of all persons to seek, obtain, and hold employment without discrimination or abridgement on account of race, religious creed, color, national origin, or ancestry."[42] Two years before the passage of Title IX of the federal Education Amendments of 1972, discrimination in employment practices on the basis of sex was likewise prohibited in California as a matter of state law.[43] Since the 1959 legislation excluded nonprofit charitable, educational or religious associations or corporations from the definition of an employer,[44] RACs were not subject to its provisions.

The current FEPC legislation is included in a comprehensive civil rights act.[45] This act repeats the purpose[46] articulated above and declares that employment without discrimination is a civil right protected by state law.[47] The definition of an employer for purposes of this statute no longer exempts all private colleges, as the 1959 legislation had done, but does exempt a nonprofit religious association or corporation.[48] RACs would qualify for this exemption only if they are reorganized under the new California corporation statute as a religious corporation rather than as a public benefit corporation.[49] If an RAC were not organized as a religious corporation, it could, nonetheless, exercise religious preference in its employment policies and practices to the extent that the religious background of an employee or prospective employee is a bona fide occupational qualification (BFOQ).[50] Unlike section 703(e)(1) of the federal Civil Rights Act of 1964, which makes the BFOQ exception applicable only to the religion, sex, or national origin[51] of the employee, the California statute appears to make the BFOQ exception available to the "race, religious creed, color, national origin, ancestry, physical handicap, medical condition, marital status, or sex of any person."[52]

Although California prohibits irrational discrimination against an otherwise qualified person solely on the basis of handicap, it does not include alcoholism or drug addiction within the definition of handicap. To the contrary, California law authorizes the dismissal, demotion, or suspension of employees at state universities and colleges for "addiction to the use of narcotics or habit-forming drugs . . . conviction of a [crime] involving moral turpitude . . . or drunkenness on duty."[53] It further directs that an application for a teaching credential be denied if the applicant has been previously convicted of a narcotics offense.[54] Since private colleges ought not to be held to a higher regulatory burden than their public counterparts, California law probably does not impede an RAC from disciplining an employee who, contrary to the ethical standards of the religious body affiliated with the college, consumes alcoholic beverages or uses illicit drugs.

RACs must comply with the minimum wage,[55] equal pay for equivalent work,[56] maximum hours,[57] and overtime wage provisions.[58]

The California Workers' Compensation and Insurance Law[59] covers any corporation[60] with one or more employees.[61] RACs are not specifically excluded.[62] However, some employees of an RAC may not be covered, either because they come under the exemptions for some student employees,[63] or for some employees covered by federal workers' compensation laws,[64] or for persons working for a religious organization in return for aid or sustenance only,[65] or for volunteers for a religious organization who receive room, board, transportation and reimbursement of incidental expenses for their services.[66] The RAC and any exempted employee, however, may jointly elect to come under the compensation provisions of this law.[67] RACs must carry insurance or become a bonded self-insurer after proving financial ability to compensate injured employees directly.[68] If an RAC fails to secure payment of compensation, it may be subject to court action for damages by an injured employee.[69]

Under the California Unemployment Insurance Code,[70] services performed for nonprofit organizations are specifically included within the definition of "employment"[71] if two conditions are met.[72] First, such service must be excluded from the definition of "employment" in the Federal Unemployment Tax Act solely due to section 3306(c)(8).[73] Second, the organization must fit the definition of "nonprofit organization" in section 501(c)(3) of the Internal Revenue Code and qualify as tax-exempt under section 501(a) of the Internal Revenue Code.[74]

The statute exempts from coverage the following services performed for RACs: (1) services performed for a church or an association of churches;[75] (2) services performed for an organization run primarily for religious purposes and controlled by a church or by an association of churches;[76] and (3) services performed by ordained ministers or members of religious orders in the exercise of their duties.[77] Because the scope of these exemptions is narrow, most services performed for RACs are covered under the state's Code. Other relevant exemptions from the statute's definition of employment include (1) services performed for a school or college by regularly enrolled students[78] or their spouses;[79] (2) services performed by a student under the age of twenty-two at an accredited nonprofit or public educational institution in a full-time program, combining academic instruction and work experience;[80] (3) services performed for which unemployment compensation is payable under a system set up by an Act of Congress;[81] and (4) domestic service for a college club or a local chapter of a college fraternity or sorority, if wages paid in any quarter of the current or preceding calendar year were less than $1,000.00.[82]

Nonprofit organizations may elect to make payments in lieu of contributions. To take advantage of this option, an organization must fit the statute's general definition of "nonprofit organization."[83] The election is effective for a period of two years upon filing of written election with the Director of the Department of Human Resources Development.[84] Required payments are equal to the amount of regular benefits plus the amount of extended benefits paid.[85] Organizations not otherwise subject to the provisions of the statute may elect to participate in the program for a minimum of two years.[86]

California has a mini-Wagner Act, protecting the rights of employees to organize and bargain collectively over terms and conditions of employment.[87] RACs are not exempted from the definition of an employer for purposes of this act.

D. Students

Although California has no statute directly regulating the admissions policies and practices of RACs or other private colleges, it has made, as was noted above, participation in the state educational facilities program conditional upon an admissions policy that does not restrict access on the basis of race or religion and upon an academic policy that would not require students to receive instruction in the tenets of a particular faith.[88] The conditioning of receipt of aid upon a policy of nondiscrimination on the basis of race has, of course, a strong parallel in Title VI of the federal Civil Rights Act of 1964.[89] But the prohibition of religious preference in student admissions has no parallel in federal legislation[90] and suggests an unwarranted interference with the measure of autonomy appropriate to RACs.

An earlier piece of state civil rights legislation prohibited discrimination in all business establishments on the basis of sex, race, color, religion, ancestry, or national origin.[91] On the ground that private schools are not "public accommodations" within the meaning of this statute, in 1959 an appellate court ruled in *Reed v. Hollywood Professional School* that this legislation did not apply to a private school that had refused to admit a black child solely on the basis of the applicant's race.[92] The California Supreme Court did not review this decision, which was subsequently undercut by the ruling of the United States Supreme Court in *Runyon v. McRary. Runyon* held that a provision of the federal Civil Rights Act of 1866 protected the rights of blacks to enter into contracts on a racially nondiscriminatory basis.[93]

The federal prohibition against discrimination on the basis of handicap in federally funded programs has generated inconclusive litigation concerning the extent to which schools receiving federal assistance must modify their facilities or programs to accommodate handicapped students, for example, by making buildings more accessible, by providing Braille collections, or by providing translators for hearing-impaired students.[94] The California civil rights legislation protecting the handicapped, however, does not require private educational institutions to provide any special services or to modify their physical facilities to accommodate the handicapped.[95]

The civil rights statute referred to above, moreover, does not explicitly include alcoholism or drug addiction within the definition of handicap.[96] The state education code, in fact, allows the disciplining of students for the use of illicit drugs,[97] and does not prohibit the disciplining of students for the consumption of alcoholic beverages.[98] California law does not, therefore, impede an RAC from disciplining a student who, contrary to the ethical standards of the religious body with which the college is affiliated, consumes alcoholic beverages or uses illicit drugs.

E. Facilities

The Fair Employment and Housing Act[99] prohibits discrimination in the sale, rental or leasing of housing accommodations. The definition of housing accommodations in this statute, however, does not include accommodations "operated by a religious, fraternal, or charitable association or corporation not organized or operated for private profit; provided, that such accommodations are being used in furtherance of the primary purpose or purposes for which the association or corporation was formed."[100] Thus, if an RAC's student admissions policy preferring applicants on the basis of religion resulted in a disproportionate number of members of a particular religion in student dormitories, the college would not be violating the state civil rights law. In addition, RACs as well as other private and public colleges in California may reserve housing accommodations "for either male or female students so long as no individual person is denied equal access to housing accommodations," and these institutions may provide "separate housing accommodations reserved primarily for married students or for students with minor dependents who reside with them."[101]

As amended in 1974, the Unruh Civil Rights Act prohibits discrimination based on sex, race, color, religion, ancestry, or national origin "in all business establishments of every kind whatsoever."[102] Whether private colleges are considered public accommodations in California is not yet certain, as discussed above. Based on the breadth of the statute, however, at least those places on RAC campuses which are open to the general public are probably subject to the civil rights law. Any facility which would *per se* be considered a "business establishment," e.g., a restaurant or bookstore, is most likely covered by the law.

California enacted an Occupational Safety and Health Act in 1973.[103] The purpose of the act is "to assure the safe and healthful working conditions . . . by authorizing the enforcement of effective standards . . . and by providing for research, information, education, training and enforcement in the field of occupational safety and health."[104] For purposes of coverage under this act, an employer is defined in the same way as in the state statute governing workers compensation: "every person, including any public service corporation which has any natural person in service."[105] An employee is defined in the OSHA statute as "every person who is required or directed by an employer to engage in any employment, or go to work or be at any time in a place of employment."[106] However, nothing in the Code requires "an employer to alter his premises to accommodate employees who have a physical handicap or medical condition . . . beyond safety requirements applicable to other employees."[107]

California grants the handicapped equal rights of access to public accommodations or facilities constructed with either public[108] or private[109] funds. The term "public accommodations or facilities" specifically includes auditoriums, restaurants, hotels, stadiums, and convention centers.[110] Every existing public accommodation *must* comply with state handicap access standards whenever repairs or alterations are made to relevant areas of its facility.[111]

F. Taxation

California taxes the net income of for-profit corporations.[112] The California Bank and Corporation Tax Law, however, exempts from the payment of this tax all "corporations . . . organized and operated exclusively for religious, charitable or educational purposes."[113] In order to maintain this exempt status, no portion of the net earnings of an RAC may benefit a private individual, and the assets of the college must remain irrevocably dedicated to the exempt functions of the institution.[114] In the case of the dissolution of an educational institution, the net assets would have to be transferred to another exempt organization, or to the local, state, or federal government for the accomplishment of similar purposes.

To qualify for the exemption, an RAC must submit an application to the Franchise Tax Board, which has discretionary power to grant the exemption. As with the parallel federal legislation, only "[c]hurches, their integrated auxiliaries, and conventions or associations of churches"[115] are exempt from filing an annual informational return with the state Franchise Tax Board. Failure to file this annual report or to adhere to other provisions in this chapter of the tax code governing exempt organizations may result in revocation of the RAC's tax-exempt status.[116]

Under the California Inheritance Tax Law,[117] transfers of property from an estate to a corporation operated exclusively[118] for religious, charitable, educational, or other exempt purposes are similarly exempt from the payment of estate tax.[119] As with the income tax exemption, this exemption carries the condition that no private individual may receive a portion of the net income of the transfer and that the recipient institution may not be substantially engaged in propaganda or similar attempts to influence legislation.[120]

Gifts to educational institutions that are designated for use as scholarships or fellowships are excluded from the gross income of the donor for state income tax purposes.[121]

Any gift to an educational institution is exempt from the California gift tax as long as no part of the institution's net earnings inures to a private individual's benefit and the institution receiving the gift does not attempt to influence legislation.[122]

The California constitution exempts from property taxation all buildings, land, equipment, and securities "used exclusively for educational purposes by a nonprofit institution of higher education."[123] This exemption has been implemented by legislation,[124] and would cover virtually all RACs. The state constitution also exempts the buildings, land on which they are located and equipment used for religious worship.[125] In *Church Divinity School of the Pacific v. Alameda County*, an appellate court ruled that a parking lot adjacent to the campus of an RAC as well as a building used to provide rent-free housing to faculty members and married students constituted property used exclusively for an educational purpose within the meaning of the constitutional provision cited above.[126]

The California constitution authorizes the exemption from property taxation of property, *inter alia*, used exclusively for religious or charitable purposes by nonprofit organizations.[127] The legislature exercised this authorization.[128] As with the income tax exemption, this property tax exemption carries a condition that the property must be "used for the actual operation of the exempt activity, and does not exceed an amount of property reasonably necessary to the accomplishment of the exempt purpose,"[129] and that the property be irrevocably dedicated to religious or charitable purposes.[130]

The gross receipts from meals served to students by RACs and other schools are exempt from sales and use taxes.[131]

G. Fund Raising

California has not enacted a general statute governing all forms of charitable solicitation.[132]

The education code provides that trustees of the state colleges may accept gratuities "which will aid in carrying out the primary functions of the state colleges."[133] RACs and other nonprofit schools are obviously not prohibited from receiving similar gifts and donations. Indeed, the article on charitable solicitations in the business and professions code defines charity to include "benevolent, educational [and] philanthropic . . ." organizations.[134] This code, moreover, requires a person soliciting for a charitable purpose to carry a "solicitation or sale for charitable purposes card."[135] The card must be signed and dated by a "principal, staff member, or officer . . ." of the organization and must show the names and addresses of the organization, the person who signed the card, and the name of the person who attempts to sell items such as advertisements or publications in any appeal for funds for a charitable purpose.[136]

Bingo games for charity[137] are excluded from the general penal provision prohibiting gambling.[138] In the unlikely event that an RAC in California might wish to raise funds by sponsoring bingo games, it would be free under California law to do so.

14. Colorado

A. Corporate Status

Colorado law has four articles under which an RAC may be incorporated: Articles 20–29, The Colorado Nonprofit Corporations Act;[1] Article 40, Corporations Not For Profit;[2] Article 50, Religious, Educational and Benevolent Societies;[3] and Article 51, Joint Stock Religious or Benevolent Associations.[4]

The first of these is the general statute intended to apply to all nonprofit corporations. The other articles regulate corporations formed before 1968[5] and contain provisions allowing for such corporations to elect to accept the provisions of the Nonprofit Corporations Act, as long as formed for purposes acceptable under the Act.[6] Any nonprofit corporation organized prior to 1968 under general law or created by a specific act of the General Assembly may also elect to accept the provisions of the Act.[7]

A corporation having no shares of capital stock may be organized under the Colorado Nonprofit Corporations Act for any lawful purpose, including educational and religious.[8]

The Uniform Management of Institutional Funds Act[9] regulates the investment funds of incorporated or unincorporated entities organized and operated exclusively for, *inter alia*, educational or religious purposes.[10] RACs are clearly governed by this act.

A nonprofit[11] private college's merger, consolidation, or dissolution is governed by the Colorado Nonprofit Corporation Act[12] if it is an educational corporation[13] organized under the Act or if it elects to accept the Act.[14] The

Colorado Supreme Court has ruled that Colorado courts may apply the doctrine of *cy pres* if that is necessary to keep a charitable gift from failing.[15]

A merger, consolidation or voluntary dissolution must be approved by the Secretary of State.[16] Any nonprofit college may be dissolved involuntarily by decree of the district court in an action filed by the attorney general because of fraud, abuse of authority, or failure to appoint or maintain a registered agent.[17] The district courts have the power to dissolve a college involuntarily and to liquidate its assets in an action properly brought by a member of the governing board or by a creditor.[18]

The Nonprofit Corporation Act[19] provides that the assets of a dissolving nonprofit corporation be distributed according to a schedule closely following that of the Model Nonprofit Corporations Act.[20] The Colorado Act allows distribution of any remaining assets to governmental entities and political subdivisions in addition to persons, societies, organizations or domestic or foreign corporations.[21]

B. State Support

The Colorado Constitution forbids the General Assembly and any other political subdivision or public corporation from making appropriations to aid any church or sectarian society or to help support any school, seminary, or college controlled by any church or sectarian society.[22] Neither the state nor any political corporation can make a grant or donation of land, money, or personal property to any church or for any sectarian purpose.[23] Still another section of the constitution forbids appropriations to private educational institutions and any denominational or sectarian institution or association,[24] but the Colorado Supreme Court has noted that "if such payments are for a public purpose, the incidental fact that the recipients are private persons does not violate this constitutional provision."[25] Although municipal governments have the statutory power to "aid and foster" associated charity organizations by appropriations, no portion of the money may be given or loaned to any entity wholly or in part under sectarian or denominational control.[26]

All of this makes clear that direct state aid to RACs is prohibited. Nonetheless, indirect state aid to RACs is authorized by Colorado student scholarship and loan[27] programs.[28]

The Student Financial Assistance Programs legislation provides that aid may go to students attending institutions of higher education that are not "pervasively sectarian or theological institutions."[29] The Colorado Incentive Grant Program[30] has a similar provision,[31] but also provides criteria for determining what is not a pervasively sectarian institution:

(a) The faculty and students are not exclusively of one religious persuasion; (b) There is no required attendance at religious convocations or services; (c) There is a strong commitment to principles of academic freedom; (d) There are no required courses in religion or theology that tend to indoctrinate or proselytize; (e) The governing board does not reflect nor is the membership limited to persons of any particular religion; (f) Funds do not come primarily or predominantly from sources advocating a particular religion.[32]

Although an RAC failing one of these criteria apparently will be deemed a "pervasively" sectarian institution rendering its students ineligible for aid, most of these provisions would not present problems for the typical RAC.[33] (a) Most RACs will not have a faculty and students *exclusively* of one religious persuasion; (b) many RACs, at least, do not have required attendance at religious services; (c) most RACs support academic freedom principles; (d) although many RACs have required religion or

theology courses, these courses are academic in nature rather than indoctrinating; (e) although this may be the most restrictive condition, many RACs do not limit their membership to persons of a particular religion either formally or de facto, and the spirit of the legislation seems aimed at exclusivity, as condition (a) makes clear. Nonetheless, it must be concluded that if the provision is construed to eliminate from the aid programs an institution fifty-one percent of whose board of trustees is of the same affiliation as the institution (on the theory that the "governing board [reflects a] particular religion), most RACs would be disqualified. Such a reading, however, would make the second part of the provision ("nor is the membership limited") extremely redundant; (f) with both the word "advocating" and the impact of tuition moneys in mind, few RACs will fail this criterion.

Although the Student Financial Assistance Programs law sets forth no such specific criteria, most likely those of the Incentive Grant Program would be used to determine whether the institution is pervasively sectarian.

The Higher and Vocational Education Loan Guarantee Act[34] and the Student Loan Guarantee Program[35] are available to students enrolled in either public or private institutions.[36] RAC students are therefore eligible to participate.

C. Personnel

It is an unfair employment practice in Colorado for an employer to "refuse to hire, to promote or demote or to discriminate in matters of compensation against any person otherwise qualified because of handicap, race, creed, color, sex, national origin, or ancestry."[37]

The legislation excludes from the term "employer" all religious organizations,[38] thus providing an exemption for a few RACs, such as seminaries and bible colleges. However, all other RACs are generally subject to the law.[39]

Colorado has no provision specifically allowing otherwise prohibited employment discrimination when based on a bona fide occupational qualification [BFOQ]. It does, however, allow job advertisements, applications and the like expressing a preference on otherwise proscribed bases when "based upon a bona fide occupational qualification."[40] This clearly reflects a legislative intent to allow employment selectivity itself on these bases. It would be ironic to allow a firm to advertise such restrictions but bar it from implementing the restrictions in the actual hiring.

The courts will, therefore, read a BFOQ into the employment law, allowing RACs to exercise religious selectivity in such positions as theology instructor, counselor and the like. For certain positions like that of a Judaism instuctor at a Christian school, the preference may be in favor of a religion different from the institutional affiliation. It is unlikely that the BFOQ will justify religious selectivity in all faculty (or staff) positions despite the institution's interest in establishing on campus a pervasive religious presence.

RACs have a legitimate interest in exercising, with regard to certain postitions, a preference with regard to sex. This interest may involve the counselor in the women's dorm, the faculty member teaching women's rights, or even the custodian of the men's locker room.

The BFOQ may justify such preferential hiring. In any event, any RAC fairly called a "religious institution" is not bound by the employment discrimination law.[41]

The employment discrimination law is enforced by the Colorado Civil Rights Division.[42]

Under Colorado law, the director of the division of labor is authorized to inquire into the wages paid to employees in any occupation and into their conditions of labor. He may do this at his own initiative, and must upon the request of twenty-five persons in that occupation.[43] Procedures by which a minimum wage for particular occupations may be established are legislatively provided.[44]

The Colorado Workmen's Compensation Act[45] applies to corporations with one or more employees.[46] Generally RACs are covered except for employees who come within the exceptions for casual employment[47] or employment covered by a federal worker's compensation law.[48] Elected or appointed employees who serve religious or charitable employers in an advisory capacity and receive less than $750.00 annually are also exempt.[49] Colorado law considers any person participating in a job training program sponsored by a private college and placed with an employer for training purposes to be an employee of the sponsoring college and covered by the workmen's compensation provisions.[50] RACs may elect to include exempted employees within the coverage of this Act by providing insurance coverage for them.[51] Prior to 1975, when Colorado repealed the provision,[52] employees could elect not to come under the provisions of this Act. In any damage action brought by a current employee who made a pre-1975 election, the employer apparently has all common law defenses available.[53] An RAC must insure its employees with the state compensation insurance fund, with an authorized insurer or by procuring a self-insurance permit from the Industrial Commission.[54]

Generally included as "employment" under Colorado's employment security legislation[55] are services for a religious, charitable, educational, or other organization "excluded from the term 'employment' as defined in the 'Federal Unemployment Tax Act' solely by reason of section 3306 (c)(8) of that act."[56]

Excluded from coverage are: (1) domestic service in a private home, local college club or local chapter of a college fraternity or sorority performed for a person paying $1,000 or less in either the current or preceding calendar year to individuals employed in such domestic service in any calendar quarter;[57] (2) services for a church or group of churches or for an organization operated primarily for religious purposes;[58] (3) services by "a duly ordained, commissioned, or licensed minister of a church" exercising his ministry or by a member of a religious order as duly required by the order;[59] (4) services performed for a school, college or university by one of its regular students[60] or by the spouse of such a student who is advised prior to the service that the employment is provided as financial assistance to the student by the institution and will not be covered by an unemployment insurance program;[61] and (5) services by a student under the age of twenty-two enrolled at a regular nonprofit or public institution of higher education in a full-time program, taken for credit, which combines academic instruction with work experience.[62] The service must be an integral part of the program, so certified to the employer, and not performed in a program "established for or on behalf of an employer or group of employers."[63]

Colorado law specifically includes within "employment" services performed for an "institution of higher education."[64] For covered institutions of higher education, however, special rules apply with regard to vacation periods, paid sabbatical leaves, weeks between successive academic years or terms, and the like.[65]

Colorado also pervasively regulates labor relations,[66] and there is no general exemption available to RACs.

D. Students

Colorado has no legislation specifically governing admissions to institutions of higher education. It is possible, however, to read the state's public accommodations law to cover admissions.[67]

E. Facilities

Colorado's Discrimination in Places of Public Accommodation[68] law makes it unlawful for anyone, on the basis of handicap, race, creed, color, sex, marital status, national origin, or ancestry to deny to another full and equal enjoyment of a place of public accommodation.[69] The law states that a place of public accommodation is:

any place of business engaged in any sales to the public and any place offering services, facilities, privileges, advantages, or accommodations to the public, including but not limited to any business offering wholesale or retail sales to the public; any place to eat, drink, sleep or rest . . . ; any sporting or recreational area and facility; . . . a barber shop, bathhouse, swimming pool . . . gymnasium . . . ; an educational institution; . . . or any public building, park, arena, theatre, hall, auditorium, museum, library, exhibit, or public facility of any kind . . . [70]

Due to the inclusion of the term "educational institution," the provision could be read to cover even admissions to institutions of higher education, since "services" and "facilities" could mean educational services and facilities. This conclusion would bar RACs from selecting students on the basis of religion or sex. The general part of the definition, however, refers to places engaged in sales "to the public" and any place offering services and the like "to the public." It is likely, therefore, that the statute was intended to cover private educational institutions only with regard to those campus facilities, such as bookstores and cafeterias, which are open to the general public and not only to their students. (It should be added that one section of the state housing discrimination law suggests an exemption for RACs which could cover admissions selectivity on the basis of religion.)[71]

At the end of the list of examples of places of public accommodation is the phrase "public building, park, arena, theatre, [etc.]." By implication, this phrase could be read to exclude from coverage privately owned arenas, theaters, and the like, although *open to* the public. Given the very broad general definition, however, and the other examples listed, it is doubtful that a court would read the provision narrowly.

Colorado law also prohibits discrimination in housing, whether sale, rental, or lease, by any "person" on the basis of handicap, race, creed, color, sex, marital status, religion, national origin, or ancestry.[72] There are, however, two possible exemptions for RACs.

First, a "person," under this legislation, does not include a "nonprofit, fraternal, educational, or social organization or club" as long as the organization does not have the purpose of promoting proscribed discrimination in housing.[73] To the extent that an RAC is a nonprofit, educational "organization," it is, of course, exempt.[74]

Should the word "organization" be read to exclude colleges and universities (on the theory, perhaps, that the phrase "organization or club" is meant to cover only societies and the like), the second possible exemption might come into play. The housing law does not:

bar any religious or denominational institution or organization which is operated or supervised or controlled by or is operated in connection with a religious or denominational organization from limiting admission to or giving preference to persons of the same religion or denomination or from making such selections of buyers, lessees, or tenants as are calculated by such organization or denomination to promote the religious or denominational principles for which it is established or maintained.[75]

To qualify for the exemption, an RAC must be either (1) a religious or denominational institution or (2) an organization run by or in connection with a religious or denominational organization. Virtually all RACs are within (1) and many are within (2). Thus, virtually all RACs are eligible for the exemption.

The exemption would allow religious selectivity in favor of the institution's religious affiliation for any or no reason. Moreover, it would allow selectivity in favor of other religions or denominations as long as it is calculated "to promote the religious or denominational principles for which it is established or maintained." Since the statute specifies that the calculation is to be made by the institution itself, the exemption does not intend courts to second-guess what will promote those principles. Indeed, this very provision may allow for selection based on lifestyle or conduct—for example, a Catholic institution not being required to rent to a divorced person or one who has had an abortion.

The use of the term "admission" (not usually found in connection with housing) may indicate the legislature's view that the housing provisions were not intended to regulate indirectly the admission of students.

Single-sex dormitories would not violate the housing law since it does not "bar any person from leasing premises only to members of one sex."[76]

Both the public accommodations and housing laws are enforced by the Colorado Civil Rights Division.[77]

Colorado's Comprehensive Occupational Safety Law was repealed on April 13, 1980.[78]

F. State Taxation

RACs exempt from federal income taxation,[79] which includes most RACs, are also exempt from Colorado state income taxation.[80] Nonetheless, any "unrelated business taxable income" of an RAC is subject to state taxation.[81]

RACs are exempt from the imposition of Colorado's inheritance and succession tax.[82] There is no limitation imposed upon the use of property received subject to the exemption.

Colorado also imposes an estate tax designed merely to channel to Colorado, by virtue of the credit allowed against the federal estate tax for state death taxes, moneys that would otherwise go to the federal government in estate taxes.[83] This tax, therefore, has no ultimate effect on the *amount* of death taxes paid.

Property transferred as a gift to a nonprofit RAC is exempt from taxation, but only if such property is used exclusively for charitable, educational, or religious purposes.[84]

If an individual itemizes deductions for state income tax purposes, his Colorado itemized deductions will equal, with a few modifications not here relevant, the total amount of the taxpayer's deductions from federal adjusted gross income, whether or not claimed on his federal return.[85] The net result, for taxpayers itemizing for state tax purposes, is to provide a state income tax deduction for contributions to nonprofit RACs, since such contributions are deductible for federal income tax purposes.[86]

Colorado's corporate income tax is calculated, with certain modifications, on the basis of "federal taxable income."[87] Since contributions to RACs by corporations are deductible, in arriving at federal taxable income, up to a limit of five percent of the corporation's taxable income (appropriately modified),[88] a parallel state deduction is in effect provided.

The Colorado Constitution provides that real and personal property used "solely and exclusively" for religious worship, schools, or charitable purposes is exempt from taxation, unless otherwise provided by the General Assembly.[89] The spirit of this provision is carried out under Colorado legislation, which exempts from general taxation real and personal property owned and used solely and exclusively for nonprofit schools.[90] Although the wording of both the constitution and the statute appears restrictive, the Colorado courts have interpreted the provisions liberally. Therefore, the exemption not only includes property *directly* connected with the school's functions, but also income-producing property, the proceeds from which are devoted solely to the institution and are reasonably necessary to carry out its purposes.[91]

The statute also exempts from general taxation real and personal property owned and used exclusively for religious worship and not for profit. The exemption is limited to buildings, the personal property located therein and land essential to the functioning of the buildings.[92] Property used for convents, monasteries and the like is specifically mentioned as tax exempt.[93]

Finally, the section regarding property used for charitable purposes specifically exempts from taxation residential buildings used as an integral part of a school and rented only to students attending that school.[94]

All sales made to nonprofit schools are exempt from the Colorado sales tax.[95] All sales of construction and building materials used in the building, erection, alteration, or repair of structures and roads owned and used by nonprofit schools, even though the sales are not directly to the schools themselves but to contractors or subcontractors, are also exempt from the sales tax.[96] The term school includes most[97] colleges and, therefore, most RACs.

All food sales in Colorado are sales tax-exempt.[98] Colorado exempts from its use tax the storage, use, consumption, or loan of tangible personal property by or to any charitable organization in the conduct of its regular charitable function.[99] Under this article a "charitable organization" is any entity organized and operated exclusively for, *inter alia*, religious or educational purposes.[100] Therefore, an RAC can be considered a charity and is exempt from the tax.

G. Fund Raising

Colorado has no comprehensive legislation specifically regulating charitable solicitation.

Under Colorado's Bingo and Raffles Law,[101] a license authorizing bingo and raffles is available to, *inter alia*, any good faith nonprofit charitable, fraternal, or educational organization in existence continually for five years immediately preceding its license application.[102] The organization must have had during the entire five-year period dues-paying members carry-

ing out its objectives.[103] Although clubs closely identified with an RAC may have no problem qualifying for the license, the "dues-paying members" requirement could be a technical bar to the RAC itself securing the license. Of course, an RAC interested in reaping the benefits of such activities could prevail upon a qualified club to conduct them for the RAC's benefit or could create such a club. In either event, of course, the club will have to have been in existence five years before being eligible for a license.

Since dues-paying memberships include "those who contribute voluntarily to the corporation or organization to which they belong for the support of such corporation or organization,"[104] alumni clubs could qualify even without regular dues. Indeed, perhaps the board of trustees, whose members make voluntary contributions, could secure the license.

In any event, the statute specifically provides that college and high school fraternities are not eligible for such licenses.[105]

Bingo and raffle activities by licensees are comprehensively regulated with regard to the equipment, the operator, the prizes, the number of events per year, and the like.[106] A quarterly report must be filed by each licensee.[107]

The licensing authority under the statute is the Secretary of State.[108]

H. Miscellaneous

Churches and private schools that conduct food service establishments are granted certificates of inspection without payment of the fee otherwise required.[109]

In 1875, the Colorado legislature enacted a consumer protection statute designed to prohibit the use of false or misleading literature, advertising, or representations by private vocational schools, and to set standards governing the educational services, fiscal responsibility, and business practices of these institutions.[110] Even if an RAC in Colorado might be deemed a vocational school, the statute clearly exempts RACs from coverage.[111]

15. Connecticut

A. Corporate Status

The incorporation, maintenance, and dissolution of religiously affiliated colleges (RACs) in Connecticut are governed by the statutes relating to church corporations and ecclesiastical societies[1] and those relating to nonstock corporations.[2] A religious corporation is established when three or more persons uniting for public worship file a certificate with the Secretary of State to form such a corporation; under its charter the corporation may exercise all forms of property rights for "any ecclesiastical, . . . charitable, or educational purpose."[3] This chapter in Connecticut's corporation code dealing with religious corporations was amended in 1969, but the new statute contains a grandfather clause allowing all religious societies in existence before that date to continue to function as a religious corporation without requiring further filing or any change in "any rule of discipline, custom or usage in respect to its policy or government,"[4] without "interfering with the lawful receipt of any grants, donations or funds, in trust or otherwise, for any charitable, educational or ecclesiastical purposes . . . by any such church or religious society,"[5] and without affecting the rights and liabilities of these not-for-profit corporations in existence prior to the statutory change. This feature of the 1969 amendment is significant because, with the exception of a single institution which no longer is functioning,[6] all RACs in Connecticut were founded prior to the 1969 revision of the corporation laws. One advantage for an RAC to function as a religious corporation is that these corporations are not required to file the biennial report with the Secretary of State required of all nonstock corporations.[7]

An RAC in Connecticut may also be organized as a nonstock educational corporation. The title in the Connecticut corporation code dealing with nonstock corporations sets forth general provisions concerning the formation of a nonprofit corporation, the powers it enjoys, the rights and liabilities of its members, and various regulations to which such corporations are subject.[8]

The Connecticut corporation code also governs the dissolution, merger and consolidation of RACs in that state. Voluntary proceedings for dissolution,[9] merger or consolidation[10] must be approved by the Secretary of State.[11] Upon the petition of a member, director, creditor or the dissolving corporation, the superior court for the county in which the principal office of the corporation is located may supervise the dissolution and distribution of the college's assets.[12] After the payment of all liabilities and obligations, the Nonstock Corporation Act provides: (1) Assets held upon a condition requiring return or transfer upon dissolution shall be returned or transferred.[13] (2) Assets held subject to limitations permitting their use only for certain charitable, religious or educational purposes shall be transferred to another domestic or foreign corporation engaged in activities which are substantially similar to those of the dissolving corporation,[14] pursuant to a plan of distribution.[15] (3) Other assets shall be distributed pro rata among the members, except to the extent that the certificate of incorporation determines the rights of members or provides for distributions to others.[16] (4) Any remaining assets may be distributed to the persons or non-profit or for-profit corporations specified in the plan of distribution adopted by the dissolving corporation.[17] In addition, Connecticut courts may apply the *cy pres* doctrine where a testator has evidenced a "dominant intent to devote his property to some charitable use but circumstances are such that it becomes impossible to fulfill the particular method he directs, and courts then sanction its use in some other way which will, as nearly as possible, approximate his general intent."[18]

B. State Support

Because the First Amendment to the United States Constitution was intended as a limit on federal authority,[19] the early states were free to maintain an officially established church. Connecticut did so until 1818, although it had allowed a certain measure of toleration for certified dissenters to the Congregationalist establishment as early as 1784.[20] After 1818 the Connecticut constitution has provided that:

[N]o person shall by law be compelled to join or support, nor be classed or associated with, any congregation, church or religious association. No preference shall be given by law to any religious society or denomination in the state. Each shall have and enjoy the same and equal powers, rights and privileges, and may support and maintain the ministers or teachers of its society or denomination, and may build and repair houses for public worship.[21]

The earlier period of Connecticut's history and of the religious character of higher education in Connecticut at that time is preserved in the current constitution's reference to the charter of Yale College.[22] Although the "Standing Order" of Congregationalism was disestablished in 1818, Professor Howard notes that "Connecticut's Constitution offers considerable room for state aid to private and sectarian education, particularly at the college level."[23]

The first major decision of the U.S. Supreme Court concerning the constitutionality of public financial assistance to RACs was *Tilton v. Richardson.*[24] In *Tilton* the Court sustained federal grants to four RACs in Connecticut, Sacred Heart University, Annhurst College, Fairfield University, and Albertus Magnus College, for construction of facilities at those institutions, provided that the facility is not used "primarily in connection with any part of the program of a school or department of divinity . . . or for sectarian instruction or religious worship."[25] The Court ruled that the statute had a valid secular purpose and that the primary effect of the legislation was neither to advance nor to inhibit religion.[26] Reasoning that the predominant mission of the four Connecticut RACs in question was not to inculcate religious beliefs but to provide a secular education, and noting that the federal aid challenged in the litigation was nonideological in character and in the form of a one-time, single-purpose construction grant, Chief Justice Burger wrote in his plurality opinion that there was little likelihood that the aid would support religious activities at the RACs and that there would not be a need for excessive governmental surveillance of the aid and entanglement with the RACs.[27]

Two years after the passage of the federal statute challenged in *Tilton,* Connecticut enacted similar legislation providing state aid to institutions of higher education, including RACs.[28] Under this program the Connecticut Health and Educational Facilities Authority may issue bonds to help with the construction or renovation of buildings on the campuses of RACs in Connecticut, provided that the facility is not used for sectarian instruction or religious worship.[29] The constitutionality of this statute has not been challenged in litigation, and the program seems clearly permissible in light of the U.S. Supreme Court's decision in *Hunt v. McNair,*[30] upholding a similar program of state assistance enacted by South Carolina.

Connecticut also maintains a grant program providing qualifying independent colleges and universities in that state with funds for student assistance.[31] An institution qualifies for participation in this program if its "primary function is not the preparation of students for religious vocation."[32] The constitutionality of this program has not been subjected to judicial scrutiny, and this program likewise seems permissible in light of the U.S. Supreme Court's decision in *Roemer v. Maryland Board of Public Works,*[33] upholding a program of non-categorical institutional assistance enacted by Maryland.

Finally, Connecticut maintains a system of state scholarships and loans for students attending any approved or accredited institution of higher education, whether in Connecticut or outside the state.[34] The constitutionality of Connecticut's programs of student aid has not been challenged, and these programs are clearly permissible under the U.S. Supreme Court's summary affirmance in *Americans United for Separation of Church and State v. Blanton,*[35] upholding similar programs in Tennessee providing aid to students even if they choose to attend an institution of higher education that is "pervasively sectarian" in character.

C. Personnel

There are three general prohibitions of unfair employment practices in Connecticut law applicable to RACs. First, like any employer with three or more employees, an RAC may not refuse to hire a prospective employee and may not discharge an employee or discriminate in an employee's compensation, terms, conditions or privileges of employment on the basis of the person's "race, color, religious creed, age, sex, marital status, national origin, ancestry, mental retardation or physical disability, including, but not limited to blindness."[36] Second, an RAC may not advertise its employment opportunities in such a way as to restrict these opportunities in a discriminatory way because of the above-mentioned classifications.[37] Third, an RAC may not engage in retaliatory treatment of its employees either because they allege an unfair employment practice or because they participate in a state proceeding concerning such a practice.[38]

The only exception to the first two prohibited practices is the bona fide occupational qualification (BFOQ) exception.[39] When this provision is compared to the parallel federal provision, it is clear that the state exception is broader in the sense of being available to a wider variety of classifications. The federal BFOQ exception is limited to religion, sex, or

national origin; the Connecticut statute makes this exception available in cases involving alleged employment discrimination because of race, color, age, marital status, ancestry, and mental retardation or physical disability.[40] Like the federal statute, however, the Connecticut statute has been construed strictly. In *Evening Sentinel v. National Organization of Women,*[41] the Connecticut Supreme Court held in 1975 that sex classifications in the help wanted section of a newspaper's classified ads constituted a per se violation of the state Fair Employment Practices Act. In one sense, this result was consistent with the ruling of the U.S. Supreme Court in *Pittsburgh Press Co. v. Pittsburgh Commission on Human Relations.*[42] But in another sense, the Connecticut court expanded on *Pittsburgh Press* by forbidding sex-designated advertising even where an employer arguably had a BFOQ exception available to it to justify a gender distinction in prospective employees. In so ruling, the Connecticut court noted that "a BFOQ exists only if no member of the class excluded is physically capable of performing the task required by the job."[43] This strict standard would not be meaningful with respect to religious preference asserted by an RAC, since physical qualities are irrelevant, for the most part, in this context.

The Connecticut Commission on Human Rights and Opportunities has not issued guidelines construing the BFOQ exception as it applies to religious preference, nor is there any case law directly ruling on this point. In light of the fact that the state statute makes available only a BFOQ exception, and in light of the narrow construction given to that kind of exception in the only relevant litigation, an RAC in Connecticut may assert religious preference in its employment policies and practices only where it can show a plausible relationship between the job in question and the religious goals or mission of the college.[44]

Finally, although Connecticut prohibits discrimination on the basis of physical disability, neither alcoholism nor drug addiction has explicitly been defined as a physical disability within the meaning of the state statute.[45] An RAC might, without violating state law, decline to hire or might discharge a chronic alcoholic or person addicted to illicit drugs, if such a person were unwilling or unable to take appropriate steps to overcome his illness or handicap.

Connecticut requires all employers with three or more employees[46] to pay a minimum wage slightly higher than the federal standard.[47] An RAC clearly falls within the statutory definition of an employer and is thus bound by this provision.

Under the Connecticut Unemployment Compensation Code,[48] services performed for non-profit organizations are specifically included within the definition of "employment"[49] if two conditions are met.[50] First, such service must be excluded from the definition of "employment" in the Federal Unemployment Tax Act solely due to section 3306(c)(8).[51] Second, the organization must employ at least one person "for some portion of a day in each of thirteen different weeks, whether or not such weeks were consecutive, within either the current or preceding calendar year, or during any thirteen weeks in any calendar year after 1970, regardless of whether they were employed at the same moment of time."[52]

The statute exempts from coverage the following services performed for RACs: (1) services performed for a church or convention or association of churches;[53] (2) services performed for an organization operated primarily for religious purposes and operated, supervised, controlled or principally supported by a church or convention or association of churches;[54] and (3) services performed by ordained, commissioned or licensed ministers or members of religious orders in the exercise of their duties.[55] Because the scope of these exemptions is narrow, most services performed for RACs are covered under the state's Code.

Other relevant exemptions from the statute's definition of employment include: (1) services performed for a school or college by regularly enrolled students[56] or their spouses;[57] (2) services performed by a student under the age of twenty-two at an accredited nonprofit or public educational institution in a full-time program, combining academic instruction and work experience;[58] (3) services performed in any calendar quarter for an organization exempt from income tax under sections 501(a) or 521, excluding any organization described in section 401(a), of the Internal Revenue Code, if re-

muneration for such services is less than fifty dollars;[59] (4) services performed for which unemployment compensation is payable under a system set up by an Act of Congress;[60] and (5) domestic services for a college club or local chapter of a college fraternity or sorority, if wages paid in any calendar quarter of the current or preceding calendar year were less than $1,000.00.[61]

Nonprofit organizations may elect to make payments in lieu of contributions. To take advantage of this option, an organization must fit the definition of 'non-profit organization' in section 501(a) of the Code.[62] The election is effective for a period of one year[63] upon filing of written notice with the Labor Commissioner.[64] Required payments are equal to the amount of regular and additional benefits plus one-half of the amount of extended benefits paid.[65] In order to take advantage of this election, however, nonprofit organizations may be required to file a surety bond or deposit money with the Labor Commissioner.[66]

RACs in Connecticut are subject to regulation under that state's Workmen's Compensation Act.[67] Covered are all RAC employees except casual workers or corporate officers who elect not to be covered.[68] Compensation will not be paid if an injury is caused by willful and serious misconduct of the employee, or by his intoxication.[69] An employer must either furnish the commission with satisfactory proof of its financial ability to pay compensation, or secure insurance from a company authorized to transact compensation business in the state.[70]

Connecticut has a mini-Wagner Act, protecting the rights of employees to organize and to bargain collectively over wages and terms and conditions of employment.[71] If an RAC in Connecticut is organized as a religious agency or corporation, it is not within the statutory definition of an employer in this statute.[72]

D. Students

Connecticut has no legislation dealing explicitly with student admissions or with discrimination in policies or practices governing student discipline. RACs in Connecticut are, therefore, free to exercise religious preference in student admissions. For example, an RAC may actively recruit for students among members of a particular religious group, and it may administer the provisions of a particular scholarship bequest limited on a religious basis, provided that the general scholarship program is nondiscriminatory in character.[73] RACs are likewise free to assert and to enforce a code of student conduct arising out of religiously grounded ethical concerns. For example, an RAC could legitimately make extramarital sex, the consumption of alcoholic beverages, or the use of illicit drugs a matter of student discipline without thereby violating state law.

E. Facilities

Thirteen years before the congressional enactment of Title II of the Civil Rights Act of 1964[74] and Title VIII of the Civil Rights Act of 1968,[75] which collectively serve as a federal warrant against discrimination in housing and in public accommodations, Connecticut had a constitutional provision[76] and had enacted civil rights legislation[77] which achieve the same end. Both the forms of prohibited discrimination[78] and the scope of dwelling units or places of public accommodations[79] are more comprehensive in the state than in the federal scheme.

Because RACs in Connecticut are not exempt from this legislation, dormitories must be made available on a nondiscriminatory basis. Religious preference in the allocation of student housing, therefore, would probably be deemed violative of the state statute. On the other hand, if a particular college had a predominance of members of a particular religious group in its rental housing which arose not out of purposeful discrimination but as a consequence of its general admissions policy, it would be overreaching for the state to rely upon the public accommodation provision in the civil rights statute to attack the right of an RAC to exercise religious preference in the selection of its student body.

Similarly, an RAC must grant nondiscriminatory access to its places of public accommodation, such as bookstores, theaters, auditoriums, inns, or dining halls. Like any private institution of higher education, an RAC might, of course, insist that a particular event such as a lecture or concert is not open to the general public and thus not governed by the civil rights statute.[80]

Finally, there can be no principled objection to uniformly applicable regulation of the facilities of an RAC, such as elevator inspection, fire safety requirements, or health standards imposed on the sale or consumption of food and beverages. RACs in Connecticut, however, are not covered by that state's Occupational Safety and Health Act,[81] which defines an "employer" as "the state and any political subdivision thereof."[82] RACs are, however, subject to state legislation articulating the duty of reasonable care owed by a master to his servants, including the duty to provide a safe workplace, safe tools, and competent coworkers.[83]

F. Taxation

Although the old Standing Order of Congregationalism was disestablished in 1818, Connecticut did not then abandon its commitment to tax exemption for religious groups, originally pressed for by Episcopalians (then a small, powerless minority) and subsequently extended to Quakers, Baptists and dissident "Separates" within Congregationalism.[84] Indeed, a year after the constitutional convention of 1818, Connecticut enacted legislation exempting church property from taxation.[85] A subsequent revision of this statute in 1821 explicitly exempted from the property tax buildings occupied as "colleges, academies, school houses, churches, or infirmaries."[86] RACs in Connecticut have enjoyed this form of tax exemption ever since,[87] as well as exemption from several other forms of state tax.

Income Tax

Connecticut's corporation business tax does not apply to corporations exempt from federal income tax.[88] Since the income of RACs is generally exempt from federal income taxation,[89] their income is also exempt from Connecticut's corporation business tax.

Inheritance, Estate and Transfer Taxes

Connecticut has no tax called an inheritance tax. The state does impose a succession and transfer tax on the right to receive property at another's death.[90] RACs, however, are exempted from this tax.[91]

Connecticut also imposes an estate tax designed merely to channel to Connecticut, by virtue of the credit allowed against the federal estate tax for state death taxes, moneys that would otherwise go to the federal government in estate taxes.[92] This tax, therefore, has no ultimate effect on the amount of death taxes paid.

Connecticut has no gift tax.

Deductions or Credits for Gifts to RACs

In computing a corporation's net income for Connecticut corporation business tax purposes, all items deductible under the federal corporation net income tax law may be deducted.[93] Since contributions to RACs are deductible for federal purposes,[94] they are deductible in determining the corporation's state income tax.

Connecticut has no true individual income tax, only a capital gains tax applicable to individuals.[95] Thus an individual's contributions to RACs have no state income tax significance.

Real, Personal and Intangibles Property Tax

As mentioned above, the real and personal property of RACs is exempt from Connecticut property tax. RACs qualify for this exemption under one or more of the following three provisions exempting:

(1) Property held or used exclusively for scientific, educational, literary, historical, or charitable purposes;[96]

(2) College property owned by or held in trust for specified institutions, including an exemption for property producing up to $6,000 of income per year for the institution;[97] or

(3) Property owned by a religious organization and used exclusively as a school.[98]

The Connecticut Supreme Court has ruled that in order to qualify as exempt property, school property must be devoted to the public use as well as being sequestered from private use or benefit.[99] This exemption is not limited to buildings used strictly for instructional purposes but extends to property incidental to the educational process, e.g. playing fields.[100]

RACs are thus afforded a broad property tax exemption in Connecticut.

Sales, Use or Meals Taxes

Sales or services to charitable and religious organizations or educational institutions are exempt from sales tax.[101] Sales not subject to sales tax are also exempt from the use tax.[102] Meals served at RACs are exempt from sales tax.[103]

Other Exemptions

Organizations exempt from the federal income tax, and therefore most RACs, need not charge an amusement tax.[104] Nor do RACs have to charge the ten percent admissions and club dues tax.[105] These exemptions also apply to any organizations controlled by nonprofit educational institutions, organizations operating under the lodge system and college fraternities.[106]

G. Fund Raising

In 1979 the state legislature enacted a new statute governing the solicitation of charitable funds.[107] This statute requires that charitable organizations, defined quite broadly in the statute,[108] register with the state Department of Consumer Protection and file an annual report, disclosing the purposes of the organization and any noncharitable uses made of funds raised, the names of professional fund raising counsel and solicitors used by the organization, and a detailed fiscal statement.[109] All documents filed with the state become public records available for inspection.[110] Furthermore, criminal sanctions are provided for violations of the statute.[111] If, however, an RAC can demonstrate that it is "owned, supervised or controlled by a religious organization or society" and if all its charitable solicitation is "conducted solely by members of [the RAC or the affiliated religious] societies or institutions without compensation therefor," a Connecticut RAC may be exempt from the provisions of this new statute.[112] Because many RACs are now structured in such a way as to cast legal doubt on the assertion that they are "owned, supervised, or controlled by a religious organization or society,"[113] and because many of them rely on professional fund raisers in their ongoing effort to survive financially, it would seem that the statute does not provide a flat, general exemption from its terms to all RACs in Connecticut.

H. Miscellaneous Provisions

Connecticut is a member of the New England Higher Education Compact,[114] the purpose of which is:

to provide greater educational opportunities and services through the establishment and maintenance of a coordinated educational program for the persons residing in the several states of New England parties to this compact, with the aim of furthering higher education in the fields of medicine, dentistry, veterinary medicine, public health and in professional, technical, scientific, literary and other fields.[115]

Although most of the state expenditures relating to this Compact support activities at state institutions of higher education, qualifying students attending RACs may participate in some of the programs funded under this scheme.[116]

16. Delaware

A. Corporate Status

RACs, under Delaware law, are incorporated pursuant to the provisions of the General Corporation Law.[1]

Two exemptions under the state's law are worthy of note. First, nonprofit religious or educational organizations are not required to register their securities nor to file copies of their sales literature or advertising communications with the Delaware Securities Commission.[2] The second exemption relates to the provision which voids a corporation's charter for failure to pay its franchise taxes.[3] A very narrow exemption provides that a religious or educational corporation whose charter has been thus revoked shall be deemed to have filed all required reports and to be relieved of all taxes and penalties and is entitled to have its certificate of incorporation or charter renewed if the corporation by its certificate of incorporation had as its object the assistance of sick, needy or disabled members, the defraying of funeral expenses of deceased members or the provision for the wants of widows and families after the death of its members.[4] For a very few RACs, this exemption could be important.

No corporation has the power to confer academic or honorary degrees unless its certificate of incorporation so provides and has been approved by the State Board of Education.[5] Approval is given only when it appears to the reasonable satisfaction of the State Board that (1) the corporation is engaged in conducting a bona fide institution of higher learning or (2) the corporation proposes to engage in that field in good faith and has or will have the resources requisite for the conduct of an institution of higher learning.[6] These provisions cover all incorporated RACs.

The merger, consolidation, and dissolution of nonprofit colleges are governed by specific sections within the Delaware General Corporation Law.[7] The *cy pres* doctrine applies in Delaware when property is given in trust for a particular charitable purpose which is or becomes impossible or impractical to carry out.[8]

A merger, consolidation, or dissolution is subject to approval by the Secretary of State.[9] Upon application of any creditor, stockholder, or other interested person, the Court of Chancery may appoint a receiver for the college's assets.[10] The Court of Chancery has jurisdiction over all questions arising from this application, and may make orders and issue injunctions required by justice and equity.[11]

The subchapter on dissolution in the General Corporation Law provides only that upon dissolution a corporation's liabilities shall be discharged and any remaining assets shall be distributed to the corporation's stockholders.[12]

B. State Support

The State of Delaware forbids the direct funding of RACs. The Delaware Constitution declares that "no man shall or ought to be compelled to . . . contribute to the erection or support of any place of worship, or to the maintenance of any ministry, against his own free will and consent . . ."[13] Although the General Assembly is directed to provide for "the establishment and maintenance of a general and efficient system of free public schools,[14] the Constitution stipulates that no portion of any fund appropriated for educational purposes shall be appropriated to, or used by, or in aid of, any sectarian, church, or denominational schools.[15] The Delaware Supreme Court, striking down a statute authorizing funds for the transportation of pupils attending free schools supported by churches, said, "The words 'sectarian, church or denominational school' as used in the Constitution mean schools which are under the control, domination or governing influence of any religious sect or denomination."[16] This interpretation serves to prohibit *direct* state support to virtually all RACs.

Financial aid is available, under certain circumstances, to qualified Delaware students to pursue courses of higher education at RACs. Scholarships at the undergraduate level are available to those students who are accepted as full-time students at accredited institutions and enrolled in a program of study which is not offered by a publicly supported Delaware college or university.[17] Scholarships at the graduate level are available to those students who meet the same requirements and are enrolled in courses of study leading to occupations and professions for which there is a reasonable expectation of job opportunity in Delaware upon completion of such study.[18]

Clearly the conditions which must be satisfied to be awarded state scholarships severely limit the number of scholarships going to students attending RACs. Few programs of study will be offered at an RAC that are not offered at state-supported institutions. For such programs at the graduate level, fewer still will be among the accepted list of courses of study leading to job opportunities in Delaware.[19] As a result, the amount of even indirect aid to RACs is relatively insignificant.

C. Personnel

In Delaware, it is an unlawful employment practice for an employer to discriminate against an individual because of that individual's race, color, age, religion, sex, or national origin.[20] "Employer" generally means any person employing four or more persons within the state.[21] However, a religious, charitable, fraternal, or sectarian corporation is not an "employer" for purposes of religious or sex discrimination.[22] Since some RACs may qualify as "religious" corporations and since Delaware case law generally holds that an educational institution can be a "charitable" institution,[23] many RACs may not be bound by the sex or religious employment provision.

In any event, the Delaware legislature has specifically exempted certain RACs from the religious discrimination prohibition:

It shall not be an unlawful employment practice for a school, college, university, or other educational institution or institution of learning to hire and employ employees of a particular religion if such school, college, university, or other educational institution of learning is, in whole or in substantial part, owned, supported, controlled or managed by a particular religion or by a particular religious corporation, association or society or if the curriculum of such school, college, university, or other educational institution or institution of learning is directed toward the propagation of a particular religion.[24]

This provision is intended to exempt certain religiously oriented educational institutions. For institutions that qualify, religious selectivity of all employees, whatever their function, would be authorized. For some RACs, however, it may be difficult to meet the religious affiliation requirements.

There is some vagueness in these requirements. There is no specific statutory or judicial guidance as to *factually* how much control by a religion or by a religious organization is sufficient. Is an institution "controlled" by a religion if it adheres to its doctrine or must there be a discernible religious entity (e.g., a formal church) in "control"? If the latter, then the "or by a particular religious [organization]" alternative is redundant. Arguably, then, an institution qualifies if it considers itself within the control of the tenets of a particular religion.

Even absent this interpretation, however, the phrasing is probably broad enough to include most RACs. Nonetheless, some institutions may lack a sufficient connection to be included within the provision, especially since the legislature did not include the words "or in connection with" between the phrases "owned, supported, controlled or managed by" and "a particular religion." This may have been a mere oversight or an indication that the legislature intended a narrower scope than that of other such statutes.

An RAC will also qualify for this exemption if its curriculum is directed toward the propagation of a particular religion. This would seem to apply only to Bible colleges, seminaries, and the like.

There is some uncertainty as to the significance of the repeated use of the phrase "a particular religion." Nonetheless, it would appear that an RAC otherwise within the exemption could prefer an employment applicant of *any* religion, not merely one of the same religion as the institution. Perhaps it was felt useful to restrict the exemption to institutions and employment applicants of identifiable and specific religious affiliations.

In any event, a separate provision establishes a bona fide occupational qualification (BFOQ) exemption for all employees:

It shall not be an unlawful employment practice for an employer to hire and employ employees . . . on the basis of his religion, age, sex, or national origin in those certain instances where religion, age, sex or national origin is a bona fide occupational qualification reasonably necessary to the normal operation of that particular business or enterprise.[25]

This provision authorizes, in BFOQ situations, selectivity on all otherwise proscribed bases save race and color. RACs will be primarily interested in the religion BFOQ, which would probably not greatly protect them in personnel decisions involving positions other than those of theology or philosophy faculty and perhaps of certain counselors. It is not likely that an RAC would be successful in arguing a right to exercise religious preference in the employment of faculty generally despite its interest in establishing on campus a pervasive presence of faculty of a certain religious persuasion.

The sex BFOQ would be especially helpful in hiring dormitory personnel and *perhaps* some counselors and teachers of courses in women's rights or women's history.

The employment provisions are enforced by the Delaware Department of Labor.[26]

For the most part, the minimum wage provisions[27] of the Delaware Code include RACs since the term "employer" means any person acting in the interest of an employer in relation to an employee.[28] The sole exemptions applicable to RACs exclude from the coverage individuals in bona fide executive, administrative or professional capacities[29] or those "engaged in the activities of an educational, charitable, religious or nonprofit organization where the employment relationship does not in fact exist or where the services are rendered to such organization gratuitously."[30]

The Delaware Workmen's Compensation Law[31] covers any corporation that has one or more employees[32] who are not expressly excluded from coverage.[33] Generally RACs are covered unless some of their employees come within the exceptions for casual employment[34] or employment covered by a federal worker's compensation law.[35] Employers who are not covered by the Act are deemed to have elected to become subject to its provisons if they carry compensation insurance for their otherwise exempted employees.[36] RACs must carry insurance or prove financial ability to compensate injured employees directly.[37] On the presentation of such proof the Industrial Accident Board will issue a revocable certificate of self-insurance to the employer.[38] The Board may require the self-insurer to deposit acceptable security with the State Insurance Commissioner.[39]

Delaware Unemployment Compensation Law[40] includes as "employment" service by an employee of a religious, charitable, educational, or other organization if the service is excluded from the definition of "employment" in the Federal Unemployment Tax Act solely by reason of Section 3306(c)(8) of that Act.[41] Service performed in the employ of a religious or educational organization described in Section 501(c)(3) of the Internal Revenue Code of 1954,[42] and thereby exempt from federal taxation, is excluded from "employment" as defined in Section 3306(c)(8) of the Federal Unemployment Tax Act.[43] Thus an RAC is subject to the unemployment compensation legislation if it qualifies for tax exempt status under Section 501(c)(3).

With regard to such covered service, federally tax-exempt nonprofit corporations may make the usual contribution[44] or elect to make "reimbursement" payments to the Unemployment Compensation Fund of an amount equal to the regular benefits plus one-half the extended benefits paid in connection with service for the nonprofit corporation.[45]

In any event, "employment" under the law does not include service performed (1) for a church or convention or association of churches;[46] (2) for an organization operated primarily for religious purposes and controlled or principally supported by a church or convention or association of churches;[47] or (3) by a "duly ordained, commissioned or licensed minister of a church in the exercise of his ministry or by a member of a religious order in the exercise of duties required by such order."[48] None of these exceptions is very broad insofar as employment at the typical RAC is concerned and, consequently, few positions at RACs will come within any of the three. This is true because (1) very few people employed by RACs can claim to be working for a church, convention, or association of churches; (2) except perhaps for institutions like seminaries and Bible colleges, few RACs can claim to be both operated primarily for religious purposes and run or principally supported by a church or group of churches; and (3) few employees on RAC campuses, save perhaps some counselors or theology teachers, will be regular ministers of a church exercising their ministry or members of a religious order performing duties required by that order.

Nonetheless, the following services, *inter alia*, are excluded from the definition of "employment" and thus are not subject to the provisions of the Unemployment Compensation law: (1) domestic service in a local college club or local chapter of a college fraternity or sorority unless performed for a person who paid more than $1,000 in any quarter in the current or preceding calendar year to individuals performing such domestic service;[49] (2) service with regard to which unemployment compensation is payable under a congressionally established system;[50] (3) service for a school, college, or university if performed by a regular student at that institution;[51] and (4) service performed by a student under the age of twenty-two, in a nonprofit or public educational institution with a regular faculty, curriculum and student body, in a full-time program for credit which combines academic instruction with work experience.[52] Such service must be an integral part of the program, this must be certified to the employer, and the program must not have been established for or on behalf of an employer.[53]

Most RACs must make unemployment compensation contributions (or "reimbursement" payments) for all employees performing service other than those excepted. However, a clarifying provision states that unemployment benefits are not paid to instructors, researchers, or principal administrators of colleges and universities for the period between successive academic years or terms, between two regular but not successive terms, or during a paid sabbatical provided for in the individual's contract, if he performs such services in the first of such academic years or terms or if there is a contract or a reasonable assurance the individual will perform service in any such capacity for any educational institution in the second academic year or term.[54] (A comparable provision controls payments for weeks commencing during established and customary vacation periods or holiday recesses.)[55]

D. Students

Delaware has no law regulating admissions to private institutions of higher education.[56]

E. Facilities

The Delaware Code prohibits discrimination in places of public accommodation against any person because of race, age, marital status, creed, color, sex, or national origin.[57] A "place of public accommodation" means any establishment which caters to or offers goods, services, or facilities to, or solicits patronage from, the general public.[58] There is no general exemption applicable to RACs. Thus, an RAC may not deny to any person, because of race, age, marital status, creed, color, sex, or national origin, full use of any of its facilities unless those facilities are closed to the general public.

Delaware's "Equal Rights to Housing" law[59] prohibits discrimination based on race, age, marital status, creed, color, sex, handicap, or national origin in the sale or rental of "dwellings offered to the public."[60] Since this phrase is interpreted to include housing of which any notice of sale or rental availability is published,[61] campus housing would likely be included. The prohibition, however, does not apply to dwellings owned and operated for other than a commercial purpose by a religious organization or any nonprofit organization operated, supervised, or controlled by, or in conjunction with, a religious organization.[62] The religious affiliation required for the exemption is loose enough to include a great many RACs.[63]

Both the public accommodations and the housing laws are enforced by the State Human Relations Commission.[64]

The Landlord-Tenant Code[65] prohibits discrimination on several bases in the renting or leasing of any real property.[66] However, this prohibition was not meant to govern residences at a private educational or religious institution.[67] This exemption is specifically applicable to all RACs.

Delaware has no occupational safety and health type of legislation.

F. State Taxation

Delaware's Corporation Income Tax[68] specifically exempts corporations created for religious or educational purposes as long as no part of the net earnings inures to the benefit of any private stockholder or individual.[69]

Under the "Inheritance Tax" provisions,[70] any property, estate or interest devised or bequeathed for educational or religious purposes will not be included in the decedent's gross estate or be subject to the inheritance tax.[71]

Delaware also imposes an estate tax designed merely to channel to Delaware, by virtue of the credit allowed against the federal estate tax for state death taxes, moneys that would otherwise go to the federal government in estate taxes.[72]

This tax, therefore, has no ultimate effect on the amount of state death taxes paid.

The Delaware Gift Tax[73] definition of "taxable gift" is the same as that for federal gift tax purposes[74] and, therefore, gifts to colleges and universities would not be taxed.[75]

Charitable contributions that an individual might have deducted for federal income tax purposes are deductible, to those who itemize on their state returns, under the Delaware income tax provisions.[76] Since contributions to nonprofit religious or educational institutions are deductible for federal income tax purposes,[77] contributions to virtually all RACs are deductible under Delaware law.

Property owned by any school or college and used for educational purposes is not subject to taxation and assessment by any county or other political subdivision of the state.[78] This would exempt from taxation all property owned by an RAC except that which was not used to further the educative function of the institution. What property furthers the educative function may not be clear, however. In one case, a Delaware court held that the residence of a school's headmaster had as its purpose furnishing a habitation for the employee and not the promotion of the efficient administration of the institution. It was not, therefore, exempt from taxation.[79] The test suggested by this case for exempt status would seem to be that the school and its administration benefit directly, as opposed to incidentally, from the property.

Delaware has no general sales or use tax.

There is a broad exemption from license fees[80] for nonprofit organizations exempt from federal income taxation under Section 501 of the Internal Revenue Code of 1954 as amended.[81] This would include virtually all RACs[82].

Any nonprofit corporation or organization created for charitable, religious or educational purposes which operates "a day care center primarily for children not over 6 years of age and not primarily as a medical or educational facility" is exempt from the payment of annual license taxes.[83]

Any nonprofit charitable, religious, or educational organization operating a nursery, rest home, or convalescent home is "exempt from any license under [the "Cost of Occupational License and Fees] chapter."[84]

G. Fund Raising

There are no provisions in the Delaware Code regulating the solicitation of funds by charitable, religious or educational organizations.

The Delaware Constitution declares the game of bingo lawful when conducted and operated by a religious or charitable organization in a district which has approved the licensing of bingo by referendum.[85] This provision is applicable to RACs insofar as such colleges can be defined as "charitable" organizations.[86]

H. Miscellaneous Provisions

The Delaware Code stipulates that all schools, colleges and other institutions of learning are to be closed on every day on which a general election is held.[87] This provision clearly extends to RACs.

17. Florida

A. Corporate Status

The creation, maintenance, and dissolution of corporations not for pecuniary profit in Florida are governed by state law.[1] (In addition, Florida courts may apply the *cy pres* doctrine if necessary.)[2] Three or more persons are required to file articles of incorporation,[3] accompanied by a thirty dollar fee,[4] with the Secretary of State for his approval.[5] Certain activities such as the issuance of shares and the payment of dividends are prohibited.[6]

RACs and other nonprofit educational institutions are required to meet minimum educational standards and to be licensed unless already accredited by a recognized accrediting agency or unless the institutions' degrees and credits are accepted by at least three accredited institutions of higher learning.[7] Accreditation is vital with regard to eligibility for tax exemptions and student scholarship funding.[8]

Voluntary dissolution of such a corporation entails five steps: (1) a petition to the local circuit court; (2) publication of direct notice; (3) a decree of dissolution by the judge; (4) the filing of the decree with the Department of State; and (5) recordation of the decree in the circuit court which approved the corporate charter.[9] The circuit judge not only must approve the dissolution, but also is charged with satisfying the claims of creditors and distributing the remaining assets.[10] The merger or consolidation of a college with another nonprofit corporation is conditioned upon the approval of articles of merger or consolidation by the Department of State.[11]

Since the governing statute is not specific in limiting distribution of assets, the court must rely on the judicial doctrine of *cy pres* and its own discretion to determine recipients.[12]

B. State Support

Direct

Public funding of RACs is expressly prohibited since Article I, Section 3 of the Florida Constitution prohibits the use of public revenue directly or indirectly to aid any sectarian institution.[13] Under Article 7, Section 10, the pledging of credit by the state or any political subdivision to aid any corporation, association, partnership, or person is also constitutionally disallowed.[14]

Despite these two constitutional prohibitions, the Florida legislature has created the "Higher Educational Facilities Authority Law," which provides for assistance to colleges and universities, sectarian and nonsectarian, for the construction of educational facilities.[15] The law creates in each county an authority empowered to issue revenue bonds whenever a need is declared in order to finance construction of facilities for higher education.[16] The Florida Supreme Court in *Nohrr v. Brevard County Educational Facilities Authority*[17] held that the "Educational Facilities Law" does violence to neither the First Amendment to the United States Constitution nor to the Florida Constitution.[18] The *Nohrr* court stated:

106

The Educational Facilities Law discloses that no aid is granted at public expense. All expenses are required to be borne by the educational institution involved and no other source of payment, which might otherwise be available for the public generally, is to be used in any manner whatsoever in connection with the project.[19]

Furthermore, the *Nohrr* opinion observes:

A state cannot pass a law to aid one religion or all religions, but state action to promote the general welfare of society, apart from any religious consideration, is valid, even though religious interests may be indirectly benefited.[20]

In the same case, the Florida court held that the Higher Educational Facilities Authority Law did not violate Article 7, Section 10 of the state constitution. Said the court:

The word "credit," as used in Fla. Const., art. VII, §10 (1968), implies the imposition of some new financial liability upon the State or a political subdivision which in effect results in the creation of a State or political subdivision debt for the benefit of private enterprises.

In order to have a gift, loan or use of public credit, the public must be either directly or contingently liable to pay something to somebody. Neither the full faith and credit nor the taxing power of the State of Florida or of any political subdivision thereof is pledged to the payment of the principal of, or the interest on, these revenue bonds.[21]

Thus, in spite of apparent constitutional barriers, the state legislature has conferred a very substantial benefit on RACs with regard to physical facilities.

Indirect

Article 7, Section 15 of the Florida Constitution declares that revenue bonds may be issued to form a fund from which loans may be made available to college students.[22] Accordingly, the legislature has created such a fund as well as several other scholarship and financial aid programs for higher education in Part IV of Chapter 240. All are administered by the State Department of Education.

The first program in this Part is the State Tuition Voucher Fund.[23] Operation of the fund is outlined as follows:

The department shall issue from the fund a tuition voucher to any full-time undergraduate student registered at a nonprofit college or university which is located in and chartered by the state, which is accredited by an agency holding membership in the Council on Postsecondary Accreditation, which grants baccalaureate degrees and whose credits are acceptable without qualifications for transfer to state universities, and which is not a state university or a pervasively sectarian institution.[24]

The phrase "pervasively sectarian institution" is not defined in the statute and no reported case has yet construed the statute since the section has been in effect less than one year.[25] Nonetheless, the use of the phrase "pervasively sectarian" rather than, for example, "sectarian" or "religiously affiliated", indicates a legislative intent not to exclude the typical RAC but rather such institutions as divinity schools, i.e., schools substantially all of whose programs are distinctly religious.

The program provides for the issuance of a voucher to the school for credit to the student's account.[26]

Another major fund created in Chapter 240 is the State Student Assistance Grant Fund.[27] This fund offers assistance grants of up to $1200 per annum on the basis of unmet need to resident full-time students.[28] Recipients must be accepted at an approved college or university, which may be an RAC, provided it is accredited.[29]

A third source of educational funds available to the student attending an RAC in Florida is the Student Financial Aid Fund.[30] Scholarship loans from this fund covering unmet need of up to $1800 are made available to full-time students attending:

any institution of higher learning in Florida, either private or public, which is a member of the Southern Association of Colleges and Secondary Schools or whose credits are acceptable for transfer to state universities in Florida or professional nursing diploma schools.[31]

"Moneys allocated for loans to students in private colleges" are not to exceed forty percent of the general revenue payments to the Student Financial Aid Trust Fund.[32]

In addition to the three general educational funds, Chapter 240 creates general scholarship loans for teachers[33] and special scholarships for nursing,[34] for Seminole and Miccosukoe Indians,[35] and for teachers in exceptional child education programs.[36] Participating institutions under the three special scholarship programs may include RACs.[37] Thus, accredited RACs have every opportunity to participate in the scholarship and loan programs.

C. Personnel

Hiring, Promoting, and Firing

Article 1, section 2 of the Florida Constitution declares that "[n]o person shall be deprived of any right because of race, religion or physical handicap."[38] The Human Rights Act of 1977[39] proclaims more specifically that

It is an unlawful employment practice for an employer . . . [t]o discharge or to fail or refuse to hire any individual, or otherwise to discriminate against any individual with respect to compensation, terms, conditions, or privileges of employment, because of such individual's race, color, religion, sex, national origin, age, handicap, or marital status.[40]

It is also an unlawful employment practice for an employer to publish any advertisement suggesting any employment preference based on such factors.[41]

For the purposes of the Human Rights Act, an "employer" is any person "employing 15 or more employees for each working day in each of 20 or more calendar weeks in the current or preceding calendar year and any agent of such a person."[42] This definition includes the typical RAC. The only exception to the Act applicable with any particularity to RACs is:

in those certain instances in which religion, sex, national origin, age, absence of a particular handicap or marital status is a bona fide occupational qualification [BFOQ] reasonably necessary for the performance of a particular employment.[43]

This exception would probably not greatly protect RACs in personnel decisions involving faculty outside the areas of theology and philosophy. It is not likely that an RAC would be successful in arguing a right to exercise religious preference in the employment of faculty generally despite the RAC's interest in establishing on campus a pervasive presence of faculty of a certain religious persuasion.

RACs receive no other exemption permitting a religious preference in hiring and promoting. It might be argued that as to certain positions, e.g., a teacher of theology, an RAC has a right under the First Amendment of the United States Constitution to limit employment to or to prefer members of a particular religious group.

Wages and Hours

The only minimum wage provision in Florida law merely prohibits unequal pay based on sex.[44] Similarly deficient is the single overtime compensation clause which vaguely requires "extra pay" for all manual labor performed in excess of ten hours daily in the absence of a contract to the contrary.[45] RACs fall within the purview of these provisions as only employers of fewer than two employees are exempted.[46]

Worker's Compensation

Florida reformed its Worker's Compensation Law in 1979, substantially rewriting the previous law to make it "suitable and contemporary."[47] At the same time, the Florida Supreme Court adopted the Florida Worker's Compensation Rules of Procedure to "govern all proceedings within its scope."[48]

The law covers all employers who have three or more employees,[49] so RACs will be included. Officers of corporations will be covered unless they choose to be exempt and file certification of the choice.[50] The law does not cover independent contractors, including employees whose work is both "casual" and "not in the course of the employer's profession."[51] "Casual" workers are those whose work is for fewer than ten days.[52]

Injuries requiring compensation under the law are any arising by accident out of and in the course of the employment.[53] Diseases covered are only those caused by or resulting from an accident; those attributable to other causes will not be covered unless an accident (but not the working conditions) aggravated them.[54] Mental or nervous injuries due to fright and excitement only, or disability due to venereal disease or the habitual use of alcohol or drugs, are specifically exempted.[55] If the employee was intoxicated, or if there was willful intention on the part of an employee to injure or kill himself or another, no compensation will be paid.[56] Willful refusal by an employee to use a safety device or observe a safety rule required by statute will cause the compensation paid to be reduced by twenty-five percent.[57]

Otherwise, compensation is payable without respect to fault as to the cause of the injury.[58]

Unemployment Compensation

Florida revised its Unemployment Compensation law in 1980, effective January, 1981.[59] The law requires all employers subject to its terms to pay unemployment benefits to any employee who has left his employment involuntarily, not due to his own misconduct, and has properly filed a claim.[60] Florida's stated intention is to meet all the requirements of the Federal Unemployment Tax Act, and its stated policy is to require a liberal construction of the law's terms. The definition of "employment" is very broad, as is the definition of "employer";[61] most RACs will be included.

There is an exclusion for services performed for "a church or convention of churches, or an organization which is operated, supervised, controlled, [or] . . . principally supported by a church or convention of churches."[62] Moreover, covered employment does not include service for a college or university by a regularly enrolled student.[63] So an RAC principally controlled by a church will not be covered.

No benefits are payable in regard to services in an instructional, research, or principally administrative capacity performed for a college for any week of unemployment which falls between two academic years, two regular terms, or during a sabbatical leave which is provided for in the person's contract.[64]

D. Students

There are no Florida laws which have any particular bearing on students attending RACs.

E. Facilities

Florida law calls for the licensing of public lodging and public food service establishments.[65] Excluded from the definition of "public lodging establishment," however, is "any dormitory or other living or sleeping facility maintained by a . . . private . . . college or university primarily for use of students, faculty, or visitors."[66] This exemption extends even to university-run hotels which cater primarily to campus guests. The definition of "public food service establishment" similarly excludes "any place maintained by . . . a private . . . college or university, either: (a) Privately for the use of students and faculty; or (b) On a temporary basis to serve such events as fairs, carnivals, and athletic contests.[67] Thus, campus eateries maintained by an RAC are likewise exempt from licensing requirements.

Florida has no comprehensive public accommodations law. RACs are exempt from the licensing requirements as noted, but, more importantly, RACs are exempt from the antidiscrimination provisions of the state code which pertain to public lodging and public food service establishments.[68]

Two other provisions which may affect RACs, however, are the equal accommodations law for the handicapped[69] and the Human Rights Act of 1977.[70] The handicapped law requires equal accommodations for the deaf, blind, and visually handicapped in all places where the general public is invited; it does not apply to facilities existing before October 1, 1974.[71] RACs are afforded no special treatment in regard to requirements concerning accessibility of facilities to the handicapped. Part V of Chapter 553—Building Construction Standards—provides for accessibility.[72] The obstruction of common or emergency exits of licensed business establishments is prohibited.[73] Much higher requirements of accessibility are set for new buildings.[74] Not only is none of the listed exceptions applicable to RACs,[75] but educational

and institutional occupancy is one of the classifications adopted for the purposes of Part V.[76]

The human rights law makes the broad policy
statement that the state is determined to secure
"freedom from discrimination because of race,
color, religion, sex, national origin, age, handicap, or marital status."[77]

Florida has no fair housing legislation.

Although Florida has no OSHA type law,
every "employer" must "furnish employment
which shall be safe for the employees therein"[78]
—including safety devices and a safe workplace. RACs are "employers" within the meaning of the term.[79] The Division of Workers'
Compensation via the State Labor Department
is authorized to prescribe safety devices and
fix reasonable safety standards in all places of
employment.[80]

F. State Taxation

Estate, inheritance, and income taxes in
Florida are limited constitutionally, but RACs
are not exempted.[81] Nor are RACs exempted
statutorily in the "Florida Income Tax Code."[82]
In fact, it is the express legislative intent of the
Code "to impose a tax upon all corporations"[83]
including corporations not for profit.[84] "Taxable income," however, in the case of an organization which is exempt from federal income
tax by reason of Section 501(a) of the Internal
Revenue Code (IRC) (This includes RACs.)[85]
means its unrelated business income as determined under the IRC.[86] The IRC in turn as a
general rule defines the term "unrelated trade or
business" as business which is not substantially
related (aside from the need or use made of the
profits derived) to the performance of the organization's charitable, educational, or other
purposes.[87] Thus, to the extent an RAC is exempt federally it is likewise exempt from the
state income tax; that is, only profits which an
RAC derives from businesses unrelated to its
educational or religious purposes will be taxed
regardless of how the profits are used. From
this general rule, it appears the profits derived
from such activities as publishing, theater productions, and bookstore sales will not be taxed
as they are "substantially related" to an RAC's
educational function, whereas an RAC's proceeds from industries such as farming, broad-

casting, or business investing will be subject to
both state and federal taxation.

There is no gift tax in Florida.

The Florida Constitution states that "[s]uch
portions of property as are used *predominantly*
for educational, . . . religious, or charitable
purposes *may* be exempted by general law from
taxation."[88] Accordingly, the state legislature
has statutorily extended such an exemption to
educational institutions within the state for real
and personal property used exclusively for
educational purposes.[89]

Exempt from the Intangible Personal Property Tax Act[90] is all intangible personal property owned by nonprofit religious or nonprofit
educational institutions.[91] "Educational Institution" for the purposes of this exemption includes "parochial, church, and nonprofit private
schools, colleges, and universities conducting
regular classes and courses of study required
for accreditation."[92]

The same definition of "educational institution" is used to exempt from taxation sales of
tangible personal property made by RACs.[93]
Under a now-repealed section,[94] every educational institution operated for a profit was taxed
a license fee of $15.00 for each place of
business.[95] Under that section, the *Albury v.
Tanner*[96] court held that a school operated by a
religious organization at a substantial financial
deficit and without any income accruing to any
church official was not "for profit" as that
phrase was used in the section.[97] The legislature, however, repealed and replaced that provision before the *Albury* case was finally decided.[98] The new provision reads:

> [W]hen used in this chapter . . .'business', 'profes-
> sion,' and 'occupation' do not include the customary
> religious, charitable or educational activities of non-
> profit religious, nonprofit charitable, and nonprofit
> educational institutions in this state.[99]

RACs are thus categorically excluded from the
"place of business" tax.

G. Fund Raising

Charitable Solicitation

Solicitation of charitable funds within Florida
is regulated.[100] The Department of State is

vested with the authority to promulgate appropriate rules and regulations governing solicitation for "charitable purposes,"[101] including religion and education.[102]

Charitable organizations intending to solicit within the state or have funds solicited on their behalf must, prior to any solicitation, file a registration application with the Department of State.[103]

An RAC may be exempted from these regulations, however, if it constitutes a "bona fide religious institution." Such institutions are the only exceptions to the general definition of charitable organization within which RACs otherwise fall.[104] "Bona fide religious institution" includes organizations which form an integral part of a church, are exempt from federal income tax under Section 501(c)(3) of the Internal Revenue Code, and are not primarily supported by funds solicited outside of their membership.[105] RACs are exempt under Section 501(c)(3).[106] But even if students, parents, and alumni are considered "members" of an RAC, it still must form an integral part of a church (or denominational organization) in order to qualify as a bona fide religious institution and consequently be free from regulation of its charitable solicitation.

Three additional exemptions from registration are specified. The first contains three conditions: the organization must not receive contributions from more than ten persons; all of its functions, including fund raising activities, must be conducted by volunteers; and no income may inure to the benefit of any officer or member.[107] An RAC may also be exempted if solicitation occurs only within its membership.[108] The final exemption is granted to organizations which receive no more than $4,000 in public contributions.[109] These three exceptions may be of help to the very small RAC, but the typical RAC must seek contributions on a large scale and outside its organizational membership.

Games of Chance

Florida law exempts nonprofit organizations which have been in existence three years or more from most regulation of bingo games, provided the proceeds are donated to, for example, religious or scholastic works.[110] Nevertheless, frequency, location, and size of such games are limited.[111]

The Florida Pari-mutuel Commission is authorized to extend time limitations on horseracing, dog racing, and jai alai operations so that a track or fronton may conduct a charity day for any charitable institution within a one-hundred mile radius.[112] For the purposes of this section, institutions of higher learning are considered "charitable institutions."[113]

H. Miscellaneous Provisions

The Department of Insurance is authorized to regulate the administration of any cooperative plan or scholarship plan in the state.[114]

18. Georgia

A. Corporate Status

Nonprofit corporations may be organized for any lawful purpose, including educational or religious.[1] Under Georgia law, no corporation may put any words or phrases into its name which indicate an affiliation with a religious organization unless that fact is certified in writing to the Secretary of State.[2]

The dissolution, merger, and consolidation of private colleges are governed by provisions of the Georgia Nonprofit Corporation Code.[3] In addition, the Georgia Supreme Court has ruled that if it is impossible to execute the terms of a validly probated will, a court of equity in Georgia must execute it by approximation.[4]

When a college dissolves voluntarily[5] or merges or consolidates with another college,[6] it must submit articles of merger, consolidation, or dissolution to the Secretary of State. If the Secretary finds the articles to be in proper form, they are approved and a certificate is issued.[7] The dissolution may be supervised by the Superior Court of the county in which the dissolving corporation's registered office is located, in an action by: (1) a member or director; (2) a creditor; or (3) the dissolving corporation. An involuntary dissolution will also be supervised by the superior courts in an action brought by the Attorney General because of fraud or violation of the Nonprofit Corporation Code.[8]

After the payment of all court costs, liabilities and obligations, the Georgia Code provides: (1) assets held upon a condition re-quiring return or transfer upon dissolution shall be returned or transferred;[9] (2) assets held subject to limitations permitting their use only for certain charitable, religious, or educational purposes shall be transferred to another domestic or foreign corporation engaged in activities which are substantially similar to those of the dissolving corporation,[10] pursuant to a plan of distribution;[11] (3) other assets shall be distributed to members or others in accordance with the provisions of the articles of incorporation or the bylaws of the dissolving corporation;[12] and (4) any remaining assets may be distributed to persons, organizations and domestic or foreign nonprofit and for-profit corporations, as may be specified in a plan of distribution.[13]

B. State Support

The Georgia State Constitution forbids any direct or indirect public aid of "any church, sect, or denomination of religionists, or of any sectarian institution."[14] Taken literally, this provision seems considerably more restrictive than its counterpart in the United States Constitution. Of course, even under the Georgia Constitution, aid to an RAC need not necessarily be deemed to be aid to any particular religion, sect, or denomination although "sectarian institutions" could easily be read to include RACs.

Chapter 32–49 creates an Authority which is empowered to deal with the financing of facilities (projects) at private, "not-for-profit" institutions of higher education. A five-member panel, appointed by the governor for staggered terms, is provided for.[15] Although the Authority may contract, sue, implead, and be sued, it is not a state instrument, department, or agency. It is an "instrumentality of purely public charity performing an essential governmental function, being a distinct corporate entity."[16] The purpose of the Authority is to assist non-profit institutions of higher education in the construction, financing, and refinancing of various projects.[17] A project is broadly defined to include all sorts of campus buildings, proposed, under construction or completed, and parking facilities, landscaping, furniture and equipment.[18] The term "project" specifically excludes "any facility used or to be used for sectarian instruction or as a place of religious worship [or] any facility which is used or to be used primarily in connection with any part of the program of a school or department of divinity for any religious denomination."[19]

The Authority will assist universities in their projects by issuing revenue bonds and lending the proceeds from the bonds under loan agreements with the institutions. The statute details such mechanics of the bond process as interest, expenses, loan agreements, and method of fixing rates.[20]

Section 32–4907 makes it clear that neither the credit of the State of Georgia nor that of its subdivisions is pledged through the bond process provided for.[21]

Chapter 32–27 of the Georgia State Code, as enacted in 1980 and revised in 1981, created the Georgia Student Finance Authority to administer all loans to students, from federal, state, or some private sources. Under the revised law, both the student and the college he or she attends must qualify to receive loans from this Authority. The qualifications for the school will eliminate some RACs from eligibility:

A nonproprietary institution of higher education located in Georgia which is not a branch of the University System of Georgia, which is accredited by the Southern Association of Colleges and Schools, which is not a bible school or college (or, at the graduate level, a school or college of theology or divinity) and which is not presently receiving State funds . . . Provided, however, that an institution which otherwise meets the requirements of this

definition and of this Chapter except for the lack of accreditation by the Southern Association of Colleges and Schools shall be deemed to be an "approved school" during the period that the institution holds candidate for accreditation status with the Southern Association of Colleges and Schools.[22]

Only fully accredited, degree-granting RACs will be eligible. A qualifying student must be a full-time (enrolled for at least ten hours) student at the undergraduate level in an approved school, and must have been a citizen of Georgia for a period of at least twelve months prior to the date of registration.[23] Aid to graduate students depends upon funds being specifically appropriated by the General Assembly.[24]

C. Personnel

An interesting religious exemption with regard to personnel arises in the context of Georgia's teacher assignment law,[25] a parallel to its student assignment law.[26] The teacher assignment provision states that:

No teacher shall be assigned to or compelled to teach at any school on account of race, creed, color or National origin, or for the purpose of achieving a certain ratio at any school of teachers of one or more particular races, creeds, colors or National origins, and no school district or school system, by whatever name known, shall be established, reorganized or maintained for any such purpose: *Provided, further, that nothing in this section shall be deemed to affect, in any way, the right of a religious or denominational educational institution to select its teachers exclusively or primarily from members of such religion or denomination or from giving preference in such selection to such members or to make such selection of its teachers as is calculated to promote the religious principle for which it is established.*[27]

It is likely that the drafters of this provision had desegregation of non-college entities foremost in their minds, but it is important to note that it is by its terms applicable to colleges and universities as well.

While any RAC would seem to fit comfortably within the phrase "religious or denominational education institution," the scope of the religious exemption is not clear. It refers to the right of an RAC, among others, to choose from or to give preference to "members of such religion or denomination." This part of the provision would indicate that the only "discrimination" that is permissible is in favor of those adhering to the religion or denomination with which the RAC is affiliated. The paragraph ends, however, with an allusion to the right "to make such selection of its teachers as is calculated to promote the religious principle for which it is established." This latter part, standing alone, would indicate that preference could be given to members of other faiths as well but, in the context of the entire provision, would seem to be limited by the earlier language restricting preference to members of that religion or denomination, which earlier language would be made meaningless if preference toward *any* religious affiliation could be exercised.

Whether or not limited to preferences toward members of the religion or denomination with which the enterprise is affiliated, the exemption is an important one in view of the fact that Georgia has no generally applicable fair employment legislation. Georgia's Fair Employment Act, effective June 1, 1978 (and repealed effective July of 1980) applies only to public employees.[28]

Except for one ambiguity, Georgia's minimum wage law[29] would seem to apply to RACs. The only likely exception would be that provided for "any employer that has sales of $40,000 per year or less."[30] If tuition is not a sale, then the RAC might well be argued to have sales of less than $40,000 per year. It would then be necessary to inquire about other sales on campus (e.g., sales in the campus bookstore) and, in that connection, whether the appropriate entity is the college or the component (e.g., the bookstore). However, it would seem that tuition moneys paid to RACs are sales within the statute. Since the minimum wage currently provided for ($1.25 per hour) is unrealistically low, its impact would be minimal in any event.

The Georgia Worker's Compensation law[31] includes all employers of three or more persons in its definition of "employer."[32] There is no exception for an educational institution, and a former exception for charitable institutions has

been eliminated;[33] all RACs in Georgia will be covered by the provisions of the law.

The law excepts from its definition of "employee" farm laborers, domestic servants, and those whose work is not in the usual trade or profession of the employer or "incidental" to it.[34]

Injuries arising out of work in the course of employment are covered, unless caused by the willful act of a third person for personal reasons or by the willful misconduct of the employee himself.[35] Diseases not arising from an accident at work are not covered, nor are heart attacks, alcoholism, or drug addiction, unless the addiction to drugs was caused by medicines prescribed for the treatment of an injury at work by an authorized physician.[36]

Every employer must insure the payment of compensation by insuring with a company licensed to provide Worker's Compensation insurance by the state of Georgia, or must furnish the State Board of Worker's Compensation proof of its financial ability to pay compensation liabilities as they occur.[37] Evidence of the employer's compliance with these requirements must be filed with the Board.[38] As usual, an employee's rights under this law exclude any common law suits against his employer.[39]

Georgia's Employment Security Tax[40] covers RACs. It defines a nonprofit corporation as one described in Section 501(c)(3) of the Internal Revenue Code[41] and a nonprofit institution of higher education as one which grants a bachelor's or higher degree, or prepares students (who have a high school degree or its equivalent) for "gainful employment in a recognized occupation."[42] RACs are therefore required to pay contributions directly to the state fund, or may elect to become liable for payments by filing a notice of such selection with the Commissioner.[43]

All employers may be experience-rated, and charged according to their payroll records.[44] The Commissioner of Labor regulates such ratings according to statutory rate tables.[45]

"Employment" under the Act does not include service performed in the employ of a church, or an organization operated primarily for religious purposes and which is "operated, supervised, controlled, or principally supported" by a church, or service by a minister in the exercise of his ministry or by a member of a religious order in the exercise of duties required by the order.[46] Casual labor not in the course of an employer's business or trade is excluded, as is service for a college or university by an enrolled student or by a student's spouse, if the spouse is notified at the start that the employment is provided by the school as part of a student financial assistance program and that such employment is not covered by any unemployment insurance program.[47]

D. Students

Sections 32–847 and 32–848 deal with compulsory assignments to certain schools on grounds of race, creed, color, national origin, or quota system. Essentially this 1970 legislation forbids busing or other forms of racial balancing in the schools. Section 32–847 permits the student's parents to choose which school the child will attend—a statutory "freedom-of-choice" plan. In *Stell v. Board of Education for the City of Savannah*,[48] the United States District Court stated that the legislation was in this regard "clearly and concededly . . . void and unenforceable,"[49] although it has yet to be repealed. It is the last part of the provision that has relevance to RACs:

[N]othing in this section shall be deemed to affect, in any way, the right of a religious or denominational education institution to select its students exclusively or primarily from members of such religion or denomination or from giving preference to [sic] such selection to such members or to make such selection of its students as is calculated to promote the religious principle for which it is established.[50]

Although Section 32–847 was probably passed with non-college entities in mind, it seems by its terms applicable to RACs.

Litigation involving Section 32–847 has not involved this religious exemption but has been limited to the racial desegregation aspects.

Since the exemption parallels that affecting teacher assignment,[51] its problems are the same. Although any RAC would tend to fit comfortably within the phrase "religious or denominational education institution," it is not clear whether preference toward members of religions or denominations other than that with which the institution is affiliated would be permitted even if the purpose of such preference was to promote the religious principle actuating the institution's establishment.

E. Facilities

Georgia has no comprehensive public accommodations law.

Georgia does have a Fair Housing Act which bars discrimination based on race, color, sex, religion, or national origin in regard to the sale, leasing, or financing of any housing accommodations by any owner, financial institution, or broker.[52] RACs, however, may be exempt from the religious discrimination aspect of this law:

Nothing in this chapter shall prohibit a religious organization, association or society, or any nonprofit institution or organization operated, supervised or controlled by or in conjunction with a religious organization, association, or society, from limiting the sale, rental, or occupancy of dwellings which it owns or operates for other than a commercial purpose to persons of the same religion, or from giving preference to such persons, unless membership in such religion is restricted on account of race, color, sex, or national origin.[53]

Virtually all RACs would fall within this exemption.

Georgia's law regarding accessibility for handicapped people applies to all "government buildings" and to those "public buildings" constructed or substantially renovated after July 1, 1977.[54]

The definitions of "government buildings" and "public buildings" are particularly important. "Government buildings" include:

all buildings, structures, streets, sidewalks, walkways, and access thereto, used by the public or in which handicapped or elderly persons may be employed, that are constructed or substantially renovated in whole or in part by use of State, county or municipal funds or the funds of any political subdivisions of the State; and, to the extent not required otherwise by federal law or regulations and not beyond the power of the State to regulate, all buildings and structures used by the public which are constructed or substantially renovated in whole or in part by use of Federal funds.[55]

"Public buildings" include:

all buildings, structures, streets, sidewalks, walkways, and access thereto, used by the public or in which handicapped or elderly persons may be employed that are constructed or substantially renovated by the use of private funds, including rental apartment complexes of 20 units or more originally constructed after July 1, 1978, and temporary lodging facilities of 20 units or more, except that the provisions of this law shall apply to only five per cent of those units or a minimum of one unit, whichever is greater: Provided that the provisions of this law shall not apply to a private single family residence, duplex, triplex or condominium: and Provided further, that section 91-1115(f) and (g), section 91-1116, section 91-1117, section 91-1118, section 91-1120 and section 91-1122 shall not apply to apartment units or to guest rooms in temporary lodging facilities.[56]

Although these definitions seem fairly broad, they are apparently limited by the following provision:

Nothing in this law shall be construed to require the equipment and facilities for handicapped persons specified by this law to be provided in public buildings which are not ordinarily open to and used by the general public.[57]

This qualification would seem to negate the disjunctive phrase "used by the public *or* in which handicapped or elderly persons may be employed" contained in the definition of "public buildings," since buildings and the like in which handicapped or elderly persons may be employed need not be "ordinarily open to and used by the general public."

Perhaps the key word in Section 91-1125 is "ordinarily," the idea being to exempt buildings such as college auditoriums that might be open to the public on relatively rare occasions.

While no specific exemption is provided for higher education, presumably the law would

apply only to those buildings constructed or substantially renovated in whole or in part with state or federal funds and which are used by the public (or in which handicapped or elderly people may be employed, if that provision survives the qualification mentioned above) or to those buildings built after July 1, 1977 that are ordinarily open to the public.

Georgia does not have OSHA type legislation, but the state does impose a duty on employers to furnish employment which is reasonably safe for the employees therein, including a duty to furnish safeguards and safety devices.[58] An RAC is an "employer" under the law as long as it employs eight or more employees.[59]

Moreover, Georgia imposes on every owner or employer of "a place of employment, place of public assembly, or public building" a duty to construct, repair, or maintain, the place so as to render it reasonably safe.[60] The phrase "public building" is not defined by the Code.

F. State Taxation

Article VII, Section I, Paragraph 4 of the Georgia Constitution[61] authorizes the General Assembly to exempt certain groups, people, or institutes from property, sales or income taxes. The specific exemptions are scattered throughout the tax legislation.

Income Tax

With two qualifications, organizations falling within categories established by Section 501(c)(3) and Section 501(d), among others, of the federal Internal Revenue Code of 1954 are exempt from state income taxes.[62] Section 501(c)(3) includes:

Corporations, and any community chest, fund or foundation, organized and operated exclusively for religious, charitable . . . or educational purposes . . . no part of the net earnings of which inures to the benefit of any private shareholder or individual, no substantial part of the activities of which is carrying on propaganda, or otherwise attempting to influence legislation, (except as otherwise provided in subsection (h)), and which does not participate in, or intervene in (including the publishing or distributing of statements), any political campaign on behalf of any candidate for public office.

Section 501(d) includes:

Religious or apostolic associations or corporations, if such associations or corporations have a common treasury or community treasury, even if such associations or corporations engage in business for the common benefit of the members, but only if the members thereof include (at the time of filing their returns) in their gross income their entire pro rata shares, whether distributed or not, of the taxable income of the association or corporation for such year. Any amount so included in the gross income of a member shall be treated as a dividend received.

RACs would generally be exempted at least under the educational or religious provisions of Section 501(c)(3).

Even if an organization fits into one of these categories, two limitations are placed on the exemption. First, the organization must request the exemption by filing a written application to the State Tax Commissioner. Until the exempt status is approved, none exists.[63] The exempt status, once approved, continues until revoked retroactively,[64] and it may be revoked if the federal Internal Revenue Service revokes the federal "exempt" status, if the organization changes its operation and is no longer in the defined group, if the organization engages in "prohibited" transactions set forth in the Internal Revenue Code or if there is a material change in the character or purpose of the organization.[65]

The second limitation involves unrelated business income, i.e., income which is derived from trade or business not related to the exempt purposes of the organization.[66] Such income is not within the tax exemption otherwise provided to organizations falling within Section 501(c)(3) and 501(d) of the Internal Revenue Code of 1945.[67]

Inheritance, Estate and Transfer Taxes

Georgia does not have an inheritance tax.

Georgia does impose an estate tax designed merely to channel to Georgia, by virtue of the credit allowed against the federal estate tax for

state death taxes, moneys that would otherwise go to the federal government in estate taxes.[68] This tax, therefore, has no ultimate effect on the amount of death taxes paid.

Georgia has no gift tax.

Deductions or Credits for Gifts to RACs.

If an individual has itemized any contributions or gifts to RACs on his federal income tax return, he may also take such a deduction on his Georgia income tax return.[69]

Property Tax

Georgia law provides several *ad valorem* property tax exemptions of interest to RACs. Exempt from taxation are, *inter alia*, "places of religious worship;"[70] "property owned by religious groups and used only for single-family residences when no income is derived from the property;"[71] "buildings erected for and used as a college, incorporated academy, or other seminary of learning;"[72] "all funds or property held or used as endowment by colleges . . . incorporated academies, or other seminaries when such funds or property are not invested in real estate;"[73] and "all books, philosophical apparatus, paintings, and statuary of any company or association which are kept in a public hall and which are not held as merchandise or for purposes of sale or gain."[74]

The most intriguing part of the section providing for these exemptions is the following:

The exemptions provided for in this section which refer to colleges . . . incorporated academies, or other seminaries of learning shall only apply to those colleges . . . incorporated academies, or other seminaries of learning *which are open to the general public.*[75]

It is not clear whether an RAC which limits its enrollment on religious grounds or one which even takes religious affiliation into account is "open to the public" within the meaning of the law. Apparently no court test of this language has yet occurred.

The section further specifies that any income from exempt property must be used only for religious, educational, or charitable purposes.[76]

Intangible Personal Property Tax

Georgia's tax on intangible personal property does not apply to such property owned by or held irrevocably in trust for the exclusive benefit of a religious, educational, or charitable institution so long as no part of the net profit from that institution's operation inures to the benefit of any private person.[77]

Sales and Use Taxes

Certain exemptions under Georgia's sales and use tax law are also of interest to RACs. Under these provisions, all purchases of goods and services made by RACs whose credits are accepted as equivalents by the University System of Georgia and its educational units would be free from tax.[78] On the other hand, sales and services provided by RACs to others (e.g., campus bookstore sales) would be subject to sales and use tax unless the sale was part of a specific charitable fund raising activity meeting the specific statutory requirements and having one of the specific purposes set out in the statute.[79] In any event, any sale or use of books "commonly recognized as being Holy Scripture" is exempt from the tax.[80]

G. Fund Raising

Charitable organizations which plan to solicit contributions within Georgia must file with the Secretary of State certain information (name, purpose, time, method, annual reports, etc.).[81]

Among those exempt from filing are religious groups (and charities connected to them) and educational institutions if the solicitations are limited to students and their families, alumni, faculty, and trustees.

With regard to contributions to RACs, Georgia law specifies that charitable trusts may be created within the regulations provided by Chapter 108. The appropriate subjects of charity for the jurisdiction of equity include "[e]very educational purpose"[82] and "[r]eligious instruction or worship."[83] The law does limit religious trusts to those involving religions which do not affirm doctrines "licentious in their tendency or inconsistent with the peace and safety of the state."[84]

Lotteries are forbidden by Article 1, Section 2 of the state Constitution.[85] The General Assembly, however, may legislate the conditions under which nonprofit Bingo type games might take place, a power which the General Assembly has exercised in detailed statutory provisions covering the licensing, operations, duties, reports, prizes, and contracts in connection with such games.[86] Reduced requirements may be available to a nonprofit tax-exempt school operating such a game only one day a year.[87]

H. Miscellaneous Provisions

The State of Georgia has a State Literature Commission which regulates various publications.[88] Religious and educational institutions, however, are not regulated with regard to reading material.[89]

19. Hawaii

A. Corporate Status

Hawaii legislation provides for the establishment of corporations for profit[1] and of nonprofit corporations.[2] Three or more persons, a majority of whom are state residents, must file a petition with the director of regulatory agencies.[3] The proposed charter of incorporation, which must accompany such a petition,[4] may contain provisions "for the distribution of assets on dissolution or final liquidation."[5]

Although a license from the Department of Education is required for private trade, vocational, or technical schools,[6] there is an exemption for religious courses given under the auspices of a religious organization.[7] Nonetheless, the Department of Education is given discretion to regulate even these.[8]

Dissolution provisions of the General Corporations chapter of the Hawaii Revised Statutes[9] apply to colleges organized as nonprofit corporations.[10] The merger or consolidation of nonprofit colleges is governed by the subchapter on Consolidation and Merger of Corporations.[11] There are no reported Hawaii decisions accepting the doctrine of *cy pres* in that jurisdiction.

Merger, consolidation, or voluntary dissolution proceedings are subject to approval by the Director of Regulatory Agencies.[12] If a college (1) fails for two years to file an annual statement; (2) ceases to have any assets and fails to function; (3) fails to apply for a renewal of its charter or articles of incorporation; or (4) is adjudicated a bankrupt, the Director of Regu-

latory Agencies may declare the corporation dissolved.[13] Upon voluntary dissolution the Director of Regulatory Agencies shall appoint a trustee to settle the affairs of the corporation, and the Director of Regulatory Agencies may do the same upon an involuntary dissolution.[14] Trustees are to settle the corporation's affairs according to statute and file a final account with the Director of Regulatory Agencies.[15] Additionally, any member or creditor may file a suit in the circuit court if the trustee account is unsatisfactory.[16] The circuit courts also have jurisdiction to dissolve and liquidate the assets of a corporation when the directors are deadlocked in the management of the corporate affairs.[17]

Hawaii statutory law does not clearly provide for the distribution of a nonprofit college's assets remaining after debts and expenses are paid. The General Corporations chapter provides only a broad power to the trustee appointed after dissolution (1) to sell and dispose of property, speedily winding up the corporation; (2) to file bills for instructions in any court of competent jurisdiction on any matters concerning the administration of assets; and (3) to divide among members money and property they are entitled to under the charter of the corporation after paying debts and expenses.[18]

B. State Support

The Hawaii Constitution prohibits the appropriation of public funds "for the support of any sectarian or private institution."[19] The Admission Act specifies that "no part of the proceeds or income from the lands granted under this Act shall be used for the support of any sectarian or denominational school, college, or university."[20]

From these provisions, it was clearly intended that Hawaii preserve a strict separation between the state and religiously oriented institutions. From a purely financial perspective, this intent has been well-honored. There is no legislation providing financial assistance to RACs for the construction or maintenance of their facilities nor to their students for tuition.[21] Such programs, and especially the former, might violate the state constitution.

The Department of Budget and Finance is statutorily authorized to contract with the United Student Aid Funds, Inc., or such other public or private nonprofit corporations "designated by or established pursuant to" federal laws relating to student loans.[22] Eligibility for loans guaranteed by the state program is determined by reference to the federal laws involved.[23] There is no state statutory restriction on student or institution eligibility based on religious affiliation.

Hawaii has established a State Post-Secondary Education Commission,[24] consisting of the members of the board of regents of the University of Hawaii and four others "broadly and equitably representative of the general public, and public and private nonprofit and proprietary institutions."[25] The Commission is authorized to act as the state recipient of certain federal funds.[26] It is stipulated that no "such funds" appropriated by the legislature may be used to aid persons attending non-state schools or to pay for staff work performed to distribute federal or private funds to such students.[27]

C. Personnel

It is unlawful under Hawaii law for an employer to discriminate on the basis of race, sex, age, religion, color, ancestry, physical handicap, marital status, or "arrest court record which does not have a substantial relationship to the functions and responsibilities of the prospective or continued employment."[28] It is specified, however, that an employer "may refuse to hire an individual for good cause relating to [his] ability . . . to perform the work in question."[29]

Also prohibited are advertisements, applications, inquiries, and the like which suggest any such discrimination "unless based on a bona fide occupational qualification."[30]

Since "employer" means any person having one or more persons in his employment,[31] RACs are clearly covered by the law. Nonetheless, several qualifications must be noted.

First, the legislature has created a bona fide occupational qualification (BFOQ) by reference to it in the provision concerning advertisements, applications, inquiries, and the like.[32] Although the same language is not contained in the provision dealing with the actual hiring, clearly the legislature did not intend to allow a BFOQ to justify advertising suggesting selectivity that could not be exercised in the actual hiring decision. Indeed, to so advertise is in fact to exercise selectivity in the hiring. Furthermore, the hiring provision does contain what is in essence a BFOQ in affirming that an employer "may refuse to hire an individual for good cause relating to [his] ability . . . to perform the work in question."[33] In any event, it is specifically provided that the discriminatory practice law is not to prohibit the "establishment and maintenance of bona fide occupational qualifications."[34] BFOQ exemptions, however, would probably not greatly protect RACs in personnel decisions involving positions beyond those of theology and philosophy faculty and perhaps of counselors. It is not likely that an RAC would be successful in arguing a right to exercise religious preference in the employment of faculty generally (let alone other staff) despite the RAC's genuine interest in establishing on campus a pervasive presence of people of a certain religious persuasion.

A second important qualification is contained in the provision stating that nothing in the discriminatory practice law is to:

[p]rohibit or prevent any religious or denominational institution or organization, or any organization operated for charitable or educational purposes, which is operated, supervised, or controlled by or in connection with a religious organization, from giving preference to persons of the same religion or denomination or from making such selection as is calculated by the organization to promote the religious principles for which it is established or maintained.[35]

Most if not all RACs may be eligible for any employment exemption created by this provision because the affiliation required between the organization and a religion is broadly worded. An institution may qualify if it is a religious or denominational organization. This part would tend to include those relatively few RACs which are seminaries or Bible colleges or the like. But an organization may also qualify if it is operated for charitable or educational purposes and "operated, supervised, or controlled by or in connection with a religious organization." The actual relationships between colleges and religious organizations vary considerably and some may not meet the "operated, supervised or controlled" portion of the requirement. That requirement, however, is considerably loosened by the addition of the phrase "or in connection with." A great many RACs can successfully argue that while their ties with religious organizations are not formal, their programs are run "in connection" with the religious organization.

Qualifying institutions are not barred from (1) limiting or giving preference in employment to persons of the same religion or denomination or (2) from making such selection as is calculated by the organization to promote the principles for which it is established or maintained.

These two subsections are of different scope. The first allows the RAC to exercise its preferences in hiring only in relation to the religion or denomination of the applicant. Even more limiting, preference can be exercised only for persons of that religion or denomination with which the RAC is affiliated. This limitation has many consequences. For example, in a situation in which an RAC might want to give preference to a member of a different religion to teach a course *in that religion*, no such preference would be allowed (unless the qualification could be established as a BFOQ). The exemption does, however, apply to all positions.

The second subsection is very broad. It does not limit itself to preference for members of the same religion, but allows any preference which promotes the RAC's religious principles. It might, however, be difficult for an RAC to justify preferring a janitor of a particular religion on the grounds that such preference furthers the religious principles of the institu-

tion. Nonetheless, this is the type of language which would allow an RAC to exercise religious preference in hiring faculty even for such nonreligious subjects as mathematics or English if the RAC appropriately feels it important to its religious principles to provide religious models and the like to its students.

It should be noted that the statute, by its use of the phrase "as is calculated by the organization," indicates that the institution should not be lightly second-guessed in the matter. The judgment is *its* to make.

Under the discriminatory practice law, a "physical handicap" means a "substantial *physical* impairment where such handicap is verified by medical findings and appears reasonably certain to continue throughout the lifetime of the individual without substantial improvement."[36] There is no indication that either people addicted to the use of alcohol or drugs or those actually using alcohol or drugs are included within the definition. In any event, with regard to users, at least, a BFOQ would apply.[37]

The discriminatory practice law is enforced by the Department of Labor and Industrial Relations.[38] Since "employer" includes any individual, association, or corporation,[39] all RACs are covered by the Hawaii Wage and Hour Law[40] which, *inter alia*, sets for certain employees a minimum wage[41] and maximum hours[42] and prohibits wage differentials based on race, religion or sex.[43] The minimum wage and maximum hour provisions do not apply to the employment of persons earning more than $700 per month,[44] of people in bona fide executive, administrative, supervisory, or professional capacities,[45] of students employed by a nonprofit school while the student attends such school,[46] and of certain persons whose compensation, and maximum workweek without overtime pay, are set by the Fair Labor Standards Act.[47]

Under Hawaii's Workers' Compensation Law,[48] "employer" means any person with one or more persons in his employment. RACs are therefore generally covered by the law. Nonetheless, excluded from covered employment is service (1) for a nonprofit religious, charitable, or educational organization if performed in a voluntary or unpaid capacity[49] or by a recipient of aid from the organization if the service is incidental to or in return for the aid;[50] (2) for a school, college, university, college club, fraternity, or sorority if performed by a regular student in return for board, lodging, or tuition furnished, in whole or in part;[51] (3) by a duly ordained, commissioned, or licensed minister, priest, or rabbi of a church in the exercise of his ministry or by a member of a religious order in the exercise of nonsecular duties required by the order;[52] or (4) covered by a federal workers' compensation law.[53] Nonetheless, employers may elect to provide coverage for employees performing such services.[54] RACs must either carry insurance, deposit adequate security with the state director of finance, or furnish the Director with satisfactory proof of financial ability to pay compensation directly to injured employees.[55]

Under Hawaii's Employment Security Law,[56] "employer" means any "employing unit which for some portion of a day within the current calendar year [has had] in employment one or more individuals"[57] and which has elected to become subject to the law.[58] Certain employment, however, is excepted from coverage unless:

a tax is required to be paid [with respect to it] under any federal law imposing a tax against which credit may be taken for contributions required to be paid into a state unemployment fund or which as a condition for full tax credit against the tax imposed by the Federal Unemployment Tax Act is required to be covered under [the state unemployment compensation law].[59]

Included within the excepted employments are (1) domestic service in a local college club or local chapter of a college fraternity or sorority "performed in any calendar quarter by an individual if the cash remuneration . . . is less than $225" and the total paid to all individuals by an employing unit for such service is less than $1,000 in each calendar quarter in both the current and preceding calendar years;[60] (2) service as to which unemployment compensation is payable under a Congressionally-established system;[61] (3) service performed in any calendar quarter for certain organizations exempted from income tax under section 501(a) of the

Federal Internal Revenue Code if the remuneration is less than $50 *or* the work "is performed by a fully ordained, commissioned, or licensed minister of a church in the exercise of his ministry or by a member of a religious order in the exercise of duties required by such order";[62] and (4) service for a school, college or university by one of its regular students.[63]

With regard to covered employment, however, a significant option is provided to nonprofit organizations and, therefore, to most RACs. Instead of the regular contribution, such organizations may elect to pay to the Director of Industrial Relations and Labor the amount of regular benefits plus one-half the amount of extended benefits paid that are attributable to employment by the organization.[64]

Most employment by RACs is covered under Hawaii's Temporary Disability Insurance Law[65] and its Prepaid Health Care Act.[66]

The Hawaii Employment Relations Act[67] authorizes employees to form or join a labor union[68] and governs the relationship among employers, employees, and labor organizations.[69] Employees of RACs are within the Act unless they are covered by the National Labor Relations Act and the National Labor Relations Board has not declined jurisdiction over them or indicated that it will not assume jurisdiction.[70]

D. Students

Hawaii has no statute regulating admissions to private institutions of higher education.

Hawaii law provides for the establishment of an annual conference of student leaders from both public and private higher education.[71] The purpose of the conference is to make recommendations concerning youth problems, and especially school-related ones.[72]

E. Facilities

Hawaii has no legislation generally prohibiting discrimination in public accommodations. It is statutorily provided that the "blind, visually handicapped, and otherwise physically disabled" are entitled to the full and equal use of, *inter alia*, hotels, lodging places, places of public accommodation, amusement, "and *other* places to which the general public is invited."[73]

Hawaii does have comprehensive legislation[74] which prohibits in real estate transactions any discrimination by any person based upon race, sex, color, religion, marital status, ancestry, or a physical handicap.[75] RACs are of course bound by this provision with regard to housing owned or controlled by them. A limited exemption is, however, provided:

It is not a discriminatory practice for a religious institution or organization or a charitable or educational organization operated, supervised, or controlled by a religious institution or organization to give preference to members of the same religion or of one sex in a real property transaction.[76]

To benefit from this provision, an RAC must qualify either as (1) a religious institution or organization *or* (2) a charitable or educational organization operated, supervised, or controlled by such a religious institution or organization. The exemption would be broader if it contained the phrase "or in connection with" after the "operated, supervised, or controlled" language.[77] Perhaps many RACs will find it difficult to meet the religious affiliation test specified by this statute.

For those that do not meet it, it can be argued that an indirect limitation on student admissions inheres in the statute. If the RAC limits housing to its own student body, as is likely, it may be unlawfully discriminating in its housing transactions to the extent to which it uses religion or sex in its student selection.

For those that do meet the test, selections based on religion or sex will be lawful. Any religious preference, however, must be in favor of a person of that religion with which the RAC is affiliated.

RACs are granted a fairly complete exemption from the rather stringent provisions of Hawaii's Residential Landlord-Tenant Code.[78] Excluded from coverage is "[r]esidence at an institution, whether public or private, where residence is merely incidental to . . . the provision of . . . educational, religious, or similar services."[79]

RACs are covered by the Hawaii Occupational Safety and Health Law[80] since it defines "employer" as any "person which has any natural person in service."[81] The Law is enforced by the Hawaii Department of Labor and Industrial Relations.[82]

F. State Taxation

Hawaii's Income Tax Law[83] exempts from such taxation "[c]orporations . . . conducted solely for charitable, religious [or] educational" purposes[84] except with regard to unrelated business taxable income.[85] With certain exceptions,[86] "unrelated business taxable income" under the Hawaii law "means the same as in the Internal Revenue Code."[87] Except for such income, therefore, all RACs would be exempt from the state income tax.

Hawaii's Inheritance and Estate Taxes Law[88] exempts from the tax for which it provides, all property transferred to any society, corporation, or institution exempted by law from taxation or "engaged in . . . charitable, benevolent, [or] educational work" so long as pecuniary profit is not one of the entity's purposes.[89] Transfers to persons or entities "in trust for or to be devoted to" such purposes are also tax-exempt.[90]

Since, under Hawaii Income Tax Law, "taxable income" means the same as it does under the Internal Revenue Code (except as otherwise provided in the state income tax chapter),[91] and since the Internal Revenue Code allows a deduction for contributions to nonprofit religious or educational institutions,[92] there is allowed to a person who itemizes deductions a state deduction for such contributions.

Hawaii has no state gift tax.

Hawaii's Real Property Tax Law[93] exempts from that tax certain real property used exclusively for nonprofit purposes.[94] Included within that exemption are junior colleges and colleges carrying on a general program of college level instruction, although the exempt property is limited to buildings for educational purposes, dormitories, housing owned by the institution and used as a residence for the institution's personnel, campus and athletic grounds, realty used for vocational purposes "incident to" the institution,[95] and property used for church purposes, including incidental activities, parsonages and church grounds.[96] The property involved must be owned in fee simple, leased, or rented for a period of one year or more, by the person using the property for the exempt purpose.[97] Property used for profit (even though the *profit* is used for an exempt purpose "or other purposes not within the conditions for exemption") is not included within the exemption.[98] Finally, a timely exemption claim must be filed with the Department of Taxation.[99]

RACs qualifying for a property tax exemption also may be exempt from improvement assessments.[100]

Hawaii's Conveyance Tax[101] imposes a tax on all sorts of conveyances of interests in real estate[102] unless the consideration involved is one hundred dollars or less.[103] There is no general exemption available to RACs.

Hawaii has a General Excise Tax Law[104] which imposes a tax on all sorts of transfers of tangible property and services.[105] There is, however, a total exemption from the tax for all corporations, associations, or societies "organized and operated exclusively for religious, charitable, scientific, or educational purposes."[106] To secure the exemption, the entity involved must file a timely written application each year with the Department of Taxation.[107] The exemption is unavailable if profit inures to any private individual.[108] Finally, if the primary purpose of the activity is to produce income, the exemption is also unavailable even if the income is used for exempt purposes.[109] Virtually all RACs, therefore, will be eligible for exemptions except as to those activities whose primary purpose is to produce income.

Hawaii's Use Tax Law,[110] presumably designed to tax transactions eluding the state excise tax,[111] incorporates the same exemptions with regard to RACs as does the excise tax law.[112]

RACs are not generally exempted from the County Vehicular Taxes provisions[113] of the Hawaii Code.

G. Fund Raising

Exempt from Hawaii's charitable solicitation provisions[114] are, *inter alia*:

[e]ducational institutions that are recognized by the director or that are accredited by a regional accrediting association or by an organization affiliated with the national commission on accrediting, any foundation having an established identity with any of the aforementioned educational institutions [and] any other educational institution confining its solicitation of contributions to its student body, alumni, faculty and trustees, and their families . . . provided that the annual financial report of the institution . . . shall be filed with the director.[115]

RACs may avoid coverage under the law, then, *either* (1) by being recognized by the director as appropriately accredited or (2) by confining its solicitation to the persons specified in the provision. Foundations having an established identity with institutions qualifying under alternative (1) are also exempt.

"Bingo" or other games of chance would easily come within Hawaii's definition of "gambling,"[116] an offense which is a misdemeanor.[117] No exception is provided for RACs.

H. Miscellaneous

Degree-granting institutions commit an unfair or deceptive act or practice[118] if they fail to disclose in all communications to the public and in all contracts to furnish instruction the fact that they are not fully accredited by any nationally recognized accrediting agency or association listed by the United States Commissioner of Education.[119]

20. Idaho

A. Corporate Status

RACs may be formed under the Idaho Nonprofit Corporation Act of 1979,[1] which provides that:

nonprofit corporations may be organized under this act for any lawful purpose or purposes . . . [which] may include, without being limited to, any of the following: . . . religious [or] educational . . . [2]

A nonprofit corporation is defined by the Act as a "corporation no part of the income of which is distributable to its members, directors, or officers."[3] The provisions of the 1979 law are to govern nonprofit corporations created under prior laws, but will not invalidate such corporations nor derogate from their rights.[4]

RACs formed under the Nonprofit Corporation Act are granted all the powers generally possessed by corporations.[5] In addition the Act provides that:

any religious . . . [or] educational corporation organized under the laws of this state may acquire, own, hold, mortgage, dispose of, and invest its funds in real and personal property for the use and benefit and under the discretion of, and in trust for any church, conference, or association . . . with which it is affiliated, or which elects its board of directors, or which controls it, in furtherance of the purposes of the member corporation.[6]

Idaho statutes also provide that a religious corporation may seek a change of its corporate name by petitioning the district court of the county in which the property of the corporation is situated.[7]

The Idaho Nonprofit Corporation Act provides that nonprofit corporations shall be governed by the Business Corporation Act[8] except when it is inconsistent with the Nonprofit Corporation Act.[9] Since the Nonprofit Corporation Act is silent on the dissolution of such corporations, the dissolution of a college is governed by the relevant provisions in the Business Corporation Act.[10] There are no reported Idaho decisions applying the *cy pres* doctrine in that jurisdiction.

If a corporation follows the statutory procedure for voluntary dissolution,[11] including the satisfaction of its liabilities and obligations and the filing of articles of dissolution, its dissolution is approved only by the Secretary of State.[12] The corporation of any creditor or any other interested person[13] may, at any time during the liquidation process, petition the Idaho district court of the county in which the registered office or principal place of business of the corporation is located to have the liquidation continued under the supervision of the court.[14] In such a case, or when the Idaho Attorney General has filed an action for involuntary dissolution because of fraud, abuse of corporate authority, or failure to maintain a registered agent,[15] the district courts have jurisdiction to supervise the dissolution[16] and will enter a decree of dissolution.[17]

The Nonprofit Corporation Act provides generally that no dividends or share of a nonprofit corporation's income shall be distributed to members, directors, or officers of the corporation except as provided for by the Nonprofit Corporation Act upon dissolution of the corporation.[18] Thus it would seem that Idaho law does not limit the class of recipients to which the assets of a private college can be distributed upon dissolution. Although, as was stated above, there are no Idaho cases dealing with the application of the doctrine of *cy pres* to charitable gifts, an Idaho court might apply that doctrine in an appropriate case, if only because of the lack of attention by the state legislature to the problem of distribution of the assets of a dissolving nonprofit corporation.

B. State Support

The Idaho Constitution prohibits direct aid by the state or any governmental or public entity to RACs controlled by religious organizations:

Neither the legislature nor any county, city, town, township, school district, or other public corporation, shall ever make any appropriation, or pay from any public fund or moneys whatever, anything in aid of any . . . sectarian or religious purpose, or to help support and sustain any school, academy, seminary, college [or] university . . . controlled by any church, sectarian or religious denomination.[19]

In *Epeldi* v. *Engelking*,[20] the Idaho Supreme Court held that this provision voided a statute providing bus service to students attending parochial schools:

[T]he framers of our Constitution intended to more positively enunciate the separation between church and state than did the framers of the United States Constitution. . . . This section in explicit terms prohibits any appropriation by the legislature or others . . . or payment from any public fund, *anything in aid* of any church to help support or sustain any sectarian school. . . .[21]

While this Constitutional provision completely bars state aid to colleges or universities controlled by a church or religious organization, it would not seem to eliminate the possibility of public assistance to religiously affiliated colleges or universities that are owned and controlled by a lay board, so long as the assistance is not for a "sectarian or religious purpose" such as for a theology course or for a campus chapel.

These grants are to be made without regard to the student's race, creed, color, sex, national origin, ancestry, age, or area of academic competence.

The Idaho Legislature has enacted a state scholarship program[22] "for the most talented Idaho secondary school graduates who will enroll in undergraduate nonreligious academic and vocational programs in eligible postsecondary institutions in the state."[23] As used in this provision, "eligible postsecondary institution" includes: "any educational organization which is operated privately and not for profit under the control of an independent board."[24] An eligible student must not be pursuing an educational program leading to a baccalaureate degree in theology or divinity.[25] Thus a student attending a nonprofit RAC is eligible for such a state scholarship if he is not studying theology or divinity, and if the RAC is controlled by an independent board.

These grants are to be awarded without regard to any student's race, creed, color, sex, national origin, ancestry, age, or area of academic competence.[26] There is serious doubt that the "creed" portion of the provision could be carried out if RAC students were not generally eligible for these grants.

C. Personnel

Freedom from discrimination in employment is a civil right under Idaho law.[27] Protection of this right is accomplished through the sanction of a criminal penalty:

Every person shall be guilty of a misdemeanor who denies to any other person because of race, creed, color, sex, or national origin the right to work: (a) by refusing to hire, (b) by discharging, (c) by barring from employment, or (d) by discriminating against such person in compensation or in other terms or conditions of employment.[28]

Curiously, "[e]very person" is defined to include any owner, lessee, proprietor, manager, agent, or employee "engaged in or exercising control over the operation of any place of public resort, accommodation, assemblage or amusement,"[29] a definition more suited to the public accommodations part of the proscription.[30] Presumably, the employment provision was intended to cover all employers, not just those in the public accommodations area.

Even if all employers are generally within the Civil Rights statutes,[31] there is an exception generally relevant to RACs: "nor shall anything herein contained apply to any educational facility operated or maintained by a bona fide religious or sectarian institution."[32]

Since this provision occurs in the subsection defining "[a]ny place of public resort, accommodation, assemblage or amusement," the provision is intended perhaps to exempt only from the public accommodations part of the law.[33]

In any event, however, the state legislature in 1969 created a Commission on Human Rights and prohibited a number of acts,[34] including discrimination in hiring and in terms of employment on the basis of race, color, religion, sex, or national origin.[35] Employers are covered by this prohibition if they employ ten or more employees[36] or perform work or furnish material as a contractor or subcontractor under a contract with "the state or governmental entity or agency of the state."[37] The Commission is empowered to adopt rules and regulations,[38] to receive and act on complaints,[39] and to appear in court and before administrative agencies.[40]

Several exemptions are relevant to RACs. First, the Commission on Human Rights Act's[41] prohibitions do not apply to a "religious corporation, association, or society with respect to the employment of individuals of a particular religion to perform work connected with the carrying on by the corporation . . . of its religious activities."[42]

The applicability of this exemption to RACs depends upon the way in which "religious corporation" and "religious activities" are interpreted. The matters of ownership and control of the RAC are important to the former qualification and the questions of the purpose and nature of the instruction by an RAC, along with their relation to the mission of the religious group, are relevant to the latter. An RAC owned, controlled, and maintained by a church or other religious group, primarily engaged in training clergy, missionaries, or other religious leaders,

might be exempt under this provision. Most RACs, however, are probably not "religious" (as opposed to "religious educational")[43] corporations and are not exempted from the Act by this provision.

A second exemption from the Act involves qualifications for the employment. It is not prohibited for:

an employer to employ an employee . . . on the basis of his religion, sex, or national origin if religion, sex, or national origin is a bona fide occupational qualification [BFOQ] reasonably necessary to the normal operation of the business or enterprise.[44]

This rather narrow exception perhaps would allow an RAC to prefer a member of a certain religious group as an instructor in theology (or perhaps as a counselor), but not in an unrelated field such as mathematics. It is not likely that an RAC could be successful in arguing a right to exercise religious preferences in faculty positions generally despite its interest in establishing on campus a pervasive presence of faculty of a certain religious persuasion.

The Commission on Human Rights Act provides a third exemption which is directly applicable to RACs. It states that "it is not a discriminatory practice for a religious educational institution . . . to limit employment or give preference to members of the same religion [in employment]."[45] Since ownership or control is not mentioned, presumably an RAC affiliated with, but not owned or controlled by a religious group could limit its employment or give preference to members of the religion with which the institution is affiliated. It would not seem to be permissible, however, for an RAC to give preference to a member of another religion even to advance its educational purposes, absent a BFOQ.

While discrimination in compensation on the basis of sex is forbidden by the Commission on Human Rights Act,[46] another statute specifically prohibits sex discrimination among employees in the payment of wages.[47] For the purpose of this provision, "employer" includes "any person acting directly or indirectly in the interest of an employer in relation to an employee."[48] Accordingly, RACs are subject to this statute and may not discriminate in the payment of wages on the basis of sex.

A BFOQ is the only exception to the prohibition against discrimination in employment on the basis of age.[49] RACs are given no further exemption from this prohibition.

An employer subject to the Minimum Wage Law[50] includes "any person employing an employee."[51] "Person" means any "association, corporation, . . . or organized group of persons."[52] Since RACs fall within these definitions, they are subject to the general provisions of the statute.

Nonetheless, certain employees are excluded from coverage, including those in good faith executive, administrative or professional capacities and certain part-time employees under the age of sixteen.[53]

Idaho law does not directly regulate the maximum number of hours to be worked per day or week by employees of RACs. The state Day's Work Law,[54] however, declares that eight hours shall constitute a day's work, except in an emergency, for all laborers, workmen, mechanics, or others engaged in manual labor employed by the state or any county, city, township, or other municipality.[55] This regulation extends to laborers, workmen, mechanics, and other similar persons employed by contractors or subcontractors in the execution of any contract with the state or a political subdivision thereof.[56] Thus laborers, workmen, mechanics, or other similar persons employed by an RAC and working under a contract or subcontract with the state or with any county, city, township, or other municipality may be within the eight-hour day restriction of the Day's Work Law.

For the purpose of the Idaho Workmen's Compensation Law, an employer is any person who has "expressly or impliedly hired or contracted the services of another,"[57] including contractors and subcontractors.[58] While RACs fit within this definition, most RACs will be exempt under the law, which excludes from coverage employment "not carried on by the employer for the sake of pecuniary gain."[59] Thus a not-for-profit RAC is exempt from the Workmen's Compensation Law unless it elects coverage by filing a "declaration in writing of himself and his surety"[60] that the provisions of the Law shall apply.[61]

Under the Idaho Employment Security Law,[62] a "covered employee" is any person who (1) in any quarter in either the current or preceding calendar year paid wages of $300 or more for covered employment; (2) for some portion of a day in each of twenty different calendar weeks employed, in either the current or preceding calendar year, at least one individual;[63] or (3) is a "nonprofit organization,"[64] defined[65] to be a religious, charitable, educational, or other organization described in section 501(c)(3) of the Federal Internal Revenue Code[66] and exempt from taxation under section 501(a) of that code.[67] An institution falling into category (3), which includes virtually all RACs, may make the usual "contributions"[68] or elect to make "reimbursements" to the unemployment fund of an amount equal to the regular benefits plus one-half the extended benefits paid in connection with service for that institution.[69]

In any event, "exempt employment" under the law includes: (1) domestic service in a local college club or local chapter of a college fraternity or sorority unless the employer, in any quarter in the current or preceding calendar year, paid $1,000 or more to individuals performing such domestic service;[70] (2) service performed by a student under the age of twenty-two, in an accredited nonprofit or public educational institution in a full-time program for credit which combines academic instruction with work experience;[71] (3) "service with respect to which unemployment compensation or insurance is payable under an unemployment compensation system established by an act of Congress other than the Social Security Act;"[72] (4) service by certain student nurses and medical interns;[73] and (5) service performed for a school or college by one of its regularly enrolled students.[74]

Also included within "exempt employment" are the following: (1) religious activities for a church or convention or association of churches;[75] (2) service for an organization run primarily for religious purposes and "operated, supervised, controlled, or principally supported" by a church or convention or association of churches;[76] (3) service for an institution of higher education devoted primarily to preparation of students for the ministry or "training candidates to become members of a religious order;"[77] and (4) service by a "duly ordained, commissioned, or licensed minister of a church in the exercise of his ministry or by a member of a religious order in the exercise of duties required by such order."[78] None of these last four exceptions is very broad insofar as employment at the typical RAC is concerned and, consequently, few positions at RACs will come within them. This is true because (1) very few people employed by RACs can claim to be working for a church or a convention or association of churches; (2) except perhaps for institutions like seminaries or bible colleges, few RACs can claim to be both run primarily for religious purposes and operated or principally supported by a church or group of churches; (3) few RACs are devoted *primarily* to training students for the ministry or for membership in a religious order; and (4) few employees on RAC campuses, save perhaps some counselors or theology teachers, will be regular ministers of a church exercising their ministry or members of a religious order performing duties required by that order.[79]

It should be noted that employers for whom services not otherwise covered are performed may with some exceptions file an election to have such services deemed covered employment.[80]

Most RACs must make unemployment compensation contributions (or "reimbursements") for all employees performing services other than those excepted. However, a clarifying provision states that unemployment benefits are not paid to instructors, researchers, or principal administrators at an "educational institution" (a phrase which includes most RACs)[81] for any week of unemployment commencing during the period between two successive academic years or between two terms, whether or not successive, if the individual involved performs services in the first of such academic years (or terms) and there is a contract or reasonable assurance that the individual will perform services in any such capacity for any educational institution in the second such academic year or term.[82] A comparable provision controls payments (and "waiting week" credit) for weeks commencing during established and customary vacation periods and holiday recesses.[83] Final-

ly, benefits are not payable for weeks beginning during a "paid sabbatical leave provided for in the individual's contract."[84]

RACs may be covered by the Injunctive Relief in Labor Disputes chapter of the Idaho Code,[85] since "labor dispute" is defined to mean any controversy between an employer and the majority of his employees in a collective bargaining unit.[86]

D. Students

The Idaho Civil Rights statute[87] sets out the right to be free from discrimination because of race, creed, color, sex, or national origin in the "full enjoyment of any of the accommodations, facilities, or privileges of any place of public resort, accommodation, assemblage or amusement."[88] The definition of the phrase "place of public resort, accommodation, assemblage or amusement," which includes restaurants, hotels, public amusements, and the like, refers specifically to "any educational institution wholly or partially supported by public funds."[89] In addition to restaurants, hotels, public amusements and the like on RAC campuses, even admission to those RACs receiving public support might be covered by this statute, which is enforceable by the sanction of the criminal law.[90] In any event, however, the statute specifically exempts any "educational facility operated or maintained by a bona fide religious or sectarian institution"[91] and, therefore, many RACs.[92] The spirit, if not the letter, of this exemption would fit most RACs.

The Commission on Human Rights legislation[93] also prohibits discrimination in the provision of public accommodations.[94] More significantly for admissions, however, the law declares it a "prohibited act" for an "educational institution," which includes private colleges,[95] to "exclude, expel, limit, or otherwise discriminate against an individual seeking admission as a student or an individual enrolled as a student in the terms, conditions, and privileges of the institution" on the basis of race, color, religion, sex, or national origin.[96] A fairly broad exemption, however, provides that it is *not* a "discriminatory practice" for:

a religious educational institution or an educational institution operated, supervised, or controlled by a religious institution . . . or organization to limit admission or give preference to applicants of the same religion. . . . [97]

This provision would allow any RAC to favor applicants of its religious affilation if the RAC could be considered a "religious educational institution," even though it might not be formally "operated, supervised, or controlled" by a church or religious group.

E. Facilities

The Civil Rights Law[98] prohibits discrimination on the basis of race, creed, color, sex, or national origin in the provision of a broad range of public accommodations.[99] This provision would clearly cover restaurants, hotels, stadium activities and the like open to the general public. (The Act specifies that the proscription does *not* apply to any "institute, bona fide club, or place of accommodation, which is by its nature distinctly private provided that where public use is permitted that use shall be covered by this section."[100]

Significantly for RACs, this legislation specifically exempts "any educational facility operated or maintained by a bona fide religious or sectarian institution,"[101] a provision broad enough to cover virtually all RACs.

The Commission on Human Rights Law[102] also prohibits the denial of "full and equal enjoyment of the goods, services, facilities, privileges, advantages, and accommodations of a place of public accommodation."[103] It too would reach campus restaurants, hotels, stadia, and the like. This legislation also exempts facilities not open to the public ("This act does not apply to a private club, or other establishment not in fact open to the public.")[104] Finally, the law specifies that it is not a discriminatory practice for:

a religious educational institution or an educational institution operated, supervised, or controlled by a religious institution . . . or organization to limit admission or give preference to applicants of the same religion.[105]

This could be read to yield a significant public accommodation exemption for a broad class of RACs. It is likely, however, that this provision was intended to apply only to student admissions, i.e., enrollments, and not to public accommodations generally.[106]

The Commission on Human Rights Law also prohibits housing discrimination on the basis of race, color, religion, sex, or national origin.[107] This broad prohibition would easily include the rental of campus housing. Curiously enough, no exemption specifically authorizes single-sex housing on campus or elsewhere. The only exemption of special interest to RACs provides that:

[i]t is not a discriminatory practice for a religious institution or organization or a charitable or educational organization operated, supervised or controlled by a religious institution or organization to give preference to members of the same religion in a real property transaction.[108]

To qualify for this exemption, the RAC must be a "religious" entity or a charitable or educational organization run by a religious entity. Loosely interpreted, virtually all RACs would be included. If, on the other hand, the typical RAC is seen as an "educational"—as opposed to a "religious"—organization, then only those RACs which are purely religious—seminaries and bible colleges, for example, and those with formal ties to a religious entity—colleges run by a religious order, for example—would qualify. The spirit of the law, if not its letter, would include virtually all RACs. This exemption works hand in hand with that provided for student admissions.[109]

It should be noted, in any event, that the exemption runs only to persons of the same religious affiliation as the institution.

Legislation requiring that public buildings, accommodations and facilities be made accessible to the physically handicapped[110] addresses itself only to action by the State and its political subdivisions[111] and does not, therefore, affect RACs.

The Idaho Industrial Commission[112] has the power to compel employers subject to the Workmen's Compensation laws[113] to maintain safe places of employment and safe tools, equipment, and machinery.[114] The Commission is empowered to establish reasonable safety standards.[115] A violation of a Commission order, after the hearing provided,[116] is punishable as a misdemeanor.[117]

There is also a Bureau of Industrial Hygiene in the Department of Health and Welfare to study, make recommendations, conduct inspections, and otherwise act in connection with industrial hazards and particularly occupational diseases.[118]

Finally, the Director of the Department of Labor and Industrial Services is empowered, *inter alia*, to acquire and disseminate information, to cooperate with the Industrial Commission and to conduct certain safety inspections.[119]

There is no comprehensive OSHA statute in Idaho. Idaho statutes do, however, provide for an Industrial Commission within the Department of Labor and Industrial Services. The Industrial Commission is empowered by the Workman's Compensation laws to prohibit employers from employing workers in areas which are not constructed and maintained in safe conditions.[120] An employer for the above purposes is defined as "any person who has expressly or impliedly hired or contracted the services of another."[121] Excepted from the definition of employee are those who work in employment which is not carried on by the employer for the sake of pecuniary gain.[122] To the extent that an RAC is not-for-profit, it may fall within this exception and thus not come within the scope of the statute.

F. State Taxation

With certain exceptions, organizations are exempt from state income taxation if they qualify for federal tax-exempt status under Section 501[123] of the Internal Revenue Code of 1954.[124] Since most RACs will qualify for such a status, they are exempt from Idaho's income tax.

The Idaho Transfer and Inheritance Tax Act[125] exempts from tax all property transferred to entities devoted to charitable or educational work if profit is not the entity's object.[126]

Idaho has no estate tax or gift tax.

Charitable contributions that an individual might have deducted for federal income tax purposes are deductible, under the Idaho income tax law,[127] to those who itemize on their state returns.[128] Since contributions to nonprofit

religious or educational institutions are deductible for federal income tax purposes,[129] contributions to virtually all RACs are deductible under Idaho law.

Idaho also provides an income tax credit for contributions to RACs:

There shall be allowed . . . as a credit against the income tax . . . an amount equal to fifty percent (50%) of the aggregate amount of charitable contributions made by such taxpayer during the year to a nonprofit corporation, fund, foundation, trust, or association organized and operated exclusively for the benefit of institutions of higher learning located within the state of Idaho, and to nonprofit private institutions of . . . higher education located within the state of Idaho.[130]

"Institution of higher learning" means only that a college or university must maintain a regular faculty, curriculum, and resident body of students, and that it must be accredited by the Northwest Association of Schools and Colleges or by the State Board of Education.[131] The credit allowed may not exceed, in the case of a taxpayer other than a corporation, twenty percent of the taxpayer's total income tax liability for the year or fifty dollars, whichever is less;[132] and, in the case of a corporation, ten percent of its total income or franchise tax liability for the year or five hundred dollars, whichever is less.[133]

All property used exclusively for nonprofit school or educational purposes is exempt from property taxation.[134] So too is "property" from which no profit is derived and which is held or used exclusively for endowment, building or maintenance purposes of schools or educational institutions.[135] Although these provisions will cover most RAC property, there is an additional exemption from property tax for the property of any religious corporation or society used exclusively in connection with public worship.[136] The exemption extends to (1) a parsonage occupied as such[137] and (2) any property "used for any combination of religious worship, educational purposes and recreational activities, not designed for profit,"[138] as long as the "parsonage" or the "property" belongs to a religious corporation or society.[139]

The Idaho Sales Tax Act[140] exempts from its

taxes, *inter alia*, (1) the sale, purchase, storage, use, or other consumption of religious literature published and sold by a bona fide church or religious denomination, as long as no profit inures to the benefit of any private individual or shareholder;[141] and (2) sales to and purchase by resident nonprofit colleges and universities whose income is "devoted solely to education and in which systematic instruction in the usual branches of learning is given."[142] The exemption does not extend to sales *by* these educational institutions.

G. Fund Raising

Idaho has no law regulating charitable solicitations or requiring disclosure concerning such solicitations.

Gambling through use of any devices whatever is a misdemeanor.[143] There is no provision under Idaho law authorizing games like bingo even when conducted by a nonprofit institution. Indeed, the state constitution provides that the "legislature shall not authorize any lottery or gift enterprise under any pretense or for any purpose whatever."[144]

H. Miscellaneous

Idaho is a participant in the Interstate Compact for Education established by the Educational Commission of the state.[145]

Under Idaho law, life insurance contracts may be made where the person paying the consideration has no insurable interest in the life of the person insured, if an educational or religious institution is irrevocably named as beneficiary.[146] The statute further provides that "such a contract shall be valid and binding between and among all of the parties thereto."[147]

Blanket disability insurance is statutorily declared to be the form of disability insurance issued to RACs.[148] A blanket policy is to be the type issued to "any religious . . . [or] educational . . . organization . . . covering participants in activities sponsored by the organization."[149]

21. Illinois

A. Corporate Status

In Illinois, there are three ways in which a religiously affiliated college (RAC) may come into existence. The General Not for Profit Corporation Act[1] provides the most basic and general manner of incorporation. Under the Act, a nonprofit corporation may be formed for charitable, educational, or religious purposes.[2] The incorporators must file articles of incorporation with the Secretary of State,[3] who issues a certificate of incorporation, thereby bringing the corporation into existence.[4]

An RAC may also come into existence by means of a statute which deals specifically with educational institutions. According to this statute, when trustees of an estate receive real or personal property by an instrument which directs them to use such property to found and establish an educational institution in the State of Illinois, it is lawful for them, so as "to better promote the establishment, maintenance and management of such institutions," to form a not for profit corporation.[5] The trustees must supply a verified copy of this will and must file articles of incorporation with the Secretary of State.[6] Moreover, the articles cannot be in violation of or inconsistent with the law or any provision of the instrument by which the property was conveyed.[7] Once the certificate of incorporation is issued and recorded, together with the articles of incorporation, the corporation is deemed fully organized and may begin to execute its corporate purposes.[8] In addition, whenever a postsecondary educational institu-

tion[9] is to be organized, a certificate of approval from the State Board of Higher Education is required.[10]

A third manner of incorporation of an RAC is implied in the statutory powers granted to trustees of a corporation formed for religious purposes, who may acquire and use real property.[11] They are empowered to develop such property as is necessary for the convenience and comfort of the religious corporation, including the maintenance and construction of schools. They must, however, use the property in the manner stipulated in the instrument of conveyance.[12]

RACs are included among the institutions covered by the Uniform Management of Institutional Funds Act. This act deals with the manner in which the governing board is to exercise its powers in relation to the management and maintenance of the institution and its fund.[13]

Under the General Not for Profit Corporation Act, an RAC may voluntarily dissolve itself by the adoption of a resolution of the board of directors to that effect. This resolution must be adopted by two-thirds of all members of the corporation entitled to vote or, in the absence of voting members, by a majority of the Board of Directors.[14] The articles of dissolution must be filed with the Secretary of State, who issues a certificate of dissolution ending the corporate existence.[15] Under some circumstances, the Attorney General may bring an action in equity to dissolve a nonprofit corporation involuntarily.[16]

Illinois law contains an explicit provision

governing the dissolution of educational institutions "under the care or patronage of any religious denomination." This provision empowers the trustees of an RAC to wind up the corporation's affairs and to sell any or all of the corporation's property. Corporate debts are then to be paid with this and other money of the corporation. All sums given to the corporation, under written conditions that they be returned should its purposes not be carried out, are returned to the donors. The religious denomination having control of the educational or charitable corporation involved is to receive, via that body of the religious denomination which nominated or elected the trustees, all funds and property remaining in the hands of the trustees.[17] In addition, the Illinois Supreme Court has ruled that Illinois courts should apply the *cy pres* doctrine to carry out the general purposes of a trust.[18] Finally, it is possible, under some circumstances, for the State Board of Higher Education to dissolve an RAC by revoking its certificate of approval following an action and hearing brought by the Board.[19]

B. State Support

In 1969 the Illinois legislature began to provide public assistance for construction and renovation of facilities at private colleges and universities, provided that such facilities not be used as a place of sectarian instruction or religious worship.[20] In addition, the state of Illinois has enacted a capitation grant program known as the Financial Assistance Act for Nonpublic Institutions of Higher Learning.[21] Under this grant program, any institution operating an educational program of at least two years applicable to a baccalaureate degree and operating in conformity with state standards of higher learning is eligible for a grant for each Illinois resident enrolled.[22] The amount of the grant varies with the year of the student.[23] As it has with the construction assistance, Illinois has conditioned participation in the capitation grant program upon an open admissions and employment policy; that is, an institution that wishes to participate in this program may not discriminate in its admissions or employment policies on the basis of race, creed, or color.[24] Illinois likewise declines to include as institutions eligible for participation in this program "any educational organization used for sectarian instruction, as a place of religious teaching or worship or for any religious denomination or the training of ministers, priests, rabbis, or other professional persons in the field of religion."[25] Again, the concern that the government not foster a particular religious perspective is legitimate, but the State of Illinois has been excessively cautious in protecting this concern by denying any assistance to an institution that trains any kind of professional, presumably including teachers, in the field of religion.

In 1972 the legislature passed the Higher Education Cooperation Act.[26] This act fosters inter-institutional cooperation with other public institutions and nonpublic institutions.[27] To encourage this cooperative, innovative concept in education, the state makes financial assistance available to the institutions participating in the program. Grants will not be given for any program entailing sectarian institutions or "designed to serve a sectarian purpose."[28]

Illinois has a comprehensive system of scholarships, grants and guaranteed loans available to students attending a qualified public or private institution of higher education within the state.[29] Scholarships for the purpose of remitting tuition and fees are granted upon the basis of financial need and competitive examination.

C. Personnel

The Illinois Constitution guarantees to all persons "the right to be free from discrimination on the basis of race, color, creed, national ancestry, and sex in the hiring and promotion practices of any employer." The General Assembly may, however, enact laws which establish "reasonable exemptions" to these rights.[30] All persons suffering from a mental or physical handicap are similarly guaranteed freedom from discrimination, not related to ability, in employment.[31]

Pursuant to this constitutional grant of authority, the Illinois legislature has enacted the Illinois Human Rights Act,[32] declaring that it is the public policy of the state to ensure that all persons within the state are not discriminated against in employment on the basis of, *inter alia*, religion.[33] Distinctions in employment policies or practices made on that basis constitute unlawful discrimination,[34] defined elsewhere in the statute as a civil rights violation.[35] The federal Civil Rights Act describes such discrimination as an "unlawful employment practice."[36] The Illinois statute affords an individual greater protection than does the federal statute in that the former covers more factors of discrimination than does the latter.[37]

The Illinois statute excludes from the definition of employer "any religious corporation, association, educational institution [or] society, . . . with respect to the employment of individuals of a particular religion to perform work connected with the carrying on by such corporation, association, educational institution [or] society . . . of its activities."[38] Since this section authorizes religious preference by a "religious . . . educational institution," i.e., an RAC, not simply in the carrying out of its *religious* activities, but in all of its activities, an RAC in Illinois is free to exercise religious preference with respect to all of its job applicants and employees. The statute does not attempt to define narrowly the practices covered in this exclusion, but grants a broad exemption covering not only the faculty and administration, but also nonprofessional positions, such as secretaries, janitors, maids, and groundskeepers.

Although the statute appears to allow such religious preference by an RAC with respect to all of its employees, it is not certain that the statute would be sustained if a constitutional attack were mounted by an applicant excluded from a nonprofessional position on the basis of his religion where there is no clear link between the job and any religious duties.[39] Hence, before exercising the rights articulated in the Illinois statute, administrators of an RAC should be aware that, in asserting a right to religious preference in all employment positions, irrespective of any connection with religious duties, they run the risk of litigation resulting in a decision invalidating the statute or limiting its applicability to jobs involving the religious activities of an RAC.[40]

This sort of limitation is contemplated in another provision of this statute, which authorizes employment distinctions on the otherwise prohibited bases when based upon a bona fide occupational qualification (BFOQ).[41] This provision is available not only to RACs, but to any employer; its scope is much narrower than the section cited above. To justify a practice of religious preference in its employment policies, an RAC may rely on the BFOQ exception, which is generally construed narrowly, only if there is a plausible connection between a particular employment position and a religious function or duty. For example, teaching positions in a religious studies or theology department and probably in a philosophy department would be covered by the BFOQ exemption, but it would be difficult for an RAC to prevail under this defense in an employment discrimination proceeding or lawsuit brought by a faculty member in another department or by an applicant for a nonprofessional position such as secretary or janitor. Title VII of the Civil Rights Act of 1964 is more explicit than the Illinois statute in that it specifies that religion constitutes a BFOQ, but it adds that the BFOQ must be "reasonably necessary to the normal operation of that particular business or enterprise."[42] Given the overall similarity between the state and the federal civil rights statutes, an Illinois court would probably construe the state BFOQ provision narrowly, as the EEOC and the federal courts have construed the federal BFOQ provision.

An employer is defined in the Illinois Minimum Wage Law[43] as "any individual, partnership, association, [or] corporation . . . for which one or more persons are gainfully employed on some day within a calendar year."[44] Under this definition RACs are clearly covered by this Act. The same act, however, excludes from its coverage an employee who works "as a member of a religious corporation or organization."[45] If an RAC is thought of as a religious corporation or organization, it might be thought to be exempt under this provision. Since, however, the legislature has differentiated between a "religious corporation" and a religiously affiliated "educational institution,"[46] most RACs are covered by the Illinois Minimum Wage Law.

This law contains special provisions for women and minors.[47] In addition, all employees are covered by the Wage Payment and Collection Act[48] which establishes, *inter alia*, the period of payment for wages earned.[49]

Illinois law provides that any employee who

works in excess of forty hours in a workweek is to receive at least one and one-half times his regular rate of compensation for the excess hours.[50] Although the Minimum Wage Law, in which this provision is found, covers most RACs, this provision is explicitly inapplicable to "any employee employed in a bona fide executive, administrative or professional capacity, as defined by the Federal Fair Labor Standards Act of 1938."[51] RACs are thus bound by this provision only with respect to their nonprofessional staff such as secretaries and janitors.

A "legal day's work" is defined in Illinois law as "eight hours of labor between the rising and the setting of the sun" in mechanical labor and other types of daily labor.[52] Judicial interpretation of this provision limits its applicability to mechanical labor and services.[53]

Another provision in Illinois employment law requires all employers to allow their employees a twenty-four hour rest period in every calendar week.[54] RACs clearly fall within the broad definition of an employer in this statute,[55] but they are not obligated to grant this benefit to their professional employees.[56]

The Illinois Worker's Compensation Act[57] applies to employers "including religious or charitable corporations"[58] who are engaged in any of the extrahazardous enterprises enumerated in the law[59] and to other employers who elect to become subject to the act.[60] Some employees of RACs, including those in food services,[61] maintenance and construction,[62] and the sale of merchandise to the public,[63] are subject to the provisions of the Act. Moreover, RACs may elect to be covered by filing proper notice with the Industrial Commission or by insuring their employees.[64] Employees covered by a federal workers' compensation law are exempt from this act.[65] An employee of an RAC that has elected coverage may, in turn, elect not to be subject to the Act's provisions by filing proper notice with the Industrial Commission.[66] RACs must carry insurance or become a self-insurer after proving financial ability to compensate injured employees directly. The Industrial Commission may require adequate security before approving an employer as a self-insurer.[67]

The Illinois Unemployment Compensation Act[68] broadly defines "employing unit" as "any individual or type of organization."[69] The statute's general definition of "employer" includes nonprofit organizations,[70] except as those organizations employ domestic-service or agricultural workers.[71] In defining "employment," the Illinois Act first provides that "any service" constitutes employment.[72] Subsequent sections specify the conditions under which service for nonprofit organizations qualifies as employment. Coverage extends to any corporation, community chest, fund, or foundation which (1) "has or had in employment four or more individuals within each of twenty or more calendar weeks . . . whether or not such weeks are or were consecutive, within the current or preceding calendar year" and (2) is "organized and operated exclusively for religious . . . or educational purposes . . . , no part of which inures to the benefit of any private shareholder or individual, no substantial part of the activities of which is carrying on propaganda, or otherwise attempting to influence legislation, and which does not participate in, or intervene in . . . , any political campaign on behalf of any candidate for public office."[73] The services in question must fall outside the definition of "employment" under the Federal Unemployment Tax Act.[74]

Certain religious and educational services do not constitute employment under the Illinois Act.[75] Within the exemptions are services performed:

(A) [i]n the employ of (1) a church or convention or association of churches or (2) an organization or school which is not an institution of higher education,[76] which is operated primarily for religious purposes and which is operated, supervised, controlled, or principally supported by a church or convention or association of churches;[77]

(B) [b]y a duly ordained commissioned or licensed minister of a church in the exercise of his ministry or by a member of a religious order in the exercise of duties required by such order.[78]

Services performed for a school, college, or university either by a full-time student or by the spouse of a full-time student are exempt from coverage under the unemployment compensation statute.[79] Also excepted from coverage are "work experience programs" provided by nonprofit or public institutions with a regular faculty and "a regularly organized body of students."[80]

The statute provides for an election of coverage by any employing unit which would ordinarily be exempt from the Act's provisions.[81] Upon approval of an organization's written application, either the unit is considered an employer under the Act[82] or services performed by employees are considered employment.[83]

The State University Civil Service System (also known as the University System) is under the control of the University Civil Service Merit Board (also known as the Merit Board).[84] Among its responsibilities, the Merit Board has the duty of prescribing the rate of compensation and authorizing the continuous recruitment of personnel.[85] Because the University System covers those colleges and universities which are under the jurisdiction of the Board of Higher Education,[86] the body from which a postsecondary educational institution must receive a certificate of approval,[87] apparently RACs fall under the regulatory jurisdiction of the Merit Board with regard to employment policies and practices.

D. Students

There is no Illinois statute which directly regulates the admission standards for students attending RACs.[88] In a 1948 decision, moreover, an Illinois appellate court ruled that unless the state, in the charter which it grants to a private educational institution, reserves for itself the power to prescribe admission standards, it cannot do so thereafter.[89] Thus RACs may prefer students on the basis of religion in their admission policy. Nonetheless, RACs in Illinois may be forced to choose between adopting a policy of religious preference in student admissions and participating in various forms of state aid.[90] In addition, RACs may not be deemed "reputable and in good standing" by the Department of Registration and Education if they refuse to admit an applicant because of the person's creed.[91]

E. Facilities

RACs may benefit from the Educational Facilities Authority Act,[92] which authorizes the Illinois Educational Facilities Authority to aid institutions of higher education in the acquisition, construction, or renovation of educational facilities.[93] Receipt of such assistance implicitly regulates RACs in a number of ways. In order to qualify as an eligible institution for participation in this program, an RAC may not utilize religion as a standard of admission.[94] Nor may it be primarily dedicated to religious or sectarian functions.[95] Indeed, no project or educational facility which is the subject of assistance may include a facility or property which is used for sectarian instruction or religious worship,[96] or which would be "used primarily in connection with any part of the program of a school or department of divinity for any religious denomination."[97]

Although, therefore, Illinois does not directly bar an RAC from implementing a policy of religious preference in student admissions, it seems clear that it inhibits the implementation of such a policy by limiting financial assistance to private colleges without such a policy. The state has a legitimate interest in avoiding direct support of religious activities. This interest is grounded in the no-establishment principle, which would, for example, bar the use of public funds for the acquisition of property to be used for a chapel or provision of support for the construction of a seminary to be used exclusively for the training of candidates for the ministry of a particular church. Because the selection of the student body so directly implicates other constitutional values such as free exercise of religion, academic freedom, and freedom of association,[98] however, the Illinois legislature exceeded the bounds of its legitimate interests when it conditioned receipt of construction grants and loans by an RAC upon the institution's forebearance of the exercise of religious preference in student admissions.

Another question relating to facilities at an RAC concerns restriction of access to campus facilities to members of its religious denomination. Under the Illinois Fair Housing Act, which allows a municipality to enact measures aimed at the prohibition of religious discrimination in residential housing transactions, an RAC may not discriminate on the basis of religion in renting dormitory space.[99] The Human Rights Act,[100] on the other hand, expressly states that an RAC may restrict access to its facilities to members of its religion as long as such facilities are not utilized for commercial purposes or as long as membership in that religion is not based on one's "race, color, or national origin."[101] If the two statutes are read *ex pari materia*, one may conclude from the explicit language of the Human Rights Act that an RAC is free to restrict accessibility to its dormitories to students who are of the same religion as the RAC. An RAC, however, may not limit its places of public accommodation, such as a theater or skating rink on its premises, to members of its religion.[102] Thus it is the private or public character of the facility which determines an RAC's freedom in limiting or extending access to buildings on its campus.

The Illinois Health and Safety Act[103] applies to all employers engaged in any occupation, business, or enterprise in the state, including the state and its political subdivisions.[104]

F. State Taxation

The Illinois State Constitution grants the General Assembly the power to "exempt from taxation only . . . property used exclusively[105] for . . . school, religious, cemetery and charitable purposes. . . . "

In keeping with its constitutional mandate, the General Assembly has enacted a number of measures which exempt RACs from state taxation. The base income of an RAC is the unrelated business taxable income of the institution as determined under section 512 of the federal Internal Revenue Code.[106]

RACs are exempt from the tax imposed by the state on the distribution of assets in an estate. This exemption extends to any property or income in which an RAC acquires a beneficial interest and which is devoted solely to "religious, educational or charitable uses and purposes."[107]

Illinois does impose an "estate tax" up to the amount of the maximum federal credit, which is designed to channel to Illinois moneys that would otherwise go to the federal government in federal estate taxes.[108] This tax has no ultimate effect on the amount of combined state and federal death taxes paid.

The Illinois Income Tax Act does not provide a deduction for taxpayers' contributions to RACs.

Illinois has no gift tax.

The General Assembly has exempted various forms of real property from state taxation as long as the title holder or the owner of the beneficial interest files a certificate in which he states whether or not there has been any change in ownership, the status of the owner-resident, or the use of the property.[109] Among the forms of property declared exempt under Illinois law is "school property," defined in the Act as all property used exclusively for school purposes and not leased or used with a view to profit.[110] Student residence halls and housing facilities for staff persons are explicitly included within the definition of tax-exempt property.

RACs, moreover, are not required to pay taxes on their intangible property. Illinois law provides an exemption from taxation on capital stock that is held by a not for profit corporation[111] and that was not taxed prior to 1978.[112] RACs are also exempt from payment of the tax on real estate transfers. This exemption extends to all property deeded "by or from" any organization devoted exclusively to charitable, religious, or educational purposes.[113] This exemption is worded broadly enough to include property used, for example, as a place of religious worship or a place of sectarian instruction.

The General Assembly has likewise exempted RACs from a number of other state-imposed taxes. For example, an RAC is exempt from the payment of use tax in connection with its retail sales of tangible personal property to its "members or students," if such property is to be used primarily for the purposes of the RAC or if the RAC is not organized for profit.[114] This provision, however, states that the retail sale of books to students is not "primarily for the purposes" of the selling school. This would deny the exemption to college bookstores unless, at least, the college was not organized for profit. Bookstores operated by most RACs would not be subject to this tax.

Illinois also excludes from the payment of a service use tax any sale or transfer of tangible personal property that is incidental to the rendering of service for or by any corporation organized and operated exclusively for charitable, religious, or educational purposes.[115] A similar provision exempts RACs from payment of the service occupation tax,[116] and persons selling tangible personal property to an RAC are exempted from payment of the retailers' occupation tax on such transactions.[117] An RAC, however, does not enjoy total exemption from the service occupation taxes; an RAC is exempt from taxation in its retail sale of tangible personal property only if it is to be used "primarily for the purposes" of the RAC or if the sale does not involve persons organized for profit.[118] As with the use tax, colleges organized for profit, at least, must pay this form of tax on the sale of school supplies to students.[119]

G. Fund Raising

RACs in Illinois are generally exempt from state regulation of their fund raising activities. Exemption from the regulatory aspects of the Solicitation of Funds for Charitable Purposes Act requires many entities that engage in charitable solicitation to register with the state Attorney General and to provide annual reports to that office.[120] These provisions, however, do not apply to any organization established for educational purposes that is "affiliated with, operated by, or supervised or controlled by a . . . religious corporation. . . . "[121] Most RACs would qualify under this exemption, and would therefore not be obliged to register with the Attorney General or to report to that office concerning their fund raising activities.[122] Even if an RAC did not for some reason qualify under this exemption, another provision specifically exempts all educational institutions "that are recognized by the Superintendent of Public Instruction or that are accredited by a regional association."[123]

The Illinois Bingo License and Tax Act[124] explicitly includes nonprofit religious and educational organizations among those which are subject to the requirements of the Act.[125]

An RAC wishing to raise funds by conducting bingo games is required to apply and pay for a license to do so.[126]

H. Miscellaneous Provisions

Because RACs are exempt from federal income taxation under §501(c)(3) of the Internal Revenue Code, they may under Illinois law establish and be the beneficiary of a trust fund created under the Religious and Charitable Risk Pooling Trust Act.[127] The purpose of the fund must be to protect and indemnify the beneficiaries against the risk of financial "loss due to damage, destruction or loss to property or the imposition of legal liability."[128]

The general statute of limitations governing personal injury suits requires that such an action be commenced within two years after the date on which the cause of action accrued.[129] In 1959, the Illinois legislature established a notice requirement of six months and a statute of limitations of one year for personal injury lawsuits brought against a public school district or a nonprofit private school.[130] In 1974, however, the Illinois Supreme Court invalidated these provisions,[131] so lawsuits of this nature may now be filed within two years of the date on which the cause of action accrued.

Under the Lobbyist Registration Act, any person who receives compensation for lobbying or whose employment includes lobbying must register with the Secretary of State.[132] The Act, however, excludes from the registration requirements a full-time employee of a religious organization if he represents the organization solely to protect the interests of its members in religious freedom.[133]

Finally, Illinois regulates the registration of securities,[134] but an RAC issuing securities is not subject to the normal requirements of registration.[135]

22. Indiana

A. Corporate Status

Indiana's Not-For-Profit Corporations Act[1] is a typical business corporation statute. There are no substantive provisions mentioning educational or religious corporations, although the definition of "not-for-profit" expressly includes ". . . any religious, civil, social [or] educational . . . association . . . which does not engage in any activities for the profit of its trustees, directors, incorporators, or members."[2]

In its provisions for the distribution of assets upon the dissolution of the corporation, the Code specifies that the assets remaining after payment of debts and liabilities are to be transferred:

to any other not-for-profit corporation, [sic] organized for purposes, [sic] substantially the same as those of the corporation being dissolved, if the laws . . . of the dissolving corporation so provide.[3]

Any Indiana corporation may choose to accept the provisions of this Act by complying with its statutory regulations.[4] Therefore, an incorporated institution of higher education may be governed either by the Not-For-Profit Corporations Act, if it falls within its parameters, or by Article 13 of Indiana's corporation laws, which specifically address the incorporation of educational institutions.[5] In its language, the former reflects business rather than educational associations. The latter addresses educational and religious institutions specifically, but its terminology is more suited to a profit-making organization.

If an RAC should be a corporation owned by stockholders, its transactions would be governed by the general statutes regulating existing Indiana institutions of learning,[6] as well as by specific legislation concerning the right to borrow money,[7] to change the number of trustees,[8] and to acquire real estate.[9] By following the Code's stipulations, a religious body may manage an educational institution by electing its governing board.[10]

In its care to uphold the state's constitutional prohibition against the use of state funds for the benefit of a religious or theological institution,[11] this part of the Indiana Code specifically requires the return of any remaining tax-levied funds kept in a separate account by a college, university, or normal school which becomes a "sectarian or religious institution or under the control of a sectarian or religious institution" if the school had been in existence for fifty years.[12]

B. State Support

The Indiana Constitution provides both for free exercise of religion and for the separation of church and state by protecting one's right to worship[13] and to express freely one's religious opinions,[14] and by prohibiting the use of state funds for religious or theological institutions.[15] These principles were intended to guarantee the same broad protection provided by the First Amendment to the United States Constitution.[16]

In sections of the state constitution having nothing to do with religion, both the counties and the state are prohibited from loaning their credit to any corporation.[17] As the clauses are worded, they might prohibit state aid to private colleges. Although there has been no challenge to state programs benefiting private educational institutions, other types of corporations have been so challenged and have kept state appropriations by arguing that they were public or quasi-public entities.[18]

In an early case,[19] Purdue University (a state-established university but also a private corporation) was allowed to keep public funds given to it for agricultural work. Noting that the organization had a public purpose, that its uses were in the public interest, and that there was no pecuniary profit, the Court concluded that the Legislature had the right to employ any agencies, "even if they could be regarded as private corporations," for public purposes.[20]

Although that case concerned a legislatively established state university, its holding has been more broadly applied to private corporations in general. It has been cited to show that:

private corporations . . . engaged in private and proprietary activities, but . . . so affected with the public interest that their activities could be considered public in another sense . . . could be the beneficiaries of subsidies raised by taxation.[21]

In other words, a private institution or corporation may be treated as a public entity and thereby receive state funds.

The Indiana Code contains a faculty oath provision triggered by public support. Teachers of all ranks in Indiana universities "supported partially or totally by public funds"[22] must take an oath swearing to support the Indiana and United States constitutions and laws.[23] Furthermore, a teacher who is an alien must pledge his support of the United States' institutions and policies during his stay in Indiana.[24]

In 1979 the state legislature passed the Indiana Educational Facilities Authority Act, whose broad purpose is to benefit the people of Indiana by providing youth "the fullest opportunity to learn and to develop their intellectual and mental capacities and skills."[25] To do this, the state pledges to assist colleges and universities in their building projects:

[I]t is the purpose of this chapter to provide a measure of assistance and an alternative method to enable institutions for higher education in the state to refund or refinance outstanding indebtedness incurred by them for the construction or acquisition of educational facilities and structures, and to provide the needed additional educational facilities and structures for the public benefit and good.[26]

A lengthy declaration of purpose was necessary to demonstrate that the legislature was not violating the Indiana constitutional provision forbidding the state to give credit to a private corporation.[27] The purpose of the Educational Facilities Authority Act, therefore, is presented as a public one, one for the benefit of the state and of its citizens.

The Act gives the educational facilities authority the power to "make loans to any private institution of higher education for the cost of a project."[28] A "private institution of higher education" is a "not for profit educational institution" which:

1. is not controlled by the state or any political subdivision;[29]
2. is an authorized postsecondary educational institution;
3. admits as regular students only high school graduates;
4. grants either a bachelor's degree, or a postgraduate degree, or two-year technical training in engineering, mathematics, or the physical or biological sciences;
5. is "accredited by a nationally recognized accrediting agency or association or . . . is an institution whose credits are accepted, on transfer, by not less than three institutions which are so accredited;"[30] and
6. "does not discriminate in the admission of students on the basis of race, color, or creed."[31]

An RAC must therefore be properly accredited and must not have a discriminatory admissions process in order to participate in this program. Religious discrimination in admissions, if otherwise allowable,[32] might well disqualify an RAC from this program.

Although a qualifying RAC may receive a loan under this Act,[33] the authority may make certain stipulations concerning the building project.[34]

The law provides that the educational facility being financed may not be used for "sectarian instruction or study or as a place for devotional activities or workshop,"[35] nor "primarily in connection with any part of the program of a school or department of divinity for any religious denomination."[36] (It would seem that any loans barred by the "divinity school" provision may well be barred under the "sectarian instruction" provision, thus making the former meaningless.) Under these relatively narrow constraints, most RACs will qualify for loans for most facilities.

Therefore, as long as an RAC qualifies under the definition of a private institution of higher education and intends to build a facility having no sectarian use, it may qualify for a loan from the state under this Act in connection with almost every type of campus facility.[37]

The Indiana Scholarships Act[38] sets out the different state scholarship and grant programs offered to qualified students attending approved institutions of higher learning. The awards are given according to academic excellence and financial need.

The definition of "approved institution of higher learning" probably includes RACs. It requires that the educational institution:

1. operate in Indiana;[39]
2. provide a "two-year or longer program of collegiate grade directly creditable toward a baccalaureate degree;"[40]
3. be either state-operated or nonprofit;[41] and
4. be accredited by a "recognized regional accrediting agency" or certified by the state department of public instruction as qualified to prepare persons to teach in the state."[42]

Under this Act, the state student assistance commission administers the scholarship programs.[43] Scholarships are offered to two or more qualified residents of each county in Indiana.[44] There are also honorary scholarships[45] and awards under the Educational Grant Program[46] and the Freedom of Choice Grant Program.[47]

For all scholarships and grants the student must attend an approved institution of higher learning;[48] the Freedom of Choice Grant recipient must attend an accredited private college or university.[49]

The State Student Assistance Commission also conducts the state's student loan programs, approving "qualified institutions" and establishing reasonable criteria for the eligibility of both the lenders and students.[50] A "qualified institution" is vaguely defined as "any post-secondary institution which is approved by the commission for the purposes of this chapter."[51] The definition specifically excludes from its parameters only correspondence or home study courses.

Scholarships and grants are given to the student recipient, but are an indirect aid to the educational institution as well. Since Article I, Section 6 of the Indiana Constitution forbids the use of state funds for religious or theological institutions, state scholarships and grants to students attending an RAC might be challenged on constitutional grounds. It might be argued that the student is merely passing the money on to the real beneficiary, the sectarian educational institution.[52]

There has been no Indiana decision concerning tuition grants for postsecondary education. However, the Indiana Attorney General has upheld state-supported busing for parochial schools, a form of financial aid to sectarian education, by arguing that the direct recipient was the student, and that any benefit to the sectarian institution or church with which he or she is associated was secondary and incidental.[53] The same argument, of course, would fully apply to student grants and loans.

The Indiana Educational Opportunity Law[54] probably will not affect RACs for two reasons: first, it is a program which provides loans for occupational education;[55] and second, the program will apparently be terminated in 1986, when all the bonds, indebtedness, and lease agreements are retired.[56] Also in 1986, the Commission for Higher Education, which develops and implements long range plans for both state and private institutions,[57] apparently will be abolished.[58]

C. Personnel

Fair Employment Practices

The Indiana Civil Rights Law[59] announces the state's public policy:

to provide all of its citizens equal opportunity for education, employment, access to public conveniences and accommodations and acquisition through purchase or rental of real property including but not limited to housing, and to eliminate segregation or separation based solely on race, religion, color, sex, handicap, national origin or ancestry.[60]

The law has the dual purpose of promoting equal opportunity without discriminatory practices[61] and of "protecting employers, labor organizations, employment agencies, property owners, real estate brokers, builders, and lending institutions from unfounded charges of discrimination."[62]

Denial of equal employment opportunity because of a person's race, religion, color, sex, handicap, national origin, or ancestry is a "discriminatory practice," and as such is unlawful unless an exemption is granted.[63] Under the Civil Rights Law, however, the term "employer":

does not include any not-for-profit corporation or association organized exclusively for fraternal or religious purposes, nor any school, educational or charitable religious institution owned or conducted by or affiliated with, a church or religious institution.[64]

This provision, covering any educational religious institution "owned or conducted by or affiliated with" a church or religious institution is extremely broad and would seem to include all RACs. The problem, however, is that the ban on general employment discrimination never uses the term "employer" and, therefore, the intended exemption seems never to come into play.

The law sets out the actions the Civil Rights Commission may take if it finds that a "person" has violated the Act by a discriminatory practice.[65] The term "person" is defined to include all organizations and corporations.[66] If the Act means to take action against all "persons" (rather than "employers") who have engaged in discrimination, the exemption found in the definition of "employer" would not apply and RACs would be liable for violation of the Civil Rights Act employment discrimination ban.

The specific exceptions to the term "employer," however, would certainly suggest a legislative intent to exclude the entities listed from the employment discrimination ban, since otherwise the exception is rendered almost meaningless.[67] Perhaps the use of the word "employment" in the paragraph describing "discriminatory practice" was meant to incorporate the definition of "employer." Under this interpretation, RACs would not be bound by any part of the ban against employment discrimination on the basis of race, religion, color, sex, handicap, national origin or ancestry.[68]

The Commission has been granted broad powers once a "person" has been found to engage in a discriminatory practice.[69]

A discrete chapter entitled "Age Discrimination" declares it to be "an unfair employment practice and to be against public policy to dismiss from employment, or to refuse to employ or rehire, any person solely because of his age" if that person is between the ages of forty and seventy.[70] Although this basic prohibition does not use the term, "employer" is defined within the chapter to exclude "religious, charitable, fraternal, social, educational, or sectarian corporations or associations not organized for private profit."[71] This provision, in order to be given significance, must be read to exclude those listed entities (which would easily include most RACs) from the age discrimination ban. Perhaps the use of the word "employment" was intended to incorporate into the prohibition the definition of "employer."[72]

The Indiana Minimum Wage Law defines "employer" as any association or corporation having during any work week four or more employees,[73] a definition which clearly includes RACs. However, the following employees are not included under the law and therefore need not be paid a minimum wage:

1. Members of any religious order performing any service for such order, any duly ordained, commissioned or licensed minister, priest, rabbi, sexton, or Christian Science reader, and volunteers performing services for any religious or charitable organization;[74]
2. Students performing services for any school, college, or university in which they are enrolled and are regularly attending class;[75]
3. Persons performing services in any camping, recreational or guidance facilities operated by a

charitable, religious, or educational not for profit organization.[76]

RACs must pay all other persons employed by them a minimum wage, and further must pay equal wages for equal work without sex discrimination.[77] Factors other than sex may be considered, however; wage rate differences may be based upon seniority, merit, or production-measuring systems.[78]

Indiana's Workmen's Compensation Act applies to RACs. An "employer" includes any association or corporation.[79] An "employee" includes "every person, including a minor, in the service of another, under any contract of hire or apprenticeship, written or implied."[80]

However, an executive officer of a "charitable, religious, educational or other nonprofit corporation" is not considered an employee under the Workmen's Compensation Act unless he is specifically brought within the corporation's insurance coverage, whereupon he is considered an employee during that coverage period.[81]

Over and above the Workmen's Compensation Act, Indiana legislation provides that any corporation doing business in the state and employing five or more persons is liable for the injury or death of an employee "where such injury or death resulted in whole or in part from the negligence of such employer, or his, its, or their agents, servants, employees or officers."[82]

Prior to 1972, under Indiana's Employment Security Act,[83] nonprofit corporations "operated exclusively for religious, charitable, scientific, literary or educational purposes"[84] were not included in the definition of "employer" and were granted a certificate of exemption after justifying to the state Director their right to be exempted from the payment of contributions. That exemption could continue until the Director would decide to cancel it. Since January 1, 1972, "employment" under the legislation includes that performed "in the employ of a religious, charitable, educational or other organization" *if* the service is excluded from "employment" as defined in the Federal Unemployment Tax Act solely by reason of Section 3306 (c)(8) of that Act[85] and if the organization has the requisite number of employees (four or more for at least part of one day in each of twenty weeks in the current or preceding calendar year).[86]

In any event, "employment" does not include service performed (1) for a "church or convention or association of churches;"[87] (2) for an organization "operated primarily for religious purposes and which is operated, supervised, controlled, or principally supported by a church or convention or association of churches;"[88] or (3) by a "duly ordained, commissioned, or licensed minister of a church in the exercise of his ministry or by a member of a religious order in the exercise of duties required by such order."[89] None of these three exceptions is very broad insofar as employment at the typical RAC is concerned and, consequently, few positions at RACs will come within any of the three. This is true because (1) very few people employed by RACs may claim to be working for a church, convention or association of churches; (2) except, perhaps, for institutions like seminaries and Bible colleges, few RACs can claim to be both operated primarily for religious purposes and run or principally supported by a church or group of churches; and (3) few employees on RAC campuses, save, perhaps, some counselors or theology teachers, will be regular ministers of a church exercising their ministry or members of a religious order performing duties required by that order.

Nonetheless, the following services, *inter alia*, are excluded from the definition of "employment" and thus are not subject to the provisions of the Unemployment Compensation law:

1. Service with respect to which unemployment compensation is payable under a congressionally established system;[90]

2. Domestic service in a local college club or local chapter of a college fraternity or sorority, unless performed for a person who paid $1,000 or more to individuals employed in the domestic service in any calendar quarter;[91]

3. Service performed for a school, college, or university by a regularly enrolled student (or by the student's spouse, if the spouse is advised at the beginning of the service that the employment is provided under a program to provide the student financial aid and that such employment is not covered by unemployment insurance);[92] and

4. Service performed by a student under the age of twenty-two in a nonprofit or public educational institution which combines academic instructions with work experience.[93]

Most RACs must make unemployment compensation contributions for all employees performing services other than those listed above. However, a clarifying provision states that unemployment benefits are not paid to instructors, researchers, or administrators of colleges and universities for the periods between terms or academic years, or during a paid sabbatical leave provided for in the individual's contract, if the individual contracts to perform services for any institution of higher education for both terms or both years (or if there is reasonable assurance the individual will perform services in the second of the academic terms or years).[94]

D. Students

The state civil rights statute has defined "discriminatory practice" as "the exclusion of a person, [sic] from equal opportunities because of race, religion, color, sex, handicap, national origin or ancestry."[95] It goes on to state that ". . . [e]very discriminatory practice relating to . . . education . . . shall be considered unlawful unless it is specifically exempted in this chapter."[96]

Under the definition of "sex," just such an exemption is given to RACs:

[I]t shall not be a discriminatory practice for a private or religious educational institution to continue to maintain and enforce a policy of admitting students of one sex only.[97]

The Code does not grant an exemption for an admissions policy which discriminates on the basis of religion. However, one opinion of the Attorney General, broadly interpreting the state's guarantee of religious freedom,[98] defended the right of a Bible college to select its enrollment on the basis of religion.[99]

The Civil Rights Law is enforced by the State Civil Rights Commission, discussed earlier.[100]

The Equal Educational Opportunity Act, following the tone of the Civil Rights Act, states Indiana's public policy of providing equal education for all "regardless of race, creed, national origin, color or sex."[101] The Code declares further that Indiana intends to:

eliminate and prohibit segregation, separation and discrimination on the basis of race, color or creed in

the public kindergartens, common schools, public schools, vocational schools, colleges and universities of the state.[102]

It is not clear whether "colleges and universities of the state" includes private colleges (and therefore RACs). Since the adjective "public" is used twice, it may be meant specifically for kindergartens and public schools only, and not intended to describe the colleges and universities. Further, the word "state" is not capitalized, and so the reference may be to *all* colleges and universities located *in* the state, rather than to *state-owned* schools. Under this interpretation the state perhaps intends to prohibit discrimination in private as well as state-owned colleges and universities.

The two following sections make this interpretation more likely. The first prohibits the board of trustees of "any college or university" from allowing any segregation "on the basis of race, color, creed or national origin of pupils," and grants to the officials the right to take "reasonable, feasible and practical" steps to bring about integration.[103] The second section focuses on the student, and forbids the denial of attendance or enrollment in "any college or university in the state because of his race, creed, color, or national origin."[104] The wording in two still later sections suggests that private colleges and universities are *not* meant to be governed by the Equal Educational Opportunity Act. The first of these expressly refers to the schools in which discrimination is prohibited ("[n]o public school, state college or state university shall segregate.")[105] and it further declares that "[a]dmission to any public school shall not be approved or denied on the basis of race, creed or color."[106] The second section prohibits teacher hiring or promotions on a discriminatory basis in any "public school, state college, or state university."[107]

The net result seems to be that RACs are not covered by the Equal Educational Opportunity Act, but are covered by the Civil Rights Law provision (discussed earlier)[108] relating to educational discrimination.

Indiana's Postsecondary Proprietary Educational Institutional Accreditation Act[109] makes state accreditation mandatory for any postsecondary proprietary educational institution,[110] but expressly excludes "any privately endowed [two or four] year degree granting institution, regionally accredited, whose principal campus is located within Indiana."[111] Most RACs would fall within this exclusionary phrase.

This Act was a revision of the Private School Accreditation Act,[112] which did not contain the above exemption. Under that previous act a private Bible college was threatened with denial of accreditation because it enrolled its students on the basis of their religious beliefs, in alleged violation of the nondiscrimination provision.[113] However, the state Attorney General upheld the Bible college's right to a selective enrollment policy, and declared that the Private School Accreditation Act's provision requiring the Bible school's loss of accreditation "inhibits the free exercise of religion by those schools which condition admission on adherence to particular doctrinal beliefs."[114]

Thus, by statute, Indiana has expressed its intent not to interfere with RACs falling within the exemption to the accreditation mandate; by official opinion it has also shown that it will not interfere with a religious school's free exercise of its religion in its admissions policy.

E. Facilities

Indiana's public policy, spelled out in its Civil Rights Act,[115] is to provide its citizens equal opportunity for "access to public conveniences and accommodations."[116] Under Indiana law, it is a discriminatory practice "to exclude from equal opportunities due to race, religion, color, sex, handicap, national origin or ancestry."[117]

Since "public accommodation" is defined as "any establishment which caters or offers its services or facilities or goods to the general public,"[118] any restaurant, store, place of amusement, or the like, open to the public on the campus of an RAC, must be made available to all on the nondiscriminatory basis specified in the law.

Although "services, facilities or goods" could even be interpreted to include the provision of education itself and, therefore, the admissions process, since "education" is separately mentioned in the Civil Rights Act,[119] it was presumably not intended to be covered by the "public conveniences and accommodations"

phrase. The public accommodations law is enforced by the State Civil Rights Commission.[120]

In its general statement of public policy, the Civil Rights Act guarantees to Indiana citizens "equal opportunity for . . . acquisition through purchase or rental of real property including but not limited to housing."[121] Since it is a "discriminatory practice" to exclude a person "from equal opportunities because of race, religion, color, sex, handicap, national origin or ancestry,"[122] RACs must not discriminate on these bases in the sale or rental of any of their real estate. This provision would presumably include all student housing. To restrict such housing to *students*, however, is not to discriminate on a prohibited basis even though *admission* might have been restricted on the basis of religion.[123]

This provision also is enforced by the State Civil Rights Commission.[124]

Anyone intentionally denying to another because of color, creed, handicap, national origin, race, religion, or sex, full use of goods, facilities, or services in an establishment serving the public or in a "housing project" owned or subsidized by a governmental entity" commits a misdemeanor.[125]

The state's Occupational Health and Safety laws are very broad, and would include RACs as employers.[126] Therefore, RACs are required to establish and maintain safe and healthful working conditions[127] and to submit annual reports of all disabling work injuries to the Safety Education and Training Bureau.[128]

The only exemption from the reporting requirements of this Act may be granted by the Bureau to those employers "for whose operations adequate records of safety experience are already available" or for whom it "would be an undue burden" and unnecessary for the Bureau's purposes.[129]

F. Taxation

The income received by nonprofit organizations and corporations formed exclusively for a religious or educational purpose is exempted from the gross income taxable under the Indiana tax provisions, as long as any income is used only for reasonable compensation and not for private gain.[130] However, any income from an "unrelated trade or business as defined in

Section 513 of the Internal Revenue Code" will not be within the exemption.[131]

A taxpayer contributing to an Indiana institution of higher education, or to a corporation or foundation operating for the benefit of such an institution, or to an association of Indiana colleges, may elect a tax credit of up to fifty percent of the charitable contribution.[132] The credit is limited to $100 for a single return ($200 for a joint return),[133] and, for a corporate donor, to either ten percent of its adjusted gross income tax or $1000, whichever is less.[134] An "institution of higher education" must have a regular faculty and curriculum and an organized student body in attendance. It must also offer education above the twelfth grade and award advanced degrees. Finally, it must be duly accredited by the North Central Association of Colleges, the Indiana Department of Public Instruction, or the American Association of Theological Schools.[135] Most if not all RACs, therefore, are qualifed donees under this tax credit.

Article X, Section 1, of the Indiana Constitution authorizes the General Assembly to exempt from property taxation any "property being used for municipal, educational, literary, scientific, religious or charitable purposes." Implementing this authorization, the Indiana Code grants a property tax exemption for buildings "owned, occupied and used . . . for educational, literary, scientific, religious, or charitable purposes."[136] (This is the "16(a) exemption.") Land is also exempt, if it meets one of the following conditions: (a) the land, including the campus and athletic grounds, must have on it a building which has a 16(a) exemption, and must not be greater than fifty acres;[137] or (b) the land must have been bought in order to build a structure which would have a 16(a) exemption, and must not be greater than forty acres.[138] Dormitories of educational institutions have been held exempt even if they are operated by a profit-making corporation.[139]

Up to one acre of land owned by a church and used as a dormitory for students of a college or university located within the state is given a property tax exemption.[140] (There is no indication that the church need have any connection to the college or university involved other than housing students attending that college or university.) But college-owned farms are not treated as tax-exempt unless they are used as "part of the educational procedure."[141]

Although these exemptions would be available to an RAC, it is important to point out that a broader property tax exemption is elsewhere provided for up to eight hundred acres in any one county of real property owned by a college incorporated within Indiana[142] and for tangible property owned by such a college.[143]

Included in this chapter is an exemption for personal property owned and used by a person for educational or religious purposes.[144]

Additional tangible property tax exemptions which may affect RACs are granted for (1) nonprofit corporations which promote the fine arts;[145] (2) a building used for worship or for a parsonage ("if it is owned by, or held in trust for the use of, a church or religious society"), the tangible property in the building used for worship, and the land (up to fifteen acres) on which the building is located;[146] and (3) land (up to one acre) owned by a fraternity or sorority, along with any building or improvement on the land and the personal property used to carry out the purpose of the organization.[147]

Nonprofit corporations "operating exclusively for religious, charitable [or] educational purposes" need not pay an intangibles tax.[148]

The Indiana gross retail tax is not applied to food furnished by nonprofit colleges and universities to their students.[149] It is also inapplicable to sales of tangible personal property made (1) to raise money for a nonprofit organization which has been exempted from gross income tax under Section 6-2-1-7(i)[150] (discussed earlier);[151] or (2) for the organization's primary purpose (educational, cultural, or religious) or for:

the improvement in the skill or professional qualifications of members of the organization for carrying on the work or practice of their trade, business or profession, and not used in carrying on a private or proprietary business.[152]

(However, this exemption does not include the sale by an accredited college or university of "books, stationery, haberdashery, supplies and other property.")[153] Exempted also are sales to nonprofit educational organizations exempted from gross income tax under Section 6-2-1-7 (discussed earlier)[154] of tangible personal property or services used by them predominantly for educational purposes or to raise money for such purposes.[155]

Indiana imposes an estate tax designed merely to channel to Indiana, by virtue of the credit allowed against the federal estate tax for state death taxes, moneys that would otherwise go to the federal government in estate taxes.[156] This tax, therefore, has no ultimate effect on the *amount* of death taxes paid regardless of the recipient institution's tax-exempt status.

Indiana has no gift tax.

Indiana also grants an inheritance and transfer tax exemption[157] for bequests, legacies, devises, and transfers "to or for the use of any corporation organized and operated exclusively for religious, charitable, scientific, literary or educational purposes"[158] and "to a trustee . . . only if such contributions or gifts are to be used . . . exclusively for religious, charitable, scientific, literary or educational purposes."[159]

G. Fund Raising

The Indiana Code states only that cities may "regulate, inspect, license and prohibit . . . solicitation for any charitable cause or purpose."[160] There are no state provisions for disclosure of donations received, for regulation of fund raising or, consequently, for exemptions for RACs.

Gambling and other games of chance are prohibited in Indiana, except at licensed racetracks.[161]

H. Miscellaneous

Any state-supported educational institution may permit its students to receive credit for:

biblical and religious instruction conducted and maintained by some association, college, seminary, foundation, or school organized for religious instruction [incorporated in Indiana and privately funded].[162]

The section stipulates that the teacher's ability and the "hours of recitation, content of instruction, requirements of attendance, and standards of work" must be equal to those required in the state school granting the credit.[163] Under this provision, RACs might consider developing programs that might appeal to substantial numbers of students attending state-supported schools.

Indiana has entered into a compact for education which provides a multistate forum for cooperative educational development.[164] No level of education is specified. The Education Commission, selected from both public and private education by representatives of the member states, is empowered to "encourage . . . research in all aspects of education, but with special reference to . . . public educational systems."[165] Therefore, educational policy concerning RACs may be encompassed by this Commission, but its interest is statutorily directed toward public education. Moreover, the Indiana Education Council, the state's representatives in the Education Commission, has been abolished and will be terminated effective June 30, 1986.[166]

All Indiana universities, including RACs, may use the state-wide telecommunications system in order to improve and advance higher educational opportunity.[167]

Indiana has a contract enforceability provision designed to prevent the evasion of property taxes by the transfer of property to an educational, literary, scientific, religious, or charitable institution if the donor seeks to control any income or proceeds therefrom.[168]

23. Iowa

A. Corporate Status

The Iowa Nonprofit Corporation Act[1] enumerates a series of requirements which would bind incorporated RACs. The corporation must have a registered office and agent;[2] it must have a board of directors[3] who must enact bylaws;[4] it must create and file articles of incorporation;[5] it is forbidden to issue shares of stock or to pay dividends.[6]

Any security issued by a nonprofit organization operated for religious or educational purposes is exempt from registration requirements.[7]

The merger, consolidation, and dissolution of nonprofit colleges are governed by the Iowa Nonprofit Corporation Act[8] if they are formed under the Act or voluntarily elect to be covered by the Act.[9] *Cy pres* is applied by Iowa courts when a charitable trust fails without any alternative disposition of the property and the general trust purposes may be accomplished by administering the property in a different but closely related way.[10]

A merger, consolidation, or voluntary dissolution is subject to approval by the Secretary of State.[11] Articles must also be filed with the recorder in the county where the college was located and in merger or consolidation proceedings where it will be located.[12] Courts of equity have jurisdiction to liquidate the assets of a college in an action brought by:

1. A member or director because of dead-locked management or directors, illegal or fraudulent acts by management or directors, or misapplication or waste of college assets;[13]

2. A creditor, when the claim has been reduced to an unsatisfied judgment or when the college has admitted in writing that the claim is due and owing and it is established that the college is insolvent;[14]

3. The dissolving college;[15] or

4. The Attorney General because of fraud, failure to file its annual report, abuse of authority, or failure to name or maintain a registered agent, when it is established that liquidation should precede a decree of involuntary dissolution.[16]

These provisions clearly follow those of the Model Nonprofit Corporation Act.

The Iowa Nonprofit Corporation Act provides that a dissolving college's assets are to be distributed according to a procedure closely following that of the Model Nonprofit Corporation Act.[17]

B. State Support

The Iowa Constitution's "separation of Church and State" clause[18] has not come into conflict with Iowa's two programs for providing aid to Iowa students in private schools: the Iowa Scholarship Program (which aids both public and private students, based on both ability and need)[19] and the Tuition Grant Program.[20]

The Tuition Grant Program, intended to help equalize the disparity in educational expenses of public and private school students, pays up to $1000 per student. The statute's definition of "accredited private institution" would not bar RACs from participation.[21] Such a grant may be given any qualified full-time student on the basis of need.[22] It is administered by the former Higher Education Facilities Commission,[23] which was established in 1964 and whose name was changed in 1981 to "College Aid Commission."[24] Its duties are to prepare and administer a state plan for higher education facilities within the state to be submitted to the federal Department of Health, Education, and Welfare (now the Department of Health and Human Services).[25] It also administers scholarship and student loan funds within the state.[26]

C. Personnel

The Iowa Civil Rights Act prohibits any discrimination against any applicant for employment or against any employee because of "age, race, creed, color, sex, national origin, religion, or disability."[27] There is a BFOQ type exception: an employer may "discriminate" if such "discrimination" is based upon the "nature of the occupation."[28] This exception would probably not greatly protect RACs in personnel decisions involving faculty outside the areas of theology and philosophy. It is not likely that an RAC would be successful in arguing a right to exercise religious preference in the employment of the faculty generally despite the RAC's interest in establishing on campus a pervasive presence of faculty of a certain religious persuasion.

The statute, however, contains another broader exception: a bona fide religious institution or educational facility may utilize qualifications based on religion when such qualifications are based on a bona fide religious purpose.[29] Furthermore, there is a presumption regarding hiring by RACs of teachers and certain administrators:

A religious qualification for instructional personnel or an administrative officer serving in a supervisory capacity of a bona fide religious educational faculty or religious institution, shall be presumed to be a bona fide occupational qualification.[30]

RACs are thus granted a substantial amount of protection in faculty and administrative hiring. Iowa's legislation is clearly one of the nation's broadest state provisions in this regard.

The term "disability" in the Iowa Civil Rights Law is defined as a "physical or mental condition of a person which constitutes a substantial handicap."[31] Under these vague terms, alcoholism and drug addiction could be considered handicaps. Nevertheless, Iowa's treatment of unrehabilitated alcoholics or drug addicts in another area related to employment can be looked to for guidance. Iowa law permits discharge of public employees for "unrehabilitated alcoholism or narcotics addiction."[32] At least these persons, therefore, are probably not under the protection of the Civil Rights Law. Whether an RAC could refuse to hire an alcoholic or drug addict who was "rehabilitated" is not certain.

The Iowa State Civil Rights Commission is responsible for conducting investigations and hearings pertaining to alleged violations of the employment provisions of the Civil Rights Act.[33] Complaints are made to the Commission, and if informal attempts to correct the situation fail, a hearing is held and an order is issued.[34] The investigating official may not preside at the hearing nor participate in deliberations regarding the issuance of an order.[35] District court review is also provided for.[36] If the Commission has taken no action on a complaint within 120 days after filing, the complainant may obtain a release from the Commission and directly commence proceedings in the district court.[27]

Iowa has no legislation mandating a minimum wage. (Federal law on the point,[38] obviously, must nonetheless be complied with).

For purposes of Iowa's Workmen's Compensation law, the term "employer" includes any person, firm, association, or corporation.[39] Since the only exemptions provided are for independent contractors and casual employees,[40] employment by RACs clearly comes within the Iowa Workmen's Compensation law.

For purposes of Iowa's Employment Security law, the term "employment" is defined as service "performed for wages or under any contract of hire, written or oral, expressed or implied."[41] "Employment" does not, however, apply to service performed

in the employ of a church or convention or association of churches, or an organization which is operated primarily for religious purposes and which is operated, supervised, controlled or principally supported by a church or convention or association of churches.[42]

Although this provision might cover some RACs, including many seminaries and Bible colleges, it would probably not cover the majority of RACs whose primary source would perhaps be viewed as educational, not religious. Furthermore, many RACs are not "operated, supervised, controlled or financially supported by a church or convention or association of churches."

"Employment" also does not apply to service by a duly ordained or commissioned minister "in the exercise of his ministry," or by members of a religious order "in the exercise of duties required by such order."[43] This provision would probably exempt from the employment security law many ministers, priests, rabbis, nuns, and brothers teaching at an RAC.

D. Students

Although there is an Iowa provision barring sex discrimination in educational programs and activities,[44] it applies only to public elementary and secondary schools and not to RACs.[45]

E. Facilities

The Civil Rights Act of Iowa forbids denial of public "accommodations, [or] advantages, facilities, services, or privileges [thereof]" on the grounds of "race, creed, color, sex, national origin, religion, or disability."[46] This section does not apply to any bona fide religious institution which imposes religious qualifications related to a bona fide religious purpose.[47] Any RAC which can meet the definition of "religious institution" (and it is not clear that all RACs can) would be able to exercise religious preference with regard to their activities and facilities so long as such preference was related to a good faith religious purpose. The Iowa public accommodations law is enforced by the Iowa State Civil Rights Commission,[48] whose procedures have been discussed earlier.[49]

It is a discriminatory practice under Iowa law to refuse to sell or rent housing or to discriminate regarding housing terms and conditions on

the basis of "race, color, creed, sex, religion, national origin or disability."[50] There are two exemptions, however, which cover two distinct needs of RACs in this area. One provides that any bona fide religious institution may impose religiously based qualifications related to a bona fide religious purpose regarding housing.[51] This exemption would enable an RAC which can meet the definition of "religious institution" (and, again,[52] it is not clear that all RACs can) to enforce religious qualifications with regard to dormitories and other housing so long as these qualifications could be related to a good faith religious purpose. The second exemption allows nonprofit corporations to place sex restrictions on housing they lease or rent.[53] This provision would enable RACs to have single-sex dormitories, floors, wings, or other areas of housing.

The housing discrimination provisions are enforced by the Iowa State Civil Rights Commission,[54] whose procedures have been discussed earlier.[55]

Iowa's Occupational Safety and Health law provides for the promulgation of health and safety standards by the State Labor Commissioner.[56] The standards are mandatory for every employer,[57] and civil penalties are provided for violators.[58] The Commissioner is only authorized to adopt and promulgate standards which have already been adopted and promulgated by the Secretary of Labor under the provisions of the federal Occupational Safety and Health Act.[59]

Employers must furnish a place of employment which is "free from recognized hazards that are causing or are likely to cause death or serious physical harm" to employees.[60] "Employer" is defined as "a person engaged in a business who has one or more employees."[61] Although RACs could be exempt from compliance if a "business" is construed to mean only a profit-making venture, the statutory definition of "person" apparently includes RACs.[62]

F. State Taxation

Under Iowa law, organizations, associations, and corporations organized for religious or educational purposes (among others) are exempt from income taxation so long as no part of the net earnings inures to the benefit of any individual.[63]

Sales of goods, wares, merchandise, or services to private, nonprofit educational institutions for use in connection with an educational purpose are exempt from the Iowa sales tax.[64]

Iowa law provides for property taxation by the taxing district at usual rates on real estate owned by any educational institution as part of its endowment fund.[65] Included as well is real estate, acquired after January 1, 1965, "upon which any income is derived or used, directly or indirectly, for full or partial payment for services rendered."[66]

When property passes to a religious, charitable, or educational institution within the state of Iowa, or outside the state if the other state would not tax property passing to similar Iowa organizations, the transfer is exempt from the inheritance tax.[67] Transfers to RACs therefore are not taxed.

Iowa also imposes an estate tax designed merely to channel to Iowa, by virtue of the credit allowed against the federal estate tax for state death taxes, moneys that would otherwise go to the federal government in estate taxes.[68] This tax, therefore, has no ultimate effect on the amount of death taxes paid.

Iowa has no gift tax.

In computing Iowa taxable income, an individual may deduct "the total of contributions, . . . deductible for federal income tax purposes."[69] Since contributions to RACs are deductible for federal income tax purposes,[70] they are also deductible on an individual's state return.

There is a very narrow property tax exemption for up to three hundred twenty acres of land held by religious institutions or societies "solely for their appropriate objects."[71] The only RAC land eligible for the exemption would be that which could fairly be said to be held by a religious institution or society. It is not clear that Iowa would consider all RACs to be religious (as opposed to educational) institutions, especially since the sales tax exemption[72] specifically mentions "educational" institutions and since there is a specific section in the property tax entitled "Property of educational institutions."[73] Land at some RACs, of course, could be said to be held by a religious society.

In any event, the exemption would cover only three hundred twenty acres. Furthermore, land held as an investment either for appreciation in value or for rental to others may not be held "solely for [the entity's] appropriate objects."

Religious institutions and societies also have a property tax exemption for moneys and credits belonging exclusively to them and devoted solely to their sustenance, so long as the amount and income are within their charter limit.[74] Also exempted are "books, papers, pictures, works of art, apparatus, and other personal property" belonging (1) to such institutions[75] and used for their appropriate objects,[76] or (2) to students in such institutions if the property is used for their education.[77] Presumably, this latter exemption would apply to the property of a person at a seminary even though used in connection with courses taken at a state university.

G. Fund Raising

Iowa law concerning charitable solicitation is at best curious. It provides that

No organization, institution, or charitable association, either directly or through agents or representatives, shall solicit public donations in this state, unless it be a corporation duly incorporated under the laws of this state or authorized to do business in this state; has first obtained a permit therefor from the secretary of state; and has filed with the secretary of state a surety company bond in the sum of one thousand dollars, running to the state and conditioned that the applicant will devote all donations directly to the purpose stated and for which the donations were given, and will otherwise comply with the laws of this state and the requirements of the secretary of state in regard thereto. The secretary of state shall have full discretion as to whom he will issue permits, and shall satisfy himself before issuing any such permit that the applicant is reputable and that the purposes for which donations from the public are to be solicited are legitimate and worthy.[78]

This provision would seem to require that any entity, charitable or otherwise, meet three conditions in order to solicit public donation: (1) that it be a corporation duly incorporated under Iowa law or authorized to do business there; (2) that it obtain the appropriate permit from the Secretary of State (who is given full discretion as to whether such a permit should issue) and who must be satisfied that the applicant is reputable and its purposes worthy; and (3) that it file with the Secretary of State a surety company bond of the indicated type.

Despite this plain indication of the statute, the Attorney General's office in 1940 stated that the word "unless" in this section should be read to mean "except."[79] According to the Attorney General, the section was not intended to require corporations duly incorporated in Iowa or authorized to do business there to obtain the permit referred to.[80]

Its purpose was to require a permit of foreign organizations, institutions, or charitable associations and of other bodies whether domestic or foreign (presumably not incorporated under Iowa law or authorized to do business there) which are not within the exemption provided for in another section.[81] That section exempts any person who, acting as an agent of a local organization, church, school (which would include an RAC), or recognized society or branch of any church or school, publicly solicits donations from within the county in which he resides or in which the entity he represents is located (or within an adjacent county if his residence or the entity's location is within six miles of the adjoining county).[82] If such an entity has a permit under the Iowa provisions (which would presumably be required for public solicitation beyond the county limits indicated unless the entity is incorporated under Iowa law or authorized to do business there) it must file with the Secretary of State a detailed report during December of each year.[83]

Since all RACs would presumably be incorporated under Iowa law or licensed to do business there, they are exempt from the permit requirement even for state-wide public solicitations.

If for some reason an RAC does not have an exemption, several problems exist. The requirement that "all donations" must be devoted "directly" to the purpose stated and for which the donations are given[84] appears to mean that one hundred percent of each contribution must go to that purpose, and that not even the slightest amount may go to administrative costs of the fund raising drive.

There could also be problems with donations exceeding the goal of a particular fund raising drive; if the college utilized it for another related purpose (e.g. a new dorm different from the one the drive was for), would it forfeit the bond or be required to return the donation?

A third concern may be even more important for an RAC: the "full discretion" of the Secretary of State in issuing permits. The statute requires an applicant who is reputable and purposes that are "legitimate and worthy."[85] If an RAC espouses ideas which are controversial or unpopular (e.g. a college espousing religious pacifism during wartime) or if a college espouses ideas or beliefs which the Secretary of State otherwise does not like, that college may be denied its permit to solicit contributions. Especially since an organization must renew its permit every year, there is a genuine reason for concern on the part of any organization with regard to its vulnerability. Under these loose criteria, a definite chilling of beliefs and statements is possible.

Since under the current interpretation of the law most if not all RACs will not need a permit, these problems remain speculative.

24. Kansas

A. Corporate Status

RACs are organized in Kansas under Article 60 ("Formation of Corporations") of Chapter 17. There is no separate chapter for nonprofit corporations. Distinctions between profit and nonprofit corporations are made as exceptions to the general provisions for all corporations.[1] Otherwise, nonprofit corporations follow the law applicable to corporations generally.

Although there is a special article applicable to religious, charitable, and other organizations,[2] "colleges, universities, academies [and] seminaries" are specifically excepted from its coverage.[3]

Kansas does allow a nonprofit corporation to issue stock.[4] Securities issued by nonprofit religious or educational associations are exempted from certain securities registration requirements[5] as long as, prior to issuance of such securities, an application for exemption is filed with the State Commissioner of Securities.[6]

Kansas institutions of postsecondary education, in order to award academic or honorary degrees, must be approved for such purposes by the state board of regents.[7] Out-of-state institutions, in order to offer in Kansas courses or programs leading to an academic degree, must register such courses or programs with the State Board of Regents.[8] The State Board of Regents is authorized to establish rules and regulations for the administration of these provisions.[9]

Any educational corporation issuing academic or honorary degrees and incorporating after July 1, 1972, must state in its articles of incorporation that it is a "bona fide institution of higher learning" and "has or will have the resources, including personnel, requisite for the conduct" of such an institution.[10] An institution incorporated prior to that date must file a certificate of amendment to the same effect.[11] In both cases, the State Board of Education must give its approval.[12] The Board thus has a virtual veto power in the creation or continuance of institutions of higher education, including RACs.

The Kansas Proprietary School Act[13] seeks to establish in a "unified and organized form" regulation of non-tax-supported educational institutions.[14] Exempted from its provisions, however, are, *inter alia*, nonprofit schools owned, controlled, operated and conducted by bona fide religious or denominational institutions exempt from Kansas property taxation (although such schools may seek a certificate of approval and thereby become subject to the Act's requirements);[15] private colleges and universities which award a baccalaureate or higher degree and maintain credit-granting programs[16] and whose credits are transferable to an appropriately accredited junior college, college, or university;[17] and any school otherwise regulated and approved under any other Kansas law.[18] Virtually all RACs, therefore, will be exempt from the provisions of the Kansas Proprietary School Act.

The merger, consolidation, and dissolution of nonprofit colleges in Kansas are governed by the state's General Corporation Code.[19] *Cy pres* doctrine applies to charitable trusts when the trust fails without any alternative disposition of the property having been made, and the general trust purposes can be accomplished by permitting administration in a different but closely related manner.[20]

A merger, consolidation, or dissolution is subject to approval by the Secretary of State.[21] Upon application of any creditor, stockholder, or other interested person, the district courts may appoint a trustee or receiver for the college's assets.[22] The district courts have broad jurisidiction over all questions arising in these proceedings, and may make orders and issue injunctions required by justice and equity.[23]

The General Corporation Code of Kansas provides only that upon dissolution a corporation's liabilities shall be discharged and any remaining assets shall be distributed to the corporation's stockholders.[24] If only because of the lack of attention paid to the complexity of this issue by the legislature, Kansas courts would undoubtedly rely on the *cy pres* doctrine in overseeing the dissolution of a college.

B. State Support

The Kansas Constitution guarantees religious liberty and provides further that no preference is to be "given by law to any religious establishment or mode of worship."[25] Although no religious sect may control public educational funds,[26] the legislature is authorized to provide for the "finance of institutions of higher education,"[27] which would seem to provide the possibility of financial aid to private institutions of higher education, including RACs. No direct aid for private higher education is in fact provided by Kansas legislation.

In Article 61 of Chapter 72, Kansas provides for tuition grants for needy students of private institutions of higher education. The institution involved must have its main campus in Kansas, must maintain an "open enrollment" and must be appropriately accredited.[28] To meet the "open enrollment" standard, the institution must have a policy of enrollment opportunity for any student meeting its academic and other reasonable enrollment requirements "without regard for race, sex, religion, creed or national origin."[29] Thus, although most RACs will be eligible to participate in the program, admissions selectivity based on religion or sex will be prohibited for those which do.

A similar program, entitled "State Scholarship Program for Students at Institutions of Post-Secondary Education," is established in Article 68 of Chapter 72. It provides for scholarships to qualified "state scholars" enrolled at "eligible institutions."[30] A qualified state scholar is a full-time in-state student who has exhibited scholastic ability[31] and financial need.[32] An eligible institution must have its main campus in Kansas and maintain an "open enrollment,"[33] i.e., it must be open to students who meet its academic and other reasonable requirements "without regard for race, sex, religion, creed or national origin."[34] Again, therefore, virtually all RACs will be eligible, but participation in the program may preclude admissions selectivity based on religion or sex.

The Kansas State Board of Regents administers a student loan guarantee program statutorily established.[35] An RAC may participate in this program if it is an:

eligible institution under the provisions of the higher education act of 1965 and acts amendatory thereof and supplemental thereto (20 U.S.C.A. 1001 *et seq.*) and the national vocational student loan insurance act of 1965 and acts amendatory thereof and supplemental thereto (20 U.S.C.A. 981 *et seq.*)[36]

Most RACs, therefore, would be eligible.

There is also provision for readers for resident blind students.[37]

Kansas law provides for enrollment without tuition or other charges, at institutions of higher education "supported by any state moneys," for dependents of prisoners of war or persons missing in action.[38] The institution is reimbursed the amount of such tuition and fees by the Kansas Veterans Commission.[39] A similar provision applies to dependents of persons killed as a result of a service-connected disability arising out of the Vietnam conflict.[40]

C. Personnel

It is an unlawful employment practice for a Kansas employer to "refuse to hire . . . to discharge . . . or to otherwise discriminate" against any person because of "race, religion, color, sex, physical handicap, national origin or ancestry."[41] Although "employer" for the purposes of the Kansas acts against discrimination includes, *inter alia*, persons with four or more employees,"[42] it specifically excludes nonprofit corporations.[43] Virtually all RACs, therefore, are exempt from the employment provisions of the Act.

For those few subject to the Act's employment constraints, Kansas has no specific provision allowing otherwise prohibited employment discrimination when based on a bona fide occupational qualification (BFOQ). Curiously, however, it does have a provision permitting job advertisements, applications and the like, expressing specifications as to race, religion, color, sex, physical handicap, national origin, or ancestry when based on a BFOQ.[44] This must reflect a legislative intent to allow employment selectivity itself on these bases. It would be ironic to allow a firm to advertise such restrictions but bar it from implementing the restrictions in the actual hiring.

For the few RACs covered by these fair employment provisions, therefore, it seems likely that courts will read a BFOQ into them, allowing such RACs to exercise religious selectivity in such positions as theology instructor, counselor, and the like. For certain positions, for example a Judaism instuctor at a Christian school, the selectivity may be in favor of a religion different from the institutional affiliation. It is unlikely that the BFOQ would justify religious selectivity in all faculty (or staff) positions despite the institution's interest in establishing on campus a pervasive religious presence.

Kansas' employment discrimination law is enforced by its Commission on Civil Rights.[45]

As indicated, few RACs are covered by the Kansas employment discrimination law, including its ban on discrimination based on handicap. However, a separate chapter requires the employment of the "blind, visually handicapped and persons who are otherwise physically disabled" if that employment is supported at least in part by public funds.[46] RACs are subject to this provision to the extent to which they have publicly supported employment. With regard to provisions dealing with handicaps and disabilities, however, the manner in which Kansas deals with alcoholism[47] and drug addiction[48] indicates it views these conditions as illnesses rather than handicaps or physical disabilities. In any event, drug or alcohol *use* (as opposed to addiction) may well be subject to a BFOQ under the fair employment provisions.[49]

Kansas' minimum wage and maximum hours law[50] applies to any "employer," which includes generally any "individual . . . association [or] corporation."[51] It also prohibits sex discrimination in compensating "employees."[52] The law sets for certain "employees" both a minimum wage[53] and a maximum number of hours[54] which may be worked without the payment of overtime compensation. "Employee," for the purpose of this legislation, excludes, *inter alia*, a person in a good faith executive, administrative or professional position;[55] one working gratuitously for a nonprofit organization;[56] and persons eighteen years of age or less, or sixty years of age or older, employed for any purpose on an "occasional or part-time basis."[57]

Two points should be made with regard to this legislation. First, it generally does not apply to situations already covered by the federal Fair Labor Standards Act of 1938[58] and its amendatory or supplemental acts.[59] Second, the minimum wage provided for is $1.60 per hour, so low as to be of little likely impact.

The Kansas Workmen's Compensation Act[60] applies to any corporation with one or more employees.[61] Any person employed by an educational, religious, or charitable organization is specifically included in the Act's coverage.[62] However, an RAC with a payroll of less than $10,000 annually is exempt from the act's provisions.[63] RACs may elect to include their exempted employees, including volunteers,[64] within the state's compensation provisions by filing notice with the Director of Worker's Compensation.[65] Injured employees not covered by the state's compensation law, however, may sue an RAC for damages.[66] RACs must carry compensation insurance or furnish the Director of Worker's Compensation with proof of financial ability to compensate injured employees directly.[67]

The Kansas employment security law applies to, *inter alia*, employing units which either (1) paid wages of $1,500 or more in the preceding or current calendar year or (2) in the same time period, had in employment at least one individual (not necessarily the same one) for some portion of a day in each of twenty separate weeks.[68]

Generally included in the Kansas employment security law is service for a religious, charitable, educational, or other organization excluded from "employment," as that term is defined in the federal Unemployment Tax Act, solely by reason of Section 3306(c)(8) of that Act.[69] Service performed in the employ of a religious or educational organization described in Section 501(c)(3) of the Internal Revenue Code of 1954,[70] and thereby exempt from federal taxation, is excluded from "employment" as defined in Section 3306(c)(8) of the federal Unemployment Tax Act.[71] Thus an RAC is subject to unemployment compensation legislation if it qualifies for tax-exempt status under Section 501(c)(3) and meets either the payroll minimum or the employee durational minimum referred to earlier.[72] Virtually all RACs will therefore be covered by the Kansas law, which does, nonetheless, provide the following exemptions: (1) service as to which unemployment compensation is payable under a system established by congressional legislation;[73] (2) service for certain federal tax-exempt organizations if the remuneration is less than $50.00;[74] (3) service for a church or for an organization operated primarily for religious purposes and "operated, supervised, controlled, or principally supported by a church or group of churches"[75] (among RACs this narrow exception would perhaps be available only to seminaries, Bible colleges or the like); (4) service by "a duly ordained, commissioned or licensed minister of a church" exercising his ministry or by a member of a religious order as duty required by the order;[76] (5) service performed for a school, college or university by one of its regular students;[77] and (6) service performed by a student under the age of twenty-two enrolled at a regular nonprofit or public institution of higher education in a fulltime program, taken for credit, which combines academic instruction with work experience.[78] The service must be an integral part of the program, so certified to the employer, and not performed in a "program established by or on behalf of an employer or group of employers."[79] Service

within these six categories is not subject to the Kansas employment security law.

D. Students

There is no legislation in Kansas dealing with fair educational opportunity, although its fair housing law could indirectly have an impact on admissions.[80]

E. Facilities

The Kansas Act Against Discrimination labels any discrimination on the basis of race, religion, color, sex, physical handicap, national origin, or ancestry in the provision of goods, services, or facilities of any place of public accommodation an unlawful discriminatory practice.[81] It is specified, however, that "public accommodations" does not include a nonprofit corporation. This clearly demonstrates a legislative intent that the public accommodations law not apply to such corporations which, of course, include virtually all RACs.

The Kansas Act Against Discrimination also makes it unlawful for any person to refuse to sell or rent real estate,[82] or to discriminate in the terms or conditions of such sale or rental,[83] or to indicate a preference in advertisements or applications concerning such sale or rental,[84] on the basis of race, religion, color, sex, national origin, or ancestry. All of the rental housing controlled by an RAC, therefore, would be generally subject to this law. One qualification must be noted, however:

Nothing in this act shall prohibit a religious organization, association or society, or any nonprofit institution or organization operated, supervised or controlled by or in conjunction with a religious organization, association or society, from limiting the sale, rental or occupancy of real property which it owns or operates for other than a commercial purpose to persons of the same religion, or from giving preference to such person, unless membership in such religion is restricted on account of race, color, national origin or ancestry.[85]

Several aspects of this statute must be highlighted. First, one may be eligible for this exception if (1) a religious organization, association, or society (this may well include such RACs as seminaries and Bible colleges) or (2) a nonprofit organization run by *or in conjunction with* such an organization, association, or society. Many more RACs would presumably be included through this alternative, since the phrase "or in conjunction with" renders the required religious affiliation quite flexible.

Second, the real property must be owned or operated for other than a commercial purpose. An otherwise qualifying RAC could use the exception for its graduate student housing but not for an apartment complex it owns and rents to the general public merely for income.

Third, the selectivity authorized must be in favor of the institution's religious affiliation. A Baptist college could not use the exception in favor of a non-Christian (or perhaps even a non-Baptist), despite the possible institutes or other programs which it might have on campus drawing staff or students of other religions.

Fourth, the exemption will not apply if the religion itself restricts membership on account of race, color, national origin, or ancestry. Presumably, this provision was intended to preclude the exercise of racial and ethnic segregation under the guise of religion.

Fifth, a more subtle but perhaps more important point lurks in the background. Normally, of course, colleges restrict their housing to their students and staff. Thus, if the statute were intended to cover housing other than that for students and staff, it would have little campus impact. Since the Kansas housing law provides an exception which the legislature must have anticipated would include RACs (among others), the law could be argued to control student admissions, at least to the extent that only students (along with staff) are eligible for the institution's housing. Otherwise, the argument would go, housing could be limited in effect on racial grounds (or whatever) so long as the institution restricted its enrollment on that basis. Fortunately, even if such an argument would prevail, the religious selectivity exemption would control for most RACs in both housing and admissions. For virtually all RACs, this is the only desirable and justifiable exception to the law.

Both the public accommodations and housing provisions of Kansas' Act Against Discrimina-

tion are enforced by its Commission on Civil Rights.[86]

Kansas has no Occupational Safety and Health Act. Its Occupational Safety and Health Advisory Board[87] was abolished effective July 1, 1976.[88]

F. State Taxation

Those organizations exempt from federal income tax are also exempt from state income taxation to the same extent. Thus, virtually all RACs will be exempt from state income taxation.[89]

Under the Kansas Inheritance Tax Act,[90] property received by entities through bequests, legacies, devises, or transfers for "public, religious, charitable . . . educational or such other uses for which deductions from federal gross estate are allowed pursuant to 26 U.S.C. 2055 as in effect on December 31, 1977" is exempt from taxation.[91]

Kansas also imposes an estate tax designed merely to channel to Kansas, by virtue of the credit allowed against the federal estate tax for state death taxes, moneys that would otherwise go to the federal government in estate taxes.[92] This tax, therefore, has no ultimate effect on the *amount* of death taxes paid.

Kansas has no gift tax.

If an individual itemizes deductions for federal income tax purposes, he may elect to do so for state income tax purposes, whereupon, subject to a few qualifications not here relevant, the Kansas itemized deduction will be the total amount of the taxpayer's federal deductions from adjusted gross income.[93] The net result, for such taxpayers, is to provide a state income tax deduction for contributions to nonprofit RACs, since such contributions are deductible for federal income tax purposes.[94]

The Kansas Constitution provides that all property used exclusively for educational or religious purposes is exempt from property taxation.[95] The Kansas legislature has implemented this provision by exempting from property or *ad valorem* taxes all real property and tangible personal property "actually and regularly used exclusively for . . . educational [or] religious purposes."[96] This exemption does not apply to property held or used as an investment even though the income or profit is used solely for such purposes.[97] All moneys and credits belonging exclusively "to universities, colleges, academies or other public schools of any kind" or to religious associations, appropriated solely to sustain them, are also exempt as long as within any limits on amount set in their charters.[98] (Presumably, the phrase "or other public schools" is not intended to suggest that the universities, colleges, and academies must be "public" in the sense of "governmentally owned.")

All revenue bonds, and interest paid to holders thereof, issued by certain Kansas nonprofit corporations for the purpose of providing a student loan program in Kansas are exempt from all taxation by the state or any of its subdivisions.[99]

The Kansas Retailers' Sales Tax Act[100] exempts from the tax imposed all sales of tangible personal property or services, including the renting and leasing of such property, purchased directly by a nonprofit educational institution, public or private, and used primarily for its nonsectarian activities or to erect, repair, or enlarge buildings for such activities.[101] This exemption does not apply with regard to buildings for human habitation.[102] A parallel exemption[103] is provided under the Kansas Compensating Tax Act,[104] an act designed to tax sales of goods eluding the sales tax because, for example, the goods were purchased out-of-state.[105]

G. Fund Raising

Charitable organizations, unless exempted,

must, in order to engage in charitable solicitations, file a registration statement with the Secretary of State.[106] An educational institution which is accredited by a regional or national accrediting association *or* which solicits only from its "student body, alumni, faculty and trustees, and their families" is exempt.[107] Most RACs, therefore, will not have to register.

Lotteries and the sale of lottery tickets are absolutely prohibited by the Kansas Constitution,[108] but the legislature is authorized to regulate, license, and tax the operation of "bingo" games by good faith nonprofit religious, charitable, fraternal, educational, and veterans organizations.[109] The legislature has provided for the issuance of licenses for the operation of "games of bingo" to, *inter alia,* bona fide nonprofit religious or educational organizations which have been in existence for at least eighteen months.[110]

H. Miscellaneous

Upon application of any college or university having an education department, incorporated under the general laws of Kansas, and requiring a four year high school course (or its equivalent) for admission, the State Board of Education may accredit it for automatic teacher certification of its graduates.[111]

No license may be issued for the retail sale of alcoholic beverages on premises within two hundred feet of any college or church.[112]

25. Kentucky

A. Corporate Status

Religiously affiliated colleges (RACs) are incorporated in Kentucky under the provisions dealing with nonstock and nonprofit corporations.[1] A nonprofit corporation is defined as a corporation in which none of the income or profit is distributable to its members, directors, or officers.[2] Kentucky law provides that a nonprofit corporation may be organized for any lawful purpose or purposes, including, without being limited to, educational or religious purposes.[3]

The process of incorporation is begun by filing the articles of incorporation with the Secretary of State.[4] The statute requires that the articles of incorporation include:

a) the name of the corporation. b) the period of duration, which may be perpetual. c) the purpose or purposes for which the corporation is organized. d) lawful provisions concerning the regulation of the corporation's internal affairs. e) the address of its registered office in the state. f) the names and addresses of those persons constituting the initial board of directors. g) the name and address of each incorporator.[5]

After all taxes, fees, and charges have been paid, the Secretary of State issues a certificate of incorporation.[6] One original copy of the articles of incorporation must also be filed with the clerk of the county in which the registered office of the corporation is located.[7]

Kentucky's nonprofit corporation law forbids RACs from having or issuing shares of stock.[8] In addition, no dividend may be paid and no part of the income or profit from RACs may be distributed to its members, directors, or officers. This provision does not, however, inhibit an RAC in Kentucky from compensating its members, directors, or officers for services rendered, or from conferring benefits upon its members in conformity with its purposes.[9]

Kentucky law requires that a nonprofit corporation be managed by a board of directors.[10] In addition, each nonprofit corporation must keep correct and complete books and records of accounts and must keep minutes of the proceedings of its members, board of directors and committees having any of the authority of the board of directors.[11] The power to alter, amend or repeal the bylaws or adopt new bylaws is vested in the board of directors unless otherwise lawfully provided in the articles of incorporation or the bylaws.[12]

Voluntary dissolution of a nonprofit educational institution in Kentucky is set in motion by a vote of at least two-thirds of the members of the governing board.[13] The governing board is likewise responsible for winding up the business of the institution and for distributing its remaining assets.[14] When proper articles of dissolution have been prepared,[15] they must be submitted in triplicate to the Secretary of State, who issues a certificate of dissolution. One of the triplicate originals of the articles of dissolution is filed with the clerk of the county court

160

in the county in which the college or university is situated.

An educational institution may be dissolved involuntarily by a decree of the circuit court when the Attorney General establishes in an appropriate action that the institution (1) is guilty of abuse or misuse of its corporate powers or has become "detrimental to the interest and welfare of the commonwealth of Kentucky or its citizens;"[16] or (2) has procured its articles of incorporation through fraud; or (3) has failed to file the annual report required under Kentucky law, or to appoint and maintain a registered agent in the state and to notify the Secretary of State of any change of its registered agent.[17]

The Kentucky statute governing distribution of assets of a dissolving college is patterned on the Model Nonprofit Corporation Act.[18] In addition, the Kentucky Supreme Court has ruled that under some circumstances the doctrine of *cy pres* is to be applied in Kentucky courts.[19]

B. State Support

Section 189 of the Kentucky Constitution provides that:

[no] portion of any fund or tax now existing, or that may hereafter be raised or levied for educational purposes, shall be appropriated to, or used by, or in aid of, any church, sectarian or denominational school.[20]

In 1917 the Kentucky Court of Appeals in *Williams v. Bd. of Trustees* stated in dictum that this provision prohibited the payment of tuition fees to a parochial school by a county school board with public school funds.[21] Professor Howard artfully distinguishes between direct payments to nonpublic schools taken from the school funds and transfer payments taken from the state's general fund, and he notes that although no case has directly ruled on the permissibility of using the general fund for this kind of aid, "the provision [section 189] on its face applies to 'any fund' raised or levied for educational purposes."[22]

Although the state constitution would appear to prohibit direct transfers from the common school fund to RACs, Kentucky has provided financial assistance for students attending RACs in Kentucky. This student aid program, consisting of grants and loans, was enacted in the 1972 Assistance to Private College Student Act.[23] This legislation was sustained by a state circuit court under both the state and federal constitutions.[24] Under this program, similar to the Tennessee legislation upheld by the United States Supreme Court in a summary affirmance,[25] qualified Kentucky residents who bear the major cost of attending accredited private colleges and universities within the state may receive a grant for tuition or educational fees as supplemental aid where need exists.[26] The amount of the tuition grant paid to a student each semester is determined by the Kentucky Higher Education Assistance Authority.[27] A student enrolled in a course of study leading to a degree in theology, divinity, or religious education is ineligible.[28] The maximum amount of aid cannot exceed fifty percent of the average state appropriation per full-time equivalent student enrolled in all public institutions of higher education.[29]

C. Personnel

Hiring, Promoting, and Firing

Kentucky law makes it an unlawful practice for an employer to refuse to hire, or to discharge any individual, or to discriminate against an individual "with respect to his compensation, terms, conditions, or privileges of employment because of such individual's race, color, religion, national origin, sex, or age between forty (40) and sixty-five (65)."[30] Discrimination is defined in the statute as "any direct or indirect act or practice of exclusion, distinction, restriction, segregation, limitation, refusal, denial or any other act or practice of differentiation or preference in the treatment of a person or persons because of race, color, religion, national origin, sex, or age."[31] RACs are clearly embraced with the broad statutory definition of an "employer."[32]

Since a stated purpose of this state civil rights act is "to safeguard *all individuals* within the state from discrimination because of race, color, religion, national origin, sex and age,"[33] RACs are bound to observe all the provisions of this legislation for which there is no explicit exemption.

Among the purposes articulated for this statute is the provision of a state remedy for enforcing within Kentucky the policies embodied in the federal civil rights legislation.[34] Consistent with this goal, the state law tracks the exemption found in section 702 of the Civil Rights Act of 1964, as well as the two exceptions found in sections 703(e)(1) and 703(e)(2) of that act. Hence RACs in Kentucky have available to them three provisions on which to ground a policy of religious preference in their employment practices. First, Kentucky law allows any employer to differentiate among employees or prospective employees on the basis of religion or national origin where either of those characteristics is a "bona fide occupational qualification reasonably necessary to the normal operation of that particular business or enterprise."[35] Second, it allows a religious corporation to "employ an individual on the basis of his religion to perform work connected with the carrying on . . . of its *religious* activities."[36] This provision follows the 1964 version of section 702 of the federal Civil Rights Act, rather than the 1972 amendment of that section which allows a broader basis for religious preference in employment practices by religious corporations.[37] Third, Kentucky provides the same exception for RACs found in section 703(e)(2) of Title VII, which allows an RAC to engage in religious preference if it regards itself as an "educational institution . . . directed toward the propagation of a particular religion."[38] The state statute, however, limits such religious preference to instances where "the choice of employees [on the basis of religion] is calculated by [an RAC] to promote the religious principles for which it is established or maintained."[39]

Wages and Hours

Every employer in the state of Kentucky, including RACs, must pay to each of his employees a minimum wage of $2.15 an hour effective July 1, 1979.[40] This statute comprehensively defines an employer as any person, i.e., individual, corporation, partnership, agency or firm, who employs an employee.[41] Under the minimum wage law, RACs would have to pay the state minimum wage to all qualified employees.[42]

Kentucky law also mandates that any employer who permits any employee to work seven days in any one workweek must pay that employee at a rate of time and a half for the time worked on the seventh day.[43] In addition, all Kentucky employers, including RACs, must pay employees at a rate at least one and one-half times their hourly wage rate for employment in excess of forty hours in one week.[44] Kentucky does not provide for a maximum hourly work load.

Consistent with the general purpose of providing a state remedy for the policies articulated in federal civil rights legislation, RACs are required to pay the minimum wage and conform to the overtime provisions with respect to most of their employees. Monetary penalties and fines of varying amounts are levied against violators of the wage and hour statutes.[45]

Kentucky likewise has a statute which, paralleling the federal Equal Pay Act of 1963, prohibits discrimination in salary on the basis of sex.[46] RACs may not pay any employee in any occupation at a rate lower than that paid any employee of the opposite sex for comparable work.[47]

Kentucky likewise prohibits employment discrimination on the basis of handicap. Unlike the parallel federal provision, which is limited to programs funded by the federal government,[48] the state law provides a blanket prohibition against such discrimination:

No employer shall fail or refuse to hire, discharge or discriminate against any handicapped individual with respect to wages, rates of pay, hours, or other terms and conditions of employment because of such person's physical handicap unless such handicap restricts that individual's ability to engage in the particular job or occupation for which he or she is eligible or otherwise provided by law.[49]

This provision is binding on all RACs.

Worker's Compensation

The Kentucky Workmen's Compensation Law[50] covers any corporation[51] that has one or more employees subject to this law.[52] Generally RACs are covered[53] unless some of their employees come within the exemptions either for persons performing services for a religious or charitable organization in return for aid or sustenance only[54] or for employment covered by a federal rule of liability for injury or death.[55] Employees who would otherwise be covered may elect to reject coverage[56] by filing a written notice with the employer prior to injury which takes effect when the employer files the employee's notice of rejection with the Workmen's Compensation Board.[57] Exempt employees may sue the RAC in court for damages.[58] However, RACs may elect to include their exempted employees (other than those employees who elect to reject coverage) within the state's compensation provisions by securing the payment of compensation to such exempted employees and by providing proper notice to both the Workmen's Compensation Board and the employees.[59] RACs must either carry insurance,[60] be certified as a self-insurer[61] or join a group self-insurers association.[62]

Unemployment Compensation

Under the Kentucky Unemployment Compensation Act[63] services performed for religious, educational, or charitable organizations constitute "employment,"[64] if two conditions are satisfied. First, such service must be exempt from the definition of employment in the Federal Unemployment Tax Act solely due to section 3306(c)(8).[65] Second, the organization must employ at least four individuals "for some portion of a day in each of twenty different weeks, whether or not such weeks were consecutive, within either the current or preceding calendar year."[66]

The Act provides the following exemptions relevant to RACs: (1) services performed for a church or for an association of churches;[67] (2) services performed for an organization run primarily for religious purposes and controlled by a church or by an association of churches;[68] and (3) services performed by ordained ministers or members of religious orders in the exercise of their religious duties.[69] Because the scope of these exemptions is narrow, most services performed for RACs are covered under the Act. Other relevant exemptions apply to: (1) services performed for a school or college by regularly enrolled students[70] or their spouses;[71] (2) services performed by a student under the age of twenty-two at an accredited nonprofit or public educational institution in a full-time program, combining academic instruction and work experience;[72] (3) services for which unemployment compensation is payable under a system set up by Congress;[73] and (4) domestic service for a college club or a chapter of a fraternity or sorority, if total wages paid in any calendar quarter of the current or preceding year were less than $1,000.00.[74] The statute also excludes from coverage certain organizations that are tax-exempt under federal statutes,[75] if the remuneration paid is less than $50.00.[76]

Nonprofit organizations, and therefore RACs, may elect to make payments in lieu of contributions.[77] To take advantage of this option, an organization must fit the definition in section 501(c)(3) of the Internal Revenue Code and qualify as tax-exempt under section 501(a) of the Code.[78] The election is effective for a two-year period[79] upon filing of written notice with the Kentucky Department for Human Resources.[80] Required payments are equal to the amount of regular benefits plus one-half the amount of extended benefits paid.[81] In addition, any electing organization may be required to file a deposit with the Secretary for Human Resources.[82] Organizations not otherwise subject to the provisions of the Act[83] may elect to participate in the program for a period of two years.[84]

Collective Bargaining

Kentucky has a mini-Wagner Act protecting the rights of workers to organize and bargain collectively with employers over terms and conditions of employment.[85] This statute provides that:

Employees may, free from restraint or coercion by the employers or their agents, associate collectively for self-organization and designate collectively representatives of their own choosing to negotiate the terms and conditions of their employment to effectively promote their own rights and general welfare.

Employees, collectively and individually, may strike, engage in peaceful picketing, and assemble collectively for peaceful purposes.[86]

Like the National Labor Relations Act, the Kentucky statute prohibits both employers or their agents and employees or associations, organizations, or groups of employees from engaging in unfair or illegal acts or practices or resorting to violence, intimidation, threats, or coercion.[87] RACs are not expressly exempted from this legislation, and would be subject to its terms unless they could succeed in persuading Kentucky courts to extend the rationale of *NLRB v. Catholic Bishop of Chicago*[88] to exempt religiously affiliated institutions of higher education from coverage under the state labor law.[89]

Indemnification and Bonding

A nonprofit corporation has the power to indemnify any director or officer against expenses actually and reasonably incurred by him in connection with the defense of any action, civil or criminal, in which he is made a party by reason of being a director or officer.[90] However, the power to indemnify does not apply to matters in which an officer or director of a college is adjudged to be liable for negligence or misconduct in the performance of his duty to the corporation.[91]

D. Students

Kentucky does not have a statute parallel to the prohibitions of discrimination on the basis of race, color, or national origin in publicly funded programs found in Title VI of the federal Civil Rights Act of 1964,[92] or a statute parallel to the similar ban on sex discrimination found in Title IX of the federal Education Amendments of 1972.[93] Kentucky law does prohibit the State Board for Proprietary Education from issuing a certificate of approval to any proprietary school that denies enrollment to any pupil on the basis of that person's race, color, or creed.[94] The statutory definition of a proprietary school, however, excludes "a parochial, denominational or eleemosynary school or institution."[95] RACs in Kentucky would thus

appear to be exempt from this provision and free to pursue a policy of religious preference in student admissions.

E. Facilities

Public Accommodations and Fair Housing Legislation

The public accommodations section of the state civil rights law prohibits any person from denying an individual the full and equal enjoyment of the goods, services, facilities, privileges, advantages, and accommodations of a place of public accommodation, resort, or amusement, on the ground of race, color, religion, or national origin.[96] A place of public accommodation is "any place, store, or other establishment, either licensed or unlicensed, which supplies goods or services to the general public, or which solicits or accepts the patronage or trade of the general public, or which is supported directly or indirectly by government funds."[97] RACs are not explicitly exempted from this legislation and must make their public accommodations available on a nondiscriminatory basis.

Kentucky has a fair housing law similar to Title VIII of the federal Civil Rights Act of 1968.[98] The state statute makes it unlawful to refuse to sell, exchange, rent, lease, or to otherwise deny to or withhold real property from an individual,[99] or to discriminate against an individual in the terms, conditions, or privileges of such sale, exchange, rental, or lease of real property because of one's race, color, religion, or national origin.[100] Under the federal provision, RACs enjoy a limited exemption for preferential rentals on the basis of the religion of the renter.[101] The Kentucky statute provides a similar exemption for religious institutions or organizations operated for charitable or educational purposes, and operated, supervised or controlled by a religious corporation, association, or society.[102] Under this exemption, a qualifying RAC may give preferential treatment to members of the same religion as that of its sponsoring body in the sale, lease, rental, assignment, or sublease of real property, if such transactions are calculated to promote the religious principles for which the organization is established and maintained.[103]

Kentucky has also enacted fair housing legislation which bars discrimination based on sex or physical handicap in the sale or rental of property.[104] Modification of a housing accommodation to suit the handicapped is not required.[105] The law does allow for single-sex dormitories.[106]

Safety Legislation

The Kentucky Occupational Safety and Health of Employees Act[107] is a comprehensive statute modeled closely on its federal counterpart.[108] Encompassing both public and private employment,[109] the act creates within the Department of Labor a Board on Occupational Safety and Health Standards, which administers the act by promulgating occupational safety and health rules, regulations, and standards[110] intended to promote the safety, health, and general welfare of all employees.[111] The broad statutory definition of an employer in the act includes RACs, which like other employers must provide their employees a place of employment free from recognized hazards likely to cause death or serious physical harm[112] and must comply with the occupational safety and health standards promulgated by the Board.[113] Any RAC willfully or repeatedly violating the provisions of the act,[114] including any standard, regulation, or order promulgated pursuant to it, is punishable in accordance with the provisions of the act.[115]

F. State Taxation

Income Tax

All nonprofit religious and educational organizations in Kentucky which are exempt from federal income taxation[116] are likewise exempt from the payment of state income tax.[117]

Inheritance, Estate and Transfer Taxes

Kentucky law also exempts from its inheritance and estate tax all transfers to educational, religious, or other institutions, societies, or associations, whose sole object or purpose is to carry on charitable, educational, or religious work.[119] Gifts and transfers to RACs are,

therefore, not subject to the state inheritance or estate tax.

Kentucky has no gift tax.

Deductions for Gifts to an Educational Institution

Kentucky's income tax law allows for deductions for gifts to RACs. Kentucky law defines net income as adjusted gross income minus the standard deduction allowed by state law or, if the taxpayer prefers, the adjusted gross income minus all the deductions allowed individuals by Chapter One of the Internal Revenue Code, which in effect allows to those itemizing on their state return a deduction for gifts to RACs.[120]

Real, Personal and Intangible Property Taxes

The Kentucky Constitution specifically exempts from taxation property used for religious worship and property held by charitable and educational institutions which use the property exclusively for their maintenance.[121] Thus, property held by RACs would not be subject to taxation to the extent that such property is used exclusively for worship or for their maintenance.

Sales, Use or Meal Taxes

The sales and use tax does not apply to sales of tangible personal property or services *to* resident, nonprofit educational, charitable, and religious institutions, provided that the property or service is to be used solely within the educational, charitable, or religious function.[122] However, sales made *by* nonprofit educational, charitable, and religious institutions are taxable and the tax may be passed on to the customer.[123] If cafeterias or dining halls operated by educational institutions are not open to the public, however, the tax does not apply to sales of food to students.[124]

G. Fund Raising

Charitable Solicitation

Kentucky has enacted a consumer protection act, prohibiting the payment by a nonprofit organization of more than fifteen percent of gross contributions to a professional fund raiser.[125] If an RAC were deemed a religious organization soliciting funds for religious purposes, however, it would be exempt from this statute.[126] In any event, charitable solicitation by RACs and all other educational institutions is exempt from this statute if the fund raising is confined to the institution's alumni, faculty members, student body and their families, and corporations.[127]

Gambling

Kentucky law prohibits gambling, which is defined broadly as any risking of something of value involving an element of chance.[128] The gambling statute used to allow gaming conducted by a charitable or religious organization, but this provision has been repealed.[129]

26. Louisiana

A. Corporate Status

The incorporation of RACs in Louisiana is governed by the provisions of the Louisiana Nonprofit Corporation Law.[1] This law defines the powers and duties of nonprofit corporations as well as the procedures which must be followed in order to acquire the status of a nonprofit corporation. It also deals with the merger, consolidation, and dissolution of nonprofit corporations.

The law makes no specific mention of nonprofit *religious* or *educational* corporations, and the statutory definition of a nonprofit corporation is unenlightening.[2] The only clue concerning the kinds of corporations considered to fall under this provision is found in the notes on the "History and Source of the Law" which follow the definitional section. Earlier laws with goals similar to those of the present Nonprofit Corporation Law contemplated application to "all corporations not designed to engage in trade . . . for profit or financial gain," including those corporations formed for "literary, scientific, religious and charitable purposes."[3]

That RACs are meant to fall within the Nonprofit Corporation Law is suggested in a section which states that title to property acquired by trustees for any unincorporated *religious, educational* or charitable association will, upon the association's incorporation, be completely vested in the new corporation regardless of whether all former trustees transferred title correctly.[4]

A merger, consolidation, or voluntary dissolution must be approved by the Secretary of State.[5] The proceeding for dissolution is commenced by a two-thirds vote of the members of the governing board or of the college's incorporators.[6]

A proceeding for involuntary dissolution may be brought in any court of competent jurisdiction by: (1) a member; (2) a creditor whose claim has been reduced to judgment and has not been paid; or (3) a receiver appointed to take charge of the college's property.[7] In an action brought by a proper party for involuntary dissolution it must appear that:

1. Assets are insufficient to pay debts or provide reasonable security to those dealing with the corporation;
2. The objects of the corporation have failed, been abandoned, or are impracticable;
3. It is beneficial to the members that the corporation be dissolved;
4. The directors or members of the governing board are deadlocked;
5. The corporation has been guilty of gross and persistent acts outside its authority;
6. The corporation's articles have been cancelled by the state because of fraud, illegality of formation or failure to name and maintain a registered agent; or
7. A receiver has been appointed to take charge of the corporation's property.[8]

The court may appoint a "judicial liquidator,"[9] and may appoint a receiver for a dissolving college or university.[10]

The Louisiana Nonprofit Corporation Law provides that the net assets of some nonprofit corporations may be distributed to members according to their respective interests.[11] Either as religious or as charitable corporations, however, nonprofit educational institutions would be excluded from this exemption and would be bound by the general norm prohibiting distribution of assets to the members of a nonprofit corporation. In the event of dissolution, Louisiana law not only provides that the *cy pres* doctrine is generally to be followed,[12] but also states more explicitly:

. . . [I]f the corporation is a religious or charitable corporation . . . the net assets shall be transferred to a public or private corporation, association, or agency having similar purposes, unless the original articles of the corporation, as initially filed with the Secretary of State, expressly authorize some other disposition of its net assets upon dissolution.[13]

According to the Louisiana *cy pres* statute, any trust donated to a charitable or religious group shall not be defeated or fail as long as there is in Louisiana a branch or society capable of administering the trust for the germane purposes for which it was created.[14]

In the unlikely event of involuntary dissolution of an RAC, the supervising court determines the distribution of any net assets.[15]

B. State Support

The Louisiana Constitution of 1921 contained two provisions that militated against any expenditure of public funds for nonpublic education. Article IV, section 8, provided: "No money shall ever be taken from the public treasury, directly or indirectly, in aid of any church, sect or denomination of religion, or in aid of any . . . teacher thereof."[16] Article XII, section 13, prohibited even the provision of credit or the loan of public funds to or for any private corporation, including RACs and other nonpublic educational institutions.[17]

In the spirit of these constitutional provisions, Louisiana enacted legislation prohibiting agreements for the combination of public and parochial schools:

The school boards of this state . . . are prohibited from entering into any contract, agreement, understanding or combination tacitly or expressly, directly or indirectly, with any church . . . or association of any religious sect or religious denomination whatsoever, with the representatives thereof or with any persons or corporation conducting a school which solicits patronage from those of any particular religious faith . . . for the purpose of running any public school . . . in connection or in combination with any private or parochial school.[18]

Three years after the 1971 decision of the United States Supreme Court in *Tilton v. Richardson* allowing federal aid for construction of facilities at RACs for nonsectarian use,[19] and a year after the Court's decision in *Hunt v. McNair* authorizing the extension of credit by South Carolina for a similar purpose,[20] Louisiana adopted a new state constitution which did not contain either of the provisions of the 1921 constitution referred to above. In place of the old prohibition against any transfer of public funds to a church or teacher of religion, the current constitution provides that no appropriation shall be made except for a public purpose.[21] The old prohibition of agreements between public and nonpublic schools gave way to a new constitutional provision authorizing cooperation between the state and nonpublic schools.[22] As Professor Howard states: "The effect of all these changes will certainly be a relaxation of the restrictions on state aid to private colleges, sectarian and nonsectarian, but the precise outlines of newly permissible aid will be unclear until there is some state judicial interpretation of the new provisions."[23]

Perhaps to give its own interpretation of the new constitutional provisions, the legislature in 1974 enacted a new "Legislative Scholarship" program.[24] By expressly providing that these scholarships could be received by students attending RACs, this legislation supersedes a 1955 opinion of the Attorney General stating that legislative scholarships could not be used at private schools.[25] The 1974 statute establishes a state scholarship fund so that needy students can attend college at any approved institution of higher education, and requires that payment of the scholarships be made directly to the approved institution.[26] Several Louisiana colleges and universities are mentioned *nominatim* as approved institutions in the statute, including RACs such as St. Mary's Dominican College, Holy Cross College, and Loyola University of New Orleans.[27]

In addition to making scholarship grants available to students attending RACs, Louisiana also includes these students in its guaranteed student loan program.[28] The only restriction placed on an RAC attended by students applying for these loans is that it be a "commission-approved privately governed institution of higher education."[29]

In 1975 the legislature moved a step further in its interpretation of the meaning of the new constitution of Louisiana by authorizing direct transfer payments to eight private colleges and universities in the state, seven of which are RACs.[30] Although no litigation has tested the constitutionality of this program, it is presumptively valid under the federal constitution, for the United States Supreme Court sustained a similar capitation grant program in *Roemer v. Maryland Bd. of Public Works*.[31]

Referring to a dubiously constitutional 1967 statute providing that no state funds shall be expended in any way to finance a communist or atheistic speaker or activity,[32] Professor Howard has expressed the concern that "pressures . . . sometimes exist for state control to follow state money."[33] Although this concern may be a legitimate one, there seems little basis for such anxiety in the post-1974 enactments discussed here. These statutes are somewhat remarkable precisely because, in granting financial support to RACs or to students attending them, they impose no serious regulatory burden on RACs as a condition of assistance.

This is not true of the Handicapped Accessibility Standards Act,[34] according to which any "building . . . utilized for purposes of education . . . which is [f]inanced in whole or in part by a grant or a loan made or guaranteed by the State"[35] must conform to state regulations governing accessibility for the handicapped.

C. Personnel

Although the 1974 constitution states that "No law shall discriminate against a person because of race or religious ideas, beliefs, or affiliations,"[36] Louisiana has not enacted any legislation prohibiting discriminatory practices in hiring based on race, sex, religion, or national origin by private employers. It does, however, have a statute prohibiting employment discrimination based on age,[37] which makes no exception for RACs in its definition of an employer.[38] Nonetheless, an employer may take the age of a prospective employee into account whenever age would be a bona fide occupational qualification (BFOQ).[39]

In the absence of any state legislation concerning private employment discrimination other than on the basis of age, RACs in Louisiana must, of course, conform their employment policies and practices to the requirements of applicable federal civil rights legislation.[40]

Louisiana has no comprehensive minimum wage legislation. It does, however, authorize the state Department of Labor to set minimum wage for girls and women not engaged in domestic work.[41] RACs are not exempt from this legislation and must follow the standards set up by the Department of Labor.

Louisiana's Workman's Compensation Act[42] also makes no special provisions for RACs, nor has judicial interpretation suggested that RACs are not "employers" under this statute. On the contrary, in *Meyers v. Southwest Region Conference Association of Seventh-Day Adventists*,[43] the Louisiana Supreme Court ruled that the "freedom of religion" clause of the state constitution did not bar the application of this statute to employees of a religious corporation. On the rationale developed in *Meyers*, the employees of an RAC would surely not be more entitled to an exemption on First Amendment grounds than would the employees of a nonprofit corporation existing solely for religious purposes.

On its own terms, the statute applies to all employees not explicitly excluded from coverage.[44] Some employees of RACs, however, may come within the exception for employment covered by a federal worker's compensation law.[45] Uncompensated executive officers and members of boards of directors of an RAC are explicitly excluded from the coverage of the act.[46] There is no explicit provision that allows employers to elect to include exempted employees within the coverage of the act. Injured persons not covered by the act may bring a civil action for damages against the employer.[47] RACs must carry insurance or qualify as a self-insurer under the act.[48] Under some circumstances, RACs may join with similar employers to form a Group Self-Insurance Association.[49]

The Louisiana Employment Security Law[50] contains a broad statutory definition of "employer" that appears to embrace RACs.[51] The statutory definition of "employment," however, which might be relied upon to ground a general exemption of RACs from the provisions of the state unemployment compensation law, excludes from coverage any service performed for a church or for any organization which is operated, supervised, controlled, or principally supported by a church or convention or association of churches.[52] Relying on this provision as the basis for exemption of employees of RACs from coverage under the Unemployment Compensation Act, however, could make an RAC vulnerable to an attack on its eligibility for public financial assistance.[53]

RACs are not forced to this choice, however, because another subsection of the definition of covered employment exempts "service performed in the employ of a corporation . . . organized and operated exclusively for religious, charitable, scientific, literary or educational purposes . . . no part of the net earnings of which inures to the benefit of any private stockholder or individual."[54] RACs may rely on this provision, applicable to all nonprofit schools, without thereby jeopardizing their eligibility for public assistance.

If an RAC claims an exemption from coverage under either or both of these provisions of the act, it must nonetheless contribute to the unemployment compensation fund for any domestic employee hired in a college club if the employer paid more than $1,000 in any quarter during the current or preceding calendar year for such services.[55]

On the other hand, even if an RAC in Louisiana does not claim a general exemption from that state's unemployment compensation law, it need not contribute to the unemployment fund for "service performed . . . by a student who is enrolled and is regularly attending classes" at the institution or for "service performed by an

individual under the age of twenty-two who is enrolled at a nonprofit . . . educational institution . . . which combines academic instruction with work experience if such service is an integral part of such program."[56]

D. Students

Far from regulating the admissions policies of RACs, Louisiana explicitly acknowledges the freedom of such institutions to exercise religious preference in the selection of their student body.[57] The 1970 act which prohibits discrimination in public schools on the basis of race, creed, color, or national origin, likewise provides:

. . . [N]othing in this Act shall be deemed to affect, in any way, the right of a religious or denominational educational institution to select its pupils exclusively or primarily from members of such religion or denomination or from giving preference in such selection to such members or to make such selection of its pupils as is calculated to promote the religious principle for which it is established.[58]

No other statutory provisions of Louisiana law restrict the independence of RACs in student admissions or discipline.

E. Facilities

Article I, section 12 of the 1974 Constitution provides that "in access to public areas, accommodations, and facilities, every person shall be free from discrimination based on race, religion, or national ancestry and from arbitrary, capricious, or unreasonable discrimination based on age, sex, or physical condition."[59] A constitutional provision such as this cannot be expected to contain definitions of terms such as "public accommodations," nor has the term been refined through the process of judicial interpretation subsequent to its adoption in 1974.

A statute enacted in 1977 to provide for equal access to public facilities for physically handicapped persons,[60] however, sheds some light on the meaning of such terms. It articulates a general policy of the state "to enable persons who are physically handicapped . . . to use and enjoy *all* buildings and facilities."[61] Moreover, it requires compliance with the building standards[62] concerning accessibility for the handicapped in any facility constructed after January 1, 1978, and utilized for purposes of education or employment,[63] any facility for public accommodation, including student dormitories constructed after January 1, 1978,[64] and any educational facility constructed or renovated with state or federal financial assistance.[65]

Although the legislature has not yet elaborated on the generic terms "public accommodations and facilities" for purposes other than accessibility for handicapped persons, the specification of those terms in the handicapped statute might serve as a guide to administrators of RACs with respect to the other obligations specified in the Louisiana constitution with respect to public accommodations. Another source of guidance for these administrators would be the public accommodations section of the federal Civil Rights Act of 1964.[66] For example, if an RAC in Louisiana were to operate a motel or inn, a restaurant, or a theater open to the general public, it could not deny any person access to those facilities on the basis of the categories enumerated in the state constitutional provision cited above. On the other hand, since, as observed above in connection with student admissions, RACs are explicitly allowed by Louisiana law to exercise religious preference in the selection of their student bodies, if a Louisiana RAC adopted such a policy resulting in a disproportionate number of students of a particular religion residing in its dormitories or served in its dining halls, it would not violate the state constitutional provision banning discrimination in public facilities.

In addition to its statute providing for equal access to public facilities for the physically handicapped,[67] Louisiana has also enacted a White Cane Law which stipulates that the blind, the visually handicapped, and the otherwise physically disabled shall have equal access to places of public accommodation[68] and to "all housing accommodations offered for rent, lease or compensation"[69] in the state. The definition of "housing accommodations" is broad enough to include RAC-owned dorms.[70] Modification of a place of public accommodation or a housing accommodation to suit the handicapped is not required.[71]

Although Louisiana has no comprehensive OSHA statute, it does empower the Commissioner of Labor to prescribe rules and regulations for the prevention of accidents in places of employment.[72] There is no definition of employer or employee and the only limitation in scope excludes private domestic and agricultural employment from the employer's duty of care.[73]

F. State Taxation

Louisiana exempts from the payment of state income tax all:

Corporations and any . . . foundation organized and operated exclusively for religious . . . or educational purposes . . . no part of the net earnings of which inures to the benefit of any private shareholder or individual and no substantial part of the activities of which is carrying on propaganda, or otherwise attempting to influence legislation.[74]

Two limits on this exemption are worthy of comment. The first limit, concerning lobbying, appears in the definition of an exempt institution cited above. The vague phrase "attempting to influence legislation" has not been judicially elaborated upon. On the one hand, the phrase should not be construed as a total ban on freedom of speech or freedom of petition for redress of grievance, for to circumscribe the associational rights of RACs to participate in the political process would offend against core societal values protected by the First Amendment of the federal Constitution.[75] On the other hand, nonprofit corporations may be held to some reasonable limits on political speech that would be inappropriate if applied to for-profit corporations,[76] precisely because of the tax-exempt status that nonprofit corporations enjoy. A prudent guideline for RAC administrators wishing to comply with the state provision granting tax-exempt status to their institutions is the newly revised federal criterion allowing 501(c)(3) organizations to expend some of the organization's funds and energies, but not a substantial amount, in efforts to influence legislation.[77]

The second limit is embodied in the provision that RACs in Louisiana must pay state income tax on unrelated business income; as with the lobbying provision, this provision is defined with reference to the parallel provision in the Internal Revenue Code.[78]

Louisiana imposes an inheritance tax on the transfer or the net estate of every resident in an amount equal to the federal credit.[79] But "legacies and donations to charitable, religious, or educational institutions located within the State of Louisiana" are exempt from this tax.[80]

Louisiana also imposes an estate transfer tax designed merely to channel to Louisiana, by virtue of the credit allowed against the federal estate tax for state death taxes, moneys that would otherwise go to the federal government in estate taxes.[81] This tax, therefore, has no ultimate effect on the *amount* of death taxes paid.

Gifts made exclusively to nonprofit charitable, religious, or educational institutions located in Louisiana are also exempt from the Louisiana gift tax.[82]

Contributions or gifts to RACs are allowed as deductions in computing Louisiana net income for both individuals and corporations.[83] Such contributions or gifts must be verified under rules and regulations prescribed by the collector[84] and, in any event, may not exceed fifteen percent of an individual's adjusted gross income or five percent of a corporation's net income as computed without the benefit of this deduction.[85]

RACs are also exempted from payment of property tax. Article VII, Section 21(B) of the 1974 Constitution exempts all:

property owned by a non-profit organization or association organized and operated exclusively for religious . . . or educational purposes, no part of the net earnings of which inure to the benefit of any private shareholder [or individual] and which is declared to be exempt from federal or state income tax.[86]

As with the state income tax, the property tax exemption is limited to property related to the exempt purposes of the nonprofit corporation.[87]

An opinion of the Louisiana Attorney General supports the validity of an exemption for property owned by religious or educational in-stitutions if it is used for school or church purposes.[88] A later opinion, refining the meaning of exempt property, states that the mere donation of the income or profits from a piece of property to a church or school will not exempt that property from taxation; in order to qualify for the exemption, the property itself must be used for church or school purposes.[89]

In *State ex rel. Cunningham v. Bd. of Assessors of Parish of Orleans,*[90] a Louisiana appellate court ruled in 1898 that a campus building housing priests not involved in the school's educative functions was not exempt and that property tax could be assessed at a value proportionate to the part of the building not being used for the educational purposes required for tax-exempt status at that time. This case was an early harbinger of the rule for pro rata assessment of income and property unrelated to the charitable purposes of a nonprofit corporation. The accrual of such income does not result in a loss of the exempt status by the nonprofit organization, but only in a payment of tax on that income.

RACs are likewise exempted from sales and use taxes on sales made by RACs when the profits and proceeds of such sales are used entirely for educational or religious purposes. Normal commercial ventures, however, are not exempt from sales and use taxes even if they are run by educational or religious corporations or associations.[91] Under applicable regulations, an RAC must apply for an exemption certificate from the collector of revenue and must provide a measure of financial disclosure to receive exempt non-profit organization status.[92] As with the property tax exemption, the sales and use tax exemption is conditioned upon a measure of political neutrality by the nonprofit organization:[93] "Any organization which endorses any candidate for political office or otherwise is involved in political activities shall not be eligible for the exemption provided herein."[94] Again, no clear guidance is given as to how far an RAC may go before it is "involved in political activities."

A related section grants the same type of sales tax exemption, with the same conditions and limitations, to nonprofit organizations such as RACs for proceeds from fairs, festivals, and expositions which they sponsor.[95]

In addition to the sales and use tax discussed above, an amusement tax may be imposed by municipalities within Louisiana on fairs and other forms of entertainment. RACs, however, are generally exempt from payment of this tax. Although the act refers primarily to religious groups, an RAC would also qualify for this exemption if the entertainment it sponsors is for a charitable purpose.[96]

G. Fund Raising

There is no charitable solicitation statute in Louisiana. The 1921 Constitution, however, required educational institutions to furnish the legislative auditor with an annual statement of "all moneys received by them, from what sources [and] all moneys expended by them and for what purposes."[97] This provision was deleted from the Constitution of 1974, but was enacted as a statute in 1975.[98]

An RAC could not legally raise money by games of chance such as casino type carnivals until quite recently. In 1956, for example, the Attorney General issued an opinion stating that religious or similar organizations could not hold bingo games or raffles, regardless of the purpose for which the proceeds are used.[99] The 1974 constitution states: "Gambling shall be defined by and suppressed by the legislature."[100] Far from suppressing all forms of gambling,

however, the legislature in 1976 enacted a statute authorizing municipalities "to license bona fide . . . charitable, educational [or] religious organizations . . . to hold and operate . . . games of chance commonly known as bingo or keno . . . when the entire net proceeds of such games of chance are to be devoted to educational, charitable [or] religious . . . uses."[101] In a municipality allowing charitable gambling within its jurisdiction, nonprofit organizations that wish to sponsor games of chance must apply to the municipality for a license to do so.[102]

According to a 1975 opinion of the Attorney General, the constitutional provision concerning the suppression of gambling is not self-executing and allows closely regulated legalization of gambling.[103] A year later an appellate court declined to rule on the issue of the constitutionality of the charitable gambling law.[104] Unless the Act is successfully challenged as violative of the state constitution, RACs may sponsor games of chance as a fund raising device if the local municipality allows it.[105]

H. Miscellaneous

The individual liability of directors, trustees, or other officers of any ". . . charitable or nonprofit hospital, organization or 'institution' " for acts or omissions of the organization is limited by statute in Louisiana.[106]

27. Maine

A. Corporate Status

Religious societies and religiously affiliated institutions may incorporate under the corporation statutes of Maine or its Nonprofit Corporation Act. A corporation may be created for any educational or religious purpose.[1] Upon written application by seven or more persons desiring to form a corporation, the county justice of the peace may issue a warrant for their first meeting.[2]

The Maine Nonprofit Corporation Act, which became effective in 1978, applies to domestic and foreign nonprofit organizations created in 1978 or later "for any lawful purpose or purposes, including educational."[3] Religious purpose is not specifically mentioned. Furthermore, it is stipulated that "parishes and societies . . . independent local churches . . . and churches organized as noncapital stock corporations under Title 13, section 901 et seq." are not included under this Act.[4]

The merger, consolidation, or dissolution of a private nonprofit college is governed by the Maine Nonprofit Corporation Act[5] if the college was created under the act or as a nonstock corporation under a prior general or special act.[6] In addition, Maine courts will apply the doctrine of *cy pres* to carry out the general charitable intention of a valid charitable trust if it is impossible or impractical to carry out the specific purpose of the trust.[7]

A merger, consolidation, or voluntary dissolution is approved by the Secretary of State.[8] Courts of equity have jurisdiction to dissolve a nonprofit corporation, to liquidate its assets, and to arrange its affairs as a result of an action brought by: (1) a member or director; (2) a creditor; (3) the corporation itself; or (4) the Attorney General. Liquidation of assets precedes the entry of a decree of dissolution.[9]

The Maine Nonprofit Corporation Act provides that in voluntary dissolution proceedings assets are to be distributed among the corporation's members according to their interests or the corporation's bylaws.[10] The assets of colleges and other educational corporations, however, shall be transferred only to one or more domestic or foreign corporations, societies, or organizations engaged in activities substantially similar to those of the dissolving college.[11] The statutory procedure for liquidating a college's assets under court supervision[12] closely follows that of the Model Nonprofit Corporation Act.[13]

B. State Support

Article II of the Constitution of Maine guarantees freedom of religion. Its education provision, Article VIII, Part 1, Section 1, places the duty of establishing and supporting public schools on the towns. The state legislature has retained some control over institutions of higher education by stipulating that it may offer a donation, grant, or endowment to any "literary institution," but that if that institution receives state funds the legislature then "has the right to grant any further powers to alter, limit, or restrain any of the powers vested in any such literary institution, as shall be judged necessary to promote the best interests thereof."[14] Nevertheless, although the state does hold this power to control educational institutions, it has seldom used it.[15]

It has been suggested that the state's retention of the right to control institutions receiving state funds may create an excessive entanglement between church and state. But as long as there is no interference which would create such a clash, state funding to private colleges (particularly student loans and grants, which are indirect grants to colleges) should remain constitutionally permissible. "In general, the test of validity of aid programs at whatever level of education seems likely to be that of the Federal Constitution."[16]

Bowdoin College, Colby College, two theological schools and twenty-five academies offering secondary education had been in existence when Maine's Constitution was written. More private schools, many of them religiously affiliated, were established in the late 1800s.[17] The constitutional provision in Article VIII allowed state aid to "literary institutions," which included colleges and academies. In 1828 a State School Fund was established, the income of which was distributed to public schools according to the number of children in attendance.[18] In the early twentieth century Bishop Walsh of Portland attempted to have some of the school funds allocated to parochial schools; he failed. Nevertheless, the legislature did continue to allow grants to religiously controlled academies and colleges.[19] When a backlash movement arose and resolutions were then introduced to cut off public funding to private and/or parochial schools, they too failed to get the percentage of votes necessary for passage. Therefore, there is at present: (1) no aid for parochial schools; (2) public funding of public schools through the School Fund and through the school committees; and (3) constitutionally granted aid to colleges and academies, with the possibility of some state control if the aid is accepted.

The state has established a Student Incentive Scholarship Program for undergraduates attending institutions of higher education in Maine.[20] North American Indians of certain tribes residing in Maine may also be given a state scholarship to attend a secondary or post-secondary institution accredited by the state department of education, a regional association of secondary schools and colleges, or the United States Veterans' Administration.[21] The institution which the Indian student attends may also receive state funds for providing support services for him.[22] In addition, the orphans, widows, or widowers of enlisted men or veterans killed or disabled in action may receive aid from the state.[23]

Maine also distributes a Tuition Equalization Fund[24] to those "Maine high school graduates who are attending as full-time undergraduates, eligible Maine private institutions of higher education."[25] As long as an RAC meets the requirements set forth in the Higher Education Act of 1965, as amended, its undergraduates may be eligible for these grants.

In 1967 Maine amended its Constitution to provide for loans to college students at both public and private colleges.[26] The legislature has the authority to grant loans to Maine students attending institutions of higher learning so long as the total number of issued and outstanding bonds covering such loans does not exceed four million dollars. The amendment reserved to the legislature the right to determine the terms and conditions for such funding. In 1968 the state legislatively established a loan program following the guidelines established in the constitutional amendment.[27]

If an educational institution of higher learning[28] intends to redevelop or rehabilitate for educational uses "land, buildings or structures located in areas adjacent to or in the immediate vicinity of federally-assisted urban renewal projects," and if such a development plan is approved under state or local law, the legislature may grant "the aggregate amount of expenditures made by an educational institution . . ." as "local grants-in-aid for federally-assisted urban renewal projects."[29]

But a charitable or educational institution which receives state or municipal grants for construction or repair must give preference to Maine workmen and bidders for the project.[30]

C. Personnel

The Maine Human Rights Act[31] recognizes as civil rights the rights to freedom from discrimination in employment, housing, use of public accommodations, and extension of credit. The Act lists a wider variety of classifications of discrimination than is found in the Federal Act: in addition to race, color, religion, sex, or national origin, Maine includes physical or mental handicap, and adds marital status as a type of discrimination to be prevented in the extension of credit.[32]

The definition of "employer" is very broad, but specifically excludes "a religious or fraternal corporation or association, not organized for private profit and in fact not conducted for private profit, with respect to employment of its members of the same religion, sect or fraternity."[33]

There is a serious question whether the statutory phrase "religious or fraternal corporation or association" would include an RAC, especially since the provision refers only to those employees who are "members" of that corporation or association. It is possible that the legislation had in mind religious orders and the like, not colleges and universities.

It should also be noted that Maine restricts the exception to employees of the faith with which the RAC is affiliated even though there are situations in which an RAC might appropriately wish to exercise preference toward one of another religious faith.

In 1975, when the Maine Human Rights Commission issued guidelines interpreting the Human Rights Act, it established a Bona Fide Occupational Qualification with respect to religious discrimination:

The Commission recognizes as a bona fide occupational qualification the requirements by a religious corporation or association, not organized for private profit and in fact not conducted for private profit, that certain of its employees be members of that religious faith.[34]

Thus, if an RAC qualifies as a nonprofit *religious* corporation or association (the definition of which is not given), it may discriminate in its employment policies on religious grounds. However, it should be noted that the examples given by the Commission narrowly construe this exception:

For example, a requirement that a Rabbi be Jewish or that a member of a Roman Catholic religious order be a Roman Catholic is valid.[35]

In general, individuals employed in any occupation must be paid a sufficient minimum wage.[36] However, exempt from minimum wage law coverage is "any individual engaged in the activities of a public-supported nonprofit organization or in a program controlled by an educational nonprofit organization."[37] Employees of RACs would fall into the latter category; therefore RACs are not obligated to meet minimum wage standards.

RACs are subject to Maine's Worker's Compensation Act.[38] Executive officers of a charitable, religious, educational or other nonprofit corporation are, however, excepted from the definition of "employees" under the act, unless the corporation elects to have them covered.[39] The defenses of employee negligence or assumption of the risk may not be used by the employer in cases of personal injury or death, except for domestic or casual employees.[40] "Casual" is defined as "occasional, irregular, or incidental."[41] RACs might have some employees in these categories and may use the common law defenses mentioned above against them in a suit brought for damages if the RAC has liability insurance of not less than $25,000, and medical payment coverage of not less than $1,000.[42]

Every employer must take out liability insurance under a Worker's Compensation policy, filing notice with the Worker's Compensation Commission, or be self-insured upon proving its solvency to the Commission and depositing such cash or security with the Commission as it requires.[43]

There is no exemption for contribution by RACs for unemployment compensation. The statutory definition of "employment" includes:

service performed in the employ of a religious, charitable, educational or other organization which is excluded from the term employment as defined in the Federal Unemployment Tax Act solely by reason of section 3306(c)(8) of that Act . . . [if] the organization had four or more individuals in employment for some portion of the day in each of 20 different weeks.[44]

Under this definition, RACs must contribute to unemployment compensation for their employees.

Nonetheless, the following types of employment are exempt from Maine's Employment Security law:[45]

1. Service performed in the employ of a church or convention or association of churches, or an organization which is operated primarily for religious purposes and which is operated, supervised, controlled, or principally supported by a church or convention or association of churches;[46]
2. Service performed by a fully ordained, commissioned, or licensed minister of a church in the exercise of his ministry or by a member of a religious order in the exercise of duties required by such order;[47]
3. Service performed in the employ of a school, college, or university, if such service is performed by a student who is enrolled and is regularly attending classes at such school, college, or university.[48]

Therefore, if an RAC would qualify as an organization operated primarily for religious purposes by a church or association of churches, it would be exempt from contribution to unemployment compensation for its employees. (Most RACs would not qualify for this exemption.) Or if an employee of that college was performing as his service to the college a duty required by his religious order, no unemployment compensation contributions would need to be provided for that employee.

D. Students

Maine has no specific legislation concerning the selection of students for admission into RACs or concerning student discipline or conduct codes.

E. Facilities

Maine's Fair Housing Law guarantees the opportunity to secure decent housing "without discrimination because of race, color, sex, physical or mental handicap, religion, ancestry or national origin."[49]

The only housing accommodation exemption pertinent to RACs is for "the rental of any dwelling owned, controlled or operated for other than a commercial purpose, by a religious corporation to its membership unless such membership is restricted on account of race, color or national origin."[50]

The Public Accommodations Law guarantees "equal access to places of public accommodation without discrimination because of race, color, sex, physical or mental handicap, religion, ancestry or national origin."[51] It is unlawful either to refuse access (directly or indirectly) to such a facility or to advertise that access to a facility shall be denied to any persons for discriminatory reasons. The definition of "place of public accommodation" lists examples of establishments which cater to or are used by the general public.[52] Although educational and religious facilities are not specifically included, there is no reason to believe that facilities included on the list (e.g., restaurants, hotels, theaters) will be exempted merely because of their presence on an RAC campus. It is thus safe to assume that all public accommodations on campus are covered by the public accommodations law. Furthermore, the list does not purport to be exhaustive.[53]

Facilities built or under construction before September, 1974, are exempted from compliance with construction standards stipulated by the Act.[54]

The Maine legislature has enacted a comprehensive occupational safety statute.[55] It appears not to cover RACs or any other employer in the private sector, however, since an employer is defined as the state or a political subdivision of the state, and an employee refers only to employees of the state or one of its political subdivisions.[56]

F. State Taxation

Property tax exemptions are granted to literary and scientific institutions for the "real estate and personal property owned and occupied or used solely for their own purposes."[57] However, certain conditions must be met:[58] the only payment directors, trustees, officers, and employees may receive is reasonable compensation for services, and all profits and sale proceeds must be used for the institution's original purpose. Furthermore, the institution must file a financial report with the tax assessors, and every five years assessors must include in their inventory "the value of all real property of literary and scientific institutions not taxed."[59]

In *Hurricane Island Outward Bound v. Vinalhaven,*[60] the courts, noticing that the legislature did not define "literary and scientific institutions" in the tax exemption statutes, turned to "the common meaning and plain meaning of those terms."[61] Although the court was interpreting only "scientific institutions," it stated in dicta its approach to legislative interpretation:

Our construction of what is a 'scientific institution' must be a narrow one, for tax exemption statutes must be strictly construed, and all doubt and uncertainty as to the meaning of the statute must be weighed against exemption.[62]

In declaring that only 'literary and scientific institutions' may qualify for tax exemption, the legislature made no provision under the penumbra of 'education,' even though it is common for taxing statutes to fashion exemptions for institutions 'organized and operated for religious, charitable, scientific, testing for public safety, literary or educational purposes.' 26 U.S.C.A. § 401(c)(3) . . . When used collectively, 'scientific' must have a meaning separate and distinct from that of 'educational.'[63]

Churches and other houses of worship, parsonages, and the personal property of a religious society have a tax exemption up to a certain value.[64] And colleges may be reimbursed the money paid as real estate taxes if the total amount of reimbursement is not greater than one thousand five hundred dollars and if the real estate was bought before April 12, 1889.[65]

Exempt from inheritance taxes under Maine law is:

[a]ll property which shall pass to or for the use of societies, corporations and institutions now or hereafter exempted by law from taxation. . . .[66] or . . . to any society, corporation, institution or association of persons engaged in or devoted to any charitable, religious, benevolent, educational, public or other like [nonprofit] work. . . .[67] or to any person, society [or] corporation . . . in trust for or to be devoted to any . . . educational . . . purpose.[68]

The only additional requirement is that the entity be organized and existing in Maine or that the property passing to it be limited to use in Maine.[69]

Maine does not have a gift tax.

Although the Maine Income Tax Act[70] does not specifically exempt RACs from taxation, it does allow individuals and corporations to incorporate into their state return their itemized, federal income tax deductions.[71] Since federal income tax law allows a deduction for contributions to RACs,[72] a state deduction is in effect provided for contributions to RACs by corporations and individuals itemizing for federal tax purposes.

Schools (the definition of which includes RACs)[73] need not pay a sales tax unless their enterprise is a commercial one.[74]

RACs are not specifically exempted from Maine's use tax.[75] Furthermore, there is no tax on the rental charged for student housing at a school.[76]

Exempt from excise taxes are "vehicles owned and used solely for their own purposes" by literary and scientific institutions and by religious societies and houses of worship.[77]

G. Fund Raising

Maine's Charitable Solicitations Act,[78] effective in 1978, requires registration and financial reporting of charitable organizations.[79] Under the definitions, a charitable organization includes any person or organization having "any charitable, benevolent, *educational*, philanthropic, humane, patriotic, religious or eleemosynary purpose."[80]

Nevertheless, an exemption (claimed by submitting a formal statement of the reason for the exemption to the Secretary of State)[81] is provided to, among others, religious corporations, societies, or organizations,[82] and educational institutions whose curriculums in whole or in part are registered or approved by the Department of Educational and Cultural Services or by an accrediting body recognized by that Department[83] and organizations operated by the student bodies of such institutions.[84] Most RACs, therefore, would be exempt from the registration statement requirements of the law.

A bona fide nonprofit charitable, educational, or religious organization in Maine may receive a license to operate a game of chance.[85]

H. Miscellaneous

Maine is a member of the New England Higher Education Compact, established in 1955 "to provide greater educational opportunities and services . . . for the persons residing in the several states of New England parties to this compact, with the aim of furthering higher education in the fields of medicine, dentistry, veterinary medicine, public health and in professional, technical, scientific, literary and other fields."[86] Its governing board is a corporate body made up of three members from each compacting state.[87] The powers of the New England Board of Higher Education include collecting data, issuing reports, and contracting in order to provide the necessary services and facilities.[88]

In 1975 Maine created a state agency called the Post-secondary Education Commission of Maine (PECOM) for the purpose of conducting:

comprehensive planning . . . in cooperation with the New England Board of Higher Education and other New England states, to assure the development, maintenance, and accessibility of diversified post-secondary educational opportunities of high quality for Maine citizens, and to seek efficient use of limited resources . . . to avoid unnecessary duplication of institutions, programs and facilities. . . . It is the intent of the Legislature that such comprehensive planning shall lead to a cohesive system of post-secondary education involving all of the public, private non-profit and proprietary post-secondary educational institutions in the State.[89]

PECOM has limited its own power and authority; it will not "infringe upon . . . the governing authority of any institution of post-secondary education."[90] (Postsecondary education would, of course, include RACs.)[91] Of the sixteen members of PECOM, three positions are held by representatives of private nonprofit institutions of postsecondary education "appointed by a subcommittee of the Higher Education Council of Maine composed of private college members."[92]

The Maine Certificate of Need Act of 1978[93] establishes standards of health care by statewide planning of health services. The only health care facilities exempted from this act are those "operated by religious groups relying solely on spiritual means through prayer for healing."[94]

Maine law requires that teachers at all levels of education, including "presidents, professors and tutors of colleges," teach "the principles of morality and justice and a sacred regard for the truth."[95]

28. Maryland

A. Corporate Status

RACs in Maryland may incorporate under the standard incorporation provisions[1] or as nonstock corporations.[2] The nonstock corporation has no authority to issue capital stock[3] and may consolidate or merge only with another nonstock corporation.[4]

Religious denominations may form religious corporations.[5] However, the tenor of the provision would indicate that its purpose is solely for the organization of churches and that it does not extend to the formation of RACs.

Any security issued by a person organized and operated not for private profit but exclusively for, *inter alia*, religious or educational purposes does not have to be registered with the Securities Commissioner.[6]

Except for an institution operating under a charter granted by the General Assembly, no institution of postsecondary education, and therefore no RAC, may commence or continue to operate without a certificate of approval from the State Board of Higher Education.[7] An institution which must obtain a certificate of approval may be required to furnish to the state a performance bond as assurance that the institution will perform faithfully all agreements or contracts it makes with its students and comply with all the provisions of the Education Article.[8]

If the State Board for Higher Education believes that an institution of postsecondary education does not meet the conditions or standards on which its certificate of approval was based, the State Board may, after following the proper procedures, order the institution to stop doing business.[9]

Before any postsecondary educational institution may discontinue its operation in Maryland, it must file with the State Board of Higher Education the original or legible copies of all essential academic records of its former students.[10]

The Maryland General Corporation Law,[11] subject to some special provisions found in the statutes regulating Nonstock Corporations,[12] governs the consolidation, merger, or dissolution of a nonprofit college or university.[13] In addition, Maryland courts are empowered both by statute and by common law decisions to apply the *cy pres* doctrine when necessary.[14]

The consolidation, merger, or voluntary dissolution takes effect when the State Department of Assessment and Taxation accepts the articles of consolidation, merger, or dissolution.[15] A private college may be dissolved involuntarily and its assets liquidated by an order of the circuit court[16] in an action authorized by the State Department of Assessments and Taxation filed by the Attorney General alleging abuse of powers.[17] The circuit court also has jurisdiction to liquidate a college's assets in an action properly brought by a member[18] of the corporation or by a creditor.[19]

The Maryland statute[20] closely follows the Model Nonprofit Corporation Act.[21] One minor variation from the Model Act is that the Maryland Nonstock Corporations Law requires that there be a plan of distribution to transfer assets held for "educational purposes only" to a corporation having a similar purpose, or to a corporation associated or connected with the dissolving college.[22]

B. State Support

The constitutionality of state funding for RACs has been tested under both the Maryland and federal constitutions. In *The Horace Mann League* v. *Board of Public Works of Maryland*,[23] the validity of four statutes granting outright matching funds to four RACs was challenged. It was argued that such grants were for private rather than public purposes in violation of the Maryland Constitution,[24] and compelled taxpayers to contribute to or maintain a place of worship or ministry also in violation of the Maryland Constitution.[25]

The Court of Appeals of Maryland ruled that the statutes did not violate the state's constitution since they manifested a public purpose, that is, the grants supported institutions whose function (the provision of postsecondary educational services) the state had failed fully to assume. The Court, however, invalidated three of the four statutes for violating the Establishment Clause of the federal constitution, using a test which antedated the three-prong test of *Lemon* v. *Kurtzman*.[26]

The *Lemon* three-prong test for the federal constitutionality of a statute authorizing aid and support for RACs, reaffirmed in *Roemer* v. *Board of Public Works of Maryland*,[27] requires (1) that the statute authorizing aid have a secular legislative purpose; (2) that its primary effect be neither the advancement nor the inhibition of religion; and (3) that the statute not foster an excessive entanglement between government and religion.[28]

In *Roemer*, noncategorical aid was given to five Maryland RACs. The Supreme Court upheld the Maryland scheme because the *Lemon* test had been met. First, all parties agreed that the statute involved had a secular legislative purpose. Second, the aid was limited in that it could only be used for secular purposes. This was sufficient to insure that the primary effect of the statute would not advance religion. Fi-

nally, the danger of excessive entanglement between government and religion because of the statute was minimal. The Supreme Court accepted the District Court's finding that occasional audits necessary to verify the sectarian purposes of expenditures would be "quick and nonjudgmental."[29]

For an RAC to be eligible for aid under the legislation[30] involved in *Roemer*, it must: (1) be a nonprofit private college or university that was established in Maryland prior to July 1, 1970; (2) be accredited by the State Board of Higher Education; (3) maintain one or more earned degree programs, other than seminarian or theological programs, leading to an associate of arts or baccalaureate degree; and (4) submit each new program and each major modification of an existing program to the State Board of Higher Education for its review and recommendation as to the initiation of the new or modified program.[31]

The money available to an RAC under this provision is computed by multiplying the number of full-time students at the RAC (minus those students enrolled in seminarian or theological programs) by a percentage of the state's general fund per full-time student appropriation to a public institution of higher learning.[32] This money is administered by the State Board of Higher Education.[33] The grants remain essentially noncategorical although aid recipients may not use the money payable or goods purchased under this provision for sectarian purposes.[34]

Students attending an RAC are eligible for Maryland's Higher Education Loan Program[35] if the RAC is recognized and approved by the State Board of Higher Education and offers a course of study leading to a postsecondary degree or diploma.[36]

Scholarships and grants awarded under Maryland's Student Financial Assistance law[37] may be used at a Maryland RAC if it is accredited by the State Board of Higher Education.[38] Although this provision does not generally affect the power of any institution over curriculum, grades, and the like, the recipient of a scholarship may not be (1) denied admission to any institution because of his religion, or (2) required to take sectarian religious courses to qualify for a degree.[39]

C. Personnel

In Maryland, it is an unlawful employment practice to fail or refuse to hire or to discharge, or to limit, segregate, or classify any employee or applicant for employment because of his race, color, religion, sex, age, national origin, marital status, or physical or mental handicap unrelated in nature and extent so as to reasonably preclude the performance of the employment.[40] However:

it is not an unlawful employment practice for a school, college, university, or other educational institution or institution of learning to hire and employ employees of a particular religion if the school, college, university, or other educational institution or institution of learning is, in whole or in substantial part, owned, supported, controlled or managed by a particular religion or by a particular religious corporation, association, or society or if the curriculum of the school, college, university, or other educational institution or institution of learning is directed toward the propagation of a particular religion.[41]

This provision is intended to exempt certain religiously oriented educational institutions. For institutions that qualify, religious selectivity of all employees, whatever their function, would be authorized. For some RACs, however, it may be difficult to meet the religious affiliation requirements.

There is some vagueness in these requirements. There is no specific statutory or judicial guidance as to factually how much control by a religion or by a religious organization is sufficient. Is an institution "controlled" by a religion if the institution adheres to the religion's doctrine or must there be a discernible religious entity (e.g., a formal church) in "control"? If the latter, then the "or by a particular religious [organization]" alternative is redundant. Arguably, then, an institution qualifies if it considers itself within the control of the tenets of a particular religion.[42]

Even absent this interpretation, however, the phrasing is probably broad enough to include most RACs. Nonetheless, some institutions may lack a sufficient connection, especially since the legislature did not include the words "or in connection with" between the phrases "owned, supported, controlled or managed by" and "a particular religion." This may have been a mere oversight or an indication that the legislature intended a narrower scope than that of other such statutes.

An RAC will also qualify for this exemption if its curriculum is directed toward the propagation of a particular religion. This would seem to apply only to Bible colleges, seminaries and the like.

There is some uncertainty as to the significance of the repeated use of the phrase "a particular religion." Nonetheless, it would appear that an RAC otherwise within the exemption could prefer an employment applicant of *any* religion, not merely one of the same religion as the institution. Perhaps it was felt useful to restrict the exemption to institutions and employment applicants of identifiable and specific religious affiliation.

In any event, a separate provision allows employment selectivity on the basis of sex, age, religion, national origin, or physical or mental qualification if it is a "bona fide occupational qualification [BFOQ] reasonably necessary to the normal operation of that particular business or enterprise."[43]

This BFOQ authorizes selectivity on all otherwise proscribed bases save race, color, or marital status. RACs will be primarily interested in the religion BFOQ, which will probably not greatly protect them in personnel decisions involving positions other than those of theology or philosophy faculty and perhaps of certain counselors. It is not likely that an RAC would be successful in arguing a right to exercise religious preference in the employment of faculty generally despite its interest in establishing on campus a pervasive presence of faculty of a certain religious persuasion.

The sex BFOQ would be especially helpful in hiring dormitory personnel and *perhaps* some counselors and teachers of courses in women's rights or women's history.

The employment provisions are enforced by the Maryland Commission on Human Relations.[44]

Maryland does have an Executive Order prohibiting state grants to recipients who engage in "discriminatory practices."[45] Presumably, however, it was not meant to apply to situations authorized under either the religious organization exemption provision or the BFOQ provision. Such an application would violate legislative intent.

Maryland's Wage and Hour Law[46] includes within the term "employer" any individual, association, or corporation[47] and, therefore, all RACs. Not included within the law's coverage, however, are those in executive, administrative, or professional capacities[48] and any "individual engaged in the activities of an educational, charitable, religious, or nonprofit organization where the employer-employee relationship does not in fact exist and where the services are rendered . . . gratuitously, with no expectation of gain."[49] Also excluded are certain part-time employees under the age of sixteen[50] or over the age of sixty-two[51] and employees of certain restaurants, cafes, taverns, drive-ins and drug stores.[52]

The law sets a minimum wage and overtime rates for covered employment.

The Maryland Workmen's Compensation Law[53] covers every corporation[54] with one or more employees.[55] Generally, then, RACs are covered. Some of their employees might fall within the exemptions for casual employment,[56] employment by a religious organization for aid or sustenance only,[57] or employment covered by federal worker's compensation laws.[58] The RAC and any exempted employee may, however, jointly elect to come under the compensation provisions of this law by filing with the Workmen's Compensation Commission.[59] RACs must carry insurance or prove financial ability to pay compensation directly to injured employees.[60]

Maryland's Unemployment Insurance Law[61] defines "employer" to include "any employing unit which for some portion of a day has in employment one or more individuals."[62] This would, of course, include RACs. "Employment," within the Act, includes service for a religious, charitable, educational, or other organization excluded from "employment," as that term is defined in the federal Unemployment Tax Act, solely by reason of section 3306(c)(8) of that Act.[63] Service performed in the employ of a religious or educational organization described in section 501(c)(3) of the Internal Revenue Code of 1954,[64] and thereby exempt from federal taxation, is excluded from "employment" as defined in section 3306(c)(8) of the federal Unemployment Tax Act.[65] Thus an RAC is subject to the unemployment insurance legislation if it qualifies for tax exempt status under section 501(c)(3).

Even for RACs within the law, however, the following service is exempted from the definition of employment: (1) service for a church or convention or association of churches, or an organization operated primarily for religious purposes and "operated, supervised, controlled, or principally supported by a church or convention or association of churches"[66] (among RACs, this narrow exception might be available only to seminaries, Bible colleges and the like); (2) service by "a duly ordained, commissioned, or licensed minister of a church" exercising his ministry or by a member of a religious order as duty required by the order;[67] (3) domestic service in a local college club or local chapter of a college fraternity or sorority if, during any calendar quarter in the current or preceding calendar year, the employer pays less than $1,000 to individuals performing the service;[68] (4) service for an employer determined, by the appropriate agency, to be subject to an unemployment insurance system established by act of Congress;[69] (5) service for certain federal tax-exempt organizations if the remuneration is less than fifty dollars;[70] (6) service performed for a school, college, or university by one of its regular students (or by the spouse of such a student if the spouse is advised, at the beginning of the service, that the employment is provided under a program of financial assistance to the student and will not be covered by an unemployment insurance program);[71] and (7) service performed by a student under the age of twenty-two enrolled at a regular nonprofit or public institution of higher education in a full-time program, taken for credit at that institution, which combines academic instruction with work experience.[72] The service must be an integral part of the program, so certified to the employer, and not performed in a "program established for or on behalf of an employer or group of employers."[73] Service within these seven categories is not subject to the Maryland Unemployment Insurance Law.

RACs may also be bound by certain provisions of the Work, Labor and Employment

Law[74] which, *inter alia*, prohibits an employer not covered by the federal Equal Pay Act of 1963 from sex discrimination in the payment of wage or salaries.[75]

D. Students

Maryland has no equal educational opportunity statute. This does not mean that the state has no leverage in urging colleges and universities not to discriminate in their admission policies. Direct financial aid is available to RACs from the state[76] and a 1976 Executive Order of the Governor forbids any state agency to approve a grant of state financial assistance to any recipient who engages in discriminatory practices.[77] Prohibited grounds of discrimination are political or religious opinions or affiliation, marital status, physical or mental handicap, race, color, creed, sex, age, or national origin.[78] The "discriminatory practices" presumably include student admissions as well as employment, since there is no indication that the term applies only to practices outlawed by legislation.[79]

It is not known to what extent this order is enforced against RACs. For instance there must be some discretion in enforcement of the order so as to allow grants to single-sex educational institutions. There is no mention of this nor of the related issue of religious selectivity in student admissions. It is difficult to believe that the Executive Order intended to bar state grants on these bases.

It should be noted that it is *statutorily* provided that recipients of scholarships under the "Student Financial Assistance"[80] title may not be denied admission to any educational institution because of religion or required to take sectarian religious courses to qualify for a degree.[81] (This provision does not apply to loan recipients). Although this legislation apparently denies even RACs the power to use religious selectivity or to require certain religious courses *vis-à-vis* such scholarship recipients, it does not purport to affect admissions or curriculum generally and, indeed, the same section of the law specifically disclaims any intent to affect the control of an institution over its "operation or curriculum" and its "rules and regulation."[82]

A person who, for compensation, engages in the business of soliciting or offering to solicit students in Maryland to enroll in or apply for any course of instruction offered by certain out-of-state postsecondary technical or vocational educational institutions must register with and acquire a permit from the State Board of Higher Education.[83]

E. Facilities

It is unlawful for an owner or operator of a place of public accommodations to deny full use of it to anyone because of race, creed, sex, age, color, national origin, marital status, or physical or mental handicap.[84] This provision would prohibit RACs from exercising any selectivity on the proscribed bases in granting admission to and use of their hotels, public cafeterias, sports arenas, lecture halls, and other such facilities open to the general public. There is no indication that the legislation is intended to affect facilities open only to enrolled students and indirectly, therefore, student admissions.

In Maryland, it is an unlawful housing practice, in the selling or renting of any dwelling, to discriminate against any person on the basis of race, color, religion, sex, national origin, marital status, or physical or mental handicap.[85] An exemption is provided for the dormitories of certain RACs:

Nothing in this subtitle shall prohibit a religious organization, association, or society, or any non-profit institution or organization operated, supervised, or controlled by or in conjunction with a religious organization, association, or society, from limiting the sale, rental, or occupancy of dwellings which it owns or operates for other than a commercial purpose to persons of the same religion, or from giving preferences to such persons, unless membership in such religion is restricted on account of race, color, or national origin.[86]

To come within the exemption, an RAC must qualify as either (1) a religious organization (perhaps Bible college and seminary type RACs would meet this standard) or as (2) a nonprofit organization "operated, supervised, or controlled by *or in conjunction with* a religious organization." Most RACs would seem to qualify under the second standard, especially due to the phrase "or in conjunction with," which seems to establish a very broad affiliation requirement.[87]

In any event, one otherwise qualifying must own or operate the dwellings for other than commercial purposes (RAC housing for students and staff would qualify); the institution may favor only those persons of the same religion; and the religion involved must not limit its membership on account of race, color, or national origin.

Although sex discrimination in the sale or rental of housing is generally prohibited, the law specifies that the sale or rental of dwellings "planned exclusively for, or occupied exclusively by, individuals of one sex"[88] may be limited to that sex. This would authorize any RAC to maintain separation of the sexes in its student housing.

The Maryland Human Relations Commission enforces both the public accommodations law and the housing discrimination law.[89]

It should be noted that institutions practicing discrimination on the basis of political or religious opinion or affiliation, marital status, race, color, sex, creed, age, or national origin in connection with their facilities or their housing may be denied state grants.[90]

Maryland has no occupational safety and health act. It does, however, have a Workmen's Compensation Commission authorized to formulate reasonable rules and regulations regarding conditions of safety and prevention of accidents in occupations covered by the Workmen's Compensation law.[91] Penalties for violation of such rules or regulations[92] and the right of entry for inspection of the premises[93] are provided.

F. State Taxation

No state income tax is imposed on the income of religious, educational, or charitable corporations not organized or conducted for profit as long as no part of the net earnings inures to the benefit of any private stockholder or individual.[94] Virtually all RACs, therefore, are exempt.

Under the Maryland Inheritance Tax law[95] no tax is imposed on property passing, in trust or otherwise, to or for the use of any corporation, trust or cummunity chest, fund or foundation,

organized and operated exclusively for religious, charitable, or educational purposes.[96] To qualify, the organization may not carry on "propaganda or otherwise [attempt] to influence legislation" and no part of its net earnings may inure to the benefit of any private stockholder or individual.[97]

Maryland also imposes an estate tax designed merely to channel to Maryland, by virtue of the credit allowed against the federal estate tax for state death taxes, moneys that would otherwise go to the federal government in estate taxes.[98] This tax, therefore, has no ultimate effect on the amount of death taxes paid.

Maryland does not have a gift tax.

An individual who has itemized his deductions from adjusted gross income on his federal income tax return may choose to deduct the sum of such deductions in determining his taxable income under the Maryland income tax law.[99] Since contributions to nonprofit religious or educational institutions are deductible for federal income tax purposes,[100] contributions to virtually all RACs are deductible under Maryland law.

Exempt from assessment and from state, county, and city ordinary taxation are real and tangible personal property (1) owned by a religious group and used exclusively for public worship (including parsonages and convents) or exclusively for educational purposes[101] and (2) property owned by any nonprofit charitable, benevolent, educational, or literary organization as long as the property is "used exclusively for and necessary for charitable, benevolent, or educational purposes (including athletic programs and activities of an educational institution) in the promotion of the general public welfare of the people of the State."[102]

Section 326 of Maryland's Retail Sales Tax Act[103] exempts from sales tax (1) sales of food for human consumption by churches, religious corporations, schools, and colleges;[104] (2) sales to nonprofit religious, charitable, or educational institutions where "the tangible personal property [involved] is purchased for use in carrying on the work of [the] institution;"[105] (3) sales by a bona fide church or religious organization where made for its general purpose[106] (an exemption available, perhaps, only to RACs like seminaries or Bible colleges); and (4) sales of tickets to places of amusement if, under the Admission and Amusement Tax legislation,[107] these are already taxed.[108] (The Admissions and Amusements Tax law exempts from taxation gross receipts derived from the charges for "admissions or refreshments, service and merchandise where [the] receipts are devoted exclusively to charitable, religious or educational purposes.")[109]

Exempted from taxation under the Maryland Use Tax Law[110] is the use, storage or consumption of tangible personal property specifically exempted from the sales tax by section 326 of the Retail Sales Tax Act.[111]

G. Fund Raising

A "charitable organization" is one "which is or holds itself out to be [*inter alia*] benevolent, educational [or] religious"[112] and which "solicits or obtains contributions solicited from the public for charitable purposes."[113] Such organizations intending to solicit contributions in Maryland (or elsewhere with regard to organizations located in Maryland) must register with the Secretary of State.[114] However, the following are not required to register if they do not employ a professional solicitor[115] *or* if they do not intend to mail out more than 500,000 solicitations in any one year: (1) an educational institution approved by the State Department of Education;[116] (2) a charitable organization not intending to solicit and not actually receiving contributions from the public in excess of $5,000 during the year for which a registration statement would otherwise be required, as long as all fund raising activities are performed by unpaid personnel and no part of its assets or income inures to the benefit of any officer or member of the organization;[117] (3) an organization soliciting only from its members;[118] and (4) a bona fide religious organization, its parent, or an affiliated school, if it has received a declaration of current tax-exempt status from the federal government.[119] Charitable organizations claiming to be exempt must nonetheless make certain simple filings[120] and maintain certain records.[121]

State law permits carnivals, raffles, and/or bingo in many Maryland counties.[122]

H. Miscellaneous

Maryland law provides criminal penalties (and the possibility of an injunction) for persons interrupting the orderly conduct of the affairs of institutions of higher education or molesting or threatening the students or personnel or such institutions.[123]

29. Massachusetts

A. Corporate Status

Corporations may be organized for educational purposes under the Corporations for Charitable Purposes Chapter of the Massachusetts statutes.[1] Securities issued by "any person organized and operated exclusively . . . for . . . religious [or] educational purposes" are exempt from state registration requirements.[2] Consolidation, merger, and dissolution are governed by this chapter if the private college concerned is nonprofit.[3] The Supreme Judicial Court of Massachusetts has ruled that Massachusetts courts should apply the doctrine of *cy pres* when necessary.[4]

A consolidation or merger takes effect when the articles of consolidation or merger are filed with the Secretary of State.[5] A voluntary dissolution takes effect when the Supreme Judicial Court issues a decree of dissolution.[6] A private college may be dissolved involuntarily and its assets liquidated by an order of the Supreme Judicial Court when petitioned by the Attorney General alleging (1) that the corporation failed to file annual financial reports; (2) that the corporation has become inactive; or (3) that dissolution is in the public interest.[7]

The Corporations for Charitable Purposes Chapter provides that the funds of a dissolving charitable corporation be administered for such similar public charitable purposes as the court may determine.[8]

B. State Support

The Massachusetts Constitution does not prohibit the use of commonwealth money for RACs, as do some state constitutions.[9] The Board of Regents of the Department of Education, charged with fostering the quality of higher education within the state, in part by "cooperative arrangements by and between public and independent institutions of higher education,"[10] administers a scholarship program intended to aid all Massachusetts students who qualify scholastically and have financial need, whether at public or independent colleges.[11] The Board is empowered to award a number of such scholarships every year, and the law specifies that not less than ten or more than twenty-five per cent of these shall be awarded to students at commonwealth-supported colleges; thus seventy-five to ninety percent of them could go to students at RACs (or other independent colleges).[12]

Twenty-five such scholarships are guaranteed each year to students in the tenth or eleventh grades, provided that they then complete high school and enroll at an approved institution of higher education in the state, public or private.[13] There are also full or partial scholarships given each year to students who have been Massachusetts residents for at least five years and who are entering medicine, dentistry, or nursing.[14]

The Department of Education offers financial aid to the children of deceased members of the armed forces up to the amount of seven hundred and fifty dollars a year for expenses of tuition, room and board, transportation, and books and supplies needed for their studies; this aid will be given students at a state institution of higher education or one approved in writing by the Chancellor of the Board of Regents.[15]

Given Massachusetts' liberal view of the values of higher education both public and private, an accredited RAC would surely be approved for a student receiving this aid.

The Board of Regents also gives education scholarships to needy high school graduates within the commonwealth entering the field of education and "who wish to attend a college other than the state college at Fitchburg."[16] Such scholarships are limited to five hundred dollars for each individual a year, and may not exceed four years.[17]

The Higher Education Facilities Commission of the Department of Education, which controls and correlates the state plan for its higher educational facilities with the federal department of Health and Human Services, including the receipt of federal aid to education, is required to have seven of its thirteen representatives from private colleges; one of them must represent a private college, operated by a religious society or order, that is "not primarily a theological seminary or institution."[18] The statute creating the Higher Education Facilities Commission specifies that "any reference in this act to a private college, university, junior college or other private institution of higher education shall be deemed to refer only to non-profit institutions."[19] As most RACs are nonprofit, they will be included in all such references.

C. Personnel

Chapter 151B of the Massachusetts Code, dealing with unlawful discrimination in employment, generally prohibits such discrimination on the basis of race, color, religious creed, national origin, sex, age, or ancestry.[20] There are three exceptions to this general rule applicable to RACs.

The first occurs in connection with the definition of "employer" as that term is used in the chapter, which definition specifically alludes to RACs:

The term "employer" does not include a club exclusively social, or a fraternal association or corporation, if such club, association or corporation is not organized for private profit, nor does it include any employer with fewer than six persons in his employ, but shall include the commonwealth and all political subdivisions, boards, departments and commissions thereof. *Nothing herein shall be construed to bar any religious or denominational institution or organization, or any organization operated for charitable or educational purposes, which is operated, supervised or controlled by or in connection with a religious organization, and which limits membership, enrollment, admission, or participation to members of that religion, from giving preference in hiring or employment to members of the same religion.*[21]

The second exception states:

Nothing herein contained shall be construed to bar any religious or denominational institution or organization, or any organization operated for charitable or educational purposes, which is operated, supervised or controlled by or in connection with a religious organization, from limiting admission to or giving preference to persons of the same religion or denomination or from making such selection as is calculated by such organization to promote the religious principles for which it is established or maintained.[22]

At first glance, one is tempted to analogize the first exception to Section 703(e)(2) of Title VII of the Civil Rights Act of 1964 and the second to Section 702 of the same Act. To an extent, such analogies are acceptable in that the first is a narrow exception permitting RACs to give hiring preference to members of the same religion while the second is a broader statement which might allow greater leeway in selection. A closer analysis, however, is necessary.

The first is a hiring exception. Preference in hiring or employment for members of the same religion is allowed if two tests are met. First, the college must be "operated, supervised or controlled by or in connection with a religious organization." Second, the college must be one which "limits membership, enrollment, admission, or participation to members of that religion." Three points must be elaborated upon.

First, the initial "operated, supervised or controlled" test leaves much to be desired.[23] The difficulty is the same as with the "owned, supported, controlled or managed" test in § 703(e)(2) of Title VII: What does it mean? The actual relationships between colleges and religious organizations vary to a large extent. Both a seminary run by the Franciscans and a "Free Christian College" with no formal links to a church but with a defined religious orientation have a legitimate sectarian purpose, but only the seminary may meet the test of being "operated, supervised or controlled by or in connection with a religious organization." The test may be too narrow. In § 703(e)(2) an alternative test is provided: "If the curriculum of such . . . college . . . is directed toward the propagation of a particular religion." While the RAC which meets this test may lose eligibility for public aid on First Amendment grounds,[24] the inclusion of the test does at least broaden the scope for colleges trying to exercise hiring preferences on religious grounds.

The second test provides less difficulty with interpretation but is extremely narrow in focus. The "and which limits membership, enrollment, admission, or participation to members of that religion" requirement is unclear. Would this mean that all students, staff, and faculty of an RAC must be of the same faith, or does it apply only to students? If the language of this test covers students, staff, and faculty, maybe only the Franciscan Seminary can qualify for the exception. It is difficult to believe that this was the legislative intent. The statute could be drafted more carefully so as to include the many institutions which must have been intended to be included, namely, religiously affiliated institutions.

Third, hiring preference is limited to members of the same religion. This means that when selecting a faculty member from a pool of applicants the RAC may favor one of that religion with which it is affiliated, but not another applicant even if the latter's religion somehow makes him better suited for the particular position. A Catholic college seeking a teacher of Judaism could not favor a Jew for the position. Ironically, a Catholic could be favored. In certain cases the religion of an applicant may be a bona fide qualification for the occupation in which case a separate exception exists.[25] However, if the religious characteristic does not rise to a BFOQ in this hypothetical case, the college could not exercise a preference for the Jew on the basis of religion even if it was somehow felt that such a selection would enhance the overall quality or religious nature of the institution.

The second is a broader exception. It is comprised of three parts: a qualification test for the RAC to meet and two kinds of preference which the qualified RAC will be entitled to exercise.

The qualification test, identical to that discussed above with regard to hiring practices, requires that the institution be "operated, supervised or controlled by or in connection with a religious organization."[26] The problems with this phraseology have already been discussed earlier and need not be further elaborated upon.

Once the test is met, the statute allows two things: (1) limiting admission to or giving preference to persons of the same religion or denomination;[27] (2) making such selection as is calculated by such organization to promote the religious principles for which it is established or maintained.[28]

It is difficult to ascertain what the legislature had in mind when using the terminology "limiting admission to or giving preference to." The crux of the matter is the meaning of "admission": hiring *per se* at RACs is discussed in Chapter 151B, Section 1.5,[29] and student admission to RACs is explicitly discussed in Chapter 151C.[30] The term could be used to refer to admission to religiously affiliated clubs, but that would not concern RACs. While the meaning is unclear it is always possible for an RAC to try to fit its selection or hiring policy under this provision's broad net if that policy is ever challenged.

The phrase "giving preference to" is arguably broader since it is conceivably more general than the word "admission." It could be said to include hiring. It is more likely, however, given its placement, that the phrase will be read to mean "giving preference in admission," so that, as indicated earlier, the crux of the matter is the meaning of the word "admission" which, in educational circles at least, commonly refers to *student* selection, not faculty or staff selection.

The language "making such selection" and "promote the religious principles for which it is established or maintained" is reminiscent of Section 702 of Title VII. Section 702 allows an RAC to make religiously oriented "employment" decisions when the work involved is "connected with the carrying on . . . of its activities." The Massachusetts statute refers to "such selection" as will "promote the religious principles for which it is established or maintained." In at least one sense, then, the Massachusetts statute is broad where Section 702 is narrow and vice-versa. The Massachusetts approach would seem to allow *any* selection, i.e., employment, admissions, and the like, as long as it promoted the institution's religious principles. Section 702 limits its applicability to employment decisions but such decisions need only involve work whose performance is connected with the carrying out of its activities.

With regard to decisions involving faculty and staff, however, the Section 702 reference to "employment" decisions seems broader than Massachusetts' reference to "such selection" since the former would include not only appointment but also promotion, tenure and the like, matters not necessarily included in the Massachusetts wording.

It is not easy to determine what the Massachusetts approach will mean in practice. None of the provisions discussed has ever been litigated and the proposed interpretations suffer as a result. Yet it seems fair to speculate that the "such selection" clause will cover both employment and admission decisions (and perhaps even promotion and tenure decisions) so long as the "religious principle" test is also satisfied. It might, therefore, be difficult for an RAC to prefer a janitor applicant of its own faith on the grounds that such selection promotes its religious principles. Nonetheless, this section might be more useful than the first exception, which is geared specifically to employment situations, in regard to matters such as hiring a religious faculty member to teach a subject such as physics or the hiring of a Jew to teach Judaism. If an RAC can argue that keeping a faculty totally of the same faith promotes its foundational religious principles, the statute would allow it to do so. At the same time such argument may not be easy to make, leaving the person not chosen for the physics job with grounds for complaint. As for the hypothetical problem involving the Catholic, Jew and Protestant all otherwise equally qualified to teach Judaism, it would seem that preference could be shown for a member of a religion other than the dominant one at the RAC if such selection

could meet the religious principle test. Meeting that test will depend on the facts in each case.

Finally, the question arises as to whether the RAC can discriminate on a basis other than religion. The answer would seem to be yes, since "such selection" can be made to promote the "religious principles" of the institution. The first exception in Chapter 151B, Section 1.5, clearly states that preference can be exercised in hiring or employment on the basis of religion. However, here we are told that the selection need only be in promotion of the "religious principles" of the institution. Presumably, then, the RAC could discriminate on the basis of race, sex, age, and the like, so long as it can relate that basis to one of its religious principles.

The third exception relates to bona fide occupational qualifications:

It shall be an unlawful practice:

1. For an employer, by himself or his agent, because of the race, color, religious creed, national origin, sex, age, or ancestry of an individual, to refuse to hire or employ or to bar or to discharge from employment such individual or to discriminate against such individual in compensation or in terms, conditions or privileges of employment, unless based upon a bona fide occupational qualification.[31]

The BFOQ exception is reiterated in other parts of the statute with regard to different organizations and practices. For example, labor organizations are prohibited from discriminating against any of their members unless based upon a BFOQ,[32] and employees or employment agencies are prohibited from using any advertisements or from making any inquiries which express any limitation or specification as to race, color, religious creed, national origin, sex, age, or ancestry unless based upon a BFOQ.[33] This broad applicability is similar to that found in the federal statement of the BFOQ exception in section 703 (e)(1) of Title VII, i.e., it applies to employers, employment agency classifications, and labor organization membership. In *The Substance of American Fair Employment Practices Legislation I: Employers*,[34] it is argued that in many states the BFOQ exception is weakened precisely because it is not given such broad applicability. The weakness is due to lack of clarity. In some states the BFOQ may only be stated in terms of advertising or pre-employment practices but not in terms of other employer practices. While it may be possible to infer a general applicability of the exception in these states, the applicability and scope of the exception will be less clear because it is not stated precisely. Massachusetts, by referring directly to employers, overcomes this problem.

Massachusetts does fail to define BFOQ. Section 703 (e)(1) uses the phrase "reasonably necessary to the normal operation of that particular business or enterprise." Massachusetts does extend the exception by applying it to race, color, religious creed, national origin, sex, age, and ancestry whereas § 703 (e)(1) applies it only to religion, sex, and national origin. It is arguable that the broader approach is better because if a qualification does rise to the level of a BFOQ it seems that it should always be respected. For example, in a case where race is such a qualification (for example, the hiring of an actor to play the role of the late Martin Luther King, Jr.) it would seem unfair not to allow discrimination or preference on the basis of race. Hence, the Massachusetts statute's broader applicability in this regard might be more realistic. Perhaps the limits on the doctrine are to make clear that certain characteristics can never be considered a BFOQ.

In any event, this exception will allow RACs to exercise religious preference whenever a BFOQ for the job is involved, although the meaning of BFOQ in regard to a RAC remains uncertain. An RAC should at least realize that unlike the other two exceptions, the Massachusetts BFOQ provisions require a genuine connection between the religious nature of the institution and the job under consideration.

The Massachusetts Commission Against Discrimination (MCAD), statutorily established,[35] has enforcement authorities with regard to the employment legislation discussed here,[36] although its ultimate power is to recommend action to other "agencies and offices of the commonwealth or its political subdivision in aid of . . . [the] policies and purposes [of Chapter 151B]"[37] and to publicize the results of its investigation and research.[38]

Massachusetts does not have any legislation prohibiting employment discrimination against the handicapped *per se.*

Massachusetts guarantees a minimum fair wage to people employed in the commonwealth.[39] The only possible exception is for certain activities said not to constitute an "occupation" under the terms of the minimum wage provision.[40] Excluded from "occupation" is work done "by persons being rehabilitated or trained under rehabilitation or training programs in charitable, educational, or religious institutions, or work by members of religious orders."[41] Hence, while there is no direct exception for RACs, people being rehabilitated or trained there and any faculty or staff members who belong to religious orders are exempted from the minimum wage requirement. For RACs, therefore, this exception is at best indirect and limited.

Massachusetts law provides that anyone employed in an occupation[42] shall receive overtime compensation at one and one half times the normal rate for employment in excess of forty hours per week.[43] However, there is an extensive list of exceptions. Specifically excluded are employees of "a non-profit school or college."[44]

The net result is that generally RACs must pay minimum wages to their employees but need not pay them at an overtime rate.

The Massachusetts Workmen's Compensation Law[45] applies to any corporation[46] with one or more employees.[47] Generally RACs are covered unless some of their employees come within the exception for employment not in the usual course of the employer's business or employment covered by a federal worker's compensation law.[48] Massachusetts has modified the provision for exemptions, providing that a person is conclusively presumed to be covered by the Act even though the employment might otherwise be exempt if: (1) the employee is injured while operating a motor vehicle or other vehicle with the general authorization of the employer; (2) the employee is injured while performing work ordered by the employer that is not in the usual course of the trade, business, or occupation in which the employee is engaged; (3) the employee receives an injury resulting from frostbite, heat exhaustion or sunstroke without having voluntarily assumed increased peril not contemplated by his contract of employment; or (4) the employee is injured by reason of the physical activities of fellow employees in which he does not participate.[49]

RACs may elect to include exempted employees within the coverage of this act by providing coverage for them.[50] Nevertheless, an employee electing to be subject to this act retains the right to sue an employer in court for damages when injured at work, if the employee gives written notice when hired that such a common law right is claimed.[51] RACs must either carry compensation insurance or obtain a self-insurer's license annually from the Division of Industrial Accidents after depositing adequate security with the State Treasurer.[52]

For an RAC to be required to make contributions to unemployment insurance, two conditions must be met. The services being performed must constitute "employment" under the terms of the Employment Security Act and the employer must meet the Act's definition of "employer."

Employment includes services:

in the employ of a religious, charitable, educational or other organization if the service is excluded from "employment" as defined in the Federal Unemployment Tax Act solely by reason of section 3306(c)(8) of the act and is not excluded from "employment" under section six of this chapter.[53]

The section provides that the services must be *excluded* from employment as defined in section 3306(c)(8) of the Federal Employment Tax Act (IRC 3306(c)(8)) and not excluded under section 6 of Chapter 151A. The rule is simpler to state than to put into practice.

First one must look to IRC 3306(c)(8) to see what services are excluded from the federal definition of employment. Under that provision, the following is not included in the definition of employment:

(8) service performed in the employment of a religious, charitable, educational, or other organization described in section 501 (c)(3) which is exempt from income tax under section 501(a);

Section 501(c)(3) includes "corporations . . . or foundations . . . organized and operated exclusively for religious, charitable, or educational purposes." RACs fit the definition given in section 501(c)(3). Hence, services for them

are excluded from the federal definition of employment. The first condition of Chapter 151A, Section 4(d), is met.

The second condition is that the services not be excluded under section 6 of Chapter 151A. Section 6, entitled "Services Not Included in Term 'Employment,' " contains four subsections relevant to RACs. They can be dealt with summarily.

Subsection (k) excludes services performed at a school, college, or university by a person who is enrolled there as a full-time student, or by the spouse of such student if the spouse is advised that the employment is provided as a means of financial assistance to the student and that the employment is not covered by unemployment insurance. Work-study employment is also excluded.

Subsection (r) excludes services performed in the employ of a church or convention or association of churches, or an organization which is operated primarily for religious purposes *and* which is operated, supervised, controlled, or principally supported by a church or convention or association of churches. RACs which fit this definition are exempted from unemployment taxes. Very few, however, will be able to qualify under such a narrow exclusion. Furthermore, since the term "educational institution" is not used in the definition, it is unlikely that the legislature had RACs in mind when drafting the statute. Hence, RACs probably are not excluded by way of this subsection.

Subsection (s) excludes services of an ordained minister or priest.

Subsection (j) excludes:

services performed in any calendar quarter in the employ of any organization exempt from income tax under section 501(a) of the Federal Internal Revenue Code, other than an organization described in section 401(a) of said Code, or exempt from income tax under section 521 of said Code, if the remuneration for such service is less than fifty dollars.

This means that services performed in any calendar quarter for an RAC (501(a) tax-exempt organization), in which the remuneration is less than fifty dollars, are excluded from the definition of employment. Sections 401(a) and 521 deal with pension plans and tax-exempt farm cooperatives respectively and are not of concern here. The gist of this is that if the services for an RAC are remunerated at less than fifty dollars for a three month period the RAC need not pay unemployment tax on those services.

Under these four subsections, most employment at RACs, such as that of staff and faculty, is not excluded under section 6 of Chapter 151A. Hence, the second condition of section 4A(d) of that Chapter is met.

Services at RACs are, therefore, generally included in the Employment Security Act's definition of employment because they are excluded from the definition of employment in IRC § 3306(c)(8) and are not excluded from the definition of employment in Section 6 of Chapter 151A. (Under the four subsections of Section 6, however, several specific types of employment at RACs are in fact excluded from the definition of employment.)

The second requirement of the Employment Security Chapter is that the employer be within the official definition of "employer."[54] The applicable definition clearly covers RACs for which, moreover, no exceptions are stated. (The requirements deal with numbers of employees and other such terms.)

The conclusion is that RACs meet the Chapter's definition of employer and that with certain enumerated exceptions most services at RACs meet the Chapter's definition of employment. Hence, for all employees performing these services, RACs are required to make contributions to unemployment insurance plans.

D. Students

Chapter 151C of the Massachusetts General Law proscribes discriminatory educational practices. While admission discrimination based on religious qualifications is generally included in the proscription, an exception is made for religiously affiliated colleges. There are three sections of Chapter 151C which are relevant.

The first[55] follows the approach of the unfair employment practices statute,[56] i.e., the RAC exception is carved out within the definition of the terms used in the Chapter:

The term "educational institution" means any institution for instruction or training, including but not limited to secretarial schools, business schools, academies, colleges, universities, primary and secondary schools, which accepts applications for admission from the public generally and which is not in its nature distinctly private, except that nothing herein shall be deemed to prevent a religious or denominational educational institution from selecting its students excusively from adherents or members of such religion or denomination or from giving preference in such selection to such adherents or members.[57]

The second is the definition of "religious or denominational educational institution":

The term "religious denominational educational institution" shall include any educational institution, whether operated separately, or as a department of, or school within the university, and which is operated, supervised or controlled by religious or denominational organizations, or in which the courses of instruction lead primarily to the degree of bachelor, master or doctor of theology, and which has so certified to the commission that it is so operated, supervised or controlled.[58]

The third states that it shall be an unfair educational practice, among other things:

[t]o cause to be made any written or oral inquiry concerning the race, religion, color or national origin of a person seeking admission, except that a religious or denominational educational institution which certified to the commission that it is a religious or denominational educational institution may inquire as to the religious or denominational affiliations of applicants for admission.[59]

The religious discrimination exception provided for religious or denominational educational institutions is limited in that the RAC can give preference only to students of the same religion with which it is affiliated. Although in most cases RACs are primarily interested in giving preference to such students, it is difficult to argue that this is a sufficient basis for the statutory limitation imposed by Massachusetts. There are legitimate reasons for which an RAC may prefer students who are members of a different religion, but will not be able to exercise such preference because of the narrow statutory exception provided.

However, counsel for the RAC should keep in mind the broad language of Chapter 151B, Section 4.15, discussed above.[60] Its language ("or from making such selection as is calculated by such organization to promote the religious principles for which it is established or maintained") might be construed to allow preference for students of other religions.

The definition of religious or denominational educational institution,"[61] which deserves careful consideration, has three parts. The first and second are qualification tests and the third is a requirement of certification by the Massachusetts Commission Against Discrimination. The second and third parts are fairly clear and should not present too much difficulty. An RAC (or an appropriate religiously affiliated division of a university) whose program leads primarily to a theology degree is easy to distinguish. Likewise, the requirement of certification is clearly stated.

The first test might prove more difficult. At first glance, it seems the same as the "operated, supervised or controlled" test which has been discussed in some detail in connection with fair employment practices.[62] The difference is that the fair employment practice test is "operated, supervised or controlled by or in connection with a religious organization,"[63] whereas here it is "operated, supervised or controlled by religious or denominational organizations."[64] The intensity of the affiliation for the employment exemption is less demanding than that for the student admissions exemption since the language "by or in connection with" does not demand as close a connection between the RAC and the religious organization as does the word "by."

There is a second difference in language. The employment exemption says "by or in connection with a *religious organization*"[65] and the educational exemption definition says "by *religious or denominational organizations.*"[66] This difference is not as significant as the first because the term "religious" is broad enough to include "denominational." Hence, the inclusion of "or denominational" in the educational admissions exemption at most provides greater specificity. In fact, the use of "denominational" could be regarded as narrowing the scope of applicability even though it is used in conjunction with the broader term "religious." Therefore, the educational admissions exception for RACs is narrower than the one governing their employment policies.

The policy behind this difference between education and employment apparently is that the state of Massachusetts is less concerned with RACs exercising employment preferences than student admission preferences. Although the policy's strength is only as great as the language difference between the two sections, there may be solid reasoning behind such a policy. For example, the state may think it more important that young people be given equal opportunity to all types of education than to have all people have such opportunity to be employed at RACs. Hence, the state makes it easier for RACs to qualify for the employment exception than for the student admission exception. An interesting problem would arise if an RAC ever qualified for the employment but not the educational exception. The likelihood of this happening is only as great as the likelihood of the courts drawing a line to indicate where the language difference between the two exceptions lies.

The educational institution must certify to the Massachusetts Commission Against Discrimination[67] that it is an organization qualified for the exception.[68]

Massachusetts does not have any legislation prohibiting admissions discrimination against the handicapped *per se*. Although Massachusetts does have specific legislation proscribing discrimination on the basis of blindness (or use of a guide dog) with regard to admission to educational institutions[69] or deafness with regard to public accommodations,[70] it has none proscribing discrimination on the basis of alcoholism or drug addiction. An RAC, therefore, on the basis of its religious teachings (or on any other basis) may "discriminate" against alcoholics or drug addicts (or those using alcohol or drugs).

The Massachusetts Commission Against Discrimination (MCAD) is also charged with the enforcement of Chapter 151C, "Fair Education Practices."[71] The Commission may issue a cease and desist order to institutions it finds to have engaged in an unfair educational practice.[72]

E. Facilities

Massachusetts' Public Accommodations statute,[73] which prohibits discrimination based on religious sect, creed, class, race, color, denomination, sex, nationality, deafness, blindness, or any physical or mental disability, must be considered in two respects. The first is whether it might apply to an RAC's admissions policy. The second is its applicability to facilities owned and operated by an RAC.

Before 1978 the statute contained a provision which read: "Provided, however, that no place shall be deemed to be a place of public accommodation, resort or amusement which is owned or operated by a club or institution whose products or facilities or services are available only to its members and their guests nor by any organization operated for charitable or educational purposes." The 1978 amendment removed this exception for educational institutions.[74]

The only case construing the exemption as it stood is *Crawford v. Robert L. Kent, Inc.*,[75] in which it was decided that a dance school run for profit did not qualify for the exception. At issue in the case was the legality of the school's decision not to admit a student on the basis of race. This case indicates that before 1978 there was an exception for educational institutions in regard to student admissions. The removal of the exception suggests that educational institutions are no longer exempt and must not therefore discriminate in admissions on any basis enumerated in the public accommodations statute. The problem, however, is that Massachusetts has a chapter dealing specifically with discrimination in admissions,[76] and nothing in the post-1978 version of the accommodations statute indicates that religious or educational organizations fall within the definition of public accommodations. Hence, it seems highly unlikely that RACs or any other educational institution will fall within this statute in regard to admissions even though prior existence of an exception for them would tend to indicate otherwise. It seems that for RACs, admissions policy with regard to discrimination is contained in the Fair Educational Practice Chapter and not in the public accommodations provision.

The second question with regard to the public accommodations law is whether it covers accommodations owned by RACs, e.g., theaters, stadia, and the like. Perhaps the pre-1978 exception applied to these as well. The *Crawford* case does not address the question of an RAC exception in regard to admission to such accommodations. Since the exception has been deleted, the statute prohibits discrimination at places such as theaters, stadia, and the like, and has no RAC exception. Hence, under Massachusetts law RACs cannot exercise preferences in use of facilities owned by them which are otherwise within the state's definition of public accommodations.

The public accommodations section is a criminal statute and thus is not enforcible by the Massachusetts Commission Against Discrimination.

Massachusetts does not have a "Fair Housing" act *per se*. Provisions prohibiting discrimination in housing are inserted in the same section which deals with employment discrimination; specific subsections govern housing.[77]

No provisions in the chapter specifically exempt RACs from the anti-discrimination subsections in the same way that Section 807 of the Civil Rights Act of 1968[78] exempts them from federal provisions. However, there is a general catchall subsection containing numerous provisions. The one with which we are concerned has been discussed previously in regard to employment and is equally applicable here:

Nothing herein contained shall be construed to bar any religious or denominational institution or organization, or any organization operated for charitable or educational purposes, which is operated, supervised or controlled by or in connection with a religious organization, from limiting admission to or giving preference to persons of the same religion or denomination or from making such selection as is calculated by such organization to promote the religious principles for which it is established or maintained.[79]

The terminology of this provision is discussed in some detail in the employment practices section.[80] Its placement at the end of the section indicates its applicability in all situations covered by the section: housing and employment. However, the real problem is the extent to which this section will be applicable to the many types of housing facilities an RAC could own. Moreover, the phrase "from making such selection as is calculated by such organization to promote the religious principles for which it is established or maintained" would tend to allow a wide range of preferences, e.g., segregation of students by sex in dormitories or student apartments. The actual scope of the statute is unknown but the language supports broad applicability.

Section 4 of Chapter 151B and Section 1 of Chapter 151C are referred to in a 1964 Attorney General's opinion[81] dealing with a private person's allegedly discriminatory housing practice. It states: "The authority of religious institutions to give preference to their own adherents . . . has not been impaired by . . . [anti-discrimination laws.]" While this quotation will not help clear up the scope of the RAC exception in housing or other practices, at least it is an official recognition of the existence of the exception.

The Massachusetts Commission Against Discrimination (MCAD) is also charged with the enforcement of the housing provisions.[82]

Massachusetts does not have any statute explicitly entitled "Occupational Safety and Health Act." There is, however, a relevant provision empowering the Department of Labor and Industries to investigate places of employment in order to determine what safety devices or other reasonable means of prevention of accidents should be adopted and to establish rules and regulations to accomplish these goals.[83] For purposes of the section, employment means any trade, occupation, or branch or industry and the service of any particular employee; a place of employment is all-inclusive. There is a statutory definition of an employer and an employee in the anti-discrimination section of the statute;[84] there is no such definition in the safety section. On the assumption that the definition found in the earlier part of the statute governs the safety section, RACs should be thought of as included within the scope of this legislation.

F. State Taxation
Income Tax

Any nonprofit corporation which is exempt from federal income taxation under section 501 of the Internal Revenue Code is also exempt from state income taxation.[85] The income of virtually all RACs, therefore, is not taxed in Massachusetts.

Inheritance, Estate and Transfer Taxes

Transfers to RACs are exempt from the Massachusetts' inheritance tax.[86]

Massachusetts imposes an estate tax designed merely to channel to Massachusetts, by virtue of the credit allowed against the federal estate tax for state death taxes, moneys that would otherwise go to the federal government in estate taxes.[87] This tax has no ultimate effect on the amount of death taxes paid.

Massachusetts has no gift tax.

Deductions or Credits for Gifts to RACs

Banks, trust companies,[88] and corporations are permitted to deduct the total of their federal deductions in computing their Massachusetts' state income tax.[89] Since contributions to RACs are deductible for federal tax purposes,[90] a similar deduction is provided under the state income tax scheme.

There appears to be no parallel deduction afforded to individuals who contribute to RACs.

Real, Personal and Intangible Property Taxes

Massachusetts exempts a charitable organization's real and personal property from taxation. "Charitable organization" is defined as "a literary, benevolent, charitable, or scientific institution or temperance society."[91] While "educational institution" is not specifically exempted, a later qualification of this charitable exemption seems to indicate that certain nonprofit educational institutions were intended to fall within this property tax exemption:

Real and personal property of an *educational institution coming within the foregoing description of a charitable organization* which is occupied or used wholly or principally as residences for officers of such institutions and which is not part of or contiguous to real estate which is the principal location of such institution shall not be exempt.[92]

Except for such residential property, therefore, the real and personal property of virtually all RACs is exempt from taxation.

Sales, Use or Meal Taxes

Sales to RACs and to other organizations which are exempt under section 501(c)(3) of the Internal Revenue Code are exempt from the Massachusetts sales tax when (1) the property sold is used to conduct the organization's exempt enterprise; (2) the organization has received a certificate from the Commissioner stating that it is entitled to such an exemption; and (3) the seller keeps a record of exempt sales.[93]

Also exempt from the state sales tax are (1) the sale of building material and supplies to an organization to construct, reconstruct, alter, remodel, or repair any building held or used exclusively for an exempt organization's exempt purposes;[94] (2) the sale of books required for instructional purposes in an educational institution; (3) the sale of materials used in religious worship; and (4) the publications of exempt organizations.[95]

Casual and isolated sales *by* RACs are tax-exempt, but any business resembling a retail operation is not generally exempt.[96]

Although the state meals tax has been repealed,[97] only meals served in primary and secondary private nonprofit schools are specifically exempted from sales tax.[98] Thus meals served at RACs are not tax-exempt.

Sales to RACs are not subject to the Massachusetts use tax since any sale exempt from sales tax is likewise exempt from the use tax.[99]

The Room Occupancy Tax does not apply to lodging accommodations at religious, charitable, educational, or philanthropic institutions.[100] Therefore, RACs are also exempt from this tax.

G. Fund Raising

Massachusetts law generally requires that charitable organizations[101] which intend to solicit funds from the public register with the Division of Public Charities in the Department of the Attorney General.[102] However, exceptions are granted to certain organizations, including:

(1) any religious corporation, trust or organization incorporated or established for religious purposes, [or] any agency or organization incorporated or established for charitable, hospital or educational purposes and engaged in effectuating one or more of such purposes, which is affiliated with, operated by, or supervised or controlled by a corporation sole or other religious corporation, trust or organization incorporated or established for religious purposes, [or] any other religious agency or organization which serves religion by the preservation of religious rights and freedom from persecution or prejudice or by fostering religion, including the moral and ethical aspects of a particular religious faith; (2) educational institutions which by ruling of the United States Treasury Department are exempt from federal income taxation.[103]

An RAC could be within either of these two exemptions. Although the second one is clear cut, the first contains interesting language: "which is affiliated with, operated by, or supervised or controlled by a corporation sole or other religious corporation." This definition of qualified organizations is much broader than the definition of organizations qualified for exceptions to the employment, education, and housing anti-discrimination statutes, under which RACs must meet the "operated, supervised or controlled" test to be excepted.[104] In particular, the language "affiliated with" used here suggests the adequacy of even minimal connections with the religious organization. It is safe to say that any RAC which meets the definitional requirements for the discrimination exceptions will also meet the requirements for this registration exception. Obviously, the policy of the state is that it should be easier for RACs to be exempted from the registration section than from the anti-discrimination sections.

Most other sections in the chapter are concerned with organizations which, unlike RACs, are required to register. For example, use of professional fund raisers by registered charities is carefully regulated. The only other section which is possibly applicable to RACs prohibits certain fraudulent practices of solicitors.[105]

Although Beano and lotteries are generally proscribed,[106] two exceptions must be dealt with.

The first[107] allows conduct of "raffles" and "bazaars" (but not Beano) by certain organizations. As the statute allows only these two, their definitions are very important for any RAC considering such methods of fund raising:

"Raffle" [is] an arrangement for raising money by the sale of tickets, certain among which, as determined by chance after the sale, entitle the holders to prizes.

"Bazaar" [is] a place maintained by the sponsoring organization for disposal by means of chance of one or both of the following types of prizes: (1) merchandise, of any value, (2) cash awards, not to exceed five dollars each.[108]

Not only does the law limit the definition of the type of activity authorized, but those who may sponsor them:

No raffle or bazaar shall be promoted, operated or conducted by any person or organization, unless the same is sponsored and conducted exclusively by (a) a veteran's organization chartered by the Congress of the United States or included in clause (12) of section 5 of chapter forty of the General Laws; (b) a church or religious organization, (c) a fraternal or fraternal benefit society; (d) an educational or charitable organization; (e) a civic or service club or organization; and (f) clubs or organizations organized and operated exclusively for pleasure, recreation and other nonprofit purposes, no part of the net earnings of which inures to the benefit of any member or shareholder.[109]

Since any RAC would clearly fall within (d), it is useless to speculate on its possible inclusion within (b) or even (f).

The statute's definitions of "raffle" and "bazaar" are augmented by a 1969 Attorney General's opinion that the statutory definitions do not allow certain activities such as the sale of lottery tickets called "Lucky Seven," "Club Vegas," or similar tickets.[110] The opinion need not be discussed in detail, but any RAC considering such activities should be sure they are within the definition of those practices declared legal.

Beano is a separate activity excepted from prosecution[111] when conducted under a license issued by the Director of the State Lottery.[112] Among the types of organizations authorized to conduct the game, an RAC could be included only as a "religious organization under the control of or affiliated with an established church of the Commonwealth."[113] Educational organizations are not specifically mentioned and it seems likely that the religious organizations the legislature had in mind were such things as parish clubs, societies, and the like.

30. Michigan

A. Corporate Status

Some RACs in Michigan have been created by specific statutes,[1] but the more typical mode of incorporation is that provided for in the educational corporations statute.[2] It is also possible for an RAC to exist as a non-incorporated private educational institution.[3]

Classification of an educational corporation is based on the size of capitalization and whether it has a religious affiliation.[4] Before being authorized to file articles of incorporation, an educational corporation must present to the Michigan Corporations and Securities Commission a statement of qualification from the State Board of Education.[5] An RAC must include in its articles of incorporation the name of the religious denomination with which it is affiliated.[6] The State Board of Education is authorized to inspect every educational corporation at least once every three years and to file a report of all matters pertaining to the school's condition, management, and instruction.[7] If the school is found not to be complying with provisions of the Act, notice will be served on it to remedy the defects. Defects not corrected within a reasonable time could subject the school to legal dissolution proceedings.[8] Each corporation must submit an annual report to the State Board of Education.[9]

Specific statutes have dissolved individual nonprofit educational corporations.[10] Corporations possess the general power to dissolve[11] according to the methods provided by statute.[12] In addition, Michigan courts will apply the doctrine of *cy pres* when necessary.[13]

The Attorney General is a necessary party to any action for dissolution before the circuit courts,[14] and notice must be provided to him by registered mail at least forty-five days prior to the filing of any document related to the dissolution.[15] The Attorney General may consent to dissolution without court proceedings,[16] in which case articles of dissolution are filed with the Corporations and Securities Commission.[17] Shares of a nonprofit corporation are not transferable absent an express provision in the corporation's bylaws.[18] Upon the dissolution of a nonprofit corporation, none of the assets may be diverted to any member, trustee, or officer.[19] Assets which are not distributed according to the nonprofit corporation's articles of incorporation or some other provision of law escheat to the state.[20]

B. State Support

Michigan's constitution provides:

No money shall be appropriated or drawn from the treasury for the benefit of any religious sect or society, theological or religious seminary; nor shall property belonging to the state be appropriated for any such purpose.[21]

Although this provision could be construed to prohibit state financial assistance to an RAC, on the theory that the RAC is of benefit to a religious sect or society, state courts have not invoked this clause to bar such aid.[22] Since most RACs provide a general education which benefits not only the churches or religious bodies with which they are affiliated, but also their students and the society into which their alumni graduate, aid to RACs and especially to their students[23] should be regarded as permissible under the Michigan constitution.

Most RACs in Michigan are eligible for direct state aid. The Higher Education Facilities Authority Act[24] gives the Michigan Higher Education Facilities Authority[25] the power to loan money to educational institutions for the purpose of assisting in the acquisition, construction, or alteration of educational facilities.[26] The statute defines an eligible institution to include any private or nonpublic, nonprofit educational institution within the state authorized by law to provide a program of education beyond the high school level.[27]

Another requirement, especially relevant to RACs, is an anti-discrimination covenant:

The authority shall require that use of educational facilities assisted under this act shall be . . . open to all regardless of race, *religion*, color or national origin, and that contractors and subcontractors engaged in the construction or alteration of such facilities shall provide an equal opportunity for employment, without discrimination as to race, religion, color or national origin. The educational institution to which any educational loan is made shall covenant with the authority that the non-discrimination provision shall be enforced.[28]

Since RACs may, under other provisions of Michigan law, exercise religious preference in student admissions,[29] a legitimate exercise of such religious preference should not be deemed a breach of the anti-discrimination covenant. To be found in breach of this covenant, an RAC should have to be engaged in irrational, invidious discrimination based on race, religion, color, or national origin.

The other source of institutional assistance available to RACs in Michigan provides payment to approved nonpublic, nonprofit institutions of higher education located within Michigan for earned degrees conferred upon Michigan residents.[30] The term "approved" is not defined in the provisions of this act. To qualify for payments under the act, however, an educational institution must "[a]dmit students without regard to race, *religion*, color, or

national origin."[31] This requirement is broader in effect than the anti-discrimination clause in the facilities act because any religious preference with regard to student admissions would apparently preclude any reimbursement under the act. Still, it could be argued that only unlawful religious discrimination was meant to be barred, not that permitted by law.

A general provision states: "To be eligible to receive funds under this act, a nonpublic institution must be eligible for state reimbursement under the provisions of the constitution of the United States and the state constitution of 1963."[32] This provision would bar aid to purely religious aspects of campus life. For example, the act excludes degrees conferred in "theology or divinity" from the reimbursement computation.[33] Similarly, the state legislature clearly would not finance the construction of a building to be used exclusively for religious worship, and it probably could not finance the training of candidates for the ordained ministry.

In addition to providing two forms of institutional assistance, Michigan provides assistance to students attending RACs in the form of loans and loan guarantees, and tuition and scholarship grants. The Michigan Higher Education Assistance Authority (MHEAA)[34] is empowered to guarantee one-hundred percent of the principal and interest of a loan of money to persons attending or accepted to attend postsecondary educational institutions to assist them in meeting educational expenses.[35] The Higher Education Loan Authority Act[36] creates an Authority consisting of members of the MHEAA[37] empowered to loan money to students who are residents of the state and attend an "eligible institution,"[38] which clearly includes all RACs.[39] No special restrictions are placed on RACs or RAC students.

The Authority also administers the State Competitive Scholarship Program.[40] Scholarships are available to students[41] who will enroll in an eligible postsecondary institution in Michigan. It is specified that the applicant shall not be restricted in the choice of an approved institution or of a course of study, although students enrolled in courses of study leading to religious degrees are ineligible.[42] Although the provision is not as clearly drafted as that authorizing loans, it is clear from actual practice that students attending RACs are eligible for scholarship assistance as well.

Michigan law[43] also provides for student tuition grants:

Tuition grants are established by the state to foster the pursuit of higher education by resident students enrolled in private, nonprofit colleges or universities in the state, which have filed with the board of education a certificate of assurance of compliance with title 6 of the civil rights act of 1964 . . . , whose instructional programs are not comprised solely of instructional programs in sectarian instruction or religious worship and which are otherwise approved by the state board of education.[44]

Since the curriculum of RACs is not "comprised *solely* of instructional programs in sectarian instruction or religious worship," RAC students are eligible for the grants as long as they meet the other statutory requirements.[45] Under the Act, a grant may not be made "to a student who is enrolled in a course of study leading to a degree in theology, divinity, or religious education or who is a religious aspirant."[46] A student receiving a state competitive scholarship may not receive a tuition grant concurrently.[47] If a student receives other scholarship awards from a private, nonprofit educational institution covering full tuition and fees, he is similarly ineligible for a tuition grant.[48]

Another act[49] gives the MHEAA the administrative authority to make a tuition differential grant to a full-time or part-time resident student enrolled in a private, nonprofit college located in Michigan if the school is approved by the State Board of Education, the instructional programs of the school "are not comprised solely of sectarian instruction or religious worship," and the school is incorporated under Michigan law[50] or is subject to the law without formal organization under the incorporation act.[51] A student is ineligible for a grant if he is "enrolled in a program of study leading to a degree in theology or divinity."[52] Grants are made to the institution on behalf of the student and credited to the individual student's account for the purposes of tuition and fees.[53]

The Legislative Merit Award Program Act[54] empowers the MHEAA to award merit scholarships to eligible Michigan students[55] who enroll in recognized postsecondary educational institutions.[56] The MHEAA is authorized to promulgate implementing rules.[57]

C. Personnel

The Elliot-Larsen Civil Rights Act[58] of Michigan forbids an employer to:

fail or refuse to hire, or recruit, or otherwise discriminate against an individual with respect to employment, compensation, or a term, condition, or privilege of employment, because of religion, race, color, national origin, age, sex, height, weight, or marital status.[59]

The comprehensive definition of an employer as any person who has four or more employees[60] clearly includes all RACs. The prohibition of discrimination on the basis of sex also includes a ban on employment discrimination related to "pregnancy [and] childbirth."[61] Any Michigan employer, however, may exercise a preference for a woman who has not undergone a nontherapeutic abortion, defined as one "not intended to save the life of the mother."[62] The Act is administered by the State Civil Rights Commission.[63]

RACs in Michigan may exercise religious preference if religion is a bona fide occupational qualification (BFOQ). Like section 703(e)(1) of the federal civil rights statute, section 208 of the Michigan statute provides a BFOQ exception if the employer determines that the BFOQ is "reasonably necessary to the normal operation of the business or enterprise."[64] Unlike the federal statute, which limits the BFOQ exception to qualifications based on an employee's religion, sex, or national origin, the Michigan statute includes these three classifications and adds three more, age, height, and weight. The RAC may ground its employment policy upon the BFOQ exception without obtaining prior approval from the Commission; but if the policy should be challenged before the Commission by a complainant, the RAC would have the burden of establishing that its preference is "reasonably necessary."[65] The term "reasonably necessary" is not defined in the act. An RAC probably could rely on the BFOQ exception to prefer faculty members employed to teach theology, religious studies, philosophy, and other matters related to the religious purpose of the institution. The language "reasonably necessary to the normal operation" might even include positions such as dean of students, counselor, and dormitory and library directors if part of their responsibilities requires decisions consistent with principles espoused by the religious body with which the RAC is affiliated, or if those persons are engaged in activity that is important to the proper religious formation of the students.

Although the statute allows RACs to exercise religious preference, at least in some of their job categories, it apparently prohibits RACs from including in any notice or advertisement concerning such positions its intention to assert religious preference.[66] On its face, it appears also to prohibit an RAC from making any inquiry concerning the religion of a prospective employee, or from making a record of a preference based on religion.[67] However, because this provision of the statute incorporates Title VII of the federal civil rights act by reference,[68] an RAC in Michigan is probably not barred by state law from doing any of the three things mentioned above, all of which seem permissible under applicable federal law.

The Michigan Handicappers' Civil Rights Act prohibits discrimination on the basis of "a determinable physical or mental characteristic . . . or the history of the characteristic which may result from disease, injury, congenital condition of birth, or functional disorder" unless it is related to the individual's ability to perform a job or utilize the facilities.[69] The statutory definition of a "mental characteristic" is limited to mental retardation.[70] Arguably, drug addiction and alcohol abuse are "determinable physical characteristics which result from diseases." But it is not clear that the legislature intended to include the consumption of alcohol and the use of illicit drugs among handicaps in this statute, for both the consumption of alcohol and the use of illicit drugs can seriously endanger the health and safety of other persons on a campus, and they can render one unable to perform one's job and incapable of using the campus facilities.[71] For these reasons, Michigan law probably does not impede an RAC

from declining to hire or from terminating an employee who, contrary to the ethical standards of the church with which the college is affiliated, consumes alcoholic beverages or uses illicit drugs.

The Michigan Worker's Disability Compensation Act of 1969[72] applies to every corporation[73] with one or more employees.[74] There is no specific exemption for RACs. Nor are there any current exemptions that apply to any employees of an RAC.[75] If, however, an RAC had exempt employees, the RAC could elect to have them come within the provisions of this act by specifically including them within the coverage of its compensation insurance policy.[76] RACs must either carry insurance,[77] pay premiums to the State Accident Fund[78] or receive authorization to become a self-insurer by furnishing the Director of the Workmen's Compensation Bureau[79] with satisfactory proof of financial ability to compensate injured employees directly.[80]

The Michigan Employment Security Act[81] broadly defines employment as "service . . . performed for remuneration or under any contract for hire."[82] It specifies that services performed for a religious, educational, or charitable organization, which are excluded from the definition of "employment in the Federal Unemployment Tax Act solely due to section 3306(c)(8)," constitute employment.[83] This coverage does not apply to the following categories of services performed in the employ of RACs and other nonprofit organizations: (1) services performed for a church or for an association of churches;[84] (2) services performed for an organization run primarily for religious purposes and controlled by a church or by an association of churches;[85] and (3) services performed by ordained ministers or by members of religious orders in the exercise of their duties.[86] Other exclusions exempt the following services from consideration as "employment": (1) services performed for a school or college by its regularly enrolled students[87] or their spouses;[88] (2) services performed by a student under the age of twenty-two, at an accredited nonprofit or public educational institution in a full-time program, taken for credit and combining academic instruction and work experience;[89] (3) domestic service for a college club or chapter of a college fraternity or sorority;[90] and (4) service for which compensation is payable under a system set up by an act of Congress.[91] The statute also excludes from coverage services performed for tax-exempt organizations,[92] if the remuneration paid is less than $50.00 in any calendar quarter.[93]

Nonprofit organizations may elect to make payments in lieu of contributions. To take advantage of this option, an organization must fit the definition of nonprofit organization in section 501(c)(3) of the Internal Revenue Code and qualify as tax-exempt under section 501(a) of the Code.[94] The election is effective for a period of two years upon filing written notice with the Michigan Employment Security Commission.[95] Required payments are equal to the amount of regular benefits plus one-half the amount of extended benefits paid.[96] Organizations not otherwise subject to the provisions of the statute may elect to participate in the program for a period of two years.[97]

Michigan's Employee Right to Know Act[98] permits an employee to review his personnel record,[99] obtain a copy of its contents,[100] and request corrections of information.[101] The act prescribes the information which may be contained in the personnel records.[102] The personnel record covered by the act does not include "[r]ecords maintained by an educational institution which are directly related to a student and are considered to be educational records under section 513(a) of Title V of the Family Educational Rights and Privacy Act of 1974, 20 U.S.C. 123g,"[103] also known as the Buckley Amendment.

Michigan labor law sustains the right of employees to organize and engage in collective bargaining.[104] RACs are not exempted from the act.

Under Michigan's Minimum Wage Law of 1964,[105] the term "employer" includes RACs.[106] The statute provides no exemption for RACs. With respect to overtime pay, the act provides that "an employee shall receive compensation at not less than 1 ½ times the regular rate at which the employee is employed for employment in a workweek in excess of 40 hours."[107]

RACs are likewise subject to the Wages and Fringe Benefits Act.[108] An employer must pay fringe benefits[109] to an employee in accordance with the terms set forth in the employment contract, and must comply with pay period schedules.[110] The Act also requires the employer to maintain payroll records which indicate total hours worked and total wages paid to his employees.[111]

An RAC is an employer for the purposes of the Youth Employment Standards Act[112] if it employs a minor person under eighteen years of age.[113] The Act does not prohibit a minor from engaging in "[e]mployment by a school, academy, or college in which the student minor 14 years of age or older is enrolled."[114]

Under the Youth Employment Clearinghouse Act,[115] private entities receiving state funds, which are sponsoring or directing youth employment programs,[116] must make "data and other nonconfidential information" available to the State Department of Labor's Youth Employment Clearinghouse.[117]

D. Students

Michigan's Civil Rights Act contains an article prohibiting certain discriminatory acts by an "educational institution." The broad statutory definition of an "educational institution" — a public or private institution, including a college, university, and professional school[118] — covers all RACs. With respect to student admissions, the article states:

An educational institution shall not:

(b) Exclude, expel, limit, or otherwise discriminate against an individual seeking admission as a student or an individual enrolled as a student in the terms, conditions, or privileges of the institution, because of *religion*, race, color, national origin, or sex.

(c) For purposes of admission only, make or use a written or oral inquiry or form of application that elicits or attempts to elicit information concerning the *religion*, race, color, national origin, age, sex, or marital status of a person, except as permitted by rule of the commission or as required by federal law, rule, or regulation, or pursuant to an affirmative action program.

(d) Print or publish or cause to be printed or published a catalog, notice, or advertisement indicating a preference, limitation, specification, or discrimination based on the *religion*, race, color, national origin, or sex of an applicant for admission to the educational institution.

(e) Announce or follow a policy of denial or limitation through a quota or otherwise of educational opportunities of a group or its members because of *religion*, race, color, national origin, or sex.[119] (emphasis added.)

The provisions related to religion, however, do not apply to a "religious educational institution or an educational institution operated, supervised, or controlled by a religious institution or organization which limits admission or gives preference to an applicant of the same religion."[120] The very fact that the statute does not further define the term "religious educational institution" suggests that the intent of the legislature was probably to include all RACs within the phrase. It is conceivable that the phrase "religious educational institution" was intended to refer narrowly to seminaries that train candidates for ministerial office.

A further difficulty is that the legislature omitted the adverbs "wholly or in part" following the phrase "operated, supervised or controlled." (The "wholly or in part" language is present in the statutory definition of an RAC in Title VII of the federal Civil Rights Act.) The consequence of this omission is that it leaves indeterminate whether the supervision or control of an RAC by a sponsoring religious body needs to be as thorough, for example, as it was in the *Hunt* case,[121] or whether a looser connection between church and campus would allow an RAC to exercise religious preference in student admissions.

The preference allowed by the statute is for students "of the same religion." The words "same religion" might be construed narrowly to mean that an RAC may prefer only students who are members of the same denomination or church body with which the college is affiliated. On this interpretation, Calvin College in Grand Rapids could prefer members of the Christian Reformed Church but not other Protestants or Roman Catholics. An even more restrictive interpretation of the phrase "same religion" would limit the availability of religious preference to students who are members of the same *synod* as that of the sponsoring religious body. For example, Concordia College in Ann Arbor could prefer students who are members of the Lutheran Church-Missouri

Synod, but not members of the American Lutheran Church. If only to avoid the constitutional difficulty of excessive entanglement of the government in religion, however, the statute should be construed broadly. On this view, "same religion" would refer not to a denomination or synod but to a world religion in a general sociological sense. Concordia College could, therefore, prefer not only Lutherans but members of any Christian church within its student body.

The statute also states that the prohibition of discrimination "relating to sex shall not apply to a private educational institution not exempt under section 403 [the religious exemption,][122] which now or hereafter provides an education to persons of one sex."[123] The obvious intent of this provision is to allow for single-sex academies in Michigan. The way in which the provision was drafted, however, achieves this result only for independent colleges and universities that are not church-related or religiously affiliated. This result apparently reflects an oversight in drafting rather than the intent of the legislature, and it could easily be rectified by subsequent legislation deleting the words, "not exempt under section 403."

The Michigan Handicappers' Civil Rights Act forbids an educational institution to:

[e]xclude, expel, limit, or otherwise discriminate against an individual seeking admission as a student or as an individual enrolled as a student in the terms, conditions, and privileges of the institution, because of a handicap that is unrelated to the individual's ability to utilize and benefit from the institution, or because of the use by an individual of adaptive devices or aids.[124]

In the event that an applicant for admission or a student who is a known alcoholic or drug addict were to claim that this statutory provision prohibits an RAC from declining to admit him or from subjecting him to some discipline or termination, the analysis suggested in the employment section of this chapter would govern.[125] The conclusion that Michigan law does not prevent an RAC from disciplining a student who consumes alcoholic beverages or who uses illicit drugs would be strengthened by a finding that such conduct is "related to the individual's ability to utilize and benefit from the institution," for the statute explicitly excludes such situtations from the definition of a handicap.[126]

E. Facilities

The public accommodation article of the Civil Rights Act[127] includes within a "place of public accommodation" any educational facility or institution "whose goods, services, facilities, privileges, advantages, or accommodations are extended, offered, sold, or otherwise made available to the public."[128] Campus facilities generally open to the public might include a motel, restaurant, bookstore, stadium, theater, and museum.

Under the public accommodations article, no one may "[d]eny an individual the full and equal enjoyment of the goods, services, facilities, privileges, advantages, or accommodations of a place of public accommodation or public service because of *religion*, race, color, national origin, age, sex, or marital status."[129] The article on educational institutions within the Civil Rights Act permits RACs a limited right to make preferences based on religion in student admissions.[130] Since many of the users of these facilities will be students, a disproportionate number of users may be members of the religion with which the RAC is affiliated. Because this would be a consequence of a legitimate student admissions policy, it would not run afoul of the Civil Rights Act. Of course, others choosing to use these facilities would be protected by the Act.

This statute does not apply to RAC facilities that are not open to the general public. Campus facilities generally regarded as private in character would include student dormitories and dining halls, classroom buildings and athletic facilities. Presumably RACs may limit use of these facilities to those who are properly associated with the RAC, such as its faculty, staff, student body, and their families.[131]

The article on educational institutions states that such an institution may not "[d]iscriminate against an individual in the full utilization of or benefit from the institution because of *religion*, race, color, national origin, or sex."[132] Even though this provision appears in the same section as the provisions concerning student admissions, nothing in the provision mentions

admissions. Its purpose is to prohibit discrimination among students, faculty, or staff in the use of the school's facilities.[133]

Although the civil rights law prohibits certain discriminatory limitations on the use and occupancy of real property, an exemption is provided for a "limitation of use on the basis of religion relating to real property held by a religious institution or organization, *or* by a religious or charitable organization operated, supervised, or controlled by a religious institution or organization, and used for religious or charitable purposes."[134]

The Michigan Public Health Code[135] contains an article on environmental health.[136] The housing provisions within Part 122 of this article give authority to the State Department of Public Health,[137] with local health department input and cooperation, to promulgate rules prescribing housing standards covering a wide range of health concerns.[138] The minimum housing standards promulgated under the housing provisions apply to multiple dwellings. A college dormitory is a multiple dwelling within the meaning of these provisions.[139]

The state Fire Safety Board[140] is authorized to promulgate rules "pertaining to fire safety requirements for schools and dormitories, including state supported schools, colleges, and universities and school, college, and university dormitories."[141] RACs are subject to these rules.

Michigan's comprehensive OSHA statute[142] applies to all places of employment except domestic employment and mines.[143] Included within the definition of a place of employment is a factory, plant, establishment, construction site or other similar area, workplace or environment where an employee is permitted to work.[144] An employee is "any person permitted to work by an employer;" and an employer is "any individual or organization [including the state] which employs one or more persons."[145]

F. State Taxation

The Michigan Income Tax Act of 1967[146] exempts from taxation persons[147] who are exempt from federal income tax. Since RACs in Michigan are generally exempt from the federal income tax under section 501(c)(3) of the federal

Internal Revenue Code, they are likewise exempt from the state income tax.[148] As with the parallel federal provision, however, Michigan imposes a tax on the taxable business income that is unrelated to the purpose for which the entity has the exemption.[149]

Transfers to charitable, religious, and educational institutions are exempt from the Michigan inheritance tax.[150]

Michigan also imposes an estate tax designed merely to channel to Michigan, by virtue of the credit allowed against the federal estate tax for state death taxes, moneys that would otherwise go to the federal government in estate taxes.[151] This tax, therefore, has no ultimate effect on the total amount of death taxes paid and neither encourages nor discourages bequests to RACs.

Michigan has no gift tax.

Michigan allows its taxpayers a credit against the state income tax in an amount, subject to applicable limitations,[152] equal to fifty percent of the aggregate amount of charitable contributions made by the taxpayer during the year to institutions of higher learning located within the state.[153] As defined in the section, "institution of higher education" would include virtually all RACs.[154] An institution receiving charitable contributions through a nonprofit corporation, fund, foundation, trust, or association organized and operated exclusively for the benefit of the institution of higher learning must file an annual report with various state legislative committees stating how the contribution is being used and any specific conditions under which a particular contribution was received.[155]

Article 9, section 4 of the Michigan Constitution provides:

Property owned and occupied by non-profit religious or educational organizations and used exclusively for religious or educational purposes, as defined by law, shall be exempt from real and personal property taxes.[156]

Pursuant to this authority, the legislature has provided for tax exemptions extending to:

Real estate or personal property . . . owned and occupied by nonprofit theater, library, benevolent, charitable, educational, or scientific institutions . . .

incorporated under the laws of this state with the buildings and other property thereon while occupied by them solely for the purposes for which the institutions were incorporated.[157]

When the constitutional provision was adopted in 1963, there already existed a statutory provision for real and personal property tax exemption. The words "as defined by law" found in the constitutional provision have been construed to validate this statutory provision.[158] The Michigan Supreme Court has held that exemption statutes are to be strictly construed in favor of the taxing unit.[159] The present statutory requirements for exempt status derive from a four-part test developed by the State Supreme Court, which ruled in 1944 that:

1. The real estate must be owned and occupied by the exemption claimant;
2. The exemption claimant must be a library, benevolent, charitable, educational or scientific institution;
3. The claimant must have been incorporated under the laws of this State;
4. The exemption exists only when the buildings and other property thereon are occupied by the claimant solely for the purpose for which it was incorporated.[160]

The second requirement has been frequently litigated and as a result the scope of an "educational institution" has been clarified. For example, in *David Walcott Kendall Memorial School v. Grand Rapids,*[161] the court inquired whether the institution assumed a portion of the burden of educating students which otherwise would fall on tax-supported schools. An educational institution apparently assumed a portion of the burden "if a substantial portion of the student body could attend a state-supported college or university and major in the same field of study."[162] The court cited several factors to be considered: the institution's admissions requirements, qualifications of the student, the student's major field of study, the time necessary to complete the prescribed course of study, and the quality and quantity of courses offered as compared with the same programs at state colleges and universities.[163] Under this test, the court found a school of design qualified for the exemption even though it was a specialized institution. *Kendall* was recently cited with approval in *Ladies Literary Club v. Grand Rapids*,[164] in which the Michigan Supreme Court denied tax-exempt status to an organization whose purposes covered a wide spectrum of civic, literary, educational, and charitable activities. Although an organization need not fit neatly into only one of the statutory categories,[165] this organization was deemed to be "essentially a social club which happens to engage in some nonprofit activities."[166] Neither did the club's programs "sufficiently relieve the government's educational burden to warrant the claimant the educational institution exemption."[167] Most RACs easily meet this second requirement. Although seminaries might have difficulty in meeting this requirement, it is clear from actual practice that they qualify for the real and personal property exemptions under other provisions.[168]

The fourth requirement has also been subject to litigation. In 1968, for example, an appellate court inquired whether the organization seeking exemption used certain parcels of property "in any appreciable *quantum*" for its stated purposes and ruled that if this "quantum" could not be met, the exemption would be unavailable.[169] In 1977, however, an appellate court held that the "quantum of use test" does not apply to educational organizations.[170] The court instead focused on whether the property "furthered the education" of the students and was used in a manner consistent with the nature of the land in such a way that the educational purpose was "plainly advanced."[171] RACs have no difficulty meeting this requirement.

A separate provision deals strictly with personal property and exempts the personal property of charitable, educational, and scientific institutions incorporated under Michigan law.[172]

The Intangibles Tax Act[173] imposes a tax upon the privilege of owning intangible personal property in Michigan. Exempted, *inter alia*, are:

a debt or obligation which is secured by a mortgage upon the real estate as may be owned and occupied by library . . . benevolent, charitable, educational

and scientific institutions, incorporated under the laws of this state, with the buildings and other property thereon, while occupied by them solely for the purposes for which they were incorporated or secured by a mortgage upon a house of public worship with the land on which it stands, the furniture therein, or any parsonage owned and occupied as a parsonage by any regularly organized religious society of this state[174] [and] [i]ntangible personal property belonging to benevolent, charitable, religious, educational, and nonprofit scientific institutions incorporated under the laws of this state.[175]

Under these provisions, RACs, and others holding certain securities issued by RACs or churches, are exempt from the tax.

The Michigan General Sales Tax Act[176] provides:

A person subject to tax under this act need not include in the amount of the gross proceeds used for the computation of the tax, sales of tangible personal property . . . [n]ot for resale, and when not operated for profit, to a[n] . . . educational . . . institution . . . operated by . . . a regularly organized church, religious, or fraternal organization . . . and when the activities of the entity . . . are carried out exclusively for the benefit of the public at large and are not limited to the advantage, interests, and benefits of its members. . . . In these cases, at the time of the transfer of the tangible personal property, the transferee shall sign a statement . . . stating that the property is to be used or consumed in connection with the operation of the institution . . . and that the institution . . . qualifies as an exempt entity.[177]

Sales of food by an educational institution not operated for profit to bona fide enrolled students are also excluded from the sales tax computation.[178]

The Michigan Use Tax Act[179] has the same exemption provision as is found in the sales tax law. Thus an RAC which is exempted from the sales tax will similarly be exempted from the use tax.[180]

Exemption from the Single Business Tax Act[181] is dependent upon the exempt status of an organization for federal income tax purposes.[182] Since all RACs are generally exempt as I.R.C. §501(c)(3) organizations, they are likewise exempt from this state tax.

G. Fund Raising

Fund raising in Michigan is governed by the Charitable Organizations and Solicitations Act,[183] which requires charitable organizations to file a license application[184] and financial statement[185] with the Attorney General before they may solicit contributions. Virtually all RACs, however, are exempted, under one or more provisions, from the license and financial statement requirements if they submit a two-page notarized questionnaire to the Attorney General. There are two relevant sections of the statute providing for the exemption of RACs. Section two states that the legislature did not intend to include within the coverage of this act:

duly constituted religious organizations or a group affiliated with and forming an integral part of a religious organization no part of the net income of which inures to the direct benefit of any individual if it has received a declaration of current tax exempt status from the United States. The affiliated group shall not be required to obtain a declaration if the parent or principal organization has obtained tax exempt status.[186]

Seminaries might exhibit such a close connection with the religious organization as not to be deemed "charitable organizations" for purposes of regulation under the Act.[187]

Section 13(d) of the act also provides that "[t]he licensing and financial statement requirements do not apply to an educational institution certified by the State Board of Education."[188] Certification simply means that the State Board of Education certifies to the Attorney General's office that the applicant is an educational institution.[189]

Also exempted from the licensing and financial statement requirements is an organization which does not "intend to solicit and receive and does not actually receive contributions in excess of $8,000.00 during a 12-month period of any year, if all of its fund raising functions are carried on by persons who are unpaid for their services," and if the organization makes available to its members and to the public a "financial statement of its activities for the most recent year."[190]

Michigan's Bingo Act[191] empowers the Commission of State Lottery to issue a bingo license to qualified organizations which include, *inter alia*, bona fide nonprofit religious and educational organizations which either have been in existence continuously as such organizations for a period of five years or are exempt from the state income tax.[192]

31. Minnesota

A. Corporate Status

The Minnesota Nonprofit Corporation Act[1] governs the creation, maintenance, and dissolution of RACs. A nonprofit corporation is one which is formed "for a purpose not involving pecuniary gain to its shareholders or members, and paying no dividends or other pecuniary remuneration, directly or indirectly, to its shareholders or members as such."[2] Creation of a nonprofit corporation requires at least three incorporators.[3] Articles of incorporation must be filed with the Secretary of State[4] and the Act requires an initial organizational meeting in order to adopt bylaws and to select officers.[5]

During its life, a corporation must maintain a registered office in Minnesota, keep books of account, and record the minutes of the meetings of the board of directors.[6] The board must have at least three directors, but they need not be members of the corporation or residents of Minnesota.[7]

A nonprofit corporation has the authority to dissolve voluntarily[8] but if it has any substantial assets, the dissolution must occur under court supervision.[9] Regardless of whether the dissolution is voluntary or not, all property and other assets "held for or devoted to a charitable, religious . . . , educational . . . or other similar use or purpose" must, under the supervision of the court, be transferred to another party that is "engaged in activities which will, as nearly as can, accomplish the general purpose of the dissolving corporation."[10] In short, a Minnesota court has broad discretion in the disposition of the assets of a dissolving RAC. Although there is no case law directly holding that a court could transfer the assets of an RAC to a public university, such a result is not foreclosed by *cy pres* principles.[11]

Minnesota has a Higher Education Coordinating Board, one of the purposes of which is to "assure the authenticity and legitimacy of private postsecondary educational institutions and programs."[12] Private schools at the postsecondary level must annually register with the Board,[13] and provide it with:

such information as the Board needs to determine the nature and activities of the school, including but not limited to, requirements for admission, enrollments, tuition charge, refund policies, curriculum, degrees granted, and faculty employed.[14]

The Board may make inspections to verify the accuracy of this information.[15]

A fee not exceeding two hundred dollars is required for initial registration with the Board, and one not exceeding one hundred fifty dollars must be paid for each annual renewal.[16] No school may grant a degree, nor may it use the designations "college," "university," "academy," or "institute," without approval from the Board.[17] All schools must maintain "permanent records of all students enrolled therein at any time."[18] In addition, the Board may require a plan for preserving records for at least ten years and a surety bond not exceeding $20,000 for the purpose of preserving records in case the school ceases to exist.[19]

A narrowly drawn exemption does exist for religious schools. Exempt from the Board's requirements are those whose programs are:

primarily designed for, aimed at and attended by persons who sincerely hold or seek to learn the particular religious faith or beliefs of that church or religious organization; and whose programs are primarily intended to prepare its students to become ministers of, to enter into some other vocation closely related to, or to conduct their lives in consonance with, the particular faith of that church or religious organization.[20]

The statute makes clear that this exemption applies only to schools such as seminaries and Bible schools. Any school which represents that the major purpose of its program is to prepare students for "a vocation not closely related to that particular religious faith," or providing the student with "a general educational program" is not exempt.[21] Thus most RACs must comply with the regulations issued by the Higher Education Coordinating Board.

B. State Support

The Minnesota Constitution twice addresses the issue of economic aid to religious institutions.[22] Section sixteen of Article One of the state constitution provides that no "money [shall] be drawn from the treasury for the benefit of any religious societies or religious or theological seminaries."[23] The words "religious societies or religious or theological seminaries" in this provision should be construed narrowly so as to refer only to institutions the primary purpose of which is to train candidates for ministerial ordination. Section two of Article thirteen is more comprehensive in scope. It provides:

In no case shall any public money or property be appropriated or used for the support of schools wherein the distinctive doctrines, creeds, or tenets of any particular Christian or other religious sect are promulgated or taught.[24]

This second provision would appear on its face to rule out direct state support not only to seminaries but to most RACs as well.

In spite of this provision in the state constitution, however, the Minnesota legislature has enacted a capitation grant program for private institutions of higher education, including RACs, in Minnesota. The grants go directly to the institution and are based on the number of Minnesota residents attending the school.[25] An institution is eligible for this assistance if it meets the following criteria: (1) it must be a nonprofit, private institution of higher education; (2) it must not be a seminary, or an institution "whose program is specifically for education of students to prepare them to become ministers of religion or to enter upon some other religious vocation;"[26] and (3) it may not require students to profess religious beliefs or to engage in religious practices.

Under the third criterion, which is the most critical and which deserves careful attention, an RAC is not rendered ineligible for participation in the capitation grant program merely by providing for "the scholarly study of religion as a discipline of knowledge in a manner similar to that provided for any other field of study,"[27] but it can be rendered ineligible by requiring students to do any of the following:

to take courses which are based on a particular set of religious beliefs, to receive instruction intended to propagate or promote any religious belief, to participate in religious activities, to maintain affiliation with a particular church or religious organization, or to attest to any particular religious beliefs.[28]

The significant feature of the statutory definition of an eligible institution is coercion or compulsion. An eligible RAC may bear witness to a particular religious tradition or heritage; it may foster certain religious beliefs and encourage the observance of certain religious practices; it may *not* coerce such beliefs or compel such practices.

Several comments are in order concerning the implications of these conditions on participation in the capitation grant program. The language of this statute appears to render ineligible for participation any RAC that asserts a right to maintain a student admissions policy in which religious preference plays a significant role. There is no adequate legislative history which can be reviewed to discover whether the legislature really intended to discourage religious preference in the student admissions policies of

RACs, but the forfeiture of participation in the capitation grant program appears to discourage such preference. This "penalty," so to speak, is also at odds with the explicit provision in the Minnesota Human Rights Act that allows a "religious or denominational institution to limit admission or give preference to applicants of the same religion."[29] It is also difficult to square this "penalty" with the constitutional value of academic freedom, which generally is regarded to protect the campus community from governmental interference in the selection of the students who make up their company.[30]

If the selection of the student body is to be protected under the rubric of academic freedom, surely the content of speech within the classroom is similarly protected, for it is at the very core of this freedom.[31] When, therefore, the Minnesota legislature conditions participation in the capitation grant program on the foregoing of instruction "based on a particular set of religious beliefs" or "intended to propagate or promote any religious beliefs," it may have moved beyond its legitimate interest in the observance of the non-establishment principle to a potentially troubling interference with the content of instruction. Since this kind of interference ought not to be tolerated on the campuses of state colleges and universities, state legislators should not be allowed to condition public support of private colleges and universities on the content of the classroom instruction.

As suggested above, however, the non-establishment principle undergirds the portion of the statute that prohibits public assistance to RACs that *require* students "to participate in religious activities, to maintain affiliation with a particular church or religious organization, or to attest to any particular religious beliefs." At least as early as the *Barnette*[32] case, public schools have been restrained from *coercing* participation in ceremonies expressive of political or religious belief. The concern reflected in *Barnette* and its progeny has likewise been reflected in cases suggesting that it is impermissible for a state to provide direct public assistance to RACs with requirements such as compulsory chapel.[33] For this reason, this portion of the statute is less objectionable.

Minnesota also provides some forms of indirect state support with more lenient eligibility requirements. The Minnesota Higher Education Facilities Authority has the power to issue tax-exempt revenue bonds in order to finance or refinance an educational institution's physical facilities.[34] After issuing the bonds, the Authority gives the school the proceeds in exchange for title to the financed project. The Authority then retains title to the project, leasing it to the school, until the school fulfills the bond obligations. At that time, the school pays the Authority a fee of $500, and title reverts to the school. In this manner, schools can finance construction projects at a lower interest rate than that offered by commercial lending institutions or other mechanisms of financing the construction. Tracking parallel provisions in the federal statute upheld in *Tilton v. Richardson*[35] and in the South Carolina scheme upheld in *Hunt v. McNair*,[36] the Minnesota statute provides that this bonding procedure may not be used to support the construction of:

any facility used or to be used for sectarian instruction or as a place of religious worship [or] any facility which is to be used primarily in connection with any part of the program of a school or department of divinity for any religious denomination.[37]

In the past, Minnesota RACs have used tax-exempt revenue bonds to finance the construction of a library, a dormitory, a student activities center, and a classroom center.[38] The use of this program by RACs was upheld as constitutional by the Minnesota Supreme Court in 1975.[39]

Minnesota also provides financial assistance to students attending RACs. This assistance is provided in the forms of loans, grants, and scholarships.[40] Financial aid is available to any eligible student attending any eligible educational institution. A student's eligibility depends on income level, academic achievement, and residency. An eligible RAC must be accredited by the state or any other national or regional accrediting board.[41] Even if a particular RAC in Minnesota were considered so "pervasively sectarian" as to be ineligible for participation in the capitation grant program described above, its students could, nevertheless, participate in the state student aid programs.[42]

C. Personnel

The Minnesota Human Rights Act[43] prohibits an employer[44] from discriminating on the basis of "race, color, creed, religion, national origin, sex, marital status, status with regard to public assistance, disability, or age."[45] In the definition section of this statute, the legislature defines a "religious or denominational educational institution" as:

an educational institution which is operated, supervised, controlled or sustained primarily by a religious or denominational organization, or is one which is stated by the parent church body to be and is, in fact, officially related to that church being represented on the board of the institution, and by providing substantial financial assistance and which has certified, in writing, to the board that it is a religious or denominational educational institution.[46]

Whether intentionally or negligently, the legislature omitted the defined phrase in the exemption provisions of the employment section of the statute. According to one staff attorney with the Minnesota Department of Human Rights, the Department regards this omission as a drafting oversight and reads the employment section as though it exempted all religious or denominational institutions. Although this interpretation may indeed be the correct one, until the legislature has clarified its intent, administrators at RACs may not with complete safety rely upon that interpretation in structuring their employment policies and practices. The more prudent course would be to conform to the law as it is drafted.

There are two exceptions contained in the statute. The first is a general exception, available to any employer and in every job category, when discrimination is "based on a bona fide occupational qualification [BFOQ]."[47] The second exception specifically addresses the ability of a religious corporation to prefer an employee or a job applicant on the basis of that person's religion. According to this provision in the statute, the generalized prohibition against religious discrimination in employment does not apply to "a religious or fraternal corporation, association, or society, with respect to qualifications based on religion, when religion shall

be a bona fide occupational qualification for employment."[48]

It is difficult to see what, if anything, a qualifying RAC gains by this second, apparently redundant BFOQ exception. It is narrower than the exemption and exceptions provided for RACs in Title VII of the federal Civil Rights Act of 1964.[49] Perhaps the Minnesota legislature wished only to emphasize the need for a religious BFOQ.

In any event, the provision appears to grant an RAC no greater power to differentiate among its employees than does the first BFOQ exception. Only those positions closely associated with a religious discipline (e.g., clergyman, religion teacher, theologian) qualify for the BFOQ exception.[50] For example, although positions like counselor or hall director might qualify under the BFOQ exception, it would probably not apply to the employment of an English professor, an admissions director, a security officer, or a custodian.

The Human Rights Act prohibits employment discrimination on the basis of disability. The statute defines "disability" as a "mental or physical condition which constitutes a handicap."[51] Since no specific mention is made of alcoholism or drug addiction in this definition, it seems plausible to conclude that Minnesota law does not impede an RAC from declining to hire or from terminating an employee who, contrary to the ethical standards of the church with which the college is affiliated, consumes alcoholic beverages or uses illicit drugs.

The Minnesota Department of Human Rights handles grievances under the Human Rights Act. After a complaint is filed, the Department Commissioner investigates the complaint. If conciliation fails, a hearing is held. A party unsatisfied with the results of the hearing may appeal to the state district court.[52]

The Minnesota Fair Labor Standards Act establishes a schedule of minimum wage standards, which are increased annually.[53] Any employee who works over forty-eight hours in one week must be paid one and a half times his normal wage for the excess hours.[54] Exempt from coverage under this act are those in bona fide executive, administrative, or professional positions, or those performing services gratuitously.[55] No general exception exists for RACs.

Minnesota's Equal Pay for Equal Work law also affects RAC employment procedures. The statute prohibits differences in pay based on sex when an employee's performance requires "equal skill, effort, and responsibility," and is performed under similar working conditions.[56] This statute does not prohibit pay differentiation between full-time and piecework employees, or pay differentiations based on seniority, merit, "or any . . . factor other than sex."

RAC employees have the right to unionize and bargain collectively under the Minnesota Labor Relations Act.[57] This act also outlines procedures for settlements of labor disputes, and describes unfair labor practices for both employers and employees. There is no statutory exception for RACs.

The Minnesota Worker's Compensation Act[58] covers any corporation[59] that employs one or more persons.[60] RACs are not specifically excluded.[61] Some employees of an RAC, however, may come within the exemption for casual employees or for employees covered by the federal Worker's Compensation Law.[62] RACs may not elect to include casual employees within the coverage of the compensation Act.[63] Injured employees not covered by the act may sue an RAC for damages.[64] RACs must carry insurance or file with the commissioner of insurance proof of financial ability to pay compensation directly to injured employees.[65]

The definition of "employment"[66] in the Minnesota Unemployment Compensation Law[67] includes services performed for a religious, charitable, educational, or other nonprofit organization, if two conditions are met.[68] First, the service must qualify for exemption from the provision of the Federal Unemployment Tax Act solely due to its section 3306(c)(8).[69] Second, the organization must have employed one or more individuals "for some portion of a day in each of twenty different weeks, whether or not such weeks were consecutive, within either the current or the preceding calendar year."[70] This definition does not apply to services performed: (1) for a church or for an association of churches;[71] (2) for an organization run primarily for religious purposes and controlled by a church or by an association of churches;[72] or by ordained ministers or by members of religious orders in the exercise of their duties.[73]

The Minnesota statute provides several other exclusions relevant to RACs. These cover services performed (1) as a domestic for a college club or a chapter of a college fraternity or sorority, if wages paid in any quarter of the current or the preceding calendar year were less than $1,000;[74] (2) for a school or college by regularly enrolled students;[75] or (3) by a student under the age of twenty-two at an accredited nonprofit or public educational institution in a full-time program, combining academic instruction and work experience.[76] Also excluded from the statute's coverage are services for which unemployment compensation is payable under a system set up by an act of Congress[77] and services for organizations exempt from tax under federal statutes,[78] if the remuneration paid is less than $50.00.[79]

Organizations not otherwise subject to the provision of this act may elect to participate in the program for a minimum of two years.[80] The election is effective upon filing of written notice with the Department of Economic Security.[81]

D. Students

The Minnesota Human Rights Act governs discrimination in the selection and retention of students. No educational institution may:

exclude, expel, or otherwise discriminate against a person seeking admission as a student, or a person enrolled as a student because of race, color, creed, religion, national origin, sex, age, marital status, status with regard to public assistance or disability.[82]

In addition, no school may make inquiries on its admission forms regarding these categories, unless the regulations of the Human Rights Department authorize an exception.[83] The Act explicitly states that its language is not to be construed to forbid a school from discriminating on the basis of "academic qualifications or achievement."[84] Sex-based restrictions on student admissions in single-sex private colleges, moreover, are explicitly permissible under the statute.[85]

The Act exempts RACs from the prohibition against religious discrimination; a religious institution may "limit admission or give preference to applicants of the same religion."[86] The words "same religion" might be construed narrowly to mean that an RAC may prefer only students who are members of the same denomination or church body with which the college is affiliated. On this interpretation, St. Olaf's College could prefer Lutheran students, but not Roman Catholics or Baptists. An even more restrictive interpretation of the phrase, "same religion," would limit the availability of religious preference for students who are members of the same *synod* (e.g., the American Lutheran Church, but not the Lutheran Church-Missouri Synod) as that of the sponsoring religious body. If only to avoid the constitutional difficulty of excessive entanglement of the government in religion, however, that statute should be construed broadly. On this view, "same religion" would refer not to a denomination or synod but to a world religion in a general sociological sense. To pursue the example offered above, if St. Olaf's College chose to prefer not only Lutherans but members of any Christian church within its student body, it would not thereby be violating the Minnesota statute.

The federal prohibition against discrimination on the basis of handicap in federally funded programs has generated litigation concerning the extent to which schools must modify their facilities in order to accommodate the disabled student (e.g., wheelchair ramps, elevators, Braille collections, and translators for students with impaired hearing).[87] The Minnesota statute, however, does not require private colleges or universities to provide any special services or to modify their physical facilities to accommodate the handicapped.[88]

The very definition of handicap, or as the Minnesota statute calls it, "disability," is itself vague. As was noted above with respect to employment discrimination, the term "disability" in Minnesota law does not explicitly include alcoholism or drug addiction. Although the term might be expanded by the legislature or the courts to include alcoholism or drug addiction, current law allows RACs to refuse to admit students who, contrary to the ethical standards of the religious body with which the college is affiliated, consume alcoholic beverages or use illicit drugs, and to discipline students on the same basis.

E. Facilities

The Minnesota Human Rights Act forbids the denial to any person of:

the full and equal enjoyment of the goods, services, facilities, privileges, advantages, and accommodations of a place of public accommodation because of race, color, creed, religion, disability, national origin, or sex.[89]

A "place of public accommodation" is broadly defined[90] and encompasses any service or facility made available to the public at large. No exemption exists in the statute for RACs. Activities of an RAC that would be affected by the statute include, *inter alia*, bookstores, public cafeterias, sports and entertainment events, movies, and lectures open to the public. For example, an RAC which makes an auditorium or convocation center available for public use would be prohibited from denying access to this event on the basis of any of the categories set forth in the statute.

Three other features of this statute deserve mention. First, the statute provides that differentiation on the basis of sex is perfectly permissible with respect to such facilities as "restrooms, locker rooms, and other similar places."[91] Second, as was suggested above, Minnesota law does not require private institutions, including RACs, to modify their places of public accommodation in order to provide access to these facilities for the handicapped.[92] Third, three categories found in other sections of the Minnesota Human Rights Act—age, marital status, and public assistance status—are omitted from the provision governing access to public accommodations.

The Minnesota Human Rights Act also contains a fair housing provision. Under this provision it is unlawful for a property owner to refuse to rent or sell his property to any person because of that person's "race, color, creed, religion, national origin, sex, age, marital status, status with regard to public assistance or disability."[93] It is also illegal to burden a lease with discriminatory provisions based on the above categories, or, in connection with the sale or lease of property, to advertise a preference or limitation based on the categories.[94]

An exception to the fair housing statute exists for "rooms in a temporary or permanent residence home run by a nonprofit organization, if the discrimination is by sex."[95] This provision permits an RAC to keep its dormitories segregated by sex. But no similar exception is found in the statute concerning religious preference in student housing. It would seem, then, that only an RAC selecting its entire student body from members of its sponsoring religious body could legally restrict access to student housing or dormitories on the basis of a student's religion. For then its "restriction" would be de facto rather than de jure, and would be the eneluctable corollary of a permissible policy. If, however, as nearly all RACs do, an RAC were to admit students of all faiths, then Minnesota law would not allow that RAC to segregate its student housing by religion.

Under the terms of the Minnesota Occupational Safety and Health Act of 1973,[96] an employer is defined broadly as a person who has one or more employees and includes any person acting in the interest of or as a representative of an employee, including the state.[97] An employee is any person permitted to work by an employer.[98] The Act provides that any standard or regulation promulgated pursuant to the act shall apply to all places of employment except those under the exclusive jurisdiction of the federal government.[99] All RACs are clearly included within the broad definition of a place of employment as any factory, plant, foundry, construction site, farm, premises, vehicle, or any other work environment where any employee is during the course of his employment.[100]

F. State Taxation

By a provision in its state constitution, Minnesota has exempted RACs, along with other nonprofit charitable organizations, from taxation.[101] The legislature has the power to tax non-educational activities and property of an RAC, but it has not yet begun to exercise this power. In keeping with the constitutional provision cited above, the Minnesota property tax statute clearly states that "all academies, colleges, and universities, and all seminaries of learning" are exempt from property taxes.[102] Similarly, RACs are likewise exempt from the state income tax,[103] although the Commissioner reserves the right to question the taxable status of any income or activity.[104] The exemption of an RAC from the state's sales tax is not as broad: only textbook sales and property purchased by an educational institution "to be used in the performance of . . . educational functions" are exempt.[105]

An individual making a gift or bequest to an RAC need not pay a state gift tax, nor must the RAC pay an inheritance tax.[106] In addition, a gift, within statutorily defined limits, can be deducted from an individual's gross income on his state income tax return.[107]

G. Fund Raising

There are registration requirements for charitable solicitation in the state of Minnesota, but an educational institution accredited by the University of Minnesota, by the North Central Association of Colleges and Secondary Schools, or by any other national or regional accrediting association is exempt.[108]

Minnesota has adopted the Uniform Management of Institutional Funds Act.[109] Its provisions regarding regulation of endowment funds apply to most RACs.

An RAC may conduct bingo games in order to raise funds, but it must first register with the state.[110] Registration and reporting procedures are contained in the state's Bingo Act.[111] In addition, an RAC may conduct any other gambling operations that might be permitted by local authorities.[112]

32. Mississippi

A. Corporate Status

The provisions in the Mississippi State Constitution relating to corporate law[1] seem to contemplate only corporations organized for "pecuniary gain."[2] The Mississippi Code, however, contains provisions for general powers of all corporations[3] and their articles of incorporation.[4] The nonprofit corporations law,[5] which would apply to most RACs, covers resident agents,[6] charters[7] and amendments,[8] and the like. Certain activities of private foundations relating to "self-dealing," "excess business holdings," and "taxable expenditures" are prohibited.[9]

The special provisions governing "religious societies" are applicable to RACs only if they are created with close structural links to a particular church, denomination, or congregation.[10] For example, Bible colleges and seminaries could probably be organized as a religious society, as could Mississippi College, an institution operated by the Mississippi Baptist Convention through its board of trustees as a mission arm of the church. Unless a religious society is incorporated, it may not hold title to property[11] or contract for work or construction.[12] Once incorporated, the society cannot divest itself of title to real property except by a majority vote of the members of the corporation.[13]

Securities issued by a corporation organized and operated exclusively for religious or educational purposes and not for profit are exempt from the state security registration laws.[14]

Permits are required for any one offering a correspondence course, with an exception only for those courses on religious instruction offered without charge by a church denomination.[15] This is a narrow exception, and may not apply to RACs without significant denominational affiliation or control.

Mississippi's Proprietary School and College Registration Law[16] applies only to those RACs which are not accredited by the State Department of Education and which offer the same level of educative advancement as public institutions of higher education.[17] This law requires a certificate of registration from a "Commission of School and College Registration" certifying that the institution has met the standards—which cover, among other things, facilities, faculty, and courses.[18] These standards are not spelled out in the statutes, but are determined by the Commission, with little indication of how much control or discretion the Commission has in its certification of RACs.

Accreditation of nonpublic schools can be accomplished through the State Board of Education or other accrediting agencies.[19] The Commission on College Accreditation, which includes members from private colleges within the state, compiles a list of approved colleges and universities.[20]

Although state institutions of higher learning are specifically under the management of their boards of trustees,[21] no state statutes specifically indicate how RACs are to be managed once they are incorporated.

The merger, consolidation, and dissolution of nonprofit colleges are governed by the chapter of the Mississippi Code dealing with nonprofit, nonshare corporations and religious societies.[22] In addition, Mississippi courts have recognized the *cy pres* doctrine and would undoubtedly apply it if necessary to preserve a charitable trust in the context of the dissolution of a college.[23]

A two-thirds majority of the governing board of a college may commence the process of dissolution by filing a petition for dissolution with the local chancery court. The court may appoint liquidators to effectuate the dissolution, but retains the responsibility of supervising the entire process of dissolution and must approve the distribution of assets before entering a decree dissolving the corporation. A certified copy of this decree is to be filed in the office of the Secretary of State.[24]

The Mississippi statute requires that the liquidators satisfy the lawful debts of the corporation before distributing the assets. The Code does not further specify who may receive the assets of the college, except to provide that any residual assets "shall revert to and become the property of the members, as co-tenants, in proportion to their rights thereto."[25] Mississippi has not adopted the Model Nonprofit Corporation Act.

B. State Support

The Mississippi Constitution contains several provisions that either prohibit or inhibit various forms of public financial assistance to RACs.[26] For example, the state constitution bars appropriations "toward the support of any sectarian school . . . or any school not conducted as a free school."[27] This provision, however, has been construed to refer to primary and secondary education.[28] The state constitution also prohibits the legislature from passing laws providing support for a particular private school or corporation,[29] and from giving state land to private corporations.[30]

In *Craig v. Mercy Hospital*, however, a provision in the state constitution inhibiting grants to private corporations was construed liberally to allow a state grant to a sectarian hospital.[31] In order to avoid characterizing the grant as one for a sectarian purpose or use, the court stressed the public welfare benefits of the grant, stating: "[M]oney may be handled by a sectarian institution and still not be devoted to a sec-

tarian purpose or use."[32] The court further noted that the constitutional prohibition of Article 8, section 208 is not against public funds *of any kind* being used for a sectarian purpose, as it is in some states. Apparently, therefore, the legislature may supply funds if there is adequate consideration in return, but true gifts may be construed as "support of sectarian institutions."[33]

Because of recent rulings of the United States Supreme Court,[34] there may be some problems of excessive governmental entanglement in the administrative oversight of educational institutions that are not present with hospitals. Mississippi courts, however, have not yet indicated how the state constitutional prohibitions referred to above are to mesh with the First Amendment. The careful consideration of the sectarian nature of the institution in the *Mercy Hospital* case suggests that an equally strict scrutiny of the sectarian puposes of an RAC would be required under the state constitution.[35] If, however, the court were to view the purpose of funds appropriated to an RAC as public rather than sectarian, then the provision against state funding will be no bar to such funding even if the recipient is a sectarian institution.[36]

Mississippi's textbook lending program[37] has been tested.[38] Although the program applies to public and private primary and secondary schools and not to RACs, the state court's reasoning would probably apply to RACs as well. Using the "child benefit" theory, the court held that the aid was incidental to the sectarian schools, and that no control of public school funds was put in their hands.[39]

Tuition grant programs to RAC students are probably constitutional under this "child benefit theory." Indeed, to exclude students attending RACs might violate the state constitution's requirement that the state show "no preference" with regard to religion.[40] Contractual considerations may further help avoid a finding that tuition grants violate the prohibition against donations for a sectarian purpose.[41] For example, the state might condition receipt of the tuition grant upon continued residence in the state after completion of schooling.

The Postsecondary Education Financial Assistance Law[42] applies to all appropriately accredited or otherwise approved[43] in-state institutions, public or private. Even ministry students are eligible to receive loans. This program is also available to eligible students enrolled out of state if the same course is unavailable in Mississippi.[44] The inclusion of ministerial candidates in the program may present a difficulty under the federal constitution, although no successful challenge to parallel provisions in the federal "G.I. Bill" has even been mounted. If ministerial candidates were not included as beneficiaries, the legislation could be justified under the "child benefit" theory. For even though payments are made directly to the institution rather than to the student,[45] the benefits of the loan program flow to individuals and, therefore, no sectarian institution is the direct beneficiary. Moreover, if the funding is through current appropriation and future repayment by the students is required, the consideration requirement is satisfied. That there is no restriction on the use of state funds by the RAC for sectarian purposes could present a constitutional problem; the matter has not yet been tested.

Loans and scholarships to medical students who contract to practice in Mississippi after graduation are available to those enrolled in schools approved by the Board of Trustees of State Institutions of Higher Learning,[46] as well as to nurses enrolled in approved institutions.[47] Students at an RAC are not barred from participation in this program. The aid is to the students, not to schools; there is consideration, there is no lending of state credit, and religion arguably plays a lesser role in hospital training than do neutral principles of public health.

Mississippi is also part of a multi-state compact for education[48] involving both private and public institutions, and permitting a state to contract with a regional education board to place its student residents in out-of-state institutions for dentistry, medicine, and other fields.[49] Students of RACs and of other colleges are presumably eligible to participate.

C. Personnel

Mississippi has no comprehensive state fair employment practice laws and no statutes concerning discrimination in hiring on the basis of race, national origin, sex, age, religion, pregnancy, or marital status.[50] Discrimination on the basis of blindness or physical handicap is prohibited in state employment, public schools, or "any other employment supported in whole or in part by public funds."[51] When this could apply to an RAC is unclear as there is no indication of the level or kind of public support required to bring this section into effect, or of whether "indirect" funding is viewed differently from "direct." There is also no indication of whether drug or alcohol addiction is included within "physical handicap."

One provision makes "any corporation doing business in this state" liable for violating any of its employees' or agents' civil, social, or political rights.[52] This broad, vague provision, however, attaches only after the process of hiring is over, and does not protect job applicants.

Mississippi also has no minimum wage or overtime laws applying to private employment. A recent amendment limits the working hours of children between ages fourteen and sixteen who are employed in factories,[53] but this limitation would have no significance to RACs.

The Mississippi Workmen's Compensation Law applies to most corporations that have five or more employees and that are not expressly excluded from coverage.[54] Although nonprofit charitable, fraternal, cultural, or religious corporations or associations are excluded from the law's coverage, there is no specific exemption for educational institutions.[55] Thus RACs are generally covered. If some RAC employees are exempt, the RAC may elect to have these employees come within the coverage of this law by purchasing compensation insurance covering such employees. RACs must carry insurance or apply to the Workmen's Compensation Commission for a self-insurance permit. The self-insurer must show financial ability to pay compensation and to comply with the provisions of the Workmen's Compensation Law. The Commission may require the self-insurer to deposit sufficient security to insure payment of claims.[56]

The definition of "employment" in the Mississippi Employment Security Law[57] includes services performed for a religious, charitable, or educational organization, if two conditions are met.[58] First, the service must be exempt from the definition of "employment" in the federal Unemployment Tax Act.[59] Second, the organization must have employed four or more individuals "for some portion of a day in each of twenty (20) different weeks, whether or not such weeks were consecutive, within the current or preceding calendar year, regardless of whether they were employed at the same moment of time."[60] This definition does not apply to services performed (1) for a church or for an association of churches;[61] (2) for an organization run primarily for religious purposes and controlled by a church or by an association or convention of churches;[62] (3) by an ordained minister or by a member of a religious order in the exercise of his duties;[63] or (4) for a school which, prior to January 1, 1978, does not qualify as an institution of higher education.[64] Thus, most services performed for RACs constitute covered employment.

The Mississippi statute provides several other relevant exemptions from the definition of employment. These include (1) domestic service for a local college club or local chapter of a college fraternity or sorority, if total remuneration in any quarter of the current or preceding calendar year was less than $1,000.00;[65] (2) service performed for a school or college by one of its regularly enrolled students[66] or by one of such students' spouses;[67] (3) service by a student under the age of twenty-two at an accredited nonprofit or public educational institution in a full-time program, taken for credit and combining academic instruction and work experience.[68] The statute also excludes from coverage certain organizations, which are tax-exempt under federal statutes,[69] if the remuneration paid is less than $50.00.[70]

Nonprofit organizations, and therefore RACs, may elect to make payments in lieu of contributions. To take advantage of this option, an organization must fit the definition in section 501(c)(3) of the Internal Revenue code and qualify as tax-exempt under section 501(a) of the Code.[71] The election is effective for a period of twelve months upon the filing of a written notice with the Mississippi Employment Security Commission.[72] Required payments are equal to the amount of regular benefits plus one-half the amount of extended benefits paid.[73] Organizations not otherwise subject to the provisions of the Mississippi unemployment compensation law may elect to participate in the program for a period of two years.[74]

Mississippi does not have a state statute protecting the rights of workers to organize and to bargain collectively, and it has enacted a "right to work" law, both in its constitution[75] and as a separate statutory enactment.[76] Mississippi does not have a statute requiring indemnification or bonding of employees at RACs.

D. Students

The state constitution states that "no preference shall be given by law to any religious sect or mode of worship; but the free enjoyment of all religious sentiments and the different modes of worship shall be held sacred."[77] No subsequent statutory enactment or judicial construction of this constitutional provision inhibits an RAC in Mississippi from maintaining a policy of religious preference in student admissions.

There is a statutory prohibition against any segregation or integration of "any school, institution or other political subdivision of the state" on the basis of race, color, or national origin in assigning persons to or restricting persons from such places.[78] The inclusion of the word "other," however, indicates that the provision applies only to state-controlled institutions.

E. Facilities

Mississippi has no fair housing legislation. Indeed, the state allows owners of public places of business, including hotels and lodging houses, "to refuse to sell to, wait upon, or serve any person that the owner, manager, or employee of such a public place of business does not desire to sell to, wait upon or serve."[79] Under this provision an RAC in Mississippi would be protected in exercising religious preference with respect to students, faculty members or other employees occupying housing owned by the RAC.

Although Mississippi has no general statute prohibiting discrimination with respect to public accommodations, it does guarantee to the visually handicapped, the deaf and other physically disabled persons the right to use public facilities, public buildings and other public places,[80] and full and equal access to the services of hotels, lodging places, places of public accommodations, amusement or resort, and other places to which the general public is invited.[81] Such facilities on RAC campuses are of course included.

The standards set by the State Building Commission for access by the handicapped to public buildings apply "to all buildings of assembly, educational institutions, . . . and other public buildings, which are constructed in whole or in part by the use of state, county or municipal funds, or the funds of any instrumentality of the state."[82] The word "other" would seem to indicate that the educational buildings referred to are those of state institutions. Even if RAC buildings open to the public are included, not many of these will be constructed with state funds due to state constitutional concern.[83]

Mississippi's Landlord Tenant Law[84] contains no indication that RACs are exempt from its provisions.

Mississippi law authorizes the State Board of Health to establish an occupational safety and health program.[85] The duties prescribed are essentially informational; the Board is authorized to collect and disseminate information helpful in preventing work-connected disabilities and to assist in safety training and education of employees. But the Board is not regulatory in the sense of its federal counterpart in the U.S. Department of Labor. Indeed, the Act expressly states that "nothing in this section shall be construed as authorizing the State Board of Health to administer or to enforce in any way the federal Occupational Safety and Health Act."[86] All other provisions of the previous act, such as the authorization of state inspection of working places, were repealed at the time of the passage of the above provisions.

There are safety regulations for "hotel and lodging house keepers" concerning fire escapes, balconies, stairs, and stair rails,[87] with special requirements for watchmen, fire detectors, and construction for hotels over two stories.[88] Student dormitories and faculty housing on a college campus would not be included in the usual sense of "hotels," but hotels or inns on campus that are open to the public would be included within the scope of these regulations.

Doors to public schoolhouses, theaters, assembly rooms, churches, and other places where the public is "wont to assemble" must open outward.[89] RACs may not be included in the words "public schoolhouses," but this regulation is clearly applicable to theaters, assembly rooms and churches at an RAC, at least if the public is invited.

Special construction regulations for school buildings, public or private, require easy egress in case of fire.[90] It is unclear whether the word "school" relates only to primary and secondary levels, or to postsecondary levels as well.

Finally, statutes require places of public accommodation or amusement to conform to fire regulation construction procedures,[91] but these provisions do not specify whether RAC buildings other than restaurants, hotels, and the like are governed by these regulations.

F. Taxation

Income received by any religious denomination or by any institution organized for religious, educational, scientific, or other purposes, if used exclusively for carrying out one or more of these purposes, is exempt from state income tax.[92] Virtually all RACs would come under this exemption, as well as that for nonprofit religious or educational institutions organized and operated exclusively for religious or educational purposes.[93]

Under Mississippi's income tax withholding law, "wages" do not include remuneration for domestic service in a college club or fraternity, or for work done by a licensed minister in ministry or by a member of a religious order in the exercise of religious duties required by the order.[94]

Nonprofit corporations, including religious and educational institutions, are exempt from the corporation franchise tax if they are organized and operated exclusively for religious or educational purposes.[95]

Deductions for the purpose of estate tax computation of a resident[96] or nonresident decedent[97] are allowed for bequests, gifts or devises to or for the use of any corporation "organized and operated exclusively" for religious or educational purposes, as long as no individual receives a part of the net earnings. This would include virtually all RACs. Mississippi has no inheritance or gift taxes.

Under Mississippi's corporate franchise tax, corporate contributions or gifts to nonprofit corporations, institutions, or organizations created solely for religious or educational purposes are deductible in an amount up to twenty percent of the donor's income.[98] Under state income tax law, an individual may either take a standard deduction,[99] or the "amount allowable for federal income tax purposes where the individual is eligible to elect, for the taxable year, to itemize deductions on his federal return."[100] Even if such an individual does take the standard deduction on the state income tax return, he can still claim a deduction for his contributions to RACs on his federal income tax return.[101]

There is no special constitutional provision for tax exemption for religious or educational property, real or personal. A statutorily created exemption, however, includes all real or personal property belonging to any religious society if used for religious or charitable purposes[102] and real property (up to six hundred forty acres) or personal property of any college if used directly and exclusively for educational purposes.[103] As discussed above,[104] not all RACs qualify as religious societies, but virtually all RACs are within the exemption for colleges.

All bonds or other evidence of debt issued by churches or church organizations are also exempt from property tax.[105] This exemption, which will apply to very few RACs, may be vulnerable to a constitutional challenge because of the apparent showing of preference to sectarian organizations.[106]

Little theaters are exempt from property tax if they are nonprofit.[107] Similarly, dormitories at RACs are exempt if they are owned by the college and used as a residence for students or employees of the college.[108]

Other tax provisions possibly applicable to RACs include a homestead exemption for a minister's home,[109] a motor vehicle tax on each church owned school bus,[110] and exemptions from property taxation on all vehicles (with a seating capacity of seven or more) owned by a nonprofit religious or educational organization and used exclusively for religious or educational purposes.[111]

Mississippi exempts from its sales tax all sales to colleges owned and operated by a nonprofit organization exempt from state income taxation.[112] This exemption does not apply if the property is not used in the ordinary operation of the school or is to be resold to students or to the public.[113] Also exempt are (1) sales of solar energy products to all colleges in the state;[114] (2) income for transporting students (including college students) under a contract with nonprofit private schools;[115] and (3) sales of daily or weekly newspapers, and periodicals or publications of scientific, literary, and educational organizations with an appropriate exemption from federal income taxation.[116]

Local privilege taxes do not apply to those operating a bazaar or festival whose profits are used exclusively for religious or educational purposes.[117] Programs advertised through church or school publications are not subject to this tax.[118]

Amusement taxes are not collected from admissions charged by religious or educational organizations when the proceeds are used solely for religious or educational purposes or to defray the costs of the organization in putting on amusements or gospel singing concerts.[119] "Amusements" include most forms of legal entertainment.

G. Fund Raising

Mississippi has no legislation requiring registration by charities or other organizations seeking donations.

Gambling[121] and lotteries[122] are illegal, but raffles held by nonprofit religious or educational organizations are exempt from the state criminal laws.[123]

Soliciting for contributions from a political candidate on behalf of an educational or religious organization is prohibited.[124] The statute also prohibits voluntary donations by candidates for political office to any educational, charitable, or religious purpose outside the county of his residence.[125]

H. Miscellaneous

Mississippi is a member of the Compact for the Operation of Regional Educational Institutions in the Southern States[126] and of the Compact for Education.[127]

Instructors and teachers hired by any higher learning institution "supported wholly or in part by public funds" are required to file affidavits of organizational membership.[128] The application of this provision to an RAC would depend on what is meant by "supported in part by public funds" and, of course, the level of public funding received by a particular RAC.

Religious societies can own certain property, including churches, educational facilities, clergy residences, hospitals, parking areas, areas for purposes of religious assembly, and denominational headquarters buildings with a "reasonable quantity of land in connection therewith."[129] The general prohibition against transacting any business on Sunday is inapplicable to religious societies or churches.[130] In any event, these two provisions would apply to very few RACs.[131]

Mississippi statutes regulating minors' entry into pool or billiard halls do not apply to such halls operated by religious or educational organizations.[132]

Motor vehicles owned or chartered by any college or religious institution and used to transport people for religious or scholastic purposes within the state are exempt from the State Motor Vehicles Commission's regulations.[133]

Public carriers may give free transportation to persons or freight for religious or scientific purposes,[134] with specific reference to ministers and secretaries of religious work.[135]

The Mississippi Bureau of Drug Enforcement may contract with any institution of higher education or private organization for research on drug abuse.[136]

Public school buildings and land may be sold or leased to any group or association for, *inter alia*, "church purposes."[137]

A public school's right of eminent domain cannot be used for the condemnation of any school or college property, private, sectarian, or denominational.[138]

No sale or consumption of alcohol is allowed on the campus of any college in Mississippi.[139]

Municipalities have the power to designate the areas surrounding churches and schools in which wine or beer may not be sold,[140] and the State Tax Commission has the power to regulate retail permits for businesses located near colleges and churches.[141]

Under a previous state constitutional provision, every devise to a religious corporation was null and void.[142] Now, by state constitution[143] and by statute,[144] a religious or educational organization can receive by will one-third of a person's estate. Any land devised can only be held for ten years.[145] If the institution does not sell or divest itself of that land within that period, it reverts to the heirs of the testator. This *mortmain* provision does not condemn all trusts for land held indefinitely for the benefit of a religious or educational organization, but only prevents accumulation of lands under that institution's control by devise. There is also no prohibition against *inter vivos* gifts to such institutions.

33. Missouri

A. Corporate Status

The Missouri Code sets forth a separate corporation statute for all religious, charitable, and educational corporations.[1] It is basically a typical corporation statute drafted to accommodate the specific needs of these noncommercial corporations.

Nonprofit organizations which are formed for religious or educational purposes are not required to register their securities or to file copies of any prospectus, advertisement, and the like with the Missouri Commissioner of Securities.[2]

The merger, consolidation and dissolution of nonprofit colleges may be governed either by the chapter of the Missouri Code relating to religious and charitable associations[3] or by the chapter containing the state's General Not For Profit Corporation Law.[4] Each chapter provides for the merger[5] and the dissolution[6] of a college incorporated under that chapter. In addition, Missouri courts will apply the doctrine of *cy pres* when necessary.[7]

The procedure for dissolution of a college organized under the chapter relating to charitable educational associations is as follows: (1) seventy-five percent of the members of the governing board must vote to dissolve the corporation and file an affidavit to this effect with the Secretary of State;[8] (2) the president or secretary of the college or a majority of its governing board must then submit to a court of general jurisdiction an application for dissolution, setting forth the reasons inducing them to desire dissolution as well as an inventory of all the assets and liabilities of the college;[9] (3) the court then enters an order requiring all persons interested in the college to show cause why the college should not be dissolved, and, when necessary, affords a hearing to those opposing the dissolution;[10] (4) if satisfied that the petition can be granted without prejudice to the public welfare, or to the interest of the members of the association or its creditors, the court then enters a decree of dissolution and vests the property of the college in court-appointed receivers;[11] (5) a certified copy of this decree is filed with the Secretary of State.[12] The procedure for involuntary dissolution of a college by way of a quo warranto or equitable proceeding brought by the Attorney General or the Circuit Attorney is set forth in the statutes.[13]

The Missouri statutes explicitly provide for the disposition of property in the event of the dissolution of a college.[14] The general scheme of the plan of distribution is as follows: (1) satisfaction of legal liabilities and obligations; (2) return of assets held upon condition requiring return; (3) transfer of assets held for charitable educational use to a corporation or society engaged in similar activities; and (4) with the approval of the Attorney General, distribution of the remaining assets to other persons, corporations, or societies specified in the articles of incorporation or in the plan of distribution.[15]

B. State Support

Initially, it should be noted that Article 9, Section 8 of the Missouri Constitution forbids any state aid to "support or sustain any private or public school, academy, seminary, college, university or other institution of learning controlled by any religious creed, church or sectarian denomination whatever."[16] Although many RACs may not be within the letter of the law if the word "controlled" is given a technical interpretation, it would seem that in spirit, at least, this provision more strictly limits state support of religiously affiliated education than does the First Amendment to the United States Constitution.[17]

One major program to provide public assistance to private higher education is the "Missouri Health and Educational Facilities Authority Act," enacted by the legislature in 1975.[18] The purpose of the Act is to assist private higher educational institutions (and others) in the construction of buildings.

The statutory procedure contemplates that the Health and Educational Facilities Authority (the "Authority" hereafter) will sell its bonds to provide funds for the construction of the buildings. After their construction, the buildings will be leased to the particular educational institutions[19] for a term not shorter than the longest maturity date of any of the bonds issued for the buildings' construction.[20] Rentals charged the educational institution are to be sufficient to pay the principal and interest on the bonds. After the bonds have been paid off, the Authority is promptly to convey all its rights, title, and interest in the buildings to the educational institution involved.[21] It is also possible (and perhaps customary) for the Authority to designate the institution involved as the Authority's agent in matters relating to the construction and subsequent maintenance of the facilities, in which case the Authority would merely provide the funding.[22]

To reconcile the program with the state constitutional prohibition against public assistance to religious organizations in Article 1, Section 6 and 7 and in Article 9, Section 8, the statute provides that the facilities involved:

shall not include any property used or to be used for sectarian instruction or study or as a place for religious worship or . . . used primarily in connection with any part of a program of a school or department of divinity of any religious denomination.[23]

Restrictions against such use must be included in each lease agreement and conveyance of title concerning any such facility.[24] To insure compliance, the statute gives the Authority the right to conduct inspections.[25]

Although the above prohibition seems to raise some question concerning the availability of assistance under the Act to RACs, facilities funding would be available to those RACs (presumably most if not all) which offer educational programs which are not religiously oriented, and so long as the buildings are not used in connection with religious education or worship.

Missouri also has a program which provides assistance to students attending such institutions. Arguments to the effect that such programs might violate constitutional prohibitions against aid to private individuals[26] or to religious organizations[27] have not prevailed.[28]

One such program allows the Missouri Department of Higher Education ("Department" hereafter) to guarantee student loans used in the pursuit of higher education.[29] Such loans may apparently be used at RACs, since "eligible institution" is defined to include:

any institution of post-secondary education . . . which has been approved for purposes of participation in the Missouri guaranteed student loan program by the department and the United States Commissioner of Education.[30]

Nowhere in the statute is there any implication that RACs would not be included. Standards of eligibility make no mention of the possible religious affiliation of the institution attended by the borrowers.[31] Further reinforcing this view is the stipulation that the "eligibility of any person for a student loan . . . shall not be determined or otherwise affected by any consideration of that person's . . . religion . . . creed . . . or choice of eligible institution."[32]

A second student aid program provides direct tuition grants to students in private or public higher education within the state of Missouri.[33] This program has a more direct effect on RACs and, in some instances, might require alterations of the school's practice before its students would be allowed to participate.

First, any such tuition grants must be used at

an "approved" institution, i.e., one which does not "discriminate in the hiring of administrators, faculty and staff or in the admission of students on the basis [*inter alia*] of . . . religion."[34] Furthermore, faculty members must be allowed to select textbooks without influence or pressure from any religious or sectarian source.[35] Although there is an exception from the sexual discrimination provision for single-sex schools,[36] there is none from religious discrimination provisions for RACs. No award may be made under this program to any student who is pursuing a course of study leading to a degree in theology or divinity.[37]

The strictness regarding religious education is perhaps primarily to avoid problems under the Missouri Constitution. Indeed, this program has survived constitutional attack.[38] It may be questioned whether the requirements need be quite so strict in light of another Missouri program which grants $300 per year to any blind student attending a college or university without regard to its religious affiliation, religious education, or religious hiring practices.[39] In the latter program, however, the money ultimately goes to the blind student's reader and would not therefore go to the institution as would a tuition grant. Apparently the validity of payments to the blind has never been challenged.

C. Personnel

Missouri law contains the typical prohibition against discrimination in hiring based upon race, creed, religion, national origin, sex, ancestry, or handicap.[40] Although applicable to "employers," some RACs may be effectively exempted since the term "employer" under that chapter "does not include corporations and associations owned and operated by religious or sectarian groups."[41] The term "owned and operated by religious or sectarian groups" would, however, especially as interpreted by state regulation,[42] exclude many RACs from the exemption if technically applied. For those within the exemption, no employment discrimination based upon religion, race, sex, ancestry, or handicap would violate state (as opposed to federal) law.

Despite this statutory exemption, however,

state anti-discrimination pressure could still be brought to bear upon an RAC in one of two ways: first, the Missouri Commission on Human Rights could administratively encourage non-discrimination.[43] Second, if an RAC does use discriminatory hiring practices, even based on religion, it may not be approved for the receipt of state tuition grants by its students under Section 173.205.[44]

Under state regulations, an employer must "make reasonable accommodation to the religious needs of employees and prospective employees" if it can be done "without undue hardship."[45]

RACs in Missouri are subject to regulation under that state's Worker's Compensation Law.[46] "Employer" is defined as any person or corporation with five or more employees.[47] "Employee" is also broadly defined, including executive officers of a corporation and independent contractors.[48] Exception is made only for farm laborers, domestic servants, and employees who are "casual or not incidental to the operation of the usual business of the employer."[49]

These excepted employees, however, may choose to be covered by so filing with the Commission, and by the employer's purchasing insurance with an authorized company.[50] Employers will be liable for all injuries to employees, whether or not negligence occurs, unless the injury is intentionally self-inflicted.[51] If an injured employee has failed to observe posted safety rules, his compensation is reduced fifteen percent.[52]

The employer must insure with an authorized insurance carrier within the state, or, upon satisfying the Commission of its ability to do so, may carry all or part of the liability itself.[53]

With regard to unemployment compensation, Missouri's Employment Security Law specifically includes work done for educational or religious organizations.[54] Work for churches[55] and work done by a student enrolled and regularly attending such an educational institution[56] (or by the student's spouse if the spouse is told that the employment is provided as financial assistance to the student and will not be covered by unemployment insurance of any kind)[57] are specifically exempted from coverage.

Nonprofit organizations are treated differently for some purposes under the law. First, a nonprofit organization "shall pay contributions equal to one percent of wages paid by it until its account has been chargeable with benefits for the period of time sufficient to enable it to qualify for a computed rate on the same basis as other employers."[58] Further, instead of paying the rate usually applicable to other employers following this period, nonprofit organizations may choose to pay into the State Division of Employment Security an amount equal to that portion of benefits paid to individuals by the Division attributable to work performed for that organization.[59] Under this alternative plan, an RAC could save to the extent that claims in connection with service performed for that RAC were below that proportionate share of all unemployment compensation paid by the typical employer.

Article I, Section 29 of the Missouri Constitution states broadly that employees have the right to organize and bargain collectively. A search of Missouri law reveals no exemption for RACs.

D. Students

Missouri has no laws directly regulating the admission of students to private colleges. As public funds are prohibited from being given to sectarian institutions by the state's constitution,[60] state anti-discriminatory laws tied to public funding will not affect RACs.

E. Facilities

Not much statutory guidance is provided with regard to the discriminatory use of facilities. There is a broad prohibition against denying access to places of public accommodation on grounds of race, sex, religion, and the like.[61] Places of public accommodation are broadly defined and would probably include such things as bookstores, auditoriums, or any other facility commonly open to the public.[62] Since the statute applies only to situations in which goods, services, or the like are held out "to the general public,"[63] nothing therein would prevent an RAC from having concerts, lectures, or other activities limited to its students and/or faculty or even to a selected group outside the campus (i.e., alumni, college officers, and the like).

In any event, an exception to the blanket provision allows places of public accommodation which are owned or operated by religious organizations to give *preference* in the use of such facilities to members of their own religious faith.[64] Presumably, after such preference is given, the facility must be opened up to the public on a nondiscriminatory basis. Note also that the "preference" allowed is only for members of the same faith, not for members of other faiths, despite the possibility that the organization might wish to give preference to one or more other religious faiths, depending upon the program involved and the like.

A provision which raises a large question is that against discriminatory rental of dwelling units.[65] Although this statute was almost certainly drafted to prevent discriminatory rental of houses and apartments to the general public, the definition of a dwelling is so broad that dormitory-type facilities would certainly fit within its scope.[66] While the definition limits "dwelling" in terms of occupancy as a residence "by one or more families," the subsequent provision specifies that the term " 'family' includes a single individual."[67]

If the provision is interpreted to include dormitories, it could conceivably preclude RACs from restricting use of their dormitories on a religious basis either directly or, indirectly, through its admissions procedure.

The physical facilities of RACs are subject to legislation that is equally applicable to other types of facilities. An example would be health regulations for facilities serving food.[68]

One major area of regulation in Missouri concerns buildings to be used as places of assembly for public amusements and gatherings. Section 316.060 provides explicit specifications concerning seating arrangements, exits, etc. There is a statutory exemption for any "church, school . . . or building used at infrequent intervals as a place of assembly of [sic] public amusement."[69] It is not clear whether exempted churches and schools must be used "at infrequent intervals" as an assembly place for public amusements or are inherently exempt. If the qualifier does apply to RACs, the applicability is uncertain since no definition of the vague term "infrequent intervals" is provided.

Another exemption is provided in conjunction with the Health and Education Facilities Authority Act, which provides that buildings constructed with the aid of the Authority are not public buildings and are specifically exempted from all requirements imposed upon *public* buildings under state law.[70] The precise extent of this exemption is unclear, however, when considered in light of Section 8.610, which provides that any building for public use constructed with any amount of state funds is subject to regulations concerning accessibility for the handicapped and the elderly. The ambiguity arises because the exemption fails to define "public buildings." Presumably that phrase relates only to publicly-*owned* buildings used for public business—e.g., courthouses, city halls, and the like. Under that interpretation, buildings owned or controlled by RACs would not be subject to "public buildings" requirements, but would be subject to the "handicapped" provision since, presumably, a building "for public use" is not necessarily a "public building." In any event, facilities constructed with the aid of the Authority would be specifically exempt from "public buildings" requirements.

Despite the above exemptions, RAC dormitories are apparently still required to meet local housing standards,[71] none of whose exemptions would include RACs.

Missouri law provides for only some specific requirements regarding the health and safety of employees,[72] and requires that every employer—including RACs[73]—provide effective means of preventing industrial diseases incident to the type of work involved.[74]

F. State Taxation

Missouri law exempts educational and religious performances from a tax which counties are authorized to impose upon public exhibitions. It is unclear whether the provision would exempt all performances at RACs or just those of an educational or religious nature. It is likely that RACs would not be faced with this tax since the exemption also includes "charitable" exhibitions, indicating that it is the sponsorship that is being described rather than the content of

the exhibition. If content were the key, commercial showings of a religious nature (e.g., *Godspell*) would be immune to this taxation, an immunity clearly not intended by the provision.

An RAC is exempt from the Missouri income tax if it is exempt from federal income taxation due to its purposes or activities.[75]

After repealing the Missouri inheritance tax from which RACs had been specifically exempted,[76] the Missouri legislature enacted an estate tax with the sole purpose of gaining the maximum benefit of the federal estate tax credit for state death taxes for the state of Missouri.[77] This tax is designed merely to rechannel to Missouri moneys which would otherwise go to the federal government.

Missouri has no gift tax.

Contributors to RACs may deduct their gifts on their Missouri income tax return, if they have done so on their federal return.[78]

The Missouri Constitution provides a property tax exemption for real or personal property used exclusively for the benefit of a religious or educational not-for-profit institution.[79] This provision is implemented in the Missouri Code.[80] The exemption does not apply to real estate not directly used for religious or educational purposes but held for investment, even though the proceeds from the investment are used for such programs. A separate provision exempts from tax property belonging to the Missouri Health and Educational Facilities Authority.[81]

All sales made by or to RACs are exempt from state and local sales taxes so long as the sales are made in connection with the carrying out of their religious or educational functions.[82]

Under Section 144.450, an exemption from the Motor Vehicle Use Tax is provided for motor vehicles and trailers purchased by religious institutions if they are used for "regular religious . . . functions and activities." This exemption might not apply to all vehicles purchased by RACs because the use might not be primarily for "regular religious functions." The statute seems to suggest the exemption was not intended to cover all RAC vehicles since there is specified an exemption for vehicles "owned and used by religious organizations in transferring pupils to and from schools supported by such organization"[83] and for those owned or used by public educational institutions. Had a pervasive exemption for RAC vehicles been intended, presumably they would have been specifically alluded to.

G. Miscellaneous

Direct institutional regulation affecting RACs is provided by the Coordinating Board for Higher Education, a Board created by Section 6 of the Omnibus State Reorganization Act of 1974[84] and heir to the powers formerly exercised by the Commission on Higher Education. The Board has little substantive control over RACs, its powers being limited essentially to requesting information[85] and recommending certain policy changes.[86] The Board is given the power to revoke an RAC's "approved institution" status, a precondition to its students' eligibility for state tuition grants, and to withhold funds.[87] This authority may be exercised only for failure to comply with lawful guidelines and orders of the State Coordinating Board[88] and it is not altogether clear from the statutory language in just what areas the Board can issue guidelines and orders.

One surprising statutory provision involves course regulation in educational institutions, presumably including RACs. Under Section 170.011, all public and private schools must offer courses of instruction in American History and Institutions, the United States Constitution and the Missouri Constitution. The Commissioner of Education is to specify the requirements. The statute further specifies that no student may be allowed to graduate from an educational institution without having successfully taken examinations in these areas.

Regulations pertaining to employment agencies specifically exempt religious and educational institutions.[89] Without such an exemption, placement offices on RAC campuses would be subject to the regulation otherwise provided for employment agencies.

34. Montana

A. Corporate Status

RACs would be organized under the Montana Nonprofit Corporation Act,[1] which contains no real surprises. One rather anachronistic piece of legislation is the Montana Religious Corporation Sole Act,[2] which authorizes the formation of a corporation solely for religious organizations whose management or ownership of property is centered in one individual.[3] The provision seems applicable to churches rather than to RACs.

Montana exempts RAC securities from registration requirements if notice is filed twenty days prior to issuance[4] and a fifty dollar fee is paid.[5] The Montana Securities Commissioner is given the authority to disallow the exemption.[6]

In an effort to prevent operation of substandard institutions,[7] the Montana Department of Business Regulation was given the responsibility for licensing institutions of higher education which meet its standards.[8] Civil and criminal penalties are provided for institutions operating in violation of the licensing requirement.[9]

Most RACs would, however, probably be unaffected by the legislation, which exempts institutions accredited by a recognized national or regional accrediting agency.[10] Also exempt is education offered by a religious or charitable organization and not leading to educational credentials.[11]

A similar provision makes it unlawful for any person or organization to grant degrees such as those normally given by colleges or universities without the approval of the regents of the Montana University System.[12] This provision also exempts institutions accredited by generally recognized accrediting agencies.[13] All Montana colleges and universities offering a degree in education must establish a course in health education which includes study in drug and alcohol education and abuse.[14] Any student who receives a degree in education is required to have successfully completed that course.[15]

Montana's Uniform Management of Institutional Funds Act[16] regulates the investment and expenditure of certain funds[17] held by, *inter alia*, educational institutions.[18]

The merger, consolidation, and dissolution of nonprofit colleges are governed by the Montana Nonprofit Corporation Act. There are no reported decisions in Montana applying the doctrine of *cy pres* in that jurisdiction.

The provisions in the Montana Code governing voluntary dissolution of a nonprofit institution are adopted from the Model Nonprofit Corporation Act.[19] Dissolution of a private college is initiated by a two-thirds vote of the governing board of the institution.[20] The governing board must also adopt an acceptable plan for the distribution of the college's assets.[21] After all debts, liabilities and obligations of the college are discharged and all property of the college transferred, articles of dissolution are prepared for the consideration of the Secretary of State; if these articles conform to Montana law, the Secretary issues a certificate of dissolution to the institution.[22]

Assets of a dissolving college in Montana are to be distributed according to a procedure closely patterned after that of the Model Act.[23]

B. State Support

The Montana Constitution prohibits the appropriation of public moneys in aid of any school "controlled in whole or in part by any church, sect or denomination."[24] (Professor Howard considers this provision to require a stricter separation between the state and denominational schools than that required by the federal Constitution.)[25] Accordingly, there are no programs providing state aid to such institutions.

Furthermore, the Montana Constitution prohibits granting state moneys "to any private individual" or "private corporation" for any religious or educational purpose.[26] It is not clear whether this provision would bar appropriations to a public agency which, in turn, would distribute the funds to private institutions or to students in the form of grants and the like. It is possible that the intent was merely to preclude direct appropriations to *specific* corporations or individuals.

Probably the nearest thing to state aid to students is provided through Montana's membership in the Western Regional Higher Education Compact.[27] The Compact aims to develop adequate graduate and professional study programs in the member states and to assist in placing students in those programs.[28] The Western Interstate Commission for Higher Education, created under this Compact, is allowed to contract with both public and private schools for placement of students in professional and graduate programs, and to assist in the payment of their tuition.[29]

Since Article IX of the Compact requires that the costs be apportioned among the member states, the program might violate the constitutional prohibition against state assistance to private individuals. It should be noted, however, that the appropriation involved is not directly to the "private individual."

In any event, a state constitutional attack may now be precluded due to the expiration of the two-year limitation on such challenges.[30]

The Commission on Federal Higher Education Programs was established "to cooperate with the Federal government in the establishment and administration of programs for higher education provided for by the Congress of the United States."[31] The Commission administers state plans under Title I of the Federal Higher Education Facilities Act of 1963, and Titles I and VI of the Federal Higher Education Act of 1965.[32] Each private college, including RACs, has its representative serving on the Commission.[33]

The Guaranteed Student Loan Program,[34] established in 1979, is administered by the Board of Regents of Higher Education within the state.[35] Funded by federal and private moneys received by the Board,[36] the program does not create any state obligation.[37] The program is available to students attending any educational institution, including an RAC, approved to participate in the guaranteed student loan program pursuant to Title IV of the Higher Education Act of 1965.[38]

A similar program, the Resident Student Financial Assistance Program,[39] aims to provide assistance to residents of Montana enrolled in postsecondary educational institutions, including RACs, approved by the state.[40] The program administers only federal and private funds.[41] Illustrative of the total separation of the state from the funding of these programs is the requirement that administrative costs of the program not provided for by federal funds be charged to the individual participants in the program.[42]

C. Personnel

The Montana state constitution broadly prohibits discrimination by the state or any person, corporation or institution against anyone in the exercise of his "civil or political rights on account of race, color, sex, culture, social origin or condition, or political or religious ideas."[43]

Whatever the reach of this constitutional provision, it is implemented by powerful statutory language. Discrimination in hiring or in terms of employment on the basis of race, creed, religion, marital status, color, sex, age, national origin, or physical or mental handicap is forbidden.[44] The only bona fide occupational qualification suggested is for age, physical or mental handicap, or sex.[45]

A separate provision outlaws advertising, circulars, employment forms and the like which indicate limitations or discrimination on the basis of sex, marital status, age, physical or mental handicap, race, creed, religion, color, or national origin "unless based upon a bona fide occupational qualification."[46] A legislative intent to allow a religious BFOQ in the actual hiring must be inferred from this since it would be anomalous to authorize an employer to advertise a religious employment requirement but preclude his actually hiring on this basis.

It must be conceded, however, that the language of the legislation is ambiguous. In the statutory provisions dealing with exemptions to the discrimination provisions,[47] there is set out the procedure one must follow for securing the required exemption from the legislation.[48] (Although not totally clear, the specific exemptions granted must apparently be within the legislatively provided exemptions.) It is clear that the legislature did not want exemptions casually granted, specifying that "grounds urged as a 'reasonable' basis for an exemption under any section of this chapter shall be strictly construed."[49] Further clouding the ability of RACs to exercise religious discrimination is a provision stipulating that "[s]ex, marital status, age, physical or mental handicap, race, *creed, religion,* color, or national origin may not comprise justification for discrimination unless the nature of the service requires the discrimination for the legally demonstrable purpose of correcting a previous discriminatory practice."[50] This provision seems strictly to limit employment selectivity on the listed bases to affirmative action situations.

Even if a BFOQ which includes religion is read into the hiring provision, it will not greatly protect RACs in personnel decisions involving positions beyond those of theology or philosophy faculty and perhaps of certain counselors. It is not likely that an RAC would be successful in arguing a right to exercise religious preference in the employment of faculty generally despite its interest in establishing on campus a pervasive presence of faculty of a certain religious persuasion.

Nonetheless, certain RACs, such as seminaries and Bible colleges, may be wholly exempt from the legislation. An "employer," under the Act, does not include a nonprofit fraternal, charitable, or religious association or corporation not organized to provide accommodations or services available on a nonmembership basis.[51]

Sex as a BFOQ is specified in the hiring and terms of employment provision.[52] Such a BFOQ would be especially helpful to an RAC in hiring dormitory personnel and perhaps some counselors and teachers of courses in women's rights or women's history.

The employment provisions are enforced by the Commission for Human Rights.[53] Violations of the Act or of the Commission's orders, or interference with the Commission's work is a misdemeanor.[54]

Title 39 of the Montana Code, "Labor,"[55] contains several chapters dealing with employment and is generally applicable to all employers, including RACs.[56] Although the legislation provides for a minimum wage[57] and for overtime compensation,[58] these do not apply, *inter alia,* to (1) "students participating in a distributive education program established under the auspices of an accredited educational agency;"[59] (2) persons who, though not regular employees thereof, "voluntarily offer their services to a nonprofit organization on a fully or partially reimbursed basis;"[60] and (3) anyone employed in a good faith executive, administrative or professional capacity.[61]

The Montana Worker's Compensation Act[62] applies to every corporation[63] with one or more employees.[64] Generally, RACs are covered unless some of their employees come within the exceptions for casual employment,[65] services performed in return for aid or sustenance only,[66] or employment covered by a federal workers' compensation provision.[67] RACs may elect to include exempted employees within the coverage of the compensation act if an insurer allows such election.[68] Injured employees working for an uninsured employer may elect either to receive compensation from the state's uninsured employers' fund or pursue a damage action in court against the employer.[69] RACs must carry insurance,[70] elect to pay premiums into a state operated workers' compensation insurance system,[71] or become a self-insurer by furnishing the Division of Workers' Compensation of the Department of Labor and Industry with satisfactory proof of financial ability to compensate injured employees directly.[72]

Services performed "in the employ of a religious, charitable, scientific, literary, or educational organization" are specifically included within the definition of employment[73] in the Montana Unemployment Insurance Law.[74] This definition does not cover services performed (1) for a church or for an association of churches;[75] (2) for an organization run primarily for religious purposes and controlled by a church or an association of churches;[76] (3) by ordained ministers or by members of a religious order in the exercise of their duties;[77] or (4) for an institution which is not an institution of higher education[78] before December 31, 1977.[79] Because these exemptions are narrow, most employees of RACs are covered by the unemployment insurance provisions. Other exemptions provided for in the statute and of relevance to RACs include (1) domestic service for a local college club or local chapter of a college fraternity or sorority, unless performed for a person who paid more than $1,000 for such services in any quarter in the current or preceding calendar year;[80] (2) service for which unemployment compensation is payable under a system set up by Congress;[81] (3) service performed for a school or college by one of its regularly enrolled students or by the spouse of such a student;[82] (4) service performed by a student under the age of twenty-two, at an accredited nonprofit or public educational institution in a full-time, credit-bearing program combining academic instruction and work experience.[83]

Employing units[84] which are exempt from the provisions of the Montana statute may elect to participate in the state's unemployment compensation program.[85] Nonprofit organizations, as defined in section 501(c)(3) of the Internal Revenue Code,[86] may elect to make payments in lieu of contributions.[87] The election is effective for a period of two years upon filing of written notice with the Employment Security Division of the Department of Labor.[88] The amount of such payments is equal to the amount of regular benefits plus one-half the amount of extended benefits paid.[89]

D. Students

Montana law prohibits any educational institution from discriminating against students or applicants for admission on the basis of race, creed, religion, sex, marital status, color, age, physical or mental handicap, or national origin "unless based on reasonable grounds."[90] An educational institution may apply to the Commission for Human Rights for a "declaratory ruling"[91] exempting it from a particular provision if "reasonable grounds" exist.[92] Under this provision, an RAC could make out a case for a single-sex school and for religious selectivity in admissions.[93]

E. Facilities

Discrimination in the provision of public accommodation services because of sex, race, age, physical[94] or mental handicap, creed, religion, color, or national origin is prohibited, except when based on reasonable grounds.[95]

A "public accommodation" is a restaurant, inn, theater, or the like[96] which caters "to the general public."[97] Clearly, therefore, an RAC's public cafeteria or theater would be included, but not facilities open only to its students. Moreover, although the law adds "all other public amusement and business establishments" after a series of specific examples, the principle of *ejusdem genesis* suggests no legislative intent to treat the college itself as a public accommodation and thus to control admissions. Even if such intent could be read into the law, an RAC could show "reasonable grounds" for an exemption with regard to religion and, in the case of single-sex schools, with regard to sex.[98]

Discrimination in the sale or rental of housing accommodations or improved or unimproved property on the basis of sex, race, creed, religion, color, age, physical or mental handicap, or national origin is also prohibited.[99] There is no indication, however, that the legislation intends to prohibit a college from restricting its housing to its students or indirectly to control admissions. Were the law read to control admissions, an RAC could still seek a "declaratory ruling" from the Commission for Human Rights that an exemption is justified with regard to religion and, for single-sex schools, with regard to sex.[100]

The Montana legislature has enacted an OSHA type statute entitled the Montana Safety Act.[101] The definitions of employer and employee are identical to those found in the worker's compensation laws.[102] An employer includes all public, quasi-public and private corporations; the definition of an employee is similarly all-inclusive.

F. State Taxation

The Corporation License or Income Tax law[103] exempts from its taxation all nonprofit religious or educational corporations[104] and, therefore, virtually all RACs. Unrelated business income, however, is taxable if it yields a federal unrelated business income tax liability of more than one-hundred dollars.[105]

Property transferred to nonprofit religious or educational organizations is exempt from the state inheritance tax.[106] Montana does impose an estate tax designed merely to channel to the state, through the federal estate tax credit for state death taxes paid, moneys that would otherwise go to the federal government. This tax is designed, therefore, not to affect the *amount* of death taxes ultimately paid.[107]

Montana does not have a state gift tax.

Under the state's Individual Income Tax Law,[108] taxpayers not using the standard deduction[109] may deduct, *inter alia*, in computing net income, those "items referred to" in section 161

of the Internal Revenue Code of 1954.[110] Since that section incorporates by reference the provision for deduction of gifts to nonprofit RACs,[111] such a deduction is available under the state income tax law for individuals who itemize. No parallel deduction seems available under the Corporation License or Income Tax law.[112]

The Montana Constitution authorizes the state legislature to exempt from taxation property used for educational purposes or religious worship,[113] and the state legislature has accepted that invitation.[114]

Montana has no sales or use taxes.

G. Fund Raising

Montana has no legislation comprehensively regulating charitable solicitation.

The Montana Constitution makes all forms of gambling illegal unless authorized by the legislature.[115] The legislature has forbidden many forms of gambling.[116] Authorized, however, are certain card games,[117] bingo and raffles,[118] and sports pools.[119]

H. Miscellaneous

Teachers, clergymen, and officers of charitable institutions may choose to be exempted from jury duty.[120]

The Montana Constitution allows perpetuities only for charitable purposes.[121]

35. Nebraska

A. Corporate Status

The Nebraska Nonprofit Corporation Act[1] provides for the incorporation and maintenance of nonprofit RACs.[2] In order to establish a private college and receive accreditation, however, one must petition the Nebraska Coordinating Commission for Postsecondary Education and receive its approval.[3] Provisional accreditation by the Commission is also available for existing private colleges which have not been previously accredited by a regional accrediting association.[4]

Securities issued by nonprofit RACs which are operated exclusively for religious or educational purposes are exempt from state registration requirements.[5]

The merger, consolidation, and dissolution of a nonprofit college in Nebraska are also governed by that state's Nonprofit Corporation Act.[6] In addition, Nebraska courts may rely on the doctrine of *cy pres* as part of their general equitable powers.[7]

The provisions in the Nebraska Code governing voluntary dissolution of a nonprofit institution are adopted from the Model Nonprofit Corporation Act.[8]

Assets of a dissolving college in Nebraska are to be distributed according to a procedure closely patterned on that of the Model Act.[9]

B. State Support[10]

The Nebraska Constitution, although providing for free exercise of religion,[11] specifies that no person may be compelled "to attend, erect or support any place of worship."[12] The Constitution also prohibits giving or loaning the credit of the state in aid of any individual, association, or corporation "except that the state may guarantee or make long-term, low interest loans to Nebraska residents seeking adult or post high school education at any public or private institutions in the state."[13] The major bar to state aid to RACs, however, except for the indirect aid provided by such long-term, low interest loans, is presented by Article VII, section 11: "Appropriation of public funds shall not be made to any school or institution of learning not owned or exclusively controlled by the state or a political subdivision thereof."[14] Indeed, the Nebraska Supreme Court has ruled unconstitutional, on federal and state grounds, a tuition grant program for Nebraska students attending Nebraska private colleges.[15] Nonetheless, Professor Howard notes that the climate for state aid to private colleges may be improving.[16]

Indeed, in 1978, the legislature enacted a second grant program, in which students at private colleges may participate.[17] The Scholarship Award Program is designed to provide financial assistance to Nebraska undergraduate residents and to establish the procedure for the administration of the federal SSIG program (under section 415 of the Higher Education Act of 1965) by the Nebraska Coordinating Commission for Postsecondary Education.[18] Participating colleges must be located in Nebraska, satisfy Nebraska law pertaining to approval, licensure, and accreditation, and offer regular courses to regular students who reside in Nebraska and have high school diplomas or the equivalent.[19] Obviously, RACs could qualify.

To be eligible, a student must be a resident undergraduate student at an eligible institution.[20] The award must be made directly to the student;[21] the student, if he has already finished the first year, must be in academic good standing;[22] the award, based on need,[23] is limited to the *lesser* of $1,800 or the student's actual tuition;[24] and award recipients may not pursue "a course of study which is pervasively sectarian and creditable toward a theological or divinity degree."[25] The program is administered by the Nebraska Coordinating Commission for Postsecondary Education.[26]

The Nebraska Investment Council is authorized to purchase from qualified lending agents all federally guaranteed student loans made to Nebraska residents attending "Nebraska institutions"[27] including, presumably, RACs. The state constitutionality of this program seems assured by the specific reference to long-term, low interest student loans in the state constitution.[28]

The State Department of Education is authorized to accept, in trust, gifts, devises, or bequests for the purpose of making loans to "worthy and needy" students who attend, *inter alia*, any college or university in the state.[29]

Cities of the second class and villages may contract with a person or his parent or guardian to loan that person money while he pursues a Doctor of Medicine or Doctor of Dental Surgery degree in exchange for a promise to repay the loan and to practice in that city or village.[30]

C. Personnel

Hiring, Promoting and Firing

It is an unlawful employment practice under the Nebraska Fair Employment Practice Act[31] for an employer[32] to discriminate in employment because of an individual's race, color, religion, sex, disability, marital status, or national origin.[33]

This prohibition does not apply, however, when religion, sex, disability, marital status, or nation origin is a bona fide occupational qualification [BFOQ] reasonably necessary to the normal operation of a particular enterprise.[34] RACs will be primarily interested in the religion BFOQ, which will probably not greatly protect them in personnel decisions involving positions other than those of theology or philosophy faculty and perhaps of certain counselors. It is not likely that an RAC would be successful in arguing a right to exercise religious preference in the employment of faculty generally despite its interest in establishing on campus a pervasive presence of faculty of a certain religious persuasion.

The sex BFOQ would be especially helpful in hiring dormitory personnel and *perhaps* some counselors and teachers of courses in women's rights or women's history.

RACs either (1) owned, supported, controlled, or managed at least in substantial part by a particular religion or religious group or (2) whose curriculum is directed toward the propagation of a particular religion may employ individuals of a particular religion.[35] Under this exception, a college at least substantially supported by a religious group (not necessarily a formal church body), or having a curriculum that seeks to reinforce or inculcate a particular religion, is entitled to grant religious preference in employment. The language indicates that the exemption applies to any position at such RACs, regardless of its direct relevance to the teaching or counseling role. Moreover, the preference need only be in favor of a "particular religion" — not necessarily that with which the institution is affiliated.

As its title suggests, the act prohibiting unjust discrimination in employment because of age[36] similarly makes employment discrimination based on age unlawful.[37] RACs are not exempted.

The discrimination in employment provisions are enforced by the Equal Opportunity Commission.[38]

Wages and Hours

Minimum wage rates are established in Nebraska's Wage and Hour Act.[39] The only exception applying specifically to RACs is for employees whose services in educational, charitable, and religious organizations are in fact voluntary.[40] Nebraska apparently extends coverage to student work-study programs.

Worker's Compensation

The Nebraska Workmen's Compensation Law[41] is an elective compensation scheme[42] with a statutory presumption of coverage[43] unless the employer and employee agree not to be subject to the law's provisions.[44] Every corporation[45] with one or more employees[46] is presumed to be subject to the compensation provisions. Thus RACs are generally presumed to be covered (unless there is an agreement to the contrary) except as to RAC employees coming within the exception for employment not in the usual course of the employer's business.[47] Injured employees not subject to the Act may sue RACs in court for damages.[48]

RACs must carry insurance or become self-insurers by paying an annual fee to the State Treasurer and also furnishing the Workmen's Compensation Court[49] with satisfactory proof of financial ability directly to compensate injured employees.[50] The Compensation Court may require the deposit of adequate security before approving an RAC as a self-insurer.[51]

Unemployment Compensation

The Nebraska Employment Security Law[52] includes within the definition of "employment"[53] services performed for nonprofit organizations if two conditions are met.[54] First, such services must be exempt from the definition of employment in the Federal Unemployment Tax Act solely due to section 3306(c)(8).[55] Second, the organization must employ at least four individuals "for some portion of a day in each of twenty different weeks . . . within either the current or preceding calendar year."[56]

The statute's coverage does not extend to (1) services performed for a church or an association of churches;[57] (2) services performed for an organization run primarily for religious purposes and controlled by a church or an association of churches;[58] (3) services performed by duly ordained ministers or members of religious orders in the exercise of their duties;[59] and (4) services performed for a school which prior to January 1, 1978, did not qualify as an institution of higher education.[60] Because the scope of these exemptions is narrow, most services performed for RACs constitute employment.

The statute, however, does provide other exclusions applicable to RACs: (1) services performed for a school or college by regularly enrolled students[61] or their spouses;[62] (2) services performed by a student under the age of twenty-two at an accredited nonprofit or public educational institution in a full-time program combining academic instruction and work experience;[63] (3) services for which unemployment compensation is payable under a system set up by Congress;[64] and (4) services performed for certain organizations which are tax-exempt under federal statutes,[65] if wages paid are less than $50.00.[66] Finally, domestic services performed for a college club or a chapter of a college fraternity or sorority are exempt from coverage, if cash wages paid in either the current or preceding calendar year were less than $1,000.00.[67]

The Nebraska statute allows nonprofit organizations to make payments in lieu of contributions.[68] The election is effective for one year upon filing written notice with the Nebraska Commissioner of Labor.[69] Required payments equal the amount of regular benefits plus one-half the amount of extended benefits paid.[70] Organizations not otherwise subject to the provisions of the Employment Security Law may elect to participate in the program for a minimum of two years.[71]

Nebraska has no comprehensive labor relations act generally applicable to private employers. (Its Court of Industrial Relations legislation[72] applies only to certain governmental and public utility entities.)[73] Nebraska's Employment Regulations legislation[74] contains a variety of provisions which, among other things, require the employer to pay for any medical examination undergone as a condition of employment[75] and which bar a "closed shop."[76]

D. Students

Nebraska has no law directly regulating the admission of students to RACs.

E. Facilities

All persons in Nebraska are entitled to full and equal enjoyment of public accommodations without discrimination as to race, color, sex, religion, national origin, or ancestry.[77] Such discrimination is punishable by imprisonment for up to thirty days and a fine of up to one-hundred dollars.[78] Public accommodations "owned by or operated on behalf of a religious corporation, association, or society," however, may give preference to members of the *same* faith in the use of the facility.[79] At least some RACs, such as Bible colleges or seminaries, may come within this exemption.

Public accommodations subject to these provisions at an RAC would include theaters, sports arenas, restaurants, hotels, and the like which are held open to the public, but not student dormitories or cafeterias.[80]

Student dormitories may well be within the scope of prohibitions against housing discrimination[81] of the Nebraska Civil Rights Act of 1969.[82] Religious organizations and nonprofit institutions "operated, supervised, or controlled" by or in conjunction with religious organizations, however, are permitted to give preference, in housing which it owns or operates for other than commercial purposes, to members of the *same* religion, unless that religion is restricted on account of race, color, national origin, or sex.[83] The flexible religious affiliation specified by the statute would probably make the exemption available to all RACs. (RACs typically limit their housing to their own students. Were the housing prohibition to apply to them, it would in effect prohibit RACs from using religious selectivity in admitting students. There is no indication that the legislature intended such a result.)

The handicapped in Nebraska are entitled to full and equal accommodations in all places of public accommodation "and other places to which the general public is invited."[84] The law also requires full and equal access to all housing accommodations offered for rent, lease, or compensation,[85] although no structural modification is demanded.[86]

Dining facilities of religious, charitable, and fraternal organizations are exempt from restaurant inspection and licensing provisions.[87] It is unclear whether this exemption extends to RACs since the usual "affiliation" language of other statutes is absent and the educational designation is similarly omitted.

Residence at private educational or religious institutions is expressly excluded from the Uniform Residential Landlord and Tenant Act,[88] which governs the rights and obligations of parties in housing rental situations.[89]

The Nebraska legislature has not passed a comprehensive OSHA statute, but Nebraska law does provide for safety codes to be established by the Commission of Labor.[90] The Department of Labor is given the power of inspection of all places of employment to determine whether the workplace is in conformance with the saftey code.[91] Although there are no definitions of "employer" or of "employee" in this section, a broad definition of those terms such as is found in the State Workmen's Compensation Law[92] may be presumed to apply to these provisions.

F. State Taxation

Income Tax

To the extent that it maintains its nonprofit tax-exempt status under the federal income tax law,[93] an RAC, under the Nebraska income tax law,[94] is also tax-exempt.[95]

Inheritance, Estate and Transfer Taxes

The Nebraska Inheritance Tax Law[96] exempts from taxation gifts and bequests to any nonprofit RAC that is organized and operated exclusively for religious, educational, or public purposes[97] if *any* of the following conditions is met: (1) the RAC is organized under Nebraska law; (2) the property is limited for use within Nebraska; or (3) the state or territory or county in which the RAC is organized in turn grants reciprocity in, or otherwise does not tax such situations.[98]

Nebraska also imposes an estate tax designed merely to channel to Nebraska, by virtue of the credit allowed against the federal estate tax, moneys that would otherwise go to the federal government in estate taxes.[99] This tax, therefore, has no ultimate effect on the *amount* of death taxes paid.

Deductions or Credits for Gifts to RACs

The Nebraska state income tax is a percentage of the federal income tax (with some modifications) the individual would be liable for.[100] Since federal income tax law allows a deduction for contributions to RACs,[101] taxpayers itemizing for federal income tax purposes are in effect provided a state income tax deduction for such contributions. A comparable arrangement is provided for corporations with regard to the franchise tax.[102]

Real, Personal and Intangible Property Taxes

Pursuant to constitutional authorization,[103] the state legislature has exempted from taxation RAC property as long as it is used exclusively for educational or religious purposes and not used for financial profit.[104] In determining exclusive use, the primary or dominant (as opposed to incidental) use is controlling.[105] Technical exclusivity, therefore, is not required.

Income from non-educational use of RAC property is still exempt as long as it is used for religious or educational purposes.[106] Moreover, if a portion of RAC property is used for a non-exempt purpose (e.g., one floor in a college building is leased to a private restaurateur), that part may be apportioned for taxation.[107]

Sales, Use or Meal Taxes

The same provision exempting nonprofit RACs from state income taxation apparently exempts them from the sales and use tax.[108] In any event, purchases by any private college or university are exempt from the Nebraska sales and use tax.[109] Construction contractors for such institutions should be appointed as purchasing agents before purchasing any materials to be incorporated into construction, improvement, or repair projects.[110] Otherwise, the institution will be required to apply formally to the Tax Commissioner to avoid taxation on the materials.[111]

Also exempted from the sales and use tax are meals and food products served by RACs during the regular school day or at approved functions provided the sales facility is not open to the general public.[112]

G. Fund Raising

Charitable Solicitation

Solicitation of funds outside the county of the organization's home office is regulated in Nebraska.[113] Certification for such solicitation from the Secretary of State is required annually.[114] All persons making solicitations must have in their possession a copy of the certificate.[115] Churches and "like charitable organizations," however, are excluded from the regulations for any solicitation in the "immediately adjoining counties where part of their membership resides or solicitation territory exists."[116] It is not clear whether at least some RACs are within the term "like charitable organizations," especially in view of their lack of a local "membership." Nevertheless, the certificate requirements are minimal and the exception would not permit widespread solicitation unless "solicitation territory" were broadly defined.

Games of Chance

Although gambling is generally prohibited in Nebraska,[117] bingo operations are permitted for lawful purposes, which include benefitting religious and educational advancement.[118] Qualifying RACs may apply to the state treasurer for an annual bingo license.[119] In order to qualify, an RAC must:

1. exist for religious or educational purposes;
2. be incorporated or organized in Nebraska as a nonprofit organization;
3. have at least ten members in good standing;
4. conduct activities other than bingo in the state;
5. be authorized in its governing document to further a lawful purpose;
6. operate without profit;
7. have at least a five year history of active membership;
8. qualify under federal and state income tax law as a donee, contributions to which are tax-deductible by the donor.[120]

The Nebraska Bingo Act[121] provides comprehensive coverage of all aspects of a bingo operation, from its definition[122] to the specification of persons having standing to bring civil suit against an operation.[123]

Nonprofit organizations which are tax-exempt under Internal Revenue Code Section 501 or whose major activities (other than conducting lotteries, raffles, or gift enterprises) are for charitable and community betterment purposes are permitted to conduct lotteries, raffles, and gift enterprises.[124] This limited gambling, like bingo, is substantially regulated.[125]

H. Miscellaneous

Nebraska has entered into and enacted the Compact for Education.[126]

To provide cooperation, coordination, and planning among the public, independent, and proprietary postsecondary institutions,[127] Nebraska has established a Coordinating Commission for Postsecondary Education,[128] whose members represent all three segments of higher education.[129]

Nonprofit corporations are provided special annual license fees for the consumption of alcoholic beverages on the premises.[130]

36. Nevada

A. Corporate Status

Nevada provides for the incorporation of nonprofit RACs.[1] Interested persons need only sign and acknowledge a certificate in writing to be filed with the Secretary of State.[2] The certificate must state, among other things, "[t]hat it is a nonprofit corporation organized solely for . . . or for a combination of educational, religious, scientific, and charitable purposes."[3] There is no charge for the filing.[4]

In addition to the general powers of a nonprofit corporation,[5] educational corporations have the power to establish educational institutions and to charge fees for instruction and use of the facilities, as well as the power to "use funds obtained from fees, private donations, devises and bequests and from all lawful sources for the construction, support and maintenance of the institution."[6]

Although not exclusively applicable to RACs, there are minimum standards for accreditation and for licensing of private, postsecondary educational institutions.[7] These standards are particularly relevant in connection with the qualifications of an "institution of higher education" for student loan purposes.[8]

The merger, consolidation, and dissolution of a nonprofit college in Nevada are governed by the provisions relating to nonprofit and cooperative corporations and associations.[9] There are no reported decisions in Nevada applying the doctrine of *cy pres*.

The sections of the Nevada Code relating to nonprofit corporations for educational, religious, scientific, charitable and eleemosynary activities do not provide for the dissolution of such corporations.[10] The sections of this chapter relating to other kinds of nonprofit corporations, however, include provisions for dissolution,[11] and would presumably be relied upon by a Nevada court faced with the dissolution of a nonprofit college in Nevada. Whether a court would get involved in the approval of dissolution of a college is, however, dubious. Nevada law grants to nonprofit educational institutions "all the powers of . . . disposal incident to the absolute ownership of property . . . by a private person"[12] and authorizes nonprofit educational institutions to exercise these powers "without the necessity of obtaining any order of court by authorization, approval or confirmation."[13]

A Nevada college seeking to dissolve would not, however, have unfettered discretion over the disposition of its assets, for the general powers of disposal mentioned above are qualified to the extent that it would remain subject to the terms of particular trusts and to the general trust that all properties and funds are held for "educational, religious, scientific, charitable or eleemosynary purposes."[14] The Attorney General is authorized to ascertain the condition of any nonprofit corporation's affairs, and to examine whether a nonprofit corporation may have failed to comply with trusts it has assumed or may have departed from the general purposes for which it was formed.[15] Because this general authority is lodged in the Attorney General, it would be prudent for a dissolving college in Nevada to submit its plan of distribution to the Attorney General for his consultation if not approval.

B. State Support

The Nevada Constitution prohibits the use of public funding of any kind (not just the public school fund) for any sectarian purpose (not just sectarian institutions).[16] Historically, "sectarian purpose" has been very strictly construed.[17] Yet in 1974, the Nevada Attorney General stated that although it was *statutorily* impermissible to allow publicly financed buses to transport students to nonpublic schools on existing bus routes, this practice would be constitutional.[18] The Attorney General relied on a United States Supreme Court decision[19] which in turn was based on an earlier Supreme Court case[20] establishing the "child benefit" theory.[21] The Attorney General's acceptance of this liberal federal theory, which "has been used extensively as an attempt to utilize public funds to diminish the financial burdens of nonpublic schools,"[22] has yet to be replicated by the Nevada courts. Nevertheless, the opinion tends to validate indirect aid to RACs such as tuition grants or student loans. Indeed, grants or loans to the RACs themselves could easily be justified as having educational purposes, not sectarian, so long as the aid does not directly support theology classes, worship activities, and the like.

Although the Nevada Constitution expressly authorizes the issuance of public credit in favor of educational corporations,[23] this benefit may be overridden in regard to RACs by the state constitutional prohibition (Article 11, Section 10) discussed above.[24]

Prohibitions of aid and lending credit in Sections 8 and 9 of Article 8 of the Nevada Constitution[25] are applicable solely with regard to companies, associations, and corporations. Therefore, loan and grant-in-aid programs to individual students attending RACs appear permissible.[26] In fact, the legislature has established the Higher Education Student Loan Program[27] to "provide loans to further the educational goals of Nevada residents who are admitted to and attending institutions of higher education."[28] The qualifications of an eligible "institution of higher education" do not exclude RACs.[29] Not only RACs within the state, but also those outside the state may satisfy the qualifications of the statute although the Nevada State Board of Education has the authority to establish policies and adopt additional regulations for the administration of the program.[30]

C. Personnel

Hiring, promoting, and firing

It is an unlawful employment practice in Nevada for an employer:

[t]o fail or refuse to hire or to discharge any individual, or otherwise to discriminate against any individual with respect to his compensation, terms, conditions or privileges of employment, because of such individual's race, color, religion, sex, age, physical or visual handicap or national origin.[31]

This rule is qualified in several ways. "Employer" is defined as:

any person who has 15 or more employees for each working day in each of 20 or more calendar weeks in the current or preceding calendar year, but does not include . . .

[a]ny private membership club exempt from taxation under section 301(c) of the Internal Revenue Code of 1954.[32]

Presumably, all RACs satisfy the minimum employee and durational requirements. However, although at first glance the ambiguity of the phrase "private membership club" in the content of Section 501(c)(3) suggests that RACs may be exempted,[33] in the final analysis it appears unlikely the Nevada legislature intended such an exclusion.

Although not categorically excluded as a "private membership club," an RAC may be afforded a limited exemption applicable "with respect to the employment of individuals of a particular religion to perform work connected with the carrying on of its religious activities."[34] Undoubtedly, this allows employment choices favoring the particular religion of a college's affiliation for the positions of campus ministers and perhaps of professors of religion, theology, and ethics, and of counselors. Indeed, this exception is sufficiently vague to support a religious preference in employment of all faculty. Since an RAC is both a religious and an educational institution, one of its principal "religious activities" is education. It is evident that religious values and faith are reflected almost as directly in nondogmatic curricula, including the sciences, as in the areas noted above. Moreover, an RAC could argue that the role model aspects of teaching require people of a certain religious persuasion. Thus, in order to maintain its religious doctrine, an RAC may discriminate in favor of its own religion in faculty hiring. This is imperative if a religious atmosphere is to pervade the extra-classroom tutelage so common and influential at the university level.

Arguably, this preference could be extended to hiring for positions of extra-curricular "religious activities", i.e., those in which religious values are instilled and promoted, for example, athletic coaches emphasizing the moral and ethical aspects of sport. It is unlikely, however, that this preference is applicable to the hiring of maintenance or staff workers who have little educational contact with the students.

The law also sets out two additional exceptions which are relevant to RACs. The first is a bona fide occupational qualification (BFOQ) exception stating that it is not unlawful to discriminate in hiring where:

religion, sex, age, physical or visual condition or national origin is a bona fide occupational qualification reasonably necessary to the normal operation of that particular business or enterprise.[35]

This allows RACs to hire selectively on the basis of religion at least for such positions as theology faculty and counselors. It would be more difficult to use this provision to justify religious preference in hiring all faculty (the role modelling idea), let alone staff positions. This exception, however, is not limited to the particular religion with which the institution is affiliated but could support, for example, the hiring of a Jew to teach Judaism at a Christian university.

The final exception applies particularly to RACs. It permits religious preference in hiring by an educational institution if (1) the institution is "in whole or in substantial part, owned, supported, controlled or managed by a particu-

lar religion, or by a particular religious corporation or society," or (2) the curriculum of the educational institution "is directed toward the propagation of a particular religion."[36] These two broad guidelines (disjunctively stated) provide a substantial immunity for RACs from the State Fair Employment Practices Law. Consequently, if an RAC is either at least substantially affiliated with a particular religion or committed to propagating a religion, it may selectively hire on religious grounds. This final exception is by far the broadest as it is not restricted to certain positions as are the "religious activities" and BFOQ exceptions.

Complaints by any person allegedly injured by an unlawful employment practice are to be filed with the Nevada Equal Rights Commission.[37] The Commission adopts the religious discrimination guidelines issued by the United States Equal Employment Opportunity Commission.[38]

Wages and Hours

There are no fair labor standards provisions in Nevada peculiar to RACs. RACs are apparently within the definition of "employer," which includes "every person, firm, corporation . . . or other person having control or custody of any employment, place of employment or any employee."[39] RACs are not listed under either the exceptions to minimum wage requirements[40] or the exceptions to overtime compensation requirements[41] and are thus bound by both.

Workmen's Compensation

Nevada law requires that "industrial insurance" be provided by employers within the state for the benefit of their employees.[42] RACs are covered by the Nevada Industrial Insurance Act,[43] as they have no applicable exemption for the purposes of the Act under the definitions of "employee"[44] or "employer."[45]

Unemployment Compensation

Employees of an RAC will not be excluded from coverage by Nevada's Unemployment Compensation Act merely because the RAC has a nonprofit, tax-free status.[46] They may, however, be excluded from coverage if the RAC is operated "primarily" for religious purposes and is "supervised, controlled, or principally supported by a church or a convention . . . of churches."[47] If an RAC does not fit into this strictly religious control and purpose definition, it must pay into the state fund for its employees, who will then receive benefits from the fund, upon proper filing, when they are unemployed.[48] Regularly enrolled students under twenty-two years of age who are performing work in connection with an academic program taken for credit are excluded.[49] A regularly enrolled student who works for a college is not covered.[50] Nor is the spouse of such a student when informed that the employment is provided under a program of financial assistance to the student and will not be covered by any unemployment insurance program.[51]

D. Students

Nevada has no legislation regulating student admission to RACs.

E. Facilities

Public Accommodations and Fair Housing Legislation

Nevada law declares that:

[a]ll persons are entitled to the full and equal enjoyment of the goods, services, facilities, privileges, advantages and accommodations of any place of public accommodation, without discrimination or segregation on the ground of race, color, religion, national origin or physical or visual handicap.[52]

"Place of public accommodation" includes any hotel, restaurant, cafeteria, theater, sports arena, or other place to which the public is invited or which is intended for public use.[53] Under the terms of the statute, such establishments open to the public although operated by an RAC may not exercise even a religious preference in catering to the public.

The Nevada Fair Housing Law[54] announces the State of Nevada's public policy that:

all people in the state shall have equal opportunity to inherit, purchase, lease, rent, sell, hold and con-

vey real property without discrimination, distinction or restriction because of race, religious creed, color, national origin, ancestry or sex.[55]

Although no "person" may conduct discriminatory housing practices,[56] RACs are not bound by the Fair Housing provisions since "person" does not include:

any nonprofit, fraternal, educational or social organization . . . unless such . . . organization . . . has the purpose of promoting discrimination in the matter of housing against any person or persons because of race, religious creed, color, national origin, ancestry or sex.[57]

RACs are similarly excluded from the applicability of the Residential Landlord and Tenant Act.[58] This Act, which outlines the obligations of both landlord and tenant, excepts "[r]esidence in an institution, public or private, incidental to . . . the provisions of medical, geriatric, educational, counseling, religious, or similar service."[59]

State law provides for the design of public buildings to accommodate the physically handicapped.[60] Although "[i]t is the intent of the legislature that insofar as possible all buildings and facilities used for the public be accessible to, and functional for, the physically handicapped,"[61] the regulations apply only to "public building[s] or facilit[ies] of the state or of a political subdivision . . . or entity of the state."[62] Hence, RACs are not bound by the requirements.

Safety Legislation

RACs are not exempt from the Nevada Occupational Safety and Health legislation.[63]

F. State Taxation

State inheritance and estate taxes are specifically forbidden by the Nevada Constitution.[64]

There is no income taxation in Nevada, therefore an RAC's income and contributions to the RAC have no state income tax consequences, either for the institution or the contributor.

There is no gift tax in Nevada.

Article 8, Section 2 of the Nevada Constitution states that "the property of corporations

formed for . . . religious, or educational purposes *may* be exempted by law."[65] Accordingly, "[a]ny corporation whose . . . purposes
are religious [or] educational and whose funds
have been derived in whole or substantial part
from public donations" has been statutorily exempted from property taxation.[66] This exemption will apply to most RACs.

"Any organization created for religious, charitable, or eleemosynary purposes" is exempt
from the state sales tax when purchasing any
tangible personal property, provided "no part of
the net earnings of [the] organization inures to
the benefit of any private shareholder or individual."[67] RACs may be eligible for this exemption on the basis of the religious purposes for
which they are formed. However, a persuasive
argument could be made to the effect that the
legislature would have used the word "educational" (rather than "religious" or even "charitable") had it intended to include RACs.[68] In any
event, those RACs in the nature of seminaries
and Bible colleges will have the best claims to
be within the statute.

Although most corporations are charged fees
by the Secretary of State for filing articles of incorporation, certificates of extension and dissolution, and other miscellaneous articles, "[N]o
fee shall be required to be paid by any religious
. . . society or educational association having
no capital stock."[69] All RACs are clearly within
this exemption.

G. Fund Raising

Charitable Solicitation

Charitable solicitation in Nevada is regulated.[70] Charitable organizations (which include RACs)[71] must file a detailed financial
report annually with the Secretary of State if
they receive their major support from public
donations whether solicited or not.[72] The
statute does not specify the level of funding at
which public donations become "major support." Presumably, one's major support would
be the majority source. When tuition, grants,
sales, and the like are taken into account, it is
unlikely that an RAC's "major support" would
be from public donations.

Games of Chance

The legislature has made exceptions in gaming laws expressly for the benefit of charitable
organizations.[73] The Nevada Racing Act[74] provides for "charity days" from which a portion of
the net proceeds are to be contributed to a
"charitable organization or society as those
terms are generally understood."[75] Again, had
the legislature intended to include colleges and
the like, it should have used the word "educational."[76] In the Nevada Gaming Control Act,[77]
the definition of a regulated "game" excludes
"games operated by charitable or educational
organizations [i.e., all RACs] which are approved by the [State Gaming Control] [B]oard."[78]
The Board, however, is authorized to approve
no more than one event or function per organization during any quarter calendar year.[79] Due
to the tight regulation (and taxation) of the legalized gambling industry, RACs are only afforded
limited exemptions.

H. Miscellaneous

To the extent that RACs in Nevada are constitutionally and statutorily denied any form of
public funding,[80] they are not subject to the
state open meeting law covering "public bodies"
supported by tax revenue.[81]

In both the Charitable Corporation Act[82] and
the Charitable Trust Act of 1971,[83] the legislature declares it:

the policy of the state . . . to maximize the funds
available for charitable purposes by minimizing, to
the greatest extent practicable, the imposition of
federal income and excise taxes upon assets otherwise available for charitable purposes.[84]

The Charitable Corporation Act encompasses
RACs since "charitable corporation" is an "organization or association described in Section
501(c)(3) and exempt from tax under Section
501(a) [of the Internal Revenue Code of 1954]."[85]
As noted above,[86] Section 501(c)(3) includes
RACs. These two acts set out certain technical prohibitions imposed on charitable corporations and charitable trusts so as to avoid increasing tax liability.[87]

37. New Hampshire

A. Corporate Status

Institutions of higher education in New Hampshire must incorporate under the Voluntary Corporations and Associations Act.[1] Articles of incorporation must be both certified by the Attorney General and approved by the postsecondary Education Commission before being recorded in the office of the Secretary of State.[2]

The dissolution of nonprofit colleges is governed by the New Hampshire Voluntary Corporations and Associations Law.[3] This statute, however, does not expressly provide for the merger or consolidation of nonprofit colleges. In addition, New Hampshire courts are empowered both by statute and by common law decisions to apply the *cy pres* doctrine when necessary.[4]

Voluntary dissolution takes effect after the corporation or one-fourth of its members petition the superior court for a decree of dissolution[5] and file the granted decree with the Secretary of State.[6] A nonprofit college may be dissolved without judicial action if the governing board files with the Secretary of State a statement that all the members of the governing board voted for dissolution.[7] The statute does not expressly provide for the involuntary dissolution of a nonprofit college.

New Hampshire law does not expressly provide for the distribution of assets when dissolution is granted by court decree. However, when dissolution is by unanimous vote the corporation must submit to the Secretary of State a plan for the distribution of its assets and satisfaction of its obligations.[8] New Hampshire law also states that nonprofit corporations organized by a special act of the legislature may provide by majority vote for the distribution of its assets upon dissolution unless limited by the special act or the bylaws of the corporation.[9]

B. State Support

The Higher Educational Building Corporation Law[10] provides for loans for "projects,"[11] i.e., buildings or structures useful to the educational program of an institution of higher education, or the refinancing of an existing indebtedness.[12] The program is applicable to public and nonprofit educational institutions[13] and is managed by the New Hampshire Higher Education and Health Facilities Authority, a public corporate body and an agency of the state.[14] The agency is expressly empowered to establish regulations for the use of any project.[15] The agency is also conferred any power of an incidental nature necessary to accomplish its purposes.[16] The inspection of an RAC's financial records as a prerequisite to project authorization would seem reasonable. Such an inquiry would render the information "public" under the Access to Public Records Act.[17]

At first glance this program seems unavailable to RACs due to the state constitutional prohibition of public aid to sectarian institutions.[18] But in light of a clear directive for liberal construction,[19] a manifest disavowal of any liability on the part of the state or any political subdivision[20] (the very basis upon which a similar Florida statute was upheld regarding RACs),[21] and the absence of an exclusion of sectarian organizations from the Act's definition of "Institution for Post-secondary Education,"[22] the legislative intent must be to benefit RACs as well as other colleges and universities.

The New Hampshire Constitution states that it is the duty of the state legislature to foster knowledge and learning by encouraging public and private education.[23] Yet the same article prohibits money raised by taxation from being "granted or applied for the use of the schools or institutions of any religious sect or denomination."[24]

The New Hampshire Supreme Court has interpreted the clause as not prohibiting grants-in-aid which accomplish a public objective even though some denomination is incidentally benefited.[25] Accordingly, the state legislature has adopted several financial aid programs for students attending institutions of higher education, including RACs:

1. State Scholarship Program[26]

The purpose of this program is to supplement funds raised by local citizens through a scholarship corporation which awards postsecondary grants to resident youths.[27] The unique feature of this plan is that awards are made on the recommendation of the voluntary citizen's scholarship corporation.[28] "Secular theology" as a course of study under such a scholarship is not allowed,[29] but any other discipline at any postsecondary educational institution is possible as long as approved by the voluntary corporation which makes the recommendation.[30]

2. Higher Education Loan Program[31]

The Higher Education Loan Program makes loans of up to $1000 per year available to resident students accepted at an approved institution.[32] Loans are based on established financial need.[33] "Approved institution" is not defined nor is the body to determine the approval indicated in the statute. Presumably, approval and the criteria therefore are left up to the three

members of the Higher Education Loan Committee which is authorized to establish the rules and regulations it deems necessary to carry out the program.[34] There is no reason to suspect that students attending RACs would not be eligible.

3. Veterinary–Medical–Optometric Educational Programs[35]

Bona fide resident students of allopathic medicine, veterinary medicine, and optometry may compete for other scholarships contracted for with the Dartmouth Medical School, any veterinary medical school accredited by the American Veterinary Medical Association, and the New England College of Optometry, respectively.[36] (Particular institutions are specified for the fields of medicine and optometry, but any RAC with a veterinary school could be selected by the governor to participate in the program for that field of study.)[37]

4. State Scholarship Program for Nursing[38]

A fourth financial aid plan in New Hampshire makes available loans on the basis of need to nursing students at institutions approved by the State Board of Nursing Education regardless of the auspices under which the program is conducted.[39]

Thus, as in many states, although state funding of sectarian education is constitutionally prohibited, loans and grants to students attending RACs are allowed.

C. Personnel

The New Hampshire Constitution was amended in 1974 to provide that "equality of rights under the law shall not be denied or abridged by the state on account of race, creed, color, sex, or national origin."[40] The New Hampshire Law Against Discrimination[41] more specifically states that "practices of discrimination against any inhabitant because of age, sex, race, creed, color, marital status, physical or mental handicap, or national origin" with respect to employment, use of places of public accommodation, or in the provision of housing accommodations are forbidden.[42]

Unlawful discriminatory practices are limited to those acts specified in Section 8 of the law and to the practices outlawed by the federal Civil Rights Act of 1964.[43] (The federal requirements incorporated by reference will not be discussed further here since they are beyond the scope of this volume.) Under the terms of Section 8, it is an unlawful discriminatory practice for an employer to refuse to hire, to discharge, or to discriminate in compensation or other employment conditions because of age, sex, race, color, religious creed, marital status, physical or mental handicap, or national origin, unless based on a bona fide occupational qualification (BFOQ).[44] It is also declared an unlawful discriminatory practice for an employer to print or circulate any statement in connection with employment which expresses any discrimination as to age, sex, race, color, marital status, physical or mental handicap, religious creed, or national origin unless based on a BFOQ.[45]

BFOQ is not defined in the law. Nevertheless, RACs are categorically exempted from all employment discrimination prohibitions,[46] since educational or religious nonprofit organizations are not included in the term "employers."[47] Consequently, RACs are exempt from all employment discrimination requirements under both the law and its implementing regulations.

RACs are similarly exempted from "protective legislation" which requires "equal pay" for equal work as between the sexes.[48] For the purposes of this section, "employers" is again defined to exclude nonprofit RACs.[49]

RACs receive no immunity from New Hampshire's Minimum Wage Law[50] nor from the definition of a "day's work."[51]

RACs will come under the definition of "employer" in the New Hampshire Workmen's Compensation Law.[52] To comply with it, an employer must see that its employees are covered either by insuring them with a company licensed to write workmen's compensation in the state, or by furnishing the Labor Commissioner with satisfactory proof of its ability to pay such compensation.[53] Employees will receive benefits to compensate them (and their

dependents, when necessary) for personal injury, death, or occupational diseases arising out of and in the course of the employment.[54] The employer will not be liable for any injury to an employee if the employee was even partly responsible for the injury due to "serious and willful misconduct," or due to intoxication, unless the employer knew of the intoxication.[55] The law covers even injuries occurring while the employee is out of the state, if the contract of employment was made in New Hampshire, and if the employee releases the employer from all liability under any other law.[56]

In general, all work performed in New Hampshire for wages or under contract is covered by the state's Unemployment Compensation Law.[57] There is, however, an exception for work in the employ of a church or group of churches, or an organization operated primarily for religious purposes and which is operated, supervised, controlled, or principally supported by a church or group of churches,[58] or by a duly ordained minister or member of a religious order exercising duties required by that order.[59] If an RAC is sufficiently controlled or supported by a church or convention of churches, its employees would generally not be covered. Otherwise, the employer must pay into the state unemployment fund a sum equal to 2.7 percent of the wages paid during a calendar year,[60] although RACs will generally have the option of making reimbursements rather than contributions.[61] The fund then pays benefits to workers who are unemployed through no fault of their own.[62]

For employees of a nonprofit college, benefits may not be payable for periods of unemployment occurring between academic years or terms, for paid sabbatical leave, or for holiday or vacation periods.[63]

Also exempted are independent contractors and casual workers, and domestic workers in a "college club," or fraternity or sorority.[64] Presumably domestic work done for the college itself would be covered. Not covered is work done for a college by one of its regularly enrolled students or by the spouse of such a student if the spouse is told at the start that the employment is provided under a program of financial assistance to the student and is not covered by any unemployment insurance program.[65] Another exemption covers certain students under twenty-two years of age whose work is part of an academic program.[66]

D. Students

New Hampshire has no statute expressly regulating student admissions or student discipline. The Law Against Discrimination,[67] however, contains two paragraphs which state that nothing contained in the Law:

shall be construed to bar any organization operated for educational purposes, which is operated in connection with a religious organization from limiting admission to or giving preference to persons of the same religion or denomination or from making such selection as is calculated by such organization to promote the religious principles for which it is established or maintained.[68]

This paragraph qualifies prohibitions of discrimination in public accommodations[69] and in housing accommodations.[70]

This exemption for religious educational institutions recognizes an RAC's right to practice a religious preference in student admissions (and certainly in the selection of other patrons and tenants, as will be elaborated upon in the next section).[71] The legislature's willingness to permit a religious preference in an RAC's student admissions is reflected in language ("limiting admission" and "making such selection") which one normally does not associate with rental and sale of a dwelling or the operation of public accommodations. Moreover, in view of the blanket exemption granted RACs from the unlawful discriminatory practices in employment,[72] which immediately precedes the provisions in question, it appears even more probable the legislature intended to allow a religious preference in student admissions to RACs. The extent of this religious preference will be discussed in the following section.

E. Facilities

The exemption for religious educational institutions provided by the Law Against Discrimination and discussed in the previous section may be read to exempt RACs from prohibitions of unlawful discrimination in both public accommodations and housing accommodations.[73] (If "admission" and "selection" refer only to choosing students for enrollment, then RACs are not otherwise exempted from the religious or other discriminatory prohibitions of the law applicable to public accommodations.) Places of public accommodation at an RAC include bars, hotels, eating establishments, theaters, bookstores, and public halls.[74] Student residence halls fall within the definition of "dwelling,"[75] covered by the statute.

Whichever of these interpretations is intended by the statute, it should be noted that the exemption is limited to religious grounds and is not, therefore, as broad as that provided in the employment area. Furthermore, the exemption is broad enough ("such selection, etc.") to allow preferences favoring a denomination other than that with which the institution is affiliated. The privilege might even authorize refusal to admit on such doctrinal bases as unwed parenthood, abortion, or abuse of alcohol or drugs.

The New Hampshire OSHA type statute[76] applies "to factories, mills, workshops, mines, quarries, or other manufacturing, commercial, mercantile establishments or building and construction occupations."[77] RACs are therefore not covered by the law.

F. State Taxation

Realty and personality owned and used directly by a college or university, organized or incorporated in New Hampshire, for the purposes for which the institution was established are exempted from taxation generally.[78] Dormitories, dining rooms, and kitchens are exempted only up to a value of $150,000 unless the exemption is increased by a vote of the host town council.[79]

As long as no benefit inures to any member of an educational or religious organization, all income used for the purposes for which the organization was established will not be taxed.[80]

Recipient educational and religious institutions are also exempt from New Hampshire inheritance taxes.[81]

New Hampshire also imposes an estate tax designed merely to channel to New Hampshire, by virtue of the credit allowed against the federal estate tax for state death taxes, moneys that would otherwise go to the federal government in estate taxes.[82] This tax, therefore, has no ultimate effect on the amount of death taxes paid.

New Hampshire has no gift tax.

Establishments owned by nonprofit corporations and associations operated exclusively for religious, charitable, or educational purposes and which do not offer sleeping accommodations to the public are not subject to the rooms tax.[83] This would, of course, exempt all student housing at RACs from the rooms tax.

Meals served on the premises of most nonprofit organizations are similarly excluded from the scope of the state meals tax.[84]

G. Fund Raising

The right to grant permits for solicitation of funds for charitable purposes is vested in the local municipal officers.[85] Bona fide religious organizations, however, are given leave to sell articles or solicit donations upon the issuance of a temporary permit by the director of the state division of welfare.[86] Whether an RAC will qualify as a religious organization will probably depend upon the intensity of its association with a church and the extent to which its curriculum is designed to propagate a religious doctrine. If the legislature had intended to include all RACs within the statute, more precise language would have been used.[87]

New Hampshire regulates the operation of "Beano" (elsewhere known as "bingo") games.[88] Public referenda are to be conducted at the local level to determine whether such games are to be allowed.[89] If so, the provisions of the chapter must be adopted locally.[90]

Assuming Beano is locally sanctioned, "charitable organizations" (i.e., "bona fide religious, charitable, civic, veterans or fraternal organizations,"[91] organized under state law, exempt from federal income tax, and in existence for at least two years) are eligible to apply for a local license.[92] A license to conduct games of Beano for not more than five days per month is to be issued by the selectmen or by the chief of police, to whom a $25.00 license fee must first be paid.[93] If an RAC is to qualify as a "charitable organization" it must be a bona fide *religious* or *charitable* organization as no provision is made for educational organizations.[94]

Similar provisions regulate the operation of raffles by charitable organizations.[95] "Charitable organizations," for the purpose of this chapter, clearly encompasses RACs since it is defined specifically to include "religious" and "educational" organizations.[96] The definition of "charitable organization" in chapter 287-A is otherwise essentially the same except that the federal tax exemption proviso is omitted.[97] With respect to raffles, a local permit is required and their operation is limited to the promotion of the purposes for which the sponsoring organization was established.[98]

A "charitable organization" which may legally conduct "games of chance" includes "any nonprofit organization [in existence at least two years] eligible to receive an Internal Revenue Service non-profit organization number."[99] (RACs are generally included in the Internal Revenue Code definition of "non-profit educational organization,"[100] provided they are operated *exclusively* for educational or religious purposes.)[101] A license valid for up to ten days of operation per year must be obtained from the chief of police in return for a $25.00 fee.[102]

38. New Jersey

A. Corporate Status

Religiously affiliated colleges (RACs) in New Jersey may be incorporated as nonprofit corporations organized for charitable or educational purposes under that state's Corporations and Associations Not for Profit Law.[1] The nonprofit corporation code likewise stipulates that:

Any college or university in this State created by special charter which limits the number of members on the board of trustees and restricts membership to members of a religious order or community, may notwithstanding such limitation and restriction appoint or elect to the board of trustees additional members including lay members in such numbers as it deems advisable.[2]

In addition to obtaining a charter under the provisions of this law, an educational institution that confers degrees in the arts, sciences, or professions must be licensed by the State Board of Higher Education.[3] In *New Jersey-Philadelphia Presybytery v. State Board of Education*, however, a federal district court enjoined a state court order prohibiting Shelton College, an institution with strong ties to a religious body that had failed to obtain such a license, from advertising or awarding collegiate degrees in the state. The court expressed the view that "all members of the public at large will ultimately benefit if the constitutional rights of a small religious minority are protected from encroachments by honorable but overly zealous public officials,"[4] but allowed the state proceedings to continue for a determination of the constitutionality of the statutory prohibition of the awarding of degrees without a license. In November of 1980 the Chancery Division of the Superior Court of New Jersey sustained that statute.[5]

In June of 1981 the college returned to the federal trial court, which issued a new preliminary injunction against the enforcements of the state court order of November, 1980, "until such time as the Supreme Court of New Jersey definitively construes the New Jersey statutes and regulations which are the subject of this action."[6] Pending the final outcome of the litigation, the college was allowed to award traditional collegiate degrees without submitting to the state licensing scheme. In August of 1982, the New Jersey Supreme Court ruled unanimously that the "application of these statutes to a sectarian college whose religious doctrine precludes state licensure does not violate the First Amendment."[7]

The merger or consolidation of a nonprofit college takes effect when a certificate of merger or consolidation approved by a majority of the members of the governing board is filed with the Secretary of State.[8]

In order to dissolve a college legally, the governing board must give public notice of the intent to dissolve and two-thirds of the members of the board of trustees must consent to the dissolution.[9] Alternatively, the board may bring a civil action in Superior Court to apply for a dissolution and for the appointment of a receiver.[10] There is no express provision for the involuntary dissolution of a nonprofit college. In a court-supervised dissolution, either the Superior Court[11] or the receiver may distribute the corporate assets among those entitled to the assets after the payment of the debts.[12] Otherwise, after the payment of lawful debts, the governing board must distribute the college's assets according to its bylaws. The corporation, however, may not divert property given in trust for a charitable purpose from the ends for which it was given.[13] The New Jersey courts are empowered to apply the *cy pres* doctrine when necessary.[14]

B. State Support

Congress enacted legislation in 1963 to provide federal funds to assist in the construction and renovation of college facilities.[15] In 1965 the Attorney General of New Jersey issued an opinion that a state program parallel to the federal program would be constitutionally permissible.[16] Recognizing the financial problems of many institutions of higher education, New Jersey passed an Educational Facilities Authority Law in 1966. In the purpose section of this legislation the legislature proclaimed that "all institutions of higher education in the state, both public and private, are an integral part of the total educational effort in the state for providing higher educational opportunities. . . . "[17] The law provides financial assistance in the construction of dormitories and other educational facilities at eligible institutions, including RACs.[18] As with the parallel federal legislation sustained in *Tilton v. Richardson*,[19] the New Jersey statute prohibits the use of a facility constructed or renovated with state funds "for sectarian instruction or as a place for religious worship."[20] The Facilities Act was sustained in *Clayton v. Kewick*,[21] in which the New Jersey Supreme Court ruled that the state program was indistinguishable from the federal program found permissible in the *Tilton* case.

In 1977 the New Jersey Attorney General issued a formal opinion concerning the use of a state-funded facility for religious worship by students at an RAC. The Attorney General expressed the view that incidental and voluntary use of a state-funded building for religious ac-

tivities organized by resident students does not violate the Establishment Clause and does not fall within the prohibition of the statute. The Attorney General stated: "By permitting voluntary religious worship among other activities in these facilities, the State has not advanced religion but is merely fulfilling their primary secular purposes."[22]

In 1979 New Jersey enacted another program of financial assistance to independent colleges.[23] Among the purposes stated for this legislation is the maximization of "educational choice among colleges and universities through the preservation of the vitality and quality of independent institutions of higher education in this state."[24]

RACs are generally eligible to participate in the program established by this legislation. Only institutions primarily dedicated to the preparation and training of "ministers, priests, rabbis or other professional persons in the field of religion"[25] are ineligible. Under authorization of this act, the Board of Higher Education is permitted to contract with eligible institutions to provide educational services to New Jersey students. Payment is based upon a ratio of independent college students to state college students and distribution is by a statutory formula. The funds given may be used for any purpose appropriate to the academic offerings, "except for purposes of sectarian instruction, the construction or maintenance of sectarian facilities, or for any other sectarian purpose or activity."[26]

New Jersey has a general prohibition against the disbursement of state monies for higher education to "any institution wholly or in part under the control of a religious denomination or in which a denominational tenet or doctrine is taught."[27] In the 1979 legislation, however, this provision is declared inapplicable to that program. The constitutionality of the program has not yet been tested.

The Department of Higher Education seeks to encourage cooperative programs among all colleges and universities in New Jersey. For example, the Board of Higher Education includes a representative of the private colleges and universities in New Jersey.[28]

New Jersey provides a variety of scholarships, grants and loans for students attending public and private institutions of higher education in that state.

New Jersey's scholarship system is coordinated and administered by the Student Assistance Board within the Board of Higher Education. The "Garden State Scholarship Act of 1977"[29] amalgamated the prior competitive scholarships. These awards are made by the New Jersey institutions upon academic merit. The monetary value of the scholarships, up to $500, is based upon financial need. The awards are made annually to each eligible New Jersey resident enrolled in a full-time capacity at an approved and accredited college.[30]

The competitive scholarships were unavailable to students attending an institution that discriminates in any of its policies on the basis of race, creed, color, or national origin, except that RACs could admit or employ any individual on the basis of religion where religion is reasonably necessary to the normal operation of the institution.[31] This provision has been repealed, and the only restrictions remaining in the Garden State Scholarship program relate to full-time participation in an accredited institution.

Junior college graduates who otherwise qualify for a competitive scholarship, but who are unable to attend a four year institution without financial assistance, may apply for a competitive scholarship.[32]

Under the Educational Opportunity Fund,[33] financially needy students are identified, recruited and given financial assistance so that they might attend institutions of higher education,[34] public or private. To be eligible for the Opportunity grants the student must not only demonstrate financial need, but must also be historically disadvantaged, a resident of New Jersey for twelve months prior to receipt of the grant and a full-time student. These grants are for no more than six years and are awarded without regard to the race, creed, or religion of the applicant.[35]

Tuition Aid Grants[36] are awarded for undergraduate study in accredited institutions. New Jersey residents who have demonstrated financial need are eligible for these grants, which can be used in collegiate level institutions either within New Jersey or in another state which has a reciprocity agreement.[37] The tuition grants are awarded without regard to race, religion, creed, or sex of the student, but a student may not participate in this program if "enrolled in a course leading to a degree in theology or divinity."[38] These awards are for at least $100, but may not exceed $1,400 in any year.[39]

New Jersey also grants full tuition in any public or private institution within the state to a dependent of a prisoner of war or a person listed as missing in action in the Vietnam War.[40] There are tuition credits available to certain veterans who are enrolled in any academic, professional or vocational school. These credits are reimbursed directly to the approved institution upon certification of enrollment.[41]

New Jersey residents attending a certified non-degree-granting postsecondary institution, whether in New Jersey or elsewhere, are eligible for educational loans through the Higher Education Assistance Authority.[42] Out-of-state students attending a New Jersey institution are also eligible.[43] In addition, the Institution of Higher Education Educational Loan Act of 1977 authorizes loans to defray the cost of collegiate attendance at any approved and accredited institution of higher education.[44]

C. Personnel

Nondiscrimination in Hiring, Promoting, and Firing

New Jersey civil rights legislation prohibits employers from discriminating against employees and prospective employees on the basis of race, creed, color, national origin, ancestry, age, marital status, or sex of any individual.[45] Until 1977, however, RACs were not bound by this statute because all nonprofit educational or religious corporations were excluded from the statutory definition of an employer.[46] In 1977 this provision was amended and "employer" was defined expansively to include all persons not otherwise specifically exempt under another section of the act.[47] The practical import of this amendment is that RACs may not discriminate in their employment policies on any basis other than religious affiliation or orientation. The statute expressly authorizes religious preference by religious associations or corporations:

it shall not be an unlawful employment practice . . . for a religious association or organization to utilize religious affiliation as a uniform qualification in the employment of clergy, religious teachers, or other employees engaged in the religious activities of the association or organization, or in following the tenets of its religion in establishing and utilizing criteria for employment of an employee.[48]

The very fact that the statute refers to religious teachers suggests that the legislature intended to include at least some RACs within the scope of a religious corporation. Some RACs like Shelton College clearly qualify under this provision, but other RACs may either not be defined in their charters as a religious corporation or not wish to be perceived primarily as a religious enterprise rather than as an educational enterprise. If these institutions wish to maintain a policy of religious preference, however, the only way they can do so is as a religious corporation. RACs in New Jersey, moreover, are prohibited from mentioning a policy of religious preference in advertisements unless the religion of a prospective employee is a bona fide occupational qualification.[49]

The New Jersey civil rights law likewise prohibits discrimination against the handicapped.[50] The statutory definition of a handicap includes "any mental, psychological or developmental disability resulting from anatomical, psychological, physiological, or neurological conditions which prevents the normal exercise of any bodily or mental functions."[51] This comprehensive definition would appear to include alcoholism and drug addiction as handicaps, but if this legislation is construed as the federal government interprets the federal Vocational Rehabilitation Act, it would not inhibit an RAC from enforcing a religiously based policy against the consumption of alcohol or use of illicit drugs on its campus.[52]

Wages and Hours

New Jersey prohibits discrimination in wages and salary on the basis of sex.[53] No RAC is exempt.[54]

New Jersey's Minimum Wage Law provides that all wage-earners must earn at least $3.35 per hour, and time and a half for all hours in excess of forty per week.[55] No RAC is exempt as an employer,[56] but full-time students employed by the college they are attending may be paid only 85% of the minimum wage.[57] RACs are likewise required to pay their ordinary wage-earners at least twice a month, and their executives or supervisors at least once a month.[58]

Worker's Compensation

The New Jersey Workmen's Compensation Act[59] is an elective compensation scheme[60] with a statutory presumption of coverage unless either the employer or the employee notifies the other party in writing to the contrary.[61] RACs electing coverage may nevertheless have employees who come within the exemption for casual employment.[62] Injured employees not covered by the compensation provision retain the right to sue their employer in court for damages.[63] Whether or not RACs elect coverage by the compensation provision, they must carry insurance or prove financial ability to pay compensation directly to injured employees.[64]

Unemployment Compensation

The New Jersey Unemployment Compensation Law[65] defines "employment"[66] to include services performed for nonprofit organizations,[67] if those services are excluded from the definition of "employment" in the Federal Unemployment Tax Act solely due to section 3306(c)(8).[68] The New Jersey statute's definition does not apply to services performed (1) for a church or for an association of churches;[69] (2) for an organization run primarily for religious purposes and controlled by a church or by an association of churches;[70] (3) or by ordained ministers or by members of religious orders in the exercise of their duties.[71] Thus, most services performed for RACs constitute covered employment.

Other exemptions relevant to RACs include services performed (1) for a school or college by one of its regularly enrolled students[72] or by their spouses;[73] (2) by a student under the age of twenty-two at an accredited nonprofit or public educational institution in a full-time program, taken for credit and combining the academic instruction and work experience;[74] or (3) as a domestic for a college club or chapter of a college fraternity or sorority.[75]

Nonprofit organizations may elect to make payments in lieu of contributions. To take advantage of this option, an organization must fit the definition in section 501(c)(3) of the Internal Revenue Code and must qualify as tax-exempt under section 501(a) of the Code.[76] The election is effective for a period of two years upon filing of written notice[77] with the Division of Unemployment and Temporary Disability Insurance.[78] The payments required equal the amount of regular benefits plus the amount of extended benefits paid.[79] The Division may require an electing organization to file an approved surety bond.[80] Organizations not otherwise subject to the provision of the statute may elect to participate in the program for a minimum of two years.

D. Students

New Jersey's civil rights law prohibits educational institutions from discriminating on the basis of race, creed, color, national origin, ancestry, marital status, or sex.[81] RACs, however, which may be characterized as being "operated or maintained by a bona fide religious or sectarian institution"[82] are exempt from this provision and may maintain a policy of religious preference in student admissions. Moreover, all-male or all-female schools are allowed to continue as single-sex academies.[83]

Although the state awards financial assistance to students without regard to race, religion, creed, age, or sex,[84] this provision in the financial aid legislation should not be construed as an implied restriction on an RAC wishing to maintain a policy of religious preference in student admissions.

E. Facilities

New Jersey's civil rights act protects access to public accommodations without discrimination because of race, creed, color, ancestry, age, marital status, or sex.[85] The definition of a public accommodation, however, generally excludes any institution which is in its nature

distinctly private. The statute specifically excludes "any educational facility operated or maintained by a bona fide religious or sectarian institution."[86]

The state civil rights act likewise contains a general prohibition against discrimination in the sale, lease, or rental of housing. But the statute also provides:

> Nothing herein contained shall be construed to bar any religious or denominational institution . . . from limiting admission to or giving preference to persons of the same religion or denomination or from making such selection as is calculated by such organization to promote the religious principles for which it is established or maintained.[87]

The first clause of this exemption applies only to religious discrimination; the second could be used for broader discrimination on the basis of "religious principles" (e.g., refusing to rent an apartment to an unmarried couple).

This exemption clearly applies to dormitories, and may even apply to off-campus property held by an RAC for the convenience of its students. An RAC may not, however, discriminate in the sale of property it has been holding solely for investment purposes. As the New Jersey Supreme Court stated in *David v. Vista:*

> the statute does not exempt all sales or rentals of real property owned by a religious organization, but only those which are calculated by such organization to promote the religious principles for which it is established or maintained.[88]

Student dormitories at RACs fall within the safety regulations issued under the Hotels and Multiple Dwellings Act,[89] but are excluded from similar safety legislation under the Rooming and Boarding Houses Act.[90]

New Jersey has a Worker Health and Safety Act,[91] but all schools, including RACs, are expressly excluded from the definition of an employer in this statute.[92]

F. State Taxation

In 1976, New Jersey enacted a new Gross Income Tax Act,[93] which imposes a tax on net profits from business.[94] This statute, however, defines the term "taxpayer" as an "individual, estate, or trust,"[95] and appears, therefore, not to refer to nonprofit corporations, including RACs.

The transfer of property to an RAC either by gift or inheritance is exempt from the payment of inheritance and estate taxes.[96] This exemption does not extend to a transfer of property to a college in another state which does not grant reciprocal exemption to New Jersey.[97]

The New Jersey constitution exempts institutions operated exclusively for a religious, educational, or charitable purpose from the payment of real and personal property taxes.[98]

New Jersey likewise exempts from the payment of sales and use tax all institutions organized and operated "exclusively for religious, charitable, scientific, testing for public safety, literary, or educational purposes."[99] The exempt sale or use must be "directly related to the purposes for which [the exempt institutions] have been organized."[100] In other words, RACs must pay the sales and use tax on transactions unrelated to their exempt purposes.

New Jersey imposes a tax on proceeds from admissions to athletic events, theatrical productions, carnivals, and the like, but such events at RACs are not subject to this tax if the proceeds go entirely to the benefit of the religious or educational corporation or organization.[101]

In calculating their liability for personal income tax, New Jersey taxpayers are allowed an additional exemption of $1,000 from gross income for each dependent under age 22 who is attending an accredited postsecondary institution on a full-time basis, and for whom the taxpayer pays at least one-half of the costs of tuition and maintenance of the dependent's attendance at college during the tax year.[102] No tax is owed on income from scholarships or fellowship grants or income to cover travel, research, or equipment incident to a scholarship or research grant.[103]

G. Fund Raising

New Jersey includes "benevolent, philanthropic, and eleemosynary organizations"[104]

within the definition of charitable organizations whose charitable solicitation is regulated. RACs, however, are exempted from registration requirements,[105] and need not file annual reports.[106] In addition, professional fund raisers engaged by RACs are not required to register with the Attorney General, as are fund raisers for other charitable organizations.[107] The Attorney General is empowered by the statute to make such rules and regulations as he deems necessary to govern charitable solicitation.[108] Among his statutory powers is the right to bring an action to enjoin a charitable organization from soliciting if it violates any provision of the Act.[109]

If an RAC were to desire to raise funds by sponsoring bingo games, it would, in some circumstances, be allowed to do so under New Jersey law. Municipalities in New Jersey may adopt a Bingo Licensing law, "making lawful the holding, operating and conducting of games of chance under licenses when the net proceeds thereof are devoted entirely to educational, . . . religious or public spirited uses."[110] If this law is adopted locally, both the governing body of the municipality[111] and the State Legalized Games of Chance Control Commission[112] control the operation of authorized games of chance.[113] For example, a charitable organization must apply for a license to the clerk of the governing board of the municipality.[114] The Commission, however, may refuse to allow the use of facilities not owned by the charitable organization for gambling purposes.[115] The state has set limits on prizes that may be awarded,[116] the price of admission,[117] and the days on which games of chance may be played;[118] and it has prohibited the serving of alcohol,[119] the participation of minors,[120] and the advertisement of such games except with a sign on the premises.[121] The act, moreover, requires licenses to be displayed while games are conducted,[122] and requires organizations to file a statement of receipts and expenses within fifteen days of a game.[123]

Raffles are also permitted.[124] The provisions are analogous to those regulating bingo except that the maximum amount allowed for prizes is different.[125]

39. New Mexico

A. Corporate Status

RACs are incorporated in New Mexico under the Nonprofit Corporation law, which defines a nonprofit corporation as one in which "no part of the income or profit is distributable to its members, directors or officers."[1] Consistent with this definition is the provision precluding the distribution of assets to present or former members, directors or officers of the nonprofit corporation.[2]

The remainder of the Chapter deals with typical corporate housekeeping matters such as the requirement of an annual report to the state[3] and the filing fee for the annual report ($1.00) and for the articles of incorporation ($10.00).

New Mexico's Post-Secondary Educational Institutions Act,[4] aimed primarily at improving the quality of, and preventing misrepresentation, fraud and collusion in postsecondary schools,[5] requires such schools, unless exempted, to obtain a permit or certificate of approval from the board of educational finance prior to operation.[6] The exceptions are so broad,[7] however, that virtually all RACs will be exempt. Exempted, *inter alia*, are private institutions which offer "a basic academic education comparable to that provided by public colleges or universities";[8] educational institutions with the specified accreditation;[9] and chartered nonprofit religious institutions whose sole purpose is religious training for religious vocations.[10]

The merger, consolidation, and dissolution of nonprofit colleges are governed by the New Mexico Nonprofit Corporation Act.[11] There is no reported decision requiring New Mexico courts to apply the *cy pres* doctrine, but in dictum the Supreme Court of that state has indicated it does not "run counter to the public policy in New Mexico."[12]

Articles of merger,[13] consolidation,[14] or voluntary dissolution[15] adoped by the governing board of a nonprofit college[16] must be filed with the state's Corporation Commission. The articles take effect when the Commission issues a certificate of merger, consolidation,[17] or dissolution.[18] The Commission may revoke a certificate of incorporation when there is fraud, abuse of authority, failure to file timely annual reports, misrepresentation, or failure to pay fees and penalties after due notice.[19] The District Courts also have jurisdiction to dissolve a nonprofit college involuntarily in an action properly brought by a member of the corporation or by a creditor.[20]

The New Mexico Nonprofit Corporation Act provides that assets of a dissolving nonprofit college shall be distributed according to a procedure identical with the Model Nonprofit Corporation Act.[21]

Under New Mexico law, any educational institution offering or representing to offer a "basic academic education," like that provided by public colleges or private accredited colleges, leading to a degree or certificate, is prohibited from terminating the program or disposing of most of its assets until it has (1) made reasonable efforts to arrange for the transfer of its students to similar institutions with minimal loss of credit;[22] (2) provided in perpetuity for the maintenance of records relating to all students who have received credit from it;[23] and (3) reported to the board of educational finance its actions in furtherance of (1) and (2).[24]

B. State Support

The framers of New Mexico's Constitution apparently intended a strict separation between the state and RACs. The Constitution is carefully drawn to prohibit any form of state support for such institutions:

[N]o part of the proceeds arising from the sale or disposal of any lands granted to the state by Congress or any other funds appropriated, levied, or collected for educational purposes, shall be used for the support of any sectarian, denominational, or private school, college or university.[25]

Another provision prohibits any appropriation for "charitable, educational or other benevolent purposes" to a "person, corporation, association, institution or community, *not under the absolute control of the state.*"[26]

In keeping with the constitutional mandate the only state financial aid available to private institutions (and therefore RACs) directly or indirectly is in the nature of loans and loan guarantees to students.

Under the Student Loan Guarantee Act,[27] the state guarantees loans (guaranteed by the United States) to eligible students through participating institutions:

consistent with Title IV, Part B, of the federal Higher Education Act of 1965, as amended; Title 45, Part 177, of the Code of Federal Regulations; and agreements with the United States Commission of Education pertaining thereto.[28]

An "eligible student" is a New Mexico resident enrolled in a participating institution and otherwise eligible for a student loan guaranteed under the Act.[29] A "participating institution" in turn is any post-high school educational institution, public or private, in or out of state, eligible to participate in the guaranteed loan program of the Higher Education Act of 1965[30] and approved by the New Mexico board of educational finance for the state's guaranteed

student loan program.[31] Students at RACs, therefore, are clearly eligible to participate in the Student Loan Guarantee Act.

C. Personnel

The New Mexico Human Rights Law[32] declares it to be an "unlawful discriminatory practice" for any employer,[33] unless based on a bona fide occupational qualification (BFOQ), to discriminate in hiring, promoting, demoting, discharging, or compensating against any person on the basis of race, age, religion, color, national origin, ancestry, sex, or physical or mental handicap.[34]

In terms of religious selectivity in employment, RACs have two possible exemptions. The first is the BFOQ which provides, of course, a very narrow exception, one likely to be helpful, at best, in its employment of faculty for certain religiously oriented courses or of certain counseling personnel. It is not likely that an RAC would be successful in arguing a right to exercise religious preference in faculty positions generally despite its interest in establishing on campus a pervasive presence of faculty of a certain religious persuasion.

The second exemption is much less explicit and, indeed, less tangible:

Nothing contained in the Human Rights Act shall . . . bar any religious or denominational institution or organization which is operated or supervised or controlled by or is operated in connection with a religious or denominational organization from limiting admission to or giving preference to persons of the same religion or denomination, or from making selections of buyers, lessees or tenants as are calculated by the organization or denomination to promote the religious or denominational principles for which it is established or maintained unless membership in the religious or denominational organization is restricted on account of race, color, national origin, or ancestry. . . . [35]

Since this provision refers to the entire Human Rights Act, it is arguable that the phrase "giving preference to" refers to employment. Three factors argue against this interpretation. First, had employment been meant, more specific language (e.g., hiring, promoting, etc.) would have been used. Second, the phrase "or giving preference to" seems to be an alternative to "limiting admission," a term more related to enrolling students or a society's members than hiring employees. Third, had employment been intended, it would have been easy to include the word "employees" after the phrase "or from making selections of." The legislature added only "buyers, lessees or tenants."

Most if not all RACs may be eligible for any employment exemption created by this provision because the affiliation required between the organization and a religion is worded extremely broadly. A qualifying institution, however, must be a religious or denominational institution or organization and it could be argued that only seminary-type colleges or Bible colleges, among RACs, are such, and that the word "educational" would have been used if most RACs had been intended to be included.

One further note about this provision. It allows preference only in favor of the religion with which the organization is affiliated. It would not justify, for example, a Jewish university's hiring of a Christian to teach a Christianity course (although, of course, the BFOQ provision discussed earlier[36] might).

The Human Rights Commission is charged with enforcing the employment discrimination law through a specified grievance procedure.[37]

New Mexico's Minimum Wage Act[38] covers, *inter alia*, any individual, association or corporation (except governmental units) employing one or more "employees" at any one time.[39] All RACs, therefore, must pay the specified minimum wages[40] to its "employees." Under the Act, "employee" does not include, *inter alia*, domestic service in a private home;[41] individuals employed in good faith executive, administrative or professional capacities;[42] foremen, superintendents and supervisors;[43] and:

any individual engaged in the activities of an educational, charitable, religious or nonprofit organization where the employer-employee relationship does not, in fact, exist or where the services rendered to such organizations are on a voluntary basis. The employer-employee relationship shall not be deemed to exist with respect to any individual being served for purposes of rehabilitation by a charitable or non-

profit organization, notwithstanding the payment of a stipend based upon the value of the work performed by the individual.[44]

The New Mexico Workman's Compensation Act[45] covers, *inter alia*, "every charitable organization employing workmen and every private person, firm or corporation engaged in carrying on for the purpose of business or trade within the state" employing three[46] or more workmen.[47] Since a "workman" is broadly defined to include anyone who has "entered into the employment of or works under a contract of service or apprenticeship with an employer,"[48] these provisions clearly suggest that RACs are included,[49] and with regard to most of their employees. However, educational institutions hiring students to enable them to pay their tuition and expenses and at which machinery or appliances are used which would subject the institution to the Workman's Compensation Act "as engaging in a hazardous calling or business" are exempted from the Act as to any liability accruing to any student so employed.[50] This does not, of course, relieve the institution from liability for damages or injuries to such a student otherwise recoverable by law.[51]

New Mexico's Unemployment Compensation Law[52] includes as "employment" service by an employee of a religious, charitable, educational, or other organization[53] if the service is excluded from the definition of "employment" in the Federal Unemployment Tax Act solely by reason of that Act's Section 3306(c)(8).[54] Service performed in the employ of a religious or educational organization described in Section 501(c)(3) of the Internal Revenue Code of 1954,[55] and thereby exempt from federal taxation, is excluded from "employment" as defined in Section 3306(c)(8) of the Federal Unemployment Tax Act.[56] Thus an RAC is subject to unemployment compensation legislation if it qualifies for tax exempt status under Section 501(c)(3).

With regard to such service, a nonprofit corporation may make the usual contribution[57] or elect to pay into the unemployment fund the amount of the regular benefits plus one-half of the extended benefits paid and attributable to service for the nonprofit corporation.[58]

"Employment" under the Act does not include

service performed by a student under the age of twenty-two enrolled at a regular nonprofit or public educational institution in a full-time program taken for credit which combines academic instruction with work experience.[59] The service must, however, be an integral part of the program, so certified to the employer, and not performed in a "program established for or on behalf of an employer or group of employers."[60]

D. Students

New Mexico has no legislation directly restricting the admission of students by RACs. Indeed, one statute, discussed at length earlier,[61] affirms the right of certain entities to make selections in favor of those of that religion with which the RAC is affiliated:

Nothing contained in the Human Rights Act shall . . . bar any religious or denominational institution or organization which is operated or supervised or controlled by or is operated in connection with a religious or denominational organization from limiting admission to or giving preference to persons of the same religion or denomination.[62]

While the provision does not specifically mention educational institutions, the language may cover the admissions of virtually all RACs.[63] The problem it creates, however, is to suggest by implication that *only* religious selectivity in favor of the religion with which the RAC is affiliated is authorized. Indeed, it would seem to suggest that Roman Catholic institutions could only favor Roman Catholics (i.e., the same religion or denominaton) and not Christians (a broader group encompassing that religion or denomination).

E. Facilities

New Mexico labels it an "unlawful discriminatory practice" for any person:

in any public accommodation to make a distinction, directly or indirectly, in offering or refusing to offer its services, facilities, accommodations or goods to any individual because of race, religion, color, national origin, ancestry, sex or physical or mental handicap.[64]

Although this provision would clearly cover RAC bookstores, hotels, theaters and the like that invite the public, there is a qualifying provision, discussed more fully earlier,[65] emphasizing the right of certain religious or denominational institutions or organizations[66] to limit admission or give preference to persons of the same religion or denomination. Although there may not be many situations in which RACs would care to so limit admission to their public accommodations, this provision may well authorize them to do so, and without any need to justify their decision.

It is possible, of course, that the phrase "limiting admission to" was intended to cover enrollment decisions[67] (rather than public accommodations decisions), in anticipation of an argument that the public accommodations law covered admissions directly (although there is no indication that an RAC itself comes within the statute's use of the term[68] or, for that matter, the term's common usage) or indirectly.[69]

It is also an unlawful discriminatory practice to discriminate in the sale or rental of any housing accommodations or real property because of race, religion, color, national origin, ancestry, sex, or physical or mental handicap.[70] This provision would seem clearly to cover student housing on RAC campuses since "housing accommodation" means any building "used or intended for use as the residence or sleeping place of any individual."[71] Nothing in the statute indicates that RACs would violate the statute by restricting its housing to students and staff and, should the institution limit its enrollment or its staff on a religious basis, New Mexico law stipulates that nothing in the Human Rights Law shall bar certain religious or denominational institutions or organizations (including perhaps RACs)[72] from:

making selections of buyers, lessees or tenants as are calculated [by such institutions or organizations] to promote the religious or denominational principles for which [the institutions or organizations are] established or maintained unless membership in the religious or denominational organization is restricted on account of race, color, national origin or ancestry.[73]

This provision provides a fairly broad exemption for qualifying organizations, enabling them (as long as their membership is not restricted on the grounds of race, color, national origin, or ancestry) to select on any ground calculated *by them* to promote their religious principles. This exemption, furthermore, is not restricted to religious preference in favor of the organization's own religious affiliation.

The Uniform Owner-Resident Relations Act,[74] *inter alia*, requires owners to comply with all housing codes materially affecting health and safety;[75] limits the ability of the landlord to enter rental premises, without lessee consent, to emergencies;[76] and prescribes the lessee's remedies upon the landlord's failure to comply with the Act.[77] Exempted from the Act's coverage is "residence at an institution, public or private, if incidental to the provision of religious, educational [,] where room and board are an entity, or similar service."[78] All RACs would be eligible for this exemption as long as *both* room and board are provided.

The New Mexico Occupational Health and Safety Act[79] is modeled upon the federal act. The Act is administered by the New Mexico Occupational Health and Safety Agency.[80] The definitions under the Act are all-inclusive, exempting only domestic employees from the definition of an employee.[81] The Act also provides that all regulations issued pursuant to the act must be at least as effective as those standards promulgated pursuant to the federal act.[82]

F. State Taxation

New Mexico exempts from its state income tax, *inter alia*, all nonprofit religious and educational organizations exempt from federal income taxation,[83] which would include almost all RACs[84] "except to the extent that such income is subject to federal income taxation as unrelated business income."[85] Virtually all RACs, therefore, are exempt from state income taxation except with regard to their unrelated business income, as defined by the federal Internal Revenue Code.[86]

New Mexico imposes an estate tax on the transfer of the net estate of every resident in an amount equal to the federal credit.[87] No specific exemption or credit is provided in the New Mexico Code for property left to RACs.

Contributions or gifts to RACs are not given any preferential income tax treatment. New Mexico does not have a gift tax.

The New Mexico Constitution provides that "all property used for educational or charitable purposes shall be exempt from taxation."[88] It is not required that the property be used *solely* for the specified purposes,[89] although it is the *primary* use of the property that controls, not the purpose for which the institution involved was organized.[90] If, therefore, a building such as a campus bookstore is used primarily for educational purposes, the entire building is exempt regardless of what other purposes it might also serve.

Although New Mexico attaches a three and three-quarter percent excise tax on the gross receipts of businesses in that state,[91] it exempts organizations that have been granted a federal income tax exemption under Section 501(c)(3) of the Internal Revenue Code,[92] except as to unrelated trade or business income as defined in the federal Internal Revenue Code.[93] Again, therefore, virtually all RACs are exempt.

The same organizations exempted under the gross receipts tax are also exempted, in the conduct of functions described in Section 501(c)(3) of the federal Internal Revenue Code, from the compensating tax,[94] a parallel tax on property and services used in the state but not subject to the gross receipt tax for various specified reasons, e.g., the property was purchased out of state.[95]

There is no state sales tax (the gross receipts and compensating taxes being the equivalent, presumably), but counties are authorized to impose a sales tax, in support of indigent hospital patients,[96] not to exceed "one-fourth of one percent on the gross receipts of all retail businesses and services within the county."[97] There is no exemption provided for RACs so any such tax enacted could apply to sales by campus restaurants and the like. Indeed, as presently drafted, the statute does not clearly exclude tuition from the tax.

It is interesting to note that for purposes of the Gross Receipts Tax Act,[98] "service" includes "all activities engaged in for other persons for a consideration."[99] Should a court interpreting this tax law have recourse to this definition, tuition at the few RACs not otherwise exempted could easily be made subject to the tax. It is true that the sales tax law refers to "retail businesses and services" and, especially if the word "retail" modifies "services," the legislature may not have intended to include professional-type services such as academic instruction.

G. Fund Raising

There is no charitable solicitation statute in New Mexico.

Under New Mexico law, gambling (which includes bets or lotteries) is a criminal offense.[100] Nothing in the "gambling" article,[101] however, is to be construed applicable to sales or drawings of prizes at fairs held:

for the benefit of any church, public library or religious society [in the state] or for charitable purposes when all the proceeds of such fair shall be expended in this state for the benefit of such church, public library, religious society or charitable purposes.[102]

It would seem that very few RACs could take advantage of this provision. Perhaps certain seminary-type colleges or Bible colleges might qualify as religious societies. It is possible that educational institutions might be included within "charitable purposes," but more likely the courts will assume that the word "educational" would have been added if colleges and the like were intended to be included.

The requirement that the lottery be held at a "fair" would seem to exclude weekly bingo games although "fair" is an ambiguous term. It is interesting to note that a 1979 piece of gambling legislation[103] specified that it was not to be construed to "prohibit the operation or continued operation of bingo programs presently conducted for charitable purposes."[104] This would seem to indicate that bingo for charitable purposes, whatever they might be, is not illegal.

H. Miscellaneous

New Mexico has a state commission on post-secondary education.[105] Made up of the board of educational finance,[106] the commission is charged with various duties of analysis, planning, and recommendation with regard to virtually all post-secondary education[107] (including private colleges and universities)[108] and, therefore, virtually all RACs.

40. New York

A. Corporate Status

An educational institution may be established in New York in one of three ways.[1] It may be created by a special act of the state legislature,[2] by a charter from the Regents of the University of the State of New York,[3] or by the approval of the Commissioner of Education for the incorporation of the institution under the Not-for-Profit Corporation Law.[4]

Although some private universities such as Cornell University have been created by a special act of the Legislature,[5] incorporation by this method is highly unusual.[6] A publication of the Office of the Counsel and Deputy Commissioner for Legal Affairs of the State Education Department[7] indicates that consent of the Commissioner of Education to incorporate under the Not-for-Profit Corporation Law will generally not be granted to colleges and universities.[8] The most appropriate method for the creation of an RAC, then, would seem to be a charter from the Regents of the University of the State of New York.[9]

An RAC seeking a charter from the Regents is subject to the same requirements imposed on all colleges and universities. It must file a petition with the Regents, and each decision is made by that body on a case by case basis. If an RAC possesses the financial resources which, in the judgment of the Regents, are "adequate to ensure satisfactory conduct of its degree program and achievement of its stated educational goals,"[10] and otherwise satisfies the Regents, a provisional charter will be granted.[11] In all other respects, creation and maintenance of an RAC is governed by the general provisions of the Education and Not-for-Profit Corporation Laws.[12]

The merger, consolidation and dissolution of nonprofit colleges are governed by the state's Not-for-Profit Corporation Law.[13] In addition, the legislature and the state courts have recognized the doctrine of *cy pres* in New York.[14]

A majority of the members of the governing board of a nonprofit college may petition for judicial dissolution if they are persuaded that the assets of the corporation are not sufficient to discharge its liabilities or that dissolution will be beneficial to the members.[15]

A nonprofit college may be dissolved in New York either judicially or nonjudicially. In the case of nonjudicial dissolution, the governing board adopts a plan for the dissolution of the corporation and for the distribution of its assets. Any college chartered by the Board of Regents must seek the approval of the Regents for its dissolution.[16]

If at the time of dissolution a nonprofit college holds assets required to be used for a particular purpose, it must seek approval for its plan of dissolution and distribution from a local Justice of the Supreme Court.[17] When the approval of the Regents and the Supreme Court has been obtained, a certificate of dissolution is delivered to the Department of State.[18] When the consent of the State Tax Commissioner is attached to the certificate, the State Department files the certificate and the college is dissolved.[19] Then the board is empowered only to wind up the affairs of the college by collecting and liquidating its assets, discharging its liabilities, and distributing its remaining assets according to the approved plan.[20]

Although this detailed procedure is entitled "nonjudicial dissolution," the Attorney General, or any single member of the governing board, or, indeed, any creditor or claimant of a college seeking to dissolve may, with the approval of the Supreme Court, suspend or annul the dissolution or continue the liquidation process under the supervision of the court.[21] The procedures for judicial dissolution of a college are similarly detailed in New York law,[22] and may be initiated by the Attorney General in case of alleged fraud either in procurement of the charter or in the conduct of the college's business,[23] by a majority of the governing board where they determine that the assets of the corporation are insufficient to discharge its liabilities or that dissolution will be beneficial,[24] or by any member of the governing board alleging that the board is deadlocked in management of the college's affairs, or so divided that dissolution would be beneficial, or that board members or college administrators have wasted the college's assets or have otherwise acted in an illegal, oppressive or fraudulent manner, or that the college is no longer able to carry out the purposes for which it was incorporated.[25] The Attorney General must be a party to any proceeding for judicial dissolution of a nonprofit college.[26]

In the case of nonjudicial dissolution the procedure for distribution of assets is closely patterned on the Model Non-profit Corporation Act.[27] In the case of judicial dissolution, the court may either distribute the college's assets or appoint a receiver to do so.[28] Six months after the date fixed for the payment of the final distribution of assets, any assets distributable to a creditor who is unknown or cannot be found are paid to the State Comptroller as abandoned property.[29]

B. State Support

New York law authorizes direct state aid to certain independent institutions of higher education located in the state.[30] Eligible institutions must be nonprofit in nature and incorporated by the legislature or the Regents of the University of the State of New York.[31] They must meet certain academic standards, including the maintenance of one or more earned degree programs,[32] and they must be eligible for state aid under the provisions of the constitutions of the United States and of the State of New York.[33] Direct state aid is also available for the support of special programs such as counseling, testing, and tutoring,[34] and for programs operating in conjunction with the state university program pursuant to a contract with the state university.[35]

The use of public property or money in aid of schools controlled by any religious group is prohibited by the state constitution. The section commonly known as the Blaine Amendment provides:

Neither the state nor any subdivision thereof shall use its property or credit or any public money, or authorize or permit either to be used, directly or indirectly, in aid or maintenance, other than for examination or inspection, of any school or institution of learning wholly or in part under the control or direction of any religious denomination, or in which any denominational tenet or doctrine is taught, but the legislature may provide for the transportation of children to and from any school or institution of learning.[36]

The restrictions of the Blaine Amendment, however, have been liberally interpreted in favor of religiously affiliated higher education. Both of the operative clauses in the Amendment were construed in *College of New Rochelle v. Nyquist.*[37] The College of New Rochelle was founded by a religious order devoted to the education of women, and described itself as "a liberal arts college for women under Catholic auspices" devoted to the Christian tradition in its uniqueness and complexity.[38] While the college required a certain number of credits in religious studies to be taken, the court described them as "courses of the type taught in any private and state institutions of higher learning which seek as an academic discipline the religious heritage of the world."[39] The faculty of the religion department included laymen and clergy of several faiths in addition to members of the sponsoring religious order.[40]

The court construed broadly the second clause in the Blaine Amendment, generally forbidding aid to an institution "in which any denominational tenet or doctrine is taught. In so doing, the court quoted from *Canisius College v. Nyquist:*

To literally interpret the provision of the Blaine Amendment that "any institution in which *any* denominational tenet or doctrine is taught" is prohibited from State aid [sic], would be absurd, since it would eliminate from State aid almost all private institutions, as well as some of the schools of the State University. The reasonable interpretation of this portion of the Blaine Amendment is that State aid should not be given to institutions which teach tenets as doctrine of a particular religious denomination to the exclusion of other denominations.[41]

A divided New York Court of Appeals reversed the Appellate Division's finding of eligibility for state aid to Canisius College.[42] Later the college "internally addressed the factors which had led the Commissioner to find [it] ineligible, reapplied, and was ultimately found eligible."[43] The College of New Rochelle, under the quoted interpretation of the Blaine Amendment, was held to be eligible.[44]

In *College of New Rochelle* the court also liberally interpreted the clause in the Blaine Amendment referring to "any school or institution . . . wholly or in part under the control of any religious denomination."[45] The court stated:

To make sense of and to give purpose to this clause of the Blaine Amendment it must be construed to proscribe State aid where the affiliated religious denomination controls or directs the institution towards a religious end; where the institution is controlled to a degree so as to enable the religious authorities to propagate and advance—or at least to attempt to do so—their religion. Mere affiliation or a sharing of administrative control by a denomination will not, in and of itself, bring the institution within the proscription of the statute; such a situation cannot be said to have caused religions to "pervade" the atmosphere of the College as to effectuate religious control or direction by a religious denomination.[46]

Thus the key to determining eligibility of an RAC under the "control" clause is not the existence of religious affiliation but rather the type of control or direction which is exercised.

In *College of New Rochelle* the court concluded that the College was not ineligible for State aid under the terms of the Blaine Amendment, and that aid was not proscribed by the United States Constitution since there was not an impermissible entanglement of the State with religion.[47]

New York provides assistance in the construction and operation of physical facilities to colleges, universities, hospitals, and other non-profit organizations through the State Dormitory Authority.[48] The definition of "dormitory" for the purpose of this legislation includes:

a housing unit for the use of students, married students, and the families of such married students, faculty and staff, an academic building, administration building, library, laboratory, classroom, health facility or other building or structure essentially necessary or useful in the academic, cultural, health or research program, including all necessary and usual attendant and related facilities and equipment at any institution for higher education located in this state and authorized to confer degrees by law or by the board of regents, other than a state-operated institution or statutory or contract college under the jurisdiction of the State University of New York.[49]

The Dormitory Authority[50] is authorized upon application of an educational institution[51] to "acquire, design, construct, reconstruct, rehabilitate and improve, or otherwise provide and furnish and equip dormitories and attendant facilities for any educational institution."[52] It may also make loans to any educational institution[53] for these purposes.[54]

It seems certain that RACs are eligible for assistance by the Dormitory Authority.[55] Notwithstanding the various methods for creating an educational institution under New York law,[56] an RAC is included within the broad definition of "any institution for higher education, other than a state-operated institution or statutory or contract college."[57]

A variety of financial aid is available to students at institutions of higher education under New York statutes.[58] Most students attending an RAC are eligible for these programs, with the exception of those students obtaining "professional instruction in theology."[59] In addition to general requirements such as forms for application,[60] a student in order to be eligible must be "matriculated in an approved program,"[61] defined to include:

collegiate level programs leading to a degree, or programs leading to a diploma or certificate that are fully creditable toward a degree program in that institution, [and] study and training programs offered by . . . an institution chartered by the regents or by the legislature for the purpose of granting degrees.[62]

Thus any accredited RAC would qualify as an "approved program" for the purpose of this legislation.

New York Education law also provides for financial assistance to students who are blind or deaf.[63] Blind or deaf citizens of New York attending a New York RAC are eligible under the statute for this assistance since the student is required only to be in actual attendance at an institution in the state authorized by law to grant degrees.[64] The assistance is paid directly to the institution on an annual basis[65] to defray the cost of readers or special facilities for a deaf student.[66]

C. Personnel

New York law makes it unlawful for an employer to discriminate on the basis of age, race, creed, color, national origin, sex, disability, or marital status.[67] There are exceptions to this general prohibition against discrimination which are applicable to RACs.

The first is the Bona Fide Occupational Qualification (BFOQ) exception, set out in the following provision:

It shall be an unlawful discriminatory practice:

(d) For any employer or employment agency to print or circulate or cause to be printed or circulated any statement, advertisement or publication, or to use any form of application for employment or to make any inquiry in connection with prospective employment, which expresses directly or indirectly, any limitation, specification or discrimination as to age, race, creed, color or national origin, sex, or disability or marital status, or any intent to make any such limitation, specification or discrimination, *unless based upon a bona fide occupational qualification.*[68]

It is repeated in another context:

1-a. It shall be an unlawful discriminatory practice for an employer . . . :

(d) To print or circulate or cause to be printed or circulated any statement, advertisement or publication, or to use any form of application for such program or to make any inquiry in connection with such program which expresses, directly or indirectly, any limitation, specification or discrimination as to race, creed, color, national origin, sex, or disability or marital status, or any intention to make any such limitation, specification or discrimination, *unless based on a bona fide occupational qualification.*[69]

In both contexts, employers are generally prohibited from advertising a preference for employees on the basis of the enumerated categories, unless the preference is based on a BFOQ. The parallel federal civil rights statute allows a BFOQ exception only with respect to religion, sex, and national origin.[70] It is possible to contrue the New York statute to imply a BFOQ exception for each of the general categories otherwise unlawful for an employer to consider, such as age, race, color, disability, or marital status. For three reasons, however, it seems preferable to narrow the availability of the BFOQ exception under the New York statute to the same three categories mentioned in the federal statute. First, the definitional section of the state statute does not authorize a BFOQ exception for the broader categories referred to in the advertisement section. Second, New York courts have applied the BFOQ exception only to a case of alleged sex discrimination, and not to any of the other categories.[71] Third, even if the New York statute were read to allow a BFOQ exception with respect to age, race, color, disability, or marital status, this would be superseded by the BFOQ provision of the federal statute both by virtue of the language in Title VII that prohibits the doing of an act which is unlawful under Title VII[72] and by virtue of the Supremacy Clause of the federal constitution.[73]

The New York State Division of Human Rights is charged with formulating policies to effectuate the purposes of the Human Rights Law, including enforcement of the fair employment legislation.[74] The Division of Human Rights has indicated that a preference is not based on a BFOQ unless the attribute in question is material to job performance and not merely the preference of employers, coworkers or customers, or the custom of the industry.[75]

The second exception to the general prohibition of employment is extremely broad:

Nothing contained in this section shall be construed to bar any religious or denominational institution or organization, or any organization operated for charitable or educational purposes, which is operated, supervised or controlled by or in connection with a religious organization, from limiting employment . . . to or giving preference to persons of the same religion or denomination or from making such selection as is calculated by such organization to promote the religious principles for which it is established or maintained.[76]

Because the actual relationships between colleges and religious organizations vary considerably, some church-related colleges might not meet the requirement that they be "operated, supervised, or controlled by" a religious organization in order to exercise religious preference in employment. These colleges, however, should qualify for this exception because the New York statute, unlike the federal parallel, only requires that the institution be operated "in connection with" a religious organization.

If the institution does meet the "operated, supervised, or controlled" test, it is not barred from (1) limiting or giving preference in employment to persons of the same religion or denomination or (2) from making such selection as is calculated by such organization to promote the religious principles for which it is established or maintained.

These two subsections are of different scope. The first allows the RAC to exercise its preferences in hiring only in relation to the religion or denomination of the applicant. Even more limiting, preference can be exercised only for members of the particular religion or denomination with which the RAC is affiliated. This limitation has many consequences. For example, in a situation in which an RAC might want to give preference to a member of a different religion to teach a course *in that religion*, no such preference would be allowed under state law, unless the qualification could be established as a BFOQ.

The second subsection is very broad. It does not limit itself to preference for members of the same religion, but allows any preference which promotes the RAC's religious principles. It might be difficult for an RAC to justify preferring a janitor of a particular religion on the grounds that such preference furthers the religious principles of the institution. However, this type of language would allow an RAC to exercise religious preference in hiring faculty even for such nonreligious subjects as mathematics or English if, for example, the RAC feels it important to its religious principles to provide religious models to its students. It should be noted that the statute, by its use of the phrase "as is calculated by such organization," indicates that the institution should not be lightly second-guessed in the matter.

As indicated earlier, the New York State Human Rights Law prohibits employment discrimination on the basis of disability.[77] The statute defines the term "disability" to mean:

a physical, mental or medical impairment resulting from anatomical, physiological or neurological conditions which prevents the exercise of a normal bodily function or is demonstrable by medically accepted clinical or laboratory diagnostic techniques, provided, however, that in all provisions of this article dealing with employment, the term shall be limited to physical, mental or medical conditions which are unrelated to the ability to engage in the activities involved in the job or occupation which a person claiming protection of this article shall be seeking.[78]

Although this statutory definition does not explicitly identify alcoholism or drug addiction as an impairment, New York's Alcoholism and Substance Abuse Act provides that:

Alcoholism as a disease can be treated. Positive results can be achieved. The magnitude of alcoholism, non-opiate substance abuse, and opiate substance abuse as health problems requires a responsive health care system.[79]

And the State Division of Human Rights has interpreted the term disability to include alcoholism and narcotics addiction, when treated by methadone maintenance.[80] Hence the question arises whether an RAC in New York may discriminate in its employment policies against alcoholics or addicts of unlawful drugs.

The State Division of Human Rights relies in part on the federal guidelines issued by the Department of Health, Education and Welfare in 1977 that define a handicapped person as "any person who has a physical or mental impairment that substantially limits one or more major life activities"[81] and that defines physical or mental impairment as including "mental retardation, emotional illness and drug addiction and alcoholism."[82] It should also be noted, however, that the section-by-section analysis of the federal regulations acknowledges a distinction between alcoholism or drug addiction as an illness or propensity and actual possession or use of alcohol or unlawful drugs in the workplace.[83] Although the memorandum issued by the State Division of Human Rights does not refer to this portion of the federal regulations, it seems plausible to construe the state statute on disability not simply as prohibiting a general employment policy discriminating against alcoholics and drug addicts, but also allowing RACs to effectuate an employment policy respecting a religiously based prohibition against consumption of alcohol or unlawful drugs.[84] This interpretation would not only conform the state definition of a disability to the federal definition, but would also be consistent with the policy of New York that allows an RAC to make "such selection as is calculated [by it] to promote the religious principles for which it is established and maintained."[85] Actual use of alcohol or illicit drugs in the workplace, moreover, is not protected by the state statute, which limits the term "disability" to "conditions which are unrelated to the ability to engage in the activities involved in the job or occupation."[86]

Research does not reveal any legislation in New York conditioning the receipt of public aid upon nondiscrimination in employment by the recipient.[87]

New York's minimum wage law covers any "employer," which includes "any individual association [or] corporation."[88] RACs, therefore, are clearly covered[89] as to any "employee," as that term is defined in the minimum wage law. Excluded from the term "employee" is any individual employed or permitted to work:

(f) as a volunteer, learner or apprentice by a corporation, unincorporated association, community chest, fund or foundation organized and operated exclusively for religious, charitable or educational purposes, no part of the net earnings of which inures to the benefit of any private shareholder or individual; (g) as a member of a religious order, or as a duly ordained, commissioned or licensed minister, priest or rabbi, or as a sexton, or as a christian science reader; (h) in or for such a religious or charitable institution, which work is incidental to or in return for charitable aid conferred upon such individual and not under any express contract for hire; (i) in or for such a religious, educational or charitable institution if such individual is a student; (j) in or for such a religious, educational or charitable institution if the earning capacity of such individual is impaired by age or by physical or mental deficiency or injury; (k) in or for a summer camp or conference of such a religious, educational or charitable institution for no more than three months annually.[90]

All employees of RACs not falling within one of these exceptions must be paid the minimum wage.

New York's Workman's Compensation Law covers all employees "except persons engaged in a teaching or nonmanual capacity in or for a religious, charitable or educational institution."[91] Furthermore, even teachers and other nonmanual employees of such institutions may be covered if the employer elects to bring his employees within the law.[92]

The unemployment insurance system in this country is run jointly by the individual states and by the federal government. The federal government imposes a tax against most employers in any state.[93] The tax is a percentage of the employer's payroll.[94] The money so collected is used to fund the unemployment benefits trust.[95] However, if a state has an unemployment tax plan of its own, and if the plan meets certain specific federal requirements, each employer is allowed a credit against his federal tax liability for a percentage of amounts contributed to the state system.[96] As this tax credit effectively provides the states with a free unemployment insurance system, they all keep in tune with federal requirements.

Since 1970 the federal government has required the states to levy unemployment insurance taxes against a category of employers which includes RACs.[97] The only relevant exceptions allowed by the federal government are for people in the employ of a church or an organization operated primarily for religious purposes which is operated, supervised, controlled, or principally supported by a church;[98] for duly ordained ministers;[99] and for certain classes of people at schools or colleges, such as work-study students and certain student spouses.[100]

New York, to remain eligible for the tax credit, has complied with the federal requirements by levying unemployment insurance taxes against nonprofit organizations.[101] The law defines nonprofit organizations in a manner which includes RACs:

A "non-profit organization" shall mean any corporation, unincorporated association, community chest, fund, or foundation organized and operated exclusively for religious, charitable, scientific, literary or educational purposes, no part of the net earnings of which inures to the benefit of any private shareholder or individual.[102]

Several types of services performed for non-profit organizations do not come within the definition of "employment" as used in the Act. Among these exceptions, the following are most significant for RACs: (1) services rendered for an educational institution by a regular student, or by the student's spouse if the spouse is told at the beginning of those services that the employment is provided under a program of financial assistance to the student and will not be covered under the unemployment insurance law;[103] (2) service by a student under the age of twenty-two, enrolled in a full-time program taken for credit at a public or nonprofit educational institution when the service is an integral part of the academic program and the institution has so certified to the employer;[104] (3) service by a regular minister of a church in the exercise of his ministry or by a member of a religious order in the exercise of duties required by the order;[105] (4) service by a lay member elected or appointed to a church office and engaged in religious functions;[106] and (5) service by one employed at a place of worship as a caretaker or for the performance of religious duties (or both).[107]

Under New York law, therefore, RACs must pay unemployment insurance taxes in connection with the employment of all persons not coming within the noted exceptions.[108]

D. Students

The policy of the state of New York is, in general, that students otherwise qualified be admitted to educational institutions without regard to race, color, religion, creed, or national origin.[109] At the same time, an exception for RACs is mentioned within the policy statement:

It is hereby declared to be the policy of the state that the American ideal of equality of opportunity requires that students, otherwise qualified, be admitted to educational institutions without regard to race, color, religion, creed or national origin, except that, with regard to religious or denominational educational institutions, students, otherwise qualified, shall have the equal opportunity to attend therein without discrimination because of race, color, or national origin. It is a fundamental American right for members of various religious faiths to establish and maintain educational institutions exclusively or primarily for students of their own religious faith or to effectuate the religious principles in furtherance of which they are maintained. Nothing herein contained shall impair or abridge that right.[110]

The second part of this provision allows a wide range in student selection, a range not limited to students of the faith with which the RAC is affiliated.

The admissions exception for RACs occurs in connection with the provision defining an unfair educational practice in the following terms:

To exclude or limit or otherwise discriminate against any person or persons seeking admission as students to such institution because of race, religion, creed, color, or national origin; except that nothing in this section shall be deemed to affect, in any way, the right of a religious or denominational educational institution to select its students exclusively or primarily from members of such religion or denomination or from giving preference in such selection to such members or to make such selection of its students as is calculated by such institution to promote the religious principles for which it is established or maintained.[111]

The language here is very broad and is structured similarly to that of section 296.11 of the Executive Law.[112] In the first part the RAC is allowed a preference for students of that religion with which the RAC is affiliated. The second part allows the RAC a much broader freedom, one to make such selection as is calculated to promote its religious principles. This type of language might allow preference for students of other religions, and it is the institution itself which is allowed to make the calculation as to which students to admit.

For the purposes of this section, a "religious or denominational educational institution" is one which is:

operated, supervised or controlled by a religious or denominational organization and which has certified to the state commissioner of education that it is a religious or denominational educational institution.[113]

This definition uses the language "operated, supervised or controlled" without the addition of "or in connection with" contained in the parallel statute discussed above in connection with employment practices.[114] The absence of "or in connection with" in this section narrows the definition's scope, thereby making it more difficult for a college to qualify for the exception in the unfair educational practice law.

Finally, it should be kept in mind that Executive Law §296.11 provides that no qualified RAC is prohibited:

from limiting . . . *admission* to or giving preference to persons of the same religion or denomination or from making such selections as is calculated by such organization to promote the religious principles for which it is established or maintained.

The overall scope of this provision and of the provision governing unfair educational practices[115] is similar, although more RACs may qualify under the former, which adds the "or in connection with" phrase. This overlap is important because different agencies enforce the two provisions. The Executive Law provision is enforced by the Division of Human Rights,[116] and the unfair educational practice provision by the State Commissioner of Education.[117] This point of overlap is discussed in *New York University*

v. New York State Division of Human Rights,[118] in which the court concluded that the Educational Department and the Division of Human Rights had concurrent jurisdiction to pass on a complaint alleging a discriminatory denial of admission to medical school.

New York Education Law does not bar admission discrimination based on disability.[119]

E. Facilities

New York's Civil Rights Law puts the proprietor of a place of public accommodation under a duty to afford all people equal access to it, i.e., he cannot deny access on the basis of "race, creed, color or national origin."[120] The Executive Law makes it an unlawful practice to discriminate at places of public accommodation on the basis of race, creed, color, national origin, sex, disability, or marital status.[121] However, the two laws have different scopes in terms of the facilities concerned. The Civil Rights law covers, *inter alia*,

public academies, colleges and universities . . . and all educational institutions under the supervision of the Regents of the State of New York; and any . . . public college, university, professional school . . . [or] other educational facility, supported in whole or in part by public funds or by contributions solicited from the general public.[122]

These very facilities are specifically excluded as places of public accommodation in New York's Executive Law,[123] which is clearly not intended "to repeal any of the provisions of the Civil Rights law."[124]

This arrangement is perhaps to make clear that the enforcement of equal access to these accommodations is not within the jurisdiction or subject to the procedure of the Division of Human Rights, which is charged with enforcing the Executive Law provisions dealing with public accommodations.[125] The Civil Rights Law provision is enforceable through both a civil and a criminal penalty.[126] No agency is specifically charged with its enforcement.

Most RACs would be affected by the provisions of the Civil Rights Law because they are "educational institutions under the supervision of the regents of the state of New York." They

would, of course, to the same extent, be exempted from coverage under Executive Law
provisions.

RACs are thus bound by the provision on
public accommodations, in the Civil Rights
Law, which bars discrimination on the basis of
race, creed, color, or national origin, but are
not bound by the Executive Law provision.
RACs may, accordingly, differentiate with respect to sex, disability, or marital status without
violating state law.

New York's Executive Law prohibits discrimination based on race, color, creed, national origin, sex, disability,[127] or marital status
in the selling, renting or leasing of private or
commercial housing property.[128] Restricting
the rental of all rooms in a housing accommodation to members of one sex is specifically excluded from the prohibition.[129]

There is, however, the following familiar
qualification:

Nothing contained in this section shall be construed
to bar any religious or denominational institution or
organization, or any organization operated for charitable or educational purposes, which is operated,
supervised or controlled by or in connection with a
religious organization, from limiting . . . sales or
rental of housing accommodations . . . to or giving
preference to persons of the same religion or denomination or from making such selection as is calculated by such organization to promote the religious
principles for which it is established or maintained.[130]

Much of the language of this section, which
also refers to employment and admissions practices, has been discussed earlier.[131] The housing provisions of the New York Executive Law,
enforced by the Division of Human Rights,
have also been discussed earlier.[132]

New York's Labor Law empowers the state
industrial commissioner to set occupational
safety and health standards and to promulgate
regulations necessary to effectuate those standards.[133] RACs are included under the definition of "employer",[134] but "employee" is defined
as a "mechanic, workingman, or laborer working for another for hire."[135] Thus, it seems that
only manual workers are covered by the law.[136]
The Labor Law only applies to employees not

covered by a federal occupational safety and
health standard.[137]

F. State Taxation

The status of RACs as tax-exempt entities is
protected by the State constitution:

Exemptions from taxation may be granted only by
general laws. Exemptions may be altered or repealed
except those exempting real or personal property
used exclusively for religious [or] educational . . .
purposes as defined by law and owned by any corporation or association organized or conducted exclusively for one or more of such purposes and not
operating for profit.[138]

The purpose of the provision is to protect
educational institutions against possible adverse
legislation.[139]

Income Tax

New York does not directly tax the income of
corporations, but it imposes an annual franchise
tax on the privilege of doing business in the
state.[140] This tax is computed on several alternative bases, but it is linked to the corporation's
net income or total capital.[141] The franchise tax
imposed by Article 9-A of the Tax Law[142] applies to all business corporations.[143] Nonstock
corporations organized and operated exclusively
for nonprofit purposes, however, are exempt.[144]
Thus most RACs[145] should be exempt from the
franchise tax.

Inheritance, Estate and Transfer Taxes

The New York Tax Law provides that certain
federal deductions and exemptions are applicable to the New York Estate Tax.[146] One of
these exemptions includes transfers to:

[a]ny corporation organized and operated exclusively
for religious . . . or educational purposes, . . . no
part of the net earnings of which inures to the benefit
of any private stockholder or individual.[147]

The exemption may be lost if the organization participates in lobbying or certain political
activities.[148]

Gift Tax and Deductions for Gifts

New York's Tax Law provides that New York adjusted gross income is, with certain modifications, federal adjusted gross income.[149] Since a deduction for gifts to a nonprofit RAC is federally allowable,[150] it is also allowable under the state law. By incorporating the federal exemption,[151] New York exempts gifts to RACs from the state gift tax.[152]

Real, Personal and Intangible Property Taxes

Real property owned by RACs is exempted by New York Real Property Tax Law:

Real property owned by a corporation or association organized or conducted exclusively for religious . . . [or] educational . . . purposes, or for two or more such purposes, and used exclusively for carrying out thereupon one or more of such purposes . . . shall be exempt from taxation as provided in this section.[153]

The term "education," as it is used in this section, is comprehensive. It includes not only mental but also physical training and the proper maintenance of those in attendance at the institution.[154] Dormitories, dining halls, hospitals, stores, and athletic fields have all been held to be tax-exempt,[155] as have residences owned by educational institutions and occupied by faculty, staff, and their families.[156] Although fraternity houses have traditionally not been given tax-exempt status,[157] a recent case has held that such property should be exempt when the fraternity houses are owned by and subject to the complete control of a university.[158]

Real property is not exempt if any member, officer or employee of the owning corporation is entitled to pecuniary profit from the operations thereof, except reasonable compensation for services rendered.[159] This seemingly simple formula, however, has been held to bar tax exempt status where the stockholders of an educational corporation were entitled to a share in the distribution of the corporation's assets upon dissolution.[160]

If any portion of the property owned by an RAC is leased or "not so used exclusively to carry out thereupon one or more of such [exempt] purposes,"[161] that portion is subject to real property tax.[162] Real property which is not in actual use because of the absence of improvements or buildings is generally taxable, but it is exempt from taxation if construction is in progress or contemplated in good faith by an RAC.[163] Unused land is exempt as well if it is held by the RAC upon condition that the title shall revert "in case any building not intended and suitable for one or more such [exempt] purposes shall be erected upon such premises or some part thereof."[164]

In addition to being exempt from real property taxation, RACs are exempt from service charges for certain governmental services.[165] These include police and fire protection; street and highway construction, maintenance and lighting; sanitation; and water supply.[166] They are also exempt from special *ad valorem* levies and special assessments.[167] According to statute, RACs are subject only to such levies and assessments made to pay for certain improvements, including sewer systems, water supply and distribution systems, waterways and drainage improvements, and street and highway improvements.[168]

Sales, Use or Meal Taxes

RACs are not subject to sales or compensating use tax under Article 28 of the New York Tax Law[169] on purchases, use or occupancy by them. A tax on the price of admissions is imposed by statute,[170] but admissions which inure exclusively to the benefit of RACs are exempt.[171] This exemption from the tax does not apply to admissions charged for athletic events,[172] rodeos, circuses, or carnivals.[173] Sales tax is not imposed on the contract sale of food or nonalcoholic beverages to a student at an establishment on the campus of an RAC, where the student does not pay cash when served;[174] thus sales tax is not imposed on a student's semester or quarter board fee.

Other Taxes

Cities, counties, and school districts are empowered to impose taxes on a variety of activities and transactions.[175] This power is dependent on the size of the population residing within the taxing entity[176] and includes the power to tax any business or trade,[177] deeds,[178] coin-operated amusement devices,[179] the privilege of selling liquor,[180] motor vehicles,[181] paper, glass, metal, or plastic containers,[182] hotel rooms in certain counties,[183] and admission charges.[184] RACs, however, are given a blanket exemption[185] from taxes imposed by these governmental entities under this subpart.[186]

RACs are exempt from a tax on commercial premises by any city having a population of one million or more[187] and from taxes on telephone service,[188] occupancy, vending machines, and on the sale of patent medicines and tobacco other than cigarettes.[189] The sale of patent medicines and tobacco by stores operated by a RAC is subject to tax, however.[190]

An RAC which maintains a normal faculty, curriculum, and student body physically in attendance is exempt from taxation on admission charges under New York Public Housing Law,[191] except those admissions charged for athletic games or exhibitions, wrestling or boxing matches, carnivals or circuses, and motion picture exhibitions.[192]

RACs are also exempt from state tax on the furnishing of utility service,[193] as long as they qualify as not-for-profit corporations organized and operated exclusively for religious or educational purposes.[194]

G. Fund Raising

A charitable organization, defined as any "benevolent, philanthropic, patriotic, or eleemosynary person or one purporting to be such,"[195] which intends to solicit contributions from persons in the state or from any governmental agency must register with the secretary of state.[196] Exempted from the entire article on charitable solicitations are certain religious entities:

This article shall not apply to corporations organized under the religious corporations law, and other religious agencies and organizations, and charities, agencies, and organizations operated, supervised, or controlled by or in connection with a religious organization.[197]

Many RACs could, of course, come within this exemption as "organizations operated, supervised, or controlled by or in connection with a religious organization,"[198] and are thereby exempt from all state regulation governing charitable solicitation.

A further exemption from the registration requirement exists specifically for:

[a]n educational institution the curriculums of which in whole or in part are registered or approved by the state education department either directly or by acceptance of accreditation by an accrediting body recognized by such department, an educational institution confining its solicitation of contributions to its student body, alumni, faculty and trustees, and their families, or a library registered by the state education department, provided that the annual financial report of such institution or library shall be filed with the state education department where it shall be open for public inspection.[199]

Thus RACs which do not qualify for total exemption under the statute referred to above are at least exempt from the requirement of registration.

A second item of concern in this area is the holding of certain games as methods of raising money. Generally, the New York Constitution prohibits such activities.[200] However, an exception to this general rule is provided for specified organizations if local municipalities so agree.

[A]ny city, town or village . . . may by an approving vote . . . authorize, subject to state legislative supervision and control, the conduct of one or both of the following categories of games of chance commonly known as: (a) bingo or lotto, in which prizes are awarded on the basis of designated numbers or symbols on a card conforming to numbers or symbols selected at random; (b) games in which prizes are awarded on the basis of a winning number or numbers, color or colors, or symbol or symbols; determined by chance from among those previously selected or played, whether determined as the result of the spinning of a wheel, a drawing or otherwise by chance. If authorized, such games shall be subject to the following restrictions, among others which may be prescribed by the legislature: (1) *only bona fide religious, charitable or non-profit organizations of veterans, volunteer firemen and similar non-profit organizations shall be permitted to conduct such games*; (2) the entire net proceeds of any game shall be exclusively devoted to the lawful purposes of such organizations; (3) no single prize shall exceed two hundred and fifty dollars; (4) no series of prizes on any one occasion shall aggregate more than one thousand dollars; (5) no person except a bona fide member of any such organization shall participate in the management or operation of such game; and (6) no person shall receive any remuneration for participating in the management or operation of any such game. The legislature shall pass appropriate laws to effectuate the purposes of this subdivision.[201]

Pursuant to this provision of the constitution, the New York legislature has passed two pieces of legislation: the bingo licensing law[202] and the games of chance licensing law.[203] These laws specify the type of games permitted, the method of municipal approval and control, and other such matters.

Although the constitutionality provided exception ("bona fide religious, charitable, or non-profit organization of veterans, volunteer firemen and similar non-profit organizations") is subject to a relatively narrow interpretation, both the bingo licensing law and the games of chance licensing law include the nonprofit "bona fide educational organization" within its list of "authorized" organizations.[204]

An "authorized organization" under both laws must have, for a period of at least three years prior to applying for a license, engaged in serving one or more of the article's specified lawful purposes,[205] which include benefiting an indefinite number of needy or deserving people by "enhancing their opportunity for religious or educational advancement."[206]

Most RACs would presumably qualify under these statutory implementations of the constitutional provision.

41. North Carolina

A. Corporate Status

North Carolina recognizes statutorily the "right of every parent to have his children attend a nonpublic school."[1] While the recognition occurs in the context of a provision dealing with "children of secondary-school age, or younger,"[2] its spirit can be extrapolated to reach higher education—and therefore religiously affiliated higher education—as well.

Such a right—and a spirit friendly to RACs—may also be read into North Carolina's Constitution, which provides that:

[a]ll persons have a natural and undeniable right to worship Almighty God according to dictates of their own conscience, and no human authority shall in any case whatever control or interfere with the rights of conscience.[3]

Obviously, the creation and maintenance of religiously affiliated institutions of higher education can be an important exercise of such rights.

Any nonpublic educational institution established after December 31, 1960, in North Carolina must, in order to be empowered to confer degrees, have sufficient income "to maintain an adequate faculty and equipment sufficient to provide" adequate instruction in the arts, science or other recognized fields of learning.[4] The board of governors is authorized to require the filing of information by such schools and to deny to or withdraw from an in-stitution not meeting the requirements its license to confer degrees.[5] (These provisions do *not* apply to a "Bible School, Bible College, or similar religious institution.")[6]

RACs are incorporated under North Carolina's Nonprofit Corporation Act.[7] A nonprofit corporation is defined as "a corporation intended to have no income or intended to have income none of which is distributable to its members, directors, or officers."[8]

The Act specifically delineates the procedure by which a nonprofit corporation is formed,[9] itemizing the contents of its articles of incorporation[10] and the registration and formation requirements.[11]

The statute prohibits the issuing of stocks and dividends, but allows reasonable compensation and benefits for services rendered to its members, directors and officers.[12]

Also set out are the methods for amending the articles of incorporation.[13] Merger, consolidation and dissolution of nonprofit private colleges are governed by this chapter.[14] In addition, both by statute and by common law, North Carolina courts are directed to apply the *cy pres* doctrine when necessary.[15]

The articles of merger, consolidation, or voluntary dissolution take effect when the Secretary of State endorses the articles of merger or consolidation[16] or issues a certificate of dissolution.[17] A private college may be dissolved involuntarily and its assets liquidated by a degree of the superior court in an action brought by the Attorney General alleging (1) fraud in procuring its charter; (2) abuse of authority; (3) failure to name or change its registered agent; or (4) refusal to comply with a court order to produce its records.[18] The Superior Court also has jurisdiction to liquidate a college's assets in an action properly brought by a member or director of the corporation, or by a creditor.[19]

The relevant provisions of the North Carolina statute closely follow the Model Nonprofit Corporation Act,[20] except that the North Carolina Nonprofit Corporation Act requires that assets distributable to an unknown or unfound creditor or member be paid to the University of North Carolina until claimed unless special limitations on the assets require disposition to an organization engaged in activities substantially similar to those of the dissolving college.[21]

B. State Support

North Carolina has set up in Article 23, entitled "State Education Assistance Authority:

a system of financial assistance, consisting of grants, loans, workstudy or other employment, and other aids, for qualified residents of the State to enable them to obtain an education beyond the high school level by attending *public or private* educational institutions.[22]

"Eligible institutions" under this legislation means, with respect to loans, the same as it does under 20 U.S.C. § 1085.[23] With respect to grants and workstudy programs, the phrase includes "private institutions" within the state (other than "a seminary, Bible school, Bible college or similar religious institution")[24] that are postsecondary and appropriately accredited.[25]

Under these provisions, therefore, students at the typical RAC will be eligible to participate in the aid program provided.

The recipients of scholarship loans under North Carolina's "Scholarship Loan Fund for Prospective Teachers"[26] may "attend any North Carolina college or university, public or private, which offers teacher training or work leading to teacher training," so long as it is approved by the State Board of Education.[27] RAC students are, therefore, eligible to participate.

Article 5 establishes a "Loan Fund for Prospective College Teachers."[28] Loans made under the program may be repaid (at a rate of $100 for each month of teaching) by teaching in a North Carolina college or other postsecondary educational institution—public or private. RACs are included within the intended beneficiaries of this program.

The Board of Governors of the University of North Carolina is authorized to contract with private institutions (again, other than seminaries, Bible schools or the like)[29] in North Carolina to provide funds to these institutions which will be devoted by them to scholarship aid for their students who are needy state residents.[30] Again, the typical RAC will be eligible to participate.

C. Personnel

In its Equal Employment Practices Act, North Carolina asserts its public policy:

to protect and safeguard the right and opportunity of all persons to seek, obtain and hold employment without discrimination or abridgment on account of race, *religion,* color, national origin, age, sex, or handicap by employers which regularly employ 15 or more employees.[31]

This public policy is to be enforced by the Human Relations Council in the Department of Administration, which is authorized to "receive charges of discrimination from the Equal Employment Opportunity Commission"[32] and to "investigate and conciliate charges of discrimination."[33]

For employers with the requisite number of employees, there is no exemption of any kind, not even one for a bona fide occupational qualification (BFOQ). Under North Carolina law, therefore, there is no explicit statement establishing an RAC's legal authority to exercise religious preference even in hiring theology faculty and the like.

The statute includes "handicap" among the discriminatory bases in employment specifically against public policy. A separate provision states:

Handicapped persons shall be employed in the State service, the service of the political subdivision of the

State, in the public schools, *and in all other employment, both public and private*, on the same terms and conditions as the ablebodied, unless it is shown that the particular disability impairs the performance of the work involved.[34]

A fair reading of this statute would surely include employment by RACs. The specification of "public schools" is not to exclude private ones, but to indicate the scope of public employment covered by the law. (No enforcement device is mentioned in connection with this statute; presumably, it was intended that the Equal Employment Practices Act be the implementing device.)

The final clause of the statute provides what is in effect a BFOQ, one which, presumably, is intended to cover the Equal Employment Practices Act provision referred to earlier,[35] since it would be absurd to exempt under this provision what is specifically stated to be against public policy in another.

Under North Carolina's provision, "handicapped persons include" those with "physical, mental and visual disabilities."[36] While the use of the word "include" could indicate a definition broader than the categories listed, it is likely that courts will restrict it to persons reasonably within those categories. Although those categories could easily be read to include alcoholics and persons *addicted* to drugs, there is no indication that the statute intended to include alcohol and drug *use* within its protection and, in any event, the BFOQ referred to would allow an employer to take such use into account in assessing a person's fitness for the particular job. Surely an RAC could rely on the BFOQ in refusing to hire or continue in employment one whose use impaired his ability to perform. Indeed, for some RACs, mere use of any amount may indicate unfitness for particular positions which the RAC deems to have role modelling aspects. (It would be much more difficult to make such an argument in the case of a rehabilitated alcoholic or drug addict.)

Most employees of RACs will be covered by the North Carolina Minimum Wage Act,[37] since employers covered include "associations" and "corporations,"[38] and employees include any "individual[s] employed by an employer."[39]

Of the several categories excepted from this definition of employee, the following is the most relevant for RACs.

Any person engaged in the activities of an educational, charitable, religious or nonprofit organization where the relationship of employer-employee does not, in fact, exist, or where the services rendered to such organizations are on a voluntary basis.[40]

This provides a very narrow exemption, covering, perhaps, the work of a member of a religious order in a school controlled by that order or the services of an alumnus volunteered to the institution.

Also excluded from coverage are employees under the age of sixteen[41] and those over the age of sixty-five.[42]

Other exceptions provided, including that for part-time employees of employers with fewer than three full-time employees,[43] are unlikely to be applicable to RACs.

The minimum wage provided for under North Carolina law ($3.10 per hour after January 1, 1982)[44] is not likely to present serious problems to any RAC.

North Carolina limits the number of hours per day and per week, and the number of days within each fourteen-day period, certain employees may work.[45] Among those exempted from the legislation are people over the age of eighteen in office, foremanship, clinical, supervisory, or executive positions, and in the learned professions.[46] Also exempt are employers of no fewer than three employees[47] and charitable institutions.[48] RACs are unlikely to have three or fewer employees and were probably not intended to be included within the term "charitable," since the legislature would have added "educational" had it so intended.[49]

North Carolina's Workmen's Compensation Act[50] applies to, *inter alia*, "all private employments in which five or more employees are regularly employed in the same business or establishment."[51] Since an RAC is an employer under the Act ("every person carrying on an employment"),[52] and will likely have five or more employees, it will be required to participate under the Workmen's Compensation Act in behalf of its employees. The only significant exception for RACs is that for executive officers elected or appointed and empowered in accordance with the charter and bylaws of a charitable, religious, educational, or other nonprofit corporation,[53] and even these executives may "be brought within the coverage of its insurance contract by any such corporation by specifically including such executive officer[s] in such contract of insurance."[54] Such executive officers are considered employees under the Act.[55]

As of January 1, 1972, an "employer" covered by North Carolina's unemployment security legislation[56] includes a nonprofit organization or corporation organized and operated exclusively for "religious" or "educational" purposes if it is exempt or may be exempt from federal income taxation under Section 501(c)(3) of the Internal Revenue Code of 1954.[57] The typical RAC will be included within this provision and will therefore be required to make unemployment compensation contributions in behalf of its employees. Among exceptions to the coverage, the following are the most significant for RACs: (1) "[d]omestic service in a private home, local college club or local chapter of a college fraternity or sorority";[58] (2) service by a regular student at a school, college or university[59] (or by the student's spouse if the spouse is advised at the beginning of such service that the employment is provided under a program of financial assistance to the student and is not covered by any unemployment insurance)[60] and (3) with regard to those nonprofit organizations organized and operated exclusively for religious or educational purposes and exempt from federal income tax under Section 501(c)(3), service performed in the employ of a church (or group of churches) or of an organization operated primarily for religious purposes which is "operated, supervised, controlled or principally supported by a church" (or group of churches)[61] or service by a "duly ordained, commissioned, or licensed minister of a church in the exercise of his ministry"[62] or by a "member of a religious order in the exercise of duties required by such order."[63]

The third exception listed is extremely narrow and would exclude only such RACs as seminaries or those employees of other RACs

who are priests, rabbis or members of religious orders.

D. Students

North Carolina statutes are silent with regard to the exercise of religious preference by RACs in student admissions. One statute ensuring every child "a fair and full opportunity to reach his full potential"[64] is limited to public schools and, in any event, specifically exempts institutions of higher education.[65] A second statute, aimed at preventing discrimination on several bases in the provision of educational services,[66] seems also directed solely at the public school systems[67] and, since it seems to implement the state policy referred to in the first statute, is easily read to exempt institutions of higher education. Finally, several provisions concerning nondiscrimination in education deal with the right of children with special needs to a free and appropriate *public* education,[68] and thus have no relevance to RACs.

It would seem, therefore, that under North Carolina law RACs are free to exercise religious preference of any kind in the selection of their students. Indeed, there seems to be no state bar to any admissions criterion the RAC deems appropriate.

E. Facilities

North Carolina does not have a general public accommodations statute. Two provisions do deal with the right of access, and the right to use, of handicapped people, who "include" those with "physical, mental and visual disabilities."[69] The first establishes the right of the handicapped to use, *inter alia*, "all other buildings and facilities, *both publicly and privately owned*, which serve the public."[70] Certainly such a provision would include any campus facility to which the public (as opposed to students, alumni or parents of students) is invited—theaters, public cafeterias, stadia. Indeed, since most RACs "invite" the general public to apply for admission, it would not be a strained reading to include the entire campus (and admission itself) as within the right established.

The second statute, largely redundant, sets

out the right of the handicapped to, *inter alia*, full use of the facilities of "hotels, lodging places, [and] places of public accommodation, amusement or resort to which the general public is invited."[71] Many campus facilities will be covered by this provision as well, but it would be much more difficult to read the entire campus (or admission itself) into the right.

It should be noted that, whatever the scope of these provisions, the right involves discrimination on the basis of the handicap. All generally applicable rules and conditions not relating to a handicap may be applied to both the ablebodied and the handicapped.

North Carolina does not have any general fair housing legislation. Like in the public accommodations area, there is a special provision dealing with rights of the handicapped.[72] That provision establishes the right of a handicapped person "to hire and reside in residential communities, homes and group homes."[73] This statute conceivably could cover dormitories and the like on RAC campuses.

Note that the statutes referred to seem to emphasize the right not to be barred from certain advantages merely because of a handicap but do not specifically require that buildings and the like be *made* accessible to the handicapped. It would seem, therefore, that those in control of covered facilities could not, for example, enforce a rule specifically directed at excluding people confined to wheelchairs, but would not be under a duty to construct or alter those facilities to accommodate such people.

Given the broad definition of "employer"[74] and "employee"[75] used in the North Carolina Occupational Safety and Health Act,[76] the typical RAC will be covered by that legislation and its implementing standards or regulations.[77] No exemption for RACs is included in the provision setting out a relatively small number of exclusions.[78]

A curious provision is included within the North Carolina Occupational Safety and Health Act:

No employer, employee, or any other person related to the administration of this Article shall be discriminated against in any work, procedure, or employment by reason of sex, race, ethnic origin, or by reason of religious affiliation.[79]

Although it appears at first blush to be a pervasive equal employment statute applicable to all employers and employees covered by the Article, use of the phrase "or any *other* person related to the administration of this Article" indicates that the provision applies only to those persons and entities which are involved in enforcing the Article. This interpretation is further borne out by the fact that North Carolina has separately provided an Equal Employment Practices Act.[80]

F. State Taxation

Nothing in the Corporate Income tax chapter[81] or in the Non-Profit Corporation[82] chapter refers to any exemption for RACs from the general income tax requirements.

Under North Carolina law, amounts received as a scholarship or as a fellowship grant — including contributed services, accommodations, and amounts received for such expenses as travel, research, clerical help and other items incident to the scholarship or fellowship, are exempt from state income taxation to the extent they are "exempt for federal income tax purposes under the provisions of Section 117 of the Internal Revenue Code of 1954 as amended."[83]

No inheritance taxes are levied on property passing to "religious, charitable or educational corporations."[84] All RACs would come within this exemption.

North Carolina does impose an estate tax equal to the maximum federal estate tax credit for state death taxes.[85] This tax, designed merely to channel to the state moneys otherwise going to the federal government, is not intended to affect the *amount* of taxes ultimately paid.

Inter vivos gifts made to or for the exclusive benefit of religious, charitable, or educational institutions are exempt from the North Carolina gift tax.[86]

Deductions from income (for the purposes of the state income tax) are allowed to corporations for amounts donated to, *inter alia*, corporations or associations organized and operated "exclusively for religious, charitable, literary, scientific or educational purposes" so long as no net earnings inure to the benefit of any individual.[87] The deduction is limited to five percent of the corporation's net income allocated to North Carolina.[88]

Deductions are also allowed to individuals, firms and partnerships for contributions to any North Carolina educational institution, no part of the net earnings of which inures to the benefit of any private stockholder or individual.[89] This deduction is not limited to any particular percentage of one's income.

All RACs would likely qualify as appropriate donees under both these deduction provisions.

Exempted from state tax is the "property of churches, religious societies, charitable, educational, literary, or benevolent institutions or orders"[90] (thus including all RACs). This exemption does not apply to property (other than state and federal lands):

held or used for investment, speculation, or rent . . . unless said rent or the interest on or income from such investment shall be used exclusively for religious, charitable, educational, or benevolent purposes, or the interest upon the bonded indebtedness of said religious, charitable, or benevolent institution.[91]

Under this provision, therefore, most property held by RACs will be exempted unless it (1) is not a federal or state bond, (2) is held for investment purposes and (3) the return is not used for religious, charitable, educational or benevolent purposes.

North Carolina exempts the following property from real property taxes:

[1] Buildings, with the land upon which they are situated, lawfully owned and held by churches or religious bodies, wholly and exclusively used for religious worship or for the residence of the minister of any such church or religious body or occupied gratuitously by one other than the owner which if it were the owner, would qualify for the exemption under this section, together with the additional adjacent land reasonably necessary for the convenient use of any such building.[92]

[2] Buildings, with the land occupied, wholly devoted to educational purposes, belonging to and exclusively occupied and used by . . . colleges, academies, industrial schools, seminaries, and any other institution of learning, together with such additional land [owned by them] as may be reasonably necessary for the convenient use of such buildings, and also such other buildings and facilities located on the premises . . . as may be reasonably necessary and

useful in the practical operation of such institutions. [To qualify for this exemption, the institution must not be organized or run for profit to any individual.][93]

While some real property on RAC campuses might come within the narrow exemption provided by the first of these two provisions, the second provides a comprehensive exemption for almost all real property used by RACs in their educational mission. Not covered by this exemption would be real property held for investment or otherwise unrelated to the ongoing educational operation. Since worship by students and staff would be reasonably incidental to an RAC's educational mission, real property used for such a purpose on an RAC campus would come within the second exemption (and perhaps the first if owned by a church or religious body).

North Carolina exempts from sales and use taxes all "meals and food products served to students in dining rooms regularly operated by State or private educational institutions or student organizations thereof."[94] This exemption would, of course, cover all RACs with regard to such transactions. The sale of Holy Bibles is also exempt.[95]

Upon filing a timely written request to the Commissioner of Revenue, nonprofit educational or religious institutions (which includes all RACs) are refunded all sales and use taxes paid by them on direct purchases of tangible personal property to be used in carrying out their work.[96] Sales and use taxes indirectly incurred by such institutions on building materials and the like which become part of a building or structure being erected, altered or repaired for the carrying on of their nonprofit activities are also refundable.[97]

G. Fund Raising

Although charitable organizations must apply for a license before soliciting funds in the state or having funds solicited in their behalf,[98] exempted from the licensing provision are (1) a religious corporation, trust, or organization incorporated or established for religious purposes, with regard to nonsecular activities, and, in any event, only if its financial support is not derived primarily from persons other than its own members, excluding sales of printed or re- corded religious materials;[99] (2) educational in- stitutions whose curricula are wholly or partly registered, approved, or accredited by either the State Department of Public Education, the University of North Carolina Board of Gov- ernors, the Southern Association of Colleges and Schools or an equivalent regional accredit- ing body;[100] and (3) any other educational in- stitution limiting its solicitation to its students, alumni, faculty, staff and trustees, and their families.[101] A "charitable organization" other- wise exempt from the licensing requirements will lose its exemption upon hiring a profes- sional solicitor.[102] Since "charitable organiza- tion" is defined as, *inter alia*, one who holds himself out to be organized or operated for any charitable purpose[103] and since "charitable purpose" is in turn defined as "any charitable, benevolent, religious, philanthropic . . . or elee- mosynary purpose for religion [or] education,"[104] it would seem that even an RAC otherwise ex- empt from the licensing requirements would lose its exemption upon the employment of a professional solicitor.

An RAC may raise money by operating either bingo games or raffles of prizes if it qualifies as an exempt organization under North Carolina's gambling laws. An exempt organization is one exempt under Internal Revenue Code Section 501(c)(3), or under similar provisions of North Carolina law for bona fide nonprofit religious organizations.[105] RACs so qualified may con- duct money-raising raffles and bingo games if they comply with the other provisions of the state law.[106] The proceeds from these games, after reasonable expenses, must be used for "re- ligious, charitable, scientific . . . literary or educational" purposes.[107]

H. Miscellaneous

A religious, educational or charitable cor- poration (*i.e.,* any RAC) may establish in- surance programs covering employees, offi- cers, contributors, students or former students "whose death or disability might cause financial loss to the corporation and to this end . . . has an insurable interest in the lives . . . of such persons."[108]

42. North Dakota

A. Corporate Status

In North Dakota, RACs are incorporated under the North Dakota Nonprofit Corporation Act.[1] This statute requires that RACs file articles of incorporation,[2] and have a registered agent,[3] certain specific officers,[4] and a board of directors;[5] RACs are prohibited from issuing stock[6] or giving loans to directors or officers.[7] The remainder of the Act deals principally with other, typically corporate matters. However, religious corporations are dealt with specifically.[8] Herein, a religious corporation, which, according to the statutory language may include RACs, is prohibited from acquiring or holding real estate of a value greater than five hundred thousand dollars, unless such is "used for educational, hospital, charitable or religious purposes."[9] If this section is violated, the religious corporation must forfeit the real estate, which shall escheat to the state.[10] A related provision regulates grants of real estate to religious corporations by providing a succession in interest in the land to subsequent officers of the particular religious corporation.[11] The wording of this section suggests, however, that it would apply more readily to church buildings and parochial schools than to RACs.

North Dakota's Postsecondary Educational Institution legislation[12] comprehensively regulates institutions through the state board of vocational education.[13] Minimum standards for these institutions are statutorily set.[14] Exempted from the law, however, are, *inter alia*, all private four-year institutions chartered or incorporated and operating in the state prior to July 1, 1977, as long as appropriate accreditation is maintained.[15]

North Dakota has enacted the Uniform Management of Institutional Funds Act.[16]

The merger, consolidation and dissolution of nonprofit colleges are governed by the North Dakota Nonprofit Corporation Act.[17] There are no reported cases in North Dakota applying the *cy pres* doctrine.

Articles of merger,[18] consolidation,[19] or voluntary dissolution[20] adopted by the governing board of a nonprofit college[21] must be filed with the Secretary of State and take effect when the Secretary of State issues a certificate of merger, consolidation,[22] or dissolution.[23] The district court has jurisdiction to dissolve a nonprofit college involuntarily in an action properly brought by the Attorney General alleging fraud, abuse of authority, failure to appoint a registered agent or to notify the Secretary of State of a change of a registered agent in the state.[24]

Courts of equity also have jurisdiction to liquidate the assets of a corporation in an action properly brought by a member of the governing board of a nonprofit college, by a creditor, or by the Attorney General.[25] In both voluntary dissolutions and court-supervised dissolutions, the North Dakota Nonprofit Corporation Act provides that assets of a nonprofit college shall be distributed according to a procedure following that of the Model Nonprofit Corporation Act.[26]

B. State Support[27]

The North Dakota Constitution, which guarantees the free exercise of religion,[28] provides that all educational institutions "supported" by a public tax must remain "under the absolute and exclusive control of the state."[29] Although the latter provision could be construed to prohibit any aid, at least if direct, to private colleges, it remains unclear that *any* amount of aid would cause a college to be "supported" by a public tax.[30] Indirect aid through grants or loans to students seem still less vulnerable to constitutional attack.[31]

A separate provision prohibits the state and its political subdivisions from loaning or giving their credit or making "donations to or in aid of any individual, association or corporation except for reasonable support of the poor."[32] The same provision does, however, allow the state and its subdivisions "to make internal improvements and engage in any industry, enterprise or business."[33] This business enterprise qualification, Professor Howard observes, might authorize certain aid programs to private higher education.[34] In any event, aid programs to the needy student, through grant or loan, are on surer footing since the constitutional provision specifically authorizes lending of credit and donation for the "reasonable support of the poor."[35]

A separate provision that "no money raised for the support of the public schools of the state shall be appropriated to or used for the support of any sectarian school"[36] seems merely to prevent funds raised specifically for public schools from being re-channelled to sectarian schools. It does not bar aid programs using different sources of funds.

In any event, North Dakota provides no direct aid to private higher educational institutions.[37] There are, however, several programs designed to aid the student.

The North Dakota student financial assistance program[38] was established to provide grants to (1) resident undergraduate students who were graduated from North Dakota high schools;[39] (2) resident students who, having attended and graduated from a high school in a bordering state pursuant to a statutorily ordained reciprocity provision,[40] attend qualified North Dakota institutions of postsecondary education;[41] and (3) physically or mentally handicapped residents who, unable to secure in North Dakota services or facilities necessary for their postsecondary educational needs, attend out-of-state postsecondary institutions.[42] Technically, only those students in the second category must attend "qualified institutions," which are not further defined in the Chapter. Presumably, RACs may be "qualified."

All students receiving such aid must be in "substantial need" of financial assistance.[43] The state board of higher education[44] administers this aid program.[45]

North Dakota also has a scholarship program "for resident persons of at least one-fourth degree of Indian blood or for enrolled members of tribes now resident in North Dakota."[46] The factors to be considered in selecting grantees are health, character, financial need, and probable and continuing success as a student.[47]

About twenty-five years ago, North Dakota enacted a scholarship loan program,[48] providing sums of up to $500 per year to North Dakota residents who were graduated from North Dakota high schools or have a North Dakota state high school general achievement certificate or have passed the entrance examination.[49] Selection was by the state board of public school education, acting as a state scholarship board.[50] The student must have needed financial aid. Loans could be received by RAC students since the statute refers to "or other institution of higher learning in the state of North Dakota."[51]

In 1969, however, the legislature discontinued loans under this Chapter and enacted a Guaranteed Loan Program[52] which, administered by the Bank of North Dakota as the "state agency,"[53] guarantees loans made in connection with the Federal Higher Education Act of 1965,[54] administers property made available to it from any source, and adopts appropriate rules and regulations for the administration of the loan program.[55]

Scholarship loans are also available for nursing education.[56]

C. Personnel

North Dakota's recently enacted general employment discrimination statute, applicable to all employers with more than fifteen employees,[57] declares:

It is the policy of North Dakota to prohibit discrimination because of race, color, religion, sex or national origin in all employment practices including hiring, firing, promotion, compensation and other terms, privileges, and conditions of employment.[58]

The Department of Labor is authorized to receive complaints and the state's district courts are authorized to try actions alleging violations.[59] The broad language of the statute seems applicable to RACs. There is no statutory provision for a bona fide occupational qualification [BFOQ]. The prohibition against religious discrimination,[60] therefore, jeopardizes any RAC employment plan based on religious selectivity.

North Dakota prohibits employment discrimination, based solely on age, against an individual who is physically and mentally competent.[61] There is in effect a BFOQ, however, since the prohibition applies only if the individual is qualified for the position and the demands of the position "do not require an age distinction."[62] Any violation of the law, which is applicable to any "person carrying on or conducting within this state any business requiring employees," constitutes a class B misdemeanor.[63]

North Dakota's established policy is to encourage the blind, the visually handicapped and other physically handicapped persons "to participate fully in the social and economic life of the state and to engage in remunerative employment."[64] Legislation calls for the employment of such persons in the state service and in any other area of employment supported in whole or in part by public funds, to the same extent that able bodied persons are employed, unless prevented by the particular handicap.[65] Although primarily intended to encourage the practice of hiring the handicapped in governmental positions, the legislation could affect RACs with regard to undertakings financially supported by the state.

North Dakota law specifies that alcoholism and drug addiction do not, *per se*, constitute mental illness, although persons suffering from these conditions may also be mentally ill.[66] It remains unclear whether the statute regards alcoholics and drug addicts as mentally rather than physically handicapped. Only the latter situation, presumably, would be within the employment discrimination provision. In any case, an RAC would be affected only to the extent that the state supported a particular area of employment under control of that RAC.

The North Dakota minimum wages and hours law defines "employer" to include any individual, association or corporation acting in the interest of an employer in relationship to an employee.[67] "Employee" includes any individual employed by an employer.[68] Similar definitions appear in the "equal pay for men and women" law.[69] Consequently, RACs, as employers, are subject to these laws and to the enforcement standards promulgated by the State Commissioner of Labor.[70]

The North Dakota Workmen's Compensation Law[71] applies to any corporation[72] engaged in "hazardous employment."[73] Hazardous employment, however, is broadly defined to mean "any employment in which one or more employees are employed regularly in the same business."[74] Therefore, employees of RACs are generally covered unless they come within the exceptions for casual employment[75] or services performed by clergy and employees of a religious organization engaged in the operation of a place of worship.[76] RACs may elect to include exempted employees within the coverage of the Act by insuring them and complying with the notice provisions of the Act.[77] Any exempt employee, nevertheless, may elect before injury to reject coverage under the compensation provisions by written notice to the Workmen's Compensation Bureau and the employer. Such an employee preserves common law and statutory rights to bring a damage suit for injuries against the employer.[78] To secure the payment of compensation for injured employees, RACs must pay a fixed premium annually into the North Dakota Compensation Fund.[79] RACs failing to comply with these insurance provisions may be sued for damages by injured employees.[80]

Under the North Dakota Unemployment Compensation Law,[81] services performed for RACs[82] constitute employment,[83] if two conditions are met.[84] First, such service must be exempt from the definition of "employment" in the Federal Unemployment Tax Act solely due to section 3306(c)(8).[85] Second, the organization must employ at least four individuals "for some portion of a day in each of twenty different weeks, whether or not such weeks were consecutive, within either the current or preceding calendar year."[86]

The statute provides the following exemptions which apply directly to RACs: (1) services performed for a church or for an association of churches;[87] (2) services performed for an organization run primarily for religious purposes and controlled by a church or by an association of churches;[88] and (3) services performed by ordained ministers or by members of religious orders in the exercise of their religious duties.[89] Because the scope of these exemptions is narrow, most services performed in the employ of RACs are covered under the Act. Other relevant exclusions from the statute's definition of employment include (1) service performed for a school or college by regularly enrolled students[90] or by their spouses;[91] (2) services performed by a student at an accredited nonprofit or public educational institution in a full-time program, taken for credit and combining academic instruction and work experience;[92] (3) services performed for which unemployment compensation is payable under a system set up by an Act of Congress;[93] and (4) domestic services for a college club or a chapter of a college fraternity or sorority, if wages paid in any quarter of the current or the preceding year were less than $1,000.00.[94] The statute also excludes from coverage certain organizations which are tax-exempt under federal statutes,[95] if the remuneration paid is less than $50.00 in any calendar quarter.[96]

Nonprofit organizations, and therefore RACs, may elect to make payments in lieu of contributions. To take advantage of this option, an organization must fit the definition in section 501(c)(3) of the Internal Revenue Code and must qualify as tax-exempt under section 501(a) of the Code.[97] The election is effective for a period of one year[98] upon filing of written notice with the North Dakota Employment and Security Bureau.[99] Required payments are equal to the amount of regular benefits plus one-half the amount of extended benefits paid.[100] Organizations not otherwise subject to the provisions of the statute may elect to participate in the program for a minimum of two years.[101]

North Dakota's Labor-Management Relations Act[102] defines "employer" to include, with few exceptions, "any person acting as an agent of an employer."[103] "Employee" is also broadly defined.[104] All RACs, therefore, are covered by the Act which, *inter alia*, gives employees the right to organize and bargain collectively with their employers or to refrain from association with fellow employees[105] and sets out unfair labor practices for employers[106] and employees.[107]

D. Students

North Dakota has no legislation directly regulating student admissions at RACs. There is no indication that the provision prohibiting discrimination in public places[108] was intended to affect such student admissions in any way.

E. Facilities

North Dakota has no comprehensive public accommodations or fair housing laws, but its policy is:

to prohibit discrimination on the basis of race, color, religion, national origin, or sex; to prevent and eliminate discrimination in employment relations, public accommodations, housing, state and local government services, and credit transactions; and to deter those who aid, abet, or induce discrimination, or coerce others to discriminate.[109]

Moreover, it is a criminal offense to injure, intimidate or interfere with anyone, on the basis of his sex, race, color, religion, or national origin, in the exercise or because of the exercise of his right "to full and equal enjoyment of any facility open to the public."[110] This law would clearly cover campus restaurants, stadia, inns, and the like open to the public. There is no indication that the law was intended to affect in any way student admission to RACs.

To promote the health and safety and the accessibility of the handicapped, North Dakota law requires certain buildings and facilities to have at least one toilet stall with a handrail, if the toilet stall is accessible from the main entrance without climbing or descending stairs.[111] This provision applies to:

[a]ll public buildings and facilities and all buildings and facilities held open to the public and used for public assemblages of any character in this state, including theatres, public halls, city halls, courthouses, factories, hotels, shopping centers, and all other public buildings wherein numbers of persons are employed or are in the habit of meeting together for any purpose.[112]

Although vague, this wording is quite comprehensive. Use of words such as "factories" and "hotels" indicates that privately owned buildings are included. Moreover, buildings in which "numbers of persons are employed" as well as those "held open to the public" are covered. In short, most if not all campus buildings, including hotels, administration buildings and dormitories,[113] must comply if they have a toilet stall accessible from the main entrance of the building or facility without climbing or descending stairs.

A separate provision requires that the same kinds of such buildings and facilities constructed after July 1, 1975, have a toilet stall with specified dimensions and features.[114]

With regard only to "public buildings and facilities and buildings and facilities held open to the public," constructed *or remodeled* after July 1, 1975, the same provision requires a toilet room with sufficient space to allow traffic of individuals in wheelchairs.[115] (Presumably, this requirement was intended to apply to fewer buildings and facilities than the other two due to its omission of such matters as the employment aspect, the assemblage aspect and the series of examples.)

There is no comprehensive statute in North Dakota regulating the conditions of labor. Under the statutory provisions governing minimum wages and hours, however, the Commissioner of Labor is empowered to investigate conditions of labor,[116] and to promulgate rules and regulations establishing standards for labor conditions.[117] The same statute makes it unlawful to employ employees under conditions which are detrimental to the health of the worker.[118] Within this section an employee is defined comprehensively as any individual employed by an employer; an employer is defined as any individual or organization acting in the interest of an employer in relation to an employee.[119]

F. State Taxation

North Dakota exempts from its income tax all "corporations organized and operating exclusively for religious, charitable, scientific, or educational purposes . . . no part of the net earnings of which inure to the benefit of any private stockholder or individual."[120] Virtually any RAC would qualify for this exemption. Such an exempt organization, however, must file an annual return containing the information needed by the tax commissioner to determine its tax exempt status.[121]

Under North Dakota's Estate Tax legislation,[122] the amount of tax imposed upon the transfer of the North Dakota taxable estate is equal to the maximum credit allowable for state death taxes against the federal estate tax imposed with respect to a decedent's estate which has a taxable situs in the state. Since the tax is ultimately credited against the federal tax, the state estate tax has no real effect on the amount of taxes paid by the estate.

North Dakota has no inheritance tax or gift tax.

North Dakota provides taxpayers an income tax credit (not merely a deduction) equal to one-half the total contributions to regular[123] nonprofit private institutions of higher education in the state or to the North Dakota independent college fund.[124] The credit for any taxable year may not, in the case of a corporation, exceed ten percent of the total income tax, or one thousand dollars, whichever is less[125] and, in the case of a taxpayer other than a corporation, forty percent of the taxpayer's total income tax, or one hundred dollars, whichever is less.[126]

The North Dakota constitution declares that "property used exclusively for schools, religious, cemetery, charitable or other public purposes shall be exempt from taxation . . . "[127] State legislation, implementing this constitutional mandate, exempts from property taxation all "colleges, institutions of learning, with the books and furniture therein, and the grants attached to such buildings necessary for their proper occupancy, use and enjoyment and not otherwise used with a view to profit."[128] Virtually all RACs would therefore be exempt from property taxes.

Also exempt are (1) all dormitories and boarding halls, land included, "owned and managed by any religious corporation for educational or charitable purposes for the use of students in attendance upon any educational institution;"[129] (2) houses used exclusively for public worship and dwellings, belonging to religious organizations, intended and ordinarily used for the minister in charge of the services of the church, together with the land on which they are situated;[130] (3) up to two acres of real property owned by a religious organization if either a building used for that organization's religious services or a dwelling intended and ordinarily used for the residence of the minister in charge of such services is located upon the land;[131] (4) all personal property of a religious organization used for worship;[132] and (5) all real and personal property of fraternities, sororities and college student organizations, used exclusively for such purposes.[133]

North Dakota exempts from its sales tax legislation,[134] *inter alia*, (1) gross receipts from educational, religious or charitable activities, unless held in a publicly owned facility, as long as all the net receipts are used for educational, religious or charitable purposes;[135] (2) gross receipts from sales of textbooks to regularly enrolled students of a private or public school and from sales of textbooks, yearbooks, and school supplies purchased by a nonprofit institution of higher learning conducting courses of study similar to those conducted by public schools;[136] (3) gross receipts from the sale of newsprint and ink used for newspaper publication;[137] (4) food purchased by a student under a boarding contract with a college, university, fraternity or sorority;[138] (5) gross receipts from the sale of Bibles, hymnals, textbooks and prayerbooks sold to nonprofit religious organizations;[139] and (6) most food sold for consumption off the premises where purchased.[140]

The North Dakota use tax specifically exempts all tangible personal property or services which would be expressly exempt from the retail sales tax if purchased in North Dakota.[141]

G. Fund Raising

North Dakota's comprehensive legislation[142] regulating charitable solicitation excludes from its definition of "charitable organization" covered by the law those organizations soliciting funds for institutions of higher learning or for churches operating and having a place of worship within the state.[143] (Also excluded are duly constituted nonprofit religious organizations and their affiliates.)[144] Virtually all RACs, therefore, would be exempt from the law's requirements.

The North Dakota Consitution bars the legislature from authorizing any game of chance, lottery, or gift enterprise except for games of chance conducted by certain bona fide nonprofit organizations, including educational or religious ones, as long as the entire net proceeds are to be devoted to public-spirited uses, including educational or religious.[145] In 1981, North Dakota enacted legislation authorizing certain games of chance by certain nonprofit organizations,[146] including religious and educational ones.[147] "Educational organizations" is defined, however, to exclude higher educational institutions.[148] A "religious organization" means a "nonprofit organization, church, body of communicants, or group gathered in common membership for mutual support and edification in piety, worship, and religious observances which has been so gathered or united in this state for two years.[149] Very few if any RACs, therefore, would be eligible to conduct authorized games of chance in North Dakota. It is possible that a religious organization affiliated with the RAC could conduct such games of chance since the proceeds of games run by *religious* organizations may go to *educational* purposes, among others.[150] Authorized games of chance are tightly regulated.[151]

This legislation does allow college fraternities and sororities to conduct raffles and bingo as long as the entire net proceeds are devoted to educational, charitable, patriotic, or other public-spirited uses under the Act.[152]

H. Miscellaneous

The State Board of Higher Education[153] is statutorily authorized to enter into agreements with public or private institutions of higher education in North Dakota or contiguous states,[154] to enable a student at one of the institutions (1) to take specialized courses at another, with or without the payment of tuition at the other,[155] or (2) to attend another institution party to the agreement without having to pay nonresident tuition.[156]

The Board is also empowered to enter into agreements with other states' institutions of higher education for the purpose of utilizing their facilities for teaching North Dakota students.[157] The Board may also enter into agreements with such institutions for the acceptance of students from other states into North Dakota institutions of higher learning.[158] Presumably RACs could be involved in such agreements.

North Dakota has entered into and enacted into law the Compact for Education.[159]

North Dakota has created a Postsecondary Education Commission,[160] one of whose members represents the governing boards of private four-year colleges and another the proprietary schools.[161] The Commission's duties include analysis and planning.[162]

43. Ohio

A. Corporate Status

The incorporation, consolidation, and dissolution of nonprofit colleges are governed by the Ohio nonprofit corporation law.[1] Any nonprofit college or university may be incorporated under this law, but any college so incorporated after October 13, 1967, must receive a certificate of authorization from the Ohio board of regents before conferring any degrees or identifying itself as a "college" or "university."[2] The standards for the certificate are established by the board of regents[3] which is also authorized to revoke certification[4] and thereby cause a college to be enjoined from awarding degrees through court action by the Attorney General.[5] Incorporated colleges "under religious influence" are permitted to state their affiliation in their articles of incorporation and to grant any ecclesiastical body the right to appoint trustees or directors.[6] Unlike public institutions, which are subject to legislative control, colleges and universities funded exclusively from private sources are relatively free from government interference into internal matters except to assure that the conditions and purposes for which funds have been donated are complied with and the funds spent in accordance with the intent of the donor and the purposes of the institution.[7]

Ohio statutes reflect this attitude. RACs are given the option of adopting statutory regulations relating to the election, term, and powers of the board of trustees.[8] Nonprofit colleges are generally authorized to hold donated property in trust[9] and to appropriate for expenditure up to fifty percent of the net appreciation of an endowment fund,[10] absent a contrary intent of the donor.[11] RACs are also subject to other regulations of the Uniform Management of Institutional Funds Act.[12]

The process of voluntary dissolution of a nonprofit college is initiated when the members of the governing board adopt by majority vote a resolution of dissolution and file a certificate of dissolution with the Secretary of State.[13] A county court of common pleas, however, may have jurisdiction to oversee the dissolution process if petitioned by the corporation, a majority of the trustees, or a creditor.[14] A corporation may be involuntarily dissolved judicially either in an action properly brought by the state in the Supreme Court or a court of appeals, or in an action properly brought by members or trustees of the corporation in a county court of common pleas.[15] The Ohio Nonprofit Corporation Law provides that assets of a dissolving nonprofit college shall be distributed according to a procedure closely following that of the Model Nonprofit Corporation Act.[16]

B. State Support

Although the Ohio Constitution forbids the lending or giving of the state's credit to any individual, association, or corporation,[18] the state Supreme Court has held that the constitution does not prohibit appropriations to private corporations for public purposes[19] as long as the private corporation is nonprofit.[20] By virtue of their educational character, private, nonprofit colleges probably qualify as having "public purposes."[21]

Due to their religious affiliation, however, RACs have an additional constitutional hurdle to clear in order to receive direct state aid. The Ohio Constitution prohibits laws giving preference to any religious society.[22] Several Ohio court decisions suggest, however, that this prohibition is no more restrictive of aid programs to RACs than is the First Amendment of the Federal Constitution.[23]

RACs have four possible sources of indirect state support: guaranteed student loans, student tuition grants, student academic scholarships, and facilities assistance.[24]

The Ohio Constitution was amended to ensure the constitutionality of the Ohio Student Loan Commission in 1965.[25] The amendment followed a restrictive construction by the Ohio Supreme Court, in *State ex rel. Saxbe v. Brand*,[26] of the constitutional prohibition against giving state "credit" to individuals, associations, and corporations.[27] The Ohio student loan commission was created to guarantee loans by private lenders to residents in order to meet the expenses of higher education.[28] The commission is directed to approve eligible institutions in which students qualifying for a guaranteed loan may be enrolled.[29] Although the statute provides no criteria on which to determine institutional eligibility, there is no reason to doubt the constitutionality of the program as applied to RACs since the benefit to the RAC is merely incidental to the direct benefit to the student.[30]

Ohio has created an instructional grant program for full-time resident undergraduate students in Ohio colleges and universities.[31] Students in private institutions may receive, depending on income, up to $1800 per academic year solely for instructional and general charges of the institution.[32] Grants are not available to students in a course of study leading to a degree in theology, religion, or any other field of preparation for a religious profession.[33]

In order for its students to qualify for grants, an RAC must hold a "certificate of authorization" from the board of regents[34] and meet the requirements of Title VI of the Civil Rights Act of 1964.[35] In view of the Supreme Court's rec-

ognition of the distinction between the primarily religious purpose of parochial schools and the primarily secular role of RACs, the Establishment Clause apparently poses no problem for this indirect state support to RACs for secular use.[36]

Resident students attending RACs in Ohio are also eligible to participate in the Ohio academic scholarship program.[37] To participate, a student must be enrolled in an Ohio RAC which holds a "certificate of authorization"[38] and meets the requirements of Title VI of the Civil Rights Act of 1964.[39] Scholarships are awarded on the basis of highest capability for successful college study.[40]

The Ohio Higher Education Facilities Commission has been created to enhance the educational opportunity of the state's residents by assisting in the provision of educational facilities at private, nonprofit institutions of higher education.[41] The commission assists primarily by issuing bonds to finance construction projects.[42] The bonds are not obligations of the state and are to be paid for solely from the proceeds derived from the constructed facility.[43] Although this program has not been tested in court, its constitutionality seems secure, the U.S. Supreme Court having upheld such revenue bonding programs benefiting RACs against challenges under the First Amendment of the Federal Constitution.[44] Thus the principal concern with the Ohio program may be whether it violates state constitutional prohibitions against pledging state credit[45] or aiding religious groups.[46] The courts in several sister states have scrutinized similar "Higher Educational Facilities" programs against their respective constitutions and found no constitutional bar to such assistance.[47] Similarly the Ohio Constitution appears inviolate as the program's limitation to nonprofit institutions for public purposes avoids the "credit clause,"[48] just as its purely secular purpose (promotion of higher education) and its restriction of funded facilities to secular use pass state entanglement muster.[49]

C. Personnel

It is an unlawful discriminatory practice under Ohio's civil rights law for any RAC[50] to refuse to hire, discharge, or otherwise discriminate in employment because of race, color, religion, sex, national origin, handicap, age, or ancestry.[51] Related practices in connection with application forms, records, advertising, and the like are also prohibited.[52] These related hiring practices, however, are the only fair employment provisions subject to a bona fide occupational qualification [BFOQ]. In order to engage in any one of these practices an RAC must seek BFOQ certification in advance from the Ohio civil rights commission.[53] BFOQs are granted to RACs only "where the position requires a member of a specific denomination or religion," presumably for such positions as professor of theology, religion, and possibly philosophy.[54] BFOQs are otherwise unavailable, particularly at the post-hiring stages, for example, of granting tenure since a BFOQ exception is available, if at all, only at the hiring stage.[55] Thus, except in limited situations, RACs in Ohio are not allowed any religious employment preference.

Moreover, RACs may even be required to pay for insurance providing health benefits for, *inter alia*, abortion where the life of the mother would be endangered and for medical complications arising from an abortion, despite possibly fundamental moral opposition to such medical procedures on the part of the RAC.[56] This is so because the statutory prohibition of discrimination based on sex includes pregnancy and any illness related to pregnancy or childbirth and specifically provides for abortion coverage *unless a contrary* agreement is made between the employer and employee.[57]

The Ohio Civil Rights Commission handles complaints of unlawful discriminatory practices.[58] Appeals from a final order by the Commission may be made to the court of common pleas.[59] Alternatively an aggrieved person may enforce his statutory civil rights by filing an original complaint in the court of common pleas.[60] Violation of the prohibitions is a misdemeanor of the third degree.[61]

RACs are in no way exempted from the minimum wage and overtime hour provisions of Ohio's Fair Wage standards.[62]

Ohio's Employment Services Law[63] defines employment to include service performed for religious institutions if that service (1) does not fall within the definition of "employment" under the Federal Unemployment Tax Act[64] and

(2) is not exempt according to the Ohio statute.[65] The statute exempts from coverage certain services[66] which are not covered under the Federal Unemployment Tax Act and are not subject to any federal tax "against which credit may be taken for contributions required to be paid into a state unemployment fund."[67] Included within the exemption are services performed:

(1) [i]n the employ of a church or convention or association of churches or in an organization which is operated primarily for religious purposes and which is operated, controlled, or principally supported by a church or convention or association of churches;[68]

(2) [b]y a duly ordained, commissioned, or licensed minister of a church in the exercise of his ministry or by a member of a religious order in the exercise of duties required by such order;[69]

(3) [b]y an individual under the age of twenty-two years who is enrolled at a nonprofit or public educational institution which normally maintains a regular faculty and curriculum and normally has a regularly organized body of students in attendance at the place where its educational activities are carried on as a student in a full-time program, taken for credit at the institution which combines academic instruction with work experience;[70]

(4) [i]n the employ of a school, college, or university . . . if such service is performed by a student who is enrolled and is regularly attending classes.[71]

The definition of "employer" is broad, covering "any individual or type of organization."[72] The statute, however, distinguishes nonprofit organizations[73] from other types of employers in two ways. First, in order to qualify as an "employer," a nonprofit organization must employ at least four people "for some portion of a day in each of twenty different calendar weeks, in either the current or the preceding calendar year."[74] Second, the fifteen-hundred dollar threshold for coverage under the statute does not apply to nonprofit organizations.[75]

An alternative to regular contribution is available to nonprofit organizations and, therefore, to most RACs. Qualifying organizations[76] may elect to pay to the Administrator of the Bureau of Employment Services an amount equal to regular benefits plus one-half of extended benefits paid that are attributable to employment in the organization.[77]

RACs in Ohio are subject to regulation under that state's Worker's Compensation Act.[78] Every employer and employee, even a casual worker if earning at least $160 in any calendar quarter, is subject to the Act.[79] An employer must pay the amount fixed by the commission into the state insurance fund semi-annually,[80] or prove its financial ability to insure itself.[81]

D. Students

Ohio has no law regulating student admissions. The autonomy and discretion of RACs with respect to discipline is very broad.[82] The faculty[83] may be charged with enforcing the rules and regulations enacted by the board of trustees for both the government and discipline of the students including suspension and expulsion of offenders.[84] "The courts will not interfere in these matters in the absence of a clear abuse of discretion by the governing board" in the formulation of the rules[85] or "unreasonable and oppressive" administration of the rules by the faculty.[86]

E. Facilities

Ohio's public accommodations and fair housing laws are incorporated in the Civil Rights Commission Law.[87] Under this law, it is an unlawful discriminatory practice for the keeper of a public accommodation to deny anyone full enjoyment of the facilities on the basis of race, color, religion, sex, national origin, handicap, age, or ancestry.[88] Public accommodation is defined to include only facilities available to the public.[89] Consequently, RACs, although serving a "public" charitable purpose as required for tax exemption,[90] are public accommodations and bound by the prohibition only to the extent their cafeterias, bookstores, museums, sporting events, and the like are open to the public. There is no reason to believe that the statute is intended to govern admissions to these private institutions.

Although generally governed by similar discrimination provisions of the civil rights act,[91] housing accommodations of certain RACs are partially exempt.[92] To qualify, the college must be "operated, supervised, or controlled by or in connection with a religious organization."[93] The religious organizations "presumably" need not be "formal denominational organizations commonly thought of as 'churches'."[94] Moreover, the degree of affiliation may be as slight as mere supervision in connection with the religious organization.

The partial exemption afforded these RACs permits them to give preference to persons of the same religion and to make any selection calculated by them to promote the religious principles for which the colleges were established.[95] This suggests that in its campus housing (and even hotel guest housing) an RAC may "prefer" not only members of its religion but also make any selection which promotes its foundational purposes and principles. The use of the phrase "as is calculated by such organization" in connection with this selection indicates that the organization's judgment is not to be lightly second-guessed.

An RAC could also limit its housing to its students under that part of the exemption which allows a "bona fide private . . . organization" to give preference to its members.[96]

In any event, it would be more than speculative to argue that the housing law was intended to require RACs to open up their campus housing to nonstudents or, conversely, to outlaw religious selectivity in admissions.

Ohio imposes a duty on all employers— which include RACs[97]—to protect employees and frequenters[98] and to furnish a safe place of employment for employees.[99] Although it is unclear whether the definition of "place of employment" includes RACs,[100] the fact that the same law gives the department of industrial relations specific authority to administer and enforce occupational safety laws as they relate to colleges[101] indicates that RACs are subject to the provisions of the legislation. The Ohio law puts upon the employer the duty "to do every other thing reasonably necessary"[102] to protect the health and safety of employees and frequenters.

F. State Taxation

Nonbusiness income of RACs is not subject to taxation in Ohio. The Ohio income tax is levied only against natural persons or their estates[103] and consequently does not apply to RACs. Moreover, RACs are not covered by the Ohio corporate excise and franchise taxes which primarily apply to "for-profit" corporations.[104] Finally, municipal corporations are prohibited from taxing otherwise exempt income of religious and educational institutions.[105]

The amount of any transfer to a corporation organized and operated exclusively for religious or educational purposes is deducted from the value of a gross estate for estate taxation purpose, provided that no part of the gift's net earnings inures to the benefit of a private individual and that no substantial part of the corporation's activity involves legislative lobbying.[106] To the extent the state estate tax exceeds the federal estate tax credit, this tax incentive would encourage private benefaction to RACs.

Ohio also imposes an "additional estate tax,"[107] which is designed to pick up the difference between the maximum federal estate tax credit for state death taxes and the amount of state death taxes paid as estate taxes. The additional estate tax merely rechannels to Ohio moneys which would otherwise go to the federal government in estate taxes. This tax, therefore, does not change the total amount of death taxes paid.

Ohio has no gift tax.

Ohio does not provide a specific state income tax deduction for contributions to RACs.

The Ohio Constitution authorizes passage of general laws exempting from taxation "institutions used exclusively for charitable purposes."[108] Accordingly, the General Assembly has passed such a law relating to real and tangible personal property.[109] This exemption includes two important elements: "charitable" purpose and "exclusive" use.

Although nonprofit colleges[110] and schools[111] were recognized as "charitable,"[112] early case law interpreting the phrase "property belonging to institutions that is used exclusively for charitable purposes" indicated such institutions must operate "without distinction as to race, color or creed" in order to be for a charitable purpose.[113] In 1969, however, the phrase "used exclusively for charitable purposes" was defined statutorily[114] to include property under the control of an educational institution for use in furtherance of or incidental to its educational purposes and

without a view to profit.[115] Since the General Assembly has undertaken to define this phrase in the tax exemption statute, prior inconsistent judicial interpretations of the phrase must yield to the statutory definition.[116] Thus the absence of any language in the defining statute excepting, for instance, RACs which exercise religious preferences suggests that property of such institutions now qualifies for "charitable purpose" treatment.

Similarly, decisions prior to the statutory definition determined that any commercial use of property, even though the proceeds went exclusively to a charitable purpose, was not "exclusive use."[117] Charges made for dormitory, cafeteria, and similar incidental services, however, did not deprive the property of religiously affiliated educational and social institutions of the tax exemption, provided such income was devoted to their charitable purposes.[118] Liberal construction of the broad language—"use in furtherance of or incidental to its . . . educational purpose"[119]—of the statutory definition appears to grant nonprofit colleges an even greater exemption.[120] Although it is not clear that this exemption is broad enough to include athletic fields used for "profitable" athletic events, such use is arguably "incidental" to a college's overall educational purpose.[121]

At least at some RACs, athletic fields and the like are probably within the scope of another statutory tax exemption covering "public colleges" and lands connected with "public institutions of learning" not used for profit.[122] "[A] private institution of learning conducted in a lawful manner without any view to profit and open to all members of the public without regard to race, creed, or nationality . . . is a public college within the meaning of [this statute]."[123] Since "exclusive" charitable use is not a prerequisite under this second statute,[124] commercially used properties such as athletic fields probably are exempt as "lands connected with institutions of learning." This second exemption, however, would still appear not to apply to RACs exercising religious or racial preferences.

Sales of otherwise taxable tangible personal property by a recognized nonprofit institution of learning made no more than six days per year nor more than one per month are exempt from taxation.[125] If the number of selling days exceeds these limits, the RAC will be considered to be engaged in business and all subsequent sales will be taxed accordingly.[126] The sale of food to students in a cafeteria, dormitory, fraternity, or sorority maintained by an RAC is separately exempted.[127] *Acquisitions* by a recognized nonprofit institution of learning are also exempt.[128] (A parallel exemption is given under the use tax.)[129] However, purchases by an RAC for use in the operation of a trade or business are not excepted from taxation.[130]

G. Fund Raising

1. Charitable Solicitation

Charitable solicitation in Ohio is regulated by law.[131] Although educational organizations in general are "charitable organizations" for the purpose of soliciting funds,[132] "religious organizations" and organizations "operated, supervised, or controlled" by religious organizations are categorically exempted from the statutory regulatory scheme.[133]

While this definition is subject to several interpretations, there is at least one indication that it includes "any organization the purpose of which is to promote religious objectives," not just "churches."[134] The Opinion of the Ohio Attorney General which gave this indication looked to the "main objective" of the organization (in that case the YMCA) as articulated in its articles of incorporation and constitution to determine that it was "religious in nature" although it conducted nonreligious services and activities.[135] RACs exercising their right to state religious affiliation in their articles of incorporation or their right to grant an ecclesiastical body the power to appoint directors, as discussed above,[136] undoubtedly qualify for this exception as do schools under actual "church" supervision. The YMCA opinion suggests that the declaration of a religious (or merely, e.g., "Christian") purpose by the controlling board of a college which has no denominational affiliation is sufficient for exemption. This exemption, therefore, will be available to most if not all RACs in Ohio.

Those RACs whose religious affiliation may be too attenuated to qualify for the blanket exemption are nevertheless exempted from the requirement of registration with the attorney general or county clerk,[137] provided solicitation is confined to alumni, faculty, trustees, or students and their families.[138] Because of this registration exemption, such RACs are also exempted from the annual financial report requirement[139] and regulations relating to professional fundraisers and solicitors.[140]

2. Games of Chance

RACs typically fulfill the three qualifications of a "charitable organization" entitled to *certain* exemptions under Ohio gambling laws.[141] The three requirements applicable to RACs are that they: 1) be tax exempt under IRC §501(c)(3);[142] 2) be an "educational organization," *i.e.*, a nonprofit organization operating a college or university whose primary purpose is to educate;[143] and 3) have been in existence for at least two years.[144]

Although gambling is generally prohibited in Ohio,[145] certain schemes of chance[146] and games of chance[147] conducted by "charitable organizations" are allowed on a limited basis.

Similarly, operation of lawful bingo games is limited exclusively to licensed charitable organizations.[148] The bingo license requires an annual application, accompanied by a license fee, to the attorney general.[149] Bingo games are subject to detailed statutory conditions.[150] Itemized records of gross receipts, expenses, prizes awarded, number of participants, and the use of the proceeds of all bingo games and schemes or games of chance must be kept by the charitable organization for at least three years.[151] Both the attorney general and local law enforcement agents are authorized to take any reasonable action necessary to assure compliance with these regulations.

H. Miscellaneous

Ohio case law accords RACs a qualified immunity from tort liability for injuries to students. As a matter of public policy an RAC will be liable for tortious injuries to a student only when the RAC has failed to exercise due care in the selection or retention of any employee.[153] This immunity is limited to nonprofit RACs and extends only to injuries to students.[154]

44. Oklahoma

A. Corporate Status

Persons wishing to form an RAC in Oklahoma are given alternative statutes of incorporation.[1] The first, chapter 14[2] of the Corporations title, allows persons associated together for religious, charitable, educational, benevolent, or scientific purposes to incorporate after electing between three and seventy-seven trustees.[3] A five-dollar fee is charged for the certificate and seal.[4] An additional five dollar fee is assessed for filing articles of incorporation.[5]

The more recent incorporation statute, chapter 19,[6] is decidedly less restrictive. Under its terms, "three or more" persons may form a nonprofit corporation "for any useful purposes"[7] upon payment of a ten dollar filing fee for the articles of incorporation.[8] The most salient difference between the two chapters is that the second flatly confers "all the general powers . . . of a domestic corporation incorporated under the Business Corporation Act"[9] on its progeny, while the former in scattered sections (1) limits its corporations' right to hold real property,[10] (2) permits them to sell or mortgage property,[11] (3) authorizes them to incur indebtedness[12] and (4) allows charitable and educational corporations to engage in business.[13]

The merger, consolidation and dissolution of nonprofit colleges are governed principally by the Oklahoma Business Corporations Act,[14] although attention should be paid to some provisions in the Nonprofit Corporations Act.[15] In addition, Oklahoma courts are empowered both by statute and by common law decisions to ap-

ply the *cy pres* doctrine when necessary.[16]

Voluntary dissolution of a nonprofit college may be conducted out of court or subject to court supervision.[17] The dissolution process is initiated when the members of the governing board adopt by unanimous consent a statement of intent to dissolve the corporation and file it with the Secretary of State.[18] The dissolution takes effect when the Secretary of State issues a certificate of dissolution or a district court enters an order of dissolution.[19] The district court also has jurisdiction to dissolve a nonprofit college involuntarily[20] in an action properly brought by a member of the corporation or a creditor.[21]

After the payment of all liabilities, the governing board must dispose of the assets to similarly exempted corporations having the same purposes as the dissolving corporation; if the governing board fails to do so, the district court supervising the dissolution process must attend to this matter.[22]

B. State Support

The Oklahoma Constitution prohibits the use, direct or indirect, of any public money or property for the benefit or support of any sectarian institution.[23] The Oklahoma Attorney General has strictly interpreted this section, declaring statutory authorization to use public funds for private educational institutions violative of the state Constitution.[24] This opinion seems more restrictive than the language of the state Constitution in that it purports to bar public funding of all private educational institutions, sectarian or nonsectarian, an issue not yet judicially resolved. In any event, the general attitude of the legislature has been to aid only state colleges and universities as evidenced by its refusal to authorize the sale of building bonds for private or sectarian colleges as other states have done through "Higher Educational Facilities Authority" laws.[25] Thus, even given court approval (which is highly improbable, especially in the case of RACs), the legislature would probably balk at any proposal of financial support for nonpublic colleges.

The Oklahoma Constitution also prohibits the pledge of state credit to RACs, as well as to any other individual corporation or municipality.[26] This prohibition extends even to organizations whose purposes promote a public interest.[27]

Oklahoma does lend indirect support to RACs through financial assistance programs for students. Under the Higher Education Tuition Act,[28] tuition grants of up to $500 per year are awarded to qualified students in accredited colleges and universities within the state.[29] The student qualifications for a grant do not exclude students attending RACs.[30] The institution attended must be of collegiate grade and approved by the Oklahoma Regents for Higher Education.[31] Although the Regents are authorized to coordinate RACs with the state system of higher education,[32] there is no reason to expect the Regents would deny approval for these purposes.

Through the Oklahoma Student Loan Act,[33] the legislature created a "Student Loan Fund"[34] from which qualified students at participating institutions may borrow money to meet educational expenses. A qualified student must be accepted for enrollment in a participating institution.[35] "Participating institution" is defined as any educational institution which qualifies under the Federal Higher Educational Act of 1965,[36] public or private.[37] Hence, students attending RACs are eligible to participate in either the grant or loan programs.

C. Personnel

Generally it is a discriminatory practice for an employer[38] to discriminate against an in-

dividual in employment on the basis of race, color, religion, sex, or national origin.[39] It is not a discriminatory employment practice, however:

for a school, college, university, or other educational institution to hire and employ an employee of a particular religion if the [institution] is, in whole or substantial part, owned, supported, controlled, or managed by a particular religion or by a particular religious corporation, association or society, or if the curriculum of [that institution] is directed toward the propagation of a particular religion.[40]

This provision is intended to exempt certain religiously oriented educational institutions. For institutions that qualify, religious selectivity of all employees, whatever their function, would be authorized. For some RACs, however, it may be difficult to meet the religious affiliation requirements.

There is some vagueness in these requirements. There is no specific statutory or judicial guidance as to factually how much control by a religion or by a religious organization is sufficient. Is an institution "controlled" by a religion if it adheres to the religion's doctrine or must there be a discernible religious entity (e.g., a formal church) in "control"? If the latter, then the "or by a particular religious [organization]" alternative is redundant. Arguably, then, an institution qualifies if it considers itself within the control of the tenets of a particular religion.

Even absent this interpretation, however, the phrasing is probably broad enough to include most RACs. Nonetheless, some institutions may lack a sufficient connection, especially since the legislature did not include the words "or in connection with" between the phrases "owned, supported, controlled or managed by" and "a particular religion." This may have been a mere oversight or an indication that the legislature intended a narrower scope than that of other such statutes.

An RAC will also qualify for this exemption if its curriculum is directed toward the propagation of a particular religion. This would seem to apply only to Bible colleges, seminaries and the like.

There is some uncertainty as to the significance of the repeated use of the phrase "a particular religion." Nonetheless, it would appear that an RAC otherwise within the exemption could prefer an employment applicant of *any* religion, not merely one of the same religion as the institution. Perhaps it was felt useful to restrict the exemption to institutions and employment applicants of identifiable and specific religious affiliation.

In any event, a separate provision allows employment selectivity on the basis of religion, sex, or national origin if it is a "bona fide occupational qualification [BFOQ] reasonably necessary to the normal operation of the business or enterprise."[41]

This BFOQ authorizes selectivity on all otherwise proscribed bases save race or color. RACs will be primarily interested in the religion BFOQ, which will probably not greatly protect them in personnel decisions involving positions other than those of theology or philosophy faculty and perhaps of certain counselors. It is not likely that an RAC would be successful in arguing a right to exercise religious preference in the employment of faculty generally despite its interest in establishing on campus a pervasive presence of faculty of a certain religious persuasion.

The sex BFOQ would be especially helpful in hiring dormitory personnel and *perhaps* some counselors and teachers of courses in women's rights or women's history.

The Oklahoma employment discrimination prohibition does not apply to a "religious corporation, association, or society with respect to the employment of individuals of a particular religion to perform work connected with the carrying on by the [entity] of its religious activities."[42] This exemption, however, is extremely narrow, applying most comfortably to entities like religious orders. The only RACs conceivably within the exemption would be seminaries and Bible colleges. In any event, the exemption would only extend to those positions related to the RAC's religious activities.

The employment provisions are enforced by the Oklahoma Human Rights Commission.[43]

The Oklahoma Minimum Wage Act[44] covers any "employer" having more than ten employees at any one location or doing a gross business of more than $100,000.00 annually.[45] The Act exempts, however, employers who, subject to the Fair Labor Standards Act of 1938, as amended,[46] pay the minimum wage provided for by that Act.[47] Also exempt are employers whose employees are (1) working as volunteers in a charitable, religious or other nonprofit organization;[48] (2) working as good faith executives, administrators or professionals;[49] (3) working as part-time (i.e., "less than twenty-five hours a week") workers; (4) less than eighteen years of age, if not a high school or vocational school graduate;[50] or (5) less than twenty-two years of age if a student regularly enrolled in a high school, college, university or vocational training program.[51] The Act sets a minimum wage of $2.00 per hour for covered employees.[52]

The Oklahoma Worker's Compensation Act[53] covers corporations engaged in enumerated hazardous[54] employments.[55] The Act also covers any employer[56] with a gross annual payroll of more than $100,000.[57] Generally, RACs are covered unless some of their employees[58] come within the exception for employment[59] covered by a federal worker's compensation law.[60] RACs must either carry compensation insurance[61] or provide the State Administrator of Worker's Compensation[62] with satisfactory proof of financial ability to directly compensate injured employees. The Administrator may require the deposit of adequate security to guarantee payment of compensation.[63]

Prior to January 1, 1972, RACs were excluded from coverage under the Oklahoma Employment Security Act[64] unless they operated for profit or were substantially involved in carrying on propaganda or otherwise influencing legislation.[65] Since that date, however, with few exceptions, service in the employ of most[66] corporations "organized or operated exclusively for religious . . . or educational purposes," and, therefore, virtually all RACs, has been subject to the Act.[67]

With regard to employment covered by the Act, a nonprofit organization may make the usual contributions[68] or elect to make payments into the unemployment compensation fund[69] of an amount equal to the regular benefits plus one-half the extended benefits paid in connection with service for the nonprofit corporation.[70]

Nonetheless, the following service is exempted from the definition of "employment": (1) service for a church or convention or association of churches;[71] (2) service for an organization operated primarily for religious purposes and "operated, supervised, controlled, or principally supported by a church or convention or association of churches";[72] and (3) service by a "duly ordained, commissioned or licensed minister of a church" exercising his ministry or by a member of a religious order as duty required by the order.[73] None of these exceptions is very broad insofar as employment at the typical RAC is concerned and, consequently, few positions at RACs will come within any of them. This is true because (1) very few people employed by RACs can claim to be working for a church, convention or association of churches; (2) except perhaps for institutions like seminaries and Bible colleges, few RACs can claim to be both operated primarily for religious purposes and run or principally supported by a church or group of churches; and (3) few employees on RAC campuses, save perhaps some counselors or theology teachers, will be regular ministers of a church exercising their ministry or members of a religious order performing duties required by that order.

In any event, the following services, *inter alia,* are excluded from the definition of "employment" and therefore are not subject to the Employment Security Act's provisions: (1) domestic service in a local college club or local chapter of a college fraternity or sorority unless performed for a person who paid $1,000 or more in the current or preceding calendar year to individuals performing such domestic service in any calendar quarter;[74] (2) service with regard to which unemployment compensation is payable under a congressionally established system;[75] (3) service performed for a school, college or university by one of its regular students (or by the spouse of such a student if the spouse is advised, at the beginning of the service, that the employment is provided under a program of financial assistance to the student and will not be covered by an unemployment insurance program);[76] and (4) service performed by a student under the age of twenty-two enrolled at a regular nonprofit or public institution of higher education in a full-time program, taken for credit at that institution, which combines academic instruction with work experience.[77] The service must be an integral part of the program, so certified to the employer, and not performed in a "program established for or on behalf of an employer or group of employers."[78] These categories are not within the coverage of the Act.

Employing units not otherwise within the Act or those having employees performing services not otherwise within the Act may elect nonetheless to be covered.[79]

A clarifying provision states that even for otherwise covered employees, unemployment benefits are not paid to instructors, researchers, or principal administrators of any educational institution for any week of unemployment beginning during the period between two successive academic years, or during a similar period between two regular but not successive terms, or during a period of paid sabbatical leave provided for in the individual's contract, if the individual performs such services in the first of such academic years or terms and if there is a contract or a reasonable assurance that the individual will perform services in any such capacity for any educational institution in the second of such academic years or terms.[80]

D. Students

Oklahoma law in no way limits or otherwise regulates the admission of students to RACs.

E. Facilities

RACs are generally not subject to the regulations prohibiting discrimination in public accommodations[81] since "places of public accommodation" includes only establishments serving the general public.[82] Of course, restaurants, cafeterias, and bookstores operated by RACs and soliciting or accepting the patronage of the general public fall within the statute.[83] Consequently, an individual may not be denied the full and equal enjoyment of such places because of race, color, religion, or national origin.[84]

Oklahoma has no fair housing act.

The state's requirements of accessibility for the handicapped apply only to "public buildings," i.e., those erected by the state or its political subdivisions or with public funds.[85] RACs are constitutionally denied public funding.[86]

Hence the accessibility standards do not apply.

The Oklahoma Health and Safety Standards Act[87] imposes a duty on each employer to "establish and maintain conditions of work which are reasonably safe and healthful for employees."[88] The OHSS Commission adopts and promulgates the standards,[89] and the Commissioner of Labor administers and enforces them.[90] RACs are included under the categories of "employer" and "employment."[91]

F. State Taxation

RACs are exempt from state income tax if they satisfy exemption requirements of the Internal Revenue Code.[92] RACs are generally exempt from federal income taxation.[93] Income derived from unrelated business, e.g., noneducational business holdings, however, is subject to the Oklahoma income tax.[94]

All transfers, gifts or bequests made to RACs are to be deducted from the value of a gross estate in order to determine the net estate subject to taxation.[95] This exemption would apply only with regard to those RACs operating under the laws of the state.[96]

Oklahoma has no inheritance tax.

Property transferred by gift to an RAC is exempt from Oklahoma's Gift Tax Code.[97]

Since "Oklahoma taxable income" means "taxable income" as the term is used for federal income tax purposes,[98] and since contributions to nonprofit RACs are deductible in arriving at federal "taxable income,"[99] there is in effect provided, at least for those who itemize federally, a state tax deduction for such contributions.

All property used exclusively by colleges as well as all property used for religious purposes is constitutionally declared exempt from taxation in Oklahoma.[100] Faithful to this constitutional exemption, Oklahoma legislation declares all property of any college used exclusively and directly for the objects of the college exempt from Oklahoma *ad valorem* taxation.[101]

RACs are not generally exempted from the state Sales Tax Code. Cafeterias and lunch rooms operated primarily for students and teachers are exempted only in public colleges.[102] Religious or educational organizations within an RAC, if operated not for profit under a lodge system, however, at least will not be taxed on their dues.[103] RACs are excepted from

the state use tax only with respect to the use of property exempt under the sales tax.[104] Oklahoma has no meals tax.

G. Fund Raising

RACs are generally exempt from the regulations of the Oklahoma Solicitation of Charitable Contributions Act[105] if they are either incorporated for religious purposes and engage in bona fide religious programs or if they are directly operated, supervised, or controlled by a religious organization.[106] These two bases for exemption would seem to cover only those RACs which are seminaries or Bible colleges. In any event, any educational institution is exempted with regards to solicitation of its students and their families, alumni, faculty, and trustees.[107]

A requirement that a telephone solicitor disclose certain information to the person called before any actual solicitation and provide, upon request, his telephone number does not apply to religious groups or to nonprofit organizations soliciting from within their memberships.[108]

Certain nonprofit organizations in existence at least two years and exempt under paragraphs (4) through (8) of section 501(c) of the federal Internal Revenue Code[109] may obtain a license to conduct bingo games from the district court clerk.[110] The proceeds of the games except actual expenses must not inure to the benefit of any individual in the organization.[111] Therefore, certain organizations may conduct bingo games for the benefit of RACs, although RACs themselves may not since they are not within the appropriate paragraphs of IRC §501(c).

The Oklahoma legislature has declared every lottery unlawful and a common public nuisance.[112] No exception is made to this rule.

H. Miscellaneous

As mentioned earlier, RACs are constitutionally subjected to the coordination of the State Regents for Higher Education.[113] The specific coordinating powers of the Regents, set out statutorily, include the powers to prescribe standards for higher education and to determine the functions and courses of study needed in the institutions to conform to the prescribed standards.[114]

45. Oregon

A. Corporate Status

The Oregon Constitution authorizes the formation of corporations under the general laws.[1] RACs would typically organize under the "Oregon Nonprofit Corporation Law."[2] There are no special exemptions for RACs under this law. A person may, however, in conformity with the constitution, canons, rules, regulations, and disciplines of any church or religious denomination, form a corporation sole.[3] A corporation sole differs from other corporations in that it has no board of directors, need not have officers and is managed by the individual constituting the corporation.[4] As of this writing, no Oregon RAC is incorporated as a corporation sole.[5]

It is unlawful for a person to offer or sell any security in Oregon unless the security is registered with the Corporations Commissioner.[6] Securities issued by nonprofit organizations which are organized and operated exclusively for, *inter alia*, religious or educational purposes are exempt from this provision.[7] This exemption applies to virtually all RACs.

No school or college may confer a degree upon any person without first having submitted the requirements for such degree to the Oregon Educational Coordinating Commission and having obtained its approval of such requirements.[8] This provision does not apply to: (1) schools which have operated and conferred degrees in Oregon since 1920; (2) schools in good standing with the Northwest Association of Schools and Colleges (NWA); or (3) schools of theology operating on a post-baccalaureate degree level.[9]

A nonprofit college in Oregon has the power to cease its activities and dissolve.[10] The dissolution process, both voluntary and involuntary, follows, with minor differences, the procedures set forth in the Model Nonprofit Corporation Act.[11] The doctrine of *cy pres* has been recognized by the state courts where necessary to effect the donor's intent.[12]

Although Oregon has generally adopted the Model Act, one slight variation in the Oregon statute is the requirement that articles of dissolution be filed with the State Corporation Commissioner.[13] The Commissioner then issues a certificate of dissolution, at which time the corporate existence ceases.[14] Involuntary dissolution procedures can be brought by the Attorney General in circuit court if a nonprofit college is allegedly involved in fraud or has failed to meet the incorporation requirements.[15] Liquidation claims may be brought in circuit court by, among others, the governing board of a nonprofit college.[16]

The Oregon scheme for distribution of a dissolving college's assets corresponds to the sequence in the Model Act.[17] This scheme for distribution of assets also applies to judicially supervised liquidation of a nonprofit college.[18] Any residual assets distributable to a person who is unknown or who cannot be found must be liquidated and the cash deposited with the Division of State Lands.[19]

B. State Support

Oregon guarantees the right of all men to worship God according to the dictates of their own consciences, free from any interference.[20] In part to insure noninterference, the Oregon constitution stipulates that "(n)o money shall be drawn from the Treasury for the benefit of any religous [sic], or theological institution."[21] However, in 1961 the Oregon Supreme Court held that this section does not in all circumstances preclude state funding of RACs.[22]

Oregon taxpayers had brought suit against a school district to enjoin it from supplying free textbooks to pupils enrolled in St. John's The Apostle parochial school, arguing that such aid violated the Oregon Constitutional provision prohibiting aid to religious institutions. The Oregon Court held for the taxpayers, observing that the teaching of the precepts of Catholicism was an inseparable part of the educational process at the parochial school.[23] Any aid to the school actually benefitted its religious functions and was therefore impermissible. The Court added, however, that "[n]either the federal nor the state constitutions prohibit the state from conferring benefits upon religious institutions where that benefit does not accrue to the institution as a religious organization. The proscription is against aid to religious functions."[24]

The Court's analysis would see the typical RAC as made up of religious and secular components.[25] State aid to the religious aspects of an institution (e.g., financial aid for divinity students or construction grants for chapels) would clearly violate the Establishment Clause of the Oregon Constitution. However, state aid to the secular aspects of an institution would be permissible.

The Oregon Legislative Assembly has recognized the important contribution of independent institutions of higher learning to post-secondary education in Oregon.[26] To sustain this contribution, the legislature authorized the Oregon State Scholarship Commission to enter into contracts with private and independent institutions of higher education for the performance of nonsectarian educational services to assist the state in providing educational opportunities to Oregon students.[27] Here, "nonsectarian educational services" means the provision of instruction in any course which is presented in the curriculum of a private and independent institution of higher education and which does not advocate the religious teachings or the morals or forms of worship of any sect.[28] As noted earlier, the State Scholarship Commission administers the Purchase of Educational Services from Independent Colleges (PESIC) program.[29]

The Oregon Legislative Assembly has appropriated funds for the construction of any building or structure for higher education.[30] However, it is the interpretation of Mr. Edward Branchfield, Oregon Assistant Attorney General, that such buildings are authorized only for institutions within the State Department of Higher Education:

To the best of my knowledge, that statute has never been used to erect buildings for any independent college. The purpose of that statute and the constitutional amendment was to allow the construction of dormitories, student union buildings and other income-producing facilities on the campuses of schools within the Department of Higher Education.[31]

Consequently, Oregon RACs are apparently not in a position to benefit from this appropriation of funds.

Most students are eligible to receive grants given by the state: need grants (awarded on the basis of the student's financial need) and scholastic grants (awarded on the basis of the student's financial need and of his academic aptitude and achievement.)[32] However, no grant may be awarded to a student enrolled in a course of study required for and leading to a degree in theology, divinity or religious education.[33] Nothing in the statutes authorizing these grants is to be construed as requiring any institution to admit a grant recipient or as attempting to control or influence the policies of the institution.[34]

Generally, all students, including those attending RACs, are eligible for loans if their institution is accredited by the Northwest Association of Secondary and Higher Education.[35]

C. Personnel

Oregon law generally prohibits discrimination in employment because of race, religion, color, sex, marital status, or national origin.[36] However, the Code does not prevent a bona fide church or sectarian religious institution, including but not limited to a school, hospital or church camp, from preferring an employee or applicant for employment of one religious sect or persuasion over another when one of three conditions is met:

(a) the religious sect or persuasion to which the employee or applicant belongs is the same as that of such church or institution;

(b) in the opinion of such bona fide church or sectarian religious institution, such a preference will best serve the purposes of that church or institution;

(c) the employment involved is closely connected with or related to the primary purposes of the church or institution and is not connected with a commercial or business activity which has no necessary relationship to the church or institution, or to its primary purposes.[37]

However, a letter from the Oregon Attorney General states that the three conditions must be read conjunctively as the "legislative history . . . indicates" and as the Bureau of Labor interprets the exemption.[38] Thus, to qualify for the exemption, an RAC would have to meet all three conditions.

It is not certain that all RACs in Oregon would be considered "sectarian religious institutions"[39] under this provision. However, the Oregon Attorney General's Office has suggested that a college merely affiliated with a religious denomination could be considered a sectarian religious institution "because the degree of ecclesiastical ownership and control of various bona fide churches and sectarian religious institutions differs and in some instances may be non-existent."[40] Such an interpretation may make the employment exemption available to all RACs in Oregon.

Oregon's minimum wage law applies generally to RACs.[41] However, the law does not cover employees employed by educational institutions at which such individuals are enrolled as students,[42] and individuals employed at a nonprofit conference ground or center operated for educational, charitable, or religious purposes.[43] This provision could be highly significant for RACs employing their students.

The Oregon Workers' Compensation Law[44] covers any corporation[45] with one or more employees[46] who are not expressly excluded from coverage.[47] Generally employees of RACs are covered unless they come within the exceptions for casual employment,[48] employment covered by the federal workers' compensation law,[49] or services performed primarily for board and lodging for a religious, charitable, or relief organization.[50] RACs may elect to include their exempt employees within the coverage of the provisions.[51] Injured employees not covered by the Act may bring suit against their employers.[52] An RAC must provide for the compensation of injured employees either by carrying insurance,[53] paying premiums into a state operated Accident Insurance Fund[54] or obtaining certification as a self-insurer from the State's Director of the Workers' Compensation Department after depositing adequate security according to the provisions of the law.[55]

The Oregon Employment Division Law[56] (the unemployment compensation statute) defines "employer" as any employing unit[57] for which one or more individuals[58] has worked "in each of 18 separate weeks during any calendar year, or in which its total payroll during any calendar quarter amounts to $225 or more.[59] The definition of "employment" under the Oregon statute applies to all "service for an employer."[60] The statute exempts certain types of services from this definition. The exemptions cover services performed (1) for a school or college by one of its regularly enrolled students or by the spouse of such a student;[61] (2) by a student under the age of twenty-two, at an accredited nonprofit or public educational institution in a full-time program, taken for credit and combining academic instruction and work experience;[62] and (3) as domestic service for a local college club or local chapter of a college fraternity or sorority, if total remuneration in any quarter of the current or preceding calendar year was less than $1,000.00.[63]

The statute provides specific exemptions for "nonprofit employing units."[64] These nonprofit employing units are organizations which fit the definition in section 501(c)(3) of the Internal Revenue Code and qualify as tax-exempt under section 501(a) of the Code.[65] The applicable exemptions apply to services performed (1) for a church or for an association of churches;[66] (2)

for an organization run primarily for religious purposes and controlled by a church or by an association of churches;[67] and (3) by an ordained minister or by a member of a religious order in the exercise of his duties.[68] The Oregon law permits organizations not otherwise subject to its unemployment compensation provisions to elect participation in the program for a period of two years.[69]

Oregon law, which guarantees the rights of employees to form, join or assist labor organizations, clearly extends to the employees of RACs.[70] It would be unlawful for a college to interfere with, restrain or coerce employees in the exercise of those rights.[71]

Oregon law does protect the nonassociation interests of an employee who, based on good faith religious tenets or teachings of his church, prefers not to join a labor union. In lieu of acquiring union membership, that employee may pay an amount equal to regular union dues and fees to any nonreligious charity or to another charitable organization mutually agreed upon by the employee and the union.[72]

D. Students

No person in Oregon will be subjected to discrimination in any higher education program or service, school or interschool activity if the program, service, or activity is financed in whole or in part by moneys appropriated by the Legislative Assembly.[73] Oregon RACs are subject to this provision only if they receive state funding.[74]

"Discrimination" under the law means "any act that unreasonably differentiates treatment, intended or unintended, or any act which is fair in form but discriminatory in operation, either of which is based on age, handicap, national origin, race, marital status, religion, or sex."[75] This particular definition of discrimination, with its use of the word "unreasonably," may, in some instances, exempt otherwise subject RACs from the law. It may be reasonable for an RAC to prefer a Jewish applicant over a Catholic one in order to create a diverse student body, or for a single-sex school to admit females only. In other words, the applicability of this provision to RACs is dependent upon both the extent of its state funding and the reasonableness of the treatment.

Interestingly, even if an RAC has violated the discrimination provision,[76] there are apparently no sanctions available. The statute specifically states that only public institutions of higher education are subject to the specified sanctions, which may include the withholding of all or part of state funding.[77]

Although state funds are available to RACs under the Purchase of Educational Services from Independent Colleges (PESIC) program,[78] Mr. Jeffrey M. Lee, executive director of the State Scholarship Commission which administers the PESIC program, writes: "No state funds have ever been withheld from a college under the PESIC program because of admissions policies."[79]

It seems evident that Oregon RACs are free to adopt any admissions policy with little or no intervention from the state.

E. Facilities

Under Oregon law, all persons are entitled to the full and equal accommodations, advantages, facilities, and privileges of any place of public accommodation, without any distinction, discrimination or restriction on account of race, religion, sex, marital status, color, or national origin.[80] Under this provision, a place of public accommodation is any place or service offering to the public accommodations, advantages, facilities, or privileges whether in the nature of goods, services, lodging, amusements, or otherwise.[81] A place of public accommodation does not include any institution, bona fide club or place of accommodation which is in its nature distinctly private.[82]

In a suit brought against the Boy Scouts of America in Oregon in 1976,[83] it was argued that the exclusion of a nine-year old girl from a scouting group was a violation of Oregon's Public Accommodations Act. The Oregon Supreme Court held that the Act was intended to prohibit discrimination by business or commercial enterprises which offer goods or services to the public. Therefore, the Act was not intended by the legislature to include a scouting group, at least to the extent of requiring it to accept membership applications by girls.

This decision suggests that the Public Accommodations Act is not applicable to RAC activities or events which are not commercial enterprises. Events or activities at which an admission fee is charged, or facilities used for commercial activities (such as a college bookstore or coffeeshop) would, however, be subject to the provisions of the Act, if open to the public.[84]

This emphasis on business or commercial activity would tend to preclude the argument that the Public Accommodations Act might even apply to RAC student admissions on the theory that educational "services" are a public accommodation under the Act. Further militating against such an argument is the fact that Oregon has a statute specifically proscribing a variety of discriminatory practices in admissions by publicly supported institutions,[85] a statute that would tend to be redundant if college admissions were within the Public Accommodations Act.

Although residence at a private or public institution, if incidental to the provision of educational or religious services, is specifically exempt from the Residential Landlord and Tenant Act,[86] campus housing is not exempt from the prohibition against discrimination on the basis of race, color, sex, marital status, religion, or national origin in the selling, renting, or leasing of real property.[87] Thus, if an RAC admitted and provided housing for Christians only, this could be considered a technical violation of the prohibition against discrimination in housing. However, it does not appear to be the policy of the state of Oregon directly to control the admissions practices of privately supported higher education,[88] and nothing indicates a legislative intent indirectly to control admissions through the housing discrimination legislation.

Construction or renovation of public buildings must provide accessibility and usability to the physically handicapped.[89] Since the term "public buildings" includes all buildings and structures used by the public that are constructed, purchased, leased, or rented in whole or in part by private funds,[90] this provision is generally applicable to RACs.

Less clear is which campus buildings are covered. Bookstores, cafeterias, and the like may obviously be "open to the public." On the other hand, dormitories, classroom buildings, student dining halls, and the like, generally restricted to students (and perhaps their guests), are open to the public only in the sense that the college invites admissions applications from the general public. It is likely that only the former category of campus building comes within the legislation.

Furthermore, the legislation *excludes* employees or tenants from the term "public" and *includes* customers and non-household guests. Students and campus employees are more like employees and tenants than customers and guests. This would indicate that many RAC buildings are not "used by the public" and are not, therefore, within the legislation.

Public buildings, i.e., buildings in which persons congregate for civic, political, educational, religious, social, or recreational purposes,[91] are subject to the provisions of the fire code.[92] Clearly this applies to many buildings on RAC campuses, as may the requirement that all "educational institutions" with an average daily attendance of fifty or more pupils conduct fire drills once a month.[93]

RACs must conform to the energy conservation standards prescribed by Oregon.[94] The provision applies to any "public building,"[95] i.e., any building which is open to the public during normal business hours or any building which provides facilities for public shelter or is used for educational, office, or institutional purposes.[96] Virtually all RAC buildings will therefore be included.

The Oregon Safe Employment Act[97] contains no exclusion for RACs from the scope of its coverage. An employee is defined broadly as any individual including minors, lawfully or unlawfully employed, who engages to furnish his services for remuneration.[98] An employer is defined as any person who has one or more employees, or any sole proprietor or member of a partnership who elects workman's compensation coverage.[99]

F. State Taxation

The Corporation Excise Tax legislation[100] exempts from the taxation provided for therein, *inter alia*, all corporations, funds, or foundations operated exclusively for religious, charitable, scientific, literary, or educational purposes.[101] No part of the net earnings of a qualifying institution may inure to the profit of any individual.[102]

The very same exemption is incorporated by reference[103] into the Corporation Income Tax[104] law. Virtually all RACs would qualify for both exemptions.

Under the Corporation Excise Tax Law, however, a specific provision imposes the tax on these otherwise exempt corporations with regard to "unrelated business income."[105] Nonetheless, a $1,000 deduction is allowed,[106] and, to be excluded from taxable "unrelated business income" are, *inter alia*, (1) dividends, interest, and annuities and otherwise allowable deductions;[107] (2) rents from real property rented by a school, college, or university to students or faculty if the property is really part of the school and the student or faculty presence is necessary to the educational function;[108] (3) income from research done for a governmental unit;[109] and (4) in the case of any organization operated primarily for fundamental research, the results of which are freely and publicly available, all income derived from research.[110]

Under Oregon's Inheritance Tax[111] legislation, a credit is allowed for the amount of the tax apportioned to any devise, bequest, legacy, or gift to or for the use of any society, association, trust, or corporation, provided the transfer is to be used solely for religious, charitable, scientific, literary, or educational purposes.[112] All such transfers to or for the use of RACs would qualify for the credit.

The Oregon Gift Tax[113] law provides a parallel exemption[114] with regard to gifts to RACs.

Oregon has no estate tax.

Under the Oregon Personal Income Tax law,[115] a deduction is in effect generally provided to taxpayers for all contributions deductible under federal income tax law.[116] (The chief exception is the taxpayer whose total amount of deductions under federal tax law is less than the state standard deduction.)[117] Since contributions to RACs are deductible under federal tax law,[118] a parallel deduction is in effect generally available under state law to taxpayers not using the state standard deduction.[119]

Under the Corporation Excise Tax Law,[120] there is allowed a deduction, up to five percent of the taxpayer's net income, for contributions to nonprofit RACs.[121] The same deduction is incorporated by reference[122] into the Corporation Income Tax Law.[123]

Buildings owned (or being purchased) by religious organizations or incorporated eleemosynary institutions which are used solely for administration, education, religious or entertainment purposes are exempt from taxation.[124] However, any building owned by such organization or institution which is used as a shop or store will be assessed and taxed.[125]

A privilege tax is levied against all amusement devices except such devices which are operated solely by or for a nonprofit corporation for the purpose of conducting a fair, festival, or trade show or special fund raising project.[126]

Oregon has no state sales or use tax.

G. Fund Raising

Charitable organizations are generally required to register and file reports concerning the assets held for charitable purposes with the Attorney General.[127] However, charitable corporations organized and operated primarily as a religious organization or an educational institution[128] are exempted from this requirement.[129] This exemption would cover virtually all nonprofit RACs.

Charitable organizations are also generally required to submit to the Attorney General reports on their fund raising activities.[130] Virtually all RACs will be excused from this requirement as well due to the exemption provided for (1) educational institutions, churches, or religious organizations soliciting funds for their own use; (2) any other similar society soliciting funds only from its own membership and (3) any religious organization soliciting only from its congregation or persons otherwise affiliated with it.[131]

Charitable, fraternal, or religious organizations (including nonprofit RACs) are permitted to operate bingo or lotto games when no other person other than the organization or a player profits in any manner from the operation of the game.[132]

H. Miscellaneous

The Insurance Code promulgated by the Oregon legislature[133] is specifically applicable to educational institutions and nonprofit corporations issuing annuity policies in compliance with the Code.[134] Under the Code, educational institutions or nonprofit corporations may receive a transfer of money or property conditioned upon an agreement to pay an annuity to the transferor or his nominee, if the institution or nonprofit corporation holds a certificate of authority issued by the Insurance Commissioner.[135]

46. Pennsylvania

A. Corporate Status

Pennsylvania's Nonprofit Corporation Law of 1972[1] governs the process of formation,[2] merger and consolidation,[3] and dissolution[4] of religiously affiliated colleges in that state. A corporation may be formed under this statute if it is organized for charitable, educational, professional, religious, scientific, or social purposes.[5] The term "charitable purposes" is defined broadly in this statute to include any object beneficial to the community, including the advancement of education or of religion.[6] The statute outlines the procedure for the formation of a nonprofit corporation[7] as well as the powers and duties of its directors and officers.[8]

The statute likewise provides that a nonprofit corporation may not use the words "college," "university," or "seminary" in its corporate title unless it has been certified by the state Department of Education as meeting the criteria for such an institution as prescribed by the Department.[9] In addition, the statute provides for a special procedure for incorporation of degree-granting educational institutions, which are required to set forth in their articles of incorporation detailed information concerning their assets, the size of the faculty, and the requirements for admission.[10]

The process of dissolution of an RAC is initiated when a majority of the governing board adopts a resolution that the college be dissolved.[11] The board then prepares articles of election to dissolve, which must be filed with the Secretary of State.[12] The statute vests broad discretion in the governing board to settle the affairs of a dissolving college.[13] The governing board may petition a court to supervise the process of dissolution,[14] and must do so with respect to the disposition of property given for charitable purposes,[15] or if the college is organized as a nonprofit corporation with "religious assets."[16] As the *Wilson College* case illustrates, a Pennsylvania court need not grant the petition of the governing board for the dissolution of a nonprofit college.[17]

B. State Support

The Pennsylvania Constitution prohibits monies raised for public schools from being "appropriated to or used for the support of any sectarian school."[18] The same article provides that no appropriations:

be made for charitable, educational or benevolent purposes to any person or community nor to any denominational and sectarian institution, corporation or association [except] in the form of scholarship grants or loans for higher educational purposes to residents of the Commonwealth enrolled in institutions of higher learning except that no scholarship, grants or loans for higher educational purposes shall be given to persons enrolled in a theological seminary or school of theology.[19]

Despite these constitutional provisions, however, Pennsylvania, recognizing the contribution of private institutions of higher education to the Commonwealth, has enacted an extensive program of assistance to these institutions, and of assistance in the form of scholarships, grants, and loans to their students.

The Pennsylvania Higher Education Assistance Agency supervises and administers the Institutional Assistance Grants allotted to private institutions to defray educational expenses.[20] Each institution receives on behalf of each Pennsylvania scholarship student an annual grant, currently valued at up to $400. Educational expenses may not include costs "for sectarian and denominational instruction, the construction or maintenance of sectarian and denominational facilities or for any other sectarian and denominational purpose or activity." Theological seminaries, schools of theology, or sectarian and denominational institutions are ineligible for participation in this program.[21] Recipient institutions, moreover, must maintain separate accounts for these grants, and may not commingle these monies with other funds.[22] These statutory provisions, similar to those found in the federal legislation sustained in *Tilton v. Richardson*[23] and in the South Carolina legislation sustained in *Hunt v. McNair*,[24] help to assure the constitutionality of the grant program if it were challenged as violative of the Establishment Clause.[25]

Through the Higher Education Equal Opportunity Act,[26] the Commonwealth provides funds for institutions to offer special programs for disadvantaged students. Grants may be awarded for remedial learning services, counseling services and tutorial programs. None of these funds may be used for tuition, room and board, or fees.[27]

Pennsylvania's Higher Educational Facilities Authority Act of 1967 created an independent corporate body to construct, furnish, and lease educational facilities for academic, research, or cultural activities at any nonprofit educational institution within the Commonwealth.[28] In order to be eligible for this assistance an institution must be recognized by the state board of education and must not discriminate in admission on the basis of race, creed, or national origin.[29]

A 1977 amendment to Pennsylvania government regulations permits "private colleges and universities to participate in or purchase off purchase contracts for materials, supplies and equipment" entered into by the Department of General Services or any other administrative department.[30]

The Pennsylvania Higher Education Assistance Agency guarantees educational loans to state residents who attend accredited institutions of higher education either inside or outside the commonwealth.[31] Loans are currently limited to a maximum of $1,500 per year and a total of $7,500 in a student's lifetime unless the loans are federally guaranteed.[32]

Pennsylvania's scholarship program seeks to provide financially needy students who show signs of academic excellence the opportunity to attend the institution of their choice.[33] Recipients of these scholarships may attend any accredited institution of higher education and may apply the funds toward tuition, room, board, books, and educational fees.[34] The awards are made without regard to race, creed, color, sex, national origin, or ancestry.[35]

Another Pennsylvania program, designed to assist children of prisoners of war or of soldiers listed as missing in action during the Vietnam war era, provides scholarships without regard to financial need or academic achievement.[36] A similar state scholarship program aids qualified veterans of the Vietnam era.[37]

C. Personnel

Unlawful Discriminatory Practices

The Pennsylvania Constitution prohibits discrimination by the state "against any person in the exercise of any civil right."[38] Since 1955, moreover, Pennsylvania has had a fair employment practices act that governs not only state action but the practices of private employers as well. This act, now called the Pennsylvania Human Relations Act,[39] proclaims the public policy of the Commonwealth "to foster the employment of all individuals in accordance with their fullest capacities regardless of their race, religious creed, ancestry, age, or national origin," and prohibits discrimination in employment and access to public accommodations and housing on the basis of those categories.[40] The act defines an employer to include any person employing four or more persons in Pennsylvania, but excludes from coverage all religious, charitable, or sectarian corporations unless they are supported, in whole or in part, by governmental appropriations.[41] The statute does not define governmental appropriations, but RACs in Pennsylvania which accept institutional assistance under any of the programs described in section II of this chapter[42] would probably be regarded as supported in part by governmental appropriations and therefore bound to observe all the provisions of the Human Relations Act, including the ban on religious preference in employment policies. In any event the statute makes unambiguously clear that RACs in Pennsylvania may not discriminate in their employment policies on the basis of race, color, age, sex, national origin, or non-job related handicap or disability.[43] The only exception provided for RACs and other religious corporations allows them to hire or employ persons "on the basis of sex in those certain instances where sex is a bona fide occupational qualification because of the religious beliefs, practices, or observances of that corporation."[44]

Although the legislature may not have intended the anomalous result that prohibits religious preference in the employment practices of RACs that accept any amount of state financial assistance, the state statute does not include any provision parallel to the exemption for religious preference allowed to religious corporations in section 702 of the federal Civil Rights Act of 1964[45] or to the exception for RACs found in section 703(e)(2) of the same act.[46] The fact that the Pennsylvania legislation included an exemption for religious corporations and RACs in the housing provisions of the state Human Relations Act,[47] but not in the section relating to employment, moreover, suggests that the legislature intended to deny to publicly supported RACs the ability to choose employees on the basis of religion.

The statute prohibits any discrimination in hiring,[48] any advertising or eliciting of information,[49] and the use of a quota system to deny or limit employment,[50] related to the categories mentioned above. The limitation of recruitment efforts with an intent to circumvent the spirit and purpose of the act is also prohibited.[51]

Although the statute does not provide any explicit exemption for religious preference by RACs, the Pennsylvania Human Rights Com-

mission has issued regulations allowing employers an exception from the ban on job discrimination where the race, color, religious creed, ancestry, age, sex, or national origin is a bona fide occupational qualification (BFOQ) of an employee reasonably necessary to the normal operation of the employer's business.[52] Since the BFOQ exception has generally been construed narrowly in equal employment law,[53] administrators of RACs in Pennsylvania may rely on this BFOQ exception only where there is a logical nexus between a prospective employee's religion and the particular job for which that person is being considered.[54] The state Human Rights Commission, moreover, has indicated that the employer would have the burden of demonstrating to the Commission the necessity for a BFOQ exception.[55] The criteria for establishing this necessity make it difficult for employers to avail themselves of this exception:

A bona fide occupational qualification allowing discrimination in employment is permissible only when the employer [can] prove a factual basis for believing that all or substantially all members of a class covered by the act would be unable to perform safely and efficiently the duties of the job involved. Absent such a showing, an applicant for a job in issue may be excluded only upon a demonstration of individual incapacity.[56]

The Human Relations Commission has also issued guidelines with regard to pregnancy and employment practices.[57] Dealing in part with whether an employer may exercise preference in employment on grounds of pregnancy, these guidelines make any preference exercised on grounds of pregnancy a *prima facie* violation of the Human Relations Act.[58] The employer has the burden of showing that discrimination on the basis of pregnancy was warranted by clearly demonstrating the factual basis relied upon. The regulations, moreover, govern all pregnancies, regardless of the marital status of the mother.[59] Disabilities caused or contributed to by pregnancy, miscarriage, abortion, childbirth and recovery therefrom are, for all job-related purposes, temporary disabilities which must be treated as such in written and unwritten employment practices and policies.[60] Some of these regulations are of dubious constitutionality as applied to certain RACs.[61]

The Human Relations Act charges the Commission to enforce the employment discrimination law and empowers it to initiate, receive, investigate, and pass upon complaints charging unlawful discriminatory practices.[62] Guidelines and orders of the Human Relations Commission, moreover, have been construed as generally binding upon the courts.[63]

Minimum Wage Law

Since 1937 Pennsylvania has regulated the minimum fair wages that may be paid to workers in the Commonwealth.[64] This protective legislation, amended repeatedly,[65] is currently enforced under the Minimum Wage Act of 1968.[66] The comprehensive definition of an employer in this statute clearly includes RACs,[67] which are currently bound to pay a minimum of $3.35 an hour to all of their employees[68] except for persons employed "in a bona fide executive, or administrative capacity"[69] or "where the employer-employee relationship does not in fact exist or where the services are rendered to such organizations gratuitously,"[70] or where "the employee is enrolled as a student, or by a related nonprofit facility, such as a fraternity, when the placement, wages and working conditions are controlled by the [nonprofit educational] institution or by such related nonprofit facility."[71]

Workers' Compensation

The Pennsylvania Workmen's Compensation Act[72] applies to most employers, including corporations that are "not for profit."[73] Generally, RACs are covered except for those employees coming within the exception for employment that "is casual in character and not in the regular course of the business of the employer."[74] An employer may file an application with the Department of Labor and Industry asking to be excepted from this Act with respect to an individual employee when that employee submits a written waiver of all benefits under this Act stating that the employee is a member of a recognized religious sect and conscientiously opposes acceptance of insurance benefits.[75] RACs must carry insurance or apply for an exemption permit for all or any part of its liability for compensation. The application for the exemption permit must show financial ability to pay compensation to injured employees.[76]

Unemployment Compensation

Pennsylvania's unemployment compensation system, adopted in 1936[77] and amended frequently since then, is currently enforced under a statute adopted in 1980.[78] RACs are included within the comprehensive definition of an employer as anyone hiring an employee subject to the act for a portion of a single day, or electing to become subject to the provisions of the act.[79] Excluded from coverage, however, are (1) "domestic service in a . . . local college club or local chapter of a college fraternity or sorority;"[80] (2) "service performed in the employ of (i) a church or convention or association of churches or (ii) an organization which is operated primarily for religious purposes and which is operated, supervised, controlled, or principally supported by a church or convention or association of churches;"[81] (3) service performed "by a duly ordained, commissioned, or licensed minister of a church in the exercise of his ministry or by a member of a religious order in the exercise of duties required by such order;"[82] (4) service performed by a student regularly attending classes at the college or by the spouse of a student under a program of financial assistance to the student by the college,[83] and (5) service performed by a student under 22 years of age who is enrolled in a program combining academic instruction with work experience.[84]

The Pennsylvania statute allows RACs and other nonprofit organizations[85] that are subject to the act the option of making reimbursement payments to the state unemployment compensation fund in lieu of regular contributions.[86] These payments must equal "the amount of regular benefits and of one-half of the extended benefits paid, that is attributable to service in the employ of [the] nonprofit organization."[87] The election of this method of payment is effective for at least two years unless the state Department of Labor terminates it sooner.[88] An employer who opted for this method of payment[89] may terminate it by filing with the department a written notice of its intention to terminate it thirty days before the beginning of the taxable year to which the termination applies.[90]

Collective Bargaining

Since 1937 Pennsylvania has had a mini-Wagner Act protecting the rights of working people to organize and bargain collectively over terms and conditions of their employment.[91] Although no explicit provision in the statute suggests that RACs are excluded from the definition of an employer[92] under the act, the Pennsylvania Supreme Court ruled in 1944 that the act did not apply to charitable organizations.[93] The Pennsylvania Supreme Court, moreover, has ruled that, in light of its previous statements that nonprofit hospitals are not covered by the act,[94] the failure of the legislature to amend the act explicitly to include these hospitals means that the act is not intended to cover this kind of nonprofit organization.[95] Pennsylvania has likewise adopted legislation similar to the federal Norris-La Guardia Act,[96] prohibiting the use of injunctions to restrain peaceful concerted activity by working people, such as strikes and picketing.[97]

D. Students

The Pennsylvania Fair Educational Opportunities Act[98] requires educational institutions in the state to afford equality in educational opportunities for otherwise qualified students, without regard to race, religion, color, ancestry, national origin, or sex.[99] RACs are bound to maintain an admissions policy which is nondiscriminatory on the basis of race, color, ancestry, national origin, or sex, but if they qualify under the statutory definition of a religious or denominational educational institution,[100] they may prefer students of a particular religion without thereby violating state law.[101] Indeed, the act explicitly states that it shall not be deemed to affect in any way the right of a religious or denominational educational institution to select its students exclusively or primarily from members of such religion or denomination, or to give preference to such members.[102]

Although, therefore, the primary legislation relating to equal educational opportunity allows RACs to exercise religious preference in student admissions, an RAC in Pennsylvania, as noted above, is ineligible for participation in the state's Higher Educational Facilities Authority Act if it discriminates in admission on the basis of race, creed, or national origin.[103]

E. Facilities

As mentioned above, the Pennsylvania Constitution prohibits state action that is discriminatory against any person in the exercise of any civil right.[104] In addition, Pennsylvania prohibits discrimination in access to public accommodations and commercial housing by private parties.[105] As suggested above, most RACs in Pennsylvania would probably be regarded as supported, at least in part, by governmental appropriations.[106] If they are, they are subject to the provisions of the Pennsylvania Human Relations Act banning discrimination in access to public accommodations and commercial housing on the basis of race, color, religious creed, ancestry, handicap or disability, age, sex, or national origin.[107] This statute, however, provides a carefully defined exception allowing RACs as well as religious organizations to take into account the religion of a potential renter or lessee of their commercial housing.[108]

As also noted above, in order to receive state grants or loans for the construction or renovation of facilities, an RAC must maintain an admissions policy that is nondiscriminatory on the basis of race, creed, or national origin, and any building constructed or renovated in part with state funds may not be used "for sectarian instruction or study, or as a place for devotional activities or religious worship."[109] For example, dormitories constructed in part with the assistance of state funds must be accessible on a nondiscriminatory basis and may not be used for sectarian religious purposes.

The Pennsylvania legislature has not enacted an OSHA statute, but Pennsylvania law requires that "[a]ll establishments be so constructed, equipped, arranged, operated and conducted as to provide reasonable and adequate protection for all persons employed therein."[110] An establishment is defined as any "room, building or place where persons are employed or permitted to work for compensation of any kind."[111] The sole exclusions from this definition are farms and private dwellings.

F. State Taxation

Income Tax

Pennsylvania has a state income tax[112] but its classes of taxable income—compensation, net profits, and net gains or income from disposition of property[113] —do not generally apply to RACs or to other nonprofit organizations. In addition, the definition of "net gains" in the statute excludes "gains or income derived from obligations which are statutorily free from state or local taxation under any other act [of Pennsylvania] or under the laws of the United States."[114] Thus, RACs that are exempt under the Internal Revenue Code are also exempt from the payment of the Pennsylvania income tax. Pennsylvania taxpayers contributing to RACs are not allowed to deduct the amount of such contributions from their gross income for purposes of state income tax.

Pennsylvania has no gift tax.

Property Tax

The Pennsylvania Constitution authorizes the legislature to exempt "institutions of purely public charity" from all forms of taxation, "but in the case of any real property tax exemptions only that portion of real property of such institution which is actually and regularly used for the purposes of the institution" may be exempt.[115] Acting on the authority of this provision, the legislature has provided an exemption for RACs as well as for all universities, colleges and institutions of learning maintained by public and private charity, with a proviso that "the entire revenue derived by the same be applied to support and to increase the efficiency and facilities thereof, the repair and the necessary increase of grounds and buildings thereof, and for no other purpose."[116] Thus, exemption of an RAC in Pennsylvania from payment of federal income tax[117] does not automatically exempt that institution from payment of all state real estate taxes,[118] and an institution seeking exemption has the burden of

showing that it is a "purely public charity."[119] Factors that a court reviewing the exempt status of a college might consider include the percent of its revenues derived from tuition, the percent of its revenues devoted to scholarship aid, and the existence of a surplus income or profit even though no person receives any pecuniary benefit from the college's revenues other than in the form of wages or payment for goods or services.[120] Some courts are inclined to construe the phrase "purely public charity" narrowly, as in the *Mercyhurst College* case, where the exemption was denied for property leased by the college to a private builder, who constructed dormitory facilities and then leased these facilities back to the college at a profit.[121]

Even if a college is generally exempt from payment of property tax, this exemption will be available only for the portions of its buildings and lands that have a necessary and direct relationship to the proper functioning of the institution.[122] The tax on unrelated business income, generally levied on the portion of a public charity's assets derived from commercial enterprises,[123] was ruled to be inapplicable to the income produced by a dairy farm operated by an RAC with student help as part of an educational program.[124] Another lower court in Pennsylvania held a fraternity building at an RAC exempt from the real estate tax because it was used to provide housing, dining, and recreational facilities for the students on the campus.[125]

Since the state constitution and implementing statutes likewise provide for an exemption for "actual places of regularly stated religious worship,"[126] RAC chapels and other facilities on the campuses of an RAC used for worship are clearly exempt from the real estate tax.

Sales and Use Tax

Pennsylvania's latest sales and use tax, entitled "Tax for Education,"[127] provides that the tax will not be imposed on retail sales or on the use of goods by any charitable organization or nonprofit educational institution. Nonetheless, the tax will be imposed "with respect to any tangible personal property or services used in any unrelated trade or business carried on by such organization or institution or with respect to any materials . . . used in construction."[128]

RACs in Pennsylvania are not exempt from payment of the tax on the sale of tobacco,[129] but they are exempt from payment of the tax on liquor sold to or used by them.[130]

Inheritance Tax

Pennsylvania exempts RACs as well as any other corporation or society "organized and operated exclusively for charitable, scientific, literary or educational purposes" from its inheritance tax on transfers of property.[131]

Pennsylvania has an estate tax designed to absorb the full federal credit for state death taxes allowed against the federal estate tax.[132] This estate tax merely channels to Pennsylvania moneys which would otherwise go to the federal government and, therefore, has no ultimate effect on the total amount of death taxes paid.

G. Fund Raising

Pennsylvania has regulated charitable solicitation since 1919. Its current statute, in force since 1963, regulates such solicitation in great detail.[133]

Neither "duly constituted" religious organizations nor groups affiliated with them, presumably including RACs, are, however, included within the definition of a charitable organization for purposes of this regulatory statute.[134] Moreover, accredited educational institutions are exempt from the registration requirements found in the statute.[135] To qualify for this exemption, however, accredited educational institutions must submit, annually, on forms supplied by the Commission on Charitable Organizations,[136] the name, address, and purpose of the organization and the reason for claiming an exemption.[137]

In addition, accredited educational institutions must file copies of annual fiscal reports with the Department of Public Instruction and with the Commission on Charitable Organizations.[138] These fiscal reports are available to the general public.[139] The Commission on Charitable Organizations confers annual letters of exemption which may be exhibited to the public.[140]

Bingo and other games of chance are not allowed in Pennsylvania.[141]

47. Rhode Island

A. Corporate Status

Rhode Island refers to nonprofit corporations as "nonbusiness corporations.[1] Such corporations may be formed for religious or educational purposes,[2] which must be stated in the articles of association.[3] The corporation must be formed by at least five persons of age[4] who write and file the articles,[5] thus beginning the corporate existence.[6] The corporation is granted powers to sue, to elect officers, to make by-laws, to contract, and to borrow money.[7] A $150,000 real and personal property limit does *not* apply to educational corporations.[8] Each corporation must file a report every two years (in February of each "even year"), stating the corporate name and location, the names, addresses and terms of officers and the date of the next annual meeting.[9] Failure to file over a four-year period may result in the forfeiture of articles of association.[10]

No college or university may be established or transact business in Rhode Island without the approval of the Board of Regents for Education,[11] which must be satisfied that the institution will comply with the provisions of the "Private Schools" chapter[12] and the Board's standards and regulations.[13]

Since Rhode Island has not adopted the Model Nonprofit Corporation Act, the merger and consolidation of nonprofit colleges are governed by that state's Nonbusiness Corporations Act,[14] and the dissolution[15] of nonprofit colleges is governed by the Business Corporations Act.[16] In addition, the state courts will

apply the doctrine of *cy pres* where necessary.[17]

The process of voluntary dissolution is indicated when the governing board files with the Secretary of State a statement of intent to dissolve. If the Secretary of State finds that the statement conforms to Rhode Island law and that all fees and franchise taxes have been paid, he endorses and officially files the statement.[18] Within thirty days after this filing, the college must cease to carry on its business except for winding up its affairs. The corporate existence of the college continues until the Secretary of State or a court issues a certificate of dissolution.[19] The governing board may petition a court of competent jurisdiction to supervise the liquidation of the college's assets.[20] After all debts of the college have been paid or provided for, all obligations discharged, and all property distributed, the president or a vice president of the corporation and the secretary must deliver articles of dissolution to the Secretary of State, who files the articles and issues a certificate of dissolution.[21] Rhode Island law likewise provides for involuntary dissolution of nonprofit corporations.[22]

According to the Business Corporations Act, after filing a statement of intent to dissolve, the governing board must collect all the college's assets, sell its properties, pay or provide for its obligations, and then distribute the remainder of its assets "among its shareholders according to their respective rights and interests."[23] Since the last element of this distribution scheme does not fit the context of the typical nonprofit college, a judge supervising the liquidation of its business[24] would probably rely on the *cy pres* doctrine to preserve the charitable purposes of gifts that a dissolving college may have received. The court may appoint a receiver in the liquidation process[25] and if there are any residual assets distributable to a creditor who is unknown or who cannot be found, they must be reduced to cash and deposited with the State Treasury to be paid to that person or his legal representative upon satisfactory proof of his right to the assets.[26]

B. State Support

The Rhode Island Constitution comfortably accommodates aid to RACs.[27] Besides a broad freedom of religion clause,[28] that Constitution authorizes legislative appropriation of public money for private purposes upon a two-thirds vote of each house.[29] Furthermore, the Rhode Island courts have construed the Rhode Island establishment clause to be no more restrictive than that of the United States Constitution and have been warm to the child benefit theory.[30] The state Constitution does, however, forbid the legislature to "pledge the credit of the state for the payment of the obligations of others."[31]

Rhode Island, in any event, provides no direct financial aid to RACs.

One comprehensive state scholarship program,[32] aiding students at RACs as well as at other colleges,[33] has been repealed effective July 1, 1981.[34] A new law, entitled "Postsecondary Student Financial Assistance,"[35] has replaced it. Aimed at helping needy students,[36] it provides funds, under a general appropriation,[37] to needy state residents enrolled or intending to enroll in a certificate or degree program at an eligible postsecondary institution.[38] To be eligible, the institution must be accredited by an agency recognized by the United States office of education or have obtained the "explicit endorsement" of the Rhode Island Higher Education Assistance Authority.[39] Students at RACs are clearly eligible, therefore, a conclusion buttressed by the fact that the aid is intended to promote "access" and to support "choice."[40] The assistance is in the form of need-based grants,[41] need-based scholarships for students of superior ability,[42] and need-based work opportunities through the provision of funds to

agencies participating in the federal work study program.[43]

The Rhode Island Higher Education Assistance Authority is authorized, *inter alia*, to guarantee student loans[44] and to accept gifts, grants, loans and the like from federal or state agencies or from other sources[45] and to establish standards for student assistance assigned by law to the authority.[46]

Presumably to avoid constitutional problems such as the pledging of state credit,[47] the authority has a "distinct legal existence" and its guarantees are specifically declared not to be obligations of the state.[48]

The Rhode Island Health and Educational Building Corporation[49] was designed to help the financing of educational "facilities" of the type *not* "customarily deemed to result in a current operating charge."[50] Facilities financed by the Corporation could include housing facilities, dining halls, student unions, administrative or academic buildings, athletic facilities, or even parking facilities.[51] The Corporation may issue bonds,[52] make loans to participating institutions to finance or to refund existing obligations related to the type of facilities coming within the legislation,[53] acquire property,[54] and accept gifts, grants or loans from federal or state agencies or from other sources.[55] Again presumably to avoid state constitutional problems, the state is not liable for any of the Corporation's bonds, pledges or other obligations.[56]

RACs are clearly eligible to participate in this program since an "institution for higher education," for purposes of the legislation, means an educational institution which, by law or charter, is a "public or other nonprofit educational institution empowered to provide a program of education beyond the high school level."[57] It must also be accredited by a nationally recognized association and either award a bachelor's or advanced degree or provide at least a two-year program which is accepted for full credit toward a bachelor's degree.[58] There is no specific restriction with regard to sectarian purposes, but "the secular, public purpose of this program seems clear: to give students 'the fullest opportunity to learn and to develop their intellectual and mental capacities.' "[59]

In related legislation, the "Gifts of Educational Facilities" act,[60] the state or any municipality is authorized to accept gifts of educational facilities from certain nonbusiness corporations (including the Health and Educational Building Corporation),[61] to sell any of its facilities at public or private sale[62] or to lease them to "any educational institution" (i.e., including RACs) as long as the lease requires the lessee to pay all operating costs.[63]

C. Personnel

Rhode Island's fair employment practices act[64] declares that all individuals "regardless of race or color, religion, sex, physical handicap, or country of ancestral origin,"[65] and regardless of age,[66] have a right to equal employment opportunities. The Act declares it to be an unlawful practice for an "employer"[67] to hire, discharge, or otherwise discriminate on these bases.[68]

There is an exemption, however: "Nothing herein shall be construed to apply to a religious corporation, association, educational institution, or society with respect to the employment of individuals of its religion to perform work connected with the carrying on of its activities."[69] Several points should be made with regard to this exemption. First, it applies to all RACs coming within the phrase "religious . . . educational institutions." This phraseology is extremely broad, compared with that of counterpart statutes in other states, and would include virtually all RACs. Second, and more narrowly, the exemption authorizes religious preference only in favor of persons of the same religion as the institution. It would not authorize, therefore, the hiring of a Christian by a Jewish institution to teach a New Testament course (although a separate provision might).[70] Third, the exemption applies to "persons performing work connected with the carrying on of its activities." It is not required that the work be related to its *religious* activities. A narrow reading might exclude jobs incidental to the institution's activities, such as those in maintenance, but would still include those related to the religious and educational objectives, e.g., teachers, counselors, and the like.

In sum, therefore, the exemption is quite far-reaching. It enables virtually all RACs to exercise religious preference in favor of persons of its religious persuasion for at least all employee positions significantly related to their religious or educational mission.

The legislature has created a bona fide occupational qualification (BFOQ) by reference to it in the provision dealing with application forms, advertisements and the like.[71] Although the same language is not contained in the provision dealing with the actual hiring, clearly the legislature did not intend to allow a BFOQ to justify advertising suggesting selectivity that could not be exercised in the actual hiring decision. Indeed, to so advertise is in fact to exercise selectivity in the hiring. Any BFOQ must be certified by the Rhode Island commission for human rights, which enforces the fair employment practices act.[72]

In any event, this BFOQ would probably not greatly protect RACs in personnel decisions involving positions beyond those of theology and philosophy faculty and perhaps of counselors. It is not likely that an RAC would be successful in arguing a right to exercise, under the BFOQ exemption, religious preference in the employment of faculty generally (let alone other staff) despite the RAC's genuine interest in establishing on campus a pervasive presence of people of a certain religious persuasion. As we have seen, however, Rhode Island grants a separate and fairly broad exemption for religious preference in favor of persons of the institution's own religious persuasion,[73] so the BFOQ is of limited importance, useful, perhaps, for the hiring of a person of a *different* religious persuasion to teach courses related to that religion.

Under the fair employment practices act, a "physical handicap" is:

any physical disability, infirmity, malformation, or disfigurement which is caused by bodily injury, birth defect or illness, including epilepsy, and which shall include, but not be limited to, any degree of paralysis, amputation, lack of physical condition, blindness or visual impediment, deafness or hearing impediment, muteness or speech impediment or physical reliance on a seeing eye dog, wheelchair, or other remedial appliance or device.[74]

There is little indication that either people addicted to the use of alcohol or drugs or those actually using alcohol or drugs are included within the definition, although, at least for some purposes, Rhode Island has suggested that both alcoholism[75] and drug addiction[76] are illnesses. Conceivably, therefore, a physical disability caused by such an illness could come within the definition. In any event, with regard to users, at least, a BFOQ would apply.[77]

Rhode Island's minimum wage act[78] sets a minimum hourly rate ($3.35 per hour as of July 1, 1982),[79] a minimum daily hours requirement[80] and overtime pay rates.[81] (The overtime provision does not apply to employees in good faith executive, administrative, professional or salaried, at a rate of not less than $200.00 per week, capacity.)[82]

An "employee" under the act, does *not* include individuals engaged in the activities of an educational, charitable, religious or nonprofit organization if the "employer-employee relationship does not, in fact, exist," or where the services are rendered to the organization on a voluntary basis.[83]

Rhode Island's Workers' Compensation Act[84] includes as an employer subject to its provisions any person or corporation with four or more employees.[85] Excluded from coverage is any employee whose employment is of a casual nature and "who is employed otherwise than for the purpose of the employer's trade or business."[86] There is no exemption generally available to RACs.

RACs may elect to include exempted employees within the coverage of this Act by filing a statement with the state's Director of Labor.[87] RACs may also choose to enter into an agreement with their employees providing for an alternative compensation scheme that has been approved by the Worker's Compensation Division of the Department of Labor as long as the coverage provides equal or greater benefits than the Act.[88] RACs will be issued a certificate of compliance[89] by the Director of Labor when they have either purchased an insurance policy or furnished the director with adequate security and satisfactory proof of financial ability directly to compensate injured employees.[90]

Rhode Island's Employment Security Act[91] defines "employer" to include virtually all RACs[92] and "employment" to include service performed on or after January 1, 1972, in the employ of virtually all RACs.[93]

Excluded nonetheless from "employment" under the Act are (1) service for a church or convention or association of churches;[94] (2) service for an organization operated primarily for religious purposes and "operated, supervised, controlled, or principally supported by a church or convention or association of churches";[95] and (3) service by a "duly ordained, commissioned or licensed minister of a church" exercising his ministry or by a member of a religious order as duty required by the order.[96] None of these exceptions is very broad insofar as employment at the typical RAC is concerned and, consequently, few positions at RACs will come within any of them. This is true because (1) very few people employed by RACs can claim to be working for a church, convention or association of churches; (2) except perhaps for institutions like seminaries and Bible colleges, few RACs can claim to be both operated for religious purposes and run or principally supported by a church or group of churches; and (3) few employees on RAC campuses, save perhaps some counselors or theology teachers, will be regular ministers of a church exercising their ministry or members of a religious order peforming duties required by that order.

Also excluded from "employment" within that act are (1) service with regard to which unemployment compensation is payable under a Congressionally-established system;[97] (2) service performed by a regular student for his school, college or university;[98] and (3) service performed by a student under the age of twenty-two enrolled at a regular nonprofit or public institution of higher education in a full-time program, taken for credit at that institution, which combines academic instruction with work experience.[99] The service must be an integral part of the program, so certified to the employer, and not performed in a "program established for or on behalf of an employer or group of employers."[100]

Employing units for which services are performed that are not "employment" under the law may, upon the approval of an appropriate filing, elect that such services be deemed employment for purposes of the act.[101]

With regard to employment covered by the act, a nonprofit organization may make the usual contributions[102] or may elect to make reimbursement payments into the employment security fund of an amount equal to the regular benefits plus one half the extended benefits paid in connection with service for that corporation.[103]

A clarifying provision states that even for otherwise covered employees, benefits are not paid to instructors, researchers or principal administrators of any educational institution for any week of unemployment beginning during the period between two successive academic years, or during a similar period between two regular but not successive terms (or during a period of paid sabbatical leave provided for in the individual's contract) if the individual performs such services in the first of such academic years or terms and if there is a contract or a reasonable assurance that the individual will perform services in any such capacity for any educational institution in the second of such academic years or terms.[104]

Rhode Island has a comprehensive labor relations act[105] and, subject to specified exceptions,[106] RACs are employers within the act.[107]

D. Students

Rhode Island has no legislation directly regulating admissions to private institutions of higher education.

E. Facilities

It is a prohibited discriminatory practice to deny directly or indirectly to any person any of the accommodations, advantages, facilities, or privileges of a public accommodation on the grounds of race, color, religion, country of ancestral origin, physical handicap, age,[108] or sex[109] or to suggest such a denial in advertising or the like.[110] Although the provisions of the law are to be liberally construed,[111] the definition of "public accommodation," which is in terms of restaurants, stores, theaters, and the like,[112] is clearly not intended to affect student admissions to private institutions. Nonetheless, facilities like restaurants, stores, and theaters open to the general public are within the definition even if situated on an RAC campus. Finally, the law does specify its inapplicability to any place of accommodation that is in "its nature distinctly private."[113]

Rhode Island's fair housing practices act[114] prohibits the refusal, directly or indirectly, to sell, rent, or lease any housing accommodation to any individual on the basis of race, color, religion, sex, marital status, country of ancestral origin, physical handicap,[115] or age.[116] Since campus housing is not excepted, and since most RACs restrict housing to their own students, it could be argued that the law regulates the admission of at least those students who reside on campus since restricting admission to whites, for example, in effect limits campus housing to whites. For virtually all RACs, however, the only significant preference likely to be exercised in admissions is with regard to religion (or, in the case of single-sex schools, sex) and, if the preference is in good faith—i.e., not merely to avoid the housing law—it is likely that the practice will be allowed.

Single-sex dorms would also technically be banned by the legislation. It is highly unlikely, however, that the legislation will be used to limit single-sex housing on campus.

These conclusions, with regard to both the admissions and the single-sex housing questions, are buttressed by the "Finding and declaration of policy" section,[117] which reflects no intent to regulate admissions or to ban single-sex housing on campus. It must be added, however, that the legislature has mandated a liberal interpretation of these provisions for the accomplishment of the intended purposes.[118]

The Rhode Island Commission on Human Rights[119] enforces both the public accommodations law[120] and the fair housing legislation.[121]

Since the Division of Occupational Safety act[122] includes within the definition of "employer" any person or corporation with one or more employees,[123] RACs (and their employees)[124] are clearly covered by this occupational safety and health legislation and any codes, regulations and the like authorized under it.[125]

F. State Taxation

Under Rhode Island's Business Corporation Tax,[126] the definition of "corporation" specifically excludes "schools, colleges and other institutions of learning not organized for business purposes and not doing business for profit and no part of the earnings of which inures to the benefit of any private stockholder or individual."[127] Virtually all RACs would be exempt from this tax, therefore.

Since the Rhode Island Franchise Tax[128] is based on the corporation's "authorized capital stock,"[129] and since, in any event, nonprofit corporations for educational purposes are included among the exemptions,[130] this tax is of no significance to virtually all RACs.[131]

In computing the value of the net estate for purposes of the Rhode Island estate and transfer tax,[132] there is deducted from the estate and exempted from the tax thereon all property or interests transferred to any corporation, association or institution in the state exempt from state taxation by charter or law.[133] This would include virtually all RACs. An identical exemption[134] is provided under the Gift Tax act.[135]

Rhode Island also imposes an additional estate tax designed merely to channel to Rhode Island, by virtue of the credit allowed against the federal estate tax for state death taxes, moneys that would otherwise go to the federal government in estate taxes.[136] This tax, therefore, has no ultimate effect on the amount of death taxes paid.

Rhode Island has no inheritance tax.

The Rhode Island personal income tax[137] is geared to the federal income tax which the person should have paid.[138] Since contributions to nonprofit religious or educational institutions are deductible for federal income tax purposes,[139] there is in effect provided a similar deduction under state income tax law to those whose federal tax liability is reached through the itemization of deductions.

The Rhode Island Business Corporation Tax legislation[140] is also geared to the federal income tax law. "Net income" means gross income as defined in the federal corporation tax law with certain modifications, one of which is a deduction for "all items deductible under the federal corporation income tax law."[141] Since contributions to RACs by corporations are deductible, for federal corporate income tax purposes, up to a limit of five percent of the corporation's taxable income (appropriately modified),[142] a parallel deduction is in effect provided under the Rhode Island law.

Rhode Island's "Property Subject to Taxation" chapter[143] provides that the following property

is exempt from taxation: (1) buildings for religious worship and "the land upon which they stand and immediately surrounding the same" (the land may not exceed five acres, and must be occupied and used for religious or educational purposes);[144] (2) certain real property owned by or held in trust for a religious organization and actually used by its officiating clergyman;[145] (3) intangible personal property owned by or held in trust for any religious or charitable organization, if the principal or income is used for religious or charitable purposes;[146] (4) buildings and personal estate owned by any corporation and used for a school, academy or seminary of learning and, to the extent of one acre, the land upon which the buildings stand and immediately surrounding them;[147] and (5) property specially exempt by charter.[148]

Exempt from the Rhode Island sales and use taxes[149] are, *inter alia*, the gross receipts from the sale, storage, use or other consumption in Rhode Island of (1) publications regularly issued at average intervals not exceeding three months;[150] (2) school meals served by colleges, universities and student organizations to the students or teachers of a school, college, or university;[151] and (3) certain food products for human consumption.[152] Also exempt are gross receipts from the rental charged to any students or teachers by an educational institution for living quarters or other accommodations required by attendance at an educational institution[153] (for purposes of this exemption an "educational institution" would include virtually all nonprofit RACs).[154] Finally, no sales or use tax is payable on the sale of tangible personal property to, and on its in-state storage, use, and other consumption by, nonprofit educational or religious institutions.[155]

G. Fund Raising

Rhode Island has comprehensive legislation dealing with charitable solicitations.[156] The law, *inter alia*, requires any "charitable organization" to file annual registration statements,[157] limits the amount a charitable organization may pay for solicitation or fund raising activities,[158] restricts the purposes for which a charitable organization may solicit funds or spend funds solicited,[159] and requires a charitable organization to maintain for three years and produce upon appropriate demand the records required by the rules and regulations of the department of business regulations.[160]

Exempt from the annual registration statement requirements (but not the rest of the law) is any educational institution whose curriculum is totally or partly registered or approved by the Board of Regents for Education.[161] This approval may be achieved through acceptance of accreditation by an accrediting body recognized by the Board.[162] Also exempt are religious organizations, societies and institutions operated, supervised, or controlled by a religious organization or society which solicit outside their own membership[163] and any organization which solicits only from its membership.[164]

Although Rhode Island comprehensively prohibits gambling and lotteries,[165] a substantial exemption is provided for, *inter alia*, religious, charitable, fraternal, or educational organizations to conduct "bingo," "beano," or similar games of chance.[166] To qualify for the exemption, the game must be promoted and conducted by members of the organization, without compensation.[167] All proceeds from admission and participation must be applied solely to the purposes of the organization except for expenses in connection with rent, heat, light, equipment, and "other reasonable expenses," which cannot exceed twenty-five percent of the gross receipts from the game.[168] A local license is required, no more than $3,000 may be awarded in any one night, only one such event may be carried on in any one calendar week, and timely reports must be filed with the licensing authority and with the Division of Taxation.[169]

A similar exemption is provided with regard to *other* games of chance.[170] The chief differences are that the game must be authorized by the Rhode Island state police, and a license must be secured, upon timely application, from the local police department, which forwards a copy of the license to the state police.[171] The reporting requirements are also different.[172]

H. Miscellaneous

The Rhode Island legislature has authorized the state Higher Education Assistance Authority to participate in the New England Higher Education Compact.[173] Rhode Island has also entered into the Compact for Education.[174]

48. South Carolina

A. Corporate Status

Nonprofit corporations having no capital stock may be organized for any lawful purpose, including religious and educational.[1] The South Carolina Constitution prohibits the General Assembly from passing any special or local law to incorporate, or to amend or extend the charter of, any educational or religious institution.[2]

Chapter 31 of Title 33 (Corporations, Partnerships and Associations) regulates nonprofit corporations[3] and contains several provisions that may be specifically applicable to RACs.

The written declaration of the proposal for organization of religious or eleemosynary institutions is exempt from the requirement of approval by the clerk of court, sheriff, probate judge, county treasurer, and county auditor of the county in which the institution proposes to have its principal place of business, and from endorsement by the freehold electors, if located within or without an incorporated town or city.[4]

Furthermore, churches, religious organizations, religious societies, and religious institutions are exempt from payment of the incorporation fee.[5]

Lastly, all charitable, social, and religious corporations created by legislative authority prior to 1900 are granted all the basic powers of corporations chartered under this chapter.[6]

While RACs clearly may be incorporated under this chapter, the phrasing used in these three sections raises some doubt as to whether they apply to all RACs. Perhaps they would apply only to seminary-type RACs or to Bible colleges.

The South Carolina Uniform Securities Act stipulates that any security issued by any person organized and operated not for private profit, but exclusively for religious or educational purposes, need not be registered and the approval of the Securities Commissioner of any advertisement, sales literature, or advertising communication addressed or intended for distribution to prospective investors is not required.[7]

The statute regulating charitable trusts specifically does *not* apply to trusts or trustees of churches, colleges or universities, and therefore has no relevance to RACs.[8]

There is an additional provision in the South Carolina Code regarding the incorporation or consolidation of corporations for religious purposes.[9] However, the tenor of the statute indicates that it is applicable only to strictly religious organizations and churches, and not to educational institutions.

The State Commission on Higher Education is the sole authority for licensing nonpublic educational institutions, within or without the State, to confer degrees in South Carolina.[10] The Commission prescribes and enforces all rules, regulations and minimum standards for licensing.[11] Most RACs are clearly included in the general definition of nonpublic educational institutions.[12] Only Bible institutions and theological schools are exempt.[13]

Any South Carolina institution of higher education offering a program of study in education must be approved by the State Board of Education, if the program is to be used for initial teacher certification or for improvement of teaching credentials.[14]

Private colleges and universities which award an associate, baccalaureate, or higher degree are exempt from the regulations pertaining to proprietary schools.[15]

South Carolina has not adopted the Model Nonprofit Corporation Act. In the chapter of the South Carolina Code relating to nonprofit corporations[16] there is no express provision governing the merger and consolidation of these kinds of institutions. The Code does provide for the voluntary dissolution of a nonprofit college.[17] In addition, the South Carolina courts will apply the doctrine of *cy pres* when necessary.[18]

By a vote of two-thirds of the members of the governing board, a college may initiate the process of dissolution by notifying the Secretary of State of this decision.[19] There is no express provision in South Carolina law requiring the Secretary of State or a state court to approve the dissolution process.

There is no statutory provision concerning the distribution of the assets of a nonprofit corporation in South Carolina. Unless otherwise bound by its charter or bylaws, a college seeking to dissolve might devise a plan of distribution of assets free from any governmental supervision or control. As noted above, however, South Carolina courts recognize the doctrine of *cy pres*. A dissolving South Carolina college, therefore, should make a genuine attempt to preserve the general charitable purpose of property it has been given in trust.

B. State Support

Direct state aid to religious or other private educational institutions is specifically prohibited by the South Carolina Constitution.[20] Prior to revision in 1973, the former section[21] prohibited both direct *and* indirect aid to any organization, of whatever kind, wholly or in part under the direction or control of any church or religious or sectarian denomination, society or organization.[22] Because of this section, the Supreme Court of South Carolina, in *Hartness v. Patterson*,[23] forbade the appropriation of

funds under the "Higher Education Tuition Grant Act"[24] to students attending RACs.[25] (Under the Act, tuition grants are made to qualified students registered at a South Carolina independent institution of higher learning.)[26] The Court voided grants to RACs, even though the Act itself specifically prohibits the student from using the grant to pursue a degree in theology, divinity, or religious education.[27]

Soon after the *Hartness* decision, the "State Education Assistance Act"[28] came under the same kind of attack. This Act empowers the State Education Assistance Authority to make, insure, and guarantee loans to South Carolina students attending eligible institutions of higher learning.[29] Such institutions need not be in South Carolina[30] and under *Durham v. McLeod*[31] also include RACs. Perhaps anticipating the change that later took place in Article XI, the South Carolina Supreme Court ruled that this Act involved no public money or credit, within the meaning of the Constitutional prohibition. The Court went on to say that even if the Act involved public funds, it would not have violated the Constitution.[32] The Court also determined that the Act passed the "*Lemon* test"[33] and therefore did not violate the Establishment Clause of the South Carolina Constitution or that of the Constitution of the United States.[34] The opinion emphasized that this Act (unlike the Tuition Grant Act) provided *loans* to students, regardless of the type of institution they attended, secular or sectarian, private or public. As such, the court reasoned, the Act had a valid purpose.[35]

Possibly in reaction to these two cases, Article XI was revised and the prohibition against indirect aid was excised. Thus the present prohibition is solely against direct aid and students attending RACs are apparently eligible for grants under the Higher Education Tuition Grant Act, as long as they abide by the limitations regarding religious courses of study.

The State Education Assistance Act, of course, remains constitutional under the revision of Article XI. The Act, however, is vague in some respects. There is no indication as to what criteria an institution must meet to become "eligible," nor whether a seminary or like institution would fall into that category. It is also interesting to note that the Court in *Durham* recognized that the Act places no restrictions on the student's course of study. It seems, therefore, that a student-borrower may be able to use the funds to pursue a degree in divinity, theology, or religious education. If indeed the funds are nonpublic, there would seem to be no reason for which that could not be done.

South Carolina's "Educational Facilities Authority Act for Private Nonprofit Institutions of Higher Learning"[36] was also the target of a constitutional attack. The purpose of the Act is to assist institutions in the construction, financing, and refinancing of projects.[37] Although RACs are not specifically mentioned, they do fit into the broad definition of an "institution of higher learning."[38] The term "project," however, does not include any facility used or to be used for sectarian instruction, religious worship, or primarily in connection with any part of a school or department of divinity.[39]

In *Hunt v. McNair*,[40] the Supreme Court of the United States upheld the validity of the statute as applied to an RAC. Using the "*Lemon* test,"[41] the Court determined that the statute was not violative of the Establishment Clause. In determining the second point of the "*Lemon* test," the principal or primary effect criterion, the court focused on the fact that the college in question (the Baptist College at Charleston) was *not* significantly oriented toward a sectarian education.[42] The opinion raises the possibility that a "more" sectarian college would be denied aid under the Act. The degree of sectarianism acceptable is not clear from the opinion, but the Court cites religious qualifications for admission, faculty religious affiliation, and the ratio of students adhering to the college's religion to the residents of the same faith in the surrounding area as relevant factors.[43]

With three exceptions South Carolina State Scholarships are limited to students attending state-supported institutions.[44] One is the South Carolina Defense Scholarship, which applies to students and institutions (public and nonprofit private) otherwise qualifying under the "Health Professions Educational Assistance Act of 1963 (P.L. 88-129) and the Nurse Training Act of 1964 (P.L. 88[581])."[45] The second exception is for scholarships given by the State Department of Health and Environmental Control to students enrolled in *any* accredited and departmentally approved medical or dental school in

the United States.[46] The last exception is the South Carolina National Guard Tuition Assistance Act, which makes grants to students attending any institution of higher learning, post secondary business school or technical education school located in South Carolina.[47]

C. Personnel

Fair Employment Practices

The South Carolina Human Affairs Law[48] prohibits discrimination in employment on the basis of race, color, religion, sex, age, or national origin. RACs are exempt in part from this law since it does not apply to:

a religious corporation, association, educational institution or society with respect to the employment of individuals of a particular religion to perform work connected with the carrying on by such corporation, association, educational institution, or society of its activities. It shall not be an unlawful employment practice for a school, college, university, or other educational institution or institution of learning to hire and employ employees of a particular religion if such school, college, university, or other educational institution or institution of learning is, in whole or in substantial part, owned, supported, controlled, or managed by a particular religion or by a particular religious corporation, association, or society, or if the curriculum of such school, college, university, or other educational institution or institution of learning is directed toward the propagation of a particular religion.[49]

This provision is somewhat vague. Perhaps a correct reading of the section is that it comprises two separate exemptions. The first sentence of the provision exempts from the act religious organizations, including educational institutions, in the hiring of employees performing work connected with the carrying on of the organizations' activities. A problem arises because there is no legislative or judicial guidance as to the proper definition of "activities." If construed narrowly, the only true activity of an RAC is education and that part of the provision would apply only to the hiring of educators, and not across the board to all employees. However, the term "activities" could also be construed broadly, and since there is a tremendous number of positions, not only educative, necessary for a school to carry out its activities, the exemption could apply to the hiring of *all* employees. It is also interesting to note that these activities need not be religious.

The next sentence narrows the focus of the provision to only religious *educational* institutions. But this exemption appears to be much broader than that in the first part, since it seems to apply to all employees, regardless of their function. Since this part of the provision is so broad in that regard, it would seem that an RAC would not be concerned with the first part and need only rely on this exemption, if its religious affiliation meets the stated requirements.

There is some vagueness in these requirements as well. The extent to which the institution must be "controlled" by a religion or by a religious organization is not clear. There again is no specific statutory or judicial guidance as to *factually* how much control is sufficient. While the phrasing is probably broad enough to include most RACs, some institutions may not have a sufficient connection to be covered by the provision. This is especially problematic since the South Carolina legislature did not include the words "or in connection with" between the phrase "owned, supported, controlled or managed by . . . " and "a particular religion." This may have been just an oversight or may indicate that the legislature was intending the provision to have a narrower scope than other statutes of its kind.

An RAC will also qualify for this second exemption if its curriculum is directed toward the propagation of religion. This would seem to apply only to Bible colleges, seminaries and the like.

Lastly, there is some uncertainty as to the significance of the repeated use of the phrase "a particular religion." It appears that under the statute an RAC could easily prefer an employee of *any* religion, not merely one of the same religion as the institution.

Workmen's Compensation

The South Carolina Workmen's Compensation Law[50] contains no specific provisions pertaining to RACs, or to any other type of non-profit or charitable organization. However, in *Caughman v. Columbia Y.M.C.A.*,[51] the Supreme Court of South Carolina declared that charitable institutions are excluded from the Act by implication, since it neither specifically includes nor expressly exempts such organizations.[52] The Court refused to extend application of the Act, leaving such a change to the legislature. Even though the Act is entirely voluntary as to nonpublic entities, this is an important decision since all employers and employees are presumed covered by the Act, unless they are specifically exempted or affirmatively opt out.[53]

In South Carolina RACs may be considered charities both under the Solicitation of Charitable Funds Act[54] and under the case law regarding the doctrine of charitable immunity.[55] Therefore, RACs would seem to be exempt from the South Carolina Workmen's Compensation Law.

Unemployment Compensation

RACs come under the South Carolina Employment Security Law[56] since their employees' service is excluded from employment as defined in the Federal Unemployment Tax Act.[57]

Article 5 of the Employment Security Law[58] provides for the financing of benefits paid to the employees of nonprofit organizations. Such organizations are those described by 26 U.S.C. 501(c)(3), and therefore include most RACs.[59] Under this article, an RAC may elect to make payments in lieu of the contributions required under the Act.[60] "Contributions" are based on a percentage of wages paid and are made by the employer to the state unemployment compensation fund.[61] "Payments," on the other hand, are paid to the Employment Security Commission for the unemployment fund, and are equal to the amount of regular benefits and one-half the extended benefits actually paid in connection with service for that particular employer.[62]

D. Students

The South Carolina Code does not regulate the admissions policies of RACs. The prohibition against discrimination in admissions on account of race, creed, color, or national origin applies only to public schools.[63] However, that section goes on to affirm that a religious or denominational educational institution may exclusively or primarily select its pupils from members of the religion or denomination of the institution. The tenor of the section and of the surrounding chapter seems to indicate that the legislature intended that this provision apply only to primary and secondary religious schools. However, the usage of the generalized term "educational institution," with no statutory guidance as to its meaning, makes it possible to include RACs within the provision.

E. Facilities

The South Carolina Board for Barrier-Free Design establishes, publishes, and enforces the minimum standards and specifications necessary to make governmental buildings, public buildings, and their facilities accessible to and usable by the aged, disabled, or physically handicapped.[64] "Public Buildings" include all buildings and structures used by the public, or in which the physically handicapped *may* be employed, that are constructed, purchased, leased, or rented by the use of private funds.[65] No such building may be constructed or renovated unless it will meet prescribed standards and regulations.[66]

While not specifically mentioning religious or educational institutions the definition of public building is certainly broad enough to include buildings owned or used by RACs. It is not clear, however, that all buildings on a campus would be covered. Surely those to which the general public is invited (e.g., a public cafeteria or bookstore) would be within the law. But those buildings open only to students may not be "used by the public," except in the sense that the public may be invited to seek enrollment as students.

In any event, if the building is one in which a handicapped person "may" be employed, it also would be covered. The statute is unclear as to whether this provision is triggered by a handicapped person actually being employed or by his potential employment. If the former, the statute would tend to discourage hiring the handicapped; if the latter, why not merely say "in which *anyone* will be employed"?

There is no public accommodations statute in South Carolina.

South Carolina's safety statute requires every employer to provide a place of employment "free from recognized hazards that are causing or are likely to cause death or serious physical harm" to the employees.[67] The law also gives the Commissioner of Labor broad powers to promulgate regulations which have legal effect "for purposes of attaining the highest degree of health and safety protection for any and all employees within the State of South Carolina, whether employed in the public or private sector."[68] RACs are "employers" under the safety law.[69]

F. State Taxation

RACs are exempt from the South Carolina "Income Tax Act of 1926" as corporations "organized for religious, charitable, scientific or educational purposes," as long as the profits are not applied to private use.[70]

Under the South Carolina Income Tax Rules, ordained ministers who teach or have administrative or management positions at RACs may, for tax purposes, exclude from their gross income the rental value of homes furnished, or the rental allowance paid, to them.[71]

South Carolina has no inheritance tax but does impose an estate tax[72] designed merely to channel to South Carolina, by virtue of the credit allowed against the federal estate tax for state death taxes, moneys that would otherwise go to the federal government in estate taxes.[73] This tax has no ultimate effect on the *amount* of death taxes paid and therefore neither encourages nor discourages private benefaction to RACs.

By incorporating the federal definition of "taxable gift" into the South Carolina gift tax scheme, the law makes transfers by gift to RACs exempt from the state gift tax.[74]

Contributions or gifts made by individuals to or for the use of an RAC may be deducted from that individual's South Carolina state income, up to twenty percent of the individual's adjusted gross income.[75]

The parallel deduction for corporations is limited to five percent of its net income.[76]

The South Carolina Constitution provides

that all property of all schools, colleges, and other institutions of learning, whose profits are not applied to private use, is exempt from *ad valorem* taxation.[77] This provision is implemented in the South Carolina Code and is broad enough to cover RACs.[78]

The gross proceeds of the sales of religious publications "are exempted from the provisions of the Sales and Use Tax Law and from the computation of the amount of tax levied, assessed, or payable thereunder."[79] "Religious publications" are those that contain "substantial" reference to belief in the existence of superior beings.[80] The exemption applies, therefore, only to specified publications and has limited applicability to RACs.

Non-profit corporations or organizations organized exclusively for religious or educational purposes are, in certain circumstances, exempt from the state license tax on paid admissions.[81] Admissions to all athletic events of postsecondary institutions of education are not included in this exemption, and neither are admission charges for the use of, or entrance to, rides at carnivals, circuses, and community fairs run by such organizations (excluding a general gate admissions charge).[82] In addition there is no admissions tax on charges made to members of nonprofit organizations for the use of the organizations' facilities.[83] Lastly, no admissions tax is charged for events run by a nonprofit corporation or organization, organized exclusively for, *inter alia*, religious or educational purposes, whose net proceeds are immediately donated to an exclusively charitable organization.[84] This exemption does not include events from which the organization receives a percentage of the gross profits or a stated fixed sum.[85]

G. Fund Raising

The South Carolina Solicitation of Charitable Funds Act regulates the solicitation of funds from the public by charitable organizations, including educational institutions.[86] This provision applies to virtually all RACs. Exempted from the provisions of the Act, however, are:

[d]uly constituted religious organizations or any group affiliated with and forming an integral part of such organization no part of the net income of which

inures to the direct benefit of any individual and which have received a declaration of current tax exempt status from the government of the United States.[87]

This category of organization has a very narrow focus, apparently intended only for church groups and other strictly religious organizations. The only RACs perhaps falling within the exemption would be seminaries, Bible colleges, and the like.

This Act also provides that an educational institution whose curriculum is in whole or in part registered or approved by the State Department of Education, either directly or by acceptance of accreditation by a recognized accrediting body, is not required to file a registration statement with the Secretary of State.[88] Such institutions, which would include most RACs, remain bound by the other provisions of the Act.

The game of bingo, when it is conducted by charitable, religious, or fraternal organizations that are exempt from federal income taxation, is exempt from the South Carolina Constitutional prohibition against lotteries.[89] While the phrasing of this section is vague, some RACs — perhaps seminaries and Bible colleges — may be included as exempted organizations.

There is also an exemption from the Code provisions regulating billiard tables and rooms for "religious orders" when no fee is charged for the use of the tables.[90]

H. Miscellaneous

Privately owned educational institutions that maintain infirmaries for the exclusive use of their students are exempt from the State Hospital Construction and Franchising Act.[91]

Every institution of higher learning in South Carolina must submit a report on the first semester accomplishments of each freshman to the state high school from which each freshman was graduated.[92]

All institutions of higher learning in the State are authorized to procure liability insurance to protect employees who may be liable to third persons as a result of negligence in the performance of their regularly assigned duties.[93] Any actions brought for damages covered by the insurance are to be brought directly against the employees insured by the policy.[94] This provision is consistent with the fact that educational institutions themselves are immune from suit under the doctrine of charitable immunity.[95] Since this section applies to all institutions of higher learning, it clearly covers RACs.

Any nonprofit educational institution not substantially involved in propaganda or "otherwise attempting to influence legislation" is not included in the term "company" for the purposes of the State Bank Holding Company Act.[96] Most RACs fit this description and are therefore exempt from the provisions of the Act.

The "Subversive Activities Registration Act" exempts any religious organization, society, or association (and its members):

whose objectives and aims do not contemplate the overthrow of the government of the United States, of this State or of any political subdivision thereof by force or violence or other unlawful means.[97]

Whatever the constitutionality of this Act, it seems that this section is useless since only organizations which advocate the overthrow of the government by force or violence or unlawful means must register.

49. South Dakota

A. Corporate Status

South Dakota's Nonprofit Corporation Act,[1] which is closely patterned after the Model Nonprofit Corporation Act, authorizes the incorporation of RACs.[2] Such corporations must have incorporators,[3] articles of incorporation,[4] a certificate of incorporation,[5] a board of directors,[6] an initial meeting for determination of bylaws,[7] a registered office[8] and agent,[9] and specific officers.[10]

Any securities issued by a corporation organized "exclusively for religious [or] educational . . . purposes and not for pecuniary gain" are exempt from South Dakota's securities registration[11] requirements.[12]

The reorganization of nonprofit colleges in South Dakota by way of merger or consolidation[13] and the dissolution[14] of these institutions are also governed by the Nonprofit Corporation Act. There are no reported South Dakota decisions applying the doctrine of *cy pres* in that jurisdiction.

The procedures for voluntary dissolution and involuntary dissolution are closely patterned after the provisions in the Model Act.[15]

Assets of a dissolving college in South Dakota are to be distributed according to a procedure closely patterned after the Model Act.[16] If there are any assets distributable to a person who is unknown or who cannot be found, they must be reduced to cash and deposited with the State Treasury, to be paid to that person or his legal representative upon satisfactory proof of his right to the assets.[17]

B. State Support

South Dakota's Constitution makes it abundantly clear that direct state aid to RACs is prohibited. Although providing for freedom of worship,[18] the Constitution bars any state, county, or municipal appropriation of land, money, or other property to help any sectarian school.[19] Another part of the Constitution specifies that taxes are to be levied and collected "for public purposes only."[20]

Professor Howard notes that there is little problem with state aid to private nonsectarian institutions since the South Dakota Supreme Court "has given the legislature great discretion in determining what is a public purpose."[21] The constitutional bars to aid to RACs, however, are considerably more formidable. Howard observes that in the last authoritative test of aid to sectarian schools,[22] in 1891, the state supreme court construed the Constitution to "prohibit the State from paying the tuition of normal students at a Presbyterian university."[23] Should that analysis prevail, Howard concludes, the state Constitutional provision will more strictly regulate state aid than the First Amendment to the federal Constitution.[24] Indeed, several recent South Dakota programs are at least vulnerable because of the state Constitution's provisions and their 1891 construction.

South Dakota provides a Student Incentive Grants[25] program which provides financial aid to needy "qualified resident students in education beyond high school in South Dakota."[26] The student must be enrolled in an "eligible institution,"[27] which generally includes "all public, and private nonprofit and proprietary institutions" beyond the high school[28] located in South Dakota. Nothing in the legislation indicates any intent to restrict the program to nonsectarian institutions. Indeed, there is no restriction with regard to the religious content of courses of study.

South Dakota also provides a Tuition Equalization Grants[29] program, which authorizes grants of up to $250 to South Dakota residents[30] attending "accredited private institutions,"[31] which means a South Dakota institution of higher learning which is privately operated and appropriately accredited by the North Central Association of Colleges and Secondary Schools.[32] There is, therefore, no legislative bar to participation in the program by RAC students. This is especially made clear in the stipulation that a "qualified student" may not be "enrolled in a course of study leading to a degree in theology or religious education."[33] The necessary implication is that students in other degree programs are eligible even though attending an RAC and even though taking some religious courses.

South Dakota's Health Profession Scholarship Loan[34] program provides loans to South Dakota residents, admitted to accredited institutions of higher education, in certain health-related courses of instruction not offered by South Dakota institutions.[35] Part or all of a loan made under the program may be forgiven in the event the borrower practices in South Dakota or in case of the borrower's death prior to repayment.[36] There is no suggestion that students at RACs are not eligible beneficiaries under the program.

The same is true of the Higher Education Law Guaranty Program,[37] authorizing the Education and Cultural Affairs Planning Commission to enter into "agreements to implement" the federally insured student loan program for higher education[38] provided by the Higher Education Act of 1965.[39]

Given the rigid 1891 construction of the South Dakota constitutional ban on aid to sectarian institutions, these programs, and especially those involving grants rather than loans or loan guarantees, could conceivably be declared unconstitutional insofar as they render assistance, however indirect, to RACs. Pro-

fessor Howard notes, however, that the 1891 case involved tuition money paid directly to the institution under a fairly elaborate contract providing for a State-dictated curriculum.[40] A modern court, especially in light of changed times and outlooks, could seize upon this fact in validating the current legislation.

The legislature seems mindful of both the problem and the possibly redeeming distinction: in the Tuition Equalization Grants Act, two separate provisions[41] specify that payments are to be made "directly to" the student.

C. Personnel

Under South Dakota's Human Rights Act,[42] it is an unfair discriminatory practice for any person to "fail or refuse to hire, to discharge . . . or to accord adverse or unequal treatment to any person" in employment because of race, color, creed, religion, sex, ancestry, or national origin.[43]

A major exemption, however, is provided to any good faith "religious institution" regarding "qualifications for employment based on religion."[44] Religious qualifications, under the exemption, must be "related to a bona fide religious purpose."[45] This broad exemption would apply to many positions at virtually all RACs, including theology teachers, history of religion teachers and perhaps counselors. Nor is the religious qualification limited to the particular affiliation of the RAC. A Christian RAC could prefer a Jew to teach a course dealing with the history of Judaism. Certainly an RAC could justify limiting at least its top administrative positions to members of its religious affiliation.

South Dakota, in its Wages, Hours and Conditions of Employment Act,[46] requires every employer to pay to each employee over the age of eighteen a minimum wage of two dollars and thirty cents an hour.[47]

The Division of Human Rights[48] enforces the employment discrimination provisions of the Human Rights Act.[49]

The South Dakota Worker's Compensation Law[50] applies to any corporation[51] employing one or more employees not expressly excluded from coverage.[52] RACs generally are covered except with regard to those employees who come within the exceptions for employment that is not in the usual course of the employer's business[53] or for employment that is covered by a federal worker's compensation law.[54] An RAC's executive officers also are exempt[55] unless the RAC elects to include them specifically in the insurance contract.[56] However, an executive officer may elect to reject coverage under this Act by giving the corporation written notice when elected or appointed.[57] An employee injured while working for an employer who is not covered by this Act may choose either to sue the employer in court for damages or to proceed against the employer under this Act as if the employer were covered.[58] An RAC must carry insurance[59] or become certified by the Department of Labor as a self-insurer after annually submitting proof of financial ability to compensate directly injured employees.[60]

Services performed for religious, charitable, or educational organizations constitute employment[61] under the South Dakota Employment Security Law,[62] if two conditions are met. First, such service must be exempt from the definition of employment in the Federal Unemployment Tax Act solely due to section 3306(c)(8).[64] Second, the organization must employ at least four individuals "for some portion of a day in each of twenty different weeks, whether or not such weeks were consecutive, within either the current or preceding calendar year."[65] This coverage does not extend to services performed (1) for a church or for an association of churches;[66] (2) for an organization run primarily for religious purposes and controlled by a church or by an association of churches;[67] or (3) by ordained ministers or by members of religious orders in the exercise of their duties.[68]

Separate sections of the Act provide further exclusions from the definition of "employment." One section applies to certain services which are peformed "in any calendar quarter in the employ of an organization exempt from income tax under section 501 of the Federal Internal Revenue Code."[69] These services include those performed (1) for a school or college by regularly enrolled students,[70] or by their spouses;[71] (2) by students under the age of twenty-two at an accredited nonprofit or public educational institution in a full-time program, combining academic instruction and work experience;[72] or

(3) for remuneration which does not exceed $52.00 in any calendar quarter.[73] A final exemption covers services for which unemployment compensation is payable under a system set up by an act of Congress.[74]

Nonprofit organizations, and therefore RACs may elect to make payments in lieu of contributions. The election is effective for a minimum period of two years upon filing written notice[75] with the Department of Labor.[76] Payments are equal to the amount of regular benefits plus the amount of extended benefits paid.[77] The Department may require electing organizations to file an approved surety bond.[78]

South Dakota has an extensive Collective Bargaining Act[79] which covers virtually all employers,[80] including RACs, and virtually all employees.[81]

D. Students

The South Dakota Human Rights Act[82] addresses itself specifically to the treatment of students by educational institutions. The legislation forbids such an institution to "include, expel, limit or otherwise discriminate" against "an individual seeking admission or an individual enrolled" because of race, color, creed, religion, sex, ancestry, or national origin.[83] A significant exemption, parallel to that provided in the employment discrimination area,[84] states that this "section shall not apply to any bona fide religious institution with respect to any qualification based on religion [if] related to a bona fide religious purpose."[85] The term "religious institution" would seem to have been intended to include virtually all RACs.

This provision would justify religious preference in admissions as long as it is not a sham — for example, to avoid racial integration. The provision does not require that the preference be in favor of the RAC's own affiliation. If in good faith, a Baptist RAC could prefer that all its students be Christian or a Christian school might prefer a certain number of Jewish students for participation in an ecumenical course of study.

The Division of Human Rights enforces this educational discrimination provision.[86]

E. Facilities

South Dakota prohibits "any person engaged in the provision of public accommodation" from "failing to provide . . . access" or equal treatment "with respect to the availability of such services and facilities" because of race, color, creed, religion, sex, ancestry, or national origin.[87] Under the law, a public accommodation is one which "offers services, facilities, or goods to the general public for a fee, charge, or gratuitously."[88] This provision would cover all campus facilities, such as bookstores, stadia, and the like, to which the general public is invited.

A related provision prohibits educational institutions from discriminating against "any individual" in the utilization of the benefits from or the services rendered by the institution.[89] This provision, not limited to potential or actual students,[90] could be argued to cover more facilities than the public accommodations section. Unlike the public accommodations section, however, the provision is specifically inapplicable to religious institutions with regard to religious qualifications related to a good faith religious purpose.[91]

It is possible (however unlikely) that the public accommodations section and the educational institution section might come into conflict. For example, an RAC might maintain a bookstore selling religious materials some of which it might not deem suitable for people of its religious persuasion. The public accommodations section would preclude a religious qualification but the educational institutions provision would provide an exemption. it seems likely that courts would construe that exemption to supersede the public accommodations prohibition as well.

It is an unfair or discriminatory housing practice for any person, on the grounds of race, color, creed, religion, sex, ancestry, or national origin, to refuse to sell, rent, lease, or assign any real property, housing accommodation "or interest therein"[92] or to discriminate in the terms or conditions of the sale, rental, or lease.[93]

Since there are no exemptions to these provisions, and since campus housing is presumably

included within the proscriptions, RACs could technically be barred from limiting such housing to students selected on a religious basis. Nonetheless, the exemptions provided for personnel[94] and student admissions decisions[95] on religious bases would surely preclude any argument that an RAC could not limit its housing to its own personnel or students.

Both the public accommodations and fair housing provisions of the Human Rights Act are enforced by the Division of Human Rights.[96]

South Dakota law entitles the handicapped to "reasonably equal accommodations" in all hotels, places of public accommodation, and other places to which the general public is invited.[97] Noncompliance with the law constitutes a misdemeanor.[98]

South Dakota has no OSHA statute, nor, apparently, any provisions governing the general quality of safety in the work place. There are provisions governing some specific safety and health hazards,[99] but there is no general statutory authority to make rules or regulations concerning occupational safety and health.

F. State Taxation

South Dakota has neither a personal income tax nor a general[100] corporate income tax. RACs are therefore not subject to any tax on income.

Under South Dakota's Imposition and Amount of Inheritance Tax legislation,[101] an exemption is allowed for all property transferred to a college, university, seminary of learning, or church within South Dakota, and to the same institutions in any other state which provides a reciprocal provision for transfers to South Dakota institutions.[102]

The South Dakota Estate Tax[103] Act provides no specific exemption or credit for property transferred to RACs.

Since South Dakota has neither a gift tax nor an income tax, contributions or "gifts" to RACs have no special state tax consequences.

The South Dakota Constitution mandates the legislature to exempt from tax property held for school or religious purposes.[104] Pursuant to the mandate, the South Dakota Code exempts from tax "all property" belonging to any charitable, benevolent, or religious society, as long as it is used exclusively for charitable, benevolent, or religious purposes.[105] Also exempt is all real or personal property belonging to any educational institution in the state and all property used exclusively for the support of such an institution.[106] Farm lands or improved town or city property not occupied or directly used in the carrying out of the primary object" of the owning institution is taxable.[107] This exemption is not as broad for profit-making institutions, being limited to property, real or personal, used *exclusively* for instructional or administrative purposes.[108]

South Dakota's Retail Sales and Service Tax[109] legislation exempts, from the tax provided for therein, certain services "enumerated in the Standard Industrial Classification Manual, 1972, as proposed by the statistical policy division of the office of management and budget, office of the President,"[110] including "educational services (major group 82)."[111] Also exempt are the gross receipts from benevolent, fraternal, or charitable activities as long as the entire amount, after the deduction of all direct costs of the activities, is devoted to educational, religious, benevolent, fraternal, or charitable purposes.[112] Receipts are not eligible for the exemption if they result from engaging "for more than five consecutive days in a business or occupation otherwise taxable."[113]

Also exempt from the retail sales and service tax are the gross receipts from sales of tangible personal property and from the sales, furnishing or service of gas, electricity, water, and communications service "to and for use by" religious educational institutions.[114] To qualify for the exemption, the purchases involved must be made by authorized officials and paid for with institution funds.[115] Title to the property must be retained in the name of the institution.[116] Quarterly reports detailing exempted purchases are required.[117] A parallel exemption[118] is provided under the Use Tax[119] legislation.

The income tax provided for under the Banks and Financial Corporations legislation[120] is calculated on the basis of "taxable income as defined in the Internal Revenue Code" in effect on January 1, 1979.[121] Since contributions to

RACs by corporations are deductible, in arriving at taxable income for federal corporate income tax purposes, up to a limit of five percent of the corporation's taxable income (appropriately modified),[122] a parallel deduction is in effect provided under the South Dakota law.

G. Fund Raising

South Dakota's Charitable and Professional Solicitation of Contributions Act,[123] which provides significant regulation of charitable solicitations, does not apply to solicitations for religious purposes,[124] to educational institutions under the general supervision of the Department of Educational and Cultural Affairs, or to such institutions accredited by the North Central Association of Colleges and Secondary Schools or by the Association of Independent Schools and Colleges.[125] The act also does not apply to professional fund raisers[126] employed for the benefit of such religious or educational organizations, except that a registration statement[127] must be filed by organizations employing such fund raisers.[128] Finally, the legislation does not apply to bingo and lottery activities otherwise permitted by law.[129]

Gambling in South Dakota is generally prohibited.[130] Nonetheless, bingo[131] and lotteries[132] are permitted if conducted by, *inter alia*, "a bona fide nationally chartered veterans, religious, charitable, educational, or fraternal organization."[133] Although it is possible to read this provision to require *all* such organizations to be "nationally chartered," the phrase was probably intended to qualify only the word "veterans," since few (if any) religious organizations, for example, are likely to be nationally chartered.

To qualify for this exemption, no proceeds may inure to the benefit of any individual,[134] no separate organization or professional person may be employed to conduct the event,[135] and the value of prizes[136] and the amount of compensation[137] for services rendered must be kept within specified limits. Finally, a written thirty-day notice of such an event must be given to the county or municipal governing body,[138] which may bar all bingo and lotteries by resolution.[139]

H. Miscellaneous

South Dakota is a member of the Midwest
Education Compact.[140]

50. Tennessee

A. Corporate Status

Under the state Constitution, general laws can be enacted by the legislature for the creation and organization of corporations.[1] The General Corporation Act[2] applies to both profit and nonprofit[3] corporations. A corporation may be organized for any "lawful purpose,"[4] its general powers including ownership of property, the making of contracts and the exercise of "all powers necessary or convenient to effect any or all of the purposes for which the corporation is organized."[5] Provisions dealing with nonprofit corporations cover membership, board actions, the prohibition of shares and dividends,[6] and, with reference to the Internal Revenue Code,[7] limitations on what private foundations may do.[8]

RACs operated "exclusively for religious [or] educational . . . purposes and not for pecuniary profit" are exempt from securities registration requirements.[9]

The Postsecondary Education Authorization Act,[10] which provides standards and regulations for institutions of higher education in Tennessee, applies to degree-granting RACs and state colleges not accredited by specified agencies.[11] Since church related schools are free from state regulation of teachers, books, and curriculum,[12] it is not clear just how much power the Tennessee Higher Education Commission, which administers the act with regard to academic degree-granting institutions,[13] has over RAC internal affairs. The idea, presumably, is to provide, for unaccredited schools, a control parallel to accreditation. Under the law, in any event, "each [non-exempt] postsecondary educational institution desiring to operate [and offer academic degrees] in this state shall make application to the [Tennessee Higher Education] commission."[14]

The provisions for management of institutional funds[15] apply to incorporated or unincorporated organizations operated exclusively for educational, religious or other eleemosynary purposes. The funds involved are those held by an institution for its exclusive use, benefit, or purposes and do not include funds held by a trustee or in which others have an interest,[16] which the governing boards of such institutions may expend, invest, or pool at their discretion.[17]

Although there are Tennessee provisions relating specifically to nonprofit corporations,[18] nothing in these provisions concerns the merger, consolidation, or dissolution of a nonprofit corporation, which are governed by the relevant provisions found in the General Corporation Act.[19] Although the doctrine of cy pres has not formally been adopted by the state courts in Tennessee, these courts have the power to interpret the substance of the donor's intent broadly rather than to adhere strictly to the form of the grant.[20]

The statute governing voluntary dissolution is written with the structure of a for-profit corporation in mind. It might intelligently be construed to mean that a majority of the governing board of a nonprofit college may initiate the process of dissolution by filing a statement of intent to dissolve with the Secretary of State.[21]

Thereafter the college must cease to do business except to wind up its affairs; the corporate existence of the college continues until the Secretary of State has issued a certificate of dissolution or until a court of competent jurisdiction has entered an order of dissolution.[22] The Tennessee Code likewise provides for involuntary dissolution of a nonprofit college.[23] In the event of a suit for involuntary dissolution, the district attorney general is to be made a party defendant.[24]

The assets of a nonprofit college in Tennessee are to be distributed according to a procedure closely patterned on the distribution scheme found in the Model Nonprofit Corporation Act,[25] except that, when the governing board in a judicially supervised liquidation fails to adopt a plan for distribution of the college's residual assets, these assets may be conveyed by the court to the State of Tennessee or its counties or municipalities for purposes similar to those of the dissolved corporation.[26] Tennessee has repealed the provision, taken from the Model Act, requiring the deposit of undistributable assets with the state treasurer,[27] providing instead that such assets escheat to the state as unclaimed property.[28]

B. State Support

Tennessee's Constitution does not specifically prohibit appropriations to RACs. Consequently, many forms of state aid to RACs may be valid under the state constitution.

The Establishment Clause of the Tennessee Constitution[29] is much less strict than its federal counterpart. The state constitutional provision on religious freedom states that "no preference shall ever be given by law, to any religious establishment or mode of worship."[30] As long as the same treatment is given to all institutions, church-related or not, state aid is allowable.[31] The constitutional statement "that no man can of right be compelled to attend, erect, or support any place of worship"[32] has been construed not to affect governmental funding of religious hospitals because no religious preference was involved in the state aid.[33] Analogously, an RAC might also be deemed not to be "a place of religious worship" under this provision.

The Constitution and state statutes prohibit the state or any county or city from giving its credit to any person or corporation or invoking its tax power to make payment on bonds issued for nonpublic purposes.[34] A public purpose is one whose end or result is public, and incidental benefits to individuals do not deprive the activity of its main public character.[35] Therefore, even direct aid to RACs not involving state or municipal credit or aid involving a public purpose is allowed.

The state legislature is authorized to establish and support postsecondary educational institutions, "including public institutions of higher learning, as it determines."[36] Although there is no direct reference to private institutions, the provision suggests that funding private institutions is allowed if not used to further religious education.

Funding of nonprofit charitable organizations by counties or by cities is allowed as long as the funds appropriated are used to promote the general welfare of the residents.[37] Although "charitable organization" is not defined, under another law it includes groups for educational, religious, or eleemosynary causes,[38] which would include most if not all RACs. Perhaps not every RAC would be seen as benefiting the "general welfare," but this would depend on how restrictive the RAC's admission and curriculum policies are.

Cities and counties may contract with and make donations to any public or tax-supported college, or to any nonprofit general welfare corporation, established for promoting educational purposes only, "at or under the supervision, authority, and direction of such [public] colleges . . . "[39] Most RACs are therefore excluded from participation.

Revenues from state sales and tobacco taxes go to the state school fund and public schools.[40] The state or common school fund is exclusively for the operation and maintenance of public schools as are the state school bonds.[41]

At one time there existed alongside the common or state school fund an educational fund which could be appropriated for any educational purpose, even through private colleges.[42] But since this fund was raised through poll taxes, which are prohibited by the Federal Constitution with regard to election of federal officials,[43] there is a question as to whether this separate fund still exists, and if it does, what its source of revenues is.

The Health and Educational Facilities Corporations Act[44] provides for public corporations authorized to finance construction of hospitals and college buildings.[45] There is no restriction on the use of the buildings constructed with this money and such corporations can lease or sell the completed project to the educational institution, profit or nonprofit, in order to pay off the bond issued to finance the project.[46] Since this law has a public purpose, aiding public health and education, and is not intended to establish or advance religious purposes, the aid does not violate the federal Constitution.[47] The test is not government ownership. The fact that the state's duty to provide educational facilities is economically served by having an RAC educate its citizens makes public the plan's primary purpose.[48]

The Tennessee Higher Education Commission's[49] purpose is to study the use of public funds for higher education and to analyze the programs and needs involved.[50] The scope of the Commission's studies and recommendations is limited to state and public colleges,[51] although the Commission is required by law to consider the programs in private institutions in its studies, and is authorized to contract with private institutions to provide needed programs.[52] In addition, the Commission can contract with private medical schools in Tennessee and pay them for each additional Tennessee resident admitted.[53] Any medical college "which annually enrolls additional Tennessee students may receive annual financial payments for each of a maximum of ten entering Tennessee students."[54]

The Tennessee state contract administrator for the Southern Regional Education Board[55] may enter into a contract, with any state or private optometry schools within the region, providing that the school, in exchange for specified payments, will reserve places for Tennessee students.[56]

The Tennessee Student Assistance Corporation was established to administer state assistance programs (tuition grants, loan guarantees, and scholarships) to any financially needy students for tuition and fees at any accredited "public or private institution."[57] This would include attendance at most RACs except perhaps in divinity programs, as even indirect support for these may be deemed an attempt to establish or advance religious purposes (rather than to aid public education) in violation of the federal Constitution.[58]

State grants, made on the basis of need, are given to Tennessee residents who are enrolled or intend to enroll in a public or nonprofit college.[59] These awards are available without regard to area of residence, race, color, creed, sex, national origin, or ancestry.[60] No influence may be placed on the applicant by the state funding agency regarding the student's selection of an institution.[61]

Fellowship and trainee grants to professional personnel desiring to work in programs for the education of handicapped children may be used at any approved institution of higher learning in the state.[62] (This program is administered by the division for the education of the handicapped.)[63]

The United Daughters of the Confederacy has a scholarship fund which is available to students attending any institution of higher education, public or private, in the state.[64] The state holds the funds in trust, paying each recipient as authorized by the UDC.[65]

The loan guarantee program administered by the Tennessee Student Assistance Corporation[66] is available to students at institutions eligible to participate as lenders, with the corporation making repayable advances to the institutions.[67] The Corporation does not make the loans itself but only aids in the processing and guaranteeing of the loans and pays administrative fees to each school for each loan made.[68] It also provides for a loan scholarship program for medical and graduate nursing students who are Tennessee residents attending approved graduate institutions anywhere.[69]

The administrator of any state or private college, if authorized by its controlling board, may accept the note or contract of a student applying for a National Defense Education Act loan or other loans provided by the college. The student may not avoid his or her obligation by use of a minority defense.[70]

C. Personnel

Tennessee's fair employment practice law[71] prohibits discriminatory practices in employment, including "any direct or indirect act or practice of exclusion, distinction, restriction, segregation, limitation, refusal, denial . . . differentiation or preference in the treatment of a person . . . because of race, color, religion, sex or national origin."[72] "Employer" under this law means any person, corporation, or organization employing eight or more people within the state.[73] The Human Development Commission established under this law[74] is given the power to enforce its provisions.[75]

Under the law, an employer may not, on the basis of race, creed, color, religion, sex, or national origin:

fail or refuse to hire or discharge or . . . otherwise discriminate . . . with respect to compensation, terms, conditions or privileges of employment . . . [or] limit, segregate or classify an employee or applicant in any way which would deprive or tend to deprive an individual of employment opportunities or otherwise adversely affect the status of an employee . . . [76]

The law does allow an employer to hire on the basis of religion or sex if either is a "bona fide occupational qualification reasonably necessary to the normal operation of that particular business or enterprise."[77]

The sex BFOQ would justify sex preference in the hiring of certain dormitory personnel and perhaps of certain counselors.

The religious BFOQ would probably not greatly protect RACs in personnel decisions involving positions beyond those of theology and philosophy faculty and perhaps of counselors. It is not likely that an RAC would be successful in arguing a right to exercise, under the BFOQ exemption, religious preference in the employment of faculty generally (let alone other staff) despite the RAC's genuine interest in establishing a particular religious environment on campus.

In a separate provision, any religious corporation, association, educational institution, or society is exempted from state anti-discrimination requirements "with respect to the employment of individuals of a particular religion to perform work connected with the carrying on of its religious activities."[78] The exemption applies to all RACs coming within the phrase "religious . . . educational institutions." This broad phraseology would include virtually all RACs. Second, the exemption arguably authorizes religious preference not only in favor of persons of the same religion as the institution, but members of other sects as well. It could authorize the hiring of a Christian by a Jewish institution to teach a New Testament course. The exemption merely requires that the work involved be related to the RAC's religious activities. (Indeed, the statutory language does not require that the persons's "particular religion" be related to the particular job, as long as the job is related to the institution's religious activities.) This qualification would most likely exclude from the exemption jobs incidental to the institution's religious activities, such as those in maintenance, and perhaps even jobs related solely to educational objectives, e.g., teachers of nonreligion courses. This exemption would probably make the religious BFOQ redundant for most if not all RACs.

It should be mentioned that sex or religious discrimination even by an RAC may make the institution ineligible for the state cooperative education program.[79]

Discrimination by any employer on the basis of "physical, mental, or visual handicap" is also illegal unless the disability prevents or impairs the performance of the work.[80] The Tennessee statute does not specify that dependency on alcohol or on illicit drugs falls within the meaning of the term "handicap." Hence, RACs are presumably free to adopt a policy that would exclude from employment a person who consumes alcoholic beverages or uses illicit drugs.

Counselors hired by any educational institution in the state, including, presumably, RACs, must possess adequate training in counseling.[81]

Sex discrimination in the payment of wages by any employer is forbidden.[82] Tennessee has no minimum wage law covering private employers and no overtime provisions. Maximum work hours were once set for women but were later repealed.[83]

The Tennessee Workmen's Compensation Law[84] covers any corporation which has five or more employees.[85] Generally RACs are covered except with regard to employees within the exception for casual or volunteer employment.[86] Corporate officers, which could include some RAC administrators, can elect to be exempt from the operation of the compensation laws if proper notice is given the state's employment commissioner.[87] RACs must pay compensation for any injury or death in the course of employment without regard to fault.[88] RACs must either carry insurance or become a self-insurer by filing an application with the department of insurance.[89] A self-insurer must deposit acceptable securities and furnish satisfactory proof of financial ability to compensate injured employees.[90]

Tennessee's Employment Security Law[91] (which has been interpreted to include students as "employees,"[92] except under certain circumstances)[93] defines an "employing unit" as "any individual or type of organization."[94] An "employer" includes any such unit which in either the current or preceding calendar year (1) paid $15,000 or more in wages in any one quarter[95] or (2) had at least one individual working for some portion of a day in each of twenty weeks, not necessarily consecutive.[96] Services performed for a nonprofit religious, charitable or educational organization constitute "employment" if two conditions are met.[97] First, the organization must have had, during either the current or preceding calendar year, four or more employees for some part of a day in each of twenty different weeks.[98] (The weeks need not be consecutive, nor do the four or more employees have to have been employed at the same moment.)[99] Second, the service must be excluded from "employment" under the federal Unemployment Tax Act solely by reason of Section 3306(c)(8) of that act.[100] Service for such organizations under the two conditions specified is not "employment" if it is: performed (1) for a church or group of churches or for an organization operated primarily for religious purposes and run or principally supported by a church or convention or association of churches[101] (among RACs, this narrow exception might be available only to seminaries, Bible colleges or the like); or (2) by a duly ordained, commissioned, or licensed minister of a church in the exercise of his ministry or by a member of a religious order in the exercise of duties required by the order.[102]

Excluded from coverage under the legislation are: (1) domestic service in private homes, local college clubs, or fraternity or sorority houses if less than $1000 in wages are paid for such services in any quarter in the current or preceding calendar year;[103] (2) services performed for a school, college, or university by one of its regular students;[104] (3) services for a school, college, or university by the spouse of a regular student.[105] (The spouse must be advised at the beginning of the service that the employment is provided under a program of financial assistance to the student and is not covered by unemployment insurance);[106] and (4) service performed by a student under the age of twenty-two enrolled at a regular nonprofit or public institution of higher education in a full-time program, taken for credit, which combines academic instruction with work experience.[107] (The service must be an integral part of the program, so certified to the employer, and not performed in a "program established by or on behalf of an employer or group of employers").[108] In general, benefits under this law are not extended to summer breaks, holidays and sabbaticals at institutions of higher education if the person involved serves in an institutional, research, or major administrative capacity, the person worked in the term prior to such a break and there is a contract or a reasonable assurance that he will perform such services after that break.[109]

In lieu of regular contributions,[110] a nonprofit organization may elect to make payments into the unemployment fund of an amount equal to the regular benefits and one-half the extended benefits paid and attributable to service for that organization.[111] This election becomes effective for a one-year period when timely written notice is approved by the state Labor Commissioner.[112]

Employing units not otherwise within the Act or those having employees performing services not otherwise within the Act may elect nonetheless to be covered.[113]

Tennessee's collective bargaining[114] and union rights[115] legislation applies to professional employees of elementary and secondary public schools. RACs are therefore not bound by these laws. However, no person or corporation may deny employment on the basis of union membership.[116]

Tennessee's corporation laws do not exclude private corporations, and therefore most RACs, from provisions regarding indemnification and bonding of corporate personnel involved in legal procedings.[117] The scope and purpose of such indemnification are expressly laid out.[118]

D. Students

Tennessee has no comprehensive legislation dealing with student admissions. Nonetheless, there is a provision entitled "Assignment of pupils by race, creed, color or national origin prohibited."[119] The use of the words "pupil" in the title, and of "student" and "school" in the operative part of the statute suggests that the provision was intended to cover elementary and secondary education. A provision at the end of the section stipulates that:

nothing in this section shall be deemed to affect, in any way, the right of a religious or denominational educational institution to select its pupils exclusively or primarily from members of such religion or denomination or from giving preference to [sic] such selection to such members or to make such selection of its pupils as is calculated to promote the religious principles for which it is established.[120]

Use of the phrase "educational institution," as opposed to "school," indicates that all religious or denominational educational institutions — primary, secondary, or higher — have the indicated right. Virtually all RACs are "religious or denominational" educational insitutions and come, therefore, within the statute.

The exemption would clearly allow an RAC to restrict its student body exclusively or primarily to those of its religion or denomination. Moreover, the latter part of the provision would even authorize religious preference in favor of other religions or denominations if the RAC calculates that to be significantly related to its establishing principle. Indeed, the statute, in using the language "or to make such selection . . . as is calculated to promote the religious principles for which it is established," indicates that the criterion used in such preference need not be a religious or denominational one. For example, an RAC whose basic religious tenets preclude the use of alcohol could refuse to admit alcohol users, as long as the selection is calculated to promote its establishing religious principle. An RAC exercising such selectivity may be ineligible for participation in certain state programs conditioned on specified nondiscrimination.[121] The better view, however, is that the legislature did not intend to disqualify from those programs institutions exercising a "right" specifically recognized by the legislature.

No pledge or oath is to be required of any student before entering any school or college that is maintained "in whole or in part by public funds of this state."[122] Whether this covers certain RACs would depend on the type (direct or indirect) or degree of state support.

E. Facilities

Any new public building and public entertainment facilities must be accessible to physically handicapped persons.[123] Public buildings would include any building or area used "primarily by the general public as a place of gathering or amusement; including but not limited to: theaters, restaurants . . . office buildings, stadiums, hospitals . . . and all other public accommodations."[124] The key word is "primarily." Depending on the kind of public use, certain RAC buildings, for example, bookstores, cafeterias, theaters, and the like, could be required to comply with the regulations. "Physically handicapped" is limited to those with sight, hearing, coordination, aging, or other disability which significantly reduces mobility, flexibility, coordination, or perceptiveness.[125]

Discrimination in public accommodations[126] (and in related advertising)[127] on the basis of race, creed, color, religion, sex, or national origin is prohibited. Public accommodations, resorts, or amusements covered under the law include any place which supplies goods or services to the general public, which solicits or accepts the patronage of the general public, or which is supported directly or indirectly by government funds.[128] Only certain private clubs are excepted.[129]

There is no indication that this law is intended to affect facilities open only to enrolled students and indirectly, therefore, student admissions. Nevertheless, facilities like restaurants, stores, and theaters open to the general public on RAC campuses are covered by the law. Moreover, any campus facility supported directly or indirectly by government funds may not discriminate, whether or not open to the general public. Again, there is no indication that this provision was intended to restrict an RAC's ability to exercise religious selectivity in admissions. Indeed, this ability seems explicitly recognized in a separate statute.[130]

These provisions presumably qualify the separate provision giving an owner the right to exclude persons from places of public accommodation for "any reason whatsoever."[131] (The latter statute in any event would cover only those offering lodging to the general public on a day-to-day basis, such as hotels, and not private colleges.[132])

The public accommodations law is enforced by the Tennessee Commission for Human Development.[133]

The terms of the Residential Landlord and Tenant Act exclude from coverage "residence at an institution, public or private, if incidental to . . . the provision of . . . educational . . . religious or similar services."[134] RACs are therefore exempted from the Act's requirements with regard to student housing. Even staff housing will be exempt if provided incident to the provision of educational services.

Statutory minimum health standards applying to the "rental of any premises" probably would cover RAC housing.[135]

The Commission on postsecondary education, through its power to set minimum standards, enforces statutory requirements that student housing maintained, owned, or approved by the institution be "appropriate, safe, and adequate."[136] In addition, minimum fire safety standards are set for the construction of any "new public or private school or other educational facility" and for additions or alterations to structures used for educational purposes.[137]

The Occupational Safety and Health Act of 1972[138] is modeled upon the federal statute. The state OSHA established an Occupational Safety and Health Review Commission to administer the act. An employer is defined broadly as "any person engaged in business and who has one or more persons in employ"; an employee is defined in similarly all-inclusive terms.[139] The exceptions to the act are narrowly defined, so RACs are included within the coverage of the statute.[140]

F. State Taxation

Income from investment stocks and bonds of an educational, religious, or other institution organized for the general welfare is exempt from income taxation, unless such income gives private individuals a profit *and* is not used for educational or religious purposes.[141] There is some question whether all RACs would be considered organized for the "general welfare."

A nonprofit corporation is not subject to the state's excise tax on corporate earnings,[142] nor is it subject to the state corporation franchise tax.[143]

The only state tax on an individual's income is imposed on income from shares of stock and from bonds; there is no provision allowing deductions for charitable contributions by the individual to institutions such as RACs.

Corporations subject to taxation may claim as deductions from income the actual charitable contributions made during the fiscal year.[144]

State inheritance tax does not apply to property transferred to an institution formed for "charitable, educational . . . or religious purposes," provided that the property is used for those purposes and not for private gain except good faith reasonable compensation.[145]

Any property given to institutions formed for "charitable, educational . . . or religious purposes" is not subject to a gift tax, provided the property is used exclusively for such purposes.[146] If any individual receives profit beyond compensation for services or if the institution is not formed in good faith for these purposes, then the exemption is lost.[147]

Tennessee also imposes an estate tax, designed merely to channel to Tennessee, by virtue of the credit allowed against the federal estate tax for state death taxes, moneys that would otherwise go to the federal government in estate taxes.[148] This tax, therefore, has no ultimate effect on the amount of death taxes paid.

An RAC would be subject to a business tax for those operations having "the object of gain, benefit, or advantage, either direct or indirect."[149] This does not include isolated sales by one not regularly engaged in the business,[150] but would apply to sales-oriented businesses.

There is a special exemption for educational services rendered by colleges, services by non-profit organizations, nonprofit educational agencies, and religious or charitable organizations, and services of operators of residential buildings other than hotels and rooming houses.[151] Any institution operated for religious or charitable purposes is exempt from this tax with respect to any profits from the sale of items "contributed to the institution or articles produced by the institution from such contributed items."[152]

The state Constitution authorizes the legislature to exempt from taxation "such [property] as may be held and used for purposes purely religious, charitable . . . or educational. . . ."[153] The word "purely" is treated the same as "exclusively" and requires that the property be used wholly for those purposes and not for profit, unless the profit is used for those purposes as well.[154]

Tennessee's legislature, accepting the state constitutional "invitation," has exempted from tax all real and personal property owned by any religious or educational institution which is occupied or used solely for the purposes for which the institution was created, even if leased by another institution.[155] Property used for social and recreational activities is exempt when it is used to advance and enlarge the purposes of the institution.[156] This would appear to apply to an RAC's athletic fields and stadia.

Dormitories owned by educational institutions are exempt from taxation,[157] but a sorority located on campus is not exempt as an educational institution just because of its association with a college.[158] Even school supplied residences for employees are exempt if it can be shown that the dominant consideration in supplying housing is to promote the efficient administration of the institution.[159]

Under state sales tax laws, the sale of religious publications *to* or *by* churches or other "religious" institutions for use in religious activities is exempt.[160] It is not clear whether all RACs would be considered "religious institutions," although this could depend on how strong the contacts are with recognized churches, or how the institutions' specific religious purposes are interpreted. The term "religious activities"

would presumably include not only church services but other activities such as bible study courses.

Other exemptions from this tax cover the sale or donation of books and any tangible personal property or services *to* any church, university or college[161] exempt from federal income tax (nonprofit institution).[162] The sale or gift must be made directly to the institution, which must have a certificate issued by the tax commissioner.[163]

G. Fund Raising

The laws regulating the solicitation of charitable funds[164] do not apply to bona fide religious or educational institutions.[165] Religious institutions are defined as "ecclesiastical or denominational organizations, churches or established physical places of worship" where nonprofit religious services and activities are conducted and include those institutions exempt from federal income tax and not primarily supported by funds solicited from outside its membership.[166] "Educational institutions" include regular postsecondary schools accredited by a recognized agency and private foundations soliciting contributions exclusively for that institution.[167] Virtually all RACs are within one of these two categories and are therefore exempt from the fund raising law's requirements.

Gambling,[168] including lotteries,[169] is illegal in Tennessee. Originally, the definition of gambling did not include bingos, lotteries, or other games of chance conducted by charities, religious groups, or nonprofit organizations exempt from federal income tax, as long as receipts were used for proper organizational purposes. But this exception was deleted from the statute[170] so that RACs may no longer use these methods to raise funds.

H. Miscellaneous

There is a cooperative education program available to higher educational institutions, public or private, within the state.[171] To participate in this "work study program," which involves the cooperation of outside businesses, the institution must be accredited and must not discriminate on the basis of sex, race, color, religion, or national origin.[172] It is doubtful, however, that the legislature meant to exclude RACs exercising the sort of religious preference in employment or admissions which it has specifically authorized.[173]

Employment agencies are prohibited from classifying or referring for employment because of race, creed, color, religion, sex, or national origin.[174] This covers both private and public agencies, thereby including an RAC's placement office. However, these agencies may classify or refer for employment any individual on the basis of religion or sex if it is a BFOQ.[175] In any event, an RAC's placement office must obtain a license, unless engaged solely in procuring employment, without charge, for public school professionals.[176]

An oath to support state and federal constitutions is required of every teacher in any " . . . school supported in whole or in part by public funds of the state, county, or municipality. . . . "[177] It is unlikely that "school" would include a college or that *any* indirect state funding an RAC might receive through scholarships and the like would place it under this provision.

All colleges have the authority to sell real property acquired by purchase, gift, or donation, with the receipts of such sales deposited in their capital outlay funds.[178]

Transportation companies may give reduced rates for shipping freight for any "religious . . . or benevolent purpose" as long as there is no discrimination among recipients of this discount."[179] Depending on the kind of freight received or shipped by an RAC, this special rate provision could benefit it.

Under state liquor laws, it is not unlawful for "any priest or minister of any religious denomination or sect" to have or be sold wine for sacramental purposes, or for any "bona fide educational institution" to have alcohol for scientific or therapeutical purposes.[180] Otherwise, the sale of alcohol is not to interfere with schools, churches, or other places of public gathering.[181] The county has the power to forbid storage, manufacture, or sale within 2,000 feet of such places.[182] Just how much effect this would have on a private school such as an RAC is not specified. Although the provision is not restricted to public institutions, it is not clear that it is meant to include institutions of higher education.

The broad condemnation powers under eminent domain procedures granted to the University of Tennessee were once granted to certain other colleges.[183] Under present law, colleges other than those in the University of Tennessee system do not have this power.[184]

51. Texas

A. Corporate Status

Creation, maintenance, and dissolution of RACs in Texas are governed by the state's Nonprofit Corporation Act,[1] which is closely patterned on the Model Nonprofit Corporation Act. In order to incorporate, three or more natural persons, at least two of whom are Texas citizens, must sign and verify the articles of incorporation.[2] The articles must be filed with the Secretary of State.[3] Corporate existence begins when the Secretary of State issues a certificate of incorporation.[4]

Another Texas statute sets forth the powers enjoyed by the governing board of an educational corporation.[5] The board of directors, or trustees, may:

make all necessary bylaws, elect and employ officers, providing for filling vacancies, appoint and remove professors, teachers [and] agents, . . . and fix their compensation, confer degrees, and do and perform all necessary acts to carry into effect the objects of the corporation.[6]

Especially significant for faculty collective bargaining in Texas after *National Labor Relations Board v. Yeshiva*,[7] the law provides that the president and professors constitute the faculty, and have the power to enforce discipline and suspend or expel any offending students.[8]

A nonprofit corporation must keep correct and complete books and records of account, and minutes of the proceedings of its board.[9] Any member of the corporation may inspect the books and records, if done for a proper purpose at a reasonable time.[10] Any RAC which holds a certificate from the Coordinating Board of the Texas College and University System is exempt from the provision requiring maintenance of more detailed financial records.[11]

The procedure for voluntary dissolution of a nonprofit college in Texas is patterned on the provisions in the Model Nonprofit Corporation Act. After observing these requirements, the governing board of the college authorizes articles of dissolution to be delivered to the Secretary of State, who officially files the articles and issues a certificate of dissolution.[12] The Attorney General may initiate the process of involuntary dissolution in a district court if a college has failed to comply with a condition precedent to its incorporation or has continued to transact business beyond the scope of the purpose of the college expressed in its charter, or has made a misrepresentation of a material matter in any document submitted to the state pursuant to the Nonprofit Corporation Act.[13] Under some circumstances the Secretary of State may order the involuntary dissolution of a nonprofit college.[14]

The assets of a dissolving college in Texas are to be distributed according to a plan closely patterned on the provisions of the Model Act.[15] The portion of assets that are distributable to a creditor or other person who is unknown or who cannot be found after the exercise of reasonable diligence is to be reduced to cash and deposited with the State Treasurer, who holds the funds for seven years for payment to the person(s) entitled to them. If after seven years no claim is made for such funds, after proper public notice the funds escheat to the General Revenue Fund of the State of Texas.[16] In addition, Texas courts will apply the doctrine of *cy pres* when necessary.[17]

B. State Support

The Texas constitution prohibits the use of state funds in order to "benefit . . . any sect, or religious society, theological or religious seminary"[18] and the use of "school fund" monies for the support of sectarian schools.[19] The Texas Attorney General has interpreted these provisions to allow some forms of public assistance to church-related schools on the ground that not all such institutions are "sectarian" in the constitutional sense.[20] Following this interpretation, the Texas legislature has enacted various programs providing financial assistance to private institutions of higher education, including RACs.[21]

The Higher Education Authority Act

Texas' Higher Education Authority Act[22] grants to municipalities the power to develop educational and housing facilities to be used by institutions of higher education. Under the Act, a city may establish a higher education authority when its governing body finds that it is to the best interest of the city to do so.[23] An authority can acquire, construct, enlarge, extend, or improve educational and housing facilities, and either operate the facilities itself or lease them to an educational institution.[24] The authorities do not have the power of taxation or eminent domain,[25] but they do have the power to issue revenue bonds to finance their activities.[26] After the bonds for a specific project have been retired, the lease or contract with the educational institution expires.[27] Although the Act does not specify the property consequences of the expiration of such a lease or contract, presumably the title to the facility funded in this way would vest in the educational institution.

Assistance under the Act is available to any RAC accredited by the Texas Education Agency.[28] Unlike parallel federal legislation,[29] the Texas statute does not explicitly restrict the use of authority-financed facilities to nonreligious activities; an educational facility is defined in Texas law as:

a classroom building, laboratory, science building, faculty or administrative office building, or other facility used exclusively for the conduct of the educational and administrative functions of an institution of higher education.[30]

Because at least some religious activities are educational in nature, the Texas statute would apparently permit such activities to be carried on in facilities constructed with state assistance. It should be noted, moreover, that *Hunt v. McNair* sustained the use of a similar revenue bonding scheme to provide public support for the construction or renovation of a building at an RAC only if that building is devoted exclusively to nonsectarian uses.[31]

Student Assistance Programs

The Texas legislature has provided for two loan programs for students who reside in Texas. The first program provides direct loans to low-income and moderate-income students who are enrolled at an eligible participating institution.[32] The statute defines a financially eligible student as one who "has established that he has insufficient resources to finance his college education";[33] to be an eligible participating institution, an RAC must be accredited and must comply with the regulations of the Coordinating Board of the Texas College and University System.[34] As with the parallel statute relating to the construction of facilities, this statute does not prohibit loans for purely sectarian training such as the formation of candidates for the ministry, but the Supreme Court has allowed state aid for students attending sectarian institutions of higher education.[35]

In 1979, Texas enacted a guaranteed student loan program.[36] Under this program, any student in good standing at an eligible institution may receive a state-guaranteed loan, regardless of his financial status.[37] Any school which is an eligible institution under the federal Higher Education Act of 1965[38] is an eligible institution under this state act,[39] so students attending any accredited RAC in Texas are eligible to participate in the guaranteed student loan program.[40]

Texas also has two student grant programs. The first, the Tuition Equalization Grant (TEG) Program,[41] is available to resident students attending private colleges and universities in Texas. Based on the student's financial need, the grants may amount to as much as one-half of the average annual appropriation for each student enrolled in the state college and university system.[42]

Although nothing in the act would prevent an RAC from qualifying as an approved institution solely because of its religious affiliation,[43] a number of other conditions are attendant to participation in this program. First, an approved institution must follow regulations promulgated by the Coordinating Board in compliance with Title VI of the Civil Rights Act of 1964 relating to nondiscrimination in admissions and employment.[44] Second, the Texas Attorney General has ruled that it would be an abuse of discretion for the Coordinating Board to fund an institution qualified to participate in the TEG program if it has a fixed policy requiring trustees, officers, faculty, and staff members to acknowledge belief in a particular and detailed religious doctrine, and refuses to hire people because of differing religious beliefs.[45] Finally, the statute states in sweeping language that any school receiving a benefit, however indirect, under the program "shall be subject to all present or future laws enacted by the legislature."[46] This sweeping conclusion is not, however, grounded on case law governing public assistance to students attending RACs.[47]

The second grant program provides grants of up to $1,000 to students attending public or private colleges in Texas.[48] Under this program, benefited schools are subject to the same regulations as under the Tuition Equalization Grant Program. Unlike the student loan program, this program explicitly excludes from participation students enrolled in theology or religious degree programs.[49]

C. Personnel

Equal Employment Opportunity

The employment policies of RACs in Texas relating to nondiscrimination are governed, of

course, by applicable federal statutes, but Texas has not enacted independent or similarly comprehensive civil rights legislation. Texas has, however, enacted a statute that protects the civil rights of the handicapped.[50] Any employer conducting business in Texas is prohibited from discriminating "against a handicapped person on the basis of the handicap if the person's ability to perform the task required by a job is not impaired by the handicap."[51] The act provides both criminal penalties for those who discriminate, and civil remedies for those who are discriminated against.[52]

In addition, those whose employment is "supported in whole or in part by public funds" must employ the handicapped "on the same terms and conditions as the able-bodied, unless it is shown that the particular disability prevents the performance of the work involved."[53] The act is open to the interpretation that student assistance in the form of the grants described above[54] would constitute public funds, and the enrollment of students participating in these grant programs would trigger the requirements of this act.[55]

The act defines a "handicapped person" as:

a person who has a mental or physical handicap, including mental retardation, hardness of hearing, deafness, speech impairment, visual handicap, being crippled, or any other health impairment which requires special ambulatory devices or services.[56]

Because the recitation of specific handicaps is prefaced by "including" rather than "including, but not limited to," the definition appears to exclude alcoholics and drug addicts from the protection of the act. Texas law, therefore, probably does not impede an RAC from declining to hire or from terminating an employee who, contrary to the ethical standards of the church with which the college is affiliated, consumes alcoholic beverages or uses illicit drugs.

Wages and Hours

The Texas Minimum Wage Act has not been revised since 1970, when the minimum wage was set at $1.40 per hour.[57] Employees performing bona fide executive, administrative, or professional services, or who are working gratuitously, are exempt from the Act.[58] In addition, the Texas act does not apply to any employee covered by the federal Fair Labor Standards Act.[59]

An employee must be paid within sixteen days of the day his wages were earned and must be paid at least twice a month.[60] Any employer who has a contract with the state must base his workday for the state work on an eight-hour day.[61] This provision would apply to RACs only in limited situations, for example, in connection with work specifically performed on a research project for the state. Texas has no other "overtime act."

It is illegal for a child under the age of fifteen to work between the hours of 10 p.m. and 5 a.m., or more than eight hours a day or 48 hours a week.[62]

Worker's Compensation

The Texas Worker's Compensation and Crime Victims Compensation Law[63] contains all the provisions for compensating employees who sustain personal injuries at work. Under the principle "*inclusio unius exclusio alterius*," the statute would cover all forms of employment not specifically excluded by the act, namely "domestic servants or casual employees engaged in employment incidental to a personal residence, farm laborers, ranch laborers and employees of interurban railways."[64] In 1973, the Attorney General of Texas underscored the broad reach of this statute, construing it to include students at a private institution of higher education working for hourly remuneration credited against their expenses, provided that the students do not fall within one of the excluded occupations mentioned above.[65] Appellate courts in Texas have ruled that the act should be construed liberally in favor of an injured worker,[66] "in order that the humane purpose of [the] enactment may be carried out."[67]

The act is administered by the State Industrial Accident Board.[68] Like other employees covered by the act, RACs may elect to become subscribers to the Employer's Insurance Association, which will pay any legal judgments against members who have complied with all the rules, regulations and demands of the association.[69] In addition, RACs may elect to cover even their exempted employees, by purchasing appropriate insurance from the association.[70]

Unemployment Compensation

Under the Texas Unemployment Compensation Act[71] a nonprofit organization is one which fits the definition of "nonprofit organization" contained in section 501(c)(3) of the Internal Revenue Code and which qualifies as tax-exempt under section 501(a) of the Code.[72] Such an organization is an "employer" under the Texas statute if it employs for some portion of a day four or more individuals "on each of some twenty (20) days during the current . . . or preceding calendar year, each day being in a different calendar week."[73]

The Act provides the following exemptions directly relevant to RACs: (1) services performed for a church or for an association of churches;[74] (2) services performed for an organization run primarily for religious purposes and controlled by a church or by an association of churches;[75] and (3) services performed by ordained ministers or by members of religious orders in the exercise of their duties.[76] Because the scope of these exemptions is narrow, most services performed in the employ of RACs are covered under the Act. Other relevant exclusions from the Act's definition of employment[77] include (1) domestic service for a local college club or local chapter of a college fraternity or sorority, if total remuneration in any quarter of the current or preceding calendar year was less than $1,000.00;[78] (2) service for which unemployment compensation is payable under a system set up by Congress;[79] (3) service performed for a school or college by one of its regularly enrolled students;[80] and (4) service performed by a student under the age of twenty-two at an accredited nonprofit or public educational institution in a full-time program, taken for credit and combining academic instruction and work experience.[81]

Nonprofit organizations, and therefore RACs, may elect to make payments in lieu of contributions. The election is effective for a period of two years upon the filing of a written notice with the Texas Employment Commission.[82] Required payments are equal to the amount of regular benefits plus one-half the amount of extended benefits paid.[83] The Commission may require an electing organization to file an approved surety bond.[84] Organizations not otherwise subject to provisions of the Act may elect to participate in the program for a minimum of two years.[85]

Collective Bargaining

The Texas legislature has enacted a law that simultaneously protects an employee's right to bargain collectively and his "right to work."[86] The statute requires that "no person shall be denied employment on account of membership or nonmembership in a labor union."[87] In addition, any contract requiring or forbidding membership in a labor union is void and against public policy.[88] A labor union may collect initiation fees, but may not "collect, receive or demand any [other] fee, assessment, or sum of money whatsoever, as a work permit or as a condition for the privilege to work from any person not a member of the union."[89] Another statute, known as the Texas Anti-Discrimination Act,[90] forbids any corporation from discriminating against "any person seeking employment on account of his having participated in a strike."[91] The same act forbids the keeping of blacklists and gives a discharged employee the right to obtain from his former employer a statement, in writing, of the reasons for his discharge.[92] The Anti-Discrimination Act applies to all RACs.

D. Students

Texas has no law directly regulating a private school's selection of its students. But as indicated in the section on state support, if a school wishes to participate in certain financial aid programs, it must comply with Title VI of the Civil Rights Act of 1964.[93] Moreoever, because of the broad definition given to "public facilities" in the Texas civil rights act for the handicapped, probably no school, including RACs, may lawfully maintain an admissions policy which discriminates against otherwise qualified persons solely on the basis of their handicaps.[94]

E. Facilities

Texas has no fair housing legislation. However, the civil rights act for the handicapped may affect the physical facilities of an RAC in Texas. The law forbids (1) denying a physically handicapped person admittance to any public facility because of his handicap;[95] (2) any discrimination through a "ruse or subterfuge calculated to prevent or discourage a handicapped person" from using a public facility;[96] and (3) denial to the handicapped of full and equal access to all housing accommodations.[97]

The definition of "public facilities" is broad, explicitly including "college dormitories and other educational facilities."[98] The act, however, also states that landlords need not modify their property in order to satisfy the "full and equal access" provision regarding housing accommodations.[99] In addition, the Texas Attorney General has limited the effect of the statute on architectural barriers only to those barriers that were intentionally designed to bar or discourage the handicapped.[100] Obviously, proving this intention would be a difficult task. Therefore, although the act attempts to provide the handicapped with greater access to public facilities, it does not lay upon employers any affirmative duties or obligations to achieve this goal.

Another Texas statute, however, requires the elimination of architectural barriers in certain categories of buildings.[101] The first category includes all buildings constructed or renovated in whole or in part by the use of public funds.[102] Any building financed by a higher education authority would probably fit into this category.[103] The other category includes all buildings or improved areas "constructed on or after January 1, 1978, in counties with a population of 50,000 or more," explicitly including "commercial business and trade schools or colleges" among a wide variety of facilities such as shopping centers, transportation terminals, theaters with a seating capacity greater than 200, hospitals and related medical facilities, office buildings, and funeral homes.[104] If the terms "commercial business and trade" are construed as an essential modifier of the substantive, "colleges," most RACs would not be covered by this statute. If, however, the intended contrast is between trade schools and traditional liberal arts colleges, then RACs that construct or improve their facilities after 1978 must do so in conformity with this statute. In any event, the clear intent of the statute is to make all of the applicable buildings accessible to the physically handicapped.[105] The statute establishes a commission to implement the act; this commission is empowered to review all plans and specifications to ascertain that the intent of the act is carried out.[106]

Texas law has created an Occupational Safety Board to administer the Division of Occupational Safety.[107] The Board is empowered to enact rules governing the safety of workers in the work place.[108] An employer is defined broadly as every person, firm, corporation, or association having control or custody of any employment, place of employment, or employee.[109] An employee is defined as any person who works for an employer for wages, compensation, or other things of value, excluding private domestics.[110] A place of employment is defined as every place where any trade, industry, or business is carried on, or where any person is employed by another for gain or profit.[111] Texas has a sunset law that provides that the Board will be abolished unless the legislature acts affirmatively to continue its existence.[112]

F. State Taxation

Texas has no personal or corporate income tax. Texas does have a franchise tax, but this tax was never intended to apply to corporations organized strictly for educational purposes or to corporations exempt from federal income taxation under §501(c)(3) of the Internal Revenue Code.[113]

The Texas inheritance tax does not apply to transfers to RACs.[114]

Texas has no gift or estate tax but does impose an additional inheritance tax designed to channel to Texas by virtue of the credit allowed against the federal estate tax for state death taxes, moneys that would otherwise go to the federal government in estate taxes.[115] This tax, therefore, has no ultimate effect on the amount of death taxes paid.

Real, Personal, and Intangible Property Tax

RACs fit within the broad definition of schools which are exempted from Texas's real and personal property taxes.[116] Property which is used incidentally to the educational function is also exempt when its use benefits the school's students or faculty.[117] Even the endowment funds of an RAC are exempt from the property tax.[118] Any property on or near RAC property which belongs to a religious organization is also exempt under the broad provisions of the statute.[119]

Sales, Use and Meals Tax

Sales to RACs are exempt from the sales and use taxes when the sale is related to the organization's exempt purpose.[120] Sales by RACs at certain fund raising events one day per year are also exempt.[121] Although there is no exemption for sales by RACs as a normal course of business, the sale of religious books and writings,[122] food products,[123] alcoholic beverages,[124] and tobacco products[125] are also exempt from the sales and use tax.

Meals served by RACs are probably subject to the sales tax since the statutory exemption from taxation on meals served by schools refers explicitly to primary and secondary schools.[126]

RACs are also exempted from the Hotel Occupancy Tax if the applicable facilities are used by employees or officers of the corporation.[127]

G. Fund Raising

Texas has not enacted a statute regulating charitable solicitation, nor does it have any other legislation which would affect the fund raising activities of RACs.[128] There is, however, a provision in the Penal Code which strictly prohibits operation of games of chance for any profit whatsoever.[129]

H. Miscellaneous

The Coordinating Board of the Texas College and University System has general authority to develop a comprehensive program for higher education in Texas.[130] Although the Board has no power to regulate RACs directly, it may enter into joint projects with private institutions.[131] The Board has the authority to approve or disapprove the granting of degrees by a private college, but any school which is accredited by a "recognized accrediting agency" is exempt from this provision.[132]

Private colleges and universities may hire private security officers to enforce the laws of Texas. These security officers enjoy the same powers, privileges, and immunities as regular peace officers.[133]

Securities issued by educational corporations are exempt from Texas blue sky laws.[134]

RACs are also exempt from the licensing requirements for coin-operated music and game machines.[135]

52. Utah

A. Corporate Status

RACs are incorporated in Utah under the Utah Nonprofit Corporation and Co-operative Association Act.[1] A nonprofit corporation in Utah is a corporation which excludes pecuniary profit and distributes no part of its income to its members, trustees or officers, or a nonprofit cooperative association.[2] Lawful purposes for organization include education and religion.[3]

As a nonprofit corporation, an RAC must file an annual report with the Secretary of State. The report must state the name and address of the RAC and the names and addresses of the RAC's governing board.[4] The law provides a penalty for failure to file an annual report[5] and sets fees for filing documents and issuing certificates.[6]

One RAC may merge with another RAC, or with another type of nonprofit corporation.[7] An RAC may voluntarily dissolve and wind up its affairs by adopting a resolution to dissolve.[8] Subject to satisfying all liabilities and obligations,[9] assets held by the RAC for religious or educational purposes not subject to return will be conveyed to similar institutions pursuant to a plan of distribution drawn up by the RAC.[10] In the case of an involuntary dissolution, the court will direct a distribution of the assets to similar institutions.[11] This is an applicaton of the common law doctrine of *cy pres* — if there has been a gift or bequest for a charitable purpose, which for some reason cannot be literally carried out, then something closely analogous is done to fulfill what appears to be the donor's intention and purpose.[12] Another RAC would, of course, be a "similar institution."

B. State Support

The Utah Constitution prohibits public aid to RACs controlled in whole or in part by any church:

Neither the Legislature nor any county, city, town, school district or other public corporation, shall make any appropriation to aid in the support of any school, seminary, academy, college, university or other institution, controlled in whole or in part, by any church, sect or denomination whatever.[13]

Nor are public funds available for religious instruction:

There shall be no union of Church and State, nor shall any church dominate the State or interfere with its function. No public money or property shall be appropriated for or applied to any religious worship, exercise or instruction, or for the support of any ecclesiastical establishment.[14]

Appropriation of public funds for courses in theology or religious studies even at an RAC not controlled in whole or in part by a church would apparently violate the Utah constitution.

Utah's Student Loan Program[15] creates a student loan fund which is available to a student resident of the state[16] attending an eligible institution of higher education,[17] which includes virtually all RACs.[18] The Utah Higher Education Assistance Authority may require students receiving a guaranteed loan to remit a fee, which may include the proportionate cost of a group life insurance premium.[19] A more recent loan program, established in the Higher Education Loan Act,[20] seems to expand loan coverage through a broader definition of eligible institution,[21] and clarifies the definition of "student" in rules promulgated by the board.[22]

The Higher Education Act of 1969[23] governs only the state system of higher education.[24] The only reference to RACs in this act states:

As a further means of attaining a well integrated and adequate system of post-high school education in Utah, the state board of higher education shall seek the co-operation of all private, denominational and other post-high school educational institutions situated in this state and which are not supported by public funds.[25]

Utah is a member of the Western Interstate Commission for Higher Education, which supports professional education in several fields, including law and medicine, by subsidizing the tuition of students at public or private professional schools, including RACs outside of a state lacking such facilities.[26]

The Utah Constitution and the almost exclusively public nature of Title 53 (education title) confirm that RACs may not obtain any direct support from the state.

Personnel

The Utah Anti-Discriminatory Act[27] prohibits an employer from deciding to hire, promote, or discharge any otherwise qualified person because of that person's color, sex, age, religion, ancestry, national origin, or handicap.[28] An "employer" includes persons employing twenty-five or more employees, but excludes religious organizations and associations, religious corporations sole, and corporations and associations constituting a wholly-owned subsidiary or agency of any religious organization or association.[29] If an RAC in Utah is structured as a wholly-owned subsidiary or agency of a religious organization, it is exempt from coverage under this Act.[30]

Because not all RACs are so structured, it is useful to compare the language of the state anti-discrimination act with the parallel provisions in the federal civil rights law. First, the exemption provided for in section 702 of the federal statute applies explicitly to RACs, referred to in the statute as a "religious . . . educational institution."[31] The Utah statute, by contrast, speaks more generally of "religious organizations and associations" and of an "agency of any religious organization or association" without explicitly mentioning educational institutions. Second, the exemption in section 702 of the federal statute refers only to religious preference in employment decisions; the legislative history of this provision requires the conclusion that racial discrimination and sex-based discrimination by RACs would be impermissible. On the other hand, if the Utah statute is intended to exclude all RACs from the definition of an employer, RACs in that state would not be prohibited by state law from engaging in racial discrimination or sex discrimination in their employment policies and practices. Third, both the federal statute and the Utah law define the exemption from otherwise applicable law in such a way as to pose a dilemma for RACs. Either they are an agency of a church and thereby arguably ineligible for public financial assistance or they are included within the statutory definition of an employer and thereby arguably prohibited from exercising any form of religious preference in their employment policies.[32] Unless an RAC in Utah is structured as a wholly-owned subsidiary or agency of a religious organization, it is generally bound to observe the provisions of the state anti-discrimination act.

Two provisions of the act, however, allow RACs in Utah freedom to establish and carry out a policy of religious preference in employment policies. Section 6(2)(a) of the Utah statute provides that it is not a discriminatory or unfair employment practice to hire on the basis of an employee's religion, sex, age, national origin, or handicap where any of these characteristics is "a bona fide occupational qualification reasonably necessary to the normal operation of that particular business or enterprise or essential to the motif, culture or atmosphere displayed, illustrated or promoted by such a particular business or enterprise."[33] The Utah statute follows the central language of section 703(e)(1) of the federal statute, but adds age and handicap as permissible categories for a BFOQ. Put simply, the BFOQ exception allows any employer, including an RAC, to take an employee's religion into account only where religion is relevant to the performance of the job. An RAC, for example, could clearly rely on the BFOQ exception to prefer faculty members employed to teach theology, religious studies, philosophy, and other matters related to the religious purpose of the institution. The language "reasonably necessary to the normal operation" might be broad enough to include positions such as dean of students and dormitory and library directors where policies and decisions, consistent with the institution's religious affiliation, are important to proper religious formation of the student.

Subsection (2)(a) goes a step further than the parallel federal legislation by permitting an employer to hire based on such a classification where it is essential to the "motif, culture or atmosphere displayed, illustrated, or promoted by such a particular business or enterprise."[34] This broad language would apparently permit a religious BFOQ in teaching and nonteaching positions, administrative positions, and any other position essential to the atmosphere. An RAC should, nonetheless, be cautious in relying exclusively on the BFOQ exception in employment policies, for even though the Utah statute is broadly couched, it would not exempt such an institution from being perceived as "pervasively sectarian," perhaps precisely because it had relied on the loose criteria of "motif" and "atmosphere" found in the statute. If an RAC were not merely perceived to be pervasively sectarian but adjudged to be so in a case brought under the Establishment Clause, it might lose its eligibility for receipt of public assistance.[35]

Section 6(2)(b) of the Utah act states that it is not a discriminatory or unfair employment practice:

[f]or a school, college, university or other educational institution or institution of learning to hire and employ employees of a particular religion if such school, college, university, or other educational in-

stitution or institution of learning is, in whole or in substantial part, owned, supported, controlled, or managed by a particular religious corporation, association or society, or if the curriculum of such school, college, university or other educational institution or institution of learning is directed toward the propagation of a particular religion.[36]

This provision closely follows section 703(e)(2) of the federal statute. It is narrower in applicability than the BFOQ exception because it is available only to religiously affiliated educational institutions. It is likewise narrower than the BFOQ exception in that it allows preference only on the basis of the religion of a job applicant or employee. But it is broader than the BFOQ in that it allows such preference not only with respect to jobs demonstrably related to the religious mission of the institution but with respect to all job positions at a qualifying RAC. Again, however, reliance on this provision as the basis for religious preference might render the institution vulnerable to a challenge of its eligibility for public assistance.[37] The phrase "of a particular religion" does not mean that religious preference by a qualifying RAC is restricted to preferring members of the same religious body with which the RAC is affiliated. Brigham Young University, for example, would be free under state law to prefer non-Mormons as well as Mormons on its faculty.

In *Larsen v. Kirkham*,[38] a plaintiff alleged that she had been discriminated against on the basis of her sex and her religion in connection with her employment as a teacher at a Mormon-related college in Salt Lake City. She challenged the exemption available to the college in both the state anti-discrimination law and the federal civil rights statute as violative of the Establishment Clause of the First Amendment. The federal district judge sustained both acts against this constitutional challenge, and suggested that these provisions should be construed to allow RACs to employ those who best promote their religious mission.[39]

In 1979 the Anti-Discriminatory Act was amended to include "handicap" among the prohibited classifications and among the classifications subject to a BFOQ.[40] "Handicap" is "a physical or mental impairment which substantially limits one or more major life activity [sic]."[41] The federal regulations accompanying Section 504 of the Vocational Rehabilitation Act include alcoholism and drug addiction within the definition of a handicap.[42] Officials within the former Department of HEW have responded that these regulations were not intended to impose upon RACs a duty to hire or to retain an employee who is a current user of alcohol or illegal drugs where the RAC has a religiously grounded reason for opposition to the consumption of alcohol and the use of illegal drugs.[43] A similar construction of the Utah statute commends itself for the following reasons. First, the statute itself does not define alcoholism or drug dependence as a handicap. Second, although there is no legislative history, administrative regulations or case law concerning this provision, this very lack of specificity favors the interpretation that the legislature meant to include only involuntary disabilities within its definition. Third, even if some state authority were to issue regulations construing the definition of handicap to include alcoholism or drug addiction, an RAC would still be free to terminate an employee who is a current user of alcohol or illicit drugs if it determined that such use rendered the employee "unqualified" within the meaning of the statute. As was mentioned above, the legislature clearly authorized employers to take into account the "motif, culture, or atmosphere" of the work environment in determining whether to exercise religious preference by way of a BFOQ exception. If administrators of an RAC could show that the consumption of alcohol or the use of illicit drugs disrupted the religious atmosphere desired by the college or university authorities, they could rely on the BFOQ exception as a complete defense to a charge that they were violating the handicap provision by terminating an employee who is a current user of alcohol or illicit drugs.

In summary, Utah law includes most RACs within the definition of an employer bound to observe the general proscription against discrimination on the basis of race, color, sex, age, ancestry, national origin, or handicap. State law, however, grants all employers, including RACs, a narrow BFOQ exception allowing them to exercise preference with respect to any position if religion, sex, or national origin is a relevant factor to the performance of the job. More broadly, it allows an RAC the freedom to exercise religious preference with respect to any of its employees.

The Utah Workmen's Compensation Law[44] applies to every private corporation.[45] Generally, RACs are covered except with regard to those employees who come within the exemption for casual employment that is not in the usual course of the employer's business.[46] RACs must secure compensation to their employees in one of three ways: (1) by insuring with the state insurance fund, (2) by insuring with any stock corporation or mutual association authorized to transact workmen's compensation insurance in the state or (3) by becoming a self-insurer.[47] The self-insurer must annually furnish satisfactory proof of financial ability to pay direct compensation. The Industrial Commission may require self-insurers to deposit acceptable security to secure payment of compensation to injured employees.[48]

The Utah Employment Security Act[49] includes within its definition of "employment"[50] services performed for a nonprofit organization,[51] if two conditions are met.[52] First, the services must be exempt from the definition of "employment" in the Federal Unemployment Tax Act solely due to section 3306(c)(8).[53] Second, the organization must employ at least four individuals "for some portion of a day in each of twenty different weeks, whether or not such weeks were consecutive, within either the current or preceding calendar year."[54]

The Act provides the following exemptions which apply directly to RACs: (1) services performed for a church, a convention or an association of churches;[55] (2) services performed for an organization run primarily for religious purposes and controlled by a church or by an association of churches;[56] and (3) services performed by ordained ministers or by members of religious orders in the exercise of their duties.[57] Because the scope of these exemptions is narrow, most services performed in the employ of RACs are covered under the act. Other relevant exemptions[58] apply to services performed (1) for a school or college by regularly enrolled students[59] or by their spouses;[60] (2) by a student under the age of twenty-two at an accredited nonprofit or public educational institution in a full-time program, combining academic instruction and work experience;[61] (3) as a domestic servant for a college club or a chapter of a college fraternity or sorority, if total wages, paid in cash, were not greater than $1,000.00 in any quarter of the current or preceding calendar year.[62]

Nonprofit organizations, and therefore RACs, may elect to make payments in lieu of contributions. To take advantage of this option, an organization must fit the definition of "non-profit organization" in section 501(a) of the Internal Revenue Code and must qualify as tax-exempt under section 501(a) of the Code.[63] The election is effective for a period of one year[64] upon filing of written notice with the Utah Department of Employment Security.[65] Required payments are equal to the amount of regular benefits plus one-half the amount of extended benefits paid.[66] In order to take advantage of this election, however, nonprofit organizations may be required to deposit money with the Utah Industrial Commission.[67] Organizations not otherwise subject to the provision of the Act may elect to participate in the program for a minimum of two years.[68]

Utah's minimum wage law and maximum hours law is contained in the chapter which deals with conditions of labor and employment for women and children.[69] The statute, designed for the health and safety of women and children, does not appear to be a general minimum wage and maximum hours law applicable to men. The Utah Anti-Discriminatory Act, however, prohibits an employer from paying "differing wages or salaries to employees having substantially equal experience, responsibilities, and competency for the particular job."[70] There is no religious exemption.[71]

Under Utah law, employees have the right to engage in collective bargaining.[72] The chapter on employment relations gives the employee the right to organize, to bargain through representatives chosen by the employees, and to engage in "concerted activities" for the purpose of mutual aid and protection.[73] Thus, labor unions may be organized, joined, or assisted by em-

ployees, RACs come under the chapter's definition of employer,[74] and in *Utah Labor Relations Board v. Utah Valley Hospital*,[75] the court held that even though the hospital was a nonprofit charitable institution, it was not immune from collective bargaining or otherwise excluded from coverage under the Utah Labor Relations Act.[76]

D. Students

The Utah Constitution provides:

Neither religious nor partisan test or qualification shall be required of any person, as a condition of admission, as teacher or student, into any public educational institution of the State.[77]

There are no reported cases interpreting this article of the Utah Constitution. But the maxim, *"inclusio unius est exclusio alterius,"* may be relied on here for the conclusion that this constitutional provision refers only to the student admissions policies and practices of publicly operated institutions such as the University of Utah at Salt Lake City and Utah State University at Logan, and not to RACs such as Brigham Young University at Provo or Westminster College in Salt Lake City. Neither the direct receipt of public institutional assistance by an RAC nor the participation by students attending these institutions in various forms of state student aid programs transforms an RAC into a public educational institution for purposes of this constitutional provision.

Although the state constitution does not prohibit an RAC from exercising religious preference in its policies governing student admission, one state statute on its face seems to prohibit such policies:

[T]he practice of discrimination on the basis of race, color, sex, religion, ancestry, or national origin in business establishments or places of public accommodation or in enterprises regulated by the state . . . violates the public policy of this state.[78]

Since RACs may in some sense be construed as "enterprises regulated by the state,"[79] this provision might arguably bar all forms of discrimi-

nation on the basis of religion at an RAC, including religious preference in student admissions. The legislature, however, probably did
not intend this provision to prohibit an institution like Brigham Young University from favoring Mormons in any of its student admissions
policies or practices. First, such an interpretation would seriously undermine the legitimate
freedom of an RAC to determine the composition of its own community.[80] Second, the statement of policy and purposes of the act requires
the act to be construed liberally with a view to
promoting justice.[81] Third, the act appears to
recognize the distinct character of religious
organizations:

Nothing in this act shall be construed to deny any
person the right to regulate the operation of a
business establishment or place of public accommodation or an enterprise regulated by the state in a
manner which applies uniformly to all persons
without regard to race, color, sex, religion, ancestry,
or national origin; or to deny any religious organization the right to regulate the operation and procedures of its establishments.[82]

Fourth, the commercial overtones of the definition of an "enterprise regulated by the state,"[83]
as well as the placement of this statute within
the Title of the Utah Code governing Commerce and Trade, suggest that the principal
concern of the Utah legislature was not with the
admissions policies of academic institutions,
but with the denial of services to persons in
places of public accommodation. Finally, the
very time of the passage of this act, shortly
after the Civil Rights Act of 1964, with its
historical prohibition in Title II upon discrimination and segregation in places of public accommodation, confirms the conclusion that the
Utah legislature intended to reinforce the national will to eliminate all forms of irrational
and invidious discrimination in places of public
accommodation such as hotels, motels, and
restaurants.[84]

Perhaps this concern about potential regulation of student admissions policies of RACs in
Utah is unwarranted in that it is highly unlikely
that state officials would behave in a heavy-
handed manner with respect to these institu-

tions.[85] The argument against federal regulation
of religious preference in student admissions at
RACs[86] is equally applicable to the state of
Utah. In any event, a simple amendment to this
statute could specify its inapplicability to
RACs.

E. Facilities

Although it was argued in the previous section that Utah's civil rights legislation does not
ban religious preference in student admissions
by an RAC, the same statute would bar RACs
from discriminating on the basis of race, color,
sex, religion, ancestry, or national origin in any
place of public accommodation. An RAC, for
example, may operate a hotel or restaurant that
is open to the public only on a nondiscriminatory basis. On the other hand, since
student dormitories and dining halls are not
normally open to the public, an RAC in Utah
would not run afoul of state law if a disproportionate number of members of a particular
religious group were users of these facilities as
a consequence of a legitimate student admissions policy. This conclusion is reinforced by
the proviso that the term "public accommodation" does not refer to any institution, church,
or place of accommodation that is distinctly
private in nature.[87]

A local housing authority, created under
Chapter 18 of the Public Welfare Title, has the
power to issue rules and regulations,[88] to determine where there is unsafe, unsanitary, or over-
crowded housing,[89] and to deal with RACs for
the provision of services, privileges, works, or
facilities, or in connection with its projects.[90]
For example, if an RAC has a certain type of
boiler system the college may be subject to the
Utah Boiler Inspection Law.[91] The State's Division of Health administers the Public Health
Code[92] and is empowered to investigate and enforce health standards.[93] The Board of Health,
entrusted with policy-making, has the power to
adopt, amend, or rescind rules, regulations,
and standards relating to the public health.[94]
RACs have no statutory immunity from such
reasonable regulations, nor, in the light of the
broad right of the state to issue such regulations

to protect the general welfare of its citizenry, should they.

The Utah Occupational Safety and Health Act of 1973[95] is a typical OSHA statute. Employer and employee are defined in all-inclusive terms, with no exceptions for RACs.[96]

F. State Taxation

Utah's Individual Income Tax Act of 1973[97] does not impose an income tax on RACs because the term "individual" subject to the tax is limited to natural persons.[98] Utah exempts from the payment of franchise and privilege taxes[99] all "[c]orporations . . . organized and operated exclusively for religious, charitable, scientific, literary, or educational purposes . . . no part of the net earnings of which inures to the benefit of any private shareholder or individual."[100] RACs, in general, are entitled to this exemption.

The Utah Inheritance Tax Reform Act[101] imposes a tax in the amount of the federal credit on the transfer of the taxable estate of every resident.[102] Utah no longer has an inheritance tax, but imposes an estate tax designed merely to channel to Utah, by virtue of the credit allowed against the federal estate tax for state death taxes, moneys that would otherwise go to the federal government in estate taxes.[103] This tax, therefore, has no ultimate effect on the amount of death taxes paid.

"Contributions" and "gifts' to RACs are deductible from an individual's income tax provided they do not exceed 15% of his gross income, the contributions are used exclusively by the RAC, and no individual will benefit from the gift.[104] Contributions are allowed as deductions only if verified under rules and regulations prescribed by the tax commission.[105] Corporations are allowed a similar deduction for their contributions to RACs, with the deduction limited to 5% of the taxpayer's net income computed without benefit of this deduction.[106]

Utah has no state gift tax.

An *ad valorem* tax is imposed on all tangible property located in the state,[107] while intangible property is exempt.[108] The Utah Constitution (Article XIII, section 2) provides that property used exclusively for either religious worship or charitable purposes is exempt from the property tax.[109] The legislature has placed few restrictions on the exemption,[110] and attempted to provide that property used exclusively for educational purposes would be deemed to be used for charitable purposes within the exemption provided by the Utah Constitution.[111]

The Utah Supreme Court rejected the attempt of the legislature to expand or amend the state constitution by means of a statute.[112] Although the court did not specifically mention the educational purposes provision of this statute, its reasoning applies to that section. On this view, tax exemption could not be based solely upon the educational purposes of an institution, but would be available to an RAC if it maintained a genuine religious purpose.[113]

The Utah courts, moreover, have had difficulty in determining the scope of the phrase "used exclusively for." One early case distinguished between parts of the property used for the charitable purpose and other parts used for production of income, the latter being subject to the tax.[114] A later case held that statutes exempting property used for educational, religious, and charitable purposes should receive a more liberal construction than those exempting private property, and allowed an exemption to an organization engaged in incidental profitable activities.[115] In 1975, the Utah Supreme Court did not strictly construe the phrase "exclusive use," but looked to the dominant use and purpose of the property.[116] In 1976, the Court held that a church parsonage used as the pastor's residence and also for some church functions, was not "used exclusively for religious worship" and thus could not be exempted from the property tax.[117]

Two other Utah Supreme Court decisions rule against the claims of a charitable organization to exempt status. In *Friendship Manor Corp. v. Tax Commission*,[118] the Court disallowed the exempt status because it found that the services provided by the nonprofit corporation were not based on charitable criteria. In *Baker v. One Piece of Improved Real Property*,[119] the court refused to recognize as a legitimate charitable organization an entity only two percent of whose total expenditures went to charitable objects. These two cases would not, of course, govern the typical RAC, which would have no difficulty in demonstrating that education is its dominant purpose and that its expenditures are generated to achieve that educational purpose.

RAC property exempt under Article XIII, section 2, of the Constitution of Utah will also be exempt from tax assessment.[120]

Although Utah has a sales tax provision,[121] gross receipts from "all sales made to or by religious or charitable institutions in the conduct of the regular religious or charitable functions and activities" are exempt.[122] One Utah case has held a charitable institution not liable to pay the sales tax even though in one activity the institution's receipts exceeded expenses and the institution was engaged in other minor income-producing activities—the thrust of the activities was nevertheless consistent with the charitable purposes.[123] While this case is subject to a broad interpretation, the sound policy seems to be that RACs are exempt from sales tax whenever their transactions are specifically related to an educational purpose.

Utah provides for a use tax, which is a tax on goods used in the state but purchased outside the state and thus initially beyond the reach of the sales tax statute. An RAC exempt from the sales tax on particular transactions should similarly be exempt from the use tax. This is reflected in the Use Tax Act of 1937,[124] which exempts property, the storage, use, or other consumption of which the state is prohibited from taxing under its Constitution or laws.[125]

In 1980, the Utah legislature passed the Gross Receipts Tax Act, Section 2 of which provides:

The purpose of this chapter is to provide for the imposition of an in lieu excise tax on the gross receipts of corporations, other than eleemosynary, religious, or charitable institutions, operating in the State of Utah who are not otherwise required to pay income or franchise taxes to the state or to declare dividends.[126]

A taxpayer under this statute is:

[a]ny corporation, other than an eleemosynary, religious, or charitable institution, nonprofit hos-

pital, [or] educational [institution] . . . engaged in business in the state that is not otherwise required to pay income or franchise tax to the state.[127]

RACs are thus exempt from the payment of the receipts tax.

G. Fund Raising

A limited regulation of charitable solicitation is found in the criminal code chapter dealing with offenses against the public welfare.[128] "Charitable organization" includes any organization that is benevolent, philanthropic, patriotic, or eleemosynary or one purporting to be such,[129] and "contribution" means the promise or grant of any money or property.[130] A charitable organization, professional fund raiser, or professional solicitor may not use another person's name without the written consent of the person, but exempted are "religious corporations or organizations, charities, agencies, and organizations operated, supervised, or controlled by or in connection with a religious corporation or organization."[131] Although most RACs would probably qualify as an "organization operated . . . in connection with a religious corporation or organization," they should, nonetheless, be cautious about securing the consent of any person whose name they intend to use in conjunction with a fund raising effort. Further, Utah law makes it illegal to use a person's name without consent for the purpose of soliciting contributions if the person's name is listed on stationery, an advertisement, or other written medium.[132] This section has no exemption for religious corporations or related entities such as RACs.

Under Utah law, gambling is a misdemeanor[133] defined as risking anything of value on a game, the outcome of which is based on chance.[134] Gambling includes such things as lotteries, raffles, and gift enterprises,[135] but not games of skill like checkers or chess.[136] In *Albertson's Inc. v. Hansen*,[137] a supermarket had run a "double cash bingo" game in which the store gave cards and number stubs free of charge and with no purchase requirement. Even though an earlier case said that players' time, attention, thought, energy, and money spent in transportation to the store for a chance to win was consideration,[138] the *Albertson* court ruled that an illegal lottery requires the payment or promise to pay "any valuable consideration for the chance of obtaining property."[139] The court adopted the rule that a participant's time, effort, and inconvenience fall short of valuable consideration.[140] Justice Maughan, however, wrote in dissent:

If consideration may be restricted to a pecuniary basis, rather than the legal definiton of the term, . . . [w]hy may not the legislature designate that any money contributed to a lottery conducted by a charitable organization be deemed a contribution and not consideration, although a sizeable prize may be awarded? The intent is clear, any scheme involving a prize, chance, and consideration is prohibited, and no matter how cleverly devised or characterized the plan . . . , the blanket constitutional proscription is applicable.[141]

Lotteries or bingo at an RAC to raise money for the college are illegal under the gambling provision. The statute provides no exemption for religious, educational, or charitable entities, and it is unlikely that the courts would create one.

H. Miscellaneous

Utah's Charitable Trust Act of 1971,[142] relating to taxation of charitable trusts, provides for amending the trust instrument to conform to changes in the federal tax law, and for the release of power to select charitable donees.[143] The statutory interpretation of the act is to encourage charitable gifts.[144]

RACs are lawfully permitted to invest in a broad range of securities under Title 33 investment provisions.[145]

53. Vermont

A. Corporate Status

RACs may be incorporated under Vermont law as nonprofit corporations. Their formation is governed by the general provisions of Chapter 19 of Title 11 of the Vermont Statutes Annotated, which provides that:

Corporations may be organized under this chapter for any lawful purpose or purposes, including, without being limited to, any one or more of the following purposes: . . . educational; . . .religious.[1]

No corporate organization fee is payable upon formation of an RAC, but there is a statutory recording fee of $10.00 payable at the time of the filing of the articles of association.[2]

The merger, consolidation and dissolution of nonprofit colleges are governed by the Vermont Nonprofit Corporations Act.[3] In addition, Vermont courts are empowered to apply the *cy pres* doctrine when necessary.[4]

The voluntary dissolution of a nonprofit college takes effect after the governing board adopts by majority vote a resolution to dissolve[5] and the Secretary of State issues a certificate of dissolution.[6] A nonprofit college may be dissolved involuntarily by a decree of the county court in an action properly brought by the Attorney General alleging fraud, abuse of authority, or failure to name a registered agent.[7] The county court also has jurisdiction to liquidate a college's assets in an action properly brought by a member of the corporation or by a creditor.[8]

The Vermont Nonprofit Corporations Act provides that assets of a dissolving nonprofit college shall be distributed according to a procedure following that of the Model Nonprofit Corporation Act.[9]

B. State Support

The Constitution of Vermont guarantees religious freedom,[10] and contains no explicit preclusion of assistance to religiously affiliated education. Indeed, the Constitution declares that laws should encourage schools and religious activities:

All religious societies, or bodies of men that may be united or incorporated for the advancement of religion and learning . . . shall be encouraged and protected in the enjoyment of the privileges, immunities, and estates, which they in justice ought to enjoy, under such regulations as the general assembly of this state shall direct.[11]

The Vermont General Assembly has created an Educational Buildings Financing Agency empowered to acquire, hold, lease, and dispose of property to assist eligible institutions.[12] While RACs are not specifically mentioned, they may receive assistance under this legislation since "eligible institutions" includes any private nonprofit college or university in the state.[13] The constitutionality of this act was tested in *Vermont Educational Building Financing Agency v. Mann*,[14] which held that permitting a church-related institution of learning to participate in the assistance provided by the act did not unconstitutionally serve the cause of religion.[15]

Vermont provides scholarships, grants, and loans to students who are state residents under a variety of provisions of Chapter 87 of Title 16. Under the statute, assistance is available to students attending colleges which are accredited.[16] No specific mention is made of the effect of religious affiliation on the granting of financial assistance, so that students attending RACs which are otherwise qualified should be eligible for these state-supported scholarships, grants and loans.

C. Personnel

RACs would seem to be included within the definition of employer for the purposes of the Vermont Fair Employment Practices statute, since that category includes any corporation "which has one or more individuals performing services for it within this state."[17] The statute makes it unlawful to discriminate against any person in employment on the basis of race, color, religion, ancestry, national origin, sex, or place of birth, unless there exists a "bona fide occupational qualification" which requires a person with certain such characteristics.[18] As a result, RACs are bound by this provision in their employment practices, absent a bona fide occupational qualification. This provides, of course, an extremely narrow exception for religious preference in employment by RACs, one likely to be helpful, at best, only in employment of faculty for religiously oriented courses or of certain counseling personnel. It is not likely that an RAC would be successful in arguing a right to exercise religious preference in faculty positions generally despite its interest in establishing on campus a pervasive presence of faculty of a certain religious persuasion.

Under the same subchapter, all contracts between the state of Vermont or any of its contracting agencies and any contractor are to include a provision obligating the contractor to comply with the nondiscrimination provision, and requiring the contractor to include a similar provision in all subcontracts.[19] Thus any RAC engaged in a contractual relationship with the state would be bound as both a contractor and as an employer.

The general provisions setting a minimum wage include any corporation within the definition of an employer, and RACs are given no exemption.[20] Since employers employing two or more employees are covered by the statute, minimum wage requirements would apply to RACs.[21]

RACs are also covered in Vermont by general worker's compensation legislation. Covered employment is defined statutorily as that "in any trade or occupation, notwithstanding that an employer may be a nonprofit corporation."[22] Workman's compensation legislation applies to all employment in the state for which such compensation is not provided by the laws of the United States.[23]

Under the chapter on unemployment compensation, a covered "employer includes:

Any employing unit for which service in employment for a religious . . . educational, or other organization as defined in (6)(A)(ix) of this section is performed after December 31, 1971.[24]

This is qualified by the following:

The term employment shall also include service for any employing unit which is performed . . . by an individual in the employ of a religious, charitable, educational or other organization but only if

(a) the service is excluded from employment as defined in the Federal Unemployment Tax Act solely by reason of section 3306(c)(8) of that act, and

(b) the organization had four or more individuals in employment for some portion of a day in each of 20 different weeks, whether or not such weeks were consecutive, within either the current or preceding calendar year, regardless of whether they were employed at the same moment of time.[25]

"Employing unit" is defined as:

Any individual or type of organization, including any . . . corporation . . . which has had in its employ, since January 1, 1936, one or more individuals performing services for it within the state.[26]

Service performed in the employ of a religious or educational organization described in section 501(c)(3) of the Internal Revenue Code of 1954,[27] and thereby exempt from federal taxation, is excluded from "employment" as defined in section 3306(c)(8) of the Federal Unemployment Tax Act.[28] Thus an RAC is generally subject to unemployment compensation legislation if it qualifies for exempt status under section 501(c)(3) and employed four or more persons for some portion of a day in each of twenty weeks during the current or previous calendar year.

D. Students

Owners or operators of places of public accommodations in Vermont are prohibited from withholding any of the facilities of the place of public accommodation from any person because of the person's race, creed, color, or national origin;[29] or because the person is blind and accompanied by a guide dog.[30]

A place of public accommodation is any "school, restaurant, store, or any other establishment which caters or offers its services or facilities or goods to the general public."[31] If it could be said that an RAC is a "school" or a place which "offers its services" to the general public, then the statute may affect the RAC's admissions policies. The word "school" is not usually used to mean "college," although colleges are conceptually included within its meaning. The statute lists "school," moreover, with "restaurant" and "store," which are profit-oriented establishments; RACs could be excluded from the law's coverage as non-profit institutions.

RACs could be exempt from the application of the public accommodations law in the case of certain religiously motivated discrimination in the admissions process:

This section shall not be construed to bar any religious denominational institution or organization or any organization, operated for education . . . which is operated or controlled by or in connection with a religious organization, from limiting admissions to or giving preference to persons of the same religion or denomination or making selections in a manner calculated by the religious organization to promote the religious principles for which the organization is established or maintained.[32]

Although this exemption clause is contained in the section which bars discrimination in real estate transactions, it suggests an intention not to interfere with RAC admissions policies.

E. Facilities

Once students are admitted to an RAC (which might be considered a place of public accommodation),[33] however, they would be protected in the use of facilities there against discrimination on the basis of race, creed, color, or national origin. Such discrimination would be barred in any restaurant or other facility owned or operated by an RAC which caters or offers its services or facilities to the general public. The language of the statute could be construed to exclude facilities on the campus of an RAC which do not cater or offer their services or facilities to the general public, such as a dining facility serving only students. Since, however, the statute was amended in 1977 specifically to include a "school" within the definition of a place of public accommodation, courts may construe the statute to apply to all facilities owned or operated by RACs.

Vermont's fair housing law bars the sale, lease, or other transfer of title, occupancy, or possession of real estate offered for sale or lease to the general public on account of race, religious creed, color, or national origin.[34] The same section, however, allows RACs an exemption to the law with respect to religiously motivated discrimination.[35]

All new buildings which are considered "public buildings" must meet certain standards for accessibility to the physically handicapped.[36] These standards are set by American National Standards Institute specification A117.1-1961, as modified by the Vermont Architectural Barrier Compliance Board.[37]

Churches, schoolhouses, and school halls are specifically included within the statutory definition of "public building."[38] While they are not specifically mentioned, new facilities constructed for use by an RAC would seem to be subject to these accessibility standards.

Under Vermont Occupational Safety and Health legislation (VOSHA), any corporation employing one or more persons is considered an "employer," and is subject to the provisions of the VOSHA Code.[39] RACs are given no exemption from this definition and are therefore subject to the regulations affecting all employers.

F. State Taxation

Corporations organized for religious or educational purposes are exempt from income taxation in Vermont.[40] All RACs would be included within this definition, and would therefore be exempt from income taxation.

In Vermont, real and personal property which is "used for public, pious, or charitable uses" is exempt from taxation[41] and land "owned or leased by colleges, academies, or other public schools is also exempt."[42] RACs are, therefore, entitled to the exemption.

Another provision of the same title, however, seems to be somewhat inconsistent.[43] According to this section, real property acquired after April 1, 1941, by any college or university which would have been exempt under § 3802(4) is to be taxed at the value fixed in the appraisal next preceding the date of its acquisition. The same section also provides, however, that the voters of any town or city may vote to exempt such property from taxation.[44]

Property owned by RACs may be exempt under a still later section. It specifically exempts under the "public, pious, and charitable uses" clause of § 3802(4) school buildings and certain adjacent land "owned or kept by a religious society" and used as a school.[45] The "owned or kept by a religious society" language makes this exemption extremely narrow and perhaps unavailable to most RACs.

Vermont has repealed its provisions relating to inheritance taxes.[46]

Vermont imposes an estate tax designed merely to channel to Vermont, by virtue of the credit allowed against the federal estate tax for state death taxes, moneys that would otherwise go to the federal government in estate taxes.[47]

This tax, therefore, has no ultimate effect on the amount of death taxes paid.

Vermont's gift tax has been repealed.[48]

Vermont allows a deduction for gifts to RACs by corporations[49] and individuals by incorporating the federal deduction.[50]

Since the Vermont personal income tax is computed as a straight percentage of the taxpayer's federal income tax liability,[51] an individual taxpayer is, in effect, given a state deduction for his federally deductible contributions to RACs.

The Vermont corporate income tax is determined by the corporation's federal taxable income[52] and "taxable income" equals gross income minus deductions like the deduction for contributions to RACs.[53] By incorporating the federal deduction, a comparable state deduction is afforded corporate contributions to RACs.

All organizations which qualify for exempt status under § 501(c)(3) of the Internal Revenue Code[54] are not subject to sales and use taxes provided that their activities are not mainly commercial enterprises, and that the sale or service is for the exempt purpose of the organization.[55] Additionally, the organization must first have obtained a certificate from the Commissioner of Internal Revenue stating that it is entitled to the exemption.[56] Presumably, most RACs would fall within the category of organizations exempt under § 501(c)(3), and would as a result be exempt from sales and use taxes for those transactions otherwise covered by the exemption.

G. Fund Raising

Vermont does not comprehensively regulate charitable solicitations.

While RACs are not specifically mentioned, nonprofit corporations are generally exempt from the prohibition against lotteries in Vermont.[57]

54. Virginia

A. Corporate Status

Virginia refers to nonprofit corporations as "non-stock corporations."[1] Such corporations may be formed for any lawful purpose[2] and are prohibited from issuing dividends or shares of stock.[3] The specific requirements for incorporation with regard to the articles of incorporation, certification by the State Corporation Commission of Virginia, membership, and boards of directors, among others, are spelled out in the Virginia Nonstock Corporation Act.[4]

The corporation is granted powers, *inter alia*, to sue, to hold real and personal property, to make bylaws, to dispose of property, to make contracts, to borrow money, to elect officers and to exercise all powers necessary to effect any of the purposes for which it was organized.[5] All nonprofit RACs would be organized under these provisions.

An incorporated educational institution which owns over a thousand acres outside of a city or town may by a majority vote of the members of the board of directors sell or convey that property in excess of one thousand acres, notwithstanding any contrary provision in charter, deed, or will.[6]

The governing body of every higher educational institution, including an RAC, has broad powers to establish regulations and rules for admissions, employment, curriculum, and administrative procedures.[7] However, Virginia has recently enacted legislation requiring the State Council of Higher Education[8] to approve the granting of traditionally secular degrees by religious institutions.[9] This legislation raises constitutional questions of free exercise and excessive governmental entanglement. The Council, which supervises public colleges primarily, also performs in an advisory capacity to private, accredited, and nonprofit colleges whose primary purpose is to provide collegiate education and not to provide religious training or theological education.[10] These services are carried out by a Private College Advisory Committee, formed by the Council, which is representative of the private sector of nonprofit higher education.[11] This committee can make suggestions about academics, administration, finance, and space utilization as well as review and advise on joint activities, including contracts for services between such private institutions (RACs included) and public institutions or state agencies.[12]

Any private institution of higher education, including an RAC, which offers certain off-campus courses, such as extension courses and other continuing education programs within the state, must register by July 1 of the preceding year with the State Council of Higher Education.[13]

Virginia has adopted the Uniform Management of Institutional Funds Act,[14] which defines "institution" as either an incorporated or unincorporated organization organized and operated exclusively for educational, religious, charitable, or other eleemosynary purposes.[15] The funds must be held by the institution for its exclusive use in order to be included within this act. Other sections cover investment authorization,[16] investment management,[17] standards of conduct[18] and the release by the donor of restrictions on use.[19]

The merger, consolidation, and dissolution of nonprofit colleges are governed by the Virginia Nonstock Corporation Act, which is closely patterned on the Model Nonprofit Corporation Act.[20] In addition, the Virginia courts are empowered to apply the *cy pres* doctrine when necesssary.[21]

The procedure for the voluntary dissolution of nonprofit colleges in Virginia is patterned on the provisions of the Model Act. After observing these provisions, the governing board of the college authorizes articles of dissolution to be delivered to the State Corporation Commission which officially files the articles and issues a certificate of dissolution.[22] Nonprofit colleges may also be automatically dissolved if for two successive years they fail to file annual reports as prescribed by law.[23] The State Corporation Commission may involuntarily dissolve a nonprofit corporation for abuse of authority or failure to maintain a registered agent in the state.[24] The circuit courts also have jurisdiction to liquidate the college's assets in an action properly brought by a member of the corporation or by a creditor.[25]

The Virginia Nonstock Corporation Act provides that assets of a dissolving nonprofit college shall be distributed according to a procedure closely following that of the Model Nonprofit Corporation Act.[26]

B. State Support

State aid to private higher education is on a relatively firm base in Virginia, with specific constitutional provisions permitting aid to students enrolled in most institutions of higher education. Essentially, only sectarian elementary and secondary schools, and *primarily religious* colleges (along with the students of each) are effectively refused state aid.[27]

Virginia's parallel to the First Amendment's religion clauses[28] is worded very broadly. It provides for free exercise and prohibits the establishment of religion.[29] It bars special privileges to any religious sect or denomination as well as the compulsion of support for any church or ministry.[30] It allows each person "to select his religious instructor, and to make for

his support such private contract as he shall please."[31] The United States Supreme Court has deemed this state constitutional section coextensive with the federal Constitution's First Amendment.[32]

Originally, the state constitution specifically authorized aid only to private, *non*sectarian institutions.[33] A later amendment, however, permits the state legislature to provide for grants or loans to students in private, nonprofit Virginia colleges, whether church-related or not, "whose primary purpose is to provide collegiate or graduate education and not to provide religious training or theological education."[34] (The provision authorizes legislation for a state agency to help such institutions in borrowing funds for facilities construction and legislation allowing public contracts with these institutions for the provision of educational and similar services.)[35] This provision, clearly intended to authorize grants and loans to students at certain sectarian institutions, has a primarily secular purpose and therefore does not violate the federal First Amendment.[36] Moreover, loans legislatively authorized pursuant to this provision are not invalid under a separate state constitutional provision[37] barring appropriations to religious bodies.[38]

The state constitution prohibits granting the state's credit, or that of any of its divisions, to any person, association, or corporation as well as involvement in internal improvements other than parks and roads.[39] This provision's effect on state aid to private education has not yet been litigated.

Some RACs would be able to obtain funding for educational facilities under the Virginia Educational Facilities Act,[40] which is specifically authorized by the state constitution.[41] Tracking the constitutional language, the act limits its benefits to *nonprofit* institutions within the state whose "primary purpose is to provide collegiate or graduate education and not religious training or theological education."[42]

The Virginia College Building Authority[43] administers this program and may float bonds backed by the credit or mortgage of the specific institution (not by the credit of the state) and payable solely out of the revenues of the authority or of the educational institution.[44] No facility acquired, built, or refinanced with help from the Authority may be used for sectarian instruction, as a place of worship, or "primarily in connection with any part of the program of a school or department of divinity for any religious denomination."[45]

All state agencies, local governments, and public educational institutions are authorized to contract wih private educational nonprofit institutions for the provision or receipt of educational and related services.[46] The primary purpose of such institutions must be educational and not religious.[47] These services encompass not only courses, but the use of professional personnel and real or personal property, or "any other activity dealing with . . . educational or related subjects, or providing public service or student service activities."[48] Approval of the State Council of Higher Education is required whenever a public college is a party to the contract.[49] Contracts between private colleges and the Commonwealth (or any of its subdivisions) must be reported to the Council.[50] The authority to contract, under this law, includes that necessary to accept gifts or matching funds to help programs.[51] This provision does not restrict or prohibit the use of any federal, state or local funds under any federal or state appropriation or grant.[52]

Any such contract for $10,000 or more would be subject to the standards outlined in the Virginia Fair Employment Contracting Act,[53] which prohibits a contractor from employment discrimination on the basis of race, religion, color, sex, or national origin, except where religion, sex, or national origin is a bona fide occupational qualification.[54]

Countries, cities, and towns in Virginia can make appropriations of funds, or personal or real property to any "charitable institution" located within their boundaries unless the institution is "controlled in whole or in part by any church or sectarian society."[55] It is doubtful that all RACs would be considered "charitable."

In any event, the "controlled" criterion, although extremely vague, would probably not cover the majority of RACs.

Article 8, section 11 of the state constitution specifically authorizes the two types of tuition grant and loan programs in the state. The first, the Tuition Assistance Grant and Loan Act,[56] is directed at private accredited and nonprofit institutions in the state whose primary purpose must be "to provide collegiate or graduate education and not to provide religious training or theological education."[57] This program, which is not based on need, authorizes a maximum award limited to the average appropriation per student for the previous year represented in state funds for public colleges, i.e., a type of tuition equalization program.[58] Participation is limited to undergraduates, and to programs not "providing religious training or theological education of an indoctrinating nature."[59] The recipient, who must be a bona fide state resident,[60] may participate no more than four years.[61] Loan repayment may take the form of money[62] or of actions beneficial to the state, including active duty in the armed forces, residence and domicile within the state, or employment by the state or by a religious, charitable or other similar society.[63] The rate of repayment generally ranges from one to two years per year of assistance received, depending on the method chosen.[64] The State Council of Higher Education administers the program.[65]

The second program, the College Scholarship Assistance Act,[66] provides for grants and loans based partly on financial need to students in accredited, degree-granting public and private colleges in the state. An eligible RAC must be nonprofit and must demonstrate that its primary purpose is not to provide religious training or theological education.[67] Eligible students must be domiciled in Virginia.[68]

Under the program, awards are limited to $1000 per year[69] and must be used for education-related expenses (including room and board).[70] The loan repayment provisions of this program[71] are the same as for the Tuition Assistance Grant and Loan Act.[72] The program is under the control of the Virginia Education Loan Authority,[73] which provides loans to resident students (and their parents) of public or private colleges in the state for educational purposes only.[74]

The State Board of Education provides teaching scholarship loans to students who, preparing to teach at Virginia public schools, attend a nonprofit college with a primarily secular purpose.[75] Repayment may be postponed or even cancelled by the Board at its discretion.[76]

Nursing scholarships are made available by

the Advisory Committee to the State Board of Health for attendance at "a school of professional nursing in this state."[77] Scholarships for dental hygienists attending any accredited school of dental hygiene in the state are also provided.[78] Scholarships for work training in fields related to mental health and retardation are available through the Department of Mental Hygiene and Hospitals, with funding provided by the legislature.[79]

C. Personnel

Virginia does not have a comprehensive fair employment practice law. However, the state of Virginia does prohibit employment discrimination on the basis of sex under its equal pay provision.[80] Discrimination in employment because of physical handicap is also prohibited where the handicap is not related to the person's qualifications and ability to perform the job.[81] There is no comprehensive definition of "physical handicap" beyond the broad categories of blindness, deafness, and physical disabilities.[82] There is therefore no indication that either people addicted to the use of alcohol or drugs or those actually using alcohol or drugs are included within the term "physically disabled," so it is quite possible that any employer, including an RAC, could refuse to hire someone with these addictions. Even if these are considered handicaps within the law, any inability to do the job because of them would remove the person from the law's protection.

The laws covering these areas describe "employer"[83] and "employee"[84] broadly enough to include virtually all RACs as employers and any person working for an RAC for pay as employee.

Beyond these specific areas of prohibited discrimination, an RAC could, under state law, exercise broad discretion, including religious selectivity, in its hiring practices.[85] There may be additional constraints, however, if the RAC contracts with a governmental unit to provide services or goods.[86]

Virginia's Minimum Wage Act[87] sets a minimum hourly rate.[88] Under this act, "employer" would include virtually all RACs.[89] An "employee," under the Act, does not include a person engaged in the activities of an educa-

tional, charitable, religious, or nonprofit organization "where the relationship of employer-employee does not, in fact, exist" or where the services rendered for such organizations are volunteered.[90] Also not protected are those under sixteen years of age,[91] those whose pay is based on the amount of work performed,[92] and those impaired by a mental or physical deficiency.[93] Students participating in a bona fide educational or apprenticeship program[94] and full-time students who work not more than twenty hours a week[95] (or who are on a work study program)[96] fall outside the act.

Virginia's maximum daily work hours law covers only children under sixteen.[97] However, child labor laws (except for the provision prohibiting cruelty and injuries)[98] do not apply to children working for a "corporation the property of which is tax exempt."[99] This exemption could include some RACs.[100]

The Virginia Workmen's Compensation Act[101] applies to corporations[102] with three or more employees.[103] Generally RACs are covered unless some of their employees come within the exceptions for executive officers,[104] for employment that is not in the usual course of an employer's business,[105] and for domestic servants and casual employees.[106] Otherwise RACs are included within the Act because a private corporation such as an RAC generally will have more than three regular employees.[107]

RACs may elect to include exempted employees within the coverage of the Act by insuring them. If, however, such an insured employee elects not to be bound by the Act, the employee must give proper notice to the Industrial Commission.[108] An employee who has exempted himself may waive such an exemption at any time by giving proper notice and thereby come under the provisions of the Act.[109]

RACs may choose to carry compensation insurance, become a self-insurer or join a licensed group self-insurance association.[110]

Under the Virginia Unemployment Compensation Act[111] services performed for religious or educational organizations and, therefore, for RACs, constitute employment,[112] if two conditions are satisfied.[113] First, such service must be exempt from the definition of employment in the Federal Unemployment Tax Act solely due to section 3306(c)(8).[114] Second, the organization must employ at least four individuals "for some portion of a day in each of twenty different weeks, whether or not such weeks were consecutive, within either the current or preceding calendar year, regardless of whether they were employed at the same moment of time."[115]

The Act provides the following exemptions which apply directly to RACs: (1) services performed for a church or for an association of churches;[116] (2) services performed for an organization run primarily for religious purposes and controlled by a church or by an association of churches;[117] (3) services performed by ordained ministers or by members of religious orders in the exercise of their duties;[118] and (4) services performed for a school which prior to January 1, 1978, did not qualify as an institution of higher education.[119] Because the scope of these exemptions is narrow, most services performed in the employ of RACs are covered under the Act. Other relevant exclusions from the Virginia Act's definition of employment include (1) domestic service for a local college club or local chapter of a college fraternity or sorority, if total remuneration in any quarter of the current or preceding calendar year was less than $1,000.00;[120] (2) service for which unemployment compensation is payable under a system set up by an act of Congress;[121] (3) service performed for a school or college by one of its regularly enrolled students;[122] and (4) service performed by a student under the age of twenty-two at an accredited nonprofit or public educational institution in a full-time program, taken for credit and combining academic instruction and work experience.[123] The statute also excludes from coverage certain organizations which are tax-exempt under federal statutes,[124] if the remuneration paid is less than $50.00.[125]

Nonprofit organizations, and therefore RACs, may elect to make payments in lieu of contributions. To take advantage of this option, an organization must fit the definition in section 501(c)(3) of the Internal Revenue Code and qualify as tax-exempt under section 501(a) of the Code.[126] The election is effective for a period of one year upon filing of written notice with the Virginia Employment Commission.[127] Required payments are equal to the amount of regular benefits plus one-half the amount of extended benefits paid.[128] Organizations not otherwise subject to the provisions of the Act may elect to participate in the program for a minimum of two years.[129]

Virginia has a comprehensive labor relations law.[130] RACs would be employers under its provisions.[131]

A non-stock corporation, and therefore virtually every RAC, is allowed to indemnify its officers, directors, employees, or agents who are parties to a suit in their corporate capacity.[132]

Under Virginia law, no employer may, as a condition of employment, require a prospective employee to answer questions in a polygraph test concerning prior sexual activities unless there has been a criminal conviction for such activities.[133]

D. Students

Virginia gives each educational institution broad powers with regard to student admissions, conduct, and dismissal;[134] no state legislation directly regulates admissions to private institutions such as RACs.

A legislative provision restricting the collection and dissemination of information concerning the religious preferences and affiliations of students[135] applies only to state institutions and not, therefore, to RACs.

High school principals may furnish lists of certain high school pupils' names and addresses to public or private colleges, but the college cannot use this information for "purposes not directly related to the academic or professional goals of the institution."[136]

E. Facilities

There is no general public accommodations law in Virginia. The handicapped are given "equal" rights of access to public places and places of public accommodation,[137] which include theaters, hotels, lodging places, and "other places to which the general public is invited."[138] This legislation would cover restaurants, stores, and the like, open to the general public, on an RAC campus.

Virginia's Fair Housing Law[139] forbids discrimination, in the sale or rental of housing, on the basis of race, sex, color, religion, or national origin.[140] Enforced by the Virginia Real Estate Commission,[141] the law allows a religious organization or any nonprofit institution "operated, supervised, or controlled by or in conjunction with a religious organization, association, or society" to limit the sale, rental, or occupancy of its housing facilities (not operated for a commercial purpose) to persons of the same religion, or to give preference to such persons in making its housing available.[142]

Not all RACs may be considered sufficiently "operated, supervised, or controlled by or in conjunction with" a religious organization to come within the exemption. It should be emphasized that use of the phrase "or in conjunction with" loosens considerably the intensity of the required affiliation. In any event, the exemption limits the basis of selectivity to the particular religious affiliation of the institution, although it is not clear how broadly the term "religion" is used. For example, is a Baptist institution limited to favoring Baptists or could it favor Christians? The spirit of the law would seem to favor the latter interpretation.

The housing facilities referred to here could include both those for students and those for staff, although that is not explained, and is not limited to on-campus housing.

A private educational institution (as well as state schools) may require that single-family residences, dorm rooms, and restrooms which it owns or operates be sexually segregated.[143] This would presumably include both on- and off-campus housing.

The handicapped are also entitled to full and equal access to housing accommodations offered for rent or lease in the state,[144] but no special modification of the property by the owner is required.[145] This broadly worded provision would seem to prohibit an RAC from refusing housing on the basis of handicaps, qualified by the RAC's right to prefer individuals of its own religion.

Since most RACs restrict housing to their own students (except perhaps for some employees), it could be argued that these laws indirectly regulate the admission of students (for example, the handicapped). This may conflict with the broad admissions power, otherwise granted colleges.[146] There is, however, no significant indication that the legislature meant to control admissions through the housing law. Moreover, for virtually all RACs, the only significant preference likely to be exercised in admissions is with regard to religion or, in the case of single-sex schools, sex. For most RACs with the required religious affiliation, such preferences are fully accommodated by the housing law exemptions.

RAC restaurants are subject to the same health standards applied to other Virginia restaurants.[147] There is no exemption for an RAC's snack bars, vending machines, or "other public eating and drinking establishments or food services areas," since public and private colleges are explicitly included.[148] However, unless the public is allowed to use the services of the student dining halls, it would appear that such eating places are exempt.

Virginia's law concerning safety in the workplace is not modeled upon the federal OSHA statute. It is intended to act in conjunction with the federal statute. The statute[149] authorizes the state Department of Labor and Industry, through the Safety and Health Codes Commission, to make rules and regulations necessary for the administration and enforcement of state occupational safety activities and the federal OSHA statute.[150] The statute, however, states that state standards shall not exceed federal standards.[151] An employer is defined broadly as any individual or business group doing business or operating in the state which employs another to work for wages, salaries, or commission and any entity that acts in the interest of an employer in relation to an employee.[152] An employee is defined as any person permitted, required, or directed to engage in employment for compensation.[153]

F. State Taxation

Incorporated nonprofit RACs are exempt from Virginia's income tax.[154]

The Virginia Franchise tax is based on the corporation's "authorized maximum capital stock."[155] Since nonprofit corporations are nonstock corporations under state law,[156] this tax is of no significance to virtually all RACs.

Under state inheritance and estate tax laws, any property devised by will to any nonprofit corporation, trust, fund, or foundation "organized and operated exclusively for religious, charitable, scientific, literary or educational purposes" is excluded from inheritance taxation and from estate taxation for estates of decedents dying before 1980.[157] This would include virtually all RACs. An identical exemption[158] was provided under the Gift Tax Law.[159] For decedents dying after January 1, 1980, there is no longer an applicable inheritance tax nor a specific estate tax deduction for property passing to institutions such as RACs.[160]

The Virginia estate tax merely channels to Virginia, by virtue of the credit allowed against the federal estate tax for state death taxes, moneys that would otherwise go to the federal government in estate taxes. This tax, therefore, has no ultimate effect on the amount of death taxes paid.

The Virginia personal income tax is geared to the individual's federal adjusted gross income, with additions and deductions as authorized.[161] Since contributions to nonprofit religious or educational institutions are deductible for federal income tax purposes,[162] a deduction for these contributions can be made from this base (the federal adjusted gross income) for state income tax purposes. An individual has two options: if he elected to itemize on his federal return he can deduct the amount allowed for itemized deductions or he can deduct the amount allowed for the standard deduction.[163] There is no corresponding deduction provision for corporations.

Implementing the state constitutional provision,[164] the Virginia Code exempts from taxation the real and personal property of a nonprofit educational institution as long as the property is used primarily for literary, scientific, or educational purposes.[165] Property owned by a church or religious association or denomination and used exclusively on a nonprofit basis for charitable, religious, or educational purposes is also exempt.[166] Under these two statutes, the real and personal property of virtually all RACs is tax-exempt. Some property of incorporated alumni associations and charitable foundations may also be exempt.[167]

The exemption is determined by the use of the property, not by the profits realized.[168] There is no limit on the amount of such property that can be held by institutions like RACs.

Private colleges are exempt from service charges that might otherwise be imposed on tax-exempt property by local government, as long as the property is used exclusively for private educational or charitable purposes and not for profit.[169] Faculty and staff housing are subject to these service charges,[170] however, as well might be stores and other profit-oriented uses of property.

Exempt under the Virginia sales and use tax law are, *inter alia*: (1) sales of school textbooks to students by a nonprofit college;[171] (2) "occasional sales";[172] (3) tangible personal property for use by a nonprofit college;[173] (4) tangible personal property (except for recording or reproduction materials) purchased by nonprofit churches "for use in religious worship services;"[174] and (5) "religious educational materials" for use in a regular school of religious education.[175]

Deeds conveying real estate to an incorporated nonprofit educational institution, when such property is to be used for educational purposes and not for profit,[176] and deeds conveying property to the trustees of any religious body to be used exclusively for religious purposes,[177] are exempt from the state recordation tax. Virtually all RACs could take advantage of this exemption.

Virginia's Motor Vehicle Sales and Use Tax[178] law exempts vehicles owned and used by a nonprofit church to transport ten or more passengers,[179] and vehicles loaned to a private nonprofit educational institution for use in its drivers training courses.[180]

A nonprofit organization, and therefore virtually any RAC, is not liable for the tax otherwise payable for conducting an auction or other sale, as long as all sales are made directly by it.[181] The charter fee for a nonstock corporation (including most RACs) is fifty dollars.[182] Nonstock corporations must also pay an annual registration fee of ten dollars.[183]

G. Fund Raising

Virginia's comprehensive legislation[184] on charitable solicitations exempts certain educational institutions from some of its provisions. To be so exempt, an RAC must be accredited by a regional accrediting association or confine its solicitation to its student body, alumni, faculty, and trustees, and their families.[185] Qualifying institutions are exempt only from registration[186] and record-keeping[187] requirements.[188] Such institutions would still be bound by the other provisions of the law,[189] including that setting out prohibited acts.[190] Although an RAC exempt from the registration requirements need not be licensed under local solicitation laws, it may obtain a local license without payment of a fee if it complies with the ordinance's requirements.[191]

Although gambling is forbidden in Virginia,[192] educational or religious organizations (including RACs) may conduct bingo games and raffles as fund raising projects.[193] A yearly permit issued by local authorities is required.[194] The twenty-five dollar fee is subject to the local governing body's discretion and may be waived.[195] Receipts must be used for the religious, charitable, community, or educational purposes which activated the organization's formation.[196] The games and raffles have prize money limits and frequency limits.[197]

H. Miscellaneous

A statutory prohibition of resales for profit of admission tickets for public events exempts "religious . . . or educational organizations where all or a portion of the admission price" reverts to the sponsoring group.[198]

Virginia, as a member of the Compact for Education,[199] has representatives on the Education Commission of the States.[200]

55. Washington

A. Corporate Status

The Washington Nonprofit Corporations Act[1] allows nonprofit corporations to be organized for any lawful purpose, including educational, religious, scientific, cultural, and literary.[2] One or more persons may incorporate a nonprofit corporation by filing articles of incorporation with the Secretary of State[3] and paying a $20.00 fee.[4] Such corporations are prohibited form issuing stock and distributing dividends.[5]

The statute provides that the affairs of the corporation shall be managed by a board of directors.[6] There are no statutory qualifications for members of the board but any qualifications imposed by the corporation must be set forth in the articles of incorporation or in the bylaws.[7] A minimum of three persons on the board of directors is required.[8]

A religiously affiliated college (RAC) not accredited by a state-recognized accrediting agency is subject to the Educational Services Registration Act.[9] The Act requires certain educational institutions to register, provide information, and file a surety bond on an annual basis, and bans misleading advertising.[10]

The merger or consolidation[11] and the dissolution[12] of nonprofit colleges in Washington are governed by that state's Nonprofit Corporation Act, which is closely patterned on the Model Nonprofit Corporation Act.[13] In addition, Washington courts will apply the doctrine of *cy pres* when necessary.[14]

The procedures for voluntary dissolution are also closely patterned on the provisions in the Model Act. After observing these requirements, the governing board of a dissolving college authorizes articles of dissolution to be delivered to the Secretary of State, who officially files the articles and issues a certificate of dissolution.[15] Under some circumstances, the Attorney General may seek a decree of involuntary dissolution from a superior court.[16]

The assets of a dissolving college in Washington are distributed according to a plan closely patterned on the provisions of the Model Act.[17] The Washington statute does not make express provision for transfer of assets of a dissolving college to the state for distribution to creditors who are unknown or who cannot be found.[18] Under some circumstances the members of the governing board are required to hold title to the property of a dissolving college as trustees for the benefit of its creditors.[19]

B. State Support

The Washington State Constitution contains a number of potential bars to state programs attempting to provide direct or indirect financial aid to RACs. The Constitution specifies that no public money shall be used to support any religious establishment or institution,[20] that schools supported in whole or in part with state funds must be free from sectarian control or influence[21] and that state credit cannot be given or loaned to any individual, association or corporation.[22]

Based on these provisions, the Washington

Supreme Court recently declared unconstitutional two programs enacted by the state legislature that would have provided indirect aid to RACs. The court rejected a tuition supplement scheme that provided each student attending a private or public institution of higher education with a grant of one hundred dollars,[23] even though students pursuing degrees in theology were excluded. The Court reasoned that the ultimate result of the aid was support of the private school and, thus, the program was violative of the state constitution.[24] The Court also rejected, on the same basis, a program creating a state agency which would purchase educational loans made by banking or educational institutions to needy students.[25]

Although these failed to pass constitutional muster, there remain in effect two programs providing indirect benefit to RACs. The state legislature has established a student financial aid program to assist financially disadvantaged students, domiciled in Washington, who are attending institutions of higher education.[26] All eligible students[27] are awarded loans or grants under a formula established by the council for postsecondary education.[28] Any aid received must be applied toward the cost of tuition, room, board, books, and fees.[29] This provision has not been tested in the state courts. It has been suggested that, if tested, this aid program would be constitutionally invalid on the same basis as those programs previously ruled unconstitutional.[30]

RACs also receive indirect financial benefit through the College Work-Study Program.[31] The program calls for a tripartite arrangement among the state, the institution of higher education and the employer. Under the program, students are given work related to their academic pursuits and the state contributes a share of the compensation paid to the student-employee.[32] Students pursuing degrees in theology are precluded from participation in the program.[33]

C. Personnel

The Washington Anti-Discrimination Law[34] prohibits discriminatory practices on the basis of race, creed, color, national origin, sex, marital status, age, or the presence of any sensory, mental, or physical handicap.[35] The Washing-

ton State Human Rights Commission enforces the act.[36]

The right to employment without discrimination is expressly enumerated as one of the civil rights protected by the anti-discrimination statute.[37] Specifically prohibited as an unfair employment practice is the refusal to hire or the discharge or discrimination in terms or conditions of employment on the basis of any of the above-mentioned protected classifications.[38] Employment notices, forms, or pre-employment inquiries referring to any of the protected classifications are also prohibited.[39] It is also an unfair employment practice to discriminate against an employee who has participated in the filing of an unfair employment practice charge.[40]

The statute permits an employer to base hiring decisions on one of the protected classifications only if it constitutes a *bona fide* occupational qualification [BFOQ].[41] Although the statute does not define BFOQ, regulations promulgated by the Washington State Human Rights Commission have indicated that the term is to be narrowly applied.[42] Thus far the Commission has recognized two areas in which race, creed, color, national origin, age, sex, marital status, or handicap may be a BFOQ: (1) where it is essential to, or will contribute to the accomplishment of the purposes for which the person is hired; and (2) where it must be considered in order to correct a condition of unequal employment opportunity.[43]

The Supreme Court of Washington has held that a handicapped person, for the purposes of the anti-discrimination law, is one with a condition which prevents, in some manner, the full and normal use of his faculties.[44] Under this nebulous definition alcoholism or drug addiction could be handicaps within the scope of the statute. (In fact, this is the position of the Washington State Human Rights Commission.)[45] Use of alcohol or drugs affecting one's job performance, however, could trigger the BFOQ exemption.

The Washington courts have determined that, for purposes of the anti-discrimination law, "marital status is not limited to conditions such as being married, single, or divorced."[46] Thus, it would seem that an employer would be prohibited from making an employment decision on the basis of abortion or single parenthood.

All of this, however, is quite immaterial to RACs since the Washington State Human Rights Commission considers all RACs to be religious or sectarian organizations,[47] and such organizations, if nonprofit, are not considered employers for purposes of the anti-discrimination law.[48] "Religious or sectarian organizations . . . are wholly exempt from the law. They are free to discriminate on the basis of handicap, race, sex, age, *et cetera*, as well as creed."[49]

Generally RACs are included within the scope of the term "employer" as it is used in the minimum wage law.[50] The minimum wage law applies to all employees who are eighteen years of age or older. The wage rate varies according to specific occupations.[51] Overtime wage rates (for more than forty hours per week) must be at least one and one-half times the regular pay rate.[52]

There are two exceptions to the minimum wage law of particular relevance to RACs. The minimum wage law is not applicable to any student employed by the institution of higher education in which he is enrolled.[53] Also, any individual engaged in activities of an educational, charitable, or religious body or agency or nonprofit organization is not within the scope of the law if, in fact, the employer-employee relationship does not exist.[54]

There is a provision for special certificates to be issued by the Director of Labor and Industries which allow employers to pay less than the minimum wage to learners, apprentices and persons whose earning capacity is impaired by age or physical or mental deficiency or impairment.[55]

There are no maximum hour laws applicable to RACs.

The Washington Industrial Insurance Law[56] contains the state's workmen's compensation provisions covering all employment[57] not specifically excluded by the law.[58] Generally, RACs[59] are covered except for those employees[60] who come within the exceptions for casual employment,[61] federal employment,[62] or the employment of any person performing services for any religious or charitable organization in return for aid or sustenance only.[63] Any private nonprofit charitable organization may elect to have volunteers covered by the Industrial Insurance Law.[64] Some college apprentices or trainees

who are registered with the state apprenticeship council are covered by the Industrial Law.[65] RACs may elect to include their exempted employees within the law by filing written notice with the Director of Labor and Industries. After receiving notice of the employer's election to participate, any exempted RAC employee may give written notice to such employer and to the director of his election not to become subject to this law.[66] RACs must either carry insurance or become certified as a self-insurer[67] after proving financial ability directly to compensate injured employees. A self-insurer may be required to deposit adequate security to guarantee payment of compensation.[68]

The Washington Employment Security Act[69] broadly defines "employment" as "personal service of whatever nature."[70] The 1971 amendment of the Act specified that any service performed by an employee of a religious, charitable, educational, or other organization, which does not constitute employment under the federal unemployment tax act due solely to section 3306(c)(8),[71] is covered under the Washington statute.[72] This coverage does not extend to (1) service performed for a school or college by its regularly enrolled students or their spouses;[73] (2) service performed by a student under the age of twenty-two, at an accredited nonprofit or public educational institution in a full-time, credit-bearing program combining academic instruction and work experience;[74] (3) service performed for a church or for an association of churches[75] or for an organization run primarily for religious purposes and controlled by a church or by an association of churches;[76] and (4) service performed by a duly ordained, commissioned, or licensed minister" or by a member of a religious order in the exercise of duties required by such a calling.[77] Separate sections of the Act exclude the following services from consideration as employment: service for which unemployment compensation is payable under a system set up by an act of Congress[78] and domestic service for a local college club or local chapter of a college fraternity or sorority, unless performed for a person who paid more than $1,000 in any quarter in the current or preceding calendar year for such services.[79]

The Act allows nonprofit organizations,[80]

and therefore most RACs, the option of making payments in lieu of regular contributions.[81] If a nonprofit organization so elects, it becomes liable to the Commissioner of the Employment Security Department[82] for the "full amount of regular and additional benefits and one-half of the amount of extended benefits paid."[83] This election is effective for a period of not less than twelve months.[84] In addition, the Commissioner may require that an organization making such an election file a surety bond or deposit money or securities with the Commissioner.[85]

Washington law bans benefits on service in an instructional, research, or principally administrative capacity for weeks commencing between academic years or terms.[86]

Washington law, recognizing the right of employees to organize and bargain collectively,[87] states that employees shall be free from interference, restraint, and coercion in the exercise of these rights and, thus, restricts the power of state courts to issue injunctions in labor disputes to certain enumerated situations.[88] Before an injunction or restraining order can issue, the court must hold a hearing in open court and must find facts set out by the statute.[89]

D. Students

No Washington laws relate directly to the admission of students to RACs. Given the exemption for RACs from the application of the law against discrimination,[90] it can be presumed that an RAC can legitimately select students on whatever basis it deems desirable.

E. Facilities

The right to full enjoyment of any of the accommodations, advantages, facilities, or privileges of any place of public resort, accommodation, assemblage, or amusement is declared to be a civil right within the Washington law against discrimination.[91] The statute deems it unfair for any person[92] to commit any act which results, directly or indirectly, in disparate treatment regarding the admission to, use of, or fee for any place of public accommodation based on race, creed, color, national origin, sex, marital status, age, or the presence of any sensory, mental, or physical handicap.[93] However, educational facilities operated or maintained by bona fide religious or sectarian institutions and places which by their very nature are distinctly private are excluded from the application of the law.[94]

Washington's fair housing legislation makes it a civil right to engage in real estate transactions without discrimination,[95] and outlines numerous unfair practices which involve discrimination based on sex, marital status, race, creed, color, national origin, the presence of any sensory, mental, or physical handicap, or the use of a trained guide dog by a blind or deaf person.[96] RACs do not appear to be exempt from this provision, but there is no indication that the law is intended to restrict admissions.[97]

The Washington legislature has also mandated that plans and specifications for certain types of buildings constructed or substantially remodeled or rehabilitated after July 1, 1976, with public or private funds, contain provisions to accommodate the needs of aged and physically handicapped persons.[98] The minimum standards are to be established by the state building code advisory council.[99] Specifically exempted from these provisions are buildings with fewer than three dwelling units[100] and apartment houses with ten or fewer units.[101] Much RAC housing would therefore be included within this legislation.

Residence at an educational institution, if the residence is incidental to the provision of educational services, is not within the scope of the Residential Landlord and Tenant Act.[102]

The Washington Industrial Safety and Health Act of 1973[103] is modeled upon the federal statute. The law is administered by the Department of Labor and Industry. The act provides that all standards promulgated pursuant to the act are to meet or exceed federal standards.[104] Charitable organizations are expressly included within the broad statutory definition of an employer as any person or business entity which engages in business activities in the state and employs or contracts for personal services.[105] An employee is defined in similarly broad terms as anyone who is employed in the business of his employer or one who is working under an independent contract, the essence of which is personal labor.[106]

F. State Taxation

There is no general state corporate or personal income tax in the state of Washington.

All property, tangible or intangible, within the jurisdiction of the state, which passes by will, statute of inheritance, trust, or conveyance in contemplation of death, is subject to an inheritance tax whether or not the property belongs to a domiciliary of Washington.[107] There is an exemption from the inheritance tax for transfers to educational institutions, provided that no part of the net earnings of the organization inures to the benefit of any private individual.[108] Washington has no estate tax.

Washington imposes a tax on the transfer of property by gift;[109] however, in computing taxable gifts, all gifts of property to or for the use of educational institutions, whether or not organized under the laws of Washington or operating within the state of Washington, are exempt from the gift tax if no part of the net earnings of the institution goes to any private person.[110]

The state legislature is permitted under the state constitution to exempt educational institutions from the property tax.[111] Accordingly, the legislature has provided a tax exemption for real and personal property (1) that is owned or used by any nonprofit educational institution solely for college or campus purposes, i.e., principally to further the educational function, or (2) the revenue from which is used exclusively for the support and maintenance of the college.[112]

The state sales tax imposes a levy on all retail sales[113] and defines a seller as every person who sells at retail.[114] Most sales tax exemptions are framed in terms of particular items sold. There are few exemptions directed to the status of the purchaser or seller. There are no exemptions for an RAC or for the types of products normally sold in a campus bookstore or snack bar.[115] The use tax provisions[116] are for all intents and purposes the same as the sales tax.

Washington has enacted a Business and Occupation Tax: "There is levied and shall be collected from every person a tax for the act or privilege of engaging in business activity."[117] Although it is difficult to comprehend how an RAC would come within the scope of such a tax, there are definite indications that this is the case, at least with respect to some of its activities.

A person within the scope of the statute includes any corporation, society, or association, whether for profit or not for profit.[118] For purposes of the statute, business includes all activities engaged in with the object of gain, benefit, or advantage, directly or indirectly.[119] It is not necessary for the activity to be engaged in for monetary gain in order for such activity to be taxed as a business.[120] In addition to the above indicators, there is reference to "future fee" and "educational institutions" in the definitions section[121] and there is an express deduction from the tax computation for amounts derived from tuition fees and endowment funds.[122] Also, there is an exemption for receipts from bazaar or rummage sales by non-profit organizations if limited to no more than two per year and if gross income does not exceed one thousand dollars per sale.[123] The tax is measured by the application of established rates against the gross income of the activity.[124]

G. Fund Raising

Charitable Solicitations

There are no broad exemptions from the regulation provisions of the charitable solicitations statute.[125] Generally, all charitable organizations intending to solicit must register with the State Department of Motor Vehicles, which is authorized to enforce the statute.[126]

A charitable organization is exempt from the *registration* provisions, however, if (1) the solicitations are conducted by its own members, who must be unpaid volunteers, and (2) if the solicitations are from the members of the organization or in the form of collections or contributions at regular meetings, assemblies, or services.[127] Also, there is an exemption if solicitations from the public are carried on by persons who are unpaid, if no part of any of the proceeds inures to any member and if the amount solicited does not exceed $10,000.[128] There is an additional exemption for tax-exempt religious organizations which solicit from members or in the form of collections at regular or special services if the solicitations are used for evangelical, missionary, or religious purposes.[129]

The statute requires that the charitable organization maintain accurate, current, and readily available books and records. All contracts with professional fund raisers must be kept on file and copies must be sent to the director of the Department of Motor Vehicles. In addition, the organization must make periodic reports setting out the gross amount pledged in any fund raising drive, the amount actually collected, the amount expended, and the use to which the funds were put.[130] Such reports are kept on file by the Department and are public records.[131]

Games of Chance

Bingo, raffles, and amusement games are not solicitations within the scope of the solicitations law. These activities are regulated under the gambling statute.[132] Bona fide charitable and nonprofit organizations, including educational institutions, are permitted to conduct bingo games when issued a license subject to regulations promulgated by the state gambling commission.[133] A license is not required if gross revenues do not exceed $5,000 per year and if participation in the games is limited to members of the organization.[134]

A city, with respect to that city, or a county, with respect to all areas of that county, may absolutely prohibit the gambling activities for which the license was issued but may not otherwise change the scope of the license.[135]

The legislative body of any county, city, or town, by local ordinance, may tax gambling activity within its jurisdiction but not by an amount greater than ten percent of the gross revenue. There is an exemption from the tax if the gross revenues do not exceed $5,000 per year.[136]

56. West Virginia

A. Corporate Status

RACs may be organized under that article of West Virginia's Corporation Code relating to nonprofit corporations.[1] This portion of the Code is closely patterned on the Model Nonprofit Corporation Act.[2]

The procedures for an RAC's merger or consolidation with another educational institution are outlined in the statute.[3] Voluntary dissolution is likewise governed by statute.[4] A majority of the members of the governing board may initiate the process of dissolution by authorizing articles of dissolution to be delivered to the Secretary of State, who officially files the articles and issues a certificate of dissolution.[5] The West Virginia Corporation Code does not include the Model Act provision authorizing the Attorney General to seek involuntary dissolution of a nonprofit corporation,[6] but it does grant the circuit courts and other courts of record with general civil jurisdiction the power to liquidate the assets of a nonprofit corporation under the circumstances specified in the Act.[7]

The assets of a dissolving college are to be distributed according to a plan closely patterned on the provisions of the Model Act.[8] In addition, West Virginia courts are directed both by statute[9] and by common law decisions[10] to apply the doctrine of *cy pres* when necessary.[11]

B. State Support

West Virginia has not enacted any program of direct support to private institutions of higher education similar to the federal program sustained in *Tilton v. Richardson*[12] or the state program sustained in *Hunt v. McNair*.[13] It has, however, enacted a variety of programs of student assistance. It has, for example, targeted funds for what has been determined to be a critical need within the state by providing scholarships for teacher training.[14] One hundred scholarships are awarded to financially needy residents of West Virginia who are interested in teaching.[15] The scholarships, currently valued at $500, may be used at any institution of higher education in West Virginia.[16] The scholarship recipient executes a note for each state payment received. If the recipient teaches in the public schools of West Virginia upon graduation, a portion of the indebtedness is remitted for each year of teaching.[17] Otherwise, the scholarship is treated as a loan which must be repaid to the fund.[18]

A similar program exists for the study of optometry.[19] The legislature has authorized the Board of Regents to contract with out-of-state institutions to pay a set amount per year for training West Virginia students in optometry.[20]

The Commission on Higher Education supervises the awarding of scholarships and it administers federal and state student loans.[21] To be eligible for a scholarship, the applicant must be a state resident who has demonstrated financial need, character, academic promise, and scholastic achievement.[22] These scholarships may be used at any institution within the state, and they are awarded without regard to race, creed, color, sex, national origin, or ancestry of the applicant. The statute explicitly provides that institutions to which a student applies for admission are free to exact compliance with their own admission requirements, standards and policies.[23]

The Board of Regents is authorized to enter into reciprocal agreements with other states and to allow recipients of scholarships or loans to use these funds for educational expenses incurred at a college or university in these states.[24]

The Board of Regents is also authorized to apply for and administer federal facilities funds or grants on behalf of public and private institutions within the state.[25] The Regents may also enter into contracts with public or private educational institutions in West Virginia or outside the state for programs, services, or facilities which will maximize educational opportunities of its citizens.[26]

The Board of Regents is authorized to guarantee student loans of West Virginia residents, but two provisions in the state constitution[27] require that the acts of the Board not be deemed to create a debt of the state.[28]

C. Personnel

Hiring, Promoting and Firing

Under West Virginia's public policy, equal opportunity in employment, without regard to race, religion, color, national origin, ancestry, sex,[29] age,[30] or blindness, is a human or civil right.[31] It is an unlawful discriminatory practice for an "employer"[32] to discriminate on these bases[33] against any individual in "compensation, hire, tenure, terms, conditions, or privileges of employment if the individual is able and competent to perform the services required."[34]

Although there is no specific exemption for RACs, the law specifically includes a bona fide occupational qualification [BFOQ].[35] This BFOQ would allow an RAC to exercise religious selectivity in hiring certain faculty (e.g., in certain theology courses) and administrators (it may be crucial to an RAC that its highest ranking officers be of its religious affiliation). Certain counselors may also come within the exemption. It is unlikely, however, that the BFOQ would allow the RAC to use religious selectivity generally in hiring faculty and the like, despite its interest in a pervasive presence on campus of people of its religious persuasion.

Sex preference in employment would clearly be a BFOQ with regard to certain counselors, locker room personnel, and perhaps even faculty (e.g., in women's history courses).

The employment provisions are enforced by the West Virginia human rights commission.[36]

Wages and Hours

Although RACs are given no general exemption from the West Virginia Minimum Wage and Maximum Hours Standards for Employees law,[37] excluded from coverage are those employees who are: (1) engaged in the activities of an educational, charitable, religious, fraternal, or nonprofit organization, as long as the employer-employee relationship does not in fact exist, or the services are rendered on a voluntary basis;[38] (2) employed in a good faith professional, executive, or administrative capacity;[39] or (3) employed on a part-time basis while a student in any recognized school or college.[40]

RACs are also bound by legislation requiring timely payment of earned wages,[41] and other legislation relating to inspections[42] and record-keeping.[43]

Worker's Compensation

The West Virginia Workmen's Compensation Law[44] applies to all corporations which are not expressly excluded from coverage.[45] Generally RAC employees come within the provisions of this law.[46] Employers not subject to the Workmen's Compensation Law may voluntarily choose[47] to come within its coverage by paying insurance premiums to the State Workmen's Compensation fund.[48] RACs subject to this law may nevertheless elect to be self-insurers after furnishing adequate security and sufficient proof to the Compensation Commissioner of financial ability to insure the payment of compensation to injured employees.[49]

Unemployment Compensation

Under the West Virginia Unemployment Compensation Law[50] services performed for religious, charitable, or educational organizations constitute "employment,"[51] if two conditions are satisfied.[52] First, such service must be exempt from the definition of "employment" in the Federal Unemployment Compensation Act solely due to section 3306(c)(8).[53] Second, the organization must employ at least four individuals "for some portion of a day in each of twenty different weeks, whether or not such weeks were consecutive, within either the current or preceding calendar year."[54]

The statute provides the following exceptions from coverage which apply directly to RACs: (1) services performed for a church or for an association of churches;[55] (2) services performed for an organization run primarily for religious purposes and controlled by a church or by an association of churches;[56] (3) services performed by ordained ministers or by members of religious orders in the exercise of their duties;[57] (4) services performed for a school which did not qualify as an institution of higher education[58] prior to January 1, 1978.[59] Because the scope of these exceptions is narrow, most services performed in the employ of RACs are covered.

Other relevant exemptions apply to services performed (1) for a school or college by regularly enrolled students[60] or by their spouses;[61] (2) by students under the age of twenty-two at an accredited nonprofit or public educational institution in a full-time program, taken for credit and combining academic instruction and work experience;[62] (3) as a domestic for a college club or a chapter of a college fraternity or sorority, if cash wages were less than $1,000.00 in any quarter of the current or preceding calendar year;[63] and (4) for which unemployment compensation is payable under a system set up by an act of Congress.[64]

Nonprofit organizations, and therefore RACs, may elect to make payments in lieu of contributions. To take advantage of this option, an organization must fit the definition of "nonprofit organization" in section 501(c)(3) of the Internal Revenue Code and must qualify as tax-exempt under section 501(a) of the Code.[65] The election is effective for a period of one year upon filing of written notice with the Department of Employment Security.[66] Required payments are equal to the amount of regular benefits plus the amount of extended benefits paid.[67] Organizations not otherwise subject to the pro-

visions of this statute may elect to participate in the program for a minimum of two years.[68]

Collective Bargaining

West Virginia's comprehensive bargaining legislation, the Labor-Management Relations Act for the Private Sector,[69] sets out the rights of employees, including the right to organize and collectively bargain,[70] and unfair labor practices of employers[71] and labor organizations,[72] respectively. The law generally applies to any employer with fifteen or more employees unless that employee is subject to the National Labor Relations Act and the National Labor Relations Board has not declined to assert jurisdiction over that employer.[73]

D. Students

West Virginia law does not directly regulate the admission of students to RACs. (Although the state does have a public accommodations law, there is no indication that it was intended to affect, directly or indirectly, RAC admissions.[74])

E. Facilities

West Virginia public policy specifies that equal access to places of public accommodations, without regard to race, religion, color, national origin, ancestry, sex, age, or blindness, is a civil and human right.[75] Accordingly, it is an unlawful discriminatory practice to deny to any individual because of his race, religion, color, national origin, ancestry, sex, age, or blindness, full use and enjoyment of a place of public accommodations.[76] A "place of public accommodations" includes any establishment or person offering services, goods, facilities, or accommodations "to the general public."[77]

Clearly, RAC restaurants, hotels, bookstores, and the like open to the general public are included within the prohibition. Arguably, indeed, RACs offer their educational services to the general public and may not, therefore, exercise religious or sexual selectivity in admissions. Admission to a college, however, is not commonly thought of as a public accommodation and, in any event, there is no persuasive indication that the law was intended to affect RAC admissions directly, or through application of the law to facilities used only by students, indirectly.

Equal opportunity in housing, without regard to race, religion, color, national origin, ancestry, sex, or blindness, is also considered a human and civil right.[78] It is an unlawful discriminatory practice for anyone controlling the ownership or possession of any housing accommodation or real property to discriminate, on any of these bases, in its sale, lease, rental, or the like.[79]

It would seem that limiting RAC housing to its own students is not to discriminate on one of the proscribed bases, even though the RAC limits its student body on the basis of religion or sex. To apply the law to RAC housing would indirectly but clearly regulate student admissions, which there is no persuasive indication that the housing law intended to do.

In any event, the housing law does provide an exception for sex selectivity "where the facilities of such housing accommodations or real property, or any portion thereof, are suitable for only one sex."[80] Single-sex campus dormitories could well be included within this exemption.

Both the public accommodations and the housing laws are enforced by the West Virginia Human Rights Commission.[81]

The Director of the Division of Vocational Rehabilitation of the State Board of Education is authorized to promulgate "reasonable" rules and regulations governing the construction of public buildings in order to facilitate their use by the handicapped.[82] A public building is one to which the public has general access and includes the travel ways to and from the building.[83]

Specifically excluded from coverage under this legislation are residence halls at colleges or universities having at least two other residence halls for men and two others for women which do provide reasonable access and use to the physically handicapped.[84] The implication of this section is that all other campus buildings are indeed covered by the law.

West Virginia requires that hotels and restaurants receive a Certificate of Inspection from the Department of Health prior to being licensed.[85]

The definition of hotel and restaurant[86] would easily cover campus hotels and restaurants open to the public. Presumably, RAC dormitories and dining halls open only to students are not within the law. In any event, an exemption is provided for, *inter alia*, "summer hotels."[87] Also exempt are temporary (not exceeding two weeks) food sales by religious, educational, charitable, or nonprofit organizations.[88]

West Virginia has not enacted a comprehensive OSHA statute. Under West Virginia law, however, the Commissioner of Labor has the power to establish standards for the prevention of accidents in the work place.[89] The law requires every employer to provide a "reasonably safe" place of employment and to do everything reasonably necessary to protect the life, health, and safety of the employer.[90] An employer is defined broadly as any business entity doing business or operating within the state; an employee is any person permitted, required, or directed by an employer to engage in employment in consideration of profit or gain.[91]

F. State Taxation

West Virginia's Corporation Net Income Tax law[92] exempts from taxation any corporation[93] which, by reason of its purpose or activities, is exempt from federal income tax.[94] The exemption does not apply, however, to federally taxed "unrelated business income," as defined in the Internal Revenue Code.[95]

Under West Virginia's Inheritance and Transfer Taxes law,[96] property transferred to a person or corporation "in trust or for the use solely for educational, literary, scientific, religious, or charitable purposes" is exempt from tax.[97]

West Virginia's Personal Income Tax law[98] allows an individual who itemized on his federal tax return to elect to deduct his "West Virginia itemized deduction" on his state return rather than take the state standard deduction.[99] With few modifications, the West Virginia itemized deduction equals the taxpayer's total federal deductions.[100] Since contributions to nonprofit RACs are deductible for federal income tax purposes,[101] there is in effect provided to individuals who itemize on the federal return and who elect to itemize on the state return, a state income tax deduction for such contributions. Under the Corporation Net Income Tax Law, a comparable arrangement obtains for corporate contributions to RACs.[102]

West Virginia exempts from taxation all property belonging to, or held in trust for, colleges and seminaries if the property is used "primarily and immediately" for educational, literary, or scientific purposes.[103] A related provision exempts all real estate up to one-half acre, and buildings on it, if used exclusively by any college or university society "as a literary hall, or as a dormitory or clubroom, if not leased or otherwise used with a view to profit."[104] (Curiously, therefore, a dormitory owned by the college and used for its students would have no acreage limit while one owned and used by a fraternity or sorority would.)[105]

Also tax-exempt are (1) property used exclusively for divine worship;[106] (2) parsonages and their houshold goods and furniture;[107] (3) certain securities issued and sold by churches and religious societies;[108] and (4) property used for charitable purposes and not leased out for profit.[109]

West Virginia's Consumer Sales Tax Act[110] covers both consumer sales and services.[111] Professional (and personal) services are exempted,[112] however, so that RAC tuition is probably not subject to the tax.[113]

Also exempt are, *inter alia*: (1) sales of textbooks required to be used in any "school"[114] (including colleges or universities);[115] (2) sales of property or services to churches and bona fide charitable organizations which do not charge for their services;[116] (3) sales of property or services to or by corporations or organizations qualified under section 501(c)(3) or (4) of the Internal Revenue Code of 1954 who make certain casual and occasional sales;[117] (5) the sale of food intended for human consumption;[118] and (6) most importantly for RACs, sales of property or services to a school authorized by the West Virginia Board of Regents to grant degrees, principally located within the state, and exempt from state and federal income tax.[119]

West Virginia's Use Tax Act[120] exempts from tax any tangible personal property the sale of which within the state is exempt from the Consumer sales tax.[121]

West Virginia's Business Franchise Registration Certificate Tax[122] exempts from taxation corporations chartered strictly for educational, literary, agricultural, scientific, religious, or charitable purposes.[123] All RACs would therefore be exempt. Exempt corporations must, however, file a required annual statement with the tax commissioner.[124]

The Business and Occupation Tax law[125] seems aimed at profit-oriented enterprises[126] and not institutions such as colleges and universities, despite some language that could so indicate.[127] In any event, there is a specific exemption for corporations, associations, and societies organized and operated exclusively for religious or charitable purposes.[128] This exemption would perhaps cover some RACs, such as seminaries and bible colleges.

G. Fund Raising

In 1977, West Virginia adopted the Solicitation of Charitable Funds Act,[129] which includes educational and religious organizations within its definition of a charitable organization.[130] Educational institutions that are registered and approved by the State Board of Education, however, are exempt from the extensive registration requirements found in the statute.[131] To qualify for this exemption, RACs must annually file with the Secretary of State the name, address, and purpose of the organization, and a statement setting forth the reason for the exemption on forms provided by the Commission for Charitable Organizations.[132] RACs are included within the general requirement that charitable organizations may raise funds only for "charitable purposes" and may not expend such funds for "noncharitable purposes."[133] They must also maintain comprehensive financial records for at least three years.[134] All material submitted to governmental officials concerning solicitations becomes part of the public record.[135]

Bingo and other games of chance are not allowed in West Virginia.[136]

H. Miscellaneous

West Virginia has enacted and entered into the Compact for Education[137] and is a party to the Southern Regional Education Compact.[138] No college fraternity or sorority may be licensed as a private club for the purpose of selling alcoholic beverages.[139]

57. Wisconsin

A. Corporate Status

As a not-for-profit corporation, the typical RAC will be organized under the Nonstock Corporation Act.[1] The Act defines a nonprofit corporation as "a corporation, no part of the income of which is distributable to its members, directors or officers."[2] A nonstock corporation is defined as "a corporation without capital stock."[3]

The corporation's legal existence begins upon the filing of duplicate originals of the articles of incorporation in the office of the Secretary of State and recordation in the office of the Register of Deeds of the county in which the corporation's principal office is located.[4] The certificate of incorporation is conclusive evidence that the corporation has been incorporated.[5]

An RAC might also be organized pursuant to the Domestic Corporations—Religious Societies Act.[6] According to this statute, three or more members, over eighteen years of age, of any church or society of a religious sect or denomination which is organized in Wisconsin and which maintains regular public worship may, with five or more persons who are over eighteen years old and not members of a religious congregation, form a corporation for religious, charitable, or educational purposes.[7] Such a corporation is to be formed in connection with a church which adheres to these members' beliefs.[8]

Inasmuch as it is a nonstock corporation, an RAC may, *inter alia*, engage in property transactions.[9] Religious societies have this same power.[10]

The merger, consolidation, and dissolution of nonprofit colleges are governed by the Wisconsin Nonstock Corporation Law, which is closely patterned on the Model Nonprofit Corporation Act.[11] In addition, the Wisconsin courts are empowered to apply the *cy pres* doctrine when necessary.[12]

The procedure for the voluntary dissolution of nonprofit colleges in Wisconsin is patterned after the provisions of the Model Act. After observing the provisions, the governing board of the college authorizes the articles of dissolution to be delivered to the Secretary of State, who officially files the articles and issues a certificate of dissolution.[13] A nonprofit college may be involuntarily dissolved in an action brought in circuit court by the Attorney General if the college is engaged in fraud or abuse of authority, or has failed to appoint a registered agent in the state, or has improperly solicited or accepted money, or has failed to comply with a court order to produce the records of the corporation.[14] Circuit courts also have jurisdiction to liquidate a college's assets in an action properly brought by a member of the corporation or by a creditor.[15]

The Wisconsin Nonstock Corporation Act provides that assets of a dissolving nonprofit college shall be distributed according to a procedure following that of the Model Nonprofit Corporation Act.[16]

B. State Support

The Wisconsin Constitution provides for the free exercise of religion,[18] and states that no person shall be "compelled to attend, erect or support any place of worship, or to maintain any ministry."[19] No money may be drawn from the state treasury "for the benefit of religious societies, or religious or theological seminaries."[20] Relevant as well to the issue of state aid to RACs in Wisconsin are state Constitutional provisions barring the giving or loaning of the credit of the state in aid of any individual or group[21] and specifying limits on and procedures for contracting public debt.[22]

Despite these and other concerns, Professor Howard suggests that direct state aid to church-related institutions would pass constitutional muster if the statute (1) limits the use of the funds involved to the secular educational function the state seeks to support; (2) prohibits any requirement that students in the supported programs or departments take religious courses for admission or graduation; and (3) does not regulate institutional policy beyond the secular educational program supported.[23] The primary effect of tuition grants and loans is to benefit the student. Since any benefit to the institution is incidental, it is likely to be permissible.[24]

The Wisconsin Higher Educational Aids Board administers scholarship and loan programs, establishes and administers plans for Wisconsin participation under federal acts relating to higher education, makes recommendations for improvements in the state's financial aid program for students, and is authorized to assign, sell, convey, or repurchase certain student loans.[25]

Tuition grants are made available to resident[26] undergraduate students, enrolled at least half-time, at an "accredited"[27] nonprofit higher educational institution in the state.[28] Under this program, no grant may exceed the lesser of $1800 per year or the difference between the student's total tuition and the amount of the resident academic fee at the University of Wisconsin—Madison,[29] whichever is less. The student's "expected family contribution" and other costs of attending the institution are also worked into the formula.[30] Members of religious orders pursuing courses of study leading to degrees in theology, divinity, or religious education are ineligible.[31]

Several other programs provide grants to students at private institutions, including grants for the "uniquely needy,"[32] for needy Indian students,[33] and for needy handicapped students.[34]

It should be noted that Wisconsin provides significant per-student funding to the Marquette University Dental School.[35] The legislation requires that the contract between the Higher Educational Aids Board and the School prohibit any courses of a religious nature in the School's curriculum and any requirement of such courses for admission to or graduation from the school.[36]

Loans are also available to students needing financial assistance for attendance at certain[37] institutions of higher education.[38]

The legislature has also provided for a guaranteed student loan program in connection with the federal student loan law,[39] a health education loan program,[40] and a medical student loan program.[41]

C. Personnel

Hiring

The Wisconsin Fair Employment Act[42] makes it unlawful for an employer to discriminate against an employee or applicant for employment[43] on the basis of age, color, handicap, sex, creed, national origin, ancestry, arrest record, or conviction record.[44] There is no bona fide occupational qualification except for handicap[45] or sex.[46]

Although "employee" would include those hired by RACs,[47] an "employer" under the legislation excludes a "religious association not organized for private profit."[48] At least certain nonprofit RACs, for example bible colleges and seminaries, would fall within this exemption and would not, therefore, be covered by the Act. Indeed, it may be argued, although with less ease, that all nonprofit RACs are "religious associations."

The Fair Employment Act is administered by the Department of Industry, Labor, and Human Relations.[49]

Each municipality is authorized to establish or to take part in "a community relations—social development commmission"[50] which shall, *inter alia*, "ensure to all municipal residents, regardless of sex, race or color," the right to equal employment opportunities.[51]

Wages and Hours

Because of the broad definition of "employer"[52] and "employee,"[53] an RAC is subject to the state's Minimum Wage Law.[54] The failure to provide a living wage[55] constitutes a violation of the law.[56]

Although an RAC may be excluded from the definition of place of employment[57] under the Employment Regulations,[58] it may still be subject to the operation of much of this legislation. Since covered employment is "any trade, occupation or process of manufacture, or any method of carrying on such trade or occupation,"[59] and a covered employer is a "person having control or custody of any employment,"[60] RACs are within the law. Consequently, the number of hours which an RAC employee may work may be regulated. The statute does not expressly state the number of hours one may work, but rather authorizes the Department of Industry, Labor and Human Relations to promulgate rules setting limits relating to time of beginning and ending work.[61] Moreover, certain hours are to be compensated for at regular rates and other at one and one-half times the regular rates.[62] Employment outside the "permissible hours" is a violation of the law.[63]

Workers' Compensation

The Wisconsin Worker's Compensation Act[64] applies to most employers with three or more employees.[65] Generally RACs are covered unless some of their employees come within the exception for employment not in the usual course of the employer's business.[66] RACs may elect to include exempted employees within the coverage of this Act by providing insurance coverage for them.[67] RACs may also elect to include volunteers within the coverage of this Act.[68] Employees who are blind or have epilepsy may elect not to be subject to this Act "for injuries resulting because of such epilepsy or blindness and still remain subject to its provisions for all other injuries."[69] Officers of corporations may also elect not to be subject to this Act. Such employees must give written notice to the employer before the election takes effect.[70] RACs must either carry compensation insurance[71] or obtain a written order of exemption from the Department of Industry, Labor and Human Relations after proving financial ability directly to compensate injured employees. The department may require the self-insurer to deposit adequate security.[72]

Unemployment Compensation

Under the Wisconsin Unemployment Reserves and Compensation Act[73] a nonprofit organization[74] meets the definition of "employer"[75] if it employs four or more individuals "for some portion of a day on at least 20 days, each day being in a different calendar week, whether or not such weeks were consecutive, in either that year or the preceding calendar year."[76] The statute's definition of "employment"[77] excludes from the law's coverage the following types of services: (1) those performed for a church or for an association of churches;[78] (2) those performed for an organization run primarily for religious purposes and controlled by a church or by an association of churches;[79] and (3) those performed by ordained ministers or by members of religious orders in the exercise of their duties.[80]

Other relevant exemptions include (1) service performed for a school or college by regularly enrolled students[81] or by their spouses;[82] (2) service performed by a student under the age of twenty-two at an accredited nonprofit or public educational institution in a full-time program taken for credit and combining academic instruction and work experience;[83] and (3) service performed in any calendar quarter for certain organizations which are tax-exempt under federal statutes,[84] if the remuneration paid is less than $200.00.[85] Wisconsin law also provides an exception for service performed by a domestic in the employ of a college club or a chapter of a fraternity or sorority.[86]

Nonprofit organizations, and therefore RACs, may elect to make payments in lieu of contributions. To take advantage of this option, an organization must fit the definition of a "nonprofit organization" in section 501(c)(3) of the Internal Revenue Code and qualify as tax-exempt under section 501(a) of the Code.[87] The election is effective for a period of one year upon filing of a written notice with the Department of Industry, Labor and Human Relations.[88] Required payments are equal to the amount of regular benefits plus one-half the amount of extended benefits paid.[89] Electing organizations must file an "assurance of reimbursement" equal to four percent of the employer's payroll for the calendar year preceding election.[90]

Collective Bargaining

Wisconsin grants employees the right to bargain collectively on matters relating to their employment.[91] Inasmuch as an RAC and persons hired by it fall within the definition of "employer"[92] and "employee,"[93] respectively, they are covered by the Employment Peace Act.[94] Employees of an RAC have the right to participate in labor organizations and collective bargaining as well as the right to refrain therefrom.[95] A violation of this right constitutes an unfair labor practice.[96]

D. Students

Student admission into postsecondary educational institutions is minimally regulated by statute. Any institution involved in postsecondary education and receiving public funds towards its support is prohibited from discriminating in admissions against any person because of a physical condition or a developmental disability.[97] Wisconsin law is silent as to the legitimacy of selecting students on the basis of religion, regardless of public funding.

E. Facilities

Public Accommodations

Wisconsin makes it a misdemeanor to deny another full enjoyment of any public place of accommodation or amusement because of sex, race, color, creed, physical condition, developmental disability, national origin, or ancestry.[98] A "public place of accommodation":

shall be interpreted broadly to include . . . places of business or recreation, hotels, motels, resorts, restaurants, taverns, barbershops, nursing homes, clinics, hospitals, cemeteries, and any place where accommodations, amusement, goods or services are available either free or for a consideration *except where provided by bona fide private, nonprofit, organizations or institutions.*[99]

It is not clear whether the italicized portion applies to the entire series (in which case even a restaurant open to the public on an RAC campus would be exempt) or only to the last item of the series (i.e., "any place where accommodations, amusement, goods or services are available either free or for a consideration . . ."). Lack of a comma after the word "consideration" supports the latter interpretation. Nonetheless, use of the phrase, "and any place" (rather than "and any *other* place") indicates a wholesale exemption of nonprofit organizations from the law's requirements.

It is also a misdemeanor for any person, club, or organization to discriminate because of sex, race, color, creed, national origin, or ancestry "regarding the use of any private facilities commonly rented to the public."[100] This provision would seem inapplicable to RAC facilities open only to its students since these are not "commonly rented to the public." This is not clear, however, since the next subsection of the law specifies that nothing in that section (which deals with both public places of accommodation and "private facilities commonly rented to the public") prohibits separate dormitories at higher educational institutions for persons of different sexes.[101] The better view, in any event, is that this qualification was inserted merely to make clear that the single-sex dormitory was not illegal rather than to suggest the total reach of the proscriptions regarding public places of accommodation and private facilities rented to the public.

Fair Housing

Virtually all forms of discrimination on the basis of sex, race, color, handicap, religion, national origin, sex or marital status of the person maintaining a household, lawful source of income, age, or ancestry are prohibited.[102] Although no exemption is provided for RACs, there is no indication that the law is intended to prohibit an RAC from limiting its housing to its own students or, alternatively, to indirectly control RAC admissions. In any event, a separate provision clearly indicates that single-sex dormitories at postsecondary institutions are lawful.[103]

The legislature has also authorized each municipality to establish or take part in "a community relations—social development commission"[104] so as to, *inter alia*, "ensure to all municipal residents, regardless of sex, race or color, the rights to possess equal housing accommodations."[105]

The Wisconsin OSHA law,[106] uniquely broad in its scope, requires every employer to furnish safe employment and a safe place of employment. This duty extends not only to employees but also to "frequenters."[107] "Employer" is defined in broad terms,[108] as is "employee," which includes every "person required or directed by an employer in consideration of gain or profit to engage in any employment or to go to work or be at anytime in any place of employment."[109] A "frequenter" is defined as every person other than an employee who may be present and who is not a trespasser; this definition expressly includes students receiving instruction at an educational institution.[110]

F. State Taxation

Wisconsin corporate franchise tax law, based on net income,[111] exempts from taxation the income of, *inter alia*, all religious, scientific, or educational corporations or associations not organized or conducted for pecuniary profit.[112] The income of virtually all RACs, therefore, is exempt.

All transfers, whether by will or by gift, to corporations, trusts, voluntary associations, or foundations "organized and operated exclusively for religious, humane, charitable, scientific or educational purposes" are exempt from the state inheritance tax[113] and the state gift tax.[114]

An individual may itemize deductions in arriving at his Wisconsin taxable income,[115] even if he used the standard deduction on his federal return.[116] Since "itemized deductions" under the Wisconsin income tax law means, with a few modifications, deductions allowable under federal income tax law,[117] and since contributions to nonprofit RACs are deductible under federal income tax law,[118] Wisconsin in effect provides a state income tax deduction for such contributions to individuals who itemize. Such contributions, when made by a corporation, are deductible, within limits,[119] from corporate gross income for purposes of the Wisconsin franchise tax on corporations.[120]

Property consisting of the grounds of "any incorporated college or university, not exceeding eighty acres" is exempt from general property taxes.[121] Any incorporated RAC would be eligible for this exemption.

The following subsection exempts from general property taxes "property" (not limited to "grounds" or even to real property)[122] owned and used exclusively by educational institutions offering regular courses six months in the year or by "churches or religious, educational or benevolent associations."[123] The exemption includes property owned and used for housing pastors and their ordained assistants, members of religious orders and communities, and ordained teachers.[124] The exemption does *not* include the property of college fraternities or sororities.[125]

Although there are acreage limits to land coming within this exemption (ten or thirty acres, depending on the nature of the owner and user),[126] these were presumably intended for noncollege situations since the earlier exemption for "colleges and universities" has an eighty acre limit. Presumably, therefore, any RAC may rely on the earlier provision to exempt up to eighty of its acres from property tax and the latter one for other types of property or for land owned and used for the specific purposes indicated when, for one reason or another[127] (e.g., the land is in excess of the eighty acre limit) the earlier exemption is insufficient.

There is a further exemption for property owned and operated by "nonprofit medical research foundations," a term broadly defined to include, for example, a corporation providing instruction for practicing physicians and surgeons.[128]

Persons claiming real property tax exemptions must, with few exceptions, file certain periodic reports with the assessor of the taxation district in which the property is located.[129]

Wisconsin's sales and use tax law[130] exempts, *inter alia*: (1) most "occasional sales" of tangible personal property and services;[131] (2) "gross receipts from sales to, and the storage, use, or other consumption of tangible personal property and taxable services," by "any nonprofit corporation or association organized and operated exclusively for religious, charitable, scientific, or educational purposes" (this would include virtually all RACs);[132] (3) gross receipts from the sale of and the storage, use or other consumption of newspapers and periodicals issued at average intervals not exceeding three months[133] (4) gross receipts from the sale of, and the storage, use, or other consumption of most food and beverages for human consumption off the premises;[134] (5) sales of meals, food, food products, or beverages pursuant to a contract or agreement by any institution of higher education;[135] and (6) certain sales of energy and fuels for residential use.[136]

Wisconsin law allows a county to add to the state sales tax a local sales tax of one-half of one percent, to be collected by the state and subject to the same laws and rules governing the state sales tax.[137]

G. Fund Raising

Wisconsin's Comprehensive Charitable Solicitations law[138] exempts from its registration[139] and reporting[140] requirements (1) corporations organized under the religious corporations law and "other religious agencies and organizations, and charities, agencies, and organizations operated, supervised, or controlled by or in connection with a religious organization" (the fairly flexible religious affiliation requirement might bring many RACs within this exemption);[141] (b) any educational institution when solicitations are limited to its student body and their families, alumni, faculty, and trustees;[142] and (3) any charitable organization not intending to solicit and receive and not actually receiving more than $3,000 in any calendar year, as long as all fund raising activities are carried on by persons unpaid for their services.[143] The legislation also regulates "professional fund raisers" and "professional solicitors."[144]

Although the Wisconsin Constitution prohibits the legislature from authorizing lotteries,[145] the same article allows the legislature to authorize licensed bingo games and raffles by "religious, charitable, service, fraternal, or veterans' organizations or those to which contributions are deductible for federal or state income tax purposes."[146] (Virtually all RACs would qualify under this broad provision.) All profits must inure to the licensed local organization and no salaries, fees, or profits may be paid to any other organization or person.[147]

Pursuant to this constitutional authorization, Wisconsin has enacted a comprehensive Bingo and Raffle Control Law,[148] and Wisconsin's gambling legislation[149] excludes authorized bingo games and raffles[150] from its definition of "lottery."[151]

H. Miscellaneous

Wisconsin has enacted into law and entered into the Compact for Education.[152]

58. Wyoming

A. Corporate Status

RACs are organized under the Wyoming Nonprofit Corporations Act.[1] The Act provides that nonprofit corporations may be organized "for any one or more lawful purposes not for pecuniary profit."[2] The term "nonprofit corporation" is defined as a corporation organized "for a purpose, other than the conduct of a business for profit, and shall include, but is not limited to, corporations organized for charitable, educational, religious, social, and fraternal purposes."[3]

The statute specifically authorizes charitable, educational, religious, and other societies to incorporate if their purpose is "to establish and maintain a college, academy, or other institution for the education of youth or for the purposes of mental and physical improvement."[4]

The Act also enumerates other requirements relating to the creation and maintenance of a nonprofit corporation generally. These provisions deal with the information to be provided in the certificate of incorporation,[5] the number, term, election and payment of directors,[6] the necessity for and character of the registered agent and resident office,[7] the amount of filing fees,[8] bylaws and amendment procedures,[9] corporate powers,[10] voting contracts[11] and voting trusts.[12]

There are also provisions dealing specifically with the incorporation of charitable, educational, religious, and other societies.[13] These provisions address questions of corporate powers,[14] the adoption and purposes of bylaws,[15]

the power to raise money,[16] the division of stock and property into shares,[17] restrictions upon dividends,[18] salaries of corporate officers,[19] and the powers of college trustees.[20]

The dissolution of nonprofit colleges is governed by the Wyoming Nonprofit Corporations Act.[21] The Wyoming Act has no explicit provision for the merger, consolidation, or involuntary dissolution of nonprofit colleges.[22] The Wyoming courts, however, are empowered to apply the *cy pres* doctrine when necessary.[23]

The voluntary dissolution of a nonprofit corporation takes effect when the governing board adopts a resolution to dissolve the corporation and files it with both the Secretary of State and the clerk of the county where the college (or nonprofit corporation) was incorporated.[24]

After paying its debts, the governing board of the dissolving college must distribute the college's remaining assets in accordance with the provisions of its certificate of incorporation.[25] Although there is no explicit statutory provision requiring that the charitable purposes of gifts be preserved when a nonprofit corporation dissolves, a Wyoming court would probably rely on the *cy pres* doctrine to effectuate this result in the event of the dissolution of a nonprofit college.

B. State Support

Two provisions in the Wyoming Constitution would prohibit any direct aid to RACs. The first states that no portion of any public school fund can "ever be used to support or assist any private school, or any school, academy, seminary, college, or other institution of learning controlled by any church or sectarian organization or religious denomination whatsoever."[26] The second provision more generally provides that "no appropriation shall be made for charitable, industrial, educational or benevolent purposes to any person, corporation or community not under the absolute control of the state, nor to any denominational or sectarian institution or association."[27] Thus, there does not appear to be any possibility for direct state financial support of RACs.

RACs may, however, receive financial assistance indirectly through loans and loan guarantees made to their students. State law provides that upon the request of the Wyoming Higher Education Council and approval by the governor, the state treasurer can invest no more than three million dollars of permanent state funds for purchasing federally insured student loans from Wyoming lending institutions.[28] Assuming that the particular RAC would qualify as a participating institution, its students would be eligible to receive the loans.

C. Personnel

Wyoming's Fair Employment Practices Act[29] makes it unlawful for an employer[30] to hire, promote, demote, discharge, or discriminate in matters of compensation against a person "otherwise qualified" on the grounds of sex, race, creed, color, national origin, or ancestry.[31] While the Act does not provide for exceptions to this general prohibition, it does specify that "employer' does not mean religious organizations or associations.[32] It is not clear, however, that all RACs would be considered religious organizations or associations. Because of the nature of their employment needs, it is unlikely that RACs would receive such a blanket exemption from the Act.

If RACs are not exempt from the Act, it would seem that they would have to assert some type of occupational qualification, under the "otherwise qualified" phrase, to justify faculty hiring based upon religious preference. This does not appear to give much protection for RAC hiring policies outside the realm of theology and perhaps some counseling personnel.[33]

The Fair Employment Commission hears complaints regarding unfair employment practices and issues orders which may be appealed to the district court of the county where the act is alleged to have occurred.[34] Direct appeal may be taken from the district court to the state supreme court.[35]

Every employer in the state of Wyoming must pay to each employee a minimum wage of $1.60 per hour.[36] While an "employee" is defined as "any individual employed by an employer,"[37] the statute specifically excepts "any individual engaged in the activities of an educational, charitable, religious, or nonprofit organization where the employer-employee relationship does not in fact exist or where the services rendered to such organization are on a voluntary basis."[38] Despite this exception, it would appear that RACs would be obliged to pay the minimum wage to most of their personnel[39] due to the "employer-employee" relationship that exists in most cases. While Wyoming does establish a minimum wage, it does not regulate overtime wages or provide for maximum hours of work, except for state and county employees and employees of certain other specialized industries.[40]

It is also the expressed policy of the state of Wyoming that organized labor should be permitted and protected:

It is hereby declared to be the policy of the state of Wyoming that workers have the right to organize for the purpose of protecting the freedom of labor, and of bargaining collectively with employers of labor for acceptable terms and conditions of employment, and that in the exercise of the aforesaid rights, workers should be free from the interference, restraint or coercion of employers of labor, or their agents in any concerted activities for their mutual aid or protection.[41]

There are no express exceptions to this general state policy.

Regarding employee indemnification, the Wyoming Business Corporation Act[42] gives a corporation the power to indemnify any director, officer, employee, or agent of the corporation, acting in good faith, from any legal action, whether civil, criminal, administrative, or investigative.[43] While no specific mention is made of nonprofit corporations, presumably

RACs could also indemnify a director, officer, employee, or agent as long as the statutory provisions and limitations are honored.[44]

The Wyoming Worker's Compensation Act[45] covers any corporation[46] having employees engaged in any extra-hazardous occupation enumerated in the Act.[47] Maintenance workers,[48] security guards,[49] printing shop workers,[50] and food service personnel[51] are some of the employees that come within the coverage of the Act. Excluded from coverage are casual employees,[52] clerical workers,[53] and employees covered by a federal worker's compensation law.[54] There is no explicit provision allowing employers to elect to include otherwise exempted employees within the coverage of the Act.

The employer must make contributions to the state director of the Workmen's Compensation Division of the state treasurer's office.[55] Under some circumstances, the employer may file an election with the director to be exempted from making continued employer contributions.[56] However, an injured employee may sue an employer who has failed adequately to insure the coverage of eligible employees.[57]

Wyoming law provides that for the purpose of unemployment compensation, "employment" does not include services "in the employ of (1) a church or convention or association of churches, or (2) an organization which is operated primarily for religious purposes and which is operated, supervised, controlled, or principally supported by a church or convention or association of churches."[58] In addition, "employment" does not include services "by a duly ordained, commissioned, or licensed minister of a church in the exercise of his ministry or by a member of a religious order in the exercise of duties required by the order."[59] Some RACs, such as seminaries and divinity schools, could be categorized as organizations which are operated primarily for religious purposes, and are, therefore, exempt. RACs which employ priests, ministers, sisters, or brothers might be able to rely upon the "exercise of ministry" or "exercise of duties required by the order" clause as an exemption. Services performed by regular college students or their spouses who are employed by the college at which the student is enrolled are also exempt.[60]

D. Students

Wyoming does not have a statute dealing with discrimination in the field of education generally. Both the constitutional provisions[61] and the specific statutory provisions of Title Twenty-one[62] address only "public education." However, there is a general anti-discrimination statute which forbids the denial of "life, liberty, pursuit of happiness, or the necessities of life because of race, color, creed, or national origin."[63] Since educational opportunity could be considered an element of "life, liberty and the pursuit of happiness" or "a necessity of life," this provision could be deemed applicable to nonpublic education.[64] It is not clear, however, what remedies would be available to aggrieved applicants nor whether this provision would prohibit RACs from exercising religious preference in the selection of students as long as public education is available.

E. Facilities

Wyoming law prohibits "any distinction, discrimination or restriction on account of race, religion, color or national origin" in all places which are public in nature.[65] There are no exceptions to this general prohibition mentioned.

While there does not appear to be a statute dealing specifically with discrimination in housing, the "necessities of life" clause previously mentioned[66] would seem to encompass the area of housing. Since there are no exceptions, RACs could not utilize religious preference in campus-related housing without violating the provision.

The Occupational Health and Safety Act[67] is the primary provision dealing with safety in the area of labor and employment, and it encompasses both public and private employment.[68] The Act creates an Occupational Heath and Safety Commission[69] which is empowered to formulate rules and regulations for the prevention, control, and abatement of unsafe and unhealthy working conditions.[70] Any employer, which would include the typical RAC, who willfully and knowingly violates any of the provisions of the Act,[71] any safety or health standards, or any rules or regulations promulgated under the Act, is punishable.[72]

The public facilities of RACs would also be

subject to the rules and regulations promulgated by the Department of Fire Prevention and Electrical safety.[73]

F. State Taxation

Wyoming has no state income tax and, therefore, there are obviously no provisions for deductions or credits for gifts to RACs.

Wyoming does exempt "gifts for state, municipal, charitable, educational or religious purposes" from its inheritance tax.[74]

Wyoming also imposes an estate tax designed merely to channel to Wyoming, by virtue of the credit allowed against the federal estate tax for state death taxes, moneys that would otherwise go to the federal government in estate taxes.[75] This tax, therefore, has no ultimate effect on the amount of death taxes paid.

Since Wyoming has no gift tax or income tax, gifts and contributions to RACs have no state gift or income tax consequences.

The legislature has provided that "property used for schools, orphan asylums or hospitals" is exempt from property tax to the extent it is not used for private profit.[76] There is also a provision which exempts centers of music or art run by a nonprofit association and open to the public, even if admission is charged.[77] An RAC's music or art center could come within this provision.

Finally, Wyoming exempts from its sales tax "sales made to religious or charitable organizations for the conduct of regular religious or charitable activities,"[78] as well as "occasional sales made by religious or charitable organizations for fund raising activities, and not in the course of any regular business."[79] Parallel exemptions are provided religious and charitable organizations regarding use taxes.[80]

G. Fund Raising

There are no charitable solicitation statutes in Wyoming.

While the state does prohibit gambling generally,[81] the gambling legislation does not apply to "games of chance known as raffles or bingo conducted by charitable or nonprofit organizations" as long as the tickets for such raffles or bingo are sold only in Wyoming.[82]

Notes

1. Corporate Status

1. Alabama, Alaska, Arizona, Colorado, Illinois, Iowa, Kentucky, Maine, Maryland, Minnesota, Montana, Nebraska, New Mexico, New York, North Carolina, North Dakota, Ohio, Oregon, Pennsylvania, South Dakota, Tennessee, Texas, Utah, Vermont, Virginia, Washington, West Virginia, Wisconsin, Wyoming.

2. See, e.g., DEL. CODE ANN. tit. 8, §§ 101 *et seq.*

3. Degree-granting RACs are regulated by a board or commission of higher education in Alabama, Arkansas, California, Delaware, Hawaii, Kansas, Maryland, Michigan, Minnesota, Mississippi, Montana, New York, North Carolina, Ohio, Oregon, Rhode Island, South Carolina, Tennessee, and Virginia.

4. See, e.g., MICH. COMP. LAWS ANN. §§ 390.751 to 390.760 (1976) (Kalamazoo College); §§ 390.701 to 390.708 (1976) (Albion College).

5. *Model Nonprofit Corporation Act*, ALI/ABA Practice Handbook § 28 (Philadelphia: American Law Institute, 1964) (Hereafter Model Act).

6. *Id.* § 31.

7. *Id.* § 4.

8. CAL. CORP. CODE §§ 5110 *et seq.* (Supp. 1980) and 9111 (Supp. 1980).

9. ALASKA STAT. §§ 10.20.011 and 10.40.101.

10. Model Act § 4.

11. N.D. CENT. CODE § 10–28–19(1).

12. ILL. ANN. STAT. ch. 32, §§ 163a3 and 163a30 (Smith-Hurd).

13. Model Act § 5.

14. *Id.* § 2.

15. *Id.* § 5 (o).

16. *Id.* § 29.

17. *Id.* §§ 33 and 34.

18. See note 3, *supra.*

19. California, Colorado, Connecticut, Delaware, Illinois, Kansas, Kentucky, Louisiana, Maryland, Massachusetts, Michigan, Minnesota, Montana, New Hampshire, New Jersey, New York, North Dakota, Ohio, Oregon, Rhode Island, Tennessee, Vermont, Virginia, Washington, West Virginia, Wisconsin. For an updated list of citations, see 7A *Uniform Laws Annotated* (hereafter cited as U.L.A.) 40 (Supp. 1982).

20. 7A U.L.A. §§ 1–11.

21. Commissioners' Prefatory Note, 7A U.L.A. 405–09.

22. 7A U.L.A. § 1(1).

23. *Id.* § 1(2).

24. *Id.* § 2.

25. *Id.* § 7.

26. *Id.* § 4.

27. *Id.* § 6.

28. See note 12, *supra.*

29. 7A U.L.A. §§ 4, 5.

30. *Id.* §§ 2, 6.

31. Alabama, Alaska, Arkansas, Colorado, Connecticut, Hawaii, Idaho, Indiana, Iowa, Kansas, Kentucky, Maryland, Massachusetts, Michigan, Minnesota, Mississippi, Missouri, Montana, Nebraska, Nevada, New Jersey, New Mexico, North Carolina, Oklahoma, Oregon, Pennsylvania, South Carolina, Utah, Virginia, Washington, West Virginia, Wisconsin, Wyoming. For an updated list of citations, see 7A U.L.A. 307 (Supp. 1982).

32. *Id.* §§ 101–419.

33. E.g., CAL. CORP. CODE §§ 25000 *et seq.* (West); ILL. ANN. STAT. ch. 121½, §§ 137.1 *et seq.* (Smith-Hurd); N.Y. GEN. BUS. LAW §§ 352 *et seq.* (McMinney).

34. 7A U.L.A. § 402(a)(9).

35. For example, RACs in Utah and Texas are exempt, UTAH CODE ANN. § 61-1-14(h); TEX. CIV. CODE ANN. tit. 19, § 581-6(j) (Vernon).

36. See Joseph P. O'Neil and Samuel Barnett, *Colleges and Corporate Change: Merger, Bankruptcy, and Closure* (Princeton: Conference-University Press, 1980). This volume contains a lengthy appendix on state regulation of the dissolution of nonprofit colleges and universities, at 127-200.

37. Model Act §§ 38 through 42; amendment requirements are at *id.* §§ 33 and 34.

38. *Id.* § 43.

39. *Id.* § 44.

40. *Id.* § 45.

41. *Id.* § 46.

42. Alabama, Boxley v. Birmingham Trust Nat'l Bank, 334 So.2d 848 (Ala. 1976); Arizona, Olivas v. Bd. of Nat'l. Missions of Presbyterian Church, Ariz. App. 543, 405 P.2d 485 (1965) (recognizing *cy pres* doctrine in dictum), and In re Hayward's Estate, 65 Ariz. 288, 178 P.2d 547 (1947); Arkansas, Sloan v. Robert Jack Post No. 1322, V.F.W., 218 Ark. 917, 239 S.W.2d 591 (1951); California, Hoyt v. College of Osteopathic Physicians and Surgeons, 61 Cal.2d 750, 394 P.2d 932, 40 Cal. Rptr. 244 (1964), and In re Loving's Estate, 29 Cal. 2d 423, 175 P.2d 524 (1946); Colorado, Dunbar v. Bd. of Trustees of Clayton College, 170 Colo. 327, 461 P.2d 28 (1969); Connecticut, Howood House, Inc. v. Trustees of Donations and Bequests for Church Purposes, 27 Conn. Supp. 176, 233 A.2d 5 (1967); Delaware, In re Will of Potter, 275 A.2d 574, 583 (Del. Ch. 1980); Florida, Jewish Guild for the Blind v. First Nat'l. Bank, 226 So.2d 414, 416 (Fla. 1969) (recognizing *cy pres* doctrine in dictum); Illinois, Community Unit School Dist. No. 4 v. Booth, 1 Ill.2d 545, 116 N.E.2d 161 (1953); Indiana, Sendak v. Trustees of Purdue Univ., 151 Ind. App. 372, 279 N.E.2d 840 (1972); Iowa, Simmons v. Parsons College, 256 N.W.2d 225 (1977); Kansas, Nelson v. Kring, 225 Kan. 499, 592 P.2d 438 (1979); Kentucky, Defenders of Furbearers v. First Nat'l. Bank and Trust Co., 306 S.W.2d 102 (Ky. App. 1957), and Kentucky Children's Home v. Woods, 289 Ky. 20, 157 S.W.2d 473 (1941); Louisiana, LA. REV. STAT. ANN. § 9:2331; Maine, Petition of Pierce, 153 Me. 180, 136 A.2d 510 (1957); Maryland, Gordon v. City of Baltimore, 258 Md. 682, 267 A.2d 98 (1970), and Wesley Home, Inc. v. Mercantile Safe Deposit and Trust Co., 265 Md. 185, 289 A.2d 337 (1972); Massachusetts, 1st Church in Somerville v. Atty. Gen., 375 Mass. 332, 376 N.E.2d 1226 (1978); Michigan, Gifford v. First Nat'l Bank, 285 Mich. 58, 280 N.W. 108 (1938),

and In re Road's Estate, 41 Mich. App. 405, 200 N.W.2d 728 (1972); Minnesota, MINN. STAT. ANN. § 501.12 (Supp. 1980), and In re Minson's Estate, 238 Minn. 358, 57 N.W.2d 22 (1953); Mississippi, Citizens' Nat'l Bank v. Longshore, 304 So.2d 287 (Miss. 1974); Missouri, Comfort v. Higgins, 576 S.W.2d 331 (Mo. 1979), and Ramsey v. Field, 237 S.W.2d 143 (Mo. 1915); Nebraska, Rohlff v. Gunman Old People's Home, 143 Neb. 636, 10 N.W.2d 686 (1943), and In re Nilson's Estate, 81 Neb. 809, 116 N.W. 971 (1908); New Hampshire, Attorney General v. Rochester Trust Company, 115 N.W. 74, 333 A.2d 718 (1975); New Jersey, Howard Savings Institution of Newark, New Jersey v. Peep, 34 N.J. 494, 170 A.2d 39 (1961); New Mexico, Farmers and Merchants Bank v. Woolf, 86 N.M. 320, 523 P.2d 1346, 1350 (1974); New York, N.Y. ESTATES AND TRUSTS LAW § 8-1.1 (McKinney Supp. 1970), and see, e.g., In re Randall's Estate, 71 Misc.2d 1063, 338 N.Y.S.2d 269 (1972), and In re Goehringer's Will, 69 Misc.2d 145, 329 N.Y.S.2d 516 (1972); North Carolina, N.C. GEN. STAT. § 36A-53 (Supp. 1979), and see, e.g., Wilson v. First Presbyterian Church, 284 N.C. 284, 200 S.E.2d 769 (1973); Ohio, Rice v. Stanley, 42 OHIO St.2d 209, 327 N.E.2d 774 (1975); Oklahoma, OKLA. STAT. ANN. tit. 60, § 602, and Estate of Campbell v. Lepley, 532 P.2d 1374 (Okla. 1975); Oregon, Matter of King's Estate, 39 Or. App. 239, 592 P.2d 231 (1979); Pennsylvania, In re Kay's Estate, 456 Pa. 43, 317 A.2d 193 (1974), and In re Christ Evangelist Lutheran Church of Monessen, 49 West 273 (Westmoreland C.C.P. 1967); Rhode Island, Industrial Nat'l Bank of R.I. v. Gloucester Manton Free Public Library, 107 R.I. 161, 265 A.2d 724 (1970); South Carolina, Furman University v. McLeod, 238 S.C. 475, 120 S.E.2d 865 (1965); Texas, Stahl v. Shriners' Hosp. for Crippled Children, 581 S.W.2d 227 (Tex. Civ. App. 1979); Utah, Gardner v. Davis County, 523 P.2d 865 (Utah, 1974); Vermont, Ball v. Hall, 129 Vt. 200, 274 A.2d 516 (1971); Virginia, Campbell v. Board of Trustees of James Barry Robinson Home for Boys, 260 S.E.2d 204 (Va. 1980); Washington, Puget Sound Nat. Bank of Tacoma v. Easterday, 56 Wash. 2d 937, 350 P.2d 444 (1963); West Virginia, W. VA. CODE § 35-2-2, and Beatty v. Union Trust and Deposit Co., 123 W. Va. 144, 13 S.E.2d 760 (1967); Wisconsin, In re Gansen's Estate, 79 Wisc. 2d 180, 255 N.W.2d 483 (1977), and In re Berry's Estate, 139 N.W.2d 72 (Wisc. 1966); Wyoming, Town of Cody v. Buffalo Bill Memorial Association, 64 Wyo. 468, 196 P.2d 369 (1948).

43. Georgia, Freedman v. Scheer, 223 Ga. 705, 157 S.E.2d 875 (1967); and Tennessee, Hardin v.

Independent Order of Odd Fellows of Tennessee, 51 Tenn. App. 586, 370 S.W.2d 844 (1963).

44. Model Act § 51.

45. See, e.g., MD. EDUC. CODE ANN. § 12–206 (Supp. 1979).

46. Model Act § 59.

47. *Id.* § 53.

48. *Id.* § 55.

49. *Id.*

50. See note 42, *supra.*

51. Model Act § 62.

2. State Support

1. The survey results are published in Edward McGlynn Gaffney, Jr., and Philip R. Moots, *Government and Campus: Federal Regulation of Religiously Affiliated Higher Education* (Notre Dame, Ind.: University of Notre Dame Press, 1982).

2. *Id.*, note 1, *supra*, pp. 11–13.

3. A. E. Dick Howard, *State Aid to Private Higher Education* (Charlottesville, Va.: Michie, 1977). The authors of the present volume are grateful to Professor Howard not only for his careful study of this theme, to which we refer in each of the ensuing chapters dealing with state support, but also for the benefit of his counsel concerning how to proceed in our own study.

4. 403 U.S. 672 (1971).

5. 20 U.S.C. §§ 751(a)(2) and 1132e(C); see also 45 C.F.R. § 170.

6. 403 U.S. at 684.

7. "Rather than focus on the four defendant colleges and universities involved in this case, however, appellants seek to shift our attention to a 'composite profile' they have constructed of the 'typical sectarian' institution of higher education. . . . Individual projects can be properly evaluated if and when challenges arise with respect to particular recipients and some evidence is then presented to show that the institution does in fact possess [such] characteristics [as to make it ineligible for aid]. We cannot, however, strike down an Act of Congress on the basis of a hypothetical 'profile.' " *Id.* at 682.

8. *Id.* at 684.

9. It should be noted, however, that the Court undermined much of the rationale underlying the prohibition in the federal statute against religious use of a federally funded building when it required, not simply allowed, the State of Missouri to make space available for religious worship by a student group on a public campus. Widmar v. Vincent, 454 U.S. 263 (1981).

10. S.C. CODE ANN. § 22–41.4.

11. *Id.* § 22–41.2.

12. *Id.* § 22–41.10.

13. *Id.* § 22–41.5.

14. Howard, note 3, *supra*, p. 40.

15. 413 U.S. 734 (1973).

16. *Id.* at 741–742.

17. *Id.* at 742–745.

18. *Id.* at 745–748.

19. 20 U.S.C. § 751(a)(2).

20. MD. EDUC. CODE § 17–102, formerly MD. ANN. CODE art. 77A, § 66.

21. MD. EDUC. CODE § 17–104, formerly MD. ANN. CODE art. 77A, § 67.

22. MD. EDUC. CODE § 17–107, formerly MD. ANN. CODE art. 77A, § 68A.

23. 426 U.S. 736 (1976).

24. *Id.* at 754.

25. *Id.* at 755–761.

26. *Id.* at 761–767. Concurring in the judgment, Justice White, joined by Justice Rehnquist, observed that the excessive entanglement test was "curious and mystifying" when announced, and remained a superfluous and "redundant exercise of evaluating the same facts and findings under a different label." *Id.* at 769. *See also* Tilton v. Richardson, 403 U.S. 602, 661–671 (1971) (White, J., concurring) and Committee for Public Education and Religious Liberty v. Nyquist, 413 U.S. 756, 813–824 (1973) (White, J., dissenting). And see Kenneth F. Ripple, "The Entanglement Test of the Religion Clauses—A Ten Year Assessment," 27 U.C.L.A. L. REV. 1195 (1980), and Edward McGlynn Gaffney, "Political Divisiveness Along Religious Lines: The Entanglement of the Court in Sloppy History and Bad Public Policy," 24 ST. LOUIS U.L.J. 205 (1980).

27. 38 U.S.C. § 1651.

28. 20 U.S.C. § 1070a.

29. 20 U.S.C. § 1070b.

30. 20 U.S.C. § 1070e.

31. 20 U.S.C. § 1087aa.

32. 20 U.S.C. § 1071.

33. 20 U.S.C. § 1070c.

34. 413 U.S. 756 (1973).

35. *Id.* at 782, note 38.

36. 429 F. Supp. 871 (W.D. N.C. 1977).

37. 433 F. Supp. 97 (M.D. Tenn. 1977).

38. 429 F. Supp. at 878.

39. 433 F. Supp. at 100 (emphasis added).

40. *Id.*

41. 434 U.S. 803 (1977).

42. 454 U.S. 464 (1982).

43. *Id.* at 468.

44. See, e.g., Tully v. Griffin, Inc., 429 U.S. 68, 74 (1976); Hicks v. Miranda, 422 U.S. 332, 343–345 (1975); Ohio ex rel. Eaton v. Price, 360 U.S. 246, 247 (1959). And see Robert L. Stern and

Eugene Gressman, *Supreme Court Practice* (Washington, D.C.: Bureau of National Affairs, 5th ed., 1978), pp. 321–325; and Charles Alan Wright, *Law of Federal Courts* (St. Paul: West Publishing Co., 3rd ed., 1976), pp. 550–551.

45. Howard, note 3, *supra*, p. 14.

46. See Everson v. Bd. of Education, 330 U.S. 1 (1947).

47. See Matthews v. Quinton, 362 P.2d 932 (Alaska 1961), cert. denied and appeal dismissed, 368 U.S. 517 (1962).

48. See, e.g., Matthews, note 47, *supra*, and Paster, note 50 *infra*. In Prune Yard Shopping Center v. Robins, 447 U.S. 74 (1980), Justice Rehnquist noted that "state constitutional provisions, which permit individuals to exercise free speech and petition rights on the property of a privately owned shopping center to which the public is invited, [do not] violate the shopping center owner's property rights under the Fifth and Fourteenth Amendments or his free speech rights under the First and Fourteenth Amendments." *Id.* at 76–77. And see William J. Brennan, "State Constitutions and the Protection of Individual Rights," 90 HARV. L. REV. 489 (1977); Jerome B. Falk, "The Supreme Court of California 1971–1972. Foreword: The State Constitution: A more than 'Adequate' Nonfederal Ground," 61 CALIF. L. REV. 273 (1973); A.E. Dick Howard, "State Courts and Constitutional Rights in the Day of the Burger Court," 62 VA. L. REV. 873 (1976); Donald E. Wilkes, "The New Federalism in Criminal Procedure: State Court Evasion of the Burger Court," 62 KY. L.J. 421, 437–443 (1974); Donald E. Wilkes, "More on the New Federalism in Criminal Procedure," 63 KY. L.J. 873 (1975); "Project Report, Toward an Activist Role for State Bills of Rights," 8 HARV. C.R.–C.L. L. REV. 271 (1973).

49. See Wolman v. Walter, 433 U.S. 229 (1977), and Bd. of Education v. Allen, 392 U.S. 236 (1968).

50. Paster v. Tussey, 512 S.W. 2d 97, 101–102 (Mo. 1974), cert. denied, 419 U.S. 1111 (1975).

51. 454 U.S. 263 (1981).

52. *Id.* at 275.

53. 12 Cal. 2d 593, 526 P. 2d 513, 116 Cal. Rptr. 361 (1974).

54. Note 15, *supra*.

55. 526 P.2d at 518.

56. *Id.* at 520–522.

57. California Teamsters' Assn. v. Riles, 29 Cal. 3d 794, 632 P.2d 953, 176 Cal. Rptr. 30 (1981).

58. N.Y. CONST. Art. 11, § 3. For a discussion of the history behind the Blaine amendment, see John Webb Pratt, *Religion, Politics and Diversity: The Church-State Theme in New York History* (Ithaca: Cornell University Press, 1967).

59. The "Bundy Law," codified at N.Y. EDUC. LAW § 6401, was sustained in College of New Rochelle v. Nyquist, 37 App. Div. 2d 461, 326 N.Y.S. 2d 765 (3d Dept. 1971). For a more thorough discussion of this issue, see Howard, note 3, *supra*, pp. 627–631.

60. See, e.g., Americans United for Separation of Church and State v. Colorado, 648 P.2d 1072 (Colo. 1982), discussed in chapter 14 on Colorado, *infra*, in text accompanying note 33.

3. Personnel Policies and Practices

1. See, e.g., Gustavus Myers, *History of Bigotry in the United States* (New York: Capricorn Books, 1960), and John Higham, *Strangers in the Land: Patterns of American Nativism, 1860–1925* (New York: Atheneum, 1963).

2. See, e.g., *Religious Discrimination: A Neglected Issue* (Washington, D.C.: United States Commission on Civil Rights, 1979).

3. Only seven states do not have such legislation: Alabama, Arkansas, Georgia, Louisiana, Mississippi, Texas and Virginia.

4. For a description of a wide variety of practices of RACs that maintain a policy of religious preference in employment, see Edward McGlynn Gaffney, Jr. and Philip R. Moots, *Government and Campus: Federal Regulation of Religiously Affiliated Higher Education* (Notre Dame, Ind.: University of Notre Dame Press, 1982), pp. 32–39.

5. *Achieving the Mission of Church-Related Institutions of Higher Learning*, Report of a Conference held Nov. 29–30, 1976 (Washington, D.C.: Association of American Colleges, 1977), pp. 6–7.

6. James Tunstead Burtchaell, C.S.C., "Sermon at Mass Inaugurating the Academic Year," Sept. 10, 1972, as cited in NOTRE DAME REPORT, vol. 2, no. 1 (1972–73), pp. 51–52.

7. NOTRE DAME MAGAZINE, Dec. 1978, p. 70; see also the final report of the Committee on University Priorities (University of Notre Dame), which recommended that "the University have a faculty and a student affairs staff among whom committed Catholics predominate" and that "appointments to the faculty and staff continue to be offered by preference to competent members of the Congregation of the Holy Cross, whose contribution to the University is a special guarantee of its Catholic character."

8. *Academic Excellence and Professional Growth: The Tenure Policy of William Jewell College* (Liberty, Mo., 1976), p. 8.

9. The leading case in which the Supreme Court gave constitutional status to freedom of association is NAACP v. Alabama ex rel. Patterson, 357 U.S. 449 (1958). For a general discussion of this freedom, see Charles Rice, *Freedom of Association* (New York:

New York University Press, 1962); Charles Rice, "The Constitutional Right of Association," 16 HASTINGS L. J. 491 (1965); Reena Raggi, "An Independent Right to Freedom of Association," 12 HARV. CIV. RTS.-CIV. LIB. L. REV. 1 (1977); Laurence H. Tribe, *American Constitutional Law* (Mineola, N.Y.: Foundation Press, 1978), pp. 700–710; and John E. Nowak, Ronald D. Rotunda, and J. Nelson Young, *Constitutional Law* (St. Paul: West Publishing Co., 1978), pp. 794–808. For an application of this area of the law to church-related colleges, see Edward Gaffney, "The Constitution and the Campus: The Case for Institutional Integrity and the Need for Critical Self-Evaluation," in John D. Mosely, ed., *Church and College: A Vital Partnership* (Sherman, Tex.: Austin College, 1980), pp. 54–56, 60–62; and W. Cole Durham, Jr., and Dallin H. Oaks, "Constitutional Protections for Independent Higher Education: Limited Powers and Institutional Rights," *id.*, pp. 69–87.

10. Pub. L. 88–352, Title VII, 78 Stat. 255, 42 U.S.C. 2000e *et seq.*

11. Pub. L. 88–352, Title VII, § 703(a), 78 Stat. 255, 42 U.S.C. 2000e–2.

12. *Id.* Title VII., § 702, 42 U.S.C. 2000e–1. For a brief discussion of the legislative history of this provision, see Philip R. Moots and Edward M. Gaffney, *Church and Campus: Legal Issues in Religiously Affiliated Higher Education* (Notre Dame, Ind.: University of Notre Dame Press, 1979), pp. 40–47.

13. Pub. L. 88–352, Title VII, § 703(e)(2), 42 U.S.C. 2000e–2(e)(2). For a brief discussion of the legislative history of this provision, see Moots and Gaffney, *Church and Campus*, note 12, *supra*, pp. 52–54.

14. Pub. L. 88–352, Title VII, § 703(e)(1), 42 U.S.C. 2000e–2(e)(1). For a brief discussion of the legislative history of this provision, see Moots and Gaffney, *Church and Campus*, note 12, *supra*, pp. 47–51.

15. See, e.g., Dothard v. Rawlinson, 433 U.S. 321, 334 (1977); McDonald v. Santa Fe Trail Transportation Co., 427 U.S. 273, 279–280 (1976); Griggs v. Duke Power Co., 401 U.S. 424 (1971).

16. See, e.g., 29 C.F.R. §§ 1604.2 (a) and 1606.1(a).

17. *Uniform Law Commissioners' Model Anti-Discrimination Act* (hereinafter designated as Model Act) § 302 (Chicago: National Conference of Commissioners on Uniform State Laws, 1960), p. 13.

18. *Id.* § 308, p. 16.

19. *Id.* § 309(2), p. 17.

20. See Gaffney and Moots, *Government and Campus*, note 4, *supra*, pp. 75–80.

21. Model Act § 309(1), note 17, *supra*, p. 16.

22. Alaska, Indiana, Missouri, North Carolina, North Dakota, Oregon, South Carolina, South Dakota, Wisconsin, and Wyoming do not provide a BFOQ exception in their civil rights statutes.

23. See, e.g., Arizona, Connecticut, Delaware, Florida, Idaho, Illinois, Kentucky, Maryland, Michigan, Nebraska, Nevada, Oklahoma, Pennsylvania, Tennessee, and Utah.

24. Colorado, Hawaii, Iowa, Kansas, Massachusetts, Minnesota, Montana, New Hampshire, New Mexico, New York, Rhode Island, and Washington.

25. See Gaffney and Moots, note 4, *supra*, pp. 47–48, 66–68.

26. See, e.g., Alaska, Arizona, California, Colorado, Delaware, Hawaii, Idaho, Illinois, Indiana, Iowa, Kentucky, Maine, Massachusetts, Minnesota, Missouri, Montana, Nebraska, New Hampshire, New Jersey, New Mexico, New York, Nevada, Oklahoma, Oregon, Pennsylvania, Rhode Island, South Carolina, South Dakota, Tennessee, Utah, Washington, Wisconsin, and Wyoming.

27. See note 26, *supra*.

28. Model Act, note 17, *supra*, § 309(2).

29. See, e.g., Nebraska, New York.

30. See, e.g., Indiana.

31. See, e.g., Georgia, Idaho.

32. See, e.g., Arizona, Hawaii, Illinois, Massachusetts, New York, Ohio, Pennsylvania.

33. See note 3, *supra*.

34. N.C. GEN. STAT. § 143–422.2.

35. Compare OHIO REV. CODE § 4112.02(H) with (K).

36. Compare MINN. LAWS ANN. § 363.01, subd. 21, with § 363.02, subd. 3. A telephone conversation with a representative of the Minnesota Department of Human Rights confirmed that it was indeed a drafting error, although she explained that the Department reads the statute as though it had been properly drafted. That, of course, provides little assurance that the next administrator or reviewing judge would follow this helpful interpretation.

37. Compare § 309(1) with § 309(2) of the Model Act, note 17, *supra*.

38. 29 U.S.C. §§ 201 *et seq.*

39. For a review of the interrelationship between federal and state hour and wage legislation, see Kent M. Weeks, ed., *A Legal Deskbook for Administrators of Independent Colleges and Universities* (Notre Dame, Ind: Center for Constitutional Studies, 1982), pp. IV–111 to IV–118.

40. See chapter 27 on Maine, *infra*.

41. See chapter 29 on Massachusetts, *infra*.

42. U.S. Dept. of Labor, Wage-Hour Publication No. 1317 (Feb. 1976).

43. NLRB v. Catholic Bishop of Chicago, 440 U.S. 490 (1979).

44. Indiana, Massachusetts, and New York.

45. 29 U.S.C. § 213(a).

46. See, e.g., Alaska, Delaware, Hawaii, Idaho, Illinois, Kansas, Maryland, Minnesota, Montana, New Mexico, Oklahoma, Pennsylvania, Rhode Island, Texas, and West Virginia.

47. See, e.g., Alaska, Arkansas, Delaware, Kansas, Maryland, Minnesota, Montana, Nebraska, New Mexico, New York, North Carolina, Oklahoma, Pennsylvania, Texas, Virginia, Washington, West Virginia, and Wyoming.

48. Employment of Full-Time Students at Subminimum Wages, 29 C.F.R., Part 519.

49. Marshall v. Regis Educational Corp., 666 F.2d 1324 (10th Cir. 1981).

50. Arkansas, Hawaii, Indiana, Montana, New Mexico, New York, Oklahoma, Pennsylvania, and Washington.

51. Virginia and West Virginia.

52. New Jersey.

53. Pub. L. 91–596, § 27, 84 Stat. 1616, 29 U.S.C. § 676. This provision was removed from the U.S. Code after the National Commission ceased to exist.

54. *Id.*

55. *The Report of the National Commission on State Workmen's Compensation Laws* (Washington, D.C.: Government Printing Office, 1972), pp. 117–130.

56. Idaho and Oklahoma exempt all nonprofit corporations from coverage under their worker's compensation statutes. South Carolina exempts all charitable institutions.

57. Illinois, Oklahoma, North Dakota, and Wyoming.

58. Hawaii, Idaho, and Mississippi.

59. Indiana, Louisiana, North Carolina, Virginia, and Wisconsin.

60. Hawaii, Kentucky, Maryland, Oregon, and Washington.

61. New York.

62. Arkansas, Arizona, Iowa, Kentucky, Ohio, Maine, Minnesota, Montana, Rhode Island, South Dakota, Virginia, Washington, Wyoming.

63. Hawaii.

64. Pub. L. 74–271, Title IX, § 907(a) and (c), 49 Stat. 642–643. FUTA is now codified at 26 U.S.C. §§ 3301–3311.

65. 26 U.S.C. § 3309(a)(1) and (c) (1979).

66. *Id.* § 3304(a) and (c) (1979). The operation of the federal-state unemployment system is explained in St. Martin Evangelical Lutheran Church v. South Dakota, 451 U.S. 772, 775–778 (1981).

67. See, e.g., Alabama, Alaska, Arizona, Arkansas, California, Colorado, Delaware, Hawaii, Idaho, Indiana, Kentucky, Michigan, Mississippi, Missouri, Montana, Nebraska, New Jersey, New Mexico, North Dakota, Ohio, Oklahoma, Pennsylvania, Rhode Island, South Carolina, Tennessee, Texas, Utah, Virginia, Washington, West Virginia, Wisconsin, and Wyoming.

68. 26 U.S.C. § 3309(a)(1).

69. *Id.* § 3306(c)(8).

70. *Id.* §§ 501(a) and 501(c)(3).

71. See, e.g., Alabama, Arizona, California, Colorado, Delaware, Florida, Illinois, Indiana, Kansas, Kentucky, Maine, Maryland, Massachusetts, Michigan, Mississippi, Nebraska, New Jersey, New Mexico, North Dakota, South Carolina, Tennessee, Utah, Vermont, Virginia, Washington, and West Virginia.

72. See, e.g., Arkansas, Idaho, New York, North Carolina, Texas, and Wisconsin.

73. See, e.g., Alaska, Connecticut, Hawaii, Iowa, Montana, New Hampshire, Oklahoma, Oregon, Pennsylvania, Rhode Island, and Wyoming.

74. See Alaska.

75. 26 U.S.C. §§ 3309(a)(1) and (c) (1979).

76. See, e.g., Alabama, Alaska, Arizona, Arkansas, California, Colorado, Delaware, Hawaii, Idaho, Illinois, Indiana, Iowa, Kansas, Kentucky, Louisiana, Maine, Maryland, Massachusetts, Michigan, Minnesota, Mississippi, Missouri, Montana, Nebraska, New Hampshire, New Jersey, North Carolina, North Dakota, Ohio, Oklahoma, Oregon, Pennsylvania, Rhode Island, Tennessee, Texas, Utah, Virginia, Washington, West Virginia, Wisconsin, and Wyoming.

77. 451 U.S. 772, (1981).

78. 102 S.Ct. 2499 (1982). The Court declined to reach the merits of the question presented, ruling that the Tax Injunction Act, 28 U.S.C. § 1341, barred the federal court from providing declaratory relief, 102 S.Ct. at 2507–2509, and noting that the appellant schools had a "plain, speedy, and efficient state remedy" for presenting their claims. *Id.* at 2509–2510.

79. This statement of the question is taken from the jurisdictional statement filed by the Solicitor General in No. 81–228.

80. 440 U.S. 490 (1979).

81. *Id.* at 504.

82. *Id.* at 508–518 (Brennan, J., dissenting). See also Gaffney and Moots, note 4, *supra*, pp. 157–161.

83. See, e.g., Notre Dame College (Ca.), 245 N.L.R.B. 386, 102 L.R.R.M. 1283 (1979), and Barber-Scotia College, Inc., 245 N.L.R.B. 406, 102 L.R.R.M. 1330 (1979).

84. 440 U.S. 490 (1979).

85. See cases cited in note 83, *supra*; and see

Gaffney and Moots, note 4, *supra*, pp. 157–161, 165; and see Weeks, note 39, *supra*, pp. IV-85 to IV-103.

86. See, e.g., Seton Hall College, 201 N.L.R.B. 1026, 82 L.R.R.M. 1434 and Niagara University, 226 N.L.R.B. 918, 94 L.R.R.M. 1001 (1976), rev'd., Niagara University v. NLRB, 558 F.2d 1116 (2d Cir. 1977); but see Nazareth Regional High School v. NLRB, 549 F.2d 873 (2d Cir. 1977); St. Francis College, 224 N.L.R.B. 907, 92 L.R.R.M. 1551 (1976), rev'd., St. Francis College v. NLRB, 562 F. 2d 246 (3d Cir. 1977).

87. See Gaffney and Moots, note 4, *supra*, pp. 161–166.

88. 444 U.S. 672 (1980).

89. *Id.* at 694–704 (Brennan, J., dissenting); and see Finkin, "Regulation by Agreement: The Case of Private Higher Education," 65 IOWA L. REV. 1119 (1980); Watkins, "AAUP to Fight Yeshiva Ruling," THE CHRONICLE OF HIGHER EDUCATION, June 30, 1980, p. 4, cols. 1–5.

90. NLRB, Office of General Counsel, Memorandum 81-19, CCH College and University Reports ¶20, 752.

91. Alabama, Alaska, Arkansas, California, Connecticut, Delaware, Florida, Georgia, Hawaii, Kentucky, Maine, Maryland, Massachusetts, Michigan, Minnesota, Missouri, New York, North Dakota, Oregon, Pennsylvania, Rhode Island, South Dakota, Tennessee, Texas, Utah, Virginia, Washington, West Virginia, Wisconsin, Wyoming.

92. Washington and Jefferson College v. Gifford, 55 Dauph. 182 (Pa. Co. Ct. 1944).

93. Alabama, Arkansas, Florida, Georgia, North Dakota, South Dakota, Tennessee, Texas, Utah, Virginia, and Wyoming.

94. Arizona, Iowa, Kansas, Louisiana, Mississippi, Nebraska, Nevada, North Carolina, and South Carolina.

4. Students

1. Arizona, Arkansas, California, Connecticut, Delaware, Florida, Hawaii, Illinois, Iowa, Kansas, Maryland, Maine, Mississippi, Missouri, Nebraska, North Carolina, North Dakota, Ohio, Oklahoma, Rhode Island, Virginia, Washington, West Virginia, Wyoming.

2. 42 U.S.C. 200d (1976).

3. See [1977] Employment Practices Guide, CCH ¶ 20,300.04 (Alaska); ALA. CODE § 16-33A-1(3) (Supp. 1980); ARK. STAT. ANN. § 80-5002(b); CAL. EDUC. CODE § 94110; ILL. ANN. STAT. § 1333 (Supp. 1981); MD. CODE of Fair Practices, art. VI (Exec.

Order, as amended effective Nov. 1, 1976).

4. See, e.g., [1977] Lab. Rel. Rep. (BNA) 453:311, § 30.170(8) (Alaska); IDAHO CODE § 18-7302(e); LA. REV. STAT. ANN. § 17:111 (B)(Supp. 1980); MASS. ANN. LAWS ch. 151C, § 1(b); N.Y. EDUC. LAW § 313(3)(a); PA. STAT. ANN. § 5004(aa)(Supp. 1981).

5. See, e.g., MASS. ANN. LAWS ch. 151C, § 1(b); MINN. STAT. ANN. § 363.02, subd. 3 (Supp. 1981); S.C. CODE § 59-63-40.

6. See also discussion of the "same religion" restriction in Student sections of Michigan, Massachusetts, and Minnesota, *infra*.

7. N.H. REV. STAT. § 354-A:8 (V-a) (Supp. 1979).

8. MONT. REV. CODES § 49-2-401; OR. REV. STAT. § 659.150(1).

9. IND. ANN. STAT. § 22-9-1-3(p)(3); MICH. COMP. LAWS ANN. § 37-2402; MINN. STAT. ANN. § 363.02, subd. 3 (Supp. 1981).

10. Publ. L. 92-318, Title IX, 86 Stat. 373, 20 U.S.C. § 1681 *et seq.*

11. See "Student" sections of Minn., Mont., Tex., and Cal., *infra*.

12. See "Student" sections of Mass. and Vt. In Missouri, the funding for readers for blind students is provided for in MO. REV. STAT. § 177.140 (Supp. 1981).

13. See "Facilities" section of individual states, *infra*.

14. See "Facilities" section of individual states, *infra*.

15. William A. Kaplin, *The Law of Higher Education: Legal Implications of Administrative Decision Making* (San Francisco: Jossey-Bass, 1978), pp. 1 and 3. For a discussion of the reasons for the increased legal intervention, see *id.* at 7 *et seq.*

16. *Id.* at 4.

17. Note, "Private Government on the Campus – Judicial Review of University Expulsions," 72 YALE L.J. 1362, 1367 (1963).

18. Lexington Theological Seminary v. Vance, 596 S.W. 2d 11, 14 (Ky. App. 1979).

19. Note, "Private Government," note 17, *supra* at 1367. (Apparently, graduate students win more often. See also *id.* at 1372). See also Note, "Expulsion of College and Professional Students – Rights and Remedies," 38 NOTRE DAME LAWYER 174 (1963).

20. Note, "Private Government," note 17, *supra*, at 1367.

21. Note, "Colleges and Universities – Dismissal of Students – Violation of Ecclesiastical Law," 8 SOUTH DAKOTA L. REV. 117 (1963).

22. Note, "Expulsion of College and Professional Students," note 19, *supra*, at 175.

23. Note 17, *supra*, at 1365; Note, "Constitutional Law—Student Academic Freedom—'State Action' and Private Universities," 44 TULANE L. REV. 184, 186 (1969).

24. See Tedeschi v. Wagner College, 49 N.Y. 2d 652, 658, 427 N.Y.S. 2d 760, 763 (1980). Note, "Judicial Intervention in Expulsions or Suspensions by Private Universities," 5 WILLAMETTE L.J. 277 (1969).

25. Note, "Private Government," note 17, *supra*, at 1365.

26. Note 21, *supra*, at 118; Note, "Mandamus—Courts Will Not Interfere With Discretion Exercised in Expelling Student on Ecclesiastical Grounds," 31 FORDHAM L. REV. 215 (1962).

27. Robert M. O'Neil, "Private Universities and Public Law," 19 BUFF. L. REV. 155, 190 (1970).

28. William Toombs and Elaine DiBiase, "College Rules and Court Decisions: Notes on Student Dismissal," 2 J. COL. & UNIV. L. 355, 364 (1975).

29. O'Neil, note 27, *supra*, at 156. "The legal system, the court's posture toward limited involvement in education, and the structure of higher education emanate from the English model where eleemosynary institutions are inviolate and those devoted to education protected even more carefully." Toombs & DiBiase, note 28, *supra*, at 358–59.

30. See Board of Curators of the University of Missouri v. Horowitz, 435 U.S. 78 (1978); Maas v. Corporation of Gonzaga University, 618 P.2d 106 (Wash. App. 1980); Tedeschi v. Wagner College, 49 N.Y. 2d 652, 657–58, 427 N.Y.S. 2d 760, 763 (1980); Jansen v. Emory University, 440 F. Supp. 1060, 1063 (N.D. Ga. 1977).

31. Note, "Private Government," note 17, *supra*, at 1391–93. See Lexington Theological Seminary v. Vance, note 18, *supra*, at 14. In Tedeschi v. Wagner College, note 24, *supra*, the court said: "Suspension or expulsion for causes unrelated to academic achievement, however, involve determinations quite closely akin to the day-to-day work of the judiciary." 49 N.Y. 2d at 658, 427 N.Y.S. 2d at 763.

32. Note, "Expulsion of College and Professional Students," note 19, *supra*, at 186.

33. Board of Curators of the University of Missouri v. Horowitz, 435 U.S. 78 (1978).

34. Maas v. Corporation of Gonzaga University, 618 P.2d 106, 109 (Wash. App. 1980); Tedeschi v. Wagner College, 49 N.Y. 2d 652, 658, 427 N.Y.S. 2d 760, 763 (1980). See Toombs and DiBiase, note 28, *supra*, at 357.

35. Toombs and DiBiase, *id.* at 362 *et seq.* In Jansen v. Emory University, 440 F. Supp. 1060 (N.D. Ga.), the court rejected the plaintiff's claim

that disciplinary procedures applied to his "academic" dismissal, which took into account failing grades entered as a result of honor code violations. See also Tedeschi v. Wagner College, 49 N.Y. 2d 652, 666, 427 N.Y.S. 2d 760, 768 (1980) (Gabrielli, J., dissenting).

36. Toombs and DiBiase, note 28, *supra*, at 363.

37. Note, "Private Government," note 17, *supra*, at 1372.

38. One commentator has noted that the doctrine led to institutional "unbridled arrogance," and "increased indifference" in the treatment of students. Eugene B. Habecker, "Students, Christian Colleges and the Law: and the Walls Come Tumbling Down," 2 J. COL. & UNIV. L. 369, 379 (1975).

39. Note, "Private Government," note 17, *supra*, at 1380. See also Kaplin, note 15, *supra*, at 5.

40. *Id.* at 8. The doctrine is still shakier when the student is married or pays his own way. Note, "Expulsion of College and Professional Students," note 19, *supra*, at 175.

41. Toombs & DiBiase, note 28, *supra*, at 356; Habecker, note 38, *supra*, at 379. See Dixon v. Alabama State Board of Education, 294 F.2d 150 (5th Cir. 1961).

42. U.S. CONST. amend. XIV, § 1 (emphasis added). The Constitution requires the federal government also to provide due process, U.S. CONST. amend. V, and equal protection, Bolling v. Sharpe, 347 U.S. 497 (1954).

43. See Jackson v. Metropolitan Edison Company, 419 U.S. 345, 349–350 (1974); Langley v. Monumental Corp., 496 F. Supp. 1144 (D.C. Md. 1980).

44. See Swanson v. Wesley College, 402 A.2d 401, 402–403 (Del. Supp. 1979).

45. Philip J. Faccenda and Kathleen Ross, "Constitutional and Statutory Regulation of Private Colleges and Universities," 9 VALPARAISO L. REV. 539, 540–41 (1975).

46. 419 U.S. 345 (1974).

47. *Id.* at 349.

48. *Id.* at 349–350.

49. *Id.* at 350.

50. *Id.* at 351.

51. *Id.* at 355, 357.

52. *Id.* at 357.

53. *Id.* at 351.

54. O'Neil, note 27, *supra*, at 155.

55. Note, "Racially-Preferential Policies in Institutions of Higher Education: State Action Limitations on 42 U.S.C. Section 1983 Complaints," 52 NOTRE DAME LAWYER 882, 889 (1977).

56. *Id.* at 923.

57. See O'Neil, note 27, *supra*, at 157 *et seq.*

58. *Id.* at 157.

59. Kaplin, note 15, *supra*, at 19. Not all would agree that there is much difference between state and private schools. See Note, "Private Government," note 17, *supra*, at 1410–1411.

60. "Student Academic Freedom," note 23, *supra*, at 190.

61. Jackson v. Metropolitan Edison Company, 419 U.S. 345, 351 (1974) (emphasis added).

62. Maas v. The Corporation of Gonzaga University, 618 F.2d 106, 110 (Wash. App. 1980).

63. Taylor v. Maryland School for the Blind, 409 F. Supp. 148, 151. (D.C.D. Md. 1976) (relying on Burton v. Wilmington Parking Authority, 365 U.S. 715 (1961)). The District Court acknowledged that other courts have applied the "particular act" analysis. 409 F. Supp. at 151. See also Note, "Legislative State Action and Indiana Private Universities," 9 VALPARAISO L. REV. 611, 616 (1975): "The participation by the state, in the partnership, must authorize or encourage the private wrongs which violate the constitution."

64. Note, "Racially-Preferential Policies," note 55, *supra*, at 916.

65. Note, "Legislative State Action," note 63, *supra*, at 623.

66. Note, "Student Academic Freedom," note 23, *supra*, at 185. See also Williams v. Howard University, 528 F.2d 658 (D.C. Cir. 1976) and Weise v. Syracuse University, 522 F.2d 397 (2d Cir. 1975). According to Kaplin, note 15, *supra*, at 25, in both *Williams* and *Weise*, the courts used a "double standard."

67. Note, "Student Academic Freedom," note 23, *supra*, at 189. This student note suggests that the student rights area is not yet one of special judicial interest. *Id.* at 189–190.

68. "The court has not adopted the notion, accepted elsewhere, that different standards should apply to state action analysis when different constitutional claims are presented." Jackson v. Metropolitan Edison Company, 419 U.S. 345, 373–374 (1974) (Marshall, J., dissenting).

69. O'Neil, note 27, *supra*, at 180.

70. *Id.* at 186.

71. Note, "Private Universities: The Right to be Different," 11 TULSA L. J. 58, 65 (1975).

72. 17 U.S. (4 Wheat.) 518 (1819).

73. *Id.* at 635.

74. Note, "Racially-Preferential Policies," note 55, *supra*, at 911; Note, "Judicial Intervention," note 24, *supra*, at 288.

75. O'Neil, note 27, *supra*, at 182.

76. Kaplin, note 15, *supra,* at 21.

77. Grossner v. Trustees of Columbia University, 287 F. Supp. 535 (S.D. N.Y. 1968), discussed in Robert M. Hendrickson, "State Action and Private

Higher Education," 2 J.L. & EDUC. 53, 60 (1973).

78. O'Neil, note 27, *supra,* at 183.

79. So argued the plaintiffs in Brown v. Mitchell, 409 F.2d 593 (10th Cir. 1969), discussed in Hendrickson, *supra* note 77, at 59.

80. See Walz v. Tax Commission, 397 U.S. 664 (1970), discussed in Note, "Racially-Preferential Policies" note 55, *supra,* at 910.

81. *Id.* at 910; and see Faccenda and Ross, note 45, *supra,* at 545.

82. Broderick v. Catholic University of America, 365 F. Supp. 147, 155 (D.D.C. 1973). (Since the defendant was located in the District of Columbia, the Fifth Amendment rather than the Fourteenth was relied upon). See note 42, *supra.*

83. 419 U.S. 345 (1974).

84. *Id.* at 371 (Marshall, J., dissenting).

85. For the suggestion that universities are "quasi-public," see note 17, *supra,* at 1382.

86. *Id.* at 1384. This may be especially true of Wisconsin's "diploma privilege" situation, which allows one awarded a law degree by a Wisconsin law school to be admitted to the bar without taking the bar examination. See O'Neil, note 27, *supra,* at 184.

87. *Id.* at 1385, quoting Judge Skelley Wright in Kerr v. Enoch Pratt Free Library, 203 F. Supp. 855, 858–859 (E.D. La.), *vacation of decision approved on appeal of new decree,* 306 F.2d 489 (5th Cir. 1962).

88. *Id.* at 1386.

89. Marsh v. Alabama, 326 U.S. 501 (1946). See also Evans v. Newton, 382 U.S. 296 (1966).

90. Note 24, *supra,* at 285.

91. Note 71, *supra,* at 65.

92. "If we were dealing with the exercise . . . of some power delegated to [the private entity] by the state which is traditionally associated with sovereignty, such as eminent domain, our case would be quite a different one." Jackson v. Metropolitan Edison Company, 419 U.S. 345, 352–353 (1974).

93. See, *e.g.,* Swanson v. Wesley College, Inc., 402 A.2d 401, 403 (Del. Super. 1979).

94. Kaplin, note 15, *supra,* at 23. In 1819, Chief Justice Marshall asked: "Does every teacher of youth become a public officer and do donations for the purpose of education necessarily become public property, so far that the will of the legislature, not the will of the donor, becomes the law of the donation?" Dartmouth College v. Woodward, note 72, *supra,* at 634.

95. Jackson v. Metropolitan Edison, 419 U.S. 345, 372 (1974) (Marshall, J., dissenting), citing Wahba v. New York University, 492 F.2d 96, 102 (2d Cir. 1974), *cert. denied,* 419 U.S. 874 (1974).

96. See Dartmouth College v. Woodward, note

72, *supra*, at 636; Hendrickson, note 77, *supra*, at 62. It has been argued that professional school licensing or chartering should be treated differently due to continuing state control over the professions and to state impact on professional school curricula. Note, "Racially-Preferential Policies," note 55, *supra*, at 907.

97. See Hendrickson, note 77, *supra*, at 55, referring to Shelley v. Kraemer, 334 U.S. 1 (1948).

98. Hendrickson, note 77, *supra*, at 65.

99. Note, "Legislative State Action," note 63, *supra*, at 614.

100. Note, "Private Universities," note 71, *supra*, at 65.

101. See Note, "The Lawmen and the Prophets: Sectarian Exercise of Police Authority in Utah and New Jersey," 1980 UTAH L. REV. 447 (1980). The Note points out that the move may be counterproductive in that the state status of the officers puts limits on them, e.g., in certain searches of rooms for drugs, that may not otherwise be present. Thus, greater power may yield less effectiveness. *Id.* at 456–457.

102. O'Neil, note 27, *supra*, at 186–187.

103. *Id.* at 187.

104. Burton v. Wilmington Parking Authority, 365 U.S. 715 (1961).

105. Note, "Student Academic Freedom," note 23, *supra*, at 188, referring to Powe v. Miles, 407 F.2d 73 (2d Cir. 1968).

106. Taylor v. Maryland School for the Blind, 409 F. Supp. 148, 151 (D. Md. 1976).

107. Jackson v. Metropolitan Edison Company, 419 U.S. 345, 360 (1974) (Marshall, J., dissenting).

108. Note, "Mandamus," note 26, *supra*, at 216.

109. See Carr v. St. John's University, 231 N.Y.S. 2d 410, 413 (1962); Note, "Expulsion by Religiously Affiliated College Upheld Where Students Married in Civil Ceremony," 37 N.Y.U.L. REV. 1164 (1962). And see Jansen v. Emory University, 440 F. Supp. 1060 (N.D. Ga. 1977); Lexington Theological Seminary v. Vance, note 18, *supra*.

110. Hendrickson, note 77, *supra*, at 59. See Lexington Theological Seminary v. Vance, 596 S.W.2d 11, 13 (Ky. App. 1979); Swanson v. Wesley College, Inc., 402 A.2d 401, 403 (Del. Super. 1979).

111. Note, "Expulsion of College and Professional Students," note 19, *supra*, at 183.

112. Kaplin, note 15, *supra*, at 179.

113. Tedeschi v. Wagner College, 49 N.Y. 2d 652, 658, 427 N.Y.S. 2d 760, 763 (1980).

114. Note, "Expulsion by Religiously Affiliated College," note 109, *supra*, at 1168; note, "Judicial Intervention," note 24, *supra*, at 281. For the reasons underlying the disparate bargaining power, see Note, "Private Government," note 17, *supra*, at 1378.

115. Note, "Expulsion of College and Professional Students," note 19, *supra*, at 179.

116. *Id.* Apparently, however, courts have not been anxious to void such contracts on such grounds. See Note, "Judicial Intervention," note 24, *supra*, at 279–280; Note, "Colleges and Universities," note 21, *supra*, at 118.

117. See Kaplin, note 15, *supra*, at 181.

118. *Id.* at 6.

119. See Note, "Expulsion by Religiously-Affiliated College," note 109, *supra*, at 1164. See also the broad clause involved in Carr v. St. John's University, 231 N.Y.S. 2d 410 (1962), discussed *infra*, in text accompanying note 161 *et seq.*

120. Note, "Private Government," note 17, *supra*, at 1370.

121. *Id.*

122. Note, "Judicial Intervention," note 24, *supra*, at 283.

123. Lyons v. Salve Regina College, 565 F.2d 200 (1st Cir. 1977); Kaplin, note 15, *supra*, at 179 (citing Slaughter v. Brigham Young University, 514 F.2d 622 (10th Cir. 1975)).

124. Jansen v. Emory University, 440 F. Supp. 1060, 1062 (N.D. Ga.) (1977).

125. Kaplin, note 15, *supra*, at 28. Most states have lowered the age of majority, which may allow college-age students greater ability to enter into binding contracts, to consent to medical treatment and the like. *Id.* at 176–177.

126. *Id.*

127. See Note, "Judicial Intervention," note 24, *supra*, at 291.

128. Kaplin, note 15, *supra*, at 7.

129. *Id.* at 27.

130. See Tedeschi v. Wagner College, 49 N.Y.2d at 659–660, 427 N.Y.S.2d at 764 (1980).

131. The fiduciary approach is discussed and rejected in favor of the contract theory in Maas v. Corporation of Gonzaga University, 618 P.2d 106, 109 (Wash. App. 1980). See also Note, "Judicial Intervention," note 24, *supra*, at 294.

132. O'Neil, note 27, *supra*, at 191.

133. *Id.*

134. Note, "Expulsion of College and Professional Students," note 19, *supra*, at 175.

135. *Id.* at 180.

136. Morale v. Grigel, 422 F. Supp. 988 (D.N.H. 1976).

137. See Faccenda and Ross, note 45, *supra*, at 633.

138. Note, "Private Government," note 17, *supra*, at 1372.

139. Cf. Jackson v. Metropolitan Edison Company, 419 U.S. 345 (1974), involving the termination of electric service to a former customer. Justice Marshall, noting the Court's possible concern about establishing complex procedures that might not benefit a large number of people, observed: "The solution to this problem, however, is to require only abbreviated pretermination procedures for all utility companies, not to free the 'private' companies to behave as they see fit." *Id.* at 373 (Marshall, J., dissenting).

140. In Swanson v. Wesley College, Inc., 402 A.2d 401 (Del. Super. 1979), the court held that the contract theory standard in disciplinary matters is that of "basic procedural fairness," the key to which is "reasonableness." *Id.* at 403.

141. De Prima v. Columbia-Greene Community College, 392 N.Y.S. 2d 348, 349 (1977).

142. Note, "Expulsion of College and Professional Students," note 19, *supra*, at 186.

143. *Id.*

144. Lexington Theological Seminary v. Vance, 596 S.W.2d 11, 12 (Ky. App. 1979); Note, "Expulsion of College and Professional Students," note 119, *supra*, at 177.

145. This discussion of the hearing will presume for the most part that the allegation involves misconduct, as presumably do most hearings. Medical unfitness and purely academic failings are typically resolved otherwise.

146. See Dixon v. Alabama State Board of Education, 294 F.2d 150 (5th Cir. 1961).

147. Note, "Private Government," note 17, *supra*, at 1406. If possible, students should be involved. *Id.* at 1409.

148. Habecker, note 38, *supra*, at 382.

149. Appeal might be appropriate if the tribunal found a regulation to be invalid, or too vague, etc.

150. See Note, "Legislative State Action," note 63, *supra*, at 633.

151. A reviewing court may only require that the school's decision be supported by "some evidence rather than substantial evidence." See Taylor v. Maryland School for the Blind, 409 F. Supp. 148 (D.C. Md. 1976), *aff'd* 542 F.2d 1169.

152. One commentator, stressing the need to think through the penalty, has asked whether expulsion, signifying the student is beyond redemption, should ever be imposed by a Christian college. He asks whether the student should be allowed to finish the term, whether we are punishing the right things, and whether we could give the student optional penalties. Habecker, note 38, *supra*, at 382–383.

153. Tedeschi v. Wagner College, 49 N.Y.2d 659, 660, 427 N.Y.S.2d 760, 764 (1980).

154. See Taylor v. Maryland School for the Blind, 409 F.Supp. 148, *aff'd* 542 F.2d 1169 (D.C. Md. 1976), where, even in a state action case, the court allowed for deviation for special situations. See also Tedeschi v. Wagner College, 49 N.Y.2d 659, 665, 427 N.Y.S.2d 760, 768 (1980) (Gabrielli, J., dissenting).

155. 551 F.2d 591 (4th Cir. 1977).

156. *Id.* at 592.

157. Note, "Private Government," note 17, *supra*, at 1393.

158. Lexington Theological Seminary, Inc. v. Vance, 596 S.W.2d 11 (Ky. App. 1979).

159. *Id.* at 12.

160. *Id.* at 14.

161. 231 N.Y.S. 2d 410, *aff'd* 12 N.Y.2d 802, 187 N.E.2d 18 (App. Div. 1962).

162. *Id.* at 413.

163. *Id.* at 412, quoting N.Y. Educ. Law § 313.

164. 231 N.Y.S. 2d at 412.

165. *Id.* at 413.

166. *Id.* at 414 (dissenting opinion).

167. Kaplin, note 15, *supra*, at 31.

168. O'Neil, note 27, *supra*, at 192. O'Neil, recognizing that "the private sector may have special needs warranting special rules . . . ," overqualifies the institution's right by adding, "so long as the differences are not too great and the Atheists are not turned away along with the Nazis." *Id.*

169. Note, "Private Government," note 17, *supra*, at 1398.

170. *Id.* at 1398–1399.

171. *Id.* at 1400. The Note suggests that if a student is dismissed for violating a religious regulation, his record so specify lest he be deemed unfit for *any* college. *Id.* at 1401.

172. Kaplin, note 15, *supra*, at 181–182.

5. Facilities

1. Wallace F. Caldwell, "State Public Accommodations Laws, Fundamental Liberties and Enforcement Programs," 40 Wash. L. Rev. 841, 843 (1965).

2. Pub. L. No. 88-352, 78 Stat. 241, 42 U.S.C. § 2000 (1964).

3. Alaska, Arkansas, Florida, Georgia, Hawaii, Mississippi, North Carolina, South Carolina, Texas, Virginia. North Dakota's statute is less than comprehensive, but it is substantive enough to label it a public accommodations law.

4. 379 U.S. 241 (1964).

5. Katzenbach v. McClung, 379 U.S. 294 (1964).

6. 42 U.S.C. §§ 2000a–3(c).

7. Caldwell, note 1, *supra*, at 869.

8. 42 U.S.C. § 2000e.

9. See, e.g., MASS. GEN. LAWS ANN. ch. 272, § 92A(10); N.Y. CIV. RIGHTS LAW § 40, and N.Y. EXEC. LAW § 296.2.

10. Nevada is the only state to prohibit an additional type of discrimination (handicap) without also prohibiting sex discrimination. NEV. REV. STAT. § 651.070.

11. E.g., ILL. ANN. STAT. ch. 68, § 1–102 (Smith-Hurd Supp. 1981); LA. CONST. art. I, § 12; OHIO CONST. art. VIII, § 4.

12. E.g., DEL. CODE ANN. tit. 6, § 4502; ARIZ. REV. STAT. § 41–1442; MICH. COMP. LAWS ANN. § 37.2302(a).

13. E.g., KAN. STAT. ANN. § 44–1009 (Supp. 1979); IND. ANN. STAT. § 22–9–1–3(1) (Supp. 1979); NEV. REV. STAT. § 651.070.

14. E.g., N.M. STAT. ANN. § 28–1–2.G; S.D. CODIFIED LAWS ANN. § 20–13–1(12); W. VA. CODE § 5–11–3(j).

15. E.g., ME. REV. STAT. ANN. tit. 5, § 4553(8); MONT. REV. CODES ANN. § 49–2–101(17); R.I. GEN. LAWS § 11–24–3.

16. E.g., R.I. GEN. LAWS § 11–24–3; ARIZ. REV. STAT. ANN. § 41–1441(2)(1974); N.J. STAT. ANN. § 10:5–4; UTAH CODE ANN. § 13–7–2(a).

17. IDAHO CODE § 67–5910(3).

18. E.g., ARIZ. REV. STAT. § 41–1441(2)(1974); DEL. CODE ANN. tit. 6, § 4501.

19. KY. REV. STAT. ANN. § 334.130; TENN. CODE ANN. § 4–21–102(j).

20. Laws in Alaska, Colorado, New Jersey, New York, and Vermont do include schools or colleges as places of public accommodation, although most of those laws also provide exceptions. See, [1980] 8A LAB. REP. (BNA) 453:321, § 30.990(2); COLO. REV. STAT. § 24–34–601(1) (Supp. 1979); N.J. STAT. ANN. § 10–5–5(1)(West); N.Y CIV. RIGHTS LAW § 40 and N.Y. EXEC. LAW § 292.9 (McKinney); VT. STAT. ANN. tit. 13, § 1451(c).

21. "Where general words follow an enumeration of persons or things, by words of a particular and specific meaning, such general words are not to be construed in their widest extent, but are to be held as applying only to persons or things of the same general kind or class as those specifically mentioned." United States v. LaBrecque, 419 F. Supp. 430, 432 (D.N.J. 1976).

22. 42 U.S.C. § 2000a(b).

23. N.H. REV. STAT. ANN. § 354–A:8(iv)(Supp. 1979).

24. 42 U.S.C. § 2000e.

25. IDAHO CODE § 67–5910(3).

26. E.g., R.I. GEN. LAWS § 11–24–3.

27. E.g., KAN. STAT. ANN. § 44–1002(h); ORE. REV. STAT. § 30.675; and see Schwentz v. Boy Scouts of America, 275 Or. 327, 551 P.2d 465 (1976); WIS. STAT. ANN. § 942.04(2)(West Supp. 1980).

28. E.g., IOWA CODE ANN. § 601A.7.2. a (West); NEB. REV. STAT. § 20–137; WASH. REV. CODE ANN. § 49.60.040 (Supp. 1979).

29. MONT. REV. CODES ANN. § 49–2–304(1); LA. CONST. art. I, § 12.

30. E.g., N.Y. EXEC. LAW § 296.11 (McKinney); VT. STAT. ANN. tit. 13, § 1452(b).

31. Pub. L. No. 90–284, title VIII, 82 Stat. 81, 42 U.S.C. §§ 3601–3631 (1968).

32. 42 U.S.C. § 3604.

33. *Id.* § 3607.

34. *Id.* § 3610(d).

35. 42 U.S.C. §§ 1981–1995.

36. *Id.* at § 1982.

37. Johnson v. Zaremba, 381 F. Supp. 165 (D. Ill. 1973).

38. E.g., McLaurin v. Brusturis, 320 F. Supp. 190 (E.D. Wisc. 1970).

39. Kentucky and Vermont do not bar sex discrimination.

40. E.g., MONT. REV. CODES ANN. § 49–2–305(1)(a); OHIO REV. CODE ANN. § 4112.02(G); R.I. GEN. LAWS § 34–37–2 (Supp. 1980).

41. E.g., COLO. REV. STAT. § 24–34.502(1)(a) (Supp. 1979); HAWAII REV. STAT. § 515–3; N.J. STAT. ANN. § 10:5–4 (West).

42. E.g., CONN. GEN. STAT. ANN. § 46a–64 (Supp. 1981); DEL. CODE ANN. tit. 6, §§ 4601 *et seq.;* IOWA CODE ANN. § 601A. 8.1 and 2.

43. MINN. STAT. ANN. § 363.03 subd. 2(1)(a)(West Supp. 1980); WIS. STAT. ANN. § 101.22(1m) and (2)(West Supp. 1980).

44. E.g., CAL. GOV'T CODE §§ 12900 *et seq.;* IDAHO CODE § 67–5909(7); IND. CODE ANN. § 22–9–1–3(1)(Supp. 1979); MD. ANN. CODE art. 49B, § 19; MO. REV. STAT. § 213.105 (Supp. 1981).

45. E.g., ALA. CODE § 11–52–75; LA. REV. STAT. ANN. § 46:195 3(A) (Supp. 1981); WYO. STAT. § 6–9–404.

46. ALASKA STAT. §§ 34.03.101 to 34.03.380 (1975 and Supp. 1980); ARIZ. REV. STAT. ANN. §§ 33–1301 to 33–1381 (1974); DEL. CODE ANN. tit. 25, §§ 5101 *et seq.;* FLA. STAT. ANN. §§ 83.40 to 83.63; HAWAII REV. STAT. §§ 521–1 to 521–77; KAN. STAT. ANN. §§ 383.505 to 383.715; NEB. REV. STAT. §§ 76–1401 to 76–1449; NEV. REV. STAT. § 118A; N.M. STAT. ANN. §§ 47–8–1 to 47–8–51; OHIO REV. CODE ANN. §§ 5321.01 to 5321.19; OR. REV. STAT.

§§ 91.710 to 91.865; Tenn. Code Ann. §§ 64–2801 to 64–2864; Va. Code §§ 55–248.2 to 55–248. 40; Wash. Rev. Code Ann. § 59.18.040 (Supp. 1979).

47. Samuel Jan Brakel and Donald M. McIntyre, "URLTA in Operation: An Introduction," 1980 A.B.F. Res. J. 559, 560.

48. *Id.* at 561.

49. E.g., Idaho Code § 55–2001 (Supp. 1981); Ill. Rev. Stat. ch. 80, § 201.

50. Twenty of thirty-six states have "religious organization" exemption clauses.

51. Mass. Gen. Laws Ann. ch. 151B, § 4.15 (West); N.H. Rev. Stat. Ann. § 354–A: 8(V–a)(Supp. 1979); N.J. Stat. Ann. § 10:5–5n (West Supp. 1980); N.Y. Exec. Law § 296.11 (McKinney); Ohio Rev. Code Ann. § 4112.02(K); Pa. Stat. Ann. tit. 43, § 955; Vt. Stat. Ann. tit. 13, § 1452(b).

52. Ohio Rev. Code Ann. § 4112.02(k)(Page).

53. E.g., Colo. Rev. Stat. § 24–34–502(3) (Supp. 1979); N.M. Stat. Ann. § 28–1–9.B (Appendix 11).

54. E.g., Hawaii Rev. Stat. § 515–8; Mich. Comp. Laws § 37.2403 (Supp. 1981).

55. E.g., Del. Code Ann. tit. 6, § 4604(1) (Supp. 1980); Ga. Code Ann. § 99–4904.

56. Ga. Code Ann. § 99–4904; Ill. Ann. Stat. ch. 68, § 3–106(E) (Supp. 1981); Kan. Stat. Ann. § 44–1018; Md. Ann. Code art. 49B, § 20; Neb. Rev. Stat. § 20–110 (Supp. 1980); Va. Code § 36–92.

57. Laws in Georgia and Nebraska require that an organization's membership not be restricted on account of sex (in addition to race, color, and national origin). See, Ga. Code Ann. § 99–4904; Neb. Rev. Stat. § 20–110 (Supp. 1980).

58. E.g., Cal. Gov't Code § 12927; Iowa Code Ann. § 601A.12–1 (West Supp. 1980); Me. Rev. Stat. Ann. tit. 5, § 4552(6)(c).

59. Alaska, Connecticut, Indiana, Minnesota, Missouri, Oregon, Rhode Island, Washington, West Virginia, Wisconsin.

60. E.g., Minn. Stat. Ann. § 363.02 subd. 2(a) (Supp. 1980); Wis. Stat. Ann. § 942.04(4) (Supp. 1980).

61. [1980] 8A Lab. Rel. Rep. (BNA) 453:321, § 30.985, and Alaska Stat. § 18.80.240 (Supp. 1980); Md. Ann. Stat. § 314.030.1 (Supp. 1980) and *id.* § 213.105 (Supp. 1981); Or. Rev. Stat. § 30.675(2), and *id.* § 659.033(1); Wash. Rev. Code Ann. § 49.60.040 (Supp. 1979); Wis. Stat. Ann. § 942.04(2) (Supp. 1980) and *id.* § 101.22 (1m) and (2) (Supp. 1980).

62. E.g., N.M. Stat. Ann. § 28–1–7.G; Wis. Stat. Ann. § 101.22 (1m) and (2) (Supp. 1980).

63. E.g., Iowa Code Ann. § 601A.8 (West); Md. Ann. Code art. 49B, § 20.

64. Cal. Gov't Code § 12927(e) (West).

65. Del. Code Ann. tit. 6, § 4601(5).

66. E.g., 42 U.S.C. § 2000a(b)(1).

67. E.g., Ohio Rev. Code Ann. § 4112.01 (10); W. Va. Code § 5–11–3(k).

68. E.g., Mont. Rev. Codes Ann. § 49–2–101(11).

69. Most laws only require that the housing accommodation be used by *one* person (or more).

70. This practice is prohibited in Ohio and Rhode Island. See, Ohio Rev. Code Ann. § 4112.02(H)(7); R.I. Gen. Laws § 34–37–4 (Supp. 1980).

71. E.g., Hawaii Rev. Stat. § 515–3(6); Minn. Stat. Ann. § 363.03 subd. 2(1)(C) (Supp. 1980); R.I. Gen. Laws § 34–37–4 (Supp. 1980); S.D. Codified Laws Ann. § 20–13–20(3); W. Va. Code § 5–11–9(f)(2).

72. E.g., Ohio Rev. Code Ann. § 4112.02(J).

73. E.g., Ky. Const. § 189; Mont. Const. art. X, § 6(1); Wash. Const. art. 1, § 11.

74. See, A.E. Dick Howard, *State Aid to Private Higher Education* (Charlottesville, Va.: Michie, 1977), p. 664. See also discussion of state financial support in chapter on Rhode Island.

75. E.g., Ala. Code §§ 16–18A–1 to 16–18A–13 (Supp. 1980); Cal. Educ. Code §§ 94100 to 94210; Va. Code §§ 23–30–39 to 23–30–51.

76. E.g., Conn. Gen. Stat. Ann. § 10–335 to 10–357; Me. Const. art. VIII, § 1; N.Y. Educ. Law, § 6401 (McKinney Supp. 1979).

77. See relevant discussion in chapters on Arizona, Idaho, Louisiana, Mississippi, and Ohio.

78. E.g., Or. Rev. Stat. § 351.160; see also Or. Const. art. XI–F(1); Tenn. Code Ann. §§ 48–1901 *et seq.*

79. E.g., Ala. Code § 16–18A–2(2) (Supp. 1980); Ga. Code Ann. § 32–4903(b) (1980 and Supp. 1981); Pa. Stat. Ann. tit. 24, § 5503(2) (Purdon Supp. 1981).

80. E.g., Cal. Educ. Code § 94.110; Ill. Ann. Stat. ch. 144, § 1333(3)(Supp. 1981); Ind. Code Ann. § 20–12–63–3 (Supp. 1979); Pa. Stat. Ann. tit. 24, § 5503(3)(Purdon Supp. 1981). Pennsylvania's restrictions apply to only one of the state's comprehensive facilities aid programs.

81. See generally Comment, "Access to Buildings and Equal Employment Opportunity for the Disabled: Survey of State Statutes," 50 Temp. L.Q. 1067–1085 (1977).

82. E.g., Alaska Stat. § 35.10.015 (1980); La. Rev. Stat. Ann. § 49:148 (West Supp. 1977); Utah Code Ann. § 26–27–1 (1976).

83. N.D. Cent. Code § 48–02–19 (Supp. 1975);

PA. STAT. ANN. tit. 71 § 1455.1 (Purdon Supp. 1977–1978); OR. REV. STAT. § 447.235 (1975).

84. E.g., DEL. CODE ANN. tit. 6, § 4604 (Supp. 1980); KAN. STAT. ANN. § 44–1009(b) (Supp. 1979); N.Y. EXEC. LAW § 296.4 (McKinney Supp. 1981).

85. Pub. L. No. 91–596, 84 STAT. 1590, 29 U.S.C. §§ 651–678.

86. 29 U.S.C. § 654(a)(1).

87. *Id.* § 652(5).

88. 29 C.F.R. § 1975.4(c)(1)(1980).

89. *Id.* § 1975.4(c)(2).

90. E.g., ALA. CODE § 25–1–1(1977); GA. CODE ANN. § 54–123; OKLA. STAT. ANN. tit. 40, § 403 (Supp. 1980); W. VA. CODE § 21–3–1.

91. E.g., LA. REV. STAT. ANN. § 23:8; MONT. REV. CODES ANN. §§ 50–70–101 to 50–70–118; and *id.* §§ 50–71–101 to 50–71–334; N.D. CENT. CODE § 34–06–02.

92. E.g., IDAHO CODE § 72–720 (1979); *id.* § 72–102 (1979); and *id.* § 72–212 (1979); ME. REV. STAT. ANN. tit. 26, § 563(7) (Supp. 1980).

93. 29 U.S.C. § 651(11).

94. *Id.* §§ 667(c)–(f).

95. Barry Brown, "State Plans Under the Occupational Safety and Health Act of 1970," 38 LAW & CONTEMP. PROB. 745, 750 (1974).

96. Mark A. Rothstein, "OSHA After Ten Years: A Review and Some Proposed Reforms," 34 VAND. L. REV. 71, 112 (1981).

97. 45 Fed. Reg. 47,542 (1980). (Alaska, California, Kentucky, New Mexico, Oregon, South Carolina, Utah, Virginia, Washington, Wyoming).

98. Only four states have safety standards which are created independently of the federal OSHA standards. Brown, note 95, *supra*, at 754.

99. CONN. GEN. STAT. ANN. § 31–367(d); N.H. REV. STAT. ANN. § 277:1.

100. 29 U.S.C. § 666.

101. E.g., CONN. GEN. STAT. ANN. §§ 19–211 *et seq.*; VA. CODE § 35–25; W. VA. CODE §§ 16–6–2 to 16–6–10.

102. E.g., ALASKA STAT. § 14.48.060(b)(11) (Supp. 1980); MD. ANN. STAT. §§ 441.500 *et seq.*, UTAH CODE ANN. § 55–18–9(7).

103. E.g., MICH. COMP. LAWS §§ 29.1 to 29.24; MISS. CODE ANN. §§ 45–11–45 to 45–11–47; TENN. CODE ANN. § 53–2562.

104. See e.g., N.M. STAT. ANN. §§ 47–8–1 to 47–8–51.

6. Taxation

1. I.R.C. §§ 511, 512, 513.

2. I.R.C. § 501(c)(3).

3. See Treas. Reg. § 1.501–1(d)(1)(ii).

4. See Bob Jones University v. Simon, 416 U.S. 725 (1974), in which an RAC's tax exempt status was revoked for excluding all blacks (or at the very least all unmarried blacks) from admission because the founding religion disapproved of interracial dating.

5. See the discussion of admissions in Chapter 4, "Students", *supra*.

6. U.S. CONST. amend. I.

7. Virtually all RACs have a federal income tax exemption.

8. Neither North Carolina nor Maine has a statute or Constitutional provision exempting nonprofit organizations from the state income tax.

9. See, e.g., CONN. GEN. STAT. ANN. § 12–214 (Supp. 1981); KY. REV. STAT. ANN. § 141.040; W. VA. CODE § 11–24–5; IDAHO CODE § 63–3026.

10. See, e.g., ALASKA STAT. § 43.20.021 (Supp. 1980); FLA. STAT. ANN. § 220.13(2)(h) (Supp. 1980); HAWAII REV. STAT. § 235–2.3 (Supp. 1979).

11. See, e.g., LA. REV. STAT. ANN. 47:121(5); N.D. CENT. CODE § 57–38–09(8); UTAH CODE ANN. § 59–13–4(4).

12. CAL. REV. & TAX CODE , § 23701(d).

13. See, e.g., TENN. CODE ANN. § 67–2610 (income from RAC stocks and bonds exempt as long as the income is used for exempt purposes); MONT. REV. CODES ANN. § 15–31–102(3) (federal unrelated business income tax liability must exceed $100 before Montana income tax applies).

14. See, e.g., N.D. CENT. CODE § 57–38–09.1 (Supp. 1979); MONT. REV. CODES ANN. § 15–31–111.

15. I.R.C. § 2055.

16. [1978] 1 FED. TAXES EST. & GIFT (P–H) ¶ 120, 552.

17. The Nevada Constitution specifically forbids state inheritance and estate taxes. NEV. CONST. art. 10, § 1.

18. *Black's Law Dictionary* (St. Paul: West Publishing Co., 1979), p. 704.

19. See, e.g., VT. STAT. ANN. tit. 32, §§ 6541 *et seq.*; LA. REV. STAT. ANN. §§ 47.2402 *et seq.*

20. CAL. REV. & TAX CODE § 14122, as limited by Cohn v. Cohn, 123 P.2d 833 (Cal. 1942).

21. [1978] 1 FED. TAXES EST. & GIFT (P–H) ¶ 120,026.

22. With the possible exception of Florida. See FLA. STAT. ANN. § 198.44.

23. *Black's Law Dictionary* note 18, *supra*, at 493.

24. See, e.g., CAL. REV. & TAX CODE §§ 13403–13408; DEL. CODE ANN. tit. 30, § 1322; MINN. STAT. ANN. § 291.03 (Supp. 1981).

25. See, e.g., CONN. GEN. STAT. ANN. § 12–391; MISS. CODE ANN. § 27–9–5 (Supp. 1981); S.D.

CODIFIED LAWS ANN. § 10–40A–3 (Supp. 1981).

26. I.R.C. § 2011(b).

27. See, e.g., HAWAII REV. STAT. § 236–13; CAL. REV. & TAX CODE § 13441; Washington, having no estate tax, enacted an additional inheritance tax, WASH. REV. CODE ANN. § 83.04.010, but did exempt transfers to RACS. See also, ILL. ANN. STAT. ch. 120, § 403a; MINN. STAT. ANN. § 291.34.

28. WYO. STAT. § 39–6–801.

29. But see VA. CODE §§ 58–154 and 58–162 (Supp. 1981), which could be read to exempt transfers to RACs from the additional estate tax.

30. See, e.g., CAL. REV. & TAX CODE § 13841; MICH. COMP. LAWS ANN. § 205.202(a) (Supp. 1981); MASS. ANN. LAWS ch. 65A, §§ 1 *et seq.*; S.D. COMP. LAWS §§ 10–40–23, 10–40A–3 (Supp. 1981).

31. See, e.g., WASH. REV. CODE ANN. § 83.58.070 (1981); CAL. REV. & TAX CODE § 15441; COLO. REV. STAT. § 39–25–104(1)(a); DEL. CODE ANN. § 1401; R.I. GEN. LAWS § 44–24–4.

32. I.R.C. §§ 2503, 2522.

33. I.R.C. § 170(c)(2)(B) and (C).

34. I.R.C. § 170(b)(1) and (2) limit such deductions to fifty percent of an individual's contribution base and five percent of a corporation's taxable income. Many states impose the same limitations on their state income tax deductions for contributions.

35. [1981] 3 FED. TAXES (P-H) ¶ 16,011.

36. Nevada, New Hampshire, South Dakota, Tennessee, Texas and Wyoming do not impose an individual income tax.

37. See, e.g., ALASKA STAT. §§ 43.20.01 *et seq.*; ILL. ANN. STAT. ch. 120.

38. See MASS. ANN. LAWS ch. 63, §§ 1 *et seq.*

39. See MONT. REV. CODES ANN. §§ 15–31–101 *et seq.*; VA. CODE § 58.151.013.

40. I.R.C. § 63.

41. See e.g., ARK. STAT. ANN. § 84–2016.3; VT. STAT. ANN. tit. 32, § 581; HAWAII REV. STAT. §§ 235–2 *et seq.*

42. See GA. CODE ANN. § 91A–3607; MD. ANN. CODE art. 81, § 281(a).

43. COLO. REV. STAT. § 39–22–113 (Supp. 1980).

44. IDAHO CODE § 63–3029A (Supp. 1980); IND. ANN. STAT. § 6–3–3–5(a) (Supp. 1979); MICH. COMP. LAWS ANN. § 206.260 (Supp. 1981).

45. See IND. ANN. STAT. § 6–3–3–5(a) (Supp. 1979) for additional limitations.

46. MICH. COMP. LAWS ANN. § 206.260 (Supp. 1981).

47. IDAHO CODE § 63–3029A (Supp. 1980).

48. IDAHO CODE §§ 63–3002 *et seq.*

49. *Id.* § 63–3024.

50. Following general statutory trends, "property"

and property tax abatement in this section refer to both real and personal property.

51. See, e.g., N.M. CONST. art. VIII, § 3.

52. See, e.g., MISS. CODE ANN. § 27–31–1(d) (Supp. 1981).

53. See, e.g., MASS. ANN. LAWS ch. 59, § 5(3).

54. UTAH CODE ANN. § 59–2–31.

55. See, e.g., ILL. ANN. STAT. ch. 120, § 500.1 and .2 and HAWAII REV. STAT. § 246–32.

56. ALASKA STAT. § 29.53.020 (Supp. 1980).

57. MICH. COMP. LAWS ANN. § 211.7(d), as construed in Ladies Literary Club v. Grand Rapids, 298 N.W. 2d 422, 425 (Mich. 1980) (see cases cited therein holding that exemption statutes are to be strictly construed in favor of the taxing unit.)

58. Arnold College for Hygiene and Physical Educ. v. Town of Milford, 144 Conn. 206, 128 A.2d 537 (1957)

59. National Music Camp v. Green Lake Township, 76 Mich. App. 608, 610, 257 N.W. 2d 188, 190 (1977).

60. FLA. CONST. art. 7, § 3.

61. MISS. CODE ANN. § 27–31–1(d) (Supp. 1981).

62. Hilger v. Harding College, Inc., 231 Ark. 686, 331 S.W. 2d 851 (1960).

63. MINN. CONST. art. 10, § 1.

64. PA. CONST. art. 8, § 2.

65. VA. CODE § 58–12.

66. TENN. CONST. art. 2, § 28.

67. WASH. REV. CODE ANN. § 84.36.050 (Supp. 1979).

68. See State v. Waggoner, 162 Tenn. 172, 35 S.W. 2d 389 (1931).

69. See Washington County v. Sullins College Corp., 211 Va. 591, 179 S.E. 2d 630 (1971); Commonwealth v. Trustees of Hampton Normal, 106 Va. 614, 56 S.E. 594 (1907).

70. See, e.g., ALASKA STAT. § 29.53.020 (Supp. 1980); HAWAII REV. STAT. § 246–32(d); McKee v. Alaska, 490 P.2d 1226, 1230 (Alaska, 1971).

71. See, e.g., GA. CODE ANN. § 91A–1102.

72. Income derived from tax-exempt property which is used for RAC educational or otherwise exempt purposes is also exempt from state income taxation.

73. ALA. CODE § 40–9–1(12) (Supp. 1980).

74. CONN. GEN. STAT. ANN. § 12–81(8).

75. See, e.g., Indiana's limit of 800 acres at IND. CODE ANN. § 6–1.1–10–20; Wisconsin's limit of 80 acres at WISC. STAT. ANN. § 70.11(3); Mississippi's limit of 640 acres at MISS. CODE ANN. § 27–31–1(d) (Supp. 1981).

76. See, e.g., HAWAII REV. STAT. § 246–32(b)(1) (B); ILL. REV. STAT. ch. 120, § 500.1; N.D. CENT. CODE § 5702–08.6 (Supp. 1979).

77. See, e.g., HAWAII REV. STAT. § 246–32(b)(1)(B); MASS. ANN. LAWS ch. 59, § 5(3).

78. See Burris v. Tower Hill School Ass'n, 36 Del. 577, 179 A. 397 (1935); State v. Waggoner, 162 Tenn. 172, 35 S.W. 2d 389 (1931).

79. See generally, Annot., 55 A.L.R. 3d 485 (1974).

80. WIS. STAT. ANN. § 70.11(4).

81. See, e.g., N.C. GEN. STAT. § 105–248.

82. See, e.g., KAN. STAT. ANN. § 79–201; MO. ANN. STAT. § 137.100(6).

83. ALASKA STAT. § 29.53.010.

84. See, e.g., MICH. COMP. LAWS ANN. § 211.9(a); IND. ANN. STAT. § 6-1.1-10-16(e) (Supp. 1979).

85. See, e.g., ILL. REV. STAT. ch. 32, §§ 163a *et seq.*; GA. CODE ANN. § 91A–1102(c); FLA. STAT. ANN. § 199.072(2)(a) (Supp. 1980).

86. There appears to be no statutory provision exempting RACs from the payment or collection of sales taxes in either New Mexico or Alaska.

87. See, e.g., MASS. ANN. LAWS ch. 64H, § 6(e); COLO. REV. STAT. § 39–26–114(1)(a)(viii) (Supp. 1979).

88. J.F. Due, *State and Local Sales Taxation* (Public Administration Service: Chicago, 1971), p. 77.

89. N.C. GEN. STAT. § 105-164.14(b).

90. See, e.g., MASS. ANN. LAWS ch. 64H, § 6(e).

91. See, e.g., MINN. ANN. STAT. § 297A.251 (Supp. 1980); MD. ANN. CODE , art. 81, § 306(i) (Supp. 1979).

92. HAWAII REV. STAT. § 237–23(b)(3).

93. MISS. CODE ANN. § 27–65–111(g) (Supp. 1979).

94. N.C. GEN. STAT. § 105-164.14(b).

95. KAN. STAT. ANN. § 79–3606(c) (Supp. 1979).

96. See, e.g., OHIO REV. CODE ANN. § 5739.02(B)(9).

97. See, e.g., MASS. ANN. LAWS ch. 64H, § 6(c).

98. TEX. TAX–GEN. ANN. art. 20.04(T).

99. MASS. ANN. LAWS ch. 64H, § 6(m).

100. W. VA. CODE § 11–15–9(3) (Supp. 1981).

101. MASS. ANN. LAWS ch. 64H, § 6(m).

102. See, e.g., W. VA. CODE § 11–15–8.

103. See MASS. ANN. LAWS ch. 64H, § 6(h).

104. *Id.* See also OHIO REV. CODE ANN. § 5739.02(B)(2); N.D. CENT. CODE 57-39.2-04.1; KY. REV. STAT. ANN. § 139–485; MD.ANN. CODE art. 81, § 326(c)(2); W. VA. CODE § 11–15–11 (Supp. 1981).

105. See, e.g., TEX. TAX–GEN. ANN. art. 20.04(L)(2)(b) and (c); IND. CODE ANN. § 6-2-1-39(b)(i)(viii)–(xiii). But see Andrews v. Tax Comm., 135 Ohio 374, 21 N.E. 2d 106 (1939) (sales tax levied only on the sale of candy and confectionary unconstitutional).

106. See, e.g., CAL. REV. & TAX. CODE § 6359(b)(c) and the application of the provision in Treasure Island Catering Co. v. State Board of Equalization, 19 C.2d 181, 120. P.2d 1 (1942) (serving a hot dog wrapped in a paper napkin from a stand with no dining facilities held to be sales tax-exempt).

107. See text accompanying notes 112–116, *infra*.

108. See MASS. ANN. LAWS ch. 64H, § 6 for a typical sales tax exemption.

109. N.D. CENT. CODE § 57–39.2–04.23 (Supp. 1979).

110. N.Y. TAX LAW § 1105(d)(ii)(b).

111. *Id.*

112. NEB. REV. STAT. § 77–2704(1)(g)(i) (Supp. 1980).

113. KY. REV. STAT. § 139.495(1)(b); IND. CODE ANN. § 6–2–1–39(b)(7) (Supp. 1979); OHIO REV. CODE ANN. § 5739.02(B)(3).

114. OKLA. STAT. ANN. tit. 68, § 1305(g) (Supp. 1979–1980).

115. MASS. ANN. LAWS ch. 64H, § 6(cc).

116. N.H. REV. STAT. ANN. § 78A:3(X)(c)(7).

117. W. VA. CODE §§ 11–13–1, and –2.

118. 20 N.Y.C.R.R. § 1–34, cited in 58 N.Y. JUR. TAX. § 514, n. 74 (Supp. 1980).

119. See VA. CODE §§ 58–456 *et seq.* and §§ 13.1–201 *et seq.*

120. MISS. CODE ANN. § 27–13–63(c) (Supp. 1979).

121. *Id.* § 27–17–55.

122. OR. REV. STAT. § 320.030(2).

123. WISC. STAT. ANN. §§ 77.70 and .71 (Supp. 1980).

124. N.Y. REAL PROP. TAX LAW § 498 (Supp. 1979).

125. NEV. REV. STAT. § 78.790.

126. VA. CODE §§ 58-64.1 and .2 (Supp. 1980).

127. ILL. ANN. STAT. ch. 120, § 1004.

128. MO. ANN. STAT. § 144.450.

129. VA. CODE § 58-685.13.

130. MD.. ANN. CODE art. 81, § 406(1) (Supp. 1981).

131. CONN. GEN. STAT. ANN. § 12-541(b).

132. MISS. CODE ANN. § 27-11-43(a) (b) and (h) (Supp. 1981).

133. S.C. CODE § 12-21-2420.

134. MO. ANN. STAT. § 178.160.

135. See, e.g., N.H. REV. STAT. ANN. § 78A:3(III)(c).

136. See, e.g., TEX. TAX CODE ANN. tit. 122A, § 23.02(c).

7. Fund Raising

1. "For Many, There Are Big Profits in Non-

Profits," U.S. NEWS & WORLD REPORT, Nov. 6, 1978, at 45.

2. Walter I. Trattner, "Private Charity in America, 1790–1900," CURRENT HISTORY, Vol. 65, No. 383 (July, 1973), at 26.

3. "Charity Battle," NEWSWEEK, May 7, 1979, at 33.

4. St. Louis Union Trust Co. v. U.S., 374 F.2d 427, 432 (8th Cir. 1967).

5. Bruce Hopkins, *Charity Under Siege: Government Regulation of Fund Raising* (New York: John Wiley & Sons, 1980), p. 9.

6. *Id.*

7. *Id.* at 13.

8. *Id.* at 8.

9. "Radix Malorem Est Cupiditas? In the Pallotine Order, Carryings On Over Cash," TIME, Jan, 23, 1978, at 75. With regard to abuses even in legalized Bingo games, see the series in the Chicago Tribune, Oct. 18, 1981, p. 1, Oct. 19, 1981, p. 1, and Oct. 20, 1981, p. 1.

10. Schaumberg v. Citizens for a Better Environment, 444 U.S. 620 (1980); see also Larson v. Valente, 456 U.S. 228 (1982).

11. International Society for Krishna Consciousness v. Rockford, 425 F.Supp. 734 (N.D. Ill. 1977).

12. NAACP v. Button, 371 U.S. 415 (1963).

13. Hopkins, note 5, *supra*, at 159.

14. Walz v. Tax Commissioner, 397 U.S. 664 (1970).

15. Harvey Katz, *Give! Who Gets Your Charity Dollar?* (Garden City, N.Y.: Doubleday, 1974), p. 41.

16. Youth for Christ International, *Summary of State Laws Regulating Charitable Solicitation by Religious Organizations* (1979).

17. Hopkins, note 5, *supra*, at 75.

18. E.g., N.Y. CONST. art. I, § 9.2: N.J. STAT. ANN. § 5:8–25 (West); DEL. CONST. art. II, § 17A.

19. E.g., N.J. STAT. ANN. § 5:8–26 (West); ME. REV. CODE ANN. tit. 17, § 332.

8. Miscellaneous

1. DEL. CODE ANN. tit. 14, § 4107.

2. MISS. CODE ANN. § 97-5-11 (Supp. 1979).

3. U.S. CONST. art. 1, § 10.

4. E.g., NEB. REV. STAT. § 79-2501; R.I. GEN. LAWS § 16-47-1; WIS. STAT. ANN. § 39.75 (Supp. 1980). See generally, THE COUNCIL OF STATE GOVERNMENTS, INTERSTATE COMPACTS, 1783-1970: A COMPILATION 18–21 (1971).

5. E.g., CONN. GEN. STAT. ANN. § 10-317 (West); R.I. GEN. LAWS § 16-41-1 (Supp. 1980).

6. E.g., S.C. CODE § 59-11-20; W. VA. CODE § 18-10C-1.

7. See, e.g., W. VA. CODE § 18-10D-1, art. 1.

8. E.g., N.M. STAT. ANN. § 173.030(2); TEX. EDUC. CODE ANN. tit. 2, § 61.064.

9. E.g., MO., TEX. boards.

10. E.g., FLA. STAT. ANN. § 240.409(2)(a)(Supp. 1980); NEV. REV. STAT. §§ 394.450 to 394.460.

11. E.g., IDAHO CODE § 41-1805(1).

12. *Id.*

13. E.g., S.C. CODE § 38-35-20(b).

14. OR. REV. STAT. § 731.026(1).

15. See, e.g., N.C. GEN. STAT. § 55A-15(b)(5).

16. I. J. Sloan, *Alcohol and Drug Abuse and the Law* (Dobbs Ferry, N.Y.: Oceana Pubs., 1980), p. 2.

17. *Id.* at 4.

18. See, e.g., KAN. STAT. ANN. § 41-710; TENN. CODE ANN. § 57-5-105(3); MISS. CODE ANN. § 67-3-65.

19. Sloan, note 16, *supra*, at 9.

20. *Id.*

21. *Id.*

22. E.g., W. VA. CODE § 60-7-4(c).

23. E.g., MISS. CODE ANN. § 67-1-37.

24. Sloan, note 16, *supra*, at 2.

25. E.g., TENN. CODE ANN. § 39-2510(1),(4); § 57-7-112. See also Sloan, note 16, *supra*, at 2.

26. E.g., CAL. GOV'T CODE § 12926(d).

27. E.g., ARIZ. REV. STAT. ANN. § 41-1461(3).

28. E.g., MD. ANN. STAT. § 289.005.

29. See generally, 3 EMPL. PRAC. GUIDE (CCH).

30. E.g., Crowley v. Bob Jones University, 268 S.C. 492, 234 S.E.2d 879 (1977); Brown v. Anderson County Hospital Assn., 268 S.C. 479, 234 S.E.2d 873 (1977); Vermillion v. Woman's College of Due West, 104 S.C. 197, 88 S.E. 649 (1916); N.M. STAT. ANN. § 42-11-1.

31. E.g., OHIO, Matthews v. Wittenburg College, 113 Ohio App. 387, 178 N.E.2d 526 (1960).

32. E.g., LA. REV. STAT. ANN. § 9:2792. See generally, William L. Prosser, *The Law of Torts* § 133 (St. Paul: West, 4th ed., 1971).

33. E.g., ILL. ANN. STAT. ch. 63, § 173; S.C. CODE § 34-23-20(d)(2).

34. E.g., MISS. CODE ANN. § 77-7-9.

35. All but eight states have passed some form of the Uniform Controlled Substances Act regulating a whole range of drug-related activities. See Sloan, note 16, *supra*, at 39–90.

36. E.g., TENN. CODE ANN. § 49-3249; MISS. CONST. art. 14, § 270; MISS. CODE ANN. § 79-11-33 (Supp. 1979).

37. MISS. CODE ANN. § 37-7-473.

38. Mo. Ann. Stat. § 170.011 (Vernon).

39. See "Comment, State Legislative Response to Campus Disorder: An Analytical Compendium" 10 Houston L. Rev. 930 (1973).

40. *Id.* at 957.

41. Me. Rev. Stat. Ann. tit. 20, § 1221.

9. Alabama

1. Ala. Code §§ 10-3-1 *et seq.* (1977, Supp. 1979).

2. *Id.* § 10-3-2(2).

3. *Id.* § 10-3-22.

4. *Id.* §§ 10-3-23 and 10-3-24.

5. *Id.* § 10-3-9.

6. *Id.* § 10-3-26.

7. *Id.* § 10-3-127.

8. *Id.* § 16-3-11.

9. *Id.* §§ 16-5-1 (Supp. 1980) *et seq.*

10. *Id.* § 16-5-10(14) (Supp. 1980).

11. *Id.* § 16-5-10(15) (Supp. 1980).

12. *Id.* § 16-46-1 *et seq.*

13. *Id.* § 16-55-4. For other examples, see also §§ 16-54-4 (Supp. 1979) and 16-51-6.

14. *Id.* § 10-3-163. The appropriate county is that of the college's principal office.

15. *Id.* § 10-3-164.

16. *Id.* §§ 10-3-161 and 10-3-166.

17. Boxley v. Birmingham Trust Nat'l Bank, 334 So. 2d 848 (Ala. 1976).

18. Ala. Code §§ 16-18A-1 *et seq.* (Supp. 1980).

19. *Id.* § 16-18A-3 (Supp. 1980).

20. *Id.* § 16-18A-4 (Supp. 1980).

21. *Id.* § 16-18A-2(3) (Supp. 1980).

22. *Id.* § 16-18A-2(2) (Supp. 1980).

23. *Id.* § 16-18A-4(5) (Supp. 1980).

24. *Id.* § 16-18A-2(5) (Supp. 1980).

25. *Id.* § 16-18A-2(2) (Supp. 1980).

26. Ala. Const. art. IV, § 93 as amended, amend. 58, and art. IV, § 94.

27. Knight v. West Alabama Environmental Improvement Authority, 246 So. 2d 903 (Ala. 1971). See also A. E. Dick Howard, *State Aid to Private Higher Education* (Charlottesville, Va.: Michie, 1977), pp. 84-85 [hereinafter cited as Howard, *State Aid*].

28. Ala. Code §§ 16-33A-1 *et seq.* (Supp. 1980).

29. *Id.* § 16-33A-4 (Supp. 1980).

30. *Id.* §§ 16-5-1 *et seq.*

31. *Id.* § 16-33A-3 (Supp. 1980).

32. *Id.* § 16-33A-2 (Supp. 1980).

33. *Id.* § 16-33A-6(d) (Supp. 1980).

34. *Id.* § 16-33A-1(4)(e) (Supp. 1980).

35. *Id.* § 16-33A-6(a) (Supp. 1980).

36. *Id.* § 16-33A-1(4) (Supp. 1980).

37. *Id.* § 16-33A-1(3) (Supp. 1980).

38. *Id.*

39. *Id.* § 16-33A-5(b) (Supp. 1980).

40. *Id.* § 16-33A-7(a) (Supp. 1980).

41. *Id.* § 16-33A-7(b) (Supp. 1980).

42. *Id.* § 16-33A-7(b) (Supp. 1980).

43. *Id.* § 16-33A-8 (Supp. 1980).

44. Opinion of the Justices, 291 Ala. 301, 280 So. 2d 547 (1973).

45. 373 So. 2d 1076, 1079 (Ala. 1979).

46. Roemer v. Maryland Public Works Board, 426 U.S. 736 (1976).

47. The Alabama Education Association v. James, 373 So. 2d 1076, 1079-1080 (Ala. 1979).

48. Ala. Const. art. XIV, § 263.

49. The Alabama Education Association v. James, 373 So. 2d 1076, 1081 (Ala. 1979).

50. Ala. Code §§ 16-33B-1 *et seq.* (Supp. 1980).

51. *Id.* § 16-33B-1(3) (Supp. 1980).

52. *Id.* § 16-33B-6 (Supp. 1980).

53. *Id.* § 16-33B-1(4) and (5) (Supp. 1980).

54. *Id.* § 16-33B-4(5) (Supp. 1980).

55. Ala. Const. art. IV, § 73: "No appropriation shall be made to any charitable or educational institution not under the absolute control of the state, other than normal schools established by law for the professional training of teachers for the public schools of the state except by a vote of two-thirds of all the members elected to each house."

56. Ala. Const. art. IV. § 93 as amended, amend. 58, and § 94.

57. Ala. Code § 16-5-11 (Supp. 1980).

58. *Id.* §§ 16-3-32 through 16-3-35.

59. Howard, *State Aid*, note 27, *supra*, at 87.

60. Ala. Code, § 16-54-6 (Supp. 1979). For other examples, see also §§ 16-55-4 and 16-51-6.

61. (1980) 8A Fair Employment Prac. Manual (BNA) ¶ 453:1. See also the Alabama statutory charts in (1979) 3 Empl. Prac. Guide (CCH) ¶ 20,080 and (1980) Lab. L. Rep. (CCH) ¶ 40,353 *et seq.*

62. Ala. Code §§ 21-5-1 *et seq.*

63. *Id.* § 21-5-1.

64. Alabama's only minimum wage law, dealing with public works contracts, expired May 19, 1980. *Id.* §§ 39-4-1 *et seq.* (Supp. 1979).

65. *Id.* §§ 37-3-7 (transportation workers), 13-6-1 *et seq.* (Sunday restrictions), and 25-8-1 *et seq.* (child labor laws).

66. *Id.* § 16-55-4. For other examples, see also *id.* §§ 16-51-6, and 16-54-6 (Supp. 1979).

67. *Id.* §§ 25-5-1 *et seq.* (1975, Supp. 1979)

(Modeled on Minnesota workmen's compensation law, MINN. STAT. ANN. §§ 176.01 *et seq.*)

68. *Id.* §§ 25-5-1(4), 25-5-51, 25-5-54.

69. *Id.* § 25-5-50 (Supp. 1979). This exception applies only when the employment is both casual and not in the usual course of the employer's business.

70. *Id.* § 25-5-35.

71. *Id.* §§ 25-5-31, 25-5-53. See, for example, Employer's Liability Act, *id.* §§ 25-6-1 *et seq.*

72. *Id.* § 25-5-50 (Supp. 1979).

73. *Id.* § 25-5-8.

74. *Id.* §§ 25-4-1 *et seq.* (Supp. 1980).

75. *Id.* § 25-4-7 (Supp. 1980).

76. *Id.* § 25-4-9 (Supp. 1980).

77. *Id.* § 25-4-8(6) (Supp. 1980).

78. *Id.* § 25-4-10(a)(3) (Supp. 1980).

79. *Id.* § 25-4-10(a)(3)b. (Supp. 1980).

80. *Id.* § 25-4-10(a)(3)a. (Supp. 1980).

81. *Id.* § 25-4-10(b)(8) (Supp. 1980).

82. *Id.* § 25-4-10(b)(21)a. (Supp. 1980).

83. *Id.* § 25-4-10(6)(21)b. (Supp. 1980).

84. *Id.* § 24-4-10(b)(11)a. (Supp. 1980). Services performed by the spouse of a student are also exempt from coverage if the spouse is informed that the employment is a form of financial aid and is not covered by unemployment insurance. *Id.* § 25-4-10(b)(11)b. (Supp. 1980).

85. *Id.* § 25-4-10(b)(12) (Supp. 1980).

86. See text accompanying notes 78 *et seq.*, *supra.*

87. ALA. CODE § 25-4-51(a)(3) (Supp. 1980).

88. The written notices must be filed by December 1. *Id.* § 25-4-51(a)(3)c. (Supp. 1980).

89. *Id.* The procedure followed in making payments in lieu of contributions is explained at *id.* § 25-4-51(b) (Supp. 1980).

90. *Id.* § 25-4-51(a)(3)b. (Supp. 1980).

91. See *id.* § 25-4-131(a) (Supp. 1980).

92. *Id.*

93. *Id.* § 25-7-6.

94. *Id.* §§ 25-7-30 *et seq.* See Carlton v. Musicians Protective Assn., 276 Ala. 128, 159 So. 2d 831 (1963); Head v. Barbers, Local 83, 262 Ala. 84, 77 So. 2d 363 (1955).

95. *Id.* § 10-3-120(14).

96. *Id.* § 10-3-121(a).

97. *Id.* § 16-33A-1(3) (Supp. 1980).

98. *Id.* § 16-33A-6(a) (Supp. 1980).

99. *Id.* § 16-5-10(14) (Supp. 1980).

100. *Id.* § 21-7-3.

101. *Id.* § 11-52-75.

102. *Id.* § 25-1-1 (1977).

103. *Id.*

104. Minyard v. Woodward Iron Co., 81 F. Supp. 414 (N.D. Ala. 1948).

105. ALA. CODE § 40-18-32(4).

106. ALA. CONST. art. XI, § 217 as amended, amend. 373(k) (Supp. 1980).

107. ALA. CODE § 40-9-16.

108. *Id.* § 340-9-1(1) (Supp. 1980).

109. *Id.* § 40-9-1(12) (Supp. 1980).

110. *Id.* § 40-9-17.

111. *Id.* §§ 40-18-15(a)(10) (Supp. 1980) and 40-18-35(10).

112. *Id.* § 40-18-25(b).

113. *Id.* § 40-15-2.

114. *Id.* § 40-23-2(1) (Supp. 1980).

115. *Id.* § 40-23-2(2) (Supp. 1980).

116. *Id.* § 40-23-2(5) (Supp. 1980).

117. *Id.* § 40-23-62(20) (Supp. 1980).

118. *Id.* §§ 13-7-20 *et seq.*

119. ALA. CONST. art. IV, § 65.

120. ALA. CODE § 13A-12-20 *et seq.*

10. Alaska

1. ALASKA STAT. §§ 10.20.216 to 10.20.450.

2. *Id.* § 10.20.005 (Supp. 1979).

3. McKee v. Evans, 490 P.2d 1226, 1230 (Alaska 1971).

4. ALASKA STAT. § 10.20.011.

5. *Id.* § 10.40.101.

6. For an assessment of a variety of relationships between colleges and sponsoring religious bodies, see Robert Rue Parsonage, ed., *Church Related Higher Education* (Valley Forge, Pa.: Judson Press, 1978), pp. 17–132; and Manning M. Pattillo and Donald M. Mackenzie, *Church Sponsored Higher Education* (Washington D.C.: American Council on Education, 1966), pp. 30–53.

7. Pub. L. 88-352, Title VII, § 702, 78 STAT. 255, 42 U.S.C. 2000e-1. For a discussion of the legislative history of this provision, see Philip R. Moots and Edward M. Gaffney, *Church and Campus: Legal Issues in Religiously Affiliated Higher Education* (Notre Dame, Ind.: University of Notre Dame Press, 1979), pp. 40–47.

8. See text accompanying notes 16 to 19, and 24 to 29, *infra.*

9. ALASKA STAT. §§ 10.20.256 and 10.20.315.

10. *Model Nonprofit Corporation Act* (Philadelphia: American Law Institute, 1964).

11. ALASKA STAT. § 10.20.325.

12. *Id.* §§ 10.20.360 and 10.20.356.

13. *Id.* §§ 10.20.295 and 10.20.395.

14. ALASKA CONST. art. I, § 4. For a comprehensive treatment of various aid programs in Alaska, see A. E. Dick Howard, *State Aid to Private Higher Education* (Charlottesville, Va.: Michie, 1977), pp. 89–99.

15. ALASKA CONST. art. VII, § 1 (emphasis supplied); see also art. IX, § 6.

16. 362 P.2d 932 (Alaska 1961), cert. denied, 368 U.S. 517 (1962).

17. 330 U.S. 1 (1947).

18. 362 P.2d at 943.

19. Howard, note 14, *supra*, at 93–94.

20. ALASKA STAT. §§ 14.40.751 *et seq.*

21. *Id.* § 14.40.763.

22. *Id.* § 14.40.767.

23. *Id.* §§ 14.40.810 *et seq.*

24. *Id.* §§ 14.40.776 *et seq.*

25. Americans United for Separation of Church and State v. Blanton, 473 F. Supp. 97 (M.D. Tenn.), *summarily aff'd.*, 434 U.S. 803 (1977). For a discussion of this case, see Moots and Gaffney, note 7, *supra*, at 35–39.

26. 599 P.2d 127 (Alaska 1979).

27. 599 P.2d at 129.

28. *Id.* at 129–31.

29. ALASKA STAT. § 18.80.255(1) (emphasis added).

30. *Id.* §§ 14.40.660 *et seq.*

31. [1977] Employment Practices Guide, CCH ¶ 20,300.04.

32. See Grove City College v. Califano, 500 F. Supp. 243 (W.D. Pa. 1980), appeal pending in Third Circuit.

33. ALASKA CONST. art. I, § 3.

34. ALASKA STAT. § 18.80.220(a)(1) (Supp. 1980).

35. *Id.* § 18.80.210.

36. *Id.* § 18.80.210 (Supp. 1980).

37. *Id.* § 18.80.220(a)(1) (Supp. 1980).

38. McLean v. Alaska, 583 P.2d 867, 869 (Alaska 1978).

39. ALASKA STAT. § 18.80.300(3) (Supp. 1980).

40. *Id.* §§ 23.10.05 to 150 (Supp. 1980).

41. *Id.* § 23.10.055(6) (1972).

42. *Id.* § 23.10.055(9).

43. *Id.* § 23.10.060(13).

44. *Id.* § 18.60 *et seq.* (Supp. 1974, 1980) (In 1980, the title of this act and all references in the Alaska statutes to workmen's compensation were changed to read "worker's compensation.")

45. *Id.* § 23.30.265(12).

46. *Id.* § 23.30.240.

47. *Id.*

48. *Id.* § 23.30.230.

49. *Id.* §§ 23.30.075, 23.30.060, 23.30.245.

50. *Id.* §§ 23.20.005 (1972 and Supp. 1980).

51. *Id.* § 23.20.165 (1972).

52. *Id.* § 23.20.276, 277 (1972 and Supp. 1980).

53. IRC § 501(a) and (c)(3).

54. ALASKA STAT. § 23.20.520(11) (1972 and Supp. 1980).

55. *Id.* § 23.20.525(a)(15) (Supp. 1980).

56. *Id.* § 23.20.526(d)(1)(5) and (6) (1972).

57. *Id.* § 14.12.115 (Supp. 1980).

58. *Id.* § 14.40.050 (1975 and Supp. 1980).

59. *Id.* § 18.80.230(17) (1974).

60. [1977] LAB. REL. REP. (BNA) 453:311, § 30.170(8).

61. See text accompanying note 31, *supra*.

62. ALASKA STAT. §§ 18.80.200(5) and 18.80.060 (1974 and Supp. 1980).

63. *Id.* § 18.80.230(1) (1974); and see note 60, *supra*.

64. [1980] 8A LAB. REL. REP. (BNA) 453:321, § 30.990(2).

65. *Id.* § 30.985.

66. ALASKA STAT. § 18.06.020 (1974).

67. *Id.* § 47.80.010 (1979).

68. *Id.* § 18.06.020(b) (1974).

69. *Id.* § 35.10.015 (1980).

70. *Id.* § 35.25.020 (1980).

71. *Id.* §§ 18.80.200 to .210 (Supp. 1980).

72. *Id.* § 18.80.240 (Supp. 1980).

73. See note 60, *supra*, and accompanying text.

74. ALASKA STAT. § 34.03.330(b)(1) (1975).

75. *Id.* §§ 34.03.010 *et seq.* (1975 and Supp. 1980).

76. *Id.* § 34.03.330(b)(5).

77. *Id.* § 14.48.060(b)(11) (Supp. 1980).

78. *Id.* § 18.35.200 (1974).

79. *Id.* §§ 18.60 *et seq.* (1974 and Supp. 1980).

80. *Id.* § 18.60.010 (1974 and Supp. 1980).

81. *Id.* § 18.60.020(a) (1974 and Supp. 1980).

82. *Id.* § 18.60.105 (1974 and Supp. 1980).

83. *Id.* § 43.20.011 (1980).

84. *Id.* § 43.20.040 (1980).

85. *Id.* § 43.20.021 (1980).

86. *Id.* § 43.20.030 (1980).

87. ALASKA CONST. art. IV, § 4 (1980).

88. I.R.C. § 501(c)(3).

89. 490 P.2d 1226, at 1230 (Alaska 1971).

90. *Id.* at 1231.

91. ALASKA STAT. § 29.53.020 (1972 and Supp. 1980).

92. Harmon v. North Pac. Union Conference Ass'n. of Seventh Day Adventists, 462 P.2d 432 (Alaska 1969).

93. Greater Anchorage Area Bur. v. Sisters of Charity, 553 P.2d 467 (Alaska 1976) (Private doctors' rented offices in a hospital owned by exempt organization).

94. Op. Atty Gen. No. 15 (1962).

95. ALASKA STAT. § 43.31.021 (1977).

96. *Id.*

97. *Id.* § 43.30.010–43.30.210 (repealed by § 1, ch. 24, Session Laws of Alaska, 1970).

98. ALASKA STAT. §§ 43.50.010 *et seq.* (1980).

99. *Id.* §§ 43.70.070 and 030 (Supp. 1980).

100. *Id.* § 43.70.010 (Supp. 1980).

101. *Id.* § 10.40.070(1) (1968). For a comprehensive treatment of governmental regulation of fund raising, see Bruce R. Hopkins, *Charity Under Siege* (New York: John Wiley, 1980).

102. ALASKA STAT. § 10.20.011(4) (1968).

103. *Id.* § 05.15.210.

104. *Id.* § 05.15.010 (1962 and Supp. 1980).

105. *Id.* § 05.15.210 (1962 and Supp. 1980).

106. *Id.* § 05.15.080 (Supp. 1980).

107. *Id.* § 05.15.150(b) (1962).

108. *Id.* § 05.15.150(a) (Supp. 1980).

11. Arizona

1. ARIZ. REV. STAT. ANN. §§ 10–1001 *et seq.* (Supp. 1979).

2. *Id.* § 10–002(21) (Supp. 1979).

3. *Id.* § 10–1028 *et seq.* (Supp. 1979).

4. *Id.* § 10–1004 (Supp. 1979).

5. *Id.* § 10–1017(a) (Supp. 1979).

6. *Id.* § 10–1018(a) (Supp. 1979).

7. *Id.* § 10–1018(a) (Supp. 1979).

8. *Id.* § 10–1045(a)(1) (Supp. 1979).

9. *Id.* § 10–1045(a)(2) (Supp. 1979).

10. *Id.* § 10–1046 (Supp. 1979).

11. See, e.g., In re Hayward's Estate, 65 Ariz. 288, 178 P.2d 547 (1947). A dictum in Olivas v. Board of Nat'l. Missions of Presbyterian Church, 1 Ariz. App. 543, 405 P.2d 481 (1965), indicates that the *cy pres* doctrine would be applied by Arizona courts to charitable trusts.

12. A good general discussion of Arizona aid to RACs can be found in A. E. D. Howard, *State Aid to Private Higher Education* (Charlottesville, Va.: Michie, Co., 1977), pp. 100–109.

13. ARIZ. CONST. art. 2, § 12.

14. *Id.* art. 9, § 10.

15. *Id.* art. 9, § 7.

16. 102 Ariz. 448, 432 P.2d 460 (1967).

17. 432 P.2d at 463, 466.

18. 1970 Ops. Ariz. Atty. Gen. 7.

19. See Roemer v. Bd. of Public Works of Md., 426 U.S. 736 (1976); Hunt v. McNair, 413 U.S. 734 (1973); and Tilton v. Richardson, 403 U.S. 672 (1971).

20. See, e.g., Americans United for Separation of Church and State v. Blanton, 433 F.Supp. 97 (M.D. Tenn.), *aff'd*, 434 U.S. 803.

21. ARIZ. REV. STAT. § 26–179 (1976).

22. *Id.* §§ 9–1151 *et seq.* (1977) (Supp. 1979).

23. *Id.* § 9–1152 (1977).

24. *Id.* § 9–1151 (Supp. 1979).

25. *Id.* § 9–1156 (Supp. 1979).

26. *Id.* §§ 41–1401 *et seq.* (1974). The Civil Rights Act covers a wide range of discriminatory practices. Employment discrimination is dealt with specifically in ARIZ. REV. STAT. §§ 41–1461 *et seq.* (1974).

27. For purposes of the employment practices section an employer is a person who has 15 or more employees for each working day in each of 20 or more calendar weeks in a calendar year. ARIZ. REV. STAT. §§ 41–1461(2) (Supp. 1979).

28. *Id.* § 41–1463(b)(1) (1974) (Emphasis added).

29. *Id.* § 41–1464(b) (1974).

30. *Id.* § 41–1464(A) (1974).

31. *Id.* § 41–1462 (1974). This section is identical with § 702 of the federal Civil Rights Act of 1964 as amended by the Equal Employment Opportunity Act of 1972, Pub. L. 88–352, 78 STAT. 255, as amended by Pub. L. 92–261, 86 STAT. 103, 42 U.S.C. 2000(e)–1.

32. *Id.* § 41–1463(F)(2) (1974). This section is the Arizona counterpart of § 703(e)(2) of the federal Civil Rights Act, Pub. L. 88–352, Title VII § 703(e)(2), 78 STAT. 255, 42 U.S.C. 2000e–2(e)(2).

33. ARIZ. REV. STAT. § 41–1463(F)(1) (1974). BFOQ is not defined. This section also tracks the federal Civil Rights Act, Pub. L., 88–352, Title VII, § 703(e)(1), 78 STAT. 256, 42 U.S.C. 2000e–2(e)(1). Sex and national origin are also within the scope of the BFOQ exception.

34. ARIZ. REV. STAT. § 41–1464(b) (1974).

35. See note 19, *supra*.

36. For a discussion concerning the meaning of the federal statute upon which the Arizona statute was based and from which these sections were largely copied, see Philip R. Moots and Edward M. Gaffney, *Church and Campus* (Notre Dame, Ind.: University of Notre Dame Press, 1979), pp. 39–54.

37. Letter of April 3, 1980, on file with the Center for Constitutional Studies.

38. See note 22, *supra*.

39. See discussion in Moots and Gaffney, note 36, *supra*.

40. *Id.*

41. ARIZ. REV. STAT. § 36–506(b) (Supp. 1979).

42. *Id.* § 36–501(17) (Supp. 1979).

43. Developmental disability means autism, cerebral palsy, epilepsy, or mental retardation. *Id.* § 36–581(1) (Supp. 1979).

44. *Id.* § 36–551.01(e) (Supp. 1979).

45. *Id.* § 23–311 (Supp. 1979). A minor is a person under the age of eighteen who is not a student.

46. *Id.* § 23–317, 236 (Supp. 1979). These provisions seem to conflict with the provisions relating to

equal opportunity for those with developmental disabilities. See note 31, *supra*.

47. The definition of employer is all-inclusive and there are no exemptions, *id.* § 23–340(3) (Supp. 1979).

48. *Id.* § 23–341(a) (Supp. 1979).

49. *Id.*

50. *Id.* §§ 23–901 *et seq.* (supp. 1979).

51. *Id.* § 23–902 (Supp. 1979).

52. *Id.* §§ 23–906 (Supp. 1979), 23–1024 (1971).

53. *Id.* § 23–901(b) (Supp. 1979). This exemption applies only when the employment is both casual and not in the usual course of business. Also exempt are domestic servants, *id.* § 23–902(a) (Supp. 1979) and some motion picture companies, *id.* § 23–909 (1971).

54. *Id.* § 23–961 (Supp. 1979).

55. *Id.* § 23–601 *et seq.* (West Supp. 1980).

56. *Id.* § 23–614A. (West Supp. 1980).

57. *Id.* § 23–613 A.2 (West Supp. 1980).

58. *Id.* § 23–613 A.6 (West Supp. 1980).

59. *Id.* § 23–613.01 A. (West Supp. 1980).

60. *Id.* § 23–615. (West Supp. 1980).

61. *Id.* § 23–615. 6. (b) (West Supp. 1980).

62. *Id.* § 23–615. 6. (b)(i) (West Supp. 1980).

63. *Id.* § 23–615. 6. (b)(ii) (West Supp. 1980).

64. *Id.* § 23–615. 6. (d) (West Supp. 1980).

65. *Id.* § 23–617. 9. (a) (West Supp. 1980).

66. *Id.* § 23–617. 9. (b) (West Supp. 1980). The spouse must be informed that the employment is part of a program of financial assistance and is not covered by an unemployment compensation plan.

67. *Id.* § 23–617. 20. (Supp. 1980).

68. *Id.* § 23–725 D. (West Supp. 1980).

69. *Id.* § 23–725 E. (West Supp. 1980).

70. See text accompanying notes 61 *et seq.*, *supra*.

71. *Id.* § 23–725 F. (1) (West Supp. 1980).

72. *Id.* § 23–725 F. (2) (West Supp. 1980). See also *id.* § 23–725 I. (West Supp. 1980).

73. *Id.* § 23–725 F. (2) (West Supp. 1980).

74. For details, see *id.* § 23–750.A.1 (Supp. 1980).

75. *Id.* § 23–750 (West Supp. 1980).

76. *Id.* § 23–750 B. 4. (West Supp. 1980).

77. *Id.* § 23–750 D. (West Supp. 1980).

78. *Id.* § 23–750 B. 1. and D. (West Supp. 1980).

79. Ariz. Const. art. 25.

80. Ariz. Rev. Stat. § 23–1302 (1971).

81. *Id.* § 41–1442(1) (1974). It should be noted that the section of the Civil Rights Act dealing with discrimination in employment (see note 14, *supra*) includes "sex" as an unlawful employment criterion but discrimination on the basis of sex is not included as an unlawful practice in the public accommoda-

tions section. Also, "no practical significance is attributed to the use of the word religious [sic] [in Ariz. Rev. Stat. § 41–1461] as opposed to creed [in Ariz. Rev. Stat. § 41–1421]." Letter from Phillip A. Austin, see note 37, *supra*.

82. *Id.* § 41–1441(2) (1974).

83. *Id.*

84. *Id.* § 34–401 (1974). The definition of places of public accommodation is identical to that in the Civil Rights Act. (See note 82, *supra*.) The physically handicapped include those who are "non-ambulatory" or "semi-ambulatory," and those with hearing and sight disabilities. *Id.* § 34–401(a) (1974).

85. *Id.* §§ 34–404, 405, 406 (1974) (Supp. 1979).

86. *Id.* §§ 33–1301 *et seq.* (1974).

87. *Id.* § 23–401(7) (Supp. 1979).

88. *Id.* § 23–40(8) (Supp. 1979).

89. *Id.* § 43–1201 (Supp. 1979).

90. *Id.* § 43–1231 (Supp. 1979). See I.R.C. § 512, 26 U.S.C. 512 ("not substantially related to the exercise or performance of the purpose or function constituting the basis for the exemption").

91. 26 U.S.C. 513(2).

92. Ariz. Rev. Stat. § 43–1212(1) (Supp. 1979). The prohibited transactions are set out at *id.* § 43–1213 (Supp. 1979).

93. *Id.* § 42–1521 (Supp. 1979).

94. *Id.* § 43–1123 (Supp. 1979).

95. *Id.* § 43–1046 (Supp. 1979).

96. *Id.* § 43–1217 (Supp. 1979).

97. Ariz. Const. art. 9, § 2.

98. Ariz. Rev. Stat. § 42–271(3) (Supp. 1979).

99. *Id.* § 42–271(6) (Supp. 1979).

100. *Id.* § 42–271(14) (Supp. 1979).

101. Verde Valley School v. Yauapai County, 90 Ariz. 180, 367 P.2d 223 (1962).

102. Ariz. Const. art. 9, § 2; State Tax Comm. v. Shattuck, 44 Ariz. 379, 38 P.2d 631 (1935).

103. Ariz. Rev. Stat. Ann. §§ 42.1382 *et seq.* (1956).

104. *Id.* § 42.1409 (1956).

105. 1964 Ops. Ariz. Atty. Gen. 7.

106. Ariz. Const. art. 20, § 1.

107. Ariz. Rev. Stat. §§ 5–401 *et seq.* (1974) (Supp. 1979).

108. Qualified organizations are defined in terms of tax-exempt status under *id.* § 43–201, which expressly includes RACs.

109. The informational requirements are at *id.* § 5–404 (Supp. 1979).

110. *Id.* § 5–404(d)(e) (Supp. 1979).

111. *Id.* § 5–401(F) (Supp. 1979).

112. *Id.* § 5–421 (Supp. 1979).

12. Arkansas

1. ARK. STAT. ANN. §§ 64–1401 *et seq.*
2. *Id.* § 64–1401.
3. *Id.* § 64–1404.
4. *Id.* § 64–1409.
5. *Id.* § 64–1402.
6. *Id.* § 64–1409.
7. *Id.* § 64–1409. There is a fee for filing and recording a charter of any educational institution. *Id.* § 64–1413.
8. *Id.* § 64–1405. RACs may also enter into cooperative relations with other educational institutions for the establishment and maintenance of such departments or schools as they may agree to correlate and make such rules for the government of such departments or schools as they may deem proper.
9. The provisions of the Nonprofit Corporations Act apply only to corporations organized under that act or under any act repealed by that act. Neither of these categories explicitly includes colleges incorporated under the Institutions of Learning chapter.
10. ARK. STAT. ANN. §§ 64–701 *et seq.* (Supp. 1980).
11. *Id.* §§ 64–901 *et seq.*
12. *Id.* §§ 64–705, 64–902.
13. *Id.* § 64–906.
14. *Id.* § 64–908 (Supp. 1980).
15. See Model Act § 51.
16. ARK. STAT. ANN. §§ 64–903, 64–908 (1966, Supp. 1980).
17. *Id.* § 64–908 (Supp. 1980).
18. Sloan v. Robert Jack Post No. 1322, V.F.W., 218 Ark. 917, 239 S.W.2d 591 (1951).
19. 403 U.S. 672 (1971). For a comprehensive treatment of the Arkansas programs of assistance to higher education, see A. E. Dick Howard, *State Aid to Private Higher Education* (Charlottesville, Va.: Michie, 1977), pp. 110–118.
20. 413 U.S. 734 (1971).
21. ARK. STAT. ANN. § 80–5001 (1980).
22. *Id.* § 80–5004.
23. *Id.* § 80–5002(b)(1).
24. *Id.* § 80–5002(b)(2).
25. *Id.* § 80–5002(b)(5).
26. *Id.* § 80–5002(b)(6).
27. *Id.* § 80–5006.
28. *Id.* § 80–5005.
29. 20 U.S.C. §§ 1070c *et seq.*, as outlined in ARK. STAT. ANN. § 80–4921 (1980).
30. ARK. STAT. ANN. § 80–4013.
31. *Id.* § 80–4032.
32. *Id.* § 80–3701.
33. Howard, note 19, *supra*, at 115.

34. ARK. CONST. art. II, § 3.
35. ARK. STAT. ANN. § 81–624.
36. *Id.* § 81–623.
37. *Id.* § 81–321(2)(3).
38. *Id.* § 81–320(g)(2).
39. *Id.* § 81–320(g)(4).
40. *Id.* § 81–320(g)(1).
41. *Id.* § 81–324.
42. *Id.* § 81–333.
43. *Id.* § 81–321(d). The provision does not apply to employees of hotels, motels, and restaurants.
44. *Id.* § 81–422. "Any employer who pays any employee less than the minimum wage to which the employee is entitled under the act, shall be liable to such employee for the full amount of such wages, less any amount actually paid, and for costs and reasonable attorney's fees as may be allowed by the court." *Id.* § 81–330.
45. *Id.* §§ 81–1301 *et seq.* (1976, Supp. 1980).
46. *Id.* § 81–1302(a).
47. *Id.* § 81–1302(c)(1).
48. *Id.* § 81–1303.
49. *Id.* § 81–1302(b) (Supp. 1980). This exception applies only when the employment is both casual and not in the course of the employer's business.
50. *Id.* § 81–1302 (Supp. 1980).
51. *Id.* § 64–1601.
52. *Id.* §§ 81–1307 and 81–1308.
53. *Id.* § 81–1336 (Supp. 1980).
54. *Id.* § 81–1336 (Supp. 1980).
55. *Id.* §§ 81–1101 *et seq.* (Supp. 1980).
56. *Id.* § 81–1103(g) (Supp. 1980).
57. *Id.* § 81–1103(h)(3) (Bobbs-Merrill Supp. 1980).
58. Any organization exempt under the Federal Unemployment Tax Act as being "organized and operated exclusively for religious, charitable, scientific, testing for public safety, literary, or educational purposes; or to foster national or international amateur sports competition . . . , or for the prevention of cruelty to children or animals" is subject to the provisions of the Arkansas statute according to this provision. *Id.* § 81–1103(i)(1)(C) (Supp. 1980).
59. *Id.*
60. *Id.* § 81–1103(i)(1)(D) (Supp. 1980).
61. *Id.* § 81–1103(i)(6)(J)(iii) (Supp. 1980).
62. *Id.* § 81–1103(i)(6)(J)(ii) (Supp. 1980).
63. A nonprofit organization is one exempt from coverage under the Federal Unemployment Tax Act (6 U.S.C. § 501 (Supp. 1980)) and for which services performed constitute employment under the Arkansas statute. See text accompanying notes 58 and 59, *supra*, ARK. STAT. ANN. § 81–1108(h) (Supp. 1980).
64. *Id.* § 81–1108(h)(1) (Supp. 1980).

65. *Id.* The procedure for making payments in lieu of contributions is detailed at § 81-1108(h)(3) (Supp. 1980).

66. ARK. STAT. ANN. § 81-1108(h)(1)(C) (Supp. 1980).

67. *Id.* This time requirement may be waived by the Director of the Arkansas Department of Labor. *Id.* § 81-1108(h)(1)(D) (Supp. 1980).

68. *Id.* § 81-332.

69. *Id.* § 81-203.

70. *Id.* § 80-5002(b).

71. Pub. L. 88-352, Title VI, § 601(a), 78 STAT. 252, 42 U.S.C. 2000d.

72. Pub. L. 92-318, Title IX, § 901, 86 STAT. 373, 20 U.S.C. §§ 1681 *et seq.*

73. See Edward M. Gaffney, Jr., and Philip R. Moots, *Government and Campus: Federal Regulation of Religiously Affiliated Higher Education* (Notre Dame, Ind.: University of Note Dame Press, 1981), pp. 86-89.

74. See Edward McGlynn Gaffney, "The Constitution and the Campus: The Case for Institutional Integrity and the Need for Critical Self-Evaluation," in John D. Mosely, ed., *Church and College: A Vital Partnership* (Sherman, Tex.: Austin College, 1980) vol. 3, pp. 47-67; and W. Cole Durham, Jr. and Dallin H. Oaks, "Constitutional Protections for Independent Higher Education: Limited Powers and Institutional Rights," *id.* at 69-87.

75. Pub. L. 88-352, Title II, 78 STAT. 243, 42 U.S.C. 2000a.

76. Pub. L. 90-284, Title VIII, 82 STAT. 81, as amended by Pub. L. 93-383, 88 STAT. 729, 42 U.S.C. §§ 3601 *et seq.*

77. ARK. STAT. ANN. § 82-2902.

78. *Id.* § 82-2905.

79. *Id.*

80. *Id.* § 82-2906.

81. *Id.* §§ 81-414 *et seq.*

82. *Id.* § 81-416 (1976).

83. *Id.* § 81-420 (1976).

84. *Id.* § 81-417 (1976).

85. ARK. CONST. art. XVI, § 5.

86. 231 Ark. 686, 331 S.W.2d 851 (1960); see also Brodie v. Fitzgerald, 57 Ark. 445, 22 S.W.29 (1893).

87. Phillips Co. v. Estelle, 42 Ark. 536 (1884).

88. ARK. STAT. ANN. § 84-206(7); see also § 84-101.

89. *Id.* §§ 84-1901 *et seq.*

90. *Id.* § 84-1904(c) and (d).

91. *Id.* § 84-1904(e).

92. *Id.* §§ 84-2004(A) *et seq.*

93. *Id.* § 84-2006(3); see I.R.C., § 501(c)(3).

94. *Id.* § 84-2006.1.

95. *Id.* § 84-2016.3.

96. *Id.* §§ 84-3101 *et seq.*

97. *Id.* § 84-3106.

98. *Id.* §§ 63-101 *et seq.*

99. *Id.* § 63-151(b). This exemption also applies to bequests to institutions outside the state of Arkansas if "the law of such other state provides an equal and like exemption for bequests made by residents of that state to such institutions, located in this State."

100. *Id.* § 64-1601.

101. *Id.* § 64-1602. The information must be filed annually, becomes part of the public record, and must include: the identity of the organization, the address, the purpose for which contributions will be used, the individual or officer who will have custody of contributions, individuals responsible for distribution, the time during which the organization will solicit, a description of the methods of solicitation, whether solicitors will be paid or unpaid and the names and addresses of professional solicitors.

102. *Id.* § 64-1603. The reports must be filed with the Secretary of State on forms provided and must include: gross amount of contributions pledged or collected, amount dedicated to the charitable purpose, amount paid or to be paid for solicitation, and the amount to be paid to professional fund raisers and solicitors.

103. *Id.* § 64-1604.

104. *Id.* § 64-1608.

105. *Id.* § 64-1614. The provisions regarding professional solicitations do not apply to "any solicitation made by or on behalf of any church, missionary or religious organization. . . ."

106. *Id.* § 64-1609.

107. *Id.* § 64-1611.

108. *Id.* § 64-1610.

109. *Id.* § 41-3262.

13. California

1. CAL. CORP. CODE §§ 9000 *et seq.* (repealed 1980), replaced by §§ 5000 to 10846 (Supp. 1980).

2. CAL. EDUC. CODE §§ 94300 *et seq.*

3. CAL. CORP. CODE §§ 5110 *et seq.* (Supp. 1980).

4. *Id.* § 9111 (Supp. 1980).

5. *Id.* § 5120 (Supp. 1980).

6. *Id.* § 5130 (Supp. 1980).

7. Metropolitan Baptist Church of Richmond, Inc. v. Younger, 48 Cal. App. 3d 850, 121 Cal. Rptr. 899 (1975).

8. CAL. EDUC. CODE § 94330. The nontransferable certification is issued to the governing body. *Id.* § 94330(e). If an institution has been in operation, it may continue, pending authorization; otherwise it must await authorization before commencing operations. *Id.* § 94330(g).

9. *Id.* § 94303(b).

10. *Id.* § 94304.

11. *Id.* § 94305.

12. *Id.* § 94339.

13. *Id.* §§ 94304 and 94305.

14. Among the factors to be considered by the Superintendent of Education in granting or withholding approval of a private college are the quality and content of courses, the adequacy of facilities, and the academic qualifications and moral character of personnel. The Superintendent must be provided with a copy of all materials given to students upon their enrollment.

15. See, e.g., Dartmouth College v. Woodward, 4 Wheat (17 U.S.) 518 (1819); and see Gaffney, "The Constitution and the Campus: The Case for Institutional Integrity and the Need for Critical Self-Evaluation," in John D. Mosely, ed., *Church and College: A Vital Partnership* (Sherman, Tex.: Austin College, 1980), vol. 3, pp. 47–67; W. Cole Durham, Jr., and Dallin H. Oaks, "Constitutional Protections for Independent Higher Education: Limited Powers and Institutional Rights," *id.* at 69–87.

16. See, e.g., New Jersey-Philadelphia Presbytery v. New Jersey State Bd. of Higher Ed., 482 F. Supp. 968 (D.N.J. 1980), final opinion and order issued May 18, 1981.

17. CAL. EDUC. CODE §§ 94320 and 94321.

18. CAL. CORP. CODE §§ 6510 *et seq.* (Supp. 1980).

19. *Id.* §§ 6713, 6715, 6716(d), and 9680(e)(1) (Supp. 1980).

20. People v. President and Trustees of the College of California, 38 Cal. 166 (1869).

21. See, e.g., Hoyt v. College of Osteopathic Physicians and Surgeons, 61 Cal. 2d 750, 394 P.2d 932, 40 Cal. Rptr. 244 (1964), and In re Loving's Estate, 29 Cal. 2d 423, 175 P.2d 524 (1946).

22. But see Queen of Angels v. Younger, 66 Cal. App. 3d 359, 136 Cal. Rptr. 36 (1977).

23. CAL. CORP. CODE §§ 6510 and 6511.

24. 403 U.S. 672 (1971).

25. CAL. EDUC. CODE §§ 94100 *et seq.*

26. *Id.* § 94100.

27. *Id.* § 94110. See 20 U.S.C. § 1163e(c) and 45 C.F.R. § 170.

28. CAL. EDUC. CODE § 94110.

29. 12 CAL. 3d 593, 526 P.2d 513, 116 Cal. Rptr. 361 (1974).

30. CAL. CONST. art. IX, § 8.

31. CAL. CONST. art. XIII, § 24 (renumbered 1966), now art. XVI, § 5 (1974).

32. 526 P.2d at 520–522.

33. CAL. EDUC. CODE § 66901.

34. *Id.* §§ 66902 and 66903.

35. *Id.* § 69700.

36. *Id.* § 69701(a).

37. *Id.* § 69535.

38. *Id.* §§ 69905 *et seq.* (Supp. 1980).

39. *Id.* § 69535 (Supp. 1980).

40. *Id.*

41. CAL. STATS. 1947, c. 42, p. 528, § 1. This legislation was introduced by Assemblyman Edward McGlynn Gaffney of San Francisco.

42. CAL. STATS. 1959, c. 124, p. 1999, § 1; CAL. LABOR CODE § 1411 (repealed).

43. CAL. STATS. 1970, c. 1508, p. 2993, § 1; CAL. LABOR CODE § 1411 (repealed).

44. CAL. STATS. 1959, c. 121, p. 2000, § 1; CAL. LABOR CODE § 1413(d) (repealed).

45. CAL. GOV. CODE §§ 12900 *et seq.*

46. *Id.* § 12920 (Supp. 1980).

47. *Id.* § 12921 (Supp. 1980).

48. *Id.* § 12926(c) (Supp. 1980).

49. See text accompanying notes 3 and 4, *supra.*

50. CAL. GOV. CODE § 12940(a) (Supp. 1980).

51. 42 U.S.C. 20003–(e)(1).

52. CAL. GOV. CODE § 12940(a) (Supp. 1980).

53. CAL. EDUC. CODE § 89535(e), (g), and (h); see also § 87009.

54. *Id.* § 87290.

55. CAL. LABOR CODE § 1197 (Supp. 1980).

56. *Id.* § 1197.5 (Supp. 1980); see also County of Washington v. Gunther, 452 U.S. 161 (1981).

57. CAL. LABOR CODE § 1198 (Supp. 1980).

58. *Id.* § 1194 (Supp. 1980).

59. *Id.* §§ 3200 *et seq.* (Supp. 1980).

60. *Id.* § 3210.

61. *Id.* §§ 3300(c); 3351 (Supp. 1980).

62. *Id.* § 3357.

63. *Id.* § 3350, note 116. And see Anaheim General Hospital v. Workmen's Compensation Appeals Bd., 83 Cal. Rptr. 495, 3 Cal. App. 3d 468 (1970).

64. CAL. LABOR CODE § 3203.

65. *Id.* § 3352(b) (Supp. 1980).

66. *Id.* § 3352(i) (Supp. 1980). But see § 3363.6 (Supp. 1980) for their inclusion by employer election. The exception for casual employment was repealed, 1977 CAL. STATS., c. 17, § 6.

67. CAL. LABOR CODE §§ 4150 *et seq.*

68. *Id.* §§ 3700 *et seq.* (Supp. 1980).

69. *Id.* §§ 3706–3708 (Supp. 1980).

70. CAL. UNEMP. INS. CODE §§ 1 *et seq.* (West Supp. 1980).

71. The general definition of "employment" is found in *id.* §§ 601, 601.5.

72. *Id.* § 608.

73. *Id.*

74. *Id.*

75. *Id.* § 634.5(a)(1).

76. *Id.* § 634.5(a)(2).

77. *Id.* § 634.5(b).

78. *Id.* §§ 642(a)(1), 642.5(a).

79. *Id.* §§ 642(b), 642.5(b). Spouses must be informed that employment is provided as a means of financial aid (*id.* §§ 642(b)(1), 642.5(b)(1)) and that they are not covered by any program of unemployment insurance (*id.* §§ 642(b)(2), 642.5(b)(2)).

80. *Id.* § 646.

81. *Id.* § 635.

82. *Id.* §§ 629, 639.

83. *Id.* § 801(a).

84. *Id.* § 801(c).

85. *Id.* § 803(b)(1). For details, see *id.* § 803.

86. *Id.* §§ 701, 702.

87. Cal. Labor Code §§ 923 *et seq.*

88. Cal. Educ. Code § 94110.

89. Pub. L. 88-352, Title VI, § 601(a), 78 Stat. 252, 42 U.S.C. 2000d.

90. See Edward McGlynn Gaffney and Philip R. Moots, *Government and Campus: Federal Regulation of Religiously Affiliated Higher Education* (Notre Dame, Ind.: University of Notre Dame Press, 1981), pp. 83-100.

91. Cal. Civ. Code §§ 51 *et seq.*

92. 169 Cal. App. 2d 887, 338 P.2d 633 (1959). "In our opinion private schools should be entitled to contract or refuse to contract with students of their choice for whatever reason if such contract or refusal does not fall within the constitutional or statutory proscription against discrimination on the basis of race or color." 169 Cal. App. 2d at 892, 338 P.2d at 638.

93. 427 U.S. 160 (1976); see also Lemon v. Kurtzman, 403 U.S. 602, 671, n.2 (1971) (White, J., concurring). In *Runyon,* the Supreme Court left open the question whether racial discrimination that was motivated by a religious teaching would be treated differently, 427 U.S. at 167, and the Court has not yet resolved that question. Brown v. Dade Christian Schools, Inc., 556 F.2d 310 (5th Cir. 1977), cert. denied, 434 U.S. 1063 (1978). But see Bob Jones University v. United States of America, 639 F.2d 147 (4th Cir. 1981), *cert. granted,* 102 S.Ct. 386 (1981).

94. See, e.g., Southeastern Community College v. Davis, 442 U.S. 397 (1979); and University of Texas v. Cumenish, 451 U.S. 390 (1981); see also Gaffney and Moots, note 90, *supra,* at 123-133.

95. Cal. Civ. Code §§ 54 *et seq.* (Supp. 1980).

96. *Id.* § 54.

97. Cal. Educ. Code § 76034.

98. *Id.* § 76032.

99. Cal. Gov. Code §§ 12900 *et seq.* (Also guaranteed by Unruh Civil Rights Act, Cal. Civ. Code § 51 (Supp. 1980)).

100. Cal. Gov't. Code § 12927.

101. *Id.* § 12995.

102. Cal. Civ. Code § 51 (Supp. 1980).

103. Cal. Labor Code §§ 6300 *et seq.* (Supp. 1980).

104. *Id.* § 6300 (Supp. 1980).

105. *Id.* § 3300.

106. *Id.* § 6304.1 (Supp. 1980).

107. *Id.* § 12994 (Supp. 1980).

108. Cal. Gov't Code § 4450 *et seq.*

109. Cal. Health & Safety Code § 19955 *et seq.* (Supp. 1978).

110. *Id.* § 19955(a).

111. *Id.* § 19959.

112. Cal. Rev. & Tax. Code §§ 23001 *et seq.*

113. *Id.* § 23701d.

114. *Id.*

115. *Id.* § 23772(a)(2)(A)(i). See I.R.C. § 6033; and see Gaffney and Moots, note 90, *supra,* at 134-150.

116. Cal. Rev. & Tax Code § 23777.

117. *Id.* §§ 13301 *et seq.*

118. But see Allen Estate, 17 Cal. App. 3d 401, 94 Cal. Rptr. 648 (1971) (incidental social activities of exempt organization do not result in loss of exempt status).

119. Cal. Rev. & Tax Code § 13841.

120. *Id.* § 13842.

121. *Id.* § 17150(a)(1).

122. *Id.* § 15441-2 (1943).

123. Cal. Const. art. XIII, § 3(e). A parallel exemption is provided in connection with such buildings under construction. *Id.* art. XIII, § 5.

124. Cal. Rev. & Tax Code § 203 (Supp. 1980). For details, see *id.*

125. Cal. Const. art. XIII, § 3(f).

126. 152 Cal. App. 2d 496, 314 P.2d 209 (1957).

127. Cal. Const. art. XIII, § 4(b).

128. Cal. Rev. & Tax Code § 214.

129. *Id.* § 214(3).

130. *Id.* § 314(6). This subsection explicitly requires that the property "upon the liquidation, dissolution or abandonment of the owner will not inure to the benefit of any private person except a fund, foundation or corporation organized and operated for religious . . . or charitable purposes."

131. Cal. Rev. & Tax Code § 6363; for the statutory definition of food products, see *id.* § 6359.

132. For a comprehensive treatment of governmental regulation of fund raising, see Bruce Hopkins, *Charity Under Siege: Government Regulation of Fund Raising* (New York: John Wiley and Sons, 1980).

133. Cal. Educ. Code § 89720.

134. Cal. Bus. & Prof. Code § 17510.2(d).

135. *Id.* § 17510.3(a).

136. *Id.* § 17510.4(a).

137. CAL. PENAL CODE § 326.5 (Supp. 1980).

138. *Id.* § 330.

14. Colorado

1. COLO. REV. STAT. §§ 7–20–101 through 7–29–106.

2. *Id.* §§ 7–40–101 *et seq.*, providing for the incorporation of any religious, educational, benevolent, charitable or other nonprofit association. *Id.* § 7–40–106.

3. *Id.* §§ 7–50–101 *et seq.* Although the use of the word "societies" suggests that RACs were not intended to be included, two provisions relate directly to institutions of higher learning. See *id.* §§ 7–50–104 and 7–50–105.

4. *Id.* §§ 7–51–101 *et seq.* Although this article allows incorporation for educational purposes, *id.* § 7–51–112, not many RACs will be organized for profit. If an association incorporated under this article elected to be bound by the Nonprofit Corporations Act, see note 11, *infra*, it would, of course, have to cancel all its stock. *Id.* § 7–24–110.

Articles 50 and 51 contain two interesting provisions allowing religious organizations to incorporate a church-operated school "in the manner and with the powers provided for the incorporation of a church" if the incorporators deem it convenient for its administrators. *Id.* §§ 7–50–109, 7–51–113. Perhaps through legislative oversight, one of these provisions is available only to a "body of Christians," *id.* § 7–50–109, while the other is available to any religious denomination, *id.* § 7–51–113. The first clearly violates the Establishment Clause of the First Amendment as well as the Equal Protection Clause of the Fourteenth Amendment to the United States Constitution. See, e.g., Larson v. Valente, 456 U.S. 228 (1982).

5. *Id.* §§ 7–40–101(2), 7–50–101(2), 7–51–101(2).

6. *Id.* § 7–20–103(1)(b).

7. *Id.* § 7–20–103(1)(C).

8. *Id.* § 7–20–104.

9. *Id.* §§ 15–1–1101 *et seq.*

10. *Id.* § 15–1–1103(5).

11. "Nonprofit corporation" means a corporation no part of the income or profit of which is distributable to its members, directors, or officers, except to a member which is another nonprofit corporation. COLO. REV. STAT. § 7–20–101(10) (1973). The basic question is whether the corporation is being exploited for direct monetary gain. People ex rel. Meiresonne v. Arnold, 37 Colo. App. 414, 553 P.2d 79 (1976).

12. COLO. REV. STAT. §§ 7–25–101 *et seq.* (1973, Supp. 1979).

13. *Id.* § 7–20–104 (1973).

14. *Id.* § 7–20–103.

15. Dunbar v. Board of Trustees of Clayton College, 170 Colo. 327, 461 P.2d 28 (1969); see discussion of *cy pres* doctrine in Chapter 1, "Corporate Status," *supra.*

16. COLO. REV. STAT. §§ 7–25–104(2), 7–26–108(1) (1973).

17. *Id.* § 7–26–111(1).

18. See *id.* § 7–26–111(2); see Model Act, § 51, and discussion in Chapter 1, "Corporate Status," *supra.*

19. COLO. REV. STAT. §§ 7–26–103, 7–26–116 (1973, Supp. 1979).

20. See discussion in Chapter 1, "Corporate Status," *supra.*

21. COLO. REV. STAT. § 7–26–103(1)(e) (Supp. 1979).

22. COLO. CONST. art. IX, § 7. See also *id.* art. II, § 4.

23. *Id.* art. IX, § 7.

24. *Id.* art. V, § 34.

25. Bedford v. White, 106 P.2d 469, 476 (Colo. 1940).

26. COLO. REV. STAT. § 31–51–901.

27. The Colorado Constitution specifically authorizes the legislature to establish a student loan program. COLO. CONST. art. XI, § 2a.

28. COLO. REV. STAT. §§ 23–3.3–101 *et seq.*

29. *Id.* § 23–3.3–101(3)(d).

30. *Id.* §§ 23–3.5–101 *et seq.*

31. *Id.* § 23–3.5–102(3)(b).

32. *Id.* § 23–3.5–105(1).

33. In Americans United for Separation of Church and State v. Colorado, 648 P.2d 1072 (Colo. 1982), the plaintiffs challenged the applicability of the State Student Incentive Grant (SSIG) program to any students attending RACs in Colorado on the ground that all of these institutions are pervasively sectarian in character. The Colorado Supreme Court sustained the legislation under the federal and the state constitution, but remanded the case to the district court for further proceedings to determine whether one of the defendant institutions, Regis College, is a statutorily eligible institution. As of the summer of 1982, the issue yet to be determined was whether the membership of the governing board of an RAC "reflected" any particular religious denominational perspective.

34. *Id.* §§ 23–3–101 *et seq.*

35. *Id.* §§ 23–3.1–101 *et seq.*

36. The Work Study Program, *id.* §§ 23–3.3–401 *et seq.*, the Scholarship and Grant Program, *id.* §§ 23–3.3–501 *et seq.*, and the Undergraduate Fellow Program, *id.* §§ 23–3.3–601 *et seq.*, apply only to students attending state institutions.

37. *Id.* § 24–34–402(a). Sex discrimination in compensation is also prohibited. *Id.* § 8–5–102. An employer also may not, in inquiries or advertisements regarding prospective employment, express directly or indirectly any limitation, specification or discrimination upon these bases unless it relates to a bona fide occupational qualification (BFOQ). *Id.* § 24–34–402(d).

The statute further provides that, with regard to a handicap, it is lawful "for an employer to act as provided in this paragraph if there is not reasonable accommodation that the employer can make with regard to the handicap, the handicap actually disqualifies the person from the job, and the handicap has a significant impact on the job." *Id.* § 24–34–402(a).

38. *Id.* § 24–34–401(3).

39. *Id.*

40. *Id.* § 24–34–402(d) (Supp. 1979). See note 37, *supra.*

41. See text at note 38, *supra.*

42. COLO. REV. STAT. § 24–34–302 (Supp. 1979).

43. *Id.* § 8–6–105 (Supp. 1979). Colorado also regulates length of pay periods and the time of payment. *Id.* § 8–4–105.

44. *Id.* § 8–6–109 (Supp. 1979). Unemancipated minors may be paid fifteen percent less, as may be "persons certified by the director to be less efficient due to a physical handicap." *Id.* 8–6–108.5 (Supp. 1979).

45. *Id.* §§ 8–40–101 *et seq.* (1974, Supp. 1979).

46. *Id.* § 8–41–105 (Supp. 1979).

47. *Id.* § 8–41–106(1)(b).

48. *Id.* § 8–41–107 (Supp. 1979).

49. *Id.* § 8–41–105(3).

50. *Id.* § 8–41–106(1)(a)(IV).

51. *Id.* §§ 8–41–105(5) and 8–43–104 (Supp. 1979).

52. *Id.* §§ 8–43–101 to 8–43–103 (Repealed, L.75, p. 311, § 62) (Supp. 1979).

53. *Id.* § 8–42–103 (Supp. 1979).

54. *Id.* § 8–44–101.

55. *Id.* §§ 8–70–101 *et seq.*

56. *Id.* § 8–70–103(10)(e). The organization must have at least four employees for some portion of a day in each of twenty weeks in either the current or preceding calendar year. *Id.*

57. *Id.* § 8–70–103(10)(f.7) (Supp. 1979).

58. *Id.* § 8–70–103(10)(g) (Supp. 1979).

59. *Id.*

60. *Id.* § 8–70–103(11)(g)(I).

61. *Id.* § 8–70–103(11)(g)(II).

62. *Id.* § 8–70–103(11)(h).

63. *Id.*

64. *Id.* § 8–70–103(10)(k). An "institution of higher education" specifically includes any college or university in Colorado. *Id.* § 8–70–103(15)(b).

65. For details, see *id.* § 8–73–107(3) (1973, Supp. 1979).

66. See *id.* Title 8, Article 1 ("Industrial Commission Division of Labor–Director"), Article 2 ("Labor Relations, Generally") and Article 3 ("Labor Peace Act").

67. See text at notes 70 *et seq., infra.*

68. COLO. REV. STAT. §§ 24–34–601 (Supp. 1979) *et seq.*

69. *Id.* § 24–34–601(2) (Supp. 1979). Related conduct in advertising and the like is also unlawful. *Id.* § 24–34–701 (Supp. 1979).

70. *Id.* § 24–34–601(1) (Supp. 1979).

71. See text at notes 75 *et seq., infra.*

72. *Id.* § 24–34–502(1)(a) (Supp. 1979). Related conduct, such as discriminatory advertising, is also prohibited. *Id.* § 24–34–502 (Supp. 1979).

73. *Id.* § 24–34–501(3) (Supp. 1979).

74. Of course, to the extent that the state public accommodations law governs admissions, see notes 70 *et seq., supra,* an RAC would have little use or need for the exemption.

75. *Id.* § 24–34–502(3) (Supp. 1979).

76. *Id.* § 24–34–502(4) (Supp. 1979).

77. *Id.* § 24–34–302 (Supp. 1979). For its composition, powers and procedures, see *id.* §§ 24–34–302 (Supp. 1979) *et seq.*

78. *Id.* §§ 8–11–100 *et seq.* (Repealed Colo. L. 80, p. 451, § 6).

79. See 26 U.S.C.A. § 501(c)(3).

80. COLO. REV. STAT. § 39–22–117(1).

81. *Id.* § 39–22–117(2).

82. *Id.* § 39–23–113 (Supp. 1979).

83. COLO. REV. STAT. §§ 39–23.5–101 *et seq.*

84. *Id.* § 39–25–104(1)(a).

85. *Id.* § 39–22–113 (Supp. 1979).

86. I.R.C. § 170(e)(2)(B) and (C).

87. COLO. REV. STAT. § 39–22–304(1).

88. I.R.C. § 170(b)(2).

89. COLO. CONST. art. X, § 5.

90. COLO. REV. STAT. § 39–3–101(f). The term "school" includes a college. *Id.* The school must have "a curriculum comparable to that of a publicly supported elementary or secondary school or college, or any combination thereof" and must require daily attendance. *Id.*

91. City and County of Denver v. Colorado Seminary, 41 P.2d 1109, 1111 (Colo. 1934); Kemp v. Pillar of Fire, 94 Colo. 41, 45–46, 27 P.2d 1036, 1037 (1933).

92. COLO. REV. STAT. § 39–3–101(1)(e).

93. *Id.*

94. *Id.* § 39–3–101(g)(I)(B) (Supp. 1979).

95. *Id.* § 39–26–114(1)(a)(viii) (Supp. 1979).

96. *Id.* § 39–26–114(1)(a)(XIX) (Supp. 1979).

97. A "school" must have a "curriculum comparable to grade, grammar, junior high, high school, or college, or any combination thereof," require daily attendance, enroll at least forty students and charge tuition. *Id.* § 39–26–102(13).

98. *Id.* § 39–26–114(1)(a)(xx) (Supp. 1979).

99. *Id.* § 39–26–203(1)(e) (Supp. 1979).

100. *Id.* § 39–26–102(2.5) (Supp. 1979).

101. *Id.* §§ 12–9–101 *et seq.*

102. *Id.* § 12–9–104(1).

103. *Id.*

104. *Id.* § 12–9–102(3).

105. *Id.* § 12–9–102(6).

106. See *id.* §§ 12–9–102 *et seq.*

107. *Id.* § 12–9–108(1). For its contents, see *id.*

108. *Id.* § 12–19–103. For powers and duties, see *id.*

109. *Id.* § 22–44–208. Churches spared the fee are limited to "serving food on less than seven consecutive days or on less than fifty-two separate days in a calendar year." *Id.*

110. *Id.* §§ 12–59–101 *et seq.*

111. *Id.* § 12–59–104(1)(b),(c) and (d).

15. Connecticut

1. CONN. GEN. STAT. ANN. §§ 33–243 *et seq.* (1958 and Supp. 1982).

2. *Id.* §§ 33–419 through 33–497 (Supp. 1982).

3. *Id.* §§ 33–264a, –264b, and –264c (Supp. 1982).

4. *Id.* § 33–264j(b) (Supp. 1982).

5. *Id.*

6. St. Basil's College in Stamford, Conn., operated for the academic year, 1976–1977.

7. CONN. GEN. STAT. ANN. § 33–435.

8. *Id.* §§ 33–423 to –432, –458 to –472.

9. The provisions for dissolution of a church corporation are found at *id.* §§ 33–264e *et seq.* (Supp. 1982). Those governing the dissolution of nonstock corporations are found at *id.* § 33–484 *et seq.*

10. *Id.* § 33–479.

11. *Id.* § 33–422 (Supp. 1982).

12. *Id.* §§ 33–491 and 492 (Supp. 1982).

13. *Id.* § 33–490(2).

14. *Id.* § 33–490(3).

15. *Id.* § 33–487 (Supp. 1982).

16. *Id.* § 33–490(4).

17. *Id.* § 33–490(5).

18. Howood House, Inc. v. Trustees of Donations and Bequest for Church Purposes, Inc., 27 Conn. Sup. 176, 233 A.2d 5 (1967).

19. "*Congress* shall make no law respecting an establishment of religion." U.S. CONST. AMEND. I (emphasis added). See also Barron v. Baltimore, 32 U.S. (7 Pet.) 243 (1833); but see Cantwell v. Connecticut, 310 U.S. 296 (1940) (applying the First Amendment to the States through the Due Process Clause of the Fourteenth Amendment).

20. See Anson Phelps Stokes, *Church and State in the United States* (New York: Harper, 1950), vol. I, pp. 186, 408–18; and A. E. Dick Howard, *State Aid to Private Higher Education* (Charlottesville, Va.: Michie, 1977), pp. 160–166.

21. CONN. CONST. art. VII.

22. CONN. CONST. art. VIII, § 3. For a sample of the religious character of Yale, see the regulations of the college concerning admission, the "religious, godly, and blameless lives" of its scholars, the "scholastical exercises" (including the study of divinity and the weekly recitation of the Westminster Confession of Faith), and its penal laws (including expulsion of any scholar "guilty of heresy or any error directly tending to subvert the fundamentals of Christianity"), in Franklin B. Dexter, *Biographical Sketches of the Graduates of Yale College with Annals of the College History* (New York, 1896), vol. II, pp. 2–18.

23. Howard, *State Aid*, note 20, *supra*, p. 182.

24. 403 U.S. 672 (1971). For a brief discussion of this case, see Edward McGlynn Gaffney, Jr., and Philip R. Moots, *Government and Campus: Federal Regulation of Religiously Affiliated Higher Education* (Notre Dame, Ind.: University of Notre Dame Press, 1982), pp. 94–96, 114–115.

25. 20 U.S.C. 751(a)(2).

26. 403 U.S. at 678–684.

27. *Id.* at 684–689. For a critical view of the Supreme Court's use of the entanglement test, see Kenneth Ripple, "The Entanglement Test of the Religion Clauses—A Ten Year Assessment," 27 U.C.L.A. L. REV. 1195 (1980). And see Edward McGlynn Gaffney, "Political Divisiveness Along Religious Lines: The Entanglement of the Court in Sloppy History and Bad Public Policy," 24 ST. LOUIS L.J. 205 (1980).

28. CONN. GEN. STAT. ANN. §§ 10–335 to 10–357 (Supp. 1982).

29. *Id.* § 10–337(b) and (3).

30. 413 U.S. 734 (1973). For a brief discussion of this case, see Gaffney and Moots, *Government and Campus*, note 24, *supra*, pp. 50–53, 94–96.

31. CONN. GEN. STAT. ANN. §§ 10–331a to 331h (Supp. 1982).

32. *Id.* § 10–331b(4) (Supp. 1982).

33. 426 U.S. 736 (1976). For a brief discussion of this case, see Gaffney and Moots, *Government and Campus,* note 24, *supra*, pp. 52–53, 95–96.

34. CONN. GEN. STAT. ANN. §§ 10–116b to 10–116 (Supp. 1982).

35. 433 F.Supp. 97 (M.D. Tenn.), *summarily aff'd.*, 434 U.S. 803 (1977); see also Smith v. Bd. of Governors of Univ. of North Carolina, 429 F.Supp. 871 (W.D. N.C.), *summarily aff'd.*, 434 U.S. 803 (1977). For a brief discussion of these cases, see Gaffney and Moots, *Government and Campus*, note 24, *supra,* pp. 55–56, 96–97, and Editorial, "Free Choice for College Students," *America* 137 (Oct. 22, 1977) 257.

36. CONN. GEN. STAT. ANN. § 31–126(a).

37. *Id.* § 31–126(f).

38. *Id.* § 31–126(d).

39. The phrase, "bona fide occupational qualification or need" recurs in subsections (a), (b), and (f) of section 126. Subsection (c), dealing with labor organizations, and subsection (g)(3), dealing with age discrimination, mention "bona fide occupational qualification," but do not include the words, "or need." Perhaps the phrase "or need" is the Connecticut legislature's attempt to paraphrase the language in the federal BFOQ exception, "reasonably necessary to the normal operation of that particular business or enterprise." 42 U.S.C. 2000e–2(e)(1).

40. CONN. GEN. STAT. ANN. § 31–126.

41. 168 CONN. 26, 357 A.2d 498 (1975).

42. 413 U.S. 376 (1973) (sustaining, against free speech and free press clause attacks, a municipal ordinance forbidding newspapers to carry "help-wanted" advertisements in sex-designated columns except where the employer or advertiser is free to make hiring or employment referral decisions on the basis of sex).

43. 357 A.2d at 505 (citing the EEOC Guidelines on the BFOQ exception, and several federal cases construing the exception narrowly).

44. See Gaffney and Moots, *Government and Campus*, note 24, *supra,* pp. 47–48, 63–69, 81–82.

45. To the extent that alcoholism and drug addiction are perceived as an illness, one might argue that an alcoholic or a drug addict is included within the general definition of a "physically disabled" person in the Connecticut Code. CONN. GEN. STAT. ANN. § 1–1f(b). See 430 Op. Atty. Gen. of U.S. No. 12, April 12, 1977; 45 C.F.R., Part 84 (defining alcoholism and drug addiction as a handicap within the meaning of section 504 of the Vocational Rehabilitation Act of 1973). Contrast Powell v. Texas, 392 U.S. 514 (1968) (not cruel or unusual to punish public drunks) with Robinson v. California, 370 U.S. 660 (1962) (invalidating criminalization of narcotic addiction as cruel and unusual). The relevant Connecticut statutes are vague; see CONN. GEN. STAT. ANN. § 31–126 (proscribing employment dis-

crimination on the basis of physical disability); see also *id.* § 53–35 (banning such discrimination in public accommodations). Perhaps because the legislature knew how to define "alcoholic" and "drug-dependent person" when it chose to, *id.* § 17–155 1(1) and (19), no litigation has been brought under Connecticut law seeking to prohibit employment discrimination on the basis of alcoholism or drug dependency.

46. *Id.* § 31–58(e).

47. "Minimum fair wage" in Connecticut is defined both in dollar amounts for calendar years 1979, 1980, and 1981, and in terms of a percentage (.5%) higher than the federal minimum wage. *Id.* § 31–58(j) (Supp. 1982).

48. *Id.* §§ 31–222 through 274.

49. *Id.* § 222(a)(1)(D).

50. *Id.*

51. *Id.* § 222(a)(1)(D)(i).

52. *Id.* § 222(a)(1)(D)(ii).

53. *Id.* § 222(a)(1)(E)(i)(I).

54. *Id.* § 222(a)(1)(E)(i)(II).

55. *Id.* § 222(a)(1)(E)(ii).

56. *Id.* § 222(a)(5)(G)(i).

57. *Id.* § 222(a)(5)(G)(ii).

58. *Id.* § 222(a)(5)(J).

59. *Id.* § 222(a)(5)(F).

60. *Id.* § 222(a)(5)(C).

61. *Id.* § 222(a)(1)(J).

62. *Id.* § 225(g).

63. *Id.* § 225(g)(1)(B).

64. *Id.*

65. *Id.* § 225(g)(2)(A).

66. *Id.* § 225(g)(3).

67. *Id.* §§ 31–275 through 31–355 (1972 and Supp. 1982).

68. *Id.* § 31–275(5)(B) (Supp. 1982).

69. *Id.* § 31–284(a).

70. *Id.* § 31–284(b).

71. *Id.* §§ 31–101 *et seq.*

72. *Id.* § 31–101(7).

73. This statement is based not on Connecticut law, but upon the opinion of the national office of the federal Internal Revenue Service. See IRS Letter Ruling, Docket No. 77–4005 (Nov. 16, 1977). A Letter Ruling lacks precedential value in court proceedings, but is indicative of prevailing national tax policy at the time it is issued. See Gaffney and Moots, *Government and Campus*, note 24, *supra,* p. 98.

74. Pub. L. 88–352, Title II, 78 Stat. 243, 42 U.S.C. 2000a *et seq.*

75. Pub. L. 90–284, 82 Stat. 81, 42 U.S.C. 3601–3619.

76. "No person shall be denied the equal protec-

tion of the law nor be subjected to segregation or discrimination in the exercise or enjoyment of his civil or political rights because of religion, race, color, ancestry, or national origin." CONN. CONST. art. I, § 20.

77. CONN. GEN. STAT. ANN. §§ 53–34 *et seq.* Portions of this 1949 statute have been repealed or transferred to other sections of the General Laws. See, e.g., §§ 46a–1 *et seq.* (Supp. 1982).

78. The federal statute bans discrimination on the basis of race, color, religion, or national origin. 42 U.S.C. 2000a(a). The state statute prohibits "any denial of [full and equal accommodation in a place of public accommodation] by reason of race, creed, color, national origin, ancestry, sex, marital status, age, mental retardation or physical disability, including, but not limited to, blindness or deafness." CONN. GEN. STAT. ANN. § 53–35(a).

79. The scope of the federal statute is quite broad, covering all places of public accommodation which "affect" commerce among the several states. 42 U.S.C. 2000a(b); see Heart of Atlanta Motel v. United States, 379 U.S. 241 (1964); Katzenbach v. McClung, 379 U.S. 294 (1964). The federal statute contains the "Mrs. Murphy boarding house" exception, 42 U.S.C. 2000a(b)(1), but the state statute applies to "any housing accommodation . . . offered for sale or rent."

80. Once a college, however, has sold a ticket to a public performance to a person, it must admit that person to the performance and may not eject the person from the performance unless the person's conduct or speech is abusive or offensive or tends to a breach of the peace. CONN. GEN. STAT. ANN. § 53–330.

81. *Id.* § 31–367 (Supp. 1982).

82. *Id.* § 31–367(d) (Supp. 1982).

83. *Id.* § 31–49.

84. See Paul R. Lauer, *Church and State in New England* (Baltimore, 1892), pp. 85–89.

85. Snyder v. Town of Newton, 147 Conn. 374, 161 A.2d 770, 776 (1960), *appeal dismissed*, 365 U.S. 299 (1961).

86. *Id.*

87. CONN. GEN. STAT. ANN. § 12–81(8). See Yale University v. New Haven, 71 Conn. 316, 42 A. 87 (1899); Yale University v. New Haven, 17 Conn. Supp. 166 (New Haven Ct. Com. Pleas. 1950). And see Alvin C. Warren, Jr., Thomas G. Kruttenmaker, and Lester B. Snyder, "Property Tax Exemptions for Charitable, Educational, Religious and Governmental Institutions in Connecticut," 4 CONN. L. REV. 181 (1971), and Howard, *State Aid,* note 20, *supra,* pp. 172–175.

88. CONN. GEN. STAT. ANN. § 12–214 (1958).

89. I.R.C. § 501.

90. CONN. GEN. STAT. ANN. § 12–341.

91. *Id.* § 12–347.

92. *Id.* § 12–391.

93. *Id.* § 12–217.

94. I.R.C. § 170.

95. CONN. GEN. STAT. ANN. § 12–505.

96. *Id.* § 12–81(7).

97. *Id.* § 12–81(8).

98. *Id.* § 12–81(14).

99. Forman Schools, Inc. v. Town of Litchfield, 14 Conn. Supp. 444, error on other grounds, 134 Conn. 1, 54 A.2d 710 (1947).

100. Arnold College for Hygiene & Physical Education v. Town of Milford, 144 Conn. 206, 128 A.2d 537 (1957).

101. CONN. GEN. STAT. ANN. § 12–412 (1958).

102. *Id.* § 12–413 (Supp. 1982).

103. *Id.* § 12–412(i) (Supp. 1982).

104. *Id.* § 12–541[b] (Supp. 1982).

105. *Id.* § 12–543[b] (1958).

106. *Id.* § 12–543[b].

107. *Id.* §§ 19–323k to 19–323z (Supp. 1982).

108. *Id.* § 19–323L(1) (Supp. 1982).

109. *Id.* §§ 19–323m, o, p, q, s (Supp. 1982).

110. *Id.* § 19–323r (Supp. 1982).

111. *Id.* §§ 19–323u to x (Supp. 1982).

112. *Id.* § 19–323L(1) (Supp. 1982).

113. See Gaffney and Moots, *Government and Campus,* note 24, *supra,* pp. 10–11, 22–23, 72.

114. CONN. GEN. STAT. ANN. §§ 10–317 to 10–320 (Supp. 1982).

115. Art. I of the New England Higher Education Compact, as cited at *id.* § 10–317 (Supp. 1981).

116. Howard, *State Aid,* note 20, *supra,* p. 181.

16. Delaware

1. DEL. CODE ANN. tit. 8, §§ 101 *et seq.*

2. DEL. CODE ANN. tit. 6, § 7309(a)(9).

3. DEL. CODE ANN. tit. 8, § 510.

4. *Id.* § 313.

5. *Id.* § 125.

6. *Id.*

7. DEL. CODE ANN. tit. 8, §§ 255, 256 (Supp. 1980), § 276 (1974).

8. In Re Will of Potter, 275 A.2d 574, 583 (Del. Ch. 1980); see also Asche v. Asche, 41 Del. Ch. 481, 199 A.2d 314, *record remanded,* 210 A.2d 306, *on remand,* 216 A.2d 272 (1964). For a discussion of the *cy pres* doctrine, see Chapter 1, "Corporate Status," *supra.*

9. DEL. CODE ANN. tit. 8, §§ 255, 256 (Supp. 1980), § 275 (1974).

10. *Id.* § 279 (1974).

11. *Id.* § 280.

12. *Id.* §§ 278, 281. Presumably, "stockholders" under § 276 would by implication include members of the governing board of an educational institution.

13. DEL. CONST. art. I, § 1.

14. *Id.* art. X, § 1.

15. *Id.* art. X, § 3.

16. State ex rel. Trant v. Brown, 6 Del (W.W. Harr.) 181, 183, 172 A.2d 835, 837 (1934).

17. DEL. CODE ANN. tit. 14, § 3404(c) (Supp. 1978).

18. *Id.* § 3404(d) (Supp. 1978).

19. *Id.*

20. DEL. CODE ANN. tit. 19, § 711.

21. *Id.* § 710(2).

22. *Id.*

23. See Jackson v. Phillips, 14 Allen 539, 96 Mass. 539 (1867), holding that a charity is for the benefit of an indefinite number of people, bringing their minds or hearts under the influence of education or religion.

24. DEL. CODE ANN. tit. 19, § 711(e)(2).

25. *Id.* § 711(e)(1).

26. *Id.* § 712. For the procedures involved, see *id.*

27. *Id.* §§ 901 *et seq.*

28. *Id.* § 901(4).

29. *Id.* § 901(5)(c).

30. *Id.* § 901(5)(e).

31. *Id.* §§ 2301 *et seq.*

32. *Id.* § 2306(a).

33. *Id.* § 2304.

34. *Id.* § 2301(8). Casual employment is defined as employment for not over two weeks or for a total salary during employment that does not exceed $100, and which is not in the regular course of the employer's business.

35. *Id.* § 2310.

36. *Id.* § 2306(b).

37. *Id.* § 2372(a).

38. *Id.* § 2375.

39. *Id.* § 2372(b).

40. *Id.* §§ 3301 *et seq.*

41. *Id.* § 3302(9)(C)(1). The organization must also have had four or more employees for some portion of a day in each of twenty different weeks during the current or previous calendar year. *Id.* § 3302(9)(C)(2).

42. 26 U.S.C.A. § 501(c)(3).

43. *Id.* § 3306(c)(8). An "employing unit" not otherwise subject to the law may elect to be so covered. DEL. CODE ANN. tit. 19, § 3343(a) and (b).

44. *Id.* § 3348.

45. *Id.* § 3345(c)(3).

46. *Id.* § 3302(9)(D)(i)(I).

47. *Id.* § 3302(9)(D)(i)(II).

48. *Id.* § 3302(9)(D)(ii).

49. *Id.* § 3302(10)(B).

50. *Id.* § 3302(10)(F).

51. *Id.* § 3302(10)(J).

52. *Id.* § 3302(K).

53. *Id.*

54. *Id.* § 3314(b)(B).

55. *Id.* § 3314(b)(D).

56. The State Board of Education may revoke the certificate of approval of a private business, trade, or vocational school refusing to admit applicants on the basis of race, color, creed, age, or sex. DEL. CODE ANN. tit. 14, § 8516.

57. DEL. CODE ANN. tit. 6, § 4502.

58. *Id.* § 4501.

59. *Id.* §§ 4601 *et seq.*

60. *Id.* § 4603 (Supp. 1980).

61. *Id.* § 4601(3) (Supp. 1980).

62. *Id.* § 4604(1) (Supp. 1980).

63. See text accompanying note 24, *supra.*

64. DEL. CODE ANN. tit. 6 §§ 4505 *et seq.*; 4605 *et seq.*

65. DEL. CODE ANN. tit. 25, §§ 5101 *et seq.*

66. *Id.* § 6503.

67. *Id.* § 5111.

68. DEL. CODE ANN. tit. 30, §§ 1901 *et seq.*

69. *Id.* § 1902(b)(2).

70. *Id.* §§ 1301 *et seq.* (Supp. 1978).

71. *Id.* § 1313 (Supp. 1978).

72. *Id.* tit. 30, § 1501 (1974).

73. *Id.* §§ 1401 *et seq.*

74. *Id.* § 1401(1).

75. See 26 U.S.C.A. § 2522(a)(2) (1976).

76. *Id.* § 1109.

77. I.R.C. § 170(c)(2)(B) and (C).

78. DEL. CODE ANN. tit. 9, § 8103.

79. Burris v. Tower Hill School Ass'n, 36 Del. 577, 179 A.397 (Del. Super. 1935).

80. See DEL. CODE ANN. tit. 30 § 2301(b) and (d) (Supp. 1978).

81. 26 U.S.C. § 501.

82. See text at notes 42 and 43, *supra.*

83. DEL. CODE ANN. tit. 30, § 2301(h) (Supp. 1978).

84. *Id.* § 2301(1) (Supp. 1978).

85. DEL. CONST. art. II, § 17A.

86. Jackson v. Phillips, 14 Allen 539, 96 Mass. 539 (1867). See note 23, *supra.*

87. DEL. CODE ANN. tit. 14, § 4107.

17. Florida

1. FLA. STAT. ANN. § 617.01–27.

2. See Jewish Guild for the Blind v. First Nat'l

Bank, 226 So. 2d 414, 416 (Fla. App. 1969) (recognizing *cy pres* doctrine in dictum). For a discussion of the *cy pres* doctrine, see Chapter 1, "Corporate Status," *supra*.

3. *Id.* § 617.013.

4. *Id.* § 617.015(1).

5. *Id.* § 617.014.

6. *Id.* § 617.0105.

7. *Id.* § 246.081 (1966 and Supp. 1980).

8. See text at notes 24, 29, 31, 92 and 93, *infra*.

9. FLA. STAT. ANN. § 617.05(1).

10. *Id.*

11. *Id.* §§ 617.051 to 617.054.

12. See note 2, *supra*.

13. FLA. CONST. art. 1, § 3.

14. *Id.* art. 7, § 10 (1968, amended 1974).

15. FLA. STAT. ANN. § 243.18–.40.

16. *Id.* § 243.21.

17. Nohrr v. Brevard County Educ. Fac. Auth., 247 So.2d 304 (Fla. 1971).

18. *Id.* at 307.

19. *Id.*

20. *Id.*

21. *Id.* at 309.

22. FLA. CONST. art. 7, § 15 (1968, amended 1972).

23. FLA. STAT. ANN. § 240.401 (Supp. 1980).

24. *Id.* § 240.401(2) (Supp. 1980).

25. *Id.*

26. *Id.* § 240.401(4)(a) (Supp. 1980).

27. *Id.* § 240.408 (Supp. 1980).

28. *Id.* § 240.409(2)(a) (Supp. 1980).

29. *Id.*

30. *Id.* § 240.415 (Supp. 1980).

31. *Id.* § 240.415(4) (Supp. 1980).

32. *Id.* § 240.419 (Supp. 1980) (emphasis added).

33. *Id.* § 240.407 (Supp. 1980).

34. *Id.* § 240.411 (Supp. 1980).

35. *Id.* § 240.413 (Supp. 1980).

36. *Id.* § 240.405 (Supp. 1980).

37. *Id.* § 240.411 (Supp. 1980); *id.* § 240.413 (Supp. 1980); *id.* § 240.405 (Supp. 1980).

38. FLA. CONST. art. 1, § 2.

39. FLA. STAT. ANN. § 23.161–167 (Supp. 1980).

40. *Id.* § 23.167(1)(a) (Supp. 1980).

41. *Id.* § 23.167(6) (Supp. 1980).

42. *Id.* § 23.162(6) (Supp. 1980).

43. *Id.* § 23.167(8)(a) (Supp. 1980).

44. *Id.* § 448.07(a) (Supp. 1980).

45. *Id.* § 448.01.

46. *Id.* § 448.07(1)(b) (Supp. 1980).

47. Publisher's note, FLA. STAT. ANN. § 440 (West, 1981).

48. FLA. STAT. ANN. § 440 (1981).

49. *Id.* § 440.02(4).

50. *Id.* § 449.02(2)(b).

51. *Id.* § 440.02(2)(d)1. For details, see *id.* For other exemptions, see *id.* § 440.02.

52. *Id.* § 440.02(3).

53. *Id.* § 440.02(6).

54. *Id.* § 440.02(8).

55. *Id.*

56. *Id.* § 440.09(3).

57. *Id.* § 440.09(y).

58. *Id.* § 440.10(2).

59. *Id.* §§ 443 *et seq.* (1981).

60. *Id.* §§ 443.091 and .101(1).

61. *Id.* § 443.021.

62. *Id.* § 443.036(17)(d)(1). Services by certain ministers are also exempt. See *id.* § 443.036(17)(d)(2).

63. *Id.* § 443.036(17)(n)9.b. See also *id.* § 443.036(17)(n)12 (service by certain student nurses).

64. *Id.* § 443.091(3)(a).

65. *Id.* § 509.241 (Supp. 1980).

66. *Id.* § 509.013(4)(a) (Supp. 1980).

67. *Id.* § 509.013(5)(6) (Supp. 1980).

68. *Id.* §§ 509.141(1), 509.142 (Supp. 1981).

69. *Id.* § 553.45–.89 (Supp. 1981).

70. *Id.* § 23.161 (Supp. 1981).

71. *Id.* § 553.46(1).

72. *Id.* § 553.45–.89 (Supp. 1980).

73. *Id.* § 553.46 (Supp. 1980).

74. *Id.* § 553.48 (Supp. 1980).

75. *Id.*

76. *Id.* § 553.47 (Supp. 1980).

77. *Id.* § 23.161(2).

78. *Id.* § 440.56.

79. *Id.* § 440.02(4).

80. *Id.* § 440.56(2).

81. FLA. CONST. art. 7, § 5(b) (1968, amended 1971).

82. FLA. STAT. ANN. § 220 (Supp. 1980).

83. *Id.* § 220.02(1) (Supp. 1980).

84. *Id.* § 220.03(b) (Supp. 1980).

85. See I.R.C. § 501(c)(3).

86. FLA. STAT. ANN. § 220.13(2)(h) (Supp. 1980).

87. I.R.C. § 513(a) (Supp. 1980).

88. FLA. CONST. art. 7, § 3 (emphasis added).

89. FLA. STAT. ANN. § 196.198.

90. *Id.* § 199 (Supp. 1980).

91. *Id.* § 199.072(2)(a) (Supp. 1980).

92. *Id.* § 199.072(2)(b)(2) (Supp. 1980).

93. *Id.* § 212.08 (Supp. 1980).

94. *Id.* § 205.491 (repealed 1972).

95. *Id.*

96. Albury v. Tanner, 264 So.2d 90 (Fla. 1972).

97. *Id.*

98. FLA. STAT. ANN. § 205.022(f) (Supp. 1980).

99. *Id.*

100. *Id.* § 496.02–.132 (Supp. 1980).
101. *Id.* § 496.021 (Supp. 1980).
102. *Id.* § 496.02(4) (Supp. 1980).
103. *Id.* § 496.03(1) (Supp. 1980).
104. *Id.* § 496.01(1)(a) (Supp. 1980).
105. *Id.* § 496.02(1)(b) (Supp. 1980).
106. I.R.C. § 501(c)(3).
107. FLA. STAT. ANN. § 491.04(1) (Supp. 1980).
108. *Id.*
109. *Id.*
110. *Id.* § 849.093(2) (Supp. 1980).
111. *Id.* § 849.093(3)–(9) (Supp. 1980).
112. *Id.* § 550.03(1) (Supp. 1980).
113. *Id.*
114. *Id.* § 617.50–.81.

18. Georgia

1. GA. CODE ANN. § 22–2201. Chapters 22–21 through 22–37 (1977, Supp. 1981) regulate non-profit corporations.
2. *Id.* § 22–301. (1977).
3. *Id.* §§ 22–2901 through 22–3120 (1977, Supp. 1980).
4. Freedman v. Scheer, 223 Ga. 705, 157 S.E. 2d 875 (1967). For a discussion of the *cy pres* doctrine, see Chapter 1, "Corporate Status," *supra.*
5. GA. CODE ANN. §§ 22–3101 through 22–3108.
6. *Id.* §§ 22–2901 *et seq.* (1977).
7. *Id.* § 22–1004 (Supp. 1980) (Merger and Consolidation); *Id.* § 22–3107 (Dissolution).
8. *Id.* § 22–3108 (Supp. 1980).
9. *Id.* §§ 22–3112(c)(2), 22–3103(b).
10. *Id.* §§ 22–3113(c)(3), 22–3103(c).
11. *Id.* § 22–3104.
12. *Id.* §§ 22–3113(c)(4), 22–3103(d).
13. *Id.* §§ 22–3112(c)(5), 22–3103(e).
14. *Id.* § 2–210 (Art. 1, Sec. II) Paragraph X: "No money shall ever be taken from the public treasury, directly or indirectly, in aid of any church, sect, or denomination of religionists, or of any sectarian institution."
15. *Id.* § 32–4902 (1980).
16. *Id.*
17. *Id.* § 32–4904 (1980, Supp. 1981).
18. For details, see *id.* § 32–4903(b) (1980, Supp. 1981).
19. *Id.*
20. See *id.* §§ 32–4905 *et seq.*
21. *Id.* § 32–4907: "Revenue bonds issued under the provisions of this Chapter shall not be deemed to constitute a debt or pledge of the faith and credit of the State of Georgia or any political subdivision thereof within the meaning of any provision of the Constitution or laws of this State, but such revenue bonds shall be payable solely from the revenues and receipts received by the Authority in connection with the financing of any project as herein permitted. Revenue bonds issued by the Authority shall not directly, indirectly or contingently obligate the State or any of its political subdivisions to levy or to pledge any form of taxation whatever therefor or to make any appropriation for the payment thereof and all such revenue bonds or other obligations of the Authority shall contain recitals on their face covering substantially the foregoing provisions of this section. No State or local public funds shall be appropriated for use of the Authority created by this Chapter."
22. *Id.* § 32–3759(1) (Supp. 1981).
23. *Id.* § 23–3752(2) (Supp. 1981).
24. *Id.*
25. *Id.* § 32–848.
26. *Id.* § 32–847 (1980). See text *infra*, at p. 285.
27. *Id.* § 32–848 (emphasis added).
28. *Id.* § 89–1701 (1980): "(e) 'Public employer' or 'employer' as used in this Chapter means any department, board, bureau, commission, Authority or other agency of the State of Georgia which employs 15 or more employees within the State for each working day in each of 20 or more calendar weeks in the current or preceding calendar year. . . ." Outside the Fair Employment Act, there are two statutes which deal with discrimination. Sex discrimination is prohibited under Section 54–1003, which applies to all employers who have ten or more employees, and who are engaged in intrastate commerce. However, Section 54–1003 is basically an equal pay for equal work statute — the primary subject is the amount of pay once one is hired, not who can be hired in the first place. The second such statute prohibits discrimination on the basis of age, *id.* § 54–1102, and applies to all employers. (1972, Supp. 1981).
29. *Id.* § 54–1202.
30. *Id.* § 54–1208(a).
31. *Id.* §§ 114–101 *et seq.* (1973, Supp. 1981).
32. *Id.* §§ 114–101, 107 (Supp. 1981).
33. Compare the 1973 version of this provision with the current version, § 114–107 (Supp. 1981).
34. *Id.*
35. *Id.* § 114–102, 105 (1973).
36. *Id.* § 114–102. (1973).
37. *Id.* § 114–602 (1973).
38. *Id.* § 114–603.
39. *Id.* § 114–103.
40. *Id.* § 54–601 through 659 (1973, Supp. 1981).
41. *Id.* § 54–622.1 (1973, Supp. 1981).
42. *Id.*
43. *Id.*
44. *Id.* § 54–622.
45. *Id.*
46. *Id.* § 54–657(h)(10)(A) (Supp. 1981).

47. *Id.* § 54–657(h)(14)(C,J) (Supp. 1981). For details see *id.*

48. 334 F. Supp. 909 (S.D. Ga. 1971).

49. *Id.* at 913.

50. GA. CODE ANN. § 32–847 (1980).

51. *Id.* See text *supra*, at p. 113.

52. *Id.* § 99–4903.

53. *Id.* § 99–4904.

54. *Id.* § 91–1105 (1980).

55. *Id.* § 91–1107(g).

56. *Id.* § 91–1107(h).

57. *Id.* § 91–1125.

58. *Id.* § 54–123(a).

59. *Id.* § 54–101.

60. *Id.* § 54–123(b).

61. *Id.* § 2–4604.

62. *Id.* § 91A–3605 (1980).

63. *Id.* § 91A–3605(b)(1).

64. *Id.*

65. *Id.* § 91A–3605(b)(2)(A)(i) through (iv). Revocation is retroactive "to the time of the occurrence of the disqualifying event or events." § 91A–3605(b)(2)(B).

66. *Id.* § 91A–3605(c)(i).

67. *Id.*

68. *Id.* § 91A–5702 (Supp. 1980).

69. *Id.* § 91A–3607.

70. *Id.* § 91A–1102(a)(2).

71. *Id.* § 91A–1102(a)(3).

72. *Id.* § 91A–1102(a)(6).

73. *Id.* § 91A–1102(a)(7).

74. *Id.* § 91A–1102(a)(9). This provision would exempt, for example, the contents of an RAC's art museum.

75. *Id.* § 91A–1102(b) (emphasis added).

76. *Id.* § 91A–1102(c).

77. *Id.*

78. *Id.* § 91A–4503. For details, see *id.*

79. *Id.* For details and further exemptions, see *id.*

80. *Id.* § 91A–4503(p).

81. *Id.* § 35–1002.

82. *Id.* § 108–203 (4605)2 (1979).

83. *Id.* § 108–203 (4605)3.

84. *Id.* § 108–205.

85. *Id.* § 2–211 (1977, Supp. 1981).

86. *Id.* §§ 91A–6301a through 91A–6313a (1980).

87. *Id.* § 91A–6313a.

88. *Id.* § 40–3110 (1975).

89. *Id.*

19. Hawaii

1. HAWAII REV. STAT. §§ 416–11 and 416–14 to 416–17.

2. *Id.* §§ 416–19 and 416–20, and chapter 419.

3. *Id.* § 416–20.

4. *Id.*

5. *Id.* Other items *must* be included. See *id.*

6. *Id.* § 300–42.

7. *Id.* § 300–41.

8. *Id.*

9. *Id.* §§ 416–121 through 416–128 (1976, Supp. 1979).

10. *Id.* § 416–2 (1976).

11. *Id.* §§ 417–51 through 417–59.

12. *Id.* §§ 417–58, 416–121.

13. *Id.* § 416–122 (Supp. 1979).

14. *Id.* § 416–123.

15. *Id.* § 416–125 (1976).

16. *Id.*

17. *Id.* § 416–128 (Supp. 1979).

18. *Id.* § 416–124 (1979).

19. HAWAII CONST. art. IX, § 1.

20. Admissions Act § 5(f), 73 Stat. 4, Public Law 86–3.

21. Hawaii's Student Loan Assistance Program, HAWAII REV. STAT. §§ 304–91 *et seq.*, is for students of the University of Hawaii and of community colleges only. *Id.* § 304–92.

22. *Id.* § 309–1.

23. *Id.* § 309–2.

24. *Id.* §§ 305H–1 *et seq.*

25. *Id.* § 305H–1.

26. *Id.* § 305H–2 (Supp. 1979).

27. *Id.* This stipulation indicates that the Commission might operate as a conduit for non-federal funds as well.

28. *Id.* §§ 378–2(1) and 378–2(2). Apprenticeship agreements are also covered. *Id.* § 378–2(7) (Supp. 1979).

29. *Id.* § 378–2(1).

30. *Id.* § 378–2(3).

31. *Id.* § 378–1(4).

32. See text at note 30, *supra.*

33. HAWAII REV. STAT. § 378–2(1).

34. *Id.* § 378–9(2).

35. *Id.* § 378–9(5).

36. *Id.* § 378–1(6) (emphasis added).

37. See text at notes 28 through 34, *supra.*

38. HAWAII REV. STAT. § 378–3 (Supp. 1979).

39. *Id.* § 378–1.

40. *Id.* §§ 387–1 *et seq.* For further provisions dealing with compensation, see "Payment of Wages and Other Compensation", §§ 388–1 *et seq.*

41. *Id.* § 387–2 (Supp. 1979). As of July 1, 1981, the minimum wage is $3.35 per hour. *Id.*

42. *Id.* § 387–3.

43. *Id.* § 387–4.

44. *Id.* § 387–1(1).

45. *Id.* § 387–1(5).

46. *Id.* § 387–1(10).

47. *Id.* § 387-1(11). People covered by the Fair Labor Standards Act may still be covered by Hawaii's law if the former does not meet the latter's standards in some respects. *Id.* The director of labor and industrial relations may set special rules for certain part-time employees, apprentices, handicapped workers, and others. *Id.* § 387-9.

48. *Id.* §§ 386-1 *et seq.*

49. *Id.* § 386-1(1) (Supp. 1979).

50. *Id.* § 386-1(2) (Supp. 1979).

51. *Id.* § 386-1(3) (Supp. 1979).

52. *Id.* § 386-1(4) (Supp. 1979).

53. *Id.* § 386-7.

54. *Id.* § 386-4.

55. *Id.* § 386-121.

56. *Id.* §§ 383-1 *et seq.*

57. *Id.* § 383-1(9)(A).

58. *Id.* § 383-1(9)(B).

59. *Id.* § 383-7 (Supp. 1979).

60. *Id.* § 383-7(2) (Supp. 1979).

61. *Id.* § 383-7(8).

62. *Id.* § 383-7(9)(A) (Supp. 1979).

63. *Id.* § 383-7(9)(B) (Supp. 1979).

64. *Id.* § 383.62(d)(1) (Supp. 1979).

65. *Id.* §§ 392-1 *et seq.* For exceptions, see *id.* § 392-5.

66. *Id.* §§ 393-1 *et seq.* For exceptions, see *id.* 393-5.

67. *Id.* §§ 377-1 *et seq.*

68. *Id.* § 377-4.

69. See, e.g., *id.* §§ 377-6 to 377-8.

70. *Id.* § 377-1(3)(D).

71. *Id.* §§ 318-1 *et seq.*

72. *Id.* § 318-1.

73. *Id.* § 347-13(a) (emphasis added). Hawaii law also protects the rights of the visually impaired to bring a guide dog into such places without payment of extra charges. *Id.* § 347-13(b).

74. §§ 515-1 *et seq.*

75. *Id.*

76. *Id.* § 515-8.

77. See text accompanying note 35, *supra.*

78. HAWAII REV. STAT. §§ 521-1 *et seq.*

79. *Id.* § 521-7.

80. *Id.* §§ 396-1 *et seq.*

81. *Id.* § 396-3 (Supp. 1979).

82. *Id.* § 396-4.

83. *Id.* §§ 235-1 (Supp. 1979) *et seq.*

84. *Id.* § 235-9(2) (Supp. 1979).

85. *Id.* § 235-9 (Supp. 1979).

86. *Id.* § 235.2.3(g) (Supp. 1979).

87. *Id.* See I.R.C. §§ 512-15.

88. HAWAII. REV. STAT. §§ 236-1 *et seq.*

89. *Id.* § 236-8.

90. *Id.*

91. *Id.* § 235-1.

92. I.R.C. § 170(c)(2)(B) and (C).

93. HAWAII REV. STAT. §§ 246-1 *et seq.*

94. *Id.* § 246-32(a).

95. *Id.* § 246-32(b)(1)(B).

96. *Id.* § 246-32(b)(3).

97. *Id.* § 246-32(b). If the property is leased or rented, the "lease or rental agreement shall be in force and recorded in the bureau of conveyances." *Id.*

98. *Id.* § 246-32(d).

99. *Id.* § 246-23. One who has been granted such an exemption is required to report to the assessor, within thirty days, his ceasing to qualify for it. *Id.* § 246-23(d).

100. See *id.* § 46.74(1).

101. *Id.* §§ 247-1 *et seq.*

102. *Id.* § 247-1.

103. *Id.* § 247-3(5).

104. *Id.* §§ 237-1 *et seq.*

105. *Id.* §§ 237-13 and 237-16.

106. *Id.* § 237-23(6).

107. *Id.* § 237-23(b)(1).

108. *Id.* § 237-23(b)(2).

109. *Id.* § 237-23(b)(3).

110. *Id.* §§ 237-1 *et seq.*

111. See *id.* § 238-3(b).

112. *Id.* § 238-1.

113. *Id.* §§ 249-1 (Supp. 1979) *et seq.*

114. *Id.* §§ 467B-1 *et seq.*

115. *Id.* § 417B-11.

116. *Id.* § 712-1220.

117. *Id.* § 712-1223.

118. See *id.* § 480.2.

119. *Id.* § 446E-2 (Supp. 1979).

20. Idaho

1. IDAHO CODE §§ 30-301 *et seq.* (1980).

2. *Id.* § 30-306(a).

3. *Id.* § 30-305-(a).

4. *Id.* § 30-304.

5. *Id.* § 30-307.

6. *Id.*

7. *Id.* § 7-802 (1979).

8. *Id.* §§ 30-1-1 *et seq.*

9. *Id.* § 30-303(a).

10. *Id.* §§ 30-1-82 (Supp. 1980) *et seq.*

11. *Id.*

12. *Id.* § 30-1-93 (1980).

13. *Id.* § 30-1-87.

14. *Id.*

15. *Id.* § 30-1-94.

16. *Id.* § 30-1-97.

17. *Id.* § 30–1–102.

18. *Id.* § 30–320.

19. IDAHO CONST. art. 9, § 5.

20. 94 Idaho 390, 488 P.2d 860 (1971).

21. *Id.* at 395, 488 P.2d at 865 (emphasis in original).

22. IDAHO CODE §§ 31–4303 (Supp. 1980) *et seq.*

23. *Id.* § 31–4305(1) (Supp. 1980).

24. *Id.* § 31–4306(1)(b) (Supp. 1980).

25. *Id.* § 31–4307(5) (Supp. 1980). For additional requirements and conditions, see *id.* § 31–4307 (Supp. 1980).

26. *Id.* § 33–4310 (Supp. 1980).

27. *Id.* § 18–7301(1).

28. *Id.* § 18–7303 (1979).

29. *Id.* § 18–7302(a).

30. *Id.* § 18–7301(2).

31. *Id.* §§ 18–7301 through 18–7303.

32. *Id.* § 18–7302(e).

33. This exemption is discussed further in the text at note 101, *infra.*

34. IDAHO CODE §§ 67–5901 *et seq.*

35. *Id.* § 67–5905.

36. *Id.* § 67–5902(6) (Supp. 1979).

37. *Id.*

38. *Id.* § 67–5906(12) (Supp. 1980).

39. *Id.* § 67–5906(8) (Supp. 1980).

40. *Id.* § 67–5906(5) (Supp. 1980).

41. *Id.* §§ 67–5901 *et seq.*

42. *Id.* § 67–5910(1) (1973).

43. See, e.g., text at note 45, *infra.*

44. IDAHO CODE § 67–5910(2)(a).

45. *Id.* § 67–5910(2)(b) (1973). The same provision speaks of the right of a religious educational institution to "give preference to applicants of the same religion," *id.* § 67–5910(4)(a), but the context indicates that this exemption refers to the admission of students rather than to employment.

46. *Id.* § 67–5909(1). See text at note 35, *supra.*

47. IDAHO CODE § 44–1702 (1977).

48. *Id.* § 44–1701(2).

49. *Id.* § 44–1602 (1977).

50. *Id.* §§ 44–1501 *et seq.*

51. *Id.* § 44–1503 (1977).

52. *Id.*

53. *Id.* § 44–1504 (Supp. 1980).

54. *Id.* §§ 44–1101 *et seq.*

55. *Id.* § 44–1101.

56. *Id.* §§ 44–1101 and 44–1102.

57. *Id.* § 72–102(10) (Supp. 1980).

58. *Id.*

59. *Id.* § 72–212(5) (Supp. 1980).

60. *Id.* § 72–213 (1973).

61. *Id.*

62. *Id.* §§ 72–1301 *et seq.*

63. *Id.* § 72–1315(a) (Supp. 1980).

64. *Id.* § 72–1315(j) (Supp. 1980).

65. In *id.* § 72–1349(A)(a) (Supp. 1980).

66. 26 U.S.C.A. § 501(c)(3) (Supp. 1980).

67. *Id.* § 501(a).

68. See IDAHO CODE § 72–1349 (Supp. 1980).

69. *Id.* § 72–1349A(a)(1)(A) (Supp. 1980). With the approval of the Director, a number of such non-profit organizations may choose to act as a group in fulfilling the law's requirements. *Id.* § 72–1349A(a).

70. *Id.* § 72–1316A9(b) (Supp. 1980).

71. *Id.* § 72–1316A(c)(3) (Supp. 1980). To qualify, the program must not have been established at the request of an employer or group of employers. *Id.*

72. *Id.* § 72–1316A(h) (Supp. 1980).

73. *Id.* § 72–1316A(i) (Supp. 1980).

74. *Id.* § 72–1316A(n) (Supp. 1980).

75. *Id.* § 72–1316A(g)(l)(i) (Supp. 1980).

76. *Id.* § 72–1316A(g)(l)(ii) (Supp. 1980).

77. *Id.* § 72–1316A(g)(2) (Supp. 1980).

78. *Id.* § 72–1316A(3) (Supp. 1980).

79. Note that service not otherwise covered by the Act may be covered if with respect to such service a tax is required to be paid (or was required to be paid in the previous year) pursuant to the federal unemployment tax act. See *id.* § 72–1316(b) (Supp. 1980).

80. *Id.* § 72–1352(c) (Supp. 1980).

81. See *id.* § 72–1322B (Supp. 1980).

82. *Id.* § 72–1366(o)(1) (Supp. 1980).

83. *Id.* § 72–1366(o)(3) (Supp. 1980).

84. *Id.* § 72–1366(o)(1) (Supp. 1980).

85. *Id.* §§ 44–701 *et seq.* (1977).

86. *Id.* § 44–712.

87. *Id.* §§ 18–7301 *et seq.*

88. *Id.* § 18–7301.

89. *Id.* § 18–7302(e).

90. *Id.* § 18–7303.

91. *Id.* § 18–7302(e).

92. See text at note 101, *infra.*

93. IDAHO CODE §§ 67–5910 *et seq.*

94. *Id.* § 67–5909(5).

95. *Id.* § 67–5902(10) (Supp. 1979).

96. *Id.* § 67–5909(6)(a). Related forms of conduct, e.g., advertising a preference on the prohibited grounds, are also outlawed. See *id.* § 67–5909(6)(a) through (d).

97. *Id.* § 67–571D(4)(a).

98. *Id.* §§ 18–7301 *et seq.*

99. *Id.* § 18–7301(2). For the list, see *id.* § 18–7302(e). Even student admissions might be covered. See text at notes 90 *et seq., supra.*

100. IDAHO CODE § 18–7302(e).

101. *Id.*

102. *Id.* §§ 67–5901 *et seq.*

103. *Id.* § 67–5909(5)(a). Related conduct in advertising, etc., is also prohibited. *Id.* § 67–5909(i).

104. *Id.* § 67–5910(3).

105. *Id.* § 67–5910(4)(a).

106. See text at notes 97 *et seq., supra.*

107. Idaho Code §§ 67–5909(7).

108. *Id.* § 67–591D9(6).

109. See text at note 97, *supra.*

110. Idaho Code §§ 39–3201 *et seq.*

111. *Id.* § 39–3201.

112. *Id.* §§ 72–501 (Supp. 1980) *et seq.*

113. See text at notes 57 *et seq., supra.* An "employer" is "any person who has expressly or impliedly hired or contracted the services of another." *Id.* § 72–102(10) (Supp. 1980).

114. Idaho Code § 72–720 (Supp. 1980).

115. *Id.*

116. *Id.* § 72–722.

117. *Id.* § 72–723.

118. *Id.* § 17–3106 (Supp. 1980).

119. *Id.* § 44–103 (Supp. 1980).

120. Idaho Code , § 72–720 (1979).

121. *Id.* § 72–102 (1979).

122. *Id.* § 72–212 (1979).

123. 26 U.S.C.A. § 501.

124. Idaho Code § 63–3026.

125. *Id.* §§ 14–401 *et seq.*

126. *Id.* § 14–408 (Supp. 1980). The entity must be organized or existing under the laws of Idaho or the transferred property must be restricted to use in Idaho or the entity must be organized under the laws of a state that grants a similar reciprocal tax exemption. *Id.* Property transferred to entities "in trust for or to be devoted to any charitable [or] educational purpose" is also exempt from tax. *Id.*

127. *Id.* §§ 63–3001 *et seq.*

128. *Id.* § 63–3022(1) (Supp. 1980).

129. I.R.C. § 170(c)(2)(B) and (C).

130. Idaho Code § 63–3029A (Supp. 1980).

131. *Id.*

132. *Id.* § 63–3029A.1 (Supp. 1980).

133. *Id.* § 63–3029A.2 (Supp. 1980).

134. *Id.* § 63–105L.

135. *Id.*

136. *Id.* § 63–105B.

137. *Id.*

138. *Id.*

139. *Id.* A similar exemption is provided for "charitable" entities. *Id.* § 63–105C.

140. *Id.* §§ 63–3601 *et seq.*

141. *Id.* § 63–3622(1) (Supp. 1980).

142. *Id.* § 63–3622(s)1 (Supp. 1980). Certain specialized schools are specifically denied the exemption. *Id.*

143. *Id.* § 18–3801. See also *id.* § 18–3809.

144. Idaho Const. art. 3, § 20.

145. Idaho Code § 33–4101 (Supp. 1980).

146. *Id.* § 41–1805(1).

147. *Id.* § 41–1805(3).

148. *Id.* § 41–2206.

149. *Id.* § 41–2206(4).

21. Illinois

1. Ill. Ann. Stat. ch. 32, § 163al(c) (Smith-Hurd) defines a not-for-profit corporation as "a corporation no part of the income of which is distributable to its members, directors or officers. . . ." This subsection does, however, allow for "reasonable compensation for services rendered and the making of distributions upon dissolution or final liquidation. . . ." See also *id.* §§ 163a2 and 163a25.

2. *Id.* § 163a3.

3. *Id.* § 163a27.

4. *Id.* § 163a30.

5. *Id.*

6. *Id.* § 14. These three additional requirements are: "(a) the name and location of the institution proposed to be operated by such corporation, (b) a verified copy of said will, deed or other instrument referred to in Section 1 hereof and (c) who shall compose the members of the corporation. . . ."

7. *Id.*

8. *Id.* ch. 155, § 15.

9. *Id.* ch. 144, § 121 defines such an institution as "a privately-operated college, junior college or university offering degrees and instruction above the high school level either in residence or by correspondence."

10. *Id.* § 122.

11. *Id.* § 183 includes among the term trustees "warden, vestrymen, or such other officers as perform the duties of trustee."

12. *Id.* §§ 181 (dealing with trustees) and 185 (dealing with the corporation itself).

13. *Id.* § 1102.03 defines a governing board as "the body responsible for the management of an institution or of an institutional fund."

14. *Id.* § 163(a) 43.

15. *Id.* § 163(a) 48.

16. *Id.* § 163(a) 49.

17. *Id.* § 201.

18. See, e.g., Community Unit School Dist. No. 4 v. Booth, 1 Ill. 2d 545, 116 N.E. 2d 161 (1953), and Bruce v. Maxwell, 311 Ill. 479, 143 N.E. 82 (1924).

19. Ill. Ann. Stat. ch. 32, §§ 125, 126.

20. See text at note 92 *et seq., infra.* For a full discussion of the Illinois programs of assistance to private higher education, see A.E. Dick Howard,

State Aid to Private Higher Education (Charlottesville, Va.: Michie, 1977), pp. 246–275.

21. ILL. ANN. STAT. ch. 144, §§ 1331 *et seq.*, (Supp. 1981).

22. *Id.* § 1332 (Supp. 1981).

23. *Id.* § 1333 (Supp. 1981).

24. *Id.*

25. *Id.* § 1332 (Supp. 1981).

26. *Id.* §§ 281 *et seq.* (Supp. 1981).

27. *Id.* § 283 (Supp. 1981).

28. *Id.* § 234 (Supp. 1981).

29. *Id.* ch. 122, § 30 (Supp. 1981).

30. ILL. CONST. art. 1, § 17.

31. *Id.* at art. 1, § 19.

32. ILL. ANN. STAT. ch. 68, §§ 1–101 to 9–102 (Smith-Hurd). The Illinois Fair Employment Practices Act, ch. 48, §§ 851 to 867, was repealed by P.A. 81–1216, § 10–108, effective July 1, 1980.

33. ILL. ANN. STAT. ch. 68, § 1–102(A).

34. *Id.* § 1–103(Q).

35. *Id.* § 2–102(A).

36. 42 U.S.C. § 2000e–2(a).

37. ILL. ANN. STAT. ch. 68, § 1–102(A) covers "race, color, religion, sex, national origin, ancestry, age, marital status, physical or mental handicap, or unfavorable discharge from military service." 42 U.S.C. § 2000e–2(a) (1978) covers "race, color, religion, sex or national origin."

38. ILL. ANN. STAT. ch. 68, § 2–101(B)(2).

39. See King's Garden v. F.C.C., 498 F.2d 51 (D.C. Cir.), *cert. denied,* 419 U.S. 996 (1974).

40. See Edward M. Gaffney and Philip R. Moots, *Government and the Campus: Federal Regulation of Religiously Affiliated Higher Education* (Notre Dame, Ind.: University of Notre Dame Press, 1981), pp. 57–65.

41. ILL. ANN. STAT. ch. 68, § 2–104(A).

42. 42 U.S.C. § 2000e–2(e)(1).

43. ILL. ANN. STAT. ch. 48, §§ 1001–1015.

44. *Id.* § 1003(c).

45. *Id.* § 1003(d)(5).

46. See, e.g., *id.*, ch. 68, § 2–101(B)(12).

47. *Id.* ch. 48, §§ 198.1 to 198.17.

48. *Id.* §§ 39m–1 to 39m–16.

49. *Id.* § 39m–3.

50. *Id.* § 1004a(1).

51. *Id.* § 1004a(2)E.

52. *Id.* § 1.

53. See, e.g., Christian County v. Merrigan, 191 Ill. 484, 61 N.E. 479 (1901).

54. ILL. ANN. STAT. ch. 48, § 8b.

55. *Id.* § 8a.

56. *Id.* § 8b(6).

57. *Id.* §§ 138.1 *et seq.* (1969, Supp. 1981).

58. *Id.* § 138.1(2) (Supp. 1981).

59. *Id.* § 138.3 (Supp. 1981).

60. *Id.* § 138.1(2) (Supp. 1981).

61. *Id.* § 138.3(14) (Supp. 1981).

62. *Id.* § 138.3(1)(2) (Supp. 1981).

63. *Id.* § 138.3(17) (Supp. 1981).

64. *Id.* § 138.2(a).

65. *Id.* § 138.1(2) (Supp. 1981).

66. *Id.* § 138.2(c).

67. *Id.* § 138.4 (Supp. 1981).

68. *Id.* §§ 300 *et seq.* (Supp. 1981).

69. *Id.* § 314 (Supp. 1981).

70. *Id.* § 315(B)(4) (Supp. 1981).

71. *Id.* § 315(K) (Supp. 1981).

72. *Id.* § 316 (Supp. 1981).

73. *Id.* § 321.2 (Supp. 1981).

74. *Id.* See 26 U.S.C. § 3306(c)(8) (Supp. 1981).

75. ILL. ANN. STAT. ch. 48, § 321.3 (Supp. 1981). Although § 331 exempts religious, charitable, scientific, literary or educational corporations from coverage, this section does not apply to any services performed for nonprofit organizations, as defined in § 321.2.

76. "Institution of higher education" is defined at *id.* § 371.

77. *Id.* § 321.3(B) (Supp. 1981).

78. *Id.*: "The term 'employment' shall not include service performed in the employ of a school, college, or university, (A) by a student who is enrolled and is regularly attending classes at such school, college, or university, or (B) by the spouse of such student if the spouse is advised, at the time the spouse commences to perform such service, that (1) the employment of the spouse to perform such service is provided under a program to provide financial assistance to the student by the school, college, or university, and (2) such employment will not be covered by any program of unemployment compensation."

79. *Id.* § 334 (Supp. 1981).

80. *Id.* § 337 (Supp. 1981).

81. *Id.* § 382 (Supp. 1981).

82. *Id.* § 382(A) (Supp. 1981).

83. *Id.* § 382(b) (Supp. 1981).

84. *Id.* ch. 24 ½, § 38bl.

85. *Id.* § 38bl; see § 38b4.

86. *Id.* § 38bl; see § 38b4.

87. *Id.* ch. 144, § 122.

88. *Id.* § 189.07 grants the Board of Higher Education the power "to establish minimum admission standards for public community colleges, colleges and state universities."

89. People ex rel. Tinkuff v. Northwestern University, 333 Ill. App. 224, 77 N.E. 2d 345, (1948), *cert. denied,* 335 U.S. 829 (1948). See ILL. ANN. STAT. ch. 144, §§ 121 to 135, which requires a private, postsecondary educational institution to obtain a certificate of approval from the Board of Higher Education. This section, however, is silent as

to whether a condition for the issuance of the certificate is that the institution refrain from implementing discriminatory admission standards for students.

90. See text at notes 94 *et seq., infra,* and notes 24 *et seq., supra.*

91. ILL. ANN. STAT. ch. 27, 560(3).

92. *Id.* ch. 144, § 1301–1326.

93. *Id.* § 1301; for the functions and powers of the authority, see *id.* §§ 1305.01 to 1305.17. This statute was sustained against an Establishment Clause challenge in Cecrle v. Illinois Educational Facilities Authority, 52 Ill. 2d 312, 288 N.E. 2d 399 (1972).

94. ILL. ANN. STAT. ch. 144, §§ 1303.07(d) and 1303.07a. For a parallel definition, see *id.* §§ 121 *et seq.*

95. *Id.* § 1303.07a.

96. *Id.* § 1303.02.

97. *Id.* § 1303.06.

98. See Edward McGlynn Gaffney, Jr., "The Constitution and the Campus: The Case for Institutional Integrity and the Need for Critical Self-Evaluation," in John D. Mosely, ed., *Church and Campus: A Vital Partnership* (Sherman, Tex: Austin College, 1980) vol. 3, pp. 47–67.

99. ILL. ANN. STAT. ch. 24, § 11–11.1–1.

100. *Id.* ch. 68, §§ 1–101 *et seq.* (Supp. 1981).

101. *Id.* § 3–106(E) (Supp. 1981).

102. *Id.* §§ 5–1–101 to 5–103 (Supp. 1981).

103. *Id.* ch. 48, §§ 137.1 *et seq.* (Smith-Hurd 1979).

104. *Id.* § 137.2 (Supp. 1981).

105. ILL. CONST. art. 9, § 6.

106. ILL. ANN. STAT. ch. 120, § 2–205(a).

107. *Id.* § 401.

108. *Id.* § 403a.

109. *Id.* § 500.

110. *Id.* § 500.1; see also *id.* § 500.2 (exemption for property of religious institutions used for school purposes).

111. *Id.* ch. 32, §§ 163a *et seq.*

112. *Id.* ch. 120, § 500.21c.

113. *Id.* § 1004.

114. *Id.* § 439.2.

115. *Id.* § 439.32.

116. *Id.* § 439.102.

117. *Id.* § 441.

118. *Id.* § 440.

119. *Id.*

120. *Id.* ch. 23, §§ 5102 and 5104.

121. *Id.* § 5703(a).

122. See Rule 24, Administrative Rules Under the Illinois Charitable Trust Act of 1961, and Rules 54 to 63, Administrative Rules Under the Illinois Solicitation Act, issued by the Office of the Attorney General.

123. ILL. ANN. STAT. ch. 23, § 5703(b)(1); see also *id.* § 5103(b)(2) (exempting educational organizations when solicitation of contributions is confined to their membership).

124. *Id.* ch. 120, §§ 1101 *et seq.*

125. *Id.* § 1101.

126. *Id.* § 1102.

127. *Id.* ch. 148, §§ 201 *et seq.*

128. *Id.* §§ 202 and 205.

129. *Id.* ch. 83, § 15.

130. *Id.* ch. 122, §§ 822 and 823.

131. Cleary v. Catholic Diocese of Peoria, 57 Ill. 2d 384, 312 N.E. 2d 635 (1974); see also Lorton v. Brown County Community Unit School Dist. 35 Ill. 2d 362, 220 N.E. 2d 161 (1966).

132. ILL. ANN. STAT. ch. 63, § 173.

133. *Id.* § 174(g).

134. *Id.* ch. 121 ½, § 137.5.

135. *Id.* § 137.3(H).

22. Indiana

1. IND. ANN. STAT. § 23–1–1.1–1 *et seq.*

2. *Id.* § 23–7–1.1–2(d) (Supp. 1979).

3. *Id.* § 23–7–1.1–33(3)(V)(b) describes the liquidation process upon voluntary dissolution. Section 23–7–1.1–65(b), concerning involuntary dissolution, states that the same procedure should be followed by the court-appointed receiver.

4. *Id.* § 23–7–1.1–37.

5. *Id.* §§ 23–13–5–1 *et seq.*
A 1974 Opinion of the Attorney General mandates that a choice be made: "[A] corporation organized under the Indiana General Corporation Act may not also be simultaneously organized under the Not-for-Profit Corporation Act." 6 Op. Att'y. Gen. 16, 19 (1974).

6. *Id.* §§ 23–13–5–1 *et seq.* Among the provisions included, Section 23–13–5–1 gives the board of directors, rather than the stockholders, the power to elect its governing body. Section 23–13–5–5 allows the capital stock to be assigned to the directors or trustees to be held and used for the benefit of the corporation, upon a two-thirds vote of the stockholders. Section 23–13–5–6 establishes dissenting shareholder rights. Section 23–13–5–8 describes the dissolution procedures and the vesting of the institution's property. Section 23–13–5–2 enumerates the information required in the Articles of Incorporation.

7. *Id.* § 23–13–12–1.

8. *Id.* §§ 23–13–13–2; 23–13–16–3; 23–13–16–4.

9. *Id.* § 23–13–15–1.

10. *Id.* §§ 23–13–6–1 *et seq.* Several specific powers granted to the governing board are found in §§ 23–13–11 *et seq.* Educational corporations with

capital stock formed after 1907 may not be able to control by resolution or by-laws the religious belief of their directors. *Id.* § 23–13–9–1.

11. IND. CONST. art. 1, § 6.

12. IND. ANN. STAT. § 23–13–7–1.

13. IND. CONST. art. 1, § 2.

14. *Id.* § 3.

15. *Id.* § 6.

16. 22 Op. Att'y. Gen. 74 (1975).

17. IND. CONST. art. 10, § 6, and art. 11, § 12.

18. A.E. Dick Howard, *State Aid to Private Higher Education* (Charlottesville, Va.: Michie, 1977), pp. 282–283.

19. Bullock v. Billheimer, 175 Ind. 428, 94 N.E. 763 (1911).

20. *Id.* at 440, 94 N.E. at 768. See also The City of Indianapolis v. The Indianapolis Home for Friendless Women, 50 Ind. 215 (1875), and School City of Gary v. State *ex rel.* Artists' League, Inc., 253 Ind. 697, 256 N.E. 2d (1970), for judicial interpretation allowing a private nonprofit corporation to be treated as a public institution because of its public purpose.

21. Department of Treasury v. City of Linton, 223 Ind. 363, 370, 60 N.E. 2d 948, 951 (1945).

22. IND. ANN. STAT. § 20–12–0.6–1 (Supp. 1979).

23. *Id.*

24. *Id.* § 20–12–0.6–2 (Supp. 1979).

25. *Id.* § 20–12–63–1 (Supp. 1979).

26. *Id.*

27. IND. CONST. art. 11, § 12.

28. IND. ANN. STAT. § 20–12–63–11(k) (Supp. 1979).

29. *Id.* § 20–12–63–3 (Supp. 1979).

30. *Id.*

31. *Id.*

32. See text accompanying notes 95 through 107, *infra.*

33. IND. ANN. STAT. §§ 20–12–63–11(k) and (1) (Supp. 1979).

34. For the function and power of the authority, see § 20–12–63–11(a) through (g) (Supp. 1979).

35. *Id.* § 20–13–63–3 (Supp. 1979).

36. *Id.*

37. For the list of facilities which the authority may approve, see *id.* § 20–12–63–3(C) (Supp. 1979).

38. *Id.* §§ 20–13–21–1 (Supp. 1979) *et seq.*

39. *Id.* § 20–12–3(2) (Supp. 1979).

40. *Id.* § 20–12–21–3(2)(a) (Supp. 1979).

41. *Id.* § 20–12–21–3(2)(b) (Supp. 1979).

42. *Id.* § 20–12–21–3(2)(c) (Supp. 1979).

43. *Id.* §§ 20–12–21–4 through 20–12–21–5.5 (Supp. 1979).

44. *Id.* § 20–12–21–7 (Supp. 1979). See *id.* at § 20–12–21–6 (Supp. 1979), for the necessary qualifications.

45. *Id.* § 20–12–21–8 (Supp. 1979).

46. *Id.* § 20–12–21–13 (Supp. 1979).

47. *Id.* § 20–12–21–15 (Supp. 1979).

48. *Id.* § 20–12–21–6(a)(4) (Supp. 1979).

49. *Id.* § 20–12–21–15(c) (Supp. 1979).

50. *Id.* § 20–12–21.1–2 (Supp. 1979).

51. *Id.* § 20–12–21.1–1(a) (Supp. 1979).

52. Howard, *State Aid*, note 18, *supra*, at 285.

53. 3 Op. Att'y Gen. 9, at 12 (1967). The opinion also states that the law providing transportation for parochial students did not violate article 1, sections 3 and 6, since the primary intent of the law was to grant educational and safety benefits directly to all children regardless of race or religion. *Id.*

54. IND. ANN. STAT. §§ 20–12–21.5–1 *et seq.*

55. *Id.* § 20–12–21.5–1(1).

56. *Id.* § 4–26–3–24(a) (Supp. 1979).

57. *Id.* § 20–12–0.5–3 *et seq.* (Supp. 1979).

58. *Id.* § 4–26–3–24(a) (Supp. 1979).

59. *Id.* § 22–9–1(a) (Supp. 1979).

60. *Id.* § 22–9–1–2(a) (Supp. 1979).

61. *Id.* § 22–901–2(b) (Supp. 1979).

62. *Id.* § 22–9–1–2(c) (Supp. 1979).

63. *Id.* § 22–9–1–3(e) (Supp. 1979).

64. *Id.* § 22–9–1–3(h) (Supp. 1979).

65. *Id.* § 22–9–1–6(k) (Supp. 1979).

66. *Id.* § 22–9–1–3(a) (Supp. 1979).

67. This interpretation is bolstered by the fact that the word "employer" is used on occasion in connection with procedures to be followed in certain employment discrimination situations. See, e.g., *id.* §§ 22–9–1–3(a) (Supp. 1979) and 22–9–1–13(a) (Supp. 1979).

68. If, perchance, RACs were held to be bound by the general employment discrimination ban, a question would arise as to whether RACs could discriminate on the basis of drug or alcohol addiction or use. Under Indiana law relating to employment discrimination, a handicap is a "physical or mental condition . . . which constitutes a substantial disability unrelated to such person's ability to engage in a particular occupation." *Id.* § 22–9–1–3(g). Although this definition could possibly be read to include alcoholics and persons addicted to drugs, there is no indication that the statute was intended to include alcohol and drug use within its protection and, in any event, the definition includes what is in effect a bona fide occupational qualification ("unrelated to such person's ability to engage in a particular occupation") which would allow an employer to take such use into account in assessing a person's fitness for the particular job. Indeed, for some RACs, mere use of any amount of alcohol or drugs may indicate unfitness for particular positions which the RAC deems to have role-modelling aspects. (It would be much more difficult to make such an argument in the case of a rehabilitated alcoholic or drug user.)

69. For details, see *id.* § 22-9-1-6(h)(i) (Supp. 1979). For a comprehensive list of the Commission's powers and duties, see *id.* §§ 22-9-1-6(a) through (n) (Supp. 1979), 22-9-1-7 and 22-9-1-11 (Supp. 1979).

Under the Indiana Civil Rights Act, state universities and colleges and "such other universities and colleges as are willing to cooperate" may participate in a "comprehensive educational program, designed to emphasize the origin of prejudice against . . . minority groups, its harmful effects, its incompatibility with American principles of equality and fair play, and violation of the brotherhood of man." *Id.* § 22-9-1-7. The program is prepared by the Civil Rights Commission. *Id.*

70. *Id.* § 22-9-2-2 (Supp. 1979).

71. *Id.* § 22-9-2-1 (Supp. 1979).

72. See the similar problem with regard to the general employment discrimination ban, discussed in the text accompanying notes 64 through 68, *supra.*

73. *Id.* § 22-2-2-3 (Supp. 1979).

74. *Id.* § 22-2-2-3(f) (Supp. 1979).

75. *Id.* § 22-2-2-3(i) (Supp. 1979).

76. *Id.* § 22-2-2-3(l) (Supp. 1979).

77. *Id.* § 22-2-2-4 (Supp. 1979).

78. *Id.*

79. *Id.* § 22-3-6-1(a).

80. *Id.* § 22-3-6-1(b).

81. *Id.*

82. *Id.* § 22-3-9-1.

83. *Id.* §§ 22-4-1-1 *et seq.*

84. *Id.* § 22-4-7-2(e).

85. *Id.* § 22-4-8-2(j)(l) (Supp. 1979).

86. *Id.* § 22-4-8-2(j)(2) (Supp. 1979).

87. *Id.* § 22-4-8-2(j)(3)(A)(i) (Supp. 1979).

88. *Id.* § 22-4-8-2(j)(3)(A)(ii) (Supp. 1979).

89. *Id.* § 22-4-8-2(j)(3)(B) (Supp. 1979).

90. *Id.* § 22-4-8-3(b) (Supp. 1979).

91. *Id.* § 22-4-8-3(d) (Supp. 1979).

92. *Id.* § 22-4-8-3(j) (Supp. 1979).

93. *Id.* § 22-4-8-3(k) (Supp. 1979).

94. *Id.* § 22-4-14-7(i) (Supp. 1979). "Institution of higher education" includes all colleges and universities in Indiana. *Id.* at § 22-4-2-31.

95. *Id.* § 22-9-1-3(1) (Supp. 1979).

96. *Id.*

97. *Id.* § 22-9-1-3(p)(3).

98. 22 Op. Att'y Gen. 76 (1975).

99. *Id.* at 74.

100. See text accompanying notes 65 through 69, *supra.*

101. IND. ANN. STAT. § 20-8.1-2-1(a).

102. *Id.* § 20-8.1-2-1(f).

103. *Id.* § 20-8.1-2-3 (Supp. 1979).

104. *Id.* § 20-8.1-2-4 (Supp. 1979).

105. *Id.* § 20-8.1-2-5 (Supp. 1979).

106. *Id.*

107. *Id.* § 20-8.1-2-6 (Supp. 1979).

108. See text accompanying notes 95 through 99, *supra.*

109. IND. ANN. STAT. §§ 20-1-19-1 (Supp. 1979) *et seq.*

110. *Id.* § 20-1-19-1(a) (Supp. 1979) defines "postsecondary proprietary educational institution" as "any person doing business in this state by offering to the public for a tuition, fee, or charge, instructional or educational services or training in any technical, professional, mechanical, business or industrial occupation, either in the recipient's home, at a designated location, or by mail."

111. *Id.* § 20-1-19-1(a)(5) (Supp. 1979).

112. *Id.*, formerly §§ 20-1-19-1 *et seq.*

113. *Id.* § 20-1-19-14.

114. 22 Op. Att'y. Gen. 74, at 76 (1975).

115. IND. ANN. STAT. §§ 22-9-1-1 *et seq.*

116. *Id.* § 2209-1-2(a) (Supp. 1979).

117. *Id.* § 22-9-1-3(1) (Supp. 1979).

118. *Id.* § 22-9-1-3(m) (Supp. 1979).

119. See text accompanying notes 95 through 99, *supra.*

120. See text accompanying notes 65 through 72, *supra.*

121. IND. ANN. STAT. § 22-9-1-2(a) (Supp. 1979).

122. *Id.* § 22-9-1-3(1) (Supp. 1979).

123. See text accompanying notes 95 through 99, *supra.*

124. See text accompanying notes 65 through 72, *supra.*

125. IND. ANN. STAT. § 35-46-2-1.

126. *Id.* § 22-8-1.1(8) (Supp. 1979). "[A]ny individual or type of organization . . . which has in its employ one or more individuals."

127. *Id.* § 22-8-1.1-2.

128. *Id.* § 22-8-1.1-43(a).

129. *Id.* § 22-8-1.1-43(b).

130. *Id.* § 6-2-1-7(i)(l) (Supp. 1979). See §§ 6-2-1-7(i)(4) and (5) for the procedure to be used for applying for the exemption.

131. *Id.* § 6-2-1-7.5 (Supp. 1979).

132. *Id.* § 6-3-3-5(a) (Supp. 1979).

133. *Id.* § 6-3-3-5(b) (Supp. 1979).

134. *Id.* § 6-3-3-5(c) (Supp. 1979).

135. *Id.* § 6-3-3-5(d) (Supp. 1979).

136. *Id.* § 6-1.1-10-16(a) (Supp. 1979).

137. *Id.* § 6-1.1-10-16(c) (Supp. 1979).

138. *Id.* § 6-1.1-10-16(d) (Supp. 1979).

139. State Board of Tax Commissioners v. International Business College, Inc., 145 Ind. App. 353, 251 N.E. 2d 39 (1969).

140. IND. ANN. STAT. § 6-1.1-10-22.
141. 1939 Op. Att'y. Gen. 146.
142. IND. ANN. STAT. § 6-1.1-10-20.
143. *Id.*
144. *Id.* § 6-1.1-10-16(e) (Supp. 1979).
145. *Id.* § 6-1.1-10-18.
146. *Id.* § 6-1.1-10-21.
147. *Id.* § 6-1.1-10-24.
148. *Id.* § 6-6-2-1 (Supp. 1979).
149. *Id.* § 6-2-1-39(b)(7) (Supp. 1979).
150. *Id.* § 6-2-1-39(b)(8) (Supp. 1979).
151. See text accompanying note 130, *supra.*
152. IND. ANN. STAT. § 6-2-1-39(b)(8) (Supp. 1979).
153. *Id.*
154. See text accompanying note 130, *supra.*
155. *Id.* § 6-2-1-39(b)(8) (Supp. 1979). For a further discussion of this provision and its applicability to private colleges and universities, see 43 Op. Att'y. Gen. 236 (1964).
156. IND. ANN. STAT. § 6-4.1-11-1.
157. *Id.* § 6-4.1-3-1.
158. 26 U.S.C. § 2055(a).
159. 26 U.S.C. § 2055(b).
160. IND. ANN. STAT. § 18-1-1.5-13(e).
161. See *id.* §§ 35-45-5-1 *et seq.*
162. *Id.* § 20-12-18-1.
163. *Id.*
164. *Id.* §§ 20-11-1-1 *et seq.*
165. *Id.* § 20-11-1-1 Art. IV, 2.
166. *Id.* § 4-26-3-24(a) (Supp. 1979).
167. *Id.* § 20-12-12-1.
168. *Id.* § 6-1.1-10-34.

23. Iowa

1. IOWA CODE ANN. Chapter 504A. Corporations organized under the older "Corporations Not for Pecuniary Profit" provision of Chapter 504 may "voluntarily elect to adopt the provisions" of the Nonprofit Corporation Act and "thereby become subject to its provisions." *Id.* § 504A.98.
2. *Id.* § 504A8.
3. *Id.* §§ 504A. 17, 18.
4. *Id.* § 504A.12.
5. *Id.* §§ 504A.29,30.
6. *Id.* § 504A.26
7. *Id.* § 502.202
8. *Id.* §§ 504A.40-504A.64 (Supp. 1980).
9. *Id.* § 504A.100.
10. See, e.g., Simmons v. Parsons College, 256 N.W. 2d 255 (Iowa, 1977). For a discussion of the *cy pres* doctrine, *see* Chapter 1, "Corporate Status," *supra.*

11. IOWA CODE ANN. §§ 504A.43, 504A.52 (Supp. 1980).
12. *Id.*
13. *Id.* § 504A.56(1).
14. *Id.* § 504A.56(2).
15. *Id.* § 504A.56(3).
16. *Id.* § 504A.56(4).
17. *Id.* §§ 504A.48, 504A.57.
18. IOWA CONST. art.I, § 3 (1972).
19. IOWA CODE ANN. § 261.2(4). (1972).
20. *Id.* § 261.9 (Supp. 1981).
21. *Id.*
22. *Id.* § 261.10.
23. *Id.* § 261.15.
24. *Id.* § 261 (Supp. 1981).
25. *Id.* § 261.2 (1972).
26. *Id.*
27. *Id.* § 601A.6(1)(a).
28. *Id.*
29. *Id.* § 601A.6(5)(d).
30. *Id.* § 601A.6(5)(d) (Supp. 1978).
31. *Id.* § 601A.2(11).
32. *Id.* § 319A.9(16).
33. *Id.* § 601A.5.
34. *Id.* §§ 601A.15(1)-(5) and (7)-(8).
35. *Id.* § 601A.15(6).
36. *Id.* § 601A.17.
37. *Id.* § 601A.16.
38. See Fair Labor Standards Act, 29 U.S.C. §§ 201 *et seq.*
39. IOWA CODE ANN. § 85.61(1).
40. *Id.* § 85.61(3)(a) and (b).
41. *Id.* § 96.19(7)(a).
42. *Id.* § 96.19.7.a(6)(a).
43. *Id.* § 96.19.7.a(6)(b).
44. *Id.* § 601A.9.
45. *Id.*
46. *Id.* § 601A.7.1.a.
47. *Id.* § 601A.7.2.a.
48. *Id.* § 601A.5.
49. See text accompanying notes 33-35, *supra.*
50. IOWA CODE ANN. §§ 601A.8.1. and 2.
51. *Id.* § 601A.12.1.
52. The same kind of exemption for public accommodations is discussed at note 47, *supra.*
53. IOWA CODE ANN. § 601A.12.4.
54. *Id.* § 601A.5.
55. See text accompanying notes 33-35, *supra.*
56. IOWA CODE ANN. § 88.1.
57. *Id.* § 88.1(3).
58. *Id.* § 88.14.
59. *Id.* § 88.5(1)(a).
60. *Id.* § 88.4.
61. *Id.* § 88.3(4).

62. *Id.* § 88.3(3).
63. *Id.* § 422.34.2.
64. *Id.* § 422.45.8.
65. *Id.* § 427.1.11.
66. *Id.*
67. *Id.* § 450.4.
68. *Id.* § 451.2.
69. *Id.* § 422.9 (Supp. 1980).
70. I.R.C. § 170(c)(2)(B) and (C).
71. Iowa Code Ann. § 427.1.9.
72. *Id.* § 422.34.2.
73. *Id.* § 427.1.11.
74. *Id.* § 427.1.10.
75. *Id.*
76. *Id.*, referring to § 427.1.9.
77. *Id.*
78. *Id.* § 122.6.
79. 1940 Op. Atty. Gen. 3.
80. *Id.*
81. Iowa Code Ann. § 122.4.
82. 1940 Op. Atty. Gen. 3.
83. Iowa Code Ann. § 122.4.
84. *Id.* § 122.1.
85. *Id.* § 122.6.

24. Kansas

1. Such distinctions are made wih regard to, e.g., the filing of an annual report and the payment of a franchise fee, Kan. Stat. Ann. § 17-7513, the information required in the report, *id.* § 17-7504, the revival of the articles of incorporation, *id.* § 17-7002(i), the dissolution of the corporation, *id.* § 17-6805, merger, *id.* § 17-6706 and voting rights, *id.*' § 17-6505.
2. *Id.* §§ 17-1701 to 17-1752.
3. *Id.* § 17-1701.
4. *Id.* § 17-6401(a).
5. *Id.* § 17-1261(h).
6. *Id.*
7. *Id.* § 74-3250 (Supp. 1979).
8. *Id.* § 74-3251 (Supp. 1979).
9. *Id.* § 74-3252 (Supp. 1979).
10. *Id.* § 17-6105.
11. *Id.*
12. *Id.*
13. *Id.* §§ 74-4916 *et seq.*
14. *Id.* §§ 72-4916.
15. *Id.* § 72-4920(b).
16. *Id.* § 72-4920(f).
17. *Id.*
18. *Id.* § 72-4920(g).
19. *Id.* §§ 17-6705, 17-6706, 17-6805 (1974).

20. Nelson v. Kring, 225 Kan. 499, 592 P.2d 438 (1979). For a discussion of the *cy pres* doctrine, *see* Chapter 1, "Corporate Status," *supra.*
21. Kan. Stat. Ann. §§ 17-6705, 17-6706, 17-6805, 17-6003 (1974).
22. *Id.* § 17-6808.
23. *Id.* § 17-6809.
24. *Id.* §§ 17-6807, 17-6810.
25. Kan. Const. Bill Of Rights § 7.
26. Kan. Const. art. 6, § 6(c).
27. *Id.* art. 6, § 6(a).
28. Kan. Stat. Ann. § 72-6107(e) (Supp. 1979).
29. *Id.* § 72-6107(f) (Supp. 1979).
30. *Id.* § 72-6811 (Supp. 1979).
31. *Id.* § 72-6810(b) (Supp. 1979).
32. *Id.* § 72-6810(a) (Supp. 1979).
33. *Id.* § 72-6810(e) (Supp. 1979).
34. *Id.* § 72-6810(f) (Supp. 1979).
35. *Id.* §§ 72-7401 *et seq.*
36. *Id.* § 72-7402 (Supp. 1979).
37. *Id.* § 76-157.
38. *Id.* § 73-1217 (Supp. 1979).
39. *Id.*
40. *Id.* § 73-1218 (Supp. 1979).
41. *Id.* § 44-1009(a)(1) (Supp. 1979).
42. *Id.* § 44-1002(b) (Supp. 1979).
43. *Id.*
44. *Id.* § 44-1009(a)(3) (Supp. 1979).
45. *Id.* § 44-1004(4) (Supp. 1979). For a list of its powers and duties, see *id.* § 44-1004.
46. *Id.* § 39-1105.
47. *Id.* §§ 65-4003 *et seq.*
48. *Id.* § 5-4601.
49. See text at note 44, *supra.*
50. Kan. Stat. Ann. §§ 44-1201 *et seq.* (Supp. 1979).
51. *Id.* § 44-1202(d) (Supp. 1979).
52. *Id.* § 44-1205 (Supp. 1979).
53. *Id.* § 44-1203(a) (Supp. 1979).
54. *Id.* §§ 44-1204(a) and 44-1204(b) (Supp. 1979).
55. *Id.* § 44-1202(e)(3) (Supp. 1979).
56. *Id.* § 44-1202(e)(4) (Supp. 1979).
57. *Id.* § 44-1202(e)(6) (Supp. 1979).
58. 29 U.S.C.A. §§ 201 *et seq.*
59. Kan. Stat. Ann. §§ 44-1202(d) (Supp. 1979); 44-1203(b) (Supp. 1979); and 44-1204(c)(1) (Supp. 1979).
60. *Id.* §§ 44-501 (Supp. 1979) *et seq.*
61. *Id.* § 44-508(a),(b) (Supp. 1979).
62. *Id.* § 44-508(b) (Supp. 1979).
63. *Id.* § 44-505 (Supp. 1979).
64. *Id.* § 44-508(b) (Supp. 1979).
65. *Id.* § 44-505(b) (Supp. 1979).

66. *Id.* § 44–564.

67. *Id.* § 44–532 (Supp. 1979).

68. *Id.* § 44–703(h)(2)(A) (Supp. 1979).

69. *Id.* § 44–703(i)(3)(F) (Supp. 1979).

70. 26 U.S.C.A. § 501(c)(3).

71. *Id.* § 3306(c)(8).

72. See text at note 68, *supra.*

73. KAN. STAT. ANN. § 44–703(i)(4)(B) (Supp. 1979).

74. *Id.* § 44–703(i)(4)(H) (Supp. 1979).

75. *Id.* § 44–703(i)(4)(I).

76. *Id.* § 44–703(i)(4)(J) (Supp. 1979).

77. *Id.* § 44–703(i)(4)(N) (Supp. 1979).

78. *Id.* § 44–703(i)(4)(O) (Supp. 1979).

79. *Id.*.

80. See text accompanying notes 81 through 86, *infra.*

81. KAN. STAT. ANN. § 44–1009 (Supp. 1979). The legislation does permit "a distinction because of sex" when necessary due to "the intrinsic nature of such accommodation."*Id.*

82. *Id.* § 44–1016(a).

83. *Id.* § 44–1016(b).

84. *Id.* § 44–1016(c).

85. *Id.* § 44–1018.

86. *Id.* § 44–1004(4). For a list of its powers and duties, see *id.* § 44–1004.

87. Created by § 44–124 (Supp. 1975).

88. *Id.* § 75–5715(a).

89. *Id.* § 79–32,113 (Supp. 1979).

90. *Id.* §§ 79–1537 *et seq.* (Supp. 1979).

91. *Id.* § 79–1537 (Supp. 1979).

92. *Id.* § 79–1540 (1975).

93. *Id.* § 79–32,120 (Supp. 1979).

94. I.R.C. § 170(c)(2)(B) and (C).

95. KAN. CONST. art. 11, § 1.

96. KAN. STAT. ANN. § 79–201.

97. *Id.*

98. *Id.*

99. *Id.* § 72–7407 (Supp. 1979).

100. *Id.* § 79–3601 *et seq.*

101. *Id.* § 79–3606(c) (Supp. 1979). Provision is made for exemption when the actual purchase is made by the contractor for the institution. *Id.* § 79–3606(d) (Supp. 1979).

102. *Id.* § 79–3606(c) (Supp. 1979).

103. *Id.* § 79–3704(d).

104. *Id.* §§ 79–3701 *et seq.*

105. See *id.* § 79–3703.

106. *Id.* § 17–1740.

107. *Id.* § 17–1741.1 (Supp. 1979).

108. KAN. CONST. art. 15, § 3.

109. *Id.* § 3a.

110. KAN. STAT. ANN. § 70–4703. For the procedures and qualifications, see *id.*

111. *Id.* §§ 72–1371; 72–1374 (Supp. 1979).

112. *Id.* § 41–710.

25. Kentucky

1. KY. REV. STAT. ANN. §§ 273.161 through 273.990 (Baldwin).

2. *Id.* § 273.161(3).

3. *Id.* § 273.167.

4. *Id.* § 273.251(1) and (2).

5. *Id.* § 273.247(1).

6. *Id.* § 273.251(1).

7. *Id.* § 273.251(2).

8. *Id.* § 273.237.

9. *Id.* § 273.237.

10. *Id.* § 273.207.

11. *Id.* § 273.233.

12. *Id.* § 273.261.

13. *Id.* § 273–300.

14. *Id.* §§ 273–300, 273.303, and 273.307.

15. *Id.* § 273.313.

16. *Id.* § 273.320.

17. *Id.*

18. *Id.* § 273.303.

19. Defenders of Furbearers v. First National Bank and Trust Co., 306 S.W.2d 102 (Ky. App. 1957); and see Kentucky Children's Home v. Woods, 289 Ky. 20, 157 S.W.2d 473 (1941).

20. KY. CONST. § 189. For a comprehensive review of the Kentucky programs of assistance to private higher education, see A. E. Dick Howard, *State Aid to Private Higher Education* (Charlottesville, Va.: Michie, 1977), pp. 323–344.

21. 173 Ky. 708, 191 S.W. 507 (1917).

22. Howard, *State Aid*, note 20, *supra,* at 336.

23. KY. REV. STAT. ANN. §§ 164.780 *et seq.*

24. Americans United for Separation of Church and State v. Pryor, Civ. No. 84114 (Franklin, Ky. Cir. Ct., judgment entered Mar. 11, 1974); see Howard, *State Aid*, note 20, *supra,* at 340–341.

25. Americans United for Separation of Church and State v. Blanton, 433 F. Supp. 97 (M.D. Tenn.) *summarily affd.*, 434 U.S. 803 (1977).

26. KY. REV. STAT. ANN. § 164.780(4).

27. *Id.* § 164.785(2).

28. *Id.* § 164.785(1)(c).

29. *Id.* § 164.785(3).

30. *Id.* § 344.040(1).

31. *Id.* § 344.010(4). To oversee and enforce the anti-discrimination laws, Kentucky law provides for the establishment of a Commission on Human Rights. *Id.* § 344.150. The Commission consists of eleven members and its general function is to "receive, initiate, investigate, seek to conciliate, hold hearings on, and pass upon complaints alleging

violations." *Id.* §§ 344.190(8), 344.180(3), (4), (5).

32. KY. REV. STAT. ANN. § 344.030(1) defines "employer" as a person who has eight or more employees within the state in each of twenty or more calendar weeks in the current or preceding calendar year and an agent of such person.

33. *Id.* § 344.020(1)(b) (emphasis added).

34. *Id.* § 344.020(1)(a).

35. *Id.* § 344.090(1).

36. *Id.* § 344.090(2).

37. Compare Pub. L. 88–352, Title VII, § 702, 78 Stat. 255, with Pub. L. 92–261, Title VII, § 702, 86 Stat. 104. For a discussion of the legislative history of these provisions, see Philip R. Moots and Edward McGlynn Gaffney, *Church and Campus: Legal Issues in Religiously Affiliated Higher Education* (Notre Dame, Ind.: University of Notre Dame Press, 1979), pp. 40–47.

38. Compare KY. REV. STAT. ANN. § 334.090(3) with Pub. L. 88–352, Title VII, § 703(e)(2), 78 Stat. 256. For a discussion of the legislative history of the federal provisions, see Moots and Gaffney, note 37, *supra*, at 52–54.

39. KY. REV. STAT. ANN. § 344.090(3).

40. *Id.* § 337.275(1).

41. *Id.* § 337.010(d).

42. An employee is "any person employed by or permitted to work for an employer, but does not include" . . . any individual employed in a bona fide executive, administrative, supervisory or professional capacity or any individual classified and given a certificate by the commissioner of labor showing a status of learner, apprentice, handicapped worker, or student under administrative procedures and administrative regulations as prescribed and promulgated by the commissioner of labor." *Id.* § 337.010(2).

43. *Id.* § 337.050(1).

44. *Id.* § 337.285.

45. *Id.* § 337.990.

46. 29 U.S.C. § 206(d). See also *County of Washington v. Gunther,* 452 U.S. 161 (1981) (allowing claims for sex-based wage discrimination to be brought under Title VIII even though no member of the opposite sex holds an equal but higher paying job, provided that the challenged wage rate is not exempted under the Equal Pay Act).

47. KY. REV. STAT. ANN. § 337.423.

48. 29 U.S.C. § 794.

49. KY. REV. STAT. ANN. § 207.150.

50. *Id.* §§ 342.001 *et seq.* (1977, Supp. 1978).

51. *Id.* § 342.620(14) (Supp. 1978).

52. *Id.* §§ 342.630 and 342.640.

53. See Opinion of the Attorney General 73–281, stating that the requirement that a minister be covered under worker's compensation does not violate the First Amendment to the U.S. Constitution. And see Meyers v. Southwest Region Conference Association of Seventh Day Adventists, 88 So. 2d 381 (La. 1956) (*accord*).

54. KY. REV. STAT. ANN. § 342.650(3) (Supp. 1978).

55. *Id.* § 342.650(4) (Supp. 1978).

56. *Id.* § 342.650(6) (Supp. 1978).

57. *Id.* § 342.395.

58. *Id.* § 342.690. Note that the employer retains all common law defenses against any action by an employee who elects not to be covered. *Id.* § 342.690(3).

59. *Id.* § 342.660.

60. *Id.* § 342.340.

61. *Id.* § 342.345.

62. *Id.* § 342.350.

63. *Id.* §§ 341.005 *et seq.*

64. "Employment" is defined at *id.* § 341.050.

65. *Id.* § 341.050(1)(e)1.

66. *Id.* § 341.050(e)2.

67. *Id.* § 341.055(19).

68. *Id.*

69. *Id.*

70. *Id.* § 341.055(16)(a).

71. *Id.* § 341.055(16)(b). Spouses must be informed that employment is provided as a means of financial aid for the students, *id.* § 341.055(16)(b)1., and that they are not covered by any program of unemployment compensation, *id.* § 341.055(16)(b)2.

72. *Id.* § 341.055(17).

73. *Id.* § 341.055(6).

74. *Id.* §§ 341.050(l)(g), (h), and 341.055(2).

75. I.R.C. §§ 501(a), 521.

76. KY. REV. STAT. ANN. § 341.055(13).

77. *Id.* §§ 341.070(9), 341.275.

78. *Id.* § 341.275(1).

79. *Id.* § 341.275(2)(c), (d). The effective period of election depends upon the date on which the nonprofit organization becomes subject to the provisions of the Act. Those organizations that became subject to the Act on January 1, 1972, are covered under the Act for a one-year period of election. *Id.* § 341.275(2)(a), (b).

80. *Id.* § 341.275(2)(a), (d).

81. *Id.* § 341.275(2), (3)(a).

82. The required deposit is described as follows: "Money equal to two percent of the organization's total wages paid for employment. . . . for the four calendar quarters immediately preceding the effective date of such election." *Id.* § 341.275(4)(a).

83. *Id.* § 341.275(4)(a).

84. *Id.* §§ 341.070(4), 341.250(3)(a), (b).

85. *Id.* § 336.130.

86. *Id.* § 336.130(1).

87. *Id.* § 336.130(2).

88. 440 U.S. 490 (1979).

89. Attempts to extend *Catholic Bishop* to colleges have been unsuccessful. See Barber-Scotia College, 245 N.L.R.B. 48, 102 L.R.R.M. 1330 (1979), and College of Notre Dame, 245 N.L.R.B., No. 44, 102 L.R.R.M. 1283 (1979).

90. KY. REV. STAT. ANN. § 273.171(14).

91. *Id.* § 273.171(14). The corporation can also make any other indemnification that is authorized by the articles of incorporation or bylaws, or by resolution adopted after notice to members entitled to vote.

92. Pub. L. 88-352, Title VI, 78 Stat. 252, 40 U.S.C. § 2000d.

93. Pub. L. 92-318, Title IX, 86 Stat. 373, 20 U.S.C. §§ 1681 *et seq.*

94. KY. REV. STAT. ANN. § 165A. 360(1).

95. *Id.* § 165A. 310(5)(b).

96. *Id.* § 344.120.

97. *Id.* § 344.130.

98. Pub. L. 90-284, Title VIII, 82 Stat. 81, 42 U.S.C. §§ 3601 *et seq.*

99. KY. REV. STAT. ANN. § 344.360(1).

100. *Id.* § 344.360(2).

101. 42 U.S.C. § 3607.

102. KY. REV. STAT. ANN. § 344.365(1)(c).

103. *Id.*

104. *Id.* § 207.180.

105. *Id.* § 207.180(2).

106. *Id.* § 207.180(5)(a).

107. *Id.* §§ 338.011 *et seq.*

108. Pub. L. 91-576, 84 Stat. 1598, 29 U.S.C. §§ 657 *et seq.*

109. KY. REV. STAT. ANN. § 338.011.

110. *Id.* § 338.051(1) and (3).

111. *Id.* § 338.011.

112. *Id.* § 338.031(1)(a).

113. *Id.* § 338.031(1)(b).

114. *Id.* §§ 338.011 through 338.991.

115. *Id.* § 338.991. Penalties for willful violations can include stiff fines and imprisonment.

116. I.R.C. § 501.

117. KY. REV. STAT. ANN. § 141.040.

118. *Id.* § 140.060.

119. *Id.* § 141.081.

120. *Id.* § 141.010(11).

121. KY. CONST. § 170. The exempt property may not exceed one-half acre in cities or towns, two acres in the country.

122. KY. REV. STAT. ANN. § 139.495(1)(a).

123. *Id.* § 139.495(1)(b).

124. *Id.* § 139.495(1)(b).

125. *Id.* §§ 367.110 *et seq.* For a comprehensive analysis of regulation of fund raising, see Bruce R. Hopkins, *Charity Under Siege: Government Regulation of Fund Raising* (New York: John Wiley and Sons, 1980).

126. *Id.* § 367.660(3).

127. *Id.*

128. *Id.* § 528.010(3).

129. *Id.* § 528.010(10) (repealed).

26. Louisiana

1. LA. REV. STAT. ANN. §§ 12:201 *et seq.* (Supp. 1980).

2. *Id.* § 12:201(7) states that: " 'Corporation' or 'nonprofit corporation' means a corporation formed under this chapter, as well as a corporation formed under the laws of this state before Jan. 1, 1969 but of a class of corporations that might be formed under this chapter."

3. La. Acts, 1870, §§ 677–679 (now repealed) and La. Acts 1914, No. 254, § 4 (now repealed by the "Non-Profit Corporation Law" discussed above).

4. LA. REV. STAT. ANN. § 12:207c.

5. *Id.* §§ 12:243(F) (Supp. 1980), 12.250 (1969).

6. *Id.* § 12:201(8) (1969).

7. *Id.* § 12:250(A) (1969).

8. *Id.* § 12:251(A) (Supp. 1980).

9. *Id.* § 12:251(E). According to § 12.252(A), the judicial liquidator may but need not be a member of the governing board.

10. *Id.* §§ 12:258 and 259 (1969).

11. *Id.* § 12:249(B) (1969).

12. *Id.* § 9:2331. Under the *cy pres* doctrine, if it has become impossible to effect literal compliance with the terms of a trust, it will be executed to accomplish those terms as nearly as practicable under existing conditions.

13. *Id.* § 12:249(B).

14. *Id.* § 9:2331.

15. *Id.* § 12:256(A).

16. LA. CONST., 1921, art. IV, § 8 (repealed).

17. LA. CONST., 1921, art. XII, § 13 (repealed). For the text of this provision and for a comprehensive discussion of Louisiana's history concerning aid to private education, see A. E. Dick Howard, *State Aid to Private Higher Education* (Charlottesville, Va.: Michie, 1977), pp. 345-360.

18. LA. REV. STAT. ANN. § 17:153.

19. 401 U.S. 672 (1971).

20. 413 U.S. 734 (1973).

21. LA. CONST. art. VII, § 10 (replacing old art. IV, § 8).

22. *Id.* art. VII, § 14(C); see LA. REV. STAT. ANN. § 17.153.

23. Howard, *State Aid,* note 17, *supra,* at 349-350.

24. LA. REV. STAT. ANN. §§ 17:1671 *et seq.* (Supp. 1980).

25. Op. Atty. Gen., Mar. 30, 1955.

26. LA. REV. STAT. ANN. § 17:1671.

27. *Id.* § 17:1672. Some special scholarship funds, such as that for children of police officers, are not available to students attending RACs. *Id.* § 17:1681(A) (Supp. 1980).

28. *Id.* §§ 17:3021 *et seq.*

29. *Id.* § 17:3023.4(1)(b).

30. *Id.* § 17:2053.

31. 426 U.S. 736 (1976).

32. LA. REV. STAT. ANN. § 17:2236.

33. Howard, *State Aid,* note 17, *supra,* at 358.

34. LA. REV. STAT. ANN. §§ 40:1732 *et seq.*

35. *Id.* § 40:1732(5)(c).

36. LA. CONST. art. I, § 3.

37. *Id.* § 23:972 (Supp. 1980). In 1978 Louisiana adopted a statute prohibiting employment discrimination on the basis of handicap, but the scope of this act does not include the private sector. *Id.* §§ 46:2111 *et seq.* (Supp. 1980); see also §§ 40:1731 *et seq.*

38. An employer is anyone who engages in an industry affecting commerce (generally, it has been considered that any RAC with more than 1,000 students "affects commerce") who has twenty or more employees for each working day in each of twenty or more weeks in the current or preceding year. *Id.* § 23:971 (Supp. 1980).

39. *Id.* § 23:972(F)(1) (Supp. 1980).

40. See Edward M. Gaffney and Philip R. Moots, *The Government and the Campus: Federal Regulation of Religiously Affiliated Higher Education* (Notre Dame, Ind.: University of Notre Dame Press, 1981), pp. 32–82.

41. LA. REV. STAT. ANN. §§ 23:354 *et seq.* This legislation may be vulnerable to an attack under the Equal Protection Clause of the Fourteenth Amendment to the U.S. Constitution.

42. LA. REV. STAT. ANN. §§ 23:1021 *et seq.* (1964 and Supp. 1980).

43. 230 La. 310, 88 So. 2d 381 (1956); but see St. Martin Evangelical Lutheran Church v. South Dakota, 451 U.S. 772 (1981) (ruling that schools that are an integral part of a church are exempt from federal unemployment compensation taxes). See discussion in chapter three, *supra,* in text accompanying notes 64–83.

44. LA. REV. STAT. ANN. §§ 23:1037 and 1045 (Supp. 1980).

45. *Id.* § 1037.

46. *Id.* §§ 1044 and 1046 (Supp. 1980).

47. *Id.* § 1045 (Supp. 1980).

48. *Id.* § 1162.

49. *Id.* § 1191.

50. *Id.* §§ 23:1471 *et seq.*

51. An employer is one who paid out $1,500 or more in wages or who employed one person in each of twenty weeks in the prior or current calendar year. *Id.* § 23:1472(11) (Supp. 1981).

52. *Id.* § 23:1472(12)(F)(III)(a) (Supp. 1980).

53. See Gaffney and Moots, note 40, *supra,* at 49–65.

54. LA. REV. STAT. ANN. § 23:1472(12)(H)(VIII) (Supp. 1980).

55. *Id.* § 23:1472(12)(F)(VI) (Supp. 1980).

56. *Id.* § 23:1472(12)(H)(XII)(b) and (c) (Supp. 1980).

57. *Id.* § 17:111(A) (Supp. 1980).

58. *Id.* § 17:111(B) (Supp. 1980).

59. LA. CONST. art. I, § 12.

60. LA. REV. STAT. ANN. §§ 40:1731 *et seq.*

61. *Id.* § 1731(B) (emphasis supplied).

62. *Id.* § 1733.

63. *Id.* § 1732(7).

64. *Id.* § 1732(8).

65. *Id.* § 1732(5); the accessibility regulations are not applicable to buildings financed with a state grant or loan made prior to September 9, 1977.

66. See Pub. L. 88-352, Title II, § 201(b), 78 Stat. 243. 42 U.S.C. § 2000a(b).

67. LA. REV. STAT. ANN. §§ 40:1731 *et seq.* (West).

68. *Id.* § 46:1952(B) (Supp. 1981).

69. *Id.* § 46:1953(A) (Supp. 1981).

70. *Id.* § 46:1953(B) (Supp. 1981).

71. *Id.* §§ 46:1952(E), 1953(c) (Supp. 1981).

72. *Id.* § 23:8.

73. *Id.* § 23:13.

74. *Id.* § 47:121(5).

75. See Edward McGlynn Gaffney, "Political Divisiveness Along Religious Lines: The Entanglement of the Court in Sloppy History and Bad Public Policy," 24 ST. LOUIS U.L.J. 205 (1980); and Gaffney, "The Constitution and the Campus: The Case for Institutional Integrity and the Need for Critical Self-Evaluation," in John D. Mosely, ed., *Church and College: A Vital Partnership* (Sherman, Texas: Austin College, 1980), vol. 3, pp. 47–67.

76. See, e.g., Con. Edison Co. v. Public Service Comm'n., 447 U.S. 530 (1980) and First National Bank of Boston v. Bellotti, 435 U.S. 765 (1978).

77. See I.R.C. § 501(c) (Supp. 1980).

78. See I.R.C. § 513(a) (Supp. 1980).

79. LA. REV. STAT. ANN. §§ 47:2401 *et seq.*

80. *Id.* § 2402(4); and see *id.* § 2402(6) (Supp. 1980).

81. LA. REV. STAT. ANN. § 47:2431.

82. *Id.* § 47:1204.

83. *Id.* § 47:57.

84. *Id.*

85. *Id.*

86. LA. CONST., art. 7, § 21(B).

87. *Id.* § 21(B)(3).

88. Op. Atty. Gen., 1920–22, at 807, 820.

89. Op. Atty. Gen., 1932–34, at 884.

90. 52 La. App. 223, 26 So. 872 (1898).

91. LA. REV. STAT. ANN. § 305:14(A).

92. *Id.* § 305:14(C).

93. *Id.* § 305:14(C).

94. *Id.*

95. *Id.* § 305:18.

96. *Id.* § 4:8; see also § 4:43.

97. LA. CONST. 1921, art. VI, § 26(2).

98. LA. REV. STAT. ANN. § 24:514 (Supp. 1980).

99. Op. Atty. Gen., 1956–58, at 130.

100. LA. CONST. art. XII, § 6.

101. LA. REV. STAT. ANN. § 33:4861.4(A) (Supp. 1980).

102. *Id.* § 33:4861.5 (Supp. 1980).

103. Op. Atty. Gen., No. 75–715, May 30, 1975; see also Op. Atty. Gen., No. 77–1657, Dec. 21, 1977.

104. Marceaux v. V.F.W. Post 2130, 337 So.2d 923 (La. App. 1976).

105. LA. REV. STAT. ANN. § 33:4861.3 (Supp. 1980).

106. *Id.* § 9:2792.

27. Maine

1. ME. REV. STAT. ANN. tit. 13, § 901.

2. *Id.* Specific provisions concerning religious societies are found at *id.* §§ 2861 through 2986.

3. ME. REV. STAT. ANN. tit. 13–B, § 201.

4. *Id.* § 201(2)(A).

5. *Id.* §§ 901–906; §§ 1101–1111 (Supp. 1980).

6. *Id.* § 103.

7. Petition of Pierce, 153 Me. 180, 136 A.2d 510 (1957). For a discussion of the *cy pres* doctrine, see Chapter 1, "Corporate Status," *supra.*

8. ME. REV. STAT. ANN. tit. 13–B, §§ 904–1104.

9. *Id.* § 1105.

10. *Id.* § 1104(d).

11. *Id.*

12. *Id.* § 1106(3).

13. See discussion in Chapter 1, "Corporate Status," *supra.*

14. ME. CONST. art. VIII, Pt. 1, § 1. The term "literary institutions" has been interpreted to include schools. See A. E. Dick Howard, *State Aid to Private Higher Education* (Charlottesville, Va.: Michie, 1977), p. 377.

15. A. E. Howard, *State Aid,* note 14, *supra,* at 365, citing E. Helmreich, *Religion and the Maine Schools: an Historical Approach* (Brunswick, Me, 1960), p. 16.

16. *Id.* at 381.

17. *Id.* at 365.

18. *Id.* at 367.

19. *Id.* at 367, citing A. Stokes, II *Church and State in the United States* (New York: Harper and Bros., 1950), p. 39, and E. Helmreich, note 15, *supra,* at 39.

20. ME. REV. STAT. ANN. tit. 20, § 2371.

21. *Id.* §§ 2205 *et seq.*

22. *Id.* § 2209.

23. ME. REV. STAT. ANN. tit. 37–A, § 50–K.

24. ME. REV. STAT. ANN. tit. 20, § 2311.

25. *Id.* § 2314.

26. ME. CONST. art. VIII, Pt. 1, § 2.

27. ME. REV. STAT. ANN. tit. 20, § 2231–2236.

28. *Id.* tit. 30, § 4902(2).

29. *Id.* § 4901.

30. *Id.* tit. 26, § 1301.

31. *Id.* tit. 5, §§ 4551 *et seq.*

32. *Id.* § 4552.

33. *Id.* § 4553(4).

34. Maine Human Rights Commission Guidelines § 3.05(c), State Fair Employment Practice Laws.

35. *Id.*

36. ME. REV. STAT. ANN. tit. 26, § 661.

37. *Id.* § 663(3)(E).

38. *Id.* tit. 39. (1978 and Supp. 1980).

39. *Id.* §§ 2.1 & 5.

40. *Id.* § 3 (1978 and Supp. 1980).

41. *Id.* § 4 (Supp. 1980).

42. *Id.* (Supp. 1980).

43. *Id.* §§ 23.1 & 2.

44. *Id.* tit. 26, § 1043(11)(A–1)(3).

45. *Id.* §§ 1041 *et seq.*

46. *Id.* § 1043(11)(F)(21)(a).

47. *Id.* § 1043(11)(F)(21)(b).

48. *Id.* § 1043(11)(F)(21)(c).

49. *Id.* tit. 5, § 4581.

50. *Id.* § 4553(6)(c).

51. *Id.* § 4591.

52. *Id.* § 4553(8).

53. *Id.*

54. *Id.* § 4593.

55. *Id.* tit. 26, §§ 561 *et seq.* (Supp. 1980).

56. *Id.* § 563 (Supp. 1980).

57. *Id.* tit. 36, § 652(1)(B).

58. *Id.* § 652(1)(C).

59. *Id.* § 707(5).

60. Hurricane Island Outward Bound v. Vinalhaven, 372 A.2d 1043 (Me. 1977).

61. *Id.* at 1046.

62. *Id.*

63. *Id.* at 1047.
64. ME. REV. STAT. ANN. tit. 36, § 652(G).
65. *Id.* § 652(I).
66. *Id.* § 3461(3).
67. *Id.*
68. *Id.*
69. *Id.*
70. *Id.* §§ 5101-5342 (1964).
71. *Id.* § 5125 (1964).
72. I.R.C. § 170(c)(2)(B) and (C).
73. ME. REV. STAT. ANN. tit. 36, § 1760(16).
74. *Id.*
75. *Id.* §§ 1861-1862 (1964).
76. *Id.* § 1760(19).
77. *Id.* §§ 1438(8) and (9).
78. *Id.* tit. 9, §§ 5001 *et seq.*
79. *Id.* § 5002.
80. *Id.* § 5003(1) and (2) (emphasis added).
81. *Id.* § 5006(2).
82. *Id.* § 5006(1)(B).
83. *Id.* § 5006(1)(E).
84. *Id.*
85. *Id.* tit. 17, § 332.
86. *Id.* tit. 20, § 2751.
87. *Id.* § 2752.
88. *Id.* § 2755(2).
89. *Id.* § 73.
90. *Id.* § 74.
91. *Id.* § 75.
92. *Id.* § 76.
93. *Id.* tit. 22, §§ 301 *et seq.*
94. *Id.* § 316.
95. *Id.* tit. 20, § 1221.

28. Maryland

1. MD. CORP. & ASS'NS CODE ANN. §§ 2-101 *et seq.*
2. *Id.* §§ 5-201 *et seq.*
3. *Id.* § 5-202(a).
4. *Id.* § 5-207(a).
5. *Id.* § 5-301.
6. *Id.* § 11-601(9)(i).
7. MD. EDUC. CODE ANN. § 12-203(a) (Supp. 1979). For criteria and procedures, see *id.* § 12-203(b) and (c). See also § 12-205. The State Board of Higher Education is charged with, *inter alia*, coordinating the overall growth and development of higher education and administering state funds for private higher education. MD. EDUC. CODE ANN. § 12-205.
8. *Id.* § 12.204. The article is former article 77A of the Maryland Annotated Code.
9. *Id.* § 12-206.
10. *Id.* § 12-207.

11. MD. CORP. & ASS'NS CODE ANN. §§ 1-103 (Supp. 1979).
12. *Id.* §§ 5-20 *et seq.* (1975, Supp. 1979).
13. *Id.* §§ 3-101 *et seq.*, and § 5-207 (Supp. 1979) (consolidations and mergers); §§ 3-401 *et seq.*, and § 5-208 (Supp. 1979) (dissolutions).
14. Maryland has adopted the Uniform Charitable Trusts Administration Act, MD. ANN. CODE § 14-302. See also Gordon v. City of Baltimore, 258 Md. 682, 267 A.2d 98 (1970), and Wesley Home, Inc. v. Mercantile Safe Deposit and Trust Co., 265 Md. 185, 289 A.2d 337 (1972). For a discussion of the *cy pres* doctrine, see Chapter 1, "Corporate Status," *supra*.
15. MD. CORP. & ASS'NS CODE ANN. §§ 3-113 and 5-207 (Supp. 1979) (consolidations and mergers); §§ 3-408 and 5-208 (Supp. 1979) (dissolutions).
16. *Id.* § 1-101(g) (Supp. 1979).
17. *Id.* § 3-514.
18. *Id.* § 1-101(t).
19. *Id.* §§ 3-413 to 3-415.
20. *Id.* § 5-208(b).
21. For a discussion of the Model Act, see Chapter 1, "Corporate Status," *supra*.
22. MD. CORP. & ASS'NS CODE ANN. § 5-208(G)(4).
23. 242 Md. 645, 220 A.2d 51 (1966).
24. See MD. CONST. art. 15 and 23.
25. See *id.* § 36.
26. 403 U.S. 602 (1971).
27. 426 U.S. 736 (1976).
28. Lemon v. Kurtzman, 403 U.S. at 612-613.
29. Roemer v. Board of Public Works of Maryland, 426 U.S at 764.
30. MD. EDUC. CODE ANN. §§ 17-701 *et seq.* Maryland also has established an eminent scholar program "to give public institutions of higher education the opportunity to attract and keep faculty who have achieved national eminence in their disciplines." *Id.* § 17-201. RACs are clearly ineligible to participate in this program.
31. *Id.* § 17-103.
32. *Id.* § 17-104.
33. *Id.* §§ 17-102; 12-105(d).
34. *Id.* § 17-707.
35. *Id.* §§ 18-1001 *et seq.*
36. *Id.* § 18-1001.
37. *Id.* §§ 18-101 *et seq.*
38. *Id.* § 18-102.
39. *Id.* § 18-103. See text at notes 80 through 82, *infra*.
40. MD. ANN. CODE art. 49B, § 16(a)(1)(2).
41. *Id.* § 16(g)(3).
42. It is interesting to note that "religion" is defined in terms of "aspects of religious observances

and practice, as well as belief . . . ," *id.* § 15(f), not in terms of entities.

43. *Id.* § 16(g). Under the law, an employer may also be authorized to disfavor one of a particular religious persuasion when his "observance, practice or belief cannot be reasonably accommodated by an employer without causing undue hardship on the conduct of the employer's business." *Id.* § 16(f).

44. *Id.* § 9. For the powers and procedures of the Commission, see *id.* §§ 1 *et seq.*

45. MD. CODE OF FAIR PRACTICES, art. VI (Exec. Order, as amended effective November 1, 1976). See text at notes 77–79, *infra.*

46. MD. ANN. CODE art. 100, §§ 81 *et seq.*

47. *Id.* § 82(d).

48. *Id.* § 82(e)(2).

49. *Id.* § 82(e)(3).

50. *Id.* § 82(e)(4) ("not more than 20 hours in any week").

51. *Id.* § 382(e)(6) ("not more than 25 hours per week").

52. *Id.* § 82(e)(10).

53. *Id.* art. 101, §§ 1 *et seq.*

54. *Id.* § 67(2).

55. *Id.* § 21(a)(1).

56. *Id.* § 21(c)(4). "Casual" employment is not defined in the statute and courts give it varied meanings. See *Winters v. Payne,* 13 Md. App. 327, 283 A.2d 807 (1971).

57. MD. CODE ANN. art. 101, § 21(c)(2).

58. *Id.* § 31.

59. *Id.* § 31.

60. *Id.* § 16.

61. *Id.* art. 95A, §§ 1 *et seq.*

62. *Id.* § 20(f)(l)(i).

63. *Id.* § 20(g)(7)(iii)(C).

64. 26 U.S.C.A. § 501(c)(3).

65. *Id.* § 3306(c)(8).

66. MD. ANN. CODE art. 95A, § 20(g)(7)(v)(B).

67. *Id.* § 20(g)(7)(v)(C).

68. *Id.* § 20(g)(7)(vii).

69. *Id.* § 20(g)(8)(iii).

70. *Id.* § 20(g)(8)(x).

71. *Id.* § 20(g)(8)(xi).

72. *Id.* § 20(g)(8)(xii).

73. *Id.*

74. *Id.* art. 100, §§ 1 *et seq.*

75. *Id.* § 55A.

76. See text at notes 30 *et seq., supra.*

77. MD. CODE OF FAIR PRACTICES, art. VI (Exec. Order, as amended effective Nov. 1, 1976).

78. *Id.*

79. Under *id.,* for example, the use of state facilities is not to be granted to groups which discriminate in membership policies, although such discrimination is not illegal in itself.

80. MD. EDUC. CODE ANN. §§ 18–101 *et seq.*

81. *Id.* § 18–103(b).

82. *Id.* § 18–103(a).

83. *Id.* §§ 12–301 and 12–302 (Supp. 1979).

84. MD. ANN. CODE art. 49B, § 5 (Supp. 1979). The sex discrimination prohibition does not apply to facilities "uniquely private and personal in nature, designed to accommodate only a particular sex." *Id.*

85. *Id.* § 20.

86. *Id.* § 24. The housing discrimination prohibition does not apply to certain nonprofit, private membership clubs. *Id.*

87. Compare the employment discrimination exemption discussed in the text at notes 41 and 42, *supra.*

88. MD. ANN. CODE art. 49B, § 20.

89. *Id.* § 9. For the powers and procedures of the Commission, see *id.* art. 49B, §§ 1 *et seq.*

90. See text at notes 77–79, *supra.*

91. MD. ANN. CODE art. 101, § 53.

92. *Id.* § 54.

93. *Id.* § 55.

94. MD. ANN. CODE art. 81, § 288(d)(5) (Supp. 1979).

95. *Id.* art. 81, §§ 149 (Supp. 1979) *et seq.*

96. *Id.* § 150(a) (Supp. 1979).

97. *Id.*

98. *Id.* art. 62A, §§ 1,2,4,5 (1957).

99. *Id.* art. 81, § 281(a).

100. I.R.C. § 170(c)(2)(B) and (C).

101. MD. ANN. CODE art. 81, § 9(c).

102. *Id.* § 9(e) (Supp. 1979). Although the exemption includes "fraternal or sororal" organizations, the statutes specify that this phrase does not include "any college or high school fraternities or sororities." *Id.*

The exemption does include property used for charitable, benevolent, or educational purposes held by a corporation, association, or trustees for the benefit of nonprofit charitable, benevolent, educational, or literary organizations. *Id.*

103. *Id.* §§ 324 *et seq.*

104. *Id.* § 326(c) (Supp. 1979).

105. *Id.* § 326(i) (Supp. 1979). A certificate of exemption must be secured from the Comptroller. *Id.*

106. *Id.* § 326.

107. *Id.* §§ 402 *et seq.*

108. *Id.* § 326(p).

109. *Id.* § 406(1) (Supp. 1979). This exemption includes receipts from charges made for admission to and use of recreational facilities and "bingo" equipment if the bingo game is "operated pursuant to § 260 of article 27 of the Annotated Code of

Maryland." *Id.* Section 260 of Article 27 deals with "bingo" in Baltimore City. Curiously, bingo is authorized by state statutes in many Maryland counties. (See text at note 122, *infra.*).

110. *Id.* art. 81, §§ 372 *et seq.*

111. *Id.* § 375(b) (Supp. 1979). See text at notes 103 to 109, *supra.*

112. *Id.* art. 41, § 103A.

113. *Id.*

114. *Id.* § 103B. For a list of the information which must be included, see *id.*

115. A bona fide salaried officer or employee of a charitable organization which maintains a permanent office in Maryland is not a "professional solicitor," *id.* art. 47, § 103A(h), or a "professional fund-raiser counsel," *id.* § 103A(i), neither of which may solicit for a charitable organization without registering with the Secretary of State, *id.* § 103A.

116. *Id.* art. 41, § 103C(a)(1). This approval may be direct or "by acceptance of its accreditation by an accrediting body recognized by that Department." *Id.* The educational institution must file with the Secretary of State a copy of the fiscal report filed with the State Department of Education. *Id.*

117. *Id.* § 103(a)(3).

118. *Id.* § 103C(a)(5). A person granted membership upon making a contribution as the result of solicitation is not a member for purposes of this exemption. *Id.*

119. *Id.* § 103C(a)(6). See I.R.C. § 501(e)(3).

120. See Md. Ann. Code art. 41, § 103C(b), (c) and (d).

121. *Id.* § 103H.

122. See *id.* art. 27, §§ 247 (Supp. 1979) *et seq.* for the counties involved and the conditions imposed.

123. Md. Educ. Code Ann. § 26-101.

29. Massachusetts

1. Mass. Ann. Laws ch. 180, §§ 1 *et seq.* See *id.* § 4 (Supp. 1979) (Michie/Law. Co-op).

2. *Id.* ch. 110A, § 402.9.

3. *Id.* ch. 180, §§ 10-11B.

4. First Church in Somerville v. Attorney General, 376 N.E. 2d 1226 (Mass. 1978); for a discussion of the *cy pres* doctrine, see Chapter 1, "Corporate Status," *supra.*

5. Mass. Ann. Laws ch. 180, §§ 10-10A, ch. 156B, § 78(d)(4).

6. *Id.* § 11A.

7. *Id.* § 11B.

8. *Id.* § 11B. Compare *Model Nonprofit Corporation Act* with Mass. Ann. Laws , ch. 180A (Management of Institutional Funds).

9. Public money has been used to pay the salaries of chaplains in Massachusetts' House of Representatives and Senate, and this has been held "not unconstitutional." Colo v. Treasurer and Receiver Gen., 392 N.E. 2d 1195 (Mass. 1979).

10. Mass. Ann. Laws ch. 15A, § 1 (Supp. 1981).

11. *Id.* § 7.

12. *Id.*

13. *Id.*

14. *Id.*

15. *Id.* ch. 69, § 7B.

16. *Id.* ch. 69, § 7D.

17. *Id.*

18. *Id.* Appendix to ch. 69, § 1.

19. *Id.* Appendix to ch. 69, § 5.

20. *Id.* ch. 151B, § 4.1.

21. *Id.* § 1.5 (emphasis added).

22. *Id.* § 4.15.

23. See Philip R. Moots and Edward McGlynn Gaffney, *Church and Campus* (Notre Dame, Ind.: University of Notre Dame Press, 1979), pp. 65-66.

24. *Id.* at 53.

25. See text accompanying note 31 *et seq., infra.*

26. Mass. Ann. Laws ch. 151B, § 4.15.

27. *Id.*

28. *Id.*

29. See text accompanying note 21, *supra.*

30. See text accompanying note 55 *et seq., infra.*

31. Mass. Ann. Laws ch. 151B, § 4.1 (emphasis added).

32. *Id.* § 4.2.

33. *Id.* § 4.1.

34. Arthur E. Bonfield, "The Substance of American Fair Employment Practices Legislation I: Employers," 61 Northwestern L. Rev. 907 (1967).

35. Mass. Ann. Laws ch. 6, § 56.

36. *Id.* ch. 151B, §§ 2 & 3.

37. *Id.* § 2.

38. *Id.* § 3.9.

39. *Id.* ch. 151, § 1.

40. *Id.* § 2.

41. *Id.*

42. As defined in *id.*

43. *Id.* § 1A.

44. *Id.* § 1A.17.

45. *Id.* ch. 152, §§ 1 *et seq.* (1976, Supp. 1980).

46. *Id.* § 1(5).

47. *Id.* § 1(4).

48. *Id.* § 1(4).

49. *Id.* § 26.

50. *Id.* § 25B.

51. *Id.* § 24.

52. *Id.* § 25A.

53. *Id.* ch. 151A, § 4A(d).

54. *Id.* § 8.

55. *Id.* ch. 151C, § 1(b).

56. See text accompanying note 21, *supra.*
57. MASS. ANN. LAWS ch. 151C, § 1(b).
58. *Id.* § 1(c).
59. *Id.* § 2(c).
60. See text accompanying note 22 *et seq., supra.*
61. MASS. ANN. LAWS ch. 151C, § 1(c).
62. See text accompanying note 23 *et seq., supra.*
63. MASS. ANN. LAWS ch. 151B, § 1.5.
64. *Id.* ch. 151C, § 1(c).
65. *Id.* ch. 151B, § 1.5 (emphasis added).
66. *Id.* ch. 151C, § 1(c) (emphasis added).
67. See text accompanying note 35, *supra.*
68. MASS. ANN. LAWS ch. 151C, § 1(c). Presumably an institution whose "courses of instruction lead primarily to the degree of bachelor, master or doctor of theology" must, to qualify as a "religious or denominational educational institution," certify that it is "so operated." *Id.*
69. *Id.* § 2(e).
70. *Id.* ch. 272, § 92 A.
71. *Id.* ch. 151C, §§ 1(a), 3, 4, 5.
72. *Id.* § 3(i).
73. *Id.* ch. 272, § 92A(10).
74. Cf. *id.* § 92A(10).
75. 341 Mass. 125, 167 N.E. 2d 620 (1967).
76. MASS. ANN. LAWS ch. 151C. See text accompanying note 55 *et seq., supra.*
77. MASS. ANN. LAWS ch. 151B, §§ 4(6), 4(7), 4(8).
78. 42 U.S.C. § 3608.
79. MASS. ANN. LAWS ch. 151B, § 4.15.
80. See text accompanying note 20 *et seq., supra.*
81. Op. Atty. Gen., 1964, at 224.
82. MASS. ANN. LAWS ch. 151B, §§ 2, 3.
83. *Id.* ch. 149, § 7.
84. *Id.* § 1 (1976).
85. *Id.* ch. 63, § 30.
86. *Id.* ch. 65, §§ 1 *et seq.*
87. *Id.* ch. 65A, §§ 1 *et seq.*
88. *Id.* ch. 63, § 1.
89. *Id.* § 30.
90. I.R.C. § 170(c)(2)(B) and (C).
91. MASS. ANN. LAWS ch. 59, § 5(3).
92. *Id.* § 5(3)(e) (emphasis added).
93. *Id.* ch. 64H, § 6(e).
94. *Id.* § 6(f).
95. *Id.* § 6(m).
96. *Id.* § 6(c).
97. *Id.* ch. 64B.
98. *Id.* ch. 64H, § 6(cc).
99. *Id.* ch. 64I, § 7(b).
100. *Id.* ch. 64G, § 2(b).
101. Charitable organizations are defined at *id.* ch. 68, § 18.
102. *Id.* § 19.
103. *Id.* § 20.

104. See text accompanying notes 21–28, *supra.*
105. MASS. ANN. LAWS ch. 68, § 27.
106. *Id.* ch. 271, §§ 1 *et seq.*
107. *Id.* § 7A.
108. *Id.*
109. *Id.*
110. Op. Atty. Gen., 1969, at 71.
111. MASS. ANN. LAWS ch. 271, § 22B.
112. See *id.* ch. 10, §§ 37 and 38.
113. *Id.* § 38.

30. Michigan

1. See, e.g., MICH. COMP. LAWS ANN. §§ 390.751 to 390.760 (1976) (Kalamazoo College); *id.* §§ 390.701 to 390.708 (1976) (Albion College).
2. *Id.* §§ 450.170 *et seq.*
3. See *id.* § 390.771 (1976).
4. *Id.* § 450.171 (1973). The section provides in relevant part: "[E]ducational corporations shall be classified as follows: (w) Those having a capital of not less than $500,000.00; (x) Those having a capital of not less than $100,000.00, and less than $500,000.00; (y) Those having a capital of $1,000,000.00 or more; (z) Those instituted and maintained by any ecclesiastical or religious order, society, corporation or corporations, retaining control of such institution for denominational purposes." *Id.* Nonetheless, "any corporation of class (z) hereafter organized under this act may enjoy the privileges provided under classes (w), (x) and (y) of section 117, on condition that it satisfies the requirements set up for corporations of these respective classes." *Id.* § 450.172(c) (1973). See Op. Atty. Gen. 1978, No. 5386, and Op. Atty. Gen. 1979, No. 5581.
5. MICH. COMP. LAWS ANN. § 450.171 (lists five qualifications).
6. *Id.* § 450.173 (1973).
7. *Id.* § 450.177 (1973).
8. *Id.*
9. *Id.*
10. See, e.g., *id.* § 450.167a (Henry Ford Trade School).
11. *Id.* § 450.1261.
12. *Id.* §§ 450.1801 *et seq.* (1973 & Supp. 1980).
13. See, e.g., Gifford v. First National Bank, 285 Mich. 58, 280 N.W. 108 (1938); In re Road's Estate, 41 Mich. App. 405, 200 N.W. 2d 728 (1972).
14. MICH. COMP. LAWS ANN. § 450.251 (1973).
15. *Id.*
16. *Id.*
17. *Id.* §§ 450.1803, .1804, .251.
18. *Id.*
19. *Id.*
20. *Id.* § 450.119a (Supp. 1980).

21. MICH. CONST. art. 1, § 4.

22. For a full discussion of Michigan law on this theme, see A. E. Dick Howard, *State Aid To Private Higher Education* (Charlottesville, Va.: Michie, 1977), pp. 438–458.

23. The leading case articulating the "child-benefit" theory in the context of governmental aid to church-sponsored education is Bd. of Ed. v. Allen, 392 U.S. 236 (1968).

24. MICH. COMP. LAWS ANN. §§ 390.921 to 390.934 (1976).

25. The Authority consists of members of the State Higher Education Facilities Commission. *Id.* § 390.923. One of the eleven members represents private colleges and universities in the state. *Id.* § 390.941(1) (Supp. 1980).

26. See *id.* §§ 390.922(c),.924(c).

27. *Id.* § 390.922(b).

28. *Id.* § 390.933 (emphasis supplied).

29. See text accompanying notes 118–120, *infra.*

30. MICH. COMP. LAWS ANN. §§ 390.1021 to 390.1027 (1976 & Supp. 1980).

31. *Id.* § 390.1022(d) (emphasis supplied). See subsections (a), (b), (c), and (e) for other requirements.

32. *Id.* § 390.1027.

33. *Id.* § 390.1023(2). Subsection (1) states: "A degree earned in a program with respect to which state reimbursement other than that established by this act is granted to a nonpublic institution is excluded from computation under section [390.1021]." *Id.* § 390.1023(1).

34. *Id.* §§ 390.951 to 390.961 (1976 & Supp. 1980) (creation and powers of the MHEAA).

35. *Id.* § 390.957(a) (Supp. 1980).

36. *Id.* §§ 390.1151 to 390.1165 (1976 & Supp. 1980).

37. *Id.* § 390.1153 (1976).

38. *Id.* § 390.1154(c).

39. *Id.* § 390.1152(d) ("eligible institution" includes an "institution of higher education").

40. *Id.* §§ 390.971 to 390.980 (1976 & Supp. 1980). See *id.* §§ 390.971–.972.

41. *Id.* § 390.974 (eligibility requirements include twelve month residency and good moral character).

42. *Id.* § 390.977 (Supp. 1980).

43. *Id.* §§ 390.991 to 390.997a (1976 & Supp. 1980).

44. *Id.* § 390.991 (Supp. 1980). The MHEAA is authorized to issue rules and regulations to carry out this act. *Id.* § 390.996 (1976).

45. See *id.* § 390.993 (Supp. 1980).

46. *Id.* § 390.994(2) (Supp. 1980).

47. *Id.* § 390.997 (Supp. 1980).

48. *Id.* § 390.997a (1976). "If a student receives other scholarship awards by a private, nonprofit institution of higher learning covering only a portion of his tuition and fees, the student may qualify for a proportionate tuition grant in accordance with the provisions of this act." *Id.*

49. *Id.* §§ 390.1271 to 390.1278 (Supp. 1980).

50. *Id.* §§ 450.62 to 450.192 (1973 & Supp. 1980) (general corporations law including educational corporations).

51. *Id.* § 390.1272(a)–(c).

52. *Id.* § 390.1274(b). See subsections (a), (c), and (d) for other criteria.

53. *Id.* § 390.1275(2).

54. *Id.* §§ 390.1301 to 390.1307 (Supp. 1980).

55. *Id.* § 390.1304(a)–(c).

56. *Id.* § 390.1304(c). There is no requirement that the college or university be located in Michigan.

57. *Id.* § 390.1307.

58. *Id.* §§ 37.2101 to 37.2804 (Supp. 1980).

59. *Id.* § 37.2202.

60. *Id.* § 37.2201(a).

61. *Id.* § 37.2201(d).

62. *Id.*

63. See *id.* §§ 37.1601 *et seq.*

64. *Id.* § 37.2208.

65. *Id.*

66. *Id.* § 27.2206 (Supp. 1979).

67. *Id.* § 37.2206(2).

68. *Id.*

69. *Id.* §§ 37.1102, .1103(b).

70. *Id.* § 37.1103(d).

71. *Id.*

72. *Id.* § 418.101 *et seq.* (Supp. 1980).

73. *Id.* §§ 418.151 and 418.111 (Supp. 1980).

74. *Id.* § 418.115 (Supp. 1980).

75. *Id.* §§ 418.115 and 418.118 (Supp. 1980).

76. *Id.* § 418.121 (Supp. 1980).

77. *Id.* § 418.611(1)(b) (Supp. 1980).

78. *Id.* § 418.701 (Supp. 1980).

79. *Id.* § 418.201 (Supp. 1980).

80. *Id.* § 418.611(1)(a) (Supp. 1980).

81. *Id.* §§ 421.1 *et seq.* (Supp. 1980).

82. *Id.* § 421.42.

83. *Id.* § 421.42(10).

84. *Id.* § 421.43(0)(1)(i).

85. *Id.* § 421.43(0)(1)(ii).

86. *Id.* § 421.43(0)(2).

87. *Id.* § 421.43(1)(i). The statute specifies that the work must be done by a person who is "primarily a student." To qualify under this classification, an individual must be enrolled, be "pursuing a course of study for academic credit," and be working thirty hours or less per week for the institution.

88. *Id.* § 421.43(1)(ii). The spouse must be given

written notice that the employment is provided as a means of financial aid and that it is not covered under any program of unemployment insurance.

89. *Id.* § 421.43(m).
90. *Id.* § 421.43(e).
91. *Id.* § 421.43(c).
92. I.R.C. §§ 501, 521.
93. Mich. Comp. Laws Ann. § 421.43(k).
94. *Id.* § 421.13a(1).
95. *Id.* § 421.13a(2).
96. *Id.* § 421.13c(1).
97. *Id.* §§ 421.25(1), (2), 421.41(4).
98. *Id.* §§ 423.501 to .512 (Supp. 1980).
99. *Id.* § 423.503.
100. *Id.* § 423.504.
101. *Id.* § 423.505.
102. *Id.* § 423.501(2)(c).
103. *Id.* § 423.501(2)(c)(vii).
104. *Id.* § 423.8 (1978).
105. *Id.* §§ 408.381 to 408.397 (1967 & Supp. 1980).
106. Section 408.382(c) provides: " 'Employer' means a person, firm, or corporation . . . who employs two or more employees at any one time within a calendar year."
107. *Id.* § 408.384a(1) (Supp. 1980).
108. *Id.* §§ 408.471 to 408.490 (Supp. 1980). Section 408.471(d) states: " 'Employer' means . . . an institution of higher education . . . who employs one or more individuals."
109. The term, "fringe benefits," means "compensation due an employee pursuant to a written contract or written policy for holiday, time off for sickness or injury, time off for personal reasons or vacation, bonuses, authorized expenses incurred during the course of employment, and contributions made on behalf of an employee." *Id.* § 408.471(e).
110. *Id.* § 408.472.
111. *Id.* § 408.479.
112. *Id.* §§ 409.101 to 409.124 (Supp. 1980).
113. *Id.* § 409.102(d).
114. *Id.* § 409.119(1)(g).
115. *Id.* §§ 409.201 to 409.205 (Supp. 1980).
116. " 'Youth employment program' means all programs both public and private, which are totally or partially funded with state or federal money, and which are organized for the purpose of alleviating the youth unemployment problem among youth 14 through 23 years of age." *Id.* § 409.202(c).
117. *Id.* § 409.205(1).
118. *Id.* § 37.2401.
119. *Id.* § 37.2402 (emphasis supplied).
120. *Id.* § 37.2403.
121. See Hunt v. McNair, 413 U.S. 734 (1973).
122. Mich. Comp. Laws Ann. § 37.2403.

123. *Id.* § 37.2404.
124. *Id.* § 37.1402(b). Compare § 37.1402(a)–(e) (section of the handicappers' civil rights act concerning educational institutions) with § 37.2402(a)–(e) (section of the civil rights act concerning educational institutions).
125. *Id.* § 37.1103(c). See text accompanying notes 69–71, *supra.*
126. Mich. Comp. Laws Ann. § 37.1103(b)(iii). See *id.* § 37.1402(b) at text accompanying note 124, *supra;* Op. Att'y. Gen. No. 5487 (May 1, 1979) (educational institutions may inquire concerning physical or mental characteristics of an applicant for admission which would prevent him from using or benefitting from the educational opportunities provided by the institution), cited in Mich. Comp. Laws Ann. § 37.2303 (article 3).
127. *Id.* §§ 37.2301 to 37.2303 (article 3).
128. *Id.* § 37.2301(a).
129. *Id.* § 37.2302(a) (emphasis supplied).
130. See text accompanying note 118 *et seq., supra.*
131. An RAC could undoubtedly require proof of authorization, such as an identification card.
132. Mich. Comp. Laws Ann. § 37.2402(a) (emphasis supplied).
133. For example, an educational institution could not prevent Hispanics or Jews or Irishmen from using the dining hall.
134. Mich. Comp. Laws Ann. § 37.2505(1) (emphasis supplied).
135. *Id.* §§ 333.1101 to 333.22190 (main text) (1980); §§ 333.25101 to 333.25211 (contains repealers, effective dates clauses) (1980).
136. *Id.* §§ 333.12101 to 333.13536.
137. "The department shall serve as the environmental health agency for this state." *Id.* § 333.12103.
138. *Id.* § 333.12211(1). Areas subject to regulation include light, maintenance, occupancy, plumbing and electrical facilities, sanitation, thermal conditions and ventilation of dwellings; the requirement of means of fire and accident prevention; and the regulation of toxic substances in building materials, and in the housing structure itself. *Id.*
139. Op. Att'y Gen. No. 5326, at 515 (1978) (interpreting Mich. Comp. Laws Ann. §§ 125.401 *et seq.* of the prior housing law), cited in Mich. Comp. Laws Ann. § 333.12202, n. 1.
140. *Id.* § 29.3b (1980) (creation).
141. *Id.* § 29.3c(1).
142. *Id.* §§ 17.50 *et seq.* (1975).
143. *Id.* § 17.50(2).
144. *Id.* § 17.50(6).
145. *Id.* § 17.50(5).

146. *Id.* §§ 206.1 to 206.532 (Supp. 1980).

147. *Id.* § 206.16 defines "person" to include corporations.

148. I.R.C. § 501(a), (c)(3).

149. MICH. COMP. LAWS ANN. § 206.201(1). See I.R.C. §§ 512(a)(1), 513(a) for the definition of "unrelated business taxable income."

150. MICH. COMP. LAWS ANN. § 205.291 (1970).

151. *Id.* § 205.202 (Supp. 1980).

152. *Id.* § 206.260(2) – (3).

153. *Id.* § 206.260(1).

154. *Id.* § 206.260(4).

155. *Id.* § 206.260(1).

156. MICH. CONST. art. 9, § 4 (1963).

157. MICH. COMP. LAWS ANN. § 211.7(d).

158. American Youth Found. v. Benona Twp., 154 N.W. 2d 554, 558–560 (Mich. App. 1967).

159. Ladies Literary Club v. Grand Rapids, 298 N.W. 2d 422, 425 (Mich. 1980) (see cases cited therein).

160. Engineering Society of Detroit v. City of Detroit, 308 Mich. 539, 550, 14 N.W. 2d 79, 83 (1944).

161. 11 Mich. App. 231, 160 N.W. 2d 778 (1968).

162. 160 N.W. 2d at 782.

163. *Id.*

164. 298 N.W. 2d 422, 426 (Mich. 1980).

165. 298 N.W. 2d at 425.

166. *Id.* at 426–427.

167. *Id.* at 426. Justice Williams, in a dissenting opinion, argued that the majority too narrowly construed the statute and thereby frustrated the legislative intent to promote the enumerated categories.

168. MICH. COMP. LAWS ANN. § 211.7(e) exempts: "Houses of public worship, with the land on which they stand, the furniture therein and all rights in the pews, and any parsonage owned by a religious society of this state and occupied as such. Houses of public worship includes buildings or other facilities owned by a religious society and used exclusively for religious services or for teaching the religious truths and beliefs of the society." Section 211.9 provides the personal property exemption corresponding to § 211.7(e).

169. Lake Louise Christian Community v. Township of Hudson, 10 Mich. App. 573, 581–82, 159 N.W. 2d 849, 854 (1968).

170. National Music Camp v. Green Lake Township, 76 Mich. App. 608, 257 N.W. 2d 188 (1977).

171. 257 N.W. 2d at 190.

172. MICH. COMP. LAWS ANN. § 211.9(a).

173. *Id.* §§ 205.131 to 205.144 (Supp. 1980).

174. *Id.* § 205.133(b)(1).

175. *Id.* § 205.133(b)(6).

176. *Id.* §§ 205.51 to 205.78 (1967 & Supp. 1980).

177. *Id.* § 205.54a(a) (Supp. 1980).

178. *Id.* § 205.54a(c) (Supp. 1980).

179. *Id.* § 205.91 to 205.111 (1967 & Supp. 1980).

180. Compare § 205.54a(a) (sales tax) with § 205.94(i) (use tax).

181. *Id.* §§ 208.1 to 208.145 (Supp. 1980).

182. *Id.* § 208.35(1)(c).

183. *Id.* §§ 400.271 to 400.294 (1976 & Supp. 1980).

184. *Id.* § 400.273 (1976).

185. *Id.* § 400.284 (1976).

186. *Id.* § 400.272(a) (Supp. 1980).

187. An official in the Charitable Trust Section of Michigan's Department of the Attorney General has stated: "Upon receipt of documentation of an organization's affiliation with a religious body, this office normally closes its file and informs the organization that it will not be required to secure a charitable solicitation license while such affiliation is in effect." Letter from Helen R. Bartlett, Administrator, Charitable Trust Section, to Center for Constitutional Studies, Notre Dame Law School (August 21, 1979).

188. MICH. COMP. LAWS ANN. § 283(d) (Supp. 1980).

189. Telephone conversation between Helen Bartlett, Administator, Charitable Trust Section, and Steven M. Zarowny, Center for Constitutional Studies, Notre Dame Law School (Aug. 15, 1979).

190. MICH. COMP. LAWS ANN. § 400.283(b) (Supp. 1980).

191. *Id.* §§ 432.101 to 432.120 (1978).

192. *Id.* § 432.103(6). " 'Educational organization' means . . . any private college, not for pecuniary profit, and approved by the state board of education." *Id.* § 432.103(1). " 'Religious organization' means an organization, church, body of communicants, or group, not for pecuniary profit . . . or a church related private school, not for pecuniary profit." *Id.* § 432.103(3). "School" usually refers to a primary or secondary educational institution rather than to a postsecondary institution.

31. Minnesota

1. MINN. STAT. ANN. §§ 317.01 *et seq.*

2. *Id.* § 317.02, subd. 5.

3. *Id.* § 317.07.

4. *Id.* § 317.10.

5. *Id.* § 317.14.

6. *Id.* §§ 317.19; 317.28.

7. *Id.* § 317.20.

8. *Id.* § 317.44.

9. *Id.*

10. *Id.* § 317.57.

11. *Id.* § 501.12 (Supp. 1981); see also In re Munson's Estate, 238 Minn. 358, 57 N.W. 2d 22 (1953).

12. Minn. Stat. Ann. § 136A.61.

13. *Id.* § 136A.63.

14. *Id.* § 136A.64.

15. *Id.*

16. *Id.* § 136A.69.

17. *Id.* § 136A.65.

18. *Id.*

19. *Id.* § 136A.68.

20. *Id.* § 136A.657, subd. 1.

21. *Id.* § 136A.657, subd. 2.

22. For a full discussion of Minnesota's aid programs, see A. E. Dick Howard, *State Aid to Private Higher Education* (Charlottesville, Va.: Michie, 1977), pp. 459–478.

23. Minn. Const. art. 1, § 16.

24. *Id.* art. 13, § 2.

25. Minn. Stat. Ann. §§ 136A.18 *et seq.* authorize the Minnesota Higher Education Coordinating Board to enter into contractual arrangements with private colleges in Minnesota for the purpose of furthering the education of state residents. At present, the Board can pay a college up to $500 for each full-time Minnesota student attending the college.

26. *Id.* § 136A.19, subd. 4.

27. *Id.*

28. *Id.*

29. *Id.* § 363.02, subd. 3(a).

30. See, e.g., Sweezy v. New Hampshire, 354 U.S. 234, 261–262 (1957) (Frankfurter, J., concurring).

31. See, e.g., Thomas I. Emerson, *The System of Freedom of Expression* (New York: Random House, 1970), pp. 593–626.

32. West Virginia State Bd. of Ed. v. Barnette, 319 U.S. 624 (1943); see also Engel v. Vitale, 370 U.S. 421 (1962); Abington Twp. School District v. Schempp, 374 U.S. 203 (1963).

33. See, e.g., Americans United for Separation of Church and State v. Bubb, 379 F. Supp. 872, 890 (D. Kan. 1974).

34. Minn. Stat. Ann. §§ 136A.25 *et seq.*

35. 403 U.S. 672 (1971).

36. 413 U.S. 734 (1973).

37. Minn. Stat. Ann. § 136A.28.

38. Minnesota Higher Education Facilities Authority v. Hawk, 232 N.W. 2d 106, 109, n. 13 (Minn. 1975).

39. *Id.*

40. See, e.g., Minn. Stat. Ann. § 136A.121

(scholarships); § 136A.121(2) (grants-in-aid on need basis); § 197.09(2) (tuition grants for dependents of prisoners of war); §§ 136A.143 *et seq.* (mitigation of tuition payment by foreign students); § 136A.16 (student loans and loan guarantees); § 136A.171 (loans for medical students agreeing to practice in rural Minnesota); and §§ 136A.232 *et seq.* (work study program).

41. See provisions cited in note 40, *supra.*

42. See, e.g., Smith v. Bd. of Governors, 429 F. Supp. 871 (W.D.N.C.), *summarily aff'd.*, 434 U.S. 803 (1977); and Americans United for Separation of Church and State v. Blanton, 433 F. Supp. 97 (M.D. Tenn), *summarily aff'd.*, 434 U.S. 803 (1977).

43. *Id.* §§ 363.01 *et seq.*

44. *Id.* § 363.01, subd. 15 (Supp. 1981) defines "employer" as "a person who has one or more employees."

45. *Id.* § 363.01, subd. 1 (Supp. 1981).

46. *Id.* § 363.01, subd. 21 (Supp. 1981).

47. *Id.*

48. *Id.* § 363.02, subd. 1 (Supp. 1981).

49. Section 702 of Title VII (42 U.S.C. 2000e-1) permits a religious educational institution to discriminate by religion in the employment of a person "connected with the carrying on [of] its activities." Section 703(e)(2) (42 U.S.C. 2000e-2(e)(2)) permits religious discrimination if an RAC is substantially controlled by a religious organization, or if its curriculum is "directed toward the propagation of a particular religion."

50. See Edward McGlynn Gaffney and Philip R. Moots, *The Government and the Campus: Federal Regulation of Religiously Affiliated Higher Education* (Notre Dame, Ind.: University of Notre Dame Press, 1981), pp. 44–49.

51. Minn. Stat. Ann. § 363.01, subd. 25 (Supp. 1981).

52. *Id.* §§ 363.04; 363.071; 363.072 (Supp. 1981).

53. *Id.* § 177.24 (Supp. 1981).

54. *Id.* § 177.25 (Supp. 1981).

55. *Id.* § 177.23 (Supp. 1981).

56. *Id.* § 181.67 (Supp. 1981).

57. *Id.* §§ 179.01 *et seq.*

58. *Id.* §§ 176.01 *et seq.* (1966, Supp. 1981).

59. *Id.* § 176.011(10).

60. *Id.* § 176.021 (Supp. 1981).

61. See Ward v. American Legion Edward B. Cutter Post 102, Anoka, 286 Minn. 81, 174 N.W. 2d 325 (1969).

62. Minn. Stat. Ann. § 176.041(1) (Supp. 1981). The casual employment exemption applies only when the employment is both casual and not in the usual course of the employer's business. Note that a nonprofit corporation not paying more than $500 in

salary a year is also exempt.

63. See *id.* § 176.012, 176.051 (Supp. 1983).
64. *Id.* § 176.031.
65. *Id.* § 176.181 (Supp. 1981).
66. *Id.* § 268.04 12. (Supp. 1981).
67. *Id.* §§ 268.011 *et seq.*
68. *Id.* § 268.04 12.(9).
69. *Id.* § 268.04 12.(9)(a).
70. *Id.* § 268.04 12.(9)(b).
71. *Id.* § 268.04 12.(10)(b).
72. *Id.*
73. *Id.* § 268.04 12.(10)(b).
74. *Id.* §§ 268.04 10.(17), 12.(14).
75. *Id.* § 268.04 12.(15)(g)(2).
76. *Id.* § 268.04 12.(15)(g)(3).
77. *Id.* § 268.04 12.(15)(f).
78. I.R.C. §§ 501(a), 521.
79. MINN. STAT. ANN. § 268.04 12.(15)(g)(1).
80. *Id.* §§ 268.04 10.(11), 268.11 3.
81. *Id.* § 268.11 3.(1), (2). Sections 268.011(1) and 268.012 provide the statutory authority for establishing the Department.
82. *Id.* § 363.03, subd. 5 (Supp. 1981).
83. *Id.*
84. *Id.* § 363.02, subd. 3 (Supp. 1981).
85. *Id.*
86. *Id.*
87. See, e.g., Southeastern Community College v. Davis, 442 U.S. 397 (1979) and University of Texas v. Camenisch, 451 U.S. 390 (1981); and see Gaffney and Moots, note 50, *supra*, pp. 123–133.
88. *Id.* § 363.02, subd. 3(a).
89. *Id.* § 363.03, subd. 3 (Supp. 1981).
90. *Id.* § 363.01, subd. 18 (Supp. 1981).
91. *Id.* § 363.02, subd. 4 (Supp. 1981).
92. *Id.* § 363.03, subd. 4a (Supp. 1981).
93. *Id.* § 363.03, subd. 2(1)(a) (Supp. 1981).
94. *Id.* § 363.03, subd. 2(1)(b) (Supp. 1981).
95. *Id.* § 363.02, subd. 2(a) (Supp. 1981).
96. *Id.* §§ 182.65 *et seq.* (Supp. 1981).
97. *Id.* § 182.651(7).
98. *Id.* § 182.651(9).
99. *Id.* § 182.652.
100. *Id.* § 182.651(10).
101. MINN. CONST. art. 10, § 1.
102. MINN. STAT. ANN. § 272.02.
103. *Id.* § 290.05, subd. 1 (Supp. 1981).
104. *Id.*
105. *Id.* § 297A.25, subd. 1 (Supp. 1981).
106. *Id.* § 291.05, subd. 1 (Supp. 1981).
107. *Id.* § 290.21, subd. 3 (Supp. 1981).
108. *Id.* § 309.515 (Supp. 1981).
109. *Id.* §§ 308.62–309.68 (Supp. 1981).
110. *Id.* § 349.
111. *Id.*
112. *Id.* § 349.26 (Supp. 1981).

32. Mississippi

1. MISS. CONST. art. 7, § 88; *id.* § 178.
2. *Id.* § 199. The establishment of *state* institutions of higher education is specifically provided for in the Mississippi Constitution. MISS. CONST. art. 8, § 213–A.
3. MISS. CODE ANN § 79–3–7.
4. *Id.* § 79–3–105.
5. *Id.* §§ 79–11–1 *et seq.*
6. *Id.* § 79–11–3.
7. *Id.* § 79–11–1.
8. *Id.* § 79–11–9.
9. *Id.* § 79–11–51 (Supp. 1981).
10. *Id.* § 79–11–31.
11. West v. State, 169 Miss. 302, 152 So.888 (1934).
12. People v. Enochs, 170 Miss.472, 153 So.796 (1934).
13. *Id.* § 79–11–31(1).
14. MISS. CODE ANN. § 75–71–51 (Supp. 1981).
15. *Id.* § 75–59–1.
16. *Id.* §§ 3.75–60–1 *et seq.* (Supp. 1981).
17. *Id.* § 75–60–5(f) (Supp. 1981).
18. *Id.* §§ 75–60–9 to 11 (Supp. 1981).
19. *Id.* §§ 37–17–7 *et seq.*
20. *Id.* § 37–101–241. There is a statutory exemption for private commercial schools. *Id.*
21. *Id.* § 37–101–1.
22. *Id.* §§ 79–11–1 *et seq.* (Supp. 1981).
23. See, e.g., Citizens' Nat'l. Bank v. Longshore, 304 So.2d 287 (Miss. 1974); for a discussion of the *cy pres* doctrine, *see* Chapter 1, "Corporate Status," *supra*.
24. MISS. CODE ANN. § 79–11–15.
25. *Id.*; see also *id.* § 79–11–23.
26. For a comprehensive treatment of Mississippi law governing aid to private education, see A.E. Dick Howard, *State Aid to Private Higher Education* (Charlottesville, Va.: Michie, 1977), pp. 479–491.
27. MISS. CONST. art. 8, § 200.
28. See State Teachers' College v. Morris, 165 Miss. 758, 144 So. 374 (1932).
29. MISS. CONST. art. 4, § 90(p).
30. *Id.* art. 4, § 95; see also art. 4, § 66, which prohibits donations or gratuity in favor of any person or object unless granted by the concurrence of two-thirds of each house of the legislature; and see art. 7, § 183, which prohibits municipalities from subscribing to any corporate stock or from making appropriations or lending their credit to a private corporation.
31. 209 Miss. 427, 45 So.2d 809 (1950).
32. *Id.* at 439, 45 So. 2d at 814.
33. See Craig v. Mercy Hosp.-St. Memorial, 209 Miss. at 451–452, 45 So. 2d at 820.

34. See, e.g., Lemon v. Kurtzman, 403 U.S. 602, 612–614 (1971). And see Kenneth F. Ripple, "The Entanglement Test of the Religion Clauses—A Ten Year Assessment," 27 U.C.L.A. L. REV. 1195 (1980).

35. See *Craig*, note 31, *supra.*, 209 Miss. at 451–452, 45 So. 2d at 820.

36. See, e.g., Craig v. North Miss. Community Hosp., 206 Miss. 11, 39 So. 2d 523 (1949).

37. MISS. CODE ANN. § 37–43–51.

38. Chance v. Miss. Textbook Rating & Purchase Bd., 190 Miss. 453, 200 So. 706 (1941).

39. The U.S. Supreme Court invalidated the loan of textbooks to students at racially segregated private schools, stating that the federal Establishment Clause permits a greater degree of state assistance to sectarian schools than may be given to private schools that engage in discriminatory practices. Norwood v. Harrison, 413 U.S. 455, 470 (1973).

40. MISS. CONST. art. 3, § 18. See Howard, *State Aid*, note 26, *supra.* at 485.

41. MISS. CONST. art. 4, § 66. See text at notes 27–33 *supra.*

42. MISS. CODE ANN. §§ 37–106–1 *et seq.* (Supp. 1981).

43. See *id.* § 37–106–5(b) (Supp. 1981).

44. *Id.* § 37–106–7 (Supp. 1981).

45. *Id.* § 37–106–21(3) (Supp. 1981).

46. *Id.* §§ 37–109–1 *et seq.*

47. *Id.* §§ 37–129–7 *et seq.*

48. *Id.* §§ 37–135–1 *et seq.*

49. Howard, *State Aid*, note 26, *supra.* at 489. See MISS. CODE ANN. § 37–135–1(c).

50. RACs in Mississippi must, of course, comply with relevant federal provisions banning unfair employment practices. See Edward McGlynn Gaffney and Philip R. Moots, *Government and Campus: Federal Regulation of Religiously Affiliated Higher Education* (Notre Dame, Ind.: University of Notre Dame Press, 1981), pp. 32–82.

51. MISS. CODE ANN. § 43–6–15 (Supp. 1981).

52. *Id.* § 79–1–11.

53. *Id.* § 71–1–21 (Supp. 1981).

54. *Id.* §§ 71–3–1 *et seq.* (Supp. 1981).

55. *Id.* §§ 71–3–3(d)(e), and 71–3–5 (Supp. 1981).

56. *Id.* § 71–3–7 (Supp. 1981).

57. *Id.* § 71–5–1 *et seq.* (Supp. 1981).

58. *Id.* § 71–5–11 I.(4) (Supp. 1981).

59. *Id.* § 71–5–11 I.(4)(a) (Supp. 1981). The definition of "employment" in the Federal Unemployment Tax Act is found at I.R.C. § 3306(c)(8).

60. MISS. CODE ANN. § 71–5–11 I.(4)(b) (Supp. 1981).

61. *Id.* § 71–5–11 I.(5)(a)(i) (Supp. 1981).

62. *Id.* § 71–5–11 I.(5)(a)(ii) (Supp. 1981).

63. *Id.* § 71–5–11 I.(5)(b) (Supp. 1981).

64. *Id.* § 71–5–11 I.(5)(c) (Supp. 1981).

65. *Id.* §§ 71–5–11 I.(7), 71–5–11 I.(15)(b) (Supp. 1981).

66. *Id.* § 71–5–11 I.(15)(h)(i) (Supp. 1981).

67. *Id.* § 71–5–11 I.(15)(h)(ii) (Supp. 1981).

68. *Id.* § 71–5–11 I.(15)(i) (Supp. 1981).

69. I.R.C. §§ 501(a) and 501(c)(3).

70. MISS. CODE ANN. § 71–5–11 I.(15)(g) (Supp. 1981).

71. *Id.* § 71–5–357 (Supp. 1981).

72. *Id.* § 71–5–357(a)(i) (Supp. 1981).

73. *Id.* § 71–5–357(a) (Supp. 1981).

74. *Id.* § 71–5–361(3)(a) (Supp. 1981).

75. MISS. CONST. art. 7, § 198–A.

76. MISS. CODE ANN. § 71–1–47.

77. MISS. CONST. art. 3, § 18.

78. MISS. CODE ANN. § 37–15–35.

79. *Id.* § 97–23–17.

80. *Id.* § 43–6–3 (Supp. 1981).

81. *Id.* § 43–6–5 (Supp. 1981).

82. *Id.* § 43–6–101 (Supp. 1981).

83. See text at notes 26 *et seq.*, *supra.*

84. MISS. CODE ANN. §§ 89–7–1 *et seq.*

85. *Id.* §§ 71–1–1 *et seq.* (Supp. 1981).

86. *Id.*

87. *Id.* §§ 45–11–21 to 27.

88. *Id.* §§ 45–11–29, 35.

89. *Id.* § 45–11–37.

90. *Id.* §§ 45–11–39 and 41.

91. *Id.* §§ 15–11–45 to 47.

92. *Id.* § 27–7–15(4)(f) (Supp. 1981).

93. *Id.* § 27–7–29(a)(3) (Supp. 1981).

94. *Id.* § 27–7–303(j)(1) to (4).

95. *Id.* § 27–13–63(c) (Supp. 1981).

96. *Id.* § 27–9–9(3).

97. *Id.* § 27–9–15(3).

98. *Id.* §§ 27–7–17(1)(h) (Supp. 1981).

99. *Id.* § 27–7–17(2)(b) (Supp. 1981).

100. *Id.* § 27–7–17(2)(a) (Supp. 1981).

101. I.R.C. § 170(e)(2)(B) and (C).

102. MISS. CODE ANN. § 27–31–1(d) (Supp. 1981). The property which a religious *society* may hold and own is limited. See *id.* § 79–11–33.

103. *Id.* § 27–31–1(d) (Supp. 1981).

104. See text at notes 10 *et seq.*, *supra.*

105. MISS. CODE ANN. § 27–31–1 (Supp. 1981).

106. Howard, *supra* note 26, at 485. But see Walz v. Tax Commission of City of New York, 397 U.S. 664 (1970).

107. MISS. CODE ANN. § 27–31–5 (Supp. 1981). Such theaters on RAC campuses may also be exempt under *id.* § 27–31–1(d) (Supp. 1981) in any event. See text at note 102, *supra.*

108. MISS. CODE ANN. § 27–37–1(d) (Supp. 1981).

109. *Id.* § 27–33–19(d).

110. *Id.* § 27–19–9(b) and (c).

111. *Id.* § 27–51–41 (Supp. 1981).

112. *Id.* § 27–65–111(g) (Supp. 1981).

113. *Id.* There is a parallel exemption for schools "supported wholly or in part" by state funds. *Id.* § 27–65–105(b) (Supp. 1981).

114. *Id.* § 27–65–105(f) (Supp. 1981).

115. *Id.* § 27–65–107(a) (Supp. 1981).

116. *Id.* § 27–65–111(b) (Supp. 1981).

117. *Id.* § 27–17–55.

118. *Id.* § 27–17–319 (Supp. 1981).

119. *Id.* § 27–11–43(a) and (b) (Supp. 1981).

120. *Id.* § 27–11–3 (Supp. 1981).

121. See *id.* §§ 97–33–1 *et seq.*

122. MISS. CONST. art. 4, § 98; MISS. CODE ANN. § 97–33–31.

123. MISS. CODE ANN. § 97–33–49 *et seq.* (Supp. 1981).

124. *Id.* § 23–3–27.

125. *Id.* § 23–1–55. This provision is constitutionally suspect after Buckley v. Valeo, 424 U.S. 1 (1976).

126. MISS. CODE ANN. §§ 37–135–1 *et seq.*

127. *Id.* § 37–135–11.

128. *Id.* § 37–101–187. This provision is constitutionally suspect after NAACP v. Alabama, 357 U.S. 449 (1958) and Gibson v. Florida Legislative Investigation Committee, 372 U.S. 539 (1963).

129. MISS. CODE ANN. § 79–11–33 (Supp. 1981).

130. *Id.* § 97–23–63.

131. See text at note 10, *supra.*

132. MISS. CODE ANN. § 97–5–11 (Supp. 1981).

133. *Id.* § 77–7–9.

134. *Id.* § 77–9–13.

135. *Id.* § 77–7–171.

136. *Id.* § 41–29–171.

137. *Id.* § 37–7–473.

138. *Id.* § 11–27–49.

139. *Id.* § 67–1–37.

140. *Id.* § 67–3–65.

141. *Id.* §§ 67–1–9; 97–31–33.

142. MISS. CONST. art. 14, § 269 (Repealed 1940).

143. *Id.* art. 14, § 270.

144. MISS. CODE ANN. § 91–5–31.

145. *Id.*

33. Missouri

1. MO. ANN. STAT. ch. 352. (Vernon 1966).

2. *Id.* §§ 409. 402(a)(9) (1979).

3. *Id.* ch. 352; *see id.* § 352.010.

4. *Id.* ch. 355; *see id.* § 355.500 (nothing contained in Missouri's general Not for Profit Corporation Law shall affect the right to organize a corporation under the chapter relating to religious and charitable associations).

5. *Id.* §§ 352.140 to 352.170, and 355.195 to 355.220.

6. *Id.* §§ 352.180 to 352.230 and 355.225 to 355.250.

7. See, e.g., Comfort v. Higgins, 576 S.W. 2d 331 (Mo. 1979), and Ramsey v. Field, 237 S.W. 2d 143 (Mo. 1915); for a discussion of the *cy pres* doctrine, see Chapter 1, "Corporate Status," *supra.*

8. MO. ANN. STAT. § 352.180; see also *id.* § 355.225 (two-thirds vote of the governing board needed to initiate voluntary dissolution).

9. *Id.* § 352.190; see also *id.* § 355.225.

10. *Id.* § 352.200; see McDaniel v. Frisco Emp. Hospital Ass'n., 510 S.W. 2d 752 (Mo. App. 1974).

11. MO. ANN. STAT. § 352.210.

12. *Id.* § 352.220.

13. *Id.* § 352.240; *see* also *id.* § 355.255.

14. *Id.* § 352.210; *see* also *id.* §§ 355.230, 355.235, and 355.245.

15. *Id.* § 355.230; *see* also *id.* § 352.210.

16. See also MO. CONST. art.1, § 7, providing that "no money shall ever be taken from the public treasury, *directly or indirectly,* in aid of any church, sect or denomination of religion, or in aid of any priest, preacher, minister or teacher thereof as such . . . " (emphasis added).

17. Poster v. Tussey, 512 S.W. 2d 97, *cert. denied,* 419 U.S. 1111 (Mo. 1974). Clearly, therefore, it would be well-nigh impossible for the state to grant any significant direct assistance, financial or in kind, to any RAC. Nonetheless, some indirect assistance is provided by state law.

18. *Id.* §§ 360.010 (Supp. 1981). *et seq.*

19. *Id.* § 360.145(7) (Supp. 1981).

20. *Id.* § 360.050 (Supp. 1981).

21. *Id.* § 360.100 (Supp. 1981).

22. *Id.* § 360.045(6) (Supp. 1981).

23. *Id.* § 360.015(3) (Supp. 1981).

24. § 360.045(7) (Supp. 1981).

25. § 360.045(15) (Supp. 1981).

26. MO. CONST. art. 3, § 38(a).

27. *Id.* art. 9, § 8.

28. See Americans United v. Rogers, 583 S.W. 2d 711, *cert. denied,* 429 U.S. 1029 (Mo. 1976).

29. MO. ANN. STAT. §§ 173.095 to 173.190 (Supp. 1981).

30. *Id.* § 173.100(4) (Supp. 1981) (emphasis added).

31. See id. § 173.170.1(1) through (12) (Supp. 1981).

32. *Id.* § 173.170.2 (Supp. 1981).

33. *Id.* §§ 173.200 through 173.230 (Supp. 1981).

34. *Id.* § 173.205.2(d) (Supp. 1981).

35. *Id.* § 173.205(2)(e) (Supp. 1981).

36. *Id.* § 173.205(2)(d) (Supp. 1981).

37. *Id.* § 173.215.1(6) (Supp. 1981).

38. Americans United v. Rogers, 538 S.W. 2d 711, *cert. denied*, 429 U.S. 1029 (Mo. 1976).

39. Mo. ANN. STAT. § 178.160 (Supp. 1981).

40. *Id.* § 296.020.1(1) (Supp. 1981). For regulations providing significant guidelines and interpretations regarding anti-discrimination laws, see generally 4 CSR 180-3.

41. *Id.* § 296.010(2) (Supp. 1981).

42. Regulations specify that for exemption under *id.* § 296.010(2), the "corporation or association must be one hundred percent (100%) owned and operated by a religious or sectarian group and being a member of that religion or sect must be a requirement for employment. . . . " See 4 CSR 180-3.010(9).

43. See Mo. REV. STAT. §§296.030 and 213.030. In *id.* § 296.030(1) (Supp. 1981), the Commission is empowered: "[t]o seek to eliminate and prevent discrimination in employment because of race, creed, color, religion, national origin, sex, ancestry, or handicap by employers or *other persons . . .* " (emphasis added).

44. See text accompanying notes 34 *et seq.*, *supra*.

45. For details see 4 CSR 180-3.050(1).

46. Mo. ANN. STAT. § 287 (1965, Supp. 1981).

47. *Id.* § 287.030.

48. *Id.* § 287.020.

49. *Id.* § 287.090.

50. *Id.*

51. *Id.* § 287.120.3.

52. *Id.* § 287.120.5.

53. *Id.* § 287.280.

54. *Id.* § 288.034.8 (Supp. 1981).

55. *Id.* § 288.034.9(1) (Supp. 1981).

56. *Id.* § 288.034.9(i) (Supp. 1981).

57. *Id.* § 288.034.9(7)(ii) (Supp. 1981).

58. *Id.* § 288.090.2 (Supp. 1981).

59. *Id.* § 288.090.3(1) (Supp. 1981).

60. Mo. CONST. art. IX, § 8.

61. Mo. ANN. STAT. § 314.030 (Supp. 1981).

62. *Id.* § 314.020 (Supp. 1981).

63. *Id.* § 314.020 (Supp. 1981).

64. *Id.* § 314.030.1 (Supp. 1981).

65. *Id.* § 213.105 (Supp. 1981).

66. *Id.* § 213.100(3) (Supp. 1981).

67. *Id.* § 213.100(4) (Supp. 1981).

68. See *id.* § 196.190 (1972).

69. *Id.* § 316.070 (1963).

70. *Id.* § 360.130 (Supp. 1981).

71. See *id.* §§ 441.500 *et seq.*

72. *Id.* § 292.010-.290.

73. *Id.* § 292.440.

74. *Id.* § 292.300.

75. *Id.* §§ 143.321, 143.441 (1976).

76. *Id.* § 145.100.

77. *Id.* § 145.011.

78. *Id.* § 143.171.

79. Mo. CONST. art. 10, § 6.

80. Mo. ANN. STAT. § 137.100.

81. *Id.* § 360.085 (Supp. 1981).

82. *Id.* § 144.030.2(19) and (20) (Supp. 1981).

83. *Id.*

84. *Id.* §§ 173.095 (Supp. 1981) *et seq.*

85. *Id.* § 173.105 (Supp. 1981).

86. *Id.* § 173.030(2) (Supp. 1981).

87. See text accompanying notes 34 *et seq.*, *supra*.

88. Omnibus State Reorganization Act of 1974, § 6.

89. *Id.* § 289.005.

34. Montana

1. MONT. REV. CODES ANN. §§ 35-2-101 *et seq.*

2. *Id.* §§ 35-3-101 *et seq.*

3. *Id.* § 35-3-201 ("bishop, chief priest or presiding elder").

4. *Id.* § 30-10-104(9).

5. *Id.*

6. *Id.*

7. *Id.* § 20-30-101.

8. *Id.* § 20-30-202.

9. *Id.* §§ 20-30-401 and 20-30-403.

10. *Id.* § 20-30-102(1).

11. *Id.* § 20-30-102(4).

12. *Id.* § 20-25-107(1).

13. *Id.* § 20-25-107(2).

14. *Id.* § 20-25-602.

15. *Id.* § 20-25-603.

16. *Id.* §§ 72-30-101 *et seq.*

17. *Id.* § 72-30-102(2).

18. *Id.* § 72-30-102(1).

19. Compare §§ 35-2-701 to 35-2-706 with §§ 45 to 50 of the Model Act.

20. MONT. REV. CODES ANN. § 35-2-701.

21. *Id.* §§ 35-2-702 and 35-2-703.

22. *Id.* §§ 35-2-705 and 35-2-706.

23. *Id.* § 35-2-702; see Model Act § 46.

24. MONT. CONST. art. X, § 6(1). This section does not apply to funds from federal sources provided to the state for distribution to nonpublic education. *Id.* art. X, § 6(2).

25. A.E. Dick Howard, *State Aid to Private Higher Education*, (Charlottesville, Va.: Michie, 1977), p. 516.

26. MONT. CONST. art. V, § 11.

27. MONT. REV. CODES ANN. § 20–25–801.

28. *Id.* § 20–25–801 (Art. VIII).

29. *Id.* § 20–25–803.

30. MONT. CONST. art. V, § 11(6).

31. MONT. REV. CODES ANN. § 20–2–402.

32. *Id.* § 20–2–403.

33. *Id.* § 2–15–15.

34. *Id.* §§ 20–26–1101 *et seq.*

35. *Id.* §§ 20–26–1102 and 1103.

36. *Id.* § 20–26–1102.

37. *Id.* § 20–26–1106.

38. *Id.* § 20–26–1101.

39. *Id.* §§ 20–26–101 *et seq.*

40. *Id.* § 20–26–103(2). The institution must be within Montana and "accredited or licensed under chapter 30 of this title [*id.* §§ 20–30–101 *et seq.*]." *Id.* § 20–26–103(2).

41. *Id.* § 20–26–201.

42. *Id.* § 20–26–202.

43. MONT. CONST. art. II, § 4.

44. MONT. REV. CODES ANN. § 49–2–303(1)(a). A separate provision makes termination and other conduct in connection with an employee's pregnancy unlawful. See *id.* § 39–7–203.

45. *Id.* (The prohibition applies when the "reasonable demands of the position do not require an age, physical or mental handicap, or sex distinction.") See also *id.* §§ 49–4–101 *et seq.*, prohibiting, under criminal and civil sanctions, employment discrimination against the physically handicapped unless "the handicap reasonably precludes the performance of the particular employment" or where the particular employment would endanger the handicapped person or his fellow employees. *Id.* § 49–4–101.

46. *Id.* § 49–2–303(1)(c).

47. *Id.* §§ 49–2–401 *et seq.*

48. *Id.* § 49–2–401.

49. *Id.* § 49–2–402.

50. *Id.* § 49–2–403.

51. *Id.* § 49–2–101(8).

52. *Id.* § 49–2–303(1)(a). See note 45, *supra.*

53. Provided for in *id.* § 2–15–1706. For its powers and procedures, see *id.* §§ 49–2–201 through 49–2–204 and §§ 49–2–501 through 49–2–508.

54. *Id.* § 49–2–601.

55. *Id.* §§ 39–1–101 *et seq.*

56. See e.g., Chapter 2 of the statute, §§ 39–2–101 *et seq.*, "The Employment Relationship."

57. *Id.* § 39–3–404.

58. *Id.* § 39–3–405. The overtime provision does not apply to employees subject to the provisions of Part I of the Interstate Commerce Act.

59. *Id.* § 39–3–406(a).

60. *Id.* § 39–3–406(e).

61. *Id.* § 39–3–406(j).

62. *Id.* §§ 39–71–101 *et seq.*

63. *Id.* § 39–72–117.

64. *Id.* §§ 39–71–401 and 39–71–118.

65. *Id.* § 39–71–401(2)(b). Casual employment means employment not in the usual course of the employer's business. *Id.* § 39–71–116(3).

66. *Id.* § 39–71–401(2)(f).

67. *Id.* § 39–710–401(2)(e).

68. *Id.* § 39–71–401(2).

69. *Id.* § 39–71–508.

70. *Id.* §§ 39–71–2201 *et seq.*

71. *Id.* §§ 39–71–2301 *et seq.*

72. *Id.* §§ 39–71–2101 *et seq.*

73. *Id.* § 39–51–203(6) (1979).

74. *Id.* § 31–51–101 *et seq.* (1979).

75. *Id.* § 31–51–204(3)(a) (1979).

76. *Id.*

77. *Id.* § 31–51–204(3)(b) (1979).

78. The current definition of "institution of higher education" appears at *id.* § 31–51–201(16) (1979).

79. *Id.* § 31–51–204(3)(c) (1979).

80. *Id.* §§ 31–51–204(1)(b), 31–51–203(9) (1979).

81. *Id.* § 31–51–204(1)(f) (1979).

82. *Id.* § 31–51–204(i) (1979).

83. *Id.* § 31–51–204(j) (1979).

84. This term is defined at *id.* § 39–51–201(11) (1979).

85. *Id.* § 39–51–1102 (1979).

86. To qualify as a nonprofit organization, the Montana statute requires that an organization fit the definition in I.R.C. § 501(c)(3) and qualify as tax-exempt under I.R.C. § 501(a). MONT. REV. CODES ANN. § 39–51–1103(4) (1979).

87. *Id.*

88. *Id.* § 39–51–1124(1) (1979).

89. *Id.* § 39–51–1125(1) (1979). A nonprofit organization making such an election may not be liable for payments with regard to services performed for a school which is not an institution of higher education. *Id.* § 39–51–1125(5) (1979).

90. *Id.* § 49–2–307(1). Related activities, e.g., in application forms or advertising, are also prohibited. See *id.* § 4–2–307(2) through (4). Sex discrimination is permitted for modesty or privacy, e.g., in lavatory facilities. *Id.* § 49–2–404.

91. *Id.* § 49–2–401.

92. *Id.* Presumably, exemptions are not to be lightly granted, since the section mandates strict construction and places on the petitioner the burden of demonstrating that the exemption should issue. *Id.*

93. Section 49–2–403, "Specific limits on

justification," seems to apply only to employment since it refers to "the nature of the service." See text at notes 50 *et seq.*, *supra*.

94. With regard to the visually handicapped, see also MONT. REV. CODES ANN. § 49–4–211.

95. *Id.* § 49–2–304(1). Related activities, e.g., with regard to advertising, are also prohibited. See *id.* § 49–2–304(2). Where reasonable grounds exist, presumably a "declaratory ruling" to that effect from the Commission for Human Rights is required. See *id.* §§ 49–2–401 *et seq.* and text at notes 91 *et seq.*, *supra*. Section 49–2–403(1), "Specific limits on justification," presumably applies only to employment cases. See note 93, *supra*.

96. For a long list of examples, see MONT. REV. CODES ANN. § 49–2–101(17).

97. *Id.*

98. For the exemption precedure, see note 95, *supra*.

99. MONT. REV. CODES ANN. § 49–2–305(1)(a). Related activities, e.g., with regard to advertising, are also prohibited. See *id.* § 49–2–305(1)(b) through (c).

100. See *id.* §§ 49–2–401 *et seq.*, and text at notes 91 *et seq.*, *supra*. (Section 49–2–403(1), "Specific limits on justification," presumably applies only to employment cases. See note 93, *supra*.) Indeed, the institution may in effect already have such an exemption in connection with the education discrimination law, see text at notes 90 *et seq.*, *supra*, or in connection with the public accommodations law, see text at notes 94 *et seq.*, *supra*.

101. *Id.* §§ 50–71–10 (1981) *et seq.* See also *id.* §§ 50–70–101 (1981) *et seq.*

102. *Id.* § 50–71–102 (1981).

103. *Id.* §§ 15–31–101 *et seq.*

104. *Id.* § 15–31–102(1)(d).

105. *Id.* § 15–31–102(3).

106. *Id.* § 72–16–312.

107. *Id.* § 72–16–901 *et seq.*

108. *Id.* §§ 15–30–101 *et seq.*

109. See *id.* § 15–30–122.

110. *Id.* § 15–30–121(1). See I.R.C. § 161.

111. I.R.C. § 170(c)(2)(B) and (C).

112. MONT. REV. CODES ANN. §§ 15–31–101 *et seq.*

113. MONT. CONST. art. 8, § 5.

114. MONT. REV. CODES ANN. § 15–6–201.

115. MONT. CONST. art. 3, § 9.

116. See e.g., MONT. REV. CODES ANN. §§ 23–5–102 *et seq.*, and §§ 23–5–203 *et seq.*

117. *Id.* §§ 23–5–301 *et seq.* For licensing, prize limits and other restrictions, see *id.*

118. *Id.* §§ 23–5–401 *et seq.* For licensing, prize

limits and other restrictions, see *id.*

119. *Id.* §§ 23–5–501 *et seq.* For licensing, prize limits and other restrictions, see *id.* Winners of a sports pool "shall receive a 100% payout of the value of the sports pool." *Id.* § 23–5–503.

120. *Id.* § 3–15–311.

121. MONT. CONST. art. 13, § 6.

35. Nebraska

1. NEB. REV. STAT. §§ 21–1901 *et seq.*

2. *Id.* § 21–1903.

3. *Id.* § 85–1105 (Supp. 1980); *id.* § 85–1111 (Supp. 1980).

4. *Id.*

5. *Id.* § 8–1110(9) (Supp. 1980).

6. *Id.* §§ 21–1937 to 1961.

7. See, e.g., Rohlff v. Gunman Old People's Home, 143 Neb. 636, 10 N.W. 2d 686 (1943), and In Re Nilson's Estate, 81 Neb. 809, 116 N.W. 971 (1908). For a discussion of the *cy pres* doctrine, see Chapter 1, "Corporate Status," *supra*.

8. NEB. REV. STAT. §§ 21–1944 to 21–1949.

9. NEB. REV. STAT. § 21–1945. See Model Act, § 46, and discussion in Chapter 1, "Corporate Status," *supra*.

10. For an excellent and thorough discussion, see A. E. Dick Howard, *State Aid to Private Higher Education* (Charlottesville, Va.: Michie, 1977), pp. 521–536.

11. NEB. CONST. art. I, § 4.

12. *Id.*

13. *Id.* art. XIII, § 3.

14. *Id.* art. VII, § 11. The legislature may authorize the state or its subdivisions to contract with institutions not wholly owned or controlled by the state to provide nonsectarian educational or other services for certain handicapped children. *Id.*

15. State ex rel. Rogers v. Swanson, 192 Neb. 125, 219 N.W. 2d 726 (1974). For details, see Howard, *State Aid,* note 10, *supra,* at 521–536.

16. *Id.* at 535.

17. NEB. REV. STAT. §§ 85–980 *et seq.*

18. *Id.* § 85–981. See text at note 127 *et seq.*, *infra*.

19. *Id.* § 85–984 (Supp. 1980). For details, see *id.*

20. *Id.* § 85–991 (Supp. 1980).

21. *Id.* § 85–994(1) (Supp. 1980).

22. *Id.* § 85–994(2)(b) (Supp. 1980).

23. *Id.* § 85–994(4) (Supp. 1980).

24. *Id.* § 85–994(3) (Supp. 1980). Grants are made for a one-year period, *id.* § 85–995 (Supp.

1980), but a student may presumably receive several consecutive grants.

25. *Id.* § 85–994(7) (Supp. 1980). For details regarding eligibility, see *id.* § 85–994 (Supp. 1980).

26. For its powers and duties, see *id.* § 85–999 (Supp. 1980).

27. *Id.* § 72–1246.01. For details, see *id. et seq.*

28. NEB. CONST. art. XIII, § 3. See text at note 13, *supra.*

29. *Id.* § 79–321.01.

30. *Id.* § 17–572.

31. *Id.* §§ 48–1101 *et seq.*

32. "Employer" includes any person employing fifteen or more individuals for twenty or more consecutive weeks in the current or preceding calendar year. For details, see *id.* § 48–1102(2) (Supp. 1980).

33. NEB. REV. STAT. § 48–1104(1).

34. *Id.* § 48–1108(1).

35. *Id.*

36. *Id.* §§ 48–1001 *et seq.*

37. *Id.* § 48–1004.

38. §§ 48–1117 (Supp. 1980) and 48–1007. For composition, powers and duties, see *id.* §§ 48–1116 *et seq.* and *id.* § 48–1007.

39. *Id.* §§ 48–1201 *et seq.*

40. *Id.* § 48–1203(3)(e).

41. *Id.* §§ 348–101 *et seq.* (1978, Supp. 1979).

42. *Id.* §§ 48–109 and 48–110.

43. *Id.* § 48–112.

44. *Id.* § 48–111 (Supp. 1979).

45. *Id.* § 48–114.

46. *Id.* § 48–106.

47. *Id.* § 48–115(2) (Supp. 1979).

48. *Id.* §§ 48–103 and 48–111.

49. *Id.* § 48–152 (Supp. 1979).

50. *Id.* § 48–145.

51. *Id.* § 48–145(1)(b).

52. NEB. REV. STAT. §§ 48–601 *et seq.* (Supp. 1980).

53. For the general definition of "employment," see *id.* § 48–604.

54. *Id.* §§ 48–603(9), 48–604(4)(b).

55. *Id.* § 48–604(4)(b)(1).

56. *Id.* § 48–604(4)(b)(2).

57. *Id.* § 48–604(6)(g)(1).

58. *Id.*

59. *Id.* § 48–604(6)(g)(2).

60. *Id.* § 48–604(6)(g)(3). "Institution of higher education" is defined at *id.* § 48–602(11).

61. *Id.* § 48–604(6)(j)(1).

62. *Id.* § 48–604(6)(j)(2). Spouses must be informed that employment is provided as a means of financial aid and that they are not covered by any program of unemployment insurance.

63. *Id.* § 48–604(6)(o).

64. *Id.* § 48–604(6)(h).

65. I.R.C. §§ 501(a), 521.

66. NEB. REV. STAT. § 48–604(6)(i).

67. *Id.* §§ 48–604(4)(d), (6)(b).

68. *Id.* § 48–660.01. Nonprofit organizations must meet the requirements of section 48–603(9) in order to take advantage of this option. *Id.* § 48–660.01. A reimbursement account is set up for each organization making payments in lieu of contributions. *Id.* § 48–652(1)(b).

69. *Id.* § 48–660.01(1)(a), (b).

70. *Id.* §§ 48–660.01(1), (2), (4).

71. *Id.* § 48–661.

72. *Id.* §§ 48–801 (Supp. 1980).

73. *Id.* § 48–801(4) (Supp. 1980).

74. *Id.* §§ 48–209 *et seq.*

75. *Id.* § 48–221.

76. *Id.* § 48–217.

77. *Id.* § 20–132.

78. *Id.* § 20–143.

79. *Id.* § 20–137.

80. See generally *id.* § 20–133.

81. *Id.* § 20–107 (Supp. 1980).

82. *Id.* §§ 20–105 *et seq.*

83. *Id.* § 20–110 (Supp. 1980).

84. *Id.* § 20–127.

85. *Id.* § 20–131.01.

86. *Id.* § 20–131.03.

87. *Id.* § 41–108.

88. *Id.* §§ 76–1401 *et seq.*, *id.* § 24–568.

89. *Id.* § 76–1408(1).

90. *Id.* § 48–412.

91. *Id.* § 48–414 (Supp. 1980).

92. *Id.* § 48–106.

93. See I.R.C. § 501(c)(3).

94. NEB. REV. STAT. §§ 77–2714 *et seq.*

95. *Id.* § 77–2714.

96. *Id.* §§ 77–2001 *et seq.*

97. *Id.* § 77–2007.04. Gifts or bequests to a trustee for the use of such an RAC are also exempt. *Id.*

98. *Id.* § 77–2007.04(3). For details, see *id.*

In a related provision, such gifts and bequests to RACs are assured validity despite indefinite designation of the beneficiary. *Id.* § 20–239. Under this section of the state code, title will vest in the district court of the proper county if no trustee is named in the transferring instrument. *Id.* The court is then empowered to appoint a trustee of the property and to make any orders or decrees necessary to carry out the benevolent purposes of the gift or bequest. *Id.*; *id.* § 20–240.

99. *Id.* § 77–2101.01 (Supp. 1980). For details, see *id.*

100. *Id.* § 77–2715 (Supp. 1980).

101. I.R.C. § 170(e)(2)(B) and (C).

102. See NEB. REV. STAT. § 77–2734(2). See also *id.* § 77–2734(1).

103. NEB. CONST. art. VIII, § 2.

104. NEB. REV. STAT. § 77–202(1)(c) (Supp. 1980).

105. Lincoln Women's Club v. City of Lincoln, 178 Neb. 357, 133 N.W. 2d 455 (1965).

106. Nebraska Conf. Ass'n Seventh Day Adventists v. County of Hall, 166 Neb. 588, 90 N.W. 2d 50 (1958).

107. Lincoln Women's Club v. City of Lincoln, 178 Neb. 357, 133 N.W. 2d 455 (1965).

108. NEB. REV. STAT. § 77–2715. See text at note 93 *et seq., supra.*

109. *Id.* § 77–2704(1)(i) (Supp. 1980).

110. *Id.*

111. *Id.*

112. *Id.* § 77–2704(1)(g)(i) (Supp. 1980).

113. *Id.* §§ 28–1440 *et seq.*

114. *Id.* § 28–1440.

115. *Id.*

116. *Id.* § 28–1446.

117. *Id.* §§ 28–1102 *et seq.*

118. *Id.* § 9–126 (Supp. 1980).

119. *Id.* § 9–141 (Supp. 1980).

120. *Id.*

121. *Id.* §§ 9–124 (Supp. 1980) *et seq.*

122. *Id.* § 9–127 (Supp. 1980).

123. *Id.* § 9–172 (Supp. 1980).

124. *Id.* § 28–1115.

125. *Id.* §§ 28–1115 *et seq.*

126. *Id.* § 79–2501.

127. *Id.* § 85–901.

128. *Id.* § 85–902.

129. *Id.* § 85–902(b). For its powers and duties, see *id.* § 85–910 (Supp. 1980).

130. *Id.* § 53–124(5)(A).

36. Nevada

1. NEV. REV. STAT. § 81.290.

2. *Id.* § 81.290.

3. *Id.* § 81.290(1)(b).

4. *Id.* § 81.290(2).

5. *Id.* § 81.310.

6. *Id.* § 81.310(9).

7. *Id.* § 394.450–460.

8. *Id.* § 385.102.

9. *Id.* §§ 81.010 *et seq.*

10. *Id.* §§ 81.290 *et seq.*

11. *Id.* §§ 81.140 (dissolution of nonprofit cooperative corporations), 81.280 (dissolution of cooperative associations), and 81.520 (dissolution of nonstock, nonprofit cooperative corporations).

12. *Id.* § 81.310(3).

13. *Id.* § 81.310.

14. *Id.* § 81.310(3).

15. *Id.* § 81.340.

16. NEV. CONST. art. 11, § 10.

17. See State ex rel. Nevada Orphan Asylum v. Hallock, 16 Nev. 373 (1882).

18. 1974 Op. Atty. Gen. 158.

19. Everson v. Board of Education, 330 U.S. 1 (1947).

20. Cochran v. Board of Education, 281 U.S. 371 (1930).

21. 1974 Op. Atty. Gen. 158.

22. *Id.*

23. NEV. CONST. art. 8, §§ 8,9.

24. See text accompanying notes 16 through 22, *supra.*

25. NEV. CONST. art. 8, §§ 8,9.

26. Nor would such aid seem to violate the Article 11, § 10 prohibition against aid for sectarian purposes. See text accompanying notes 16 through 22, *supra.*

27. NEV. STAT. ANN. § 385.102–106.

28. *Id.* § 385.104.

29. *Id.* § 385.102.

30. *Id.* § 385.104(3).

31. *Id.* § 613.330(1).

32. *Id.* § 613.310(1).

33. The only mention of clubs in I.R.C. § 501(c) is in part (F), which refers to nonprofit pleasure and recreational clubs. Since the Nevada legislature did not refer specifically to § 501(c)(F) and chose to create its own phrase rather than borrow the Internal Revenue Code language, it is possible that the intent was to exempt all § 501(c) organizations including RACs under § 501(c)(3). But, in view of the "private membership" description, this interpretation seems unlikely.

34. NEV. REV. STAT. § 613.320.

35. *Id.* § 613.350(1). There is a BFOQ provision as well with regard to hiring discrimination on the basis of a physical or visual handicap. *Id.* at § 613.350(2).

36. *Id.* § 613.350(3).

37. *Id.* § 613.405.

38. [1977] 8A Lab. Rel. Rep. (BNA) 455:2351.

39. NEV. REV. STAT. § 608.010(2).

40. *Id.* § 608.250(4).

41. *Id.* § 608.018.

42. *Id.* § 616.395.

43. *Id.* § 616.

44. *Id.* § 616.060.

45. *Id.* § 616.090(2).

46. *Id.* § 612.121.1.

47. *Id.* § 612.121.2.

48. The definition of total and partial unemployment is left to the director. *Id.* § 612.185.

49. *Id.* § 612.118. For details, see *id.*

50. *Id.* § 612.119.1.

51. *Id.* § 612.119.2.

52. *Id.* § 651.070.

53. *Id.* § 651.050.

54. *Id.* § 118.010–.120.

55. *Id.* § 118.020.

56. *Id.* § 118.100 (emphasis added).

57. *Id.* § 118.080(2).

58. *Id.* § 118A.

59. *Id.* § 118A.180(2)(d).

60. *Id.* § 338.180.

61. *Id.* § 338.180(1)(b).

62. *Id.* § 338.180(3).

63. *Id.* § 618.315(2).

64. Nev. Const. art. 10, § 1.

65. *Id.* art. 8, § 2 (emphasis added).

66. Nev. Stat. Ann. § 361.140.

67. *Id.* §§ 374, 330, 375, 325.

68. See, e.g., *id.* § 463.011.

69. *Id.* § 78.790.

70. *Id.* § 81.630.

71. "Charitable organization" is not defined in *id.* § 86, but is defined earlier in *id.* § 81.590 so as to include RACs. See text accompanying note 85, *infra.*

72. *Id.* § 86.190.

73. See note 71, *supra.*

74. *Id.* § 466.

75. *Id.* § 466.160.

76. See, e.g., *id.* § 463.011.

77. *Id.* § 466.

78. *Id.* § 463.011.

79. *Id.* § 463.409.

80. See text accompanying notes 16 and 17, *supra.*

81. Nev. Rev. Stat. § 241.020.

82. *Id.* § 81.550–660.

83. *Id.* § 163.430–550.

84. *Id.* § 81.560; *Id.* § 163.430.

85. *Id.* § 81.590.

86. See note 33, *supra.*

87. Nev. Rev. Stat. § 81.630; *id.* § 163.520.

37. New Hampshire

1. N.H. Rev. Stat. Ann. § 292.

2. *Id.* at § 292:8–C.

3. *Id.* § 292.1 *et seq.* (1977, Supp. 1979).

4. *Id.* § 498.4c (Supp. 1979); Attorney General v. Rochester Trust Company, 115 N.W. 74, 333 A.2d 718 (1975).

5. N.H. Rev. Stat. Ann. § 292.9.

6. *Id.* § 292.10.

7. *Id.* § 292.10–a (Supp. 1979).

8. *Id.* § 292.10–a (Supp. 1979).

9. *Id.* § 292.8–1.

10. *Id.* § 195–D.

11. *Id.* § 195–D:5 (XII).

12. *Id.* § 195–D:5 (XVII) (Supp. 1979).

13. *Id.* § 195–D:3 (V).

14. *Id.* § 195–D:4.

15. *Id.* § 195–D:5 (VIII).

16. *Id.* § 195–D:5.

17. *Id.* § 91–A.

18. N.H. Const. pt. 2, art. 83.

19. N.H. Rev. Stat. Ann. § 195–D:24.

20. *Id.* § 195–D:11.

21. Nohrr v. Brevard County Educational Facilities Authority, 247 So. 2d 304 (Fla. 1971).

22. N.H. Rev. Stat. Ann. § 195–D:3 (V).

23. N.H. Const. part. 2, art. 83.

24. *Id.*

25. See Opin. of the Justices, 99 N.H. 519, 113 A.2d 114 (1955).

26. N.H. Rev. Stat. Ann. § 200–D.

27. *Id.* § 200–D:1.

28. *Id.* § 200–D:4.

29. *Id.* § 200–D:10.

30. *Id.* § 200–D:7.

31. *Id.* § 186:54–57.

32. *Id.* § 186:55.

33. *Id.* § 186:55 (I).

34. *Id.* § 186:54.

35. *Id.* § 200–J (Supp. 1979).

36. *Id.* § 200–J:2 (Supp. 1979).

37. *Id.* § 200–J:2(I) (Supp. 1979).

38. *Id.* § 326–B:20 (Supp. 1979).

39. *Id.*

40. N.H. Const. pt. 1, art. 2.

41. N.H. Rev. Stat. Ann. § 354–A.

42. *Id.* § 354–A:1 (Supp. 1976).

43. *Id.* § 354–A:3(4).

44. *Id.* § 354–A:8(I) (Supp. 1979).

45. *Id.* § 354–A:8(III) (Supp. 1979).

46. *Id.* § 354–A:3(5).

47. *Id.*

48. *Id.* § 275:37.

49. *Id.* § 375:36.

50. *Id.* § 279.

51. *Id.* § 275:15.

52. *Id.* § 281:2(I) (1977).

53. *Id.* § 281:9.

54. *Id.* § 281:2(V).

55. *Id.* § 281:15.

56. *Id.* § 281:13.

57. *Id.* § 282 (1978).

58. *Id.* § 282.1(H)(4)(s)(1). The organization must be one described in section 501(c)(3) of the Internal Revenue Code and exempt under section

501(a) of that Code. For details, see *id.*

59. *Id.* § 282.1(H)(4)(s)(2).

60. *Id.* § 282.6.

61. *Id.*

62. *Id.* §§ 282.3 and 282.4.

63. *Id.* § 282.3.F. (Supp. 1979). For details, see *id.*

64. *Id.* § 282.1(H)(3) & (4).

65. *Id.* § 282.1(H)(4)(h)(1).

66. *Id.* § 282.1(H)(4)(h)(2). For details, see *id.*

67. *Id.* § 354–A.

68. *Id.* § 354–A:8 (V–a) (Supp. 1979); *id.* § 354A:8(IV) (Supp. 1979).

69. *Id.* § 354–A:8(IV) (Supp. 1979).

70. *Id.* § 354–A:8(V) (Supp. 1979).

71. See text accompanying note 73 *et seq., infra.*

72. See text accompanying note 46 *et seq., supra.*

73. See text accompanying note 68 *et seq., supra.*

74. N.H. Rev. Stat. Ann. § 354–A:3(9).

75. *Id.* § 354–A:3(10).

76. *Id.* § 277.

77. *Id.* § 277:1.

78. *Id.* at § 72:23(IV) (Supp. 1979).

79. *Id.*

80. *Id.* § 77:8.

81. *Id.* § 86:6(II)(e).

82. *Id.* § 88–A:1 (1959).

83. *Id.* § 78–A:3(III)(c).

84. *Id.* § 78–A:3(X)(c)(1), 2 and 7.

85. *Id.* § 31–91.

86. *Id.* § 320:20.

87. See, e.g., the employment discrimination statute discussed in text accompanying note 47, *supra.*

88. *Id.* § 287.

89. *Id.* § 287:7.

90. *Id.*

91. *Id.* § 287:1(II).

92. *Id.* § 287:2.

93. *Id.* § 287:3.

94. For discussion of a similar limitation in connection with charitable solicitations, see text accompanying note 86 *et seq., supra.*

95. *Id.* § 287–A.

96. *Id.* § 287–A:1(II).

97. *Id.*

98. *Id.* § 287–A:7.

99. *Id.* § 287–D:1(II).

100. I.R.C. § 4057(6).

101. *Id.* § 501(c)(3) (emphasis added).

102. N.H. Rev. Stat. Ann. § 287–D:5(I).

38. New Jersey

1. N.J. Stat. Ann. §§ 15.1–1 *et seq.* (Supp. 1980) (West).

2. *Id.* § 18A:68–3.

3. 482 F. Supp. 968 (D.N.J. 1980), *aff'd on other grounds,* 654 F.2d 868 (3d Cir. 1981).

4. 482 F. Supp. at 979.

5. New Jersey State Bd. of Higher Education v. Bd. of Directors of Shelton College (Super. Ct. Cape May Co., Chancery Div., Docket No. C–1088–79E, Nov. 1980).

6. New Jersey–Philadelphia Presbytery of the Bible Presbyterian Church v. New Jersey State Bd. of Higher Education, 514 F. Supp. 506, 515 (D.N.J. 1981).

7. New Jersey Board of Higher Education v. Bd. of Directors of Shelton College, 90 N.J. 470, 448 A.2d 988, 989 (1982).

8. N.J. Stat. Ann. § 15.1–17.

9. *Id.* § 15.14–4.

10. *Id.* § 15.14–1 (Supp. 1980).

11. *Id.* § 15.14–3 (Supp. 1980).

12. *Id.* § 15.14–5 (Supp. 1980).

13. *Id.* § 15.1–20.

14. Howard Savings Institution of Newark, New Jersey v. Peep, 34 N.J. 494, 170 A.2d 39 (1961); see also Howard Savings Institution v. Trustees of Amhearst College, 61 N.J. Super 119, 160 A.2d 177 (1960).

15. Higher Education Facilities Act of 1963, 20 U.S.C. §§ 781 *et seq.*

16. 1965 Op. Atty. Gen. No. 2. For an excellent discussion of New Jersey aid to independent colleges, see A. E. Dick Howard, *State Aid to Private Higher Education* (Charlottesville, Va.: Michie, 1977), pp. 570–595.

17. N.J. Stat. Ann. § 18A:72A–1 (1968).

18. *Id.* § 18A:72A–3.

19. 403 U.S. 672 (1971).

20. N.J. Stat. Ann. § 18A:72A–3.

21. 52 N.J. 138, 244 A.2d 281 (1968), 56 N.J. 523, 267 A.2d 503 (1970), vacated, 403 U.S. 945, on remand, 59 N.J. 583, 285 A.2d 11 (1971).

22. 1977 Op. Atty. Gen. No. 21.

23. Independent College and University Assistance Act of 1979, N.J. Stat. Ann. §§ 18A:72B–15 *et seq.* (Supp. 1980).

24. *Id.* § 18A:72B–16.

25. *Id.* § 18A:72B–17(2).

26. *Id.* § 18A:72B–18.

27. *Id.* § 18A:62–2 (1968).

28. *Id.* § 18A:3–6.

29. *Id.* §§ 18A:71–26.1 *et seq.* (Supp. 1980).

30. *Id.* § 18A:71–26.5.

31. *Id.* § 18A:71–10 (repealed).

32. *Id.* § 18A:71–7.2.

33. *Id.* §§ 18A:71–28 *et seq.*

34. *Id.* § 18A:71–31.

35. *Id.* §§ 18A:71–37 and 71–38.

36. *Id.* §§ 18A:71–41 *et seq.*
37. *Id.* § 18A:71–47.
38. *Id.*
39. *Id.*
40. *Id.* § 18A:71–62.
41. *Id.* §§ 18A:71–64 *et seq.*
42. *Id.* §§ 18A:72–1 *et seq.*
43. *Id.* § 18A:72–10 (Supp. 1980).
44. *Id.* §§ 18A:68–11 *et seq.* (Supp. 1980).
45. *Id.* §§ 10:5–1 *et seq.*
46. *Id.* § 10:5–5(e) (1976).
47. *Id.* § 10:5–5(e) (Supp. 1980).
48. *Id.* § 10:5–12(a).
49. *Id.* § 10:5–12(c).
50. *Id.* § 10:5–4 (Supp. 1980).
51. *Id.* § 10:5–5(q) (Supp. 1980).
52. See Edward M. Gaffney and Philip R. Moots, *Government and the Campus: Federal Regulation of Religiously Affiliated Higher Education* (Notre Dame, Ind.: University of Notre Dame Press, 1981), pp. 123–133.
53. N.J. STAT. ANN. § 34:11–56.2.
54. *Id.* § 34:11–56.1.
55. *Id.* § 34:11–56a4 (Supp. 1980).
56. *Id.* § 34:11–56al(g) (Supp. 1980).
57. *Id.* § 34:11–56a4 (Supp. 1980).
58. *Id.* § 34:11–4.2 (Supp. 1980).
59. *Id.* §§ 34:15–1 *et seq.* (1959, Supp. 1980).
60. *Id.* § 34:15–7 (Supp. 1980).
61. *Id.* § 34:15–9.
62. *Id.* § 34–15–36 (Supp. 1980). "Casual employment . . . shall be defined, if in connection with the employer's business, as employment the occasion for which arises by chance or is purely accidental; or if not in connection with any business of the employer, as employment not regular, periodic or recurring."
63. *Id.* § 34:15–1.
64. *Id.* §§ 34:15–71, 34:15–72, 34:15–77 (Supp. 1980).
65. *Id.* §§ 43:21–1 *et seq.* (Supp. 1980).
66. The definition of "employment" is found at *id.* § 43:21–19(i).
67. The statute refers to a "religious, charitable, educational or other organization." *Id.* § 43:21–19(i)(1)(C).
68. *Id.*
69. *Id.* § 43:21–19(i)(1)(D)(i)(I).
70. *Id.* § 43:21–19(i)(1)(D)(i)(II).
71. *Id.* § 43:21–19(i)(1)(D)(ii).
72. *Id.* § 43:21–19(i)(7)(T)(i). This exemption applies when the student is attending school fulltime or "completing such educational program leading to a degree at any of the several recognized levels." *Id.*
73. *Id.* § 43:21–19(i)(7)(T)(ii). Spouses must be informed that employment is provided as a means of financial aid and that they are not covered by any program of unemployment insurance.
74. *Id.* § 43:21–19(i)(7)(U).
75. *Id.* §§ 43:21–19(i)(1)(J), (i)(7)(B).
76. *Id.* § 43:21–7.2(a).
77. *Id.* §§ 43:21–7.2(a)(2), (a)(3).
78. *Id.* § 43:21–7.2(a)(1).
79. *Id.* § 43:21–7.2(h).
80. *Id.* § 43:21–8(C)(1).
81. *Id.* § 10:5–12(f) (Supp. 1980).
82. *Id.* § 10:1–3 (Supp. 1980); see also *id.* § 10:5–5L.
83. *Id.*
84. *Id.* §§ 18A:71–26.7 and 71–45 (Supp. 1980).
85. *Id.* § 10:5–4.
86. *Id.* § 10:5–5L.
87. *Id.* § 10:5–5n (Supp. 1980).
88. 45 N.J. 301, 308, 212 A.2d 345, 353 (1977).
89. N.J. STAT. ANN. §§ 55:13A–1 *et seq.* (Supp. 1981); see Blair Academy v. Sheehan, 149 N.J. Super. 113, 373 A.2d 418 (1977).
90. N.J. STAT. ANN. §§ 55:13B–1 *et seq.* (Supp. 1981).
91. *Id.* §§ 34:6A–1 *et seq.* (Supp. 1981).
92. *Id.* § 34:6A–22 (Supp. 1981).
93. *Id.* §§ 54A:1–1 *et seq.* (Supp. 1981).
94. *Id.* § 54A:5–1(b) (Supp. 1981).
95. *Id.* § 54A:1–2(1); see also *id.* § 54:8A–8 (definition of "taxpayer" for purposes of commuters' income tax explicitly excludes corporations).
96. *Id.* § 54:34–4(d) (Supp. 1981).
97. *Id.*
98. N.J. CONST. art. 8, § 1, par. 2.
99. N.J. STAT. ANN. § 54:32B–9.
100. *Id.*
101. *Id.*
102. *Id.* § 54A:3–1.1 (Supp. 1981).
103. *Id.* § 54A:6–8 (Supp. 1981).
104. *Id.* § 45:17A3. For a comprehensive analysis of governmental regulation of fund raising, see Bruce R. Hopkins, *Charity Under Siege* (New York: John Wiley and Sons, 1980).
105. N.J. STAT. ANN. § 45:17A5(a) exempts religious corporations and "other religious agencies and organizations operated, supervised or controlled by or in connection with such a religious organization" from registration requirements. *Id.* § 45:17A5(b)(1) exempts educational institutions that are accredited or that confine solicitations to the student body, alumni, faculty, and trustees and their families.
106. *Id.* § 45:16A6; only organizations registered pursuant to *id.* § 45:17A4 are penalized for failure to file reports. Section 45:17A5 exempts RACs from registration requirements.
107. *Id.* § 45:17A8(a).

108. *Id.* § 45:17A–15.
109. *Id.* § 45:17A–14.
110. *Id.* §§ 5:8–24 *et seq.*
111. *Id.* § 5:8–30.
112. *Id.* § 5:8–49.9. The Commission, a state administrative agency, makes rules and regulations and hears appeals. *Id.* § 5:8–39.
113. *Id.* § 5:8–25.
114. *Id.* § 5:8–26. Applications must include information regarding the nature of the charitable organization, the places and dates games are to be held, the items of expense intended to be incurred, and the purposes to which net proceeds will be directed, and must verify prizes, salaries, and compensation.
115. *Id.* § 5:8–49.3.
116. *Id.* § 5:8–27.
117. *Id.* § 5:8–35.
118. *Id.* § 5:8–35.
119. *Id.* § 5:8–33.
120. *Id.* § 5:8–32.
121. *Id.* § 5:8–36.
122. *Id.* § 5:8–29.
123. *Id.* § 5:8–37.
124. *Id.* §§ 5:8–50 *et seq.*
125. *Id.* § 5:8–62.

39. New Mexico

1. N.M. Stat. Ann. §§ 53–8–1 *et seq.* (1978, Supp. 1981).
2. *Id.* § 53–8–48.
3. *Id.* § 53–8–82.
4. *Id.* §§ 21–23–1 through 21–23–14.
5. *Id.* § 21–23–2.
6. *Id.* § 21–23–5.
7. See *id.* § 21–23–4.
8. *Id.* § 21–23–4.F.
9. *Id.* § 21–23–4.H. New Mexico's "Out-of-State Proprietary Schools" chapter, regulating such schools offering correspondence or in-person instruction to students in New Mexico, also exempts educational institutions with certain kinds of accreditation. *Id.* § 21–24–3.
10. *Id.* § 21–23–4.J.
11. *Id.* §§ 53–8–1 *et seq.* (1978, Supp. 1981).
12. Farmers and Merchants Bank v. Woolf, 86 N.M. 320, 523 P. 2d 1346, 1350 (1974).
13. N.M. Stat. Ann. §§ 53–8–40 and 53–8–43 (1978).
14. *Id.* §§ 53–8–41 and 53–8–43.
15. *Id.* § 53–8–51.
16. *Id.* § 53–8–42 (merger or consolidation), § 53–8–47 (dissolution).
17. *Id.* § 53–8–44.
18. *Id.* § 53–8–52.

19. *Id.* §§ 53–8–53 and 53–8–54.
20. *Id.* §§ 53–8–55 and 53–8–54.
21. *Id.* §§ 53–8–48 and 53–8–49; see Model Act, § 46; for discussion of the Model Act, see Chapter 1, "Corporate Status," *supra.*
22. *Id.* § 21–23–15.A(1) (Supp. 1981).
23. *Id.* § 21–23–15.A(2).
24. *Id.* § 21–23–15.B.
25. N.M. Const. art. XIII, § 3.
26. *Id.* art. IV, § 31 (emphasis added). One state constitutional provision authorizes the legislature to establish a scholarship program for Vietnam veterans "who are post-secondary students at educational institutions *under the exclusive control of the state.*" *Id.* art. IX, § 14 (emphasis added).
27. N.M. Stat. Ann. §§ 21–21–14 through 21–21–24. Its predecessor was the Student Loan Act, *id.* §§ 21–21–1 through 21–21–13. Although no new loans are to be made under the Student Loan Act, it remains in effect for the administration of loans already made, and for the retirement of bonds issued under it. *Id.* § 21–21–14.
28. *Id.* §§ 21–21–3 through 21–21–15. Title IV, Part B, of the Higher Education Act of 1965 is 20 U.S.C. §§ 1071 to 1087–4.
29. *Id.* § 21–21–16.B.
30. 20 U.S.C. §§ 1001 *et seq.*
31. N.M. Stat. Ann. § 21–21–16.E.
32. *Id.* §§ 28–1–1 *et seq.*
33. Since "employer" includes anyone hiring four or more persons, virtually all RACs are included. *Id.* § 28–1–7.A.
34. *Id.* § 28–1–7.A. Discrimination on these bases in admitting to apprenticeship or training programs is also an unlawful discriminatory practice. *Id.* § 28–1–7.C.
35. *Id.* § 28–1–9.B. (Appendix II).
36. See text at notes 33 *et seq., supra.*
37. N.M. Stat. Ann. § 28–1–10 (1978 Supp. 1981).
38. N.M. Stat. Ann. §§ 50–4–19 to 50–4–30 (Supp. 1981).
39. *Id.* § 50–4–21.B (Supp. 1981).
40. See *id.* § 50–4–22 (Supp. 1981) for minimum regular wages and overtime wages.
41. *Id.* § 50–4–21.C(1) (Supp. 1981).
42. *Id.* § 50–4–21.C(2) (Supp. 1981).
43. *Id.*
44. *Id.* § 50–4–21.C(4) (Supp. 1981).
45. *Id.* §§ 52–1–1 through 52–1–69.
46. *Id.* § 52–1–6. Indeed, such employers with fewer than three employees may apply for coverage. *Id.* § 52–1–6.
47. *Id.* § 52–1–2.
48. *Id.* § 52–1–16. Excepted is "a person whose employment is purely casual and not for the purpose

of the employer's trade or business." *Id.*

49. This is confirmed by the fact that another provision of the law exempts *certain* employees of educational institutions, *id.* § 52-1-63, indicating by implication that other employees are covered.

50. *Id.*

51. *Id.*

52. *Id.* §§ 51-1-1 through 51-1-54.

53. *Id.* § 51-1-42.F(8).

54. *Id.* § 51-1-42.F(8)(a). The organization must also either have paid out $450.00 in wages in any calendar quarter in the current or previous year or have hired at least one individual for some portion of a day in each of twenty different calendar weeks in the current or preceding calendar year.

55. 26 U.S.C.A. § 501(c)(3).

56. *Id.* § 3306(c)(8).

57. See *id.* § 51-1-9.

58. *Id.* § 51-1-13.A.

59. N.M. STAT. ANN. § 51-1-42.F(i).

60. *Id.*

61. See text at notes 35 *et seq., supra.*

62. *Id.* § 28-1-9.B (Appendix II).

63. For a discussion of which RACs may be included, see text at notes 35 *et seq., supra.*

64. *Id.* § 28-1-7.F.

65. See text at notes 35 *et seq., supra.*

66. As to whether these include RACs, see text at notes 35 *et seq., supra.*

67. See text at notes 62 *et seq., supra.*

68. The statutory language does not clearly exclude RACs themselves, either, since it defines "public accommodation" as "any establishment that provides or offers its services, facilities, accommodations or goods to the public, but does not include a bona fide private club, or other place or establishment which is by its nature and use distinctly private." *Id.* § 28-1-2.G.

69. It could be argued that through its admissions decisions based on religion the use of a facility on campus which might be a public accommodation is restricted religiously.

70. N.M. STAT. ANN. § 28-1-7.G(i). It is also an unlawful discimination practice to indicate any such preference or limitation through advertisement, inquiries, and the like. *Id.* § 28-1-7.G(3).

71. *Id.* § 28-1-2.(H).

72. See text at notes 35 *et seq., supra.*

73. N.M. STAT. ANN. § 28-1-9.B.

74. *Id.* §§ 47-8-1 through 47-8-51.

75. *Id.* § 47-8-20.A.

76. *Id.* § 47-8-24.

77. *Id.* § 47-8-19A.

78. *Id.* § 47-8-9.A. (emphasis added).

79. N.M. STAT. ANN. §§ 50-9-1 *et seq.* (1978).

80. *Id.* § 50-9-4.

81. *Id.* § 50-9-3(6).

82. *Id.* § 50-9-7.

83. See I.R.C. § 501(a).

84. See I.R.C. § 501(c)(3).

85. N.M. STAT. ANN. § 7-2-3.

86. I.R.C. § 513(a) (Supp. 1980).

87. N.M. STAT. ANN. § 7-7-3. For the nonresident estate tax, see *id.* § 7-7-4.

88. N.M. CONST. art. VIII, § 3. Any pre-existing tax lien or assessment survives, however. *Id.*

89. 1914 Op. Atty. Gen. 225.

90. 1961-62 Op. Atty. Gen. 62-66; 1959-60 Op. Atty. Gen. 60-63.

91. N.M. STAT. ANN. § 7-9-4.

92. *Id.* § 7-9-29.

93. See I.R.C. § 513(a) (Supp. 1980).

94. N.M. STAT. ANN. § 7-9-15.

95. *Id.* § 7-9-7.

96. *Id.* § 7-21-3.A.

97. *Id.* § 7-31-3.B. Municipalities are also authorized to impose certain taxes. *Id.* § 3-18-2.D.

98. See text at notes 91 *et seq., supra.*

99. N.M. STAT. ANN. § 7-9-3.K.

100. *Id.* §§ 30-19-2 and 30-19-3.

101. *Id.* §§ 30-19-1 through 30-19-4.

102. *Id.* § 30-19-6. The entire proceeds must go to the organization or charitable purpose, *id.*, not just the net proceeds. Harriman Institute of Social Research v. Carrie Tingley Crippled Children's Hospital, 43 N.M. 1, 84 P.2d 1088 (1938).

103. *Id.* § 30-19-15 (Supp. 1980).

104. *Id.* § 30-19-15.B (Supp. 1980).

105. *Id.* § 21-2-3.

106. *Id.*

107. See *id.* § 21-2-2.

108. *Id.* § 21-2-2.A(2)(d).

40. New York

1. Leonard W. Krouner, "The Incorporation of Educational Institutions in New York State," 48 N.Y.S.B.J. 370, 371 (1976).

2. E.g., N.Y. EDUC. LAW § 4301 (McKinney 1970) (N.Y. State School for the Blind); *Id.* § 5701 (McKinney 1972) (Cornell University).

3. *Id.* § 216 (McKinney Supp. 1979). The University of the State of New York is not a university with a campus, faculty, and students, but rather is a corporation whose objects "shall be to encourage and promote education, to visit and inspect its several institutions and departments, [and] to distribute to or expend or administer for them such property or funds as the state may appropriate." *Id.* § 201 (McKinney 1969).

4. *Id.* § 216 (McKinney Supp. 1979).

5. See note 2, *supra.*

6. Krouner, note 1, *supra,* at 371–372.

7. LAW PAMPHLET 9—Incorporation Of Educational Institutions By The Regent (cited in Krouner, note 1, *supra,* at 372).

8. *Id.* at 9, n. 7.

9. See discussion in note 3, *supra.*

10. N.Y. EDUC. LAW § 218 (McKinney Supp. 1980), as amended by chapter 48 of the Laws of 1918.

11. *Id.* § 217 (McKinney 1969).

12. Applicability of New York's NOT-FOR-PROFIT CORP. LAW to educational corporations chartered by the Regents is determined by *id.* § 216-a (McKinney Supp. 1979).

13. *Id.* § 216-a; N.Y. NOT-FOR-PROFIT CORP. LAW §§ 1101 *et seq.* (McKinney Supp. 1979).

14. N.Y. ESTATES AND TRUSTS LAW § 8-1.1 (McKinney 1970); and see, e.g., In Re Randall's Estate, 71 Misc. 2d 1063, 338 N.Y.S. 2d 269 (1972), and In Re Goehringer's Will, 69 Misc. 2d 145, 329 N.Y.S. 2d 516 (1972).

15. N.Y. NOT-FOR-PROFIT CORP. LAW § 1001 (McKinney Supp. 1979).

16. *Id.* § 1002(c).

17. *Id.* § 1002(d) (Supp. 1979).

18. *Id.* § 1003.

19. *Id.* § 1004.

20. *Id.* § 1005.

21. *Id.* § 1008.

22. *Id.* §§ 1103 to 1114.

23. *Id.* § 1101(a).

24. *Id.* § 1102(a)(1).

25. *Id.* § 1102(a)(2).

26. *Id.* § 1102(b).

27. See Committee on Corporate Laws of the American Bar Association, *Model Nonprofit Corporation Act* (Philadelphia: American Law Institute, 1964), §§ 46 and 47.

28. N.Y. NOT-FOR-PROFIT CORP. LAW § 1111.

29. *Id.* §§ 1005(a)(4), 1008(a)(14), and 1115(a) and (b).

30. N.Y. EDUC. LAW § 6401 (McKinney Supp. 1979).

31. *Id.* § 6401(2)(a).

32. *Id.* § 6401(2)(b) and (c).

33. *Id.* § 6401(2)(d).

34. *Id.* § 6451.

35. *Id.* § 358.

36. NEW YORK CONST. Art. 11, § 3.

37. 37 A.D. 2d 461, 326 N.Y.S. 2d 765 (1971).

38. *Id.* at 466, 326 N.Y.S. 2d at 771.

39. *Id.* at 465, 326 N.Y.S. 2d at 770.

40. *Id.*

41. 36 A.D. 2d 340, 344, 320 N.Y.S. 2d 652, 656 (1971).

42. 29 N.Y. 2d 928, 329 N.Y.S. 2d 195, 279 N.E. 2d 860 (1972), *reargument den.,* 30 N.Y. 2d 751, 333 N.Y.S. 2d 177, 284 N.E. 2d 160 (1972).

43. Letter from Robert D. Stone, Counsel and Deputy Commissioner for Legal Affairs for the University of the State of New York, State Education Department, Aug. 24, 1981.

44. College of New Rochelle, 37 A.D. 2d at 465, 326 N.Y.S. 2d at 770.

45. See note 36, *supra,* and accompanying text.

46. 37 A.D. 2d at 466, 326 N.Y.S. 2d at 771.

47. *Id.* at 470–471, 326 N.Y.S. 2d at 775. See generally Tilton v. Richardson, 403 U.S. 672, 684–685 (1971); Lemon v. Kurtzman, 403 U.S. 602, 613 (1971).

48. N.Y. PUB. AUTH. LAW §§ 1676 *et seq.* (McKinney Supp. 1979).

49. *Id.* § 1676(2)(b).

50. *Id.* § 1677.

51. "Educational Institution" is defined in language identical to that found in the statute set out in the text accompanying note 49, *supra. Id.* § 1680(1) (McKinney Supp. 1979).

52. *Id.* § 1680(2)(a).

53. *Id.* § 1680(1).

54. *Id.* § 1680(3)(a).

55. Of course, any RAC seeking assistance from the Dormitory Authority would be subject to federal and state constitutional restraints on the use of public money to aid religious organizations. See, e.g., Tilton v. Richardson, 403 U.S. 672 (1971), Hunt v. McNair, 413 U.S. 734 (1973), and text accompanying notes 82–93, *infra.*

56. See text accompanying notes 1–9, *supra.*

57. N.Y. PUB. AUTH. LAW § 1680(1) (McKinney Supp. 1979).

58. N.Y. EDUC. LAW §§ 601 *et seq.,* §§ 661 *et seq.* (McKinney Supp. 1979).

59. *Id.* § 661(6)(a).

60. *Id.* § 661(2). A statutory "citizenship" requirement, *id.* § 661(3), is unconstitutional. Nyquist v. Mauclet, 432 U.S. 1 (1977).

61. *Id.* § 661(4).

62. *Id.* § 601(4).

63. *Id.* § 4210 (McKinney 1970).

64. *Id.* § 4210(1).

65. *Id.* § 4210(2).

66. *Id.* § 4210(1).

67. N.Y. EXEC. LAW § 296.1(a). A similar prohibition applies to employment agencies and labor organizations in regard to their respective practices. *Id.* §§ 296.1(b), 296.1(c).

68. *Id.* § 296.1(d) (emphasis added).

69. *Id.* § 296.1–a(d) (emphasis added).

70. 42 U.S.C. § 2000e–2(e)(1).

71. See State Division of Human Rights on Complaint of Cox v. New York State Department of Correctional Services, 61 A.D. 2d 25, 401 N.Y.S. 2d 619 (1978); see also State Division of Human Rights v. Averill Park Central School District, 59 A.D. 2d 499, 399 N.Y.S. 2d 926 (1977) (interpreting the definition of a disability to include physical, mental, or medical conditions unrelated to ability to perform a job).

72. 42 U.S.C. § 2000e–7.

73. U.S. Const., Art. VI.

74. N.Y. EXEC. LAW § 292.21.

75. See BNA SOURCEBOOK ON STATE EMPLOYMENT PRACTICE LAWS.

76. N.Y. EXEC. LAW § 296.11. The same provision also applies to "sales or rental of housing accommodations" and "admission."

77. *Id.* § 296.1.

78. *Id.* § 292.21.

79. N.Y. MENTAL HYGIENE LAW § 19.01.

80. New York State Division of Human Rights, Memorandum of Law No. 803.

81. 45 C.F.R. § 85.31(a).

82. 45 C.F.R. § 85.31(b).

83. 45 C.F.R. Part 84, p. 376 (1977).

84. See Edward M. Gaffney and Philip R. Moots, *Government and the Campus: Federal Regulation of Religiously Affiliated Higher Education* (Notre Dame, Ind.: University of Notre Dame Press, 1982), pp. 123–133.

85. N.Y. EXEC. LAW § 296.11.

86. *Id.* § 292.21.

87. Discrimination by industries involved in defense contracts is specifically prohibited. N.Y. CIVIL RIGHTS LAW § 44. Furthermore, any contract for or on behalf of the state or a municipality for construction, repair or alteration of any public building must contain a clause prohibiting employment discrimination. N.Y. LABOR LAW § 220–e.

88. *Id.* § 651.6.

89. Indeed, it is specified elsewhere that nonprofitmaking institutions are covered by the law. *Id.* § 6512.3.

90. *Id.* § 651.5. Note that while all RACs are within the exceptions relating to "educational" institutions, it may be more difficult for an RAC to bring itself within an exception limited to a "religious or charitable" (as opposed to "educational") institution. See *id.* § 651.5(h) in text accompanying this note.

91. *Id.* § 3 (Group 18).

92. *Id.* § 3 (Group 19).

93. 26 U.S.C. § 3306(a).

94. *Id.* § 3301.

95. 42 U.S.C. § 1101(b)1.

96. 26 U.S.C. § 3302(a).

97. *Id.* § 3304(6)(A).

98. *Id.* § 3309(b)(1).

99. *Id.* § 3309(b)(2).

100. *Id.* § 3306(c)(10)(B).

101. N.Y. LABOR LAW § 563.3(2).

102. *Id.* § 563.1.

103. *Id.* § 511.15.

104. *Id.* § 511.17. This exception will not apply "to service performed in a program established by or on behalf of an employer or group of employers." *Id.*

105. *Id.* § 563.2(a).

106. *Id.* § 563.2(b).

107. *Id.* § 563.2(c).

108. Federal law requires states to allow nonprofit organizations to elect to provide reimbursement to state funds for compensation actually paid, in lieu of taxation. 26 U.S.C. § 3309(a)(2). See N.Y. LABOR LAW § 563.4.

109. N.Y. EDUC. LAW § 313(1).

110. *Id.*

111. *Id.* § 313(3)(a).

112. See text accompanying note 76, *supra.*

113. N.Y. EDUC. LAW § 313(2)(b).

114. N.Y. EXEC. LAW § 296.11. See text accompanying note 76, *supra.*

115. N.Y. EDUC. LAW § 313(3)(a).

116. N.Y. EXEC. LAW §§ 293, 294. See text accompanying note 74, *supra.*

117. N.Y. EDUC. LAW §§ 301 *et seq.* Any person seeking admission who claims to be aggrieved by an unfair educational practice may file a petition so alleging with the Commissioner, who is charged with investigating and otherwise pursuing the complaint. *Id.* § 313(5)(a). He may also initiate investigations when he has reason to believe that an applicant has been discriminated against. *Id.* § 313(5)(b). The procedures for enforcement are set out at *id.* § 313(5) through (8).

118. 84 Misc. 2d 702, 278 N.Y.S. 2d 842 (1975).

119. See N.Y. EDUC. LAW § 313(3)(a).

120. N.Y. CIVIL RIGHTS LAW § 40.

121. N.Y. EXEC. LAW § 296.2.

122. N.Y. CIVIL RIGHTS LAW § 40.

123. N.Y. EXEC. LAW § 292.9.

124. *Id.* at § 300.

125. See text accompanying note 74, *supra.*

126. N.Y. CIVIL RIGHTS LAW § 41.

127. With regard to the disability provision, see text accompanying note 77 *et seq., supra.*

128. N.Y. EXEC. LAW § 269.5.

129. *Id.* § 296.5(a).

130. *Id.* § 296.11.

131. See text accompanying note 76 *et seq.*, *supra*.

132. See text accompanying notes 125 and 126, *supra*.

133. N.Y. Lab. Law § 27 (McKinney) (Supp. 1980).

134. *Id.* § 2(6).

135. *Id.* § 2(5).

136. This conclusion was confirmed by Metropolitan Life Ins. Co. v. New York State Labor Relations Board, 168 Misc. 948, 6 N.Y.S. 2d 775, *aff'd.* 255 App. Div. 840, 7 N.Y.S. 2d 1007, *aff'd.* 280 N.Y. 194, 20 N.E. 2d 390 (1938).

137. N.Y. Lab. Law § 27(1) (McKinney) (Supp. 1980).

138. N.Y. Const. art. 16, § 1 (McKinney 1969).

139. Riverdale Country School, Inc. v. City of New York, 13 A.D. 2d 103, 213 N.Y.S. 2d 543 (1961), *aff'd.* 11 N.Y. 2d 741, 226 N.Y.S. 2d 445, 181 N.E. 2d 457 (1962).

140. N.Y. Tax Law § 209(1) (McKinney Supp. 1979). At least constitutionally, however, the "net income tax" is the same as a tax imposed on the "privilege of doing business." See Complete Auto Transit, Inc. v. Brady et al., 430 U.S. 274 (1977).

141. *Id.* § 210(1).

142. *Id.* §§ 208 *et seq.*

143. Article 9-A of the Tax Law is entitled "Franchise Tax on Business Corporations." Business corporations are defined at N.Y. Tax Law § 208(1).

144. 20 NYCRR § 1-3.4(6), cited in 58 N.Y. J. Taxation § 514, n. 74 (Supp. 1980).

145. An educational institution was held to be a business corporation subject to the franchise tax in Rye Country Day School v. Lynch, 239 App. Div. 614, 269 N.Y.S 761 (1934), *aff'd* 266 N.Y. 549, 195 N.E. 194 (1935), where the school was not operated for profit but issued shares of stock entitling the holder to share in its assets upon dissolution.

146. N.Y. Tax Law § 955(a) (McKinney 1966).

147. I.R.C. § 2055(a)(2). "RAC," as used in the remainder of this section, refers to a religiously affiliated college entitled to the exemption under I.R.C. § 2055(a)(2).

148. *Id.*

149. N.Y. Tax Law § 3612(a).

150. See I.R.C. § 170(c)(2)(B) and (C).

151. See I.R.C. § 2522.

152. 59 N.Y. Tax Law §§ 1002–1004.

153. N.Y. Real Prop. Tax Law § 421(1)(a) (McKinney 1972).

154. University of Rochester v. Wagner, 63 A.D. 2d 341, 408 N.Y.S. 2d 157 (1978), *aff'd* 47 N.Y. 2d 833, 418 N.Y.S. 583, 392 N.E. 2d 569 (1979).

155. *Id.*

156. Pratt Institute v. Boyland, 16 Misc. 2d 58, 174 N.Y.S. 2d 112 (1958), *aff'd* 8 A.D. 2d 625, 185 N.Y.S. 2d 753 (1959).

157. Cornell University v. Board of Assessors of City of Ithaca, 24 A.D. 2d 526, 260 N.Y.S. 2d 197 (1965).

158. University of Rochester v. Wagner, 63 A.D. 2d at 355–356, 408 N.Y.S. 2d at 165.

159. N.Y. Real Prop. Tax Law § 421(1)(d) (McKinney 1972).

160. People ex. rel. Rye Country Day School v. Schmidt, 266 N.Y. 196, 194 N.E. 405 (1935).

161. N.Y. Real Prop. Tax Law § 421(2) (McKinney 1972).

162. *Id.*

163. *Id.* § 421(3).

164. *Id.*

165. *Id.* § 498(d) (McKinney Supp. 1979).

166. *Id.* § 498(b) (McKinney 1972).

167. *Id.* § 490(1).

168. *Id.*; See Op. State Compt. 78–964; 5 Op. Counsel S.B.E.A., No. 105.

169. N.Y. Tax Law §§ 1101 *et seq.* (McKinney 1975, Supp. 1979).

170. *Id.* § 1105(f) (McKinney 1975).

171. *Id.* § 1116(d)(1)(a) (McKinney Supp. 1979).

172. *Id.* § 1116(d)(2)(A) (McKinney 1975).

173. *Id.* § 1116(d)(2)(B).

174. *Id.* § 1105(d)(ii)(B). This provision also requires that an RAC be created by one of the three methods discussed in the text accompanying notes 1–9, *supra*.

175. N.Y. Tax Law §§ 1201–1204 (McKinney 1975).

176. *Id.*

177. *Id.* § 1201(a).

178. *Id.* § 1201(b).

179. *Id.* § 1201(c).

180. *Id.* § 1201(d).

181. *Id.* § 1201(e), (g).

182. *Id.* § 1201(f).

183. *Id.* § 1202-a, 120-b (McKinney Supp. 1979).

184. *Id.* § 1201(i) (McKinney 1975).

185. *Id.* § 1230(d) (McKinney 1974).

186. *Id.* §§ 1201–1204.

187. N.Y. Unconsol. Laws § 9447(7)(d) (McKinney 1974).

188. N.Y. Tax Law § 804(4)(d) (McKinney 1975); N.Y. Pub. Hous. Law, § 113(1)(d) (McKinney 1955).

189. N.Y. Pub. Hous. Law § 113(1)(d), 110(c), (d) and (e) (McKinney 1955).

190. *Id.* § 113(2).

191. *Id.* § 113(3)a(1)(b) (McKinney 1955).

192. *Id.* § 113(3)b(1)–(4).

193. N.Y. Tax Law § 186–a(2)(a) (McKinney Supp. 1979).

194. *Id.* § 186–a(2)(b).

195. N.Y. Exec. Law § 171.1.

196. *Id.* § 172.1.

197. *Id.* § 172–a.1.

198. See the identical language in the statute accompanying note 76, *supra,* and the following exploration of that language.

199. N.Y. Exec. Law § 172–a.2(a).

200. N.Y. Const. art. 1, § 9.1.

201. *Id.* at § 9.2 (emphasis added).

202. N.Y. Gen. Mun. Law §§ 475–499.

203. *Id.* §§ 185–195–h.

204. *Id.* §§ 476.4 and 186.4, respectively.

205. *Id.* One or more of those purposes must be among the institution's "dominant" purposes. *Id.*

206. *Id.* at §§ 476.5 and 186.5, respectively. Among other "lawful purposes" which RACs might claim are assistance in establishing people as worthy and useful citizens, increasing people's comprehension of and devotion to the nation's foundational principles, enhancing people's loyalty to the government, and otherwise lessening the burdens of government or augmenting or supplementing services normally rendered by the government. *Id.*

41. North Carolina

1. N.C. Gen. Stat. § 115–255.

2. *Id.*

3. N.C. Const. art. I, § 13.

4. N.C. Gen. Stat. § 116–15(b).

5. *Id.* § 116–15(c).

6. *Id.* § 116–15(e). On February 15, 1980, the North Carolina Dept. of Justice issued a formal opinion with regard to the scope of this licensure exemption, concluding that (1) a religious institution is subject to the licensure requirements only with regard to any secular degree program it offers; (2) that an institution of higher education that does not designate itself a religious institution is nonetheless not subject to the licensure requirement as to religious degree programs; and (3) subjecting the secular degree program of a religious institution of higher education to the licensure requirement does not violate the First Amendment. This exemption is, of course, too narrow to include the great majority of RACs.

7. *Id.* at Chapter 55A. Chapter 61, entitled "Religious Societies," apparently does not apply to educational institutions. Thornton v. Harris, 140 N.C. 498, 53 S.E. 341 (1906); Allen v. Baskerville, 123 N.C. 126, 31 S.E. 383 (1898).

8. N.C. Gen. Stat. § 55A–2(8).

9. Note that religious, educational, or charitable associations formed prior to January 1, 1894 and acting since that date "as a corporation, exercising the powers and performing the duties of religious, educational or charitable corporations" are conclusively presumed to have been organized as a corporation on January 1, 1894. *Id.* § 55A–88.

10. *Id.* § 55A–7.

11. *Id.* §§ 55A–8 through 55A–14.

12. *Id.* § 55A–28.

13. *Id.* §§ 55A–35 through 55A–37.1.

14. *Id.* §§ 55A–38 to 55A–57.

15. *Id.* § 36A–53 (Supp. 1979); and see, e.g., Wilson v. First Presbyterian Church, 284 N.C. 284, 200 S.E. 2d 769 (1973); for discussion of the *cy pres* doctrine, see Chapter 1, "Corporate Status," *supra.*

16. N.C. Gen. Stat. §§ 55A–41(c), 55A–41(b).

17. *Id.* § 55A–49.

18. *Id.* §§ 55A–50, 55A–53(e).

19. *Id.* § 55A–53.

20. *Id.* §§ 55A–45, 55A–57; see Model Act, § 46; for a discussion of the Model Act, see Chapter 1, "Corporate Status," *supra.*

21. N.C. Gen. Stat. § 55A–57.

22. *Id.* § 143–422.2 (emphasis added).

23. *Id.* § 116–201(5). The federal legislation referred to would include most, if not all, RACs. 20 U.S.C. § 1085(a) and (b).

24. N.C. Gen. Stat. § 116–20(8).

25. *Id.* § 116–20(6).

26. *Id.* §§ 116–171 *et seq.*

27. *Id.* § 116–174(1). The loans may not be used to obtain credit through correspondence or extension courses, however. *Id.*

28. *Id.* §§ 116–71 *et seq.*

29. *Id.* § 116–122(1).

30. *Id.* § 116–119.

31. *Id.* § 143–422.2 (emphasis added).

32. *Id.* § 143.422.3.

33. *Id.*

34. *Id.* § 168–6 (emphasis added).

35. See text at note 31, *supra.*

36. N.C. Gen. Stat. § 168–1.

37. *Id.* §§ 95–85 *et seq.*

38. *Id.* § 95–86(2).

39. *Id.* § 95–86(3).

40. *Id.* § 95–86(3)c.

41. *Id.* § 95–86(3)i.

42. *Id.* § 95–86(3)k.

43. *Id.* § 95–87.

44. *Id.*

45. *Id.* § 95–17.

46. *Id.*

47. *Id.*

48. *Id.*

49. See the Minimum Wage Act provision accompanying note 44, *supra.*

50. *Id.* §§ 97–1 *et seq.*

51. *Id.* § 97–2(1).

52. *Id.* § 97–2.

53. *Id.* § 97–2(2).

54. *Id.*

55. *Id.*

56. *Id.* § 96–1 *et seq.*

57. *Id.* § 96–8.k.

58. *Id.* § 96–8.g.5.

59. *Id.* § 96–8.g.15(i).

60. *Id.* § 96–8.g.15(ii).

61. *Id.* § 96–8.g.17(i).

62. *Id.* § 96–8.g.17(ii).

63. *Id.*

64. *Id.* § 116–1.1(a).

65. *Id.*

66. *Id.* § 115–1.1(b)(3).

67. *Id.*

68. *Id.* §§ 115–373 *et seq.*

69. *Id.* § 168–1. See text accompanying note 36, *supra.*

70. *Id.* § 168–2.

71. *Id.* § 168–3. The visually handicapped have the right to bring a specially trained guide dog into any of the places mentioned in the statute. *Id.* § 168–4.

72. *Id.* § 168–9.

73. *Id.*

74. *Id.* § 95–127(9).

75. *Id.* § 95–127(10).

76. *Id.* §§ 95–216 *et seq.*

77. *Id.* § 95–128.

78. *Id.* Exclusions from coverage include: "[e]mployees whose employer is within the class and type of employment which does not permit federal funding, on a matching basis, to the State in return of State enforcement of all occupational safety and health issues." *Id.* § 95–128(6).

79. *Id.* § 95–151.

80. See text accompanying note 31, *supra.*

81. *Id.* §§ 105–130 *et seq.*

82. *Id.* §§ 55A–1 *et seq.*

83. *Id.* § 105–145(b)(10). "Educational institution" for the purposes of this provision means one which normally maintains a regular faculty and curriculum, and normally has a regularly organized student body in attendance. *Id.* § 105–135. This would include most, if not all, RACs.

84. *Id.* § 105–3(2).

85. *Id.* § 105–7.

86. *Id.* § 105–188(h).

87. *Id.* § 105–130.9(1).

88. *Id.* § 105–130.9(1) and (3).

89. *Id.* § 105–147(16). For purposes of the provisions governing corporate or individual deductions for such contributions, the donee educational institution must maintain a regular faculty and curriculum, and a regular student body in attendance. *Id.* The donee may be any of the entity's components (departments, etc), a group of such institutions, or any organization "organized and operated exclusively to receive, hold, invest and administer property and to make expenditures to or for the sole benefit" of such an institution or group of such institutions. *Id.*

90. *Id.* § 105–248.

91. *Id.*

92. *Id.* § 105–278(3).

93. *Id.* § 105–278(4). A similar exemption is provided for real property owned by "religious educational assemblies, retreats and similar organizations, associations, and corporations." *Id.* § 105–278(4a).

94. *Id.* § 105–164.13(27).

95. *Id.* § 105–164.13(14).

96. *Id.* § 105–164.14(b).

97. *Id.*

98. *Id.* § 108–75.6.

99. *Id.* § 108–75.7(a)(1).

100. *Id.* § 108–75.7(a)(2). Included within the exemption is any foundation or department with an established identity in such an educational institution. *Id.*

101. *Id.*

102. *Id.* § 108–75.7(b): A good faith full-time salaried officer or employee of a charitable organization maintaining a permanent establishment within the State or the bona fide salaried officer or employee of a parent organization certified tax exempt shall not be deemed to be a professional solicitor. *Id.*

103. *Id.* § 108–75.3(1).

104. *Id.* § 108–75.3(2).

105. *Id.* § 14–292.1.

106. See *id.* at (g) *et seq.*

107. *Id.* (d).

108. *Id.* § 55A–15(b)(5).

42. North Dakota

1. N.D. CENT. CODE §§ 10–24 *et seq.*

2. *Id.* § 10–24–30.

3. *Id.* § 10–24–08.

4. *Id.* § 10–24–23.

5. *Id.* § 10–24–17.

6. *Id.* § 10–24–26.

7. *Id.* § 10–24–27.

8. *Id.* §§ 10–28–19(1), 10–28–19(2).

9. *Id.* § 10–28–19(1).

10. *Id.*

11. *Id.* § 10–28–19(2).

12. *Id.* §§ 15–20.4–01 (Supp. 1977) *et seq.*

13. See its powers and duties at *id.* § 15–20.4–03 (Supp. 1977).

14. *Id.* § 15–20.4–04 (Supp. 1977). Much of the statute is in the nature of consumer protection law. See, e.g., §§ 15–20.4–06 (Supp. 1977) *et seq.*

15. *Id.* § 15–20.4–02.6 (Supp. 1977). For details, see *id.*

16. *Id.* §§ 15–67–10 (Supp. 1977) *et seq.*

17. *Id.* §§ 10–24–01 *et seq.* (Supp. 1979).

18. *Id.* §§ 10–25–01 and 10–25–04.

19. *Id.* §§ 10–25–02 and 10–25–04.

20. *Id.* § 10–26–05.

21. *Id.* §§ 10–25–03 (merger or consolidation) and 10–26–01 (dissolution).

22. *Id.* §§ 10–26–04 and 10–25–05.

23. *Id.* § 10–26–06.

24. *Id.* §§ 10–26–07 and 10–26–08.

25. *Id.* § 10–26–10.

26. *Id.* §§ 10–26–02 and 10–26–10; see Model Act § 46; for a discussion of the Model Act, see Chapter 1, "Corporate Status," *supra.*

27. For an excellent and comprehensive discussion, see A.E. Dick Howard, *State Aid to Private Higher Education* (Charlottesville, Va.: Michie, 1977), pp. 653–667.

28. N. D. CONST. art. I, § 4.

29. *Id.* art. VIII, § 152.

30. See Howard, note 27, *supra*, at 658–659.

31. See *id.* at 659.

32. N. D. CONST. art. XII, § 185.

33. *Id.*

34. Howard, note 27, *supra*. at 657.

35. See *id.* at 657–658.

36. N. D. CONST. art. VIII, § 152.

37. Howard, note 27, *supra* at 664.

38. N. D. CENT. CODE §§ 15–62.2–01 (Supp. 1979) *et seq.*

39. *Id.* § 15–62.2–01.1 (Supp. 1979).

40. See *id.* § 15–40.2–10, (Supp. 1979).

41. *Id.* § 15–62.2–01.2 (Supp. 1979).

42. *Id.* § 15–62.2–01.3 (Supp. 1979).

43. *Id.* § 15–62.2–01 (Supp. 1979).

44. For powers and duties, see *id.* § 15–62.2–02 (Supp. 1979). An advisory board made up of representatives from North Dakota educational institutions is also provided for. *Id.* § 15–26.2–03 (Supp. 1979).

45. *Id.* § 15–62.2–01 (Supp. 1979).

46. *Id.* § 15–63–03 (Supp. 1979).

47. *Id.* § 15–63–04 (Supp. 1979).

48. *Id.* §§ 15–62–01 (1971 Rep. Vol.) *et seq.*

49. *Id.* § 15–62–02 (1971 Rep. Vol.).

50. *Id.* § 15–62–01 (1971 Rep. Vol.).

51. *Id.* § 15–62–02 (1971 Rep. Vol.).

52. *Id.* §§ 15–62.1–01 (Supp. 1979) *et seq.*

53. *Id.* § 15–62.1–01 (Supp. 1979).

For power and duties, see *id.* § 15–62.1–02 (Supp. 1979).

54. 20 U.S.C. §§ 1001 *et seq.*

55. N. D. CENT. CODE § 15–61.1–02 (Supp. 1979).

56. *Id.* §§ 43–12–27 (Supp. 1977) *et seq.*

57. *Id.* § 34–01–19.

58. *Id.* § 34–01–19.

59. *Id.* For details, see *id.*

60. *Id.*

61. *Id.* § 34–01–17. For details, see *id.*

62. *Id.*

63. *Id.*

64. *Id.* § 25–13–01.

65. *Id.* § 25–13–05.

66. *Id.* § 25–03.1–02(10).

67. *Id.* § 34–06–01(3).

68. *Id.* § 34–06–01(2).

69. *Id.* §§ 34–06.1 *et seq.* An employee is "any individual employed by an employer including individuals employed by the state or any of its political subdivisions including public bodies." *Id.* § 34.06.1–02.2. An employer is "any person acting directly or indirectly in the interest of an employer in relation to one or more employees of each sex." *Id.* § 34.06.1–02.4.

70. *Id.* §§ 34–06–03; 34–06.1–04.

71. *Id.* §§ 65–01 *et seq.* (1960, Supp. 1979).

72. *Id.* §§ 65–01–02(3) and 65–01–02(7) (Supp. 1979).

73. *Id.* § 65–01–01.

74. *Id.* § 65–01–02(4)(a) (Supp. 1979).

75. *Id.* § 65–01–02(5)(b)(1) (Supp. 1979).

76. *Id.* § 65–01–02(4)(a)(4) (Supp. 1979).

77. *Id.* § 65–04–29.

78. *Id.* § 65–04–29.

79. *Id.* § 65–04–04 (Supp. 1979).

80. *Id.* § 65–09–01 (Supp. 1979).

81. *Id.* §§ 52–01–01 *et seq.* (Supp. 1979).

82. The statute refers to a "religious, charitable, educational or other organization." *Id.* § 52–01–01.13 (g) (Supp. 1979).

83. The general definition of "employment" is found at *id.* § 52–01–01.13 (Supp. 1979).

84. *Id.* § 52–01–01.13 (g)(Supp. 1979).

85. *Id.* § 52–01–01.13 (g)(1) (Supp. 1979).

86. *Id.* § 52–01–01.13(g)(2) (Supp. 1979).

87. *Id.* § 52–01–01.13(h)(1)(a) (Supp. 1979).

88. *Id.* § 52–01–01.13(h)(1)(b) (Supp. 1979).

89. *Id.* § 52–01–01.13(h)(2) (Supp. 1979).

90. *Id.* § 52–01–01.15(i)(5) (Supp. 1979).

91. *Id.* § 52–01–01.15(i)(5) (Supp. 1979). Spouses must be informed that employment is provided as a means of financial aid and that they are not covered by a program of unemployment insurance. *Id.*

92. *Id.* § 52–01–01.15(i)(10) (Supp. 1979).

93. *Id.* § 52–01–01.15(h) (Supp. 1979).

94. *Id.* §§ 52–01–01.13(n) (Supp. 1979), 15.b (Supp. 1979).

95. I.R.C. §§ 501(a), 521.

96. N. D. CENT. CODE § 52–01–01.15(i)(1) (Supp. 1979).

97. *Id.* § 52–04–18.

98. *Id.* § 52–04–18.1(b).

99. *Id.* The Bureau ("job service North Dakota") is established at *id.* § 52–02–01 (Supp. 1979).

100. *Id.* § 52–04–18. 1.

101. *Id.* § 52–05–02.

102. *Id.* §§ 34–12–01 *et seq.*

103. *Id.* § 34–12–01.3.

104. *Id.* § 34–12–01.2 ("includes any employee").

105. *Id.* § 34–12–02. See also *id.* § 34–01–14, protecting the "right of persons to work" whether or not members of labor unions or labor organizations.

106. *Id.* § 34–12–03.1.

107. *Id.* § 34–12–03.2.

108. *Id.* § 12.1–14–04 (Supp. 1975). See the discussion of this statute in the text accompanying note 110, *infra*.

109. N. D. CENT. CODE § 14–02–11 (Supp. 1981).

110. *Id.* § 12.1–14–04 (Supp. 1975). The law applies whether or not the actor is acting under color of law. *Id.*

111. *Id.* § 23–13–12.

112. *Id.*

113. Groups of people meet in dormitories; a number of people are employed in dormitories and, indeed, since an RAC tends to accept applications from the general public, a dormitory could be argued, however persuasively, to be open to the public.

114. *Id.* § 23–13–13. For details, see *id.*

115. *Id.*

116. *Id.* § 34–06–02(1).

117. *Id.* § 34–06–03(2).

118. *Id.* § 34–06–05(2).

119. *Id.* § 34–06–01.

120. *Id.* § 57–38–09.

121. *Id.* § 57–38–09.1 (Supp. 1979).

122. *Id.* §§ 57–37.1–01 (Supp. 1979) *et seq.*

123. The institution must normally maintain a regular faculty and curriculum, normally have a regularly organized student body in attendance "at the place where its educational activities are carried on" and must regularly offer post-twelfth-grade education. *Id.* § 57–38–01.7.3 (Supp. 1979).

124. *Id.* § 57–38–01.7.1. (Supp. 1979).

125. *Id.* § 57–38–01.7.1(a) (Supp. 1979).

126. *Id.* § 57–38–01.7.1(b) (Supp. 1979).

127. N. D. CONST. art. XI, § 176.

128. N. D. CENT. CODE § 57–02–08.6 (Supp. 1979).

129. *Id.* Exempt dormitories and boarding halls must not be managed or used for making any profit beyond maintenance and operation costs. *Id.*

130. *Id.* § 57–02–08.7 (Supp. 1979).

131. *Id.* § 57–02–08.9 (Supp. 1979). Such property may be in one or more. tracts. *Id.*

132. *Id.*

133. *Id.* § 57–02–08.11 (Supp. 1979).

134. *Id.* §§ 57–39.2–01 (Supp. 1979) *et seq.*

135. *Id.* § 57–39.2–04.1 (Supp. 1979). Tuition receipts would presumably be exempt under this section.

136. *Id.* § 57–39.2–04.5 (Supp. 1979).

137. *Id.* § 57–39.2–04.16 (Supp. 1979). For the parallel use tax exemption, see *id.* § 57.40.2–04.6 (Supp. 1979).

138. *Id.* § 57–39.2–04.23 (Supp. 1979).

139. *Id.* § 57–39.2–04.25 (Supp. 1979). For the related use tax exemption, see *id.* § 57–40.2–04.11 (Supp. 1979).

140. *Id.* § 57–39.2–04.1 (Supp. 1979). For details, see *id.* For the related use tax exemption, see *id.* § 57–40.2–04.1 (Supp. 1979).

141. *Id.* § 57–40.2–04.15 (Supp. 1979).

142. See *id.* §§ 50–22–01 (Supp. 1979) *et seq.*

143. *Id.* § 50–22–01.2 (Supp. 1979).

144. *Id.*

145. N. D. CONST. art. XI, § 25.

146. N. D. CENT. CODE §§ 53–06.1–01 (Supp. 1981) *et seq.*

147. *Id.* § 53–06.1–02 (Supp. 1981).

148. *Id.* § 53–06.1–01.7 (Supp. 1981).

149. *Id.* § 53–06.1–01.16 (Supp. 1981).

150. *Id.* § 53.06.1–02 (Supp. 1981).

151. See *id.* §§ 53.06.1–03 (Supp. 1981) *et seq.* See also *id.* §§ 53–04–03 (Supp. 1981) *et seq.* and § 53–04.1–01 (Supp. 1981).

152. *Id.* § 53–06.1–04 (Supp. 1981). For details and procedures, see *id. et seq.*

153. See *id.* §§ 15–10–01 (Supp. 1977) *et seq.*

154. *Id.* § 15–10.1–02.

155. *Id.* § 15–10.1–02.1.

156. *Id.* § 15–10.1–02.2.

157. *Id.* § 15–10–28 (Supp. 1977).

158. *Id.* See also, with regard to medical education, *id.* § 15–52–08 (Supp. 1977) and § 15–52–30 (Supp. 1977).

159. *Id.* §§ 15–64–01 *et seq.*

160. *Id.* §§ 15-20.3-01 (Supp. 1977) *et seq.*
161. *Id.* § 15-20.3-01 (Supp. 1977).
162. *Id.* § 15-20.3-02 (Supp. 1977).

43. Ohio

1. OHIO REV. CODE ANN. §§ 1702 *et seq.* (Supp. 1978). See also *id.* § 1713, "Educational Corporations."
2. *Id.* § 1713.02. Colleges established before October 13, 1967, *may* also apply for a certificate of authorization, *id.*, which is required for eligibility in many "indirect" state support programs. See text accompanying notes 34 and 38, *infra.*
3. OHIO REV. CODE ANN. § 1713.03.
4. *Id.* § 1713.04.
5. *Id.* § 1713.06.
6. *Id.* § 1713.22. For example, bishops or other church officials may be designated *ex officio* members. Previously incorporated RACs may also avail themselves of these provisions. *Id.* § 1713.23.
7. 54 O. Jur. 2d § 27.
8. OHIO REV. CODE ANN. § 1713.12.
9. *Id.* § 1713.07. See *id.* § 1719 for incorporation, regulation, and management of charitable trusts, defined at *id.* § 109.23(a).
10. *Id.* § 1715.52.
11. *Id.* § 1715.53.
12. *Id.* §§ 1715.51 *et seq.*
13. OHIO REV. CODE ANN. § 1702.47.
14. *Id.* § 1702.50.
15. *Id.* § 1702.52.
16. *Id.* § 1702.49. *See* Model Act, § 46, and discussion of the Model Act, in Chapter 1, "Corporate Status," *supra.*
17. For a general discussion of Ohio aid to private higher education, see A.E. Dick Howard, *State Aid to Private Higher Education* (Charlottesville, Va.: Michie, 1977), pp. 668–85.
18. OHIO CONST. art. VII, § 4.
19. State ex. rel. Dickman v. Defenbacher, 164 Ohio St. 142, 128 N.E. 2d 59 (1955).
20. State ex. rel. Saxbe v. Brand, 176 Ohio St. 44, 197 N.E. 2d 328 (1964).
21. See Gerke v. Purcell, 25 Ohio St. 229 (1874) (dictum) (Private college corporation is devoted to public use.)
22. OHIO CONST. art. I, § 7.
23. See Howard, note 17, *supra*, at 75. For a discussion of First Amendment limitations on government aid to RACs, see Philip R. Moots and Edward McGlynn Gaffney, *Church and Campus* (Notre Dame, Ind.: University of Notre Dame Press, 1979), pp. 19–25.
24. For a detailed compilation of the facts and

figures of Ohio support of private higher education, see Association of Independent Colleges and University of Ohio, *Fact File* (1979–80).
25. OHIO CONST. art. VI, § 5.
26. 176 Ohio St. 44, 197 N.E. 2d 328 (1964).
27. OHIO CONST. art. VIII, § 4.
28. OHIO REV. CODE ANN. § 3351.05.
29. *Id.* § 3351.07(B)(2).
30. See notes 44 and 47, *infra.*
31. OHIO REV. CODE ANN. § 3333.12.
32. *Id.*
33. *Id.*
34. See text accompanying note 2, *supra.*
35. OHIO REV. CODE ANN. § 3333.12.
36. See Howard, note 17, *supra*, at 682.
37. OHIO REV. CODE ANN. §§ 3333.21 *et seq.*
38. See text accompanying note 2, *supra.*
39. OHIO REV. CODE ANN. § 3333.21.
40. *Id.*
41. *Id.* § 3377.02.
42. *Id.* § 3377.04(C).
43. *Id.* §§ 3377.05 and 3377.15.
44. Hunt v. McNair, 413 U.S. 734 (1973).
45. OHIO CONST. art. VIII, § 4.
46. *Id.* art. I, § 7.
47. See, e.g., Nohrr v. Brevard County Educational Facilities Authority, 247 So.2d 304 (Fla. 1977) Vermont Educational Buildings Financing Agency v. Mann, 127 Vt. 262, 247 A.2d 68, *app. dismissed* 396 U.S. 801 (1968); Hunt v. McNair, 255 S.C. 71, 177 S.E.2d 362, *vacated*, 403 U.S. 945, *aff'd. on remand* 258 S.C. 97, 187 S.E. 2d 645, *aff'd.* 413 U.S. 734 (1970); California Educational Facilities Authority v. Priest, 12 Cal.3d 593, 116 Cal.Rptr. 361, 526 P.2d 513 (1974); Minnesota Higher Educational Facilities Authority v. Hawk, 305 Minn. 97, 232 N.W.2d 106 (1975). See generally 95 A.L.R. 3d 1000.
48. See discussion of the Ohio Constitution's "credit clause," art. VIII, § 4, at text accompanying notes 18–21, *supra.* The bonds themselves state that they do not constitute a debt or pledge of the credit of the state. OHIO REV. CODE ANN. § 3377.15.
49. See notes 22 and 23 and accompanying text, *supra.*
50. As long as the RAC has four or more employees in Ohio. OHIO REV. CODE ANN. § 4112.01(A)(2).
51. *Id.* § 4112.02(A).
52. *Id.* § 4112.02(E).
53. *Id.*
54. Telephone conversation with Mr. Frank Gibb of the Ohio Civil Rights Commission, August 9, 1979.
55. Post-hiring employment practices are covered

by the first "unlawful practice" mentioned above, which "practice" includes "tenure, terms, conditions, or privileges, and any matter directly or indirectly related to employment." *Id.* § 4112.02(A).

56. *Id.* § 4112.01(B).

57. *Id.*

58. *Id.* § 4112.04(A)(G).

59. *Id.* § 4112.06.

60. *Id.* § 4112.051.

61. *Id.* § 4112.99.

62. *Id.* §§ 4111.01 *et seq.*

63. *Id.* §§ 4141.01 *et seq.* (Supp. 1979).

64. 26 U.S.C. § 3306(c)(8) (Supp. 1978).

65. OHIO REV. CODE ANN. § 4141.01(B)(2)(6) (Supp. 1979).

66. *Id.* § 4141.01(B)(3) (Supp. 1979).

67. *Id.* § 4141.01(B)(2)(j) (Supp. 1979).

68. *Id.* § 4141.01(B)(3)(h)(i) (Supp. 1979).

69. *Id.* § 4141.01(B)(3)(h)(ii) (Supp. 1979).

70. *Id.* § 4141.01(B)(3)(e)(ii) (Supp. 1979).

71. *Id.* § 4141.01(B)(3)(e)(i) (Supp. 1979).

72. *Id.* § 4141.01(A)(1) (Supp. 1979).

73. The Ohio statute looks to I.R.C. § 501(C) (3) for its definition of "nonprofit organization." OHIO REV. CODE ANN. § 4141.01 (Supp. 1979).

74. *Id.* § 4141.01(A)(1) (Supp. 1979).

75. *Id.* § 4141.01(A)(1)(b) (Supp. 1979).

76. See notes 73 *et seq.*, *supra.*

77. § 4141.241(A)(1) (Supp. 1979).

78. OHIO REV. CODE ANN. § 4123 (1980).

79. *Id.* § 4123.01.

80. *Id.* § 4123.35.

81. *Id.*

82. See also discussion of tort immunity of RACs for injuries to students, at text accompanying notes 153–154, *infra.*

83. The President and professors constitute the faculty. OHIO REV. CODE ANN. § 1713.08.

84. *Id.*

85. Schoppelrei v. Franklin College, 11 Ohio App. 2d 60, 62, 228 N.E. 2d 334, 336 (1967).

86. Koblitz v. Western Reserve University, 11 Ohio Dec. 515, 524 (1901).

87. OHIO REV. CODE ANN. §§ 4112.01 *et seq.*

88. *Id.* § 4112.02(G).

89. *Id.* § 4112.01(A)(9).

90. *Id.* § 5709.121. See text accompanying notes 108 *et seq.*, *infra.*

91. *Id.* § 4112.02(H).

92. *Id.* § 4112.02(K).

93. *Id.*

94. Ohio Op. Att'y. Gen. No. 6579, p. 406 (1956) (construing the phrase "operated, supervised, or controlled by a religious organization," found in the charitable solicitation statute). It should be noted that

the housing discrimination language is even less rigid, since it adds "or in connection with" after the phrase "controlled by."

95. *Id.*

96. *Id.*

97. OHIO REV. CODE ANN. § 4101.01(c) (Page).

98. *Id.* § 4101.011.

99. *Id.* § 4101.12.

100. The language suggests that a "place of employment" is a place utilizing mechanical power for the most part. *Id.* § 4101.01(A).

101. *Id.* § 4101.02(B).

102. *Id.* §§ 4101.11, 4101.12.

103. OHIO REV. CODE ANN. § 5747.02. The "individual" subject to the tax is "any natural person." *Id.* § 5747.01(G).

104. *Id.* § 5733.01. Nonprofit agricultural cooperative corporations are subject to the tax, however.

105. *Id.* § 718.01.

106. *Id.* § 5731.17(A)(2).

107. OHIO REV. CODE ANN. § 5731.18.

108. OHIO CONST. art. XII, § 2.

109. OHIO REV. CODE ANN. § 5709.12.

110. See, e.g., Little v. United Presbyterian Theological Seminary, 72 Ohio St. 417, 74 N.E. 193 (1905).

111. See, e.g., College Preparatory School v. Bratt, 144 Ohio St. 408, 59 N.E. 2d 142 (1945).

112. Privately maintained schools and colleges have long been recognized as "charitable institutions" for tax purposes. Gerke v. Purcell, 25 Ohio St. 229, 243 (1874).

113. Goldman v. Friars Club, 158 Ohio St. 185, 107 N.E. 2d 518 (1952).

114. See Galvin v. Masonic Toledo Trust, 34 Ohio St. 2d 157, 296 N.E. 2d 542 (1973).

115. OHIO REV. CODE ANN. § 5709.121.

116. Galvin v. Masonic Toledo Trust, 34 Ohio St. 2d 157, 296 N.E. 2d 542 (1973).

117. Wehrle Foundation v. Evatt, 141 Ohio St. 467, 49 N.E.2d 52 (1943). Under this view, a parking lot could be exempt property, University Circle Development Foundation v. Perk, 32 Ohio App.2d 213, 200 N.E. 2d 897 (1964), but college property issued to a fraternity for construction of a fraternity house was not, Denison Univ. v. Bd. of Tax Appeals, 173 Ohio St. 429, 183 N.E.2d 773 (1962). Partial use of buildings for charitable purposes has been dealt with by apportioning and taxing the nonexempt floors, Huntington Ass'n. Inc. v. Tax Comm., 21 Ohio St. 526 (Common Pleas Court 1941).

118. Goldman v. Friars Club, 158 Ohio St. 185, 107 N.E.2d 518 (1952).

119. At least with regard to federal taxation,

"[t]he exemption from taxation granted to organizations created and operated for charitable purposes . . . should be liberally construed in determining the exempt status. . . . " Davis v. United States, 201 F. Supp. 92, 95 (S.D. Ohio 1961).

120. See Galvin v. Masonic Toledo Trust, 34 Ohio St. 157, 296 N.E.2d 542 (1973).

121. Compare the separate statutory exemption of "[a]ll property . . . of the . . . state universities." OHIO REV. CODE ANN. § 3345.17.

122. *Id.* § 5709.07.

123. Denison University v. Board of Tax Appeals, 2 Ohio St. 2d 17, 20, 206 N.E.2d 896, 898 (1965). RAC dormitories are included within the exemption. Thomas v. Board of Tax Appeals, 5 Ohio St. 2d 182, 214 N.E.2d 231 (1966).

124. Denison University v. Board of Tax Appeals, 2 Ohio St. 2d 17, 28, 205 N.E.2d 896, 903 (1965).

125. *Id.* § 5739.02(B)(9).

126. *Id.*

127. *Id.* § 5739.02-B(3).

128. *Id.* § 5739.02(B)(12).

129. *Id.* § 5741.02(C)(2).

130. *Id.* §§ 5739.02(B)(12) and 5741.02(C)(2).

131. *Id.* §§ 1716 *et seq.* ("Charitable Organizations.")

132. *Id.* § 1716.01(A) and (C).

133. *Id.* § 1716.03(A).

134. Ohio Op. Att'y Gen. No. 6593 (1956).

135. *Id.*

136. See note 6 and accompanying text, *supra.*

137. *Id.* § 1716.02.

138. *Id.* § 1716.03(B)(1). This exception applies to non-RACs as well.

139. *Id.* § 1716.04.

140. *Id.* §§ 1716.05 *et seq.*

141. *Id.* §§ 2915.01 (Supp. 1979) *et seq.* ("Gambling").

142. *Id.* § 2915.01(H) (Supp. 1979).

143. *Id.* § 2915.01(J) (Supp. 1979).

144. *Id.* § 2915.01(H) (Supp. 1979).

145. *Id.* § 2915.02 (Supp. 1979).

146. *Id.* § 2915.02(D)(1) (Supp. 1979). For detailed conditions, see *id.*

147. *Id.* § 2915.02(D)(2) (Supp. 1979). For detailed conditions, see *id.*

148. *Id.* § 2915.04 (Supp. 1979).

149. *Id.* § 2915.08(A) (Supp. 1979).

150. *Id.* § 2915.09 (Supp. 1979).

151. *Id.* § 2915.10(A) (Supp. 1979).

152. *Id.* § 2915.10(B) (Supp. 1979).

153. Matthews v. Wittenberg College, 113 Ohio App. 387, 178 N.E.2d 526 (1960).

154. *Id.*

44. Oklahoma

1. Sections 851 *et seq.* of title 18 — Corporations — provide a new and alternative avenue of corporate organization for religious, educational, and benevolent purposes. Op. Att'y. Gen., No. 68-261 (Sept. 11, 1968).

2. OKLA. STAT. ANN. tit. 18, §§ 541-91.

3. *Id.* § 541 (Supp. 1979-80).

4. *Id.*

5. *Id.*

6. *Id.* §§ 851-64 (Supp. 1979-80).

7. *Id.* § 853 (Supp. 1979-80).

8. *Id.* § 857 (Supp. 1979-80).

9. *Id.* § 856 (Supp. 1979-80).

10. *Id.* § 543.

11. *Id.* § 545.

12. *Id.* § 550 (Supp. 1979-80).

13. *Id.* § 549.

14. *Id.* § 1.3.

15. *Id.* §§ 851 (Supp. 1979) *et seq.* See also title 18, chapter 14, of the Oklahoma Code relating to Educational Corporations.

16. OKLA. STAT. ANN. tit. 60, § 602. See also Estate of Campbell v. Lepley, 532 P.2d 1374 (Okla. 1975).

17. OKLA. STAT. ANN. tit. 18, § 1.77.

18. *Id.* § 1.181.

19. *Id.* tit. 16, § 1.177.

20. *Id.* tit. 18, § 1.195.

21. *Id.* § 1.196.

22. *Id.* § 864 (Supp. 1979).

23. OKLA. CONST. art. 2, § 5. For an excellent discussion of state aid, see A. E. Dick Howard, *State Aid to Private Higher Education* (Charlottesville, Va.: Michie, 1977), pp. 686-700.

24. Op. Att'y Gen., No. 70-128 (Feb. 12, 1970).

25. Compare OKLA. STAT. ANN. tit. 70, §§ 4001 (Supp. 1979-80) and 4002 with, e.g., the Florida Higher Education Facilities Authority Law. See FLA. STAT. ANN. § 243.18-40.

26. OKLA. CONST. art. 10, § 15.

27. VFW v. Childers, 1979 Okla. 331, 171 P.2d 618 (1946).

28. OKLA. STAT. ANN. tit. 70, §§ 626.1 *et seq.*

29. *Id.* § 626.7(2).

30. *Id.* § 626.6.

31. *Id.* § 626.7.

32. OKLA. CONST. art. 13-A, § 4; OKLA. STAT. ANN. tit. 70, § 3206(g).

33. OKLA. STAT. ANN. tit. 70, §§ 695.1 *et seq.*

34. *Id.* § 695.5.

35. *Id.* § 695.2(4).

36. 20 U.S.C.A. §§ 1001 *et seq.*

37. OKLA. STAT. ANN. tit. 70, § 695.2(3).

38. "Employer," under the employment discrimination legislation, includes, *inter alia*, persons having "for each working day in each of twenty or more calendar weeks in the current or preceding calendar year" fifteen or more employees. See *id.* tit. 25, § 1301(1) (Supp. 1979–80).

39. *Id.* §§ 1302 and 1306(a) (Supp. 1979–80). Sex discrimination in the payment of wages is specifically prohibited in a separate title. *Id.* art. 40, § 198.1.

40. *Id.* tit. 25, § 1308(2) (Supp. 1979–80).

41. *Id.* § 1308(1) (Supp. 1979–80).

42. *Id.* § 1307 (Supp. 1979–80).

43. *Id.* §§ 1501 *et seq.* (Supp. 1979–80). For its powers and procedures, see *id.*

44. *Id.* tit. 40, §§ 197.1 *et seq.* (Supp. 1979–80).

45. *Id.* § 197.4(d) (Supp. 1979–80).

46. 29 U.S.C.A. §§ 201 *et seq.*

47. OKLA. STAT. ANN. tit. 40, § 197.4(d) (Supp. 1979–80). A parallel exemption exists when the employee is subject to that Act or one like it. See *id.* § 197.4(e)(7) (Supp. 1979–80).

48. *Id.* § 197.4(e)(4) (Supp. 1979–80).

49. *Id.* § 197.4(e)(8) (Supp. 1979–80).

50. *Id.* § 197.4(e)(9) (Supp. 1979–80).

51. *Id.* § 197.4(e)(10) (Supp. 1979–80).

52. *Id.*

53. *Id.* tit. 85, §§ 1 *et seq.* (Supp. 1980).

54. *Id.* § 2(B)(1) (Supp. 1980).

55. *Id.* § 2(A) (Supp. 1980).

56. *Id.* § 3(3) (Supp. 1980).

57. *Id.* § 2(C) (Supp. 1980).

58. *Id.* § 3(3) (Supp. 1980).

59. *Id.* § 3(5) (Supp. 1980).

60. *Id.* § 2.1(2) (Supp. 1980).

61. *Id.* § 61(a)(b)(c) (Supp. 1980).

62. *Id.* § 3(1) (Supp. 1980).

63. *Id.* § 61(d) (Supp. 1980).

64. *Id.* § 3(5) (Supp. 1979–80).

65. *Id.* tit. 40, §§ 211 *et seq.*

66. Compare *id.* § 229(f)(1) (Supp. 1979–80) with *id.* § 229(6)(m) (amended 1971).

67. For the exceptions, see *id.* § 229(f)(1)(D) (Supp. 1979–80).

68. *Id.*

69. See *id.* § 217 (Supp. 1979–80).

70. *Id.* § 237 (Supp. 1979–80). For details on such elections, see *id.*

71. *Id.* § 229(G)(i)(II) (Supp. 1979–80).

72. *Id.* § 229(G)(i)(II) (Supp. 1979–80).

73. *Id.* § 229(G)(ii) (Supp. 1979–80).

74. *Id.* § 229(F) (Supp. 1979–80).

75. *Id.* § 229(f)(6)(f) (Supp. 1979–80).

76. *Id.* § 229(f)(6)(n) (Supp. 1979–80).

77. *Id.* § 229(f)(6)(n) (Supp. 1979–80).

78. *Id.*

79. See *id.* § 218(c) (Supp. 1979–80).

80. *Id.* § 214(j) (Supp. 1979–80). For service prior to January 1, 1978, see *id.* § 214(i) (Supp. 1979–80).

81. See *id.* tit. 25, §§ 1401 *et seq.* (Supp. 1979–80).

82. *Id.* § 401(1) (Supp. 1979–80).

83. *Id.*

84. *Id.* § 1402 (Supp. 1979–80).

85. *Id.* tit. 61, § 12.

86. OKLA. CONST. art. 2, § 5.

87. OKLA. STAT. ANN. tit. 40, § 401 (Supp. 1980).

88. *Id.* § 403 (Supp. 1980).

89. *Id.* § 407 (Supp. 1980).

90. *Id.* § 410 (Supp. 1980).

91. *Id.* § 402 (Supp. 1980).

92. *Id.* tit. 68, § 2359(A) (Supp. 1979–80).

93. See I.R.C. § 501(c)(3).

94. OKLA. STAT. ANN. tit. 68, § 2359(B) (Supp. 1980).

95. *Id.* § 808(i).

96. Osborn v. Tax Commission, 279 P.2d 1096 (Okla. 1954). See also In Re Noble's Estate, 183 Okla. 148, 80 P.2d 243 (1938).

97. OKLA. STAT. ANN. tit. 68, § 903(a)(1) (Supp. 1979–80).

98. *Id.* § 2353.12 (Supp. 1979–80).

99. I.R.C. § 170(e)(2)(B) and (C).

100. OKLA. CONST. art. 10, § 6.

101. OKLA. STAT. ANN. tit. 68, § 2405(c).

102. *Id.* § 1305(g) (Supp. 1979–80).

103. *Id.* § 1305(d) (Supp. 1979–80).

104. *Id.* § 1404(e).

105. *Id.* tit. 18, §§ 552.1 *et seq.* (Supp. 1979–80).

106. *Id.* §§ 552.4(1) (Supp. 1979–80). See text accompanying note 40, *supra.*

107. OKLA. STAT. ANN. tit. 18, § 552.4(2) (Supp. 1979–80).

108. *Id.* tit. 21, § 1861(A) (Supp. 1979–80).

109. See 26 U.S.C.A. (I.R.C. 1954) § 501.

110. OKLA. STAT. ANN. tit. 21, § 995.1 (Supp. 1979–80).

111. *Id.* For further requirements and procedures, see *id.* tit. 21, §§ 995.1 *et seq.*

112. *Id.* § 1052.

113. OKLA. CONST. art. 13–A, § 4.

114. OKLA. STAT. ANN. tit. 70, § 3206.

45. Oregon

1. OR. CONST. art. XI, § 2.

2. OR. REV. STAT. §§ 61.005 *et seq.*

3. *Id.* § 61.055.

4. *Id.*

5. Letter from Mr. William F. Hoelscher, Oregon Assistant Attorney General and Counsel, July 29, 1980.

6. OR. REV. STAT. § 59.055.

7. *Id.* § 59.025(11).

8. *Id.* § 348.835(1).

9. *Id.* § 348.835(2).

10. *Id.* §§ 61.051, 61.061(14) (1979).

11. Compare §§ 61.525 to 61.600 with §§ 45 to 51 of the Model Act. For a discussion of the Model Act, see Chapter 1, "Corporate Status," *supra.*

12. See, e.g., Matter of King's Estate, 39 Or. App. 239, 592 P.2d 231 (1979); for a discussion of the *cy pres* doctrine, see Chapter 1, "Corporate Status," *supra.*

13. OR. REV. STAT. § 61.550 (1979).

14. *Id.*

15. *Id.* §§ 61.556, 57.585 (1979). The Attorney General may also institute involuntary dissolution proceedings if a nonprofit college procured its franchise through fraud or continues to exceed or abuse its legal authority. *Id.* § 57.585(3)(6).

16. *Id.* § 61.565 (1979).

17. *Id.* § 61.530 to 535 (1979); see Model Act § 46, and see discussion of the Model Act in Chapter 1, "Corporate Status," *supra.*

18. OR. REV. STAT. § 61.570 (1979).

19. *Id.* §§ 61.595, 57.625 (1979). For further details, see *id.* §§ 61.595 and 57.625 (1979).

20. OR. CONST. art. I, §§ 2,3.

21. *Id.* art. I, § 5.

22. Dickman v. School District, 366 P.2d 533 (Or. 1961).

23. *Id.* at 536.

24. *Id.* at 542–543.

25. *Id.* at 543–544.

26. OR. REV. STAT. § 352.710.

27. *Id.* § 352.730.

28. *Id.* § 352.720.

29. Letter from Mr. Jeffrey M. Lee, executive director of the State Scholarship Commission, July 21, 1980.

30. OR. REV. STAT. § 351.160; see also OR. CONST. art. XI-F(1).

31. Letter from Mr. Edward Branchfield, Assistant Attorney General and Counsel, July 16, 1980. The constitutional provision referred to is OR. CONST. art. XI-F(1).

32. OR. REV. STAT. §§ 348.205 *et seq.*

33. *Id.* §§ 348.240(5), 348.260(5).

34. *Id.* § 348.250(5).

35. *Id.* § 348.040.

36. *Id.* §§ 659.010 *et seq.*

37. *Id.* § 659.020(2).

38. Letters of October 8, 1981, from Attorney General Dave Frohnmayer, on file with the Center for Constitutional Studies, Notre Dame Law School.

39. OR. REV. STAT. § 659.020(2).

40. Letter from Mr. Hoelscher, July 29, 1980. Mr. Hoelscher notes that there is no substantive law supporting this interpretation, and he recommends that the reader rely on his own interpretation.

41. OR. REV. STAT. §§ 653.010(3), 653.025.

42. *Id.* § 653.020(5).

43. *Id.* § 653.020(13).

44. *Id.* §§ 656.001 *et seq.* (1979).

45. *Id.* § 656.005(25).

46. *Id.* § 656.023.

47. *Id.* § 656.027.

48. *Id.* § 656.027(3).

49. *Id.* § 656.027(4).

50. *Id.* § 656.027(8).

51. *Id.* § 656.039.

52. *Id.* §§ 656.006 and 656.020.

53. *Id.* §§ 656.401(1)(a) and 656.005(5).

54. *Id.* §§ 656.411 and 656.005(10).

55. *Id.* §§ 656.407(2) and 656.005(13), (26).

56. *Id.* §§ 657.005 *et seq.*

57. *Id.* § 657.030(2).

58. "Employee" is defined at *id.* § 657.015 (1979).

59. *Id.* §§ 657.025 (1979).

60. *Id.* § 657.030(1) (1979).

61. *Id.* § 657.030(2)(a) (1979).

62. *Id.* § 657.030(2)(d) (1979).

63. *Id.* § 657.050(1) (1979). The 1981 Oregon Legislature added exemptions for theatrical personnel and others "for or on behalf of a nonprofit organization when the remuneration consists solely of a gratuity, prize, scholarship or reimbursement of expenses." 1981 Or. Laws 162, c.636, § 22(1). See also *id.* § 2(2)(d) for the definition of scholarship.

64. *Id.* § 657.072 (1979).

65. *Id.* § 657.072(2) (1979).

66. *Id.* § 657.072(1)(a)(A) (1979).

67. *Id.* § 657.072(1)(a)(B) (1979).

68. *Id.* § 657.072(1)(b) (1979).

69. *Id.* § 657.420(1) (1979). This section was repealed in 1981, with its substance being incorporated, with major additions, into *id.* § 657.425. See 1981 Or. Laws 12, c.5, §§ 3 and 4.

70. *Id.* § 663.110.

71. *Id.* § 663.120.

72. *Id.* § 663.110.

73. *Id.* § 659.150(2).

74. See "State Support," Oregon, Part II, *supra.*

75. OR. REV. STAT. § 659.150(1).

76. *Id.* § 659.150.

77. *Id.* § 659.155(2).

78. *Id.* §§ 352.710 *et seq.*

79. Letter from Jeffrey M. Lee, executive director of the State Scholarship Commission, July 21, 1980.

80. Or. Rev. Stat. § 30.670.

81. *Id.* § 30.675(1).

82. *Id.* § 30.675(2).

83. Schwenk v. Boy Scouts of America, 275 Or. 327, 551 P.2d 465 (1976).

84. From the discussion in *Schwenk*, 551 P.2d at 468, the definition of the term "distinctly private" as used in Or. Rev. Stat. § 30.675(2) apparently remains unsettled. Thus, it is not clear that the term would apply to, and completely exempt, RACS.

85. See text at note 73, *supra.*

86. Or. Rev. Stat. § 91.710. Presumably, faculty, administrator and staff housing—as well as that of students—could come within the exemption.

87. *Id.* § 659.033(1).

88. See text at note 73 *et seq.* and at note 84 *et seq., supra.*

89. Or. Rev. Stat. § 447.220.

90. *Id.* § 447.210(9). Buildings with fewer than 4,000 square feet, or lower than twenty feet are not covered. *Id.* Parking spaces for the disabled may be required. *Id.* § 447.233(1).

91. *Id.* § 479.101(1)(i).

92. *Id.* §§ 479.101 *et seq.*

93. *Id.* § 336.072. The use of the "average daily attendance" concept, and of the term "pupil" may, despite the inclusion of both "school" and "educational institutions," indicate an intent that the provision *not* apply to higher education.

94. *Id.* §§ 456.744 *et seq.*

95. *Id.* § 456.744.

96. *Id.* § 456.746(3).

97. *Id.* §§ 654.001 *et seq.* (1979).

98. *Id.* § 654.005(5).

99. *Id.* § 654.005(6).

100. *Id.* §§ 317.005 *et seq.*

101. *Id.* § 317.080(4).

102. *Id.*

103. *Id.* § 318.030.

104. *Id.* §§ 318.010 *et seq.*

105. *Id.* § 317.920. Although there are no comparable "unrelated business income" sections in the Corporation Income Tax law, they might be read into that law since the legislative intent is that both laws "be administered as uniformly as possible," with few exceptions. *Id.* § 318.030.

106. *Id.* § 317.930(8).

107. *Id.* § 317.930(1).

108. *Id.* § 317.930(2).

109. *Id.* § 317.930(3).

110. *Id.* § 317.930(4).

111. *Id.* §§ 118.005 *et seq.*

112. *Id.* § 118.020(1)(b).

113. *Id.* §§ 119.010 *et seq.*

114. *Id.* § 119.035.

115. *Id.* §§ 316.002 *et seq.*

116. *Id.* § 316.068.

117. *Id.*

118. I.R.C. § 170(e)(2)(B) and (C).

119. For details and variations, see Or. Rev. Stat. § 316.068.

120. *Id.* §§ 317.005 *et seq.*

121. *Id.* § 317.295(1)(b) and (c).

122. *Id.* § 318.030.

123. *Id.* §§ 318.010 *et seq.*

124. *Id.* §§ 307.140 *et seq.* See also § 307.460.

125. *Id.* § 307.140(1).

126. *Id.* § 320.030(1).

127. *Id.* §§ 128.650 *et seq.*.

128. Under the law an "educational institution" is a "school, college or other institution with an established curriculum, student body and faculty, conducting classes in buildings adapted for that purpose." *Id.* § 128.620(5).

129. *Id.* § 128.640.

130. *Id.* § 128.805.

131. *Id.* § 128.825(1).

132. *Id.* § 167.117(4)(d). Such organizations must comply with the provisions of *id.* § 465.100(2). *Id.* § 167.117(4)(d).

133. *Id.* §§ 731.004 *et seq.*

134. *Id.* § 731.026(1).

135. *Id.* § 731.704(1). Virtually all RACs would be eligible. See *id.* § 731.704(5).

46. Pennsylvania

1. Pa. Stat. Ann. tit. 15, §§ 7301 *et seq.* (Purdon) (Supp. 1981).

2. *Id.* §§ 7311 *et seq.* (Supp. 1981).

3. *Id.* §§ 7921 *et seq.* (Supp. 1981).

4. *Id.* §§ 7961 *et seq.* (Supp. 1981).

5. *Id.* § 7311 (Supp. 1981).

6. *Id.* § 7103 (Supp. 1981).

7. *Id.* §§ 7311 *et seq.* (Supp. 1981).

8. *Id.* §§ 7721 *et seq.* (Supp. 1981).

9. *Id.* § 7313(c)(1) (Supp. 1981).

10. *Id.* § 7211.

11. *Id.* §§ 7962(1) and 7964(a).

12. *Id.* § 7965.

13. *Id.* § 7967.

14. *Id.* § 7968(a).

15. *Id.* § 7968(b).

16. *Id.* § 7968(c).

17. Zehner et al. v. Alexander et al., 3 Franklin Co. Legal J. 27 (Orphans Ct., Franklin County, Pa.,

May 25, 1979). For a discussion of this case, see Joseph C. Gies, "The Wilson College Case," *AGB Reports*, vol. 22, no. 4 (July–Aug. 1980), pp. 3–5; Elisabeth Hudnut Clarkson, "Ten Misconceptions About the Wilson College Case," *id.* at 6–11; and G. Philip Anderson and Kent M. Weeks, "The Lessons of Wilson," *id.* at 12–15.

18. PA. CONST. art. III, § 15.

19. *Id.* § 29.

20. PA. STAT. ANN. tit. 24, §§ 5181 *et seq.* (Purdon) (Supp. 1981).

21. *Id.* § 5183 (Supp. 1981).

22. *Id.* § 5186 (Supp. 1981).

23. 403 U.S. 672 (1971).

24. 413 U.S. 756 (1973).

25. For a comprehensive treatment of Pennsylvania's programs of financial assistance to independent colleges and their students, see A. E. Dick Howard, *State Aid to Private Higher Education* (Charlottesville, Va.: Michie, 1977), pp. 730–767.

26. PA. STAT. ANN. tit. 24, §§ 2510–301 *et seq.* (Purdon) (Supp. 1981).

27. *Id.* § 2510–304 (Supp. 1981).

28. *Id.* §§ 5502 *et seq.* (Supp. 1981).

29. *Id.* § 5503.

30. *Id.* tit. 71, § 633 (Supp. 1981).

31. *Id.* tit. 24, §§ 5101 *et seq.* (Supp. 1981).

32. *Id.* § 5104 (Supp. 1981).

33. *Id.* §§ 5151 *et seq.* (Supp. 1981).

34. *Id.* § 5154 (Supp. 1981).

35. *Id.* §§ 5154 and 5157 (Supp. 1981). These awards are currently valued at a minimum of $100 and a maximum of $1,500 per year.

36. *Id.* §§ 5161 *et seq.* (Supp. 1981). These scholarships are currently valued at a maximum of $1,200 per year.

37. *Id.* §§ 5171 *et seq.* (Supp. 1981).

38. PA. CONST. art. I, § 26.

39. 1961 Pa. Laws, No. 47, Feb. 28, 1961, amending 1955 Pa. Laws, No. 744, Oct. 27, 1955.

40. PA. STAT. ANN. tit. 43, § 952(b) (Purdon).

41. *Id.* § 954(b) (Supp. 1981).

42. See text accompanying notes 20–37, *supra.*

43. PA. STAT. ANN. tit. 43, § 954(b) (Purdon) (Supp. 1981).

44. *Id.* § 955(a) (Supp. 1981).

45. Pub. L. 88–352, 78 Stat. 255, as amended by Pub. L. 92–261, 86 Stat. 104, 42 U.S.C. 2000e–1. For a discussion of the legislative history of this provision see Philip R. Moots and Edward McGlynn Gaffney, *Church and Campus: Legal Issues in Church Related Higher Education* (Notre Dame, Ind.: University of Notre Dame Press, 1979), pp. 40–47.

46. Pub. L. 88–352, 78 Stat. 256, 42 U.S.C.

2000e–2(e)(2). For a discussion of the legislative history of this provision, see Moots and Gaffney, *Church and Campus*, note 45, *supra,* at 52–54.

47. PA. STAT. ANN. tit. 43, § 955(j) (Purdon) (Supp. 1981); see also Pub. L. 90–284, 82 Stat. 84, 42 U.S.C. § 3607.

48. PA. STAT. ANN. tit. 43, § 955(a) (Purdon).

49. *Id.* § 955(b)(1) and (2).

50. *Id.* § 955(b)(3).

51. *Id.* § 955(b)(4).

52. 16 Pa. Code § 41.71(b), as cited in Fair Employment Practices 457:877.

53. See, e.g., 29 C.F.R. §§ 1604.2(a) and 1606.1(a); see also Dothard v. Rawlinson, 433 U.S. 321, 334 (1977); McDonald v. Santa Fe Trail Transportation Co., 427 U.S. 273, 279–280 (1976); and Griggs v. Duke Power Co., 401 U.S. 424, 434 (1971).

54. See Moots and Gaffney, *Church and Campus*, note 45, *supra,* at 47–51.

55. 16 Pa. Code § 41.71(d), as cited in note 52, *supra.*

56. 16 Pa. Code § 41.71(c).

57. *Id.* §§ 41.101 *et seq.*, as cited in Fair Employment Practices (BNA) 457:880.

58. 16 Pa. Code § 41.102.

59. *Id.* § 41.101.

60. *Id.*

61. See Edward McGlynn Gaffney, "The Constitution and the Campus: The Case for Institutional Integrity and the Need for Critical Evaluation," in John D. Mosely, Ed., *Church and College: A Vital Partnership* (Sherman, Tex.: Austin College, 1980), vol. 3, pp. 47–67; and W. Cole Durham, Jr. and Dallin H. Oaks, "Constitutional Protection for Independent Higher Education: Limited Powers and Institutional Rights," *id.* at 69–87.

62. PA. STAT. ANN. tit. 43, § 957 (Purdon).

63. Rankin v. School District of Pittsburgh, 33 Pa. Commw. Ct. 129, 381 A.2d 195 (1977).

64. Pa. Laws 1937, No. 917, codified in PA. STAT. ANN. tit. 43, §§ 331a *et seq.* (Purdon).

65. See, e.g., Pa. Laws 1961, No. 1313, codified in PA. STAT. ANN. tit. 43, §§ 333.1 *et seq.* (Purdon).

66. PA. STAT. ANN. tit. 43, §§ 333.101 *et seq.* (Purdon) (Supp. 1981).

67. *Id.* § 333.103(g) (Supp. 1981).

68. *Id.* § 333.104(a)(4) (Supp. 1981).

69. *Id.* § 333.105(a)(5) (Supp. 1981).

70. *Id.* § 333.105(a)(6) (Supp. 1981).

71. *Id.* § 333.105(a)(8) (Supp. 1981). A provision in this statute requires worker's compensation coverage if the student employee is engaged in an activity that is not part of a school function or that is open to the public; see also *id.* § 333.105(a)(7) (ex-

empting seasonal employees under eighteen years of age and employees of a nonprofit health or welfare agency who are under twenty-four years of age and who are engaged in activities dealing with handicapped or exceptional children.)

72. *Id.* tit. 77, §§ 1 *et seq.* (Supp. 1981).

73. *Id.* § 21.

74. *Id.* § 22 (Supp. 1981).

75. *Id.* § 484 (Supp. 1981).

76. *Id.* § 501 (Supp. 1981).

77. 1936 Pa. Laws, No. 2897, Dec. 5, 1936, codified in PA. STAT. ANN. tit. 43, §§ 751 *et seq.*

78. 1980 Pa. Laws, No. 521, July 10, 1980.

79. PA. STAT. ANN. tit. 43, § 753(j)(1) (Purdon) (Supp. 1981).

80. *Id.* § 753(1)(4)(2) (Supp. 1981).

81. *Id.* § 753(1)(8)(a) (Supp. 1981).

82. *Id.* § 753(1)(8)(b) (Supp. 1981).

83. *Id.* § 753(1)(10)(b) (Supp. 1981).

84. *Id.* § 753(1)(10)(c) (Supp. 1981).

85. The statutory definition of a nonprofit organization includes religious, charitable, and educational organizations that are exempt from payment of federal income tax. *Id.* § 901 (Supp. 1981).

86. *Id.* § 904(a) (Supp. 1981).

87. *Id.*

88. *Id.* § 904(b) (Supp. 1981).

89. *Id.* § 905 (Supp. 1981).

90. *Id.* § 907 (Supp. 1981).

91. *Id.* §§ 211.1 *et seq.*

92. *Id.* § 211.3.

93. Petition of Salvation Army, 349 Pa. 105, 36 A.2d 479 (1944); see also Washington and Jefferson College v. Gifford, 55 Dauph. 182 (1944).

94. Pennsylvania Labor Relations Bd. v. Mid–Valley Hospital Assn., 385 Pa. 344, 124 A.2d 108 (1956); Western Pennsylvania Hospital v. Lichliter, 340 Pa. 382, 17 A.2d 306 (1941).

95. In re Employees of Uniontown Hospital Assn., 432 Pa. 146, 247 A.2d 621 (1968).

96. 29 U.S.C. §§ 101 *et seq.*; see Felix Frankfurter and Nathan Greene, *The Labor Injunction* (New York: Macmillan, 1930).

97. PA. STAT. ANN. tit. 43, §§ 191 *et seq.* (Purdon).

98. *Id.* tit. 24, §§ 5001 *et seq.*

99. *Id.* § 5002 (Supp. 1981).

100. " 'Religious or denominational educational institution' means an educational institution which is operated, supervised, controlled or sustained primarily by a religious or denominational organization, or is one which is stated by the parent church body to be and is, in fact, officially related to that church by being represented on the board of the institution, and by providing substantial financial assistance and which has certified, in writing, to the [Pennsylvania Human Relations] Commission that it is a religious or denominational institution." *Id.* § 5003(2).

101. *Id.* § 5004(aa) (Supp. 1981).

102. *Id.* § 5004(c).

103. *Id.* § 5503. See text accompanying notes 28 and 29, *supra.*

104. PA. CONST. art. I, § 26.

105. PA. STAT. ANN. tit. 43, §§ 951 *et seq.* (Purdon).

106. *Id.* § 954(b); and see text accompanying notes 18–37, *supra.*

107. PA. STAT. ANN. tit. 43, §§ 952(a) and 953 (Purdon) (Supp. 1981).

108. "Nothing in [the] subsection [relating to the sale, leasing, and financing of commercial housing] shall bar any religious or denominational organization or any charitable or educational organization, which is operated, supervised, or controlled by or in connection with a religious organization . . . from giving preference to persons of the same religion or denomination . . . or from making such selection as is calculated by such organization to promote the religious principles or the aims, purposes or . . . principles for which it is established or maintained." PA. STAT. ANN. tit. 43 § 955(j) (Purdon) (Supp. 1981).

109. *Id.* tit. 24, § 5503(2) (Supp. 1981).

110. *Id.* tit. 43, § 25–2.

111. *Id.* § 25–1.

112. *Id.* tit. 72, §§ 7301 *et seq.* (Supp. 1981).

113. *Id.* § 7303(a) (Supp. 1981).

114. *Id.* § 7303(a)(3) (Supp. 1981).

115. PA. CONST. art. VIII, § 2.

116. PA. STAT. ANN. tit. 72, § 5020–204(a)(1) (Purdon); see also *id.* § 5453–202.

117. I.R.C. § 501(c)(3).

118. See, e.g., Pittsburgh Institute of Aeronautics v. Bd. of Property Assessment, 435 Pa. 618, 258 A.2d 850 (1969).

119. In re Appeal of Doctor's Hospital, 51 Pa. Commw. Ct. 31, 414 A.2d 134 (1980).

120. See, e.g., Robert Morris College v. Bd. of Property Assessment, 5 Pa. Commw. Ct. 648, 291 A.2d 567 (1972); see also Appeal of Woods School, 406 Pa. 579, 178 A.2d 600 (1962); but see In re Hill School, 370 Pa. 21, 87 A.2d 259 (1952); and Appeal of Hospital Council of Western Pennsylvania, 439 Pa. 295, 266 A.2d 619 (1969).

121. Appeal of Mercyhurst College, 56 Erie 89 (1973); see Lutheran Home at Tapton v. Bd. for Assessment and Revision of Taxes, 6 Pa. Commw. 199, 293 A.2d 888 (1972).

122. Appeal of East Pennsylvania Conference, 62 Berks. 227 (1920).

123. *Id.*; see also Philadelphia v. Barber, 160 Pa. 123, 28 A. 644 (1894).

124. In re Property of East Pennsylvania of Seventh Day Adventists, Inc., 2 Pa. Commw. 281, 278 A.2d 180 (1971), reversing Appeal of East Pennsylvania Conference, cited in note 122, *supra*; but see Pittsburgh v. Third Presbyterian Church, 10 Pa. Super. 302 (1899) (janitor's residence on church lot not exempt) and Pittsburgh v. Third Presbyterian Church, 20 Pa. Super. 362 (1902) (vacant lot intended for future construction of church but not currently used for religious worship not exempt).

125. Appeal of Muhlenberg College, 44 D. and C. 2d 579 (Lehigh Co. 1966).

126. PA. CONST. art. VIII, § 2(a)(i).

127. PA. STAT. ANN. tit. 72, §§ 7201 *et seq.* (Purdon) (Supp. 1981).

128. *Id.* § 7204(10).

129. *Id.* §§ 3169-101 *et seq.* (Supp. 1981).

130. *Id.* tit. 47, § 763.

131. *Id.* tit. 72, § 2485-302 (1964 and Supp. 1981).

132. *Id.* § 2484-421 (1964).

133. 1919 Pa. Laws, No. 505, § 1-14, June 20, 1919, amended by 1925 Pa. Laws, No. 644, §§ 1-11, May 13, 1925; amended by 1963 Pa. Laws, No. 628, Aug. 9, 1963, PA. STAT. ANN. tit. 10, §§ 160-1 *et seq.* (Purdon). See also *id.* tit. 10, §§ 141 to 151. For a comprehensive analysis of government regulation of fund raising, see Bruce R. Hopkins, *Charity Under Siege* (New York: John Wiley and Sons, 1980).

134. PA. STAT. ANN. tit. 10, § 160-2 (Purdon).

135. *Id.* § 160-4(2)(1).

136. *Id.* § 160-5.

137. *Id.* § 160-4(a)(1).

138. *Id.* § 160-4(a)(1).

139. *Id.* § 160-9.

140. *Id.* § 160-4(b).

141. "Games of bingo as here conducted constituted an unlawful gambling operation in that prizes were to be won, winners were determined by chance and a consideration was paid by players." Appeal of North End Republican Ass'n., Inc., 37 North. 239 (1966).

47. Rhode Island

1. See "Nonbusiness Corporations" chapter, R.I. GEN. LAWS §§ 7-6-1 *et seq.*

2. *Id.* § 7-6-2.

3. *Id.* § 7-6-3.

4. *Id.*

5. *Id.* § 7-6-4 (Supp. 1980).

6. *Id.* § 7-6-5.

7. *Id.* § 7-6-7.

8. *Id.* § 7-6-8 (Supp. 1980).

9. *Id.* § 7-6-14 (Supp. 1980).

10. *Id.* § 7-6-16 (Supp. 1980).

11. For its creations, powers, etc., see *id.* §§ 16-49-1 (Supp. 1980) *et seq.*

12. See *id.* §§ 16-40-1 (Supp. 1980) *et seq.*

13. *Id.* § 16-40-1 (Supp. 1980). When articles of association seeking to establish a college or university are received by the Secretary of State, he transmits them to the Board and does not issue the certificate of incorporation until the Board approves the incorporation application. *Id.* Certain of the provisions of the "Private Schools" chapter, namely *id.* §§ 16-40-1 through 9 (Supp. 1980), do not apply to, *inter alia*, colleges and universities operated in Rhode Island for at least the ten years prior to April 13, 1932 or established by special act of the general assembly. *Id.* § 16-40-10.

14. *Id.* § 7-6-18.

15. *Id.* § 7-6-13 (Supp. 1980).

16. *Id.* §§ 7-1.1-1 *et seq.* (1956 and Supp. 1980).

17. See, e.g., Indust. Nat. Bank of R.I. v. Gloucester Manton Free Public Library, 107 R.I. 161, 265 A.2d 724 (1970). For a discussion of the *cy pres* doctrine, see Chapter 1, "Corporate Status," *supra.*

18. R.I. GEN. LAWS §§ 7-1.1-77 and 7-1.1-78.

19. *Id.* § 7-1.1-79.

20. *Id.* § 7-1.1-80.

21. *Id.* §§ 7-1.1-85 and 7-1.1-86.

22. *Id.* §§ 7-1.1-87 (Supp. 1980) *et seq.*

23. *Id.* § 7-1.1-80(b).

24. *Id.* § 7-1.1-80(c).

25. *Id.* § 7-1.1-97.1 (Supp. 1980).

26. *Id.* § 7-1.1-97; see Model Act § 61.

27. For a discussion of Rhode Island aid to private higher education generally, see A. E. Dick Howard, *State Aid to Private Higher Education* (Charlottesville: Michie, 1977), pp. 768-789.

28. R.I. CONST. art. I, § 3.

29. *Id.* art. IV, § 14. This power was confirmed by the Rhode Island Supreme Court in Opinion to the Governor, 79 R.I. 305, 88 A.2d 167 (1952). See Howard, *State Aid,* note 27, *supra,* at 773-774.

30. Howard, *supra,* note 27, at 788.

31. R.I. CONST. amend. XXXI, § 1.

32. R.I. GEN. LAWS §§ 16-37-1 *et seq.*

33. *Id.* § 11-37-1.

34. See P.L. 1977, ch. 238, § 4.

35. R.I. GEN. LAWS §§ 16-56-1 (Supp. 1980) *et seq.*

36. *Id.* § 16-56-1 (Supp. 1980).

37. *Id.* § 16-56-2 (Supp. 1980).

38. *Id.* § 16–56–3.1 (Supp. 1980).

39. *Id.* § 16–56–3.2 (Supp. 1980). The authority's creation, powers and duties are provided for in *id.* §§ 16–57–1 (Supp. 1980) *et seq.* The purpose of the authority is to enable resident students to attend "public *or private* educational institutions." *Id.* § 16–57–2 (Supp. 1980) (emphasis added).

40. See *id.* § 16–51–4 (Supp. 1980).

41. *Id.* § 16–56–4.1 (Supp. 1980).

42. *Id.* § 16–56–4.2 (Supp. 1980).

43. *Id.* § 16–56–4.3 (Supp. 1980).

44. *Id.* § 16–57–6(a) (Supp. 1980).

45. *Id.* § 16–57–6(f) (Supp. 1980).

46. *Id.* § 16–57–6(g)(3) (Supp. 1980).

47. See text accompanying note 31, *supra.*

48. R.I. GEN. LAWS § 16–57–12 (Supp. 1980). See Howard, *State Aid*, note 27, *supra,* at 776.

49. R.I. GEN. LAWS §§ 45–38.1–1 *et seq.*

50. *Id.* § 45–38.1–3.

51. *Id.*

52. *Id.* § 45–38.1–5(6).

53. *Id.* § 45–38.1–5(12) and (13).

54. *Id.* § 45–38.1–6.

55. *Id.* § 45–38.1–5(15).

56. *Id.* § 45–38.1–19.

57. *Id.* § 45–38.1–3(f).

58. *Id.*

59. Howard, *State Aid*, note 27, *supra,* at 776 (quoting R.I. GEN. LAWS § 45–38.1–1).

60. R.I. GEN. LAWS §§ 45–38–1 *et seq.*

61. *Id.* § 45–38–3(1). See *id.* § 45–38–5 for the procedures required prior to such acquisition.

62. *Id.* § 45–38–3(3).

63. *Id.* § 45–38–3(2).

64. *Id.* §§ 28–5–1 *et seq.*

65. *Id.* § 28–5–5 (1979).

66. *Id.* § 28–5–5.2 (Supp. 1980). The term "age," however, "means anyone who is at least forty . . . but not seventy . . . years of age." *Id.* § 28–5–6(I) (Supp. 1980). In any event, it is not unlawful, from July 1, 1980, through July 1, 1982, for an institution of higher education to retire compulsorily an employee who has reached the age of sixty-five but not of seventy years old and who is serving under a contract (or similar arrangement) providing for unlimited tenure. *Id.* § 28–5–7(G) (Supp. 1980).

67. "Employer" is defined to include any person employing four or more employees, *id.* § 28–5–6(B), therefore including virtually all RACs.

68. *Id.* § 28–5–7(A). (See also *id.* § 28–6–18, also prohibiting wage differentials based on sex.) Certain related activities, e.g., with regard to application forms, are also prohibited. *Id.* § 28–5–7(D).

69. *Id.* § 28–5–6(B).

70. See text accompanying note 71, *infra.*

71. R.I. GEN. LAWS § 28–5–7(D).

72. For its powers and duties, see *id.* §§ 28–5–8 *et seq.* The legislative authority for the Commission's existence ceases as of June 30, 1975. *Id.* § 22–14–5(F)(3) (Supp. 1980).

73. See text accompanying note 69, *supra.*

74. R.I. GEN. LAWS § 28–5–6(H).

75. See §§ 40.1–4–1 *et seq.*

76. See §§ 21–28.2–1 (Supp. 1980) *et seq.*

77. See text accompanying note 71, *supra.*

78. R.I. GEN. LAWS §§ 28–12–1 *et seq.*

79. *Id.* § 28–12–3 (Supp. 1980). A lower rate is provided for minors. *Id.* § 28–12–3.1 (Supp. 1980). Under special licenses, lower rates may be paid to certain handicapped workers, *id.* § 28–12–9, and to certain learners and apprentices, *id.* § 28–12–10.

80. *Id.* § 28–12–4.2.

81. *Id.* §§ 28–12–4.1 and 4.2.

82. *Id.* § 28–12–4.3(d).

83. *Id.* § 28–12–2(g)(5).

84. *Id.* §§ 28–29–1 *et seq.*

85. *Id.* § 28–29–6. Employers with fewer employees may come under the Act if the employment is hazardous or if the employer elects to be covered. See *id.* §§ 28–29–5 and 28–29–8.

86. *Id.* § 28–29–2(b) (Supp. 1980).

87. *Id.* § 28–29–8 and 28–29–5. An employee may preserve his right of action at common law to recover damages for personal injuries by timely written notice to his employer and to the Director of Labor. *Id.* § 28–29–18.

88. *Id.* § 28–29–22.

89. *Id.* § 28–36–2.

90. *Id.* § 28–36–1.

91. *Id.* §§ 28–42–1 *et seq.*

92. See *id.* § 28–42–3.(5).

93. See *id.* § 28–42–3(7).

94. *Id.* § 28–42–8(4)(a)(A) (Supp. 1980).

95. *Id.* § 28–42–8(4)(a)(B) (Supp. 1980).

96. *Id.* § 28–42–8(4)(b) (Supp. 1980).

97. *Id.* § 28–42–8(5) (Supp. 1980).

98. *Id.* § 28–42–10.

99. *Id.* § 28–42–8(12) (Supp. 1980).

100. *Id.*

101. *Id.* § 28–42–12. For the procedures involved, see *id.*

102. See §§ 28–43–1 *et seq.*

103. *Id.* § 28–43–29. For the procedures involved, see *id.* §§ 28–43–29 and 28–43–30.

104. *Id.* § 28–44–68.

105. *Id.* §§ 28–7–1 *et seq.*

106. See *id.* § 28–7–45.

107. See *id.* § 28–7–3(2).

108. "Age" in this context means "anyone over the age of eighteen." *Id.* § 11–24–3.2 (Supp. 1980).

109. The "sex" prohibitions do not apply to restrooms, bath houses and dressing rooms. *Id.* § 11–24–3.1 (Supp. 1980).

110. *Id.* § 11–24–2 (Supp. 1980).

111. *Id.* § 11–24–5 (Supp. 1980).

112. *Id.* § 11–24–3.

113. *Id.*

114. *Id.* §§ 34–37–1 (Supp. 1980) *et seq.*

115. Although the legislation prohibits denial of housing to the handicapped, it does not require renters or lessors to modify their property or exercise a greater degree of care for the handicapped. *Id.* § 34–37–4(D) (Supp. 1980).

116. *Id.* § 34–37–4(B) (Supp. 1980).

117. *Id.* § 34–37–1 (Supp. 1980).

118. *Id.* § 34–37–9.

119. For its procedures, etc., see *id.* §§ 28–5–1 *et seq.* and §§ 34–37–5 *et seq.* The legislative authority for its existence ceases June 30, 1985. See *id.* § 22–14–5.

120. *Id.* § 11–24–5.

121. *Id.* § 34–37–5.

122. *Id.* §§ 28–20–1 *et seq.*

123. *Id.* § 28–20–1(b).

124. *Id.* § 28–20–1(i).

125. See *id.* §§ 28–20–8 and 9.

126. *Id.* §§ 44–11–1 *et seq.*

127. *Id.* § 44–11–1(a)(4).

128. *Id.* §§ 44–12–1 *et seq.*

129. *Id.* § 44–12–1.

130. *Id.* § 44–12–11 exempts corporations mentioned in *id.* § 7–6–2, which includes educational nonprofit corporations.

131. For corporations or persons with business corporation or income tax liability, a deduction may be available for costs incurred in connection with new research and development facilities. See *id.* §§ 44–32–1. *et seq.*

132. *Id.* §§ 44–22–1 *et seq.*

133. *Id.* § 44–22–1(c) (Supp. 1980). A parallel exemption exists for out-of-state corporations which would be so tax-exempt if situated in Rhode Island and whose home state grants a reciprocal exemption. *Id.*

134. *Id.* § 44–24–4.

135. *Id.* §§ 44–24–1 *et seq.*

136. *Id.* § 44–22–13 (Supp. 1980).

137. See *id.* §§ 44–30–1 *et seq.*

138. *Id.* § 44–30–2(b).

139. I.R.C. § 170(c)(2)(B) and (C).

140. R.I. Gen. Laws §§ 44–11–1 *et seq.*

141. *Id.* § 44–11–11.

142. I.R.C. § 170(b)(2).

143. R.I. Gen. Laws §§ 44–3–1 *et seq.*

144. *Id.* § 44–3–3(5) (Supp. 1980).

145. *Id.* § 44–3–3(6) (Supp. 1980). For particular conditions, see *id.*

146. *Id.* § 44–3–3(7) (Supp. 1980).

147. *Id.* § 44–3–3(8) (Supp. 1980). The exemption is unavailable if any part of the income or profits from the property "or of the business carried on thereon" is divided among owners or stockholders. *Id.*

148. *Id.* § 44–3–3(10) (Supp. 1980).

149. See *id.* §§ 44–18–1 *et seq.*

150. *Id.* § 44–18–30(B) (Supp. 1980).

151. *Id.* § 44–18–30(C) (Supp. 1980).

152. *Id.* § 44–18–30(J) (Supp. 1980).

153. *Id.* § 44–18–30(S) (Supp. 1980).

154. See *id.*

155. *Id.* § 44–18–30(E) (Supp. 1980).

156. *Id.* §§ 5–53–1 (Supp. 1980) *et seq.*

157. *Id.* § 5–53–2 (Supp. 1980). For the information required in the statement, see *id.*

158. *Id.* § 5–53–4 (Supp. 1980).

159. *Id.* § 5–53–5 (Supp. 1980).

160. *Id.* § 5–53–8 (Supp. 1980). For additional prohibited acts, see *id.* § 5–53–1 (Supp. 1980).

161. *Id.* § 5–53–3(1) (Supp. 1980).

162. *Id.*

163. *Id.* § 5–53–3(2) (Supp. 1980).

164. *Id.* § 5–53–3(6) (Supp. 1980). "The term membership shall not include those persons who are granted a membership upon making a contribution as the result of a solicitation." *Id.* For further exemptions, see *id.* § 5–53–3 (Supp. 1980).

165. See *id.* §§ 11–19–1 (Supp. 1980) *et seq.*

166. See *id.* § 11–19–30 (Supp. 1980).

167. *Id.*

168. *Id.*

169. *Id.* For further details, see *id.*

170. *Id.* § 11–19–30.1 (Supp. 1980).

171. *Id.*

172. *Id.*

173. *Id.* §§ 16–41–1 (Supp. 1980) *et seq.*

174. *Id.* §§ 16–47–1. The legislative authority for the entity created by this provision ceases as of June 30, 1983. *Id.* § 22–14–5(D)(16) (Supp. 1980).

48. South Carolina

1. S.C. Code § 33–31–10.

2. S.C. Const. art. III, § 9.

3. S.C. Code §§ 331–31–10 *et seq.*

4. *Id.* § 33–31–40.

5. *Id.* § 33–31–50.

6. *Id.* § 33–31–110.

7. *Id.* § 35–1–310(8).

8. *Id.* § 21–31–50.

9. *Id.* §§ 33–33–10 *et seq.*

10. *Id.* § 59–46–20 (Supp. 1977). See Rules 62–1 through 62–22 (Supp. 1978) for regulations pertaining to this chapter.

11. S.C. CODE § 59–46–30 (Supp. 1977).

12. *Id.* § 59–46–10(3) (Supp. 1977).

13. *Id.* § 59–46–90 (Supp. 1977).

14. Rule 43–90 (Supp. 1976).

15. Rule 43–112(F).

16. S.C. CODE §§ 33–31–10 *et seq.*

17. *Id.* § 33–31–150.

18. See, e.g., Furman Univ. v. McLeod, 238 S.C. 475, 120 S.E. 2d 865 (1965). For a discussion of the *cy pres* doctrine, see Chapter 1, "Corporate Status," *supra.*

19. S.C. CODE § 33–31–150.

20. S.C. CONST. art. XI, § 4.

21. S.C. CONST. art. XI, § 9.

22. Hartness v. Patterson, 255 S.C. 503, 179 S.E.2d 907 (1971).

23. *Id.*

24. S.C. CODE § 59–113–10 *et seq.*

25. 179 S.E.2d at 909.

26. S.C. CODE § 59–113–20(d).

27. *Id.* § 59–113–20(e).

28. *Id.* §§ 59–115–10 *et seq.*

29. *Id.* § 59–115–40(2).

30. *Id.*

31. 259 S.C. 409, 192 S.E.2d 202 (1972).

32. 192 S.E.2d at 203.

33. Lemon v. Kurtzman, 403 U.S. 602 (1971). The three-prong *"Lemon test"* is used to determine if a particular statute is violative of the Establishment Clause: "First, the statute must have a secular legislative purpose; second, its principal or primary effect must be one that neither advances nor inhibits religion . . .; finally, the statute must not foster 'an excessive governmental entanglement with religion.' " 403 U.S. at 612–613.

34. 192 S.E.2d at 204.

35. *Id.*

36. S.C. CODE §§ 59–109–10 *et seq.*

37. *Id.* § 59–109–50. Under the law a "project" is: "a structure or structures available for use as a dormitory or other housing facility, including housing facilities for student nurses, a dining hall, student union, administration building, academic building, library, laboratory, research facility, classroom, athletic facility, health care facility, and maintenance, storage or utility facility and other structures or facilities related thereto or required or useful for the instruction of students or the conducting of research or the operation of an institution for higher education, including parking and other facilities or structures essential or convenient for the orderly conduct of such institution for higher education, and shall also

include landscaping, site preparation, furniture, equipment and machinery and other similar items necessary or convenient for the operation of a particular facility or structure in the manner for which its use is intended but shall not include such items as books, fuel, supplies or other items the costs of which are customarily deemed to result in a current operating charge. . . ." *Id.* § 59–109–30(b).

38. *Id.* § 59–109–30(e).

39. *Id.* § 59–109–30(d).

40. 413 U.S. 734 (1973).

41. See note 33, *supra.*

42. 413 U.S. at 744–745.

43. *Id.*

44. S.C. CODE §§ 59–111–10; 59–111–20 (Supp. 1978); 59–111–30. *Id.* §§ 59–111–10 and 59–111–320 (Supp. 1978).

45. *Id.* § 59–111–40.

46. *Id.* § 59–111–520.

47. *Id.* § 59–114–20 (Supp. 1979).

48. S.C. CODE §§ 1–13–10 *et seq.* (Supp. 1979).

49. *Id.* § 1–13–80(h)(5) (Supp. 1979).

50. *Id.* §§ 42–1–10 *et seq.*

51. 212 S.C. 337, 47 S.E.2d 788 (1948).

52. *Id.* at 341, 47 S.E.2d at 789.

53. S.C. CODE § 42–1–310.

54. See text accompanying notes 86–90, *infra.*

55. See Crowley v. Bob Jones University, 268 S.C. 492, 234 S.E.2d 879 (1977); Brown v. Andersen County Hospital Assn., 268 S.C. 479, 234 S.E.2d 873 (1977); Vermillion v. Woman's College of Due West, 104 S.C. 197, 88 S.E. 649 (1919).

56. *Id.* § 41–27–230(3) (Supp. 1977).

57. 26 U.S.C. 3306(c)(8). This section exempts employment in organizations described under 26 U.S.C. § 501(c)(3) and therefore includes most RACs.

58. S.C. CODE §§ 41–31–610 *et seq.*

59. *Id.* § 41–31–610.

60. *Id.* § 41–31–620 (Supp. 1977).

61. *Id.* § 41–27–200.

62. *Id.* § 41–31–620 (Supp. 1977).

63. *Id.* § 59–63–40.

64. *Id.* § 10–5–250 (Supp. 1978).

65. *Id.* § 10–5–220(2).

66. *Id.* § 10–5–260.

67. *Id.* § 41–15–80.

68. *Id.* § 41–15–210.

69. *Id.* § 41–27–210,–220.

70. *Id.* § 12–7–330(3).

71. Rule 115–87.59 (Supp. 1979).

72. S.C. CODE § 12–15–10 *et seq.* (1976).

73. *Id.* § 12–15–410.

74. *Id.* § 12–17–40 (Supp. 1980).

75. *Id.* § 12–7–700(10) (1976).

76. *Id.* § 12–7–700(5).

77. S.C. Const. art. X, § 3.

78. S.C. Code § 12–37–220(A)(2) (Supp. 1978). An additional provision exempts any "religious, charitable, eleemosynary, educational or literary society, corporation, or other association, when the property of such society, corporation or association is used by it primarily for the holding of its meetings and the conduct of the business of such society, corporation or association and no profit or benefit therefrom shall inure to the benefit of any private stockholder or individual." *Id.* § 12–37–220(B)(16) (Supp. 1979). Because the initial exemption is so broad, RACs would probably not have to resort to this provision, which seems to be directed at literary societies and the like.

79. Rule 117–174.188 (Supp. 1979).

80. *Id.*

81. S.C. Code § 12–21–2420.

82. *Id.* § 12–21–2420(4).

83. *Id.*

84. *Id.* § 12–21–2420(11) (Supp. 1978).

85. *Id.*

86. *Id.* § 33–55–20(1).

87. *Id.*

88. *Id.* § 33–55–60(2).

89. S.C. Const. art. XVII, § 7.

90. S.C. Code § 52–11–200.

91. S.C. Code § 44–7–140.

92. *Id.* § 59–101–130.

93. *Id.* § 29–101–170.

94. *Id.*

95. See note 55, *supra.*

96. S.C. Code § 34–23–20(d)(2).

97. *Id.* § 23–29–40.

49. South Dakota

1. See S.D. Codified Laws Ann. §§ 47–22–1 *et seq.*

2. *Id.* § 47–22–4.

3. *Id.* § 47–22–5.

4. *Id.* § 47–22–6.

5. *Id.* § 47–22–12.

6. *Id.* § 47–23–13.

7. *Id.* § 47–22–31.

8. *Id.* § 47–22–42.

9. *Id.* § 47–22–43.

10. *Id.* § 47–23–24.

11. See *id.* § 47–31–9.

12. *Id.* § 47–31–76.

13. *Id.* §§ 47–25–1 *et seq.* (1967 and Supp. 1980).

14. *Id.* §§ 47–26–1 *et seq.*

15. Compare *id.* §§ 47–26–1 *et seq.* with §§ 45 to 50 of the Model Act.

16. Compare S.D. Codified Laws Ann. §§ 47–26–5 and 47–26–6 with § 46 of the Model Act; and see discussion in Chapter 1, "Corporate Status," *supra.*

17. S.D. Codified Laws Ann. § 47–26–38; see Model Act, § 61.

18. S.D. Const. art. VI, § 3.

19. *Id.* art. VII, § 16. (See also *id.*, art. VI, § 3, prohibiting the gift of any state property "for the benefit of any sectarian or religious society or institution.") Nor may any state, county or municipality even accept any gift to be used for sectarian purposes. *Id.*

20. *Id.* art. XI, § 2.

21. A. E. Dick Howard, *State Aid to Private Higher Education* (Charlottesville, Va.: Michie, 1977), p. 813.

22. Synod of Dakota v. State, 2 S.D. 366, 50 N.W. 632 (1891).

23. Howard, *State Aid,* note 21, *supra,* at 816.

24. *Id.*

25. S.D. Codified Laws Ann. §§ 13–55A–1 *et seq.*

26. *Id.* § 13–55A–1. For the amounts available, see *id.* § 13–55A–4.

27. *Id.* § 13–55A–2(4). For other qualifications and for procedures, see *id.* §§ 13–55A–2 *et seq.*

28. *Id.* § 13–55A–2(5). For a detailed description, see *id.*

29. *Id.* §§ 13–55B–1 (Supp. 1980) *et seq.*

30. The student must have been a South Dakota resident twelve months prior to registration at the institution. *Id.* § 13–55B–3 (Supp. 1980).

31. *Id.* § 13–55B–3 (Supp. 1981).

32. *Id.* § 13–55B–1(3) (Supp. 1980).

33. *Id.* § 13–55B–1(2) (Supp. 1980).

34. *Id.* §§ 13–56A–1 *et seq.*

35. *Id.* § 13–56A–3 (Supp. 1980). The specified fields are osteopathic medicine, veterinary medicine, chiropractic, physical therapy, optometry, podiatry and dentistry. *Id.*

36. *Id.* § 13–56A–5 (Supp. 1980). The forgiveness rate is higher if the borrower practices in South Dakota counties with no city over 5,000 in population. *Id.*

37. *Id.* §§ 13–56–1 (Supp. 1980) *et seq.*

38. *Id.* § 13–56–1 (Supp. 1980).

39. See 20 U.S.C. §§ 1071 through 1087–4.

40. Howard, *State Aid,* note 21, *supra,* at 821.

41. S.D. Codified Laws Ann. §§ 13–55B–3 (Supp. 1980). and 13–55B–5 (Supp. 1980).

42. *Id.* §§ 20–13–1 *et seq.*

43. *Id.* § 20–13–10. (Related activities such as discriminatory employment applications and advertising are prohibited in *id.* §§ 20–13–11 through 13.)

44. *Id.* § 20–13–18.

45. *Id.*

46. See *id.* §§ 60–11–1 *et seq.*

47. *Id.* § 60–11–3. For the few exceptions, see *id.* and *id.* § 60–11–5.

48. See *id.* § 20–13–2.1.

49. *Id.* § 20–13–28. For its powers and duties, see *id.* chapter 20–13, *passim.* Under its control is the Commission on Human Rights. *Id.* § 20–13–2.1.

50. *Id.* §§ 62–1–1 *et seq.* (1978, Supp. 1980).

51. *Id.* § 62–1–2.

52. *Id.* § 62–1–3.

53. *Id.* § 62–1–3.

54. *Id.* § 62–3–4.

55. *Id.* § 62–1–7.

56. *Id.* § 62–1–8. See also § 62–3–17.

57. *Id.* § 62–3–5.1.

58. *Id.* § 62–3–11.

59. *Id.* § 62–5–2.

60. *Id.* §§ 62–5–4 and 62–5–5.

61. The definition of "employment" is found in sections throughout Chapter 61–1, Title 61, S.D. CODIFIED LAWS ANN. § 61–1–1 to 61–1–43 (1978).

62. *Id.* §§ 61–1–1 *et seq.*

63. *Id.* § 61–1–10.3.

64. *Id.* § 61–1–10.3(1). As this subsection indicates, I.R.C. § 3306(c)(8) excludes from the definition of "employment" services performed for a religious or educational organization as described in § 501(c)(3). Such services are exempt from federal taxation under § 501(a). See also S.D. CODIFIED LAWS ANN. § 61–1–21.

65. *Id.* § 61–1–10.3(2).

66. *Id.* § 61–1–10.4(1)(a).

67. *Id.* § 61–1–10.4(1)(b).

68. *Id.* § 61–1–10.4(2).

69. *Id.* § 61–1–22.

70. *Id.* § 61–1–22(2)(a).

71. *Id.* § 61–1–22(2)(b). Spouses must be informed that employment is provided as a means of financial aid and that they are not covered by a program of unemployment insurance.

72. *Id.* § 61–1–22(2)(c).

73. *Id.* § 61–1–22(1).

74. *Id.* § 61–1–18.

75. *Id.* §§ 61–5A–6, 61–5A–7.

76. *Id.* The Department is established at *id.* § 61–1–2.

77. *Id.* § 61–5A–18.

78. *Id.* § 61–5A–12.

79. *Id.* §§ 60–9A–1 *et seq.* The act is part of Title 60, "Labor and Employment."

80. *Id.* § 60–9A–1(3).

81. *Id.* § 60–9A–1(4).

82. *Id.* §§ 20–13–1 *et seq.*

83. *Id.* § 20–13–22(2). Related conduct with

regard to application forms and the like is also forbidden. See *id.* § 20–13–22(3).

84. See text at note 44, *supra.*

85. S.D. CODIFIED LAWS ANN. § 20–13–22.

86. *Id.* § 20–13–28. See note 49, *supra.*

87. S.D. CODIFIED LAWS ANN. § 20–13–23. "The blind, the visually handicapped and otherwise physically disabled" are entitled to "reasonably equal" public accommodations. *Id.* § 20–13–23.1. The visually impaired may be accompanied by a guide dog, without extra charge. *Id.* § 20–13–23.2 (Supp. 1980).

88. *Id.* § 20–13–1(12).

89. *Id.* § 20–13–22(1).

90. Compare the provision set out in the text at note 83, *supra.*

91. S.D. CODIFIED LAWS ANN. § 20–13–22. See text at notes 44 and 85, *supra.*

92. S.D. CODIFIED LAWS ANN. § 20–13–20(1).

93. *Id.* § 20–13–20(2). A related provision forbids advertising or otherwise indicating a preference on any such ground. *Id.* § 20–13–20(3).

94. See text at note 44, *supra.*

95. See text at note 85, *supra.*

96. S.D. CODIFIED LAWS ANN. § 20–13–28. See note 49, *supra.*

97. *Id.* § 20–13–23.1.

98. *Id.* § 20–13–23.3.

99. See, e.g., *id.* §§ 32–13–1 *et seq.* (highway safety), 32–16–1 *et seq.* (interstate vehicle equipment safety), 34–28–5 *et seq.* (building safety), 34–30 and 34–33 to 34–39 (fire safety), and 45–46 (mining safety).

100. South Dakota does tax the income of certain businesses. See, e.g., the Income Tax on Banks and Financial Corporations act, §§ 10–43–1 (Supp. 1980) *et seq.*

101. *Id.* §§ 10–40–1 *et seq.*

102. *Id.* § 10–40–23(2) (Supp. 1980).

103. *Id.* §§ 10–40A–1 (Supp. 1980) *et seq.*

104. S.D. CONST. art. XI, § 6.

105. S.D. CODIFIED LAWS ANN. § 10–4–9. An application must be filed with the county director of equalization. See *id.* § 10–4–15. See also *id.* § 10–4–19. If buildings used by such a society or institution are upon agricultural lands, there is an eighty-acre limit. *Id.* § 10–4–10. With regard to property with revenue purposes, see §§ 10–4–11 and 10–4–12.

106. *Id.* § 10–4–13. An application must be filed with the county director of equalization. See *id.* § 10–4–15. See also § 10–4–19.

107. *Id.* § 10–4–13.

108. *Id.*

109. *Id.* §§ 10–45–1 (Supp. 1980) *et seq.*

110. *Id.* § 10–45–12.1 (Supp. 1980).

111. *Id.*

112. *Id.* § 10–45–13 (Supp. 1980). Organizations claiming exemption must pay the tax otherwise due on all goods and services used in the conduct of these activities. *Id.* In this connection, however, see text at notes 114 through 119, *infra.*

113. S.D. CODIFIED LAWS ANN. § 10–45–13 (Supp. 1980).

114. *Id.* § 10–45–14.

115. *Id.*

116. *Id.* The exemption does not apply to "sales to or purchases of tangible personal property for the personal use of officials, members or employees" of those institutions, or to such "sales to or purchases of" such property "used in the operation of a taxable retail business." *Id.*

117. *Id.*

118. *Id.* § 10–46–15.

119. *Id.* §§ 10–46–1 (Supp. 1980) *et seq.*

120. See note 100, *supra.*

121. S.D. CODIFIED LAWS ANN. § 10–43–10.1 (Supp. 1980).

122. I.R.C. § 170(b)(2).

123. S.D. CODIFIED LAWS ANN. §§ 37–27–1 *et seq.*

124. *Id.* § 37–27–3.

125. *Id.* § 37–27–4. Also exempt under the chapter are foundations having an established identity with any such institutions, *id.,* and fraternal, social, educational and alumni associations whose solicitations are directed only to members with voting eligibility, *id.* § 37–27–8.

126. A professional fund raiser is one who, for financial compensation or profit, solicits contributions from the public for any charitable organization. *Id.* § 37–27–1(6). A member or employee of the organization is not a professional fund raiser unless his compensation is based on the amount of money raised or to be raised. *Id.*

127. See *id.* § 37–27–12 for the contents required.

128. *Id.* § 37–27–5.

129. *Id.* § 37–27–11. Referred to here are *id.* §§ 22–25–23 through 22–25–25.

130. See *id.* §§ 22–25–1, 22–25–3, 22–25–6, 22–25–13, 22–25–14, and 22–25–6.

131. As defined in *id.* § 22–25–23.

132. As defined in *id.* § 22–25–24.

133. *Id.* § 22–25–25(1).

134. *Id.* § 22–25–25(2).

135. *Id.* § 22–25–25(3).

136. *Id.* § 22–25–25(5). No prize for any one play of bingo may be in excess of $500.00, and no lottery prize may be worth more than $5,000.00. *Id.*

137. *Id.* § 22–25–25(4). No person may receive more than fifteen dollars for any one session of bingo or for any one lottery. *Id.*

138. *Id.* § 22–25–25(6).

139. *Id.*

140. *Id.* § 13–53A–1 (Supp. 1980).

50. Tennessee

1. TENN. CONST. art. 11, §§ 8 and 12.

2. See "Corporations," TENN. CODE ANN. §§ 48–101 *et seq.*

3. A corporation is nonprofit when "no part of the net earnings . . . inures or may lawfully inure to the benefit of any private shareholder or individual." *Id.* § 53–1202(s). The definition tracks the language of the federal Internal Revenue Code. I.R.C. § 501(c)(3).

4. TENN. CODE ANN. § 48–401.

5. *Id.* § 48–402.

6. *Id.* § 48–103(2).

7. I.R.C. § 509(a).

8. TENN. CODE ANN. §§ 48–601 to 604.

9. *Id.* § 48–1619(E).

10. *Id.* §§ 49–3901 *et seq.*

11. *Id.* § 49–3904(f). Institutions operated solely as law schools and subject to the approval of the Tennessee Board of Law Examiners are also exempt. *Id.* § 49–3904(h).

12. *Id.* § 49–5202.

13. See *id.* § 49–3906.

14. *Id.* § 49–3909.

15. *Id.* §§ 35–1101 to 1109.

16. *Id.* § 35–1102(2).

17. *Id.* § 35–1105.

18. *Id.* §§ 48–601 *et seq.* (1979).

19. *Id.* §§ 48–901 *et seq.* (merger and consolidation) and §§ 48–1001 *et seq.* (dissolution).

20. See, e.g., Hardin v. Order of Odd Fellows of Tenn., 51 Tenn. App. 586, 370 S.W. 2d 844 (1963). For a discussion of the *cy pres* doctrine, see Chapter 1, "Corporate Status," *supra.*

21. TENN. CODE ANN. § 48–1002.

22. *Id.* § 48–1003.

23. *Id.* § 48–1008.

24. *Id.* § 48–1015.

25. *Id.* § 48–1004(c); see Model Act § 46, and discussion in Chapter 1, "Corporate Status," *supra.*

26. TENN. CODE ANN. § 48–1009.

27. Acts 1968, ch. 523, § 1 (repealed 1978); *see* Model Act § 61.

28. TENN. CODE ANN. § 64–2901.

29. TENN. CONST. art. 1, § 3.

30. *Id.*

31. For a general discussion of Tennessee aid to private higher education, see A.E. Dick Howard, *State Aid to Private Higher Education* (Charlottesville, Va.: Michie, 1977), pp. 825–839.

32. TENN. CONST. art 1, § 3.

33. Fort Sanders Presbyterian Hospital v. Health & Educ. Facil. Bd., 224 Tenn. 240, 453 S.W. 2d 771 (1970).

34. TENN. CONST. art. 2, §§ 29 and 31; TENN. CODE ANN. § 6-2-302.

35. Chattanooga v. Harris, 223 Tenn. 51, 442 S.W. 2d. 602 (1969).

36. TENN. CONST. art. 11, § 12.

37. TENN. CODE ANN. §§ 5-9-109(b); 6-54-111 (b).

38. *Id.* § 48-2201.

39. *Id.* § 49-3233.

40. *Id.* §§ 67-3047 *et seq.* (Supp. 1979).

41. *Id.* § 49-601. Established under the Tennessee Constitution, art. 11, § 12. See State v. Knoxville, 115 Tenn. 175, 90 S.W. 289 (1905). See TENN. CODE ANN. §§ 49-3501 *et seq.* (Supp. 1979).

42. Lynn v. Polk, 76 Tenn. 121, 76 Tenn. 328 (1881).

43. U.S. CONST. amend. 24.

44. TENN. CODE ANN. §§ 48-1901 *et seq.*

45. *Id.* § 48-1908.

46. *Id.* §§ 48-1901 *et seq.*

47. Fort Sanders Presbyterian Hospital v. Health and Educ. Facil. Bd., 224 Tenn. 240, 453 S.W. 2d 771 (1970).

48. *Id.* at 243, 453 S.W.2d at 774.

49. TENN. CODE ANN. § 49-4201.

50. *Id.* §§ 49-4202 *et seq.*

51. *Id.* § 49-4204.

52. *Id.* § 49-4214 (Supp. 1981).

53. *Id.* § 49-4212.

54. *Id.* § 49-4212(1).

55. See the Southern Regional Education Compact legislation at *id.* §§ 49-3601 *et seq.*

56. *Id.* § 49-3606. For details, see *id.*

57. *Id.* § 49-5003 (Supp. 1979).

58. See Lemon v. Kurtzman, 403 U.S. 602, 612-613 (1971).

59. TENN. CODE ANN. § 49-5013(1) (Supp. 1979).

60. *Id.* § 49-5013(2).

61. *Id.* § 49-5017.

62. *Id.* § 49-2952.

63. *Id.*

64. *Id.* §§ 49-4901 *et seq.*

65. *Id.* § 49-4901.

66. See text at note 57, *supra.*

67. TENN. CODE ANN. § 49-5402 (Supp. 1979).

68. *Id.* § 49-5405.

69. *Id.* §§ 49-5005, 49-5006.

70. *Id.* § 49-3228.

71. *Id.* §§ 4-21-101 *et seq.* A state executive order prohibits employment discrimination on the basis of handicap, race, color, religion, sex, or national origin by the state or any agency, department or institution of the state. See [1977] 8A LAB. REL. REP. (BNA) 457:1865.

72. TENN. CODE ANN. § 4-21-102(e).

73. *Id.* § 4-21-102(b) and (g).

74. *Id.* § 4-21-103.

75. *Id.* § 4-21-104.

76. *Id.* § 4-21-105(1) and (2). Related practices are also prohibited, such as discrimination in job advertisements. See *id.* §§ 4-21-108 *et seq.* Sex discrimination in compensation by any employer is forbidden. See text at note 82, *infra.*

77. TENN. CODE ANN. § 4-21-110(1)(A). There is a parallel exemption for advertising. *Id.* § 4-21-108(2). Curiously, the Commission's "Rules of Practice and Procedures" states that religion, *national origin* or sex may be a BFOQ in advertising.[1980] Emp. Prac. Guide (CCH) ¶27, 965.10.

78. TENN. CODE ANN. § 4-21-109.

79. *Id.* §§ 49-5301 *et seq.* See text accompanying notes 171-172, *infra.*

80. TENN. CODE ANN. § 8-50-103.

81. *Id.* § 8-50-105.

82. *Id.* §§ 50-320 *et seq.*

83. See Acts 1949, ch. 200, § 1; C. Supp. 1950, § 5323; Acts 1953, ch. 242, § 1; TENN. CODE ANN. § 50-718 (Repealed 1969).

84. TENN. CODE ANN. §§ 50-901 *et seq.*

85. *Id.* § 50-906(b)(c) and (d).

86. *Id.* § 50-906(b). "Casual employment" means without regularity, occasional or incidental unless in the usual course of business. Smith v. Lincoln Memorial Univ., 202 Tenn. 238, 304 S.W. 2d 70 (1957). See also Gibbons v. Roller Estates, Inc., 163 Tenn. 373, 43 S.W. 2d 198 (1931); Murphy v. Gaylord, 160 Tenn. 660, 28 S.W. 2d 348 (1930).

87. TENN. CODE ANN. § 50-904.

88. *Id.* § 50-903.

89. *Id.* § 50-1205(a) (Supp. 1980).

90. *Id.* § 50-1205(b) (Supp. 1980).

91. *Id.* §§ 50-1301 *et seq.*

92. Wiley v. Higgins, 192 Tenn. 65, 237 S.W. 2d 555 (1951).

93. TENN. CODE ANN. § 50-1309(6)(I) and (J) (Supp. 1979). See also text accompanying note 104, *infra.*

94. TENN. CODE ANN. § 50-1307 (Supp. 1979).

95. *Id.* § 50-1308(1)(A) (Supp. 1979).

96. *Id.* § 50-1308(1)(B) (Supp. 1979). Included

also is any employing unit, not otherwise qualifying as an employer, "for which within either the current or preceding calendar year services in employment are or were performed in respect to which such employing unit is liable for any federal tax against which credit may be taken for contributions required to be paid into a state unemployment compensation fund." *Id.* § 50–1308(3) (Supp. 1979).

97. *Id.* § 50–1309(1)(C)(i)–(ii) (Supp. 1979).
98. *Id.* § 50–1309(1)(C)(ii) (Supp. 1979).
99. *Id.*
100. *Id.* § 50–1309(1)(C)(i) (Supp. 1979); see I.R.C. § 3306(c)(8). Except for services for these organizations under the two conditions specified, the legislation excludes from "employment" services performed for a nonprofit corporation organized and operated exclusively for religious, charitable, literary, or educational purposes. TENN. CODE ANN. § 50–1309(6)(G).
101. *Id.* § 50–1309(1)(D)(i) (Supp. 1979).
102. *Id.* § 50–1309–(1)(D)(ii) (Supp. 1979).
103. *Id.* § 50–1309(1)(J) (Supp. 1979).
104. *Id.* § 50–1312(6)(I)(i) (Supp. 1979).
105. *Id.* § 50–1312–(6)(I)(ii) (Supp. 1979).
106. *Id.*
107. *Id.* § 50–1312(6)(J) (Supp. 1979).
108. *Id.*
109. *Id.* § 50–1323(G)(1) and (3) (Supp. 1979). For details, see *id.*
110. See *id.* §§ 50–1326 *et seq.*
111. *Id.* § 50–1328(6)(a)(A).
112. *Id.*
113. *Id.* § 50–1330(D)(1) and (2).
114. *Id.* §§ 49–5501 *et seq.*
115. *Id.* §§ 49–5504 *et seq.*
116. *Id.* § 50–208.
117. *Id.* §§ 48–406 *et seq.*
118. *Id.* §§ 48–407 to 411.
119. *Id.* §§ 49–1771.
120. *Id.*
121. See the state cooperative education program at *id.* §§ 49–5301 *et seq.*, and the state grant-in-aid program at § 49–5013(2) (Supp. 1979). See also text at notes 59–60, *supra*, and 171–172, *infra.*
122. TENN. CODE ANN. § 49–3213.
123. *Id.* § 53–2547(a),(b) (Supp. 1979).
124. *Id.* § 53–2546 (Supp. 1979).
125. *Id.*
126. *Id.* § 4–21–111. The law does not apply to bathrooms, health clubs, rooms for sleeping or changing clothes, or other places of public accommodation the Commission specifically exempts on the basis of bona fide considerations of public policy. *Id.* § 4–21–113.
127. *Id.* § 4–21–112.

128. *Id.* § 4–21–102(j).
129. *Id.*
130. See text at notes 119 *et seq., supra.*
131. TENN. CODE ANN. § 62–710.
132. *Id.* § 62–707(1)(2).
133. *Id.* § 4–21–104. For its powers and duties, see *id.*
134. *Id.* § 64–2804(a).
135. *Id.* § 53–5502.
136. *Id.* §§ 49–3906, 3907(xi).
137. See *id.* § 53–2562.
138. *Id.* §§ 50–501 *et seq.* (1977).
139. *Id.* § 50–583.
140. *Id.* § 50–504.
141. *Id.* § 67–2610. The stocks and bonds involved must be exempt from property tax under *id.* § 67–513.
142. *Id.* § 67–2702.
143. *Id.* § 67–2902.
144. *Id.* § 67–2704(a)(5) and (b)(5) (Supp. 1980). These donations are subtracted from the charitable contributions deduction claimed under I.R.C. § 170.
145. TENN. CODE ANN. § 30–1608 (Supp. 1979).
146. *Id.* § 67–2503.
147. *Id.*
148. *Id.* § 30–1701–20.
149. *Id.* § 67–5804(h).
150. *Id.* § 67–5805 (Supp. 1979).
151. *Id.*
152. *Id.* § 67–5812(f) (Supp. 1979).
153. TENN. CONST. art. 2, § 28.
154. Cumberland Lodge, No. 8 v. Mayor of Nashville, 127 Tenn. 248, 154 S.W. 1141 (1912).
155. TENN. CODE ANN. § 67–513.
156. *Id.* § 67–513(e).
157. *Id.* § 67–514.
158. Metro. Gov. v. Nashville Pi Beta Phi House, 56 Tenn. App. 330, 467 S.W. 2d 179 (1966).
159. State v. Waggoner, 162 Tenn. 172, 35 S.W. 2d 389 (1931).
160. TENN. CODE ANN. § 67–3010.
161. *Id.* §§ 67–3012, 67–3014 (Supp. 1979).
162. *Id.* § 67–3014 (b) and (c) (Supp. 1979); see I.R.C. § 501(c)(3).
163. TENN. CODE ANN. § 67–3014(d) and (e) (Supp. 1979).
164. *Id.* §§ 48–2201 *et seq.*
165. *Id.* § 48–2202.
166. *Id.*
167. *Id.*
168. *Id.* § 39–2032.
169. TENN. CONST. art. 11, § 55; TENN. CODE ANN. §§ 39–2017 *et seq.*
170. Acts 1979, ch. 358, § 9 (amending TENN. CODE ANN. § 39–2033(8)(1979).

171. TENN. CODE ANN. §§ 49–5301 *et seq.*

172. *Id.* § 49–5304(a).

173. See text at notes 77 *et seq.* and at notes 119 *et seq., supra.*

174. TENN. CODE ANN. § 4–21–107.

175. *Id.* § 4–21–110(1)(B).

176. *Id.* §§ 50–1403 *et seq.* (Supp. 1979).

177. *Id.* § 49–1304.

178. *Id.* § 49–3249.

179, *Id.* § 65–510.

180. *Id.* § 39–2510(1),(4); § 57–7–112.

181. *Id.* § 57–5–105(3).

182. *Id.*

183. *Id.* § 23–1506 (1959) (amended 1978).

184. *Id.* § 23–1506.

51. Texas

1. TEX. REV. CIV. STAT. ANN. art. 1396, §§ 3.01 *et seq.* (Vernon 1980). Cf. §§ 45 to 51 of the Model Nonprofit Corporation Act, discussed in Chapter 1, "Corporate Status," *supra.*

2. TEX. REV. CIV. STAT. ANN. art. 1396, § 3.01. The Act provides a sample form for the articles of incorporation of a nonprofit corporation. *Id.* § 3.02.

3. *Id.* § 3.01. There is a fee for filing the articles of incorporation. *Id.* § 9.03.

4. *Id.* §§ 3.03 and 3.04.

5. *Id.* art. 1302, § 3.02.

6. *Id.* § 3.02(A).

7. 444 U.S. 672 (1979). For a discussion of this case, see Edward McGlynn Gaffney and Philip R. Moots, *Government and Campus: Federal Regulation of Religiously Affiliated Higher Education* (Notre Dame, Ind.: University of Notre Dame Press, 1982), pp. 151–166.

8. TEX. REV. CIV. STAT. ANN. art. 1396, § 3.02(B).

9. *Id.* § 2.23.

10. *Id.*

11. *Id.* § 2.23A.

12. *Id.* § 6.06.

13. *Id.* § 7.01(A).

14. *Id.* § 7.01(B) and (C).

15. *Id.* §§ 6.02 and 6.03.

16. *Id.* § 7.11.

17. See e.g., Stahl v. Schriners' Hosp. for Crippled Children, 581 S.W. 2d 227 (Tex. Civ. App. 1979).

18. TEX. CONST. art. 1, § 7.

19. *Id.* art. 7, § 5.

20. Op. Atty. Gen. 1973, No. H–66.

21. For a thorough discussion of legislation in Texas providing financial assistance to private institutions of higher education, see A.E. Dick Howard, *State Aid to Private Higher Education* (Charlottesville, Va.: Michie, 1977), pp. 840–863.

22. TEX. EDUC. CODE ANN. §§ 53.01 *et seq.* (Vernon 1972).

23. *Id.* § 53.11.

24. *Id.* § 53.33.

25. *Id.* §§ 53.31 and 53.32.

26. *Id.* §§ 53.34 *et seq.*

27. *Id.* § 53.44.

28. *Id.* § 53.02(5).

29. See e.g., the Higher Education Act of 1963, 20 U.S.C. § 711–21, sustained in Tilton v. Richardson, 403 U.S. 672 (1971).

30. TEX. EDUC. CODE ANN. § 53.02(6).

31. See Hunt v. McNair, 413 U.S. 734 (1973).

32. TEX. EDUC. CODE ANN. §§ 52.01 *et seq.*

33. *Id.* § 52.32.

34. *Id.* § 52.31.

35. See Americans United for Separation of Church and State v. Blanton, 433 F.Supp. 97 (M.D. Tenn.), *affd.*, 434 U.S. 803 (1977); but see Roemer v. Bd. of Public Works, 426 U.S. 736, 740–742 (1976).

36. TEX. EDUC. CODE ANN. §§ 57.41 *et seq.* (Supp. 1980).

37. *Id.* § 57.44.

38. 20 U.S.C. §§ 1001 *et seq.*; see *id.* § 1085 for the eligibility requirements.

39. TEX. EDUC. CODE ANN. § 57.46.

40. See Americans United for the Separation of Church and State v. Blanton, note 35, *supra.*

41. TEX. EDUC. CODE ANN. §§ 61.221 *et seq.* (Supp. 1980).

42. *Id.* § 61.227. These grants, however, cannot be made without specific appropriations from the legislature.

43. *Id.* § 61.222 grants to the Coordinating Board the power to approve institutions for purposes of student participation in this program.

44. *Id.* § 61.223.

45. Op. Atty. Gen. 1973, NO. H–66.

46. TEX. EDUC. CODE ANN. § 61.226 (Supp. 1980).

47. See., e.g., Americans United for the Separation of Church and State v. Blanton, note 35, *supra.*

48. TEX. EDUC. CODE ANN. §§ 56.031 *et seq.* (Supp. 1980).

49. *Id.* § 56.014.

50. TEX. HUMAN RESOURCES CODE ANN. tit. 8, §§ 121.001 *et seq.* (Supp. 1980).

51. *Id.* § 121.003(f).

52. *Id.* § 121.004. The criminal penalty if a fine of not more than $300 nor less than $100. Damages for an injured party are presumed to be at least $100.

53. *Id.* § 121.003(g).

54. See text accompanying notes 41–49, *supra*.

55. See, e.g., Grove City College v. Harris, 500 F. Supp. 253 (W.D. Pa. 1980), reversed in part and remanded, 687 F. 2d 684 (3d Cir. 1982), *cert. pending*, No. 82–792.

56. TEX. HUMAN RESOURCES CODE ANN. tit. 8, § 121.002(4) (Vernon, 1980).

57. TEX. REV. CIV. STAT. ANN. art. 5159d (Vernon, 1971).

58. *Id.* § 4(b).

59. *Id.* § 4(a).

60. *Id.* art. 5155 (Vernon, 1971).

61. *Id.* art. 5165.1–3 (Supp. 1980).

62. *Id.* art. 5181(d) (Supp. 1980).

63. *Id.* art. 8306 to 8309 (Supp. 1980).

64. *Id.* art. 8306, § 2 (Supp. 1980).

65. Op. Atty. Gen. 1973, No. H–33.

66. Consolidated Cas. Ins. Co. v. Jackson, 419 S.W. 2d 232 (Tex. Civ. App. 1967).

67. Texas Empire Ins. Assn. v. Thomas, 415 S.W.2d 18 (Tex. Civ. App. 1967).

68. TEX. REV. CIV. STAT. ANN. art. 8307.

69. *Id.* art. 8308, §§ 7 and 21.

70. *Id.* § 18 (Supp. 1980).

71. TEX. LABOR CODE ANN. tit. 83, §§ 522lb–1 *et seq.* (Vernon Supp. 1980).

72. *Id.* § 522lb–17(f)(3) (Vernon Supp. 1980). See *id.* § 522lb–6(b)(1) (Vernon Supp. 1980).

73. *Id.* § 522lb–17(f)(3) (Vernon Supp. 1980).

74. *Id.* § 522lb–17(g)(5)(E) (Vernon Supp. 1980).

75. *Id.*

76. *Id.* § 522lb–17(g)(5)(N) (Vernon Supp. 1980).

77. Employment is broadly defined as "any service . . . performed for wages or under any contract of hire, written or oral, express or implied." *Id.* § 522lb–17(g)(L) (Vernon Supp. 1980).

78. *Id.* tit. 83, §§ 522lb–17(f)(9), 522lb–17(g)(5)(C) (Vernon Supp. 1980).

79. *Id.* § 522lb–17(g)(5)(A) (Vernon Supp. 1980).

80. *Id.* § 522lb–17(g)(5)(S) (Vernon Supp. 1980).

81. *Id.* § 522lb–17(g)(5)(T) (Vernon Supp. 1980).

82. *Id.* § 522lb–6(b)(1), (b)(2) (Vernon Supp. 1980). The Commission is established at *id.* § 522lb–8(a) (Vernon Supp. 1980).

83. *Id.* § 522lb–5a(a), (b) (Vernon Supp. 1980).

84. *Id.* § 522lb–5a(j) (Vernon Supp. 1980).

85. *Id.* § 522lb–6(b)(6) (Vernon Supp. 1980).

86. TEX. REV. CIV. STAT. ANN. art. 5207a; see also *id.* art. 5154g, and TEX. BUS. & COM. CODE ANN., §15.03(a)94).

87. TEX. REV. CIV. STAT. ANN. art. 5207a, § 2.

88. *Id.* art. 5207a § 3.

89. *Id.* art. 5154a, § 8a.

90. *Id.* art. 5196 *et seq.*

91. *Id.* art. 5196(6).

92. *Id.* art. 5196(5).

93. See text accompanying notes 41–49, *supra*.

94. See text accompanying notes 95–98, *infra*.

95. TEX. HUMAN RESOURCES CODE ANN. tit. 8, § 121.003(c) (Vernon, Supp. 1980).

96. *Id.* § 121.003(d).

97. *Id.* § 121.003(h).

98. *Id.* § 121.002(3).

99. *Id.* § 121.003(i).

100. Op. Atty. Gen. 1974, No. H–420.

101. TEX. REV. CIV. STAT. ANN. art. 60lb., §§ 7.01 *et seq.* (Vernon Supp. 1980).

102. *Id.* art. 60lb, § 7.02(a).

103. See text accompanying notes 22–30, *supra*.

104. TEX. REV. CIV. STAT. ANN. art. 60lb, § 7.02(d) (Vernon Supp. 1980).

105. *Id.* art. 60lb, § 7.03.

106. *Id.* art. 60lb, § 7.05.

107. *Id.* art. 5182(a), § 4.

108. *Id.* art. 5182(a), § 8.

109. *Id.* art. 5182(a), § 2(5).

110. *Id.* art. 5182(a), § 2(6).

111. *Id.* art. 5182(a), § 2(9).

112. *Id.* art. 5182(a), § 4(d) (Vernon Supp. 1980).

113. TEX. TAX. CODE ANN., tit. 122A, § 12.03(1)(g) (Supp. 1980).

114. *Id.* tit. 122A, § 14.015 (2) (Supp. 1980).

115. *Id.* tit. 122A, § 14.12 (1965).

116. *Id.* tit. 122A, § 11.21 (Pamphlet 1979).

117. *Id.* tit. 122A, § 11.21(b) (Pamphlet 1979).

118. *Id.* tit. 122A, § 11.21(c) (Pamphlet 1979).

119. *Id.* tit. 122A, § 11.20 (Pamphlet 1979).

120. *Id.* tit. 122A, § 20.04(h)(5) (Supp. 1980).

121. *Id.* tit. 122A, § 20.04 (GGX1) (Supp. 1980).

122. *Id.* tit. 122A, § 20.04(T) (1969).

123. *Id.* tit. 122A, § 20.04(L) (1969).

124. *Id.* tit. 122A, § 20.04(D)(5) (Supp. 1980).

125. *Id.* tit. 122A, § 20.04(D)(1)(c)(d) (1969).

126. *Id.* tit. 122A, § 20.04(F)(1) (1969).

127. *Id.* tit. 122A, § 23.02 (1969).

128. For a comprehensive treatment of governmental regulation of fund raising, see Bruce R. Hopkins, *Charity Under Seige* (New York: Wiley, 1980).

129. TEX. PENAL CODE ANN. tit. 10, §§ 47.02, 47.03 (Vernon, 1974). Op. Atty. Gen. 1976, No. H–820 ruled that a lottery held even for charitable purposes is illegal.

130. TEX. EDUC. CODE ANN. tit. 3, § 61.064 (1972).

131. *Id.* This chapter explicitly permits a contractual arrangement with Baylor University (a Baptist-

related RAC) for the purpose of educating Texas medical students, *id.* § 61.091. On the other hand, a contractual arrangement contemplated among three RACs and a Texas junior college, which would require the RACs to accept junior college students, was forestalled by the Texas Attorney General because in his opinion such an arrangement would require "excessive entanglements between church and state." Op. Atty. Gen. 1972, No. M–1036.

132. Tex. Educ. Code Ann. tit. 3, § 61.303 (Supp. 1980). An exempt institution may be issued a certificate to grant degrees if it so desires.

133. *Id.* § 51.212.

134. Tex. Rev. Civ. Stat. Ann. arts. 581–5(k); 581–6(e) (Vernon Supp. 1980).

135. Tex. Tax. Code Ann., tit. 122A, § 13.17(8) (Supp. 1981).

52. Utah

1. Utah Code Ann. §§ 16–6–18 to –6–53 (1953, Supp, 1979). See generally, Paul G. Kauper and Steven C. Ellis, "Religious Corporations and the Law," 71 Mich. L. Rev. 1499, 1554–1557 (1973). For the exemption of an RAC from securities registration and related provisions, see Utah Code Ann. §§ 61–1–1 (1953, Supp. 1979) *et seq.* and *id.* §§ 63–55–1 to 63–55–7.

2. *Id.* § 16–6–19(3).

3. *Id.* § 16–6–21.

4. *Id.* §§ 16–6–97(1)–(3), –6–98.

5. *Id.* § 16–6–99 (notice of delinquency, notice of suspension date—unless the annual report is filed on or before the suspension date the charter of the corporation will be suspended as of that date).

6. *Id.* § 16–6–100.

7. *Id.* § 16–6–54 (merger). See also *id.* § 16–6–55 (consolidation).

8. *Id.* § 16–6–62.

9. *Id.* § 16–6–63(1)–(2).

10. *Id.* § 16–6–63(3). Indeed, the subsection refers to a conveyance to other nonprofit corporations, societies or organizations engaged in "substantially similar" activities.

11. *Id.* § 16–6–70(3).

12. Gardner v. Davis County, 523 P.2d 865, 868 (Utah 1974).

13. Utah Const. art. X, § 13. See Grubler v. Utah State Teachers' Retirement Bd., 113 Utah 188, 192 P.2d 580 (1948), upholding the constitutionality of a statute interpreted to permit teachers to receive credit in computing retirement benefit for prior services performed as teachers in parochial schools.

The court said: "We have not overlooked the caveat that this court should be ever mindful not to abridge, in the name of education, the complete division of religious and civil authority which our forefathers made. Were we convinced that this act in the slightest degree introduced sectarian education and observance into the public schools, had a tendency to aid or support religious schools or a religious faith, we would cast it aside." 192 P.2d at 586.

14. Utah Const. art. I, § 4. See *Grubler*, note 13, *supra.*

15. Utah Code Ann. §§ 53–47–1, –2.

16. *Id.* § 53–34–2.2 (Supp: 1980) contains the definition of "resident" student.

17. *Id.* § 53–47–2. See *id.* § 53–47a–1(1).

18. Section 53–48–24(4) provides: "An eligible institution . . . shall mean an institution authorized to provide post-high school education which (a) is a nonprofit or public institution or (b) is accredited by a nationally recognized accrediting agency or association or (c) is determined by the U.S. Commissioner of Education to be an eligible institution under any student loan insurance program supported in whole or in part by federal funds." See *id.* § 53–47a–1(4).

19. *Id.* § 53–47a–1(6).

20. *Id.* §§ 53–47b–1 to –14 (Supp. 1979).

21. *Id.* § 53–47b–2(4) provides: " 'Eligible institution' means: an institution of higher education; a vocational school; or, with respect to students who are citizens of the United States, an institution outside the United States comparable to institutions of higher education, or vocational schools which are approved by the [state] board [of regents] and the United States commissioner of education for purposes of the guaranteed loan program."

22. *Id.* § 53–47b–2(6) says: " 'Student' means a person who, under the rules promulgated by the board, is enrolled or accepted for enrollment at an eligible institution and who is making suitable progress in his education toward obtaining a degree or other appropriate certification in accordance with standards acceptable to the board."

23. *Id.* §§ 53–48–1 to –25 (1953 & Supp. 1979).

24. *Id.* § 53–48–2 (Supp. 1979).

25. *Id.* § 53–48–22.

26. *Id.* §§ 63–7–12 *et seq.* (Supp. 1979).

27. *Id.* §§ 34–35–1 to –35–8 (Supp. 1979).

28. *Id.* § 34–35–6(1).

29. *Id.* § 34–35–2(5): " 'Employer' . . . does not include religious organizations or associations, religious corporations sole, nor any corporation or association constituting a wholly owned subsidiary or agency of any religious organization or association or religious corporation sole. . . . "

30. In a letter of November 12, 1981, Frank V.

Nelson, Assistant Attorney General of Utah, suggested that an RAC is not an employer under the anti-discrimination act.

31. 42 U.S.C. § 2000e–1, § 702 of Title VII of the Civil Rights Act of 1964, as amended by the Equal Employment Opportunity Act of 1972.

32. Philip R. Moots and Edward McGlynn Gaffney, *Church and Campus: Legal Issues in Religiously Affiliated Higher Education* (Notre Dame, Ind.: University of Notre Dame Press, 1979), pp. 53–57.

33. UTAH CODE ANN. § 34–35–6(2)(a).

34. *Id.*

35. Moots and Gaffney, *Church and Campus*, note 32, *supra*, at 35.

36. UTAH CODE ANN. § 34–35–6(2)(b).

37. Moots and Gaffney, *Church and Campus*, note 32, *supra*, at 48.

38. See N.M. STAT. ANN. § 28–1–9.B (Appendix II).

39. Moots and Gaffney, *Church and Campus*, note 32, *supra*, at 55.

40. UTAH CODE ANN. § 34–35–6(1)–(2).

41. *Id.* § 34–35–2(14) (Supp. 1979).

42. *Id.* § 34–35–6(1)(a).

43. See Mormon Church v. United States, 136 U.S. 1, 50 (1889).

44. UTAH CODE ANN. §§ 35–1–1 *et seq.* (1974, Supp. 1981).

45. *Id.* § 35–1–42(2) (Supp. 1981).

46. *Id.* § 35–1–43(2) (Supp. 1981).

47. *Id.* § 35–1–46 (Supp. 1981).

48. *Id.* § 35–1–46(3) (Supp. 1981).

49. *Id.* § 35–4–1 *et seq.* (Supp. 1981).

50. The definition of "employment" is found at *id.* § 35–4–22(j).

51. This section refers specifically to a "religious, charitable, educational, or other organization." *Id.* § 35–4–22(j)(2)(E).

52. *Id.*

53. *Id.* § 35–4–22(j)(2)(E)(i).

54. *Id.* § 35–4–22(j)(2)(E)(ii).

55. *Id.* § 35–4–22(j)(6)(H)(i)(aa).

56. *Id.* § 35–4–22(j)(6)(H)(i)(bb).

57. *Id.* § 35–4–22(j)(6)(H)(ii).

58. These state exemptions require that such services be exempt from coverage under the Federal Unemployment Tax Act. *Id.* § 35–4–22(j)(6).

59. *Id.* § 35–4–22(j)(6)(F)(i)(aa).

60. *Id.* § 35–4–22(j)(6)(F)(i)(bb). Spouses must be informed that employment is offered as a means of financial aid and that their services are not covered by any program of unemployment compensation.

61. *Id.* § 35–4–22(j)(6)(F)(ii).

62. *Id.* §§ 35–4–22(j)(6)(E), (j)(2)(K).

63. *Id.* § 35–4–7.5(a).

64. *Id.* § 35–4–7.5(a)(3).

65. *Id.* § 35–4–7.5(b). The Department is established at *id.* § 35–4–13.

66. *Id.* § 35–4–7.5(a)(1).

67. *Id.* § 35–4–7.5(d).

68. *Id.* §§ 35–4–8(c)(1), 35–4–22(j).

69. *Id.* §§ 34–22–8 to –11, –13, –16, to –18.

70. *Id.* § 34–35–6(1)(a).

71. The only exception is an increase in pay, uniformly available to all employees, as a result of longevity with the employer. *Id.*

72. *Id.* §§ 34–20–7, –19–1.

73. *Id.* § 34–20–7.

74. *Id.* § 34–20–2(2).

75. 120 Utah 463, 235 P.2d 520 (1951).

76. 235 P.2d at 521, 524–525.

77. UTAH CONST. art. X, § 12.

78. UTAH CODE ANN. § 13–7–1 (Supp. 1979).

79. *Id.* § 13–7–2(c) (Supp. 1979): "Enterprises regulated by the state" are defined as "(1) All institutions subject to regulation under the Utah Uniform Commercial Credit Code, Title 70B. . . ." Under § 70B–1–301(11), an organization is defined as any corporation.

80. See W. Cole Durham, Jr. and Dallin H. Oaks, "Constitutional Protections for Independent Higher Education: Limited Powers and Institutional Rights," in John D. Mosely, ed., *Church and College: A Vital Partnership* (Sherman, Tex.: Austin College, 1980), vol. 4, pp. 69–87.

81. *Id.* § 13–7–2(a).

82. *Id.* § 13–7–3 (Supp. 1979).

83. *Id.* § 13–7–2(c) (Supp. 1979).

84. Compare Pub. L. 88–352, 78 Stat. 243, Title II, § 201(a), 42 U.S.C. 2000a, sustained in Heart of Atlanta Motel v. United States, 379 U.S. 241 (1964), with UTAH CODE ANN. § 13–7–3.

85. See letter of Frank V. Nelson, note 30, *supra.*

86. See Edward McGlynn and Philip R. Moots, *Government and Campus: Federal Regulation of Religiously Affiliated Higher Education* (Notre Dame, Ind: University of Notre Dame Press, 1981), Chapter 3.

87. UTAH CODE ANN. § 13–7–2(a) (Supp. 1981). See text accompanying note 81, *supra.*

88. UTAH CODE ANN. § 55–18–9(7).

89. *Id.*

90. *Id.* §§ 55–18–9(4).

91. *Id.* §§ 35–7–5 to –9 (1953 & Supp. 1979).

92. *Id.* §§ 26–15–1 to 15–90 (1953 & Supp. 1979).

93. *Id.* § 26–15–4(3)–(11).

94. *Id.* §§ 26–15–1, –5 (1953 & Supp. 1979).

95. *Id.* § 35–9–1 *et seq.* (1974).

96. *Id.* § 35–9–3.

97. *Id.* §§ 59–14A–1 to –38.

98. *Id.* § 59–14A–4(b).

99. *Id.* §§ 59–13–1 to 13–97.

100. *Id.* § 59–13–4(4).

101. *Id.* §§ 59–12A–1 to –12A–15.

102. *Id.* § 59–12A–3(1).

103. *Id.* § 59–12A–2(4).

104. *Id.* § 59–14–5.

105. *Id.*

106. *Id.* § 59–13–7.

107. *Id.* § 59–1–1.

108. *Id.*

109. Utah Const. art. XIII, § 2; Utah Code Ann. § 59–2–1.

110. Utah Code Ann. § 59–2–30(1)–(4).

111. *Id.* § 59–2–31.

112. Salt Lake County v. Tax Comm'n, 548 P.2d 630 (Utah 1976).

113. See letter of Frank V. Nelson, note 30, *supra.*

114. Parker v. Quinn, 23 Utah 332, 64 P. 961 (1901).

115. Salt Lake Lodge No. 85 v. Groesbeck, 40 Utah 1, 120 P. 192 (1911) (fraternal order clubhouse partly used as a buffet and café only incidental to charitable purpose of the order).

116. B.P.O.E. No. 85 v. Tax Comm'n, 536 P.2d 1214 (Utah 1975).

117. Salt Lake County v. Tax Comm'n, 548 P.2d 630 (Utah 1976).

118. Friendship Manor Corp. v. Tax Comm'n, 26 Utah 2d 227, 487 P.2d 1972 (1971) (nonprofit corporation not exempt as a charity where senior citizen residents paid for services and rent not based on need, but based on amount necessary to cover the facility's expenses and mortgage).

119. Baker v. One Piece of Improved Real Property, 570 P.2d 1023 (Utah 1977) (organization's expenditures on charitable objects amounted to only slightly more than 2% of total expenditures—organization more like a social club).

120. Utah Code Ann. § 59–5–1 (Supp. 1979).

121. *Id.* §§ 59–15–1 to 15–22.

122. *Id.* § 59–15–6(1).

123. Youth Tennis Foundation v. Tax Comm'n, 554 P.2d 220 (Utah 1976).

124. Utah Code Ann. §§ 59–16–1 to 16–25 (1953, Supp. 1979 & Supp. 1980).

125. *Id.* § 59–16–4(b).

126. 1980 Utah Laws, ch. 67, §§ 1–6 (codified at Utah Code Ann. §§ 59–17–1 to –17–6 (Supp. 1980).

127. Utah Code Ann. § 59–17–3(5).

128. *Id.* §§ 76–10–601 to –10–604 (1978).

129. *Id.* § 76–10–601(4).

130. *Id.* § 76–10–601(5).

131. *Id.* § 76–10–602.

132. *Id.* § 76–10–603. Nor may a person's name be listed or referred to as one who has contributed to, sponsored, or endorsed the charitable organization or its activities. *Id.*

133. *Id.* §§ 76–10–1101 to 1109.

134. *Id.* § 76–10–1101(1).

135. *Id.* § 76–10–1101(2).

136. D'Orio v. Startup Candy Co., 71 Utah 410, 266 P. 1037 (1928).

137. 600 P.2d 982 (Utah 1979).

138. Geis v. Continental Oil Co., 29 Utah 2d 452, 511 P.2d 725 (1973), citing Schillberg v. Safeway Stores, Inc., 75 Wash. 2d 339, 450 P.2d 949 (1969).

139. Albertson's, Inc. v. Hansen, 600 P.2d 982, 985–986 (Utah 1979) (Emphasis omitted).

140. *Id.*

141. 600 P.2d at 986–987 (Maughan, J., dissenting). Section 27 of article VI of the Constitution of Utah reads: "The Legislature shall not authorize any game of chance, lottery or gift enterprise under any pretense or for any purpose."

142. Utah Code Ann. §§ 59–23–1 to 13.

143. *Id.* §§ 59–23–7, –8.

144. *Id.* § 59–23–12.

145. *Id.* § 33–1–1 (Supp. 1979).

53. Vermont

1. Vt. Stat. Ann. tit. 11, § 2531.

2. *Id.* tit. 32, § 8001.

3. *Id.* tit. 11, §§ 2301 *et seq.* (1973, Supp. 1980).

4. Ball v. Hall, 129 Vt. 200, 274 A.2d 516 (1971).

5. Vt. Stat. Ann. tit. 11, § 2601.

6. *Id.* § 2606.

7. *Id.* §§ 2607 and 2608.

8. *Id.* § 2610.

9. *Id.* § 2602. For a discussion of the Model Act, see Chapter 1, "Corporate Status," *supra.*

10. Vt. Const. ch. I, art. 3.

11. *Id.* ch. II, § 68.

12. Vt. Stat. Ann. tit. 16, § 3853(3).

13. *Id.* § 3851(c).

14. 127 Vt. 262, 247 A.2d 68 (1968), *appeal dismissed,* 396 U.S. 801 (1969).

15. *Id.* at 266, 247 A.2d at 71.

16. Vt. Stat. Ann. tit. 16, §§ 2822(h) and 2531a(a)(1). Accreditation is by the State Board of Education, the New England Association of Colleges and Secondary Schools or any comparable agency, or the State Board of Nursing.

17. *Id.* tit. 21, § 495(d).

18. *Id.* § 495.
19. *Id.* § 495a.
20. *Id.* § 302.
21. *Id.* § 382.
22. *Id.* § 601(4).
23. *Id.* § 616.
24. *Id.* § 1301.
25. *Id.* § 1301(5)(A)(ix).
26. *Id.* § 1301(4).
27. 26 U.S.C.A. § 501(c)(3).
28. *Id.* § 3306(c)(8).
29. VT. STAT. ANN. tit. 13, § 1451(a) (Supp. 1980).
30. *Id.* § 1451(b).
31. *Id.* § 1451(c).
32. *Id.* § 1452(b).
33. See text accompanying note 31, *supra.*
34. VT. STAT. ANN. tit. 13, § 1452(a).
35. See note 32 and accompanying text.
36. VT. STAT. ANN. tit. 18, § 1322.
37. *Id.*
38. *Id.* § 1301.
39. *Id.* tit. 21, § 203(7), (8).
40. *Id.* tit. 32, § 5811(3)(J).
41. *Id.* § 3801(4).
42. *Id.*
43. *Id.* § 3831(a).
44. *Id.* Presumably the power of the voters to exempt such property extends only to property within that town or city.
45. *Id.* § 3832(2).
46. See *id.* § 6541 (repealed).
47. *Id.* § 7442a.
48. *Id.* § 7412 (Supp. 1980).
49. There is no general provision dealing with the power of corporations or public utilities to make charitable contributions. (The provision formerly in effect, *id.* tit. 11, § 107, was repealed in 1973.) Banks, trust companies, and mutual insurance companies, however, may make contributions for religious or educational purposes which are authorized by their directors or stockholders. *Id.* tit. 11, § 108.
50. I.R.C. § 170(c)(2)(B) and (C).
51. VT. STAT. ANN. tit. 32, § 5822 (Supp. 1980).
52. *Id.* § 5831 (Supp. 1980).
53. I.R.C. § 63.
54. 26 U.S.C. § 501(c)(3).
55. VT. STAT. ANN. tit. 32, § 9743(3).
56. *Id.*
57. VT. STAT. ANN. tit. 13, § 2143(a).

54. Virginia

1. VA. CODE § 13.1–202(c).
2. *Id.* § 13.1–204.
3. *Id.* § 13.1–229.
4. *Id.* §§ 13.1–201 *et seq.*
5. *Id.* § 13.1–204.1.
6. *Id.* § 13.1–246.1
7. *Id.* § 23–9.2.3.
8. *Id.* §§ 23–9.3 *et seq.*
9. *Id.* §§ 23–265 *et seq.* (1980). For details, see *id.*
10. *Id.* § 23–9.6:1(1).
11. *Id.* § 23–9.10:2.
12. *Id.* § 23–9.10:3.
13. *Id.* § 23–8.2(b).
14. *Id.* §§ 55–268.1 *et seq.*
15. *Id.* § 55–268.1(1).
16. *Id.* § 55–268.4.
17. *Id.* § 55–268.5.
18. *Id.* § 55–268.6.
19. *Id.* § 55–268.7.
20. Compare VA. CODE §§ 13.1–201 *et seq.* (1978, Supp. 1980) with §§ 45–51 of the Model Act. For a discussion of the Model Act, see Chapter 1, "Corporate Status," *supra.*
21. See, e.g., Campbell v. Board of Trustees of James Barry Robinson Home for Boys, 260 S.E.2d 204 (Va. 1980). For a discussion of the *cy pres* doctrine, see Chapter 1, "Corporate Status," *supra.*
22. VA. CODE §§ 13.1–248 and 13.1–253.
23. *Id.* § 13.1–254 (Supp. 1980).
24. *Id.* § 13.1–256.
25. *Id.* § 13.1–257.
26. *Id.* §§ 13.1–249 and 13.1–250.
27. See generally A. E. Dick Howard, *State Aid to Private Higher Education* (Charlottesville, Va.: Michie, 1977), pp. 889–910.
28. VA. CONST. art. 1, § 16.
29. *Id.*
30. *Id.*
31. *Id.*
32. See Everson v. Board of Education, 330 U.S. 1, 13 (1947).
33. VA. CONST. art. 8,, § 10.
34. *Id.* art. 8, § 11.
35. *Id.*
36. Miller v. Ayres, 213 Va. 251, 191 S.E.2d 261 (1972).
37. VA. CONST. art. 8, § 11.
38. Miller v. Ayres, note 36, *supra.*
39. VA. CONST. art. 10, § 10.
40. VA. CODE §§ 23–30.39 *et seq.*
41. VA. CONST. art. VIII, § 11. See text at note 35, *supra.*
42. VA. CODE § 23–30.41(e).
43. *Id.* § 23–30.25.
44. *Id.* § 23.30.47.
45. *Id.* §§ 23–30.41(b) and 23–30.41(e).

46. *Id.* § 23-9.10:3. The authority to contract also includes that to accept gifts to facilitate or advance programs. *Id.* § 23-9.10:3.E.
47. *Id.* § 23-9.10:3.A.1.
48. *Id.* § 23-9.10:3.A.3.
49. *Id.* § 23-9.10:3.B.1.
50. *Id.* § 23-9.10:3.C.
51. *Id.* § 23-9.10:3.E.
52. *Id.* § 23-9.10:3.F.
53. *Id.* § 2.1-374-77.
54. *Id.*
55. *Id.* § 15.1-24.
56. *Id.* §§ 23-38.11 *et seq.*
57. *Id.* § 23-38.12.
58. *Id.* § 23-38.14.
59. *Id.* § 23-38.16.
60. *Id.* § 23-38.15.
61. *Id.* § 23-38.16.
62. *Id.* § 23-38.15(cl).
63. *Id.* § 23-38.15(c2)(1) through (5). See Howard, *State Aid,* note 27, *supra,* at 902-903.
64. Va. Code § 23-38.15(c2)(1) through (5).
65. *Id.* § 23-38.13.
66. *Id.* §§ 23-38.45 *et seq.*
67. *Id.* § 23-38.46.
68. *Id.* § 23-38.46(b).
69. *Id.* § 23-38.48.
70. *Id.* § 23-38.50.
71. *Id.* § 23-38.49.
72. *Id.* §§ 23-38.11 *et seq.* See text at note 56, *supra.*
73. *Id.* § 23-38.30.
74. *Id.* § 23-38.33:1. The constitutional prohibition against using the state's credit, Va. Const. art. 10, § 10, is honored here by stipulating that the revenue of the Authority is the funding source and that no obligation of the Authority constitutes a debt or pledge of credit of the Commonwealth. Va. Code § 23-38.31.
75. *Id.* § 22.1-290.
76. State Bd. Of Education, Regulations For Administering Regular Term State Teacher Scholarships Loans (1972-1974). See Howard, *State Aid,* note 27, *supra,* at 906.
77. Va. Code § 23-35.9. For limits on the awards, see *id.*
78. *Id.* § 23-37.1. For details, see *id.*
79. *Id.* § 23-38.2. The scholarships, which run for one year, require the recipients to agree to work for the state upon completion of training. *Id.* § 23-38.2(b)(1) and (2).
80. *Id.* § 40.1-28.6.
81. *Id.* § 40.1-28.7.
82. *Id.* § 63.1-171.2.
83. *Id.* § 40.1-2(3).

84. *Id.* § 40.1-2(4).
85. See text at note 7, *supra.*
86. See text accompanying notes 53 and 54, *supra.*
87. Va. Code §§ 40.1-28.9 *et seq.*
88. *Id.* § 40.1-28.10. ($2.65 per hour, effective 1980).
89. *Id.* § 40.1-28.9(A). Employers with fewer than four non-family employees are excluded. *Id.* § 40.1-28.9(B)(15).
90. *Id.* § 40.1-28.9(B)(3).
91. *Id.* § 40.1-28.9(B)(9).
92. *Id.* § 40.1-28.9(B)(10).
93. *Id.* § 40.1-28.9(B)(13).
94. *Id.* § 40.1-28.9(B)(14).
95. *Id.* § 40.1-28.9(B)(16).
96. *Id.* § 40.1-28.9(B)(16A).
97. *Id.* § 40.1-80 (Supp. 1980).
98. *Id.* § 40.1-103.
99. *Id.* § 40-1-79 (Supp. 1980).
100. See text at note 167, *infra.*
101. Va. Code §§ 65.1-1 *et seq.* (1980).
102. *Id.* § 65.1-3.
103. *Id.* § 65.1-28.
104. *Id.* § 65.1-23.
105. *Id.* § 65.1-4.
106. *Id.* § 65.1-28.
107. *Id.*
108. *Id.* § 65.1-35.
109. *Id.* § 65.1-25.
110. *Id.* § 65.1-104.1.
111. *Id.* §§ 60.1-1 *et seq.* (Supp. 1980).
112. Tests for determining what constitutes employment are found at *id.* § 60.1-1(6) (Supp. 1980).
113. *Id.* § 60.1-14(1)(c) (Supp. 1980).
114. *Id.* § 60.1-14(1)(c)(i) (Supp. 1980). I.R.C. § 3306(c)(8) excludes from the definition of "employment" services performed for a religious or educational organization as described in I.R.C. § 501(c)(3). Such services are exempt from federal taxation.
115. Va. Code § 60.1-14(1)(c)(ii) (Supp. 1980).
116. *Id.* § 60.1-14(1)(d)(i)(I) (Supp. 1980).
117. *Id.* § 60.1-14(1)(d)(i)(II) (Supp. 1980).
118. *Id.* § 60.1-14(1)(d)(ii) (Supp. 1980).
119. *Id.* § 60.1-14(1)(d)(iii) (Supp. 1980). "Institution of higher education" is defined at *id.* § 60.1-14.1 (Supp. 1980).
120. *Id.* § 60.1-14(1)(d2) (Supp. 1980).
121. *Id.* § 60.1-14(7)(c) (Supp. 1980).
122. *Id.* § 60.1-14(7)(j) (Supp. 1980).
123. *Id.* § 60.1-14(7)(r) (Supp. 1980).
124. I.R.C. §§ 501(a), 521.
125. Va. Code § 60.1-14(7)(i) (Supp. 1980).

126. *Id.* § 60.1–89 (Supp. 1980).

127. *Id.* § 60.1–89(2) (Supp. 1980). The Commission is established by *id.* § 60.1–31 (Supp. 1980).

128. *Id.* § 60.1–89(1) (Supp. 1980).

129. *Id.* § 60.1–100(a) (Supp. 1980).

130. *Id.* §§ 40.1–58 *et seq.*

131. *Id.* § 40.1–58.1.

132. *Id.* § 13.1–205.1.

133. *Id.* § 40.1–51.4:3 (Supp. 1980).

134. *Id.* § 23–9.2.3.

135. *Id.* § 23–2.1.

136. *Id.* § 22.1–288.

137. *Id.* §§ 63.1–171.1 *et seq.*

138. *Id.* § 63.1–171.2.

139. *Id.* §§ 36–86 *et seq.*

140. *Id.* § 36–88(1). Related practices are also prohibited. *Id.*

141. *Id.* § 36–94.

142. *Id.* § 36–92. This sort of preference is prohibited, however, if membership in the religion is restricted on grounds of race, color, national origin, or sex. *Id.*

143. *Id.*

144. *Id.* § 63.1–171.7.

145. *Id.* § 63.1–171.7(c).

146. *Id.* § 23–9.2.3. See text at note 134, *supra.*

147. *Id.* §§ 35–25 *et seq.*

148. *Id.* § 35–25.

149. *Id.* §§ 40.1 *et seq.*

150. *Id.* § 40.1–1.

151. *Id.* § 40.1–6.

152. *Id.* § 40.1–2.

153. *Id.*

154. *Id.* § 58–151.03.

155. *Id.* § 58–456 (Supp. 1980).

156. *Id.* § 13.1–201. See text at note 1, *supra.*

157. *Id.* §§ 58.154. (Supp. 1980), 58–157 (Supp. 1980).

158. *Id.* § 58–220.

159. *Id.* §§ 58–218 (Supp. 1980) *et seq.*

160. *Id.* § 58–238.1 (Supp. 1980).

161. *Id.* § 58.151.013. (Supp. 1980).

162. I.R.C. § 170(c)(2)(B) and (C).

163. Va. Code § 58.151.013(d)(1), (2) and (3) (Supp. 1980).

164. Va. Const. art. 10, § 6.

165. Va. Code § 58–12.

166. *Id.* § 58–12.24 (implementing Va. Const. art. X, § 6(a)(6)).

167. Va. Code § 58–12.25. For details, see *id.*

168. Washington County v. Sullins College Corp., 211 Va. 591, 179 S.E.2d 630 (1971); Commonwealth v. Trustees of Hampton Normal, 106 Va. 614, 56 S.E. 594 (1907).

169. Va. Code § 58.16.2(ii) (Supp. 1980).

170. *Id.*

171. *Id.* § 58–441.6(1) (Supp. 1980). The exemption applies to other book dealers if the book involved has been appropriately certified as "required." See *id.*

172. *Id.* § 58–441.6(m) (Supp. 1980).

173. *Id.* § 58–441.6(t) (Supp. 1980).

174. *Id.* § 58–441.6(gg) (Supp. 1980). The church (or its property) must be appropriately tax-exempt. For details, see *id.*

175. *Id.*

176. *Id.* § 58–64.1 (Supp. 1980).

177. *Id.* § 58–64.2 (Supp. 1980).

178. *Id.* §§ 58–685.11 *et seq.*

179. *Id.* § 58–685.13(14).

180. *Id.* § 58–685.13(15). The drivers education instruction must be part of the school's curriculum for full-time students. *Id.*

181. *Id.* § 58–381.1 (Supp. 1980).

182. *Id.* § 58–443.

183. *Id.* § 58–450.

184. *Id.* §§ 57–48 *et seq.*

185. *Id.* § 57–60.

186. See *id.* § 57–49.

187. See *id.* § 57–53.

188. *Id.* § 57–60.

189. *Id.*

190. See *id.* § 57–57.

191. *Id.* § 57–63(a)(2) (Supp. 1980).

192. *Id.* § 18.2–325.

193. *Id.* § 18.2–334.2 (Supp. 1980).

194. *Id.* § 18.2–340.2 (Supp. 1980).

195. *Id.*

196. *Id.* § 18.2–340.9 (Supp. 1980).

197. *Id.* § 18.2–340.4 and § 18.2–340.9(D) and (G) (Supp. 1980).

198. *Id.* § 15.1–29.3.

199. *Id.* § 22.1–336.

200. *Id.* § 22.1–337.

55. Washington

1. Wash. Rev. Code Ann. §§ 24.03 *et seq.* (1969).

2. *Id.* § 24.03.015 (1969). A "not for profit corporation is defined as a corporation no part of the income of which is distributed to its members or directors." *Id.* § 24.03.005 (1969).

3. *Id.* § 24.03.02 (1969). The items to be listed in the articles of incorporation are set out in § 24.03.025 (1969).

4. *Id.* § 24.03.405 (Supp. 1979).

5. *Id.* § 24.03.030 (1969).

6. *Id.* § 24.030.005(7).

7. *Id.* § 24.03.095 (1969).

8. *Id.* § 24.03.100 (1969).

9. *Id.* § 28B.05. (Supp. 1980).

10. For details, see *id.* § 28B.05.040(5) (Supp. 1980).

11. *Id.* §§ 24.03.195 *et seq.* (1969 and Supp. 1980).

12. *Id.* §§ 24.03.220 *et seq.*

13. Compare, e.g., *id.* § 24.03.220 (voluntary dissolution) with Model Act, § 45.

14. See, e.g., Puget Sound Nat. Bank of Tacoma v. Easterday, 56 Wash. 2d 937, 350 P.2d 444 (1963). For a discussion of the *cy pres* doctrine, see Chapter 1, "Corporate Status," *supra.*

15. WASH. REV. CODE ANN. §§ 24.03.220, 240, and 245; see Model Act, §§ 45, 49 and 50.

16. WASH. REV. CODE ANN. § 24.03.250 (Supp. 1980); see Model Act, § 51.

17. WASH. REV. CODE ANN. §§ 24.03.255 and 230 (Supp. 1980); see Model Act, §§ 46 and 47.

18. See Model Act § 61.

19. WASH. REV. CODE ANN. § 24.03.302 (Supp. 1980).

20. WASH. CONST. art. 1, § 11.

21. *Id.* art. 9, § 4.

22. *Id.* art. 8, § 5.

23. Weiss v. Bruno, 509 P.2d 973 (Wash. 1973).

24. *Id.* at 988.

25. Washington State H.E.A.A. v. Graham, 84 Wn. 2d 813, 529 P.2d 1051 (1974).

26. WASH. REV. CODE ANN. §§ 28B.10.800 *et seq.* (Supp. 1979). An "institution of higher education" includes all accredited colleges and universities. *Id.* § 28B.10.802(1) (Supp. 1979).

27. Students who are pursuing degrees in theology are ineligible. *Id.* § 28B.10.814 (1970).

28. *Id.* § 28B.10.808 (Supp. 1979).

29. *Id.* § 28B.10.816 (1970).

30. A. E. Dick Howard, *State Aid to Private Higher Education* (Charlottesville, Va.: Michie, 1977), p. 926.

31. WASH. REV. CODE ANN. § 28B.12.101 (Supp. 1979).

32. *Id.* § 28B.12.040 (Supp. 1979). The compensation paid by the state may not exceed eighty percent of the total compensation. *Id.*

33. *Id.* § 28B.12.060(2)(c) (Supp. 1979).

34. *Id.* §§ 49.60. *et seq.* (1962).

35. *Id.* § 49.60.010 (Supp. 1979).

36. *Id.* § 49.60.051 (Supp. 1979).

37. *Id.* § 49.60.030(1)(a) (Supp. 1979).

38. *Id.* § 49.60.180 (Supp. 1979).

39. *Id.* § 49.60.180(4) (Supp. 1979).

40. *Id.* § 49.60.210 (Supp. 1979).

41. *Id.* § 49.60.150(1) (Supp. 1979).

42. *Id.* § 162.16.130 (1975).

43. *Id.* § 162.16.020 (1975).

44. Chicago, M., St. P. & Pac. R. v. Washington St. Comm., 87 Wash. 2d 802, 557 P.2d 307 (1976).

45. Letter of May 20, 1980, from Morton M. Tytler, Senior Assistant Attorney General, for the Washington State Human Rights Commission, on file with the Center for Constitutional Studies: "The Human Rights Commission does consider alcoholism and drug addiction to be mental or physical handicaps if they are the basis for employer action adverse to an employee who can do the job."

46. Wash. Water Power v. Wash. State Human Rights Comm., 91 Wash. 2d 62, 586 P.2d 1149 (1978).

47. "The Commission has not distinguished between direct and indirect control of the employer by a church. The Commission looks to the question of the institution and considers it to be religious or sectarian if it has a religious orientation and mission." Letter from Morton M. Tytler, note 45, *supra.*

48. WASH. REV. CODE ANN. § 49.60.040 (Supp. 1981).

49. Letter from Morton M. Tytler, note 45, *supra.*

50. *Id.* §§ 49.46. *et seq.* (1962). An employer includes any individual, partnership, association, or corporation acting directly or indirectly in the interest of an employer in relation to an employee. *Id.* § 49.46.010 (Supp. 1979).

51. *Id.* § 49.46.050 (Supp. 1979). The minimum wage for minors is to be set by the Industrial Welfare Committee and may not exceed the prescribed minimum wage for adults. *Id.* § 49.12.121 (Supp. 1979).

52. *Id.* § 49.46.130 (Supp. 1979).

53. *Id.* § 49.46.025 (1962).

54. *Id.* § 49.46.010(d) (Supp. 1979).

55. *Id.* § 49.46.060 (1962).

56. *Id.* § 51.04.010 *et seq.* (1962, Supp. 1981).

57. *Id.* § 51.12.010 (Supp. 1981).

58. *Id.* § 51.12.020 (Supp. 1981).

59. *Id.* § 51.08.070 (Supp. 1981).

60. *Id.* § 51.08.185 (Supp. 1981).

61. *Id.* § 51.12.020(3) (Supp. 1981).

62. *Id.* § 51.12.060 (Supp. 1981).

63. *Id.* § 51.12.020(4) (Supp. 1981).

64. *Id.* § 51.12.035(2) (Supp. 1981).

65. *Id.* § 51.12.130 (Supp. 1981). With regard to whether RAC apprentices are covered, see *id.* § 51.08.012 (Supp. 1981).

66. *Id.* § 51.12.110 (Supp. 1981).

67. *Id.* § 51.14.010 (Supp. 1981).

68. *Id.* § 51.14.020 (Supp. 1981).

69. *Id.* § 50.01.005 *et seq.* (Supp. 1980).

70. *Id.* § 50.04.100 (Supp. 1980). The statute sets forth three tests for employment. *Id.* § 50.04.140 (Supp. 1980).

71. Section 3306(c)(8) of the Federal Unemployment Tax Act excludes from the definition of "employment" services performed for a religious or educational organization as described in I.R.C. § 501(c)(3). Such services are exempt from federal taxation.

72. WASH. REV. CODE ANN. § 50.44.010 (Supp. 1980).

73. *Id.* § 50.44.040(8) (Supp. 1980).

74. *Id.* § 50.44.040(9) (Supp. 1980).

75. *Id.* § 50.44.040(1)(a) (Supp. 1980).

76. *Id.* § 50.44.040(1)(b) (Supp. 1980).

77. *Id.* § 50.44.040(2) (Supp. 1980).

78. *Id.* § 50.04.160 (Supp. 1980).

79. *Id.* § 50.04.220 (Supp. 1980).

80. "Nonprofit organization" is defined by referring to *id.* § 50.44.010 (Supp. 1980). *Id.* § 50.44.060 (Supp. 1980). An organization for which service does not constitute employment according to I.R.C. § 3306(c)(8) is considered a nonprofit organization under the Washington statute.

81. WASH. REV. CODE ANN. § 50.44.060 (Supp. 1980).

82. This department is established at *id.* § 50.08.101 (Supp. 1980).

83. *Id.* § 50.44.060(1) (Supp. 1980).

84. *Id.* § 50.44.060(2) (Supp. 1980).

85. *Id.* § 50.44.070 (Supp. 1980).

86. For details, see *id.* § 50.44.050 (Supp. 1980). For similar provisions relating to personnel in other capacities or to vacation periods, see *id.*

87. *Id.* § 49.32.020 (1962). Cf. *id.* § 49.36.010 (1962), establishing the legality of unions.

88. *Id.* § 49.32.050 (1962).

89. *Id.* § 49.32.072. (1962). The Court must establish that unlawful acts have been threatened and will be committed unless restrained; that substantial and irreparable injury to property will result; that there is no adequate legal remedy; that public authorities are unable or unwilling to provide adequate protection; and that the injury to property will outweigh the injury to the rights of those restrained. *Id.*

90. See text accompanying notes 47 *et seq., supra.*

91. WASH. REV. CODE ANN. § 49.60.030 (Supp. 1969). The definition of a place of public accommodation is all-inclusive, expressly including any place kept for gain where charges are made for entertainment, housing, lodging, recreation, rest, rendering of personal services, public conveyance, or sale of food or medical services or wherever the public gathers. The definition includes educational institutions. *Id.* § 49.60.040 (Supp. 1979).

92. RACs are not excepted from the definition of a "person" covered by the law. *Id.* § 49.60.040 (Supp. 1979).

93. *Id.* § 49.60.010 (Supp. 1979).

94. *Id.* § 49.60.040 (Supp. 1979). RACs are within the concept of religious or sectarian institutions. See note 47, *supra.*

95. WASH. REV. CODE ANN. § 49.60.030(c) (Supp. 1981).

96. *Id.* § 49.60.222 (Supp. 1981).

97. See text accompanying notes 47, 48, 90, 94 and 102.

98. WASH. REV. CODE ANN. § 70.92100 (Supp. 1979). "Substantially remodeled or rehabilitated" refers to any alteration or restoration which exceeds sixty percent of the appraised valuation. *Id.* § 70.92.130 (Supp. 1979). Buildings included within the scope of this section are those within group A through H occupancies as defined in the Washington State Building Code. *Id.* § 70.92.110 (Supp. 1979). See *id.* §§ 19.27 *et seq.* for the State Building Code.

99. *Id.* § 70.92.140 (Supp. 1979).

100. *Id.* § 70.92.110(3) (Supp. 1979).

101. *Id.* § 70.92.110(5) (Supp. 1981).

102. *Id.* § 59.18.040 (Supp. 1979).

103. *Id.* §§ 49.17 *et seq.* (Supp. 1979).

104. *Id.* § 49.17.050(2).

105. *Id.* § 49.17.020(3).

106. *Id.* § 49.17.020(4).

107. *Id.* § 83.04.010 (Supp. 1979).

108. *Id.* § 83.20.010(5) (Supp. 1981).

109. *Id.* § 83.58.020 (Supp. 1979).

110. *Id.* § 83.58.070 (Supp. 1979).

111. WASH. CONST. art. VII, § 1 (amend. 14).

112. WASH. REV. CODE ANN. § 84.36.050 (Supp. 1979). Such purposes include, but are not limited to educational, social, athletic and housing facilities, the need for which would be non-existent without the presence of the educational institution. *Id.*

113. *Id.* § 82.08.020 (Supp. 1979).

114. *Id.* § 82.08.010(2) (Supp. 1979).

115. *Id.* § 82.08.030 (Supp. 1979).

116. *Id.* §§ 82.12. *et seq.* (1962).

117. *Id.* § 82.04.220 (1962).

118. *Id.* § 82.04.030 (Supp. 1979). In Young Men's Christian Ass'n. v. State, 62 Wash. 2d 504, 383 P.2d 497 (1963), "person" was deemed broad enough to include a charitable institution such as the Y.M.C.A.

119. WASH. REV. CODE ANN. § 82.04.140 (1962).

120. Young Men's Christian Ass'n. v. State, 62 Wash. 2d 504, 383 P.2d 497 (1963).

121. WASH. REV. CODE ANN. § 82.04.170 (Supp. 1979).

122. *Id.* § 82.04.430(2) (Supp. 1979).

123. *Id.* § 82.04.365 (Supp. 1979).

124. *Id.* § 82.04.220 (1962).

125. *Id.* § 819.09.030 (1978).

126. *Id.* § 19.09.060 (1978). The registration provisions are set out at *id.* § 19.09.070 (1978).

127. *Id.* § 19.09.030(2) (1978).

128. *Id.* § 19.09.030(4) (1978).

129. *Id.* § 19.09.030(1) (1978).

130. *Id.* §§ 19.09, 200, 210 (1978).

131. *Id.* § 19.09.170 (1978).

132. *Id.* §§ 9.46. *et seq.* (1977).

133. *Id.* § 9.46.020(3) (Supp. 1979).

134. *Id.* § 9.46.030(2) (Supp. 1979).

135. *Id.* § 9.46.295 (1977).

136. *Id.* § 9.46.110 (Supp. 1979).

56. West Virginia

1. W.Va. Code §§ 31–1–136 *et seq.* (1975).

2. American Law Institute–American Bar Association, *Model Nonprofit Corporation Act* (Philadelphia: American Law Institute, 1964). For a discussion of this act, see Chapter 1, "Corporate Status," *supra.*

3. W.Va. Code §§ 31–1–34 to 38, 31–1–150 and 151.

4. *Id.* §§ 31–1–39 and 40; 31–1–154 to 158.

5. *Id.* § 31–1–40; see Model Act, § 50.

6. See Model Act, § 51.

7. W.Va. Code § 31–1–41; see Model Act, § 54.

8. W.Va. Code §§ 31–1–155 to 158; see Model Act, §§ 46 and 47.

9. W.Va. Code § 35–2–2.

10. See, e.g., Beatty v. Union Trust and Deposit Co., 123 W. Va. 144, 13 S.E.2d 760 (1967).

11. For a discussion of the *cy pres* doctrine, see Chapter 1, "Corporate Status," *supra.*

12. 403 U.S. 672 (1971). For a comprehensive treatment of West Virginia's programs of assistance to private higher education, see A. E. Dick Howard, *State Aid to Private Higher Education* (Charlottesville, Va.: Michie, 1977), pp. 945–951.

13. 413 U.S. 734 (1973).

14. W.Va. Code §§ 18–21–1 *et seq.*

15. *Id.* §§ 18–21–3 and 18–21–4.

16. *Id.* § 18–21–5.

17. *Id.* § 18–21–7.

18. 50 Op. Att'y Gen. 373 (1963).

19. W.Va. Code § 18–26–15a.

20. *Id.* §§ 18–26–15a.

21. See *id.* §§ 18–22B–4 *et seq.*

22. *Id.* § 18–22B–5.

23. *Id.* § 18–22B–6.

24. *Id.* § 18–22B–6. (Supp. 1983). West Virginia has an agreement with Pennsylvania and is a member of the Southern Regional Education Compact.

25. *Id.* § 18–26–10.

26. *Id.* § 18–26–10a.

27. W.Va. Const. art. X, §§ 4 and 6.

28. W.Va. Code § 18–26–17.

29. A separate provision specifically bars sex discrimination in wages. W.Va. Code § 21–5B–1.

30. "Age," under the law, means age forty through sixty-five, inclusively. *Id.* § 5–11–3(q).

31. *Id.* § 5–11–2.

32. An employer includes any person other than a private club, employing twelve or more people. *Id.* § 5–11–3(d).

33. *Id.* § 5–11–3(h).

34. *Id.* § 5–11–9(a). Related conduct, e.g., in application forms and advertising, is also prohibited. *Id.* §§ 5–11–9(b) *et seq.*

35. *Id.* § 5–11–9. An exception is also provided for federal and state security requirements. *Id.*

36. *Id.* §§ 5–11–4 and 5–11–8(c). For its composition, powers and duties, see §§ 5–11–5 *et seq.* Court action is also possible. *Id.* §§ 55–11–13; 5–11–11.

37. *Id.* §§ 21–5C–1 *et seq.*

38. *Id.* § 21–5C–1(f)(2).

39. *Id.* § 21–5C–1(f)(6).

40. *Id.* § 21–5C–1(f)(14).

41. *Id.* § 21–5–3 (Supp. 1979). For details, see *id.* See also *id.* §§ 21–5–1 *et seq.*

42. *Id.* § 21–1–3.

43. *Id.*

44. *Id.* §§ 23–1–1 *et seq.* (1978, Supp. 1980).

45. *Id.* § 23–2–1.

46. *Id.* § 23–2–1a.

47. *Id.* § 23–2–1.

48. *Id.* § 23–2–5.

49. *Id.* § 23–2–9.

50. *Id.* §§ 21A–1–1 *et seq.* (Supp. 1979).

51. The definition of "employment" is found at *id.* § 21A–1–3 (Supp. 1979).

52. *Id.*

53. *Id.*

54. *Id.*

55. *Id.*

56. *Id.*

57. *Id.*

58. "Institution of higher education" is defined at § 21A–1–3 (Supp. 1979).

59. *Id.*

60. *Id.*

61. *Id.* Spouses must be informed that employment is provided as a means of financial aid and that they are not covered by any program of unemployment insurance. *Id.*

62. *Id.*

63. *Id.*

64. *Id.*

65. *Id.* § 21A-5-3a.

66. *Id.* § 21A-5-3a(1)(a)(b). The Department is established by *id.* § 21A-1-4.

67. *Id.* § 21A-5-3a(1).

68. *Id.* § 21A-5-3(1).

69. *Id.* §§ 21-1A-1 *et seq.*

70. *Id.* § 21-1A-3. For details, see *id.*

71. *Id.* § 21-1A-4(a).

72. *Id.* § 21-1A-4(b).

73. *Id.* § 21-1A-2(a)(2).

74. See text accompanying notes 75 *et seq., infra.*

75. W.Va. Code § 5-11-2.

76. *Id.* § 5-11-9(f)(1). Related conduct, e.g., with regard to advertising, is also prohibited. *Id.* § 5-11-9(f)(2).

77. *Id.* § 5-11-3(j). The term does not include "any accommodations which are in their nature private." *Id.* This presumably is intended to allow sex separation in lavatories and the like.

78. *Id.* § 5-11-2.

79. *Id.* § 5-11-9(g)(1) and (2). Related activities, e.g., with regard to advertising and inquiries, are also prohibited. *Id.* §§ 5-11-9(g)(3) *et seq.*

80. *Id.* § 5-11-9(g)(1).

81. See note 36, *supra.*

82. *Id.* § 18-10F-1.

83. *Id.* § 18-10F-1.

84. *Id.* § 18-10F-1(8).

85. *Id.* § 16-6-7. Annual inspections are required. *Id.* § 16-6-8.

86. See *id.* § 16-6-3.

87. *Id.*

88. *Id.*

89. *Id.* § 21-3-1.

90. *Id.*

91. *Id.* § 21-3-17.

92. *Id.* §§ 11-24-1 *et seq.*

93. "Corporation" includes a joint stock company or any association taxed as a corporation under federal income tax law. *Id.* § 11-24-3(b)(2) (Supp. 1979).

94. *Id.* § 11-24-5.

95. *Id.*

96. *Id.* § 11-11-1 (Supp. 1979) *et seq.*

97. *Id.* § 11-11-4 (Supp. 1979). When the transferee is in another jurisdiction, the exemption applies only if that jurisdiction would exempt the reciprocal situation. *Id.*

98. *Id.* §§ 11-21-1 *et seq.*

99. *Id.* § 11-21-15(a).

100. See *id.* § 11-21-15(a) and (c).

101. I.R.C. § 170(c)(2)(B) and (C).

102. W.Va. Code § 11-24-3 (Supp. 1979).

103. *Id.* § 11-3-9.

104. *Id.*

105. A March, 1980, letter from David C. Hardesty, Jr., State Tax Commissioner, suggests that even college-owned dormitories would have a half-acre limit under the exemption: "To qualify for exemption based upon educational purposes, the educational use must be primary and immediate, such as a classroom building or laboratories. Dormitories and social clubs are not viewed as primarily and immediately educational. Therefore, private college dormitory complexes exceeding one-half acre in extent would, at least in theory, be subject to property taxes." Letter on file, Center for Constitutional Studies, Notre Dame Law School.

Whatever the merits of the assertion that dormitories are not a primary and immediate educational use, the one-half acre limit under the statute applies only to real estate used by a college or university "society." W.Va. Code § 11-3-9. It does not, therefore, apply to a dormitory used by the college or university itself for its students.

106. W.Va. Code § 11-3-9.

107. *Id.*

108. *Id.* For details, see *id.*

109. *Id.*

110. *Id.* §§ 11-15-1 *et seq.*

111. *Id.* § 11-15-1.

112. *Id.* § 11-15-8.

113. Although "professional" service is not limited to that performed by lawyers, ministers, doctors, or the like, one claiming an exemption must establish that the services are performed by a member of a clearly established profession. Wooddell v. Dailey, 230 S.E.2d 466 (W. Va. 1976). See W.Va. Code § 11-15-6.

114. *Id.* § 11-15-9(3) (Supp. 1979).

115. Letter of March, 1980, from David G. Hardesty, Jr., State Tax Commissioner, on file, Center for Constitutional Studies, Notre Dame Law School. The word "school" is used to include "college" in another subsection of the same provision. See W.Va. Code § 11-15-9(18) (Supp. 1979).

116. *Id.* § 11-15-9(6) (Supp. 1970). The property or services must be used or consumed by the specified organization itself. *Id.*

117. *Id.* The property or services must be used or consumed by the specified organization itself. *Id.* § 11-15-9(6) and (16) (Supp. 1979).

118. *Id.* § 11-15-11(a) (Supp. 1979). For details see *id.* § 11-15-11(c) (Supp. 1979) *et seq.*

119. *Id.* § 11-15-9(18) (Supp. 1979). The federal exemption must be by virtue of I.R.C. § 501(c)(3). *Id.*

120. *Id.* §§ 11-15A-3 *et seq.* (Supp. 1979).

121. See *id.* § 11-15A-3(2) and (5) (Supp. 1979).

122. *Id.* §§ 11–12–5 *et seq.*

123. *Id.* § 11–12–89.

124. *Id.* §§ 11–12–89 and 11–12–83 (Supp. 1979).

125. *Id.* §§ 11–13–1 *et seq.*

126. See, e.g., *id.* § 11–13–1, *passim.*

127. See, e.g., *id.* § 11–13–2h.

128. *Id.* § 11–13–3 (Supp. 1980).

129. *Id.* § 29–19–1 *et seq.*

130. *Id.* § 29–19–2.

131. *Id.* § 29–19–6(a)(1).

132. *Id.* § 29–19–6(b). The Commission on Charitable Organizations includes seven members and determines rules, regulations and procedures for charitable organizations, enforces the rules, and holds necessary hearings. *Id.* § 29–19–3.

133. *Id.* § 29–19–8.

134. *Id.* § 29–19–11.

135. *Id.* § 29–19–10.

136. *Id.* § 61–10–5 provides: "if any person, at any place, public or private, shall bet or wage money or other thing of value on any game of chance or shall knowingly furnish any money or other thing of value to any other person to bet or wage on any such game, he shall be guilty of a misdemeanor . . ." There is no exemption in this statute for RACs or other charitable organizations.

137. *Id.* §§ 18–10D–1 *et seq.*

138. *Id.* §§ 18–10C–1 *et seq.* The Southern Regional Educational Board is scheduled to terminate on July 1, 1982. *Id.* § 4–10–4 (Supp. 1979).

139. *Id.* § 60–7–4(c).

57. Wisconsin

1. Wis. Stat. Ann. §§ 181.01 *et seq.* (West).

2. *Id.* § 181.02(4).

3. *Id.* § 181.02(3).

4. *Id.* § 181.32 (Supp. 1980).

5. *Id.* § 181.33.

6. *Id.* §§ 187.01 *et seq.*

7. *Id.* § 187.01(1) (Supp. 1980).

8. *Id.* § 187.01(1) (Supp. 1980). "Every religious or religious educational and charitable society organized or attempted to be organized under [previous statutes] and which . . . has acted as a religious or religious educational and charitable corporation in pursuance thereof, shall be deemed to be legally incorporated and shall have all the powers and be subject to all the liabilities of religious corporations under the provisions of this chapter." *Id.* § 187.09.

9. *Id.* § 181.04 (Supp. 1980).

10. *Id.* § 187.01(3) (Supp. 1980).

11. Compare *id.* §§ 181.01 *et seq.* with §§ 45–51 of the Model Act. For a discussion of the Model Act, see Chapter 1, "Corporate Status," *supra.*

12. See, e.g., In re Gansen's Estate, 79 Wisc. 2d 180, 255 N.W.2d 483 (1977); In re Berry's Estate, 139 N.W.2d 72 (Wisc. 1966).

13. Wis. Stat. Ann. §§ 181.50, 181.54, and 181.55.

14. *Id.* § 181.56 (Supp. 1980).

15. *Id.* § 181.57.

16. *Id.* § 181.51.

17. For an excellent and thorough discussion, see A. E. Dick Howard, *State Aid to Private Higher Education* (Charlottesville, Va.: Michie, 1977), pp. 952–981.

18. Wis. Const. art. 1, § 18.

19. *Id.*

20. *Id.*

21. *Id.* art. 8, § 3.

22. *Id.* art. 8, § 6.

23. Howard, *State Aid,* note 17, *supra,* at 980.

24. *Id.* at 977–978, 980.

25. Wis. Stat. Ann. § 39.28 (Supp. 1980). The Council on Financial Aids advises the Board on matters pertaining to the state's student financial aid programs. *Id.* § 39.27.

26. See *id.* § 39.30(1)(e) (Supp. 1980).

27. There are various ways of being "accredited" for purposes of the law. For example, a nonprofit institution qualifies if its credits are accepted on transfer by no fewer than three regularly accredited institutions. *Id.* § 39.30(1)(d) (Supp. 1980).

28. *Id.* § 39.30. (Supp. 1980).

29. *Id.* § 39.30(3) (Supp. 1980). For details, see *id.*

30. *Id.* § 39.30(3)(b) and (c) (Supp. 1980).

31. *Id.* § 39.30(2)(d) (Supp. 1980).

32. *Id.* § 39.435(4) (Supp. 1980).

33. *Id.* § 39.38 (Supp. 1980).

34. *Id.* § 39.435(5) (Supp. 1980).

35. *Id.* § 39.46 (Supp. 1980). For the history, details, and constitutionality of this arrangement, see Howard, *State Aid,* note 17, *supra,* at 970–974.

36. Wis. Stat. Ann. § 39.46(2)(a) (Supp. 1980). See State ex rel. Warren v. Nusbaum(I), 55 Wis. 2d 316, 198 N.W.2d 650 (1972).

37. See Wis. Stat. Ann. § 39.32(1)(a) (Supp. 1980).

38. *Id.* § 39.32 (Supp. 1981). For details, see *id.*

39. *Id.* § 39.33 (Supp. 1980).

40. *Id.* § 39.325 (Supp. 1980). These loans may be "forgiven". See *id.* § 39.377 (Supp. 1980).

41. *Id.* § 39.34 (Supp. 1980).

42. *Id.* §§ 111.31 *et seq.*

43. *Id.* § 111.325.

44. *Id.* § 111.32(5)(a) (Supp. 1980).

45. See *id.* § 111.32(5)(g)1 (Supp. 1980) *et seq.*

46. See *id.* § 111.32(5)(f) (Supp. 1980).

47. *Id.* § 111.32(2).

48. *Id.* § 111.32(3) (Supp. 1980).

49. *Id.* § 111.33. For its duties, powers and procedures, see *id.* §§ 111.35 *et seq.*

50. *Id.* § 66.433(2) (Supp. 1980).

51. *Id.* § 66.433(3)(c)1.b. (Supp. 1980).

52. *Id.* § 104.01(1).

53. *Id.* § 104.01(2).

54. *Id.* §§ 104.01 *et seq.*

55. *Id.* § 104.02. A "living wage" is "sufficient to enable the employee receiving it to maintain himself or herself under conditions consistent with his or her welfare." *Id.* § 104.01(5). "Welfare means "reasonable comfort, reasonable physical well-being, decency, and moral well-being." *Id.* § 104.01(4).

56. *Id.* § 104.11.

57. *Id.* § 103.01(1) (Supp. 1980).

58. *Id.* §§ 103.01 *et seq.*

59. *Id.* § 103.01(2) (Supp. 1980).

60. *Id.* § 103.01(3) (Supp. 1980).

61. *Id.* § 103.02 (Supp. 1980).

62. *Id.*

63. *Id.* § 103.03 (Supp. 1980). For the law on frequency of payments, see Wage Payments, Claims And Collections, *id.* §§ 109 *et seq.*

64. *Id.* §§ 102.01 *et seq.*

65. *Id.* § 102.04 (Supp. 1980).

66. *Id.* § 102.07(4).

67. *Id.* § 102.05(2).

68. *Id.* § 102.07(11) (Supp. 1980).

69. *Id.* § 102.08.

70. *Id.* § 102.08.

71. *Id.* § 102.28(2)(a) (Supp. 1980).

72. *Id.* § 102.28(2)(b) (Supp. 1980).

73. *Id.* §§ 108.01 *et seq.*

74. "Nonprofit organization" is defined at § 108.02(26).

75. The definition of "employer" is found at § 108.02.

76. *Id.* § 108.02(4)(b) (Supp. 1980).

77. The definition of "employment" is found at § 108.02(5).

78. *Id.* § 108.02(5)(h)(1) (Supp. 1980).

79. *Id.* § 108.02(5)(h)(2) (Supp. 1980).

80. *Id.* § 108.02(5)(h)(3) (Supp. 1980).

81. *Id.* § 108.02(5)(i)(1) (Supp. 1980).

82. *Id.* § 108.02(5)(i)(2) (Supp. 1980). Spouses must be informed that such employment is provided as a means of financial aid and that they are not covered by unemployment insurance.

83. *Id.* § 108.02(5)(j)(1) (Supp. 1980).

84. See I.R.C. §§ 501(a), 521.

85. WIS. STAT. ANN. § 108.02(5)(j)(5) (Supp. 1980).

86. *Id.* § 108.02(5)(k)(2) (Supp. 1980). This exemption is not available to any organization which pays $1,000.00 or more for domestic services in any calendar quarter of the current or preceding calendar year.

87. *Id.* § 108.151(2).

88. *Id.* § 108.151(2)(b). The Department is established at §§ 108.02(2m), 108.14.

89. *Id.* § 108.151(5)(b).

90. *Id.* § 108.151(4) (Supp. 1980).

91. *Id.* § 103.57. See also *id.* § 111.01(3).

92. *Id.* § 111.02(2).

93. *Id.* § 111.02(3).

94. *Id.* §§ 111.01 *et seq.*

95. *Id.* § 111.04.

96. *Id.* § 111.06(1)(a).

97. *Id.* § 101.223.

98. *Id.* § 942.04(1)(a) (Supp. 1980). Related conduct, e.g., with regard to advertising, is also prohibited. See *id.* § 942.04(1)(b) through (c) (Supp. 1980).

99. *Id.* § 942.04(2) (Supp. 1980) (Emphasis added).

100. *Id.* § 942.04(3) (Supp. 1980).

101. *Id.* § 942.04(4) (Supp. 1980). Indeed, this provision could suggest that the exemption for nonprofit institutions in connection with public places of accommodation, see text at note 99 *et seq., supra,* was *not* intended to be "wholesale."

102. *Id.* § 101.22(1m) and (2) (Supp. 1980).

103. See text accompanying note 101, *supra.*

104. WIS. STAT. ANN. § 66.433(2) (Supp. 1980).

105. *Id.* § 66.433(3)(c)1.b (Supp. 1980).

106. *Id.* §§ 101.01 *et seq.*

107. *Id.* § 101.11.

108. *Id.* § 101.01(2)(c).

109. *Id.* § 101(2)(d).

110. *Id.* § 101.01(2)(e).

111. *Id.* § 71.01(2) (Supp. 1980).

112. *Id.* § 71.01(3) (Supp. 1980).

113. *Id.* § 72.15(1)(a) (Supp. 1980). A reciprocity provision is attached. *Id.* § 72.15(1)(b) (Supp. 1980).

114. *Id.* § 72.76(1)(h) (Supp. 1980). A reciprocity provision is attached. See *id.* and *id.* § 72.15(1)(b) (Supp. 1980). Wisconsin's *estate* tax, *id.* §§ 72.60 (Supp. 1980) *et seq.,* seeks merely to secure to Wisconsin "the benefit of the maximum credit allowable upon the United States estate tax . . ." *Id.* § 72.60 (Supp. 1980).

115. *Id.* § 71.02(2)(d).

116. *Id.* § 71.05(3).

117. *Id.* § 71.02(2)(f) (Supp. 1980).

118. I.R.C. § 170(c)(2)(B) and (C).

119. See WIS. STAT. ANN. § 71.04(5)(a) and (c).

120. *Id.* § 71.04(5)(a) and § 71.045(d)(2) (Supp. 1980).

121. *Id.* § 70.11(3). "The leasing of land by a university or college, for educational or charitable purposes, shall not render it liable to taxation provided the income derived therefrom is used for the maintenance of the institution or for charitable purposes." *Id.* § 70.11(3)(b).

122. It could be argued that only "real" property is covered due to the existence of a separate provision specifically exempting certain "personal" property. See *id.* § 70.111.

123. *Id.* § 70.11(4).

124. *Id.*

125. *Id.*

126. *Id.*

127. Interestingly, the earlier exemption uses the word "grounds," which may or may not include buildings, whereas the second uses "land," which specifically includes buildings. *Id.* § 70.03. Given the specific language of the second exemption, moreover, all *buildings* of RACs, on whatever acreage, would be exempt as "property . . . owned and used exclusively by educational institutions," even though the *land* involved may not be exempt if beyond the acreage limit.

128. *Id.* § 70.11(25).

129. See *id.* § 70.337 (Supp. 1980).

130. *Id.* §§ 77.51 (Supp. 1980) *et seq.*

131. *Id.* § 77.54(7) (Supp. 1980).

132. *Id.* § 77.54(9a)(f) (Supp. 1980).

133. *Id.* § 77.54(15) (Supp. 1980).

134. *Id.* § 77.54(20) (Supp. 1980). For exceptions, see *id.* § 77.54(20)(b) (Supp. 1980). See also *id.* § 77.54(20)(c)(2) (Supp. 1980), taxing certain items, e.g., meals, sandwiches, soda fountain items, and candy, even if for off-premises consumption. Gross receipts from most sales of food for direct on-premises consumption are taxable, *id.* § 77.54(20)(c)(1) (Supp. 1980). For exceptions relating to hospitals, nursing homes, day care centers, etc., see *id.* § 77.54(20)(c)(4) (Supp. 1980).

135. *Id.* § 77.54(20)(c)(5) (Supp. 1980). Cf. Kollash v. Adamany, 99 Wis. 2d 533, 299 N.W.2d 891 (Wis. Ct. App. 1980) (holding that sales tax on meals served to groups at Centers run by religious orders are not a violation of the free exercise right).

136. See § 77.54(30)(a)(1) and (2) for details. Such sales to RACs for use in campus housing would be exempt from tax. See *id.* § 77.54(30)(d) (Supp. 1980).

137. *Id.* §§ 77.70 (Supp. 1980) and 77.71 (Supp. 1980).

138. *Id.* §§ 440.41 *et seq.*

139. For details, see *id.* § 440.41(2).

140. For details, see *id.* § 440.41(4).

141. *Id.* § 440.41(3)(a).

142. *Id.* § 440.41(3)(b).

143. *Id.* § 440.41(c) (Supp. 1980). For details, see *id.*

144. *Id.* §§ 440.41(5) (Supp. 1980) *et seq.* For definitions of "professional fundraisers" and "professional solicitors," see *id.* § 440.41(c) (Supp. 1980) and (d), respectively.

145. WIS. CONST. art. IV, § 24. (Supp. 1980).

146. *Id.* § 24(1) and (2) (Supp. 1980). For the parallel legislation, see WIS. STAT. ANN. § 163.11(1).

147. WIS. CONST. art. IV, § 24(1) and (2) (Supp. 1980).

148. See WIS. STAT. ANN. §§ 163.02 (Supp. 1980) *et seq.*

149. *Id.* §§ 945.01 (Supp. 1980) *et seq.*

150. As defined in *id.* § 163.03 (Supp. 1980), and as long as conducted according to the provisions of Chapter 163. *Id.* § 945.01(2)(a).

151. *Id.*

152. *Id.* § 39.75 (Supp. 1980).

58. Wyoming

1. WYO. STAT. §§ 17-6-101 *et seq.*

2. *Id.* § 17-6-101.

3. *Id.* § 17-6-111.

4. *Id.* § 17-7-101.

5. *Id.* § 17-6-102.

6. *Id.* § 17-6-105.

7. *Id.* § 17-6-113.

8. *Id.* § 17-6-15.

9. *Id.* § 17-6-112.

10. *Id.* § 17-6-103.

11. *Id.* § 17-6-116.

12. *Id.* § 17-6-117.

13. *Id.* §§ 17-7-101 *et seq.*

14. *Id.* § 17-7-103.

15. *Id.* § 17-7-104.

16. *Id.* § 17-7-105.

17. *Id.* § 17-7-106.

18. *Id.* § 17-7-108.

19. *Id.* § 17-7-109.

20. *Id.* § 17-7-111.

21. *Id.* §§ 17-6-101 *et seq.* (1977).

22. The statutes governing merger, consolidation, (*id.* §§ 17-1-401 *et seq.*) and involuntary dissolution (*id.* §§ 17-1-614 *et seq.*) are found in the Wyoming Business Corporation Act which is written with the structure of a for-profit corporation in mind. It might intelligently be construed to mean that Wyoming will also apply these procedures when a nonprofit college merges, consolidates, or is involuntarily dissolved.

23. Town of Cody v. Buffalo Bill Memorial Association, 64 Wyo. 468, 196 P.2d 369 (1948). See

also, First National Bank and Trust Company of Wyoming v. Brimmer, 504 P.2d 1367 (Wyo. 1973).

24. Wyo. Stat. § 17–6–109.

25. *Id.*

26. Wyo. Const. art. 7, § 8.

27. *Id.* art. 3, § 36.

28. Wyo. Stat. § 21–16–101.

29. *Id.* §§ 27–9–103 through 27–9–108.

30. Defined to include persons with two or more employees. *Id.* § 27–9–102(b).

31. *Id.* § 27–9–105.

32. *Id.* § 27–9–102(b).

33. *Id.* § 6–9–404 provides that "no person of good deportment shall be denied the right of life, liberty, pursuit of happiness, or the necessities of life because of race, color, creed, or national origin." This statute might also serve as a means to attack discriminatory employment practices.

34. *Id.* § 27–9–107.

35. *Id.* § 27–9–108.

36. *Id.* § 27–4–202.

37. *Id.* § 27–4–201.

38. *Id.*

39. An exception may be made for teachers who are members of the religious community such as sisters or brothers.

40. See *id.* §§ 27–5–10 through 27–5–107.

41. *Id.* § 27–7–101.

42. *Id.* §§ 17–1–101 through 17–1–1011.

43. *Id.* § 17–1–105.

44. The Wyoming legislature has also empowered the board of trustees of each public school district to indemnify teachers and other personnel against liability for negligence. While private schools are not mentioned, it appears that the same policy would apply to RACs. See *id.* § 21–3–128.

45. *Id.* §§ 27–12–101 *et seq.* (1977, Supp. 1980).

46. *Id.* § 27–12–102(a)(xx).

47. *Id.* § 27–12–106.

48. *Id.* §§ 27–12–102(a)(i) and 27–12–106(xxvi).

49. *Id.* § 27–12–102(a)(xv).

50. *Id.* § 27–12–106(a)(iv).

51. *Id.* § 27–12–106(a)(xxvii).

52. *Id.* § 27–12–102(a)(viii). This exception applies only when the employment is both casual and not for the purpose of the employer's usual business.

53. *Id.* § 27–12–102(a)(viii). This exception applies if the clerical worker is not subject to the hazards of the business. *Id.* § 27–12–102.

54. *Id.* § 27–12–102(a)(i).

55. *Id.* § 27–12–204.

56. *Id.* § 27–12–204(c).

57. *Id.* § 27–12–103.

58. *Id.* § 27–3–102(f)(I).

59. *Id.* § 27–3–102(f)(II).

60. *Id.* § 27–3–102(m). For details, see *id.*

61. Wyo. Const. art. 7, § 10.

62. Wyo. Stat. §§ 21–7–302 and 21–4–303.

63. *Id.* § 6–9–404.

64. Any person, firm, or corporation who violates *id.* § 6–9–404 is guilty of a misdemeanor and, upon conviction, shall be fined no more than one hundred dollars or imprisoned in the county jail for a term not to exceed six months or both. See *id.* § 6–9–405.

65. *Id.* § 6–4–610.

66. See text accompanying note 63, *supra.*

67. Wyo. Stat. §§ 27–11–101 through 27–11–114.

68. *Id.* § 27–11–102.

69. *Id.* § 27–11–104.

70. *Id.* § 27–11–105.

71. See note 44, *supra.*

72. Wyo. Stat. § 27–11–107.

73. *Id.* §§ 35–9–101 through 35–9–615.

74. *Id.* § 39–6–801(c)(vi) and (vii).

75. *Id.* § 39–6–801.

76. *Id.* § 39–1–201(a)(xxv).

77. *Id.* § 39–1–201(a)(xxvii).

78. *Id.* § 39–6–405(a)(xii).

79. *Id.* § 39–6–405(a)(xiv).

80. *Id.* § 39–6–505(a)(vi).

81. *Id.* § 6–9–101.

82. *Id.* § 6–9–111.